HUMAN RIGHTS IN THE
WORLD COMMUNITY

Pennsylvania Studies in Human Rights
Bert B. Lockwood, Jr., Series Editor
A complete list of books in the series is available from the publisher.

HUMAN RIGHTS in the WORLD COMMUNITY

Issues and Action

THIRD EDITION

Edited by

Richard Pierre Claude

and

Burns H. Weston

with the assistance of Gavin H. Boyles and Jessica L. Downs

PENN

UNIVERSITY OF PENNSYLVANIA PRESS

Philadelphia

10 9 8 7 6 5 4 3 2 1

Published by
University of Pennsylvania Press
Philadelphia, Pennsylvania 19104-4112

Human Rights in the world community : issues and action / edited by Richard Pierre Claude
and Burns H. Weston with the assistance of Gavin H. Boyles and Jessica L. Downs.—3rd ed.
    p.   cm. — (Pennsylvania studies in human rights)
  Includes bibliographical references and index
  ISBN-13: 978-0-8122-1948-7 (alk. paper)
  ISBN-10: 0-8122-1948-1 (alk. paper)
1. Human rights. I. Claude, Richard Pierre, 1934–. II. Weston, Burns H., 1933– III. Series.
Published/Created: Philadelphia : University of Pennsylvania Press, c2006.
K3240 .H8573   2006
341—dc22   2006042172

To our grandchildren

Nicholas

Angela

Julian

Christopher

Timothy

and

Tiana

&

Leah

Elijah

Emma

and

Isabella

Contents

CHAPTER 8   **PRIVATE SECTOR APPROACHES TO HUMAN RIGHTS IMPLEMENTATION**   **413**

POSTSCRIPT: HUMAN RIGHTS AND HUMANE GOVERNANCE   **455**

Preface

This is the third edition of *Human Rights in the World Community: Issues and Action*. Since its first publication in 1989, students of human rights have witnessed in every hemisphere and on every continent a large array of states undertaking reform, becoming "emerging" or "re-emerging" democracies, and proclaiming support for the promotion and protection of international human rights. The second edition, published in 1992 soon after the dismantling of the Berlin Wall, reflected a post-Cold War aspiration, widely shared, to displace the sterile ideological posturing of superpower rivalry with a lively and constructive global human rights culture. This hope was manifest at the World Conference on Human Rights held in Vienna in 1993. Among other things, the Conference called "on all States and institutions to include human rights, humanitarian law, democracy and rule of law as subjects in the curricula of all learning institutions in formal and non-formal settings."[1]

This third and wholly revised edition is intended to facilitate human rights education and to do so in support of the international resolves voiced in the 2000 "Millennium Declaration," according to which member states of the United Nations said they would spare no effort to promote democracy and strengthen the rule of law as well as respect for internationally recognized human rights and fundamental freedoms.[2] Since then, small networks of non-state actors organized as terrorists have made even the most powerful states feel vulnerable, tempting some to conclude that countering terrorism should displace human rights as a priority on the global agenda. Moreover, within only six years after the Millennium Declaration, more than 40 countries, by UN accounts, have been scarred by violent conflict. Challenges to human rights worldwide have featured wars, genocides, crimes against humanity, and reports of torture attributable to many countries, including the United Kingdom and the United States, two countries that have long espoused the world rule of law. These deadly assaults on the roots of civilization and budding prospects for a humane world order tell us that it is time to relearn the message of the UN Charter and the Universal Declaration of Human Rights (UDHR):[3] the global struggle for justice undertaken through peaceful means centrally includes everyone working for the recognition and implementation of human rights as the fundamental foundation of world peace.

1. World Conference on Human Rights, "Vienna Declaration and Programme of Action" (referenced in Documentary Appendix B); endorsed by the 48th session of the General Assembly at its 85th plenary meeting by Resolution 48/121 of Dec. 20, 1993, available at http://www.un.org/Depts/dhl/res/resa48.htm.
2. Adopted by the UN General Assembly Sept. 8, 2000, referenced in Documentary Appendix B.
3. Adopted by the UN General Assembly Dec. 10, 1948, reprinted and referenced in Documentary Appendix A.

In 2005, in a report entitled *In Larger Freedom*, United Nations Secretary General Kofi Annan, taking both challenges and opportunities into account, sought to set a direction for our time:

> We have it in our power to pass on to our children a brighter inheritance than that bequeathed to any previous generation. We can halve global poverty and halt the spread of major known diseases in the next 10 years. We can reduce the prevalence of violent conflict and terrorism. We can increase respect for human dignity in every land. And we can forge a set of updated international institutions to help humanity achieve these noble goals. If we act boldly—and if we act together—we can make people everywhere more secure, more prosperous and better able to enjoy their fundamental human rights.[4]

The time is now to take these words seriously, and one important—indeed paramount— way to do so is to encourage and facilitate human rights education on a widespread basis.[5] Recognizing that bequeathing a bright inheritance to future generations is in significant measure done through education, the UN General Assembly, with help from UNESCO and the Office of the UN High Commissioner for Human Rights (OHCHR), thus has called for the development, beginning in 2006, of a World Programme of Human Rights Education. Included is the development of appropriate texts and teaching materials—plowshares essential for tilling the groundwork of peace through justice.

This book brings such human rights materials together in one place for classrom use in many disciplines, including but not limited to political science, international law and relations, history, sociology, philosophy, religion, and of course education itself. Relying upon a broad distinction between *issues* associated with international human rights problems (Part I) and *action* that seeks to implement human rights norms and standards (Part II), each of the eight chapters contains essays by leading scholars and activists, preceded by an editors' introduction designed to spotlight the larger context within which the essays fit. To save on limited space, we have abridged most of the essays substantially; and to facilitate ease of use as well as save space, we have largely dispensed with distracting ellipses and bracketed editorializing, footnotes, and website visitation dates, which in every case may be assumed to be current to at least 1 March 2006. In all instances, however, we have remained otherwise faithful to the original language and intent of each author, and indeed rely on that language and intent to formulate "Questions for Reflection and Discussion" following each of the essays—questions that we hope will be helpful in analyzing the essays, prodding new thinking, and stimulating fresh research beyond the scope of the existing literature. They have been devised, too, with the general reader as well as the classroom student in mind. We hope the book will be of interest to the general reading public as well.

At the end of the book is a human rights bibliography that emphasizes relatively recent publications as well as selected "classics" in the field. On the theory that human rights is made tangible by eyewitness experience, an annotated filmography following the bibliography is likewise set out.[6] In 2005, the movie *Lord of Wars*, starring Nicholas Cage,

---

4. Report of the Secretary-General for Decision by Heads of State and Government in September 2005, *In Larger Freedom: Towards Development, Security and Human Rights for All*, available at http://www.un.org/largerfreedom, at para. 1.
5. See, e.g., the Dec. 10, 2004 "Global Appeal for Human Rights Learning" of the People's Movement for Human Rights Education, available at http://www.pdhre.org/global-appeal.html
6. Persons interested in using such films should consult Internet sources (e.g., Netflix, TiVo), video film outlets, and libraries for mailing addresses of nonprint media distributors.

graphically portrayed the multiple human rights violations flowing from international arms trading and illegal gun running. Films are an important teaching device in our television age when, by way of international satellite hookups and online transmissions, Madonna and Paul McCartney show up on our TV and computer monitors kicking off London's "Live 8" concert to prompt the "Group of 8" economic summit meeting in Scotland to respond generously to hunger in Africa, and top performers (e.g., U2 in Ireland and Chris de Burgh and Green Day in Berlin) rally support for international human rights. One way or another, we all have become eyewitnesses to human rights problems. Because the promotion and protection of human rights depends on everyone, readers should familiarize themselves with the many NGOs and other groups that serve human rights causes. They are easy to join and need the help of new members.

Human rights is not an abstract field of study. It is a field of work and way of life. It requires everyone's committment, effort, and support. Thankfully we do not have to begin from scratch. The United Nations took the first step with the Universal Declaration in 1948, formulating internationally defined norms to which all states and peoples could commit. These standards form the basis on which the study of human rights is rooted. Hence, this volume concludes with two documentary appendices. The first (Documentary Appendix A) reprints and references the leading instruments known as the International Bill of Human Rights. The second (Documentary Appendix B) identifies both the original and primary digital references for the many human rights and human rights related instruments that, in addition to the International Bill of Human Rights, specify the doctrines, principles, and rules upon which the world seeks to build a community respectful of human dignity.

Of course, whether the world is up to the task of building a world community respectful of human dignity remains to be seen. That it should try to do so, however, is imperative and beyond debate. A credible case for this view can be made by those who have seen its opposite. An Argentine judge who served on the court that convicted military rulers in his country for human rights violations between 1976 and 1983 has argued that it is time to view human rights from a global perspective. According to Justice Judge Antonio Bacqué,

> It has become obvious that technological idiocy, unbridled fanaticism and Realpolitik have pushed humanity, for the first time in its history, to the brink of a precipice where the mode and conditions of life are at risk. This danger may be averted only by paying unconditional respect to human dignity.[7]

We agree.

---

7. Supreme Court of Argentina, Buenos Aires, Judgment of June 22, 1987 (*Causa No. 547 incoada en virtue del Decreto No. 280/84 del Poder Ejecutivo Nacional*). Constitutionality of the Law of "Due Obedience," Justice Jorge Antonio Bacqué, dissenting. The full opinion is published in English in "Supreme Court of Argentina, Buenos Aires," *HRLJ* 8 (1987): 430–71.

Acknowledgments

As with our first two editions, we are greatly indebted to a number of very generous people—at The University of Iowa, the University of Maryland, the Vermont Law School, and the Blue Mountain Lake Center—who gave invaluably of their time, resourcefulness, and skill to the realization of this third edition. We cannot thank them enough. But we do gratefully and proudly acknowledge them here.

A number of colleagues and friends have served us grandly with valuable comments and other scholarly first aid, many of them users of the first two editions, some of them authors in this edition: George Andreopoulos, Anne Bayefsky, Ellen Dorsey, Patricia Weiss Fagan, Richard Falk, David Forsythe, Laurie Handrehan, Stephen Hansen, Hidetoshi Hashimoto, Rhoda Howard-Hassmann, Bernardo Issel, Edy Kaufman, Allen Keller, George Kent, Shulamith Koenig, Maivân Lâm, J. Paul Martin, Rachel Neild, Jordan Paust, Michael Ratner, Jon Van Dyke, Justin van Fleet, Richard Alan White, and Adrien Wing.

We importantly acknowledge, too, John Crees for his insightful and selfless compilation and composition of our filmography. John is living proof of the old truism that there are no limits to what one can accomplish when one cares not who gets the credit.

We are indebted also to Dean Emeritus N. William Hines and Dean Carolyn Jones of The University of Iowa College of Law and to Dean Geoffrey Shields, former Vice Dean Bruce Duthu, and Vice Dean Stephanie Willbanks of the Vermont Law School for availing us of indispensible research assistant support. Also deserving of grateful recognition are the law librarians of The University of Iowa College of Law, especially Mary Sexton, and of the Vermont Law School, especially Carl Yirka.

On final analysis, however, it is those selfless hands behind the scenes that make it possible for the play to go on, among them Konstanz Kuraz and Vassiliki Tsitsopoulou, each of whom volunteered their time in important ways on our behalf because of their passionate commitment to human dignity. To student research assistants and associates of the past two years years—Jonathan Amarilio, Anne Burmeister, Maureen De Armond, Megan Dempsey, Jessica Downs, Kara Hartzler, Amy Lammers, and Casie Shorey at The University of Iowa College of Law, and Gavin Boyles and Alexandra Goncalves at the Vermont Law School—we owe special thanks also. Their energy and enthusiasm supplied us not only with a satisfying endorsement of our enterprise, but, as well, with friendships about which we care deeply. Anne Burmeister and Kara Hartzler are particularly to be thanked for their diligence, creativity, and generosity in the early stages. Most of all, however, we thank Gavin Boyles and Jessica Downs for their extraordinarily acute, sensitive, and tireless help that went way beyond the proverbial call of duty. As a measure of their contributions and our appreciation of them, we pay them tribute by recognizing them on our title page. They deserve no less. And probably more.

Finally, we thank Grace Tully and Laura Gillen, Burns Weston's secretarial assistants at The University of Iowa College of Law and the Vermont Law School respectively, for coming to our rescue on countless occasions, always with a dedication, perfectionism, and smiles that are, quite simply, wonderful. Any eccentricities or errors in this volume, however, are our copyright alone.

In sum, we have been exceedingly lucky. To everyone mentioned, thank you. And to those authors on whom we leaned and from whom we gleaned much insight and wisdom, know that your work in the cause of human rights is profoundly appreciated and that we salute you.

Abbreviations

ACHR	American Convention on Human Rights
AIR SC	All India Reporter, Supreme Court
AU	African Union (formerly the Organization of African Unity or OAU)
AJIL	*American Journal of International Law*
APSR	*American Political Science Review*
ASIL	American Society of International Law
BYBIL	*British Yearbook of International Law*
CAT	Convention against Torture and Other Cruel, Inhuman or Degrading Treatment or Punishment; *also* Committee against Torture
CEDAW	Convention on the Elimination of All Forms of Discrimination against Women; *also* Committee on the Elimination of All Forms of Discrimination against Women
CERD	Committee on the Elimination of Racial Discrimination
CESCR	Committee on Economic, Social and Cultural Rights
CHR, UNCHR	United Nations Commission on Human Rights
CRC	Convention on the Rights of the Child; *also* Committee on the Rights of the Child
DFR	Declaration on Principles of International Law concerning Friendly Relations and Co-operation among States in Accord with the Charter of the United Nations
ECHR	European Convention on Human Rights and Fundamental Freedoms
ECOSOC	Economic and Social Council
EHRR	European Human Rights Reports
ESC	European Social Charter
ETS	European Treaty Series
EU	European Union
HHRJ	*Harvard Human Rights Journal*
HILJ	*Harvard International Law Journal*
HRC	Human Rights Committee
HRLJ	*Human Rights Law Journal*

HRQ	*Human Rights Quarterly*
ICC	International Criminal Court
ICCPR	International Covenant on Civil and Political Rights
ICERD	International Convention on the Elimination of All Forms of Racial Discrimination
ICESCR	International Covenant on Economic, Social and Cultural Rights
ICJ	International Court of Justice
ICRC	International Committee of the Red Cross
ICLQ	*International and Comparative Law Quarterly*
ILM	*International Legal Materials*
ILO	International Labour Organization
ILO CR	International Labour Organization Conventions and Recommendations 1919–66
IMF	International Monetary Fund
LNTS	League of Nations Treaty Series
OAS	Organization of American States
OASTS	Organization of American States Treaty Series
OAU	Organization of African Unity (now the African Union or AU)
OHCHR	Office of the High Commissioner for Human Rights
OJEC	Official Journal of the European Communities
TLCP	*Transnational Law and Contemporary Problems*
UDHR	Universal Declaration of Human Rights
UNDP	United Nations Development Programme
UNEP	United Nations Environment Programme
UNGA	United Nations General Assembly
UNHCHR	United Nations High Commissioner for Human Rights
UNHCR	United Nations High Commissioner for Refugees
UNSC	United Nations Security Council
UNTS	United Nations Treaty Series
USC	United States Code
VJIL	*Virginia Journal of International Law*
YBUN	*Yearbook of the United Nations*
YJIL	*Yale Journal of International Law*
WCED	World Commission on Environment and Development
WFS	World Food Summit
Weston and Carlson	Burns H. Weston and Jonathan C. Carlson, *International Law and World Order: Basic Documents*, 5 vols. (Ardsley, N.Y.: Transnational Publishers, 1994–).

What we must offer

is a vision of human rights

that is foreign to no one

and native to all.

—KOFI ANNAN

Part I
ISSUES

Chapter One

International Human Rights: Issues Overviews

THE idea of human rights has wings. It has found its way around the globe, and we are reminded often of its importance everywhere. On any given day, we are likely to be confronted by one or more news stories about individual heroics on behalf of human rights—at home and in every other reach of the world: Americans demanding better conditions for the homeless, adequate health insurance for all, and an end to torture on U.S. military bases near and far; Cuban citizens petitioning for free speech, fair elections, and the rule of democratic law; Brazilian and other indigenous peoples fighting to safeguard their native homelands against colonization and dispossession; Bulgarian women protesting international sex trafficking; Ukrainians standing up to corrupt autocracy in favor of political democracy; Indian and other children marching against abusive and exploitative child labor; Tibetan monks demonstrating against Chinese meddling with cherished customs; Burmese peasants challenging enslavement and forced labor by their military government to build a gas pipeline for a multinational corporation; Congolese women demanding an end to rape and other violence against women in war-torn central Africa; Sudanese minorities appealing—to anyone who will listen—for rescue from widespread atrocity in Darfur; and so forth. The fact that we increasingly classify such issues as human rights problems not only makes moral philosophers of us all but supports also the hunch that we are traversing a twenty-first century in which the idea of human rights shapes the aspirations of people no matter who or where they may be.

Even if human rights are on people's minds all over the world, however, the full realization of human rights worldwide is a distant dream. A truly just world order is not easily or quickly achieved. But the drive for social justice on a global scale, spurred by the experience of Nazi atrocity and ever more revealed in internationally defined human rights norms and procedures, persists nonetheless. As Adolfo Pérez Esquivel put it on receiving the Nobel Peace Prize as long ago as 1980, "The last few decades have seen a more extended and internationalized conscience in respect of human rights, such that we are confronted with and increasingly forced toward a deeper understanding of what the struggle for human rights means."[1]

1. Adolfo Pérez Esquivel, "Afterword," in Paul Williams ed., *The International Bill of Rights* (Glen Ellen, Calif.: Entwhistle Books, 1981), 105–8, at 105.

In this introductory chapter, we seek to provide a "deeper understanding of what the struggle for human rights means" by looking at the topic from four broad vantage points. First, we review human rights in the context of changing historical concepts and international law. Burns Weston, in the opening essay, explores the concept and content of human rights as the idea of human rights has evolved over the ages and especially since World War II. His underlying presupposition is that human rights, while having achieved widespread consensus about their meaning and application, are nonetheless not a corpus of fixed thought and action but, rather, a set of assumptions and choices that are open to constant rethinking because of ever evolving ideas, conditions, and needs. Second, and illustrating such rethinking, is an essay by Martha C. Nussbaum that introduces us to the "capabilities approach" to human rights, laying out a framework for understanding the Universal Declaration of Human Rights (UDHR)[2] in terms of the ways its provisions may be understood to enable people to achieve their individual promise and community-based potential. Her concern is to conceptualize and use human rights as a tool for empowerment, especially in the context of those "capabilities" that help to define what it means to be human.

Next, we look to the argument, prominent in the post-Cold War 1990s and early twenty-first century, between those who insist that local practices and traditions should determine the existence and scope of rights promised to individuals and groups versus those who contend that no amount of difference among diverse individuals and cultures should be allowed to obscure the essential universality of human rights. In his essay, "The Universality of Human Rights in a Multicultured World," Burns Weston asserts that proponents of the universality of human rights, a viewpoint to which he subscribes, cannot convincingly succeed without approaching cultural pluralism in a manner that is consistent with the core value of human rights: respect. To this end, he therefore posits a "methodology of respect" for the resolution of competing relativist-universalist claims. Finally, Rhoda Howard-Hassmann focuses on our rapidly changing global political economy captured by the term "globalization." In "The Second Great Transformation: Human Rights Leapfrogging in the Era of Globalization," she challenges us—as thinking, acting agents in world history—to consider the possible long-range human rights outcomes of globalization and particularly whether "The global human rights regime, and the global human rights process, can perhaps remedy some of the dangers of the global economic system."

All four of these readings are intended to provoke rather than soothe. The reader is urged to reflect, discuss, and debate after studying them critically and carefully, taking into account the questions posed at the end of each.

To deepen our understanding of the struggle for global justice, it is important to appreciate at the outset that international human rights bespeak, at bottom, a multidimensional program of legal and political struggle that takes human suffering seriously. As Weston's opening essay suggests, the term "international human rights," far from defining a static or monolithic state of affairs, is code language for a number of different—ever expanding, ever accelerating—initiatives: (a) an attack upon the concept of state sovereignty as traditionally conceived; (b) a goal-setting agenda for global policy; (c) a standard for assessing national behavior and therefore for judging political legitimacy; and (d) a spirited movement of concerned private individuals and groups that transcends political boundaries (an increasingly significant factor in international relations). Let us take an exploratory look at some aspects of these four meanings of international human rights.

2. Adopted Dec. 10, 1948, reprinted and referenced in Documentary Appendix A.

HUMAN RIGHTS AS A CHALLENGE TO STATE SOVEREIGNTY

International law, a complex process of authoritative and controlling decision operating across national and equivalent frontiers, exists, at a minimum, to maintain world order. To this end, by way of an interpenetrating medley of command and enforcement structures both internal and external to nation-states, classical international law has come to rely upon a variety of doctrines, principles, and rules to minimize interstate conflict and otherwise guarantee a world order system of separate territorial states.[3]

Many, if not most, of these doctrines, principles, and rules—and the institutions and procedures that apply them—have been altered in meaning, challenged in usage, and otherwise thrown into question by the field of international human rights. Consider, for example, the classical international law doctrine of state sovereignty and its corollary of nonintervention, the central props of our inherited state-centric system of world order. The values associated with this doctrine (a legal license to "do your own thing") and corollary (an injunction to "mind your own business") rest in uneasy balance with human rights concerns (which seem to tell us that "you are your brother's and sister's keeper"). The problem typically arises in the context of the question: Is it appropriate or inappropriate for one state to criticize or interdict the human rights performance of another?

During the 1970s and 1980s, South African diplomats from Pretoria protested when the case of Nelson Mandela (a black political leader long imprisoned because of his opposition to that country's practice of racial apartheid and discrimination) was publicized at the United Nations. They pointed to Article 2(7) of the UN Charter,[4] which says that the United Nations may not intervene "in matters which are essentially within the domestic jurisdiction of any state." Many countries use this ploy. The governments of China, Iran, Myanmar (Burma), Sudan, Syria, Zimbabwe, and others ritually call upon the doctrine of state sovereignty and the principle of nonintervention, particularly when they are on the defensive in respect of their international human rights obligations.[5] Those governments that abuse human rights (or are accused of doing so) typically plead for restraint, asking outsiders to refrain from interfering, directly or indirectly, individually or collectively, with their internal or external affairs.

The tension between the claims of those who criticize human rights violations and those who protest such interference was the topic of extended analysis by the late legal scholar Sir Hersch Lauterpacht of the United Kingdom. A dominant trend of the last half of the twentieth century, he observed, was one that involved the sovereign state yielding to the "sovereignty of humankind." In Lauterpacht's words,

---

3. It is useful in the human rights context especially to consider a modern, process-oriented definition of international law: "a Hydra-headed [transnational] process of social decision, involving persons at all levels and from all walks of public and private life who, with authority derived both explicitly and implicitly from community consensus or expectation, and supported by formal and informal sanction, effect those codes or standards of everyday conduct by which we plan and go about our lives." Burns H. Weston, "The Role of Law in Promoting Peace and Violence: A Matter of Definition, Social Values, and Individual Responsibility," in W. Michael Reisman and Burns H. Weston, eds., *Toward World Order and Human Dignity: Essays in Honor of Myres S. McDougal* (New York: Free Press, 1976), 114–31, at 117.
4. The UN Charter is excerpted in Documentary Appendix A.
5. Similarly, the government of the United States has invoked, at least by implication, Article 2(7) in defense of its continued imposition of capital punishment despite widespread international abandonment and condemnation of the practice. It may be asked whether this invocation of the doctrine of state sovereignty might not be also an example of the invocation of the doctrine of cultural relativism which the United States generally has opposed.

Insofar as the denial of fundamental human rights has been associated with the nation-state asserting the claim to ultimate reality and utterly subordinating the individual to a mystic and absolute personality of its own, the recognition of these rights is a brake upon exclusive and aggressive nationalism, which is the obstacle, both conscious and involuntary, to the idea of a world community under the rule of law.[6]

This claim is readily understood when we note some of the major historical trends upon which Lauterpacht relied.

With the inception of the modern state system in the mid-seventeenth century, the relation of citizen ("subject") to government was seen to fall within the exclusive jurisdiction of the territorial state, although absolute sovereignty was by no means an historical accident. Religious jealousies and rivalry between kingdoms made the 1600s a century fraught with war, including one of the most destructive civil and international wars in the annals of human history: the Thirty Years War (1618–48). This calamity led princes and potentates to decide that the cycle of violence had to be broken; the territorial integrity of kingdoms had to be insulated from interference from without.[7]

The sixteenth-century French social and political philosopher Jean Bodin (1530?-1596) is best remembered for giving the notion of state sovereignty its classic formulation: The sovereign prince exercises power simply and absolutely and cannot be subject to the commands of another, for it is the sovereign prince who makes the law for the subject. It is only by voluntary agreement that the sovereign can incur an obligation from abroad.

So conceived, the late seventeenth-century world of nation-states would provide each kingdom with a defense of absolute power to overcome the centrifugal forces of jealousy and threat from without. Of course, though this new safety barrier between nations served the cause of human rights by reducing arbitrary killings based on religious and political rivalries, it also was an arrangement that suited well the interests of European monarchs who sought to expand their power often at the expense—indeed the abuse—of their subjects.

Yet, just as the pre-seventeenth-century forces of political centrifugalism provided the counterpoint of sovereign absolutism, so also did the unchecked and commonly abusive displays of sovereign absolutism provoke their own counterpoint. As Weston points out in his opening essay, the philosophy of natural rights associated with John Locke and others began to take hold in much of Enlightenment Europe and America before the nineteenth century. Against unlimited claims of power in the guise of "the divine right of kings," philosophers began to speak of natural rights. In this spirit, Thomas Jefferson wrote from Paris to James Madison: "A bill of rights is what the people are entitled to against every government on earth."[8] Jefferson's Lockean turn of mind made him realize that natural rights were of limited value if they were not reflected in the fundamental structure of a nation's laws. It was not until after World War II—after the rise and fall of Nazi Germany—that the doctrine of state sovereignty changed dramatically, taking its most radical turn since the Peace of Westphalia (1648) when the state system first emerged. In *Beyond Sovereignty*, Marvin Soroos notes that, in stark contrast to an earlier reverence for the state sovereignty doctrine that "discouraged outside efforts to intervene on behalf of populations victimized by

6. Hersch Lauterpacht, *International Law and Human Rights* (New York: Garland, 1973), 47.
7. James A. Caporaso, "Changes in the Westphalian Order: Territory, Public Authority, Sovereignty," in James A Caporaso, ed., *Continuity and Change in the Westphalian Order* (Malden, Mass.: Blackwell, 2000), 1–28.
8. Thomas Jefferson, *Writings of Thomas Jefferson*, ed. Paul Leicester Ford, 10 vols. (New York: G.P. Putnam, 1892–99), 4: 477.

even the most cruel and tyrannical of rulers,"[9] the defense of unrestricted sovereignty was increasingly challenged during the twentieth century, "especially in the aftermath of revelations of the horrors of the atrocities committed by the Nazis against the Jews during World War II, which led many commentators to conclude that state sovereignty was not an absolute principle, but rather was subject to certain limitations in regard to human rights."[10]

In short, as Weston makes clear, human rights came of age as a legitimate international concern with the close of World War II, the founding of the United Nations, and the adoption of the Universal Declaration of Human Rights by the UN General Assembly in 1948,[11] and as a consequence such weighty issues as the proper limits of state sovereignty came to occupy a central place on the agendas of most governments and international institutions. Since World War II and its immediate aftermath, individuals have become subjects of international concern, not only as the charges of a sovereign state, but directly and in their own right; and on this radical foundation the scaffolding of contemporary international human rights law and policy has been erected. It is a modern structure, cantilevered and often fundamentally at odds with the classical international law doctrine of state sovereignty. No longer can it be said, in the early twenty-first century, that the state may treat its own citizens however it may wish, unaccountable to the international community beyond. No longer can it be said internationally that "the king can do no wrong." Whatever perception may have prevailed when the Westphalian system first gave rise to the notion of state sovereignty in the mid-seventeenth century, today that notion clearly carries with it the obligation of a state to protect the welfare of its own people and to meet its obligations to the wider international community.

HUMAN RIGHTS AS AN AGENDA FOR PREFERRED WORLD POLICY

The field of international human rights has achieved the comprehensive and elevated global status of preferred world public policy. It supplies a framework for a world order of human dignity.

Such is the thesis, at any rate, of international human rights scholars Myres S. McDougal, Harold Lasswell, and Lung-chu Chen, who have led the way in urging others to facilitate the development of global policy with reference to the values that "are being ever more insistently expressed in the rising common demands . . . of people everywhere"[12] and that consequently supply the menu for global human rights study and action. Demands for *respect* (insisting, for example, on nondiscrimination), for *power* (reflected in appeals for wider political participation), and for *wealth* (including calls to accumulate and employ wealth for productive developmental purposes) are among the more obviously important value demands recognized. But also important and sometimes primary are those relating to *enlightenment* (involving the enjoyment of knowledge and information), *well-being* (embracing

9. Marvin S. Soroos, *Beyond Sovereignty: The Challenge of Global Policy* (Columbia: University of South Carolina Press, 1987), 230.
10. Ibid. See generally Paul Gordon Lauren, *The Evolution of International Human Rights: Visions Seen*, 2nd ed. (Philadelphia: University of Pennsylvania Press, 2003).
11. See generally Aryeh Neier, *Taking Liberties: Four Decades in the Struggle for Rights* (New York: Public Affairs, 2003).
12. Myres S. McDougal, Harold Lasswell, and Lung-chu Chen, *Human Rights and World Public Order: The Basic Policies of an International Law of Human Dignity* (New Haven, Conn.: Yale University Press, 1980), 90.

assurances of individual and group health and survival), *skills* (for example, seeking to opti-
mize talents and to overcome handicaps), *affection* (including the freedom to give and
receive loyalty to groups of one's choice), and *rectitude* (requiring, optimally, a public order
in which one can act responsibly for the common interest). Human rights, conceived in
terms of these eight values, involve the underlying concerns of a world public order of
human dignity, and they delineate the focus for intellectual inquiry and appraisal in the field
we have come to call human rights. According to McDougal and his colleagues, we live in
an era characterized by "an overriding insistence, transcending all cultures and climes,
upon the greater production and wider distribution of all basic values, accompanied by
increasing recognition that a world public order of human dignity can tolerate wide differences in the specific practices by which values are shaped and shared, so long as all
demands are effectively appraised and accommodated in terms of common interest."[13]

Complementing the eight values underlying the human rights world of McDougal,
Lasswell, and Chen is a more reductive model that concentrates on three sets of values.
Described by Weston in his essay in this chapter and referred to throughout this book, the
model invokes the notion of three accumulating "generations" of human rights elaborated
by French human rights specialist Karel Vasak[14] and tracking the French revolutionary
slogan: *liberté, égalité, et fraternité*. The civil and political rights of pre-nineteenth-century
origin belong to the first (*liberté*) generation. The economic, social, and cultural rights sur-
facing largely in the last one hundred years comprise the second (*égalité*) generation. The
third generation of rights, which is currently emerging from both the rise and decline of
the nation-state in the dawning of the twenty-first century, parallels the notion of *fraternité* (and *sororité*). The notion is born of the kinship and indispensable solidarity of men
and women everywhere—for example, claims of right to political and economic self-
determination; claims of right to the "common heritage of [hu]mankind"; claims of right
to a clean and healthy global environment; and claims of right to national and international peace. Of course, the three-generations perspective is not meant to undermine the
holistic nature of the human rights agenda. Nor is it meant to suggest that one set of rights
is more important than the other or to deny that all human rights are inextricably interconnected and interdependent. Rather, the generational categories simply draw attention
to the sequence whereby the agenda has evolved and to the range and scope of human
needs that are linked to human rights.

The connections among law, politics, and values implied by the global human rights
agenda relative to human needs have stimulated considerable scholarly analysis by such
philosophers as Martha C. Nussbaum, Henry Shue, and Amartya Sen, and such social
scientists as Michael Freeman, Adamantia Pollis, and Peter Schwab.[15] Johan Galtung and
Anders Helge Wirak also have elaborated a model of human values linked to human needs

---

13. Ibid., 6. See also Jonathan Glover, *Humanity: A Moral History of the Twentieth Century* (New Haven,
Conn.: Yale University Press, 1999).
14. Karel Vasak, "A 30-Year Struggle: The Sustained Efforts to Give Force of Law to the Universal
Declaration of Human Rights," *UNESCO Courier* (Nov. 1977): 29–32. See the related analysis by Stephen
P. Marks: "The Peace-Human Rights-Development Dialectic," *Bulletin of Peace Prosposals* 4 (1980): 339–
47; "Emerging Human Rights: A New Generation for the 1980s?" *Rutgers Law Review* 33 (1981):
435–52.
15. See Martha C. Nussbaum, *Sex and Social Justice* (New York: Oxford University Press, 1999); Henry
Shue, *Basic Rights: Subsistence, Affluence, and U.S. Foreign Policy* (Princeton, N.J.: Princeton University
Press, 1996); Amartya Sen, *Poverty and Famines: An Essay on Entitlement and Deprivation* (Oxford:
Oxford University Press, 1981), and "Justice Across Borders," in Pablo De Greiff and Ciaran Cronin,
eds., *Global Justice and Transnational Politics* (Cambridge, Mass.: MIT Press, 2002), 37–52; Michael Freeman, *Human Rights: An Interdisciplinary Approach* (Cambridge: Polity Press, 2002); Adamantia Pollis
and Peter Schwab, eds., *Human Rights: Cultural and Ideological Perspectives* (New York: Praeger, 1979).

and concepts of rights that is particularly useful in the analysis of economic and political development.[16] Their model is set out in the introduction to Chapter 3 of this text, where it helps guide our thoughts about basic human needs relative to second- and third-generation human rights, with special attention to issues vital to developing countries, the particular focus of the annual United Nations *Human Development Report*. The official responsible for the UN Report, Sakiko Fukuda-Parr, noted that "while human rights are rooted in the concept of human dignity, human development is rooted in the concept of 'capability and function'— the valuable things that a person can do."

This practical action-based perspective focuses on what people are able to do to improve their lot under diverse conditions. The special concern of the second essay in this chapter is to introduce us to Nussbaum's "capabilities approach" to human rights, which is helpful in assessing development efforts, welfare, and quality of life issues. The utility of the "capabilities approach" becomes evident when we look at a political system such as that under Taliban-ruled Afghanistan where women had a nominal right of freedom of movement, without having the right in the sense of capability; for example they were routinely threatened with violence should they leave the home unaccompanied by a man, a circumstance said to be justified by local culture.

Not everyone agrees on the importance of cultural difference in relation to global human rights standards. Adamantia Pollis and Peter Schwab, for example, have forcefully argued that efforts to paper over differences from society to society with rhetoric about universal human rights is bound to generate skepticism and frustration. In "Human Rights: A Western Construct with Limited Applicability," they rely on theories of cultural relativism to assert that

> The cultural patterns, ideological underpinnings and developmental goals of non-Western and socialist states are markedly at variance with the prescriptions of the Universal Declaration of Human Rights. Efforts to improve the Declaration as it currently stands not only reflect a moral chauvinism and ethnocentric bias but are also bound to fail.[17]

An unintended political result of reliance upon cultural relativism, however, is that the notions associated with it can easily give comfort to tyrants who justify abusive practices by virtue of historical sanction in local custom: for example, amputation of limbs as punishment for crime in some countries or the cruel practice of "female genital mutilation" in others. The complex problems of universal versus local standards of civility have been carefully explored by researchers associated with the Sudanese legal scholar Abdullahi Ahmed An-Na`im in *Human Rights in Cross Cultural Perspectives*.[18] They seek to explore human rights issues in anthropological terms through multiple viewpoints, both cross-cultural and indigenous, in a quest for consensus. An-Na`im acknowledges that universalizing western concepts can serve (and historically in his native Africa has served) as a tool for colonial

16. Johan Galtung and Anders Helge Wirak, "Human Needs and Human Rights—A Theoretical Approach," *Bulletin of Peace Proposals* 1 (1977): 251–58.
17. Adamantia Pollis and Peter Schwab, "Human Rights: A Western Construct with Limited Applicability" in *Human Rights: Cultural and Ideological Perspectives*, note 15, at 14. Cf. Micheline R. Ishay, *The History of Human Rights: From Ancient Times to the Era of Globalization* (Berkeley: University of California Press, 2004).
18. Abdullahi Ahmed An-Na`im, ed., *Human Rights in Cross Cultural Perspectives: A Quest for Consensus* (Philadelphia: University of Pennsylvania Press, 1991). See also Abdullahi An-Na`im and Francis M. Deng, eds., *Human Rights in Africa: Cross Cultural Perspectives* (Washington, D.C.: Brookings Institution, 1990). Cf. Makau Mutua, *Human Rights: A Political and Cultural Critique* (Philadelphia: University of Pennsylvania Press, 2002).

penetration. He acknowledges as well that cultural relativism has been used by some African, Asian, and Latin American rulers to justify their domination and abuse of the people. The comparable conclusion has been offered by the Japanese scholar Yoshikazu Sakamoto: "Both Western universalism and non-Western specificity are capable of being distorted in such a way as to prevent international application of human rights."[19]

In his essay on this topic presented in this chapter as Reading 3, Burns Weston addresses these issues with special attention to theories of justice in the cross-cultural setting. He asserts both that cultural diversity does not alone convincingly serve as justification for failure or refusal to honor internationally defined human rights and that the international law of human rights as ordinarily espoused does not alone convincingly serve as justification for failure or refusal to honor cultural diversity. In "The Universality of Human Rights in a Multicultural World: Toward Respectful Decision-Making," he relies on the "policy-oriented approach" of McDougal, Lasswell, and Chen and the "veil of ignorance" perspective of John Rawls to provide a framework within which to accept or reject cultural claims favoring exemptions from universal standards.[20] Weston's objective is to lay out the elements of a methodology that treats diverse cultural claims respectfully and demonstrates that cross-cultural decision-making bearing on human rights issues—the relativist-universalist debate in this instance—can by no means be a "simpleminded affair." Dialogue across cultures and societies is an essential component of any international project and brings to life every single major human rights covenant, convention, and declaration containing a nondiscrimination clause, including Article 3 of the UN Charter on which this positive law and norm is premised. Article 3 states that a major purpose of the organization is to achieve and promote respect for human rights and fundamental freedoms for all without discrimination as to race, sex, language, and religion. Indeed, abhorrence of all kinds of unfair and unequal treatment of people pervades the entire field of the international law of human rights—a leitmotif—and sets up important barriers to claiming that culturally based customs justify discrimination irrelevant to merit and need.

HUMAN RIGHTS AS A STANDARD FOR ASSESSING NATIONAL BEHAVIOR

In an essay surveying positive international human rights law, Theo C. van Boven, former Director of the UN Division of Human Rights, correctly notes that the mandate extended to the UN Commission on Human Rights in 1946 to prepare an "international bill of rights" was inspired by, among other things, "the desire to establish a comprehensive system for the promotion and protection of human rights."[21] The resulting 1948 UDHR, the 1966 International Covenant on Economic, Social and Cultural Rights (ICESCR),[22] and 1966

19. Yoshikazu Sakamoto, "Human Rights Are Universal," *UNESCO Courier* 6 (Aug.–Sept. 1982): 19–22. This issue is extensively analyzed by Alison Dundes Renteln, *International Human Rights: Universalism Versus Relativism* (Newbury Park, Calif.: Sage, 1990). See also Joanne R. Bauer and Daniel A. Bell, *The East Asia Challenge for Human Rights* (Cambridge: Cambridge University Press, 1999).
20. For related and contrasting views, see John Rawls, *A Theory of Justice* (Cambridge, Mass.: Harvard University Press, 1971). Cf. William F. Schultz, *In Our Own Interest: How Defending Human Rights Benefits Us All* (Boston: Beacon Press, 2002); Alan Dershowitz, *Rights from Wrongs: The Origin of Human Rights in the Experience of Injustice* (New York: Basic Books, 2004).
21. Theo C. van Boven, "Survey of the Positive Law of Human Rights," in Karel Vasek, ed., *The International Dimensions of Human Rights*, 2 vols., rev. and ed. Philip Alston (Westport, Conn.: Greenwood Press for UNESCO, 1982), 1: 85–110, at 87.
22. Concluded Dec. 19, 1966, reprinted and referenced in Documentary Appendix A.

International Covenant on Civil and Political Rights (ICCPR),[23] which together have come to be called the international bill of rights, went a long way toward this end.

But these trailblazing instruments were clearly only the beginning, not the end, of international human rights law-making in the United Nations and elsewhere. Supplementing the Universal Declaration and the two covenants, in the years preceding and since, have been literally scores of other human rights conventions (treaties) and law-making declarations less well known to the general public but nonetheless representative, in their totality, of what is considered the international *"corpus juris* of social justice."[24] These include, *but are not limited to,* treaties that fall into the following four categories of human rights instruments:[25]

1. General conventions, which concern all or a large portion of human rights and adopted at the global or regional level.
2. Topically specific conventions, which are intended to guard against particular human rights abuses, e.g., genocide, war crimes, and crimes against humanity, slavery, traffic in persons, forced labor, and torture.
3. Conventions on group protection, which correspond to the special needs of distinct groups, such as children, indigenous peoples, migrants, refugees, stateless persons, women, workers, and combatants, prisoners, and civilians in time of armed conflict.
4. Conventions prohibiting discrimination, based on race or sex, and in education, employment, and occupation.

In van Boven's words, "International human rights law," since World War II especially, "has been developing in an unprecedented way and has become a very substantive part of international law as a whole."[26]

Proof that international human rights law "has become a very substantive part of international law as a whole," serving as a standard against which to measure national behavior, is found, of course, in the human rights protestations of states, international governmental institutions, transnational professional associations, corporations, trade unions, churches, nongovernmental organizations (NGOs), and others who variously respond to distress signals from abroad on the basis of these instruments. Mindful that human rights assessments can be politically as well as juridically significant because they can appreciably enhance or detract from the legitimacy upon which governments depend to retain and exercise power, all of these actors believe themselves to be, particularly in this age of relatively easy access to the Internet and other sophisticated communications technologies, more or less free to

---

23. Concluded Dec. 19, 1966, reprinted and referenced in Documentary Appendix A.
24. Van Boven, "Survey of the Positive Law," note 21, at 88.
25. Starting with the American Declaration on the Rights and Duties of Man (March 30-May 2, 1948), referenced in Documentary Appendix B, and shortly thereafter the UDHR, a lengthy list of declarations and resolutions has shaped and defined the content of fundamental rights. While declarations and resolutions, adopted by such international organizations as the United Nations or the Organization of American States (OAS), do not always give rise to "rights" in the positive law sense that treaties are said to do, they invariably contain "rights" in the aspirational sense that are expected to be respected globally and consequently afford a basis for evolving standards of *customary* international human rights law. For convenient sources of international human rights instruments, including declarations and resolutions as well as treaties, see Documentary Appendixes A and B. See also United Nations, Office of the High Commissioner for Human Rights, *International Human Rights Instruments* (New York: United Nations Publications, 2004) (hereafter *UN Instruments*), Available on the UN Web site: http://www.unhchr.ch/html/intinst.htm and on CD-ROM, *Human Rights: A Compilation of International Instruments*, UN Sales # E.03.XIV.6. Additionally, see Burns H. Weston and Jonathan C. Carlson, eds., *International Law and World Order: Basic Documents*, 5 vols. (Ardsley, N.Y.: Transnational Publishers, 1994–), esp. vol. 3.
26. Van Boven, "Survey of the Positive Law of Human Rights," note 21, at 87.

criticize governments for their human rights failings and to use state assent to treaties and other sources of international human rights law as the warrant of their disapproval.

Fault-finding, however, can be a dangerous enterprise, marred by dogmatism and self-righteousness and consequently capable of exacerbating international tensions in the most severe ways. International human rights law, therefore, ought not to be invoked for the imposition of one set of values to the detriment of others. With the advent of improved international communications, global politics is a highly pluralized debate, and that debate includes the issue of how, in a world of diverse cultures, basic demands for human dignity can be satisfied while simultaneously accommodating widely differing views of what human dignity means. It is well to be skeptical of the popular wisdom that internationally prescribed human rights are common to all cultural traditions and adaptable to a great variety of social systems and structures.[27] As Michael Freeman reminds us, human rights universalism has to compete with "the view that there are different cultural interpretations of human rights."[28]

Still, while no political regime is without its shortcomings where human rights performance is concerned, neither is any political regime today inclined to disavow intentionally prescribed human rights standards—at least not publicly—as if to confirm La Rochefoucauld's wise observation that "hypocrisy is the homage which vice pays to virtue." Even though the human rights achievements of different political regimes vary and even though they do not yet represent the realization of a comprehensive conception of human dignity, the human rights standards that have been adopted internationally have become a major feature of the world's political landscape. These standards, representing the most inclusive recognition of rights possible within the political, ideological, and cultural constraints of our current global system, reflect a consensus among states as to the existence of certain minimal individual and group rights within their respective jurisdictions, rights that member states of the UN have agreed to recognize, promote, and protect, and for which, therefore, the states are properly held accountable. Today, the legitimacy of political regimes—hence their capacity to rule non-coercively—is judged less by the old standards of divine right, revolutionary heritage, national destiny, or charismatic authority, and more by new standards informed and refined by the language of international human rights.

HUMAN RIGHTS AS A POPULIST WORLDWIDE MOVEMENT INFLUENCING INTERNATIONAL RELATIONS

In concluding that international human rights law has been generated largely in response to "political or social concerns of a widely-felt character," Theo van Boven cites the work of many NGOs.[29] The persistent pressure of Amnesty International on the UN General Assembly to adopt a Convention against Torture and Other Cruel, Inhumane, or Degrading Treatment or Punishment, for example, or of the American Jewish Committee to win the General Assembly's acceptance of a Declaration on the Elimination of All Forms of Intolerance and of Discrimination Based on Religion or Belief, for another, lends credence to the

27. See Jack Donnelly, *Universal Human Rights*, 2nd ed. (Ithaca, N.Y.: Cornell University Press, 2002); Rhoda E. Howard and Jack Donnelly, "Human Dignity, Human Rights, and Political Regimes," *APSR* 80 (Sept. 1986): 801–18. For a vigorous reply to the authors' thesis that internationally defined human rights require the existence of a liberal regime, followed by a spirited rejoinder by the authors, see Nell Mitchell, "Liberalism, Human Rights and Human Dignity," *APSR* 81 (Sept. 1987): 921–27.
28. Freeman, *Human Rights*, note 15, at 103.
29. Van Boven, "Survey of the Positive Law of Human Rights," note 21, at 88.

conclusion that international human rights law has been greatly advanced by global popular support. In van Boven's words, "one of the specific traits of international human rights law is that this branch of international law extends well beyond the domain of international judicial decisions and intergovernmental practice."[30] It is directly influenced and advanced by an international movement; and as states and the United Nations fall short in the defense of human rights, as James Avery Joyce has written, "it is the non-governmental groups who are steadily forming a global if not yet systematized movement of investigation, protest and reform."[31] Such groups, in no way bound by the norms of nonintervention applicable to states, maximize the free flow of information across borders, spreading the word on human rights violators. While governments dally with "quiet diplomacy," nongovernmental human rights groups turn up the volume on complaints to "mobilize shame" in the relationship of offender states to the world community and to enlist world public opinion against egregious rights violations.[32] Such human rights interest groups have proliferated and continue to do so.

In the decades since 1945, the cold war, nationalism, and power politics have largely undermined any expectation that states would police each other, and that the United Nations would somehow enforce and protect internationally defined human rights. But NGOs have begun to fill the gap. Claude E. Welch, Jr., who has written extensively about NGOs, reports that the number of "conventional" NGOs, which stood at 973 in 1956, has roughly doubled each decade since.[33] International groups such as Amnesty International and strictly national groups such as the Cambodian Health and Human Rights Network or the Ethiopian Professionals Action Group, for example, use the politics of information gathering and advocacy to maximize the free flow of information across borders, spreading the word on human rights violations around the globe. All of these organizations greatly increase the numbers of people worldwide who are engaged in human rights activities. The international law of human rights has, in other words, an attentive global constituency.

These human rights interest groups are also diverse. They include trade unions and business organizations, professional societies, single-issue and policy reform groups, political organizations, and ethnic, ideological, and religious entities. A minority deal exclusively in the human rights field. Most are human rights "part-timers," special purpose groups that make human rights activities a significant but not exclusive part of their concerns: trade unions and political parties as well as religious organizations (such as the Simon Weisenthal Center, the Human Rights Office of the National Council of Churches in Korea, Pax Romana, the International Movement of Catholic Lawyers, the Society of Friends, the International Human Rights Program of the Disciples of Christ, and so forth). Indeed, the humanitarian concerns of various churches, including Bahá'í, Buddhist, Hindu, and Muslim groups, have drawn their faithful into promoting human rights through action as well as through education. As one observer of the international human rights movement, José Zalaquett, has remarked, "a union, by virtue of its own nature, will have the central objective to advance the interest and labor rights of its members; a political party will aspire, by definition, to

30. Ibid., 110.
31. James Avery Joyce, *The New Politics of Human Rights* (New York: St. Martin's Press, 1978), chap. 3, "Mobilization of Shame," 79. See also Robert F. Drinan, S.J., *The Mobilization of Shame: A World View of Human Rights* (New Haven, Conn.: Yale University Press, 2001); Claude E. Welch, Jr., ed., *NGOs and Human Rights: Promise and Performance* (Philadelphia: University of Pennsylvania Press, 2002).
32. For pertinent discussion, see Reading 31 by Richard Pierre Claude in Chapter 8 of this volume.
33. Welch, *NGOs and Human Rights*, note 31, at 1 (quoting from the Union of International Associations, *Yearbook of International Organizations 1996–97*, available at http://www.uia.org/uiastats).

political power; any given church will not regard the task of defending and promoting human rights as necessarily its exclusive or central programme."[34]

In fact, however, numerous trade unions and political parties and church groups do have goals and programs that touch significantly upon human rights concerns as a matter of routine. As Zalaquett himself observes, many such organizations, with memberships and affiliations crossing national frontiers, have in recent years reformulated existing projects or started new ones using the language of human rights or invoking international standards. Many of these and equivalent transnational groups, such as the American Association for the Advancement of Science, have incorporated human rights objectives into their scheme of goals, and many have institutionalized these interests by setting up human rights offices to monitor the problems of their counterparts, confreres, or co-religionists in distant lands.[35]

This proliferation and diversification of human rights groups lends support, logically, to a new perspective on international relations. This new viewpoint emphasizes the significance of nonstate actors and rejects the conventional wisdom of international law and relations defined exclusively or nearly exclusively by the behavior of states and of international organizations composed of states. Modern communication and transportation technologies have made the classical notion of world politics obsolete. Territorial boundaries, however much bolstered by doctrines of sovereignty, are no longer impregnable—indeed, they are downright porous. Drugs, pollutants, illegal aliens, and terrorists manage to get through these boundaries, to be sure; but so too, and more importantly in the long run, does information. No longer does the world consist of independent sovereign states, impenetrable to anything but the influence of other states in direct proportion to the size and resources of such other states (what British international relations theorist John W. Burton has called "billiard-ball-like states").[36]

Many view some features of the new international relations format as favorable to international human rights. According to Abid Hussain of India, former Special Rapporteur of the UN Commission on Human Rights on the Promotion and Protection of the Right to Freedom of Opinion and Expression, global communication via the Internet has been beneficial for human rights, transforming "the lives of people, including those who have previously been ignored by societies or disinherited of their rights."[37] By delivering cheap access to information, and by providing forums for debate in countries where the media are monopolized, the Internet offers the disenfranchised an opportunity to participate in solutions to their own misery. The Internet can be used to mobilize people locally. For example, electronic mail campaigns against corruption influenced Korea's 1999 elections and played a key role in publicizing the scandals that ultimately deposed President Joseph Estrada of the Philippines in 2000. E-mail and the Internet can also surmount international barriers.

---

34. José Zalaquett, *The Human Rights Issue and the Human Rights Movement* (Geneva: Commission of the Churches on International Affairs, World Council of Churches, 1981), 30–31. See also Pontifical Commission, "Justicia et Pax," *The Church and Human Rights*, Working Paper 1 (Vatican City, 1975); Lutheran World Federation, *Theological Perspectives on Human Rights: Report of an LWF Consultation on Human Rights* (Geneva: Lutheran World Federation, 1977).

35. See, e.g., Richard Pierre Claude, *Science in the Service of Human Rights* (Philadelphia: University of Pennsylvania Press, 2002), chap. 10, "Emerging Governance Among Transnational Organizations," 178–96.

36. In Michael Banks, "The International Relations Discipline: Asset or Liability for Conflict Resolution?" in Edward A. Azar and John W. Burton, eds., *International Conflict Resolution: Theory and Practice* (Boulder, Colo.: Lynne Rienner, 1986), 5–27, at 18–19. See also R. J. Vincent, *Human Rights and International Relations* (Cambridge: Cambridge University Press, 1986).

37. Steven Hick, Edward F. Halpin, and Eric Hoskins, eds., *Human Rights and the Internet* (New York: St. Martin's Press, 2000), x.

NGOs, working within and outside countries with tyrannical regimes, can use communications technology to bypass government control and communicate directly with ordinary citizens to send data on human rights violations to concerned NGOs overseas. Where governments exert tight control over Internet use by their own citizens, as in Vietnam or Burma, web sites communicate with expatriate communities, sympathetic foreign audiences, and also with internal groups who are able to access the Internet illegally by dialing out of the country using mobile telephony. The United Nations Human Development Report estimates that in 2005 one billion people have access to the Internet, although distribution shows the North greatly advantaged over the South.[38] The *Report* comments: "Connecting a major portion of the population will be a challenge in developing regions. But the digital divide need not be permanent if technological adaptations and institutional innovations expand access."[39]

Twenty-first-century conditions have rushed us into a new, more interconnected world of far reaching rapid change that scholars and activists call "globalization," a term that refers to, inter alia, the interaction of information technology and the global economy.[40] Globalization spans not only the growing interdependence of economic relations—trade, investment, finance, and the organization of production globally—but also social and political interactions among organizations and individuals across the world. As the modern Internet and the worldwide web proved popular by the turn of the century, it became tempting, especially for those who overlooked the "digital divide," to see technological developments as the key to understanding the meaning of change in our time and to deciphering its historical direction as both benign and inevitable.[41] Rhoda E. Howard-Hassmann gives pause to such optimism in her contribution to this volume (Reading 4): "The Second Great Transformation: Human Rights Leapfrogging in the Era of Globalization." She brings insight and prudent scepticism to these issues in a wide ranging exercise in "scenario analysis" that helps readers envision alternative futures, both benign and adverse for the prospect of human rights in the context of globalization. A grand speculative inquiry addressed to the future, her essay is concerned with our shrinking world, ever more interdependent environmentally,

---

38. United Nations, "Today's Technological Transformation—Creating the Network Age," in *Human Development Report, 2001* (New York: Oxford University Press for the United Nations Development Programme, 2001), chap. 2, 35.

39. Responding to fears that the Internet will not serve less developed countries, OneWorld, an NGO, and the Dutch development aid agency, Hivos, have joined forces to help organizations based in developing countries to use the Internet for sustainable development and human rights. The initiative includes helping hundreds of South-based NGOs to go online, connect to sources of support and training, and to build online gateways promoting regional perspectives from civil society in Africa, Latin America, and South Asia. In a comparable initiative, in 2004, the University Human Rights Network headquartered in São Paulo, Brazil, began publishing *SUR*, an international journal on human rights designed to promote scholarly interchange in the Southern Hemisphere and to do so by making it *fully* available in English, Spanish, and Portuguese on the Internet at http://www.Surjournal.org. From the extreme top of the home page, select "English | Español | Português."

40. The literature on "globalization" is vast. It is also contentious and multidisciplinary. See, e.g., Zbigniew Brzezinski, *The Choice: Global Domination or Global Leadership* (New York: Basic Books: 2004); Steve Chan and James R. Scarritt, *Coping with Globalization: Cross-National Patterns in Domestic Governance and Policy Performance* (Portland, Ore.: Frank Cass, 2002); Ian Clark, *Globalization and International Relations Theory* (Oxford: Oxford University Press, 1999); Pablo De Greiff and Ciaran Cronin, eds., *Global Justice and Transnational Politics* (Cambridge, Mass.: MIT Press, 2002); Richard A. Falk, *Human Rights Horizons: The Pursuit of Justice in a Globalizing World* (New York: Routledge, 2000) and *Predatory Globalization: A Critique* (New York: Polity Press, 1999); Carol C. Gould, *Globalizing and Democracy and Human Rights* (Cambridge: Cambridge University Press, 2004); Mahmood Monshipouri, Neil Englehart, Andrew J. Nathan, and Kavita Philip, eds., *Constructing Human Rights in the Age of Globalization* (Armonk, N.Y.: M.E. Sharpe, 2003).

41. See Hick, Halpin, and Hoskins, *Human Rights and the Internet*, note 37.

economically, politically, culturally, and socially. Her thesis—that the effects of globalization, so understood, may take on positive or negative connotations depending upon what we make of them—challenges us to take responsibility for whether our growing interconnectivity will nurture a global community committed to humane governance and shared human rights for all or whether, instead, it will produce an Orwellian scenario of centralized control of the levers of technology by self-serving elites tied to a nightmare process of enriching the North while impoverishing the South. Of course, there are alternative futures in between, beneficial, adverse, and mixed. The question is: have we the imagination and will to choose and shape wisely?

In Howard-Hassmann's view, globalization is inevitable, neither good nor bad in and of itself, but good or bad or in between depending upon how we respond to it. If globalization is to be directed toward positive ends, we have at hand, she argues, a powerful tool in contemporary international human rights law. Astutely applied to policy processes in a globe webbed by networks of interconnected and interconnecting state and nonstate actors, the human rights cause can benefit greatly. In the context of politics as an integrated process operating in a single community, states constitute an important subsystem in the global social community. But they are by no means the only, or even the principal, actors. Nonstate actors, such as human rights NGOs, have significant influences on the international scene. If gross violations of human rights in one part of the globe drive refugees in unmanageable numbers elsewhere in search of asylum, human rights groups, sometimes more reliably than governments, may send the early warning signals. Church groups may supply essential sanctuary despite government apathy or hostility. Private organizations and research institutions may supply the most reliable accounts of the social costs of these and similar events. And all those involved will have the capacity to allocate blame and urge responsibility for the displaced.

The idea of human rights, then, has talons as well as wings. It increasingly shapes the aspirations of people around the globe. However, new issues linked to globalization raise questions about whether human rights can not only shape aspirations of people world wide but also fulfill them.

In 2000, heads of state and government gathered in New York to mark the dawn of the new millennium by reaffirming faith in the goals of the UN Charter and to resolve that the evolving processes of globalization should become a positive force for everyone.[42] In 2004, following up on the Millennium Declaration, the World Commission on the Social Dimension of Globalization, an independent creation of the International Labor Organization (ILO), issued an in-depth assessment of globalization and reported, inter alia, that, in the long run, globalization harbors, potentially, an ever-widening commitment to shared humane values that "can be channeled to build enlightened and democratic governance in the interests of all."[43] However, in the short run, the Report warned, while established and emerging market economies are clearly creating unprecedented wealth as a result of their new interconnectedness, "too few countries and peoples are sharing in [the] benefits" and "the revolution in global communications heightens awareness of [the] disparities." All of which leaves us, at the very least, with a wide range of issues at the global level that need urgently to be addressed. Whether or not international human rights law and policy can succeed at playing a constructive and moderating role when facing these issues cannot yet be told. But taking into account the ensuing contributions of Weston, Nussbaum, and Howard-Hassmann is a good place to begin.

42. United Nations Millennium Declaration (Sept. 8, 2000), referenced in Documentary Appendix B.
43. Report of the World Commission on the Social Dimension of Globalization, *A Fair Globalization: Creating Opportunities for All* (Geneva: International Labor Organization, 2004), x.

1. BURNS H. WESTON, *Human Rights: Concept and Content*

It is a common observation that human beings everywhere demand the realization of diverse values or capabilities to ensure their individual and collective well-being. It also is a common observation that this demand is often painfully frustrated by social as well as natural forces, resulting in exploitation, oppression, persecution, and other forms of deprivation. Deeply rooted in these twin observations are the beginnings of what today are called "human rights" and the national and international legal processes that are associated with them.

HISTORICAL DEVELOPMENT

The expression "human rights" is relatively new, having come into everyday parlance only since World War II, the founding of the United Nations in 1945, and the adoption by the UN General Assembly of the Universal Declaration of Human Rights in 1948.[1] It replaced the phrase "natural rights," which fell into disfavour in part because the concept of natural law (to which it was intimately linked) had become a matter of great controversy; and it replaced as well the later phrase "the rights of Man," which was not universally understood to include the rights of women.

ORIGINS IN ANCIENT GREECE AND ROME

Most students of human rights trace the origins of the concept to ancient Greece and Rome, where it was closely tied to the doctrines of the Stoics, who held that human conduct should be judged according to, and brought into harmony with, the law of nature. A classic example of this view is given in Sophocles' play *Antigone*, in which the title character, upon being reproached by King Creon for defying his command not to bury her slain brother, asserted that she acted in accordance with the immutable laws of the gods.

In part because Stoicism played a key role in its formation and spread, Roman law similarly allowed for the existence of a natural law and with it—pursuant to the *jus gentium* ("law of nations")—certain universal rights that extended beyond the rights of citizenship. According to the Roman jurist Ulpian, for example, natural law was that which nature, not the state, assures to all human beings, Roman citizens or not.

It was not until after the Middle Ages, however, that natural law became associated with natural rights. In Greco-Roman and medieval times, doctrines of natural law concerned mainly the duties, rather than the rights, of "Man." Moreover, as evidenced in the writings of Aristotle and St. Thomas Aquinas, these doctrines recognized the legitimacy of slavery and serfdom and, in so doing, excluded perhaps the most important ideas of human rights as they are understood today—freedom (or liberty) and equality.

For the idea of human rights qua natural rights to gain general recognition, therefore, certain basic societal changes were necessary, changes of the sort that took place gradually, beginning with the decline of European feudalism from about the thirteenth century and continuing through the Renaissance to the Peace of Westphalia (1648). During this period, resistance to religious intolerance and political and economic bondage; the evident failure of rulers to meet their obligations under natural law; and the unprecedented commitment to individual expression and worldly experience that was characteristic of the Renaissance all combined to shift the conception of natural law from *duties* to *rights*. The teachings of Aquinas and Hugo Grotius on the European continent, and the Magna Carta (1215), the Petition of Right of 1628, and the English Bill of Rights (1689) in England, were proof of this change. Each testified to the increasingly popular view that human beings are endowed with certain eternal and inalienable rights that never were renounced when humankind "contracted" to enter the social from the primitive state and never diminished by the claim of the "divine right of kings."

1. Adopted Dec. 10, 1948, reprinted and referenced in Documentary Appendix A.

NATURAL LAW TRANSFORMED INTO NATURAL RIGHTS

The modern conception of natural law as meaning or implying natural rights was elaborated primarily by thinkers of the seventeenth and eighteenth centuries. The intellectual—and especially the scientific—achievements of the seventeenth century (including the materialism of Hobbes, the rationalism of Descartes and Leibniz, the pantheism of Spinoza, and the empiricism of Bacon and Locke) encouraged a belief in natural law and universal order; and during the eighteenth century, the so-called Age of Enlightenment, a growing confidence in human reason and in the perfectibility of human affairs led to the more comprehensive expression of this belief. Particularly important were the writings of John Locke, arguably the most important natural-law theorist of modern times, and the works of the eighteenth-century philosophes centred mainly in Paris, including Montesquieu, Voltaire, and Jean-Jacques Rousseau. Locke argued in detail, mainly in writings associated with the English Revolution of 1688 (the "Glorious Revolution"), that certain rights self-evidently pertain to individuals as human beings (because these rights existed in "the state of nature" before humankind entered civil society); that chief among them are the rights to life, liberty (freedom from arbitrary rule), and property; that, upon entering civil society, humankind surrendered to the state—pursuant to a "social contract"—only the right to enforce these natural rights and not the rights themselves; and that the state's failure to secure these rights gives rise to a right to responsible, popular revolution. The philosophers, building on Locke and others and embracing many and varied currents of thought with a common supreme faith in reason, vigorously attacked religious and scientific dogmatism, intolerance, censorship, and social and economic restraints. They sought to discover and act upon universally valid principles governing nature, humanity, and society, including the inalienable "rights of Man," which they treated as a fundamental ethical and social gospel.

Not surprisingly, this liberal intellectual ferment exerted a profound influence in the Western world of the late eighteenth and early nineteenth centuries. Together with the Revolution of 1688 in England and the resulting Bill of Rights, it provided the rationale for the wave of revolutionary agitation that swept the West, most notably in North America and France. Thomas Jefferson, who had studied Locke and Montesquieu, gave poetic eloquence to the plain prose of the seventeenth century in the Declaration of Independence, proclaimed by the 13 American colonies on July 4, 1776: "We hold these truths to be self-evident, that all men are created equal, that they are endowed by their Creator with certain unalienable Rights, that among these are Life, Liberty and the Pursuit of Happiness." Similarly, the marquis de Lafayette, who won the close friendship of George Washington and who shared the hardships of the U.S. War of Independence, imitated the pronouncements of the English and American revolutions in the Declaration of the Rights of Man and of the Citizen of August 26, 1789, proclaiming that "men are born and remain free and equal in rights" and that "the aim of every political association is the preservation of the natural and imprescriptible rights of man."

In sum, the idea of human rights, though known by another name, played a key role in late eighteenth- and early nineteenth-century struggles against political absolutism. It was, indeed, the failure of rulers to respect the principles of freedom and equality that was responsible for this development.

"NONSENSE UPON STILTS": THE CRITICS OF NATURAL RIGHTS

The idea of human rights as natural rights was not without its detractors, however. In the first place, because it was frequently associated with religious orthodoxy, the doctrine of natural rights became less attractive to philosophical and political liberals. Additionally, because they were conceived in essentially absolutist terms, natural rights were increasingly considered to conflict with one another. Most importantly, the doctrine of natural rights came under powerful philosophical and political attack from both the right and the left.

In England, for example, conservative political thinkers such as Edmund Burke and David Hume united with liberals such as Jeremy Bentham to condemn the doctrine, the former out of fear that public affirmation of natural rights would lead to social upheaval, the latter out of concern lest declarations and proclamations of natural rights substitute for effective legislation. In his *Reflections on the Revolution in France* (1790),

Burke—a believer in natural law who nonetheless denied that the "rights of Man" could be derived from it—criticized the drafters of the Declaration of the Rights of Man and of the Citizen for proclaiming the "monstrous fiction" of human equality, which, he argued, serves but to inspire "false ideas and vain expectations in men destined to travel in the obscure walk of laborious life." Bentham, one of the founders of Utilitarianism, was no less scornful. "Rights," he wrote, "is the child of law; from real law come real rights; but from imaginary laws, from 'law of nature,' come imaginary rights. . . . Natural rights is simple nonsense; natural and imprescriptible rights (an American phrase) . . . [is] rhetorical nonsense, nonsense upon stilts." Agreeing with Bentham, Hume insisted that natural law and natural rights are unreal metaphysical phenomena.

This assault upon natural law and natural rights intensified and broadened during the nineteenth and early twentieth centuries. John Stuart Mill, despite his vigorous defense of liberty, proclaimed that rights ultimately are founded on utility. The German jurist Friedrich Karl von Savigny, England's Sir Henry Maine, and other "historicalist" legal thinkers emphasized that rights are a function of cultural and environmental variables unique to particular communities. The English jurist John Austin argued that the only law is "the command of the sovereign" (a phrase of Hobbes). And the logical positivists of the early twentieth century insisted that the only truth is that which can be established by verifiable experience and that therefore ethical pronouncements are not cognitively significant. By World War I, there were scarcely any theorists who would defend the "rights of Man" along the lines of natural law. Indeed, under the influence of nineteenth-century German Idealism and parallel expressions of rising European nationalism, there were some—the Marxists, for example—who, though not rejecting individual rights altogether, maintained that rights, from whatever source derived, belong to communities or whole societies and nations preeminently.

THE PERSISTENCE OF THE NOTION

Although the heyday of natural rights proved short, the idea of rights nonetheless endured. The abolition of slavery, the implementation of factory legislation, the rise of popular education and trade unionism, the universal suffrage movement—these and other examples of nineteenth-century reformist impulses afford ample evidence that the idea was not to be extinguished, even if its a priori derivation had become a matter of general skepticism. But it was not until the rise and fall of Nazi Germany that the idea of human rights truly came into its own. Many of the gruesome atrocities committed by the Nazi regime had been officially authorized by Nazi laws and decrees, and this fact convinced many that law and morality cannot be grounded in any purely Idealist or Utilitarian or other consequentialist doctrine. Certain actions, according to this view, are absolutely wrong, no matter what the circumstances; human beings are entitled to simple respect, at least.

Today, the vast majority of legal scholars and philosophers—particularly in the liberal West—agree that every human being has, at least in theory, some basic rights. Indeed, except for some essentially isolated late nineteenth-century and early twentieth-century demonstrations of international humanitarian concern to be noted below, the last half of the twentieth century may fairly be said to mark the birth of the international as well as the universal recognition of human rights. In the charter establishing the United Nations, for example, all member states pledged themselves to take joint and separate action for the achievement of "universal respect for, and observance of, human rights and fundamental freedoms for all without distinction as to race, sex, language, or religion." In the Universal Declaration of Human Rights, representatives from many cultures endorsed the rights therein set forth "as a common standard of achievement for all peoples and all nations." And in 1976, the International Covenant on Economic, Social and Cultural Rights and the International Covenant on Civil and Political Rights, each approved by the UN General Assembly in 1966, entered into force and effect.[2]

DEFINING HUMAN RIGHTS

To say that there is widespread acceptance of the principle of human rights is not to say that there is complete agreement about the nature

2. Each of these documents is reprinted and referenced in Documentary Appendix A.

and scope of such rights—which is to say, their definition. Among the basic questions that have yet to receive conclusive answers are the following: whether human rights are to be viewed as divine, moral, or legal entitlements; whether they are to be validated by intuition, culture, custom, social contract, principles of distributive justice, or as prerequisites for happiness; whether they are to be understood as irrevocable or partially revocable; and whether they are to be broad or limited in number and content.

THE NATURE OF HUMAN RIGHTS: COMMONLY ACCEPTED POSTULATES

Despite this lack of consensus, a number of widely accepted (and interrelated) postulates can assist in the task of defining human rights. Five in particular stand out, though not even these are without controversy.

First, regardless of their ultimate origin or justification, human rights are understood to represent both individual and group demands for political power, wealth, enlightenment, and other cherished values or capabilities, the most fundamental of which is respect and its constituent elements of reciprocal tolerance and mutual forbearance in the pursuit of all other such values or capabilities. Consequently, human rights imply both claims against persons and institutions impeding the realization of these values or capabilities, and standards for judging the legitimacy of laws and traditions. At bottom, human rights qualify state sovereignty and power, sometimes expanding the latter even while circumscribing the former (as in the case of certain economic and social rights, for example; see *Égalité* below).

Second, human rights are commonly assumed to refer, in some vague sense, to "fundamental," as distinct from "nonessential," claims or "goods." In fact, some theorists go so far as to limit human rights to a single core right or two—for example, the right to life or the right to equal freedom of opportunity. The tendency is to emphasize "basic needs" and to rule out "mere wants."

Third, reflecting varying environmental circumstances, differing worldviews, and inescapable interdependencies within and between different value or capability systems, human rights refer to a wide continuum of claims, ranging from the most justiciable to the most aspirational. Human rights partake of both the legal and the moral orders, sometimes indistinguishably. They are expressive of both the "is" and the "ought" in human affairs.

Fourth, most assertions of human rights—though arguably not all—are qualified by the limitation that the rights of individuals or groups in particular instances are restricted as much as is necessary to secure the comparable rights of others and the aggregate common interest. Given this limitation, which connects rights to duties, human rights are sometimes designated prima facie rights, so that ordinarily it makes little or no sense to think or talk of them in absolutist terms.

Finally, if a right is determined to be a human right, it is understood to be quintessentially general or universal in character, in some sense equally possessed by all human beings everywhere, including in certain instances even the unborn. In stark contrast to the divine right of kings and other such conceptions of privilege, human rights extend in theory to every person on Earth, without discriminations irrelevant to merit or need, simply for being human.

In several critical respects, however, all these postulates raise more questions than they answer. Granted that human rights qualify state power, do they also qualify private power? If so, when and how? What does it mean to say that a right is fundamental, and according to what standards of importance or urgency is it so judged? What is the value of embracing nonjusticiable rights as part of the jurisprudence of human rights? Does it harbor more than rhetorical significance? If so, how? When and according to what criteria does the right of one person or group of people give way to the right of another? What happens when individual and group rights collide? How are universal human rights determined? Are they a function of culture or ideology, or are they determined according to some transnational consensus of merit or value? If the latter, is the consensus regional or global? How exactly would such a consensus be ascertained, and how would it be reconciled with the right of nations and peoples to self-determination? Is the existence of universal human rights incompatible with the notion of national sovereignty? Should supranational norms, institutions, and procedures have the power to nullify local, regional, and national laws on capital punishment, corporal punishment of children, "honor killing," veil wearing, female genital cutting, male circumcision, the claimed right to bear arms, and other practices? How would such a situation comport with Western conceptions of democracy and representative government?

In other words, though accurate, the five foregoing postulates are fraught with questions about the content and legitimate scope of human rights and about the priorities, if any, that exist among them. Like the issue of the origin and justification of human rights, all five are controversial.

THE CONTENT OF HUMAN RIGHTS: THREE "GENERATIONS" OF RIGHTS

Like all normative traditions, the human rights tradition is a product of its time. Therefore, to understand better the debate over the content and legitimate scope of human rights and the priorities claimed among them, it is useful to note the dominant schools of thought and action that have informed the human rights tradition since the beginning of modern times.

Particularly helpful in this regard is the notion of three "generations" of human rights advanced by the French jurist Karel Vasak. Inspired by the three themes of the French Revolution, they are: the first generation of civil and political rights (*liberté*); the second generation of economic, social, and cultural rights (*égalité*); and the third generation of solidarity rights (*fraternité*). Vasak's model is, of course, a simplified expression of an extremely complex historical record, and is not intended to suggest a linear process in which each generation gives birth to the next and then dies away. Nor is it to imply that one generation is more important than another. The three generations are understood to be cumulative, overlapping, and, it is important to note, interdependent and interpenetrating.

Liberté: Civil and Political Rights

The first generation of civil and political rights derives primarily from the seventeenth- and eighteenth-century reformist theories noted above (i.e., those associated with the English, American, and French revolutions). Infused with the political philosophy of liberal individualism and the related economic and social doctrine of

laissez-faire, the first generation conceives of human rights more in negative terms ("freedoms from") than positive ones ("rights to"); it favors the abstention over the intervention of government in the quest for human dignity. Belonging to this first generation, thus, are rights such as those set forth in Articles 2–21 of the Universal Declaration of Human Rights, including freedom from gender, racial, and equivalent forms of discrimination; the right to life, liberty, and security of the person; freedom from slavery or involuntary servitude; freedom from torture and from cruel, inhuman, or degrading treatment or punishment; freedom from arbitrary arrest, detention, or exile; the right to a fair and public trial; freedom from interference in privacy and correspondence; freedom of movement and residence; the right to asylum from persecution; freedom of thought, conscience, and religion; freedom of opinion and expression; freedom of peaceful assembly and association; and the right to participate in government, directly or through free elections. Also included are the right to own property and the right not to be deprived of it arbitrarily—rights that were fundamental to the interests fought for in the American and French revolutions and to the rise of capitalism.

Yet it would be wrong to assert that these and other first-generation rights correspond completely to the idea of "negative" as opposed to "positive" rights. The right to security of the person, to a fair and public trial, to asylum from persecution, and to free elections, for example, manifestly cannot be assured without some affirmative government action. What is constant in this first-generation conception is the notion of liberty, a shield that safeguards the individual— alone and in association with others—against the abuse of political authority. This is the core value. Featured in the constitution of almost every country in the world and dominating the majority of international declarations and covenants adopted since World War II, this essentially Western liberal conception of human rights is sometimes romanticized as a triumph of the individualism of Thomas Hobbes and John Locke over Hegelian statism.

Égalité: Economic, Social, and Cultural Rights

The second generation of economic, social, and cultural rights originated primarily in the socialist tradition, which was foreshadowed among adherents of the Saint-Simonian movement of early nineteenth-century France and variously promoted by revolutionary struggles and welfare movements that have taken place since. In large part, it is a response to the abuses of capitalist development and its underlying and essentially uncritical conception of individual liberty, which tolerated, and even legitimized, the exploitation of working classes and colonial peoples. Historically, it is a counterpoint to the first generation of civil and political rights, conceiving of human rights more in positive terms ("rights to") than in negative ones ("freedoms from") and requiring more the intervention than the abstention of the state for the purpose of assuring the equitable production and distribution of the values or capabilities involved. Illustrative are some of the rights set forth in Articles 22–27 of the Universal Declaration of Human Rights, such as the right to social security; the right to work and to protection against unemployment; the right to rest and leisure, including periodic holidays with pay; the right to a standard of living adequate for the health and well-being of self and family; the right to education; and the right to the protection of one's scientific, literary, and artistic production.

But in the same way that all the rights embraced by the first generation of civil and political rights cannot properly be designated "negative rights," so all the rights embraced by the second generation of economic, social, and cultural rights cannot properly be labeled "positive rights." For example, the right to free choice of employment, the right to form and to join trade unions, and the right to participate freely in the cultural life of the community (Articles 23 and 27) do not inherently require affirmative state action to ensure their enjoyment. Nevertheless, most of the second-generation rights do necessitate state intervention because they subsume demands more for material than for intangible goods according to some criterion of distributive justice. Second-generation rights are, fundamentally, claims to social equality. However, partly because of the comparatively late arrival of socialist-communist and compatible "Third World" influence in international affairs, the internationalization of these rights has been relatively slow in coming, and with free-market capitalism in ascendancy under the banner of globalization at the turn of the twenty-first century, it is not likely that these rights will come of age any time soon. On the other hand, as the social inequities created by unregulated national and transnational capitalism become more and more evident over time and are not accounted for by explanations based on gender or race, it is probable that the demand for second-generation rights will grow and mature, and in some instances even lead to violence. This tendency is apparent already in the evolving European Union and in wider efforts to regulate intergovernmental financial institutions and transnational corporations to protect the public interest.

Fraternité: Solidarity Rights

Finally, the third generation of solidarity rights, while drawing upon and reconceptualizing the demands associated with the first two generations of rights, is best understood as a product of both the rise and the decline of the nation-state in the last half of the twentieth century. Foreshadowed in Article 28 of the Universal Declaration of Human Rights, which proclaims that "everyone is entitled to a social and international order in which the rights set forth in this declaration can be fully realized," this generation appears so far to embrace six claimed rights. Three of these rights reflect the emergence of Third World nationalism and its "revolution of rising expectations" (i.e., its demand for a global redistribution of power, wealth, and other important values or capabilities): the right to political, economic, social, and cultural self-determination; the right to economic and social development; and the right to participate in and benefit from "the common heritage of mankind" (shared Earth and space resources, scientific, technical, and other information and progress, and cultural traditions, sites, and monuments). The other three third-generation rights—the right to peace, the right to a healthy and sustainable environment, and the right to humanitarian disaster relief—suggest the impotence or inefficiency of the nation-state in certain critical respects.

All six of these rights tend to be posed as collective rights, requiring the concerted efforts of all social forces, to a substantial degree on a planetary scale. However, each of them also manifests an individual dimension. For example, while it may be said to be the collective right of all countries and peoples (especially developing countries and non-self-governing peoples) to secure a "new international economic order" that would eliminate obstacles to their economic and social development, so also may it be said to be the individual right of every person to benefit from a developmental policy that is based on the satisfaction of material and nonmaterial human needs. It is important to note too that the majority of these solidarity rights are more aspirational than justiciable in character, and that their status as international human rights norms remains ambiguous.

Thus, at various stages of modern history, the content of human rights has been broadly defined not with any expectation that the rights associated with one generation would or should become outdated upon the ascendancy of another, but expansively or supplementally. The history of the content of human rights reflects evolving perceptions of which values or capabilities stand, at different times, most in need of responsible attention and, simultaneously, humankind's recurring demands for continuity and stability.

LEGITIMACY AND PRIORITY: LIBERTÉ VERSUS ÉGALITÉ

The fact that the content of human rights has been broadly defined should not be taken to imply that the three generations of rights are equally acceptable to everyone. Nor should it suggest that they or their separate elements have been greeted with equal urgency. The debate about the nature and content of human rights reflects, after all, a struggle for power and for favoured conceptions of the "good society."

First-generation proponents, for example, are inclined to exclude second- and third-generation rights from their definition of human rights altogether or, at best, to regard them as "derivative." In part this is because of the complexities involved in putting these rights into operation. The suggestion that first-generation rights are more feasible because they stress the absence over the presence of government is somehow transformed into a prerequisite of a comprehensive definition of human rights, such that aspirational claims to entitlement are deemed not to be rights at all. The most compelling explanation, however, has more to do with ideology or politics. Persuaded that egalitarian claims against the rich, particularly where collectively espoused, are unworkable without a severe decline in liberty and equality, first-generation proponents, inspired by the natural law and laissez-faire traditions, are partial to the view that human rights

are inherently independent of organized society and are individualistic.

Conversely, second- and third-generation defenders often look upon first-generation rights, at least as commonly practiced, as insufficiently attentive to material—especially "basic"—human needs and, indeed, as instruments in service to unjust social orders, hence constituting a "bourgeois illusion." Accordingly, if they do not place first-generation rights outside their definition of human rights, they tend to assign such rights a low status and to treat them as long-term goals that will come to pass only after the imperatives of economic and social development have been met, to be realized gradually and fully achieved only sometime vaguely in the future.

This liberty-equity and individualist-collectivist debate was especially evident during the period of the Cold War, reflecting the extreme tensions that then existed between Liberal and Marxist conceptions of sovereign public order. Although Western social democrats during this period, particularly in Scandinavia, occupied a position midway between the two sides, pursuing both liberty and equity—in many respects successfully—it remains true that the different conceptions of rights contain the potential for challenging the legitimacy and supremacy not only of one another, but, more importantly, of the sociopolitical systems with which they are most intimately associated.

THE RELEVANCE OF CUSTOM AND TRADITION

With the end of the Cold War, however, the debate took on a more North-South character and was supplemented by a cultural-relativist critique that eschews the universality of human rights doctrines, principles, and rules on the grounds that they were Western in origin and therefore of limited relevance in non-Western settings. The viewpoint underlying this assertion—that the scope of human rights in any given society is fundamentally determined by local, national, or regional customs and traditions—may seem problematic, especially when one considers that the idea of human rights and many of its precepts are found in all the great philosophical and religious traditions. Nevertheless, the historical development of human rights demonstrates that it cannot be wholly mistaken. Nor is it surprising that it should emerge soon after the end of the Cold War. First prominently expressed at an Asian preparatory meeting to the second UN World Conference on Human Rights convened in Vienna in June 1993, it reflects the end of a bipolar system of alliances that had discouraged independent foreign policies and minimized cultural and political differences in favour of undivided Cold War loyalties. Against the backdrop of increasing human rights interventionism on the part of the UN and by regional organizations and deputized coalitions of states (as in Bosnia and Herzegovina, Somalia, Liberia, Rwanda, Haiti, and Serbia, including Kosovo, for example), the viewpoint serves as well as a functional equivalent of the doctrine of respect for national sovereignty and territorial integrity, which had been declining in influence not only in the human rights context but as well in the contexts of national security, economics, and the environment. As a consequence, there remains sharp disagreement about the legitimate scope of human rights and about the priorities that are claimed among them.

INHERENT RISKS IN THE DEBATE

On final analysis, however, this legitimacy-priority debate can be dangerously misleading. Although useful for pointing out how notions of liberty and individualism have been used to rationalize the abuses of capitalism and Western expansionism and how notions of equality, collectivism, and culture have been alibis for authoritarian governance, in the end it risks obscuring at least three essential truths that must be taken into account if the contemporary worldwide human rights movement is to be objectively understood.

First, one-sided characterizations of legitimacy and priority are very likely, at least over the long term, to undermine the political credibility of their proponents and the defensibility of the rights they regard as preeminently important. In an increasingly interdependent global community, any human rights orientation that does not support the widest possible shaping and sharing of values or capabilities among all human beings is likely to provoke widespread skepticism. The last half of the twentieth century is replete with examples.

Second, such characterizations do not accurately reflect reality. In the real world, virtually all societies, whether individualistic or collectivist in essential character, consent to, and even promote, a mixture of all basic values or capabilities. President Franklin Delano Roosevelt's Four Freedoms (freedom of speech and expression, freedom of worship, freedom from want, and freedom from fear) is an early case in point. A more recent demonstration is found in the Declaration and Programme of Action of the Vienna conference mentioned above, adopted by representatives of 171 states. It proclaims that, "[w]hile the significance of national and regional particularities and various historical, cultural and religious backgrounds must be borne in mind, it is the duty of States, regardless of their political, economic and cultural systems, to promote and protect all human rights and fundamental freedoms."

Finally, none of the international human rights instruments currently in force or proposed says anything about the legitimacy or priority of the rights it addresses, save possibly in the case of rights that by international covenant are stipulated to be "nonderogable" and therefore, arguably, more fundamental than others (e.g., freedom from arbitrary or unlawful deprivation of life, freedom from torture and from inhuman or degrading treatment and punishment, freedom from slavery, and freedom from imprisonment for debt). To be sure, some disagreements about legitimacy and priority can derive from differences of definition (e.g., what is "torture" or "inhuman treatment" to one may not be so to another, as in the case of punishment by caning or by death). Similarly, disagreements also can arise when treating the problem of implementation. For instance, some insist first on certain civil and political guarantees, whereas others defer initially to conditions of material well-being. Such disagreements, however, reflect differences in political agendas and have little if any conceptual utility. As confirmed by numerous resolutions of the UN General Assembly and reaffirmed in the Vienna Declaration and Programme of Action,[3] there is a growing consensus that all human rights form an indivisible whole and that the protection of human rights is not and should not be a matter of purely national jurisdiction. The extent to which the international community actually protects the human rights it prescribes, on the other hand, is a different matter.[4]

---

3. Adopted June 25, 1993, referenced in Documentary Appendix B.
4. This discussion is continued in Reading 23 by Burns Weston in Chapter 5 of this volume.

QUESTIONS FOR REFLECTION AND DISCUSSION

1. Members of indigenous cultures in Africa and elsewhere believe that individual rights do not exist independently of a group structure; witness the Xhosa saying, "umntu ngumntu ngabantu" (a person is a person because of other people). Other, including Marxist, societies agree. Judeo-Christian and Islamic societies contend, on the other hand, that individual rights and duties are derived from divine sanction or nature. Given such radically different assumptions about the origins of rights, is it possible for the world's cultures to arrive at mutually comprehensible human rights accords? Indeed, might it not be argued that the individualistic ontology of the contemporary West has led not only to the development of individual human rights, but also to the abrogation of those rights by the West among peoples who do not share the same precepts?

2. Why is it important to inquire into the nature and scope of human rights? Do the following two statements by Burns Weston provide any guidance?

> [I]f a right is determined to be a human right it is quintessentially general or universal in character, in some sense equally possessed by human beings everywhere, including in certain instances even the unborn.

> [T]he legitimacy of different human rights and the priorities claimed among them are necessarily a function of context. Because different people located in different parts of the world both assert and honor different human rights demands according to many different procedures and practices, these issues ultimately depend on time, place, institutional setting, level of crisis, and other circumstance.

Can these two statements be reconciled? Does the latter statement imply that the universalist project reflected in the former is illegitimate?

3. If, as Weston contends, human rights "qualify state power" and, in addition to being "quintessentially universal," are "fundamental" in character, addressing needs rather than "mere wants," why is it considered permissible to place limits on them? Consider, for example, Article 29 of the Universal Declaration of Human Rights (UDHR) and Article 4 of the International Covenant on Civil and Political Rights (ICCPR), each reprinted in Documentary Appendix A. By the same token, under what circumstances, if any, is it permissible to sit by while human rights are violated?

4. It has been argued that the idea of universally applicable human rights is essentially a modernist idea, and that cultural relativism and contextuality critiques have undermined its theoretical foundations. If, as Andrei Sakharov once wrote, "The defense of human rights is a clear path toward the unification of people in our turbulent world," might one not rightly object that this "defense" is on the (offensive) march as, for example, Makau Mutua has done in *Human Rights: A Political and Cultural Critique* (Philadelphia: University of Pennsylvania Press, 2002)? Might the "defense" of human rights in fact result in a new imperialism, albeit one imposed with the best of intentions? How might traditional modernist notions of universal human rights be reimagined to respond to this critique? See, in this connection, Jack Donnelly, *Universal Human Rights in Theory and Practice*, 2nd ed. (Ithaca, N.Y.: Cornell University Press, 2002).

5. Are economic, social, and cultural rights really "rights"? Is it better to think of these second-generation "rights" as social "goals"? Why? Why not? See Reading 13 by Asbjørn Eide in Chapter 3 of this volume.

6. If economic, social, and cultural rights are rights, is the right to property—important in the liberal West and proclaimed in Article 17 of the Universal Declaration of Human Rights (UDHR)—among them? If so, why is it not recognized in the International Covenant on Economic, Social and Cultural Rights (ICESCR)? Is it because economic, social, and cultural rights really are not rights after all and that the right to property should be treated the same as life and liberty and thus be considered among first-generation civil and political rights? If so, why is the right to property also not recognized in the International Covenant on Civil and Political Rights (ICCPR)? Is it because civil and political rights are not really "rights" either and that they, too, are better thought of as social "goals"? If so, is the right to property a right?

7. Are so-called "communitarian" or "solidarity" (third-generation) rights really "rights"? Or is it better to think of them as social "goals"? Why? Why not? Consider Philip Alston, "A

Third Generation of Solidarity Rights: Progressive Development or Obfuscation of International Human Rights Law?" *Netherlands International Law Review* 29 (1992): 307–22, at 322:

> In many respects the concept of third generation rights smack rather too strongly of a tactical endeavor to bring together, under the rubric of human rights, many of the most pressing concerns on the international agenda and to construct an artificial international consensus in favour of human rights by appealing to the "favorite" concerns of each of the main geopolitical blocs. . . . In sum, the concept of third generation solidarity rights would seem to contribute more obfuscation than clarification in an area which can ill afford to be made less accessible to the masses than it already is.

Consider also the conundrum posed in Question 6, above, and reflect upon how your answers to it compare with Professor Alston's observation.

8. It has been suggested that there exists a "fourth generation" of human rights consisting of women's rights, the rights of future generations, rights of access to information, and the right to communicate. Does this make sense? Is a "fourth generation" of human rights a valid category of rights? If so, how is it defined, what other rights might be included, and would it pose redundancy with certain first, second, or third generation rights? John Locke (1632–1704) once suggested in inevitably dated language that everyone has "property in his own person" and that "nobody has a right but to himself." Does it make sense to expand the notion of property rights to rights in one's person? Would such an expansion make property rights redundant with other rights? How might your answer to this question affect your answer to the issue of a "fourth generation" of rights? Is possible redundancy necessarily a liability?

9. In "The International Human Rights Movement: Part of the Problem?" *HHRJ* 15 (1999): 101–25, at 108, David Kennedy has argued that the human rights movement has achieved a level of hegemony that has effectively crowded out other, possibly more effective, modes of understanding, communicating, and acting. Kennedy also notes that human needs not framed in the vocabulary of the human rights movement often go unattended. Do you agree? If so, with which? And why? How might the human rights movement respond to Kennedy's critique? Consider Reading 2 by Martha Nussbaum, next in this chapter.

10. Is it possible and/or desirable to set a hierarchy of rights or categories of rights? Should economic, social, and cultural rights be secured before civil and political rights? Before solidarity rights? The other way around? Some other sequence? Why? Why not?

11. Former Indian Prime Minister Indira Gandhi once said that "it is not individuals who have rights but states." Do you agree? Disagree? What arguments can you make for this assertion? Is the claim that the state is a substitute for the traditional communal group—ergo the embodiment of the people—sufficient to justify the statement?

12. Where do human rights come from and for whom are they intended? In *The End of Human Rights: Critical Legal Thought at the Turn of the Century* (Oxford: Hart, 2000), Costas Douzinas comments that "it is not so much that humans have rights but that rights make human" (372). This implies, Douzinas notes, that the granting and/or denial of rights results in a hierarchy of humanity, with those at the bottom accorded few rights and those at the top many or more. Does this reflect an understanding of what rights are that is meaningfully different from Weston's rationale for human rights, which, as stated in Reading 1, is essentially in agreement with that of Rhoda Howard (now Howard-Hassman) in *Human Rights and the Search for Community* (Boulder, Colo.: Westview Press, 1995): "Human rights are rights that one holds merely by virtue of being human" (1). Which rationale for the justification of human rights makes the most sense to you? Why? Or do you agree with Michael Freeman, *Human Rights: An Interdisciplinary Approach* (Cambridge: Polity Press, 2002) that it is not enough to say that human beings possess human rights simply for being human because "It is not clear why one has any rights simply because one is a human being" (61)? If you agree with Freeman, what theoretical rationale for human rights do you propose? Given that human rights are presumed to be, in Weston's words, "quintessentially universal in character," bear in mind the importance (necessity?) of a rationale to which all peoples and cultures can subscribe. Is such a rationale or theory possible?

13. In *The End of Human Rights* Douzinas also comments that the twentieth century "has witnessed more violations of [human rights] principles than any of the previous and less 'enlightened' epochs" (2). He goes on to ask whether this gap between the theory and practice of human rights should lead us to question the principles of human rights. What do you think?

2. MARTHA C. NUSSBAUM *Capabilities, Human Rights, and the Universal Declaration*

On December 10, 1948, forty-eight states voted for the Universal Declaration of Human Rights (UDHR).[1] The rhetorical consensus on this enunciation of human aspirations in the language of rights was consolidated on the Universal Declaration's twentieth anniversary, when the first United Nations International Conference on Human Rights, meeting in Teheran in 1968, proclaimed the Declaration to express "a common understanding of the peoples of the world concerning the inalienable and inviolable rights of all members of the human family and constitutes an obligation for the members of the international community."[2] For the Universal Declaration's 45th anniversary, the second UN World Conference on Human Rights, meeting in Vienna in 1993, proclaimed the text to constitute "a standard of achievement for all peoples and all nations."[3] More significant is the vast array of international conventions and national constitutions that refer explicitly to the Declaration and purport to give legally binding character to the propositions it contains. The governments and international agencies engaged in this process express people's basic political and economic entitlements in the language of rights, singling out a group of particularly urgent interests that deserve special protection. The language of rights, especially of human rights, is regularly preferred.

The language of rights has a moral resonance that makes it hard to avoid in contemporary political discourse. But it is certainly not on account of its theoretical and conceptual clarity that it has been preferred. There are many different ways of thinking about what a right is, and many different definitions of "human rights." For example, rights are often spoken of as entitlements that belong to all human beings simply because they are human, or as especially urgent interests of human beings as human beings that deserve protection regardless of where people are situated. Within this tradition there are differences. The dominant tradition has typically grounded rights in the possession of rationality and language, thus implying that non-human animals do not have them, and that mentally impaired humans may not have them. Some philosophers have maintained that sentience, instead, should be the basis of rights; thus, all animals would be rights-bearers. In contrast to this entire group of natural-rights theorists, there are also thinkers who treat all rights as artifacts of state actions. The latter position would seem to imply that there are no human rights where there is no state to recognize them. Such an approach appears to the holders of the former view to do away with the very point of rights language, which is to point to the fact that human beings are entitled to certain types of treatment whether or not the state in which they happen to live recognizes this fact.

There are many other complex unresolved theoretical questions about rights. One of them is the question whether the individual is the only bearer of rights, or whether rights belong, as well, to other entities, such as families, ethnic, religious, and linguistic groups, and nations. Another is whether rights are to be regarded as side-constraints on goal-seeking action, or as parts of a goal that is to be promoted. Still another unresolved question is whether rights—thought of as justified entitlements—are correlated with duties. If A has a right to S, then it would appear there must be someone who has a duty to provide S to A. But it is not always clear who has these duties—especially when we think of rights in the international context. The Universal Declaration, for example, stipulates that the aim of its proclamation is "that every

Reprinted with changes from Martha C. Nussbaum, "Capabilities, Human Rights, and the Universal Declaration," in Burns H. Weston and Stephen P. Marks, eds., *The Future of International Human Rights* (Ardsley, N.Y.: Transnational Publishers, 1999), 25–64. Copyright © 1999 Transnational Publishers, Inc. Reprinted by permission.

1. Exclusive of South Africa, Saudi Arabia, and six states in the Soviet bloc, all of which abstained. The Universal Declaration of Human Rights (hereinafter UDHR) is reprinted and referenced in Documentary Appendix A.
2. Final Act of the United Nations International Conference on Human Rights at Teheran (May 13, 1968), Preamble, referenced in Documentary Appendix B.
3. Vienna Declaration and Programme of Action (June 25, 1993), 20 (hereinafter Vienna Declaration), referenced in Documentary Appendix B.

individual and every organ or society, keeping this Declaration constantly in mind, shall strive . . . to secure their universal and effective recognition and observance."[4] Even accepting that specific obligation of a legal character was supposed to await what eventually became the two 1966 international covenants,[5] this text reveals ambiguity as to who is the duty-holder. The reference to "organs of society" suggests that state agents have duties to secure observance of the declared rights. But so do ordinary citizens and probably noncitizens since the text is directed also at "every individual." Thus the vagueness of these terms could be interpreted to create obligation[s] both on agents of the state in dealing with individuals and on individuals in their relations with other individuals.

Finally, there are difficult theoretical questions about what rights are to be understood as "rights to." When we speak of human rights, do we mean, primarily, a right to be treated in certain ways? A right to a certain level of achieved well-being? A right to certain resources with which one may pursue one's life plan? A right to certain opportunities and capacities with which one may, in turn, make choices regarding one's life plan? Political philosophers who debate the nature of equality commonly tackle a related question head on, asking whether the equality most relevant to political distribution should be understood primarily as equality of well-being, or equality of resources, or equality of opportunity, or equality of capabilities. The language of rights to some extent cuts across this debate and obscures the issues that have been articulated, particularly in distinguishing between "positive" and "negative" rights.

Thus, one might conclude that the language of rights, including that of the Universal Declaration, is not especially informative, despite its uplifting character, unless its users link their references to rights to a theory that answers at least some of these questions. It is for this reason, among others, that a different language has begun to take hold in talk about people's basic

entitlements. This is the language of capabilities and human functioning which was in some ways anticipated in the Universal Declaration even though its authors came from diverse cultural backgrounds and did not use this language *per se*. As this essay seeks to demonstrate, rethinking the Universal Declaration in terms of human capabilities and functioning enhances rather than questions the validity of most of the normative pronouncements of that text and suggests public policy directions for the Declaration's second fifty years.

The application of the capabilities approach to international human rights standards has accelerated in recent years. Since 1993, the Human Development Reports of the United Nations Development Programme (UNDP) have assessed the quality of life in the nations of the world using the concept of people's capabilities, or their abilities to do and to be certain things deemed valuable. Under the influence of economist/ philosopher and Nobel laureate Amartya Sen, they have chosen that conceptual framework as basic to inter-country comparisons and to the articulation of goals for public policy. In 1997, this concern with human capabilities merged into a new policy of a rights-based approach to development, approved in November 1997, and set out in the UNDP publication *Integrating Human Rights with Sustainable Human Development*.[6]

Along with Sen, I have been among those who have pioneered what is now called the "capabilities approach," defending its importance in international debates about welfare and quality of life. In a variety of contexts, we argue that the capabilities approach is a valuable theoretical framework for public policy, especially in the international development context. We commend it to both theoreticians and practitioners as offering certain advantages over approaches that focus on opulence—GNP per capita, or welfare—construed in terms of utility or desire-satisfaction, or even the distribution of basic resources. Similar efforts using different theoretical starting-points have been articulated in the

4. UDHR, Preamble.

5. International Covenant on Economic, Social and Cultural Rights (hereinafter ICESR) and International Covenant on Civil and Political Rights (hereinafter ICCPR)(both Dec. 16, 1966), each reprinted and referenced in Documentary Appendix A.

6. See *Integrating Human Rights with Sustainable Human Development—A UNDP Policy Document* (UNDP, Jan. 1998), available at http://magnet.undp.org/Docs/policy5.html

7. See, e.g., Myres S. McDougal, Harold D. Lasswell, and Lung-chu Chen, *Human Rights and World Public Order: The Basic Policies of an International Law of Human Dignity* (New Haven, Conn.: Yale University Press, 1980).

public policy approach of the so-called New Haven School of Jurisprudence[7] and research on the intersection of basic needs and human rights.[8]

[*Eds.*—The author next traces the recent application of the capabilities approach by various human rights theorists, then continues:]

But there still are some large questions to be answered. The relationship between the two concepts [of capabilities and rights] remains as yet underexplored. Does the capabilities view supplement a theory of rights, or is it intended to be a particular way of capturing what a theory of rights captures? Is there any tension between a focus on capabilities and a focus on rights? Are the two approaches competitors? On the other hand, is there any reason why a capabilities theorist should welcome the language of rights—that is, is there anything in the view itself that leads naturally in the direction of recognizing rights? Would a natural-law Catholic theorist who used an Aristotelian language of capability and functioning, but rejected liberal rights-based language, be making a conceptual error? Does the capabilities view help us to answer any of the difficult questions which have preoccupied theorists of rights? Does the capabilities view incline us to opt for any particular set of answers to the various questions about rights, or any particular conception of rights? Finally, is there any reason, other than a merely rhetorical one, why we should continue to use the language of rights in addition to the language of capabilities?

[*Eds.*—The author next considers the "antecedents and argument" of the "capabilities approach," describing the approach and the motivation for its introduction, asking how it contrasts with other ways of thinking about entitlements, and briefly clarifying the connection between it and liberal theories of justice. In particular, she stresses "the essential element of equality," asking: "What is the relevant type of equality that we should consider in political planning? What does it mean when the Universal Declaration affirms that 'Everyone is entitled to all the rights and freedoms set

forth in this Declaration, without distinction of any kind, such as race, colour, sex, language, religion, political or other opinion, national or social origin, property, birth or other status'"? She concludes: "I believe that the most illuminating way of thinking about the capabilities approach is that it is an account of the space within which we make comparisons between individuals and across nations as to how well they are doing. This idea is closely linked with the idea of a theory of justice, since one crucial aim of a theory of justice typically is to promote some desired state of people." Thereafter critiquing a variety of frameworks used to assess a person's quality of life, including Gross National Product per capita, utilitarianism, and a list of "primary resources," the author continues:]

We argue that the most appropriate space for comparisons is the space of capabilities. Instead of asking "How satisfied is person A," or "How much in the way of resources does A command," we ask the question: "What is A actually able to do and to be?" In other words, about a variety of functions that would seem to be of central importance to a human life, we ask: Is the person capable of this, or not? This focus on capabilities, unlike the focus on GNP, or on aggregate utility, looks at people one by one, insisting on locating empowerment in this life and in that life, rather than in the nation as a whole. Unlike the utilitarian focus on satisfactions, it looks not at what people feel about what they do, but about what they are actually able to do. Finally, unlike the focus on resources, it is concerned with what is actually going on in the life in question: not how many resources are sitting around, but how they are actually going to work in enabling people to function in a fully human way.[9]

The distinction just made between the subjective acceptance of a given level of satisfaction and a more objective standard of empowerment for each individual to understand and achieve capabilities has practical implications for human rights action strategies. Recent approaches to human rights education stress the distinction between the static teaching of abstract human

---

8. See, e.g., Johan Galtung, *Human Rights in Another Key* (Cambridge, Mass.: Blackwell, 1994); Johan Galtung and Anders H. Wirak, "Human Needs, Human Rights and the Theories of Development," in Johan Galtung and R. G. Cant, eds., *Indicators of Social and Economic Change and Their Applications*, Reports and Papers in Social Science 37 (Paris: UNESCO, 1976).

9. In this sense, the approach takes its inspiration from Marx's discussion of fully human functioning in several early works in which he was, in turn, much influenced by Aristotle. . . .

rights concepts and the transformative pedagogy that engages learners in analyzing the causes of their deprivation and in taking control of the transformation of that reality until they attain a higher level of capability. This idea was captured in a definition agreed upon at a regional workshop on human rights education in the Asia-Pacific region in 1994: "Human rights education is a participative process of developing knowledge, values and skills that will enable people to develop their potentials and emancipate themselves from oppressive social realities."[10] Similarly, Richard Claude defines human rights education as "a process through which people and/or communities increase their control or mastery of their lives and the decisions that affect their lives."[11] Such transformative pedagogies have been developed and applied especially in community based human rights education and for the secondary level as well. Their aim is the practical realization of the theoretical potential revealed by the capabilities approach to human rights insofar as they teach affected populations to reject as inadequate the utilitarian goal of the greatest good and even the liberal goal of Rawls's primary goods and advocate instead the empowerment of each individual to become capable of actually functioning in the fully human way defined in the international human rights texts. Enabling people to develop their potential captures the essence of the capabilities approach.

[*Eds.*—The author next addresses the "central human capabilities" and their correlation to human rights. In so doing, she introduces a list which she contends "can be convincingly argued to be of central importance in any human life, whatever else the person pursues or chooses."]

The central capabilities are not just instrumental to further pursuits; they are held to have value in themselves, in making a life fully human. But they are held to have a particularly central importance in everything else we plan and choose. In that sense, central capabilities play a role similar to that played by Rawls's primary goods; they support our powers of practical reason and choice, and have a special importance in making any choice of a way of life possible. They thus have a special claim to be supported for political purposes in societies that otherwise contain a great diversity of views about the good. The basic point of the account is to put forward something that people from many different traditions, with many different fuller conceptions of the good, can agree on as the necessary basis for pursuing their good life.

The list is therefore an attempt to summarize the empirical findings of a broad and ongoing cross-cultural inquiry. As such, it is open-ended and humble; it can always be contested and remade.

The current version of the list,[12] presented here, is revised as a result of recent visits to development projects in India. Most of the central capabilities correspond to the essence of the rights proclaimed in the Universal Declaration which, in turn, have been reaffirmed by the expanding membership of the international community and resoundingly reaffirmed in their entirety on the fiftieth anniversary of the Universal Declaration. Their mention in the international texts contributes to the cross-cultural basis of the list, and in this sense the Declaration becomes a source, an evidentiary element, in defining the good. To illustrate this correlation, the list records both the basic capabilities that I have identified and the corresponding article of the Universal Declaration.

This list is, emphatically, a list of separate and indispensable components. We cannot satisfy the need for one of them by giving a larger amount of another. All are of central importance and all are distinct in quality and thus may be understood,

10. Quoted in Richard Pierre Claude, *Educating for Human Rights: The Philippines and Beyond* (Quezon City: University of the Philippines Press, 1996), 198.

11. Richard Pierre Claude, *The Bells of Freedom—With Resource Materials for Facilitators of Non-Formal Education and 24 Human Rights Echo Sessions* (Addis Ababa: Action Professionals Association for the People, 1996), 7; Claude, *Popular Education for Human Rights: 24 Participatory Exercises for Facilitators and Teachers* (Cambridge, Mass.: Human Rights Education Associates, 2001), in English, Chinese, Dutch, and Arabic, available at http://www.hrea.org/pubs/claude00.html. See also Reading 17 by Richard Pierre Claude in Chapter 3 of this volume.

12. The list is compatible with, but less abstract and more detailed than, the four "welfare values" (wealth, well-being, skills, enlightenment) and four "deference values" (power, respect, rectitude, affection) upon which the so-called New Haven School of Jurisprudence is premised. See McDougal et al., *Human Rights and World Public Order*, note 7.

1. *Life.* Being able to live to the end of a normal length; not dying prematurely, or before one's life is so reduced as to be not worth living

Article 3 on right to life.

2. *Bodily Health.* Being able to have good health, including reproductive health; to be adequately nourished; to have adequate shelter

Article 25, further defined in Article 12 of the ICESCR as the "highest attainable level of physical and mental health."

3. *Bodily Integrity.* Being able to move freely from place to place; to be secure against violent assault, including sexual assault and domestic violence; having opportunities for sexual satisfaction and for choice in matters of reproduction.

Articles 3, 4, 5, and 13, although domestic violence, sexual satisfaction, reproductive choice were not sufficiently well established in 1948 for the overwhelmingly male drafters to include them.

4. *Senses, Imagination, and Thought.* Being able to use the senses; being able to imagine, to think, and to do these things in a "truly human" way, a way informed and cultivated by an adequate education, including, but by no means limited to, literacy and basic mathematical and scientific training. Being able to use imagination and thought in connection with experiencing and producing expressive works and events of one's own choice, religious, literary, musical, and so forth. Being able to use one's mind in ways protected by guarantees of freedom of expression with respect to both politica and artistic speech and freedom of religious exercise. Being able to have pleasurable experiences and to avoid non-beneficial pain.

Article 18 on freedom of thought, conscience, and religion; Article 19 on freedom of opinion and expression; Article 26 on the right to education, which "shall be directed to the full development of the human personality"; Article 27 on participation in cultural life.

5. *Emotions.* Being able to have attachments to things and people outside ourselves; to love those who love and care for us, to grieve at their absence; in general, to love, to grieve, to experience longing, gratitude, and justified anger. Not having one's emotional development blighted by fear and anxiety. Supporting this capability means supporting forms of human association that can be shown to be crucial in their development.

Articles 12 and 16, although privacy, non-interference with family and the right to marry and found a family are manifestations of a much broader idea of capabilities regarding emotions.

6. Being able to form a conception of the good and to engage in critical reflection about the planning of one's life. This entails protection for the liberty of conscience and religious observance.

Article 18 on freedom of thought, conscience, and religion.

7. *Affiliation*
A. *Friendship.* Being able to live for and to others, to recognize and show concern for other human beings, to engage in various forms of social interaction; to be able to

Article 1, mentioning "spirit of brotherhood [*sic*]"; Article 18 on thought and conscience; Article 19 on opinion and expression; Article 20 on peaceful

imagine the situation of another and to have compassion for that situation; to have the capability for both justice and friendship. Protecting this capability means, once again, protecting institutions that constitute such forms of affiliation, and also protecting the freedom of assembly and political speech.

B. *Respect*. Having the social bases of self-respect and non-humiliation; being able to be treated as a dignified being whose worth is equal to that of others. This entails provisions of non-discrimination on the basis of race, sex, ethnicity, caste, religion, and national origin.

8. *Other Species*. Being able to live with concern for and in relation to animals, plants, and the world of nature.

9. *Play*. Being able to laugh, to play, and to enjoy recreational activities.

10. *Control over One's Environment*
A. *Political*. Being able to participate effectively in political choices that govern one's life; having the right of political participation, protections of free speech and association.

B. *Material*. Being able to hold property (both land and movable goods); having the right to employment; having freedom from unwarranted search and seizure.

assembly and association; Article 29 on duties to the community and respect for the rights of others and "just requirements of morality, public order and general welfare in a democratic society."

Article 1, on equality in dignity and rights; Article 2 on non-discrimination.

This concern is found in international environmental instruments and in several draft texts on human rights and the environment, but not in the Universal Declaration, except by implication in Article 28.

Article 24 relative to rest and leisure.

Article 21 on political participation; Article 19 on speech; Article 20 on association.

Article 17 on property; Article 23 on right to work and free choice of employment; Article 12 on non-interference in privacy, family, home or correspondence.

in the official language of rights of the United Nations, as "universal, indivisible and interdependent and interrelated,"[13] which is often ritualized rhetoric in compromise resolutions on human rights but which, in the context of central human capabilities, acquires practical significance. Practical reason and affiliation are of special importance because they both organize and suffuse all the other capabilities, making their pursuit truly human. The individual importance of each component limits the trade-offs that it will be reasonable to make, and thus limits the applicability of quantitative cost-benefit analysis. At the same time, the items on the list are related to one another in many complex ways. One of the most effective ways of promoting women's control over their environment,

and their effective right of political participation, is to promote women's literacy. Women who can seek employment outside the home have more resources in protecting their bodily integrity from assaults within it.

[*Eds.*—The author next discusses what she calls "capability of goal," i.e., "rights as entitlements" and "rights as policy objectives."]

"Reflecting varying environmental circumstances, differing world views, and inescapable interdependencies within and between value processes," writes Burns Weston, "human rights refer to a wide continuum of value claims ranging from the most justiciable to the most aspirational. Human rights partake of both the legal and the

13. Vienna Declaration, note 3, para. 5.

moral orders, sometimes indistinguishably. They are expressive of both the 'is' and the 'ought' in human affairs."[14] In practice, human rights are viewed either as legal entitlements that are immediately justiciable before courts or as guiding aspirational principles that all branches of government should keep in mind as general propositions even if not as specific prescriptions to resolve specific cases. Commonly, the issue of these competing approaches to human rights is erroneously reduced to the distinction made at the time of the elaboration of the two 1966 covenants between, on the one hand, civil and political rights which supposedly are freedoms from state interference and immediately applicable and justiciable, and, on the other hand, economic, social, and cultural rights which are claims against the state for benefits to be provided progressively as resources allow. Rightist thinkers have attempted a philosophical justification of this approach. A more recent development assumes that all human rights—civil, cultural, economic, political, and social—are not only interdependent but of equal legal and moral validity, and thus focuses on the nature of obligations to realize rights. According to this view, the duty-holder (usually the state) has the triple obligation to "respect" (not to commit a violation), to "ensure respect" or to "protect "(not to allow others to violate), and to "fulfill" (provide the means to realize). Depending on the object of the right (freedom from torture or access to education, for example), one or the other of these obligations predominates. Without all three, human rights remain abstractions that the right-holder possesses in theory but does not enjoy in practice. The distinction between capability and functioning underlies this approach to obligation in the human rights field.

But how are capability and functioning related? If we were to take functioning itself as the goal of public policy, the liberal would rightly judge that we were precluding many choices that citizens may make in accordance with their own conceptions of the good, and perhaps violating their human rights. A deeply religious person may prefer not to be well-nourished, but instead prefer to engage in strenuous fasting. Whether for religious or for other reasons, a person may prefer a celibate life to one containing sexual expression. A person may prefer to work with an intense dedication that precludes recreation and play. Am I declaring, by my very use of the list, that these are not fully human or flourishing lives? And am I instructing government to nudge or push people into functioning of the requisite sort, no matter what they prefer?

It is important that the answer to these questions is no. Capability, not functioning, is the political goal. Capability must be the goal because of the great importance the capabilities approach attaches to practical reason. It is perfectly true that functionings, not simply capabilities, are what render a life fully human: if there were no functioning of any kind in a life, we could hardly applaud it, no matter what opportunities it contained. Nonetheless, for political purposes it is appropriate for us to strive for capabilities, and those alone. Citizens must be left free to determine their course after they have the capabilities. The person with plenty of food may always choose to fast, but there is a great difference between fasting and starving, and it is this difference that we wish to capture.

I can make the issue clearer by pointing out that there are three different types of capabilities that figure in my analysis. First, there are what I call *basic capabilities*: the innate equipment of individuals that is the necessary basis for developing the more advanced capability. Most infants have from birth the basic capability for practical reason and imagination, though they cannot exercise such functions without a lot more development and education. Second, there are *internal capabilities*: that is, states of the person herself that are, so far as the person herself is concerned, sufficient conditions for the exercise of the requisite functions. A woman who has not suffered genital mutilation has the internal capability for sexual pleasure; most adult human beings everywhere have the internal capability to use speech and thought in accordance with their own conscience. Finally, there are *combined capabilities*, which I define as internal capabilities combined with suitable external conditions for the exercise of the function. A woman who is not mutilated but is secluded and forbidden to leave the house has internal but not combined capabilities for sexual expression—and work, and political participation. Citizens of repressive nondemocratic regimes have the internal but not the combined

14. Burns H. Weston, "Human Rights," in *Encyclopædia Britannica* (15th ed., 1998), 20: 714–22, at 714; also Reading 1 by Burns H. Weston in this chapter.

capability to exercise thought and speech in accordance with their conscience.

The aim of public policy is the production of combined capabilities. This idea means promoting the states of the person by providing the necessary education and care, as well as preparing the environment so that it is favorable for the exercise of practical reason and the other major functions. The Universal Declaration expresses this idea clearly in Article 28: "Everyone is entitled to a social and international order in which the rights and freedoms set forth in this declaration can be fully realized." The most philosophically coherent interpretation of this article, and potentially the most powerful exhortation of the Universal Declaration for the second half century of its life, is based on the capabilities approach. Specifically, the human rights of the Universal Declaration and its progeny cannot be realized unless and until the social, economic, and political conditions prevailing domestically and internationally ensure each rights-holder the combined capability to exercise the rights he or she may desire. This means that their internal capabilities (called "human potential" in many human rights texts) are combined with the social order, including the legal regime and the economic and social conditions, so that they can express a controversial idea, attain sexual pleasure, secure free public education, or escape from poverty if they wish.

This explanation of the types of capability clarifies the link between capabilities and human rights. I am not saying that public policy should rest content with internal capabilities, but remain indifferent to the struggles of individuals who have to try to exercise these capabilities in a hostile environment. In that sense, my approach is highly attentive to the goal of functioning, and instructs governments to keep functioning always in view. On the other hand, I am not pushing individuals into the function; once the stage is fully set, the choice is up to them.

The matter is confused when human rights texts also enumerate duties, thus shattering the distinction between capabilities and functioning. Once a text purporting to affirm rights stipulates duties, the factor of choice is eliminated. The expression of duties in the Universal Declaration does not suffer this defect as it states in Article 29 that "Everyone has duties to the community in which alone the free and full development of his personality is possible." The problem arises more commonly in constitutional texts that enumerate a set of duties along with rights, usually to pay taxes, to defend the fatherland, to support the government's development policy or socialist system, to protect the constitution against all enemies foreign and domestic, etc.

[*Eds.*—In the next and concluding discussion, the author explores the "different relationships" that capabilities have to human rights.]

How, then, are capabilities related to human rights? We can see, by this time, that there are two rather different relations that capabilities have to the human rights traditionally recognized by international human rights instruments. In what follows, I shall understand a human right in the same way as the Universal Declaration, namely as involving an especially urgent and morally justified claim that a person has, simply by virtue of being a human, and independently of membership in a particular nation, or class, or sex, or ethnic or religious or sexual group.

First, there are some areas in which the best way of thinking about rights is to see them as combined capabilities to function in various ways. The right to political participation, the right to religious free exercise, the freedom of speech, the freedom to seek employment outside the home, and the freedom from unwarranted search and seizure are all best thought of as human capacities to function in ways that we then go on to specify. The further specification will usually involve both an internal component and an external component: a citizen who is systematically deprived of information about religion does not really have religious liberty, even if the state imposes no barrier to religious choice. On the other hand, internal conditions are not enough: women who can think about work outside the home, but who are going to be systematically denied employment on account of sex, or beaten if they try to go outside, do not have the right to seek employment. In short, to secure a right to a citizen in these areas is to put them in a position of capability to go ahead with choosing that function if they should so desire.

Of course, there is another way in which we use the term "right" in which it could not be identified with a capability. We say that A has "a right to" seek employment outside the home, even when her circumstances obviously do not secure such a right to her. When we use the term "human right" this way, we are saying that just by virtue of being human, a person has a justified claim to have the capability secured to her: so a right in that sense would be prior to capability, and a ground for the securing of a capability. "Human rights" used in this sense lie very close to what I have called "basic capabilities," since typically human rights are thought to derive from some actual feature of human persons, some untrained power in them that demands or calls for support from the world.

On the other hand, when we say, as we frequently do, that citizens in country C "have the right of free religious exercise," what we typically mean is that this urgent and justified claim is being answered, that the state responds to the claim that they have just by virtue of being human. It is in this sense that capabilities and rights should be seen to be equivalent: As I have said, combined capabilities are the goals of public planning.

Why is it a good idea to express rights, so understood, in terms of capabilities? I think this approach is a good idea because we then understand that what is involved in securing a right to people is usually a lot more than simply putting it down on paper. We see this very clearly in India, for example, where the Constitution is full of guarantees of Fundamental Rights that are not backed up by effective state action. Thus, since ratification women have had rights of sex equality, but in real life they are unequal not only *de facto*, but also *de jure*. In short, thinking in terms of capability gives us a benchmark in thinking about what it is really to secure a right to someone.

There is another set of rights, largely those in the area of property and economic advantage, which seem to me analytically different in their relationship to capabilities. Take, for example, the right to a certain level of income, or the right to shelter and housing, expressed in [Article 25(1) of] the Universal Declaration as the "right to a standard of living adequate for the health and well-being of himself and of his family, including food, clothing, housing and medical care." These are rights that can be analyzed in a number of distinct ways, in terms of resources, or utility, or capabilities. We could think of the right to a decent level of living as a right to a certain level of resources; or, less plausibly, as a right to a certain level of satisfaction; or as a right to attain a certain level of capability to function.

Once again, we must distinguish the use of the term "right" in the sentence "A has a right to X," from its use in the sentence "Country C gives citizens the right to X." All human beings may arguably have a right to something in the first sense, without being in countries that secure these rights. If a decent living standard is a human right, then American citizens have that right although their state does not give them, or secure to them, such a right. So far, then, we have the same distinctions on our hands that we did in the case of the political liberties. But the point I am making is that at the second level, the analysis of "Country C secures to its citizens the right to a decent living standard" may plausibly take a wider range of forms than it does for the political and religious liberties, where it seems evident that the best way to think of the secured right is as a capability. The material rights may, by contrast, plausibly be analyzed in terms of resources, or possibly in terms of utility.

An interesting controversy erupted during the Second United Nations Conference on Human Settlements (Habitat 11) in Istanbul, in June 1996. The United States delegation strongly resisted efforts to include in the final document any reference to the "right to housing" as such. It proposed instead that the text refer to "adequate shelter for all" and "enablement." While the concept of "enablement" may be seen as an element of the concept of capabilities and functionings, it does not address the responsibility of the state when the real estate industry, acting under the law of supply and demand, fails to make a significant dent in the problem of homelessness. It is here that the link between the human rights language and capabilities makes practical sense. The concept of "enabling environment" leaves open the possibility that an environment that holds out the potential for alleviating homelessness fails to do so in fact. The state is off the hook because the enabling environment—here the free operation of the real estate industry—exists. The concept of capabilities restores the obligation of result and makes it possible to talk of a right to housing.

Indeed this is the approach of the International Covenant on Economic, Social and Cultural Rights. The right in question is expressed in [Article 11(1) in] language similar to the Universal Declaration: the "right of everyone to an adequate standard of living himself and his family, including adequate food, clothing and housing, and to the continuous improvement of living conditions." However, the Covenant further stipulates [in the same article] that the "States Parties will take appropriate steps to ensure the realization of this right, recognizing to this effect the essential importance of international cooperation based on free consent." The first part of this provision suggests that states parties must place persons within their jurisdiction in the position of being capable of having shelter, while suggesting, in the second part, that voluntarily given foreign aid and technical cooperation through Specialized Agencies is most likely going to be necessary for poor countries to realize this right. Moreover, [as provided in Article 2(1)], the entire Covenant is conditioned by the general obligation of each state party

> to take steps, individually and through international assistance and cooperation, especially economic and technical, to the maximum of its available resources with a view to achieving progressively the full realization of the rights recognized in the present Covenant by all appropriate means, including particularly the adoption of legislative measures.

The reference to resources is crucial. The adoption of legislative measures, except with regard to legislation allocating resources for the national budget, is only marginally relevant to the issue of capabilities expressed in terms of allocation of resources.

Here again, however, I think it is valuable to understand these rights, insofar as we decide we want to recognize them, in terms of capabilities. That is, if we think of a right to a decent level of living as a right to a certain quantity of resources, then we get into the very problems I have pointed to; that is, giving the resources to people does not always bring differently situated people up to the same level of functioning. If you have a group of people who are traditionally marginalized, you are probably going to have to expend more resources on them to get them up to the same living standard—in capability terms—than you would for a group of people who are in a favorable social situation.

Analyzing economic and material rights in terms of capabilities would thus enable us to understand, as we might not otherwise, a rationale we might have for spending unequal amounts of money on the disadvantaged, or creating special programs to assist their transition to full capability. This way of thinking has also practical implications for understanding what states parties must do to comply with their obligations under the International Covenant on Economic, Social and Cultural Rights. The acknowledgment on paper of the right is not sufficient; securing the right as a capability is closer to meeting the duties imposed on the state by the Covenant.

If we have the language of capabilities, do we still need, as well, the language of rights? The language of rights still plays, I believe, four important roles in public discourse, despite its unsatisfactory features. When used in the first way, as in the sentence "A has a right to have the basic political liberties secured to her by her government," rights language reminds us that people have justified and urgent claims to certain types of urgent treatment, no matter what the world around them has done about that. I have suggested that this role of rights language lies very close to what I have called "basic capabilities," in the sense that the justification for saying that people have such natural rights usually proceeds by pointing to some capability-like feature of persons that they actually have, on at least a rudimentary level, no matter what the world around them has done about that.

At the second level, when we are talking about rights guaranteed by the state, the language of rights places great emphasis on the importance and the basic role of these things. To say, "Here's a list of things that people ought to be able to do and to be" has only a vague normative resonance. To say, "Here is a list of fundamental rights," means considerably more. It tells people right away that we are dealing with an especially urgent set of functions, backed up by a sense of the justified claim that all humans have to such things, by virtue of being human. This is the essence of the role of the Universal Declaration; it reaffirms in a list of normative propositions the claims that people may consider fundamental to their humanness.

Third, rights language has value because of the emphasis it places on people's choice and autonomy. The language of capabilities, as I have said, was designed to leave room for choice, and to communicate the idea that there is a big difference between pushing people into functioning in ways you consider valuable and leaving the choice up to them. At the same time, if we have the language of rights in play as well, I think it helps us to lay extra emphasis on this very important fact: that what one ought to think of as the benchmark are people's autonomous choices to avail themselves of certain opportunities, and not simply their actual functionings.

Finally, in the areas where there is disagreement about the proper analysis of right talk—where the claims of utility, resources, and capabilities are still being worked out—the language of rights preserves a sense of the terrain of agreement, while we continue to deliberate about the proper type of analysis at the more specific level. Rights language thus limits the areas that can be bargained away in a policy compromise. For example, a wide range of justifiable limitations

may be placed on freedom of speech for reasons of public safety, order, morals, national security, and other reasons, but rights language precludes the policy option of replacing freedom of speech with a residual principle of censorship.

The capabilities approach discussed in this essay builds on an understanding of human rights only vaguely alluded to in the Universal Declaration of Human Rights. Nevertheless, it fits well within the normative framework of the Declaration and offers a valuable tool for assessing compliance with the rights it reaffirms and that are set out in the numerous instruments that have built upon it.

QUESTIONS FOR REFLECTION AND DISCUSSION

1. Martha Nussbaum, a philosopher, observes that "There are many . . . complex unresolved theoretical questions about rights," among them "whether the individual is the only bearer of rights, or whether rights belong, as well, to other entities, such as families, ethnic, religious, and linguistic groups, and nations"; "whether rights are to be regarded as side-constraints on goal-seeking action, or as parts of a goal that is to be promoted"; "whether rights—thought of as justified entitlements—are correlated with duties." She also comments that "it is not always clear who has these duties—especially when we think of rights in the international context." Do you agree with Nussbaum? Why? Why not? Is it possible that the bearers of human rights may be both the individual and groups? that they may be regarded as both "side-constraints" and "goal-seeking action"? that they implicate both "entitlements" and "duties"? that every person from the most global to most local—natural and legal, public and private—is or should be a human rights duty-bearer? While human rights discourse would be theoretically defective if it addressed none of these issues, is it defective if it answers all of these questions in the affirmative? Does it answer all of them in the affirmative?

2. In "The International Human Rights Movement: Part of the Problem?" *HHRJ* 15 (2002): 101–25, David Kennedy theorizes that the human rights movement may create more harm than good, stating that

> The human rights movement proposes itself as a vocabulary of the general good—as knowledge about the shape of emancipation and human possibility that can be "applied" and "enforced." As an emancipatory vocabulary, it offers answers rather than questions, answers that are not only outside political, ideological and cultural differences, but also beyond the human experience of specificity and against the human capacity to hope for more, in denial of the tawdry and uncertain quality of our available dreams about and experience with justice and injustice. Rather than enabling a discussion of what it means to be human, of who is human, of how humans might relate to one another, it crushes this discussion under the weight of moral condemnation, legal adjudication, textual certainty and political power. (111)

Do you agree with Kennedy? Would a capabilities approach avoid the issues he raises? That is, would it enhance the discussion of human rights (i.e., increase the number of questions asked) or would it hurt the discussion (i.e., provide too many answers)? If so, how?

3. Nussbaum observes also that "there are difficult theoretical questions about what rights are to be understood as 'rights to.'" She continues: "When we speak of human rights, do we mean, primarily, a right to be treated in certain ways? A right to a certain level of achieved well-being? A right to certain resources with which one may pursue one's life plan? A right to certain opportunities and capacities with which one may, in turn, make

choices regarding one's life plan?" One of these? All of them? How do you answer these questions?

4. A leitmotif that runs through the entirety of human rights, and which therefore is at the center of the foregoing questions, is the value of nondiscrimination or equality. Nussbaum acknowledges that the language of rights "cuts across [the] debate [about] the nature of equality," but argues that, in the process, it "obscures" important issues embedded in it—for critical example, "whether the equality most relevant to political distribution should be understood primarily as equality of well-being, or equality of resources, or equality of opportunity, or equality of capabilities." She concludes, therefore, that "the language of rights . . . is not especially informative, despite its uplifting character, unless its users link their references to rights to a theory that answers at least some of these questions." Accordingly, she recommends (together with her long-time collaborator Amartya Sen) "a different language [to] talk about people's basic entitlements," to wit, "the language of capabilities and human functioning." What is the language of capabilities and human functioning? How does it differ from human rights discourse?

5. Do you agree with Nussbaum that a different language or approach is needed, one that is based on capabilities as opposed to rights? If so, does this mean that talk about people's basic entitlements in terms of rights is fundamentally a waste of time? Note Nussbaum's assertion that "rethinking the Universal Declaration in terms of human capabilities and functioning enhances rather than questions the validity of most of the normative pronouncements of that text and suggests public policy directions for the Declaration's second fifty years." Does this not imply an acceptance of rights and rights talk not simply as a fact of life but perhaps even a necessity? If so, what, precisely, is the relationship between rights and capabilities? How do capabilities enhance rights?

6. Might the answer to the immediately foregoing questions be found in the "policy-oriented jurisprudence" of the late Yale law scholars Myres S. McDougal and Harold D. Lasswell (founders of the so-called "New Haven Approach" to law and society) who, when contemplating human rights (as well as other law-policy subjects), distinguished between "goal values" (the "deference" values of power, respect, rectitude, and affection, and the "welfare values" of wealth, well-being, skills, and enlightenment—all defined as *desired* goods) and "base values" (the same values—all defined as *instrumental* goods)? See, e.g., Myres S. McDougal, Harold D. Lasswell, and Lung-chu Chen, *Human Rights and World Public Order: The Basic Policies of an International Law of Human Dignity* (New Haven, Conn.: Yale University Press, 1980). That is, may it not be said that capabilities are the base values (the instrumental goods) we must have satisfied to secure the goal values or rights (the desired normative goods) we need to be considered fully functioning humans and to which, therefore, we believe we are fundamentally entitled? If so, may it not then be said also that capabilities (instrumental goods) and rights (normative goods) are but two interdependent sides of the same human rights coin—that each are, in their own way, human rights when considered in basic or fundamental terms (i.e., more "needs" than "wants")? If so, is it that we need a different language to talk about peoples's basic entitlements or that we need a broader and deeper understanding of what those entitlements are, why they are important, and how to secure them?

7. Nussbaum asks: "is there any reason, other than a merely rhetorical one, why we should continue to use the language of rights in addition to the language of capabilities?" Taking into account the questions for reflection and discussion posed so far, what is your answer? Why?

8. Fundamentally, the capabilities approach to human rights and functioning is about empowerment. "Citizens must be left free to determine their course after they have the capabilities," Nussbaum states. Is it fair to suggest that this injunction has a distinctly Western individualistic ring to it, perhaps inappropriate for communitarian (usually non-Western) cultures? And what about citizens who do not have the requisite empowerment capabilities? For example, does an Islamic woman living in, say, Saudi Arabia have a right to be free from physical abuse by her husband if she has no capability to exercise such a right? What are Nussbaum's answers to these questions?

9. Nussbaum argues that the language of human capabilities and functioning should be used to ensure that a person is *not* forced to exercise a right against her or his will. Is this to say that there is a human right not to partake of a human right? If so, why is the language

of human capabilities and functioning used? Also, do you think the term "right" implies that an option *must* be exercised?

10. Does the capabilities approach contain an inherent endorsement of affirmative action programs? An inherent requirement? If so, does the failure to provide such programs constitute a violation of human rights? If so, whose?

11. Who, in the capabilities approach to human functioning, is the enabler of individual and group capabilities? The state? International institutions? Sub-national entities? The private sector (corporations, trade unions, professional associations, nongovernmental organizations, academic institutions, faith-based groups)? The family? The individual? Some of the above? All of the above?

3. BURNS H. WESTON *The Universality of Human Rights in a Multicultured World*

DELIMITATION OF THE PROBLEM

Values are preferred events, "goods" we cherish; and the value of respect, "conceived as the reciprocal honoring of freedom of choice about participation in value processes,"[1] is "the core value of human rights."[2] In a world of diverse cultural traditions that is simultaneously distinguished by the widespread universalist claim that "human rights extend in theory to every person on earth without discriminations irrelevant to merit,"[3] the question thus unavoidably arises: when, in international human rights decision-making, are cultural differences to be respected and when are they not?

This question was perhaps most famously posed in the late 1980s when Iran's Ayatollah Khomeini issued a death threat against British novelist Salman Rushdie for publication of *The Satanic Verses* and a *fatwa* to suppress its distribution. The Rushdie affair, however, is only one of a long history of occasions in which the universal validity of moral judgments has been called into question. Table 1, listing cultural practices well known for the cross-cultural controversies they can and often do generate, demonstrates how this is so.[4] And the more global modernization unfolds and "culture contact" grows, the more are such occasions likely to arise and insist upon answers.

By way of illustration, consider the practices of child betrothal and fixed marriage widespread in the "Third World." Sooner or later one must ponder Article 16 of the Universal Declaration of Human Rights (UDHR) proclaiming that "[m]en and women of full age, without any limitation due to race, nationality or religion, have the right to marry and found a family" and "only

Reprinted with changes from Burns H. Weston, "The Universality of Human Rights in a Multicultured World: Toward Respectful Decision-Making," in Burns H. Weston and Stephen P. Marks, eds., *The Future of International Human Rights* (Ardsley, N.Y.: Transnational Publishers, 1999), 65–99. Copyright © 1999 Transnational Publishers, Inc. Reprinted by permission.

1. Myres S. McDougal, Harold D. Lasswell, and Lung-chu Chen, *Human Rights and World Public Order: The Basic Policies of an International Law of Human Dignity* (New Haven, Conn.: Yale University Press, 1980), 7.
2. Ibid., 451. The authors impose an individualistic perspective on the meaning of this "core value." They write: "respect is defined as an interrelation *among individual human beings* in which they reciprocally recognize and honor each other's freedom of choice about participation in the value processes of the world community or any of its component parts" (emphasis added).
3. Burns H. Weston, "Human Rights," in *Encyclopædia Britannica* (2005), *Encyclopaedia Britannica Online* at http://www.britannica.com/eb/article?tocId=219350. Reconsidering this phrase, I am today inclined to add "capability" to "merit" (and possibly also "basic need" insofar as it is not a function of "capability") as potentially a permissible basis for discrimination in otherwise equal arenas of claim and decision.
4. The practices—neither exhaustively nor altogether unambiguously stated—are listed in alphabetical order according to the physical and behavioral dimensions of human existence. The inner existential (spiritual) dimension of human existence does not seem apt for separate categorization inasmuch as all cultural practices for which relativist claims have been or might be made appear to affect the human psyche in some way, mental or psychological torture most directly of course.

TABLE 1

PHYSICAL PRACTICES	BEHAVIORAL PRACTICES
1. Abortion	1. Banishment, "ethnic cleansing," ostracization
a. Mandatory	2. Discrimination, segregation
b. Permitted, prohibited	a. Age
2. Cannibalism	b. Caste/Class
3. Corporal disfigurement	c. Ethnicity
a. Foot binding	d. Gender, sexual orientation
b. Genital cutting	e. Health (e.g., HIV, lepers)
(1) Male (e.g., circumcision)	f. Merit/Basic need
(2) Female (FGC, aka FGM, FGS)*	g. Nationality
c. Scarring, tattooing	h. Political opinion
4. Corporal punishment	i. Race
a. Public (state imposed/sanctioned)	j. Religion
(1) Amputation	3. Divorce, separation
(2) Caning, flogging, lashing, spanking,	a. Unilateral
whipping	4. Dress codes
(3) Death/Execution	a. Body covering
(a) Electric chair	b. Veil wearing
(b) Firing squad	5. Marriage
(c) Hanging	a. Arranged child marriage
(d) Lethal injection	b. Bride price, dower
(e) Stoning	c. Forced marriage
b. Private (e.g., familial)	d. Homosexual
(1) Spanking, slapping, whipping	e. Polygamy/polygyny
(2) "Honor killing"	6. Slavery, forced labor
5. Euthanasia	7. State-sponsored deprivations
6. Genocide, "ethnic cleansing"	a. Civil/political deprivations
7. Imprisonment	(1) Assembly, association
a. Life	(2) Expression, opinion, speech
b. Solitary	(3) Other
c. Hard labor	b. Economic/social deprivations
8. Infanticide	(1) Education
9. Torture (physical, mental)	(2) Employment
	(3) Other

* "Female genital cutting" (FGC) is a value-neutral term that I borrow from the *New York Times* and other media to avoid the pre-judgment bias of "female genital mutilation" or FGM. I choose the term in lieu of "female genital surgery" because this latter implies a greater degree of precision and refinement in the practice than I believe is empirically warranted overall.

with the free and full consent of the intending spouses." Similarly, in light of the communitarian traditions prevalent in sub-Saharan Africa of defining an individual's existence and status primarily with reference to birthright, sex, age, and group membership, or, alternatively, the occasional Hindu and Muslim traditions of segregating women (*harem, purdah*), one must puzzle over the reach of the UDHR's guarantees of equality and nondiscrimination irrespective of "race, colour, sex, language, religion, political or other opinion, national or social origin, property, birth or other status" (art. 2). Such illustrations of the possible non-universality of alleged universal human rights are of course many and in no way restricted to "Third World" settings. The long-standing resistance of the capitalist countries, particularly the United States, to economic

and social rights, and of the communist countries, past and present, to civil and political rights, attest to this fact. So too do the abortion and nuclear weapons policies in the industrialized world, challenging the "right to life" set forth in UDHR Article 3 just as do the practices of infanticide and female sacrifice (e.g., *sati*) in "pre-modern" societies. And when one adds to the mix that disagreements over claimed universal human rights exist not only in respect of their substantive identification but, as well, with regard to their interpretation and enforcement, the argument of cultural relativism—that there are no overarching moral truths and that local customs and traditions therefore fundamentally determine the existence and scope of rights in any given society—may be seen to loom large.

The issue remains with us today. Since 1989

especially, when cultural variabilities were freed from the silencing grip of Cold War loyalties, there has ensued not a little debate among governmental officials, scholars, and others about the extent to which cultural particularities should be allowed to determine the existence and scope of rights promised to individuals and groups by the UDHR and related universalist human rights instruments. The interplay between the landmark 1993 Vienna Declaration and Programme of Action,[5] adopted by 172 states participating in the UN World Conference on Human Rights that produced it, and the provocatively relativist Bangkok Declaration that emanated the same year from an Asia-Pacific preparatory meeting to the Conference[6] makes this clear. The Bangkok Declaration, after reaffirming in its preamble a "commitment to principles contained in the Charter of the United Nations and the Universal Declaration of Human Rights," stresses "the urgent need to . . . ensure a positive, balanced and confrontational approach to addressing and realizing all aspects of human rights" (¶ 30); emphasizes "the principles of respect for national sovereignty and territorial integrity as well as non-interference in the internal affairs of States, and the non-use of human rights as an instrument of political pressure" (¶ 5); and recognizes that "while human rights are universal in nature, they must be considered in the context of a dynamic and evolving process of international norm-setting, bearing in mind the significance of national and regional particularities and various historical, cultural and religious backgrounds . . . " (¶ 8). In language renunciative but reminiscent of this Bangkok Declaration, the 1993 Vienna Declaration provides in its paragraph 5 that "All human rights are universal, indivisible and interdependent and interrelated. The international community must treat human rights globally in a fair and equal manner, on the same footing, and with the same emphasis."

This outcome, Dianne Otto observes, "can be read as supporting either the universalist or relativist position."[7] It "reflects the paralysis of the debate," she adds, "and leaves the issue firmly on the international human rights agenda for another day." While Otto exaggerates, I think, the impact of the relativist position on the Vienna Declaration, she correctly judges that the relativist-universalist debate itself remains strong on the human rights agenda.

A survey of the literature reveals that the vast majority of commentators, most of them intellectually indebted or sympathetic to Western thought and tradition, come down on the side of universalism.[8] Cultural relativism, if not criticized for preventing transnational moral judgments altogether, is repeatedly denounced as "a new excuse for an old strategy,"[9] used "to justify limitations on speech, subjugation of women, female genital mutilation, amputation of limbs and other cruel punishment, arbitrary use of power, and other violations of international human rights conventions."[10] Where once the old Adam of territorial sovereignty served generally to prevent foreign "humanitarian intervention" into "the domestic jurisdiction," now cultural relativism is seen increasingly to substitute in this role, invoked to prevent transnational judgments about genocide, ethnic cleansing, torture, rape, and other such acts of human violation wherever they occur.

Are these choices and conclusions unequivocally favoring universalism over relativism legitimate? In a critical sense, I think not, though not because they are the result of simplistic a priori reasoning or even that they are wrong. To the contrary, as Martha Nussbaum has pointed out, relativism, as a normative thesis about how we should make moral judgments, suffers from major conceptual problems of its own making:

First, it has no bite in the modern world, where the ideas of every culture are available, internally, to every other, through the

---

5. Adopted June 25, 1993, referenced in Documentary Appendix B.
6. Adopted Mar. 29-Apr. 3, 1993, UN Doc. A/CONF/93, reprinted in *HRLJ* 14 (1993): 370.
7. Dianne Otto, "Rethinking the 'Universality' of Human Rights Law," *Columbia Human Rights Law Review* 29 (1997): 1–46, at 11.
8. See, e.g., Michael Freeman, *Human Rights: An Interdisciplinary Approach* (Cambridge: Polity Press, 2002), chap. 6 and the references cited therein.
9. Anne E. Bayefsky, "Cultural Sovereignty, Relativism, and International Human Rights: New Excuses for Old Strategies," *Ratio Juris* 9 (1996): 42–59.
10. Jerome J. Shestack, "The Philosophical Foundations of Human Rights," *HRQ* 20 (1998): 201–34, at 231.

internet and the media. . . . Many forms of moral relativism . . . use an unrealistic notion of culture. They imagine homogeneity where there is really diversity. . . . Second, it is not obvious why we should think the normative thesis true. Why should we follow the local ideas, rather than the best ideas we can find? Finally, normative relativism is self-subverting; for, in asking us to defer to local norms, it asks us to defer to norms that in most cases are strongly relativistic. Most local traditions take themselves to be absolutely, not relatively true. So in asking us to follow the local, relativism asks us not to follow relativism.[11]

Furthermore, sympathetic (Westerner) as I am to the expansion and invigoration of universal human rights norms and practices, I am much taken by the idea that universalist international human rights law can and should serve as a basis for rendering cross-cultural normative judgments.

My concern is that, without an analytically neutral approach for deciding when cultural differences are to be respected and when not, the pro-universalist choices and conclusions undermine the credibility and defensibility of their own particularistic objectives and thus make the idea of international human rights law as a basis for rendering moral judgments very difficult, perhaps even unworkable on occasion. One-sided assertions of legitimacy and priority, by definition discounting the centrality of the value of respect in human rights, invite countervailing charges of cultural imperialism (defending against real or imagined claims of cultural superiority—"colonizing") and cultural ethnocentrism (defending against real or imagined claims of cultural bias—"Westernizing"), and thus defeat the core goals they seek to achieve. True, cultural relativists also express themselves in ways that subvert their own credo—as when, for example, non-Western and sometimes even Western proponents of cultural pluralism evince absolutist outrage at the supposed moral decay of the West. But this is only to prove my point. Any human rights orientation that is not genuinely in support of the widest possible embrace of the value of respect in the prescription and application of human rights norms in a multi-cultured world is likely to provoke widespread skepticism if not unreserved hostility.

It is of course tempting to argue that international human rights law itself settles the issue. In human rights convention after human rights convention, after all, states have committed themselves to the universality of human rights, and as required by the foundational international law principle *pacta sunt servanda* they are duty-bound to uphold that universality. This, argument, however, falls woefully short of the cross-cultural challenge, and there are at least four reasons why.

First, not all states, certainly not all "relativist states," have ratified even some of the core international human rights instruments, thus thwarting the *pacta sunt servanda* argument *ab initio*. Second, much of international human rights law, particularly as it relates to such "first generation" rights as are reflected in the International Covenant on Civil and Political Rights (ICCPR),[12] is Western inspired, thus fueling the conflict rather than resolving it. Third, all human rights instruments are filled with ambiguity and indeterminacy, sometimes deliberately to ensure signature and ratification, and thus require interpretation to inform the *content* of universalism even when the *concept* of it has been accepted. Finally, when their plenipotentiaries are not signing human rights treaties and voting for human rights resolutions merely for public relations purposes, states, including states that profess the universality of human rights, typically hedge their bets by resort to reservations, statements of understanding, and declarations so as to ensure that certain practices deemed central to their legal or other cultural traditions will not be rendered unlawful or otherwise anachronistic.

In sum, the invocation of international human rights law does not of itself settle the relativist-universalist debate; and there is, thus, no escaping that claims of cultural relativism demand and deserve reasoned, respectful response to them. But how is this to be done in the particular case? How do we reach the conclusion that a particular claim of universalism should trump a competing claim of cultural relativism or vice versa?

The remainder of this essay explores this question, detailing a *methodology of respect* according to which competing relativist-universalist

---

11. Martha C. Nussbaum, *Women and Human Development: The Capabilities Approach* (Cambridge: Cambridge University Press, 2001), 49.
12. Concluded Dec. 16, 1966, reprinted and referenced in Documentary Appendix A.

claims can be assessed objectively and thereby escape, hopefully, charges of cultural imperialism and ethnocentrism. I begin by delineating the observational standpoint that I believe is needed to render human rights judgments about particular cultural practices in transnational settings in an objectively respectful manner.

DELINEATING THE OBJECTIVE OBSERVATIONAL STANDPOINT

The observational standpoint required to resolve a relativist-universalist controversy in a genuinely respectful manner is, I believe, that of rational persons of diverse identity (creed, gender, race, etc.) acting privately (i.e., not as state representatives) and in their personal self-interest relative to the policies or values they believe should define the world public order of which they are a part, but behind a "veil of ignorance" as to the particular circumstances of their own personal condition within that order. Persons familiar with legal philosophy will recognize the influence here of neo-Kantian John Rawls. The true principles of justice, Rawls argues, are those of "fairness"—to wit, those that "free and rational persons concerned to further their own interests would accept in an *initial position* of equality as defining the fundamental terms of their association."[13] The assumption is of thinking men and women who, each in their private capacity in some original social setting, but without knowledge of the details of their own physical and social identity, freely choose a public order that is fair to all in its distribution of benefits (rights) and burdens (duties) because, rationally contemplating their own self-interests, they choose a public order that will not cause anyone, including of course themselves, to be disadvantaged in the real world; they choose principles of governance that are good for all, not simply for some or a few. The result is a set of public order value preferences that transcend parochial interest and selfish motive, a map of basic values or blueprint of fundamental laws that can win the assent of persons everywhere, and thereby facilitate respectful decision when it comes to legal and moral judgments about particular cultural practices across national boundaries.

Is this proposed observational standpoint subject to criticism for being too Western inspired, too individualistically oriented? I think not. Rational people acting individually behind a "veil of ignorance" can foresee the possibility that they may belong to social groups not necessarily Western in origin or outlook. The essential thrust of the observational standpoint is its dedication to a world public order that will most guarantee the fairest distribution of benefits and burdens among all social groups as well as all individuals and thereby ensure that groups as well as individuals benefit as much as possible and suffer the least possible disadvantage.

In short, an observational standpoint that identifies more with the human species as a whole than with the primacy of any of its individual or group parts constitutes, at least for anyone committed to global justice, an ideal to be pursued even if it is never to be fully realized. Hence the observational standpoint recommended here. Absent the core value of respect at the center of all inquiry into the relativist-universalist debate, there is no extending human rights values of any kind without rancor, possibly even violence. As stated above, one-sided characterizations of legitimacy and priority, by definition discounting the centrality of the value of respect in human rights, are likely, over the long term at least, to undermine the moral credibility of their proponents and the defensibility of their particularistic objectives.

THE POSTULATION OF BASIC WORLD PUBLIC ORDER GOALS

So what map of basic values, what fundamental principles of decision-making, should our "initial position" decision-makers choose to guide their transnational judgments about particular cultural practices? If they are to be consistent with the observational standpoint recommended above, such values or principles cannot represent only the exclusive interests of a particular segment of the world community; they must reflect an inclusive approach to humankind's great diversity.

[*Eds.*—The author begins with Rawls's proposition that decision-makers in the "initial position" would intuitively choose two "principles of justice"—liberty and equality. While not

13. See John Rawls, *A Theory of Justice* (Cambridge, Mass.: Belknap Press of Harvard University Press, 1971), 11.

discounting the importance of these ordering principles, however, he observes that "cultural practices for which relativist claims have been or might be made commonly reach beyond the values of liberty and equality that Rawls stresses." Therefore, concluding that "neither liberty nor equality are sufficient to serve adequately as the exclusive determinants of relativist-universalist contests," the author, quoting McDougal, Lasswell, and Chen,[14] urges consideration of all "the basic values of human dignity or of a free society"—i.e., "those [values] which have been bequeathed to us by all the great democratic movements of humankind and which are being more insistently expressed in the rising common demands and expectations of peoples everywhere." Even this alternative, however, is seen by the author to betray "a distinct Western bias that appears . . . to prejudge the outcome of . . . relativist-universalist controversies in the first place"; and thus he advocates a compromise, drawing from both Rawls and McDougal-Lasswell-Chen.]

The map of basic values or decision-making principles that should guide transnational judgments about particular cultural practices should be both more expansive or inclusive than that proposed by Rawls and less vulnerable than the McDougal-Lasswell-Chen formulation to accusations of Western/universalist bias, ergo one that embraces the following self-interested *desiderata*:

- the widest possible shaping and sharing of *all* the values of human dignity, including but not limited to (political) liberty and (socioeconomic) equality,
- without discrimination of any kind save that of merit and basic need (e.g., physical/mental handicap, rank poverty) in many though not necessarily all instances,
- consistent with the truism that in a world of finite possibility, "most assertions of human rights . . . are qualified by the limitation that the rights of any particular individual or group in any particular instance are restricted as much as is necessary to secure the comparable rights of others and the aggregate common interest."[15]

It need here be added only that, in choosing this policy guide to respectful relativist-universalist decision, our "initial position" decision-makers might substitute Martha Nussbaum's (and Amartya Sen's) language of "capabilities"[16] for the more commonly used language of "rights"—i.e., thinking upon all the values of human dignity not in terms of *abstract goals* but rather in terms of the concrete and more readily *measurable needs* that all people must have satisfied to fulfill at least the minimal requirements of human dignity however defined.

THE INTELLECTUAL TASKS OF RELATIVIST-UNIVERSALIST DECISION

It is tempting to argue that local practices that are indisputably destructive of the values (or capabilities) of human dignity must be altogether rejected and that such rejection should not be confused with disrespect for cultural differences or the principles of sovereignty that afford them protection. I have in mind such policies and practices as genocide, ethnic cleansing, imposed starvation, torture, systematic rape, arbitrary execution, slavery, forced labor, and racial *apartheid*. If they are not entirely without cultural basis in the first place, these policies and practices are now so widely condemned that they no longer can be justified by any local custom or rationale.

However, to ensure fully respectful cross-cultural judgment generally, it is, I believe, essential first to embrace *all* the intellectual tasks that seem required to resolve, from an "initial position" policy-oriented perspective, a particular relativist-universalist controversy: (1) the clarification of community policies relevant to the specific cultural practice at issue, (2) the description of past trends in decision relevant to that practice, (3) the analysis of factors affecting these trends, (4) the projection of future trends in decision relevant to the specific cultural practice in question, and (5) the invention and evaluation of policy alternatives to that practice. An analytical flow chart of these relevant intellectual tasks looks as follows:

Clarification of Community Policies

↕

Description of Past Trends in Decision

14. McDougal, Lasswell, and Chen, *Human Rights and World Public Order*, note 1, at 90.
15. Weston, "Human Rights," note 3.
16. See Reading 2 by Martha Nussbaum in this chapter.

↕
Analysis of Factors Affecting Decision
↕
Projection of Future Trends in Decision
↕
Invention and Evaluation of Policy Alternatives

Although they are presented in logically sequenced order here, they must be applied configuratively (as the two-way arrows suggest), each task informing and being informed by the others, to achieve as comprehensive a contextual analysis as possible. The goal is to test each dimension of policy-oriented inquiry for its ability to contribute to rational but respectful choice in decision, and to obtain guidance in the development of international community policy relative to the practices in question. Of course, a preliminary issue is the threshold question of whether or not the practice in question is a *cultural* practice as distinct from one that might be, say, *idiosyncratic* to the particular governing elite involved. If the latter, then the relativist-universalist issue is by definition not implicated, and a decision about the practice may be taken according to potentially different policy criteria.

CLARIFICATION OF COMMUNITY POLICIES

In Table 3.1 above are listed cultural practices well known for the cross-cultural controversies they generate or might generate. The policy issue most fundamentally underlying each of the two existential categories concerns the intensity and scope of power being exercised—more particularly, the necessity of each—by one group of people (public or private) in relation to another in the administration of the practice in question. This comes as no surprise, of course, because it is alleged abuses of power that characterize most if not all human rights controversies.

Spanning the two categories, however, though not coextensive with them, are at least two other dimensions of human experience that merit attention because they suggest yet more precise ways to identify the principal policies that are at stake when cross-cultural normative judgments are attempted: the societal functions of (1) punishment and (2) social differentiation. Regarding punitive practices, relativist-universalist disagreement centers essentially on the severity of the punishment in question or, alternatively, its

proportionality relative to the alleged precipitating transgression, thus on community policies that regulate resort to coercion in the administration of cultural practices. Regarding socially differentiating practices, relativist-universalist disagreement centers mainly on the justification given for the differentiation in question, thus on community policies that regulate the legal and moral rationales of cultural administration—which, as it happens, tend significantly to favor men over women (patriarchy) in many if not most instances. Women's issues lie both directly and indirectly at the heart of many relativist-universalist controversies, particularly at the intersection between masculine hegemony and women's sexual and reproductive identities.

From a policy-clarifying standpoint, some of these practices are less easily diagnosed than others. Exceedingly difficult, for example, is the matter of abortion, though less because of the emotional politics that surround the practice (in the United States at least) than because of fundamental disagreement on what it means to be human, thus disagreement on whether it is the human rights of the fetus that are at stake (the right to life or "pro-life" position) or the human rights of the mother (the right to liberty or "pro-choice" position). Adding to the complexity is the matter of mandatory or forced abortion as a function of population control. It is likely that both pro-life and pro-choice proponents would agree that forcing a woman to have an abortion without her consent is a clear violation of human rights—but whose human rights espoused by whom?

Also complicating policy clarification are the competing philosophical traditions of individualism and communitarianism. In addition to being invoked to prioritize civil and political ("first generation" or "negative") rights, on the one hand, or economic and social ("second generation" or "positive") rights, on the other, even to the complete denial of one generation in favor of the other, they have served to rationalize most, perhaps even all, of the physical and behavioral practices that have proven controversial in the cross-cultural setting. Exalting liberty (individualism) and equality (communitarianism) to the disregard of other principles or values, they have diverted responsible attention from the centrality of respect in human rights decision-making and thus thwarted clear-headed thinking about the relativist-universalist choice.

Consider, for example, a cultural practice that privileges one group over another. If equality is to serve as our policy guide, it follows that relativist defenses of the practice must be rejected. All of which will seem reasonable enough if the local differentiation is based on, say, gender or race and we shun gender- or race-based discrimination or segregation as incompatible with equality. But what if it is based on, say, age, basic need, capability, or merit? What decision then? The point is, of course, that notions of equality do not of themselves provide a reliable exit from the relativist-universalist conundrum. Caught up in a swirl of normative tautology, we are no closer to the objective understanding we seek. For this we must be guided by something else.

Similar confusion sometimes accompanies the cross-cultural assessment of physical practices (at least in theory). Consider, for example, the Islamic practice of hand amputation (*qisas*) for thievery in formerly theocratic Afghanistan and imprisonment for thievery in the secular United States. Clearly each practice contradicts the individualist value of liberty. But it is not this infringement that inclines us to reject a relativist defense of the theocratic culture in the first instance and possibly accept a relativist defense (depending on other variables) vis-à-vis the secular culture in the second instance. The issue here is not whether liberty may be infringed, but to what extent, in what proportion. Thus, just as notions of equality do not of themselves provide reliable exit from the relativist-universalist conundrum, neither do notions of liberty. For this we again must be guided by something else.

This "something else" (or guide to respectful decision) is, of course, that map of basic values or fundamental principles of decision-making that our hypothetical "initial position" decision-makers would choose behind a "veil of ignorance" to ensure the greatest possible equal distribution of rights and duties within the public order of which they are a part. Only by relating these broad goals to specific instances of relativist-universalist controversy—be it hand amputation in the former Afghanistan or outright execution in the United States—will it be possible to ensure respectful decision about the competing values of cultural pluralism and universalist principle. True, the task of relating these goals to specific cultural practices is no easy one. Nor is it made easier by the fact that behind the relativist-universalist debate lurks a desire, evident

on *both* sides of the debate, less to ensure cultural pluralism than to further the interests of the private and public governing elites who currently are engaged in a grand global struggle for economic and political influence (to the shameful disregard of the interests of the "Other" who typically are the victims of globalization's highly uneven—unjust—distribution of economic benefits and burdens and whose pain always must be central to human rights discourse and action). The relativist-universalist debate is not merely a conflict between differing cultural and universal norms. It is, often, a high-level confrontation between competing conservative and liberal versions of capitalism, none of which is a priori superior to the other, especially when expressed in cultural terms. Neither the relativist nor the universalist, therefor, may dismiss the other's claims without a reasoned response. The policies that underwrite their claims must be understood for what they are and properly measured for their compatibility with the wider public order goals that our neutral "initial position" decision-makers would have chosen to ensure respectful decision when rendering cross-cultural moral judgments.

DESCRIPTION OF PAST TRENDS IN CROSS-CULTURAL DECISIONS

A key task in cross-cultural decision-making is to describe past trends in decision relevant to the particular cross-cultural controversy. An understanding of past cross-cultural decision can reveal the extent to which the world community has actively denounced/supported, passively opposed/tolerated, or otherwise disapproved/condoned the particular practice across space and time, and thus reveal as well the extent to which one should or should not take objection to it seriously. The essentially passive official response to the caning of a young U.S. national for adjudged vandalism in Singapore in the mid-1990s, for example, might usefully be examined from this perspective. In addition, assuming a desire to repeal or reform a local practice in keeping with some universalist perspective, past trends can instruct us on the cross-cultural difficulties that are likely to be encountered when subjecting provisional formulations of the desirable to the discipline of the possible, and thus encourage sensitivity to the potential for excessively burdensome demands for change, a particularly important concern where developing countries may be involved.

ANALYSIS OF FACTORS AFFECTING CROSS-CULTURAL DECISIONS

Next it is important to analyze the factors that have influenced decisional trends in relativist-universalist controversy and thus also the case at hand. It is important because such analysis helps us to understand not only how and why relevant precedents were reached but also what factors are likely to serve as useful indicators for present and future decisions, particularly as they may prove useful in guiding our evaluation and recommendation of policy alternatives. The following impressionistic forays, organized around the principal elements of social process, should help to clarify what I have in mind—understanding that it is seldom the investigation of one conditioning factor alone but, rather, the in-depth exploration of all of them that is going to provide the comprehensive knowledge that is needed to reach a respectful decision, our objective.

Participants

In all cultural practices, individual human beings are the ultimate actors, either because they are themselves the *masters* of the practice or its *servants*, or because they are affiliated with a group that is either way directly involved.[17] If only just to comprehend the practice, therefore, it is important to ask, as an anthropologist or historian might do, such descriptively-oriented questions as: Who are the key participants in the practice? Who is responsible for the practice, who are its principal masters? Who is the object of it, who are its primary servants? What biological characteristics (race, sex, age, sexual orientation), culture (ethnicity, nationality), class (wealth, power), interest (group membership), or personality (authoritarian, submissive) may

be attributed to each? And so forth. But participatory questions such as these, helping us to understand the identity and roles of the different participants involved, can also greatly assist the issue of whether or not to honor a cultural practice, particularly where the resolution of that issue turns on the legal and moral rationales given for social differentiation. Indeed, together with other considerations, they may, in such instances, prove decisive in the given case. Consider, for example, the practice of racial *apartheid* in pre-1990 South Africa. In addition to violating our general "initial position" postulate of nondiscrimination in the shaping and sharing of all values, the fact that it privileged minority whites of European origin over majority blacks of indigenous origin obviously had much to do with the world's having outlawed it. Might similar conclusions be reached vis-à-vis the Hindu and Muslim traditions in Central and South Asia and in the Middle East of segregating women (*harem, purdah*)? Of veil wearing (*chador, hijab, niqab*) and total body covering (per the Shari'a doctrine of *urf*)? Of the erstwhile Chinese practice of female foot binding were it still exercised today? In light of our nondiscrimination postulate, surely the participatory (patriarchal) dynamics of such practices (privileging men over women) are important, sometimes perhaps even decisive, to the issue of whether they should or should not be honored in cross-cultural judgment. For example, if the practice involves a broad cross-section of society participating in decision-making about it, including its servants as well as its masters, we might tentatively conclude that the practice has some at least *prima facie* legitimacy. If, on the other hand, only privileged persons make the relevant decisions about it, we would apply, in light of the postulated public order goal values of our "initial position" decision-makers, a higher level of scrutiny to the cultural practice. Likewise, if only one group benefits—particularly if the benefit is at the expense of another group or if only one group "loses"—the practice, according to the same criteria, should be called into question.

17. There are no perfect words of common usage to identify the key participants in cultural practices. Therefore, for lack of more suitable alternatives and for purely descriptive purposes (i.e., free of bias or preference), I adopt the term "master" to refer to those persons who define, execute, administer, and otherwise govern cultural practices and the term "servant" to refer to those persons who follow or who are expected to follow such practices. It must be understood, however, that neither the masters nor servants of cultural practices are restricted to their most distinctive participatory characteristics. On many occasions, the same participant or participants perform both roles simultaneously.

Perspectives

Individuals and groups who participate in cultural practices bring to them predispositional variables or perspectives—objectives (value demands), identities (for whom values are demanded), and expectations (about the fulfillment or nonfulfillment of demanded values)—which, together with environmental factors, affect cross-cultural judgment about the legitimacy of a given practice from the standpoint of our "initial position" decision-makers. Those objectives and perspectives, be they of the masters or the servants of the cultural practice in question, are important in the relativist-universalist judgmental setting as well: What are the objectives, identities, and expectations of the master(s) of the practice? The servant(s)? To what extent do the former affect the fulfillment or nonfulfillment of the latter and *vice versa*? Are the perspectives of the master(s) constructive and expansionist, believed to increase aggregate values for all, or are they defensive, intended to protect the existing values of exclusive groups? Are the perspectives of the servant(s) opposed to the given practice, or are they in support of it? Does the master of a given practice seek power, wealth, or some other value at the expense of the servant? Does the servant willingly acquiesce to such demands? Unwillingly? Do the identities of the participants relate to the common interest of all members of the culture or only to the interests of a few? Do all or some of the participants, masters and servants alike, perceive an intrinsic value in fulfilling one's role in the cultural practice? If so, which ones? Are they conditioned to personal/social security or insecurity as part of their daily routine? Consider in these lights the death threat and literary suppression imposed by Iran's theocratic government upon Salman Rushdie for his Shiite apostasy, claimed necessary for the promotion and protection of religious rectitude; or the imposition of the death penalty in the United States, professedly to deter crime and otherwise promote civic virtue.

It is of course not only the express or stated perspectives of the participants that must be taken into account. In a world where processes of socialization commonly promote the internalization and toleration of patterns of inequality, it is of utmost importance to question the extent to which acquiescence to the given practice in issue is freely given. While by no means the exclusive determinant of cross-cultural judgment, it is in this light that one should assess, for example, the female dress codes in certain Islamic societies and the tradition of arranged child betrothal in South Asia and elsewhere. In such cases, if we are to be consistent with the postulated public order goals of our "initial position" decision-makers, a high level of scrutiny is warranted.

Situations

Spatial, temporal, institutional, and crisis-level features of social process also set the parameters within which cultural practices must be judged. Is the practice confined to a single country or subnational unit or does it extend across national frontiers to embrace whole regions or continents? Is it of long-standing or short duration, sporadic or continuous, thriving or dying out? Does it operate exclusively in the private sphere—say, as part of the institution of the nuclear family or clan—or is it initiated and/or sanctioned by governmental, religious, or other institutions of national scope and sway? Is it a function of emergency situations or is it an everyday organic occurrence? Consider in these lights, for example, resort to the death penalty in the United States; female genital cutting (FGC) recently outlawed in Egypt and reportedly on the decline in Kenya and the Côte d'Ivoire; female "honor killings" in Jordan in violation of Jordanian public policy; and the curtailment of civil liberties in the presence of civil conflicts or terrorism or in the wake of national disasters. If the practice extends broadly geographically, or has been around for centuries or is growing in use, or is sponsored or actively supported by national governmental or religious institutions, or is a function of normal everyday life, might it not deserve at least *prima facie* deference? By the same token, if it is geographically confined, relatively new or dying out, carried out without church/state participation or approval, and/or implemented only or mainly during "manufactured crises," surely greater skepticism regarding claims of "cultural tradition" would be warranted. Guiding our assessment of the answers to these questions are, of course, the public order goals postulated by our "initial position" decision-makers.

Bases of Power

Potentially, all values (the "welfare values" of wealth, well-being, skills, and enlightenment, on the one hand, and the "deference values" of power, respect, rectitude, and affection, on the other[18]) may be, alone or in combination, bases of power to ensure the continuity or discontinuity of given cultural practices. They are, indeed, the essential components of empowerment in any social process such that careful scrutiny of their availability to the masters and servants of a cultural practice in any given case would seem axiomatic. Notably requiring attention is the availability or non-availability of particular values in the absolute sense, as often this will explain both the intensity and the character of selected courses of action or inaction—that is, the enforcement (execution or maintenance) of a cultural practice, on the one hand, and/or its reception (acceptance or toleration), on the other—and thus the cross-cultural deference that should or should not be extended to it. Even more important, perhaps, are the relative value positions of the masters and servants of a cultural practice since significant disparities between them, relative to each other and to the wider community of which they are a part, might well tip the scales of cross-cultural judgment. It is well known, for example, that such masters of cultural practices as family clans, ethnic and religious groups, and governments commonly possess greater effective influence (power) and control more resources and personnel (wealth, enlightenment, skill) than the servants of such practices. In such circumstances, one's evaluative guard must be up. Bearing in mind the postulated public order goals of our "initial position" decision-makers, a cultural practice that continues because those with the most resources are able to force others to submit to it should be subject to intense scrutiny, as in the case, for example, of caste-based social arrangements in which only "upper" caste members may hold positions of power and influence while "lower" caste members are relegated to laborious jobs and poor living conditions. The examples are of course legion.

Strategies

The strategies employed by both the masters and the servants of cultural practices commonly embrace the whole range of instruments of policy—diplomatic, ideological, economic, and military—that invariably are available to public and private officials. Typically the masters of cultural practices will resort to some or all of them to ensure the vitality and continuity of such practices, and the servants of them will do likewise either for the same reasons or, alternatively, to resist their continued exercise. Thus, because the type of strategy employed may sometimes shape cross-cultural judgment about a given practice and thus its acceptability within the social framework within which it is exercised, it is useful to ask what strategies the participants employ to secure their objectives. For example, again recalling the public order goals postulated by our "initial position"decision-makers, one might legitimately look askance at cultural practices whose continued maintenance depends upon, say, bribery and other corrupt measures (economic instrument) or resort to the use of force (military instrument). However, as implied, the type of strategy employed is less relevant than the differing degrees of coerciveness and persuasiveness with which they are employed. From the standpoint of the masters of cultural practices, this calls for responsible attention to alleged abuses of power that manifest coercive or disproportionate means of enforcing cultural practices. All other things being equal, again recalling the public order goals of our "initial position" decision-makers, practices implemented largely through highly coercive or arguably disproportionate uses of power—amputation and stoning in the Middle East? the death penalty and solitary confinement in the United States?—should come under greater scrutiny than those that are characterized mainly by persuasion and with all or most of the participants freely choosing to take part in the practice in question. From the standpoint of the servants of cultural practices, it is well to consider the intensity of commitment or resistance to the practice, thus to the degree of persuasiveness or coerciveness

18. For this typology, I am indebted to the germinal work, Harold D. Lasswell and Abraham Kaplan, *Power and Society: A Framework for Political Inquiry* (New Haven, Conn.: Yale University Press, 1950). Lasswell and Kaplan write, at 55–56: "By 'welfare values' we mean those whose possession to a certain degree is a necessary condition for the maintenance of the physical activity of the person. * * * Deference values are those that consist in being taken into consideration (in the acts of others and of the self)."

with which it is greeted by them. If a practice is carried out or served voluntarily, all other things being equal, it warrants at least *prima facie* deference or respect in cross-cultural decision-making. Likewise, if it is violently resisted, its legitimacy is in doubt.

Outcomes and Effects

Perhaps most important to cross-cultural judgment about given cultural practices are the short-term outcomes and long-term effects of the interactions between the masters and servants of the cultural practice in question. When all is said and done, it is the balance sheet of net value gains and losses, both short- and long-term, absolute and relative, that results from the practice that commonly determines whether that practice is to be honored or dishonored in cross-cultural judgment; for hovering over that balance sheet is the issue of necessity—that is, the necessity of the value losses relative to the gains for cultural diversity or pluralism.

The following kinds of "outcome" questions are thus exceedingly pertinent: Does the continued exercise of the practice spell a "win-win" outcome for the participants involved? A "win-lose" outcome? If the latter, who "wins" and who "loses," and in what ways? In other words, if the continued exercise of the cultural practice can be seen essentially to reflect the shared aspirations of persons engaged in a cooperative community enterprise (a "win-win" outcome), then at least preliminary deference should be shown that practice. If, on the other hand, its continued exercise may be concluded to benefit only a small group of "winners," say, at the expense of a large group of "losers," then a high degree of scrutiny is warranted, particularly when the "losers" manifest distinctive "minority" identity. Even if the masters of a cultural practice do not intend a discriminatory result, the postulated public order goals of our "initial position" decision-makers compel us to account for the fact of discriminatory deprivation or nonfulfillment as such.

As for the long-term effects of the cultural practice in dispute, which potentially can impact beyond the immediate participants involved, again cross-cultural decision-making must take heed. Suppose, for example, that the continued exercise of a given cultural practice were to result in racially discriminatory outcomes that would spark instability and violent uprisings in large parts of the country involved, even perhaps beyond. What then? If we are faithful to the postulated public order goals of our "initial position" decision-makers, then, logically, cross-cultural decision-making should look upon the practice with skepticism. Suppose, however, that the opposite were true, i.e., that the continued exercise of the cultural practice—say, discriminations based on merit or basic need—were to have a net positive effect for the society in question as a whole. Then, just as logically and based on the same criteria, cross-cultural decision-making should display at least initial great deference.

The point is, of course, that cultural practices can have both beneficial and detrimental outcomes and effects relative to the postulated public order goals of our "initial position" decision-makers. Precise characterization of them and therefore cross-cultural judgment about them will hinge at least in part on whether and how one appraises their short- and long-term consequences.

General Conditions

If cross-cultural decision-making is to respond adequately to the vicissitudes of our times, it must account not only for the primary characteristics of the particular relativist-universalist case, but also for those influential general conditions of the larger global context within which those characteristics live. Of course, the wider context is ever-changing. Moreover, what may be relevant in that context for one relativist-universalist controversy may not be germane for another. Nevertheless, certain features of the current world scene, many of them contradictory, may prove especially significant and therefore worthy of at least passing consideration when attempting cross-cultural judgment at the present time—for example: the accelerating socio-economic "globalization" of the world, commonly on unequal terms as between "modern" and "traditional" peoples and cultures; or transnational messianic terrorism and responses to it that pit fundamentalist Islamic values against Western Judeo-Christian values and vice versa. Comprehensive assessment of such "secondary" contextual conditions would seek richer indication of their specific relevance to diverse cultural practices and to the fundamental policies that are deemed pertinent in relation to them.

THE PROJECTION OF FUTURE TRENDS IN CROSS-CULTURAL DECISIONS

The projection of probable future developments relative to given cultural practices—in the sense of the broad trend, not the particular instance—is an important variable in cross-cultural decision-making for at least two reasons. First, it can help us see whether continuation of the practice will reveal movement toward or away from the postulated public order goals of our "initial position" decision-makers. If so, the practice merits at least *prima facie* deference; if not, then the opposite. Second, to minimize the diminution of cultural pluralism where continuation of a given practice reveals movement away from the postulated goals of our "initial position" decision-makers, it can help creativity in the invention and evaluation of alternatives to the manner in which the given cultural practice is exercised so as to make it comport with our postulated public order goals while simultaneously preserving its essence. This is no easy decisional task. No simpleminded extrapolation of the past, it requires a disciplined analysis of all the relevant features of the practice under scrutiny and of the primary and secondary contextual factors that condition it.

THE INVENTION AND EVALUATION OF ALTERNATIVES

The final intellectual task of respectful decision-making in relativist-universalist controversies relates to the deliberate search for, and assessment of, alternatives either to the given cultural practice itself or to the manner in which it is exercised in cases where it may be found that the practice or, more precisely, its manner of exercise is at odds with the postulated public order goals of our "initial position" decision-makers. It is the last task toward which all the preceding intellectual tasks accumulate and therefore the one to be pursued after all of its predecessors have been credibly exhausted. The point is that the ultimate goal of respectful decision-making in the relativist-universalist context is not to declare a "winner," but, rather, to enhance the possibility of ensuring the world's

rich diversity (cultural pluralism) while at the same time serving the values of *human* dignity as defined by the postulated public order goals of our "initial position" decision-makers. Thus, where a particular cultural practice is found, on final analysis, to conflict with those goals in the manner of its exercise but not necessarily in its innate purpose or social function, one would look to encourage or reward initiatives that can make the practice consistent with the values of human dignity embedded in the goals. A recent case in point is found in the rites of female passage and sexual purification in sub-Saharan Africa, where for generations these rites have been administered via female genital cutting (FGC). Recently in Kenya and the Côte d'Ivoire, for example, the focus of responsible attention has shifted to emphasize the innate purpose of the ritual rather than the modality of its implementation and thus to preserve the ritual and simultaneously lessen or eliminate its severity. To the extent feasible, respectful decision-making in cross-cultural context should seek integrative solutions characterized by maximum gains and minimum losses for all sides of the relativist-universalist debate; it should seek diversity in unity.

APPRAISAL AND RECOMMENDATION

In the preceding pages, I have sought to outline in at least impressionistic fashion the key intellectual tasks and inquiries required to serve respectful decision in relativist-universalist contests. To say that they are the *key* intellectual tasks and inquiries, however, is not to say that they constitute *all* the study that is needed. Additionally critical is an honest assessment of the very decision process pursuant to which that judgment is being rendered. As any sophisticated law student knows, who decides what, why, when, where, and how often has as much and sometimes more to do with the resolution of legal controversies as the facts and pertinent doctrines, principles, and rules themselves. Indeed, for precisely this reason, a thorough approach to respectful decision in the relativist-universalist context would identify and analyze that process just as it would identify and analyze the process of decision in any controversy—that is, not simply as just one more factor generally conditioning the controversy, but, rather, as a separate yet intimately interrelated central part of the total social process surrounding the controversy that merits discrete analysis in its own right.

In any event, one thing is certain: if one is to take seriously the proposition that respect is the core value of all human rights, cross-cultural decision-making about relativist-universalist controversies must reflect the complexity of life itself, implicating a whole series of interrelated activities and events that are indispensable to effective inquiry and, thus, rational and respectful choice in decision. Accordingly, I join other human rights theorists and activists in advocating dialogue across cultures and societies. But not only ethical or moral dialogue. Also needed is that kind of cross-cultural dialogue that can yield substantial consensus on the many factual and policy-oriented questions that absolutely must be asked—hopefully in keeping with the *methodology of respect* that I have urged here—so as to guarantee that the core value of respect will be present in all relativist-universalist decision-making. This essay is offered as a modest preliminary contribution to that end.

QUESTIONS FOR REFLECTION AND DISCUSSION

1. Human rights, it is said, are the rights to which everyone is entitled simply for being human; they are universal by definition. How, then, is it possible to talk about cultural relativism in relation to them? Can the notions of universal human rights and cultural relativism logically coexist? Does the right of self-determination provide an answer? If so how? Consider in this light Reading 12 by Maivân Clech Lâm and Reading 19 by Hurst Hannum in this volume, each of them addressing the right to self-determination. What would Weston say?

2. In "Cultural Relativism and Universal Human Rights," *HRQ* 6, no. 4 (1984): 400–419, at 400, Jack Donnelly identifies cultural relativism as "a doctrine that holds that (at least some) variations [in the observance of human rights] are exempt from legitimate criticism by outsiders, a doctrine that is strongly supported by notions of communal autonomy and self-determination." In "International Human Rights and Cultural Relativism," *VJIL* 25, no. 4 (1985): 869–98, Fernando R. Tesón argues that the right of self-determination should not be allowed to deny human rights, that the relativist version of self-determination is a rationalization for oppression. Who is right? What would Weston say?

3. The Dalai Lama has observed that

> We are at the dawn of a new age in which extreme political concepts and dogmas may cease to dominate human affairs. We must use this historic opportunity to replace them by universal human and spiritual values and ensure that these values become the fibre of the global family which is emerging. * * * It is our collective and individual responsibility to protect and nurture the global family, to support its weaker members and to preserve and tend to the environment in which we all live. (International Institute of Human Rights, *Universality of Human Rights in a Pluralistic World: Proceedings of the Colloquy Organized by the Council of Europe in Co-operation with the International Institute of Human Rights, Strasbourg, 17–19 April 1989* [Arlington Va.: N.P. Engel, 1990], 20–21)

In what way or ways, if at all, does the doctrine of cultural relativism countermand this viewpoint? Is it possible to ensure cultural pluralism and at the same time insist on cultural universalism? Does Weston's "methodology of respect" provide an answer?

4. Weston observes that the value of respect is the core value of all human rights. What does this mean? What are its implications for the theory and practice of human rights? What is its relevance to the relativist-universalist debate? To cross-cultural decision-making?

5. According to one observer, the expectation of equal cultural recognition is inherent in all modern democratic societies because it is grounded in the Enlightenment value of "equal dignity." Charles Taylor, "The Politics of Recognition," in Amy Gutmann, ed., *Multiculturalism and the "Politics of Recognition"* (Princeton, N.J.: Princeton University Press, 1992), 25–73, at 27. However, equal dignity means different things politically. It is synonymous with extending to all citizens the same entitlements or rights regardless of their differences, which is the basis of liberalism. But it also means extending the same respect to the unique cultural identity of all individuals or groups in a society, which Taylor considers a legitimate but dangerous challenge to liberalism. The legitimate challenge of recognition, according

to Taylor, is all too often coopted by the "politics of difference," which demands the same respect for all cultures based merely on the fact that they are different. Do you agree with Taylor? How do we know when the "politics of difference" is coopting the "challenge of recognition"? What are the criteria? Does Reading 18 by Stephen A. Hansen in Chapter 2 of this volume tell us? Does Weston?

6. Weston's "methodology of respect" is an attempt to formulate an "analytically neutral approach for deciding when cultural differences are to be respected and when they are not." Why is neutrality important? Is it possible? Does he succeed?

7. By asserting the uniqueness of their cultures, non-Western countries or groups may be reclaiming their dignity and national self-esteem from their past experiences of colonial domination by the West and its attendant cultural denigration of the colonized. Does Weston address this possibility? How? How not?

8. To apply Weston's methodology premised on respect for the cultures of other peoples, it is helpful, arguably even necessary, to know these cultures well. However, as Michael Freeman remarks in *Human Rights: An Interdisciplinary Approach* (Cambridge: Polity Press, 2002), it is difficult for outsiders to have this knowledge because "governments and intellectual elites often act as 'gatemasters,' offering an official version of the people's culture to the outside world" (110). Does Weston's methodology overcome this difficulty? How? How not?

9. Consider the wearing of the *burka* by women practiced in some Islamic traditions. Proceed through Weston's five-step model for evaluation. At what decision do you arrive? Why?

10 It often has been argued that Western responses to grave human rights violations in non-Western countries have been selective and inconsistent, contradicting the West's claimed universalist approach to human rights. Can you cite examples? How, if at all, does Weston's "methodology of respect" handle such situations?

11. Would it profit Westerners to apply Weston's "methodology of respect" to cultural practices of their own countries that arguably are in violation of universal human rights principles? Why? Why not? If so, what might some of these practices be?

4. RHODA E. HOWARD-HASSMANN *The Second Great Transformation: Human Rights Leap-Frogging in the Era of Globalization*

THE SECOND GREAT TRANSFORMATION

Globalization is the final assault of capitalism on all those areas of the world that previously escaped it. It is changing the conditions under which all countries and societies are integrated into the world economy.

Among human rights activists and some human rights scholars, thus, there is a debate about whether globalization is "good" or "bad" for human rights. I suggest that this is a false debate. The question is not whether globalization is a "thing" out of control, eating up traditional societies, local values, and local economies. This is inevitable. Globalization cannot be stopped, and its forces will undermine what is left of purely local societies. The question is the kinds of changes that globalization is likely to cause, and how societies and individuals will react to those changes. To debate whether globalization as a process is "good" or "bad" is as irrelevant as arguing whether the transition from an agrarian to an industrial society in the Western world from the eighteenth to the twentieth century was good or bad.

There have been earlier rounds of "globalization," such as the creation of the Roman Empire, or the opening up of European trade with China. This round is truly global, however, as no area of the world can now escape capitalism's grasp without severe cost to its economy (as in the case of North Korea, for example). Globalization is not only inevitable, it is the only path to long-term economic growth.

There are, however, many severe short-term costs along this path. The potential for harm is not to be minimized. At the same time, the "leapfrogging" of human rights across time and space may partially alleviate the problems globalization causes. The global human rights regime, and the global human rights process, can perhaps remedy some of the dangers of the global economic system.

The following analysis addresses globalization's possible long-range human rights outcome. It considers both an "optimistic" and a "pessimistic" model of social change generated by globalization.

Karl Polanyi wrote *The Great Transformation*[1] to explain the economic, social, and political changes that occurred in Europe, particularly Britain, from the end of the eighteenth century to the Second World War. This was a period of about 160 years, known to have radically transformed the way people lived. Peasants became artisans, industrialists, or workers; they migrated from villages to cities; they moved from closed, church-based societies to open, secular communities. Most important, to Polanyi, was the newness of a society based only on gain, and the very rapid end of the "social," in which previously mankind had always been embedded. A society in which all members had relations of obligation and reciprocity to all others gave way to one in which individuals in their different roles were cut off from each other, and related to each other only within the marketplace.

Globalization is the *Second Great Transformation*. It is affecting societies that earlier in the modern era escaped capitalism's grip, either because of explicit communist or socialist politics, because of national policies of withdrawal from the world economy, or because capitalism had no interest in the region as a source of resources or workers or as a market. All over what was formally the non-capitalist or only partly capitalist worlds, the social is giving way to the profit motive, as it did in Western Europe two centuries ago. The transnational corporations (TNCs) that are the symbols of globalization seem to feel no obligation to their local employees or their local suppliers, or to the local communities in which they make investments. Individuals' and families' security now depends on their capacities to find scarce employment, obtain insecure property rights, or invest in erratic and incalculable international capital markets. The protections of belonging, however materially poor the community to which you belong, are giving way to the feeling that no one cares, that no one is there to help, that no one knows who you are. Billions of people are experiencing what Polanyi called an "avalanche of social dislocation."[2]

Globalization is defined by Malcolm Waters as "a social process in which the constraints of geography on social and cultural arrangements recede and in which people become increasingly aware that they are receding."[3] The information explosion, the world-wide reach of mass media, and ease of communications affect local cultures. Similarly, ease of travel, migration, and circulation among ancestral and new homes change social arrangements. Nevertheless, the chief impetus and beneficiary of globalization is capitalism. Capitalism is the economic system behind new technologies of information and communication, behind unprecedented large and quick capital flows, and behind the capacity of TNCs to spread all over the world. In 1997, Jeffrey Sachs pointed out that, whereas twenty years earlier only about 20 percent of the world's population had been living under capitalism, by the time he wrote the percentage had increased to 90.[4] As societies are incorporated into the world capitalist system, many social changes occur.

In a sermon in the English city of York in 1014, Archbishop Wulfstan said: "The world is in a rush, and is getting close to its end."[5] This is the reaction of many people to the current era. Integration of the "rest" of the world—Asia, Africa, and Central and Latin America—into the global economy has been occurring since World

---

1. Karl Polanyi, *The Great Transformation: The Political and Economic Origins of Our Time* (Boston: Beacon Press, 1944).
2. Ibid., 40.
3. Malcolm Waters, *Globalization* (New York: Routledge, 1995), 3.
4. Jeffrey Sachs, "New Members Please Apply," *Time*, July 7, 1997, 11–12, cited in Richard Falk, *Predatory Globalization: A Critique* (Malden, Mass.: Polity Press, 1999), 141.
5. Quoted in Anthony Giddens, *Runaway World: How Globalization Is Reshaping Our Lives* (New York: Routledge, 2003), 1.

War II, and has been dramatically speeded up by globalization. Russia and the ex-Soviet "transitional" societies are also integrating into the world economy. The leaders of China in 1979 decided to adopt a controlled capitalism. All these societies hope that by joining the world economy their own standards of living will improve.

Economic policies change quickly with international institutions such as the World Bank to guide the changes, and foreign consultants available to teach the rules and practices of capitalism to willing policy-makers and entrepreneurs. Political changes are guided by constitutional and legal consultants. Social changes are influenced by international and transnational social movements, some of which strive to protect human rights at the very time that powerful political and economic forces undermine them. These manifold changes impel a human rights debate. Will globalization improve or undermine individuals' access to economic benefits? Will it erode local cultures completely, or will it leave them some space to flourish? Will it improve or undermine the state of civil and political rights? To understand the Second Great Transformation, we must look at the interactions among economic, cultural, and social change, political organization, and social movements.

We must also look at the long term to understand the consequences for human rights of this enormous social upheaval. A period of about fifty years permits us to look back to the recent past to analyze social, cultural, political, and economic changes that have occurred as a result of what we now call globalization. South Korea provides a model of almost complete transition from a peasant to an urban society, from a dictatorship to a democracy, over fifty years. China has rapidly changed from a collectivist, command economy to an individualist, entrepreneurial one, yet with a party-bureaucratic dictatorship still in place. In former Eastern Europe and the Russian Empire, there are multiple examples of greater and lesser success in integrating into the world capitalist system, and in adopting democracy, since 1989.

Modern democratic states buttressed by the rule of law and by a civic culture of activism and political freedom are more likely than any other type of political system to protect human rights. Democratic principles of government, the rule of law, and a civic culture took centuries to emerge in Western Europe and North America, with intervening episodes of dictatorship and fascism.

Until well into the twentieth century, the vast majority of Westerners did not enjoy what are now known as human rights. Rights-based liberal democratic societies certainly did not emerge through some easy, predictable, and inevitable coincidence of capitalism and rights.

The eventual outcome of the Industrial Revolution could certainly not have been predicted in Europe in 1780: so too the outcome of globalization cannot be predicted anywhere in the world in the early twenty-first century. It is unwise to think that the benefits of democracy, the rule of law, and a human rights culture will inevitably be reaped in all societies affected by globalization. In most societies entering the world capitalist economy, there will be severe social disruption, and much exploitation of newly available labor. Nor will this be confined to "Western" or "Northern" exploitation of the "non-Western" or "Southern" worlds. Capitalists and governments in the former "Third World" are as capable as were the early English industrialists of exploiting their own workers and citizens.

Whether for good or ill in human rights terms, social relations will change in the new global society. Societies will become more fluid; individuals will be more mobile, social norms will change, and traditional roles will give way to new ideas of how to behave. Persons formerly holding authority will find they are unheeded, while hitherto disreputable individuals will gain credence as role models in a new entrepreneurial world. Guns and drugs will be considered as legitimate objects of exchange, much as they were during the period of European expansion. Some people will be confused by these changes, and long for a simpler time with a stricter normative order. Among them, some will—and do—fight viciously to retain the older world from which they are being so abruptly torn. In such situations of flux, there will be no necessary correlation between the processes of globalization and the entrenchment of human rights, either positive or negative.

How then, does a society change from a global system of capitalism that results in deep inequalities and social exploitation, to a system than promotes relatively equal social relationships and relatively equal distribution of wealth? Such a change is not inevitable. If it does occur, it will do so because of multiple changes—some economic, some political or legal, some cultural or social—that may result from globalization.

Below, I suggest two models of such social change. I first propose a "positive" model of how globalization might result in economic development and better protection of human rights. I follow this with a "negative" model of how globalization might undermine human rights. In both cases my starting point is investments by TNCs. Neither of these models suggests any inevitable relationships, nor is either a complete picture. But they do show how very complex and contingent is the transition to a rights-protective society.

AN OPTIMISTIC MODEL OF THE RELATIONSHIP BETWEEN GLOBALIZATION AND HUMAN RIGHTS

Figure 1 starts with one, and only one, factor: namely, transnational investment in a society that is not democratic and does not respect human rights. Transnational investment promotes some changes in such a society.

On the economic front, the most obvious change is the provision of new employment opportunities. A small and growing number of people now work in the modern, industrial sector. Some pay taxes to the government, as does the transnational corporation itself (unless it is allowed a complete tax holiday in perpetuity). Increased national revenue is associated with improvement in human rights.[6] It results in a small increment in governmental capacity: with more tax revenue, the government can pay its civil servants more regularly. Regular pay gives civil servants an incentive to stay in their offices and abide by bureaucratic rules of fairness and impartiality, rather than wander off to eke out a living in the informal sector, or ask for bribes every time they encounter a citizen with a request. New economic opportunities also lessen resistance to political democracy. Holders of both political and bureaucratic office are less frightened by the possibility of losing that office if they can maintain their standard of living in the private sector.

TNC investment also helps establish the rule of law. Investors want predictable laws and competent judicial systems to enforce their contracts and property rights. The rule of law also provides private citizens the opportunity to legally own property. De Soto has argued that one of the biggest stumbling blocks to development in Latin America, Asia, and Africa today is that the poor are not legal owners of their houses, land, and mini-enterprises. Without legal title, they are at the mercy of corrupt bureaucrats who demand bribes not to evict them from their homes and businesses. Further, without evidence of legally enforced property, they have no collateral to offer banks for loans.[7] Thus, enforcement of property law permits citizens to pursue their private interests. TNC investment results in business opportunities to supply locally made inputs to the TNCs, or to provide goods and services for workers who have established new communities in the areas of TNC investment. A new middle class develops.

The new middle class wants its children to be educated, so that they can join their parents in business and later manage the property they inherit. It also desires a more educated population, so that it can employ individuals with the skills it needs. TNCs may eventually join in a demand for more education, or provide their own educational systems, if they discover they need a more literate or numerate labor force.

As the new middle class becomes more aware of its own interests, it will become less willing to live in an undemocratic political structure. It will establish the rudiments of a civil society, organizing to protect its own interests. This civil society will in turn feed back into the educational system. It will promote ideals of social equality, so as to enhance its own chances of advancement. It will also enhance governmental capacity, demanding fairness and efficiency, and displaying some willingness to pay taxes in order to obtain them. A more secure bureaucracy will be more willing to respond to the concerns of its citizenry. As it does so, it will learn that it is possible to make changes in policy, even to disburse more funds, without losing control of the state. It will be easier to adhere to the principles of accountability and transparency, key aspects of good governance, in state institutions that are properly funded and in which bureaucrats are well trained and adequately paid.

6. See Kathleen Pritchard, "Human Rights and Development: Theory and Data," in David P. Forsythe, ed., *Human Rights and Development: International Views* (London: Macmillan, 1989), 329–45.
7. See Hernando de Soto, "The Mystery of Capital," *Twenty-First Morgenthau Memorial Lecture on Ethics and Foreign Policy* (New York: Carnegie Council on Ethics and World Affairs, 2002).

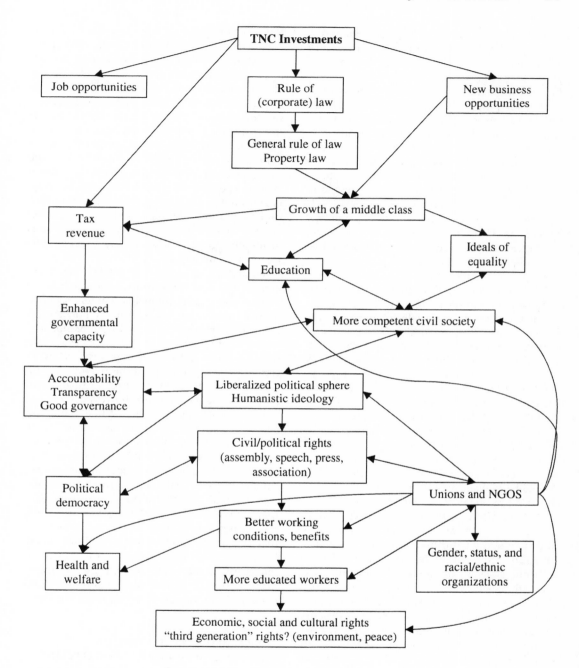

Figure 1. The Second Great Transformation: an optimistic model.

An emergent civil society also demands a more liberalized political sphere. Citizens start to make their interests known, and expect their government to take these interests into account. Citizens want the rule of law to cover areas of life beyond property and contract: they demand regularity, fairness, and predictability in other spheres of life. A government less reliant than previously on corruption, and more used to bureaucratic procedure, becomes more willing to entertain the possibility of liberalizing, gradually opening up to freedoms of speech, press, and association. A more humanistic ideology develops along with the more liberalized political sphere. As the market spreads and impersonal market relations become commoner, market trust helps to build the social trust necessary for a functioning political democracy.[8]

The entrenchment of economic rights for ordinary people requires a different and expanded set of social actors, especially members of the working class. People working in the modern, industrialized sector start to make demands. They demand independent trade unions. As they attain small incremental improvements in working conditions, so they are emboldened to ask for more rights, such as better access to education. They also learn how to take part in large, bureaucratized organizations and how to lobby and bargain. As they become more educated and experienced, they enter other spheres of civil society, generalizing the idea that social welfare should be available to all citizens. Improvements in education, health, and welfare in turn spiral backward, affecting the capacity of citizens to take part in political democracy. Both workers and members of the middle class, now living under the rudiments of the rule of law and political democracy, absorb the idea that with rights, they are legally equal citizens of their country. This idea spreads to groups such as women, persons occupying lower castes or statuses, or ethnic, religious or racial minorities. They in turn form their own civic associations, and learn the same lobbying and bargaining techniques as other groups.

The above is not so much a prediction as a rough description of what happened in the West during and after the First Great Transformation.

None of the social changes discussed above is inevitable during the Second Great Transformation. One indication that some of these changes might occur, however, is that almost all countries of the world now accept capitalism. Capitalism is a necessary, though not sufficient, prerequisite for democracy.[9] For democracy to emerge from capitalism requires class action and organization. But the class action required to wrest democracy from capitalism arises only if the structural conditions are appropriate. Class action is made possible by transformations in social organization, especially by improvements in education and communication, and by urbanization and the concentration of population. This results in the emergence of civil society as a counterweight to state power.

Capitalism does not inevitably result in democracy—much less human rights—as some of its ideologically minded promoters seem to believe. But without capitalism, democracy appears to be impossible, and without democracy, human rights cannot be protected. Far more than an economic system, capitalism relies on certain presumptions about the rule of law, and capitalism creates modern citizens who demand human rights. Once again, however, these are not inevitable relationships. While there can be no democracy without capitalism, there can certainly be capitalism without democracy. A state elite can command resources such as decision-making power over investment and tax conditions that make it worthwhile for the international capitalist class to ally itself with that elite, blocking any changes that the lower classes might try to demand. We cannot be sure that the happy model presented above of the West's first Great Transformation will be an accurate representation of the second Great Transformation. Thus, it is necessary to also consider a pessimistic model of the present transformation.

A PESSIMISTIC MODEL OF THE RELATIONSHIP BETWEEN GLOBALIZATION AND HUMAN RIGHTS

What happened in the past may not happen in the future. Globalization of capitalism may

---

8. See G. B. Madison, *The Political Economy of Civil Society and Human Rights* (New York: Routledge, 1998).
9. See Dietrich Rueschemeyer, Evelyne Huber Stephens, and John D. Stephens, *Capitalist Development and Democracy* (Chicago: University of Chicago Press, 1992).

not result in globalization of democracy and human rights. Decisions by international organizations that are imposed from above and that restrict the political dynamic that might otherwise occur between a state's government and citizens' movements, can undermine human rights. Human actions and human decisions will affect any transformation that occurs in the less wealthy parts of the world.

A key difference between the earlier development in the West of capitalist, democratic and eventually rights-protective societies, and development occurring in the twenty-first century, is the role of global financial institutions in managing investments. Joseph Stiglitz is extremely critical of the way the International Monetary Fund (IMF) encourages "hot money" investments without regard to national governments' economic goals. He defines hot money as "money that comes into and out of a country, often overnight, often little more than betting on whether a currency is going to appreciate or depreciate."[10] This rapid movement of money is possible in part because of the tremendous advances in communications that are a characteristic of the present era of globalization. Hot money can destabilize an economy without providing any economic or human rights benefits. Stiglitz explains how this policy contributed to the South-East Asian economic melt-down of 1997. Without claiming a knowledge of economics sufficient to verify Stiglitz's argument, I attempt below to schematize his explanation, and to extrapolate from it to a more general model of how a society that is both growing economically and becoming more politically open can regress.[11]

In the pessimistic model of the Second Great Transformation, hot money flows into a country as a result of IMF pressure to reduce controls on capital mobility. Hot money looks for quick earnings opportunities on the financial market, not for longer-term earnings requiring investment in infrastructure or manufacturing. There is then an economic crisis, and the hot money flees the country as quickly as it entered. Without capital, businesses cannot pay their debts, and many of them fail. This causes job loss, within both the foreign investment sector and the local sector of businesses geared to servicing foreign-owned corporations. The middle class's savings are reduced as disinvestment results in lower valuations on locally owned investments.

As a result of capital flight, governments' tax revenue and overall capacity declines. Governments react by disinvesting in the civil service, causing further job loss. Governments also disinvest in social services, especially in education and health. The quality of human capital declines, thereby rendering the country less attractive to future investors who might be looking for workers.

Whatever democratization and development of civil society might have previously occurred is also now subject to threat. Society begins to distrust the rule of law, as it becomes obvious that the law has been used to protect the interests of the hot money investors. Distrust in the rule of law generates distrust in government as an institution capable of reforming a disintegrating economy. Thus, communities and individuals retreat from the state. Distrust in law and government expands into a generalized social distrust. Ethnic and communal groups start to compete for jobs, business opportunities, and government benefits, and men try to force women back into the home. There are food riots, and other political manifestations of extreme social unrest. Fundamentalist political parties, or parties advocating populist or fascist solutions to political crisis, quickly arise. They recruit especially from among unemployable men.

The result of such economic and social crises is often a reversion from democracy to autocratic political policies. As they attempt simultaneously to meet outsiders' economic demands that they pay their debts, and to restore civic order, governments impose controls on civil and political rights and on civil society. Attempting to attract international capital back to the country, they offer a weakened labor force, imposing controls on trade unions. Less educated than previously and less able to exercise their basic civil and political rights, workers are less capable of pressuring either governments or employers for their economic rights, which consequently decline. "Third generation" rights such as the right to development and the right to a clean environment also suffer, without active labor movements and civil society organization to pay attention to them.

10. Joseph E. Stiglitz, *Globalization and Its Discontents* (New York: W.W. Norton, 2002), 7.
11. Ibid., 89–132.

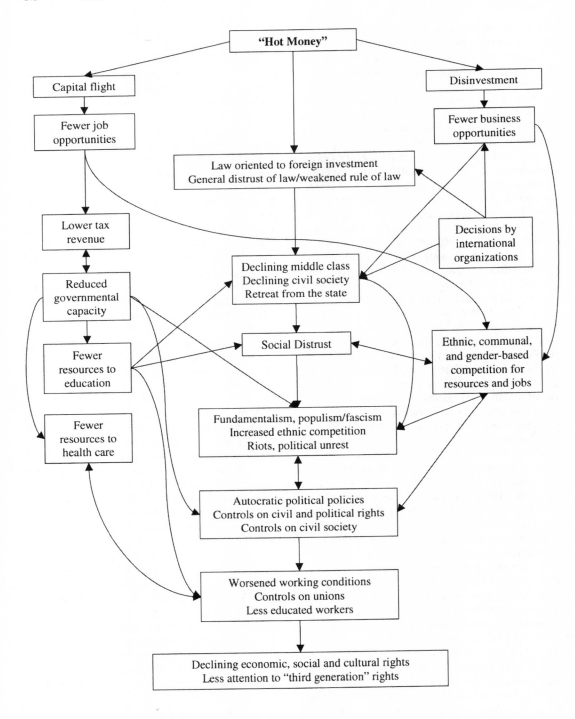

Figure 2. The Second Great Transformation: a pessimistic model.

Stiglitz's description of the meltdown in Asia refers to the very short period of 1997–99. He describes problems that preoccupy the anti-globalization forces. These problems make clear that class action and organization are necessary to connect capitalism, democracy and human rights. As the world globalizes, no positive transformation of the human rights situation of ordinary people will occur without a social movement for those rights. This is so even when all economic indicators are positive, and when the rule of law and democracy seem "naturally" to evolve. It is even more so when economic indicators are negative, and when the rule of law and democratic politics disappear.

HUMAN RIGHTS LEAPFROGGING

Above, I have discussed human rights only as dependent consequences of globalization. But the principles, laws, and practice of human rights also independently affect both the elite implementation of globalization and social action in favor of, or against, it. A major difference between the first and second Great Transformations is the existence the second time around of the international human rights regime, and the international human rights social movement.

The happy predictions made above in Figure 1, schematizing the optimistic model of the Second Great Transformation, rely on similarities to the social evolution of the West. None of this suggests, however, an easy or inevitable transition in the "Rest" of the world from poverty to wealth. Formerly colonized countries in what used to be called the Third World do not have access to one of the most important advantages the West had during its own period of capitalist growth. That advantage was human rights lawlessness. Neither states nor entrepreneurs had to think about the rights of their citizens or workers, or the rights of those inhabiting the worlds they conquered.

During the West's period of growth, there were no international laws to prevent slavery or colonialism. Imperialists used the people and resources of the conquered territories as they saw fit. As there were no laws against slavery or colonialism, so also there were no laws against massive population transfers. Governments in Europe and North America could deport their citizens to the colonies, or deprive them of the lands they traditionally owned. Finally, no international law prohibited genocide and ethnic cleansing. Colonists could do as they pleased to wipe out the "primitive" populations occupying territories that they sought.

Human rights lawlessness, then, gave industrializing Western powers several advantages not enjoyed by industrializing regimes in the early twenty-first century. None of these advantages however, assured the prosperity of the Western world, without the social changes diagramed in Figure 4.1. Not all colonial powers became equally prosperous, nor did all slave-trading economies become equally wealthy. Internal changes in habits, laws, entrepreneurial activities and relations among social groups were also important determinants of capitalist growth.

Therefore, in a global world now characterized by human rights constraints, less-developed countries will be at some disadvantage compared to their Western predecessors. On the other hand, citizens of these less-developed countries are at an advantage in demanding their rights, as compared to citizens of the West until well into the twentieth century. Citizens in places now being reached by globalization need not wait 150 or 200 years before attaining their rights. Figure 3 shows the many aspects of the global order that now promote human rights.[12]

To begin with, the entire world is now constrained by the international human rights regime, a set of norms and laws which most countries have formally said they respect. These norms and laws mean newly industrializing countries are not supposed to engage in the same wealth-creating activities as their Western predecessors: they are not supposed to engage in slavery, colonialism, genocide, massive population transfers, or deportations of citizens they do not want. Nor are they supposed to ignore citizens' basic economic needs.

A global communications network supports the spread of information about the global human rights regime. Once they encounter this information, more and more citizens demand their governments respect international human rights law. It is easy for citizens of all nations of the world to communicate with each other instantaneously. Citizens are no longer mere

12. Ibid., 89–132.

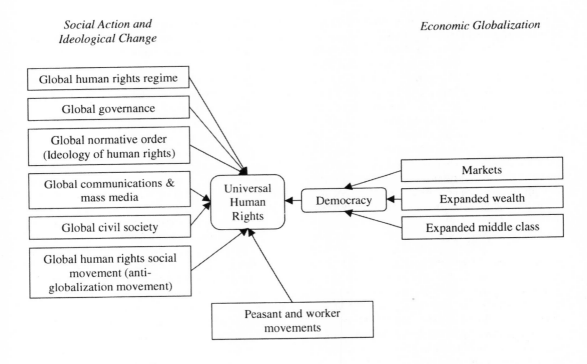

*Social Action and
Ideological Change*

Economic Globalization

Figure 3. Social action and human rights.

consumers of information: they are generators of knowledge and debaters about social issues. Civil society actors have immediate access to knowledge and immediate capacity to criticize public policy decisions by governments and international agencies. The civil society actors who now populate global public space link the developed and nondeveloped parts of the globe, the democracies with authoritarian states, in a discussion of human rights that only the most draconian restrictions on access to the international communicative media can control.

This communications network in turn enables the formation of global social movements in favor of human rights, which also benefits from ease of travel. People living in remote parts of the globe form alliances with civil society actors in the developed world, and persuade the mass media to take up their cause. If the capitalist-owned mass media ignore a particular problem, the technology of global communications nevertheless allows discussion of it through the formation of independent media groups, chat rooms, and websites. As global communication erodes geographical remoteness, the universal

principle of human rights becomes one upon which local actors can base their demands for justice.

An important aspect of the global social movement to protect human rights is the movement to protect workers' rights. Global consumer campaigns against child labor have been particularly successful. There are also now voluntary international codes of conduct for TNCs. And there is a movement among international lawyers to bring TNCs under the constraints of the international human rights regime. The International Labor Organization and the Organization for Economic Co-operation and Development have elaborated minimum labor standards and voluntary guidelines for multinational enterprises.

The international human rights movement is also assisted by an unprecedented level of global governance. States voluntarily dilute their sovereignty in favor of international treaties and regulations. Both the reach and the depth of international law have been significantly extended. The argument that economic growth requires a free hand both for capitalists and governments without regard to political democracy or the rule of law, has little credence in the early twenty-first century. But global governance is not only a matter of formal institutional development, or proclamation of new treaties and laws. It is also a matter of new space for citizens' movements. Global space is densely populated, and within it there is much pressure for cosmopolitan democracy.[13] Thus globalization speeds up the processes not only of capitalist expansion, but also of resistance to capitalism.

In the game of leapfrog, little children line up in a row, then leap over each other's backs, the child at the end starting first. In the human rights world, rights now leap over much larger obstacles. Oceans are crossed and centuries ignored in the debate about what human rights are or ought to be, what people are entitled to, and who is expected to implement those rights. Over the Atlantic and Pacific Oceans, the Mediterranean and Black Seas, human rights leap from developed to underdeveloped regions. Over the centuries of the first Great Transformation, human rights leap to the second Great Transformation. And as in the children's game of leapfrog, the last are often first. Those who are most deprived demand to go to the head of the line. They demand enjoyment of all the rights to which they are told by international law they are entitled, despite the relative economic

underdevelopment and political and legal backwardness of their own societies. Patience is not enjoined upon them: they are not told their time will come.

Human rights leapfrogging is one positive aspect of globalization, but it is no guarantee of ultimate global respect for human rights. The final human rights outcome of globalization cannot now be predicted. It is no more sensible to pass judgment on globalization as an instrument of social change that it would have been sensible to pass judgment on the Industrial Revolution in 1780 or 1800. Now, as then, the short-term detrimental consequences are obvious. Now, as then, humanitarians must strive to overcome the harms of dispossession, underemployment, and poverty. Now, as then, we do not know the final outcome.

But we do know that economic globalization must be tempered by social action. Groups and individuals in societies being affected by globalization must insist on democracy and on respect for human rights laws and principles. National governments, international organizations, and private corporations must also respect human rights. Human rights are the only path to a globalization that is humane, respects local cultures and societies, and improves economic conditions without dehumanizing those affected by its reach.

QUESTIONS FOR REFLECTION AND DISCUSSION

1. Howard-Hassmann contends that "the debate whether globalization . . . is good or bad is as irrelevant as arguing whether the transition from an agrarian to an industrial society in the Western world from the eighteenth to the twentieth century was good or bad." Do you agree? Disagree? Are societies that are fighting to retain their unique identities and practices simply tilting at windmills?

2. Does Howard-Hassmann's vision of "human rights leapfrogging" square with what you know to be the lived experience of the global poor? Do "those who are most deprived" (say, the impoverished, displaced, and starving of Sudan) truly "demand to go to the head of the line," as Howard-Hassmann asserts? If so, how? And do they truly "demand enjoyment of all the rights to which they are told by international law they are entitled"? Is it the *right* to food or the *right* to employment they demand, or is it food and jobs? Is there a difference? What about the right to vote? To freedom of speech and assembly?

3. Does Howard-Hassmann's vision of "human rights leapfrogging" adequately address the seemingly contrary concerns of those working ardently to protect the right of indigenous peoples to self-determination and their own culture? Compare, for example, Reading 12 by Maivân Clech Lâm in Chapter 2 of this volume. Choose a specific indigenous culture fighting for autonomy and ask whether members of the culture will find more protection of their rights in Lâm's approach or in Howard-Hassmann's. Can the two approaches work in concert?

13. See James N. Rosenau, "Governance and Democracy in a Globalizing World," in Daniele Archibugi, David Held, and Martin Kohler, eds., *Re-imagining Political Community: Studies in Cosmopolitan Democracy* (Stanford, Calif.: Stanford University Press, 1998), 28–57, at 42.

4. Howard-Hassmann notes that "National governments, international organizations, and private corporations must . . . respect human rights" if human rights are to be universally (or even widely) enjoyed worldwide. She also recognizes that, while the reach and depth of international law are expanding, they do not yet extend to strict legal governance of multinational/transnational corporations, which are subject primarily to voluntary codes of conduct and guidelines. How do you think multinational/transnational corporations should be regulated? By whom? Does a human rights framework provide meaningful guidance for how that regulation should be structured? Why? Why not? For pertinent discussion, see Reading 32 by Mahmood Monshipouri, Claude E. Welch, Jr., and Evan T. Kennedy in Chapter 8 in this volume.

5. If "class action and organization are necessary to connect capitalism, democracy, and human rights," as Howard-Hassmann suggests, what do you make of the concern, expressed by anti-globalization activists, that multinational/transnational corporations have the power effectively to prevent both class action and organization from occurring in countries where they operate? If class action and organization do not happen on a meaningful scale in those countries, how else might human rights be protected there?

6. Multinational/transnational corporations have increasing influence over international treaties, including human rights treaties. If this is true, even only partially, how does it square with Howard-Hassmann's assertion that "The international human rights movement is also assisted by an unprecedented level of global governance"? Is that governance always on the side of human rights? If not, what interests does it serve and how might the human rights movement respond?

7. In *Human Rights Horizons: The Pursuit of Justice in a Globalizing World* (New York: Routledge, 2000), Richard Falk suggests that the era of neoliberal economic growth and globalization, coupled with privatization of resources and a widening gap between rich and poor (perhaps with concomitant human rights neglect and abuses), will be followed by a reempowerment of the state. In your opinion, is the first stage likely to be marked by more or fewer human rights problems than the second? Why? Why not? Based on which historical precedents?

8. In *The End of Human Rights: Critical Legal Thought at the Turn of the Century* (Oxford: Hart, 2000), Costas Douzinas calls into question Howard-Hassmann's assertion that the "modern democratic state buttressed by the rule of law and by a civic culture of activism and political freedom is more likely than any other type of political system to protect human rights," asserting instead that the advent of a global human rights culture has not prevented suffering from becoming more widespread in the twentieth century than ever before. Do you agree with Howard-Hassmann or Douzinas in this regard? Does Howard-Hassmann's assessment imply that pre-industrial societies cannot protect human rights?

9. Howard-Hassmann imagines both an "optimistic" and a "pessimistic" scenario in the relationship between globalization and human rights. Which is the more likely? Why? Is an in-between scenario possible? Probable? Why?

10. On final analysis, what does Howard-Hassmann propose to ensure that globalization will turn out to be, from a human rights perspective, a good thing?

Chapter Two

Basic Decencies and Participatory Rights

IN this chapter, we consider some grave problems raised by recent world history: genocide, torture, threats to the rule of law, and discrimination based on race, sex, and religion, as well as that directed against refugees and indigenous peoples. Our concern is with the root value of simple human respect or, more precisely, with those modern-day deprivations of human respect that show contempt for the basic decencies of life—personal survival and security—and for claims to equality in the pursuit of life.

Suffering characterizes much of human history, but during the twentieth century and the early years of the twenty-first we have managed to propagate misery of the most grotesque sort on a global scale. Two world wars, complete with fire bombings and atomic blasts, claimed sixty million lives. Through genocide, mass purges, arbitrary killings, and barbarous torture (at the hands of such persons as Adolf Hitler, Josef Stalin, Idi Amin, Pol Pot, Slobodan Milosevič, Saddam Hussein, Augustin Bizimungu, and, most recently, Janjaweed militia leader Musa Hilal), through the abuse of powerless minorities of all descriptions, and through racial, sex-based, and other forms of arbitrary discrimination, the processes of dehumanization have further revealed themselves in all their stark obscenity. These patterns of indecency and invidious marginalization continue.

Against this appalling background, however, there is some good news. Though unparalleled in its perfidy, our era is also the first in which people are trying to do something about these treacheries on a global and regional scale. In the name of human rights, insistence upon basic decency and equality has established a minimum global standard that is now an integral part of contemporary international law even if not always national and international policy. Thus does the Preamble to the UN Charter, responding to death camps, torture chambers, abused minorities, and helpless peoples fleeing misery and oppression, "reaffirm faith in fundamental human rights, in the dignity and worth of the human person, in the equal rights of men and women and of nations large and small."

A first step from preambulary rhetoric to legal action was taken at Nuremberg in 1945, when Nazi leaders captured as criminals of war were convicted not only for violations of the laws and customs of war, a time-honored standard imposed by military victors, but also for "crimes against humanity." They were convicted for political, racial, and religious persecutions committed against *any* civilian population (i.e., German citizens as well as other nationals) and their convictions were justified "whether or not in violation of the domestic law of the country where perpetrated."[1] In other words, in contrast to pre-World War II times when "international law allowed each equal sovereign an equal right to be monstrous to his [sic] subjects,"[2] the law of Germany, however authoritative, constituted no defense. As the late Leo Gross put it, "these (Nuremberg) trials were in a profound sense a demonstration against the totalitarian subjection of the individual to 'nationalized' truth; they were a protest against the erasure of the individual as a subject, mediate or immediate, of international law, and as a responsible member of the international community."[3]

THE CRIME OF GENOCIDE

Drawing upon the principles of Nuremberg, the United Nations developed the Convention on the Prevention and Punishment of the Crime of Genocide.[4] The Convention defines genocide as "acts committed with intent to destroy in whole or in part, a national, ethnical, racial, or religious group as such,"[5] and the Contracting Parties to it "confirm" that, even if perpetrated by a government against its own inhabitants, it "is a crime under international law which they undertake to prevent and punish."[6] Genocide is a violation of human rights on the most hideous scale, and as Samantha Power argues in *"A Problem from Hell": America and the Age of Genocide*, the United States, like all countries, has a responsibility to "call it like it is."[7]

In 2004, in an act without precedent since the UN Genocide Convention was adopted in 1948, a government accused another sitting government of genocide when U.S. Secretary of State Colin L. Powell asserted that the "Arab" (light-skinned) Government of Sudan undertook a war of ethnic extermination against the "African" (darker-skinned) Fur, Masalit, and Zaghawa inhabitants of the western Sudanese province of Darfur. Speaking before the U.S. Senate Foreign Relations Committee, Powell asserted: "I [have] concluded that genocide has been committed in Darfur and that the Government of Sudan and the Janjaweed [paramilitary terrorists] bear responsibility—and genocide may still be occurring."[8]

Secretary Powell's assertion set in motion an inquiry with the potential for official as well as public condemnation, sanctions, and even war crimes trials. How this works—that is, how an authoritative response to humans exterminating one another is operationalized—is analyzed by international law scholar Diane Orentlicher. In her essay on "Genocide" (Reading 5), she presents the methods by which the Convention can be enforced and clarifies the definition of genocide which importantly raises issues about the intentions of the perpetrators.

1. Article 6(c) of the Agreement for the Prosecution and Punishment of the Major War Criminals of the European Axis Powers and Charter of the International Military Tribunal (Aug. 8, 1945), referenced in Documentary Appendix B.
2. Tom J. Farer, "Introduction," in Paul Williams, ed., *The International Bill of Human Rights* (Glen Ellen, Calif.: Entwhistle Books, 1981), xiii.
3. Leo Gross, "The Punishment of War Criminals: The Nuremberg Trial," *Netherlands International Law Review* (1954): 34.
4. Concluded Dec. 9, 1948, referenced in Documentary Appendix B.
5. Ibid., art. 2.
6. Ibid., art. 1.
7. Samantha Power, *"A Problem from Hell": America and the Age of Genocide* (New York: Basic Books, 2002). See also Eric D. Weitz, *A Century of Genocide: Utopias of Race and Nation* (Princeton N.J.: Princeton University Press, 2003).
8. Quoted in Glenn Kessler and Colum Lynch, "U.S. Calls Killings in Sudan Genocide," *Washington Post*, Sept. 10, 2004, A1.

Political scientists such as Ted Gurr and Barbara Harff have sought to develop advance warning indicators for genocide, attempting to anticipate its onset.[9] Others, such as international criminal law specialists M. Cherif Bassiouni and Michael Scharf, have worked to prevent future genocides by focusing on the identification, arrest, trial, and conviction of the perpetrators of genocide.[10] And still others have looked retrospectively at the historical record, explaining genocide, at least in part, by what sociologist Helen Fein has described as the tendency of people to act within a restricted "universe of obligation" (i.e., that circle of people with reciprocal obligations to protect one another) set by friendship, family, tribe, nation, culture, religion, or other bonds of fraternity and to dehumanize "outside others."[11] Also, because it is so atrocious, genocide raises fundamental questions about whether other acts contemptuous of human life are properly within the scope of survival rights. What other life-threatening acts, it may be asked, are today sought to be prevented and punished, if any? Does the *desideratum* of basic decency include survival rights beyond the right to be free from genocide?

CONFRONTING TORTURE AND DISAPPEARANCES

Torture, it may be assumed, is within the scope of survival rights under contemporary international law, customary and conventional. Both the Universal Declaration of Human Rights (UDHR) and the International Covenant on Civil and Political Rights (ICCPR) specify that "no one shall be arbitrarily deprived of his [sic] life."[12] In his book, *The Right to Life in International Law*, former Deputy High Commissioner for Human Rights B. G. Ramcharan shows that the word "arbitrarily" was carefully chosen "with the intention of providing the highest possible level of protection to the right to life and to confine permissible deprivations therefrom to the narrowest of limits."[13] He asserts that today there is an international consensus as to deprivations of life that are manifestly arbitrary and that they include torture-related deaths and those resulting from degrading treatment or punishment in prison or other detention (as well as genocide, crimes against humanity, war crimes, deaths resulting from acts of aggression, executions carried out in the absence of due process, and enforced or involuntary "disappearances"). In remarks to the Committee against Torture in April 2001, in which he ably reviews some relevant historical literature and recounts an important 12-point torture prevention program adopted as a model guide by Amnesty International, Dr. Ramcharan concluded unequivocally: "No exceptional circumstances whatsoever, whether a state of war or a threat of war, internal political instability or any other public emergency, may be invoked as a justification of torture."[14]

9. See Barbara Harff, "No Lessons Learned from the Holocaust? Assessing Risks of Genocide and Political Mass Murder Since 1955," *APSR* 97, no. 1 (Feb. 2003): 57–73. See also Barbara Harff and Ted Robert Gurr, "Victims of the State Genocides and Politicides and Group Repression Since 1945," *International Review of Victimology* 11 (1989): 23–41.
10. See M. Cherif Bassiouni, *Crimes Against Humanity in International Criminal Law*, 2nd rev. ed. (The Hague: Kluwer Law, 1999). See also the "War Crimes Research Portal" of the Case School of Law Frederick K. Cox International Law Center, directed by Professor Scharf, at http://www.law.case.edu/war-crimes-research-portal/ links.asp?id=34
11. Helen Fein, *Accounting for Genocide: National Responses and Jewish Victimization During the Holocaust* (New York: Free Press, 1979), 7–9.
12. Each of these instruments, the first adopted Dec. 10, 1948 and the second concluded Dec. 16, 1966, is reprinted and referenced in Documentary Appendix A.
13. B. G. Ramcharan, *The Right to Life in International Law* (The Hague: Nijhoff, 1985).
14. Remarks of Dr. Bertrand Ramcharan, Deputy High Commissioner for Human Rights, Committee

In "Torture and the Future" (Reading 6), Professor Lisa Hajjar reports that "today, people are being tortured in two thirds of the world's countries," that U.S. and British practices at their military prisons in Iraq (and Guantánamo Bay, Cuba, as well, in the case of the United States) are but the most recently notorious examples of this reality, and thus she reveals that Dr. Ramcharan's assertion, if taken as a statement of fact, may be wide of the behavioral mark—and notwithstanding adherence to the 1984 Convention against Torture and Other Cruel, Inhuman or Degrading Treatment or Punishment[15] by 141 or almost 74 percent of the world's states as of this writing, the United Kingdom and the United States included. "No torturing regime defends or even acknowledges its own torture as torture," Hajjar observes, thus implicitly endorsing Ramcharan's assertion as a statement of principle. But, she insists, "torture is not a relic of our past" and provides "[no] meaningful geographical or cultural demarcation between 'civilized' and 'uncivilized' societies." As Eyal Press has pointed out, even a celebrated criminal law professor at the Harvard Law School, Alan Dershowitz, contends that torture practices are warranted in the face of the "ticking bomb" scenario whereby "torture is justified to extract potentially life-saving information" (as in the "war against terrorism," for example)—in stark contrast, however, to Justice Robert Jackson of the Nuremberg Tribunal who favored a legal "bright line" against the use of torture in order to uphold the integrity of U.S. law and set an example for other countries.[16]

In July 2004, the International Committee of the Red Cross (ICRC) presented a confidential report to the United States government saying that its military intentionally used psychological and sometimes physical coercion "tantamount to torture" on prisoners at Guantánamo Bay, Cuba. The inspection team also asserted that some doctors and other medical workers were participating in planning for coercive interrogations, in what the report called "a flagrant violation of medical ethics." The *New York Times*, which did not say how it received the secret report, noted that the government rejected the charges: "The United States," the government claimed, "operates a safe, humane, and professional detention operation at Guantánamo that is providing valuable information in the war on terrorism."[17] As philosopher Henry Shue queries: If the most powerful country in the world has to torture, how are we supposed to convince anyone else that they shouldn't torture?[18]

That the travesty of government reliance on torture is not a thing of the past and is a most serious issue in international affairs today is underscored by three responsive United Nations initiatives. Each merits notice.

First, as a result of an intensive campaign by nongovernmental organizations (NGOs), especially Amnesty International, the UN General Assembly adopted, in 1975, the Declaration on the Protection of All Persons from Being Subjected to Torture and Other Cruel, Inhuman or Degrading Treatment or Punishment.[19] In 1984, building upon the Declaration, it adopted the above-mentioned Convention against Torture and Other Cruel, Inhuman or Degrading Treatment or Punishment.[20] The Convention entered into force on June 26, 1987, thereby moving state-sponsored torture into the poisoned circle of "crimes against

---

Against Torture, 26th Sess., April 30, 2001, available at http://www.unhchr.ch/ huricane/huricane.nsf/0/AFA592526C883257 C1256A400056D579?opendocument.
15. Concluded Dec. 10, 1984, referenced in Documentary Appendix B.
16. Eyal Press, "Tortured Logic: Thumbscrewing International Law," in *Amnesty Now*, available at http://www.amnestyusa.org/ amnestynow/tortured.html
17. Neil A Lewis, "Red Cross Finds Detainee Abuse in Guantánamo," *New York Times*, Nov. 30, 2004, 1.
18. Henry Shue, "Torture," *Philosophy and Public Affairs* 7, no. 2 (Winter 1978): 124–43, at 133.
19. Adopted Dec. 9, 1975, referenced in Documentary Appendix B.
20. See note 15.

humanity," and it does so with a tough provision recognizing "universal criminal jurisdiction" (which is to say that any state party apprehending a torturer may bring her or him to justice). Specifically, per Convention Articles 6 and 7, the states parties are required to take alleged offenders into custody, make preliminary inquiries, notify the state from which the accused comes, and, unless the accused is to be extradited by the arresting state, submit the accused to her or his own state authorities for prosecution.

Second, the UN Commission on Human Rights established the office of Special Rapporteur on Torture. The person assuming that position is authorized to respond to complaints of torture on an "urgent action" basis by questioning governments about reliance on cruelty. The Rapporteur's confidential challenges on specific allegations have made a difference. The first Special Rapporteur on Torture, Professor P. H. Kooijmans of the Free University of Amsterdam, after reporting to the United Nations in 1985, commented auspiciously "on people who had been released and not been tortured" as follows:

> Whenever one approaches a government with a concrete case, that action by the UN Rapporteur is considered at least by the government involved, as an activist attitude. . . . Yet, I never received a reply that it was none of my business, and (that) I was interfering with the internal situation. The general shame felt for the practice of torture obviously is so great that no government at this time feels that the most appropriate reply is to make a reproach of interference. . . . Even when governments flatly deny that torture has taken place, it means that they feel they are subject to the rule that torture is prohibited. If you compare that response with the situation of a few years ago, when governments would protest interference in internal affairs, it is real progress.[21]

Even the Chinese Government, steadfast in protesting external queries about torture, responded to Special Rapporteur Theo van Boven in 2004 by acknowledging the "sudden death of Falun Gong [religious dissident] practitioners in its custody" although at the same time insisting that "allegations of their torture and ill-treatment are unfounded."[22]

Finally, in recent years, the United Nations has sought also to help the victims of torture. In 1981, the General Assembly set up a Voluntary Fund for Victims of Torture, relying upon contributions of governments, private groups, and individuals. Among the Fund's projects are grants to psychiatric and medical centers for the treatment and rehabilitation of victims of torture.[23] For example, the International Rehabilitation Center for Torture Victims, established in Denmark in 1985, maintains facilities at the University Hospital of Copenhagen which treats both victims and their families, and trains health professionals from other countries in the latest methods of therapy. By 2005, the Danish Center had collaborated with more than 200 clinics and programs worldwide, especially in refugee receiving cities such as Bangkok, Toronto, Paris, and Stockholm. In the United States, 30 such programs operate in 19 states. Illustrative is the Minneapolis Center for Victims of Torture where health professionals operate an outpatient clinic serving traumatized persons, many from the large refugee community in the Minneapolis-St. Paul area. Center staff help

---

21. Interview with Professor Kooijmans, Special Rapporteur on Torture for the UN Commission on Human Rights," *SIM Newsletter* (Netherlands Institute of Human Rights) 16 (Nov. 1986): 6–7. See also Marina Svensson, *Debating Human Rights in China: A Conceptual and Political History* (Lanham, Md.: Rowman and Littlefield, 2002).
22. Reports by the Falun Gong Human Rights Working Group are accessible at www.flghrwg.net. By 2004, the NGO passed along to the UN tens of thousands of reports on torture of its member in China. "UN Rapporteur on Torture Highlights China, Falun Gong," *Epoch Times*, June 3, 2004.
23. Hans Danelius, "The UN Fund for Torture Victims," *The Review* (International Commission of Jurists) 37 (Dec. 1986): 35–42. For updated information, visit the Web site of the International Rehabilitation Council for Torture Victims at www.irct.org

torture victims to recover their mental and physical health and to find housing, seek political asylum, and adjust to daily life. Consulting psychiatrists, physicians, and volunteers follow strict rules of confidentiality, giving patients a needed sense of safety and trust.

A problem related to torture is the phenomenon of "disappearances" whereby a government criminally assumes the power to end life without cause, public notice, or responsibility. The problem was most common in the 1970s, but it persisted, tragically, into the 1990s in Kenya, Sri Lanka, and Guatemala, and into the twenty-first century as well. On the occasion of the International Day of the Disappeared (August 30) in 2004, the UN Working Group expressed concern for 890 cases in Colombia, 270 in the Russian Federation, and 130 cases in Nepal. The "desaparecidos" or "disappeared" (a term first used by the Guatemalan press and intended to refer to presumed victims of political violence) in reality have not disappeared. Even though their fate is, typically, violent (often illegal) arrest, torture, secret detention, and death,[24] their whereabouts are ordinarily well known to the governments or vigilantes responsible for their "disappearance." Evidence collected by Amnesty International, the International League for Human Rights, and the United Nations Working Group on Involuntary Disappearances, among others, documents the point ad nauseam. The uncovering of mass graves of people previously believed to have "disappeared" and the testimony of survivors of secret detention camps have helped not only to fill in the factual vacuum left by each individual "disappearance" but also to refute denials of accountability on the part of the governmental authorities in countries such as Argentina where the practice once was widespread.[25]

CLAIMS TO EQUALITY IN THE PURSUIT OF LIFE AND HAPPINESS

The two essays in this chapter by the late Richard B. Lillich and Rachel Neild (Readings 7 and 8) track the range of those governmental acts other than and in addition to torture and "disappearances" that show contempt for the basic decencies of life and for claims to equality in the pursuit of life.

Lillich sets out the international standards designed to safeguard the rights to life, liberty, and security of the person as well as the civil rights to equality implicit in the rule of law. He explains how these and other rights—the right to a remedy, the right to a fair trial, the presumption of innocence, the right to freedom of movement, the right to nationality, the right to marry and found a family—are protected under international law so as to ensure everyone's claims for respect and equal participation in the fundamental freedoms set forth in the Universal Declaration of Human Rights. These first generation rights, he asserts, are "commonly considered to be the most basic and fundamental of all human rights."

Rachel Neild in "Human Rights and Crime" is concerned with the implementation and application of the standards described by Lillich but her analysis goes beyond concern with state violations of civil rights and takes into account also the rights of victims of crimes committed by non-state actors. Neild focuses on twenty-first-century conditions in countries undergoing transition from authoritarianism and repression to peace and democracy.

---

24. See, e.g., Amnesty International, *Disappearances: A Workbook* (New York: Amnesty International, 1981).
25. Reed Brody and Felipe González, "*Nunca Más*: An Analysis of International Instruments on "Disappearances," *HRQ* 19, no. 2 (1997): 365–405. See *Nunca Más! (Never Again): A Report by Argentina's National Commission on Disappeared People* (London: Faber and Faber, 1986), with Index on Censorship.

The contrast is especially acute among the new post-Cold War democracies where international civil rights are challenged by significantly rising crime rates. Referencing experience in Africa, Asia, Eastern Europe, and Latin America, the author argues the importance of improving police accountability and effectiveness and working against criminal impunity (especially when tied to state violence) while simultaneously safeguarding the civil rights of citizens.[26]

Remaining essays in this chapter focus on state obligations to afford equal protection of the laws to all without discrimination irrelevant to merit or need. The topic of racial discrimination is introduced by Paul Gordon Lauren in his "First Principles of Racial Equality" (Reading 9). He recounts the contentious first efforts to come to normative terms with racism internationally. A signal advance was made in 1967 when the United Nations Educational, Scientific and Cultural Organization (UNESCO) convened a committee of distinguished experts to assess issues of racial discrimination worldwide, to disseminate scientific facts about race, and to combat racial discrimination. The committee agreed that racist doctrines lack scientific foundation altogether and adopted the position that racism stifles the development of those who suffer it, perverts those who apply it, divides nations within themselves, aggravates international conflict, and threatens world peace.[27] The UNESCO experts confirmed the obvious, of course: racial discrimination, however widespread and wherever found, degrades and fetters all humans. Accordingly, defining "racial discrimination" as constituting "any distinction, exclusion, restriction or preference based on race, color, descent, or national or ethnic origin which has the purpose or effect of nullifying or impairing the recognition, enjoyment or exercise, on an equal footing, of human rights and fundamental freedoms in the political, economic, social, cultural or any other field of public life" (and whether or not an actual or potential victim of discrimination is, like the Roma of Europe, itinerant or permanently situated), the 1965 International Convention on the Elimination of All Forms of Racial Discrimination (ICERD),[28] to combat this social abomination, authorizes such remedies as penal sanctions in some cases and education and community action in others. Under the Convention, too, is mandated a Committee on the Elimination of Racial Discrimination (CERD) to (a) review and analyze state reports; (b) examine state complaints relative to the performance of other states parties, and subject to appropriate recognition of the competence of the committee; and (c) consider and act upon complaints and communications from individuals and groups claiming to be victims of racial discrimination.

26. See also Niels Uildriks and Piet van Reenen, *Policing Post-Communist Societies: Police-Public Violence, Democratic Policing, and Human Rights* (New York: Open Society Institute, 2003); Andrew Coyle, Allison Campbell, and Rodney Neufeld, *Capitalist Punishment: Prison Privatization and Human Rights* (London: Zed Books, 2003).

27. See UNESCO, *Statement on Race and Racial Prejudice* (Paris: UNESCO, 1967). The UNESCO experts reached a consensus also on the following propositions:
- All people living today belong to the same species and descend from the same stock.
- The division of human species into "races" is partly conventional and partly arbitrary and does not imply any hierarchy whatsoever.
- Current biological knowledge does not permit us to impute cultural achievements to differences in genetic potential. The peoples of the world today appear to possess equal biological potentialities for attaining any level of civilization.
- The human problems arising from so-called "race relations" are social in origin rather than biological. Racism involves antisocial acts and beliefs that are based on the fallacy that discriminatory intergroup relations are justifiable on biological grounds.

See also Raphael Walden, *Racism and Human Rights* (Amsterdam: Nijhoff Law Special, 2004); David Wippman, *International Law and Ethnic Conflict* (Ithaca, N.Y.: Cornell University Press, 1998).

28. Concluded Dec. 21, 1965, referenced in Documentary Appendix B. For wide ranging analysis on related topics, see Kevin Reilly, Stephen Kaufman, and Angela Radino, *Racism: A Global Reader* (Armonk, N.Y.: M.E. Sharpe, 2003).

As of April 2006, the Race Convention (as it is sometimes called) had been ratified by 170 states, and in its 65th session in 2004 when the states parties totaled only one less, the 18-member CERD, noting Sudan's adherence to the Convention, announced its alarm about events in Sudan's western province of Darfur (mentioned above in relation to accusations of genocide). The Committee demanded prompt cessation of reported large-scale violations of human rights there, calling particular attention to violations of the Race Convention in the form of the massive displacement, terrorizing, and killing of "African" (dark-skinned) ethnic groups. In response, the "Arab" (lighter-skinned) Government of Sudan asserted that the violations were the work of private Janjaweed paramilitary forces and thus not government sponsored. In turn, the Committee called the Sudanese government's attention to the Race Convention's Article 5(b) guarantee of "The right to security of [the] person and protection by the State against violence or bodily harm, whether inflicted by government officials *or by any individual group or institution*" (emphasis added).

Extreme forms of racism cast a pall upon modern history, having been used to justify colonial exploitation, scapegoat Jews in Nazi Germany, exile Asians from Uganda, and repress blacks in South Africa, to name a few examples. Until recently, South Africa, both internally and in its former UN trust territory of South West Africa (now independent Namibia), rejected outright the notion that it should seek justice, equality, and other human rights protections for all its citizens. The doctrine of apartheid systematized racial segregation and, through elaborate arrangements, restricted all aspects of the domestic, social, political, and economic life of nonwhites who, in South Africa proper, constitute four-fifths of the population[29]—arrangements not identical but similar to what obtained in the United States prior to the 1960s, especially in the American south, and what continue in important respects to this day throughout American society, "still a residentially segregated society."[30]

Carried out with harsh rigor and determination, apartheid has been condemned by the United Nations as a policy that amounted to "the organization of society on the principles of slavery." In South Africa and South West Africa (Namibia), blacks were denied political rights, freedom of movement and residence (forced to live in conditions of humiliating indignity and squalor), freedom to work, and freedom to marry. In addition, every African over age sixteen was compelled to carry a "pass book" so the Government could maintain tight control. Beginning in 1962, with a growing demand for the adoption of anti-apartheid enforcement measures by the United Nations, the General Assembly recommended, by a more than two-thirds majority, the imposition of economic and diplomatic sanctions against South Africa, and the Security Council called upon all member states not to supply arms to the country.[31] Ultimately, the pressures of economic sanctions, a changing political climate, and the mutual cooperation of South African President F. W. de Klerk and the United Nations during Namibia's transition from trust territory administration by Pretoria to sovereign independence in March 1990 lessened long-time antagonisms. On June 17, 1991, President de Klerk dramatically declared that the legal foundation of apartheid "now

29. See Julian Kunnie, "A Comprehensive History of the South African Struggle," in Kunnie, *Is Apartheid Really Dead? Pan-Africanist Working-Class Cultural Critical Perspectives* (Boulder, Colo.: Westview Press, 2000), 1–54. Comparative analysis can usefully be found in Charles V. Hamilton, *Beyond Racism: Race and Inequality for Brazil, South Africa and the United States* (Boulder, Colo.: Lynne Reinner, 2001).
30. Douglas S. Massey and Nancy A. Denton, *American Apartheid: Segregation and the Making of the Underclass* (Cambridge, Mass.: Harvard University Press, 1993), 1.
31. The history of UN action is presented analytically in the framework of "regimes analysis" by Newell M. Stultz, "Evolution of the United Nations Anti-Apartheid Regime," *HRQ* 13, no. 1 (Feb. 1991): 1–23.

belongs to history." When Nelson Mandela came to office as president of South Africa in 1994, however, he faced daunting challenges, preeminently involving the stabilization of political and social order. In "The New South Africa: A Decade Later," historian Antoinette Handley observed in 2004: "A society that had been organized on the basis of separate and inequitable access to the most basic needs has been restructured into an open and democratic system in which all South Africans enjoy the right to representation and services." She also observed that, while issues of discrimination in many forms continue with sad results in South Africa, the state is nonetheless making progress in setting aside the legal apparatus of "social inequalities that apartheid created."[32] Even with apartheid laws abolished, however, it remains to be seen whether tolerant attitudes will dissolve compartmentalization in everyday life, in schools, jobs, and neighborhoods—another point of troubling comparison with the United States.[33] Such progress faces the daunting task of changing attitudes and behavior. With this challenge in mind and with the guidance of the new South African Human Rights Commission, the Ministry of Education has incorporated human rights education into the secondary school curriculum. A number of cooperating NGOs have extended it to the police, prisons, and public service as well.

Although the end of apartheid in South Africa is hailed as a victory for human rights, the country remains home to one of the world's highest levels of violent crime. According to psychologist Christopher Harper in 2003, "The legitimization of violence under apartheid, as a means both of enforcing apartheid and as a form of resistence, has contributed to [post-apartheid] high levels of violence";[34] and a shocking degree of such brutality, it must be noted, is directed at women.[35] In this respect, an innovative South African human rights education project described by Harper targets men—not just perpetrators, but nonviolent men also—who become active in the struggle for gender equality and for the eradication of violence against women and girls.

For the reader new to human rights or who has not considered gender issues, an extended quotation from Martha Nussbaum should spark new thoughts while appropriately representing most of the significant factors that make gender/women's human rights a discrete category within human rights. In "The 'Capabilities' Advantage to Promoting Women's Human Rights," Nussbaum writes:

> Women in much of the world are less well nourished than men, less healthy, more vulnerable to physical violence and sexual abuse. They are less likely than men to be literate, and still less likely to have preprofessional or technical education. Should they attempt to enter the workplace, they face greater obstacles, including intimidation from family members, discrimination in hiring, and sexual harassment—all, frequently, without effective legal recourse. Similar obstacles often impede their participation in political life, and in many nations women are not full equals under the law. Often burdened with the "double day" of taxing employment and full responsibility for housework and child care, they lack opportunities for play and cultivation of their imaginative and cognitive faculties. All these factors take their toll on emotional well-being; women have fewer opportunities than men to live free from fear and to enjoy rewarding types of

32. Antoinette Handley, "The New South Africa: A Decade Later," *Current History* 103, no. 673 (May 2004): 195–201. See also Kristin Henrad, *Minority Protection in Post-Apartheid South Africa: Human Rights, Minority Rights, and Self Determination* (Westport, Conn.: Praeger, 2002).
33. Massey and Denton, *American Apartheid*, note 30.
34. Interview with Christopher Harper, "Rights for All in the New South Africa," *Violence Against Women, Human Rights Dialogue* special issue 2, no. 10 (Fall 2003): 8–10, at 8.
35. See, e.g., Fiona C. Ross, *Bearing Witness: Women and the Truth and Reconciliation Commission in South Africa* (London: Pluto Press, 2003).

love—especially when, as is often the case, they are married without choice in child-hood and have no recourse from a bad marriage.[36]

"In all these ways," Nussbaum concludes, "unequal social and political circumstances give women unequal human capabilities."

An important step toward the attainment of the goal of equal rights for women was taken on December 18, 1979, when the UN General Assembly adopted the Convention on the Elimination of All forms of Discrimination against Women (CEDAW).[37] The 30-article convention, reflecting the extent of the exclusions and restrictions inflicted on women solely because of their sex, calls for equal rights for women, regardless of their marital status, in all fields—civil, political, economic and social (including health), and cultural. In addition, for international supervision of the obligations accepted by the states parties, the Convention provides for machinery comparable to that of the Race Convention. A committee of experts, elected by the states parties and serving in their personal expert capacity (i.e., not under instructions from their respective governments), monitors progress made toward the objectives of equal rights. In feminist Fran Hosken's opinion, "there is no doubt that in the international context, this convention is the single most important document speaking for the human rights of women that has ever been devised."[38]

The important proposition that "women's rights are human rights" is given astute analytical clarity by Eva Brems in "Protecting the Rights of Women" (Reading 10). A Belgian human rights scholar, she relies on insightful feminist scholarship to explore the core dimensions of women's human rights: (1) where women's rights are the same as men's human rights; (2) where "women's specificity" warrants special and distinctive women's rights; and (3) where key issues hold out the potential for a "feminist transformation of human rights for all." Leading to a future in which women build coalitions in support of economic, social, and cultural rights, this latter dimension, Professor Brems argues, "fits best in a conception of universality based on all-inclusiveness.

The importance of context as a fundamental component of taking human rights seriously is true also for the right to freedom of religion and conscience. Like race and gender discrimination, religious bigotry is an affront to human dignity and a disavowal of the principles of the International Bill of Human Rights, a viewpoint reaffirmed by the UN General Assembly in its 1981 Declaration on the Elimination of All Forms of Intolerance and Discrimination Based on Religion or Belief.[39] In propounding a right to "freedom of thought, conscience and religion," the Declaration proclaims in Article 1: "This right shall include freedom to have a religion or whatever belief of [one's] choice, and freedom, either individual or in community with others and in public or in private, to manifest [one's] religion or belief in worship, observance, practice and teaching." In Article 2, it defines "intolerance and discrimination based on religion or belief" to include "any distinction, exclusion restriction or preference" based on religion and intended or having as its effect

---

36. Martha Nussbaum, "The 'Capabilities' Advantage to Promoting Women's Human Rights," in *Silence Breaking: The Women's Dimension of the Human Rights Box, Human Rights Dialogue* special issue 2, no. 3 (Summer 2000): 10–14, at 10. See also Catherine Kingfisher, ed., *Western Welfare in Decline: Globalization and Women's Poverty* (Philadelphia: University of Pennsylvania Press, 2002).
37. Concluded Dec. 18, 1979, referenced in Documentary Appendix B.
38. Fran P. Hosken, "Toward a Definition of Women's Human Rights," *HRQ* 3, no. 2 (Spring 1981): 1–10, at 6. See also Marjorie Agosín, *Women, Gender, and Human Rights: A Global Perspective* (New Brunswick, N.J.: Rutgers University Press, 2001); Rebecca J. Cook, ed., *Human Rights of Women: National and International Perspectives* (Philadelphia: University of Pennsylvania Press, 1994); Katie Holmes Grimshaw and Marilyn Lake, eds., *Women's Rights and Human Rights: International Historical Perspectives* (New York: Palgrave, 2001).
39. Adopted Nov. 25, 1981, referenced in Documentary Appendix B.

the "nullification or impairment of the recognition, enjoyment or exercise of human rights and fundamental freedoms on an equal basis." In thus placing religious liberty squarely in the context of human rights—and in so doing, reflecting an underlying presumption that one need not be a "believer" to acknowledge religious freedom as a basic human right—the Declaration affirms the seamless fabric of all human rights.[40] In contexts wherein religious fundamentalism honors patriarchy and religious extremism fosters violence, this core truth begs to be taken seriously.

THE DISPOSSESSED, THE DISPLACED, THE DISENFRANCHISED

Invidious discrimination of all kinds has directly or indirectly caused wars and great suffering. Racism, sexism, and religious bigotry also have contributed to the flood of refugees that currently besets the world community. Since most of the world's refugees are women and their children, it is ironic that a woman is the symbol of freedom and refuge in the United States: the Statue of Liberty, "Mother of Exiles."

The human rights issues of those unfortunate enough to fall in the refugee category are the focus of Maryellen Fullerton's essay on "The International and National Protection of Refugees" (Reading 11). The author supplies a clear and sweeping historical introduction to one of the world's most persistent tragedies: the loss of one's home prompted by fear and force. The central focus is on the 1951 Convention Relating to the Status of Refugees as modified by the 1967 Protocol, which contains the most widely accepted definition of "refugee."[41] At this writing, 143 countries have ratified the Convention and its 1967 Protocol. While this large number suggests that there is a consensus concerning who qualifies as a refugee, the Convention and Protocol, according to Fullerton, contain major weaknesses—for example, failing to empower one who claims refugee status to protest its denial by a ratifying state. Despite this and other flaws she identifies, the author concludes that the Convention and Protocol remain the most significant international instruments for the protection of refugees. Accordingly, her essay searches the components of the Convention's definition of "refugee" as interpreted by the Office of the UN High Commissioner for Refugees (UNHCR) to supply a people-oriented guide for saving the lives of the world's uprooted and rejected who seek escape under desperate conditions.

Fleeing for their lives, refugees generally are unable to select their destinations, often traveling instead to areas bereft of services, good land, roads, and water. Typically, private humanitarian agencies and international organizations are unable to plan adequate relief when catastrophes and civil conflict strike quickly. Such was the case in early 2003 when refugees and displaced people began to escape fighting that erupted in Sudan's western region of Darfur. According to the UNHCR, more than 170,000 Sudanese fled across the border to neighboring Chad and an estimated one million were displaced within Darfur where paramilitary groups reportedly killed, raped, and forced hundreds of thousands from their homes, which then were destroyed on a massive scale. Near the border in strife-torn

---

40. On the political implications of this proposition for religious groups, see Claude E. Welch, Jr., "Mobilizing Morality: The World Council of Churches and Its Programme to Combat Racism, 1969–1994," *HRQ* 23, no. 4 (2001): 863–910.
41. The Convention and Protocol were concluded on, respectively, July 28, 1951 and Jan. 31, 1967. Each is referenced in Documentary Appendix B.

Darfur itself, UNHCR showed heroic action in working to improve the lives of hundreds of thousands of displaced Sudanese in UNHCR camps. For the UNHCR, life-saving principles are at work under the most arduous and difficult circumstances.

The sheer numbers of refugees and displaced persons worldwide have been such as to cause increasing concern in receiving nations such as Canada, Chad, Honduras, Jordan, Pakistan, Thailand, the United States, and the countries of Scandinavia. According to the UN High Commissioner for Refugees, the global number of such persons by the end of 2004 exceeded 19 million refugees and internally displaced persons, all of whom hope, like all of us, not unreasonably, to be able to participate equally in the global system. Notwithstanding these colossal numbers, however, the UNHCR persists in pursuing its core mandate under the 1951 Convention to protect the basic human rights of vulnerable persons and to ensure that refugees will not be returned involuntarily to a country where they face persecution. Longer term, the organization helps civilians repatriate to their homeland, integrate in countries of asylum, or resettle in third countries. Using a worldwide field network, it also seeks to provide at least a minimum of shelter, food, water, and medical care in the immediate aftermath of any benighted refugee exodus.

The fact remains, however, that without home and commonly even country, refugees are severely marginalized from effective participation in the global system. At the same time, they are not the only people who today suffer marginalization on a large scale worldwide. Also to be counted are those who live outside the periphery of modern civilization and who generally are recognized to be the largest (300 to 500 million) and most disadvantaged group whose status has not yet been fully addressed by international legal standards and mechanisms pertinent to the values of basic decency and equality. We refer to indigenous peoples—aboriginals, Native Americans, and other tribal peoples referred to by the Minority Rights Group (London) as the "Fourth World"[42]—whose very survival, let alone the protection of their basic decency and equality rights, struggles constantly for responsible attention. Far too often, they are forgotten or, for economic reasons, deliberately ignored. For this reason, the United Nations in 1971 appointed a Special Rapporteur to study the policies pursued in various countries toward their indigenous populations. Additionally, in 1982 the UN Human Rights Commission authorized the establishment of a Working Group on Indigenous Populations to review developments pertaining to the promotion and protection of indigenous rights and to submit its conclusions to the UN Sub-Commission on Minorities.[43]

We learn about what followed these initiatives in Maivân Clech Lâm's essay, "Indigenous Peoples' Rights to Self-Determination and Territoriality" (Reading 12). She investigates the various tools available within international law to indigenous persons wishing to obtain the rights to self-determination and territoriality. The article examines various UN documents dating from 1945 on and traces the subsequent amendments that have rendered them either more or less helpful to indigenous persons. The author concludes by offering suggestions on ways in which international law could be reformed better to serve indigenous communities in their struggles for self-determination and territoriality.

42. See Ben Whitaker, ed., *The Fourth World: Victims of Group Oppression* (New York: Schocken, 1972). See also Bradley Reed Howard, *Indigenous Peoples and the State: The Struggle for Native Rights* (Dekalb: Northern Illinois Press, 2003); Ronald Niezen, *The Origins of Indigenism: Human Rights and the Politics of Identity* (Berkeley: University of California Press, 2003).
43. See José R. Martinez-Coba, UN Special Rapporteur, *Study on Indigenous and Tribal Populations*, UN Doc. E/CN.4/sub.2/1986/7; Asbjørn Eide, "Indigenous Populations and Human Rights: The United Nations Efforts at Mid-Way," in Jens Brosted, ed., *Native Powers: The Quest for Autonomy and Nationhood of Indigenous Peoples* (Bergen: Universitetsforlegt, 1985), 196–212.

The readings in this chapter explore a broad array of issues affecting people everywhere: civil liberties, equality rights, and standards of decency that reject genocide, torture, "disappearances," and multiple affronts to human dignity. All these issues, in the present day as in earlier eras, are dealt with by cultural prohibitions, religious norms, and elite standards of noblesse oblige. But as our world has become more interdependent and interpenetrating, the emerging international law of human rights has sought to rise above parochialism by fixing a minimum normative foundation of basic decency and to establish a range of claims defining everyone's participation in basic human rights. Fewer and fewer of humankind's compelling problems have solutions that are viable in national isolation. Increasingly they call for cooperative global solutions, solutions that recognize that we are a single species and that each of us has a stake in the human interests emerging globally alongside national and regional interests. The discovery that human interests can best be fostered by united action is beginning—but only beginning—to have major impact on political thinking. Minimal norms of basic decency and equal participation by all in the enjoyment of human rights is moving increasingly to the center of the international agenda. No ideology has refuted nor has any national action effectively taken exception to the proclamation in the 1948 Universal Declaration of Human Rights that basic freedoms and human rights represent "the highest aspiration of the common people."

5. Diane F. Orentlicher *Genocide*

Invoked with a frequency, familiarity, and reverence rarely associated with instruments of law, the 1948 Convention on the Prevention and Punishment of the Crime of Genocide[1] has come to embody the conscience of humanity.

Its moral force is surely ironic. For the record of the Genocide Convention since its adoption has been notable above all for States' nearly wholesale failure to enforce its terms. Although the treaty envisages (but does not require) the creation of an international court to punish genocide, forty-five years passed before the first international criminal tribunal was established. Its jurisdiction was limited to crimes, including genocide, committed in the former Yugoslavia since 1991. A similar, more circumscribed, tribunal was created for Rwanda one year later. It was not until September 2, 1998—a half-century after the United Nations General Assembly adopted the Genocide Convention—that the first verdict interpreting the Convention was rendered by an international tribunal following a

trial (one other defendant had previously pleaded guilty to genocide). On that day the Rwanda Tribunal found Jean-Paul Akayesu guilty on nine counts for his role in the 1994 Rwandan genocide.[2]

Nor did any State bring a case under the Genocide Convention to the World Court until 1993, and this was scarcely a milestone in international enforcement efforts. The case was brought by a State that had endured genocidal crimes—Bosnia-Herzegovina—against a State allegedly responsible—the former Yugoslavia—and not by other States determined to enforce the law of universal conscience on behalf of desperate victims beyond their borders.

To the contrary, when those same crimes were being committed—and gruesomely portrayed in the daily media—legal experts in the U.S. government were asked, in the words of a former State Department lawyer, "to perform legal gymnastics to avoid calling this genocide." And as Rwandan Hutus slaughtered hundreds of

Reprinted with changes from Diane F. Orentlicher, "Genocide," in Roy Gutman and David Rieff, eds., Kenneth Anderson, legal ed., *Crimes of War: What the Public Should Know* (New York: W.W. Norton, 1999), 153–57. Copyright © 1999 by the Crimes of War Project. Reprinted by permission.

1. Concluded Dec. 9, 1948, referenced in Documentary Appendix B.
2. *The Prosecutor v. Jean-Paul Akayesu*, United Nations International Criminal Tribunal for Rwanda (Chamber 1), Case No. ICTR-96–4-T, available at http://www.un.org/ictr/english/judgements/akayesu.html

thousands of Tutsis, the Clinton administration instructed its spokespeople not to describe what was happening as genocide lest this "inflame public calls for action," according to the *New York Times*. Instead, the State Department and National Security Council reportedly drafted guidelines instructing government spokespeople to say that "acts of genocide may have occurred" in Rwanda.

Five decades of nonenforcement have left the Genocide Convention's core terms shrouded in considerable ambiguity, making it that much easier for recalcitrant politicians to equivocate. (Such equivocations nonetheless fly in the face of the Convention, which requires States parties not only to punish genocide—a measure that does demand legal certainty—but also to prevent and repress the crime—action that by its nature must not await the certain knowledge that genocide has occurred.)

The definition of genocide set forth in the Genocide Convention is authoritative and has been incorporated verbatim in the statutes of the Yugoslavia and Rwanda tribunals as well as that of a permanent International Criminal Court (ICC) that [was] created [on July 1, 2002] after sixty states . . . ratified the statute adopted in Rome in July 1998.[3] After affirming that genocide is a crime under international law whether committed in time of peace or war, the 1948 Convention defines genocide as "any of the following acts committed with intent to destroy, in whole or in part, a national ethnical, racial or religious group, as such: killing members of the group; causing serious bodily or mental harm to members of the group; deliberately inflicting on the group conditions of life calculated to bring about its physical destruction in whole or in part; imposing measures intended to prevent births within the group; forcibly transferring children of the group to another group."

In the 1948 Convention, then, the crime of genocide has both a physical element—comprising certain enumerated acts, such as killing members of a racial group—and a mental element—those acts must have been committed with the intent to destroy, in whole or in part, a national, ethnic, racial, or religious group "as such." In its verdict in the Akayesu case, the Rwanda Tribunal found that the systematic rape

of Tutsi women in Taba Province constituted the genocidal act of "causing serious bodily or mental harm to members of the [targeted] group." In addition to the crime of genocide itself, the 1948 Convention provides that the following acts shall be punishable: conspiracy to commit genocide, direct and public incitement to commit genocide, attempt to commit genocide, and complicity in genocide.

What was left out of the Convention is as important as what was included. Although earlier drafts of the Convention listed political groups among those covered by the intent requirement, this category was omitted during final drafting stages. Too many governments, it seemed, would be vulnerable to the charge of genocide if deliberate destruction of political groups fell within the crime's compass.

Also excluded was the concept of cultural genocide—destroying a group through forcible assimilation into the dominant culture. The drafting history makes clear that the 1948 Convention was meant to cover physical destruction of a people; the sole echo of efforts to include the notion of cultural extermination is the Convention's reference to forcibly transferring children of a targeted group to another group.

In this and other respects the conventional definition of genocide is narrower than the conception of Polish scholar Raphael Lemkin, who first proposed at an international conference in 1933 that a treaty be created to make attacks on national, religious, and ethnic groups an international crime. Lemkin, who served in the U.S. War Department, fashioned the term *genocide* from the Greek word *genos*, meaning race or tribe, and the Latin term for killing, *cide*. [In his 1944 book, *Axis Rule in Occupied Europe*, Lemkin noted that the same idea could also come from the term "ethnocide," consisting of the Greek word "ethnos"—nation—and the Latin word "cide."]

Although Lemkin's conception included the physical extermination of targeted groups, this was, in his view, only the most extreme technique of genocide:

> By "genocide" we mean the destruction of an ethnic group. . . . Generally speaking, genocide

---

3. See Rome Statute of the International Criminal Court (July 17, 1998), referenced in Documentary Appendix B.

does not necessarily mean the immediate destruction of a nation, except when accomplished by mass killings of all members of a nation. It is intended rather to signify a coordinated plan of different actions aiming at the destruction of essential foundations of the life of national groups, with the aim of annihilating the groups themselves. The objectives of such a plan would be disintegration of the political and social institutions, of culture, language, national feelings, religion, and the economic existence of national groups, and the destruction of the personal security, liberty, health, dignity, and even the lives of the individuals belonging to such groups. . . .

Genocide has two phases: one, destruction of the national pattern of the oppressed group; the other, the imposition of the national pattern of the oppressor. This imposition, in turn, may be made upon the oppressed population which is allowed to remain, or upon the territory alone, after removal of the population and colonization of the area by the oppressor's own nationals.[4]

Four years would pass before Lemkin's crime was recognized in an international treaty, but the legal foundation was laid during the 1945 Nuremberg and other postwar prosecutions. Although the Nuremberg Charter did not use the term *genocide*, its definition of crimes against humanity overlapped significantly with Lemkin's conception of *genocide*. The term *genocide* was used in the indictment against major war criminals tried at Nuremberg, who were accused of having "conducted deliberate and systematic genocide, viz., the extermination of racial and national groups, against the civilian populations of certain occupied territories in order to destroy particular races and classes of people and national, racial or religious groups." Nuremberg prosecutors also invoked the term in their closing arguments, and it also appeared in the judgments of several U.S. military tribunals operating in Nuremberg.

Shortly after the trial of major war criminals at Nuremberg, the UN General Assembly adopted a resolution affirming that genocide is a "crime under international law."[5] In its preamble, the 1946 resolution termed genocide "a denial of the right of existence of entire human groups, as homicide is the denial of the right to live of individual human beings."

The comparatively narrow terms of the 1948 Convention—in particular, its exclusion of political groups and its restrictive intent requirement—have enabled political leaders to raise doubts about whether probable genocides satisfy the Convention's stringent criteria. Did the authors of the Anfal campaigns of 1988, in which at least fifty thousand Iraqi Kurds are estimated to have been massacred, intend to kill Kurds "as such" or, in the words of one leading scholar, was their aim to eliminate "the Kurdish movement as a political problem"?[6] Did Serb perpetrators of ethnic cleansing in Bosnia intend to destroy Muslims and Croats "as such," or did they "merely" seek to establish homogeneous Serb control over coveted territory?

As these questions suggest, a key source of ambiguity is the meaning of the 1948 Convention's intent requirement. Although the drafting history is somewhat ambiguous, I believe that it is a mistake to treat the Convention's use of the term *intent* as though it were synonymous with motive. That Serb perpetrators of ethnic cleansing may have slaughtered Muslims so that they could obtain control over territory does not negate their intent to destroy Muslims "as such" in order to achieve their ultimate goal.

The Genocide Convention imposes a general duty on States parties "to prevent and to punish" genocide. Those charged with genocide are to be tried either in the State where the crime occurred or "by such international penal tribunal as may have jurisdiction . . . with respect to those Contracting Parties which shall have accepted its jurisdiction." Although the Convention does not mention a third possibility—prosecution in a third State—it is now well established that any State can assert jurisdiction over crimes of genocide, wherever the crimes occurred and whatever the nationality of the perpetrators and victims.

4. Raphael Lemkin, *Axis Rule in Occupied Europe* (Washington, D.C.: Carnegie Endowment for International Peace, 1944).
5. Affirmation of the Principles of International Law Recognized by the Charter of the Nuremberg Tribunal (Dec. 11, 1946), referenced in Documentary Appendix B.
6. Martin van Bruinessen, "Genocide in Kurdistan," in George Andreopolous, ed., *Genocide: Conceptual and Historical Dimensions* (Philadelphia: University of Pennsylvania Press, 1994), 156.

In addition to individual criminal responsibility for genocide, the Convention also establishes State responsibility—that is, international legal responsibility of the State itself for breaching its obligations under the Convention. Parties to the Convention can bring a case before the International Court of Justice alleging that another State party is responsible for genocide. As noted above, the first case of this sort was brought against Yugoslavia by Bosnia-Herzegovina in 1993. . . .

Article 8 of the Convention contemplates measures not only to punish genocide, but also to stop it in its tracks: "Any Contracting Party may call upon the competent organs of the United Nations to take such action under the Charter of the United Nations as they consider appropriate for the prevention and suppression of acts of genocide or any of the other acts enumerated in article 3." States that are parties to the Convention could, for example, seek Security Council authorization to use military force to stop genocide being committed in another country. Finally, although treaties themselves are binding only on States that are parties to the treaties, in a 1951 advisory opinion the International Court of Justice observed that the principles underlying the Genocide Convention are part of customary international law, which binds all states.

GENOCIDE IN HISTORY

Although Lemkin implied that Nazi crimes were fundamentally different from any previously committed, Hitler's "Final Solution" was not the first campaign of extermination that would meet Lemkin's definition of genocide. The systematic extermination of Armenians by the Young Turks beginning in April 1915 was the first genocide in this century. Emboldened by the world's acquiescence in the slaughter of Armenians—over 1 million are estimated to have been put to death—Hitler is famously reported to have reassured doubters in his ranks by asking, "Who after all is today speaking of the Armenians?"

Among more recent episodes of wholesale slaughter, at least some scholars have concluded that the Turkish massacre of Kurds in the district of Dersim in 1937–1938, the massacre of Hutus by Tutsi perpetrators in Burundi in 1972, the Khmer Rouge campaign of extermination in the mid-1970's, and the 1988 Anfal campaign against Iraqi Kurds meet the legal definition of genocide.

Among these cases, perhaps none better illustrates the complexities of the 1948 Convention's definition of genocide than the case of Cambodia. In view of the magnitude of the carnage there—1.5 million out of Cambodia's 7 million citizens are believed to have died as a result of Khmer Rouge policies—there has been a keen desire to affix the term *genocide* to their crimes. Since, however, both the perpetrators and the majority of victims were Khmer, reaching this conclusion has required agile legal reasoning. Some scholars have invoked the concept of *autogenocide*, arguing that it is possible to satisfy the 1948 Convention's definition even when the perpetrators sought to kill a substantial portion of their own ethnic/national group. Others, more conservatively, have conceded that the vast majority of victims were killed for reasons that may be broadly termed political, but note that certain minority groups, such as the Muslim Cham and Khmer Buddhists, were specially targeted for destruction and argue that at least the crimes against these groups were genocidal.

While some campaigns of extermination more clearly qualify as genocide than others—the Holocaust and the 1994 Rwandan genocide are instances—the truth is that plausible arguments can be raised with respect to most cases of possible genocide. In the absence of judicial resolution or political resolve, virtually any case of genocide can be questioned. The first defendant tried before the Rwanda Tribunal argued, for example, that the massacres in Rwanda were politically motivated, a gruesome manner of waging civil war. In response the tribunal concluded that, "alongside the conflict . . . genocide was committed in Rwanda in 1994 against the Tutsi as a group." That the execution of this genocide "was probably facilitated by the conflict" did not negate the fact that genocide occurred.

The dearth of precedents enforcing the Convention—a grim testament to the international community's failure of will—has for decades left experts able to do little more than argue knowledgeably about whether well-known candidates for the label "genocide" meet the legal definition. The ambiguities built into the Genocide Convention can finally be resolved only when States are willing to acknowledge forthrightly that genocide has occurred and to enforce the law of conscience.

QUESTIONS FOR REFLECTION AND DISCUSSION

1. In Leo Kuper, *Genocide: Its Political Use in the Twentieth Century* (New Haven, Conn.: Yale University Press, 1981), 167, the author quotes a Ugandan official asking: "Is systematic genocide an internal matter or a matter for all mankind [sic]?" How would you answer this question and why? If you think it is a matter for all humankind, what would be the appropriate action by the international community to stop genocidal activity within the boundaries of a sovereign state? Or do you think the absolute sovereignty of the state should be maintained? Why?

2. The UN Commission on Human Rights (UNCHR) has on numerous occasions failed to condemn acts of genocide, due in part to some of its members being states known or alleged to have committed genocide. Does this failure of the UNCHR have the effect of condoning genocidal activity? Or is it merely a coincidence of UNCHR membership without normative consequence? In any event, do you agree that membership on the UNCHR should be restricted to states without a genocidal history? Why? Why not?

3. As Orentlicher notes, the 1948 Convention on the Prevention and Punishment of the Crime of Genocide (referenced in Documentary Appendix B) defines "genocide" in Article 2 as follows:

> In the present Convention, genocide can mean any of the following acts committed within intent to destroy, in whole or in part, a national, ethnical, racial or religious group, as such:
> (a) Killing members of the group.
> (b) Causing serious bodily or mental harm to members of the group.
> (c) Deliberately inflicting on the group conditions of life calculated to bring about its physical destruction in whole or in part.
> (d) Imposing measures intended to prevent birth within the group.
> (e) Forcibly transferring children of the group to another group.

Orentlicher observes that political groups, though as vulnerable and identifiable as ethnic groups, are not protected by the Convention. Why might this be so? Should they be? Why? Why not?

4. Given how frequently the Genocide Convention has been breached (as evidenced by the number of genocides by states parties to the Convention, including genocides by states parties presently ongoing—in Sudan, for example), what legal or other significance does the Convention have? Is it law today, or merely the illusion of law? What does Orentlicher say? Are you persuaded? What is the use of a convention that isn't enforced by the international community?

5. What motivates political elites to engage in genocide? What rationales do they use to excuse their acts? Are any of their rationales convincing? During the Inquisition of the twelfth and thirteenth centuries, largely because the Inquisitors charged by the Catholic church to eradicate heresies sincerely believed that God was directing them to murder the Infidels, whole populations were slaughtered for departing from orthodoxy. Is it reasonable to expect any of the contending factions in, say, the Israeli-Palestinian dispute, to act any differently toward their adversaries, given that they appear to believe, too, that their ultimate political legitimacy is derived from divine authority?

6. Russia and the United States are parties to the Genocide Convention. Yet each day, in keeping with the strategy of nuclear deterrence, each maintains the capacity to annihilate the other and others with nuclear weapons. A similar circumstance obtains in China, India, Israel, North Korea, and Pakistan. Does this amount to genocidal intent? Does the capacity for "nuclear overkill" afford proof of this intent? Did the US atomic bombings of Hiroshima and Nagasaki during World War II constitute acts of genocide?

7. Were the saturation bombings, widespread defoliation, and rural "pacification" programs used by the United States in Vietnam evidence of genocidal activity? Do Russian actions in Chechnya today qualify as genocide? American actions in Fallujah? For factual details, consult the many informational sources available on the Internet.

8. The Cambodian, Rwandan, and Yugoslav genocides could be labeled civil wars or internal political conflicts. Orentlicher offers several rationales to define each as a genocide under the Genocide Convention. Where in the Convention can you find support for these

conclusions? Does it matter? Is it not sufficient that the mass murders could be prosecuted under the humanitarian rules of armed conflict, e.g., 1977 Protocol Additional (No. II) to the Geneva Conventions of August 12, 1949, and Relating to the Protection of Victims of Non-International Armed Conflicts (referenced in Documentary Appendix B)?

9. Given the mixed success of the ad hoc Yugoslav and Rwandan tribunals, is it possible to enforce the Genocide Convention and punish violators justiciably? What alternatives might be more appropriate? What about the new *permanent* International Criminal Court (ICC)? Note that the United States has not only refused to ratify the 1998 Rome Statute of the International Criminal Court (referenced in Documentary Appendix B) but even has withdrawn its signature. Why?

6. LISA HAJJAR *Torture and the Future*

There is a popular belief that Western history constitutes a progressive move from more to less torture. Iron maidens and racks are now museum exhibits, crucifixions are sectarian iconography and scientific experimentation on twins is History Channel infotainment. This narrative of progress deftly blends ideas about time, place and culture. In the popular imagination, "civilized societies" (aka "us") do not rely on torture, whereas those societies where torture is still common remain "uncivilized," torture being both a proof and a problem of their enduring "backwardness."

George W. Bush epitomizes and mines the American popular imagination with his mantra of "spreading freedom," which carries a strong implication of stopping torture. . . . On April 30, 2004, Bush said, "A year ago I [gave a] speech . . . saying that we had achieved an important objective, that we'd accomplished a mission, which was the removal of Saddam Hussein. And as a result, there are no longer torture chambers or rape rooms or mass graves in Iraq."[1]

Even as Bush spoke those words, he and millions of newspaper readers and television viewers across the world were aware that torture chambers, rape, and sexual abuse of detainees in Iraq are not a thing of the past. The public exposure of torture of Iraqi detainees by U.S. soldiers, working in interrogation wings run by military intelligence and American "security contractors," at Abu Ghraib prison outside of Baghdad—as well as allegations of torture of other Iraqis by British

soldiers—are headline news. The shocking revelations and photographs provide stark proof that torture is not a relic of our past. Nor does torture provide a meaningful geographical or cultural demarcation between "civilized" and "uncivilized" societies.

IMPLICATORY DENIAL

The fact is that, today, people are being tortured in two thirds of the world's countries. Yet if one were to accept the rhetoric of the world's states at face value, there is no torture in the world. No torturing regime defends or even acknowledges its own torture as torture. Stanley Cohen, author of *States of Denial*, identifies three common forms of denial of torture and other atrocities.[2] "Literal denial" is when a state accused of torture responds by saying that nothing happened and that those who claim something happened are liars or "enemies of the state." "Interpretative denial" is when a state refutes allegations by saying that what happened is not torture but "something else"—like "moderate physical pressure" or "stress and duress." "Implicatory denial"—that is, denial by implicating others—occurs when a state acknowledges torture but blames it on "aberrant agents," claiming that rogue elements have breached official norms and policies. Official U.S. responses to the Abu Ghraib prison photos are a classic example of implicatory denial.

Reprinted with changes from Lisa Hajjar, "Torture and the Future," *Middle East Report Online* (May 2004), available at http://merip.org/mero/interventions/hajjar_interv.html. Copyright © 2004 by MERIP. Reprinted by permission.

1. "President Bush Welcomes Canadian Prime Minister Martin to White House," Dec. 23, 2005, available at http://www.whitehouse.gov/news/releases/2004/04/print/2004043
2. Stanley Cohen, *States of Denial: Knowing About Atrocities and Suffering* (Cambridge: Polity Press, 2001), 103.

In the story on CBS *60 Minutes II* that exposed the abusive U.S. practices in Abu Ghraib, Brig. Gen. Mark Kimmitt said, "All of us are disappointed by the actions of the few. The acts that you see in these pictures may reflect the actions of individuals, but by God, it doesn't reflect my army." Secretary of State Colin Powell agreed with Kimmitt when he condemned the six soldiers who have been arrested in the Abu Ghraib incidents: "But I want to remind the world it was a small number of troops . . . compared to the hundreds of thousands who have served around the world, who have come to build hospitals and schools and restore civil society." These implicatory denials were echoed, with a grander sweep, by Defense Secretary Donald Rumsfeld, who in Congressional testimony described the abuses depicted in the now infamous photos as "un-American."

Many Americans can doubtless relate to Rumsfeld's attempt to relegate the Abu Ghraib torturers—all, apparently, Americans—to another discursive time, place, and culture. But before Rumsfeld spoke, investigative journalist Seymour Hersh, writing in the *New Yorker*, had already rebutted the implicatory denials so ambient in the Pentagon and the media sphere.[3] Hersh obtained a copy of a report from another U.S. Army general, Antonio Taguba, who investigated prisons and interrogation centers in Iraq between October and December 2003 and found "sadistic, wanton and criminal abuses" that were systemic and rampant. According to Hersh, "Taguba saved his harshest words for the military intelligence officers and private contractors." Brig. Gen. Janis Karpinski, who oversaw 16 prisons in Iraq and has been relieved of those duties because of the scandal, said, "The [Abu Ghraib] prison, and that particular cell block where the events took place, were under the control of the MI [military intelligence] command." Karpinski lay the blame elsewhere when she noted that military intelligence officers went "to great lengths to try to exclude the International Committee of the Red Cross from access to that interrogation wing."

Denial of torture is articulated in many ways, but all states deny it for the same reason. Torture must be practiced in secret and denied in public because, in the mid-twentieth century, torture became an international crime. Irrespective of what penalties the arrested soldiers may face under the Uniform Code of Military Justice, the pictures from Abu Ghraib—whose authenticity no one has denied—document offenses of an especially heinous kind.

LAW AND (INTERNATIONAL) ORDER

The international criminalization of torture is inextricable from the history of human rights. The unprecedented horrors and violence of World War II provided the negative inspiration for a revolution in international law to forge the principle that people should have rights as humans, and not merely as protected classes of subjects, such as citizens, civilians, or prisoners of war. However, the creation of international human rights did not undermine or substantially alter the power of states. Rather, it entailed the elaboration of new internationalized norms of government to which all states would be expected to adhere, while preserving states' sovereign rights. Human rights obtained their "universalizing" character from the fact that people are subjects of states and states are subjects of international law.

The right not to be tortured became a human right when international law prohibited the practice, and established legal liabilities and penalties.[4] The right not to be tortured is one of many human rights, but it is stronger than almost any other human right because the prohibition of torture is absolutely nonderogable and because the law recognizes no exceptions.[5] What this means is that no one—ever, anywhere—has a "right" to torture, and that everyone—always, everywhere—has a right not to be tortured. It also means that anyone who engages in or abets torture is committing a crime.

3. Seymour Hersh, "Torture at Abu Ghraib," *New Yorker*, May 10, 2004.
4. Torture is defined and prohibited in a number of international instruments, including the Universal Declaration of Human Rights (Dec. 10, 1948), the Geneva Conventions (Aug. 12, 1949) and the Convention against Torture or Other Cruel, Degrading or Inhuman Treatment or Punishment (Dec. 10, 1984). The Universal Declaration is reprinted in Documentary Appendix A. The Geneva Conventions and the Convention against Torture are referenced in Documentary Appendix B.
5. The only other absolutely nonderogable rights are the right not to be enslaved and the right not to be prosecuted for something that was not a crime at the time it was done.

The international prohibition of torture illuminates something very important about the rights of human beings. The right not to be tortured represents an ideal type of human rights norm because it invests people, regardless of their social status, political identity, or affiliations, with a kind of sovereign right over their bodies and minds, albeit limited to situations that fall within the legal definition of torture. In contrast, the right of persons not to be exterminated through genocide hinges on a collective identity as members of a national, religious, or ethnic group. The right not to be deliberately targeted in war hinges not on one's humanity but rather on one's status as a civilian or noncombatant, or a surrendered or captured soldier.

The prohibition of torture is customary international law and therefore attaches universal jurisdiction. Universal jurisdiction means that if a perpetrator is not prosecuted in his or her own country, he or she can be prosecuted in any competent legal system anywhere in the world. Therefore, the right not to be tortured is accorded greater weight in law than the sovereign rights of states because torture is prohibited under all circumstances, including the "ticking bomb" scenario. In the words of the Convention against Torture and Other Cruel, Inhuman or Degrading Treatment or Punishment (1984), "No exceptional circumstances whatsoever, whether a state of war or a threat of war, internal political instability or any other public emergency, may be invoked as a justification for torture." The U.S. ratified this convention in 1994.

[*Eds.*—The author next provides, as "vivid illustration of the strength of the prohibition on torture and of the universal jurisdiction that attaches to it," the tale of former Chilean dictator Augusto Pinochet. Pinochet, the author notes, never personally tortured anyone, but his control over those who did rendered him liable for torture under international law. Pinochet's liability attached even outside his own country, when the British government acted on an indictment issued by a Spanish judge. Thanks to the extradition of Pinochet from Britain to Chile and to a Chilean court ruling on December 13, 2004, there is a good chance that the former military dictator, 90 years old at this writing, will go on trial for crimes committed decades ago. The author concludes by noting that the Pinochet case illustrates that the right not to be tortured is "substantially stronger" than the right to life, which is derogable in certain circumstances.]

WHY IS THE PROHIBITION OF TORTURE SO STRONG?

Torture refers to purposefully harming someone who is in custody—unfree to fight back or protect himself or herself and imperiled by that incapacitation. Other violent practices, like domestic violence and battery, also involve the purposeful causing of pain, and in some ways these practices might "look like" torture. But they lack the public dimension of custodianship. The distinction does not turn on what happens, because if it did, torture would be difficult if not impossible to distinguish from domestic violence and battery. Pain and suffering, humiliation and injury are common to all. But, legally, severe pain, suffering, humiliation, and injury constitute torture only if they serve some public purpose and if the status and role of the torturer emanates from a public authority and if the person being harmed is in custody.[6]

Contrary to the implications of some, the forced public nakedness, forced public masturbation, and forced simulation of homosexual acts depicted in the Abu Ghraib photos do not qualify as torture or as "especially" torturous because the Iraqi detainees are Arab and, presumably, Muslim. . . . Would persons of any ethnicity or culture find such abuse anything other than severely and sadistically humiliating? What was done to the Iraqi detainees was torture because the detainees were in the custody of the U.S. military and private contractors, because they were compelled by their captors to assume the humiliating positions and because they were powerless to resist their humiliation. While the detainees' cultural sensitivities were undoubtedly offended, the relevant point is that the most inalienable of their human rights was violated by their American jailers.

Notwithstanding these qualifications, there is

---

6. Precise definitions of torture are still a subject of intense debate among the international human rights community, with many advocates arguing for a more expansive definition. The definition here—the most widely accepted formulation—comes from the Convention against Torture or Other Cruel, Degrading or Inhuman Treatment or Punishment.

no bright line empirically distinguishing torture from "everything else." Rather, torture is like a core within layers of violence. For example, being beaten while being arrested changes from "cruel treatment" to "torture" only when "custody" has been achieved, obviously a very blurry and contestable line. The combination of "torture" and "cruel, inhumane and degrading treatment" in the same laws contributes to this confusion, which is further compounded by the exclusion of painful—but lawful—punishments such as floggings, amputations, or the death penalty. Many forms of violence may lead to torture and many forms of violence may result from torture, but the core violence that is torture—and what makes torture a "core international crime"—is violence (physical or psychological) against a person already in the custody of an authority.

An "authority" is a category that obviously would include states and their agents, but it would not exclude nonstate groups and their agents, or civilians. Torture is not contingent on legitimacy, jurisdiction, or international recognition. It is contingent on an organized rather than individualized capacity to take people into custody and then harm them for a purpose that is public rather than personal.

On this point, the use of private contractors to run prisons and conduct interrogations in Afghanistan and Iraq has been a subject of confusion. American media are reporting, and many people are assuming, that because these private contractors are civilians, they are not subject to military or international laws. Peter W. Singer of the Brookings Institution, writing in the May 2 *Los Angeles Times*, quotes Phillip Carter, a former Army officer now at UCLA Law School, as saying that, "Legally speaking, [military contractors in Iraq] actually fall into the same gray area as the unlawful combatants detained at Guantánamo Bay." Carter may be correct in some respects, but the contractors have been hired and authorized to fulfill a public function of handling and interrogating detainees on behalf of the U.S. government. As another military analyst, Paul C. Forage, told the *Baltimore Sun* on May 4, the private contractors could be prosecuted under either the Military Extraterritorial Jurisdiction Act of 2000 or a 1996 federal law. "I

think it's a pretty clear case," Forage concluded. "It's not an area of legal limbo."

TORTURE AND TERROR

If torture is so strongly prohibited, and denied by all states because it is fundamentally illegitimate, why is it so common in today's world? While states torture people for numerous reasons, one common reason invoked by many states is that they claim to be engaged in conflicts with "terrorists."[7]

Terrorism is a broad and flexible concept, and there is no clear, internationally accepted definition. It is used, variously, to describe certain kinds of actions, including attacks on civilians, hijackings, organized resistance or repression, and to identify certain types of actors. In U.S. national security discourse, the term *terrorism* typically is used to refer to nonstate actors or organizations engaged in attacks or struggles against the state, emphasizing but not necessarily limited to violence, to which the state responds with "counter-terrorism."

Terrorism is not a figment of the politically paranoid imagination. The September 11, 2001 attacks were indisputably terrorist attacks, and al-Qaeda operates as a terrorist organization. Any and every instance of deliberately targeting civilians or civilian infrastructures as a tactic in the furtherance of some cause, whatever the political or ideological motivation and whomever the targeting agents, is terroristic. If the deliberate targeting of civilians constitutes terrorism, then we must acknowledge that states can be as culpable as nonstate groups. However, as Richard Falk explains,

> With the help of the influential media, the state over time has waged and largely won the battle of definitions by exempting its own violence against civilians from being treated and perceived as "terrorism." Instead, such violence was generally discussed as "uses of force," "retaliation," "self-defense" and "security measures."[8]

National security is a legitimate interest of any state, and states have a responsibility to provide for the security of their citizens. But the tendency to characterize and treat all "enemies" as "terrorists" or "terrorist sympathizers" contributes

---

7. See the extensive background in Human Rights Watch, *In the Name of Counter-Terrorism: Human Rights Abuses Worldwide* (October 2003), accessible at http://www.hrw.org/un/chr59/counter-terrorism-bck.htm
8. Richard Falk, *The Great Terror War* (New York: Olive Branch Press, 2002), xix.

to the delineation between "legitimate" and "illegitimate" communities, leaving the latter vulnerable to state violence, and enabling the state to justify that violence as a necessary reaction to terror. Pointing out the limits and obfuscations of national security discourse is not an *apologia* for terrorism. Rather, it is an effort to understand, evaluate, and criticize violence in a manner that is not glazed by partisan or statist ideology.

Around the world, some of the most egregious human rights violations have been perpetrated by states in the name of counter-terrorism. Terrorism is, by definition, a violation of human rights. Michael Ignatieff, director of the Carr Center of Human Rights Policy at Harvard, writes:

> The two terms—human rights and terror—look like a simple antithesis: human rights good, terror bad. [But] the antithesis is not so simple. Of course, human rights and terror stand opposed to each other. Terrorist acts violate the right to life, along with many other rights. But equally, human rights—notably the right to self-determination—have constituted major justification for the resort to violence, including acts of terror.[9]

Ignatieff correctly points out that it is not international human rights law—which is inherently pacifist—but rather, international humanitarian law that obtains in any war, including a war on terrorism. The Geneva Conventions, which compose the main body of international humanitarian laws, are agnostic about the causes of war or the justness of the aims of adversaries. Rather, they govern what is legally permissible in war. Their aim is to minimize suffering and destruction, and to provide guidelines for the detention and treatment of enemy civilians and combatants. International humanitarian law is not pacifist, but on the issue of torture it concurs with human rights law. Even in war, the right not to be tortured is absolutely nonderogable, and the use of torture in the context of conflict can constitute a war crime.

Since September 11, the Bush administration has articulated positions and pursued policies that blatantly contravene the Geneva Conventions, on the grounds that terrorists do not deserve legal rights and protections. These policies include the invention of a category, "unlawful combatants," that does not exist in international law. These unlawful combatants are being held *incommunicado*, at Guantánamo Bay and other locations, and subjected to years of interrogation with no judicial oversight, no public accountability, and virtually no visitation by representatives of the International Committee of the Red Cross. Although the U.S. government claims that no torture is used in the interrogation of these detainees, these clandestine and extralegal conditions are an invitation for abuse. The Abu Ghraib images are a piece of hard evidence indicating that the U.S. has joined the list of countries—Egypt, Israel, Uzbekistan—that are fighting wars on terrorism partly through the use of torture.

Still, because torture is illegal, it remains necessary for states to deny torture, even the torture of terrorists. In the U.S., the terrorist attacks of September 11 have raised for debate several vexing and related questions: should "terrorists" have a right not to be tortured? Is torture a necessary and effective tactic in the fight against terrorism? If so, why deny torture?

A DISTINCTION IS BORN

Israel was the first state in the world to break the "torture taboo" by publicly authorizing interrogation practices that constitute torture. Israel has been in an official state of emergency and war since it was established in 1948. In the 1967 Arab-Israeli war, Israel captured and occupied the West Bank and Gaza and established a military administration to rule the Palestinians residing in these areas. A military court system was established to prosecute Palestinians suspected of violating Israel's military and emergency laws. These laws criminalized not only violence, sabotage, and militancy, but also a vast array of political and nonviolent activities. Israel used prosecution as one of its key strategies to rule Palestinians and to thwart and punish resistance to the occupation. Since 1967, over half a million Palestinians have been prosecuted in the military court system, out of a population that now numbers 3.2 million. There have been periods when incarceration rates in the West Bank and Gaza were among the highest in the world.

For two decades, allegations that Israeli soldiers and interrogators were routinely torturing

---

9. Michael Ignatieff, "Human Rights, the Laws of War, and Terrorism," *Social Research* 69, no. 4 (2002).

Palestinian detainees were consistently refuted by Israeli officials as lies and fabrications of "enemies of the state." Then in 1987, for reasons unconnected to the interrogation of Palestinians, the Israeli government established an official commission of inquiry to investigate the General Security Services.

The report produced by the Landau Commission was path-breaking in a number of ways. It confirmed that, in fact, GSS agents had used violent interrogation methods routinely on Palestinian detainees since at least 1971, and that they had routinely lied about such practices when confessions were challenged in court on the grounds that they had been coerced. The Landau Commission was harsh in its criticism of GSS perjury, but adopted the GSS's own position that coercive interrogation tactics were necessary in the struggle against "hostile terrorist activity." The Landau Commission accepted the broad definition of "terrorism" utilized by the GSS, which encompassed not only acts or threats of violence, but virtually all activities related to Palestinian nationalism.

The most path-breaking aspects of the Landau report were its conclusions and recommendations. The report's authors argued that national security requires physical and psychological coercion in the interrogation of Palestinians, and that the state should sanction such tactics in order to rectify the problem of perjury. The Landau Commission's justification for this recommendation was based on a three-part contention: that Palestinians have no right to legal protections given their predisposition for terrorism, that the GSS operates morally and responsibly in discharging its duties to preserve Israeli national security, and that GSS interrogation methods do not constitute torture. The Landau Commission offered a way for the state to engage in torture while simultaneously denying it by renaming it as "moderate physical pressure."

This euphemism traces back to British torture of Irish prisoners in Northern Ireland, but the Landau report adds a distinctive wrinkle. A legal challenge was mounted against Britain's "five techniques" in the interrogation of suspected Irish Republican Army members on the grounds that they violate the European Convention on Human Rights. The majority decision by the European Court of Human Rights ruled that the five techniques (wall standing, hooding, subjection to noise, sleep deprivation, and

deprivation of food and drink) do not amount to "torture" but to the lesser—and also prohibited—category of "inhumane and degrading treatment." But the British government accepted the minority opinion of the Court that the techniques constitute (or come close to) torture, and decided to forego their use. The Landau Commission, noting that Israeli interrogation tactics resembled the five techniques, embraced the Court's majority decision that they do not constitute "torture." Thus was born the euphemization of "moderate physical pressure" as "not torture."

The Israeli government adopted the Landau Commission's recommendations to "legalize" torture, and this stimulated enormous debate and criticism in Israel. Since 1987, there has been a concerted campaign by Israeli lawyers and human rights organizations to end Israeli interrogation practices that constitute torture. One of the main sites of struggle was the Israeli High Court of Justice which, in 1999, finally issued a ruling prohibiting the routine use of "pressure" tactics (though not calling these tactics "torture") while preserving the option to use such tactics in "exceptional circumstances."

In the U.S. today, many of the people who point to Israel as a model for good interrogation tactics are pointing implicitly to the Landau Commission report, rather than the struggles, scandals and changes that have emanated in its wake. The Landau Commission had adopted an apocalyptic view of the world where nothing less than survival of the Israeli state and the Jewish nation were deemed to be at stake in the interrogation of "hostile terrorists." It concluded that survival and security trump other valued considerations, including due process and the right not to be tortured. Read on its own terms, the Landau Commission report is a blueprint for "absolute security" in a war on terror.

"STRESS AND DURESS"

In a sense, the U.S. already has its own Landau Commission report. On December 26, 2002, Dana Priest and Barton Gellman published a lengthy story in the *Washington Post* revealing that U.S. security agents were utilizing "stress and duress" tactics in the interrogation of people captured in Afghanistan and elsewhere. The tactics they described are identical to Israeli "moderate physical pressure." Priest and Gellman wrote that: "Those who refuse to cooperate inside this secret CIA interrogation center [at the Bagram air base in Afghanistan] are sometimes kept standing or kneeling for hours, in black hoods or spray-painted goggles, according to intelligence specialists familiar with CIA interrogation methods. At times, they are held in awkward, painful positions and deprived of sleep with a 24-hour bombardment of lights—subject to what are known as 'stress and duress' techniques."

Priest and Gellman also reported that detainees who could not be broken by the "restrained" stress and duress tactics might be given mind-altering drugs or "turned over—'rendered,' in official parlance—to foreign intelligence services whose practice of torture has been documented by the U.S. government and human rights organizations." They continued, "While the U.S. government publicly denounces the use of torture, each of the current national security officials interviewed for this article defended the use of violence against captives as just and necessary. They expressed confidence that the American public would back their view. The CIA . . . declined to comment."

Like the Landau Commission report when it was published in Israel in 1987, this *Washington Post* story dramatically altered both what is known about American interrogation and how torture is talked about in the U.S. Human rights advocates assailed official admissions of "stress and duress" as defenses of torture. On January 11, 2003, in a letter to the *Washington Post*, two former Justice Department officials who served under Presidents Ronald Reagan and George Bush cited the European Court ruling as evidence that "stress and duress" is not torture. "Indeed," they retorted to the human rights advocates, "to say these practices do [constitute torture] ultimately trivializes the torture that does take place in so many areas of the world." So far, the pictures of grinning American soldiers forcing nude Iraqis into sexual positions seem to have dimmed the vigor of this particular defense for the "stress and duress" at Abu Ghraib.

More to the point, the use of tactics by U.S. officials that arguably constitute torture, and the rendering of prisoners to states with well-established records of torture—including Jordan, Egypt, Syria, Morocco, Pakistan, and the Philippines—illuminate the conundrum of what to do about terrorism. Priest and Gellman recounted the testimony of Cofer Black, former head of the CIA Counterterrorist Center, before Congress on September 26, 2002, to the effect that the CIA and other security agencies need "operational flexibility," and therefore cannot be held to the "old" standards. Black said, "There was before 9/11, and there was an after 9/11. After 9/11 the gloves come off."

TALE OF TWO CLICHÉS

Taking the gloves off in interrogation is a thinly veiled reference to torture, but calling torture "stress and duress" or "abuse" is the homage paid to the still current imperative of denial. The presumptions that torture is both necessary and effective, and the implications of breaking the torture taboo by legalizing torture are shaping debates in the U.S. This debate circles around two clichés: the slippery slope and the lesser evil.

Jeremiads against the slippery slope argue that no cause or crisis justifies the erosion of the absolute prohibition against torture. Variations on this theme include: (1) there is no such thing as just a "little torture"; (2) once you start torturing "terrorists" you open the door to torturing anyone in the future; and (3) using torture makes you no better than your enemy. Defenders of the lesser evil argue that the absolute prohibition on torture is immoral if it ties the hands of security agents from finding that "ticking bomb" and saving innocent lives. On CNN's *Crossfire*, conservative commentator Tucker Carlson said, "Torture is bad. But some things are worse. And under some circumstances, it may be the lesser of two evils. Because some evils are pretty evil."

Interestingly, the example of Israel is invoked to bolster each case. The slippery slopers point to the realities of torture in Israel-Palestine, where torturing tens of thousands of people has neither ameliorated the conflict nor enhanced Israeli security; rather it has exacerbated conflict and thus contributed to Israeli insecurity. According to Yael Stein, a researcher at the Israeli human rights organization B'tselem, "Israel's experience shows you can't stop the slippery slope: they tortured almost all the Palestinians they could. It was in the system. The moment you start, you can't stop."[10] The lesser evilers argue that Israel has preserved its "democratic character" by bringing torture "into the law" and that its security services have a fabulous success rate of averting many "ticking bombs" by torturing terrorists.[11]

While coercive Israeli interrogation tactics have provided information about militant organizations and arms caches and foiled plans of some would-be bombers, there is no public record that the use of torture has ever averted an actual ticking bomb in Israel—that is, a bomb that was imminently set to explode.[12] American lesser evilers who invoke the Israeli example either misunderstand or misrepresent the fact that Israeli officials use the "ticking bomb" scenario loosely, not literally. But American lesser evilers like Alan Dershowitz invoke the literal ticking bomb—not the future bomb, not the general danger, not the malevolent enemy—to argue that the U.S. should follow Israel's example and legalize torture. Dershowitz writes:

> If American law enforcement officers were ever to confront the law school hypothetical case of the captured terrorist who knew about an imminent attack but refused to provide the information necessary to prevent it, I have absolutely no doubt that they would try to torture the terrorists into providing the information. Moreover, the vast majority of Americans would expect the officers to engage in that time-tested technique for loosening tongues, notwithstanding our unequivocal treaty obligations never to employ torture, no matter how exigent the circumstances. The real question is not whether torture would be used—it would—but whether it would be used outside of the law or within the law.[13]

Dershowitz offers a suggestion as to how torture can be brought "into the law": "torture warrants" issued by judges. He also offers a helpful suggestion for tactics: sterilized needles under the fingernails. He told an interviewer for *Salon.com*, "I wanted to come up with a tactic that can't

possibly cause permanent physical harm but is excruciatingly painful. . . . [T]he point I wanted to make is that torture is not being used as a way of producing death. It's been used as a way of simply causing excruciating pain . . . I want maximal pain, minimum lethality."

Lesser evilers like Dershowitz criticize the slippery slopers as human rights fundamentalists who would sacrifice innocent civilians to preserve a legal principle. They are not suggesting that we forsake the principle that torture is illegal, but rather that we suspend that principle in the handling of some people on the grounds that they are necessarily and legitimately "torturable." The implicit rationale is that terrorists are not human, and therefore are undeserving of inclusion in the universe of human beings covered by international and constitutional law that categorically prohibits torture. But the most glaring problem with this argument, as many critics have pointed out, is the implausibility of knowing with absolute certainty that the torture candidate possesses information about an imminent threat. The speculation would translate into a license to use violence on a person assumed to be guilty. Following Dershowitz's suggestion to involve judges in the dispensing of torture warrants would, at best, narrow the pool of candidates.

Oren Gross refines the lesser evil position by arguing for what he terms an "extralegal model."[14] This model would uphold the illegality of torture while enabling it to be used at the discretion of authorities. They would then be potentially subject to punishment, which they could avoid by gaining the approval of the public ex post facto. In some ways, this "extralegal model" already characterizes U.S. policies in the war on terrorism. Depending on how the Supreme Court rules, it might very well become the controlling norm for executive power. The extralegal model proposes that the U.S. have its rule of law cake while eating its unfettered executive power, too. Many legal issues are at

10. Quoted in Flore de Preneuf, "Time to Torture?," Salon.com, November 16, 2001.
11. See, for instance, Mark Bowden, "The Dark Art of Interrogation: A Survey of the Landscape of Persuasion," *Atlantic Monthly* (October 2003): 51–76.
12. The Public Committee Against Torture in Israel, Israel's premier watchdog organization for torture, confirmed this fact on May 4, 2004.
13. Alan Dershowitz, "Let America Take Its Cues from Israel Regarding Torture," *Jewish World Review*, January 30, 2002.
14. Oren Gross, "Chaos and Rules: Should Responses to Violent Crises Always Be Constitutional?" *Yale Law Journal* 112 (March 2003): 1011–1134.

stake, including habeas corpus, incommunicado detention, the right to counsel, and the transparency and accountability of government agents and agencies. But torture is a distinct issue of concern because the prohibition against it is so strong.

NO ROOM FOR MISTAKES

The slippery slopers present a valuable and worthy defense of taking the moral and legal high road. Those who invoke the slippery slope tend to focus on the tortured and worry—with good cause, as the Abu Ghraib photos have shown—that they are defenseless and susceptible to abuse in custody. But making slippery slope arguments against torture to a public gripped by fear of "evildoers" and willing to sacrifice the rights of "enemies" is not an effective rebuttal to advocates of torture as a lesser evil.

Those who invoke the lesser evil tend to focus on the public that is vulnerable to terrorism and violence. Their arguments have appeal because many people are willing to accept the legitimacy of torturing terrorists as necessary and effective. Much of the public is willing to trust that government agents empowered to decide whom to torture are capable of discerning real from imagined threats, and restricting torture to the former. But at least 22 Guantánamo Bay detainees—people described as "the worst of the worst" by Rumsfeld—have been released, an implicit acknowledgment that their very detention—in a place where torture is likely being used—had been a mistake. On May 5, the *New York Times* published an interview with an Iraqi advancing a credible claim to be the man infamously pictured naked and hooded in Abu Ghraib prison, a female soldier pointing jokingly at his genitalia—was the torture that he is now compelled to relive also a "mistake"? Without effective oversight by a judicial body, the public cannot know or trust that other such "mistakes" will not be made. When it comes to torture, there is no room for a mistake.

Naturally, it is important to focus both on the tortured and on the vulnerable public, but the case of Abu Ghraib shows that it is most important to focus on the torturers. They are representatives of the public they serve. If torture is practiced by agents of a state that claims to be a democracy, then "we the people" are responsible for torture. Citizens of a democracy cannot or at least should not be comforted by blaming a few "aberrant agents" if torture is systemic and routine. Those citizens cannot or should not be quiescent as democratic values and laws are being trampled in a panic. "We the people" are responsible for stopping, protesting and preventing torture.

Keeping torture illegal and struggling to enforce the prohibition are the front lines, quite literally, of a global battle to defend the one core right that all human beings can claim. If torture is legitimized and legalized in the future, it is not "the terrorists" who will lose but "the humans." Should proponents of torture as a lesser evil succeed in regaining legitimacy for the execrable practice, there would be no better words than George Orwell's from *1984*: "If you want a picture of the future, imagine a boot stamping on a human face—forever."

QUESTIONS FOR REFLECTION AND DISCUSSION

1. In what is today impolitic gendered language, the 1984 Convention against Torture and Other Cruel, Inhuman or Degrading Treatment or Punishment (referenced in Documentary Appendix B) defines "torture" to include the following six elements:

[1] any act [2] by which severe pain or suffering, whether physical or mental [3] is intentionally inflicted [4] by or at the instigation of a public official [5] on a person for such purposes as [5.1] obtaining from him or a third person information or confession, [5.2] punishing him for an act he has committed or is suspected of having committed, or [5.3] intimidating him or other persons. [6] It does not include pain or suffering arising only from, inherent to or incidental to, lawful sanctions to the extent consistent with the [1955 United Nations] Standard Minimum Rules for the Treatment of Prisoners.

Assessing this definition, consider the following:

1.1. Does "any act" encompass a related series of acts which together "intentionally inflict severe pain or suffering"? What difference would it have made had the drafters used the words "any systemic infliction" instead of "any act"?

1.2. Does the qualification of *"severe* pain or suffering" imply that torture is a question of degree, distinguishable from "cruel, inhuman or degrading treatment or punishment"? What standards should be applied or variables used to establish "severe" pain or suffering?

1.3. Does the fact that severe pain or suffering must be "intentionally inflicted" imply that there must be a specific intent to inflict severe pain or suffering? Or is it sufficient that the torturer know or have known that severe pain or suffering might result from her or his acts?

1.4. Article 1 refers to the intention of state or governmental officials. Which ones? Lower as well as higher officials? The reverse? Might low-level officials be insulated from responsibility if they have acted under orders? Should they be? Might high-level officials be insulated from responsibility for the unauthorized acts of their subordinates? Should they be? And what about terrorists or vigilantes? By the term "public official," does Article 1 exempt them from responsibility under the Convention? What if the terrorist or vigilante is a former state or governmental official? Can you think of any way in which "public official" might legitimately be construed to cover such persons? Might the U.S. constitutional doctrine of "state action" be helpful (a limitation on private conduct, mostly in relation to racial discrimination)? See, e.g., *Shelley v. Kraemer,* 334 U.S. 1 (1948); *Evans v. Newton,* 382 U.S. 296 (1966); *Evans v. Abney,* 396 U.S. 435 (1970); *Burton v. Wilmington,* 365 U.S. 715 (1971); *Moose Lodge v. Irvis,* 407 U.S. 163 (1972); and *Edmonson v. Leesville Concrete,* 500 U.S. 614 (1991). Should it be possible for individuals, acting alone and for various reasons, to be prosecuted for torture? Would this strengthen or weaken the prohibition on torture?

1.5. Is an "act" not torture if it does not serve one of the purposes listed in the fifth element of Article 1? Is the enumeration of purposes exhaustive? Too restrictive?

1.6. The 1955 United Nations Standard Minimum Rules for the Treatment of Prisoners (referenced in Documentary Appendix B) are open to interpretation by state officials, and their enforcement depends on the good faith of penal officials. How might these facts prove problematic relative to the definition of "torture"? Would repeated administration of electric current for the purpose of killing a prisoner as punishment for a crime constitute torture? If so, what might be the implications for capital punishment as practiced in the United States and elsewhere? What about other forms of capital punishment? Does capital punishment without pain escape the definition of torture? What about the mental suffering leading up to the killing regardless of the means chosen?

How would Lisa Hajjar answer the foregoing questions?

2. In "The Protection of Universal Human Rights: The Problem of Torture," *Universal Human Rights* 1, 4 (1979): 25–55, Matthew Lippman lists a myriad techniques then utilized in over 60 countries, which he characterized as "torture," including: unsedated tooth extraction; prolonged suspension of the body by the victim's feet; immersion of the victim's head in a tub of urine; electric shock to sensitive portions of the body; sexual abuse; nudity; strapping the victim to a bed with wet sheets that dry out and suffocate the victim; placing a hood over the victim's head; and the use of drugs that cause depression, headaches, vomiting, cramps, and paralysis (33–35). Do you agree with Lippman that these acts constitute torture? What about, in addition, throwing suspects against a wall, sleep deprivation, subjection to extreme temperatures, forced uncomfortable positions, and repeated strip searches? What would Lisa Hajjar say? How would you define torture?

3. Lippman (see Question 2) condemns the practices he enumerates, but concludes that it is "futile to attempt to protect individuals from torture through treaties and legal instruments" (55) when governments systematically using torture are already outside the community of law-abiding states. Do you agree? What about the cumulative effect of being identified as a torturing country, being condemned for your official acts, being forced by international agencies, public and private, to defend your actions? Consider the following observation by Louis Henkin: "Rhetoric is important, . . . and even some hypocrisy may be tolerable as a first step. Acceptances of human rights in principle make respect for human rights the norm, violation illegitimate. It unleashes forces for compliance, forces both official and unofficial, internal and external." "International Instruments for the Protection of Human Rights," *Acta Juridica* (1979): 224–35, at 232–33. What do you think?

4. Are acts that constitute torture culturally determined or universal—that is, do acts that constitute torture vary from culture to culture? From gender to gender? Religion to religion? If so, how is it possible to enforce the 1984 Torture Convention meaningfully?

5. When, on October 27, 1990, the U.S. Senate consented to ratification of the 1984 Torture Convention, it did so subject to a declaration stating that the substantive provisions of the Convention (arts. 1–16) are not "self-executing," meaning that a further act of Congress would be required to make those provisions part of the "supreme law of the land." See *Foster v. Neilson*, 27 U.S. 253 (1829). Also, the Senate inserted a reservation stating that the United States has an obligation to prevent "cruel, inhuman or degrading treatment or punishment" only insofar as this language means the "cruel and unusual punishment" prohibited by the Eighth Amendment to the U.S. Constitution. Does the declaration strengthen or weaken the Convention? Why? Does the reservation strengthen or weaken the Convention? Why? Should the United States hold itself to a lower standard than other nations with respect to torture? The same standard? A higher standard? Which of these alternatives is the United States presently pursuing? Why? What are the consequences of each?

6. Lisa Hajjar describes the post-9/11 mistreatment by United States officials of Afghani, Iraqi, and other prisoners suspected or alleged to be terrorists or cooperating with terrorists. For further details, including the George W. Bush administration's establishment of a network of detention centers lacking accountability, see Michael Ratner and Ellen Ray, *Guantánamo: What the World Should Know* (Adlestrop, UK: Arris Books, 2004) and David Rose, *Guantánamo: America's War on Human Rights* (London: Faber and Faber, 2004). What problems does this behavior pose for the United States? For the world? For international law?

7. In its "war on terrorism," the United States has transferred prisoners to countries known to use torture techniques for interrogation purposes. Is this permissible under international law? Should it be permissible? Why? Why not?

8. Article 4(1) of the International Covenant on Civil and Political Rights (reprinted and referenced in Documentary Appendix A) permits the derogation of certain enumerated rights "in time of public emergency which threatens the life of the nation and the existence of which is officially proclaimed." The right to be free from torture (art. 7) is among those—including, *inter alia*, the right to be free from arbitrary killing (art. 6), slavery (art. 8), and the right to be recognized everywhere as a person before the law (art. 16)—from which there may be no derogation under any circumstances. To what extent has the United States, citing the exigencies of the "war on terror" abrogated these rights? Should the United States have done so? What recourse and remedies should be available to those whose nominally nonderogable rights have been violated? What recourse do Iraqi prisoners tortured by U.S. citizens currently have? What recourse should they have? What recourse do U.S. citizens tortured by Iraqi captors have? What recourse should they have?

9. Under current international law, Hajjar notes, torture "is prohibited under all circumstances, including the 'ticking bomb' scenario." Do you think the U.S. should abide by the law as it stands, or would you side with Harvard law professor Alan Dershowitz and others who have asserted that torture might be justified under certain circumstances and when certain procedural safeguards are met? Dershowitz proposes a system of publicly known "torture warrants" (i.e., licenses to commit torture for interrogation purposes) signed by either the President or a Supreme Court Justice. Do you agree with this view? Why? Why not? Would torture warrants adequately protect human rights? Why? Why not? Would they facilitate reliable interrogation? Why? Why not?

10. Many experts on torture have observed that information extracted from a person through torture is unreliable. If this is true, why is torture so apparently tempting to governments the world over?

11. The UN Committee Against Torture and Special Rapporteur on Torture are, according to some, so underfunded as to be ineffectual. Civil society must therefore fill the void or, according to Winston Nagan and Lucie Atkins, "The International Law of Torture: From Universal Proscription to Effective Application and Enforcement," *Harvard Human Rights Law Journal* 14 (2001): 87–122, at 120, "those committed to the future of human indignity undoubtedly will." Do you agree, or is this an unduly pessimistic view? Will torture inevitably occur if it is not actively resisted by third parties?

12. In *Torture and Truth: America, Abu Ghraib, and the War on Terror* (New York: New York Review Books, 2004), Mark Danner, a staff writer for the *New Yorker* and contributor to the *New York Review of Books*, recounts in detail, with documents, photographs, and his

own text the shocking tale of torture of prisoners by American soldiers in Baghdad. At the close of his Introduction, he writes:

> To date the true actors in those lurid scenes [at Abu Ghraib], who are professionals and no doubt embarrassed by the garish brutality of their apprentices in the military police, have remained offstage. None has testified. The question we must ask in coming days . . . , as young Americans face public courts-martial in Baghdad, is whether or not we as Americans can face a true revelation. We must look squarely at the photographs and ask: Is what has changed only what we know, or what we are willing to accept?

What do you think? Why?

13. Hajjar concludes her essay by quoting George Orwell's *1984*. Why? Is at least a partial answer found, perhaps, in Mark Danner's comment quoted in Question 12, above?

7. RICHARD B. LILLICH *Civil Rights*

A decade ago this writer, surveying the development of international human rights law subsequent to the adoption of the UN Charter, observed that "the progress in the area of human rights has been almost exclusively in the direction of clarifying and codifying the substantive law norms. . . ." During the intervening years, which have seen considerable progress in the implementation area, this trend has continued apace. Yet, upon reflection, one may conclude that perhaps more codification than clarification has occurred. As Professors McDougal, Lasswell, and Chen conclude in their magnum opus, "It is in the substantive definition of human rights that the greatest confusion and inadequacy prevail. Little effort has been made to create a comprehensive map of the totality of human rights, and there has been little discussion of the detailed content of particular rights."[1]

This [essay], as its title indicates, is not intended to be a comprehensive map of all international human rights norms. Rather, it is basically a description *cum* commentary of those international norms which purport to guarantee and protect one bundle of rights: the civil rights of individuals. These rights, commonly considered the most basic and fundamental of all human rights, will be familiar to readers versed in United States constitutional law, for, as Professor Henkin has recalled:

> Americans were prominent among the architects and builders of international human rights, and American constitutionalism was a principal inspiration and model for them. As a result, most of the Universal Declaration of Human Rights, and later the International Covenant on Civil and Political Rights, are in their essence American constitutional rights projected around the world.[2]

Since these rights find their expression in articles 3–18 of the Universal Declaration of Human Rights (UDHR)[3]—restated, supplemented, and occasionally modified by companion articles in the International Covenant on Civil and Political

Reprinted with changes from Richard B. Lillich, "Civil Rights," in Theodor Meron, ed., *Human Rights in International Law: Legal and Policy Issues* (New York: Oxford University Press, 1984), 1: 115–69. Copyright © 1983 by Richard B. Lillich. Reprinted by permission.

1. Myres S. McDougal, Harold D. Lasswell, and Lung-chu Chen, *Human Rights and World Public Order: The Basic Policies of an International Law of Human Dignity* (New Haven, Conn.: Yale University Press, 1980), 64.
2. Louis Henkin, "Rights: American and Human," *Columbia Law Review* 79 (1979): 405–25, at 415. See also *Message of the President Transmitting Four Treaties Pertaining to Human Rights*, S. Exec. Doc. No. 95-C, D, E, and F, 95th Cong., 2d Sess. XI (1978): "The International Covenant on Civil and Political Rights is, of the [four] treaties submitted, the most similar in conception to the United States Constitution and Bill of Rights. The rights guaranteed are those civil and political rights with which the United States and the western liberal democratic tradition have always been associated. The rights are primarily limitations upon the power of the State to impose its will upon the people under its jurisdiction."
3. Adopted Dec. 10, 1948, pmbl, reprinted and referenced in Documentary Appendix A.

Rights (ICCPR)[4]—for the sake of convenience they will be considered in the order they appear in the Universal Declaration. Before beginning this survey, however, the human rights to be reviewed must be placed in proper juridical perspective. Specifically, what is their status under contemporary international law, and what restrictions may states impose upon their enjoyment? Unless these questions can be answered satisfactorily, human rights, no matter how nicely phrased, can have little real meaning in or effect upon the lives of individuals.

As to the first question, it now may be argued persuasively that substantial parts of the Universal Declaration, a UN General Assembly resolution adopted in 1948 without dissent and originally thought not to give rise to international legal obligations, have become part of customary international law binding upon all states. This view, first advanced solely by legal scholars but subsequently supported by the statements of international conferences, by state practice, and even by court decisions,[5] now appears to have achieved widespread acceptance. Indeed the suggestion has even been made that the Universal Declaration has "the attributes of *jus cogens*,"[6] a statement that, in the opinion of this writer,

goes too far if intended to imply that all rights enumerated in it have this character.[7] There is little doubt, however, that many of the human rights to be discussed—the prohibition of slavery being just one example—not only reflect customary international law but also partake of the character of *jus cogens*. This conclusion is particularly valid when the right in question appears in both the Universal Declaration and the Political Covenant. The latter, of course, is binding conventional law only between states parties to it, but many of its provisions now can be said to have helped create norms of customary international law—including ones having *jus cogens* status[8]—binding even states which have yet to ratify it.[9] Dramatic evidence of this process at work may be found in the U.S. Memorial to the International Court of Justice in the *Case Concerning United States Diplomatic and Consular Staff in Tehran*,[10] where, after citing four articles of the Political Covenant—to which, ironically, Iran [was] a party and the United States . . . merely a signatory—the United States argued that Iran had violated not only conventional law but also "fundamental principles . . . of customary international law. . . ."

With respect to the second question, the

---

4. Concluded Dec. 16, 1966, reprinted and referenced in Documentary Appendix A.

5. See, e.g., *Filártiga v. Peña-Irala*, 630 F.2d 876, 882 (2d Cir. 1980), where the Court of Appeals for the Second Circuit held that "the right to be free from torture . . . has become part of customary international law, *as evidenced and defined by the Universal Declaration of Human Rights*" (emphasis added). [For discussion of this important decision and its aftermath, see Reading 29 by Michael Ratner in Chapter 7 of this volume.]

6. Meaning "compulsory law" in Latin, *jus cogens* denotes a peremptory norm of international law binding on all states at all times and so fundamental that it may not be overridden by any rule that any one or more states may seek to establish by treaty or custom (e.g., prohibitions on aggression, slavery, genocide).

7. Roslyn Higgins [now judge of the International Court of Justice], "Derogations Under Human Rights Treaties," *BYBIL* 48 (1976–77): 281–320, at 282, writing about human rights treaties but reasoning along lines applicable to the Universal Declaration as well, makes a similar point:

> the suggestion has been made that human rights treaties have the character of *jus cogens*. There certainly exists a consensus that certain rights—the right to life, to freedom from slavery or torture—are so fundamental that no derogation may be made. And international human rights treaties undoubtedly contain elements that are binding as principles which are recognized by civilized States, and not only as mutual treaty commitments. Some treaties may focus almost exclusively on such elements—such as the Genocide Convention—while others may cover a wider range of rights, not all of which may have for the present a status which is more than treaty-based. This being said, neither the wording of the various human rights instruments nor the practice thereunder leads to the view that all human rights are *jus cogens*.

8. In seeking to determine what human rights protected by the Political Covenant have achieved *jus cogens* status, a good starting point is the list of rights which art. 4(2) makes nonderogable, i.e., rights which a state may not suspend even in time of war or national emergency.

9. There is ample language in the decisions of the International Court of Justice to support the late Judge Baxter's conclusion that "Treaties that do not purport to be declaratory of customary international law at the time they enter into force may nevertheless with the passage of time pass into customary international law." Richard Baxter, "Treaties and Custom," *Recueil des Cours* 129 (1970-II): 25, 57.

10. 1980 ICJ 3.

restrictions which a state may impose upon an individual's internationally protected human rights come in two tiers, both of which must be kept in mind in determining the protection afforded by particular guarantees. On the first tier of restrictions, both the Universal Declaration and the Political Covenant contain provisions limiting the rights guaranteed therein. The former contains a general limitations clause, article 29(2), which provides that

> In the exercise of his rights and freedoms, everyone shall be subject only to such limitations as are determined by law solely for the purpose of securing due recognition and respect for the rights and freedoms of others and of meeting the just requirements of morality, public order and the general welfare in a democratic society.

In the Political Covenant, as Professor [now Judge] Higgins has pointed out, the references to the need for rights to be exercised in conformity with morality, public order, general welfare, etc., appear not as a general clause but as qualifications to specific freedoms.[11] The specific limitations (or, as she aptly terms them, "clawback" clauses[12]) in the Political Covenant relating to civil rights are contained in articles 12(3), 14(1), and 18(3). One can only endorse [the] warning that such limitations can be "highly dangerous (from the point of view of human rights) . . . ."

On the second tier of restrictions which is relevant to the Political Covenant alone, article 4(1) thereof permits states parties to derogate from, i.e., suspend or breach, certain obligations "In time of public emergency which threatens the life of the nation and the existence of which is officially proclaimed. . . ." No derogation may be made, however, from the human rights

contained in articles 6, 7, 8(1), 8(2), 11, 15, 16, and 18, evidence that at least some of these rights may have "attributes" of *jus cogens*.[13] Nevertheless, as in the case of the limitation clauses discussed in the preceding paragraph, the fact that a wide variety of important rights—for example, the right to liberty and security of person guaranteed by article 9(1)—may be rendered temporarily "inoperative" by means of derogation is extremely troublesome from the human rights viewpoint. Certainly the existence of both tiers of restrictions—limitations and derogations—must be kept in mind when assessing the degree of protection actually afforded individuals by the language of articles 3–18 of the Universal Declaration.[14]

[*Eds.*—The author next analyzes the civil rights of individuals set forth in the Universal Declaration: rights to life, liberty, and security of person (art. 3); prohibition of slavery and servitude (art. 4); prohibition of torture and cruel, inhuman, or degrading treatment of punishment (art. 5); right to legal recognition (art. 6); rights to equality before the law and to nondiscrimination in its application (art. 7); right to a remedy (art. 8); prohibition of arbitrary arrest, detention, or exile (art. 9); right to a fair trial (art. 10); presumption of innocence and prohibition of *ex post facto* laws (art. 11); right to privacy (art. 12); right to freedom of movement (art. 13); right to asylum (art. 14); right to a nationality (art. 15); right to marry and found a family (art. 16); right to own property (art. 17); and freedom of thought, conscience, and religion (art. 18). Noting that these rights are set forth also in the International Covenant on Civil and Political Rights (1966), the European Convention on Human Rights and Fundamental Freedoms (1950),[15] and

11. Higgins, "Derogations Under Human Rights Treaties," note 7, at 283.
12. By a "clawback" clause is meant one that permits, in normal circumstances, breach of an obligation for a specified number of public reasons. Ibid., at 281. It thus differs from a derogation clause, e.g., art. 4(1) of the Political Covenant, "which allows suspension or breach of certain obligations in circumstances of war or public emergency."
13. Reservations to the Political Covenant, to the extent that they are directed to the rights guaranteed in these seven articles, presumably have no force or effect if these rights actually have acquired *jus cogens* status.
14. An issue is raised by the use of the words "arbitrary" or "arbitrarily" throughout the UDHR and the ICCPR. These words, it now seems clear, should be construed to prohibit not only "illegal" but also "unjust" acts. Thus, despite the fears of some observers, a state cannot impinge upon an individual's internationally protected human rights simply by enacting legislation making its acts legal on the domestic plane.
15. Concluded Nov. 4, 1950, referenced in Documentary Appendix B.

the American Convention on Human Rights (1969),[16] the author points out their complexity and frequent ambiguity. He also opines that only the following rights may be considered part of customary international law: right to life; freedom from slavery and involuntary servitude; freedom from torture and cruel, inhuman, or degrading treatment or punishment; rights to equality before the law and to nondiscrimination in its application; freedom from arbitrary arrest and detention; presumption of innocence; and freedom of thought, conscience, and religion. The author concludes by emphasizing, *inter alia*, the international community's rank-ordering of these rights in terms of those that in the Political Covenant made nonderogable, that is, rights that may not be suspended by a state even in time of public emergency, declared or otherwise: right to life; freedom from torture and cruel, inhuman, or degrading treatment or punishment; freedom from slavery and involuntary servitude; freedom from debtor prison; freedom from *ex post facto* laws; and freedom of thought, conscience, and religion. The author's discussion makes clear that even basic procedural due process rights are seen to be a part of customary international law and nonderogable only exceptionally.]

RIGHTS TO EQUALITY BEFORE THE LAW AND TO NONDISCRIMINATION IN ITS APPLICATION (ARTICLE 7)

Equality before the law and nondiscrimination in its application are provided for by this article, which reads: "All are equal before the law and are entitled without any discrimination to equal protection of the law. All are entitled to equal protection against any discrimination in violation of this Declaration and against any incitement to such discrimination." Language almost identical with the first sentence of article 7 is found in the first sentence of article 26 of the Political Covenant; the second sentence of

article 26, however, contains the following variation: "*In this respect*, the law shall prohibit any discrimination and guarantee to all persons equal and effective protection on any ground. . . ." Language paralleling the first sentence of article 7 is found in article 24 of the American Convention, while the European Convention contains no directly corresponding provision.

Almost from the beginning, the words "equal protection of the law" caused confusion. According to one member of the Third Committee during debates on the draft Declaration, "it was not clear whether they meant that there should be laws which should be applied equally or that all were equally entitled to the protection of whatever laws existed." This lack of clarity, in the view of some observers, persists under the Political Covenant. Professor Robertson analyzes and evaluates the alternative interpretations as follows:

> Broadly speaking, two quite different meanings seem possible: that the substantive provisions of the law should be the same for everyone; or that the application of the law should be equal for all without discrimination. The former interpretation would seem unreasonable; for example, in most countries women are not required to perform military service, while it is unnecessary that the law should prescribe maternity benefits for men. It would seem, therefore, that the meaning rather is to secure equality, without discrimination, in the application of the law, and this interpretation is borne out by the *travaux préparatoires*.[17]

He acknowledges that the second sentence of article 26, "if it stood alone, would constitute an important and far-reaching commitment and a general protection against discrimination," but points out that "in the Third Committee the words 'in this respect' were added at the beginning of this sentence . . . so that its scope is now limited to the general statement of equality and equal protection contained in the preceding sentence."[18]

16. Concluded Nov. 22, 1969, referenced in Documentary Appendix B. The United States, while a party to the ICCPR, is not a party to the American Convention.
17. Arthur H. Robertson and J. G. Merrills, *Human Rights in the World: An Introduction to the Study of the International Protection of Human Rights*, 4th ed. (Manchester: Manchester University Press, 1996), 39.
18. Ibid. "As a result, the phrase is, in the view of one expert, largely tautologous." Idem, citing Egon Schwelb, "The International Convention on the Elimination of All Forms of Racial Discrimination," *ICLQ* 15 (1966): 996–1068, at 1019:

> The second sentence as amended . . . , makes the article an accumulation of tautologies. It now says, inter alia, that the law shall prohibit any discrimination in respect of the entitlement not to

This interpretation is consistent with the approach taken in article 2 of the Universal Declaration and article 2(1) of the Political Covenant, both of which mandate nondiscriminatory treatment, but only insofar as the rights set out in the respective human rights instrument are concerned. Articles 7 and 26, therefore, while specifically guaranteeing one important civil right to all persons on a nondiscriminatory basis, surely cannot be read to constitute a general norm of nondiscrimination invocable in other contexts. Properly limited, however, the right considered in this subsection probably now has become customary international law.

RIGHT TO A REMEDY (ARTICLE 8)

This unique article, added at the last minute by the Third Committee to fill a supposed lacuna in the draft Declaration, guarantees all persons "the right to an effective remedy by the competent national tribunals for acts violating the fundamental rights granted him *by the constitution or by law.*" Although, as one commentator has observed in an analogous context, "there is a certain anomaly in the right to a remedy itself being classed among the rights guaranteed,"[19] that fact has not prevented the inclusion of roughly similar provisions in article 2(3) of the Political Covenant and article 13 of the European Convention.

Since, as Professor Humphrey has remarked, "human rights without effective implementation are shadows without substance,"[20] there is no doubt that the right to a remedy is an extremely important one. For this reason, despite assertions that such a right was superfluous or would prove of little value, it has been included not only in the Universal Declaration and the Political Covenant, but, as indicated above, in the

European Convention and American Convention as well. Its importance, however, depends greatly upon the scope of the "substantive" rights it is designed to protect. Here there is considerable variation in the language of the relevant articles.

The Universal Declaration, quoted above, guarantees an effective domestic remedy for acts which violate rights granted by the constitutions or laws of the various states. Thus, in contrast with article 7, whose reach extends only to acts in violation of the Universal Declaration, article 8's scope is potentially much broader. Since the ambit of the rights granted by [domestic constitutions and domestic law] generally is larger (at least on paper) than that of the rights enunciated in the Universal Declaration, the right to a remedy contemplated by article 8 may be regarded as a broad one indeed.

Unfortunately, both the Political Covenant and the European Convention are more restrictive in this regard. Effective remedies are guaranteed by article 2(3)(a) of the Political Covenant only to vindicate the "rights or freedoms as herein recognized," that is, recognized by the Political Covenant. Similarly, article 13 of the European Convention guarantees an effective remedy only for "rights and freedoms as set forth in this Convention. . . ." The American Convention, on the other hand, provides the person seeking relief the best of all possible worlds: article 25(1) combines the approaches of the Universal Declaration, Political Covenant, and European Convention, requiring states to accord prompt and effective relief "against acts that violate . . . fundamental rights recognized by the constitution or laws of the state concerned or by the Convention. . . ."

To date only article 13 of the European Convention has been interpreted and, in Professor Fawcett's words, its interpretation has revealed

---

be discriminated against. It says further that the law shall guarantee to all persons equal and effective protection against discrimination in respect of their entitlement to equal protection of the law. In other words: the second sentence has no normative content at all and the prohibition of "any discrimination" has, in fact, disappeared from the provision.

19. Francis G. Jacobs, *The European Convention on Human Rights* (Oxford: Oxford University Press, 1975), 215.
20. John Humphrey, "Report of the Rapporteur of the International Committee on Human Rights," in International Law Association, *Report of the Fifty-Third Conference Held at Buenos Aires, August 25th to August 31st, 1968* (London: the Association, 1969), 437–58, at 457. His remarks echo the more poetic words of Justice Holmes: "Legal obligations that exist but cannot be enforced are ghosts that are seen in the law but are elusive to the grasp." *The Western Maid*, 257 U.S. 419, at 433 (1922).

"a basic confusion of thought as to the real purpose and function of the Article."[21] Is article 13, he asks, "concerned with the international or the domestic implementation of the Convention, with the collective guarantee, or with internal remedies?"[22] Does the article, from the claimant's perspective, mandate that an effective domestic remedy be in place ready to consider any alleged violation of the European Convention, or does it become applicable only after there has been a determination (by the Committee of Ministers, the European Court of Human Rights, or a domestic court applying the Convention as part of domestic law) that another, "substantive" article of the Convention actually has been violated? For textual and other reasons, Professor Fawcett leans away from the former ("domestic" or "internal") and toward the latter ("international" or "collective") view of the article. This view, which greatly minimizes the importance of the right to a remedy, has not been explicitly adopted by the European Court of Human Rights and hopefully will be rejected by the UN Human Rights Committee and the American Commission and Court of Human Rights when the issue arises under the Political Covenant and the American Convention respectively. In any event, so much confusion exists about the scope of this right that it can be said with reasonable assurance that it is not part of customary international law.

PROHIBITION OF ARBITRARY ARREST, DETENTION OR EXILE (ARTICLE 9)

Article 3, it will be recalled, establishes not only the right to life, but also the right to liberty and security of person. The Political Covenant handles these rights in two articles, 6(1) and 9(1), the latter of which, in addition to guaranteeing "the right to liberty and security of person," provides, *inter alia*, that "No one shall be subjected to arbitrary arrest or detention." "Protection against arbitrary arrest and detention,"

Professor Jacobs rightly notes, "is clearly the central feature of any system of guarantees of the liberty of the individual."[23] Indeed, the drafters of the Universal Declaration considered the prohibition of arbitrary arrest and detention so important that rather than treating it as just one liberty interest, they devoted a separate article to it, demonstrating their intention to establish it as an independent human right. Thus, article 9 of the Universal Declaration provides that "No one shall be subjected to arbitrary arrest, detention or exile."

The *travaux préparatoires*, revealing an understandable reluctance to define "arbitrary" and an enthusiastic endorsement of an amendment adding "exile" to the draft Declaration's proscription against "arbitrary arrest or detention," indicate that most members of the Third Committee were pleased with the article's "eloquent brevity" and content to leave it to the Political Covenant to spell out its general terms. The Political Covenant, in article 9, fulfills their expectations by elaborating in considerable detail the rights to be accorded a person who has been arrested or detained. Most of these rights also are protected by article 5 of the European Convention and article 7 of the American Convention in "substantially similar terms."

After the language quoted above, article 9(1) of the Political Covenant concludes with the following sentence: "No one shall be deprived of his liberty except on such grounds and in accordance with such procedure as are established by law." The purpose of this provision is to require states to spell out in legislation the grounds on which an individual may be deprived of [her or] his liberty and the procedures to be used. With the freedom of action of the executive branch of government thus restricted, Dinstein observes, "Not every policeman (or other state functionary) is entitled to decide at his discretion, and on his own responsibility, who can be arrested, why and how."[24] Nor is any detention allowed by law permissible, as a literal interpretation of the provision might suggest. Just as an arrest may

21. James E. S. Fawcett, *The Application of the European Convention on Human Rights* (Oxford: Clarendon Press, 1969), 232.
22. Ibid., 229.
23. Jacobs, *The European Convention*, note 19, at 75.
24. Yoram Dinstein, "The Right to Life, Physical Integrity and Liberty," in Louis Henkin, ed., *The International Bill of Rights: The Covenant on Civil and Political Rights* (New York: Columbia University Press, 1981), 114–37, at 130.

not be arbitrary—defined as "unjust" and not merely "illegal"—so too must a detention not be arbitrary. The deprivation of liberty therefore must be not only in accordance with law, but also in conformity to the principles of justice.

The balance of article 9 defines certain guarantees applicable in case of any arrest or detention, plus certain special guarantees applicable when a person is arrested or detained on a criminal charge. Space dictates that these guarantees be listed rather than fully evaluated [here]. In the first, general category are following:

> Article 9(2). "Anyone who is arrested shall be informed, at the time of arrest, of the reasons for his arrest and shall be promptly informed of any charges against him."

> Article 9(4). "Anyone who is deprived of his liberty by arrest or detention shall be entitled to take proceedings before a court, in order that court may decide without delay on the lawfulness of his detention and order his release if the detention is not lawful."

> Article 9(5). "Anyone who has been the victim of unlawful arrest or detention shall have an enforceable right to compensation."

In the second category—special guarantees applicable to persons arrested or detained on criminal charges—article 9(3) provides that such persons "be brought promptly before a judge" and thereafter "be entitled to trial within a reasonable time or to release." Additionally, it establishes a presumption that persons awaiting trial shall not be detained in custody; their release, however, may be made subject to guarantees of appearance, the most common of which presumably would be bail.

Interpretative guidance as to the meaning of most of the above provisions can be obtained from the nascent practice of the UN Human Rights Committee [established under the Political Covenant] as well as the more developed practice of the European Court of Human Rights under article 5 of the European Convention. Given the differences in wording, however, the latter must be used with care. In any event, taking into account uncertainties about the contours and content of the prohibition of arbitrary arrest and detention, plus the fact that states may derogate therefrom under article 4(2) of the Political Covenant, it seems unlikely that little more than the basic core prohibition can be said

to constitute part of customary international law at present.

RIGHT TO A FAIR TRIAL (ARTICLE 10)

This article, which along with its companion, article 11, guarantees individuals "the basic right to a fair trial [in] both civil and criminal matters," enunciates a very important right, for the implementation of all other rights depends upon the proper administration of justice. In its entirety article 10 reads as follows: "Everyone is entitled in full equality to a fair and public hearing by an independent and impartial tribunal, in the determination of his rights and obligations and of any criminal charge against him." Two preliminary points should be made with respect to this language. First, it lumps together both criminal and civil proceedings, despite cogent arguments for their being treated separately, the potential for abuse of state power obviously being greater where the rights of an accused—as opposed to a mere party in civil lawsuit—are concerned. Second, it is so terse that it offers little help when applied to the facts of particular cases. Hence, here more than elsewhere, guidance as to the meaning of the right must be obtained from parallel provisions in subsequent international human rights instruments and the decisions of competent bodies interpreting them.

The requirements of a fair trial in criminal proceedings, the sole concern of this subsection, can be divided somewhat arbitrarily into four general categories: the character of the tribunal, the public nature of the hearing, the rights of the accused in the conduct of his defense and, lastly, a miscellaneous collection of other prescriptions.

The first category, the character of the tribunal, obviously is of prime importance. Article 10 requires tribunals to be "independent and impartial," as do article 14(1) of the Political Covenant and articles 6(1) and 8(1) of the European Convention and American conventions, respectively. As Professor Harris has put it,

> These are obvious and overlapping requirements. The primary meaning of "independent" is independence of other organs of government in the sense of the doctrine of the separation of powers: in particular, a judge must not be subject to the control or influence of the executive or the legislature. . . .

The requirement that the court must be "impartial" needs little implication. It is reflected in the "universally accepted doctrine" that no man may be a judge in his own cause and is an obvious characteristic for a court to possess.[25]

Whether such independence and impartiality can be assured when a state resorts to ad hoc or special tribunals, as frequently occurs after revolutions or in national emergencies, is a doubtful proposition: for this reason, it is disappointing that article 10 does not speak directly to this point. In contrast, article 14(1) of the Political Covenant and article 8(1) of the American Convention add the requirement that the tribunal be "competent," a word which, according to the *travaux préparatoires* of the former, "was intended to ensure that all persons should be tried in courts whose jurisdiction had been previously established by law, and arbitrary action so avoided." Article 8(1) of the American Convention goes one step further, specifically stating that a trial must be conducted by a tribunal "previously established by law. . . ." Arguably, this requirement can be read into the "independent and impartial" language of the Universal Declaration.

The second category, the public nature of the hearing, also is of importance in protecting individuals from arbitrary proceedings. The drafters of article 10 of the Universal Declaration inserted the words "and public" between the words "fair" and "hearing" to insure the openness of trials, a procedure conducive to their fairness. Moreover, despite language in the *travaux préparatoires* that "There were circumstances in which a secret trial might be acceptable," article 10 itself acknowledges no such exception. Article 14(1) of the Political Covenant, however, closely tracked by article 6(1) of the European Convention, contains a wide range of exceptions. . . . Article 14(1) reads, in part, as follows: "The Press and the public may be excluded from all or part of a trial for reasons of morals, public order (*ordre public*) or national security in a democratic society, or when the interest of the private lives of the parties so requires, or to the extent strictly necessary in the opinion of the court in special circumstances where publicity would prejudice the interests of justice. . . ." Such language, as Professor Fawcett remarks with respect to article 6(1) of the European Convention, is so broad that "it is doubtful whether the requirement of public hearing under the Convention is likely in practice to yield much protection."[26]

The rights of the accused in the conduct of [her or] his defense, the third category, presents the converse of the above. Rather than the Political Covenant undercutting a broad and unqualified right found in the Universal Declaration, here the Political Covenant spells out at length in article 14(3) just what rights an accused has in a criminal proceeding. In brief, they are the right to be informed promptly of the charge against him; the right to have adequate time and facilities to prepare a defense and to communicate with counsel; the right to be tried without undue delay; the right to be tried in his presence and to defend himself in person or through counsel; the right to cross-examine witnesses against him and to summon witnesses on his own behalf; the right to an interpreter; and the right not to be compelled to testify against himself. Roughly similar guarantees are found in article 6(3) of the European Convention and article 8(2) of the American Convention. As is apparent, they generally reflect the procedural due process rights developed by the U.S. Supreme Court from the fifth and fourteenth amendments to the U.S. Constitution.

The fourth and final category comprises a number of miscellaneous rights, none of which are set out in the Universal Declaration, which generally are thought to contribute to a fair trial in criminal proceedings. In the order in which they appear in article 14 of the Political Covenant, they are: the right of juveniles to be tried under special procedures; the right to appeal one's conviction and sentence; the right to compensation when one is convicted through a miscarriage of justice; and the right not to be subjected to double jeopardy. The fact that none of these rights are mentioned in the European Convention (and only three are guaranteed by the American Convention) suggests that they are part of conventional rather than customary international law, a status they are likely to retain until the Political Covenant becomes so widely accepted as to be generally norm-creating. Moreover, without the interpretative assistance of the Political Covenant, the right to a fair trial provided for in article 10 of the Universal Declaration

---

25. David J. Harris, "The Right to a Fair Trial in Criminal Proceedings as a Human Right," *ICLQ* 16 (1967): 352–78, at 354–56.

26. Fawcett, *The Application of the European Convention*, note 21, at 150.

seems too generally phrased to constitute a customary international law rule capable of application in concrete cases.

PRESUMPTION OF INNOCENCE AND PROHIBITION OF EX POST FACTO LAWS (ARTICLE 11)

This article, closely related to article 10 of the Universal Declaration, also is concerned with the rights of the accused in criminal proceedings. It establishes the presumption of innocence and proscribes *ex post facto* offenses. These important and distinct guarantees will be discussed separately.

Article 11(1) provides that "Everyone charged with a penal offence has the right to be presumed innocent until proved guilty according to law in a public trial at which he has had all the guarantees necessary for his defense." Since the latter part of this sentence is redundant, in view of the rights accorded accused by article 10, it was omitted when the language of article 11(1) was adopted, almost *in haec verba*, as article 14(2) of the Political Covenant. Language almost identical to article 11(1) is contained in articles 6(2) and 8(2) of the European Convention and American Convention respectively. Thus, there is unanimous consensus supporting the presumption of innocence in criminal proceedings; surely therefore it has become part of customary international law.

Little difficulty has been encountered so far in applying the principle under the European Convention, although, as Professor Jacobs cautions, it has a slightly different meaning in the civil law than it has at common law.

> The principle of the presumption of innocence is reflected in English law in the rule placing the burden of proof on the prosecution. But it cannot be equated with that rule, to which there are in any event numerous exceptions. Under the inquisitorial system of criminal procedure found in many of the Contracting Parties [to the European Convention], it is for the court to elicit the truth in all cases. What the principle of the presumption of innocence requires here is first that the court should not be predisposed to find the accused guilty, and second that it should at all times give the accused the benefit of the doubt, on the rule *in dubio pro reo*.[27]

While the principle thus concerns primarily the behavior of judges, admissibility in evidence of prior convictions and the effect of pretrial publicity have been alleged, so far unsuccessfully, to violate the right to be presumed innocent. Other such allegations can be anticipated as this right is tested under the Political Covenant and the American Convention.

Article 11(2), which proscribes *ex post facto* offenses, requires quoting in full. It states:

> No one shall be held guilty of any penal offence on account of any act or omission which did not constitute a penal offence, under national or international law, at the time when it was committed. Nor shall a heavier penalty be imposed than the one that was applicable at the time the penal offence was committed.

Two points here are worth noting: first, the reference to international law, inserted "to exclude doubts as to the Nuremberg and Tokyo trials" and "to ensure that no one shall escape punishment for a criminal offense under international law by pleading that his act was legal under his own national law;" and, second, the extension, in the second sentence, of the nonretroactivity principle to increased penalties.

Article 15(1) of the Political Covenant, from which there may be no derogation according to article 4(2), closely follows article 11(2); thus it may be argued convincingly that customary international law now prohibits both *ex post facto* offenses and penalties. Moreover, article 15(1) adds a sentence designed to guarantee an accused the benefits of *ex post facto* legal reforms: "If, subsequent to the commission of the offence, provision is made by law for the imposition of a lighter penalty, the offender shall benefit thereby." Article 15(2) of the Political Covenant also adds an entirely new and arguably superfluous provision justifying past and authorizing future international war crimes trials: "Nothing in this article shall prejudice the trial and punishment of any person for any act or omission which, at the time when it was committed, was criminal according to the general principles of law recognized by the community of nations." Articles 7 and 9 of the European Convention and American Convention respectively are based upon article 11(2) of the Universal Declaration and article 15 of the Political Covenant, albeit both contain one or more variations.

27. Jacobs, *The European Convention*, note 19, at 113.

While the primary purpose of such *ex post facto* provisions is to prohibit retrospective penal legislation, a secondary purpose is to preclude "the courts from extending the scope of the criminal law by interpretation." Thus the European Commission, construing article 7 of the European Convention, noted that it "does not merely prohibit—except as provided in paragraph (2)—retroactive application of the criminal law to the detriment of the accused," but it "also confirms, in a more general way, the principle of the statutory nature of offences and punishment . . . and prohibits, in particular, extension of the application of the criminal law *'in malam partem'* by analogy. . . ."[28] It further added that,

> although it is not normally for the Commission to ascertain the proper interpretation of municipal law by national courts . . . , the case is otherwise in matters where the Convention expressly refers to municipal law, as it does in Article 7. . . . [U]nder Article 7 the application of a provision of municipal penal law to an act not covered by the provision in question directly results in a conflict with the Convention, so that the Commission can and must take cognisance of allegations and of such false interpretation of municipal law. . . .

The above remarks, according to Castberg, "clearly keep the door open for preventing under Article 7 not only the application of criminal law by analogy, but also extensive interpretations."[29] The various proscriptions against *ex post facto* offenses certainly offer an opportunity to develop a similar body of restraints against retroactive judicial as well as legislative action.

QUESTIONS FOR REFLECTION AND DISCUSSION

1. Richard Lillich says that the civil and political rights of individuals are "commonly considered to be the most basic and fundamental of all human rights." Do you agree? Should they be? Why? Why not? Would persons in developing countries agree? In communist or socialist countries? Would persons from economically low social classes in any given country agree? If civil and political rights are so basic, why did it take more than a quarter century for the United States to become a party to the 1966 International Covenant on Civil and Political Rights (ICCPR, reprinted and referenced in Documentary Appendix A)?

2. In "Distinguishing Criteria of Human Rights," in Karel Vasak, ed., *The International Dimensions of Human Rights* (Westport, Conn.: Greenwood Press for UNESCO, 1982), 43–59, at 50, Theo C. van Boven recounts the discussion of the drafters of the two international covenants on human rights (each reprinted and referenced in Documentary Appendix A):

> those who favoured the drafting of two separate instruments argued that civil and political rights were enforceable, or justiciable, and immediately applicable, while economic, social and cultural rights were to be progressively implemented. . . . [T]hey drew attention to the fact that civil and political rights, being "legal" rights, required different means and methods of implementation (namely through complaints procedures) than economic, social and cultural rights, which were "programme" rights and could best be implemented through a system of periodic reports.

Is it this distinction between first- and second- generation rights that is the basis of Lillich's assertion that civil and political rights are "commonly considered to be the most basic and fundamental of all human rights"? If so, should it be? Are first generation rights more "legal" than second generation rights? Also, should means or relative efficiency of implementation of rights be the basis for deciding what are "most basic and fundamental" among human rights"? Why? Why not?

3. Lillich is at pains to identify which treaty-prescribed civil and political rights have become part of customary international law. Why? What is the juridical effect of treaty law? Customary law?

4. Among the rights that Lillich determines to have become part of customary international law is the right to equal protection of the law, as expressed in UDHR Article 7 and ICCPR Article 26 as well as in regional human rights charters. In discussing the meaning

28. *X v. Austria*, 1965 *Yearbook of the European Convention on Human Rights* (Eur. Ct. Hum. Rts.), 190, 198.
29. Frede Castberg, *The European Convention on Human Rights* (Dobbs Ferry, N.Y.: Oceana Publications, 1974), 130.

of "equal protection of the law," proclaimed in UDHR Article 7 and ICCPR Article 26, Lillich quotes Arthur Robertson to the effect that "two different meanings seem possible: that the substantive provisions of the law should be the same for everyone; *or* that the application of the law should be equal for all without discrimination" (emphasis added). Both Lillich and Robertson favor the second (and dominant) interpretation. The first interpretation, they contend, is "unreasonable," citing the fact that in most countries women are not required to perform military service and that it is unnecessary to provide men with maternity benefits. But does this interpretation of "equal protection of the law," which allows states to determine how the law should be applied and to whom it should apply, lead to genuine equality or nondiscrimination in general? Consider, for example, Saudi Arabia's refusal to allow the vote to women. Is this equal protection of the law qua equal application of the law as the law is stated in Saudi society? If so, is it possible that "equal protection of the law" is not the same as equality under the law? What is the difference? How would you define "equal protection of the law" and "equality under the law"?

5. Lillich writes that, while guaranteeing an important civil right on a nondiscriminatory basis, UDHR Article 7 and ICCPR Article 26, guaranteeing the right to equal protection of the law, "cannot be read to constitute a general norm of nondiscrimination invocable in other contexts." To ensure or at least facilitate equality or nondiscrimination in all contexts, Lillich writes, one must take seriously the right to a remedy as proclaimed in UDHR Article 8, ICCPR 2(3), and elsewhere. But whose duty is it to secure equality under the law? Does it depend on the ability of individuals to secure a remedy to guarantee them? If so, what are the chances of real equality for people most deprived of it? If it is the duty of the state to supply a remedy, how far should the state be required to go to ensure that individual rights are truly protected? If it is the duty of the international community, how is it fulfilled without trampling national sovereignty? If it is a combination of all three, how is the responsibility distributed and shared? See generally Dinah Shelton, *Remedies in International Human Rights Law*, 2nd ed. (Oxford: Oxford University Press, 2005).

6. Lillich notes the presence of "derogation" and "limitation" (or "clawback") clauses in the ICCPR and analogous regional instruments, allowing states to excuse themselves from their obligations under these agreements. What is the difference between these two types of clauses? Why do they exist? What is their utility? Are they desirable? Necessary? Do they not seriously undermine the effectiveness of the human rights instruments of which they are a part? From the standpoint of wanting to enhance human rights, which type is better? Why?

7. Lillich cites ICCPR Article 29(2) as an example of a rights-limiting provision: "In the exercise of his [sic] rights and freedoms, everyone shall be subject only to such limitations as are determined by law solely for the purpose of securing due recognition and respect for the rights and freedoms of others and of meeting the just requirements of morality, public order and the general welfare in a democratic society." Does this provision lean towards the protection or the destruction of human rights? Consider Article 29's exception for "morality," a concept that is not only culturally variable but one that varies even among closely situated individuals. How limiting is this provision? Whose meaning of morality does one use as a gauge?

8. It is necessary, surely, that states be able to function effectively during public emergencies. But is it necessary that they be allowed to suspend or curtail human rights guarantees in the process? Note that some states—for example, Chile under Augusto Pinochet or the Philippines under Ferdinand Marcos—operated under states of emergency for years with little or no regard for the rights of their peoples. Who defines "emergency" and what deference should be given to the definition? A customary international law "doctrine of margin of appreciation" extends to states a certain latitude in determining the existence of a public emergency. Is such a doctrine desirable? Why? Why not?

9. Express exemptions to rights, such as derogation, clawback, and state of emergency provisions suggest the manipulability of international human rights instruments. For example, while the prohibition against slavery and servitude may be said to achieved the status of *jus cogens* (i.e., a norm of fundamental world public policy from which no derogation is permitted), forced or compulsory labor is not so uniformly condemned. Indeed, according to ICCPR Article 8(3)(c), the phrase "forced or compulsory labor" expressly does not preclude the performance of hard labor:

(i) Any work or service, not referred to in subparagraph (b), normally required of a person who is under detention in consequence of a lawful order of a court, or of a person during conditional release from such detention;

(ii) Any service of a military character and, in countries where conscientious objection is recognized, any national service required by law of conscientious objectors;

(iii) Any service exacted in cases of emergency or calamity threatening the life or well-being of the community;

(iv) Any work or service which forms part of normal civil obligations.

What difficulties might be encountered in restricting this preclusion? What constitutes an "emergency or calamity"? What are "normal civil obligations"?

10. While it is true that vague or overly broad words and phrases can be used to manipulate against particular human rights guarantees, might it not also be true that such words and phrases can allow penumbral rights to be protected? Consider, for example, the word "treatment" in ICCPR Article 7 prohibiting "cruel, inhuman or degrading treatment of punishment." Decisions from the European Court of Human Rights, interpreting analogous language in the European Convention on Human Rights and Fundamental Freedoms (referenced in Documentary Appendix B) have held allegations of brutality by prison officials or police officers, inadequate conditions of detention, and even discrimination on the basis of race to constitute "degrading treatment." Might not the term be expanded, additionally, beyond the boundaries of criminal institutions to other state-sponsored activities such as hospitals, mental institutions, foster homes, and other centers of confinement? Would such an interpretation of "treatment" be desirable? Undesirable? Note that it is not found in the Eighth Amendment to the U.S. Constitution, the equivalent language of which is restricted to the words "cruel and unusual punishments." Is this a good or a bad thing? Should the U.S. Constitution be further amended? Why? Why not?

11. Rights cast at high levels of abstraction, such as "the right to life," also present problems. Does such a guarantee protect against, for example, capital punishment, voluntary euthanasia, or abortion? Should it? All? Some? If only some, according to what differentiating criteria?

12. Considering all the ways in which civil and political guarantees can be lawfully circumvented, what is their status under contemporary international law?

8. Rachel Neild *Human Rights and Crime*

The end of the twentieth century witnessed historic transitions to peace and democracy, albeit often tentative and partial, in Latin America, Eastern Europe, Africa, and Asia. For the global human rights movement, it might have been a time for ushering in a new era focused on securing the national and international mechanisms of accountability that would be the foundation for a new culture of rights within and across borders. Yet in many countries human rights groups barely had time to draw breath before finding themselves facing a new set of threats to human rights in the growth of common crime and social violence, and in particular in the public and political reactions to these crime waves.

Crime and violence appear to be rising in a wide range of countries. In its examination of available data, the World Health Organization found a staggering 50 percent increase in homicides around the world between 1985 and 1994. Regionally, Africa and Latin America vie for first place with the highest homicide rates in the world. The growth in violence crosses all regions, but while industrialized countries saw a 15 percent increase, the jump was more than 80 percent in Latin America and 112 percent in the Arab world.

Overall, low- and middle-income countries have homicide rates more than double those of high-income countries. Such data hide tremendous variations among gender and age cohorts, urban and rural or rich and poor communities,

Reprinted with changes from Rachel Neild, "The New Face of Impunity," in *Human Rights Dialogue* 28 (Fall 2002). Copyright © 2002 Carnegie Council on Ethics and International Affairs. Reprinted by permission.

and ethnic and racial groups. While poverty does not necessarily correlate with high crime, many demographic, economic, and social trends are feeding real increases in crime rates. The youth factor is particularly clear (globally, violence is the cause of 14 percent of male deaths between the ages of fifteen and forty-four) and deeply troubling for the many developing countries with "youth bubbles" and few youth employment opportunities. Other studies indicate that rapid and high-density urbanization cultivate violence, while a World Bank study of fifty countries found a clear relationship between inequality and increasing homicide rates. Expanding global trade in arms and drugs also creates opportunity and means for violent crime.

In transitional contexts, specific political factors also come into play. Armed groups can metamorphose into criminal gangs. Criminal justice systems molded by authoritarian regimes for the purposes of social control and regime protection are poorly equipped to tackle crime. Efforts by police and politicians to confront crime often lead to proposals that undermine rights, such as the expansion of police powers, a tolerance of torture, and the increasing of penalties—even reintroducing the death penalty. Even as the state again resorts to repression, private responses may erode the state's sphere of influence. The boom of private security companies and, in some cases, the appearance or expansion of vigilantes and lynching are outgrowths of state incapacity to deal with crime.

Some analyses posit a continuum of violence from authoritarianism through the transition to democracy, with state violence replaced by private violence. State impunity for political crimes undergoes a perverse metamorphosis into criminal impunity. In developing countries already struggling with economic, social, and political challenges, crime and the ineffective and authoritarian responses to it further reduce the expected "democracy dividend." This dynamic has a profoundly negative impact on public support for human rights. Surveys sometimes show massive support for abusive responses to crime, even among the poor who bear the brunt of both crime and police abuse. In some cases, people's support for democracy itself has eroded.

For human rights organizations, the obvious strategy might be a relatively straightforward effort to stand up against policies that violate human rights norms and to take up the banner for due process rights and an end to police violence. International human rights instruments, both global and regional, have long protected fundamental rights to life and physical integrity, to due process including the right to be represented by an attorney, and to humane conditions of detention. Work to confront police abuse is supported by an evolving array of instruments that specifically address police conduct and clearly delineate the parameters for the police's legitimate use of their coercive powers: for example, the 1979 United Nations Code of Conduct for Law Enforcement Officials,[1] the 1990 UN Basic Principles on the Use of Force and Firearms by Law Enforcement Officials,[2] and the extensive Council of Europe European Code of Police Ethics of 2001.[3]

1. Adopted Dec. 17, 1979, referenced in Documentary Appendix B.
2. Adopted by the Eighth United Nations Congress on the Prevention of Crime and the Treatment of Offenders, Havana, Cuba, Aug. 27-Sept.7, 1990, available on the website of the Office of the UN High Commissioner for Human Rights at http://www.unhchr.ch/html/menu3/b/h_comp43.htm. Article 9 sets a precise framework for police use of deadly force: "Law enforcement officials shall not use firearms against persons except in self-defence or defence of others against the imminent threat of death or serious injury, to prevent the perpetration of a particularly serious crime involving grave threat to life, to arrest a person presenting such a danger and resisting their authority, or to prevent his or her escape, and only when less extreme means are insufficient to achieve these objectives. In any event, intentional lethal use of firearms may only be made when strictly unavoidable in order to protect life."
3. Council of Europe, Recommendation Rec 10 (2001) of the Committee of Ministers to Member States on the European Code of Police Ethics, adopted by the Committee of Ministers, 765th mtg. of the Ministers' Deputies, Sept. 19, 2001, available at http://cm.coe.int/ta/rec/2001/2001r10.htm. Articles 54 and 55 of the European Code of Police Ethics stipulate that the police should only exercise their powers of arrest and deprivation of liberty when it is absolutely necessary and when the person deprived of her or his liberty is informed of the reasons for the deprivation, a guarantee that is found also in Article 5(2) of the European Convention for the Protection of Human Rights and Fundamental Freedoms (Nov. 4, 1950), referenced in Documentary Appendix B. The European Code of Police Ethics also ensures the right for detained persons to be provided with appropriate safety, health, hygiene and nourishment by the police and the right to have access to legal assistance and medical care.

To date, however, such instruments have not been created in other regional human rights forums. Also, in many transitions human rights groups have not immediately recognized the challenges crime waves and abusive state responses pose, perhaps expecting or hoping that democratic governments would rein in violent police and improve the courts. Often, groups were fighting other authoritarian legacies, or moving on to confront underlying socio-economic injustice. In adapting their strategies to a new environment, they were following the lead of key donors, who did not see that crime would emerge as a human rights concern.

In many countries, rights organizations have stopped systematically documenting individual cases of police violations. This reduction of human rights groups' role as police watchdog also relates to the identity of the new victims of police abuse who are (alleged) common criminals—both perpetrators and victims of crime. In the past human rights organizations defended the innocent victims of state repression (in many cases activists were colleagues and family members of the victims). While few rights organizations have reflected upon the issues in these terms, it is clear that the idea of defending the new "guilty victims" is increasingly discomforting to them. Human rights groups face denunciation by politicians for coddling criminals and must contend with the argument that tough-on-crime policies entail a necessary trade-off in the abrogation of some rights. Since September 11, human rights advocates in the North have engaged in this debate's various forms, and, sadly, in the United States for example, we see it strike a public chord across ideological and political party lines. In transitional societies, where rights are far more fragile in both public consciousness and political discourse, this hard-line appeal threatens a loss of public support for hard-won rights values.

When human rights groups do resume the watchdog role, security information tends to be classified and inaccessible, requiring human rights groups to develop new strategies to obtain information on the full range of victims of police abuse. Rights groups in Argentina have used *leyes de amparo*—a kind of habeas corpus instrument—to obtain data from the police. In Brazil, groups have mapped police abuse demonstrating the prevalence of police violence against the poor. In both countries, groups have analyzed patterns of abusive police practice by using press accounts to build databases of police abuse. In South Africa, NGOs used the new Freedom of Information Law to require the police to end a moratorium on the release of national crime statistics. As such laws are being passed in an increasing number of countries, they may offer a new avenue for increasing the transparency of policing. Other organizations have chosen to work on miscarriages of justice in which the defendants are clearly wrongly accused. The cases of the new innocent victims of the war on crime generally have far greater media and political resonance.

At the same time, human rights activists have come to understand that simply denouncing the bad practices of the criminal justice system ignores the very real suffering of crime victims and other citizens whose lives are ever more constrained by both real and perceived threats of crime. One important strategy for rights organizations reflects a lesson learned earlier in struggles for transitional justice. Just as early truth commissions were criticized for their focus on offenders and neglect of the reparative needs of the victims, criminal justice systems also often pay little heed to the needs and rights of crime victims.

Rights groups, for their part, have also sometimes focused on violations of due process without sufficiently recognizing the plight of crime victims. In part, this may be a reflection of international standards, the bulk of which focus on protecting the rights of the person against state-perpetrated abuses. However, standards affirming the duty of the state to provide basic safety and security to citizens, i.e., protections against the criminal acts of private persons, are starting to emerge.[4]

National criminal justice systems are also often

4. In the *Velásquez Rodríguez* Case, Judgment of June 26, 1987, Inter-Am. Ct. H.R. (Ser. C) No. 1 (1987), the Inter-American Court of Human Rights held that the state of Honduras could be held liable for the disappearance of Velásquez even if state agents were not proven responsible because of the Honduran government's "lack of due diligence to prevent or respond to it as required by the Convention." For example, the Human Rights Committee explicitly recognized the importance of protecting women's rights to protections from domestic violence in General Comment No. 20; as has the Inter-American Convention for the Prevention, Sanction and Eradication of Violence against Women (Belem do Pará Convention) and subsequent decisions interpreting the treaty.

strongly perpetrator-focused, and give little attention or solace to the plight of crime victims. Many victims and witnesses refuse to cooperate with criminal proceedings because, at best, it is time consuming, frustrating, expensive, and often a waste of time; at worst, cooperation with unsympathetic or hostile officials can be psychologically traumatic (particularly in cases of violence against women) or even dangerous when there is no protection against violent reprisals. Some organizations are starting to examine the treatment of crime victims and advocate for more attention and sensitivity to their needs, particularly the very poor whose livelihoods are desperately fragile. Others seek to increase access to justice through legal aid and other mechanisms. Through this work, advocates confront the remoteness, lack of consideration, and irrelevance of formal justice to the lives of the poor, and seek to build justice systems defined by and based in human rights standards—fundamentally concerned with protecting victims and victims' rights, be they victims of crime or of police abuse.[5]

Another fundamental challenge—and perhaps the area where most work remains to be done—lies with the police. The abysmal lack of public trust in and cooperation with the police has been well documented across Africa, Asia,

and Latin America. Human rights activists have far more experience with the workings of the courts than of the closed, sometimes military-dominated, and often hostile police forces. Yet the police are on the frontline of crime fighting, and, despite research indicating that abusive and discriminatory policing reduces effectiveness, efforts to introduce community policing and other responsive and prevention-oriented approaches often collapse, criticized as being "soft on crime." The challenge of crafting reforms that can address both police accountability and effectiveness lies at the heart of human rights engagement with the need to confront both crime and ongoing state violence.

Few criminal justice policies are made on the basis of consultation or debate with broad sectors of society, and few are informed by solid data and analysis. All too often, perceptions and emotions dictate policies. Human rights groups can and should play a role in shaping the tone and content of policy debates, shifting the model of criminal justice from the retributive to the restorative and engaging with institutional reform processes. Without intervention by the human rights community, it is more likely that policy responses will undermine rights and perpetuate injustice.

QUESTIONS FOR REFLECTION AND DISCUSSION

1. The issue of crime tends to take on an entirely domestic character. What makes this an issue of international human rights? Are criminal law issues such as capital punishment or police brutality international human rights issues? Why? Why not? What determines your answer?

2. Which of the rights enumerated in the Universal Declaration of Human Rights (UDHR, reprinted and referenced in Documentary Appendix A) are implicated by high crimes? For the victims? For the perpetrators?

3. Given that low- and middle-income countries have more than double the crime rates of more developed countries, do you agree with Neild that poverty "does not necessarily correlate with high crime"? What about regime types? Do governments that do not guarantee civil and political rights spur higher crime rates? If so, how do you explain the high crime rates of the United States? Could these be attributable, at least in part, to the lack of economic, social, and cultural rights? If so, how does this square with Neild's assessment? What factors might explain the high United States crime rate?

4. Neild observes that in developing countries already struggling with socioeconomic and political challenges, "crime and the ineffective and authoritarian responses to it . . . has [had] a profoundly negative impact on public support for human rights. Surveys," she says, "sometimes show massive support for abusive responses to crime, even among the poor who bear the brunt of both crime and police abuse. In some cases, people's support for democracy itself has eroded." What reasons does Neild give for this state of affairs? Are

---

5. Here, also, there are international standards in the General Assembly Declaration of Basic Principles of Justice for Victims of Crime and Abuse of Power, adopted Nov. 29, 1985, referenced in Documentary Appendix B.

human rights activists to blame? If so, does this mean that a human rights approach to crime reduction is a waste of time? What does Neild say?

5. Neild states that "the challenge of crafting reforms that can address both police accountability and effectiveness lies at the heart of human rights engagement with the need to confront both crime and ongoing state violence." How do you suggest that a state balance the need to institute social order with necessary human rights protections? Should there be an international oversight committee to police state-sanctioned crime? Would this be a good or bad idea? Is this an issue that is best handled at the domestic level? The international level? Both? How?

6. If a human rights approach to crime is to be pursued on the international plane, one may assume that states and intergovernmental organizations both global and regional would be involved. What role might there be, if any, for human rights NGOs? Should NGOs be involved? Why? Why not?

7. What insights from Neild's essay might be helpful to combat the crime of terrorism? Is a terrorist deserving of a human rights approach to her or his arrest, detention, prosecution, and punishment? If so, how? Has the United States pursued such an approach? How? How not?

9. PAUL GORDON LAUREN *First Principles of Racial Equality*

Repulsed by atrocities and shocked by the slaughter of millions, representatives from many countries gathered immediately after World War II to assess the cause of the catastrophe they had just experienced. Of all the possible explanations they could have used, these diplomats felt compelled to focus upon only one. "The great and terrible war which has now ended," they poignantly concluded, "was a war made possible by the denial of democratic principles of the dignity, equality, and mutual respect for men, and by the propagation, in their place, through ignorance and prejudice, of the doctrine of the inequality of men and races."[1] The horrors of this war represented neither the first case of discrimination and the denial of human rights in international politics, nor the last. But their blatant, widespread, and abhorrent nature brought into focus "the problem of the century"[2]: the deep and difficult problem of human rights and racial discrimination.

[*Eds.*—In parts I and II, the author recounts the history of racial discrimination and its effects on human rights enforcement in the years prior to and including World War II, noting in particular the dilatory impact the legacy of slavery in the United States had on the drafting and ratification of instruments opposing racial discrimination. During the war years, human rights treaties (including the first drafts of the UN Charter) were routinely stripped of their enforcement provisions, which were widely viewed, particularly among the western powers, as "unacceptable at the present time." In early Autumn 1944, at the Dumbarton Oaks estate in Washington, D.C., where representatives from the Republic of China, the Soviet Union, the United Kingdom, the United States, and other delegates to the "Washington Conversations on International Peace and Security Organization" formulated and negotiated the creation of the United Nations, a provision proposed by the Chinese delegation, stating that "The principle of equality of all states and all races shall be upheld," was strongly resisted by the other nations present and, at the second stage of the conference, removed. The end product of Dumbarton Oaks was a proposal

Reprinted with changes from Paul Gordon Lauren, "First Principles of Racial Equality: History and the Politics and Diplomacy of Human Rights Provisions in the United Nations Charter," *HRQ* 5 (1983): 1–26 (copyright © 1983 Johns Hopkins University Press); Addendum reprinted from Paul Gordon Lauren, *The Evolution of International Human Rights: Visions Seen*, 2nd ed. (Philadelphia: University of Pennsylvania Press, 2003), 243–45, 258–59 (copyright © 2003 University of Pennsylvania Press). Each reprinted by permission.

1. UNESCO, *Conference for the Establishment of the United Nations Educational, Scientific, and Cultural Organization*, ECO/CONF./29 (Nov. 16, 1945), 93.
2. Mr. Driberg, M.P., in the House of Commons, May 6, 1949, PRO/FO, 371/78946.

containing only one deeply buried, veiled reference to human rights, and no reference to racial equality whatsoever. This proposal was submitted to the broader coalition of delegates who met in San Francisco in Spring 1945 for the purpose of creating the United Nations.]

THE SAN FRANCISCO CONFERENCE

The opening speeches of the delegates at San Francisco conveyed a spirit of unparalleled euphoria. Flushed with success against their military enemies and with the excitement of participating in one of the century's most historic events, hundreds of representatives of 50 participating countries eagerly anticipated creating a new world order that would guarantee peace and security. The gathering was described as a "landmark" and a "milestone in the long march of man to a better future." The participants were urged to rise above their own national interests and to promote the common international good, to put past practices behind them, and to create an organization founded upon justice. "If we should pay merely lip service to the inspiring ideals and then later do violence to simple justice," said President Harry Truman, "we would draw down upon us the bitter wrath of generations yet unborn . . .. We must build a new world . . . in which the eternal dignity of man is respected."[3]. . . Such words sounded marvelous, but the delegate from India rose to be more specific. "We are all asked to be realists, we are asked to recognize various factors in the world set up as it is today," he stated.

> There is one great reality, one fundamental factor, one eternal verity which all religions teach, which must be remembered by all of us, the dignity of the common man [sic], the fundamental human rights of all beings all over the world. Those rights are incapable of

segregation or of isolation. There is neither border nor breed nor color nor creed on which those rights can be separated as between beings and beings. And, speaking as an Asiatic, may I say that this is an aspect of the question which can never be forgotten, and if we are laying the foundations for peace we can only lay them truly and justly . . ... Those fundamental human rights of all beings all over the world should be recognized, and men and women treated as equals in every sphere, so far as opportunities are concerned.[4]

This concern with human rights and racial equality was not unexpected. Indeed, various delegations had anticipated it for months. The Inter-American Conference on Problems of War and Peace, held in March 1945, had already passed a resolution condemning racial discrimination and requesting a draft declaration of the international rights and duties of men.[5] Others, however, reacted differently. One of the delegates, U.S. Senator Arthur Vandenberg (R-Mich.), stated for the record his pleasure in seeing the word "sovereign" in the statement of principles, for it was a matter "dear to our hearts" and would prevent international interference in domestic affairs.[6] Australia shared this concern; as one official in London wrote, "if 'racial equality' is once written into a basic treaty, it will be easier for China or India in [the] future to challenge the 'White Australia' policy, and an Australian may well see in such an apparently harmless statement of principle the thin edge of a dangerous wedge."[7] The British Foreign Office therefore predicted, correctly, that "the racial equality question will come up again in some form in the postwar settlement."[8]

As feared by some, and as hoped by others, the question of race came up immediately at the San Francisco Conference. The mood and interests of the delegates differed sharply from those of the Americans, British, and Soviets at

---

3. Harry S Truman, "Verbatim Minutes of the Opening Session" (Apr. 25, 1945), in United Nations Information Organization, *Documents of the United Nations Conference on International Organization, San Francisco, 1945*, 22 vols. (New York: United Nations Conference on International Organization, 1946–55), 1: 113–15 (hereinafter "UNIO, *Documents*").
4. Ramaswami Mudaliar, "Verbatim Minutes of the Third Plenary Session" (Apr. 28, 1945), UNIO, *Documents*, 1:245.
5. See PRO/FO, 371/45016; see also Ruth B. Russell, *History of the United Nations Charter: The Role of the United States, 1940–1945* (Washington, D.C.: Brookings Institution, 1953), 568–69.
6. "Minutes of the Sixth Meeting of the U.S. Delegation" (Apr. 10, 1945), in U.S. Department of State, *Foreign Relations of the United States, 1945*, 9 vols. (Washington, D.C.: Government Printing Office, 1966), 1: 228 (hereinafter "U.S. Dept. State, *FRUS, 1945*").
7. "Comments of G. T. Hudson," Mar. 19, 1945, PRO/FO, 371/46324.
8. Ibid.

Dumbarton Oaks. As voiced by the noted publicist of the National Association for the Advancement of Colored People, W. E. B. Du Bois,

> Today as we try in anticipation to rebuild the world, the propositions of Dumbarton Oaks center their efforts upon stopping war by force and at the same time leaving untouched, save by vague implication, the causes of war, especially those causes which lurk in rivalry for power and prestige [and] race dominance.[9]

So long as these exist, he declared, "there can be neither peace on earth nor goodwill toward men." Now was the time, he argued, to shift from the old "for white people only" policies and to recognize that "The day has dawned when above a wounded tired earth unselfish sacrifice, without sin and hell, may join thorough technique, shorn of ruthless greed, and make a new religion, one with new knowledge, to shout from the old hills of heaven: 'Go down, Moses'."[10] Du Bois and other active observers and participants wanted definite changes in international behavior, and said so. In opening speeches to the conference, representatives of India, Haiti, and Uruguay argued the necessity of realizing the ideals for which so many had suffered and died during the war, particularly the "repudiation of doctrines of racial division and discrimination."[11]

Many delegates were by no means satisfied with the vague statements of purpose and stark omissions of the Dumbarton Oaks proposals. The stated purposes of the new United Nations, they maintained, should go beyond the general ideas of peace and security. Consequently, the representatives of Egypt, India, Panama, Uruguay, Brazil, Mexico, the Dominican Republic, Cuba, and Venezuela, among others, forcefully argued that clear and explicit provisions supporting human rights should be placed in the very beginning of the charter and perhaps throughout, to replace the relatively meaningless statement buried deep within the text. Added to these

official declarations were those of numerous nongovernmental organizations encouraging their national representatives to take more determined action on human rights.

These voices—and, in many cases, votes—wanted not only articles on human rights but provisions about racial equality and nondiscrimination as well. Fundamental liberties should be guaranteed, in the words of the formal amendment submitted by India, "for all men and women, irrespective of race, color, or creed, in all nations and in all international relations and associations of nations one with another."[12] Others actively supported these and similar propositions calling for the prohibition of discrimination on the basis of race. These included Brazil, the Dominican Republic, Mexico, Panama, France, and the Soviet Union. Given the previous Soviet opposition to human rights at Dumbarton Oaks, the United States representatives interpreted this action as being motivated by the politics and diplomacy of the emerging Cold War and as "playing up to the small nations."[13]

Yet it was precisely these "small nations" that had suffered so much from racial discrimination and been excluded from participation in international deliberations. In the past, they had been the victims, the subjects, and the pawns in the chess game of diplomacy, and now they wanted change. This determination surfaced with particular emotion on one issue, described in advance by one observer as "loaded with explosive material"[14]: the fate of colonial territories. Few in the West wanted to discuss the controversial issue of territorial possessions overseas with its obvious racial dimensions, but at San Francisco it could no longer be ignored. Arguing against proposals for new trusteeships, the Chinese declared, "Nothing in the Charter should contravene the principle of the equality of all races, and their right to self determination" in the postwar world.[15] Others from former colonial

---

9. W. E. B. Du Bois, *Color and Democracy: Colonies and Peace* (New York: Harcourt, Brace, 1945), 103.
10. Ibid., 143.
11. José Serrato, "Verbatim Minutes of the Fourth Plenary Session" (Apr. 28, 1945), in UNIO, *Documents*, 1: 299.
12. "Suggestions Presented by the Government of India for the Amendment of the Dumbarton Oaks Proposals," Document 2, G/14 (h), May 4, 1945, in UNIO, *Documents*, 3: 527.
13. "Review of Amendments to Dumbarton Oaks Proposals as Suggested by the Soviet Delegation," in U.S. Department of State, *FRUS, 1945*, 1: 546 (statement by Leo Pasvolsky). The formal amendment by the United States, China, Britain, and the Soviet Union supporting these principles came after these other proposed amendments and not before.
14. Pertinax, "France Joining Big Four Envisaged," *New York Times*, Mar. 21, 1945.
15. "Summary Report of Sixth Meeting of Committee II/4," Document 404, II/4/17 (May 18, 1945), in UNIO, *Documents*, 10: 453.

possessions joined together in asserting that it "was essential that the Conference get away from all ideas of racial superiority and racial inferiority if peace were to be achieved."[16] Iraq argued that racial discrimination was a "Nazi philosophy" that had to be "discarded forever" in international relations.[17] General Carlos Romulo of the Philippines reiterated this theme by reminding all the delegates that many different races had fought in the Second World War together declaring it a victory for the whole world, not for one race, one nation, or one leader, but for all men.[18]

The negotiating power of those states determined to insert provisions on human rights and racial nondiscrimination was [considerable], and accounts for the numerous modifications of the Dumbarton Oaks proposals made at San Francisco. As a result of this influence and that of nongovernmental organizations a number of new provisions were added to the Charter.[19] Article 1 listed among the major purposes that of achieving human rights and fundamental freedoms "for all without distinction as to race, sex, language, or religion." Article 13 repeated the same basic provision when discussing the activities of the General Assembly. Similarly, Article 55 spoke of respect "for the principle of equal rights and self-determination of peoples" and the promotion of human rights without discrimination. Articles 62 and 68 reiterated these objectives in terms of the programs of the Economic and Social Council. Finally, articles 73 and 76, referring to the United Nations trusteeship system, stated that administration of these territories should be regarded as "a sacred trust" where there would be "just treatment" for individuals, "protection against abuses," and respect "for human rights and fundamental freedoms for all without distinction as to race, sex, language, or religion."

Many delegates enthusiastically greeted these provisions and the fact that, for the first time in history, they would appear in a negotiated international document. They prided themselves in obtaining so many references to human rights

and nondiscrimination throughout the Charter. These advocates were soon to be disappointed, however, for the politics and diplomacy of human rights had not yet run its course.

Although countries might have been willing to consent to the inclusion of words and statements of principle, few were prepared to commit themselves to practical or effective means of implementation. All the proposals that the United Nations actively be required to "safeguard," "protect," "guarantee," "implement," "ensure," "assure," or "enforce" those provisions died a sudden death. Instead, the only verbs that could gain majority acceptance were relatively innocuous ones such as "should facilitate," "assist," "encourage," and "promote." Even here, delegates carefully explained that they did not want these words to assume any greater meaning than they already possessed. Human rights and racial nondiscrimination foundered on the rock of national sovereignty.

The tension between national and international law revolved around the issue of domestic jurisdiction. Few states were willing to sacrifice elements of their sovereignty for the sake of human rights by authorizing the international community to intervene in their own internal affairs. Any number of individuals and groups urged leaders of the world to use this unique occasion to advance respect for human beings by changing practices and policies of the past. "We have taught the layman to worship the fiction of the sovereign state," warned international legal scholar Philip C. Jessup before the conference even began, "and thereby have built a Maginot line against the invasion of new ideas in the international world, and behind that rampart the demagogue and the reactionary are enthroned."[20] James T. Shotwell of the Commission to Study the Organization of Peace joined in arguing for a minimum international standard to uphold human rights. "Each state, jealous of its sovereignty, has regarded any expression of foreign interest in the welfare of

16. Document 712, II/4/30 (May 31, 1945), in UNIO, *Documents*, 10: 497.
17. "Verbatim Minutes of Third Meeting of Commission II," Document 1144, II/16 (June 21, 1945), in UNIO, *Documents*, 8: 134.
18. Ibid., 138–39.
19. Charter of the United Nations (June 26, 1945), selected provisions reprinted and referenced in Documentary Appendix A.
20. Philip C. Jessup, as cited in Commission to Study the Organization of Peace, *Fundamentals of the International Organization*, Fourth Report, vol. 4, *International Safeguard of Human Rights* (New York: the Commission, 1944), 16. [Jessup later served as a judge of the International Court of Justice at The Hague, 1961–70.]

its citizens at home, as an interference in its own affairs," he stated. "Now as a result of the Second World War, it has become clear that a regime of violence and oppression within any nation of the civilized world is a matter of concern to all the rest."[21] The spokesman of Uruguay similarly asserted that guaranteeing human rights was "the basic problem which this Conference will have to solve."[22]

This problem was not solved, for the delegates at San Francisco remained either unwilling or unable to be convinced. When John Foster Dulles wondered aloud among his American colleagues in the delegation whether the human rights and nondiscrimination provisions might not create difficulties for "the Negro problem in the South,"[23] he was told that the inclusion of a domestic jurisdiction provision would preclude this possibility. When Herbert Evatt, Minister for External Affairs of Australia, wanted to voice his concern about immigration policy, he received the advice that it would be "embarrassing to India and would provoke an awkward debate in the Conference on the color question," and would be "unnecessary as long as the Charter included domestic jurisdiction safeguards."[24] Similarly, when the British worried about the implications of the provisions about human rights and race, their Foreign Office prepared a special memorandum, entitled "World Organization: Racial Equality and Domestic Jurisdiction," which stated that internal policy would be protected by the inclusion of an article regarding domestic jurisdiction.[25] Consequently, article 2, paragraph 7 was included in the United Nations Charter and read: "Nothing contained in the present Charter shall authorize the United Nations to intervene in matters which are essentially within the domestic jurisdiction of any state or shall require the Members to submit such matters to settlement . . . ."[26] In the words of Senator Tom Connally (D-Tex.) of the United States delegation, this article "was sufficient to overpower all other considerations."[27]

The resulting provisions dealing with human rights and racial discrimination in the United Nations Charter evoked a variety of reactions. To many, they marked an unprecedented accomplishment and a culmination of efforts to realize individual dignity in the world. To others, those same articles produced either anxiety at having said too much or frustration at having said too little. A number of British officials worried about what all this would mean for restrictive immigration quotas in the dominions and their own policies in colonial areas. During hearings in Washington Senator Eugene Millikin (R-Colo.) asked: "Would the investigation of racial discrimination be within the jurisdiction of this body?" In quick response to this question Senator Vandenberg assured him that the domestic jurisdiction clause would prohibit such an action, would prevent any compulsion or enforcement whatever, and would retain for the various states the right either to accept or reject even recommendations for a change in behavior. Statements such as these confirmed the worst fears and frustrations of those who, like Du Bois, viewed the results of the United Nations conference as nothing but a compromise between "the national interests, the economic rivalries, and the selfish demands" of the powers. Du Bois argued that the new organization should serve "not only white peoples of English descent, but Latins and Slavs, and the yellow, brown, and black peoples of America, Asia, and Africa." "The proposed Charter," he declared,

> should, therefore, make clear and unequivocal the straightforward stand of the civilized world for race equality, and the universal application of the democratic way of life, not simply as philanthropy and justice, but to save human civilization from suicide. What was true of the United States in the past is true of world civilization today—we cannot exist half slave and half free.[28]

Other participants and observers viewed the Charter, including its human rights provisions,

21. Ibid., 23–24.
22. "Statement of Uruguayan Delegation," Document 995, I/1/41 (June 15, 1945), in UNIO, *Documents*, 6: 627.
23. Minutes of the Fifty-First Meeting of the U.S. Delegation (May 23, 1945), in U.S. Dept. State, *FRUS, 1945*, 1: 855; see also 853–54.
24. Ibid.
25. "World Organization: Racial Equality and Domestic Jurisdiction" (June 8, 1945), PRO/FO, 371 /46324.
26. UN Charter, art. 2, para. 7, reprinted in Documentary Appendix A.
27. Minutes of the Fifty-First Meeting of the U.S. Delegation (May 23, 1945), note 23, 1: 854.
28. "Statement of W. E. B. Du Bois," July 11, 1945, Senate Committee on Foreign Relations, *The*

neither as a magnificent achievement nor as a horrendous tragedy, but rather as a first step toward the future. They considered the practice of politics and diplomacy as being the art of the possible, and believed that they had accomplished about as much as could be expected given the circumstances, traditions, and prejudices of the time. In his concluding statement before the entire conference, President Harry Truman spoke of the accomplishments as "only a first step." "This Charter, like our Constitution," he said,

> will be expanded and improved as time goes on. No one claims that it is now a final or a perfect instrument. It has not been poured into a fixed mold. Changing world conditions will require readjustments—but they will be readjustments of peace and not of war. . . . The Charter is dedicated to the achievement and observance of human rights and fundamental freedoms. Unless we can attain those objectives for all men and women everywhere—without regard to race, language, or religion—we cannot have permanent peace and security in the world.[29]

What had been achieved, in the words of one delegate, were "the beginnings of a long and challenging endeavor."[30]

SEQUEL TO THE CHARTER

The creation of the Charter of the United Nations did, indeed, represent the beginnings— the genesis—of practical accomplishments and genuine change, dashed hopes and cynicism, frustrations and conflicts, tension between national and international law, and an insight into the politics and diplomacy of human rights for the remaining years of the twentieth century. In all of the efforts that followed, the specific issues and the relative bargaining positions first taken at the end of the war would be repeated, refined, reinforced, and, by some, readjusted to

fit particular circumstances. This both blessed and cursed the movement for human rights set into motion by the Charter in 1945.

In 1946 the General Assembly entered into an intense debate about race and equality and called for "prompt and energetic steps" to end racial and religious discrimination, while the Economic and Social Council established the Commission on Human Rights and directed it to submit proposals, recommendations, and reports regarding an "international bill of rights." Enormously encouraged by these developments, and determined that this momentum not be lost, the majority of members in the United Nations subsequently adopted the Universal Declaration of Human Rights (UDHR)[31] and the 1948 Convention on the Prevention and Punishment of the Crime of Genocide;[32] the 1965 International Convention on the Elimination of All Forms of Racial Discrimination (ICERD);[33] the 1966 International Covenant on Economic, Social, and Cultural Rights (ICESCR)[34] and International Covenant on Civil and Political Rights (ICCPR) with its Optional Protocol;[35] and the 1973 International Convention on the Suppression and Punishment of the Crime of Apartheid,[36] among many other provisions.

During all of the negotiations surrounding these instruments and resolutions, human rights and racial discrimination became inextricably intertwined in many of the century's most critical and controversial problems. The Cold War led the Soviet Union to exploit American internal racial discrimination for propaganda purposes and prompted the United States to draw world attention to Soviet violations of human rights in Eastern Europe and the USSR. International human rights norms influenced the domestic and foreign policies of federal states confronting civil rights violations by state or local governments. The conflicting claims of Israelis and Palestinians in the Middle East led to the General Assembly's description of Zionism as "a form of racism

---

Charter of the United Nations: Hearings Before the Committee on Foreign Relations, 79th Cong., 1st Sess., July 1945, 392.
29. Harry S Truman, "Verbatim Minutes of the Closing Plenary Session" (June 26, 1945), in UNIO, *Documents*, 1: 715–16.
30. Lord Halifax, ibid., 1: 698.
31. Adopted Dec. 10, 1948, reprinted and referenced in Documentary Appendix A.
32. Concluded Dec. 9, 1948, referenced in Documentary Appendix B.
33. Concluded Dec. 21, 1965, referenced in Documentary Appendix B.
34. Concluded Dec. 16, 1966, reprinted and referenced in Documentary Appendix A.
35. Concluded Dec. 16, 1966, reprinted and referenced in Documentary Appendix A.
36. Concluded Nov. 30, 1973, referenced in Documentary Appendix B.

and racial discrimination."[37] In addition, human rights principles helped promote decolonization, as well as the North-South dialogue between the developed and the developing states, which was in many cases a dialogue between white and nonwhite countries.

Moreover, the human rights and racial discrimination provisions first introduced in the Charter also marked the beginning of serious jurisdictional disputes and legal controversies. Despite the determined efforts to insert the "domestic jurisdiction" clause in the text of the Charter, and the subsequent confident assertions that it would prohibit internal interference, many individuals and groups quickly asserted that the "spirit and purpose" of the Charter imposed important obligations. Even those governments most insistent upon protecting the prerogatives of national sovereignty agreed when pressed that in signing the Charter states assumed certain minimum responsibilities to honor its provisions. The Netherlands explicitly raised this issue by asking:

> Does an obligation—at least a moral obligation—result from this Chapter and the Charter as a whole for the states members concerned to eliminate, in the territories under consideration, all discrimination resulting from feelings of racial superiority and to combat such feelings by education and by other adequate means?

The United States representative briefly and tersely responded, "[y]es, there is a moral obligation to endeavor to overcome the evils to which you refer."[38]

Others asserted that these provisions constituted solemn, legally binding obligations, and not simply statements of public morality. They argued that the Charter, as a legal document, recognized fundamental rights of the individual, and thereby for the first time in history transformed individuals from mere objects of international compassion into subjects of international law. India immediately tested this proposition in its long-standing dispute with South Africa,

claiming before the United Nations that as a result of discriminatory laws directed against Indians and other Asiatic, the South African government violated the provisions of the Charter regarding human rights. South Africa responded, of course, that her laws were her business and that the entire matter remained within her jurisdiction. This defense provoked a sharp reaction by the General Assembly and in particular by the representative of Panama who declared:

> Are human rights essentially within the domestic jurisdiction of the State? My answer is no, and a hundred times no. I submit that by the San Francisco Charter human rights have been taken out of the province of domestic jurisdiction and have been placed within the realm of international law.[39]

These tensions between national and international law occurred not only between states, but perhaps more importantly, within them as well. Here aggrieved parties sought to challenge and redress domestic discrimination by appealing directly to the provisions in the Charter. As early as 1945 in Canada, the High Court of Ontario in the *Re Drummond Wren* case dismissed racially restrictive real estate covenants and cited the human rights and fundamental freedoms articles in the Charter as the reason for doing so.[40] Shortly thereafter, Du Bois and the National Association for the Advancement of Colored People used the provisions of the Charter as the basis for submitting a formal petition entitled "A Statement on the Denial of Human Rights to Minorities in the Case of Citizens of Negro Descent in the United States of America and an Appeal to the United Nations for Redress." This caused, as might be expected, enormous reaction at home and abroad. Four justices of the United States Supreme Court noted the importance of the Charter's nondiscrimination provisions in *Oyama v. California*.[41] The Court found that a California statute which excluded Japanese from certain categories of land ownership violated the fourteenth amendment. In a concurring opinion Associate Justice

---

37. United Nations General Assembly Resolution 3379 on the Elimination of All Forms of Racial Discrimination, Nov. 10, 1975, referenced in Documentary Appendix B.
38. Draft Report of the Rapporteur of Committee III4, Document 1091, 1114–44, Annex B (June 19, 1945), in UNIO, *Documents*, 10: 586.
39. Mr. Alfaro, in United Nations, *Journal of the United Nations*, No. 54, Supplement A-A/P.V./50, Dec. 9, 1946, 368.
40. See *Re Drummond Wren*, Ontario Reports 4 (1945): 778.
41. 332 U.S. 662 (1948) (Murphy, J., concurring).

Murphy described the law as "designed to effectuate a purely racial discrimination." Justices Black, Douglas, and Rutledge joined Murphy in maintaining that as a matter of national policy the United States should honor its pledge to respect the United Nations Charter's human rights provisions.

Within only months of this decision, the United States Supreme Court decided the famous *Shelley v. Kraemer* case.[42] This dispute, which concerned racially restrictive private real estate covenants, attracted the attention of the nation. Throughout the proceedings, the petitioners continually cited the human rights and nondiscrimination provisions in the United Nations Charter, as did the many briefs filed as *amici curiae* by the Department of Justice, American Association for the United Nations, and the American Civil Liberties Union. The Attorney General and Solicitor General even referred to the opinion of the Legal Advisor of the State Department who wrote that "the United States has been embarrassed in the conduct of foreign relations by acts of discrimination taking place in this country."[43] The Court, although not explicitly citing the Charter in its official opinion, for the first time refused to allow judicial agencies to enforce restrictive covenants based upon race. In the judgment of international legal authority Hersch Lauterpacht, this decision was strongly influenced by the Charter, and its subsequent impact came to be of "revolutionary importance" for the cause of human rights.[44]

These political, diplomatic, and legal controversies were soon followed by many others. The Charter of the United Nations and the events and cases surrounding it provided only "the start of a revolution in the development of new approaches to human rights issues."[45] Prior to this document, the international community in its practices, institutions, and laws remained deathly silent on the subject of individual liberties. Since then, the world has experienced a virtual explosion of instruments, procedures, declarations, and decisions designed to confront the global issue of basic human rights. The politics and diplomacy of this remarkable and dramatic movement have been filled with hopes and frustrations, careful calculations and emotions, harmony and tension, successes and failures. Throughout it all, however, the significance has been not only in the answers the movement toward adoption of international human rights provides, but in the questions it raises—questions about ourselves, our values, our past, and perhaps even our future.

ADDENDUM

[Both during and after the UN Charter process described above, Asian and African delegates to the United Nations who struggled to achieve independence for colonial countries and peoples] never lost sight of the related issue certain to bring them together: the right to racial equality. A long and heavy history of subjugation, exploitation, enslavement, segregation, and exclusion had long since convinced them of the pattern of human rights violations by white Western powers on the basis of race. They returned to this theme without ceasing and consistently cited the Universal Declaration when they met at the Asian-African Conference in Bandung, the All African Peoples' Conference in Accra, the Summit Conference of Independent African States creating the Organization of African Unity in Addis Ababa, the Afro-Asian Peoples' Solidarity Organization in Cairo, and in meetings of the United Nations in New York and Geneva. The intensity of their feeling grew even more as they watched the determined refusal of whites to give up power in territories controlled by Portugal, Southern Rhodesia, and South Africa; the continual marginalization of indigenous peoples and immigration policies of "White Australia,"

42. 334 U.S. 1 (1948).
43. Ernest A. Gross, Legal Advisor to State Department, to Attorney General, Nov. 4, 1947, as cited in "Brief of the United States as Amicus Curiae," in Philip B. Kurland and Gerhard Casper, *Landmark Briefs and Arguments of the Supreme Court of the United States: Constitutional Law* (Washington, D.C.: University Publications of America, 1975-), 46: 251.
44. "Extract from Professor Lauterpacht's Paper Read Before the Meeting of the International Law Association," Aug. 30, 1948, in Letter from George T. Washington, Assistant Solicitor General, to Ernest A. Gross, Sept. 14, 1948, RG 59, Box 2258, 501.BDHuman Rights/9-1448, National Archives, Washington, D.C.
45. The words are those of the U.S. House Subcommittee on International Organizations, *Human Rights in the International Community and in U.S. Foreign Policy, 1945–76* (Washington, D.C.: Government Printing Office, 1977), 1.

"White New Zealand," and "White Canada"; and the emergence of the civil rights movement and Martin Luther King, Jr., struggling against discrimination within the United States. Of particular importance was the unrelenting practice of racial persecution and segregation known as apartheid against an overwhelming majority of blacks by a small, white minority regime in South Africa. When police attacked an unarmed crowd gathered at Sharpeville in 1960 and massacred black civilians, it proved to be more than the Asian and African countries would tolerate. They called for a special emergency session of the Security Council to consider the dangers that apartheid presented for world peace and to condemn racial discrimination. This prompted the white South African prime minister to lash out at what he called the "international forces interfering within his country's domestic jurisdiction." In sharp contrast, the charismatic black leader Nelson Mandela embraced such external pressure, declaring before being imprisoned for twenty-seven years: "The Universal Declaration of Human Rights provides that all men are equal before the law."[46]

With all these violations of racial equality, the new majority of Asian and African countries decided that it was time for them to do whatever they possibly could to help transform this particular feature of the vision of the Universal Declaration into reality. They began by creating the Special Committee on the Policies of Apartheid and called on all member countries to pressure South Africa by severing diplomatic relations, boycotting its products, embargoing goods (including weapons), and enacting legislation prohibiting its ships or aircraft from using port facilities. Casting a broad net, they then went on to adopt an important document known as the Declaration on the Elimination of All Forms of Racial Discrimination, condemning any ideology or policy that resulted in racial segregation or apartheid and calling for concrete action against them. "We are not forgetting for a single instant," said one delegate, "that even the best resolutions are of value only in so far as they are effectively applied. . . . The hour for decisive action has struck. Let us not allow it to pass by."[47] Toward this end, and again citing the Universal Declaration by name, they worked to create the ground-breaking International Convention on the Elimination of All Forms of Racial Discrimination (ICERD) in 1965.[48] For the first time in history, states negotiated a standard-setting and binding treaty that defined racial discrimination,[49] pledged themselves to adopt all

46. Nelson Mandela, Oct. 22, 1962, as cited in Thomas Karis and Gwendolen Carter, eds., *From Protest to Challenge: A Documentary History of African Politics in South Africa, 1882–1990*, 4 vols. (Stanford, Calif: Hoover Institution Press, 1977), 3: 725–31.
47. Diallo Telli, Nov. 20, 1963, in UN/GA, *Official Records, Plenary Meetings*, 1963, at 13.
48. Concluded Dec. 21, 1965, referenced in Documentary Appendix B.
49. *Eds.*—"According to [ICERD] . . . , race encompasses color, descent, and national or ethnic origin. 'Descent' suggests social origin, such as heritage, lineage, or parentage. 'National or ethnic origin' denotes linguistic, cultural, and historical roots. Thus, this broad concept of race clearly is not limited to objective, mainly physical elements, but also includes subjective and social components. The ingredients considered central to a person's race may, in fact, vary from place to place. Some may emphasize linguistic and cultural factors while others emphasize social determinants. Certain castes, for example, are discriminated against for social reasons, but not ethnic reasons. Furthermore, nothing is permanent about all these aspects of race. Anthropologists have shown that environmental influences can profoundly change even the physical appearance of a human being in a relatively short time. * * * Therefore, race, most certainly, cannot be understood simply in terms of skin color. Racial classifications, racist bigotry, and racial hatred often have not relied on skin color. Historical examples abound. The German Nazis' belief that the Russians (as white as the Germans) were subhuman led to a massacre of millions of Russian citizens. The white Irish farmers looked like the white British landlords in Ireland in the 1840s. Yet, the white British elite exported food and gave no concessions to the white Irish farmers and laborers after crop failures in 1846–1847, and thus, 'imposed' the Irish potato famine. The issue here was not skin color, but political power. The white Irish farmers had no political or economic power. The powerful white British elite exported the food that could have saved hundreds of thousands of Irish lives. It was easier for the British to justify these policies by classifying the Irish as a backward and inferior people. * * * A definition and understanding of race and racial discrimination analysis should, therefore, include more than a mere difference of skin color. Race is also tied to power differentials, social status, and other distinctions. Differences in power give one group the ability to declare the less powerful group 'inferior.' In fact, those in power may share the same skin color and ethnic characteristics as those they oppress, yet use 'race' and 'ethnic' differences to consolidate their rule." William F. Felice, "The UN Committee on the Elimination of All Forms of Racial Discrimination: Race and Economic and Social Human Rights," *HRQ* 24, no. 1 (2002): 205–36, at 205–7.

necessary measures to prevent and eradicate it, agreed that they could be subject to criticism from other states party to the convention and individual petitioners, and, significantly, authorized the creation of the first international machinery for any United Nations sponsored human rights instrument to implement compliance with the treaty itself.

These actions finally broke the stalemate that had prevented completion of any work on the covenants. They proved that if the political will existed among the majority, the United Nations could move forward in extending rights and setting standards. Consequently, and with the full and active support of an ever-growing number of NGOs, work now started in earnest to complete the international bill of human rights that would make respect for the proclaimed rights a legal responsibility of states. An indication of the intensity of this new determination can be seen in the fact that it took only the single, pivotal year of 1966 for both the historic International Covenant on Civil and Political Rights and the International Covenant on Economic, Social and Cultural Rights to move through the General Assembly and finally to be adopted and opened for signature. Both treaties begin by referring to the Universal Declaration. They unequivocally state that human rights are essential matters of international concern, hence no longer reside within the exclusive confines of the domestic jurisdiction of those states parties to the covenants. They also prohibit discrimination based on race, color, gender, language, religion, political or other opinion, national or social origin, property, birth, or other status. In addition, both covenants provide not just for the human rights of individuals but also for "peoples" or "collective" rights relating to the right of self-determination and the right to control their natural resources and means of subsistence. Moreover, each establishes a distinct and compulsory international enforcement system designed to ensure that the parties comply with their obligations. Participants thus described them as marking a "historic event," "a new era, a new epoch, in the development of positive international concern for human rights," and a "major advance" toward realizing the vision proclaimed by the Universal Declaration of Human Rights.

These remarkable changes occurred at such a rapid pace that serious assessment was frequently difficult. The many achievements and benefits were not always fully appreciated or understood, nor were the problems. Consequently, in order to address these issues, the General Assembly, with strong support from many NGOs, declared 1968 as the International Year for Human Rights. In doing so, its members specifically cited the vision of the Universal Declaration as being "of the highest importance," called on all states to ratify the human rights treaties and accept the incumbent obligations, and agreed to make their effort "truly universal." Toward this end, they created a committee composed of representatives from different geographical areas, ideological orientations, religious faiths, cultures, and stages of development and charged them with organizing a major conference on human rights.

The resulting International Conference on Human Rights was held in Teheran during 1968 and attended by delegations from eighty-four countries, staff from the United Nations and its specialized agencies, officials from regional organizations such as the League of Arab States and the Organization of African Unity, and members of NGOs ranging from the International Alliance of Women and the League of Red Cross Societies to the World Council of Churches and the World Muslim Congress. With vast and worldwide media attention, the participants evaluated the effects of the Universal Declaration, called upon all states to ratify the existing treaties, and devoted considerable effort to analyzing the specific problems of racial and religious discrimination, apartheid, self-determination, humanitarian law in armed conflicts, discrimination against women, and protection for families and children. Significantly, the delegates went on to declare that "since human rights and fundamental freedoms are indivisible, the full realization of civil and political rights without the enjoyment of economic, social, and cultural rights is impossible." They urged "all peoples and governments to dedicate themselves" to the Universal Declaration and to "redouble their efforts" to transform its vision into reality.

Toward this end, the members of the United Nations then decided to begin a series of promotional activities in which particular issues would be the focus of attention for an entire decade. Not surprising, given the intensity of emotion on the subject, the General Assembly declared that 1973 marked the beginning of the Decade to Combat Racism and Racial Discrimination "to promote human rights and fundamental freedom for all, without distinction of any kind on grounds of race, color, descent, or national or ethnic origin," and with the aim of eliminating the persistence of racist beliefs, policies, and practices wherever they might exist. To achieve this, they agreed on a specific and ambitious Plan of Action that included such concrete measures as providing assistance to victims, denying political and diplomatic support to governments that practiced racial discrimination, seeking ratification and implementation of relevant standard-setting instruments, and sponsoring the World Conference to Combat Racism and Racial Discrimination. Both the successes of this program, which eventually saw the creation of ICERD as a treaty-monitoring body and the end of apartheid in South Africa, as well as the emergence of new problems, such as "ethnic cleansing" in

the former Yugoslavia and genocide in Rwanda, caused the members of the United Nations to twice renew the decade's theme and to rededicate themselves to its goals.

These efforts on race encouraged others on gender, and the international community therefore launched the Decade for Women in 1976 following the World Conference of the International Women's Year held in Mexico City. Working closely with the Commission on the Status of Women and with many NGOs, the participants successfully worked to gain adoption of the Convention on the Elimination of All Forms of Discrimination against Women (CEDAW),[50] to secure the necessary number of ratifications for it to enter into force, and then to create the treaty-monitoring body of the Committee on the Elimination of Discrimination against Women.

QUESTIONS FOR REFLECTION AND DISCUSSION

1. Given that both the ICESCR and ICCPR (each reprinted and referenced in Documentary Appendix A) expressly ensure freedom from racial, sexual, and religious discrimination, why has it been deemed necessary to draft other agreements to ensure the same freedoms? Consider, for example, the 1965 ICERD, the 1979 CEDAW, and the 1981 Declaration on the Elimination of All Forms of Religious Intolerance (all referenced in Documentary Appendix B). Should not states be free to apply the principles expressed in the general instruments in their own way rather than being directed by provisions that arguably may be poorly tailored to a particular place, time, and context?

2. According to ICERD Article 1, a person in the U.S. whose family is originally from Latin America would be considered a "racial minority" even if her/his skin color is the same as a European-American's. Do you agree that a person's "race" should not necessarily be synonymous with her/his skin color? Are we in danger of broadening the definition of "race" to include elements that are overly subjective?

3. Some of the most extreme racially motivated violence in recent memory occurred in Rwanda, between the Tutsis and Hutus, two groups that would be classified as "African American" if born in the United States. Does your answer to Question 2, above, help you resolve this apparent dichotomy?

4. South African apartheid was internationally condemned as a gross violation of the human right to racial equality of the people of South Africa, and it was rejected by the United States. Yet the U.S. hesitated to deal truly firmly with South Africa. For example, it was reluctant to assist in South Africa's total economic isolation through full-scale economic embargoes and boycotts. Some of the reasons given were national security interests in mineral resources and geostrategic location, the ability to better influence policy by maintaining contacts, and the need to protect corporate investments. Similar reasons have been given, more recently, for U.S. human rights policy toward China. Are they persuasive? All of them? Some? Should a country's national interests be measured against such a denial of human rights? Are there arguments to be made that it is not in the U.S. national interest or that of other governments to cooperate with countries with poor human rights records? If so, what are they?

5. In "Why More Africans Don't Use Human Rights Language," *Human Rights Dialogue* 2 (2000): 3–4 (available from the Carnegie Council on Ethics and International Affairs at

50. Concluded Dec. 18, 1979, referenced in Documentary Appendix B.

http://www.cceia.org/ viewMedia.php/prmTemplateID/8/prmID/602), Chidi Anselm Odin-kalu eloquently argues that, with limited exceptions, "The current human rights movement in Africa appears almost by design to exclude the participation of the people whose welfare it purports to advance." Odinkalu notes that native human rights activists in Africa live primarily in cities, enjoy much higher standards of living than the people on whose behalf they work, and rely almost exclusively on Western donations for their operating expenses. Does this suggest that the human rights movement is itself racist? Privileged? Or merely short-sighted? Odinkalu argues that the human rights movement in Africa should look to the "popular mobilization and inclusivity" of successful social justice movements of the past. Is this necessary for the long-term success of human rights in Africa and elsewhere? If so, how is it to be achieved?

6. At the time of *Brown v. Board of Education*, 347 U.S. 483 (1954), ICERD did not exist. However, the UN Charter did, and it contains several provisions that seek to ensure freedom from racial, sexual, and religious discrimination (see Documentary Appendix A). What would have been the United States obligation as a party to the Charter if, in *Brown* in 1954, the U.S. Supreme Court had concluded that domestic constitutional law tolerated racial discrimination in the schools? Would the United States, under the Charter, have been obliged to correct the condition? The Supreme Court's opinion in *Brown* does not mention international law. Should the Court have considered it? Would the inclusion of international-law-based arguments have made the Brown decision more or less controversial? And what if ICERD, to which the U.S. is a party, had entered into force in time for Brown? What would have been the obligation of the U.S. Supreme Court then? Of the U.S. government as a whole? Note that U.S. participation in ICERD is subject to several declarations and reservations, including a declaration stating that "nothing in the Convention shall be deemed to require or to authorize legislation or other action by the United States of America incompatible with the provisions of the Constitution of the United States of America," and another declaration stating that "The United States declares that the provisions of the Convention are not self-executing." What result? For guidance, see Burns H. Weston, "Treaty Power," in Leonard W. Levy, Kenneth L. Karst, and Adam Winkler, eds., *Encyclopedia of the American Constitution*, 6 vols., 2nd ed. (New York: Macmillan, 2000), 6: 2721–22.

7. Do you believe that affirmative action should continue in the United States? What, if anything, do international human rights instruments such as the UDHR, the ICESCR, the ICCPR, ICERD, and CEDAW have to say about the question? Consider how useful comparative research might focus on how other countries deal with disparities resulting from past discrimination.

8. Do you think racism is an inevitable aspect of human relations? Has the widespread elimination of "formal" racism (i.e., *de jure* segregation, discrimination) had as profound an effect on the lives of minorities as was expected? Consider John A. Powell's argument that those who would end race-based discrimination must "put aside . . . the pursuit of formal equality" and "focus on real equality by concentrating on the underlying conditions and causes of racial disparity." Powell, "Is Racism Permanent? A Symposium," *Poverty & Race* (Nov./Dec. 1993), available at http://www.prrac.org/news.php. Do you agree? Why? Why not? Also, does a focus on the "underlying conditions" of discrimination tend to lead to a less race-based view of racism?

9. ICERD Article 4 requires the states parties to "declare an offence punishable by law all dissemination of ideas based on racial superiority or hatred, incitement to racial discrimination, as well as all acts of violence or incitement to such acts against any race or group of persons of another colour or ethnic origin, and also the provision of any assistance to racist activities." It also requires the states parties "To declare illegal and prohibit organizations, and also organized and all other propaganda activities, which promote and incite racial discrimination." Do these Article 4 provisions contradict the First Amendment to the U.S. Constitution providing that "Congress shall make no law . . . abridging the freedom of speech, or of the press; or the right of the people peaceably to assemble, and to petition the Government for a redress of grievances." If so, should the U.S. Constitution be further amended? Is there any reason why racially based hate speech and the Ku Klux Klan, the Aryan Brotherhood, neo-Nazis, and other racist groups should not be banished from, or severely restricted by, a democratic society that professes racial harmony as a matter of fundamental public policy? For further pertinent insight, see Question 10, below.

10. Throughout modern history, racial and religious hatred have provided justifications for actions ranging from private discrimination to government-sanctioned genocide. Occupying a middle ground between these extremes is mass media hate speech against racial groups. Do you think such speech should be criminalized under international law? Under domestic law? For a consideration of how the International Criminal Tribunal for Rwanda has dealt with the question in the context of genocide, see Note, "UN Tribunal Finds That Mass Media Hate Speech Constitutes Genocide, Incitement to Genocide, and Crimes Against Humanity," *Harvard Law Review* 117 (2004): 2769–76. For further pertinent insight, see Question 9, above.

11. The USA Patriot Act (P.L. 107–56, October 26, 2001, 115 Stat. 272), passed in the wake of the September 11, 2001, terrorist attacks in New York City, has been widely criticized as racist. The Act has been used, its critics argue, as a justification for widespread abrogations of the civil rights of Arab-Americans. But the Act itself contains no mention of race or ethnicity. Should such facial neutrality provide a defense for the drafters of laws? Or should the foreseeable discriminatory uses of the law be considered as well?

12. Some writers describe the evolution of stereotypes between different peoples as a cycle of misunderstandings, communication breakdowns, and conflicts that arise when emotional images or habitual thinking becomes a substitute for knowledge. Consider the following account by Andreas Fuglesang in "The Myth of People's Ignorance," *Development Dialogue* 1–2 (1984): 60–61:

> The Dorobo [of East Africa] are scattergroups composed of persons dispersed by war, famine or natural disasters. They eke out a living on the periphery of the larger tribal societies, assimilating the language of their closest tribal neighbour. Of interest here is the image the settled farmers or the herders have developed of the Dorobo. Since the Dorobo do not farm or herd, their humanity is held in question by those who do. For the Masai, a Dorobo means a poor man because he does not own cattle; for the Kikuyu, because he does not own land. In the eyes of men, the Dorobo are women-like. In the eyes of the guardians of tribal morale, they are practisers of witchcraft. In the eyes of the tribal establishment, they are considered devious, unreliable and conniving, as well as generally ignorant.
>
> The litany of traits ascribed to the Dorobo is common to the folklore of social outcasts in cultures the world over. The names of these subterranean creatures may vary— sirens, gnomes or trolls are but a few examples—but they belong to the no-man's-land between human beings and goods, devils and spirits.
>
> Evidently all societies have their barbarians, savages, poor people, workers . . . , or Dorobo. Whatever constitutes the responsible, moral, orderly, normal, progressive, knowledgeable, and well-dressed citizen in a given society, these people are its opposite. Our world view is stuck in a dichotomy. Conceptually, it is a negative film without which we cannot process as positive images of ourselves.

"How," Fuglesang asks, "are we to change this attitude and linguistic habit that so viciously labels other peoples as ignorant? Isn't the term ignorance just one culture's judgment on the knowledge of another culture?" How do you answer these questions?

10. EVA BREMS *Protecting the Rights of Women*

A feminist perspective on international human rights law and politics emerged during the last decade of the twentieth century. . . . The United Nations World Conference on Human Rights, held in Vienna in 1993, was a major turning point. Women's groups from around the world with multiple agendas sharpened their skills of coalition making and lobbying and experienced the strength of their combined forces. Earlier efforts, particularly the series of UN conferences on the advancement of women that had started in 1975, were part of a period of gestation;

Vienna marked the birth of an international women's human rights movement.

Feminist critiques have for some time been applied to crucial areas of domestic law. Many of the analytical and methodological tools developed in the domestic context are now being applied to international human rights law. In this chapter, I examine how feminist claims are transforming international human rights and suggest where this growing impact may lead. Three different approaches to the protection of women's rights will be addressed. The first is based on what might be called the "sameness" of women and men, while the other two take women's "specificity" as a starting point, one leading to a claim for special human rights for women and the other to a claim for the feminist transformation of human rights for all.

There is a certain chronological order in this presentation in that the "sameness" approach historically came first, and the idea of a feminist transformation of human rights is relatively recent. Yet the three approaches are not intended to reflect the viewpoints of specific persons or groups but rather should be seen as theoretical models, or analytical tools, to facilitate discussion of different ways in which women's human rights can be approached. In the real world, hardly anyone promotes a purely "sameness" approach. What is known as "liberal feminism" comes closest, yet it includes some elements of a "specificity" approach. Moreover, most proponents of a specificity model support both certain proposals for special women's rights, and certain "feminist transformations" of human rights. We are faced not so much with a choice among three models as with a choice between different combinations of measures linked to the three approaches.

All three approaches are as relevant today as they are for the future. However, this chapter will focus most strongly on feminist transformations of international human rights. . . . [Additionally], within the specificity approach, [it] will promote the transformative approach more than special women's rights, because [the transformative approach] fits best in a conception of universality based on all inclusiveness. Finally, the claim for the recognition of women's specificity in international human rights cannot be considered in isolation since identity based claims are being launched by others, notably minorities, indigenous peoples, and representatives of non-Western societies. Though similar to the feminist demands in form and in their underlying rationale, these other claims are often at odds with feminist views when it comes to their substance. Managing multiple specificities is another huge challenge for international human rights in the next fifty years.

SAMENESS

In the simplest of terms, both women and men are human, which means that in many respects they are the same and they want to be treated in the same way. The principle of the universality of human rights and the ensuing rule of nondiscrimination in the enjoyment of human rights are meant to assure such equal treatment.[1] When human rights first appeared on the international scene, with the Universal Declaration of Human Rights (UDHR) in 1948,[2] they had a strong emphasis on natural law. The idea of universality was based on that of an essential "human" nature. It was believed that human rights captured the common denominator of all human beings. . . . Hence the ambition to apply the same rights, in the same way, to everybody regardless of their gender, class, and so forth. The ideal of equality of the sexes was that of formal, gender-blind equality.

Formal equality of the sexes was a huge challenge in 1948, a time when, in many states, women had only recently obtained the right to vote. Formal equality only gradually became a reality, and it is still not realized today. Discrimination against women in all areas of life is widespread. The number of laws still on the books that formally and explicitly discriminate against women is extensive. According to the Sudanese Personal Law for Muslims Act, enacted in 1991, for example, a woman needs a male guardian to

1. Equal treatment does not always mean "the same treatment." There are many different conceptions of equality and nondiscrimination, including those that recognize that equal treatment requires different treatment when there are relevant differences. . . . In the context of the present analysis, such conceptions fall under the "specificity" rubric. Under "sameness," a conception of equality is discussed which focuses on the common humanity of men and women, in the light of which the differences between them are considered irrelevant.

2. Adopted Dec. 10, 1948, reprinted and referenced in Documentary Appendix A.

contract her own marriage. During marriage, she is required to obey her husband, and while her husband can divorce her at will, she can divorce him only on certain grounds and after a court procedure. In South Africa, women married under customary law are considered minors and cannot enter into any legal contract without the consent of their husbands or guardians. And in Saudi Arabia, women are not allowed to drive cars.

Even where the laws protecting women against discrimination exist, the practice is often one in which the rules are flagrantly violated on a daily basis. Recently Human Rights Watch reported how abuses against women have been carried out frequently and with virtual impunity in states such as Russia, South Africa, Pakistan, and Jordan. . . . In the United States, Human Rights Watch identified violence by custodians against women in prisons and in Bosnia, discrimination against women with regard to loans and training programs in reconstruction programs.[3] The organization also accused the Mexican government of not protecting the rights of pregnant women that are guaranteed under domestic legislation but violated by transnational corporations in the export-processing sector.[4]

As these examples show, the sameness approach toward women's human rights remains highly relevant. Such discriminatory practices deny the sameness of women and men on the basis of patriarchal constructions of difference, which do not necessarily view women as inferior but are almost inevitably distortions brought on by the interpretation of the specificity of women by men (i.e., by outsiders in a dominant position). Activists for women's rights thus need to continue to focus on eliminating patriarchal constructions of difference and on achieving formal equality before the law through the abolition of discriminatory laws and the enforcement of anti-discrimination legislation. This type of feminist activism rests within mainstream human rights rules and institutions and has been called the "doctrinal" or "institutional" approach or, in an analogy with feminist approaches to domestic law, "liberal feminism."[5] It may seem too limited to many living in Western countries where its goals have largely been reached, but it is a necessary step, which can make an enormous difference in the lives of women.

Another consequence of the sameness of women and men is that women experience many of the same human rights violations as men. If a political party or a religious sect is outlawed, female and male members are equally affected. If a village is burned down and the crops are destroyed, all its inhabitants suffer. There is no need for different rules for men and women, nor is there any need for different control mechanisms. Yet in those situations as well, a women's perspective on human rights may make sense simply because women are often not aware of their entitlement [to human rights protections]. There is a need to make women more aware of their rights in many societies and provide them with access to human rights discourse and remedies.

SPECIFICITY

Biological differences between men and women lead to different personal experiences, as do role patterns in the family and in the broader society. Beyond these differences, some feminists also claim that there are inherent psychological differences between the sexes. At the same time, men have dominated the history of international human rights since the [UDHR]. Today, the natural law approach to human rights no longer prevails. The concept of "human nature" is under fire, and considerable dispute persists about whether a neutral perspective is possible at all. We realize now that however well intentioned the drafters of the declaration, their attempt to assume a common human nature inevitably resulted in a projection of their own experiences, needs, and values onto the rest of humanity. Despite the participation of Eleanor Roosevelt, those were predominantly the experiences, needs, and values of well-off white Western men. The same holds true for developments in human rights theory and practice since 1948.

As social groups emerge from domination, they become aware of this distortion within international human rights, and they advance

3. Human Rights Watch, *World Report 2000*.
4. Ibid.
5. Kathleen Mahoney, "Theoretical Perspectives on Women's Human Rights and Strategies for Their Implementation," *Brooklyn Journal of International Law* 21 (1996): 799–856, at 802–8.

claims to correct it. After the end of the Cold War . . . , [e]mancipation movements, such as the women's movement, became aware of the increased potential of international human rights to realize their agendas. As a result, the claims to correct the biases of international human rights have become louder, in particular those from the women's movement and those from non-Western societies. Those claims are based on a different conception of universality and equality. They start from a realization that neutrality and objectivity are, practically speaking, impossible and, as a consequence, formal equality is not sufficient when there are relevant differences, such as there are between men and women.

From that perspective, equality can no longer be realized by eliminating all context-related factors but rather by deliberately taking some such factors into account. If human rights are to be universal in the sense that they apply in an equal manner to all women and all men, they must take some gender-based differences into account instead of stressing their irrelevance. This is not necessarily at odds with the earlier view of universality and equality, which purports to eliminate differences. The difference to be eliminated in that first conception is difference as constructed by dominant outsiders, *in casu* by men. The difference to be recognized in this second view, however, is difference as experienced by the insiders. In this case: by women themselves.

The main focus of this [essay] is on the adaptation of international human rights law to the specific needs and experiences of women. Although the specificity approach may obviously be linked to a strand of feminism known as "cultural feminism,"[6] it should not be interpreted as taking sides in the feminist debate between "sameness" and "difference." Particularly when discussing the future of international women's human rights over the next several decades, the emphasis on specificity simply offers a more fruitful approach.

The theoretical framework within which these issues will be addressed is that of "inclusive universality."[7] Inclusive universality is based on the inclusion of all people in the human rights framework. It accepts the critique that the pretended neutrality of human rights is inherently biased and, as a result, insists that formal applicability of standards is not enough to guarantee general inclusion in human rights protection. It recognizes that people who do not correspond to the implicit reference point of human rights (the human being in its male and Western manifestation) experience a form of exclusion because their needs, concerns, and values are not taken into account to the same extent as those of Western men. Inclusive universality proposes to correct this situation by accommodating particularist claims from those who are excluded.

With regard to women, this means listening to what women have to say about how the present system of international human rights does not sufficiently protect them, does not correspond to their needs, and does not reflect their priorities. There is now a strong and well-organized women's movement advancing such arguments and making very concrete proposals for changes to standards, organizations, mechanisms, and policies. If human rights are to be universal, they should respond to these claims, for several reasons. In the first place, from a democratic perspective, inclusion requires participation . . . , [and this] means that women should be present when human rights standards are formulated and when agendas are set. They should be there in fact, and they should be there in the sense that they are being fully taken into account with all their gender-specific concerns.

Human rights should also respond to the claims of women (or others who have been excluded) for pragmatic reasons. The connection between human rights standards and practice, on the one hand, and the life experiences of people, on the other, is crucial. Human rights make no sense unless they are relevant to the experience of people. They only work if the people activate them; they strongly rely on an active civil society. Women make up at least half of the human population. If a significant group of women feel disconnected from human rights, this undermines not only their significance as "human" rights but also their effectiveness.

[*Eds.*—The author next asks how "women's specificity" (in contrast to "women's sameness") can

6. Ibid., 808–14.
7. The concept of inclusive universality was developed to deal with non-Western particularist claims about human rights. See Eva Brems, "Human Rights: Universality and Diversity," Ph.D. dissertation, K.U. Leuven, 1999.

be accommodated within international human rights law. In search of answers, she proposes two methods of analysis involving: (a) "'flexibility,' or differentiation of human rights standards, depending on the context (the relevant specificities)," such that, "with regard to women the creation of special 'women's human rights' is the main expression of 'flexibility'"; and (b) "'transformation' of human rights standards, with general norms or institutions being changed in response to the particularist claims of those who have been excluded," contending that, "[i]n many respects, the transformation of general human rights standards in response to the claims of women holds the most promise for the future." She then turns to a discussion of each approach, beginning with the observation that, together with the "sameness approach" to women's human rights, the "flexibility" and "transformation" approaches "reflect the three types of claims that may be addressed to rights discourse from the perspective of identity politics."[8] She explains: "The sameness approach reflects the complaint of groups 'that they are inappropriately defined as different.' The flexibility approach deals with the complaint of groups 'that their distinctiveness is inappropriately ignored or disrespected by the majority.' Finally, the transformation approach is the most radical, expressing 'an alternative Universalist vision that challenges the foundational commitments of the majority'" Brems adds: "Yet however radical some of the arguments may be, they remain internal to our human rights framework in that they accept the aspirations of the existing scheme at a general level but argue that those aspirations have been improperly defined in some cases and inadequately met in others.'"[9]]

Flexibility: Human Rights for Women

It is logical that the initial response to feminist demands for the inclusion of women's specificity in international human rights should have been to add specific human rights for women. For one thing, additions to human rights standards and institutions targeted at those excluded

are more readily interpreted as a response to that group than are modifications of a general nature. "When women complain, let's do something for them" is the straightforward reasoning of the flexibility approach. . . . Second, the creation of specific women's human rights standards and institutions leaves the mainstream system intact. When claims for important changes have to be met, adding something new is a much less drastic intervention than questioning and reshaping what already exists. Hence the flexibility approach is, at once, less drastic and more visible than the transformation approach.

In many ways, the international movement for the advancement of women dates back to before World War II and was initiated quite apart from the human rights movement. In the 1920s, feminist activists from the Americas pressured their governments into creating the Inter-American Commission of Women (Commission Interamericana de Mujeres [CIM]). The CIM drafted the Inter-American Convention on the Nationality of Women (1933)[10] and promoted an Equal Rights Treaty (1928). With the creation of the Organization of American States (OAS) in 1948, the CIM became an autonomous specialized commission of the OAS. It drafted two more women's conventions in 1948: the Inter-American Convention on the Granting of Political Rights to Women and the Inter-American Convention on Granting Civil Rights to Women.[11] After shifting its efforts to problems of education and development, the CIM returned to the question of women's rights in the 1980s, with its work on the Inter-American Convention on the Prevention, Punishment, and Eradication of Violence against Women, adopted by the General Assembly of the OAS on June 9, 1994.[12]

The CIM was also influential in the creation of the United Nations Commission on the Status of Women (CSW) in 1946. Until the early 1970s, the CSW was mainly oriented toward the promotion of equal rights for women, drafting the Convention on the Political Rights of Women (1952), the Convention on the Nationality of Married Women (1957), the Convention on Consent to Marriage, Minimum Age for Marriage,

---

8. Citing Tracy E. Higgins, "Regarding Rights: An Essay Honoring the Fiftieth Anniversary of the Universal Declaration of Human Rights," *Columbia Human Rights Law Review* 30 (1999): 239.
9. Ibid., 241.
10. Concluded Dec. 26, 1933, referenced in Documentary Appendix B.
11. Each concluded, May 2, 1948, referenced in Documentary Appendix B.
12. Concluded June 9, 1994, referenced in Documentary Appendix B.

and Registration of Marriages (1962), and a number of declarations.[13] The CSW also drafted the Convention on the Elimination of All Forms of Discrimination against Women (CEDAW, 1979),[14] the most important expression of the "human rights for women" approach. The CEDAW has its own supervising body, the Committee for the Elimination of Discrimination against Women (CmEDAW).

Within the structure of the United Nations, the Division for the Advancement of Women (DAW) is the secretariat for both CSW and CmEDAW. Other "bureaucratic spaces" for women's issues within the UN include UNIFEM (United Nations Development Fund for Women) and INSTRAW (International Research and Training Institute for the Advancement of Women). There are also a number of International Labor Organization (ILO) conventions [responsive in various ways to women's issues].

What has thus been developed within the international system are specific instruments and institutions dealing with women's rights that are expressions of a "flexibility" approach to the issue of human rights for women. Yet within this approach, different attitudes can be distinguished toward the issue of gender. Several of the older instruments, for example, reflect a "sameness" approach. Texts such as the UN Convention on the Political Rights of Women (1952) and the ILO Equal Remuneration Convention (1951)[15] are based on a concept of formal equality that elevates women to the same level of rights as men. Because they use a male reference point, however, such texts cannot (nor are they intended to) do justice to the specific needs and experiences of women. They are gender-specific in form but not in substance.

Other texts are based on women's specificity, yet they interpret it in a way that leads to the exclusion of some women. In line with traditional role patterns, these "protective" instruments see women as especially vulnerable and in need of protection. . . . While many women may agree with such views of femininity and many also may benefit from these provisions,

others feel that this approach does not do justice to them as persons capable of making their own choices.

In the more recent texts, the goal is to include an array of women's perspectives that is as complete as possible. In the first place, they try to address the ways in which the experience of human rights violations, whether suffered by men or women, is influenced by gender. For example, denial of the right to food or adequate housing in a society where women bear the primary responsibility in these fields affects women differently than men. Another typical situation occurs when women are subjected to arbitrary violence—for example, in detention, where this frequently takes the form of sexual assault. *A fortiori*, these texts also address violations in which gender is a determining factor, such as relating to the sexuality of women or their reproductive capacity.

Texts on women's rights that adopt this approach have been labeled "corrective" instruments and include conventions that address trafficking in women, the UN Convention on Consent to Marriage, Minimum Age for Marriage, and Registration of Marriages (1962), the UN Declaration on the Elimination of Violence against Women (1993), and the Inter-American Convention on the same subject (1994). The latter texts particularly reflect the perspective of women by extending protection against violence that is committed in the private sphere and violence that results from cultural factors.

The CEDAW contains elements of all three approaches. As largely an anti-discrimination convention, it has a strong sameness component as many provisions give women "equal rights with men." Other provisions have a protective character, in particular with regard to wo reproductive function (articles 11(1)(f (2)(d)). And there is a strong corrective in the provisions that deal with issues i women are not treated equally. . . : T ment also devotes an article to the speci. lems of rural women (article 14) and another to trafficking in women and prostitution (article 6).

---

13. Concluded Mar. 31, 1953, Feb. 20, 1957, and Dec. 10, 1962, respectively, each referenced in Documentary Appendix B. See also UN General Assembly Declaration on the Elimination of Discrimination Against Women (1967), UN General Assembly Declaration on the Protection of Women and Children in Emergency and Armed Conflict (1974), and Declaration on the Participation of Women in Promoting International Peace and Co-operation (1982, drafted by the Third Committee of the General Assembly, after an initial proposal was considered by the CSW), all referenced in Documentary Appendix B.
14. Concluded Dec. 18, 1979, referenced in Documentary Appendix B.
15. Concluded June 29, 1951, referenced in Documentary Appendix B.

In these areas, the CEDAW imposes specific obligations on states, which would not necessarily be read under gender-neutral provisions. For example, in the field of education, states are required to eliminate stereotyped concepts of the roles of men and women (article 10(c)) and to reduce female student dropout rates (article 10(f)), and in the field of employment, specific measures are required to prevent discrimination against women on the grounds of marriage and maternity (article 11(2)). Moreover, the concept of equality in the CEDAW goes beyond formal equality. It recognizes affirmative action measures (article 4), extends protection to all aspects of life (article 1), and stresses the need to modify discriminatory cultural patterns (article 5).

In recent years, especially since the UN world conferences of Vienna (human rights, 1993) and Beijing (women, 1995), the idea of special instruments has, nevertheless, lost the support of many women. Specialization has come to be seen as marginalization or ghettoization with the existence of specific treaties leading to a neglect of women under the mainstream human rights regime. At the same time, mechanisms created under specific treaties are underfunded and lack strong enforcement. The concerns of women, it is argued, should be at the center of human rights, not on their periphery, and gender-specific violations should be addressed through the mainstream instruments, using the mainstream supervisory mechanisms.

For the future, there may be good arguments to limit the creation of new specialized instruments. Yet it would be foolish to totally reject those that exist. The CEDAW, in particular, has much potential that has not yet been fully used and should not be abandoned, especially the ~tional Protocol, which was opened for signa- · on December 10, 1999,[16] and entered into · on December 22, 2000. This protocol has ~tential to dramatically strengthen the role of the CmEDAW. It provides a complaint procedure for individuals and groups and a process of inquiry into grave or systematic abuses. The absence of an individual complaint procedure was a major deficiency in the original CEDAW, and with its inclusion, the convention deserves a new chance in the coming decades.

TRANSFORMATION: WOMEN'S RIGHTS ARE HUMAN RIGHTS

The argument for "mainstreaming" calls for the full integration of women's rights into the international regime so that the problems that women face are taken into account whenever human rights are on the agenda. For example, monitoring gender-specific issues should not be left to the CmEDAW but should be taken up also by other supervising committees such as those established under the [1966] International Covenant on Civil and Political Rights (ICCPR), the [1966] International Covenant on Economic, Social, and Cultural Rights (ICESCR), the [1984] Torture Convention, and the [1989 Convention on the Rights of the Child (CRC)].[17] Thus far, the situation has varied with the Committee on Economic, Social and Cultural Rights and the Committee on the Rights of the Child being most responsive, and the Committee on the Elimination of Racial Discrimination and the Committee against Torture the least. "Mainstreaming" also means that the perspectives of women can bring about a transformation of the system of protection, with "a reappraisal of and a qualitative change in the relevant institutions, laws, and procedures."[18] Charlotte Bunch has noted that the transformative approach is increasingly the choice of women who are now actively working on human rights.[19]

Both the flexibility model and the transformation model propose changes in human rights norms and institutions, or at least in the way norms are interpreted and applied in response to women's specific gender experiences. Both assert that the human rights regime developed in a male-dominated environment and that insufficient female input explains some gaps in the system that need to be remedied. The difference

16. Concluded Oct. 19, 1999, referenced in Documentary Appendix B.
17. Each of these instruments is referenced in Documentary Appendix B.
18. Anne Gallagher, "Ending the Marginalization: Strategies for Incorporating Women into the United Nations Human Rights System," *HRQ* 19 (1997): 288.
19. Charlotte Bunch, "Feminist Visions of Human Rights in the Twenty-First Century," in Kathleen A. Mahoney and Paul Mahoney, eds., *Human Rights in the Twenty-First Century* (Dordrecht: M. Nijhoff, 1993), 976.

between them is in the scope of the remedy. The flexibility model proposes to complete the human rights system with specific "women's" norms or institutions. It rests on the supposition that the gaps discovered through women's gender experience are relevant only for women, and it tailors the cure to that diagnosis. The transformation model, on the other hand, attributes a more universal value to women's claims, arguing that they reflect general deficiencies in the human rights regime, applicable as much to men as to women. . . . In the transformation model, changes in rights brought on by women apply equally to both men and women. A good example is the right to parental leave that generally emerges from the hardship that women have in combining a career with a family. Women usually take the initiative in ensuring the right of parental leave, but men experience the problem of the double burden as well, and where the right to parental leave exists, many men are happy to make use of it, even though more women do so.

There are two strong arguments for preferring a transformation approach to a flexibility approach in advancing the human rights of women. First, the transformation approach is more inclusive and shows more respect for difference. How seriously will the claims of women be taken if they are applicable to women alone? Real participation implies the power to change the general parameters, the power to contribute to the definition of what human rights are about, not only for women but also for all. If it is true that, thus far, human rights reflect a male bias, then the inclusion of women must lead to questioning some of the concrete features of human rights that manifest this bias. [Hilary] Charlesworth rightly states that "unless the experiences of women contribute directly to the mainstream international legal order . . . , international human rights law loses its claim to universal applicability: it should be more accurately characterized as international men's rights law."[20] * * * The assertion that "women's rights are human rights" expresses both a demand to be included "in the project of human rights and a radical redefinition of what that project entails."[21]

Second, the integration of a women's perspective in international human rights should not lead to new types of exclusion. A flexibility approach runs the risk of excluding men from new types of human rights protection. Today much of the critical thinking about law and politics comes from one or another specific perspective such as race or gender. However, innovative solutions proposed on the basis of such analysis may often be as pertinent outside as well as within that specific context. The principle of universality of international human rights requires that additional human rights protection, from wherever it emerges, apply to all human beings.

[*Eds.*—The author notes that, while the project of transformation must take account of men's and women's different modes of interacting with the private and public spheres, the project must not, in taking such account, enshrine the status quo, which is itself not something "most feminists want to preserve." The author further argues that the "breach of the public/private divide" is a good example of a project in which the transformational feminist perspective can (and, she argues, should) have a profound impact on international human rights law writ large. Brems notes that traditional international human rights law has concerned itself primarily, if not exclusively, with the actions of nations and public officials. The transformation suggested by such gender-specific instruments as CEDAW and the UN Declaration on the Elimination of Violence Against Women, Brems contends, is at a minimum to hold states accountable for the actions of private actors that violate human rights norms in the private sphere. Further, she notes, "the possibility of holding private actors directly accountable should not be excluded." Steps in this direction have been made both by the European Court of Human Rights and the Inter-American Court of Human Rights. Relatedly, Brems observes that the feminist transformation of human rights suggests strongly that international human rights should direct its focus more towards the historically-neglected social and economic rights, rather than continuing to focus on civil and political rights.]

20. Hilary Charlesworth, "Human Rights as Men's Rights," in Julie Peters and Andrea Wolper, eds., *Women's Rights, Human Rights: International Feminist Perspectives* (New York: Routledge, 1995), 105.
21. Christine Bell, "Women's Rights as Human Rights: Old Agendas in New Guises," in Angela Hegarty and Siobhan Leonard, eds., *Human Rights: An Agenda for the 21st Century* (London: Cavendish, 1999), 139.

EMERGING STANDARDS

Integrating the needs and experiences of women can affect general human rights standards either through new formulations or through innovative interpretations of existing standards. Together, according to Coomaraswamy, they constitute a "fourth generation" of human rights[22] that is emerging in such areas as reproductive rights, sexual violence, the right of asylum, and rights connecting to slavery and slavery-like practices. These are examples of a transformative approach rather than a flexibility approach, because the situations they bring within the focus of human rights attention do not exclusively concern women, and the normative changes thus inspired concern general standards, applicable to both men and women.

REPRODUCTIVE RIGHTS

Reproduction is an area in which many states intervene when they pursue nationalist, economic, religious, or other interests to control population growth through pronatalist or antinatalist policies. These invariably focus on regulating the reproductive capacities of individuals. These policies affect both women and men, yet women are most directly concerned. Over the years, women's movements have increasingly focused on reproduction as a human right, an issue that was first brought to the international scene at the International Conference on Human Rights in Teheran in 1968. In its Final Act, the conference recognized that "parents have a basic human right to determine freely and responsibly the number and spacing of their children."[23]

This language was significantly expanded in the World Population Plan of Action adopted in Bucharest in 1974: "All couples and individuals have the basic right to decide freely and responsibly the number and spacing of their children and to have the information, education and means to do so; the responsibility of couples and individuals in the exercise of this right takes into account the needs of their living and future children, and their responsibilities towards the community."[24] In 1979, under article 16(1)(e), CEDAW recognized the same right in a legally binding fashion: "States Parties . . . shall ensure, on a basis of equality of men and women . . . the same rights to decide freely and responsibly on the number and spacing of their children and to have access to the information, education and means to enable them to exercise these rights." Other CEDAW articles are also relevant to reproductive rights.

A major breakthrough came with the 1994 Cairo Population Conference, where the international women's health movement, greatly expanded since the 1970s and 1980s, became a major player.[25] The Cairo Programme of Action contains a chapter on reproductive rights and reproductive health. Reproductive health is a comprehensive concept that includes the "full spectrum of health needs associated with women's reproductive and sexual activities"[26] and that embraces reproductive rights. * * * The 1995 Beijing Declaration and Programme of Action, adopted at the Fourth United Nations World Conference on Women, reconfirms the Cairo definitions of reproductive health and reproductive rights,[27] adding a specific emphasis on the rights of women. . . .

The CEDAW provisions aside, reproductive human rights have not yet been included in other legally binding documents. Nonetheless, the Cairo and Beijing Declarations, both based on a broad worldwide consensus, provide strong authority to guide the interpretation of existing human rights, including the right to health and

22. Radhika Coomaraswamy, *Reinventing International Law: Women's Rights as Human Rights in the International Community* (Cambridge, Mass.: Human Rights Program, Harvard Law School, 1997), 20. She is recommending adding to the frequently made subdivision of three "generations" of human rights. The first generation are civil and political rights; the second are social, economic, and cultural rights; and the third are the so-called solidarity rights. See Reading 1 by Burns Weston in Chapter 1 of this volume.
23. Adopted May 13, 1968, referenced in Documentary Appendix B.
24. UN Doc. E/CONF.60/19 (1974), 7.
25. Amy J. Higer, "International Women's Activism and the 1994 Cairo Population Conference," in Mary K. Meyer and Elisabeth Prügl, eds., *Gender Politics in Global Governance* (Lanham, Md.: Rowman & Littlefield, 1999), 122–41.
26. Paula Abrams, "Reservations About Women: Population Policy and Reproductive Rights," *Cornell International Law Journal* 29 (1996): 1–23, at 32.
27. UN Doc. E/CONF.177/20, SS 94–95.

the right to privacy (which encompasses sexual and reproductive freedom).[28] Further developments in this area could lead to the recognition of "sexual rights" that are broader than reproductive rights but failed to gain general acceptance at the Cairo and Beijing conferences. The enjoyment of reproductive rights is, moreover, continuously influenced by medical advances, so much so that radical feminists already accuse reproductive technology of subjecting women to patriarchal control. Strengthening reproductive rights is a way of guaranteeing that whatever developments may occur, the dignity, equality, and freedom of individuals both men and women—remain central.

SEXUAL VIOLENCE

[*Eds.*—The author chronicles the historical development and future prospects of the protections afforded by international human rights law against sexual violence. In particular, Brems notes that "international law has been slow in recognizing the seriousness of this type of violence," criticizing the 1949 Geneva Conventions on the Laws of War[29] in particular as embodying a paternalistic view of sexual violence and its prevention. Later instruments and judicial decisions have, Brems contends, reflected laudable improvements in the conception of sexual violence as a human rights issue. Brems further argues, as presaged above in her consideration of the private/public divide generally, that the treatment of sexual violence provides an apt forum in which that divide might be breached; that is, *private* actors might be held to account for sexual violence as a form of torture.]

RIGHT TO ASYLUM

The right to [seek and enjoy] asylum from persecution is a human right (article 14 UDHR). The international law in this regard is found in the 1951 Convention Relating to the Status of Refugees as modified by the 1967 Protocol Relating to the Status of Refugees.[30] The convention defines a refugee as a person who, "owing to well-founded fear of being persecuted for reasons of race, religion, nationality, membership of a particular social group or political opinion, is outside the country of his nationality and is unable or, owing to such fear, is unwilling to avail himself of the protection of that country."

Under these provisions, persecution on the basis of gender is not grounds for asylum, an omission that has long been a serious issue for women's rights activists. Gender-based persecution, they insist, is systematic and widespread and no less serious than persecution based on race or other criteria. Again, the public/private divide seems to be the main obstacle, as gender-based persecution is suffered mainly at the hands of private persons. Gradually it has nonetheless come to be recognized that gender-based persecution may be recognized by including groups of women under the category of membership of a particular social group, and several countries have taken important steps in this direction. Yet in the present state of international law, the right to asylum of women fleeing from such ordeals as forced marriage, massive rape, and genital mutilation depends on the goodwill and changing policies of a small number of states. Changes along these lines are slow and uncertain. In the long run, the only solution offering adequate protection to these women is the inclusion of gender as a category of persecution in the international texts.

SLAVERY

[*Eds.*—Brems notes that international law has historically been explicitly attentive to slavery's impact on women, but that this attention has perhaps been too focused on one aspect of women's enslavement: forced prostitution. While forced prostitution remains a real (and perhaps growing) problem worldwide, it is accompanied by enslavement of women in other forms and

---

28. Other relevant human rights include the right to life (e.g., death caused by unsafe abortion); the prohibition of sex discrimination (e.g., when women are forced to undergo abortion or family planning, or when they need the approval of a husband or a male relative to do so), the right to family life, the prohibition of torture and inhuman or degrading treatment, the right to education, and the right to enjoy the benefits of scientific progress. . . .
29. Referenced in Documentary Appendix B.
30. Each referenced in Documentary Appendix B.

for other purposes. International human rights law should, Brems concludes, explicitly account for such horrible practices as forced marriages, trafficking in women for commercial and/or domestic labor, and the genital mutilation and other profound mistreatment of young women.]

PROPOSALS FOR ADDITIONAL STANDARDS

There are other feminist proposals for new human rights standards, but these are farther from gaining general acceptance. One proposal is that international humanitarian law no longer focus [exclusively] on direct violence but rather also take into account the long-term effects of armed conflicts, which often disproportionately affect women. Charlesworth, for example, argues that "conflict exacerbates the globally unequal position of women and men in many ways. We know," she continues, that "distinctive burdens [are] placed on women through food and medical shortages caused by conflict. When food is scarce, more women than men suffer from malnutrition, often because of cultural norms that require men and boys to eat before women and girls. Humanitarian relief for the victims of conflict regularly fails to reach women, as men are typically given responsibility for its distribution. Economic sanctions imposed before, during, or after armed conflict have had particular impact on women and girls, who are disproportionately represented among the poor. Although the effect of these practices falls heavily on women, they are not understood by international law to be human rights abuses that would engage either state or individual responsibility."[31]

Still another proposition is to expand the definition of genocide to include the generally culturally determined practice of female infanticide whether committed through direct killings or through neglect of female children (with their consequent death frequently due to malnutrition). A completely different proposal is that of restricting the scope of the freedom of expression, so that it no longer protects pornography. In this context it should be noted, however, that present international standards already allow for the restriction and even prohibition of pornography by national—or, for that matter,

international—authorities. It seems that those who desire stricter measures in this area should aim their arrows not at international human rights standards but rather at political decision makers.

OTHER FEMINIST TRANSFORMATIONS OF HUMAN RIGHTS

The women's human rights movement is extremely diverse, encompassing groups and individuals campaigning for a wide range of different issues. One such issue is the language of human rights. Many women have trouble with the consistent use of male pronouns in almost all international human rights texts. The Convention on the Rights of the Child is an exception; wherever possible, it uses the gender-neutral "the child," and where the use of the possessive pronoun is necessary, it uses "his or her." The importance of language in gender equality has been analyzed in many different contexts, and the argument has been made that it operates at both a direct and a subtle level to exclude women by constructing and reinforcing their subordination. The language in the Convention on the Rights of the Child is a model for future international texts.

Even more important is the representation of women in international bodies dealing with human rights issues. Equal representation is not only a matter of democratic participation but also a necessary requirement if the needs and experiences of women are to be incorporated into the activities of international organizations. Despite strong insistence from activists, the representation of women in mainstream human rights bodies is still unacceptably low.

Another crucial matter involves integrating a woman's perspective into the methodologies used for investigating and enforcing human rights norms. Gallagher finds that "when human rights abuses against women are identified, the wider context of the violation is almost invariably ignored. There is a subsequent failure to explore and acknowledge the root causes of violations against women and to develop effective responses."[32] . . . Methodologies developed within feminist studies may have broader applicability.

31. Hilary Charlesworth, "Feminist Methods in International Law," *AJIL* 93 (1999): 386–94, at 388.
32. Gallagher, "Ending the Marginalization," note 18, at 292.

Feminist analysis has been described as "contextual, experiential, and inductive. Whereas much social theory is hierarchical, abstract, and deductive, the feminist starting point is from actual human experience and the implications of that experience."[33]. . .

Some feminists also criticize the individualist character of international human rights. They argue, on the one hand, that women have a relational world-view, which is not adequately expressed in terms of individual rights and, on the other, that violations of a woman's human rights are, in many cases, structural problems which are also not accounted for. This criticism, however, does not have to lead to an advocacy for group rights, especially since group rights under international law are largely conceived in terms of ethnic groups that often subordinate women. The rights of women as a group have received some attention in domestic law in connection with issues like affirmative action, but they have rarely been recognized under international law. In the years to come, the collective dimension of women's rights may come to the forefront, for example, as a framework for addressing the root causes of gender discrimination. However, from an inclusive perspective, this would be a step in the wrong direction, as the same structural problems usually also affect men, and remedies created in response to women's group claims risk excluding them. The final example is the claim for the inclusion of women's human rights, or at least the prohibition of gender discrimination, in the category of *jus cogens*. This fits perfectly in the mainstreaming concept: women's human rights are to move from the periphery to the core of international human rights, and the core of the core consists of those human rights with *jus cogens* value. In substance, this claim is not absurd, either, as there is a clear parallel with the prohibition of racial discrimination, which is a *jus cogens* rule. The symbolic value of this transformation cannot be overestimated. Eliminating gender bias from the inner core of international human rights would be a major victory for women's human rights. However, as *jus cogens* per definition changes slowly, this is not to be expected in the short term.

MULTIPLE SPECIFICITIES

If human rights are to be all-inclusive, they should take into account the relevant differences between men and women. Yet caution is needed to avoid efforts designed to fully include women resulting in the exclusion of some of them.

When the "women's movement" reacts against the invisibility of women in the conception of "humans" in dominant human rights discourse, it puts forward an image of "woman" that inevitably reflects the experiences of the dominant group in that movement. Within the organized women's movement acting on the international scene, the most powerful lobbying and agenda setting is generally done by white Western women. Minority women and non-Western women have strongly criticized their invisibility in the dominant feminist discourse. Even in face-to-face encounters, Western feminists often fail to listen to their sisters from the South.

For many non-Western women, Western feminism focuses too narrowly on gender discrimination. As one writer emphasized:

> The point is that factors other than gender figure integrally in the oppression of Third World women and that, even regarding patriarchy, many Third World women labour under indigenous inequitable gender relationships exacerbated by Western patriarchy, racism, and exploitation. . . .Third World women can embrace the concept of gender identity, but must reject an ideology based solely on gender. . . . We must create a feminist movement which struggles against those things which can clearly be shown to oppress women, whether based on race, sex, or class or resulting from imperialism.[34]

A certain degree of generalization is inherent in any group-based emancipation movement, and all generalizations are in some way exclusionist. Yet if generalization becomes essentialism, if internal diversity within the group is ignored, the exclusion becomes particularly serious. In the women's movement, this risk can be avoided if, in addition to the central theme of gender, other factors are taken into account. The contextualization of human rights in the pursuit of inclusive

---

33. Gayle Binion, "Human Rights: A Feminist Perspective," *HRQ* 17 (1995): 509–26, at 512. . . .
34. Cheryl Johnson-Odim, "Common Themes, Different Contexts: Third World Women and Feminism," in Chandra Talpade Mohanty, Ann Russo, and Lourdes Torres, eds., *Third World Women and the Politics of Feminism* (Bloomington: Indiana University Press, 1991), 32.

universality should, in principle, extend to all specificities that have been the basis for exclusion from the dominant model. For example, the claim of non-Western people to see the particularity of their economic situation and of their culture integrated in human rights is as strong as women's claim with regard to their gender specificity. Non-Western women find themselves at the crossroads of both sets of claims. Contemporary feminist discourse on international human rights recognizes the diversity of women around the world and embraces in principle the claims of women from the South for a stronger focus on development-related rights.[35] Still, in the overall picture of women's human rights claims, these claims remain underexposed. . . .

In principle, the above-discussed human rights claims of women and non-Western people are claims of groups, based on the communal features of their members that distinguish them from the dominant group. Yet, since the specificities of different groups are combined in individuals, the only way to avoid exclusion is to replace the group perspective with the perspective of the individuals concerned. Contrary to the abstract individuals on which the enlightenment conception of human rights relies, these should be contextualized individuals, with their relevant specificities. Hence, a consequence of inclusive universality in terms of method is that the perspective should be that of the (actual or potential) victim of human rights violations. This does not a priori exclude a conception of women's rights (or cultural rights for that matter) as group rights, but they must be conceived in function of the individual. As a result, on concrete issues involving a conflict between different specificities, the perspective of the individual(s) concerned is crucial. Some of the most problematic of these issues involve conflicts between the rights of women (as constructed by the dominant discourse) and cultural or religious rules or practices.

It is important to realize that Western feminist interpretations of a cultural practice may be totally disconnected from the experience of women who are "on the inside." Moreover, even if they experience a practice as discriminatory or repressive, adult women are capable of balancing any pain they might suffer against the positive benefit they derive from participating in their own culture. The right to make their own choice has to be protected by international human rights. This means that the human rights movement has to come out strongly in support of women's participation in the internal cultural debate about such rules and practices. If such debate results in changes that eliminate the oppressiveness of the rule or practice, a perfect solution is reached. It also means that individual women's right to opt out of certain practices or cultures has to be supported. The fact is that while forcing women to wear Islamic dress or to endure genital mutilation may be considered human rights violations, their right to choose to participate in such practices has to be respected. From an "insider" perspective, laws outlawing such practices can no more be supported than laws imposing them.

Going further, there is the issue of strategies and priorities. Female genital mutilation (FGM) is an example of an issue on which feminists have blundered immensely in the past. Without attempting to understand the perspective of "insider," they have called it "torture" and "barbaric" and alienated and angered African women who may be opposed to the practice yet demand respect for their culture. African women who have joined the fight against practices such as FGM should decide how to proceed and how to set priorities. . . . It is also a matter of strategy. Respect for other cultures is not incompatible with campaigning against certain cultural practices. Yet this campaigning has to give culture its due and be directed from inside, at the grassroots level. Moreover, the reasons for opposing the practice must be close to the experiences of the women who are most concerned. In most cases it is advisable to leave feminist theories of patriarchy at home. Sometimes it may even be advisable to leave human rights discourse at home.

Again, the importance of the "insider" perspective is not only a matter of democratic participation but also a matter of pragmatism.

35. See Adetoun O. Ilumoka, "African Women's Economic, Social and Cultural Rights," in Rebecca J. Cook, ed., *Human Rights of Women: National and International Perspectives* (Philadelphia: University of Pennsylvania Press, 1994); Nadia H. Youssef, "Women's Access to Productive Resources: The Need for Legal Instruments to Protect Women's Development Rights," in Peters and Wolper, *Women's Rights*, note 20, 279–88.

Feminist analysis has long been developing methodologies to deal with the diversity of voices in women's rights discourse in both domestic and international settings and with the complexity of real-life situations. In particular, feminist scholars have addressed not only the conflicting loyalties of women in traditional societies to gender equality, on the one hand, and cultural practices, on the other, but also the multiplicity of oppressions suffered by poor women, minority women, and homosexual women. More than most approaches, feminism should be able to overcome the dilemma between universality and diversity.[36] Among the many benefits of feminist analysis to be integrated in mainstream human rights, this capacity is crucial.

THE NEXT FIFTY YEARS

What developments can be expected over the next fifty years? Formal equality of women and men before the law (the "sameness" approach) is no longer contested yet still has to be realized over much of the world. It should be a realistic goal to eradicate all formal gender discrimination over the foreseeable future. At the same time, education and increasing activism should substantially enhance an awareness among women about their rights and an understanding on the part of men how the conditions under which women live regularly subject them to gross violations.

It is unlikely that many new "women's human rights" instruments will be created. Yet those already set up have some unexplored potential. In particular, CEDAW should prove more effective [now that its] Optional Protocol [has entered] into force. The individual complaint mechanism not only will benefit many individual women but will also lead to the development of a case law that will elaborate and strengthen international women's rights norms and that is likely to inspire domestic judges.

We can also anticipate that women will increasingly favor "transforming" human rights to respond to their special experience while remaining universally applicable. This is to be preferred over the "special rights" approach, because it shows more respect for women's diversity and

because it does not exclude men from innovations in the field of human rights protection.

Recent transformations that have been taking shape will likely be strengthened. The public/private divide should no longer be considered a legal obstacle, yet the extension of human rights protection in the private sphere still needs to gain general recognition and acceptance. The standard-setting developments in the area of domestic violence are promising, yet it is unfortunate that they are restricted to women.

Moreover, it is likely that private perpetrators will increasingly be held responsible for human rights violations in international (criminal) tribunals, in domestic courts and in extrajudicial human rights campaigns. With regard to upgrading and reorienting economic and social rights, the women's movement has been less successful. . . . In the light of the expected strengthening of the position of non-Western activists within the women's movement, it is possible that feminists will build a coalition with others, including the third and fourth world movements and organized labor, in support of economic and social rights.

The new standards that have been developing in the areas of reproductive rights, sexual violence, asylum, and slavery-like practices are likely to be more solidly established in the near future. It is hoped that their benefits will be extended to men as well as women. Furthermore, improvements are also likely in the use of gender-sensitive language, the representation of women in human rights bodies, and the integration of a gender perspective in human rights methodologies. These improvements will in turn have an indirect positive effect on many other issues. Non-Western women from developing countries will certainly be more effective in international activities, arguing that issues of peace and economic development are critical to advancements in human rights and that those directly affected, the "insiders," have to resolve conflicts that arise between human rights and cultural practices, on their own terms rather than on any abstract notion of right and wrong. The future, as always, is difficult, if not impossible, to predict. Nonetheless, there is considerable hope that the forces of change already unleashed will greatly improve the lives of millions of women all over the world.

36. On cultural relativism versus universalism, see Reading 3 by Burns Weston in Chapter 1 of this volume.

QUESTIONS FOR REFLECTION AND DISCUSSION

1. What, according to Eva Brems, are the "rights of women," how are they understood and implemented, and what are the failures of the existing international legal order in achieving genuine equality for women?

2. Brems writes: "Equal treatment does not always mean 'the same treatment.' There are many different conceptions of equality and nondiscrimination, including those that recognize that equal treatment requires different treatment when there are relevant differences." Is it possible to read UDHR Article 2(1) in this way? In any event, given the biological differences between men and women, is it, on final analysis, *equality* that women seek or should seek? Or is it *equity*? For example, do women in general wish to forgo maternity rights to be equal with men in all respects? Or might they prefer, not the loss of maternity rights but, rather, the extension of birthing rights such that men might have paternity rights of comparable worth? What are the implications of this line of reasoning for CEDAW and other women's rights instruments that are based on the principle of equality? What does Brems say?

3. A leading feminist legal scholar writes that "many of the relationships of subordination sanctioned by the law are so deeply engrained that they appear quite natural." Hilary Charlesworth, "What Are 'Women's International Human Rights?,'" in Rebecca Cook, ed., *Human Rights of Women: National and International Perspectives* (Philadelphia: University of Pennsylvania Press, 1994), 58–84. A leading feminist social scientist and activist writes that "much of the abuse against women is part of a large socioeconomic web that entraps women, making them vulnerable to abuses which cannot be delineated as exclusively political or solely caused by states. . . . Female subordination runs so deep that it still is viewed as inevitable or natural rather than as a politically constructed reality maintained by patriarchal interests, ideology, and institutions." Charlotte Bunch, "Women's Rights as Human Rights: Toward a Re-Vision of Human Rights," *HRQ* 12 (1990): 486–512, at 488, 491. Are women not adequately protected by gender neutral guarantees such as the right to vote? What does Eva Brems say? What do you think? Why? Should women's rights be considered a separate category of human rights? What does Eva Brems say? What do you think? Why?

4. Consider the three main approaches to the protection of women's rights cited by Brems—*sameness*, *specifity/flexibility*, and *specificity/transformation*. Which one is best suited to address practices such as the following and why: (a) female feticide in India and China; (b) child marriage; (c) the Islamic law rule that a daughter inherit one-third of what a son inherits; (d) customary Afghani law that permits the family of a criminal to transfer young girls or women to the family of his victim as reparation for the crime; (e) the common Turkish judicial practice of reducing a rapist's sentence if he marries his victim; (f) American women's lack of access to paid maternity leave with job security, a benefit to which European women generally are entitled by law; (g) rape and forced pregnancies suffered by women in armed conflicts around the world; (h) trafficking in women and girls; (i) voting-by-proxy laws authorizing husbands to vote on behalf of their wives; (j) barring women from passing on their nationality to their children; (k) polygamy. Can the approaches cited by Brems contribute to the eradication of the human rights violations listed above? The advancement of women's human rights generally?

5. The author argues that for women to have their human rights fully realized and protected, it is necessary to examine and question the basis of value orientation of human rights law itself, national as well as international . What does she mean by this? Why does she consider this task important? Do you agree with her? Why? Why not?

6. Most of women's international human rights law, Brems observes, reflects the traditional (Western) liberal understanding of rights and freedoms. Founded on the principle of "nondiscrimination, it pursues equal treatment with men in the public arena (education, employment, health care, legal standing, etc.) but leaves the private sphere (family, home, intimate personal relations) largely outside its purview. Do you agree with this analysis of the liberal understanding of women's rights? Should not the state be disallowed from intervening in the private sphere as a general matter? What about spousal abuse, for example? What are or should be the limits of state intervention in the home, if any?

7. The principle of nondiscrimination is enshrined in American law. Has it helped American women enjoy their full human rights? In any event, given that both CEDAW and

American law are founded on the liberal principle of equal rights or nondiscrimination, why does the United States resist ratifying CEDAW, remaining the only Western country that has yet to do so? What are possible points of conflict between the CEDAW text and American law that might contribute to the U.S. government's reluctance to ratify CEDAW? Or is that reluctance simply reflective of a wider mistrust of international instruments of binding effect?

8. Try to imagine a CEDAW in which the rights of women are defined by the criterion of what women fear will happen to them. What would such a text look like? Would it be different from the current CEDAW? How? How not?

9. Brems contends that the very boundaries of traditional human rights law must be redefined if international legal measures that address the rights of women and girls (e.g., CEDAW) are to have real effect. There appears to be room for optimism in this regard. See, e.g., Georgina Ashworth, "The Silencing of Women," in Tim Dunne and Nicholas J. Wheeler, eds., *Human Rights in Global Politics* (Cambridge: Cambridge University Press, 1999), 259–78. Before the 1980s, Ashworth notes, not even human rights NGOs were inclined to treat women's rights as human rights, and specific references to women in international institutions were limited to their procreative function, echoing a long European tradition of jurisprudence in which women were systematically denied legal personhood. But since the late 1980s, according to Ashworth, women's human rights are no longer "invisible" in international bodies and among the human rights community, and a women-oriented "reconceptualization" of international human rights law has started to take place. Ashworth credits a small number of dedicated NGOs for changing the international climate by taking it upon themselves in both official and unofficial circles to record the terrible discrepancies between the realities of women's daily lives and human rights standards. Does Brems agree? Do you? What evidence? What future role should NGOs play? Should UN bodies rely on them? If so, how? What does Brems say? On human rights NGOs generally, see Reading 31 by Richard Pierre Claude in Chapter 8 of this volume.

10. The 1999 Optional Protocol to the Convention on the Elimination of all Forms of Discrimination Against Women (referenced in Documentary Appendix B) affords enforcement mechanisms through which individual complaints, fact-finding, and inquiry processes in support of women's rights may proceed. But how likely is this to happen? According to Ursula O'Hare, "Realizing Human Rights for Women," *HRQ* 21, no. 2 (1999): 364–402, at 373, "mechanisms in place for enforcing women's human rights remain weak" in comparison to those available for "mainstream" international law. For one example, states parties to CEDAW have lodged many reservations to specific articles in it. Most of these, according to O'Hare, are incompatible with CEDAW's object and purpose because, she says, they effectively exempt the states parties from enacting the kinds of legal reforms that are most needed to ensure the equality of their male and female populations as required by CEDAW (for pertinent information about these reservations, see the website of the UN's Division for the Advancement of Women at http://www.un.org/womenwatch/daw/cedaw/reservations.htm. Reservations incompatible with the purposes of international treaties are impermissible according to the Vienna Convention on the Law of Treaties. Yet, however incompatible and therefore invalid, such reservations nevertheless require the inconvenience of challenge. What explains this state of affairs? Is there value in allowing state parties such latitude in fulfilling their treaty obligations? Why? Why not? Does it risk leaving women's human rights law without serious bite? Why? Why not?

11. A number of decisions by the European Court of Human Rights extend the state's responsibility beyond the negative obligation not to violate individual human rights to a positive obligation to ensure that human rights can be enjoyed. In one such case, the Court ruled that in failing to assist a woman financially in her escape from her violent spouse, the State of Ireland violated her right to respect for her family life. *Airey v. Ireland*, 30 Eur. Ct. H.R. (ser. B) at 3 (1979). In other cases, the court has extended the state's positive obligations in the private sphere relative to the right to be free from torture, inhumane, and degrading treatment and the right to life. See, e.g., O'Hare, "Realizing Human Rights for Women, Question 10. In June 2003 the U.S. Supreme Court ruled that same-sex intimate behavior in the home was constitutionally protected. See *Lawrence v. Texas*, 539 U.S. 558 (2003). In so doing, the Court cited for the first time in its history a decision of the European Court of Human Rights in which homosexual acts in the home were judged to

be protected by the right to respect for private and family life. See *Dudgeon v. United Kingdom*, 40 Eur. Ct. H.R. (ser. B) at 573 (1983). Do the above-cited cases redefine the private sphere and the concept of privacy? If so, how? Do they constitute hopeful signs for the future of women's human rights in the U.S. and internationally? Why? Why not?

12. Compare CEDAW with the Declaration on the Elimination of All Forms of Intolerance and of Discrimination Based on Religious Belief (each referenced in Documentary Appendix B). Jack Greenberg has asked: "If a religion relegates women to a certain societal or familial status which otherwise would be deemed discrimination on the basis of sex, which convention [sic] governs?" "Race, Sex, and Religious Discrimination in International Law," in Theodor Meron, ed., *Human Rights in International Law: Legal and Policy Issues* (New York: Oxford University Press, 1984), 2: 307–39, at 330. Putting aside the legal distinction between a convention and a declaration, how do you answer Greenberg's question?

13. In "The Rights of Women and International Law in the Muslim Context," *Whittier Law Review* 9 (1987): 491–516, at 516, Abdullahi An-Na`im has observed that many Muslim countries have ratified at least one of the three main instruments related to women's rights. He offers three alternative explanations:
(a) They do not feel bound by Shari`a [Islamic religious law].
(b) They do not take their international obligations very seriously.
(c) They have taken a view of the relevant principles of Shari`a which is consistent with these international obligations
An-Na`im favors the third explanation, and urges a critical reexamination of Shari`a by Muslims, working toward a synthesis of Islamic law and women's rights. In defense of this gradualist approach, he argues that "It is irresponsible and inhumane to encourage these women to move too fast too soon and to repudiate many of the established norms of their culture or religious law, without regard to the full implications of such action." Do you agree with An-Na`im? Why? Why not? Can you think of any analogous gender-based practices in the West, the eradication of which might arguably require a gradualist approach?

14. Harold Hongju Koh argues in Reading 24 in this volume that international human rights laws are imperfectly "enforced" through a "transnational legal process" in which, ultimately, international norms are "internalized by domestic legal systems" and thereby given effect in ways that respond to the particularized concerns of domestic governments. Viewed through this lens, how have women's human rights been "enforced" in the United States since the drafting of CEDAW? Does the U.S. failure to ratify CEDAW *necessarily* mean that the U.S. is not enforcing its terms? What would Koh say? Does his understanding of "enforcement" militate in favor of a relativistic approach to international standards?

---

11. MARYELLEN FULLERTON *The International and National Protection of Refugees*

HISTORICAL BACKGROUND

Since ancient times people have been forced to flee their homes and seek refuge in other lands. The Bible describes places of asylum for those who are persecuted. The Greeks and Romans similarly set aside certain areas to provide refuge to individuals fleeing for their lives. In medieval times, history records that whole populations sometimes were forced to flee and seek refuge. Religious intolerance led to the expulsion of thousands of Jews from Spain in 1492, followed ten years later by the expulsion of thousands of Muslims. Protestants fled France after the Saint Bartholomew Day massacres in 1572 and again after the repeal of the Edict of Nantes in 1685. More Protestants were expelled from Salzburg in 1731; thousands of Jews were forced out of Bohemia in 1744.

Political persecution also played a part. For

example, the British Governor of Nova Scotia, suspicious of the political sympathies of French-Acadian farmers, deported thousands from their homes in 1755. The expansionist policy of the U.S. government in the 19th century resulted in mass deportations of Native Americans from their ancestral lands to government reservations on the other side of the continent. The Balkan Wars generated forced migrations of large populations of Greeks, Bulgarians, and Turks. The Russian Revolution triggered waves of refugees. The Nazi regime in Germany reached new depths in the expulsion of national groups and the forced transfer of whole populations from lands their families had inhabited for centuries.

Despite the international consensus, codified in the Charter of the International Military Tribunal at Nuremberg, that forced deportation of civilian populations constitutes a crime against humanity, refugee movements have continued unabated in the post-World War II era. The victorious allies expelled millions of Germans from densely populated territory that was awarded to Poland. Huge national groups were deported from the European portion of the Soviet Union to Central Asia. Millions of Muslims fled to Pakistan and Hindus fled to India at the time of the partition of British India in 1947. The Hungarian revolt in 1956 triggered many refugees, as did the overthrow of Salvador Allende in Chile in 1973 and the fall of Saigon in 1975. Africa witnessed the expulsion of large numbers of noncitizens from Ghana in 1969, Asians from Uganda in 1972, Egyptians from Libya in 1976, Rwandans from Uganda in 1982, and nearly two million individuals from Nigeria in 1983. The civil wars in Sudan and Sri Lanka generated substantial numbers of refugees throughout the 1980s and 1990s, as had the civil war in East Pakistan (now Bangladesh) in the 1970s.

At the century's close, widespread violence produced millions of refugees and displaced persons. The conflict in the Persian Gulf was followed by the dissolution of former Yugoslavia, where war and "ethnic cleansing" in Croatia and Bosnia-Herzegovina displaced more than three million people. Several years later, nearly one million fled from Kosovo to Montenegro, Macedonia, Albania, and other countries. In Africa, the genocide in Rwanda and Burundi forced millions more to flee, an exodus of biblical proportions, and the violence and refugee movements spread to other countries in the Great Lakes region of Central Africa. West Africa was not spared, as armed conflict engulfed Sierra Leone, Liberia, and the Ivory Coast, and created many more refugees.

The beginning of the twenty-first century brought some positive developments. More than two million refugees returned to Afghanistan; close to one million ethnic Albanians returned to Kosovo; and 400,000 Bosnians returned to their homeland. Due to these and other repatriations, the world-wide refugee population numbered roughly twelve million in 2002, compared to fifteen million in 1995. This was offset, however, by a huge rise in the number of internally displaced people. These individuals, forced from their homes by persecution, armed conflict, and other violence, numbered almost twenty-five million in 2003, approximately twelve million of whom were in Africa. Although they did not cross an international border, they suffered the age-old fate of refugees: they were uprooted, dispossessed, and vulnerable.

Although refugees are an age-old phenomenon, societal responses to refugees during the past century have differed substantially from those in earlier times. Before the emergence of industrialized societies and the rise of the welfare state, rulers often welcomed refugees into their realm, anticipating that artisans would benefit the society they joined, while others seeking refuge would increase the taxpayer rolls and enlarge the pool of those who could be conscripted for military service. There was no corresponding public duty to care for refugees from another land. Private charity might sustain refugees for a short time, but quasi-permanent government-supported refugee camps were unknown. Refugees became self-supporting fairly quickly or perished.

During the nineteenth and twentieth centuries, governments grew more wary of refugees. The growth of "nation-states" and the creation of national identities led to the view that refugees and other outsiders threatened a society's security and cultural cohesion by introducing disease, subversive ideas, and foreign traditions. Simultaneously, post-Enlightenment societies gradually assumed greater responsibility for the poor but did not want to see their numbers swelled by large groups of outsiders. The ironic result was that, as governmental obligations to assist the helpless and indigent became a fundamental tenet of society, states began to impose extremely restrictive conditions on those who sought to enter. This tension between generosity toward those at home and wariness of those from abroad still persists and, in many ways, characterizes the responses of developed nations to the millions of refugees in the world today. The turn of the century has been characterized by "compassion fatigue" in the industrialized world, with many nations enacting laws to restrict the access of refugees to their territory and to reduce the legal and social protections available to those already within their territory.

INTERNATIONAL PROTECTION OF REFUGEES

The disintegration of the Turkish, Russian, and Austro-Hungarian empires in the early twentieth century emphasized the international scope of refugee movements. Millions of refugees fled in all directions. International organizations dedicated to refugee assistance were created; with them came attempts to define legally who is a refugee. Early definitions tended to describe refugees in terms of their nationality, implicitly recognizing that political events had triggered the flight of certain groups of people. The cataclysm of World War II and the streams of humanity that it displaced gave impetus to the 1951 Convention Relating to the Status of Refugees[1] (referred to throughout this chapter simply as the Convention), which defined a refugee as follows:

> any person who . . . owing to well-founded fear of being persecuted for reasons of race, religion, nationality, membership of a particular social group or political opinion, is outside the country of his nationality and is unable, or owing to such fear, is unwilling to avail himself of the protection of that country, or who, not having a nationality and being outside the country of his former habitual residence as a result of such events, is unable or, owing to such fear, is unwilling to return to it.

This definition diverged from earlier definitions in several important respects. It took a more universal approach by specifying five different bases for persecution that can occur in any society, rather than listing specific national or religious groups at risk in certain societies. It also has been interpreted as rejecting a group determination approach, indicating instead that refugee status should be decided on an individual basis. The definition's World War II origin is revealed in its implicit vision of persecution as actions by a totalitarian state systematically oppressing individuals deemed undesirable due to their personal characteristics and in its restriction to refugee situations caused by events which occurred prior to 1951. This last restriction, however, was removed by the 1967 Protocol to the Convention Relating to the Status of Refugees,[2] which has been ratified by most of the countries that ratified the 1951 Convention.[3]

[*Eds.*—The author notes the promulgation by the African Union of the 1969 Convention Governing the Specific Aspects of the Refugee Problem in Africa,[4] in which the definition of "refugee" was expanded to include persons forced to seek refuge by internal public order disturbances, however caused. Further, she notes the adoption by a group of Latin American states of the 1984 Cartageña Declaration which similarly expanded the definition to include those threatened by "generalized violence, foreign aggression, internal conflicts, massive violations of human rights or other circumstances which have seriously disturbed public order." The African Union Convention has been adopted only by states in Africa; similarly, only "a relatively small number of countries," albeit including the General Assembly of the OAS, has adopted the Cartagena definition. The author then discusses the 1951 Convention and its 1967 Protocol.]

THE CONVENTION AND PROTOCOL RELATING TO THE STATUS OF REFUGEES

More than [141] countries have ratified the Convention and its 1967 Protocol. Although this indicates that there is a consensus concerning

---

1. Concluded July 28, 1951, referenced in Documentary Appendix B.
2. Concluded Jan. 31, 1967, referenced in Documentary Appendix B.
3. The United States is a party to the 1967 Protocol (with qualification). It is not a party to the 1951 Convention. For a comprehensive up to date list of all the states parties to each of these instruments, see Weston and Carlson, 3: Appendix I, III.G.4 (Convention) and III.G.8 (Protocol).
4. Concluded Sept. 10, 1969, referenced in Documentary Appendix B

who qualifies as a refugee, the Convention and Protocol contain major weaknesses. Neither provides a mechanism under which individuals can protest the denial of refugee status by a ratifying state. Even more significantly, neither imposes an obligation to allow refugees to enter and reside in the territory of a state. Despite these flaws, the Convention and Protocol remain the most significant international instruments for the protection of refugees. Accordingly, it is useful to examine the components of the Convention refugee definition, as interpreted by the Office of the United Nations High Commissioner for Refugees (UNHCR).[5]

Well-Founded Fear of Persecution

To gain Convention refugee status, individuals must show that they subjectively fear persecution and that their fear is rational or reasonable, based on objective facts. Past persecution, or credible threats of future persecution, directed at an individual or at similarly situated persons would support a conclusion that a well-founded fear exists.

A refugee must fear *persecution*, as opposed to conditions such as poverty or natural disaster. The concept of persecution is flexible. Threats to life, bodily harm, torture, prolonged detention, repeated interrogations and arrests, internal exile, and other serious human rights violations constitute persecution. Discrimination generally does not unless it entails serious restrictions on important rights. Persecution typically stems from action by government authorities, but it also may include action by private individuals if government officials cannot or will not protect the victims.

Bases of Persecution

Recognition as a refugee is predicated on persecution based on one of five grounds: race, religion, nationality, membership in a particular social group, or political opinion. Any combination of these reasons suffices, but persecution based solely on a different ground, such as purely personal dislike, does not.

Race is used in the broadest sense and includes ethnic groups and social groups of common descent.[6]

Religion also has a broad meaning, including identification with a group that tends to share common traditions or beliefs, as well as the active practice of religion.

Nationality obviously includes an individual's citizenship, lack of citizenship, or former citizenship. In many parts of the world, though, nationality refers not to formal citizenship, but to the language, culture, and ethnic background of a group. For these reasons, persecution of ethnic, linguistic, and cultural groups within a population also may be deemed persecution based on nationality.

A particular social group refers to people who share a similar background, habits, or social status. This category often overlaps with persecution based on one of the other four grounds. It has been applied to families of capitalists, landowners, entrepreneurs, former members of the military, students, tribal groups, and individuals who violate the caste system. Recently, some refugee authorities have recognized certain groups defined by gender and sexual orientation as protected social groups.

Political opinion refers to ideas not tolerated by the authorities, including opinions critical of government policies and methods. It includes opinions attributed to an individual by the authorities, even if the individual does not, in fact, hold that opinion. Persecution based on political opinion presupposes that the authorities are aware—or will become aware—of the opinion. Individuals who conceal their political opinions until after they have fled their countries may be eligible for refugee status, if they can show that their views are likely to subject them to persecution if they return to their homeland.

Outside the Country of Nationality or Former Habitual Residence

Applicants for refugee status must be outside the country of their nationality [or] their former habitual residence. The 1951 Convention does not require that refugees must be outside their

---

5. See UN Office of the High Commissioner for Refugees, *Handbook on Procedures and Criteria for Determining Refugee Status Under the 1951 Convention and the 1967 Protocol Relating to the Status of Refugees*, rev. ed. (Geneva: UNHCR, 1992).

6. For helpful discussion on the meaning of "race," see note 49 in Reading 9 by Paul Gordon Lauren in this chapter.

countries due to persecution. Individuals may have left their country for purely private reasons, such as to study abroad, but circumstances may have changed since departure so that the individuals now fear persecution if they return.

Unable or Unwilling to Return to the Former Country

Refugee applicants are unable to return to their former country when the country denies passport facilities or refuses to accept the individuals or when the absence of diplomatic relations prevents their return. Refugees also may be unable to avail themselves of the protection of the country of their nationality if a war or other serious disturbance prevents the country from offering effective protection.

Individuals who are able to return to their former country, but are unwilling to do so, may qualify for refugee status in certain instances. Their unwillingness must be due to a well-founded fear of persecution based on race, religion, nationality, membership in a social group, or political opinion. Other reasons for unwillingness to return do not satisfy the refugee situation.

Loss of Refugee Status

The Convention and Protocol list six circumstances under which individuals recognized as refugees may lose that status because they no longer need international protection:

- A refugee has voluntarily [and not merely temporarily] accepted the protection of the country of nationality.
- A refugee has voluntarily reacquired his or her nationality, which had previously been lost.
- A refugee has acquired a new nationality and enjoys the protection of the country of new nationality.
- A refugee has voluntarily [and permanently] "reestablished" in the country where persecution was previously feared.
- The reasons for becoming a refugee have [permanently] ceased to exist.
- The reasons for a stateless person to seek refuge have ceased [and return to the refugee's former country of residence is possible].

Persons Excluded from Refugee Status

The Convention and Protocol explicitly exclude from refugee status those individuals who, despite satisfying the refugee definition, fall into the following categories:

- Persons who already receive protection or assistance from UN agencies other than the UN High Commissioner for Refugees. This currently applies to Palestinian refugees who fall within the mandate of the UN Relief and Works Agency (UNRWA).
- Persons who have been granted the rights and obligations of nationals in the country in which they have gained residence. This would include, for example, ethnic Germans from other lands who have the right to resettle and exercise the rights of citizens in Germany.
- Persons who have committed crimes against peace, war crimes, or crimes against humanity.
- Persons who have committed a serious nonpolitical crime outside the country of refuge prior to admission as a refugee. A serious crime means a capital offense or a grave act punishable by a severe sentence [but not political crimes unless disproportionate to the political objective].
- Persons guilty of acts contrary to the purposes and principles of the United Nations. This includes criminal acts undertaken by persons in positions of power in their states.

With respect to the last three categories, there is no requirement of proof of criminal prosecution and conviction; it is sufficient that there are serious reasons for believing that the refugee applicant committed the proscribed acts.

- Recently, former child soldiers pressed into service by insurgent groups or by government security forces have faced challenges during asylum proceedings.

Non-Refoulement and Other Limitations on Rejection and Expulsion of Refugees

Although the Convention and Protocol do not expressly require state parties to admit refugees to their territory, they do contain specific provisions that limit the discretion enjoyed by a state. Article 33 contains the most significant limitation, the principle of *non-refoulement*, which explicitly prohibits a state from expelling or returning a refugee "in any manner whatsoever to the frontiers of territories where his life or freedom would be threatened on account of his race, religion, nationality, membership of a particular social group or political opinion."

There are only two exceptions: refugees who are reasonably believed to be a danger to the security of the receiving country and refugees who have been convicted by a final judgment of a particularly serious crime and are a danger to the receiving country. Many now view non-refoulement as a principle of customary international law that is binding on all states, even those that have not ratified the Convention and Protocol.

Article 31 prohibits states from penalizing refugees who enter or remain illegally, provided that (1) the refugees have come directly from a land where their lives or freedom were threatened, and (2) the refugees present themselves to the authorities without delay and show good cause for their illegal entry or presence. Article 32 prohibits states from expelling a refugee lawfully present in a country, unless there are compelling reasons of national security or public order.

Although they do not guarantee refugees the right to permanent lawful residence, these three articles, taken together, have effectively provided protection to millions of refugees who have crossed frontiers in search of safety.

Rights of Those Granted Refugee Status

The Convention and Protocol require that states grant certain substantive rights to individuals that the state has recognized as refugees. All refugees must be granted *identity papers and travel documents* that allow them to travel outside the country.

Refugees must receive *the same treatment as nationals of the host country* with regard to the following rights: free exercise of religion and religious education; free access to the courts, including legal assistance; protection of industrial property, such as inventions and trade names; protection of literary, artistic, and scientific work; access to elementary education [and] public relief and assistance; access to rationed goods; pro-tection provided by labor legislation [and] social security; and equal treatment by taxing authorities.

Refugees must receive the *most favorable treatment provided to nationals of a foreign country* with regard to the following rights: the right to belong to trade unions; the right to belong to other nonpolitical nonprofit organizations; and the right to engage in wage-earning employ-ment. Restrictions applicable to foreign nationals regarding wage-earning employment do not apply to refugees in the following circumstances: (1) the refugee was exempt from such restrictions when the Convention entered into force in the host country; (2) the refugee has resided in the host country for three years; or (3) the refugee's spouse or child is a national of the host country.

Refugees must receive the *most favorable treatment possible, which must be at least as favorable as that accorded foreigners generally in the same circumstances*, with regard to the following rights: the right to own property; the right to practice a liberal profession; the right to self-employment in agriculture, industry, handicrafts, and commerce, including the right to establish companies; access to housing; and access to higher education, including eligibility for scholarships and fee waivers.

Refugees must receive the *same treatment as that accorded to noncitizens generally* with regard to the following rights: the right to choose their place of residence; the right to move freely within the country; and all other rights not explicitly provided in the Convention.

ROLE OF THE UNITED NATIONS HIGH COMMISSIONER FOR REFUGEES

In 1950, the UN General Assembly established an international agency to assist refugees, the Office of the United Nations High Commissioner for Refugees (UNHCR). Initially, the mandate of the UNHCR was generally coextensive with the refugee definition adopted by the 1951 Convention. The UNHCR acted to provide material assistance and legal protection to individuals with a well-founded fear of persecution based on race, religion, nationality, membership in a social group, or political opinion.

Refugee movements do not always correspond to legal definitions, however, and in 1959 the General Assembly authorized the UNHCR to use its "good offices" to assist refugees who did not fall strictly within the Convention definition. In pursuing its expanded mandate to help refugees, the UNHCR eschewed the individualized approach generally adopted by parties to the Convention. This enabled the UNHCR to respond quickly and effectively to large-scale refugee movements [and] to assist groups of refugees without criticizing the political conditions in the country of origin.

The UNHCR is active in all phases of refugee work. It provides the institutional framework for coordinating international refugee efforts. It organizes material assistance to refugees around the globe, establishing refugee camps, delivering food, and arranging for medical care. In addition to responding to emergency conditions, the UNHCR undertakes longer-term assistance, such as education and training programs. The UNHCR is particularly active in countries of first asylum, i.e., countries such as Thailand and Tanzania that have received refugees from nearby lands and allowed them to remain on a temporary basis. This aspect of the UNHCR effort has led to serious dilemmas in recent years, as refugee camps administered by UNHCR have sometimes been effectively controlled by militias who obstruct resolution of the crisis and use the refugees as tools to further their political and military goals.

The UNHCR's primary mission, the voluntary repatriation of refugees, requires it to focus much of its energy and resources on arranging the return of refugees from countries of first asylum to their homelands and monitoring their safety and welfare after their return. When repatriation is not possible, the UNHCR works to integrate refugees into the local community and its economy. As a last resort, the UNHCR coordinates efforts to resettle refugees in other countries.

[*Eds.*—The author goes on to observe that these tasks are fraught with difficulty, as evidenced in particular by the gruesome events in and around Central African refugee camps in the mid-1990s].

In addition to providing direct assistance to refugees, the UNHCR spearheads the development of international and national legislation and policies to improve the legal protection of refugees. The UNHCR offers training programs on international law for immigration officials, lawyers, and refugee advocates; participates in the refugee determination process in some countries; helps asylum seekers locate *pro bono* legal counsel; intervenes in domestic cases that raise important issues of refugee law; and provides information in support of refugee applications.

NATIONAL PROTECTION OF REFUGEES

As the Convention does not require states to grant asylum, legal protection for refugees is generally found in national laws. It is significant,

then, that many of the states that have ratified the Convention and Protocol have not adopted domestic legislation to implement these agreements. This is not to say that all of these countries have turned their backs on refugees. Many states without refugee legislation have provided refuge to tremendous numbers of individuals fleeing persecution, and this humane response has been essential in saving the lives of millions. However, it has rarely resulted in legal protection, and refugees in these countries often remain in limbo, unable to regularize their status and proceed with a normal life.

Those states that have enacted domestic legislation to implement the Convention and Protocol have created a wide variety of measures concerning refugees. Although the details of refugee legislation vary enormously from state to state, there are certain themes that recur.

Almost all states with national legislation regarding refugees have adopted the basic Convention refugee definition, although variations exist with respect to the bases for exclusion from or loss of refugee status. Generally, national legislation entitles those individuals recognized as refugees to official identification documents and to lawful residence. A recent worrying trend, often referred to as the "safe third country" principle, is the denial of refugee status and the residence permits associated with it to individuals who satisfy the refugee definition but who passed through a state in which they did not fear persecution en route to the state in question.

PROCEDURES FOR DETERMINING REFUGEE STATUS

The Convention and Protocol require no particular procedure for determining refugee status [but the UNHCR] recommends the following basic guidelines:

1. The competent official . . . to whom applicants address themselves at the border or in the territory of a state should have clear instructions for dealing with [refugee] cases. . . . The official should be required to act in accordance with the principle of *non-refoulement* and to refer such cases to a higher authority.
2. Applicants should receive necessary guidance as to the procedure to be followed.
3. There should be a clearly identified authority . . . with responsibility for examining requests for refugee status and taking a decision in the first instance.

4. Applicants should be given all facilities necessary, including the services of a competent interpreter, to submit their cases to the appropriate authorities. Applicants should also be given the opportunity . . . to contact a representative of UNHCR.

5. If applicants are recognized as refugees, they should be so informed and issued documents certifying their refugee status.

6. If applicants are not recognized, they should be given a reasonable time to appeal from the decision . . . according to the prevailing system.

7. Applicants should be permitted to remain in the country pending a decision on their initial request by the competent authority referred to in paragraph (3) above, unless it has been established by that authority that the request is clearly abusive. Applicants should also be permitted to remain in the country while an appeal to a higher administrative authority or to the courts is pending.[7]

Although these standards are not part of a legally binding international instrument, they can be extremely useful politically in encouraging states to improve their refugee determination procedures. These standards also might be considered to constitute the minimum norms of due process, which, according to other international instruments, must be extended to all persons.

States that have enacted national legislation to implement the Convention and Protocol generally have designated a central authority with jurisdiction over requests for refugee status, although the details vary significantly from state to state. Many countries provide some role for the UNHCR in their refugee determination process. Often, a UNHCR representative is a regular observer or advisor to the government body that decides refugee cases, and UNHCR representatives may assist individual refugee applicants. In other instances, the UNHCR role is more limited and may be restricted to activities such as providing letters in support of selected individual applications.

In a majority of the states with implementing legislation, the authorities must provide reasons for negative decisions, and rejected refugee applicants have a right to seek a reconsideration or appeal of the decision. The grounds for pursuing

an appeal vary, as do the bodies to which an appeal can be made. Some states allow appeals based on factual or legal contentions; others will reconsider a decision only if newly discovered facts are alleged. Some states provide no judicial review; others allow appeals to both administrative and judicial tribunals. National legislation also varies widely as to whether a refugee applicant may remain in the country while an appeal is pending.

DE FACTO REFUGEES

Although, as mentioned earlier, national implementing legislation generally adopts the 1951 Convention refugee definition, a number of states have concluded that this definition does not provide sufficient protection. As a result, some states have created additional categories of persons that deserve protection. *De facto*, or humanitarian, refugees are those who do not meet the Convention definition but nonetheless have a compelling need for protection. For example, persons fleeing generalized violence or internal turmoil may not be able to demonstrate that they are likely to be targeted for persecution, but they may be able to show that their lives would be at great risk if they were to return to their homeland. They might be permitted to remain in states that recognize *de facto* or humanitarian refugees.

This concept takes many different forms. Some legal systems distinguish between *de facto* refugees and humanitarian refugees, using the first term to denote applicants whose cases are quite similar to, but not as compelling as, those that fall within the 1951 Convention definition, and using the second term to denote applicants who are at serious risk but whose fear is based on conditions not enumerated in the Convention definition. Other countries make further distinctions. For example, German legislation recognizes multiple refugee categories: Convention refugees who have not passed through a safe country en route to Germany (asylum status), Convention refugees who have passed through a safe country but cannot be returned there (lesser asylum status), refugees who do not satisfy the Convention definition but would

---

7. These standards were recommended by the Executive Committee of the High Commissioner's program, Report on the 28th Session, Conclusion on International Protection, UN Doc. A/32/12/Add.1 (1977), 12–16.

face torture or serious threats to their life or freedom if returned (humanitarian residence permit status), and war refugees (temporary protection status granted for periods of six months).

In other states, there are fewer gradations. The distinctions [can nevertheless] be dizzying, and it behooves refugee advocates to master the details of this concept in their country.

The development of the concept of *de facto* refugee has been controversial. Many believe that its existence encourages governments to apply the Convention definition in an excessively strict manner, thus denying traditional refugee status to many who deserve it. Nonetheless, it is useful to remember that the purpose behind the *de facto* or humanitarian refugee concept is a benevolent one, and, as this concept is strongly entrenched in some states, it is crucial for all those dealing with refugees to be aware of it.

RECENT DEVELOPMENTS

The waning years of the twentieth century witnessed a growth in restrictive measures affecting refugees. The initially progressive refugee efforts that accompanied the dissolution of communist regimes [in the early 1990s in Eastern Europe] have gradually changed to more restrictive policies, as the newly emerging democracies have followed the developed countries' lead in adopting measures to limit and deter refugees and asylum seekers.

During the 1990s, Western European countries joined together in several efforts that have had major impacts on refugees. Most of the European Union (EU) countries worked to abolish internal borders and simultaneously raise external barriers to entry to the region. Most EU countries also ratified guidelines to determine which state is responsible for examining an asylum application. As the twenty-first century dawned, the EU expanded its membership from fifteen to twenty-five states and simultaneously began to develop a common EU policy on asylum and migration. EU officials drafted directives on minimum standards for asylum procedures and for qualification of non-EU nationals as refugees or persons in need of protection. Hotly debated and criticized as diluting refugee law principles, the proposals [underwent] multiple rounds of consultations and discussion.

Imposing advance visa requirements on nationals from many refugee-producing countries has become commonplace in the EU and elsewhere in the industrialized world. Refugees and asylum seekers who lack a valid entry visa are prevented from even boarding an airplane or ship heading for safety. Carrier sanctions have also become common, and airline and shipping companies face fines if they board asylum seekers without entry documents for the destination.

Those who manage to travel to developed countries increasingly face an array of devices that turn them away at the border either immediately or within a matter of days: The development of the "safe third country" principle, an expanding network of readmission agreements, the growth of the "manifestly unfounded" concept, accelerated hearings, and curtailed judicial review all play a role. Under the "safe third country" rubric, some states turn away asylum seekers, no matter what countries they fled or what persecution they fear, if they passed through a country en route to the destination state that the destination state considers to be "safe." There is no examination of the merits of the asylum claims and, generally, no examination of whether the so-called "safe" country will admit the asylum seekers under its own refugee procedures. As more countries adopt this "safe" third country approach, each applying its own notions of what is "safe" and each party to different bilateral readmission agreements, the chances of chain deportation leading to *refoulement* increases dramatically.

Asylum seekers not rejected on "safe third country" grounds may find their claims denied as "manifestly unfounded." An elastic concept in many national systems, the "manifestly unfounded" notion provides decision-makers with great discretion [and provides minimal procedural protections].

Expedited proceedings held at airports, as in the United States, Germany, and Spain, are another measure devised to turn away asylum seekers quickly and to deter potential future applicants. To accomplish similar goals, the five largest EU states (Germany, France, Italy, Spain, and the United Kingdom) banded together in early 2004 to develop a "safe country of origin" list. Citizens of such "safe" countries will not be eligible to seek refugee status in any of the five states.

Asylum seekers allowed to enter and remain during the refugee determination process often face harsh treatment designed to make their stay so unpleasant that others, in turn, will hesitate to come. Many countries have reduced social support for asylum seekers during the asylum process, and most prohibit asylum seekers from working. Thus, refugees and asylum seekers who can barely make ends meet are prevented from helping themselves, which can easily lead to people becoming increasingly dysfunctional. At the same time, negative public perceptions that refugees and asylum seekers are lazy and unwilling to contribute to society are reinforced.

More draconian yet is the increasing use of detention as a response to asylum seekers. The United States now detains all who request asylum at the border, although thus far the number of asylum seekers has outstripped available detention facilities and overwhelmed the policy. Various European countries have begun to use detention at the end of the asylum process, incarcerating those whose applications are denied. Whether detention occurs at the beginning or the end of the asylum process, it poses major problems. The conditions of the detention facilities are often deplorable. Even worse, asylum seekers who have not been charged with a crime often are housed with those convicted of serious criminal acts.

The repercussions of the September 11, 2001, attacks on the United States have been widespread and negative. The United States has enacted multi-faceted anti-terrorist legislation, which has had negative impacts on many non-citizens, including asylum seekers.[8] A heightened concern with controlling the borders and preventing future terrorist attacks has led to expanded government authority to detain suspected terrorists, including those who have been granted asylum. Special registration requirements were imposed on adult males from designated countries, mostly Arab and Muslim states.

This post-September-11 phenomenon has not been confined to the United States. The discovery of terrorist cells in Europe has led Germany, France, and the United Kingdom, among other countries, to adopt anti-terrorist laws and administrative measures that impose new burdens on asylum seekers and other migrants. They reveal the current fear of foreigners, frustration with attempts to create effective and efficient asylum procedures in EU states, and awareness of the increasing role of professional human smugglers.

Such measures also indicate that the atmosphere in Europe has become increasingly focused on managing migration, and rhetoric has often confused immigration and asylum. This has led to criticism of the 1951 Convention as outmoded.

Although many recent legal developments concerning asylum seekers have been retrogressive, there have been some positive steps. Refugee authorities in Canada, followed by those in the United States, Australia, and the United Kingdom, have developed guidelines concerning female asylum seekers which recognize and work to overcome many of the difficulties that have been experienced by women who claim asylum. In addition, refugee advocates in many countries are becoming more knowledgeable about the potential of other international human rights instruments to protect refugees and asylum seekers in certain instances. In particular, the Convention against Torture has been a genuine source of protection against *refoulement* of rejected asylum seekers. Article 3 of the European Convention on Human Rights offers another powerful tool.

It is clear, though, that human rights practitioners at the start of the 21st century must understand the basic international and regional human rights framework, in addition to knowing the sources of international refugee law and the national refugee laws in the states where they work.

QUESTIONS FOR REFLECTION AND DISCUSSION

1. What is at the root of the refugee problem? Economics? Maldistribution of resources? Politics? War? Corruption? Other factors? Why?

2. The 1951 Convention Relating to the Status of Refugees (referenced in Documentary Appendix B) protects only persons classified as political refugees. Economic refugees or migrants are clearly not protected. As W. R. Smyser has put it in "Refugees: A Never-Ending Story," *Foreign Affairs* 64, no. 1 (1985): 154–68, at 164, "Migrants seek opportunity.

8. The USA Patriot Act of 2001, P.L. 107–56, is perhaps the best known of the recent anti-terrorist laws adopted by the United States.

Refugees seek haven. A migrant does not wish to return home; a refugee does not dare."
What is the theory behind not allowing "economic refugees" the same or similar privileges
as "political refugees"? Should such a distinction exist? Why? Why not?

3. Historically, refugees have had no legal right to sanctuary, only the right to *request*
sanctuary. Hence Article 14(1) of the Universal Declaration of Human Rights (reprinted and
referenced in Documentary Appendix A): "Everyone has the right to seek and enjoy in
other countries asylum from persecution." One is free to *seek* asylum but not *enjoy* it unless
it is granted, at the discretion of the receiving state. In recent times, however, principles
such as the right to territorial asylum and the right not to return (*non-refoulement*) to a
country where there is a reasonable expectation of persecution have been asserted as bases
for extending legal rights to refugees. Which of these asserted rights—to asylum or to *non-
refoulement*—appears stronger from the standpoint of the refugee—that is, which seems
most likely to have binding effect on the host state? Why?

4. What about refugees fleeing war, pestilence, natural disasters, or other such calami-
ties—so-called "humanitarian refugees? To what rights are they entitled, if any? What does
Fullerton say?

5. Fullerton distinuishes between *de facto* and humanitarian refugees, the former denoting "applicants whose cases are quite similar to, but not as compelling as, those that fall
within the 1951 Convention definition," the second denoting "applicants who are at serious
risk but whose fear is based on conditions not enumerated in the Convention definition."
The U.S. has utilized a number of administrative measures for granting "safe haven" to
aliens from China (after the Tiananmen Square massacre), Afghanistan (1980), Iran (1997),
and Nicaragua (1979), but refused to extend the same measure to refugees from Salvador and Guatemala. More recent beneficiaries include Bosnians, Lebanese, Liberians,
Kuwaitis, and Somalis. A common justification for these preferential treatments—known
by acronyms such as EVD (Extended Voluntary Departure), TPS (Temporary Protected
Status) and DED (Deferred Enforced Departure)—is that the home countries of their beneficiaries were undergoing civil war. It has been said that foreign policy considerations were
the real reasons for extending "refugee-like" status to these populations. Is it appropriate
to use foreign policy as a guide for distinguishing refugee claims? Given the foundational
human rights principle of nondiscrimination, is it even lawful?

6. In the 1990s the UN High Commission for Refugees (UNHCR) recognized that women
refugees—who, with their children, comprise the majority of the world's refugees—face
numerous unique problems "which interfere with the ability to obtain a meaningful determination of claims [for asylum]." Carolyn Patty Blum and Nancy Kelly, "The Protection of
Women Refugees," in Kelly D. Askin and Dorean M. Koenig, eds., *Women and International
Human Rights Law* (Ardsley, N.Y.: Transnational Publishers, 1999), 3: 197–239, at 223. To
inform all parties involved in asylum adjudication about these problems, the UNHCR issued
Guidelines for the Protection of Refugee Women (1991) and *Guidelines on Sexual Violence Against
Refugees* (1995). The Guidelines acknowledged that, as Karen Musalo, Director of the Center for Gender and Refugee Studies at the University of California, has put it: "the way we
think about refugees is a male paradigm. If a man is tortured with electric shock during
war, most people would say of course he deserves asylum. If a woman is raped during war
. . . we don't consider it a form of persecution." Edwidge Danticat, "A Crime to Dream,"
The Nation (May 2, 2005), 13–16, at 15. What would Eva Brems (Reading 10 in this chapter) say about this? How do you assess Musalo's statement? Is it necessary that the "male
paradigm" to which she alludes be shifted to a *human* paradigm? If not, why not? If so,
how?

7. Acknowledging that only refugees have access to internationally recognized rights,
as opposed to migrants and internally displaced peoples who have no legal status whatsoever, Nira Yuval-Davis describes the current international trend on the treatment of
refugees:

> While complying with the rights and regulations of international law concerning refu-
> gees, most states these days have created a situation in which it is becoming more and
> more difficult, if not virtually impossible, to acquire [the] legal status [of refugee]. There-
> fore, more and more people who could, some years ago, be entitled to the rights and
> protection of the status of the refugee have no legal means to obtain it today and are
> pushed into becoming part of the other, unprotected, forms of migration.

Nira Yuval-Davis, "Human Security and Asylum Seeking," *Bristol Lecture Series 2004: The Politics of Belonging* (Bristol University, June 2004), 35–36, available at http://www.bristol. ac.uk/sociology/ethnicity citizenship/nyd3.pdf. What are the causes and consequences of this *de facto* dismissal of refugee status? Don Flynn has noted that the British Labor government in the 1990s has been increasingly liberalizing its policies to facilitate "economic migration" while at the same time imposing draconian access restrictions on people who go to the UK as asylum seekers. See Don Flynn, "Tough as Old Boots? Asylum, Immigration and the Paradox of New Labour Policy," *Discussion Paper* (London: Joint Council for the Welfare of Immigrants, Nov. 2003): "For most practical purposes" he argues "there are now no legal routes to Britain for people fleeing persecution in their own countries. . . . [T]he old world order of universal rights is obsolete. . . . In the new world of globalized reality, the old concept of 'rights,' if it is applicable at all, should be reserved for those who have made themselves useful" (1–2). Consider Fullerton's analysis of contemporary trends in refugee policies in light of Yuval-Davis's and Flynn's views. What considerations, economic and otherwise, work against the recognition of refugee rights?

8. It has been observed that the 1990s and the first years of the twenty-first century saw an increasing "securitization" of migration. Refugees are conflated with terrorists, drug smugglers, and economic migrants in a new dominant preoccupation with "security," more and more seen as "security problems" rather than "humanitarian problems"—potential impostors or unwitting instruments of armed rebels mingling undetected amongst them and taking advantage of refugee camp services. Refugees are seen also as sources of ethnic strife and political unrest in host countries. See Michael E. Brown, ed., *Grave New World: Security Challenges in the 21st Century* (Washington, D.C.: Georgetown University Press, 2003). What consequences can this new language of security have for the rights of refugee asylum seekers?

9. Since the administration of President Jimmy Carter, asylum-seekers from Haiti have been consistently portrayed by the U.S. government as fraudulent asylum-seekers (mere economic migrants) and denied proper adjudication of their claims. See Lucas Guttentag, "Haitian Refugees and U.S. Policy," in Alan B. Simmons, ed., *International Migration, Refugee Flows and Human Rights in North America: The Impact of Free Trade and Restructuring* (New York: Center for Migration Studies, 1996). In the 1970s and 1980s, the U.S. enforced an interdiction program that prevented asylum seekers from reaching U.S. territorial waters. U.S. immigration officers were stationed aboard Coast Guard cutters determining the credibility of claims while on the high seas. After the military coup against popularly elected president Bertrand Aristide in 1991, Aristide supporters fleeing political persecution were brought to the U.S. Guantánamo military base in Cuba, where they were prescreened by asylum officers pressured by the U.S. Department of State to limit approvals. Despite the danger of indefinite detention under harsh conditions, Haitians continued to flood Guantánamo. In 1992, president G. H. W. Bush issued a special order (the Kennebunkport Order) stopping the Guantánamo screening process and imposing an automatic repatriation of all interdicted Haitians with no opportunity to apply for asylum. President Clinton did not repeal the Kennebunkport Order. The Supreme Court held that the U.S. government and Immigration and Naturalization Service (INS) did not violate any U.S. or international law in the processing of Haitian asylum-seekers. *McNary v. Haitian Centers Council, Inc.*, 506 U.S. 996 (1992). The Court held that neither U.S. nor international refugee law applies to acts of the U.S. government taken outside U.S. territory. Should the Supreme Court's decision be reversed? Why? Why not? Compare the international legal implications of the use of Guantánamo for the detention of Haitian refugees and Iraqi and Afghan prisoners in the "war on terror."

10. Solutions to the refugee problem, suggested by many, include voluntary repatriation, resettlement in the country of first asylum, and resettlement in a third country. Are there other solutions? Might they include other ways of conceptualizing the refugee and the refugee problem? In "We Refugees" (trans. Michael Rocke), available at http://www.egs. edu/faculty/agamben/agamben-we-refugees.html, the political philosopher Giorgio Agamben has written:

> in the context of the inexorable decline of the nation-state and the general corrosion of traditional legal-political categories, the refugee is perhaps the only imaginable figure of the people in our day. At least until the process of the dissolution of the nation-state

and its sovereignty has come to an end, the refugee is the sole category in which it is possible today to perceive the forms and limits of a political community to come. Indeed, it may be that if we want to be equal to the absolutely novel tasks that face us, we will have to abandon without misgivings the basic concepts in which we have represented political subjects up to now (man and citizen with their rights, but also the sovereign people, the worker, etc.) and to reconstruct our political philosophy beginning with this unique figure.

Refugees, according to Agamben, reveal what we have chosen to overlook, namely, that the human creature has no legal-political existence outside the confines of the nation-state. The original 1789 French Declaration of the Rights of Man conflated the "nativity" of human beings—that is, their biological birth—with the exercise of citizenship and with state power (sovereignty). The refugee is disquieting to us, according to Agamben, because he or she shows us that the "identity between man and citizen, between nativity and nationality," which we have come to take for granted, allows no room for the rights of the human being as such, the rights of those who have lost all other attributes and capabilities except their humanness. Agamben argues that the "permanently resident mass of noncitizens" that advanced Western states face today is the reverse mirror image of their native residents who divest themselves of their citizenship by withdrawing from political life into apathy. Citizens and noncitizens are thus joined as refugees and must reclaim their human rights and political agency in the face of xenophobia and arbitrary state power. Should we therefore do away with the notion of asylum, as Agamben argues, and reconsider the meaning of citizenship and the utility of the status of "statelessness"? See further Giorgio Agamben, *Homo Sacer: Sovereign Power and Bare Life*, trans. Daniel Heller-Roazen (Stanford, Calif.: Stanford University Press, 1998).

12. MAIVÂN CLECH LÂM *Indigenous Peoples' Rights to Self-Determination and Territoriality*

The white man's dead forget the country of their birth when they go to walk among the stars. Our dead never forget this beautiful earth, for it is the mother of the red man. We are part of the earth and it is part of us. . . . We know that the white man does not understand our ways. One portion of land is the same to him as the next, for he is a stranger who comes in the night and takes from the land whatever he needs. The earth is not his brother, but his enemy, and when he has conquered it, he moves on. . . . His appetite will devour the earth and leave behind only a desert.[1]

In July 1944, representatives of 45 states, most dominated at the time by either the United States or the United Kingdom, met in Bretton Woods to lay out a postwar economic world order, manifest today as global capitalism, that would safeguard the extensive extraterritorial economic interests of the West against the threat potentially posed to them by the possible convergence of two ideologies then on the rise: Soviet socialism and Third World nationalism. To date, the Bretton Woods scheme, comprised of the World Bank, the IMF, and the GATT (now the WTO), has served its promoters exceedingly well. Global capitalism runs the world, generating exces-sive wealth for some, comfortable sufficiency for many, and unbearable poverty for the rest, all the while re-arranging natural and cultural landscapes at will or as aided by the American imperium. In the process, what ties there remain in the postcolonial world that still bind human beings close to the lands of their birth—ties spun from cultural communities' intimate knowledge of, and profound dependence

Reprinted with changes from Maivân Clech Lâm, "Remembering the Country of Their Birth: Indigenous Peoples and Territoriality," *Journal of International Affairs* 57, no. 2 (2004):129–50. Copyright © 2004 The Trustees of Columbia University. Reprinted by permission.

1. Chief Seattle, "Speech," reproduced in Roger Moody, ed., *The Indigenous Voice: Visions and Realities* (London: Zed Books, 1988), 2: 41–43. While some have questioned the authenticity of the speech, the preeminent Native American historian Vine DeLoria assured the author that its genre and tone reflect the discursive style of his forebears of the period.

on, their natural environments—are mindlessly slashed, if not severed.

In this story, indigenous peoples, comprising over 350 million individuals and 5,000 ethnolinguistic groups, are in essence those last wrenched from, or harassed in, their native spaces. They consequently assert more vigorously than others earlier displaced their attachments and rights to homelands still experienced, or remembered, as sufficient, animate, and meaningful. José R. Martinez Cobo, the Special Rapporteur appointed in 1971 by the UN Commission on Human Rights (UNCHR) to conduct its first-ever study of indigenous peoples, recognized this land-rootedness as the primary marker of indigenous identity:

Indigenous communities, peoples and nations are those which, having a historical continuity with pre-invasion and pre-colonial societies that developed on their territories, consider themselves distinct from other sectors of the societies now prevailing in those territories, or parts of them. They form at present non-dominant sectors of society and are determined to preserve, develop and transmit to future generations their ancestral territories, and their ethnic identity, as the basis of their continued existence as peoples, in accordance with their own cultural patterns, social institutions and legal systems.[2]

Simultaneously, Cobo's description captured the fundamental message that, since the 1960s, indigenous delegations from around the world have carried to international fora where they seek legal and institutional protection, impelled there by the depredations that global capitalism visits on their territories and the attendant impotence if not connivance of their enclosing states.[3] The message indigenous peoples deliver is quite simple: their ability to survive as distinctive peoples is inextricably tied to their right to occupy their traditional territories and control their resources. Translating the rights language of the message into its political correlate, indigenous peoples are in fact claiming territoriality, an attribute normally associated with sovereign statehood to which, paradoxically, only a few of them aspire.[4] This paper assesses the response of the international law-making community to this message.

DEVELOPMENTS IN INTERNATIONAL FORA[5]

In 1957, the International Labor Organization adopted the well-intentioned but decidedly assimilationist Convention (No. 107) Concerning the Protection and Integration of Indigenous and Other Tribal and Semi-Tribal Populations in Independent Countries (ILO C107).[6] Notwithstanding its limitations, ILO C107 performed the valuable task of inscribing for the first time in international law the category of indigenous and tribal peoples, whom it correctly represented as deserving of special attention. Over the next two decades, advocacy for indigenous interests unfolded in primarily NGO fora where indigenous representatives, alone or in combination with academic, church, and other allies, publicized the plight of their communities and pleaded for protection. By 1982, the UN Commission on Human Rights (UNCHR), urged on by ever more effective indigenous, academic, and NGO advocates, as well as by the findings of its own Special Rapporteur Cobo, set up a Working Group on Indigenous Populations (WGIP) composed of five independent experts charged with a dual mandate: to monitor developments affecting indigenous peoples, and to formulate standards to guide the behavior of states toward them.

Very early on, the WGIP attracted an impressive number of indigenous participants, but remarkably few states, to its summer sessions in Geneva. As a result, when, in 1994, the WGIP experts completed and unanimously recommended their standard-setting UN on the Rights

---

2. *Study of the Problem of Discrimination Against Indigenous Populations* (New York: United Nations, 1987), 5: ¶ 379, UN Doc. E/CN.4/Sub.2/1986/7/Add.4.

3. The Copenhagen-based International Work Group for Indigenous Affairs (IWGIA) has for decades carefully documented the circumstances and struggles of indigenous peoples in three sets of publications: an annual report entitled *The Indigenous World*, a journal called *Indigenous Affairs*, and a monographic series that now exceeds 100 titles.

4. Serious independence movements exist in Kanaky/New Caledonia, Ka Pae'Aina/Hawai`i, Tahiti/French Polynesia, and West Papua/Irian Jaya.

5. I have described these developments through 1999 in some detail in *At the Edge of the State: Indigenous Peoples and Self-Determination* (Ardsley, N.Y.: Transnational Publishers, 2000).

6. Concluded June 26, 1957, referenced in Documentary Appendix B.

of Indigenous Peoples[7] to the Sub-Commission on Prevention of Discrimination and Protection of Minorities,[8] which in turn unanimously passed it on to the UNCHR, the text was found to have incorporated the main demands of indigenous representatives. From the indigenous perspective, the 's most prized provisions are those relating to self-determination and territoriality.

Two articles, placed far apart, specifically mention self-determination. Article 3 reproduces the standard formulation of the right of self-determination contained in prior instruments of international law:[9]

> Indigenous peoples have the right of self-determination. By virtue of that right they freely determine their political status and freely pursue their economic, social and cultural development.

Article 31, on the other hand, if adopted, would constitute the first time that the term "right to autonomy" appears in an international norm-building instrument.

> Indigenous peoples, as a specific form of exercising their right to self-determination, have the right to autonomy or self-government in matters relating to their internal and local affairs, including culture, religion, education, information, media, health, housing, employment, social welfare, economic activities, land and resources management, environment and entry by non-members, as well as ways and means for financing these autonomous functions.

Articles 25 to 30 address territorial issues. The first two of these are foundational:

> *Article 25.* Indigenous peoples have the right to maintain and strengthen their distinctive spiritual and material relationship with the lands, territories, waters and coastal seas and other resources which they have traditionally owned or otherwise occupied or used, and to uphold their responsibilities to future generations in this regard.

> *Article 26.* Indigenous peoples have the right to own, develop, *control* and use the lands and territories, including the total environment of the lands, air, waters, coastal seas, sea-ice, flora and fauna and other resources

which they have traditionally owned or otherwise occupied or use. (emphasis added)

Remaining articles 27-30 forbid military activities and placement of hazardous materials on indigenous territory; legitimize indigenous land-tenure systems; obligate states to guarantee these rights; and, most importantly, require in articles 27 and 30 that states obtain the "free and informed consent" of indigenous peoples prior to any project that affects what the Draft Declaration calls, in a tripartite rubric, their "lands, territories and resources."

Given that states have long reserved to themselves the legal and political attribute of territoriality, it should come as no surprise that these articles on self-determination and territories are now generating serious controversy in the body that the UNHCR created in 1995 to advise it on the Draft Declaration: the Working Group on the (WGDD). The WGDD, unlike the WGIP, is controlled by states rather than independent experts. Like the WGIP, however, it draws a large and seasoned group of indigenous participants to its annual fall sessions in Geneva. Reprising the practice they first developed in the WGIP, these participants coalesce as an Indigenous Caucus that speaks, as much as possible, with a single forceful voice on key issues. The original WGDD mandate expired at the end of 2004, with only two of the document's 45 articles having gained consensual approval. Happily, the UNCHR renewed the WGDD mandate in spring 2005. At the following WGDD session in late 2005, more than 20 preambular and operative provisions were adopted, leaving many now to expect a completion of the review process in early 2006, such that a document acceptable to both states and indigenous representatives could well be submitted to the UNCHR, and thereafter the General Assembly, as early as 2006 or 2007.

The fate of the Draft Declaration remains of utmost concern to indigenous activists around the world given its prospectively universal, albeit nonbinding, reach as a UN declaration. At the same time, indigenous peoples promote their rights to self-determination and territoriality in

7. Referenced in Documentary Appendix B.
8. Now known as the Sub-Commission on the Promotion and Protection of Human Rights.
9. See the Declaration on the Granting of Independence to Colonial Countries and Peoples (Dec. 14, 1960), referenced in Documentary Appendix B; and the International Covenant on Economic, Social and Cultural Rights and International Covenant on Civil and Political Rights, each concluded Dec. 16, 1966, reprinted and referenced in Documentary Appendix A.

a number of other bodies that generate or implement international or regional laws and norms. For groups that live in states that have ratified the 1989 ILO Convention (No. 169) Concerning Indigenous and Tribal Peoples in Independent Countries (ILO C169)[10] which renounces the assimilationism of the earlier ILO C107 and also replaces it in states that have signed both, the ILO secretariat itself is a key site of activism as it proffers mechanisms for investigating indigenous peoples' complaints against noncompliant states. ILO C169, however, offers less generous territorial control to indigenous peoples than the later born Draft Declaration proposes. Nonetheless, what ILO C169 offers are enforceable treaty rights, which a declaration, being essentially aspirational, does not, even if it is eventually adopted by the General Assembly. In the key area of lands, territories, and resources, ILO C169 recognizes a range of cognizable rights in indigenous peoples: of possession, co-use, co-management, co-conservation, and only in cases of nonremoval or relocation, the right to give or withhold "free and informed consent." Unlike the Draft Declaration, then, ILO C169 stops short of conferring on indigenous peoples a unilateral right to give or withhold their free and informed consent, i.e., a veto right, over all activities affecting the spaces they call home. A number of other treaties, which can only be mentioned here, provide indirect support for the territorial claims of indigenous peoples: the widely ratified 1948 Convention on the Prevention and Punishment of the Crime of Genocide;[11] the 1966 International Covenant on Civil and Political Rights (ICCPR);[12] and the 1966 International Convention on the Elimination of All Forms of Racial Discrimination (ICERD).[13]

Recognition of the territoriality of indigenous peoples is simultaneously spreading through the Organization of American States (OAS) system. In 1997, the Inter-American Commission on Human Rights, composed of seven independent experts appointed by states, submitted a Proposed American Declaration on the Rights of Indigenous Peoples (PADRIP) to the Permanent Council of the OAS. The latter entrusted its review to a Working Group to Prepare the Draft American Declaration on the Rights of Indigenous Peoples (OAS WG), a body made up of member states. As in the WGDD, indigenous representatives from the Americas do not hold decision-making powers in the OAS WG but participate vigorously all the same in its meetings, collectively as an Indigenous Caucus, and also autonomously as spokespersons of particular communities. Indeed, many indigenous attendees are veterans of both the UN and OAS processes. Not surprisingly they insist, in both venues, on the primacy of the same two foundational rights: self-determination and territoriality.

Succinctly put, a key difference between the PADRIP and the UN Draft Declaration article 27, which broadly recognizes indigenous peoples' right to withhold consent for all occupation or use of their territory, lies in the fact that the PADRIP specifically vests the state with the task of designating indigenous territory. Only thereafter do indigenous peoples exercise full control therein. The Draft Declaration, on the other hand, specifies no such prior designation by the state, though arguably that is understood. Either way, given a state's potential for abuse of its power to designate, indigenous peoples will need a share in that power, or at least an impartial review mechanism for the designation. Finally, it should be noted that the OAS process, which began well after the UN one, is moving faster than the latter, and will likely yield a hemispheric declaration ahead of a universal one.

Notwithstanding the uncertain prospects of both the OAS and the UN, OAS jurisprudence on indigenous peoples' rights to their lands is moving forward with remarkable alacrity and effect. The impetus here springs from both the complaints that indigenous plaintiffs diligently bring to the Inter-American Commission of Human Rights (the Commission) alleging violations of the 1969 American Convention on Human Rights (ACHR),[14] and to the principled behavior of the Commission itself in pleading cases it finds meritorious to the Inter-American Court of Human Rights (the Court). On 31 August 2001, in a case initiated by the U.S.-based Indian Law Resource Center, the Court issued a path-breaking decision regarding one

10. Concluded June 27, 1969, referenced in Documentary Appendix B.
11. Referenced in Documentary Appendix B..
12. Concluded Dec. 16, 1966. reprinted and referenced in Documentary Appendix A.
13. Concluded Dec. 21, 1965, referenced in Documentary Appendix B.
14. Concluded Nov. 22, 1969, referenced in Documentary Appendix B.

such complaint: *Case of the Mayagna (Sumo) Community of Awas Tingni v. Nicaragua.*[15] The Court, applying Article 21 of the ACHR (guaranteeing the right of property), which it read in conjunction with the Constitution of Nicaragua (recognizing the right of indigenous peoples to maintain their communal forms of land ownership, use, and enjoyment), as well as Nicaraguan domestic legislation (requiring the demarcation of indigenous territories), wrote:

> Given the characteristics of the instant case, some specifications are required on the concept of property in indigenous communities. Among indigenous peoples there is a communitarian tradition regarding a communal form of collective property of the land, in the sense that ownership of the land is not centered on an individual but rather on the group and its community. Indigenous groups, by the fact of their very existence, have the right to live freely in their own territory; the close ties of indigenous people with the land must be recognized and understood as the fundamental basis of their cultures, their spiritual life, their integrity, and their economic survival.[16]

With that important foundation laid, the Court went on to confirm that the community of Awas Tingni held rights to their lands and resources in common, which accorded with the land-tenure system of their culture, which in turn governed in their territory. The state of Nicaragua violated the community's property rights protected by the ACHR by failing to demarcate the community's territory and issuing title thereon as required by its own legislation, and by unilaterally granting a logging concession in the territory to an outside timber company.

Awas Tingni is the last in a trio of remarkably innovative and far-reaching judicial opinions on the territorial rights of indigenous and tribal peoples that have been handed down over the last three decades by international, regional, and national tribunals. The first was the 1975 International Court of Justice (ICJ) *Western Sahara* Advisory Opinion,[17] and the second was the 1992 Australian High Court's *Mabo v. Queensland* judgment.[18] Together with *Awas Tingni*, these cases profoundly reorient normative thinking in

the area. However, ICJ advisory opinions are only that: advisory. Thus, even though the ICJ ruled—on the basis of, *inter alia*, anthropological information attesting to the historical depth and ecological logic of the cultures of the nomadic tribes involved—that the inhabitants of the Western Sahara, while not necessarily showing conventional indices of past or incipient statehood, were a people entitled to the exercise of self-determination under international law, the Court lacked the authority, let alone power, to interdict or reverse Morocco's physical assertion of hegemony over the territory. Likewise, while the *Mabo* decision—holding null and void the notorious *terra nullius* (land belonging to no one) doctrine that underlay the settler society's property regime—certainly binds Australia, the High Court there gave the federal and state governments so much leeway to adjust their property laws in response to its ruling that the aboriginal peoples of the continent have yet to reap real benefit from the decision. Of the three cases, then, perhaps only *Awas Tingni* will be implemented in good faith.

From a normative perspective, however, the three cases cumulatively effect a sea change in the standing of indigenous peoples in international law. First, local ethnographic data, as much as universal political formula, were privileged by the ICJ as a basis for validating the self-determination claim of the nomadic tribes of the Western Sahara. Second, the *terra nullius* doctrine was laid to rest: indirectly in *Western Sahara*, definitively in *Mabo*. The legal doctrine's conceit that inhabited spaces later settled by Westerners either did not shelter human beings before, or that these human beings possessed no evidence of social order such as a normative land tenure construct, was exposed for the blatant racism and pitiful ignorance that it embodied. *Awas Tingni* contributed a further piece in this rectificatory legal evolution: A prior indigenous social order does not yield automatically to a later statist order, particularly when, as is the case today, modern international law has repudiated the doctrine that territory may be lawfully acquired through conquest or other forms of coercion.

Beyond treaty law and the judicial opinions

15. Inter-Amer. Ct. H.R., Judgment of August 31, 2001 (Series C, No. 79).
16. Ibid. See note 24, ¶ 149.
17. 1975 ICJ 12.
18. 175 CLR 1 (1992); 107 ALR 1 (1992).

that interpret it lie additional matrices of international norms and rules. The practice of states, intergovernmental bodies and, increasingly, agents of international civil society such as NGOs potentially generate incremental norms and rules of customary international law that evolve in response to aspects of life in the global village that tend to be relational and fluid (such as indigenous-state relations), in contrast to those that present themselves as largely repetitive or technical (such as trade or civil aviation), which invite regulation via treaty law. As ICJ Judge C. G. Weeramantry has written, customary international law plays a key role in fashioning a community, as opposed to a mere collection, of states.[19] Indeed, it is outside the formal treaty-making sites that states control, and in the practice-accumulating and norm-developing spaces of international society where indigenous peoples and independent or semi-independent "experts" increasingly interface, that the territorial prerogative of indigenous peoples is now being most actively and creatively negotiated. . . .

An example of this is presented by discussions regarding indigenous communities at the World Bank which, typically, bears responsibility for financially enabling the mega-projects, particularly dams, that have delivered the unkindest cuts of all in the last half-century to settled communities and fragile ecologies. Left to its own devices, the World Bank would accumulate an uninterrupted history of activities that showcase rationalist, universalist, and high modernist thinking that presumes to see long into the future exactly what it is that human societies need, even when the affected themselves fail to share that vision." But, fortunately, external voices sometimes reach the divine ear. Pressured to appreciate "the special vulnerabilities of indigenous peoples," the Bank has subscribed to the principle that its projects should shield indigenous communities from coercion and injury. And such pressure, it is proposed, tends to be alchemized in, among other places, the intersectoral workshops of the global village where new knowledge and fresh resolve sometimes take root, without which the predatory form of

capitalism now prowling the world requisitioning laissez-faire mats of welcome might already have left behind only a desert.

In this regard, the inauguration of the UN Permanent Forum on Indigenous Issues in New York in May 2002 represented an ambitious effort by the UN to institutionalize a maximally productive interface between representatives of indigenous communities, states, UN agencies, other IGOs, and NGOs. The Permanent Forum is composed of 16 commissioners nominated in equal number by states and indigenous organizations and appointed by the president of the Economic and Social Council (ECOSOC). It is charged with advocating for the interests of indigenous peoples throughout the UN system as well as cooperating bodies such as the World Bank. Notwithstanding the real promise inherent in its creation, however, the Permanent Forum will need far more resources than currently it receives from the cash-strapped UN if it is to realize its mandate.

ISSUES AND PARADIGMS

Because the rights to self-determination and to territoriality are worded more favorably for indigenous peoples in the UN Draft Declaration than in the OAS PAD, the debate around them has also been more engaged, thorough, and indeed vehement in the older UN process than the younger OAS one. This section therefore discusses the debate on the two rights as it crystallized in the WGDD after Norway submitted, in 2002, a proposal calling for changes to the provisions that address the right of self-determination.[20]

First, the Norway proposal added a qualifier (italicized below) to the previously unqualified reference to the right of self-determination contained in paragraph 15 of the Draft Declaration's preamble:

> Bearing in mind that nothing in this Declaration may be used to deny any peoples their right of self-determination, *yet nothing in this Declaration shall be construed as authorizing or*

19. C. G. Weeramantry, "The Contemporary Role of Customary International Law," in *Imagining Tomorrow: Rethinking the Global Challenge* (Merrill Corporation, unpublished collection compiled on the occasion of the United Nations Millennium Assembly, 2000), 351–71.
20. It was a blow to indigenous representatives that Norway, which had hitherto declared itself able to live with the original text, took this position. Its representatives explained to the Indigenous Caucus, without success, that it did so to bring oppositional states like the U.S. on board the Declaration.

encouraging any action which would dismember or impair, totally or in part, the territorial integrity or political unity of sovereign and independent States conducting themselves in compliance with the principle of equal rights and self-determination of peoples. . . .

Second, the proposal moved article 31—which states that "Indigenous peoples, as a specific form of exercising their right to self-determination, have the right to autonomy"—from its unremarkable location toward the end of the to a prominent position immediately following article 3 which, standing alone, extends the classic, unqualified right of self-determination contained in international law instruments to indigenous peoples. Thus juxtaposed, the two articles potentially support an argument that article 31 reduces the scope of article 3 to that of autonomy, or what some confusingly call internal self-determination. Interestingly, the U.S. offered a proposal at the same session of the WGDD that explicitly merged the right of self-determination with that of autonomy by simply absorbing article 31 into an emasculated article 3:

> Indigenous peoples have the right to internal self-government. By virtue of that right, they may negotiate their political status within the framework of the existing nation-state to pursue their economic, social and cultural development. Indigenous peoples, in exercising their internal right of self-determination, have the internal right to autonomy or self-government. . . .[21]

As can be seen, the U.S. text employs the terms "internal self-government" and "internal right to autonomy" interchangeably. At the moment, neither term figures as a term of art in international law for the simple reason that international law does not, in principle, concern itself with internal political subdivisions. The international law right of self-determination is a unitary one that has not been subdivided into internal and external components in either conventional or customary international law (except, arguably, in the case of apartheid South Africa when the General Assembly called apartheid a violation of self-determination which, under the circumstances, could only have meant internal self-determination). A jurist close to the subject,

Gudmundur Alfredsson, decries the cosmetic use of the term: "political participation and autonomy . . . fall short of granting the right of self-determination. . . . [W]e should call the rights offered by their correct names and not try to advance their image by doubtful labeling."[22]

As set out in treaty law, the right of self-determination simply enunciates a people's right to choose, among other things, its political status, the form of which international law neither prescribes nor proscribes. The General Assembly made this quite clear in its 1960 Resolution 1541—which accompanied 1960 Resolution 1514, known as the Declaration on the Granting of Independence to Colonial Countries and Peoples[23]—wherein it is stated that the political status a people chooses in its exercise of self-determination may range from incorporation with an existing state, through free association with it, to total independence. Furthermore, as indigenous peoples never tire of pointing out, the five WGIP independent experts who crafted the Draft Declaration and the much larger group of independent experts who endorsed it in the Sub-Commission could not have constructed a lesser right of self-determination for indigenous peoples than for other peoples without violating the UN Charter's Article 1 mandate "requiring respect for the principle of equal rights and self-determination of peoples."

At the same time, the WGIP experts—who unambiguously established, in Article 3, the formal equality of indigenous peoples with all other peoples relative to self-determination—understood that virtually all indigenous peoples seek a freely negotiated partnership with states rather than independence. They thus ingeniously constructed a paradigm for just such a partnership in the rest of the Draft Declaration. In effect, the WGIP experts anticipated that, to the extent that international law guarantees indigenous peoples' right to self-determination, it will also: (1) motivate states to negotiate with them in good faith; and (2) motivate indigenous peoples, heretofore rightfully wary of states, to entertain new arrangements with them where minimal standards are guaranteed by international law, and where, should states prove intransigent, the choice to seek alternative

21. Document distributed by the U.S. delegation to the 2002 session of the WGDD.
22. "The Right of Self-Determination and Indigenous Peoples," in Christian Tomuschat, ed., *Modern Law of Self-Determination* (Dordrecht: Martinus Nijhoff, 1993), 53.
23. Note 9.

arrangements as set out in G.A. Resolution 1541 remains. The Norwegian and U.S. proposals, if adopted, would jettison this fundamental nexus, or inspired balance, between the right of indigenous peoples to self-determination, on the one hand, and the high likelihood that they will exercise it to negotiate a partnership with states, on the other.

The U.S. (typically seconded by other Western anglophonic countries) and Norway (followed by other Nordic countries that have signed on to its 2002 proposal) rationalize their opposition in the WGDD to an unencumbered right of self-determination for indigenous peoples on two closely related grounds: (1) that international law does not permit secession; and (2) that it affirmatively protects the territorial integrity of states which, they contend, Article 3 threatens.

While literally accurate, the first proposition misleads: international law says nothing whatsoever about secession, for or against. However, international law does say that "peoples," which it does not define, may exercise their right of self-determination to claim independence, an action that certainly entails separation from an existing state. So, a people's separation from an existing state—whether or not called "secession," indigenous peoples representatives insisting that the term be used only to describe the repudiation of a state by an entity that previously agreed to join it (not their case)—is not as such forbidden in international law.

The related proposition that international law protects the territorial integrity of states is likewise literally true. But the question must be asked: from whom? The answer, given international law's simultaneous support for the self-determination of peoples, can only be: from other states. Norway's proposal, which constructs the principle of territorial integrity as a limitation on the right of a people to self-determination, is thus a wholly novel move in international law. No previous instrument of this system indicates that the principle of territorial integrity bars a state's own constituents from challenging its borders. Indeed, the qualifier language, which the Norway proposal lifts from the 1970 UN General Assembly Declaration on Principles of International Law Concerning Friendly Relations and Co-operation among States in Accordance

with the Charter of the United Nations (DFR), is taken out of context.[24] The DFR is a declaration concluded by states in which, as its name intimates, they mutually agree, among other things, not to disturb one another's borders. Nowhere does the DFR allude to secession. Indeed, Western states, more than others, should be embarrassed to suggest otherwise; for when they collectively pronounced on "equal rights and self-determination of peoples" in Helsinki in 1975, in the context of the restiveness then spreading through the USSR and Eastern Europe, they in fact extended its reach beyond its classic expression. "By virtue of the principle of equal rights and self-determination of peoples," they agreed in the Helsinki Final Act, "all peoples *always* have the right, *in full freedom*, to determine, *when and as they wish their internal and external political status*, without external interference, and to pursue as they wish their political, economic, social and cultural development."[25]

Raising the bar of state territorial integrity against self-determination for indigenous peoples is jurisprudentially faulty for another reason. The right of self-determination is generally considered to be *jus cogens*—i.e., of the highest order and nonderogable—in international law. Territorial integrity, on the other hand, while a fundamental principle that shields states from other states, does not enjoy this status. Thus, the invocation by some states in the WGDD of the principle of territorial integrity as a limitation on the right of self-determination of indigenous peoples caused great concern in the Indigenous Caucus which saw it not as a move to keep international borders inviolate (since these were not being particularly threatened) but as a way for states to maintain their traditional and increasingly intrusive jurisdiction—i.e., their "internal" territorial integrity—over all lands, territories, and resources within their borders. Now, state and global market intrusion and control in indigenous homelands are, of course, precisely what drove indigenous activists to seek out international fora in the first place, in the hope that international law could and would help their communities retain or regain control of the homelands that long ago shaped their distinctive identities and that still could guard them against the shock of physical and

---

24. Adopted Oct. 24, 1970, referenced in Documentary Appendix B.
25. Final Act on Security and Co-Operation in Europe (Helsinki Final Act) (Aug. 1, 1975), referenced in Documentary Appendix B.

cultural dissipation in the present globalizing moment.

States regularly urge indigenous peoples to accept the autonomy offered in the UN and OAS Draft Declaration as an alternative to the full right of self-determination that they seek. For a number of reasons, indigenous peoples just as consistently reject the offer. First, as explained above, "autonomy," like "secession," carries no technical meaning in international law; it therefore is a concept whose content is filled in by enclosing states according to their domestic laws, will, or whim. Thus, whether called autonomous, self-governing, internally self-determining, or nation-within-a-nation, tribes in the U.S., for example, remain, under U.S. domestic law, subject to the ever-elastic "plenary power of Congress." Benedict Kingsbury has proposed that international law develop a new norm of autonomy that is accepted and honored by states.[26] Indeed, the description of what, at a minimum, an indigenous peoples/state relationship should look like may generate just such a development. However, unless the balance that the Draft Declaration strikes for indigenous peoples between the right of self-determination and the practice of autonomy is simultaneously retained, and international oversight additionally mandated, states could easily turn floor into ceiling, putting indigenous peoples right back where they started before they reached international fora. International civil society has a continuing role to play here, in clarifying issues and proposing better paradigms.

Looking back now on the decades-long exchange between indigenous peoples, independent experts, and state representatives—an exchange in which the author participated sporadically—it is possible to decipher a principled approach that could resolve the impasse at the WGDD. The approach involves a limited textual change to the Draft Declaration, and a more ambitious paradigm shift in prevailing assumptions regarding the nature of peoples, states, international society, and international law, as set out below. In brief, amendments to the preamble of the Draft Declaration could be added to: (a) require the right of self-determination to be exercised, in conformity with international law, so as not to cause the partial or total disruption of the national unity and territorial integrity of any other state or country; and (b) create an "oversight" duty on the part of the United Nations to facilitate the peaceful resolution of conflicts and disputes between indigenous peoples and states that, for the most part, would be asked to transform in good faith their relationship into a partnership in which indigenous peoples hold the right to "prior free and informed consent" regarding any activity affecting their territories and resources. Indeed, the second amendment could simply elaborate on preambular paragraph 17, which already names the UN as the protector of indigenous peoples' rights.

Paradigmatic chasms. However, it is context rather than text that likely stands in the way of the completion of the Draft Declaration at this time. That is, representatives of states and indigenous peoples are conditioned by divergent experiences and thus paradigms regarding the nature of identity, the state, international society, and international law. These paradigmatic chasms need to be surfaced if they are to be overcome:

(a) Representatives of governments, accustomed to seeing the state as the exclusive subject of international law and retainer of domestic jurisdiction, remain hesitant to accommodate nonstate actors in substance, even when they do so in form.

(b) Indigenous peoples know the state more as enemy than friend. Global capitalism has worsened this perception because, while states continue to invoke sovereignty to shield their own human rights violations from international scrutiny, they concurrently plead loss of sovereignty vis-à-vis global capital's depredations within their borders.

(c) In light of the above, indigenous peoples are driven to seek international legal personality, albeit a *sui generis* one, and not secession, so as to influence decisions that affect them, whether these emanate from international or national fora.

(d) A complex issue concerns the relationship between culture and citizenship. Since the French Revolution, modern states have tried to solidify their hold over citizens by merging the two affiliations—one thick (culture), the other thin (citizenship). The attempt is misdirected in general, and

26. Benedict Kingsbury, "Reconstructing Self-determination: A Relational Approach," in Pekka Aikio and Martin Schienin, eds., *Operationalizing the Right of Indigenous Peoples to Self-Determination* (Turku/Åbo: Åbo Akademi University Institute for Human Rights, 2000).

especially unsuccessful in the case of indigenous peoples.[27]

(e) As states submit to globalization's demand for ultra-fungibility, indigenous peoples more and more seek affective refuge in the original homeland, the one portion of land that is not the same as the next, the place that remains, from mixed portions of memory and experience, distinctive, sufficient, animate, meaningful, and validating of their worth. At the same time, this very attachment to their homeland is what appears unfathomable, unrealistic, indeed irrational to the persons who represent states, whose very utility to states may have required their own suppression of memory and attachment.

(f) Finally, the interstate system in some respects is a small village of under 200 inhabitants[28] who know each other's idiosyncrasies well, and could afford to accommodate some of them. That is, in several areas, it may need courts and rules less than wise elders and flexible norms. Significantly, indigenous activists who come from small communities may be adept at precisely this form of order-building that is long on norms and short on operational rules. Opposed to them in the drafting processes are states' lawyers, short on norms but chock-full of positivist legal training, who insist on clear definitions and "operational" rules. Not surprisingly, the interface between indigenous peoples and the less legalistic members of expert committees has been more productive.

CONCLUSION

Should the processes, now in the control of states, fall significantly short of the positive developments that indigenous peoples are gaining in fora controlled by independent experts, the Indigenous Caucuses involved may well choose to repudiate the processes rather than lend legitimacy to instruments that undermine practices that, increasingly, confirm their status as subjects of international law with a stake in the activities that affect their traditional homelands, hence with a territorial prerogative to control and regulate those activities. The term "prerogative," not "imperative," is used advisedly here, for even states have lost the prior absolutism of their sovereignty over peoples and territory. This is a loss that represents a challenge to our times, no doubt, but perhaps is also a harbinger that other absolutisms—of capitalism, religion, hegemony—will follow suit as we discover the necessity and also fertility of perpetual conversation and mediation in the global village.

QUESTIONS FOR REFLECTION AND DISCUSSION

1. Do indigenous peoples have a right to self-determination? If so, on the basis of what authority and what is the nature of this claimed right? Also, assuming that this right exists for indigenous peoples, what responsibilities to ensure what measure of self-determination should be imposed upon national and provincial governments, if any? For discussion of the right to self-determination, see Reading 19 by Hurst Hannum in Chapter 4 of this volume.

2. Colin Samson argues that most discussions of indigenous peoples' rights sidestep the fact that American states like the U.S. and Canada, relative to their native populations, are illegitimate because they were founded on colonial expropriation. The political status and cultural difference of native peoples are linked to the fact that they have never been decolonized, according to Samson. "Although contemporary procedures for the recognition of native rights are couched in the politically correct language of participation and citizenship," they fail to address that link. As a result, the price of rights for Native Americans according to Samson, is acceptance of a territorial occupation to which they never consented. "Rights and the Reward for Simulated Cultural Sameness: The Innu in the Canadian Colonial Context," in Jane K. Cowan, Marie-Bénédicte Dembour, and Richard A. Wilson, eds., *Culture and Rights: Anthropological Perspectives* (Cambridge: Cambridge University Press, 2001), 201.

27. See Benedict R. Anderson, *Imagined Communities: Reflections on the Origin and Spread of Nationalism* (London: Verso, 1991).

28. *Eds.*—At present, 191 states are members of the United Nations, not counting Niue (part of New Zealand which sometimes functions as a state) and Taiwan (arguably part of China but which ordinarily functions as a state).

Does the right to self-determination as stated in articles 3 and 25-31 of the UN Draft Declaration on the Rights of Indigenous Peoples (referenced in Documentary Appendix B) pose a threat to the stability of states with indigenous populations? Why? Why not? What is to be concluded from Lâm's comment that most indigenous peoples make claims to territoriality, not to sovereign statehood? What does this mean? What are its economic and political implications? Its legal implications? Are Norway's concerns about preserving its territorial integrity valid?

3. Is there a middle ground between the right to self-determination *qua* statehood (i.e., full self-determination) and the complete subordination of indigenous peoples to the territorial jurisdiction of the state? Would tensions associated with this extreme choice be alleviated by some form of local autonomy? If so, would this be an acceptable compromise for indigenous peoples? For states? If so, should there be an international legal definition of "autonomy"? Or should defining the concept be left to the individual states? Alone? In cooperation with the people affected?

4. If indigenous peoples are entitled to be somehow left alone to determine their lives for themselves, does this mean that they would have no right to demand the affirmative activation of national and/or provincial economic and other resources to assist them in attaining higher levels of physical and material well-being? Should it? What if national or provincial inaction were to lead to the group's destruction?

5. Is it wise to place all or most responsibility for the protection of indigenous peoples on national and/or provincial governments? If so, what happens when there are not sufficient resources to ensure the well-being of the peoples at risk? Is it then the responsibility of international institutions to come to the rescue? If so, how is such responsibility to be met without encroaching upon the prerogatives of state sovereignty?

6. An underlying tension in respect of indigenous peoples' rights lies between (a) the right to preserve one's culture and way of life and (b) the right to development which commonly encroaches upon it. When "maximum growth" developmental policies, usually involving large-scale business interests, conflict with indigenous rights, how is the conflict to be resolved? Is it a matter simply of striking a balance between the two or is it best to opt for one or the other? If the latter, which?

7. What is the current impasse between states and indigenous people in respect of the UN Draft Declaration? What does Lâm say, and do you agree that her suggestions will resolve this impasse? Why? Why not? If not, what do you recommend? A UN oversight committee? Something else?

8. The report of the Third Session of the Permanent Forum on Indigenous Issues 2004, entitled "Report of the American Indian Law Alliance and the Teton Sioux Nation Treaty Council (available at http://www. ailanyc.org/PF2004.htm), reads in pertinent part as follows:

> The right to self-determination must be enshrined in any international forums as the most critical right of Indigenous peoples. This just and equitable principle available to all peoples has remained unavailable to Indigenous peoples within the United Nations system. Due to the absence of political will of a few states determined to deny basic rights to over 370 million of the world's peoples, the right to self-determination has remained inaccessible during the International Decade on the Rights of the World's Indigenous Peoples.
>
> We believe that only the highest levels of informed influence will be able to convince some states of their responsibilities to uphold international law and standards and create sufficient international pressure to convince them of these obligations. It has been abundantly clear to most states, agencies and Indigenous representatives that the majority of the world is cooperating on the issue of Indigenous peoples right to self-determination. Only a few nations stand in the way of the equal, just and fair application of international law and standards. . . .
>
> It is therefore recommended that in order to meet the declared goals of the International Decade on the World's Indigenous Peoples, a strong, unqualified and unwavering declaration of this right for Indigenous peoples must be enshrined within the foundational documents of the United Nations system. Passage of the Draft Declaration on the Rights of the World's Indigenous Peoples, as drafted in consultation with Indigenous peoples, is therefore the most logical and direct method to achieve this goal.

Does it appear that the AILA would agree with Lâm's suggestions to add amendments to qualify the right to self-determination so as not to cause, in Lâm's words, "the partial or total disruption of the national unity and territorial integrity of any other state"?

9. Lâm observes that "in several areas, [the interstate system] may need courts and rules less than wise elders and flexible norms [and that] indigenous activists who come from small communities may be adept at precisely this form of order-building that is long on norms and short on operational rules." Is Lâm saying that the self-determination of indigenous peoples is a matter best left outside the reach of law or is she saying that, in this realm at least, law must be conceived and applied in more adaptive terms? If the latter, is this compatible with the self-determination statement of American Indian Law Alliance in Question 8, above? In any event, how might "wise elders and flexible norms" be in a state's interests? How not?

Chapter Three

Basic Human Needs as Security Rights

IN this chapter, we turn to a set of values—basic human needs as security rights—that concerns the right of individuals and groups to expect that governments, through domestic and international policy, will do something positive to help realize those values. In contrast to the preceding chapter, in which we were concerned primarily with so-called "first generation" human rights conceived mainly in terms of the abstention of government ("freedom from" or "negative" rights), here we are concerned largely with so-called "second generation" human rights conceived mainly in terms of the affirmative intervention of government ("rights to" or "positive" rights).

Basic human needs encompass those "social goods" that are essential to human subsistence—for example, food, clothing, shelter, medical care, schooling. Public policies that affect these goods are critically important. Basic human needs imply the duty of governments to satisfy the welfare requirements involved, taking into account the constraints of limited resources. Indeed, such a duty exists, at least in principle, even and perhaps most especially when natural disasters take place. According to the International Committee of the Red Cross, the victims of droughts, floods, and monsoons—even tsunamis—have a human right to basic disaster relief from the international community.

Security rights refer to the rights of individuals and groups to enjoy reasonably reliable prospects of well-being and survival—for example, relying on their rights as workers, and rights to food, health, education, and culture (the topics selected for special attention in this chapter, not least because they often are discounted as "rights" in modern-day neoliberal economies which tend generally to favor the achievement of social justice through the workings of the free market rather than via governmental interventions). Because these essentially "second generation" rights are interconnected with others in holistic, interdependent, and interconnected ways, it is appropriate to acknowledge them in the context of the full array of human rights articulated by the Universal Declaration of Human Rights (UDHR).[1]

---

1. Adopted Dec. 10, 1948, reprinted and referenced in Documentary Appendix A.

THE ARCHITECTURE OF HUMAN RIGHTS

The framers of the UDHR recognized that it should be taught to people worldwide for its thirty articles to take hold. To do so, French Nobel Laureate René Cassin said that, for learning purposes, the structure of human rights can be visualized as a temple (or Asian pagoda, or African meeting hut) founded on four pillars.[2] Shown in Figure 1 are, first, *civil and personal rights*—the right of equality, rights to life and liberty (arts. 1–11); then the *social rights* that belong to the individual in her or his relationships with the groups in which they participate—the rights to privacy, to family life and to marry, to freedom of movement within or outside the national state, to have a nationality, to asylum in case of persecution, to property, to freedom of religion (arts. 12–17); next the third pillar of *political rights*, exercised to contribute to the formation of government institutions or to take part in decision-making processes—freedom of conscience, thought, and expression, freedom of association and assembly, the right to vote and to stand for election, the right of participation in government (arts. 18–21). Finally, the fourth category or pillar: *rights exercised in the economic and cultural area*—the rights to social security, to work and its employment rights, to rest and leisure and an "adequate" standard of living, to health care, to education, to participate freely in the cultural life of the community (arts. 22–27).

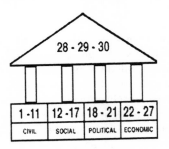

Figure 1.

Erected on these four pillars and found in the remaining three articles of the Universal Declaration, there is a fifth section—what Cassin called the "pediment of the temple"—that encompasses harmonizing provisions designed to hold the structure together and calling upon governments to make arrangements in support of human rights. Article 28 proclaims the "entitlement" of "Everyone . . . to a social and international order in which the rights and freedoms set forth in the Declaration can be fully realized"—the premise being that governments have duties to foster a favorable social structure within which human rights can take root, and that international duties also call on prosperous states to assist the economic development of poorer states. Articles 29 and 30 set out, further, principles to harmonize rights, e.g., that they must be exercised in ways that do not transgress the rights of others and that do not conflict with other UN objectives (e.g., free speech should not be misused to disseminate war propaganda). Seeing economic, social, and cultural rights in relation to other rights enhances our analytical skills in this complex area, helping us to avoid the harm that is done by approaching a right's content with reference to a single category of rights exclusively—a simplistic exercise fraught with danger. Indeed, according

2. René Cassin, "Historique de la Déclaration Universelle de 1948," in *La pensée et l'action* (Paris: Centre National de la Recherche Scientifique, 1981), 109–21, at 114.

to Toronto Professor Craig Scott, for those aiming to work as human rights activists, policy-makers, or as scholars dealing with economic, social, and cultural rights issues, problem-solving is enhanced by understanding the holistic bundle of rights and by being "prepared to engage in category crossing and category combining."[3] Two perspectives can assist in this regard.

First, simply by imagining the partial or total collapse of just one of the rights pillars in our four-pillared human rights temple, we can see quickly the fundamental interdependence of the various pillars of rights that jointly hold up the temple. Consider, for example, the consequences to the right to health (Pillar 4) if all or part of pillars 1–4 were to collapse or be demolished, having theretofore provided: *equality* to safeguard access to medical care for all without regard to race, sex or other status factors (Pillar 1, art. 3); *privacy*, essential for the security of one's health records (Pillar 1, art. 12); *freedom of movement*, necessary for health professionals to attend international conferences to improve their skills (Pillar 2, art. 13); *freedom of thought*, essential for scientific creativity in support of medical science advances (Pillar 3, art. 18); the *right to information and freedom of expression*, central to everyone's right to inquiry as pharmaceutical consumers and to criticize public health policy (Pillar 3, art. 19); everyone's *right to enjoy the advancements of science* (Pillar 4, art. 27). And what, indeed, might be the consequences if the temple's pediment itself were damaged or destroyed—for example, Article 28's promise of an *international order promotive of international cooperation*, including technology transfer?

Second, in addition to imagining how the loss of one right may lead to the loss of others, one must also understand that these various categories ("generations," "pillars," or otherwise) of rights, while distinct, often display significant overlap and connection. For example, freedom of speech, perhaps the ultimate symbol of individualism (freedom from governmental intervention), necessarily takes place in a group or social setting and, in any event, requires courts and other decision-making institutions (commonly at large public expense) to be safeguarded. The collective right to social and economic development is meaningless if it does not embody education rights for individuals. A people's cultural identity is preserved only if individuals are protected in their customary practices. And so on. In other words, the commonplace suggestion that traditional civil and political rights are individual rights (ostensibly "negative rights") and that socioeconomic and cultural rights are collective rights (ostensibly "positive rights") breaks down when one analyzes the content of human rights. Classifying rights as individual or collective, negative or positive, or in any other such categorical way is a useful first step in understanding their scope and in distinguishing between rights that are associated with, say, political liberty on the one hand and socioeconomic equality on the other, and, moreover, reflects ideological preferences that are real and significant. But it is precarious theoretically and therefore hazardous operationally when it comes to the "nuts and bolts" hard work of implementing human rights "on the ground." As Burns Weston emphasizes in Reading 1 of Chapter 1, in an increasingly interdependent and interpenetrating global community, any human rights orientation that fails to recognize the essential interrelatedness of all human rights is likely to provoke widespread skepticism.

Still, while human rights in the early twenty-first century may be seen increasingly as embodying interrelated values, the connections between them are perceived variously by different people depending on their respective philosophical or ideological viewpoints. Not

---

3. Craig Scott, "Toward the Institutional Integration of the Core Human Rights Treaties," in Isfahan Merali and Valerie Oosterveld, eds., *Giving Meaning to Economic, Social, and Cultural Rights* (Philadelphia: University of Pennsylvania Press, 2001), 7–38, at 7.

at all trivial in their implications for human rights are the disparate perspectives of, say, a free market Canadian, an ardent Cuban Marxist, or a Kenyan official, each preoccupied with issues of modernization.[4]

BASIC NEEDS AND HUMAN RIGHTS

The interrelatedness of individual and collective rights and of political liberty and economic equality—valuable in understanding second generation rights and perhaps nowhere so evident as in the debate over appropriate goals for modernization in developing countries—is depicted in a basic needs/human rights approach to balanced human development proposed by Johan Galtung and Anders Wirak,[5] partially extrapolated in Table 1.

Projected onto the national plane, the Galtung-Wirak approach points to the duty of governments to respect fundamental civil and political rights (the principal focus of Chapter 2 in this volume) and to provide needed goods and services to all on the basis of equality (the principal focus of this chapter). Moreover, the approach assumes that the purpose of development (a primary focus in Chapter 4) is to enhance the lives of "men and women everywhere" rather than "things, systems, and structures"[6] and, to that end, to serve the humane values of security, welfare, freedom, and identity.

The classic debate as to whether capitalism or socialism or some combination of the two affords the most promising route to the fulfillment of this duty as a function of national governance is sometimes broadly characterized as a contest between freedom and bread. But with the collapse of the Soviet Union and the demise of most authoritarian socialist regimes, the successor free and mixed market democracies must still attend to the issue of whether choices between freedom and bread must be made with a consequent imbalance in overall human development. Writing in 2002, Michael Freeman noted that "there is now a widespread belief that free markets will do a better job" in meeting basic human needs, to which he tersely replied: "It is clear unregulated markets will almost certainly not."[7] Similarly, echoing Rhoda Howard-Hassmann in Reading 4 of Chapter 1, Jack Donnelly has staked out a strong position on this theme, arguing that human rights are required to modulate and "tame" both majoritarian democracy and markets, restricting their operation to "a limited rights-defined domain."[8] That is, majoritarian democracy must respect minority rights and market economies must be tempered by the duty to short-change no one's basic needs.[9] Donnelly concludes: "Only when the pursuit of prosperity is tamed by

4. See Adamantia Pollis, "Liberal, Socialist and Third World Perspectives on Human Rights," in Peter Schwab and Adamantia Pollis, eds., *Toward a Human Rights Framework* (New York: Praeger, 1982).

5. See Johan Galtung and Anders Helge Wirak, "Human Needs, Human Rights and the Theories of Development," in Johan Galtung and R. G. Cant, eds., *Indicators of Social and Economic Change and Their Applications*, Reports and Papers in Social Science 37 (Paris: UNESCO, 1976), 7–34 (hereafter "Human Needs, Human Rights"). See also Galtung and Wirak, "Human Needs and Human Rights—A Theoretical Approach," *Bulletin of Peace Proposals* 8 (1977): 251–58 (hereafter "Theoretical Approach"). For a differently derived (human evolutionary biology) but similar model of human needs and human rights, see John O'Manique, *The Origins of Justice: The Evolution of Morality, Human Rights, and Law* (Philadelphia: University of Pennsylvania Press, 2003).

6. Galtung and Wirak, "Human Needs, Human Rights," note 5, at 2, 8.

7. Michael Freeman, *Human Rights: An Interdisciplinary Approach* (Cambridge: Polity Press, 2002), 166.

8. Jack Donnelly, "Human Rights, Democracy, and Development," *HRQ* 21, no. 3 (1999): 608–32, at 630.

9. See Amy Chua, *World on Fire: How Exporting Free Market Democracy Breeds Ethnic Hatred and Global Instability* (New York: Anchor Books, 2004). Cf. Andrew J. Nathan, "The Dynamics and Counterdynamics of Globalization," in Mahmood Monshipouri, Neil Englehart, Andrew J. Nathan, and Kavita Philip, eds, *Constructing Human Rights in the Age of Globalization* (Armonk, N.Y.: M.E. Sharpe, 2003), 2: 111–236.

TABLE 1.
THE GALTUNG-WIRAK MODEL OF BASIC NEEDS AND HUMAN RIGHTS AND THE
CORRESPONDING GOVERNMENT DUTIES TO PROVIDE GOODS AND SERVICES

VALUES	NEEDS/RIGHTS	GOODS/SERVICES
Security	Individual: against attack	Personal security
	Collective: against war and group` destruction	Peace
		Self-determination
Welfare		
Physiological	Individual and collective	Food, water,
Ecological	Climatic	Clothing, housing
	Somatic	Medical treatment
	Collective	Clean environment
Sociocultural	Self-expression, dialogue, preservation of group values	Schooling
		Cultural preservation
Freedom		
Mobility	Right to travel	Transportation
Exchange	Right to exchange information	Communication
Politics	Right to participate, choose, mobilize	Elections, parties, assemblies, meetings
	Right of due process	Courts
Legal work	Right to work	Jobs
Identity		
Relation to self	Need for self-expression, creativity	Leisure
(individual needs)	Need for self-actualization to realize personal potential	Vacation
Relation to others	Need for sense of purpose	Religion, ideology, culture
(collective needs)	Need for affection, love, sex	Primary groups
	Need for association, support from others	Secondary groups

economic and social rights, such as when markets are embedded in a welfare state does a political economy merit our respect."[10]

Projected onto the international plane, particularly in relation to "Third World" development issues (presented in Chapter 4 below), the Galtung-Wirak approach raises key questions about the prospects for a world order rooted in mutual respect for the needs and rights of everyone and about patterns of interstate cooperation designed to promote self-reliant socioeconomic development as a means of preserving identity values that, as Galtung has observed, are based on the needs of people in their own societies. "Self-reliance," he writes, "implies reliance on one's own resources."[11] In short, the Galtung-Wirak approach begs us to seek ways to harness global cooperation for human development in order to minimize exploitative and dominance relationships among peoples and nations.

In addition to pointing up the essential interconnectedness of all human rights at the individual, collective, and global levels, the Galtung-Wirak approach encourages us to acknowledge that economic, social, and cultural rights are interdependent and that "rights are the means and that the satisfaction of needs is the end of holistic human development"[12] and everyone's right to an adequate standard of living. Like all other means-end relations, the relationship is complicated,[13] and the achievement of most needs/rights will

10. Donnelly, "Human Rights, Democracy, and Development," note 8, at 630.
11. Johan Galtung, *True Worlds* (New York: Free Press, 1980), 154.
12. Galtung and Wirak, "Theoretical Approach," note 5, at 258.
13. See Philip Alston, "Making Space for New Human Rights: The Case of the Right to Development," *Harvard Human Rights Yearbook* (1988), 1: 3–40.

require, especially in the developing Third World, integrated as well as enlightened and resolute responses on the national and international planes. Thus food, commonly conceived in the language of rights, becomes, in this new context, both an individual and collective physiological need.

Most of the selections in this chapter emphasize the ways in which the Galtung-Wirak perspective on needs and rights clarifies the concept of holistic human development with particular attention to "second generation" socioeconomic and cultural rights. For example, in his essay on "Economic, Social and Cultural Rights as Human Rights" (Reading 13), the Norwegian human rights scholar Asbjørn Eide argues that economic and social rights cannot be considered apart from development which, in turn, means the realization of human rights in all their aspects. To monitor this process of realization, Eide associates himself with the work of Bard-Anders Andreassen and other Nordic scholars who seek to identify measurement indicators appropriate to represent minimum supporting levels to meet human needs, including nutrition, health, employment, a clean environment, and so forth.[14] These scholars concede that cooperation of various social institutions and the social sciences is essential for the daunting tasks of identifying peoples' needs from country to country and for ensuring that the participation of those groups with the greatest barriers enjoy social and economic rights. But Eide makes clear his conclusion that the interdependent relationships identified among various rights imply that the weakest in society deserve to have their basic needs and related human rights guaranteed, at least in terms of definable minimum thresholds.

WORK, FOOD, HEALTH, EDUCATION, AND CULTURE

The philosopher James W. Nickel, asking whether there is a human right to employment, identifies work as "the central means to many of the essential goals of life."[15] The importance of work as a human right is also reflected in the history of the concept. Among the array of economic, social, and cultural rights specified in 1948 by the framers of the Universal Declaration of Human Rights, workers' rights and the rights of labor predated the post-World War II instruments, the International Labour Organization (ILO) having been organized in Washington, D.C., in 1919. Since that time, although seldom invoking the language of human rights as such, the ILO has initiated a system for defining and protecting labor rights ("standards"), and today operates as a specialized agency affiliated with the United Nations. The ILO has adopted over 180 conventions constituting standards to which member states pledge adherence, respect, and protection. Both the UDHR and the ICESCR build on the work of the ILO in their provisions regarding the right to an adequate standard of living and to social security in the event of unemployment. In his essay below on "Workers Rights Are Human Rights" (Reading 14), Lee Swepston invokes ILO standards that are designed to look out for the benefit of workers' rights including "core human rights standards." These cover the subjects of freedom of association and protection of the right to organize, and protection against forced labor, child labor, and discrimination in relation to work. On these topics and with regard to equal pay for equal work,

14. See United Nations Development Programme, *Human Development Report 1991* (New York: Oxford University Press, 1991).

15. James W. Nickel, "Is There a Human Right to Employment?" *Philosophical Forum* 10 (1978–79): 158–70. See also James A. Gross, *Workers' Rights as Human Rights* (Ithaca, N.Y.: Cornell University Press, 2003); Richard Lewis Siegel, *Employment and Human Rights: The International Dimension* (Philadelphia: University of Pennsylvania Press, 1994).

healthy workplaces, and protection against the effects of unemployment, ILO standards develop in more depth many of the concepts found in the International Bill of Rights.[16] With such standards, Lee Swepston looks critically at American labor law. Viewing workers' rights as human rights, he finds the United States lags behind other modern market economies.

Swepston's analysis draws upon human rights standards that tie workers' rights to other related human rights reflecting basic human needs which the UDHR categorizes in terms of the right to an adequate standard of living. Consider, for example, the language of UDHR Article 25 and note how several economic rights tied to human needs are interconnected: "Everyone has the right to a standard of living adequate for the health and well-being of himself and of his family, including food, clothing, housing and medical care and necessary social services, and the right to security in the event of unemployment, sickness, disability, widowhood, old age or other lack of livelihood in circumstances beyond his control." The ILO played a leading role in drafting this language in 1947–48 and in promoting the concept of an "adequate standard of living" as the "hook" on which to hang the right to health, medical care, and the right to food. The drafters of Article 25 conceded that implementation of these rights would vary depending on the public, private, or mixed nature of economic organization and also with state capacity relative to [available] national resources. But they also aspired to implementation of these rights augmented by "international co-operation."[17] Such cooperation includes collaboration and support among governmental, intergovernmental, and nongovernmental organizations, and, as well, professional societies working in support of human rights across national boundaries.

The need for and right to food is among the human rights linked to everyone's right to an adequate standard of living. In his essay "Food Is a Human Right" (Reading 15), George Kent acknowledges the importance of international cooperation in satisfying global food needs. However, he dissents from people working to end hunger and malnutrition who use the slogan "food first"; the phrase or concept, he argues, appears to assume that the issue of food should overshadow other human rights with which it is interconnected and/or with which it is interdependent. The right to food (and nutrition), as important as it is, constitutes but one of the dimensions of adequate livelihood specified in Article 25. Thus, Kent says, it is inappropriate to argue that nutrition is necessarily more important than, say, health, housing, or education. Kent aligns his holistic perspective with that of Asbjørn Eide in arguing that all aspects of livelihood are interrelated and should be kept in balance.

Like food, the right to health is among those the framers of the UDHR linked to the right to an "adequate standard of living." Paul Hunt, in "The Right to Health: Key Objectives, Themes, and Interventions" (Reading 16), provides the reader with an insider's view of how to assess the right to health from an international perspective. As the UN Special Rapporteur on the Right to Health, Hunt clarifies key objectives of the right, as well as related themes and interventions. Since the UN's adoption of the Universal Declaration, its canons have become globally pervasive, influencing related areas of law and professional standards, including medical ethics and policy analysis, especially in the field of public health.[18]

16. ILO standards can be accessed from the ILO web site http://www.ilo.org under "International Standards and Human Rights."
17. United Nations Commission on Human Rights, 3rd Sess., Summary Record of the 65th Meeting, UN Doc. E/CN.4/SR.65, at 5.
18. Jonathan M. Mann, Sofia Gruskin, Michael A. Grodin, and George J. Annas, eds., *Health and Human Rights: A Reader* (New York: Routledge: 1999); British Medical Association, *The Medical Profession and Human Rights: Handbook for a Changing Agenda* (London: Zed Books with BMA, 2001).

A human rights perspective applied to public health scrutinizes inequalities in the distribution of health resources and identifies institutional discrimination against disfavored minorities and immigrants. It prompts us to ask whether medical research funds are allocated fairly to issues of women's health, contributing to morbidity, mortality, and lack of well-being. The UDHR reinforces our understanding that among the essential steps in responding to the HIV/AIDS pandemic is recognizing and ensuring the human rights of those at risk. Moreover, human rights analysis calls on us not only to look at war with abhorrence but to monitor the extent to which modern war and civil strife take a toll on civilians, including children. In short, human rights analysis drawing on internationally defined standards discloses how rights violations contribute to ill-health and even undermine the right to life.[19]

Over a half century after the adoption of the UDHR, violations of the right to health, the right to medical care, and the right to share in the benefits of scientific advances have proliferated far beyond that imagined in 1948. In addition to the related violations of human rights with which we are all familiar, the UDHR drafters could not have foreseen such present-day issues as the maldistribution of medical services for life-saving drugs based on ethnic, racial, and national differences; DNA testing without regard to privacy; gene patenting that does not benefit gene contributors; pharmaceutical fraud and dumping in less developed countries; and discrimination in access to education in the health professions and medicine. For these and myriad other such contemporary problems, we look to the UDHR to begin—but hardly to conclude—inquiry into applicable normative standards and enforcement mechanisms.

In "The Right to Education and Human Rights Education" (Reading 17), Richard Pierre Claude examines the importance of education in the UDHR cluster of internationally defined human rights. The right to education is multifaceted. As a social right in the community context, it promotes the full development of the human personality. As an economic right, it facilitates economic self-sufficiency through employment or self-employment. And as a cultural right, now that the international community has directed education toward the building of a universal culture of human rights, it serves all levels of human civilization from the most local to the most global. In his essay, Claude describes the three goals for education stipulated by UDHR Article 26: the full development of the human personality, the promotion of understanding and tolerance among diverse groups, and the promotion of world peace. Examples of programs of human rights education directed to each of the three goals are described, both with respect to programs of formal education (involving the customary tripartite academic structure) and nonformal or "popular education" undertaken by NGOs in their efforts to respond to the needs of particular targeted groups such as street children and illiterate women in rural areas of the "Global South." In an important related essay, anthropologist Stephen A. Hansen writes about "The Right to One's Own Culture" (Reading 18). He observes that several international instruments refer to the right to culture, cultural development, and cultural life, and at the same time notes that cultural rights remain among the least understood and the least legally developed of all human rights.[20] He introduces the reader to a number of conceptual issues relating to the right to culture and problems of implementation. These include the nature and scope of culture within a human rights context, individual and collective rights, and the recognition of unique cultural groups with special needs.

19. Paul Farmer, "Pathologies of Power: Rethinking Health and Human Rights," *American Journal of Public Health* 89, no. 10 (1999): 1486–96.
20. Rhoda E. Howard-Hassmann, *Human Rights and the Search for Community* (Boulder, Colo.: Westview Press, 1995).

Across the globe, as Rhoda Howard-Hassmann (Reading 4) has reminded us, human societies have established progressively closer contacts and, in our new post-Cold War world, at a pace that has accelerated dramatically, confronting us with the new facts of globalization. In 2002, the ILO empaneled a World Commission on the Social Dimensions of Globalization whose 15 independent experts addressed, among many other things, the prospective impact of the worldwide expansion of market economies on human rights, including those discussed in this chapter—work, food, health, education, and culture.[21] In defining their task, leading to recommendations, they said:

> We seek a globalization with a social dimension which sustains human values and enhances the well-being of people in terms of their freedom, prosperity and security. Globalization is seen through the eyes of women and men in terms of the opportunity it provides for decent work; for meeting their essential needs for food, water, health, education and shelter and for a livable environment. Without such a social dimension, many will continue to view globalization as a new version of earlier forms of domination and exploitation.[22]

The World Commission offered numerous recommendations, but recognized as fundamental the need of people to see that solutions to many of the problems that affect them can be found no longer, certainly not exclusively, at the national level alone. This fact requires that people resist cultural nationalism as a barrier to living together in an interconnected and ever more integrated world while, at the same time, they nurture and celebrate traditional symbols, ancient customs, and all else that makes them distinct culturally.[23] However worthy of veneration peoples' cultural origins from area to area, we live in a new—experimental—global society in which the United Nations has called on the international community to cooperate in the "building of a universal culture of human rights."[24] As ancient cultures invoked sailing ships as symbols to reference their origins and address their shared fate, so today modern science gives us photos of "Spaceship Earth" that help us to visualize our planet as the unique carrier vessel of all humanity that it is and thus to embrace a new global ethic of species identity that perceives our common human needs as human rights.

21. *A Fair Globalization: Creating Opportunities for All*, Report of the World Commission on the Social Dimension of Globalization (Geneva: International Labour Organization, 2004).
22. Ibid., 5.
23. In this connection, Burns Weston's essay on the tension between cultural relativism and universalism (Reading 3 in Chapter 1) is especially relevant and helpful.
24. UN General Assembly Resolution on the United Nations Decade for Human Rights Education (Dec. 23, 1994), referenced in Documentary Appendix B.

13. ASBJØRN EIDE *Economic, Social, and Cultural Rights as Human Rights*

THE HUMAN RIGHTS SYSTEM AND THE PLACE OF ECONOMIC, SOCIAL, AND CULTURAL RIGHTS

Obligations undertaken by states, and consequently by the international community, under international human rights instruments shall be implemented in good faith.[1] This standard applies to all parts of the contemporary human rights system. However, many obstacles must be overcome in fulfilling this standard, including that of the relative neglect of economic, social, and cultural rights. Another problem has been the slow process in clarifying the content of these rights and their corresponding obligations. Greater and more detailed precision has been obtained during later years, however, by way of the "general comments" interpreting the relevant international instruments by the UN Committee on Economic, Social and Cultural Rights.

Internationally recognized human rights are those included in the International Bill of Human Rights or those elaborated on in subsequent instruments adopted by the UN General Assembly. The International Bill includes the Universal Declaration of Human Rights (UDHR) and the two Covenants adopted on the basis of that Declaration, that is, the International Covenant on Civil and Political Rights (ICCPR) and the International Covenant on Economic, Social and Cultural Rights (ICESCR).[2] The International Bill of Human Rights has since been extensively elaborated through the adoption of numerous conventions and declarations, both at the universal level (by the United Nations and specialized agencies) and at the regional level. The rights contained in these instruments form a wide-ranging, but interrelated, normative system.

The UDHR, adopted in 1948, contains nearly the whole range of human rights within one consolidated text. The subsequent division of human rights into two main categories resulted from a controversial and contested decision made by the UN General Assembly in 1951, during the drafting of the ICCPR and ICESCR. The General Assembly decided that two separate human rights covenants should be prepared.

Underlying this decision were several assumptions, not all of them well-founded. It was argued and subsequently often repeated that the two sets of rights were of a different nature and therefore needed different instruments. Civil and political rights were considered to be "absolute" and "immediate," whereas economic, social, and cultural rights were held to be programmatic, to be realized gradually, and therefore not a matter of rights. A related assumption was that civil and political rights were "justiciable" in the sense that they could easily be applied by courts and similar judicial bodies, whereas economic, social, and cultural rights were of a more political nature. It was further believed that civil and political rights were "free" in the sense that they did not cost much. Their main contents were assumed to be obligations of states not to interfere with the integrity and the freedom of the individual. The implementation of economic, social, and cultural rights, in contrast, was held to be costly since they were understood as obliging the state to provide welfare to the individual. Thus, the arguments centered around the issue of the differences in state obligations arising from the two sets of rights. For this reason, it was expected that states who did not want to undertake the obligations arising from economic, social, and cultural rights would be willing to ratify an instrument which contained only civil and political rights.

In hindsight, many of the assumptions have been overstated or mistaken. It will be shown below that there are considerable similarities in state obligations with regard to both sets of rights.

---

1. This is expressly provided by Article 26 of the 1969 Vienna Convention on the Law of Treaties: "Every treaty in force is binding upon the parties to the treaty and must be performed by them in good faith."
2. Each of these instruments is reprinted and referenced in Documentary Appendix A.

The proclamation of the universality of human rights understandably met resistance from representatives of different cultures and ideologies. Within some societies in the West, cultural traditions persist based on a strong faith in full economic liberalism and a severely constrained role for the state in matters of welfare. This gives rise to some cultural and ideological resistance to economic and social rights, but it has not proved itself strong enough to prevent the ratification of the ICESCR by the vast majority of Western states.

Resistance to parts of the human rights system, including some aspects of economic, social, and cultural rights, may also be found in other cultures. In many Islamic states, paternalism remains strong and causes cultural resistance to equal enjoyment of economic and social rights for men and women, in particular equal access to education, equal pay for equal work, and equality in inheritance laws and thereby equality in the right to property.

While cultural resistance to parts of the universal rights system can be found in both Western and non-Western societies, the evolution has over time gone in the direction of greater integration between the different sets of rights. In human rights instruments adopted in later years, building on and further developing the International Bill of Human Rights, the different sets of rights are included side by side. The best example of this integration is the Convention on the Rights of the Child (CRC),[3] where freedom of expression and information (Article 13), freedom of thought, conscience, and religion (Article 14) and other civil rights are found together with the right to health (Article 24), to social security (Article 25), to an adequate standard of living (Article 27), to education (Article 28), and to protection from economic exploitation (Article 32). The CRC has now been ratified by approximately 192 states, which constitutes [almost the totality] of the world community of states.

Both the International Convention on the Elimination of All Forms of Racial Discrimination (ICERD) and the International Convention on Elimination of All Forms of Discrimination against Women (CEDAW)[4] include express references to the right to equal enjoyment of economic, social, and cultural rights as well as to civil and political rights.

The Preamble of the UDHR (1948) points out that "the highest aspiration of the common people" is the "advent of a world in which human beings shall enjoy freedom of speech and belief and freedom from fear and want." The intention to integrate the different sets of rights were obvious. Forty-five years later, in 1993, representatives of 171 governments assembled in Vienna at the World Conference on Human Rights and reiterated that all human rights are universal, indivisible, and interdependent and interrelated.[5]

EVOLUTION OF HUMAN RIGHTS AND THE EXPANDING ATTENTION TO ECONOMIC, SOCIAL, AND CULTURAL RIGHTS

Throughout the evolutionary history of human rights, three aspects of human existence have sought to be safeguarded: human integrity, freedom, and equality. Axiomatic to these three aspects is the respect for the dignity of every human being. The way in which these issues have been addressed has matured over time, from initial idealistic assertions of vague principles to the adoption of the comprehensive, international normative system now in existence. The existing system contains a wide range of specific rights and to some extent also the corresponding obligations of states. The latter aspect, however, is still underdeveloped.

When the UDHR was adopted in 1948, there was not much doubt that economic and social rights had to be included. Its great contribution is that it extended the human rights platform to embrace the whole field—civil, political, economic, social, and cultural—and made the different rights interrelated and mutually reinforcing. One of the main sources of the broad approach to human rights was the "Four Freedoms Address" by Franklin D. Roosevelt, then president of the United States, in his State of the Union Address in January 1941. This approach was widely supported by others in the United States and elsewhere in what is normally referred to as "the West." One of the four freedoms on which President Roosevelt envisaged

---

3. Concluded Nov. 2, 1989, referenced in Documentary Appendix B.
4. Both ICERD (Dec. 21, 1965) and CEDAW (Dec. 18, 1979) are referenced in Documentary Appendix B.
5. World Conference on Human Rights, Vienna Declaration and Programme of Action (June 25, 1993), Pt. I, ¶5, referenced in Documentary Appendix B.

the post-war world order to be built was the freedom from want.

The initial planning of the United Nations was mainly carried out within the United States administration, influenced to a large extent by the aims contained in the Four Freedoms Address. In his 1944 State of the Union Address, Roosevelt advocated the adoption of an "Economic Bill of Rights," saying that "[w]e have come to the clear realization of the fact that true individual freedom cannot exist without economic security and independence"; "necessitous men are not free men." People who are hungry and out of job are the stuff of which dictatorships are made.[6] He proposed including many of those economic and social rights which subsequently came to be included in the UDHR and later in the ICESCR. The impact of the "Four Freedoms Address" gives reason to assume that Roosevelt's address articulated visions widely shared in many countries by those who were struggling against the devastating effects of extremist nationalism and totalitarianism, while simultaneously fighting against the effects of callous economic laissez-faire, which had ushered in the Great Depression and in turn had fueled the emergence and appeal of authoritarian nationalism.

When the Division on Human Rights of the United Nations secretariat, directed by Canadian professor John Humphrey, prepared its first draft of the Universal Declaration, one of the main texts used was the one prepared by the American Law Institute. The realization, particularly in the West, that the political upheavals and the emergence of totalitarian regimes in the period between the two World Wars had been due to the widespread unemployment and poverty led to a genuine interest in securing economic and social rights, not only for their own sake but also for the preservation of individual freedom and democracy. These concerns are equally important in the present time, in light of escalating unemployment, increasing poverty and growing disparities in income, not only in the Third World but also in Central and Eastern Europe and in the West. It is necessary, therefore, to increase the efficiency of international mechanisms in this field and possibly to develop new ones.

The UDHR envisaged that the rights contained therein shall be enjoyed by everyone, throughout the world. This required both absorption and global institutionalization. Absorption here means that within all national societies, the rights contained in the Declaration shall be recognized as achievable ideals to be implemented in national law and administration, and through necessary political and social reforms. Global institutionalization means the development of mechanisms at the international level which, on the one hand, can monitor the implementation of human rights worldwide and, on the other hand, can generate the necessary cooperation in the fields of economic, social, and cultural matters required to establish conditions for their full enjoyment worldwide.

Obligations undertaken by states under [the two Covenants adopted in 1966] include taking steps with a view to achieving progressively the rights, including the adoption of legal measures.[7] The adoption of such legislation constitutes a process of positivization of economic, social, and cultural rights at the national level. The transformation of economic, social, and cultural rights into positive law, whether in constitutions or in statutory law, is, however, not enough. The rights must be realized in fact, which may require comprehensive administrative measures and social action. The success of the transformation depends on the evolution of a human rights culture where individuals accept both their own rights and their duties to the community which make the enjoyment of rights possible.

WHAT RIGHTS AND WHOSE RIGHTS?

The sources of economic, social, and cultural rights in international law can be found in numerous declarations and conventions. While the UDHR is the initial foundation and the ICESCR constitutes a more elaborate framework for these rights, they are also contained in numerous other instruments partly adopted by the UN General Assembly, partly by specialized agencies, and partly by regional organizations. A brief review of the main categories of economic, social, and cultural rights and the groups of persons who are their beneficiaries, with reference to some

6. For details on this statement by Roosevelt, see Philip Alston, "U.S. Ratification of the Covenant on Economic, Social and Cultural Rights: The Need for an Entirely New Strategy," *AJIL* 84 (1990): 365–93, at 387.
7. ICESCR, art. 2.

of the main instruments adopted by the United Nations, will be made.

Economic, social, and cultural rights constitute three interrelated components of a more comprehensive package. The different components also have links to civil and political rights. At the core of social rights is the right to an adequate standard of living (UDHR, Article 25; ICESCR Article 11; CRC, Article 27). The enjoyment of this right requires, at a minimum, that everyone shall enjoy the necessary subsistence rights—adequate food and nutrition rights, clothing, housing, and the necessary conditions of care. Closely related to this right is the right of families to assistance (ICESCR Article 10; CRC, Article 27). In order to enjoy these social rights, there is also a need to enjoy certain economic rights. These are the right to property (UDHR, Article 17), the right to work (UDHR, Article 23; ICESCR, Article 6) and the right to social security (UDHR, Articles 22 and 25; ICESCR, Article 9; CRC, Article 26).

The economic rights have a dual function, most clearly demonstrated in regard to the right to property. On the one hand, this right serves as a basis for entitlements which can ensure an adequate standard of living, while on the other hand it is a basis of independence and therefore of freedom. The initial concern with the right to property, articulated by John Locke and others, was directed against the feudal order where control over land and other resources were based on a hierarchical system constituting profound inequality and dependencies. It is therefore understandable that the right to property became a crucial element in the early quest for freedom and equality. The right to property in the traditional understanding of the word cannot be enjoyed on an equal basis by all. The right to property therefore has to be supplemented by at least two other rights: the right to work which can provide an income ensuring an adequate standard of living, and the right to social security which can supplement, and where necessary fully substitute for, insufficient income derived from property or from work—insufficient, that is, in regard to the enjoyment of an adequate standard of living.

The right to work is also a basis of independence, provided the work is freely chosen by the person concerned, that sufficient income is obtained from it, and provided the workers can protect their interests through free trade unions (Article 8 of the ICESCR and several ILO conventions).

The right to social security is essential, particularly when a person does not have the necessary property available, or is not able to secure an adequate standard of living through work, due either to unemployment, old age, or disability (UDHR, Articles 22 and 25).

The notion of cultural rights is more complex.[8] Under Article 27 of the UDHR and Article 15 of the ICESCR, cultural rights contain the following elements: the right to take part in cultural life, the right to enjoy the benefits of scientific progress and its applications, the right to benefit from the protection of the moral and material interests resulting from any scientific, literary or artistic production of which the beneficiary is the author, and the freedom indispensable for scientific research and creative activity.

It is closely linked, however, to other rights such as the right to education (UDHR, Article 26; ICESCR, Articles 13 and 14; CRC, Articles 28 and 29), but that right is also an essential element in economic and social rights.[9] Education is increasingly important in order to make optimal use of property to secure an adequate standard of living, in order to obtain satisfactory work and to perform well in work, as well as to be able to use income derived from property, work, or social security in an optimal way for an adequate standard of living. Education, however, should also be a tool for creative participation in society, in the overall cultural evolution and in the development of respect for human rights and a world order based on law as envisaged in the Charter of the United Nations. One important aspect of cultural rights is the right to preserve the cultural identity of minority groups (ICCPR, Article 27; CRC, Article 30) which has implications for civil and political as well as economic and social rights.

In principle, everyone is the beneficiary of human rights. In practice, however, two sets of issues must be addressed. First, some groups are more vulnerable than others or have traditionally been subject to discrimination; they may require special protection of their rights, sometimes

---

8. On cultural rights and their complexities, see Reading 18 by Stephen A. Hansen in this chapter.
9. On the right to education, see Reading 17 by Richard Pierre Claude in this chapter.

through the adoption of affirmative action or other special measures. Second, who is the duty-holder, or responsible, with regard to particular groups of rights. The latter problem arises, in particular, with regard to migrant workers and other aliens (non-nationals), where the division of responsibility between the host country and the country of origin may sometimes create difficulties. Those who are stateless or who have lost their link to their country of origin, including asylum-seekers and refugees, may be in a particular predicament.

The first set of questions are addressed by special instruments seeking to ensure equality among all groups in society: The International Convention on the Elimination of All Forms of Discrimination against Women (CEDAW) and other instruments seeking to ensure equality for women, also in the economic, social, and cultural fields, if need be by affirmative action, the International Convention on the Elimination of All Forms of Racial Discrimination (ICERD), which similarly requires measures to ensure equality—in the economic, social, and cultural field as well as in the civil and political field—for everyone irrespective of racial or ethnic origin; the CRC which addresses the special needs of the child, including its economic and social rights. For minorities and indigenous peoples, two issues arise: one is to ensure equality in the enjoyment of economic and social rights; the other is to ensure conditions for the maintenance of their cultural identity, which in some cases may make it necessary to ensure that they control their own land and other resources and to ensure their standard of living in ways which correspond to their own traditions. This is of particular importance to indigenous peoples. The UN General Assembly has adopted a Declaration on the Rights of Persons Belonging to National or Ethnic, Religious and Linguistic Minorities (1992)[10] and a Declaration on the Rights of Indigenous Peoples is under preparation.[11]

The second aspect is even more complicated: rights require the existence of some duty-holders, and the primary responsibility for the realization of human rights rests with the state in which the persons concerned live. Can everyone present on a given territory demand that their economic, social, and cultural rights be ensured by that state?

With regard to economic and social rights there is clearly a need to distinguish between different groups of persons who are not nationals of the country concerned. In one category are persons who lawfully resided in a territory as citizens of a larger entity comprising that territory, and who subsequent to a political change become aliens without having moved, because of a change in borders, or because new states emerge or reemerge as independent entities [e.g., inhabitants of former Soviet territories or of the successor states to the former Yugoslavia]. Such residents must be entitled to all human rights, with only one qualification: until they are citizens, they are not entitled to vote and be elected in national elections. Another group of persons are those aliens who are temporary sojourners in the state, who arrive in full knowledge that it is not their state, and whose enjoyment of economic, social, and cultural rights must be dependent on the nature and length of their stay in that country, on conditions set by the host government.

More detailed rules for migrant workers and their families are contained in the International Convention on the Protection of All Migrant Workers and Their Families of 1990.[12]

DUTY-HOLDERS AND THEIR OBLIGATIONS

Rights require correlative duties. These are not spelled out in great detail in the main human rights instruments, but are gradually clarified through additional, more specific instruments, and through the practice of monitoring bodies. An inventory of the obligations contained in the many specific international instruments now adopted would show that a wide range of concrete obligations have already been undertaken, and that the treaty bodies are also contributing to the clarification of the obligations.

At the national level, many states have comprehensive and detailed legislation concerning economic, social, and cultural rights.

10. Adopted Dec. 18, 1992, referenced in Documentary Appendix B.
11. United Nations Draft Declaration on the Rights of Indigenous Peoples, referenced in Documentary Appendix B.
12. Concluded Dec. 18, 1990, in force July 1, 2002, referenced in Documentary Appendix B.

Under international law, obligations for human rights are primarily held by states. When states seek to implement these obligations in national law, they are required to impose duties on persons subject to their jurisdiction. Duties to respect the right of other persons, and duties to contribute to the common welfare, make it possible for the state to assist and to provide in ways which enable everyone to enjoy their economic, social, and cultural rights.

The UDHR imposes at least a moral obligation, if not more, on all states to seek to realize social, and economic rights. More importantly, under Article 2 of the ICESCR, States Parties have undertaken legally binding obligations to take steps to the maximum of their available resources to "achieve progressively" the full realization of the economic and social rights in that Covenant. It should be noted that the CRC, which includes many economic and social rights and corresponding state obligations, does not contain the qualifying clause "progressive realization." Under the CRC, the obligations arise immediately, only qualified by the phrase "within their means." This shows that what is special about economic, social, and cultural rights is only the question of the availability of means when such are required; the obligations are otherwise as immediate as are those relating to civil and political rights.

A widely spread misunderstanding has been that all economic, social, and cultural rights must be provided by the state, and that they are costly and lead to an overgrown state apparatus. Fundamental to a realistic understanding of state obligations is that the individual is the active subject of all economic and social development, as stated in the Declaration on the Right to Development (Article 2).[13] The individual is expected, whenever possible through his or her own efforts and by use of one's own resources, to find ways to ensure the satisfaction of his of her own needs, individually or in association with others. Use of his or her own resources, however, requires that the person has resources that can be used—typically land or other productive capital, or labour. This could include the shared right to use communal land, and the land rights held by indigenous peoples. Furthermore, the realization of economic, social, and cultural rights of an individual will usually take place within the context of a household as the smallest economic unit, although aspects of female and male division of labour and control over the production, as well as various forms of wider kinship arrangements may present alternative alliances.

State obligations must be seen in this light. Human rights impose three types or levels of obligations on States Parties: the obligations to *respect*, to *protect*, and to *fulfill*. In turn, the obligation to *fulfill* incorporates both an obligation to *facilitate* and an obligation to *provide*. States must, at the primary level, *respect* the resources owned by the individual, her or his freedom to find a job of preference and the freedom to take the necessary actions and use the necessary resources—alone or in association with others—to satisfy his or her own needs. In regard to the latter, collective or group rights can become important: the resources belonging to a collective of persons, such as indigenous populations, must be respected in order for them to be able to satisfy their needs. Consequently, as part of the obligation to respect these resources the state should take steps to recognize and register the land rights of indigenous peoples and land tenure of small holders whose title is uncertain.

State obligations consist, at a secondary level, of, for example, the protection of the freedom of action and the use of resources against other, more assertive or aggressive subjects—more powerful economic interests, protection against fraud, against unethical behavior in trade and contractual relations, against the marketing and dumping of hazardous or dangerous products. This protective function of the state is the most important aspect of state obligations also with regard to economic, social, and cultural rights, and it is similar to the role of the state as protector of civil and political rights.

At the tertiary level, the state has the obligations to fulfil the rights of everyone under economic, social, and cultural rights, by way of facilitation or direct provision. The obligation to fulfil by facilitation takes many forms, some of which are spelled out in the relevant instruments. For example, under the ICESCR, Article 11(2), the state shall take measures to improve measures of production, conservation, and distribution of food by making full use of technical and scientific knowledge and by developing or reforming agrarian systems. The obligation to fulfil by way of provision could consist in making

13. Adopted Dec. 4, 1986, referenced in Documentary Appendix B.

available what is required to satisfy basic needs, such as food or resources which can be used for food (direct food aid, or social security) when no other possibility exists, such as, for example: (1) when unemployment sets in (such as under recession); (2) for the disadvantaged, and the elderly; (3) during sudden situations of crisis or disaster (see below); and (4) for those who are marginalized (for example, due to structural transformations in the economy and production).

It may now have become clearer why the allegation that economic and social rights differ from the civil and political is that the former requires the use of resources by the state, while the obligation for states to ensure the enjoyment of civil and political rights does not require resources. This is a gross oversimplification. The argument is tenable only in situations where the focus on economic and social rights is on the tertiary level (the obligation to fulfill), while civil and political rights are observed on the primary level (the obligation to respect). This scenario is, however, arbitrary. Some civil rights require state obligations at all levels—also the obligation to provide direct assistance, when there is a need for it. Economic and social rights, on the other hand, can in many cases best be safeguarded through non-interference by the state with the freedom and use of resources possessed by the individuals.

In light of the complexity of the issue, and the need for flexibility to respond to different situations, it now becomes understandable that the basic provisions (ICESCR, Articles 2 and 11) were drafted more in the form of obligations of result rather than obligation of conduct. It is also understandable that some of these obligations when taken at their highest and most general level, cannot easily be made justiciable (manageable by third party judicial settlement). It is only when they are broken down into their more specific components that justiciability becomes practicable.

State obligations for economic and social rights were elaborated by a group of experts, convened by the International Commission of Jurists, in Limburg (the Netherlands) in June 1986. The outcome of the meeting is the so-called Limburg Principles, which is the best guide available to state obligations under the ICESCR.[14]

Among them we find the following Principle 8: "Although the full realization of the rights recognized in the Covenant is to be attained progressively, the application of some rights can be made justiciable immediately while other rights can become justiciable over time."

A decade later, experts on economic, social, and cultural rights met in Maastricht to adopt a set of guidelines on violations of human rights.[15] Many of these guidelines have since been taken into account in the practice of the treaty monitoring bodies.

When Article 2(1) of the ICESCR requires each State Party to take steps, individually and through international assistance and cooperation "to the maximum of its available resources" to "achieve progressively the full realization of the rights," it raises a number of fundamental questions: What resources are available to the state? Obviously, different states have vastly different amounts of resources available. This, however, does not depend solely on the GNP of the society concerned, but also on the amount of resources made available to the state for the pursuit of its obligations under international human rights law. An additional question, however, is the way in which privately held resources are distributed in society. Where income is fairly evenly distributed and opportunities therefore reasonably equal, the individuals are in a better position to take care of their own needs, and there could be a lesser need for public expenditures for the state—except for those expenditures which can more effectively be organized by the state. When, on the other hand, income is unevenly distributed, the requirement of equal opportunities and equal enjoyment of economic, social, and cultural rights may require more public expenditures, based on progressive taxation and other sources of state income. Paradoxically, however, there appears to be a greater willingness to accept taxation for public spending in egalitarian societies than in those societies where income is highly unequally distributed.

Strategies to improve the conditions for the poorer part of such societies must seek to ensure for them an opportunity to take charge of their own destiny, which is often blocked by the more powerful and assertive members of society. In such cases, economic, social, and cultural rights

14. Adopted Jan. 8, 1987, referenced in Documentary Appendix B.
15. Maastricht Guidelines on Violations of Economic, Social and Cultural Rights, referenced in Documentary Appendix B.

can be better safeguarded by land reform and other ways of redistributing basic resources, than through high levels of public expenditure. In industrialized and post-industrial societies, however, where agriculture is an insignificant part of the economy, economic, social, and cultural rights require the existence of a relatively strong state serving both to facilitate avenues towards equal opportunity for those who otherwise would become marginalized, and to ensure social security for those who cannot manage on their own.

With specific reference to the right to food,[16] the Committee on Economic, Social and Cultural Rights has observed that violations of the ICESCR occur when a state fails to ensure the satisfaction of, at the very least, the minimum essential level required to be free from hunger. In determining which actions or omissions amount to a violation, it is important to distinguish the inability from the unwillingness of a State Party to comply. Should a State Party argue that resource constraints make it impossible to provide access to food for those who are unable by themselves to secure such access, the state has to demonstrate that every effort has been made to use all the resources at its disposal in an effort to satisfy, as a matter of priority, those minimum obligations. This follows from Article 2(1) of the Covenant, which obliges a State Party to take the necessary steps to the maximum of its available resources, as previously pointed out by the Committee in its General Comment No. 3, paragraph 10. A state claiming that it is unable to carry out its obligation for reasons beyond its control therefore has the burden of proving that this is the case and that it has unsuccessfully sought to obtain international support to ensure the availability and accessibility of the necessary food.

The immediate obligations of states under Article 2 imply that countries with more resources have a higher level of core content or immediate duties than those with more limited resources. Objectively this should be possible to determine on the basis of GNP per capita. The question is not what resources are in the hands of the government as compared to privately owned resources—that is a political question which cannot be used as an excuse—but on the total resources of the country as a whole. How the implementation is to be carried out, either

by reliance on what people manage themselves when income distribution is relatively equal, or by redistribution through the government when resources are unevenly distributed, depends on the conditions which will vary in the different countries.

While the core content of the obligations are higher for states with more resources than those with less, all states must set benchmarks to move progressively beyond the core content and to harness the national resources for that purpose.

Any discrimination on the grounds of race, colour, sex, language, age, religion, political or other opinion, national or social origin, property, birth, or other status with the purpose or effect of nullifying or impairing the equal enjoyment or exercise of economic, social, and cultural rights constitutes a violation of the Covenant.

Violations can occur through the direct action of states or other entities insufficiently regulated by states, including failure to regulate activities of individuals or groups so as to prevent them from violating the rights of others, or the failure of a state to take into account its international legal obligations regarding economic and social rights when entering into agreements with other states or with international organizations.

A second question concerns the choices made by the state: What part of its resources are allocated to the realization of economic, social, and cultural rights compared to other purposes? By way of illustration it is important to grasp the part played by military expenditure in international relations as well as national policies. Sophisticated arms are mainly produced in high-tech countries and sold at great cost to Third World countries, whose main possibility to exchange often is to export agricultural products (not necessarily food, but also coffee, tea, flowers, etc.) at very low prices compared to the armaments they import. The exchange is profoundly destructive to the development of these countries. Wealthy countries nevertheless actively market armaments, which are imported by Third World governments—for prestige or for reasons of self-preservation. The "expenditure of death" should be turned into "expenditure of life" (public action to combat poverty) which could solve many of the problems now said to be insoluble owing to lack of resources, at the international as well as national level.

---

16. On the right to food, see Reading 15 by George Kent in this chapter.

QUESTIONS FOR REFLECTION AND DISCUSSION

1. Are economic, social, and cultural rights really *legal* rights? Is it not better to think of these second-generation "rights" as *moral* rights? Why? Why not? In *Basic Rights: Subsistence, Affluence, and U.S. Foreign Policy* (Princeton, N.J.: Princeton University Press, 1996), 13, Henry Shue writes that a "moral right provides (1) the rational basis for a justified demand (2) that the actual enjoyment of a substance be (3) socially guaranteed against standard threats." What is a "justified demand"? Are not legal as well as moral rights responses to justified demands? What is the "actual enjoyment of a substance"? Cannot such enjoyment be the outcome of legal as well as moral process? What does it mean to be "socially guaranteed"? Is not a purpose of law as well as morality to provide social guarantees? What are examples of "standard threats"? Are they any different from what provokes legal as well as moral action? Now, how do you answer the first two questions?

2. In *Making Sense of Human Rights: Philosophical Reflections on the Universal Declaration of Human Rights* (Berkeley: University of California Press, 1987), 149, James W. Nickel argues that to have an adequate understanding of economic rights we must recognize both "production-related rights" and "consumption-related rights." The former include, he says, the rights to liberty, health, and safety for people engaged in production, rights needed for effective production, and the right to employment, while the latter include the right to adequate nutrition and the right to protection of activities such as shopping, purchasing, renting, borrowing, contracting, storing, using, sharing, giving, receiving, inhabiting, eating, and drinking. Is this a useful dichotomy? If so, how? If not, why not?

3. Eide notes a "widely spread misunderstanding . . . that all economic, social, and cultural rights must be provided by the state, and that they are costly and lead to an overgrown state apparatus." He continues: "Fundamental to a realistic understanding of state obligations is that the individual is the active subject of all economic and social development [and that] the individual is expected, whenever possible through his or her own efforts and by use of one's own resources, to find ways to ensure the satisfaction of his or her own needs, individually or in association with others." He then remarks: "Use of his or her own resources, however, requires that the person has resources that can be used—typically land or other productive capital, or labour." Compare this statement with the "capabilities approach" advocated by Martha Nussbaum in Reading 2 of Chapter 1 in this volume. Is Eide promoting the "capabilities approach"? How are Eide and Nussbaum alike or different?

4. State parties to the International Covenant on Economic, Social and Cultural Rights (ICESCR, reprinted and referenced in Documentary Appendix A) are required "to take steps [toward] achieving progressively the full realization of the rights recognized in the . . . Covenant" (art. 2(1)). Why are economic, social, and cultural (ESC) rights qualified by a progressive realization standard while civil and political rights are not? Should this qualification be? Does not the progressive realization standard provide an opening for states to sign and ratify the ICESCR without implementing its legal obligations? Does not this treatment of ESC rights encourage the belief that these rights are more aspirational goals than legal obligations?

5. ICESCR Article 2(1) provides also that a state party is obligated under the Covenant "to the maximum of its available resources." Is it intuitive that states with greater capabilities are expected or required to implement ESC rights sooner than states with lesser capabilities and arguably greater need for the fulfillment of such rights? Note that Article 2(1) provides that the achievement of ESC rights shall be done not only individually but also "through international assistance and co-operation, especially economic and technical." If this provision were taken seriously by the international community, would there be any need for the resource availability qualification? Does it suggest a duty on the part of the world's wealthy to help the world's poor? In any event, how are a state's capabilities to be measured?

6. In "A Violations Approach to Monitoring the International Covenant on Economic, Social, and Cultural Rights," *Human Rights Dialogue* (New York: Carnegie Council on Ethics and International Affairs, Fall 1997), Ser. 1, no. 10, at http://www.cceia.org/viewMedia.php/prmTemplateID/8/prmID/580, Audrey R. Chapman argues for abandoning the progressive realization approach in favor of a violations-based approach (critically analyzing

the number of actual violations of the ICESCR of member states), largely because of the data-retrieval and statistical complexity of monitoring state progress on implementation under the progressive realization approach. She writes:

> A "violations approach" is more feasible precisely because it does not depend on the availability and public release of extensive and appropriate statistical data or on major improvements in states' statistical systems. The monitoring of human rights is not an academic exercise; it is intended to ameliorate human suffering resulting from violations of international human rights standards. It follows that identifying violations in order to end and rectify abuses deserves a higher priority than promoting progressive realization. An added benefit of focusing on the identification of violations is that it may prove a more effective path to conceptualizing the positive content of ESC rights than the more abstract legal or philosophical analyses attempted thus far.

Then, after remarking that a "violations approach" would also make it easier to identify and specify violations," Chapman proposes "a tripartite categorization of violations": (a) "state violations resulting from government actions, policies, and legislation"; (b) "violations related to patterns of discrimination"; and (c) "violations related to the state's failure to fulfill minimum core obligations of enumerated rights." Do you agree with Chapman that a "violations approach" would make implementation of the ICESCR less complicated than the "progressive realization approach"? Which system do you think would be the most effective? Why?

7. Imagine a state party to the ICESCR truly committed to fulfilling its obligations under the Covenant but without resources and access to resources sufficient to fulfill all the rights enumerated in the ICESCR. Should such a state prioritize the rights it can at least attempt to fulfill? If so, which ones should be prioritized? Sacrificed? Should civil and political rights that can be implemented relatively inexpensively, such as freedom from torture or the right to political participation, rank above or outweigh ESC rights such as the right to food or to education, which usually are costly? The reverse?

8. What, if any, compromises in civil and political rights should a state be authorized to make to ensure the economic well-being of its people? A capitalist state? A socialist state? An economically developed state? An economically developing state? To what extent, if at all, does or should economic well-being depend on the limitation of civil and political rights? By the same token, to what extent, if at all, does or should political freedom depend on the limitation of ESC rights?

9. Do ESC rights apply only to poor persons and poor countries? If not, what ESC rights might wealthy persons or countries lack and therefore seek?

10. Eide asks: "Can everyone present on a given territory demand that their economic, social, and cultural rights be ensured by that state?" His question is posed with reference to the distinction between nationals and non-nationals in a given state. Should the state provide for everyone? How do you answer the question? Why?

11. The ICESCR is meant to regulate state action. But what about acts by individuals acting independent of state action that deny others economic, social, and cultural rights—like employment, education, and housing discrimination. Do these activities fall within the purview of the ICESCR? If not, should they?

12. What would it take to get the United States officially to recognize ESC rights? To implement them domestically? Are either of these prospects realistic? Why? Why not? Should they be? Why? Why not? Is it, in any event, appropriate for the United States to deny the existence of such rights in its relations with countries that recognize them? Given the large U.S. influence worldwide, what implications does such a denial have for the justness of the global economy?

14. LEE SWEPSTON *Worker Rights Are Human Rights*

ILO STANDARDS AND GENERAL HUMAN RIGHTS

International labor law is very much a part of international human rights law. It is dealt with principally but not exclusively by the International Labour Organization (ILO). It is also dealt with under broader international human rights law, which is in turn based on the ILO standards.

Almost all the relevant United Nations human rights standards were adopted after the ILO conventions on the four basic human rights subjects of concern to the ILO.

[*Eds.*—Citing pertinent ILO conventions,[1] the author identifies these "four basic human rights" as: freedom of association and the right to organize and bargain collectively; freedom from forced labor; freedom from discrimination in employment and remuneration; and freedom from child labor (defined in terms of both minimum age and abusive/exploitative/hazardous work).]

WHAT DOES INTERNATIONAL LABOR LAW COVER?

International labor law is a wide and interesting field, which until lately has usually been ignored by writers on international law generally and on human rights particularly. It was in fact the first international law and human rights subject, with the campaign in the 1830s to eliminate slavery, and it is one of the fundamental subjects of international law.

These days the ILO is calling the basic content of international labor law "decent work." This is of course, a new expression for the ILO's traditional rallying cry of social justice, with some new elements. It is meant to address the changing environment for labor in the broader framework of globalization and the basic rules that should govern working life. Even though globalization has resulted in some real gains in the world's economies, it has also left behind very many of the world's working people, including the small employers and entrepreneurs whose success is essential for economic development around the world. Unemployment has risen and conditions of work have worsened especially in areas not directly caught up in export industries. So one of the ILO's goals in its legal and promotional work is to ensure that no one is left behind—or at least to reduce the negative impact of globalization on vulnerable workers.

The labor law of most of the world is based on ILO standards which were often incorporated directly into the labor legislation of newly independent countries that wanted to separate themselves from their colonial masters in the period beginning in the 1960s. As these countries became more sophisticated, they again turned to the ILO for help in reforming and updating their standards, and now at any one time the ILO is usually working with forty or fifty countries on their labor legislation. Needless to say, the ILO's advice on labor legislation is either based directly on its standards, or at least ensures that its advice is consistent with those standards.

In some cases the influence may be the other way around. When the ILO adopts new standards, its basis is the best national standards worldwide, and it tries not to establish international standards that are too high for developing countries to ratify. Thus the international standards are based on the best practice and most recent trends in its member states.

International labor law is not much known in the United States, as the U.S. system works very much in its own context. The fact that the U.S. system is different from the rest of the world has led to the decision of the U.S. government not to ratify most of the ILO's basic human rights standards, though the ILO and the U.S. government have been working on some of them.

The ILO constitution (adopted in 1919 and

---

1. See note 2 and accompanying text.

updated in 1946) includes the basic expression of human rights—though the term was not in use then—which includes equal pay for work of equal value; freedom from discrimination on the basis of race, creed, and sex; and of course freedom of association. Beyond the constitution, the ILO's traditional method of addressing social problems is through international labor standards, or conventions and recommendations adopted by the International Labor Conference, sometimes characterized as the International Labor Code. These international instruments lay down requirements of international law that are similar to national labor codes—hours of work, minimum wages, social security systems, safety and health, and the like. But they also contain guidance for larger questions of social policy that do not normally appear in national labor law. These include such matters as dedicating governments to the concept of full, productive, and freely chosen employment, the needs that should be met by statistical systems, the virtues of good labor administration, the requirements for labor inspectorates, and many other questions.

Given below is a sketch of the basic ILO standards, forming international labor law.

BASIC RIGHTS

The ILO has always seen several categories of rights as fundamental for all workers. This has been progressively formalized over the last few years. These are the four categories of rights mentioned above, all based on concepts found in the ILO constitution. There are two conventions considered as fundamental for each of the basic rights.

Forced Labor

The basic ILO documents about forced labor are the 1930 Forced Labor Convention (No. 29) and the 1958 Abolition of Forced Labor Convention (No. 105).[2] The Forced Labor Convention, adopted shortly after the League of Nations

adopted the Slavery Convention of 1926,[3] established protection against this most basic of human rights problems. This convention prohibits all forced or compulsory labor, with a few common-sense exceptions (compulsory military service, prison labor in most situations, emergencies, etc.). After World War II, and in the face of the horror of the concentration camps and the mass forced labor programs of the Communist states, the ILO adopted the Abolition of Forced Labor Convention in 1957, supplementing the basic protection laid down in Convention 29. Convention 105 prohibits forced labor for political or development purposes, as a punishment for expressing political opinions or participating in strikes, and in other related circumstances.

Freedom of Association and Collective Bargaining

The basic ILO covenants covering these issues are the 1948 Freedom of Association and Protection of the Right to Organize Convention (No. 87) and the 1949 Right to Organize and Collective Bargaining Convention (No. 98).[4] Convention 87 establishes principles and guarantees concerning the right to organize vis-à-vis the state, and Convention 98 protects workers and their organizations especially from employers. Convention 98 also promotes voluntary collective bargaining to determine conditions of employment. The two instruments taken together contain the essential elements for the creation, administration, and functioning of employers' and workers' organizations. They were adopted just before and after the adoption of the Universal Declaration of Human Rights (UDHR) in December 1948 and well before the United Nations had begun to adopt conventions. Indeed, in addition to taking up the theme of freedom of association and the right to organize in terms compatible with ILO standards, there is an explicit reference to Convention 87 in both 1966 international human rights covenants [Article 23(2) of the 1966 Civil and Political Rights Covenant (ICCPR) and Article 8(3) of the Economic, Social and Cultural Rights Covenant (ICESCR)].[5]

2. Concluded June 28, 1930, and June 25, 1957, respectively, each of these instruments is referenced in Documentary Appendix B.
3. Concluded Sept. 25, 1926, referenced in Documentary Appendix B.
4. Concluded July 9, 1948, and July 1, 1949, respectively, each of these instruments is referenced in Documentary Appendix B.
5. The UDHR (Dec. 10, 1948) and the two covenants (Dec. 16, 1966) are reprinted and referenced in Documentary Appendix A.

Discrimination

In 1951 the International Labor Conference adopted the Equal Remuneration Convention (No. 100) to protect the right of women and men to equal remuneration for work of equal value, going beyond the principle of equal pay for equal work laid down in 1948 in the Universal Declaration of Human Rights (UDHR). It went on in 1958 to adopt the Discrimination (Employment and Occupation) Convention (No. 111) which laid down the right to protection against discrimination in the world of work, on the basis of a wide range of grounds. These standards were then supplemented by the United Nations conventions that addressed the theme of equality in the broader context, including labor: the 1965 International Convention on the Elimination of all Forms of Racial Discrimination (ICERD); the 1966 International Covenant on Economic, Social and Cultural Rights (ICESCR); the 1973 International Convention on the Suppression and Punishment of the Crime of Apartheid; and the Convention on the Elimination of All Forms of Discrimination against Women (CEDAW), adopted in 1979.[6]

Child Labor

The international community, including the ILO, was slower to adopt human rights standards concerning child labor, the fourth of the ILO's principal human rights concerns. The ILO had traditionally treated child labor as a technical subject, involving a long series of instruments regulating the age of entry into employment and work of young people in various economic sectors. This way of dealing with the subject culminated in 1973 with the Minimum Age Convention (No. 138).[7] The adoption of the UN Convention on the Rights of the Child in 1989[8] was crucial in giving expression in a convention to the notion that the rights of children, including the right to protection against economic exploitation, fell properly into the human rights

sphere. The ILO filled the gap in its own human rights standards on child labor by adopting the 1999 Worst Forms of Child Labor Convention (No. 182),[9] and this has followed the lead of the Convention on the Rights of the Child in gathering ratifications faster than any other in ILO history.

The foregoing four sets of rights were endorsed as fundamental by the World Summit on Social Development in Copenhagen in 1995, which stated that all states should ratify these standards and apply them if they could not yet ratify them. The ILO then launched a ratification campaign for them, and [hundreds of] ratifications of these eight conventions have been registered since then, with many more in the pipeline. More than 139 countries had ratified the conventions on freedom of association, forced labor, and discrimination [as of 2003] . . . , meaning that they are approaching virtually universal ratification fairly rapidly. This also puts them among the most ratified international human rights standards.

On child labor, the ILO had not earlier promoted Convention 138 aggressively, as there was a feeling among the constituents that its technical nature made it difficult to ratify, but since 1995 it has gone from [few to many adoptions] with assiduous promotional work by the ILO and a real effort by the member states. In 1999, the ILO completed its human rights panoply with the adoption of Convention 182, which has the fastest ratification pace of any convention the ILO has ever adopted.

In 1994, the ILO devised an innovative new approach, which the U.S. government and employers especially supported enthusiastically. This became the Declaration on Fundamental Principles and Rights at Work,[10] a pledge by all members to "respect, promote and realize in good faith" the principles and rights relating to:

1. freedom of association and the effective recognition of the right to collective bargaining;
2. the elimination of all forms of forced or compulsory labor;

---

6. The ICESCR (Dec. 16, 1966) is reprinted and referenced in Documentary Appendix A. ICERD (Dec. 21, 1965), the Apartheid Convention (Nov. 30, 1973), and CEDAW (Dec. 18, 1979) are referenced in Documentary Appendix B.
7. Concluded June 26, 1973, referenced in Documentary Appendix B.
8. Concluded Nov. 2, 1989, referenced in Documentary Appendix B.
9. Concluded June 17, 1999, referenced in Documentary Appendix B.
10. Adopted June 18, 1998, referenced in Documentary Appendix B.

3. the effective abolition of child labor; and
4. the elimination of discrimination in respect of employment and occupation.

Under the declaration's follow-up mechanism, governments that have not ratified all the ILO's fundamental conventions on each of these subjects must provide annual reports indicating how they are implementing the principles involved. An annual Global Report on one of these four principles is to be prepared by the director-general to examine how it is being implemented and to analyze ILO assistance. The result is to be an action plan adopted at each November session of the ILO Governing Body, to serve as the basis for targeted ILO assistance to correct the problems encountered. The innovation is that the declaration is a purely promotional and not a supervisory instrument. Reports under it are not a new form of complaints mechanism, but a basis for finding out what is happening in the world in these four areas and for carrying out another new feature of the declaration: an obligation for the ILO to assist its members in reaching these goals.

[*Eds.*— As of 2003, ILO reports based on country reports were published on freedom of association and collective bargaining in 2000; forced labor in 2001; child labor in 2002; and discrimination in 2003—each followed by action plans adopted by the ILO Governing Body, before starting the cycle again.]

OTHER STANDARDS

The standards adopted by the ILO, and by others, cover a great number of subjects other than fundamental rights including on all the matters that would be covered by a national labor code, and beyond.

[*Eds.*—The author next lists the subjects covered and the ILO conventions that address them, including: • *employment* (promotion of full, productive, and freely chosen employment; maintenance of employment services; abolition of fee-charging employment and private employment agencies; vocational guidance and training; vocational rehabilitation and employment of the disabled; and termination of employment by employers); • *wages* (including minimum wage fixing "machinery," a system of minimum wages; payment of wages; and labor clauses in public contracts); • *general conditions of work* (hours of work; night work; and rest periods); • *occupational safety and health* (general policy, legislation, and implementation; establishment of occupational health services; prevention of major industrial accidents; protection against risks or processes such as carcinogenic agents or substances, noncarcinogenic chemicals that endanger health, dangerous machinery, air pollution, noise and vibration; and health and safety standards for particular branches of activity, such as commerce and offices, the construction industry, dock work, work at sea, mines, agriculture; and compensation for injury due to occupational accidents and diseases); • *social security* (minimum basic income; comprehensive medical care; sickness benefit; unemployment benefit; old-age, invalidity and survivors' benefits; employment injury benefit; family benefit; maternity benefit; and equality of treatment of nationals and non-nationals in social security, workers compensation for industrial accidents, and in the maintenance of rights acquired in the course of acquiring social security and related benefits); • *social policy* (basic aims and standards); and • *industrial relations* (e.g., voluntary conciliation and arbitration; cooperation at the level of the undertaking; consultation at the industrial and national levels; and communications and examination of grievances). The author then turns to consider the ILO's policies and practices relative to categories of workers.]

Employment of Women

Originally, the desire to protect women against excessively arduous conditions of work was the ruling factor. Subsequently, this was supplemented and partly replaced by the concern to ensure equality of rights and of treatment between women and men.[11] The basic ILO approach now is that women should be provided special protection only in so far as conditions of work place them specifically at risk with relation to reproduction.

One form of prohibition over the years has concerned night work for women. Most countries now consider these standards to be inconsistent

---

11. On the controversial issue of gender equality, see Reading 10 by Hilary Charlesworth in Chapter 2 of this volume.

with the principle of equality, and they have been widely denounced. At the same time, the ILO conference adopted standards to regulate the conditions of night work for workers generally. Protective standards for women are also contained in the conventions on maternity protection and on underground work in mines, as well as in certain conventions dealing with occupational safety and health (e.g., lead poisoning, benzene, maximum weight for the manual transport of loads).

Migrant Workers

The principal instruments are the 1949 Migration for Employment Convention (Revised) (No. 97) and the 1975 Migrant Workers (Supplementary Provisions) Convention (No. 143).[12] The former provides for assistance and information to migrants for employment, for regulation of recruitment, and for granting to lawful immigrants treatment not less favorable than that applied to nationals in respect of labor matters and social security. The latter provides for the suppression of trafficking in migrant workers and of illegal employment of such workers, and for measures to promote equality of opportunity and treatment of migrant workers lawfully within the national territory. . . . In a general survey of 1998, the ILO Committee of Experts found that these instruments had such a great level of detail that many states could not ratify them, and those that had could not apply all their provisions. The ILO experts found that many of the same concerns applied to the United Nations convention on the same subject . . .[13] The experts proposed that consideration be given to revising them in the fairly near future.

Other Special Categories of Workers

In general, ILO conventions apply to all workers falling within their scope, irrespective of nationality. However, conventions or recommendations have been adopted to deal with particular problems arising in various areas.

[Eds.—The author then details the conventions adopted to deal with seafarers, fishermen, dockworkers, nurses, public servants, part-time workers, and agricultural workers of various types.]

Indigenous and tribal peoples are protected under the 1989 Indigenous and Tribal Peoples Convention (No. 169), which replaced Convention 107 of 1957 on the same subject.[14] These standards were adopted in collaboration with the UN and other interested specialized agencies and deal comprehensively with the situation of these peoples. The earlier standards had an integrationist approach. Convention 169 provides for action to protect the rights of these peoples and to guarantee respect for their integrity, based on the principles of consultation and participation.

[Eds.—The author next alludes briefly to ILO conventions relating to nursing personnel, labor relations in the public sector, part-time workers, and to "a series of other instruments on particular categories of workers." He also alludes briefly to provisions on labor administration, including standards relating to labor inspection and labor statistics. He then continues.]

THE IMPLEMENTATION OF INTERNATIONAL LABOR STANDARDS

All these standards are, of course, of limited use if there is no way of supervising their implementation. The ILO has an extensive scheme for doing this.

OBLIGATIONS IN RESPECT OF STANDARDS

The ILO constitution requires member states to submit all ILO conventions and recommendations to their competent authorities (normally the legislature) within a year to eighteen months of adoption, for consideration of implementing action and, in the case of conventions, of ratification. This obligation—unique to the ILO—means that new ILO standards may be taken into account by national legislatures even if they are not in a position to ratify a convention.

12. Concluded July 9, 1948 and June 24, 1975, respectively, each of these instruments is referenced in Documentary Appendix B.
13. Entered into force July 1, 2003.
14. For discussion of indigenous peoples' rights, see Reading 12 by Mâivan Lâm in Chapter 2 of this volume.

Under Article 22 of the constitution, all states must submit reports on the conventions they have ratified, and also must send copies of those reports to the national employers' and workers' organizations. This is a very important provision, as it gives these other ILO constituents the possibility of supplementing or contradicting the governments' reports and gives the ILO other sources of information it is allowed to take officially into account.

Governments must supply reports not only on conventions they have ratified but also, when requested by the Governing Body, on unratified conventions and on recommendations, to indicate the position of their law and practice, the difficulties encountered, and future prospects. The latter reports yield a "general survey" by the Committee of Experts.

Supervisory System for Ratified Conventions

Since its founding, the ILO has had a system for supervising the manner in which governments apply the conventions they have ratified. The principal bodies are the Committee of Experts on the Application of Conventions and Recommendations, and the Conference Committee on the Application of Standards. There are also various complaint mechanisms, as well as a special system for examining freedom of association even when the countries concerned have not ratified the conventions.

Regular Supervision

The Committee of Experts [comprised of jurists appointed for their expertise, not their politics] carries out the first part of the regular supervisory procedure. The committee was created for the purpose of "making the best and fullest use" of the reports submitted on ratified conventions and for "securing such additional data as may be provided for in the forms approved by the Governing Body and found desirable to supplement that already available." In 1947 the committee's terms of reference [were expanded]. Since then, the committee covers the examination of reports on ratified conventions (art. 22 of the constitution); reports on unratified conventions and on recommendations (art. 19); information on submission of instruments to the

competent national authorities (art. 19); and reports and information on the application of conventions in nonmetropolitan territories (arts. 22 and 35).

The committee is required to examine, with complete impartiality and objectivity, whether states comply with their obligations under the constitution on standards-related matters, and in particular to examine the degree to which the legal and factual situation complies with the terms of ratified conventions. It examines some two thousand government reports each year. It makes comments on these reports in two forms. Observations are used for the most serious or persistent cases of noncompliance and are published in the committee's report. The committee may add a footnote inviting the government to "supply full particulars to the Conference" at its next session, or to send a detailed report before it would otherwise be due, or both. Direct requests are used to request information, clarify questions, or deal with technical points or questions of minor importance. They are not published, but are sent directly to governments. They are, however, available on request.

The committee's report, containing the observations and general comments, is submitted to each session of the International Labor Conference.

The conference creates each year a Committee on the Application of Standards. Like most ILO bodies, it is tripartite [i.e., including government and employer and worker organization representatives]. It examines the report of the Committee of Experts and selects about thirty cases each year in which it requests the government concerned to appear before it and discuss the situation. In 1957, the committee decided that in some cases the discrepancies noted were so fundamental or had been discussed for so long a time, it should call the attention of the conference to them. Since then the committee has pointed out in its report the cases it considers most important, or other special cases of noncompliance.

The report is submitted to the conference for adoption. Important cases of noncompliance are pointed out in the general part of the report, according to various criteria. One category covers failure to comply with formal obligations, concerning, for instance, reporting or submission of conventions and recommendations to the competent national authorities. The report also deals with cases of failure to apply ratified conventions. Some special cases, which are considered by the committee to be sufficiently serious for it to express special concern, are summarized in "special paragraphs," along with a conclusion or recommendation by the committee. Other cases may be mentioned under the severest criterion of "continued failure to apply," when serious deficiencies have been encountered in the application of a convention for a given country. Cases are mentioned under this criterion only on rare occasions.

SPECIAL PROCEDURES ON FREEDOM OF ASSOCIATION

In 1947, the ILO conference adopted a resolution by which it invited the Governing Body to examine the possibility of creating a special body for the protection of trade union rights. This was based on the fact that, on the one hand, the procedures contemplated in the ILO constitution were only applicable for ratified conventions, and, on the other, that the question of freedom of association was so important and often so specific (since the problems that arose were often more of fact than of law) that it was necessary to create a special procedure that could be applied independently of the ratification of the conventions on the subject.

The Governing Body decided in January 1950 to create the Fact-Finding and Conciliation Commission on Freedom of Association. The commission's mandate was to examine complaints submitted to the ILO Governing Body, whenever it considered an inquiry justified and the government concerned had consented (if it had not ratified the conventions on freedom of association). The latter requirement prevented the commission from functioning expeditiously. The Governing Body therefore decided in November 1951 to create a special committee from among its own members to carry out prior examinations of the cases submitted.

The Committee on Freedom of Association was originally conceived as a "filtering body" for the Fact-Finding and Conciliation Commission, but in practice it shortly began to recommend to the Governing Body that it bring to the attention of governments the anomalies that it had noted. In fact, it turned into a specialized body that regularly examines complaints, without the consent of the government concerned being required. It has developed its procedures over the years, with the approval of the Governing Body. The committee has examined [thousands of] cases, and it has developed a "jurisprudence" that clarifies and develops the principles and standards of the freedom of association conventions.

The committee is composed of nine titular and nine substitute members, and meets three times each year in Geneva. Complaints may be presented only by governments or by employers' and workers' organizations which may be international organizations that have consultative status with the ILO (International Confederation of Free Trade Unions, World Confederation of Labor, World Confederation of Trade Unions, and International Organization of Employers), or other international organizations when the questions concerned directly affect national organizations affiliated to them.

The committee examines cases related to trade union legislation, collective bargaining strikes, and, most frequently, problems associated with the right to strike and to bargain collectively, the dissolution or suspension of organizations, and measures of anti-union discrimination.

The committee's action has often led, directly or indirectly, to the release of trade unionists from prison or their return from exile. Its activities also have a preventive impact. The mere presentation of complaints often leads governments to resolve a trade union problem or to refrain from measures that violate principles of freedom of association, in order to avoid the case being aired publicly at the international level.

[*Eds.*—The author then notes that governments cooperate with the committee in the great majority of cases, either to avoid publicity or to demonstrate that the accusations are unfounded.]

THE FACT-FINDING AND CONCILIATION COMMISSION

The commission is composed of independent personalities appointed by the Governing Body and may convene between three and five of its members to examine a complaint. Complaints may be submitted to it by the Governing Body under the procedure described earlier, by the conference (on the recommendation of its Credentials Committee), or by a government that complains against another government. Only governments and organizations of employers or of workers may submit complaints.

COMPLAINTS SYSTEMS

The ILO constitution provides two systems for complaints of violations of ratified conventions. Representations are covered in articles 24 and 25. This procedure may only be initiated by an organization of employers or of workers that alleges that a country has not taken measures to ensure the satisfactory observance of a convention it has ratified. It was used only rarely until the end of the 1970s, but since that time representations have been received far more frequently.

The procedure also provides that the Governing Body may decide at any time that the representation shall be examined under the complaints procedure laid down by articles 26 et seq. of the Constitution. This procedure was not used successfully until 1961, but frequency of submission of complaints has increased.

A complaint may be submitted by one country against another alleging that the latter has not taken measures for the effective observance of a convention, if both countries have ratified the convention. The Governing Body may also follow this procedure on its own motion or on a complaint from a conference delegate (the method used most frequently in recent years). The Governing Body may communicate the complaint to the government against which the allegations are made, so that it may make any comments it wishes. If the Governing Body does not consider this communication necessary, or if it does not receive a satisfactory answer within a reasonable time, it may appoint a commission of inquiry to consider the complaint and to report on it.

This procedure does not require the consent of the government concerned and may take place even when the government of the country against which the allegations are made decides not to participate in it. The commission of inquiry examines the case, often holding hearings and making on-the-spot visits. It submits a report in which it sets out its findings, makes recommendations on the steps that should be adopted to meet the complaint, and indicates the time limits within which these measures should be taken (art. 28).

The report is communicated to the Governing Body and to the governments concerned, and is published. The governments concerned should indicate, within three months, whether or not they accept the recommendations of the commission of inquiry and, in case they do not, whether they desire to submit the case to the International Court of Justice. The court may confirm, modify, or annul the conclusions or recommendations of a commission of inquiry, and the court's decision is not subject to appeal. This, however, has never happened.

If a country does not comply with the recommendations or conclusions of the court within a defined period of time, the Governing Body may propose to the conference the measures it considers necessary to secure compliance. Until recently this provision was entirely theoretical, but in an exciting new development it [recently was] applied to Myanmar (Burma). The commission of inquiry appointed for this case found in 1998 that—as was already well known—there is massive and systematic forced labor in the country, violating the 1930 Forced Labor Convention (No. 29). When the government refused to accept that this was true and failed to take measures to correct it, the Governing Body began to consider the application of Article 33 in 1999, and in June 2000 the conference adopted a set of measures which were to go into force on 30 November 2000 unless the Governing Body declared itself satisfied that the measures taken complied with the recommendations of the commission of inquiry.

However, the Governing Body did not find that the government had complied, and the measures went into force. [*Eds.*—The author notes that these measures encouraged ILO and UN member states to review their relations with Myanmar and to take measures to ensure that those relations did not encourage continued violations. In March 2002, an agreement was concluded between the ILO and Myanmar providing for the stationing of an ILO officer there.]

After a complaint procedure is completed, the government may inform the Governing Body that it has taken the measures necessary to apply the recommendations of the commission cf inquiry or the court's decision and may request that another commission of inquiry be convened to verify these assertions. If this report is favorable, the Governing Body may recommend to the conference that it cease whatever measures were taken under its earlier proposals. Normally the results of commissions of inquiry are simply followed up through the regular supervisory procedures for the application of ratified conventions.

DOES THE ILO SYSTEM WORK?

The ILO has been seriously remiss in not analyzing how well it works. In large part this was because for many years the system itself was its own justification, especially during the Cold War. It was set up and maintained as a bulwark against the Communist system, especially for its insistence that freedom of association required the possibility of trade union pluralism and that such fundamental rights as freedom from discrimination applied also to political opinion.

But concerns with budgets allied with a renewed concern for greater integration among the UN system organizations, have changed this. There has resulted an affirmation of the basic validity of the system, but also changes to concentrate on the most important problems, to reinforce connections between the supervision of the application of standards and their implementation at the national level, and in a few other adjustments. From the viewpoint of a practitioner, I can say that it works—not always, but certainly more frequently than any other international supervisory system.

First, as a source for law: most countries in the world—and the United States and China are the two big exceptions—have ratified most of the fundamental instruments. They form a common basis of law throughout the world and are rarely challenged openly these days. On child labor, the boom in commitment to the elimination of this terrible practice—and the money being made available to the ILO and others to fight it—is incredible, with the 1999 Convention 182 gathering ratifications at a record rate, and the International Program for the Elimination of Child Labor being given so much money that it is often difficult to spend it wisely as fast as the donors want.

Freedom of association is the other principal question for the ILO, a difficult subject, and there are problems with its implementation everywhere. The United States has found that it cannot ratify the international standards on the subject—as it has said in its communications to the ILO, it is committed to the principles of conventions 87 and 98, but is unable to ratify them because of some technical differences. I am not evaluating that statement here, but it is not the opinion of everyone that these differences with international law are minor.

Nevertheless, there is constant vigilance by the ILO, and the Committee on Freedom of Association has been able to document hundreds of releases of trade unionists from prison and returns from exile among its accomplishments. The ILO has established a body of law and a reference point for freedom of association throughout the world, and the work being done to promote the declaration and its underlying standards is having a real effect, even if this is yet too small.

On the basis of the signs the ILO is getting it is conducting studies and training sessions around the world on labor standards and human rights.

[*Eds.*—The author then cites a number of concrete projects, several with United States funding, for abolishing forced and bonded labor in Nepal, for ending the trafficking of women and child in the Mekong Delta ("the only major human rights project in which China is cooperating"); for setting up mechanisms in Brazil and Namibia under which workers can make effective discrimination complaints; for eliminating child labor; and so forth. He also notes that "There are many other instances in which countries are asking the ILO to come and help improve workers' rights." He then concludes:]

The [genesis of this essay in its original form] was characterized by a discussion of the ILO's dental characteristics: does the ILO have teeth? Could it get teeth? Should we let someone else have teeth for our mouth? It is an interesting discussion, and one that has been going on for a while. But in fact no international organization is likely in the near future to adopt a sanctions-based approach to violations of labor standards, unless it be in such a severe case as Myanmar. The ILO will just have to keep "gumming" violators and letting them feel the effects more gradually, with the support of partners in the United States and elsewhere.

QUESTIONS FOR REFLECTION AND DISCUSSION

1. Swepston alludes to criticism of the ILO, particularly to the lack of enforcement mechanisms ("does the ILO have teeth?"), which he blames on the ILO's failure to publicize "how well this system works." Since its inception in 1919, the ILO has promoted

international standards in the form of legally binding conventions, intended for incorporation into national labor legislation and including conventions addressing "core" rights, e.g., the right to organize, bargain collectively, and strike. Many of the ILO Conventions have remained unratified by key ILO member states, however. Also, in the 1990s, the ILO shifted from its traditional convention-oriented, standard-setting system in favor of less binding instruments such as the 1998 Declaration on Fundamental Principles and Rights at Work (referenced in Documentary Appendix B), "a purely promotional and not a supervisory instrument," according to Swepston, but a shift made necessary, he says, because the ILO system "had grown heavy." How do you evaluate this shift? Is it a sign that the ILO system works well? The U.S. government and employers have been particularly vocal in supporting the nonbinding form of these same standards in the Declaration of Fundamental Principles and Rights. Yet in a Human Rights Watch report published in 2000 under the title "Unfair Advantage: Workers' Freedom of Association in the United States Under International Human Rights Standards" (available at http://www.hrw.org/reports/2000/uslabor), Lance Compa found numerous examples of violation of international labor standards by the United States, especially with regard to freedom of association. Given that the right to freedom of association is expressly reaffirmed in the Declaration, does the promotion of the Declaration by the United States enhance the credibility and validity of ILO basic rights? Will China, a country with tremendous influence on global trade flows and labor conditions today, be more or less likely to discontinue its systematic violation of all four fundamental labor rights proclaimed in the Declaration?

2. In 1977, in recognition of the fact that ILO law was designed to hold only governments responsible for workers' rights violations, not private employers such as multinational enterprises, the ILO adopted a Tripartite Declaration on Principles Concerning Multinational Enterprises and Social Policy, referenced in Documentary Appendix B. Like the Declaration of Fundamental Rights (Question 1 above), the Tripartite Declaration is a voluntary, not legally binding set of recommendations. In "'Form Follows Function': Formulations of International Labor Standards—Treaties, Codes, Soft Law, Trade Agreements," in Robert J. Flanagan and William B. Gould IV, eds., *International Labor Standards: Globalization, Trade, and Public Policy* (Stanford, Calif.: Stanford University Press, 2003), 179–205, at 194–95, Virginia Leary writes:

> the adoption of the Declaration as a voluntary nonbinding instrument was essentially due to political obstacles. The regulation of multinational enterprises remains today a controversial subject on which it is difficult to obtain agreement. Legal difficulties also created obstacles to adoption as a binding agreement: the definition of "multinational enterprise" was deliberately left vague, and attempting to affect the policies of nonstate entities, not subjects of international law, was also perceived as an obstacle.

Despite the difficulties, however, the Declaration established a set of procedures for monitoring and reporting, and in 2001 the ILO published its "Seventh Survey on the Effect Given to the Tripartite Declaration." Based on responses from governments, workers, and employers to an ILO questionnaire, the report provided considerable information on the activities of multinational corporations, much of it, according to Leary, revealing of violations of worker rights and their social consequences and often mentioning offending corporations by name. But the ILO took it upon itself to erase the names of the multinationals from the Report. How accountable is the ILO? Why would the ILO hesitate to reveal the names of multinationals that violate labor rights? Why would it hesitate to clearly define what a multinational corporation is? "It is not clear," Leary comments, "why the ILO, a public international organization, feels called upon to omit part of the replies provided by its constituents." Leary also notes that the Report's conclusions and recommendations are vague and innocuous. If the ILO cannot police nonstate actors, who will? Are governments able to do so under the current free-trade regime?

3. It has been argued that international labor conditions are linked to international trade regimes and that violations of workers' rights cannot be properly addressed without the cooperation of international trade institutions such as the World Trade Organization (WTO), the World Bank, and the International Monetary Fund (IMF). Since the inception of the ILO, there have been efforts to outlaw the abuse of worker rights for competitive advantage and punish offending countries with trade sanctions. The "trade/labor linkage"

(or "social clause") is extremely controversial, however. See Sarah H. Cleveland, "Why International Labor Standards?" in Flanagan and Gould (*International Labor Standards*, Question 2 above), 129–78. It is said that developing countries object to the trade/labor linkage because they fear it would deprive them of the competitive advantage they derive from low wages and be used by the West for protectionist purposes. From a human rights perspective, are these legitimate concerns? And just how sincere is Western commitment to the trade/labor linkage? In *Trade Law and Global Governance* (London: Cameron, 2002), 287–88, Steve Charnovitz, a former U.S. government official with high-level involvement in formulating U.S. trade and labor policy in the 1980s and 1990s, writes:

> Using trade sanctions to promote [workers'] freedom may not be an effective course. For one thing, it is self-contradictory to deny the individual's freedom to trade in order to promote other freedoms. Moreover, such sanctions will reduce the amount of trade, thus making everyone worse off. Asking the WTO to restrict trade in products made by child labor is even more problematic. These abuses are heinous, but are carried out by employers, not by governments. Empathetic citizens in rich countries have a much more direct way to curtail child labor than to enlist the WTO: they can send money to children in poor countries (or to NGOs helping the children).

But is it really possible to separate labor from trade and still protect workers' basic rights? Are not forced labor, child labor, and the prohibition of unions unfair trade practices as well as violations of core labor rights? Is Western responsibility for violations of labor rights in developing countries limited to the "remedies" proposed by Charnovitz? Are developing countries alone responsible for ameliorating working conditions for their populations? WTO rulings are reciprocally binding and allow for costly sanctions if breached. ILO conventions and declarations have no comparable enforcement mechanisms. Are developing countries justified in their suspicion of Western countries' declared opposition to child labor?

4. Many labor law experts, particularly from Europe, are concerned about the separation of trade law from human rights law. According to Mireille Delmas-Marty, "Commerce mondial et protection des droits de l'homme," in Institut International des Droits de l'Homme, *Commerce mondial et protection des droits de l'homme/World Trade and the Protection of Human Rights* (Bruxelles: Bruylant, 2001), two mutually incompatible and clashing sets of international norms have evolved, one for markets and one for human rights, both operating at the expense of the old universal rights from which they were selectively detached. Trade law, embodied not only in the WTO and the IMF but also in the EU and other regional bodies of economic cooperation like NAFTA, operates globally, independently from territorial states whose jurisdiction it transcends. It is devoted exclusively to the liberalization of markets and the expansion of commercial transactions rendering the state increasingly irrelevant and, it is argued, increasing social inequality. Human rights law also aspires to a global reach but in pursuit of equality and social justice for which it holds states accountable. At the global level, the commercial priorities of the WTO are kept apart from the ethical aspirations of the UN and the ILO, and at the regional level we find, for example, the separate existence of the European Union and the Council of Europe each represented by a separate court: the Court of Justice of the European Communities situated in Luxembourg and constituted for matters of economic integration; and the European Court of Human Rights, situated in Strasbourg. These two legal realms do in fact interact, Delmas-Marty argues, but in the form of irresolvable conflicts that produce the wrong kinds of universalization, increasing the lack of accountability of both states and nonstate actors and subordinating human rights to the primacy of the market and "globalized American law." The rights propounded in Universal Declaration of Human Rights, Delmas-Marty argues, presuppose the fundamental *indivisibility* of the economic, civil, political, and cultural realms and are capable of being realized only if trade law and human rights law are *integrated*. Delmas-Marty hopes that the December 2000 European Charter of Fundamental Rights (referenced in Documentary Appendix B) will transcend the dualism of the economic and the ethical and thus help remedy the current division of international law. In "Episodes on the Path Towards the European Social Model: The EU Charter of Fundamental Rights and the Convention on the Future of Europe," in Catherine Barnard, Simon Deakin, and Gillian S. Morris eds., *The Future of Labour Law* (Oxford: Hart Publishing,

2004), 179–99, at 179, Brian Bercusson expresses the same hope. The European Charter, he contends, "has the potential to renew labour law in the Member States and at EU level [because] it breaks new ground by including in a single list of fundamental rights not only traditional civil and political rights, but also a long list of social and economic rights." Do you think the European Union can change the balance of power between the ILO, the UN, and the WTO? Do you agree that the current system of international law, favoring trade over human rights, reflects the excessive influence of the United States? If not, what is the explanation for it?

5. As Swepston notes, the current ILO system does not cover migrant workers. Yet labor migration has been one of the most important consequences of globalization. Migrant female labor, in particular, has become such an important international economic force that scholars have begun to talk about the "feminization of migration." See Barbara Ehrenreich and Arlie Russell Hochschild, *Global Woman: Nannies, Maids, and Sex Workers in the New Economy* (New York: Metropolitan, 2003). According to Ehrenreich and Hochschild,

> The lifestyles of the First World are made possible by a global transfer of the services associated with a wife's traditional role—child care, home-making, and sex—from poor countries to rich ones. . . . Today, while still relying on Third World countries for agricultural and industrial labor, the wealthy countries also seek to extract something harder to measure and quantify, something that can look very much like love. Nannies . . . bring the distant families that employ them real maternal affection, no doubt enhanced by the heartbreaking absence of their own children in the poor countries they leave behind. Similarly, women who migrate from country to country to work as maids bring not only their muscle power but an attentiveness to detail and to the human relationships in the household that might otherwise have been invested in their own families. Sex workers offer the simulation of sexual and romantic love, or at least transient sexual companionship. It is as if the wealthy parts of the world are running short on precious emotional and sexual resources and have had to turn to poorer regions for fresh supplies. (4–5)

A "global redivision of women's traditional work" is under way, according to Ehrenreich and Hochschild, prompted by the globalization of capital. As the middle-class household in the West now needs two paychecks to maintain the same standard of living that in the 1950s and 1960s could be achieved by the husband's earnings alone, working women find themselves working double shifts. The new economic conditions have not changed men's expectations that women do all the housework, so Western women now work both outside and inside the home. Persistent poverty of the Third World, meanwhile, coupled with development policies guided by international financial institutions like the WTO, the IMF, and the World Bank, are creating conditions that push more and more Third World women to migrate in search of foreign work. No law currently exists to protect these women and the real impact of their labor—both on Western societies and on their home countries and families—cannot be fully "monetized" based on existing economic measures. Should international human rights law make special provision for female migrant workers? If not, why not? If so, how?

15. GEORGE KENT *Food Is a Human Right*

ECONOMIC, SOCIAL, AND CULTURAL RIGHTS

Economic, social, and cultural rights include the right to an adequate standard of living. Article 25(1) of the Universal Declaration of Human Rights (UDHR)[1] says:

Everyone has the right to a standard of living adequate for the health and well-being of himself and of his family, including food, clothing, housing and medical care and necessary

Reprinted with changes from George Kent, *Freedom from Want: The Human Right to Adequate Food* (Washington, D.C.: Georgetown University Press, 2005), 45–59. Copyright © 2005 Georgetown University Press. Reprinted by permission.

1. Adopted Dec 10, 1948, reprinted and referenced in Documentary Appendix A.

social services, and the right to security in the event of unemployment, sickness, disability, widowhood, old age or other lack of livelihood in circumstances beyond his control.

This was elaborated upon in Article 11 of the International Covenant on Economic, Social and Cultural Rights (ICESCR).[2] Paragraph 1 says:

The States Parties to the present Covenant recognize the right of everyone to an adequate standard of living for himself and his family, including adequate food, clothing and housing, and to the continuous improvement of living conditions.

The human right to adequate food is explicitly recognized as part of the broader human right to an adequate standard of living. While the focus here is on food, we have much to learn from the work that has emerged on health, education, housing, and other issues relating to an adequate standard of living.

Individuals and organizations working to end hunger and malnutrition sometimes use the slogan "food first." The concept expresses their feelings that the food issue should be given high priority. However, it should be recognized that food and nutrition constitute just one of the dimensions of adequate livelihood; it would be inappropriate to argue that nutrition is more important than, say, housing or education. All aspects of livelihood are interrelated, and should be kept in balance.

The point may be clarified by asking: can the human right to adequate food be fulfilled by an authoritarian regime? It is certainly possible to assure that individuals' biological nutritional needs are fulfilled through authoritarian measures. Even chained prisoners can have their minimum required daily allowances of nutrients delivered to them. But fulfilling one's *need* for food in the biological sense is different from fulfilling one's *right* to food. It is true that many human needs can be met by authoritarian powers without consulting with the people. Certainly one can provide food for individuals that will meet their basic nutrient requirements, as in a prison or an army. However, if people have no chance to influence what and how they are

being fed, if they are fed prepackaged rations or capsules or are fed from a trough, their right to adequate food is not being met, even if they get all the nutrients their bodies need. Serving pork to a Muslim prisoner would violate his human rights, even if it contained the nutrients he needed.

Human rights are mainly about upholding human dignity, not about meeting physiological needs. Dignity does not come from being fed. It comes from providing for oneself. In any well-structured society, the objective is to move toward conditions under which all people can provide for themselves.

One of the major critiques of humanitarian assistance programs has been that "Aid processes treat lives to be saved as bare life, not as lives with a political voice."[3] The human rights approach responds directly to this concern. One can assure that people are treated like dignified human beings, rather than like animals on a feedlot, by making sure that they have some say in how they are being treated. This is why, in a human rights system, the people *must* have some institutionalized remedies available to them that they can call upon if they feel they are not being treated properly. There must be some meaningful action they can take if they feel their rights are not being acknowledged.

Saying that people must have actions they can take if they feel their rights are not being acknowledged is another way of saying that they must be free to participate in shaping the conditions in which they live. This refers not only to the quality of relationships between individuals and their governments, but also to the quality of their relationships with one another. Human rights are not only about the potentialities of isolated individuals. People must be recognized as social beings with a need and a right to share in shaping not only their individual futures but also the futures of their communities. At one level human rights may appear to be individualistic, but it should be recognized that the basis of the realization of individual human rights is the quality of our social relationships.[4] This is the essence of democracy.

On the basis of this formulation, democracy

---

2. Concluded Dec. 16, 1966, reprinted and referenced in Documentary Appendix A.
3. Jenny Edkins, *Whose Hunger? Concepts of Famine, Practices of Aid* (Minneapolis: University of Minnesota Press, 2000), xvi.
4. See A. Belden Fields, *Rethinking Human Rights for the New Millennium* (New York: Palgrave Macmillan, 2003).

is required for the full realization of the human right to adequate food and all other human rights. The fulfillment of human rights requires a democratic social order, one in which individuals can play an active role in shaping the conditions under which they live. Democracy is about participation.[5]

Just as the human right to adequate food must be seen in the context of the right to adequate livelihood, that cluster of rights, in turn, must be viewed in the broader context of all human rights. Livelihoods may be adequate in terms of specific measures of income, health care, housing, etc., but this must not be achieved through means that violate other human rights. Human rights are indivisible.

FOOD IN INTERNATIONAL HUMAN RIGHTS LAW

Historically, national and international responses to problems of malnutrition have been based on compassion and the recognition that reducing malnutrition can be of considerable benefit to the society as a whole. These responses have ranged from small local feeding programs to large-scale international actions involving the United Nations Children's Fund (UNICEF), the World Bank, the World Food Program, and many nongovernmental organizations. Now, however, there is increasing recognition that adequate food is a human right, and thus there is a legal *obligation* to assure that all people get adequate food.

As indicated above, the articulation of the human right to adequate food in modern international human rights law arises in the context of the broader human right to an adequate standard of living. The 1948 UDHR asserts in Article 25(1) that "everyone has the right to a standard of living adequate for the health and well-being of himself and his family, including food . . . ." And the 1966 International Covenant on Civil and Political Rights (ICCPR),[6] which came into force in 1976, says, in Article 1, Paragraph 2: "In no case may a people be deprived of its own means of subsistence." In addition, ICCPR

Article 6 says, "Every human being has the inherent right to life." This clearly implies the right to adequate food and other necessities for sustaining life.

The human right to adequate food was affirmed explicitly in two other major and binding international agreements. In the 1966 ICE-SCR, which came into force in 1976, Article 11 provides that "The States Parties to the present Covenant recognize the right of everyone to an adequate standard of living for himself and his family, including adequate food, clothing, and housing" and also recognize "the fundamental right of everyone to be free from hunger." In the 1989 Convention on the Rights of the Child (CRC),[7] which came into force in 1990, two provisions address the issue of nutrition. Article 24 says that the "States Parties recognize the right of the child to the enjoyment of the highest attainable standard of health" (para. 1); that they pledge to "take appropriate measures . . . to combat disease and malnutrition . . . through the provision of adequate nutritious foods, clean drinking water, and health care" (para. 2c); and that they pledge also to "take appropriate measures . . . [t]o ensure that all segments of society, in particular parents and children, are informed, have access to education and are supported in the use of basic knowledge of child health and nutrition [and] the advantages of breastfeeding . . ." (para. 2e). Article 27(e) says that States Parties "shall in case of need provide material assistance and support programmes, particularly with regard to nutrition, clothing, and housing."

Even if the human right to adequate food had not been stated directly, it would be strongly implied in other provisions such as those asserting the right to life and health, or the CRC's requirement that the States Parties shall "take appropriate measures to diminish infant and child mortality"(art. 24, para. 2a). Other binding international human rights agreements, such as the 1979 Convention on the Elimination of All Forms of Discrimination Against Women (CEDAW),[8] contribute to the articulation of relevant rights. The Food and Agriculture Organization of the United Nations (FAO) has identified a large number of authoritative international

---

5. On democracy itself as a human right, see Thomas M. Franck, "The Emerging Right to Democratic Governance," *AJIL* 86 (1992): 46–91.
6. Concluded Dec. 16, 1966, reprinted and referenced in Documentary Appendix A.
7. Concluded Nov. 2, 1989, referenced in Documentary Appendix B.
8. Concluded Dec. 18, 1979, referenced in Documentary Appendix B.

instruments that address the human right to adequate food.[9]

The human right to adequate food has been reaffirmed at the international level in many different settings. On reviewing the hunger data, Philip Alston and Katarina Tomaševski observe that "statistics make hunger by far the most flagrant and widespread of all serious human rights abuses"; to which Alston adds that "the right to food has been endorsed more often and with greater unanimity and urgency than most other human rights, while at the same time being violated more comprehensively and systematically than probably any other right."[10]

There really is no need to propose the human right to adequate food; it is already well established in international law. Henry Shue defines basic rights as those necessary for the enjoyment of all other rights.[11] In these terms, there can be no question that the human right to adequate food is a basic right. The task now is to assure the universal recognition and realization of that right.

FOOD IN INTERNATIONAL HUMANITARIAN LAW

Food plays a special role in international humanitarian law—that part of international law that is particularly concerned with conflict situations. In a statement on *The Right to Food* made to the UN Commission on Human Rights in April 2001, the International Committee of the Red Cross described the major relevant rules:[12]

- International humanitarian law expressly prohibits starvation of civilians as a method of combat in both international and non-international armed conflict. This prohibition is violated not only when lack of food or denial of access to it causes death, but also when the population suffers hunger because of deprivation of food sources or supplies.

- It should be noted that intentional starvation of civilians as a method of warfare is a war crime when committed in international armed conflict under the 1998 Rome Statute establishing a permanent International Criminal Court.[13] Intentional starvation of civilians is a serious violation of international humanitarian law when committed in internal armed conflict as well.

- In elaboration of the prohibition of starvation, international humanitarian law specifically prohibits attacking, destroying, removing, or rendering useless objects indispensable to the survival of the civilian population. Such objects include foodstuffs, agricultural areas for the production of foodstuffs, crops, livestock, drinking water installations, drinking water supplies, and irrigation works.

- It is fairly obvious that population displacement is a major cause of hunger and starvation in war. International humanitarian law prohibits the forced displacement of civilians unless their security or imperative military reasons so demand in both international and non-international armed conflict. Forced movement of civilians is a war crime in both types of conflict under the Rome Statute.

- Last, but by no means least, international humanitarian law contains specific rules on assistance to civilian populations in armed conflict situations. Parties to an armed conflict must allow humanitarian and impartial relief operations—including those aimed at providing food—when supplies essential for the civilian population are lacking.

The ICRC pointed out that "the strength of humanitarian law lies also in the fact that its prescriptions must be applied immediately, rather than progressively, that it unequivocally binds both state and nonstate actors and that it permits no derogations whatsoever."[14]

The Special Rapporteur on the Right to Food of the UN Commission on Human Rights

9. FAO, *Extracts from International and Regional Instruments and Declarations, and other Authoritative Texts Addressing the Right to Food*, Legislative Study 69 (Rome: FAO, 1999), available at http://www.fao.org/Legal/Rtf/legst68.pdf

10. Philip Alston and Katarina Tomaševski, eds., *The Right to Food* (The Hague: Nijhoff, 1984), 7, 9.

11. Henry Shue, *Basic Rights: Subsistence, Affluence, and U.S. Foreign Policy*, 2nd ed. (Princeton, N.J.: Princeton University Press, 1996), 19.

12. ICRC, *The Right to Food: Official Statement to the Commission on Human Rights* (Geneva: ICRC, 2001), http://www.icrc.org/Web/eng/siteeng0.nsf/iwpList78/3FB7E0D8B82A07DEC1256 B66005FD4ED

13. Rome Statute of the International Criminal Court (July 17, 1998), referenced in Documentary Appendix B.

14. ICRC, *The Right to Food*, note 12.

highlighted the role of food in international humanitarian law:[15]

> 75. The starvation of civilians as a method of warfare is prohibited in both international and non-international armed conflict. That prohibition is violated not only when denial of access to food causes death, but also when the population suffers hunger because of deprivation of food sources or supplies. The prohibition of starvation is elaborated upon in provisions prohibiting attacks against or destruction of items necessary for the survival of the civilian population, including foodstuffs and drinking water:
>
> Starvation of civilians as a method of combat is prohibited. It is therefore prohibited to attack, destroy, remove or render useless, for that purpose, objects indispensable to the survival of the civilian population, such as foodstuffs, agricultural areas for the production of foodstuffs, crops, livestock, drinking water installations and supplies and irrigation works.
>
> 76. Physical destruction includes the destruction of crops by chemical defoliants or the pollution of water reservoirs. Violations would also occur if landmines were to render agricultural areas useless. Under the Rome Statute of the International Criminal Court, intentionally using starvation of civilians as a method of warfare by depriving them of objects indispensable to their survival is considered a war crime in international armed conflict.

Strictly speaking, the rules relating to food in international humanitarian law are not cast as human rights. They are seen, rather, to complement the human right to adequate food in international human rights law. However, as summarized in an ICRC study on the right to food in armed conflict situations, the practical results are the same. "While the rules are primarily formulated as obligations of parties to an armed conflict, rather than as rights," writes Jelena Pejic, "the results desired by both humanitarian and human rights law are the same—the ability of individuals to obtain or receive adequate food."[16]

GLOBAL DECLARATIONS AND COMMITMENTS

Alongside the developments in international law described in the preceding sections, numerous conferences and theoretically nonbinding international declarations and resolutions have helped to shape the emerging international consensus on norms regarding the human right to adequate food. Several are notable.

In 1974, the World Food Conference issued the Universal Declaration on the Eradication of Hunger and Malnutrition, asserting that "Every man, woman and child has the inalienable right to be free from hunger and malnutrition in order to develop fully and maintain their physical and mental faculties."[17] The Declaration was subsequently endorsed by the UN General Assembly.[18]

The constitution of the World Health Organization (WHO) says that "the enjoyment of the highest attainable standard of health is one of the fundamental rights of every human being . . . ," clearly implying the human right to adequate food.[19] In response to concerns about inappropriate marketing and promotion, the International Code of Marketing of Breastmilk Substitutes was adopted by the World Health Assembly (WHA) in 1981.[20] The WHA has approved a series of resolutions in subsequent years to further clarify and strengthen the code.

15. United Nations Economic and Social Council, Commission on Human Rights, *Economic, Social and Cultural Rights; The Right to Food; Report by the Special Rapporteur on the Right to Food, Mr. Jean Ziegler, Submitted in Accordance with Commission on Human Rights Resolution 2000/25,* UN Doc. E/CN.4/2002/558 (Jan. 10, 2002), available at http://www.unhchr.ch/Huridocda/Huridoca.nsf/TestFrame/832c9dd3b2f32e68c1256b970054dc89?Open document

16. Jelena Pejic, "The Right to Food in Situations of Armed Conflict: The Legal Framework," *International Review of the Red Cross* (2001), 83(844):1097–1110, 1109, available at http://www.icrc.org/Web/eng/siteeng0.nsf/htmlall/57JRLG/$FILE/ 1097–1110_Pejic.pdf

17. Adopted Nov. 16, 1974, referenced in Documentary Appendix B.

18. GA Res. 3348 (XXIX), UN GAOR, 29th Sess., Supp. No.31, at 75, UN Doc. A/RES/29/3348 (1994).

19. See Gro Harlem Brundtland, *Nutrition, Health, and Human Rights: ACC/SCN Symposium on The Substance and Politics of a Human Rights Approach to Food and Nutrition Policies and Programmes* (Geneva: WHO, Apr 12, 1999, updated Sept.15, 2000), available at http://www.who.int/director-general/speeches/1999/english/19990412_ nutrition.html

20. International Code of Marketing of Breast-Milk Substitutes, available at http://www.ibfan.org/english/resource/who/fullcode.html

An International Conference on Nutrition organized by the FAO and the WHO was held in Rome in December 1992. In the Conference's concluding World Declaration on Nutrition, the nations of the world agreed that "access to nutritionally adequate and safe food is a right of each individual."[21]

In November 1996 the World Food Summit concluded with agreement on the Rome Declaration on World Food Security and World Food Summit Plan of Action,[22] the first paragraph of which declares: "We, the Heads of State and Government, or our representatives, gathered at the World Food Summit at the invitation of the Food and Agriculture Organization of the United Nations, reaffirm the right of everyone to have access to safe and nutritious food, consistent with the right to adequate food and the fundamental right of everyone to be free from hunger." The Summit called for further specification of the meaning of the right to food, through a process described below.

Paragraph 2 of the 1996 Rome Declaration states: "We pledge our political will and our common and national commitment to achieving food security for all and to an ongoing effort to eradicate hunger in all countries, with an immediate view to reducing the number of undernourished people to half their present level no later than 2015." This pledge was repeated in Paragraph 7 of the Declaration's accompanying Plan of Action. However, apart from a minor mention in Paragraph 60, the thirty pages of commitments, objectives, and actions that followed made no further reference to this specific time frame.

In the late 1990s, work on the human right to adequate food centered on a mandate from the 1996 Rome World Food Summit. In the Summit's concluding Plan of Action, Objective 7.4 called upon the UN High Commissioner for Human Rights, "in consultation with relevant treaty bodies, and in collaboration with relevant specialized agencies and programmes of the UN system and appropriate inter-governmental mechanisms, to better define the rights related to food in Article 11 of the Covenant [ICESCR] and to propose ways to implement and realize these rights. . . ."[23]

Several initiatives were taken in response to this call, including supportive resolutions from the Commission on Human Rights; a Day of Discussion on Right to Food held by the UN Committee on Economic, Social and Cultural Rights; and Expert Consultations on the human right to adequate food held in Geneva, Rome, and Bonn. In April 1999 the United Nations System Standing Committee on Nutrition (then known as the United Nations Administrative Committee on Coordination/Sub-Committee on Nutrition) focused its annual meeting on the human right to adequate food. In May 1999, the United Nations Committee on Economic, Social and Cultural Rights released its landmark General Comment 12 on the Right to Adequate Food, described below.

All of these efforts were given further impetus at the Millennium Summit of the United Nations in 2000. The eight Millennium Development Goals, supported by all 189 nations at the Millennium Summit,[24] were led off by goal 1: eradicate extreme poverty and hunger. The final report of the Millennium Task Force on Hunger[25] argues that developed countries should contribute more generously to development in poor countries. It does not argue that they have any legal obligation to do so.

A follow-up to the World Food Summit of 1996, titled "World Food Summit: Five Years Later" (though actually held in 2002 because of the events of September 11, 2001), produced a final declaration that called for the creation of an International Alliance Against Hunger and called upon the FAO Council (the executive governing body of the FAO) to establish

an Intergovernmental Working Group, with the participation of stakeholders, in the context of the WFS follow-up, to elaborate, in a period of two years, a set of voluntary guidelines to support Member States' efforts to achieve the progressive realisation of the right to adequate food in the context of national food security; we ask the FAO, in close collaboration with relevant treaty bodies, agencies and programmes of the UN System, to assist the Intergovernmental Working Group,

21. World Declaration on Nutrition, ¶1, available at http://www.fao.org/docrep/U9920t/u9920t0a.htm
22. Adopted Nov. 13–17, 1996, referenced in Documentary Appendix B.
23. Ibid.
24. See United Nations Millennium Declaration (Sept. 8, 2000), referenced in Documentary Appendix B.
25. Available at http://www.unmillenniumproject.org/reports/reports2.htm

which shall report on its work to the Committee on World Food Security.[26]

This was a disappointment to many because the idea of voluntary guidelines appeared to move away from acknowledging any sort of firm obligation on the part of the international community relative to the human right to adequate food. The United States had a sharply different view:

> The United States believes that the issue of adequate food can only be viewed in the context of the right to a standard of living adequate for health and well-being, as set forth in the Universal Declaration of Human Rights, which includes the opportunity to secure food, clothing, housing, medical care, and necessary social services. Further, the United States believes that the attainment of the right to an adequate standard of living is a goal or aspiration to be realized progressively that does not give rise to any international obligation or any domestic legal entitlement, and does not diminish the responsibilities of national governments towards their citizens. Additionally, the United States understands the right of access to food to mean the opportunity to secure food, and not guaranteed entitlement. . . . [W]e are committed to concrete action to meet the objectives of the World Food Summit, and are concerned that sterile debate over "Voluntary Guidelines" would distract attention from the real work of reducing poverty and hunger.[27]

The United States has consistently resisted not only the human right to food but also the more comprehensive human right to an adequate livelihood. Even before the UDHR was adopted by the UN General Assembly in December 1948, Eleanor Roosevelt told that body that the United States government did not consider economic, social, and cultural rights to "imply an obligation on governments to assure the enjoyment of these rights by direct government action."[28] The United States failure to ratify either the ICESCR or the CRC reflects its long-standing resistance to the idea of economic and social rights.

The Intergovernmental Working Group established by the FAO Council functioned as a subgroup of FAO's Committee on Food Security. In two years of hard discussion, some governments pressed for keeping the guidelines in the form of soft recommendations, while some, supported by a group of nongovernmental organizations led by FIAN (FoodFirst Information and Action Network)[29] emphasized the need to recognize firm obligations. In the final compromise, the obligations under international human rights law remained in place, and the guidelines showed that governments had choices in the means through which they were fulfilled. The Intergovernmental Working Group approved its text on September 23, 2004 and, later on the same day, it was approved by the Committee on World Food Security.[30] It was adopted by the FAO Council on November 23, 2004.

GENERAL COMMENT 12

On May 12, 1999, the UN Committee on Economic, Social and Cultural Rights released its interpretative General Comment 12 (GC12) on the right to adequate food.[31] This statement constitutes a definitive contribution to international jurisprudence.

GC12 begins by citing the foundation of the legally binding right to food: the two paragraphs that comprise 1966 ICESCR Article 11. It draws a distinction between the first paragraph reference to an adequate standard of living (including adequate food) and the second paragraph which calls for ensuring "the fundamental right

---

26. FAO, *Declaration of the World Food Summit: Five Years Later* (Rome: FAO, 2002), ¶ 10.
27. FAO, *Explanatory Notes/Reservation to the Declaration of the World Food Summit: Five Years Later* (Rome: FAO, 2002).
28. Quoted in Mary Ann Glendon, *A World Made New: Eleanor Roosevelt and the Universal Declaration of Human Rights* (New York: Random House, 2001), 186.
29. Based in Heidelberg, Germany, FIAN has its website at http://www.fian.org/fian/index.php
30. See Food and Agriculture Organization of the United Nations, *Committee on World Food Security Adopts Right to Food Guidelines* (2004), available at http://www.fao.org/newsroom/en/news/2004/50821/index.html. The text is available at ftp://ftp.fao.org/unfao/bodies/council/cl127/J3345e1.pdf
31. UN. Economic and Social Council (Committee on Economic, Social and Cultural Rights), *Substantive Issues Arising in the Implementation of the International Covenant on Economic, Social and Cultural Rights: General Comment 12 (Twentieth Session, 1999), The Right to Adequate Food (art. 11)* (Geneva: ECOSOC Doc. E/C.12/1999/5), available at http://www.unhchr.ch/tbs/doc.nsf/MasterFrameView/3d02758c707031d58025677f003b73b9?Opendocument

to freedom from hunger and malnutrition," stating that "more immediate and urgent steps may be needed to ensure" the fundamental right to freedom from hunger and malnutrition. Hunger and malnutrition signify, thus, more acute, more urgent problems than inadequate food in itself, a distinction that is addressed again in GC12's paragraph 6: "The *right to adequate food* will have to be realized progressively. However, States have a core obligation to take the necessary action to mitigate and alleviate hunger as provided for in paragraph 2 of article 11, even in times of natural or other disasters." It is important to distinguish the broad concern with food supplies from the immediate need to deal with hunger and malnutrition. The food supplies approach focuses attention on what is in the family's or the nation's cupboard; the focus on hunger and malnutrition focuses attention on the condition of people's bodies.

GC12's paragraph 4 highlights the linkage of the right to adequate food to "the inherent dignity of the human person" and points out that it is indispensable for the realization of other human rights. It is also inseparable from social justice.

Paragraph 5 observes that "Fundamentally, the roots of the problem of hunger and malnutrition are not lack of food but lack of *access to* available food, *inter alia* because of poverty, by large segments of the world's population." This sentence might have been clearer if the phrase "lack of food" had been followed by something like "in the community." The reference here is to the fundamental distinction between *availability* (is there food around?) and *access* (can you make a claim on that food?).

Paragraph 6 of GC12 presents the core definition:

> The right to adequate food is realized when every man, woman and child, alone or in community with others, has physical and economic access at all times to adequate food or means for its procurement.

The paragraph goes on to emphasize that the right to adequate food "must not be interpreted in a narrow or restrictive sense which equates it with a minimum package of calories, proteins and other specific nutrients." In other words, simply delivering prepackaged meals in the way one might deliver feed pellets to livestock cannot fulfill the right. That sort of approach would be incompatible with human dignity. Delivering such meals might be sensible in a short-term

emergency, but it cannot be the means for realizing the human right to adequate food over the long run.

GC12's paragraph 7 explains that *adequacy* means that account must be taken of what is appropriate under given circumstances. Food *security* implies food being accessible for both present and future generations. *Sustainability* relates to long-term availability and accessibility. Thus, as explained in GC12's paragraph 8, the core content of the right to adequate food implies:

> The availability of food in a quantity and quality sufficient to satisfy the dietary needs of individuals, free from adverse substances, and acceptable within a given culture; [and]

> The accessibility of such food in ways that are sustainable and that do not interfere with the enjoyment of other human rights.

These terms are then explained further in paragraphs 9–13.

Paragraph 14 summarizes the obligations of States as follows:

> Every State is obliged to ensure for everyone under its jurisdiction access to the minimum essential food which is sufficient, nutritionally adequate and safe, to ensure their freedom from hunger.

The obligation applies to everyone under the state's jurisdiction. Thus, it is not permissible to exclude immigrants or refugees, even if they are in the country illegally. The obligation cannot be limited only to citizens, or only to particular ethnic groups. If a group of people is under military occupation, the obligation extends to them as well.

Paragraph 15 spells out the different kinds or levels of state obligations. These may be categorized as follows:

> *respect*—"The obligation to *respect* existing access to adequate food requires States parties not to take any measures that result in preventing such access."

> *protect*—"The obligation to protect requires measures by the State to ensure that enterprises or individuals do not deprive individuals of their access to adequate food."

> *fulfil (facilitate)*—"The obligation to fulfil (facilitate) means the State must pro-actively engage in activities intended to strengthen people's access to and utilization of resources and means to ensure their livelihood, including food security."

fulfil (provide)—"Finally, whenever an individual or group is unable, for reasons beyond their control, to enjoy the right to adequate food by the means at their disposal, States have the obligation to fulfil (provide) that right directly. This obligation also applies for persons who are victims of natural or other disasters."

General Comment 12 should be consulted for its analyses on these and other themes, including the issues of implementation at the national level, framework legislation, monitoring, remedies and accountability, international obligations, etc. The key point is that people should be provided with food directly only under very limited conditions. The major obligation is to facilitate, which means that people should be provided with enabling conditions that allow them to provide for themselves. Dignity comes not from being fed, but from being able to provide for yourself.

GLOBAL GOVERNANCE

Human rights are international in the sense that they apply to all persons. But they are really *inter*national—in the sense of transcending national borders—only if, upon the failure of a national government to assure realization of those rights, the international community is *obligated* to step in to do what is necessary. There is now no mechanism and no firm commitment to such an obligation when it comes to the human right to adequate food. In current law and practice, human rights obligations are primarily domestic, affecting relationships between national governments and their own people and others living under their jurisdictions. However, people who do not have adequate food are people not only of particular nations; they are people of the world as well, and they have claims of rights not only in relation to their own governments but in relation to the world as a whole. The human right to adequate food means very little if obligations to honor that right are limited only to one's own government or nation. Children born into poor countries are not born into a poor world.

There is abundant recognition of obligations beyond national jurisdiction in human rights law—for example, in Article 22 of the UDHR providing that economic, social, and cultural rights should be achieved "through national effort and international cooperation"; in UDHR Article 28 stating that "Everyone is entitled to a social and international order in which the rights and freedoms set forth in this Declaration can be fully realized"; in Article 2(1) of the ICESCR calling on each state party to take steps "individually and through international assistance and cooperation, especially economic and technical, to the maximum of its available resources, with a view to achieving progressively the full realization of the rights recognized in the present Covenant"; and in ICESCR Article 11 requiring states parties individually and through international cooperation to take the measures needed to implement "the fundamental right of everyone to be free from hunger"—*everyone*, not just the people of their own countries.

International human rights law is fundamentally a project of articulating universally accepted standards of governance that favor the protection and promotion of human dignity. It connotes some level of obligation to everyone everywhere, not only to persons under a state's jurisdiction; and it connotes also that the world community through its international institutions is subject to human rights obligations similar to those of states. If a particular action by a national government is viewed as a human rights violation, then a similar action by, say, the World Bank should be viewed as a human rights violation as well. International governmental agencies, as creations of nation states and acting in their behalf, are subject to much the same obligations as those states.

Under truly democratic global governance, the world community's attention and resources would be devoted to addressing the concerns of poor people everywhere. We must not reduce the obligations of the international community merely to that of assuring equality in the dispensation of international assistance. An identical nickel into everyone's tin cup won't do the job. Moreover, we should not suggest that the solution is to come in the form of handouts, soup kitchens on a global scale. The Millennium Development Task Force on Hunger reduces the role of the international community to that of a donor, and leaves the strategic planning to the separate nations. This amounts to an evasion of responsibility. The task is not to feed people, but to provide enabling conditions for all people, everywhere, so that they can provide for themselves. Everyone has a right to that. And we all have an obligation to make sure that right is realized everywhere.

QUESTIONS FOR REFLECTION AND DISCUSSION

1. When discussing the "right to food," what food are we talking about? Gourmet food? A meat and potatoes or comparable vegetarian diet? Fundamental nutrients? Article 11 of the International Covenant on Economic, Social and Cultural Rights (ICESCR, reprinted and referenced in Documentary Appendix A), proclaims "the right of everyone to . . . adequate food." What is "adequate food"? Would ensuring everyone (or at least everyone in need) access to basic multi-vitamins on a daily basis satisfy the requirements of the right to food?

2. Does the right to food vary from country to country? From time to time? Does it vary based on gender? Age? Class, caste, or economic status? How would Kent answer these questions? How would Eleanor Roosevelt?

3. Is the right to food best understood as an independent right or as a part of another right such as the right to health (see Reading 16 by Paul Hunt next in this chapter) or the right to development (see Reading 20 by Arjun Sengupta in Chapter 4 of this volume)? Note also the pertinent language of ICESCR Article 11(1): "the right of everyone to an adequate standard of living for himself and his family [sic], *including adequate food*" (emphasis added). Must rights be independent to be viable, useful?

4. Kent states that "it would be inappropriate to argue that nutrition is more important than, say, housing or education"? Do you agree? If you had to construct a hierarchy of rights including, for example, all the rights enumerated in the table of contents of this volume, where would the right to food rank? Why?

5. ICESCR Article 11(2) recognizes "the fundamental right of everyone to be free from hunger." Kent writes that "dignity does not come from being fed . . . [but] from providing for oneself." Is freedom from hunger a matter of dignity or health and survival? Are starving people concerned with dignity or simply with eating, by whatever means food is obtained? How would Kent answer these questions? How do you?

6. Which of the following two approaches better protects the human right to food as articulated by Kent: (a) the approach taken by The Heifer Project (see http://www.heifer.org), in which community needs are ascertained in concert with the recipients of aid and in which aid consists of animals (chickens, cows, goats, water buffalo, etc., depending on the identified needs) capable of providing long-term access to food; or (b) the approach of the United Nations World Food Programme (see http://www.wfp.org), in which foodstuffs (typically bags of grain or rice, tins of meat or other protein, and cooking oil) are delivered to identified "hunger hotspots"? Or is this a false dichotomy? Are both approaches necessary? When?

7. Kent quotes Philip Alston's and Katarina Tomaševski's observation that "statistics make hunger by far the most flagrant and widespread of all serious human rights abuses." But who, exactly, is doing the abusing? The producers? The distributors? International institutions? Governments? All of the above? Some of the above? Is the assignment of duty or responsibility more problematic with respect to the right to food than other rights?

8. In "Realization of Social and Economic Rights and the Minimum Threshold Approach," *HRLJ* 10, no. 1–2 (1989): 35–51, at 41–42, Asbjørn Eide writes: "Nonaccess to food and other material substance needs is in most cases related to poverty. * * * The factors underlying this poverty are partly exogenous, influenced by the structure of the international economic system as it has evolved over centuries, and partly endogenous, influenced by the internal distribution of resources and of unequal opportunities." In what way or ways does Eide's observation implicate the responsibility of the duty-bearers of the right to food under international law?

9. More than five years after the World Food Summit concluded with the Rome Declaration on World Food Security and World Food Summit Plan of Action, Zambia and Angola, both famine-stricken, refused offers of food aid containing unmilled genetically engineered (GE) corn from the United States. See "Better Dead Than GM Fed?" *The Economist*, Sept. 19, 2002, also available at http://www.economist.com/science/displayStory.cfm?story_id=1337197. Did the Zambian and Angolan governments violate their citizens' human rights by refusing the proffered aid? Or were their actions in keeping with the Rome Declaration's affirmation of the right to access to "safe and nutritious food"? Did the U.S. offer, made with the knowledge that many Zambians and Angolans strongly object to genetic engineering on spiritual grounds, violate international law?

10. The United States resists the imposition of legal obligations on states to provide food for people. Why? Similarly, why does the U.S. refuse to recognize economic and social rights in general? What effect has the continued U.S. resistance on both fronts had on progress at the UN? On the people whose rights in these realms the U.S. refuses to recognize?

11. Is the right to food an individual or collective right? Is it perhaps both? Who are the right's duty-bearers in each case and why? The family? The business sector? Government? International institutions? How would the duty be enforced in respect of these or other potential duty-bearers?

12. Has the United States fulfilled its obligations even under the very limited right to food it has recognized—that is, has the United States made a good-faith effort to provide an "opportunity to secure food" to all of its citizens? Has the United States fulfilled its obligations under paragraph 14 of General Comment 12: "Every State is obliged to ensure for everyone under its jurisdiction access to the minimum essential food which is sufficient, nutritionally adequate and safe, to ensure their freedom from hunger"? In the city or town in which you live, what has the government done to alleviate hunger among, for example, the homeless? The elderly?

13. Kent argues that "an identical nickel into everyone's tin cup won't do the job" of alleviating hunger. Is there any amount of money, evenly distributed, that would? $100 per person? $1,000? If, for example, all nations redirected their military spending to filling Kent's hypothetical tin cup, each person could receive about $124 per year. What, in your view, would be the best way to spend this money to have the most lasting impact on world hunger?

14. Kent concludes with a call for international institutions such as the World Bank to be held to the same human rights standards as national governments. Do you agree? How has the World Bank helped or hindered "the right of everyone to . . . adequate food" and "to be free from hunger," per ICESCR Article 11? Do "restructuring" programs which require nations to severely limit government spending, including spending to provide food to the hungry, violate international law by abrogating the right to food?

16. PAUL HUNT *The Right to Health: Key Objectives, Themes, and Interventions*

In September 2002, I was appointed Special Rapporteur on the Right to Health by the Chairperson of the UN Commission on Human Rights.[1] A few months after my appointment, I presented my preliminary report to the Commission. Because space does not permit an in-depth examination of the content of that report, I have chosen to focus here on some of the key objectives, themes, and interventions arising from the contemporary realization of the right to health. The full report, which includes an examination of the sources, contours, and

Reprinted with changes from Paul Hunt, "The UN Special Rapporteur on the Right to Health: Key Objectives, Themes, and Interventions," *Health and Human Rights* 7 (2003): 1–27. Copyright © 2003 by the President and Fellows of Harvard College. Reprinted by permission.

1. *Eds.*— In this capacity, the author writes at pp. 2–3: "I am requested to do the following: • Gather, request, receive, and exchange right to health information from all relevant sources. • Dialogue and discuss possible areas of cooperation with all relevant actors, including governments; UN bodies; specialized agencies and programs, in particular the World Health Organization [WHO] and the joint UN Program on HIV/AIDS, as well as nongovernmental organizations (NGOs); and international financial institutions. • Report on the status of the realization of the right to health throughout the world, including laws, policies, good practices, and obstacles. • Make recommendations on appropriate measures to promote and protect the right to health. The Special Rapporteur is also mandated to apply a gender perspective, to pay special attention to the needs of children in the realization of the right to health, to take into account the relevant provisions of the Durban Declaration and Program of Action [see Documentary Appendix B], and to bear in mind, in particular, General Comment No. 14 of the Committee on Economic, Social, and Cultural Rights [CESCR] and General Recommendation No. 24 of the Committee on the Elimination of Discrimination Against Women (CEDAW)."

content of the right to health, can be read in its entirety on the UN Commission on Human Rights web site.[2] I would like to emphasize briefly four crucial jurisprudential elements of the right to health that inform this discussion.

First, the right to health includes, but goes beyond, the right to health care: The right to health is an inclusive right, extending not only to timely and appropriate health care, but also to the underlying determinants of health, such as access to safe and potable water and adequate sanitation, healthy occupational and environmental conditions, and access to health-related education and information, including information on sexual and reproductive health.

Second, the right to health contains both freedoms and entitlements: Freedoms include the right to control one's health, including the right to be free from nonconsensual medical treatment and experimentation. Entitlements include the right to a system of health protection (i.e., health care and the underlying determinants of health) that provides equality of opportunity for people to enjoy the highest attainable standard of health.

Third, the right to health imposes some immediate obligations: Although subject to progressive realization and resource constraints, the right to health imposes various obligations of immediate effect. These immediate obligations include the guarantees of nondiscrimination and equal treatment, as well as the obligation to take deliberate, concrete, and targeted steps toward the full realization of the right to health, such as the preparation of a national public health strategy and plan of action. Progressive realization means that states have a specific and continuing obligation to move as expeditiously and effectively as possible toward the full realization of the right to health.[3]

Fourth, the right to health gives rise to responsibilities in relation to international assistance and cooperation: States have an obligation to take steps, individually and through international assistance and cooperation, toward the full realization of the right to health. For example, states are obliged to respect the enjoyment of the right to health in other jurisdictions, to ensure that no international agreement or policy has an adverse impact on the right to health, and to make certain that their representatives in international organizations take due account of the right to health, as well as the obligation of international assistance and cooperation, in all policy-making matters.[4]

BROAD OBJECTIVES

Given the state of the right to health today, three broad interrelated objectives deserve particular attention:

1. *To promote—and to encourage others to promote—the right to health as a fundamental human right, as set out in numerous legally binding international human rights treaties, resolutions of the Commission on Human Rights, and the Constitution of the [World Health Organization (WHO)].* Although the right to health is a fundamental human right that has the same international legal status as freedom of religion or the right to a fair trial, it is not as widely recognized as these and other civil and political rights. Many different actors, such as governments, international organizations, and civil-society groups, can help to raise the profile of the right to health as a fundamental human right. While it may take some years before the right to health enjoys the same currency as other, more-established human rights, a crucial goal should be to ensure that the right to health receives widespread recognition as a fundamental human right.

---

2. See http://www.ohchr.org/english/issues/health/right.

3. The UNCESCR General Comment 14 [infra note 6] also uses the term "core obligations." On core obligations, see Audrey R. Chapman and Sage Russell, eds., *Core Obligations: Building a Framework for Economic, Social and Cultural Rights* (Antwerp: Intersentia, 2002).

4. Note Judge Weeramantry's dissenting opinion in the Advisory Opinion of the International Court of Justice on the Legality of the Threat or Use of Nuclear Weapons, in which he cited [Article 12 of the International Covenant on Economic, Social and Cultural Rights (hereinafter ICESCR)] and then stated, in relation to this article, that "it will be noted here that the recognition by States of the right to health is in the general terms that they recognize the right of 'everyone' and not merely of their own subjects. Consequently, each State is obligated to respect the right to health of all members of the international community." *ICJ Reports* 1 (1996): 144. For an overall assessment of the Court's Advisory Opinion, see Burns H. Weston, "Nuclear Weapons and the World Court: Ambiguity's Consensus," *TLCP* 7 (1997): 371–99.

2. *To clarify the contours and content of the right to health in jurisprudential terms. What does the right to health mean? What obligations does it give rise to?* Although national and international jurisprudence on the right to health is growing, the legal content of the right is not yet well established. This is not surprising, given the historic neglect of the right to health, as well as other economic, social, and cultural rights. Thus, a second key objective is to clarify and explore the contours and content of the right to health by drawing first on the evolving national and international jurisprudence and second on the basic principles that animate international human rights law, such as equality, nondiscrimination, and dignity of the individual.

3. *To identify good practices for operationalizing the right to health at the community, national, and international levels.* Once human rights are recognized and their legal content understood, their legal provisions must be operationalized. In other words, national and international norms must be translated into effective policies, programs, and projects. How to go about such a transition for the right to health is not readily evident, any more than it is for a number of other human rights. Fortunately, different jurisdictions can provide examples of good laws, policies, programs, and projects that reflect the right to health. While what works in one context might not necessarily work in another, lessons can be learned. Thus, collecting, analyzing, and promoting good practices on the right to health are important steps. These good practices may be found at the community, national, and international levels and may be related to various actors including governments, courts, national human rights institutions, health professionals, civil-society organizations, and international organizations.

MAIN THEMES

The right to health extends across a wide, diverse, and at times highly complex range of issues. To make promoting the right to health more manageable, I suggest focusing on two interrelated themes: (a) poverty and the right to health and (b) discrimination, stigma, and the right to health.

As affirmed in the UN Millennium Declaration, poverty eradication has become one of the key, overarching policy objectives of the UN, as well as of other international organizations and many states.[5] Discrimination and stigma both continue to seriously constrain and undermine progress in the field of health. The themes of poverty, discrimination, and stigma especially affect issues of gender, children, and racial discrimination. These themes also lend themselves to an examination of other important issues, such as those relating to mental health and HIV/AIDS.

POVERTY, HUMAN RIGHTS, AND THE RIGHT TO HEALTH

A growing body of literature and practice has emerged that focuses on the impact of human rights on poverty reduction. In brief, human rights empower the poor; help tackle discrimination and inequality; require the participation of the poor; underscore the importance of all rights in the struggle against poverty; render some policy choices (e.g., those with a disproportionately harmful impact on the poor) impermissible; emphasize the crucial role of international assistance and cooperation; and introduce the notion of obligation and thus the requirement of effective, transparent, and accessible mechanisms of accountability.

Less literature and practice exist on the contribution that the right to health specifically has made to poverty reduction—and it is this issue that demands particular attention. A poverty reduction strategy based on the right to health would, for example, focus on improving poor populations' access to health services by, perhaps, identifying diseases that are particularly prevalent among the poor and creating immunization and other programs that are specifically designed to reach the poor; improving the effectiveness of public health interventions by, for instance, implementing basic environmental controls, especially for waste disposal in areas populated by the poor, reducing the financial burden of health protection on the poor, e.g., by reducing or eliminating user fees for the poor; and promoting policies in other sectors that bear positively on the underlying determinants of

5. Referenced in Documentary Appendix B.

health, e.g., supporting agricultural policies that have positive health outcomes for the poor.

Ultimately, exploring the specific contribution the right to health makes to reducing poverty is important. This contribution has to be understood in the overall context of the contributions human rights—including nondiscrimination, participation, international cooperation, and accountability—make to reducing poverty.

DISCRIMINATION AND STIGMA AND THE RIGHT TO HEALTH

Discrimination and stigma is a second key theme relevant to the right to health. Discrimination on the grounds of gender, race, ethnicity, and other factors is a social determinant of health. Social inequalities, fueled by discrimination and marginalization of particular groups, shape both the distribution of diseases and the course of health outcomes among those afflicted. As a result, the burden of ill health is borne by vulnerable and marginalized groups in society. At the same time, discrimination and stigma associated with particular health conditions, such as mental disorders, and diseases, such as HIV/ AIDS, tend to reinforce existing social divisions and inequalities. Nondiscrimination is among the most fundamental principles of international human rights law. The International Covenant on Economic, Social and Cultural Rights (ICESCR) proscribes

> any discrimination in access to health care and underlying determinants of health, as well as to means and entitlements for their procurement, on the grounds of race, colour, sex, language, religion, political or other opinion, national or social origin, property, birth, physical or mental disability, health status (including HIV/AIDS), sexual orientation and civil, political, social or other status, which has the intention or effect of nullifying or impairing the equal enjoyment or exercise of the right to health.[6]

As well as prohibiting discrimination on a range of specified grounds, such as race, color, sex, and religion, international human rights instruments also prohibit discrimination on the grounds of "other status." The Commission on Human Rights has interpreted this term to include health status. Thus, the Commission and UNCESCR agree that states have an obligation to take measures against discrimination based on health status, as well as in relation to other prohibited grounds. With respect to the right to health, states have an obligation to ensure that health facilities, goods and services—including the underlying determinants of health—are accessible to all, especially the most vulnerable or marginalized sectors of the population, without discrimination.

The links between stigma, discrimination, and denial of the right to enjoy the highest attainable standard of health are complex and multifaceted. Together, discrimination and stigma amount to a failure to respect human dignity and equality by devaluing those affected, often adding to the inequalities already experienced by vulnerable and marginalized groups. This increases people's vulnerability to ill health and hampers effective health interventions. The impact is compounded when an individual suffers double or multiple forms of discrimination based, for example, on gender, race, poverty, and health status.

Effectively promoting the right to health requires identifying and analyzing the complex ways in which discrimination and stigma have an impact on the enjoyment of the right to health of those affected, particularly women, children, and marginalized groups, such as racial and ethnic minorities, indigenous peoples, persons with disabilities, people living with HIV/AIDS, refugees, the internally displaced, and migrants. Promoting the right to health also requires gathering and analyzing data to better understand how various forms of discrimination are determinants of health, recognizing the compounding effects of multiple forms of discrimination, and documenting how discrimination and intolerance affect health and access to health care services. It will also require carefully balancing the need to address discrimination and stigma in relation to health by encouraging the desegregation of data and the development of policies and strategies to combat discrimination, while also ensuring that publication of such data does not perpetuate stigma. The impact of stigma and discrimination on the enjoyment of the right

---

6. UNCESCR, General Comment 14 on the Right to the Highest Attainable Standard of Health, Aug. 11, 2000, UN Doc. E/C.12/2000/4, ¶18.

to health is best understood in relation to particular populations, such as women, racial and ethnic minorities, people with disabilities, and people living with HIV/AIDS.

SPECIFIC PROJECTS, ISSUES, AND INTERVENTIONS

Given the three previously identified objectives, as well as the themes of poverty and discrimination/stigma, what are examples of specific right-to-health projects, issues, and interventions that might be usefully pursued? Below, six possible interventions are briefly discussed that, in my opinion, deserve increased attention. Of course, many other compelling right-to-health interventions could and should be undertaken by various actors. The following illustrations are designed to signal how the general objectives and themes already identified can be taken forward and made more specific.

POVERTY-REDUCTION STRATEGIES

Poverty is a global phenomenon experienced in varying degrees in all nations. An increasing variety of nations—higher-income, lower-income, and those in transition—are formulating strategies to reduce poverty. Thus, one intervention is to examine a selection of poverty-reduction strategies through the prism of the right to health with a view to suggesting ways in which the health component might more effectively benefit the poor and reduce poverty.

Poverty Reduction Strategy Papers (PRSPs), derived from the Heavily Indebted Poor Countries (HIPC) initiative, are one category of antipoverty strategy. WHO recently carried out a desk review of 10 full PRSPs and three interim PRSPs. This preliminary study found little evidence of attempts to adapt national health strategies to meet the needs of the poorest populations. Very few PRSPs have built in any health indicators that would monitor their impact on poor people or regions. No PRSPs contain plans to include poor people in a participatory monitoring process. All of these shortcomings would have been, at least, attenuated if the right to health had been taken into account during the

formulation of the relevant PRSP. Not surprisingly, the study also found that no PRSP mentions health as a human right.

An examination of antipoverty strategies should not only include [the world's poorest countries] and lower-income states, but should also extend to some antipoverty strategies [of higher-income states addressing] two different constituencies: their own jurisdiction and developing states. In light of its obligation of international assistance, a higher-income state should consider what contribution it is making to reduce poverty in the countries of the South. Accordingly, one project or intervention is to examine, through the prism of the right to health, higher-income states' strategies for the reduction of poverty in both their jurisdictions and in countries of the South.

NEGLECTED DISEASES

Broadly speaking, diseases fall into three categories. Type I diseases, such as hepatitis B, occur in rich and poor countries alike, with large numbers of populations vulnerable to these diseases found in each. Type II, or "neglected," diseases include HIV/AIDS and tuberculosis and are found in both rich and poor countries but are disproportionately present in poor countries.

Type III, or "very neglected," diseases, such as river blindness and sleeping sickness, overwhelmingly or exclusively plague lower-income countries. According to a recent WHO report, *Global Defence Against the Infectious Disease Threat*, the "health impact of these . . . diseases is measured by severe and permanent disabilities and deformities in almost 1 billion people. . . . Their low mortality despite high morbidity places them near the bottom of mortality-tables and, in the past, they have received low priority."[7] The report continues:

> [These] diseases form a group because they affect almost exclusively poor and powerless people living in rural parts of low-income countries. While they cause immense suffering and often life-long disabilities, these diseases rarely kill and therefore do not receive the attention and funding of high-mortality diseases, like AIDS, tuberculosis, and malaria. They are neglected in a second sense as well. Confined as they are to poor populations all

7. WHO, *Global Defence Against the Infectious Disease Threat* , ed. Mary Kay Kindhauser (Geneva: WHO, 2002), iv.

have traditionally suffered from a lack of incentives to develop drugs and vaccines for markets that cannot pay. Where inexpensive and effective drugs exist, demand fails because of inability to pay. Neglected diseases impose an enormous economic burden in terms of lost productivity and the high costs of long-term care. . . . [These] diseases can help to guarantee that the next generation remains anchored in poverty. . . . The disabilities caused by most of these diseases are associated with great stigma.[8]

The lines separating these three disease categories are not rigid: Some diseases straddle two categories. Malaria, for instance, falls between types II and III.

In the case of type I diseases, incentives for research and development exist in rich countries, e.g., the market mechanism, public funding of basic research, and patent protection for product development. Products get developed, and the main policy issue for poor countries is gaining access to those technologies, which tend to be high priced and patent protected. Although many vaccines for type I diseases have been developed during the past 20 years, there is little incentive to widely introduce them into poor countries because of anticipated low returns on such an investment.

Incentives for research and development of type II diseases do exist in rich-country markets, but funding globally is not commensurate with the disease burden. A particularly accurate example of this involves vaccines for HIV/AIDS. Substantial research and development for these vaccines is underway because of rich-country market demand, but not in proportion to global need or addressed to the specific disease conditions of poor countries.

Type III diseases receive extremely little research and development, with essentially no commercial funding taking place in rich countries. Because of poverty, the market mechanism fails. Moreover, governments of poor countries lack the means to subsidize the needed research and development. Thus, research and development

for diseases specific to poor countries tend to be grossly underfinanced. As the report from the WHO Commission on Macroeconomics and Health puts it: "The poor countries benefit from R&D (research and development) mainly when the rich also suffer from the same diseases."[9]

The imbalance between research on diseases of the poor (type II and especially type III) and on diseases of the rich has been documented for more than a decade. In 1990, the Commission on Health Research and Development noted what has become known as the "10/90 disequilibrium": only 10% of research and development spending goes into health problems that affect 90% of the world's population. Initiatives have been launched to address this imbalance and some progress has been made—but the initiatives remain profoundly underfunded. Recently, neglected diseases—a problem arising from market and public-policy failures—have been given fresh impetus by a number of welcome developments, including adoption of the Declaration on the Trade-Related Aspects of Intellectual Property Rights (TRIPS Agreement) and Public Health and the work of the Global Fund to Fight AIDS, Tuberculosis, and Malaria.[10]

In the final analysis, particular attention must be paid to the numerous right to health implications of neglected [including very neglected] diseases and the 10/90 disequilibrium, including nondiscrimination, equality, the availability and accessibility of health facilities, goods and services (including drugs), international assistance and cooperation, and so on. Neglected diseases, very neglected diseases, and the 10/90 disequilibrium are human rights issues.

IMPACT ASSESSMENTS

Before a state introduces a new law or policy, it has to ensure that the new initiative is consistent with its existing national and international legal obligations, including those relating to human rights.[11] If a state has adopted poverty reduction as a major policy objective, it must

8. Ibid., 96.
9. WHO, *Macroeconomics and Health: Investing in Health for Economic Development* (Geneva: WHO, 2001), 77.
10. WTO, Declaration on the TRIPS Agreement and Public Health, adopted by the Fourth Ministerial Conference, Doha, Nov. 14, 2001, WT/MIN(01)/DEC/2.
11. According to the Vienna Declaration and Program of Action: "Protection and promotion of human rights and fundamental freedoms is the first responsibility of Governments." See Vienna Declaration and Programme of Action, June 25, 1993, UN Doc. A/CONF.157/24, pt. 1, ¶ 1, Weston and Carlson, 3: III.U.2, referenced in Documentary Appendix B.

ensure that any new law or policy is consistent with that policy goal. Rigorous policy making demands that the distributional impact of reforms on the well-being of different groups in society, especially the poor and vulnerable, is analyzed. Such an analysis has to consider—before, during, and after implementation of any relevant policy—the intended and unintended consequences of an initiative, with a view to identifying appropriate mitigating or other measures. This socially responsible impact analysis is required of states and other actors in the context of national and international policies.

Of course, there are obstacles to preparing such rigorous analyses. According to authors of a recent International Monetary Fund (IMF) publication, these obstacles include "Data limitations, weak national capacity, and a lack of donor coordination."[12] They recommend that poverty and social-impact analyses should be strengthened and suggest the international community should do more to develop institutional capacity at the national level for the "development of alternative policy scenarios" and "the preparation of poverty and social-impact analysis."[13]

Despite these and other difficulties, different forms of impact analysis are increasingly common at the national and international levels. In the context of the European Union, there is a requirement to check that some policy proposals do not have an adverse impact on health—and this has contributed to a growing literature on health-impact assessments. In addition, the World Bank has recently prepared a lengthy guide, entitled *User's Guide to Poverty and Social Impact Analysis*.[14] Some civil-society organizations have advocated the introduction of "poverty impact assessments" within the framework of the PRSP process. Human rights impact assessments have been suggested for many years, most prominently in the Vienna Declaration and Program of Action, and a few actors have sought to put them into practice.

Appropriate impact analyses are one way of ensuring that the right to health—especially of marginalized groups, including the poor—is given due weight in all national and international policy making processes. Accordingly, in the context of the right to health, continuing attention should be given to the different types of impact analyses with a view to identifying good practice for states and other actors.

THE WORLD TRADE ORGANIZATION AND THE RIGHT TO HEALTH

It is not possible in a commentary of this nature and length to adequately scrutinize TRIPS and the General Agreement on Trade in Services (GATS) through the prism of the right to health, an exercise begun by the former High Commissioner for Human Rights in her reports of June 2001 and 2002. What is clear, however, is that both agreements have crucial bearings on the right to health. TRIPS, for example, affects issues of access to essential drugs and also international cooperation. As the Commission on Human Rights has observed: "Access to medication in the context of pandemics such as HIV/AIDS is one fundamental element for achieving progressively the full realization of the right of everyone to the enjoyment of the highest attainable standard of physical and mental health."[15]

The Declaration on the TRIPS Agreement and Public Health, adopted at the WTO Fourth Ministerial Conference in Doha during November 2001, is a significant development.[16] The Doha Declaration recognizes "the gravity of the public health problems afflicting many developing and least-developed countries, especially those resulting from HFV/AIDS, tuberculosis, malaria and other epidemics."[17] The Declaration stresses that TRIPS "can and should be interpreted and implemented in a manner supportive of WTO members' right to protect public health and, in particular, to promote access to medicines for all."[18] In this way, the Declaration

---

12. Sanjeev Gupta, Mark Plant, Benedict Clements, Thomas Dorsey, Emanuele Baldacci, Gabriela Inchauste, Shamsuddin Tareq, and Nita Thacker, "Is the PRGF Living Up to Expectations? An Assessment of Program Design," Occasional Paper 216 (Washington, D.C.: International Monetary Fund, September 2002), 32.

13. Ibid., 35.

14. World Bank, *A User's Guide to Poverty and Social Impact Analysis* (Washington, D.C.: World Bank, 2003).

15. UNCHR Res. 2002/32, ¶ 1.

16. WTO, Declaration on the TRIPS Agreement and Public Health, note 10.

17. Ibid., ¶ 1.

18. Ibid., ¶ 4.

reflects human rights perspectives, especially the right to health and the right to enjoy the benefits of scientific progress.

In a recent resolution, the UN Commission on Human Rights called on all states

> to ensure that their actions as members of international organizations take due account of the right of everyone to the enjoyment of the highest attainable standard of physical and mental health and that the application of international agreements is supportive of public health policies which promote broad access to safe, effective and affordable preventive, curative and palliative pharmaceuticals and medical technologies.[19]

In these circumstances, it is important to monitor and examine trade rules and policies in the context of the right to health, including implementation of the Doha Declaration.

THE RIGHT TO MENTAL HEALTH

In 2001, WHO estimated that 450 million people suffered from mental or behavioral disorders and that these disorders accounted for 12% of the global burden of disease.[20] Mental disorders, including schizophrenia, bipolar disorder, depression, mental retardation, and Alzheimer's disease and other dementias, are common in all countries. Poor and other marginalized groups tend to be disproportionately affected by these disorders in both higher-income and lower-income countries.

For a majority of the world's population, mental-health care is geographically and economically inaccessible. Where it is accessible, there are significant disparities in the standards of care between and within countries. In many countries, mental-health care often consists primarily of large psychiatric institutions that have limited provisions for community-based treatment and care.

A wide range of human rights violations reportedly occur in some institutions designated for the care and treatment of persons with mental disorders. These violations include torture and other cruel, inhuman, or degrading treatment, such as sexual exploitation. Stigma and discrimination surround those with mental disorders, including the real or perceived incapacity, of persons with mental disorders to make decisions about the treatment of their illness. It is the combination of these interrelated issues that makes persons with mental disabilities particularly vulnerable to violations of their human rights.

Thus, more attention should be devoted to this neglected element of the right to health: the right to mental health.

HEALTH PROFESSIONALS

As providers of health services, health professionals play an indispensable role in the promotion and protection of the right to health. This role, as well as the difficulties impeding their practice, must not be overlooked.

In many countries, health professionals are poorly paid, work long hours, and must make do with shortages of equipment and obsolete facilities. Poor terms and conditions of employment are a major cause of "brain drain": the migration of medical practitioners mainly from the South to the North, but also from rural areas to urban settings within countries. While the exporting countries may accrue some benefits (e.g., financial remittances from expatriates), the potential adverse outcomes, including shortages of health professionals, absence of compensation, and a decline in quality of health care, are likely to outweigh the benefits. Poor terms and conditions also create incentives for better-trained medical practitioners to seek more favorable situations, often in the private sector, thereby depleting public health systems.

In some countries, professional activities have made health workers victims of discrimination, arbitrary detention, killings, and torture. These worker have also had their freedoms of opinion, speech, and movement curtailed. At particular risk are health professionals who work with victims of torture. Some health professionals have participated, often under duress, in human rights abuses, including torture and the preparation of false medical documentation to cover up human rights abuses.

Corruption is a problem in the provision of health services in some jurisdictions. While in some cases this problem derives from unsatisfactory employment terms and conditions, corruption in health services is not confined to

---

19. UNCHR, Res. 2002/32, note 15, ¶ 6(b).
20. WHO, *Mental Health: New Understanding, New Hope*, World Health Report 2001 (Geneva: WHO, 2001), 3.

health workers. Nor is it confined to one region of the world. Corruption is clearly disadvantageous to the poor and corrodes the right to health. "In many countries poor people report that they are asked to pay for medicine that should be available to them at no charge."[21] Interestingly, a recent IMF study of corruption in healthcare services concludes: "Participation of the poor in the decisions that influence the allocation of public resources would mitigate corruption possibilities."[22] Although there are no quick solutions, corruption should be understood as an issue of both poverty and the right to health.

CONCLUSION

International human rights law, including the right to health, should be consistently and coherently applied across all relevant national and international policy making processes. In the context of international policy making, this fundamental principle is reflected in the Vienna Declaration and Program of Action, as well as in the Secretary-General's reports *Renewing the United Nations: An Agenda for Reform* (1997), *Strengthening of the United Nations: An Agenda for Further Change* (2002), and *Roadmap Toward Implementation of the United Nations Millennium Declaration* (2001).[23] Moreover, the principle is also reflected in positions taken by the UN Commission on Human Rights, such as its resolution calling on States parties to the ICESCR to "ensure that the Covenant is taken into account in all of their relevant national and international policymaking processes."[24]

At the national level, the right to health can enhance health policies and also strengthen the position of health ministries. At the international level, the right to health can contribute to the realization of the Millennium Declaration's vision of global equity and shared responsibility. Thus, the consistent and coherent application of the right to health across all national and international policy making processes is one of the most important challenges confronting those committed to the promotion and protection of this fundamental human right.

QUESTIONS FOR REFLECTION AND DISCUSSION

1. What is health? According to the World Health Organization (WHO), health is *a state of complete physical, mental and social well-being and not merely the absence of disease or infirmity.* What is the right to health? According to General Comment 14 on Article 12 of the ICESCR, it is the right of all people *to the highest attainable standard of health as a prerequisite for the full enjoyment of all other human rights.* Are these definitions too broad? Too narrow? Should they be downsized? Expanded? If so, how?

2. Hunt writes that "the right to health includes, but goes beyond, the right to health care." What else does it include? What else should it include? What does Hunt say? What does Article 12 of the International; Covenant on Economic, Social and Cultural Rights (ICESCR, reprinted and referenced in Documentary Appendix A) say? Are Hunt and Article 12 in agreement? Is one more expansive or inclusive than the other? If so, which one and how?

3. Is it reasonable to think of the right to health as involving, in addition to health care, the improvement of all the cultural, economic, environmental, and sociopolitical conditions that determine health status—e.g., inequality and poverty; race, gender, and minority relations; discrimination, and marginalization (especially in relation to HIV/AIDS); global

21. Deepa Narayan-Parker with Raj Patel et al., *Can Anyone Hear Us! Voices of the Poor Series* (New York: Oxford University Press, 2000), 111.
22. Sanjeev Gupta, Hamid Davoodi, and Erwin Tiongson, "Corruption and the Provision of Health Care and Education Services," in George T. Ahed and Sanjeev Gupta, eds., *Governance, Corruption, and Economic Performance* (Washington, D.C.: International Monetary Fund, 2002), 272.
23. UN, *Renewing the United Nations: An Agenda for Reform, Report of the Secretary-General*, July 14, 1997, UN Doc. A/51/950, ¶¶ 78–79; UN General Assembly, *Strengthening of the UN: An Agenda for Further Change, Report of the Secretary-General*, Sept. 9, 2002, UN Doc. A/57/387, ¶ 48; *Roadmap Toward the Implementation of the UN Millennium Declaration, Report of the Secretary-General*, Sept. 6, 2001, UN Doc. A/56/326, ¶¶ 202, 204.
24. UNCHR, Res. 2002/24, ¶ 7.

environmental threats; labor; militarism; and consumerism and meaninglessness/disease-inducing lifestyles? Such was the position taken in April 2001 at The University of Iowa by a Global Assembly on Advancing the Human Right to Health in its "Iowa City Appeal on Advancing the Human Right to Health," expressly informed by the Declaration of the International Conference on Primary Health Care of the World Health Organization meeting in Alma Ata, Kazakhstan (USSR) in September 1978, and building on the more recent achievements of the UN Committee on Economic, Social and Cultural Rights in its March 2000 General Comment 14 interpreting Article 12 of the ICESCR; see http://www.uichr. com. Participants in the Global Assembly numbered more than 275 persons comprised of leading U.S. and foreign health care providers, legal professionals, and community activists together with faculty and students in public health, medicine, law, and the social sciences, including top officials from the WHO. Do you agree? Disagree? Why?

4. Paul Hunt begins his essay by emphasizing briefly "four crucial jurisprudential elements of the right to health." What are these "four crucial jurisprudential elements"?

5. As noted in Ichiro Kawachi and Bruce Kennedy, *The Health of Nations: Why Inequality Is Harmful to Your Health* (New York: New Press, 2002), 45, economic historians and epidemiologists who have been examining the correlation between health and wealth/poverty have suggested that

> the requirements for maintaining good health are finite and do not keep rising with the level of economic development. . . . Up to a level of national income of about $5,000 per head (in 1990 US dollars), there is a steep linear relationship between money and higher life expectancy. Beyond that point, however, further growth does not produce more health, and the relationship between income and life expectancy flattens out.

Despite being the wealthiest country in the world, the U.S. does not compare well with other less wealthy countries in terms of life expectancy: American men ranked 22nd out of 28 OECD countries in 1996 and American women ranked 19th. Also, Americans rank near the bottom in terms of infant mortality and potential years of life lost to premature mortality. Rather than wealth per se, researchers found, it is the absence of extreme disparities in income distribution that makes for better overall health across the societal spectrum (Kawachi and Kennedy, *The Health of Nations*, Question 5, 49–50). These findings suggest that poverty reduction alone may not be the best strategy for improving health in developing countries and that the most important consequence of WTO, IMF, and World Bank economic prescriptions for these countries is an increase in wealth disparities. In fact, the "health gap" between the world's rich and the world's poor is widening. See David Legge, "Health Inequalities in the New World Order," in Richard Eckersley, Jane Dixon, and Bob Douglas, eds., *The Social Origins of Health and Well-Being* (Cambridge: Cambridge University Press, 2001). How are these difficulties to be overcome?

6. In 1999, WHO's World Health Assembly instructed WHO's Director General to monitor the public health impact of international trade agreements (the WHO having been represented in the 1999 Seattle WTO Conference for the purpose of linking public health concerns to trade). While affirming its support for drug patent protection under the Agreement on Trade-Related Aspects of Intellectual Property Rights (TRIPS), 1869 UNTS 401, reprinted in 33 ILM 1197 (1994) and Weston and Carlson, 4: IV.C.2d. WHO voiced its concern with the "obvious market failures that lead to hundreds of millions of people being left without access to essential drugs." Quoted in Yves Beigbeder, *International Public Health: Patients' Rights vs. the Protection of Patents* (Aldershot: Ashgate, 2004), 64. WHO pushed for delays in the implementation of TRIPS in favor of developing and least-developed countries and, with the help of key NGOs, fought to permit poor countries to import desperately needed patented drugs at reduced prices ("parallel imports") and to manufacture generic drugs without the agreement of the patent holder ("compulsory licensing"). In the following years, however, the implementation of these concessions was obstructed by developed countries and the pharmaceutical industry. The 2001 Doha WTO Ministerial Conference reaffirmed the inviolability of patent rights even in cases of extreme public health emergencies and created serious doubts as to whether parallel imports and compulsory licensing were permissible. In 2002, the U.S. representative to the WHO Executive Board was particularly critical of the WHO's emphasis on access to essential medicines and refused to support differential drug pricing for poorer countries on the grounds that it would stifle

American research and innovation. Should trade laws be above international public health? Why? Why not?

7. As observed by David Wikler and Richard Cash, "Ethical Issues in Global Public Health," in Robert Beaglehole, ed., *Global Public Health: A New Era* (Oxford: Oxford University Press, 2003), there are pressing ethical dilemmas that arise in the context of global public health projects. They write at 237, for example:

> In international health research involving developing countries, the treatment given to participants in the research is often superior to that available to their fellow-citizens. Nevertheless, a number of international collaborative trials have been subjected to vociferous ethical criticism. In the critic's view, the basic question is whether scientists are using a single standard of ethical conduct. If they are, according to this view, any experiment they would perform in a poor country must be one that would be permitted in their home countries. The studies that were most criticized did not meet that standard.

Do these dilemmas arise from the fact that health is not considered a human right? Would a human rights orientation to health provide alternative solutions and vantage points?

8. In 2004, there were estimated to be 6.63 infant deaths per 1,000 live births in the United States—ranking 185th in the world behind, for example, Singapore (2.28), Sweden (2.77), Japan (3.28), the Czech Republic (3.97), Germany (4.2), France (4.31), Slovenia (4.5), Australia (4.76), Canada (4.82), Netherlands (5.11), United Kingdom (5.22), Greece (5.63), Cuba (6.45), and Taiwan (6.52). See *CIA World Fact Book, 2004*, at http://www.cia.gov/cia/publications/factbook/rankorder/2091rank.html. In 2004, $2,400 was needed to purchase a new cancer drug—Campath—in the United States compared to $500 in Italy, $570 in Britain, $660 in Canada and Sweden, and $760 in France. See ABC News, 2003, at http://abcnews.go.com/sections/wnt/Living/healthcare031022_canada.html. In 2004, approximately 43,000,000 US citizens were without health insurance and many more had only limited coverage. See Physicians for National Health Program, at http://www.pnhp.org. The United States does not officially recognize the right to health? Why? What are the consequences of this posture? Does it make any difference to wealthy Americans? To poor Americans without health insurance?

17. RICHARD PIERRE CLAUDE *The Right to Education and Human Rights Education*

Education is intrinsically valuable as humankind's most effective tool for personal empowerment. Education takes on the status of a human right because it is integral to and enhances human dignity through its fruits of knowledge, wisdom, and understanding. Moreover, for instrumental reasons education has the status of a multifaceted social, economic, and cultural human right. It is a social right because in the context of the community it promotes the full development of the human personality. It is an economic right because it facilitates economic self-sufficiency through employment or self-employment. It is a cultural right because the international community has directed education toward the building of a universal culture of human rights. In short, education is a prerequisite for individuals to function as fully human beings in modern society.

In positing a human right to education, the framers of the Universal Declaration of Human Rights (UDHR)[1] axiomatically relied on the notion that education is not value-neutral. In this spirit, Article 26 lays out a set of educational goals analyzed in this essay along with discussion focusing on education *about* human rights in the light of Article 26.

Human rights education (HRE) is a long-term strategy with sights set on the needs of coming generations. Such education for our future will

Reprinted with changes from Richard Pierre Claude, "The Right to Education and Human Rights Education," *SUR, International Journal on Human Rights* 2, no. 1 (São Paulo, 2005), 37–60, available also at http://www.surjournal.org/eng/?PHPSESSID=59eb818edd9759689e0065a0c22d84b8. Reprinted by permission.

1. Reprinted and referenced in Documentary Appendix A.

not likely draw support from the impatient and the parochial, but it is essential to construct innovative education programs to advance human development, peace, democracy, and respect for rule of law. Reflecting these aspirations, the UN General Assembly proclaimed a United Nations Decade of Human Rights Education (1995–2004).[2] In so doing, the international community referred to human rights education as a unique strategy for the "building of a universal culture of human rights."

THE RIGHT TO EDUCATION IN THE UDHR

In the wake of World War II, the globe lay in shambles, torn by international violence from Poland to the Philippines, from the tundra to the tropics. Discussion about the importance of education as indispensable for post-World War II reconstruction emerged in the earliest work of the United Nations Human Rights Commission set up in 1946 by the UN Economic Social and Cultural Council (ECOSOC). It was established to make recommendations for promoting the observance of human rights on the untested theory that human rights-respecting regimes do not make war on other such regimes. Thus to bring peace to the world, members began their work in 1947, electing Mrs. Eleanor Roosevelt to chair the Commission. The Commission's Rapporteur, Dr. Charles Malik (Lebanon), said that, from the beginning, all the Commission members knew that their task of composing a declaration of human rights was itself an educational undertaking. He said: We "must elaborate a general declaration of human rights defining in succinct terms the fundamental rights and freedoms of [everyone] which, according to the Charter, the United Nations must promote." He concluded: "This responsible setting forth of fundamental rights will exert a potent doctrinal and moral and educational influence" on the minds and behavior of people everywhere.[3] Malik's statement echoed the Preamble to the Universal Declaration proclaiming the instrument a common standard of achievement for all

peoples and all nations who should "strive by teaching and education to promote respect for these rights and freedoms. . . ." This entirely new global "bottom up" program of educating people regarding their human rights marked a challenge to the "top down" strategies of diplomatic state-craft, balance of power manipulations, and *réal politique* that were insufficient to forestall the calamity of two world wars.

FORMULATING THE RIGHT TO EDUCATION

The Universal Declaration shows its framers realized that education is not value-neutral, and in drafting the document, the Soviets, being most ideologically sensitive, were the first to speak on this point. Mr. Pavlov for the USSR argued that one of the fundamental factors in the development of fascism and Nazism was "the education of young people in a spirit of hatred and intolerance."[4] As it finally turned out, Article 26 took up Pavlov's point that education inescapably has political objectives, but ignored his ideologically rigid ideas substituting several goals in positive terms. Thus Article 26, in its most contentiously debated section, says that the right to education should be linked to three specific educational goals: (1) the full development of the human personality and the strengthening of respect for human rights and fundamental freedoms; (2) the promotion of understanding, tolerance, and friendship among all nations, racial, or religious groups; and (3) the furthering of the activities of the United Nations for the maintenance of peace.

THE FIRST GOAL

This arresting notion of the development of the human being's full personality, while abstract, is important as a thematic thread running throughout the UDHR. Its significance in framing a holistic concept of human nature as essentially free, social, potentially educated, and entitled to participation in critical decision-making is bolstered by repetition at several points:

---

2. Adopted Dec. 23, 1994, GA Res. 49/184, UN GAOR, 94th Sess., Supp. No. 49, at 202, UN Doc. A/49/49 (1994).
3. Charles Malik, *These Rights and Freedoms* (Lake Success, N.Y.: United Nations Department of Public Information, 1950), 4–5.
4. UN Doc. E/CN.4/SR.67, Commission on Human Rights, Third Sess., *Summary Record of the 69th Meeting* (Lake Success) June 11, 1948, 13.

- Article 22 says everyone's rights to social, economic and cultural rights are "indispensable" for the "free development of his personality."
- Article 26 posits a right to education, and says "Education shall be directed to the full development of the human personality. . . ."
- Article 29 repeats the holistic vision of human rights, saying: "Everyone has duties to the community in which alone the free and full development of his personality is possible."

Given the goal of the full development of the human personality in the context of society—the only context in which this can occur, it follows that the right to education is a social right, a social good, and a responsibility of society as a whole.

Latin Americans took a leading role in framing the right to education. The Brazilian delegate provided a keynote statement on the importance of value-based education and was the first to argue that education provides the individual with the wherewithal "to develop his [sic] personality, which was the aim of human life and the most solid foundation of society."[5] An Argentine proposal put substance on these abstractions, mimicking Article 12 of the American Declaration of the Rights and Duties of Man: "Every person has the right to an education that will prepare him [sic] to lead a decent life, to raise his [sic] standard of living, and to be a useful member of society."[6] Calling for greater conciseness, Mrs. Roosevelt cautioned against language that would overload the right to education. In this spirit, the framers settled on alternative simpler language: "education shall be directed to the full development of the human personality."[7]

The "full development" goal was intended to capture the enabling qualities of the right to education, and of education about human rights to capacitate people to their potential faculties so as to ensure human dignity. This view follows from a close reading of the key phrase: "full development of the human personality"—which

is immediately followed without so much as a comma by the phrase: "and to the strengthening of human rights and fundamental freedoms." Using a standard canon legal interpretation, one might fairly conclude that the joining of the two elements was deliberate and meaningful, especially in view of Mrs. Roosevelt's injunction toward conciseness. The logic of the two ideas in combination tells us that education promoting the full development of the human personality and the dignity it entails also promotes human rights. And for such full development, education for dignity should take into account the total menu of human rights: personal rights like privacy; political rights like participation and the right to seek and disseminate information; civil rights like equality and nondiscrimination; economic rights like a decent standard of living; and the right to participate in the community's cultural life. This analysis pre-figures Brazilian Paulo Freire's views advocated in his book, *The Pedagogy of the Oppressed*.[8] Freire emphasizes the connections between popular empowerment and self-realization as the consequence of people learning and exercising their human rights.

THE SECOND GOAL

Article 26 calls for education to "promote *understanding*, *tolerance* and *friendship* among all nations, racial or religious groups. . . ."[9] This idea started out under different language. Professor René Cassin, the influential French delegate and Vice President of the Human Rights Commission, drew support for asserting that one goal of education should involve "combating the spirit of intolerance and hatred against other nations and against racial and religious groups everywhere."[10] But again the Latin American delegations had the last word, showing their voting strength in supporting the view that educational goals should be framed in positive terms instead of negative goals such as "combating hatred." Mr. Campos Ortiz of Mexico convincingly said that Article 26

---

5. *Official Record of the 3d Session of the General Assembly*, Part I, "Social Humanitarian and Cultural Questions," 3d Committee, Summary Records of Meeting, Sept. 21-Dec. 8, 1948 (reporting the 147th Meeting of the Commission, held at the Palais de Chaillot, Paris, November 19, 1948), 597.
6. Ibid.
7. Cuban Amendment (A/C.3/261).
8. Paulo Freire, *Pedagogy of the Oppressed* (New York: Seabury Press, 1973).
9. Emphasis added.
10. *Official Record*, note 5, 587.

should link the right to education with the positive goal of "the promotion of understanding, tolerance and friendship among all nations and racial and religious groups."[11]

THE THIRD GOAL

Article 26 says education should "further the activities of the United Nations for the maintenance of peace." In the final consideration of the Declaration before the General Assembly, the Mexican delegate said that the right to education should be connected to the peaceful objectives of United Nations activities. Mr. Watt from Australia promptly objected and urged support for a broader reference to all the "purposes and principles of the United Nations."[12] Again, Mrs. Roosevelt expressed a distaste for any formulation lacking conciseness and specificity, and said for that reason she associated herself with the simpler Mexican proposition. She thought that *for educational purposes*, United Nations activities for the maintenance of peace should be recognized as "the chief goal of the United Nations."[13] True to pattern, other Latin American voices chimed in supporting the Mexican initiative. Mr. Carrera Andrade of Ecuador lyrically concluded that when the world's youth became imbued with "the guiding principles of the United Nations, then the future [would promise] . . . greater hope for all nations living in peace."[14]

Finally, the reference to UN peace activities was adopted and all dissent was swept away with the final version of Article 26 winning a unanimous 36 votes with 2 abstentions. As a result, Article 26, with three separate sections, now reads as it does.[15]

On December 10, 1948, the General Assembly solemnly adopted and proclaimed the UDHR. That body was alerted by several framers that the document could have little effect unless people everywhere knew about it and appreciated its significance for every human being. Therefore,

the Assembly also passed Resolution 217 D urging that the widest possible publicity be given to the Declaration and inviting the Secretary General and UN specialized agencies and nongovernmental organizations to do their utmost to bring the Declaration to the attention of their members.[16] One present-day result is that the Universal Declaration can be obtained from the United Nations in any of 300 languages.[17]

HUMAN RIGHTS EDUCATION TODAY

As noted, the educational directives of Article 26 point to three distinguishable goals. Using this tripartite framework affords a glimpse at present day examples of human rights education.

Education involves more people than any other institutionalized activity worldwide, according to the UN Special Rapporteur on the Right to Education. In her 2002 report to the UN Commission on Human Rights, Katarina Tomaševski said that while a commitment to institutionalized education is globally ubiquitous, the commitment everywhere is "to 'hardware' at the expense of 'software.'"[18] In these terms Tomaševski lamented a "disequilibrium between the formal institutional structure and contents of schooling on the one hand and the value-oriented substance of teaching and learning on the other." She concluded, the "disequilibrium" is manifested in "fierce disputes about the orientation and content of schooling [which] are thus endless."

While the obligation for states, schools, and all of us to promote human rights through education is a 50-year-old internationally defined duty, it has only recently become more lively and widely accepted. Among the several reasons, perhaps none is more important than the end of the Cold War which made more realistic than before the announcement of the UN Decade for Human Rights Education whereby the United Nations intervened in the "fierce disputes"

11. Ibid., 584.
12. Ibid., 594.
13. Ibid.
14. Ibid., 589.
15. See UDHR, art. 26(1), (2), and (3), reprinted and referenced in Documentary Appendix A.
16. GA Res. 217D, UN GAOR, 3d Sess., Pt. I, Resolutions, at 78, UN Doc. A/810 (1948).
17. See the website of the Office of the High Commissioner for Human Rights at http://www.unhchr.ch/udhr/index. htm
18. Annual Report of the Special Rapporteur on the Right to Education, Katarina Tomaševski, submitted pursuant to Commission on Human Rights Resolution 2001/29, para. 46, UN Doc. E/CN.4/2002/60.

referenced by Tomaševski, calling for the insertion of human rights content into the orientation and material dealt with in the classroom.

In 1993, the World Conference on Human Rights held in Vienna asked the UN to accelerate the promotion of human rights. One important result was that the UN General Assembly proclaimed the years 1995–2004 as the World Decade for Human Rights Education.[19] The UN proclamation says the decade has as its aim "the full development of the human personality in a spirit of peace, mutual understanding, and respect for democracy and the rule of law." The resolution says that such education should be introduced at all levels of formal education (the conventional school system) and should be adopted in nonformal education (called "popular education" as promoted by NGOs). The resolution also speaks to issues of methodology, favoring interactive, participatory, and culturally relevant learning methods.

There are many examples of programs embracing these goals and methods. It is instructive to link recent HRE programs with each of the Declaration's goals. The thumbnail profiles that follow draw from both formal and nonformal education where various activist groups target specialized constituencies. Examples are chosen to illustrate how wide-ranging the human rights education project has become since its recent inception. The "software" is diverse. Some of these projects are, for example, short-term and others reflect long-term educational commitments; some are addressed to values clarification and cognitive development, others to analytical skills and problem-solving; and others emphasize changing attitudes and behavior. Some are embedded in formal educational programs and others in programs of popular education. All manifest one or more of the educational goals specified in Article 26 of the Universal Declaration.

FULL PERSONAL DEVELOPMENT AND RESPECT FOR HUMAN RIGHTS

Popular Education on the Rights of the Child in Nepal

The United Nations Convention on the Rights of the Child (CRC) was adopted by the General Assembly in 1989[20] and rapidly came into force.

States Parties are obliged to make its principles and provisions widely known to both adults and children and to file a report on such activities with the UN Committee on the Rights of the Child, a ten-person group of experts. Nepal is one of 192 countries which have ratified the treaty as of January 1, 2005. Despite episodes of civil strife, NGOs in the Himalayan kingdom have shown ingenuity in propagating its provisions and in seizing the state's reporting duties as an opportunity to launch a nationwide educational program on the rights of children.

In 1992, many Nepali NGOs, along with the United Nations Children's Fund (UNICEF), organized a workshop on the CRC in the capital of Kathmandu. The workshop supplied educational opportunities to inform policy-makers, to prompt questions from members of the media, and to raise the consciousness of the general public regarding children's issues and Nepal's duties under the Convention. The workshop was replicated in five administrative regions of the country and finally in all 75 provincial districts. Drawn from many localities, children also participated in a National Seminar of NGOs, after which they went back to their communities to share their learning and then return to the capital with friends. The resulting Children's Seminar discussed the status of children and their responsibilities as well as the related duties of parents, the community, local government bodies, and political parties. As an outcome, the government's National Planning Commission, as required by the CRC, prepared Nepal's treaty report by forming a joint committee with NGO representation. Thus the National NGO Workshop and Children's Seminar, as well as various declarations and plans of action developed in their wake, became the basis for NGO input in the national report to the United Nations. The resulting report was important, but no less so than the nationwide NGO-led process of education on the subject of the rights of the child.

The NGO objective of values enhancement and clarification took place at many levels as Nepal prepared to take up its responsibility under the CRC, including the incorporation of human rights and the rights of the child into the formal school curricula. The Convention provides that such education shall be directed to "the development of the child's personality, talents and

---

19. GA Res. 49/184, referenced in Documentary Appendix B.
20. Concluded Nov. 2, 1989, referenced in Documentary Appendix B.

mental and physical ability to their fullest potential" as well as "the development of respect for human rights and fundamental freedoms and for the principles enshrined in the Charter of the United Nations."[21]

Women's Rights in Ethiopia

A project in Ethiopia initiated by a group called Action Professionals Association for the People stresses the importance of education for full personal development with particular attention to respect for the human rights of women. In 1995, Action Professionals sought a teaching program to promote women's rights, taking into account that Ethiopia had ratified the UN International Convention on the Elimination of All Forms of Discrimination Against Women (CEDAW).[22] This author documented their work, observing them setting up community-based programs of human rights, including one called "Bringing CEDAW Home." Their curriculum planning was meticulous, and the resulting training manual, *The Bells of Freedom*, is accessible at the University of Minnesota online Human Rights Library.[23]

The CEDAW exercise begins with the announced objective of promoting behavioral change and women's empowerment through community-based nonformal education to break the old curse of domination by one gender over the other and to take action to eliminate discrimination. They designed simple ways and simple language to introduce CEDAW, article by article, explaining that the Government has promised to abide by its provisions. Thereafter, people were asked to speak from experience about any specific provision of CEDAW, such as Article 5 stating that customary practices based on the idea of the inferiority of the sexes should be eliminated.

Most important, using a problem-solving approach, participants designed programs of action and selected the one action plan, among several they designed, that all actually were willing to put into effect, including one specifically addressed to removing barriers to the full development of the woman's personality. In one significant outcome, women agreed to stop using coercion and even force to back up arranged marriages among their pre-teenage daughters, thus to abide by UDHR Article 16 stating that everyone has a right freely to choose a spouse.[24]

PROMOTING TOLERANCE AMONG GROUPS AND INTERNATIONAL FRIENDSHIP

The Minnesota B.I.A.S. Program

Minnesota Advocates for Human Rights is a coalition of educators, activists, and global rights specialists who promote the incorporation of human rights standards and practices into their state's public and private school curricula. They also create, pilot, and disseminate curricular resources for use in human rights education throughout the United States. Their shared work is based on field-tested human rights educational projects done locally and regionally. They developed a program to introduce human rights and responsibilities to K-12 teachers who work in diverse educational environments and use the framework of the UDHR and the CRC to help students understand common human values, prompt them to apply such standards to their own lives, and advocate and assist positive student action to remedy human rights violations in their own communities.

A leading immigration-receiving state, Minnesota benefits from one such initiative dealing with discrimination in a socially diversifying environment. Designed for "promoting tolerance among groups and international friendship," consistent with UDHR Article 26, the BIAS Project (Building Immigrant Awareness and Support) is an educational campaign designed to help Minnesotans deal responsibly with the substantial migration to Minnesota that took place after the Vietnam War. Since the 1980s, aided by local churches, thousands of refugees from Southeast Asia have resettled in Minnesota communities. Originally comprised of Native Americans, the state has a population predominantly of Scandinavian descent, other Western European

---

21. Ibid., art. 29.
22. Concluded Dec. 18, 1979, referenced in Documentary Appendix B.
23. Action Professionals Association for the People (APAP), *The Bells of Freedom* (Addis Ababa: APAP, 1995), available at http://www.umn.edu/humanrts/education/belfry.pdf
24. UDHR, art. 16(1), reprinted and referenced in Documentary Appendix A.

immigrants, and African Americans. Today, Minnesota's largest immigrant populations are Vietnamese, Hmong, and Somali. With 55 languages spoken by students in the state's public schools, an appropriate educational priority is thus advanced by the B.I.A.S. Project. The Project supplies educational resources, teacher training, and technical assistance to welcome and support new immigrants and refugees. The curriculum guide, entitled "The Energy of a Nation: Immigrants in America," highlights immigrants' personal testimony and, through role play and research, explores immigration from historical, political, economic, demographic, and human rights perspectives. These educational activities and projects include substantial follow-up programs relying on a speakers bureau, interactive student workshops, continuing legal education for attorneys, and other resources reported on the website of Minnesota Advocates for Human Rights.[25]

Arab-Israeli Education Planning

In 2003, the Council of Europe brought together educators from Northern Ireland, Israel, and Palestine to compare educational techniques for advancing tolerance. Israeli and Palestinian participants, involved in preparing school textbooks, learned how education authorities in Northern Ireland try to overcome the problems of teaching in a divided society. The Council's Rapporteur on the Situation in the Middle East, Mikhail Margelov (Russia), hailed the "spirit of tolerance" that prevailed during the meetings, suppressing inflammatory language and incitements to hatred in school textbooks.[26] Participants heard examples of provocative language used in current Israeli and Palestinian schoolbooks, and agreed to make changes to promote tolerance. Taking into account the fact that the majority of hostile interactions (acts of violence and destruction) in Israel and Palestine are conducted by and against the young, too often prompted by adults, the Rapporteur observed: "What makes me optimistic is the level of self-criticism and cooperation we have heard."

For their part, Arab and Israeli educators were able to share a positive example of educational planning directed at the promotion of intergroup understanding among youth at the secondary school level in Israel. "The Rules of the Game" is called by its designers a "bottom-up" curriculum, developed with the full participation of an equal number of Arab and Jewish high school teachers. The objective of the group of 20 educators was to cooperate in developing a curriculum to foster understanding of human rights and democratic principles, including both majority rule and minority rights. The teachers' planning phase encompassed a year of debate and discussion with intensive workshops drawing materials from Al-Haq and B'Tselem, respectively Arab and Jewish human rights NGOs.

The teachers' participatory learning project is supposed to build and reinforce attitudes of tolerance, mutual respect, and individual freedom. To these ends, the curriculum emphasizes a cognitive approach aimed at helping students distinguish empirical findings from value judgments, eye-witness evidence from hearsay, and a logical argument from an emotional one. The teacher-planners of the project expressed the hope that "a 'grass roots' curriculum, introduced by the very same teachers by whom it was developed, might secure good will and cooperation that are so direly needed in order to overcome negative attitudes and resistance to change."[27] In the Israeli example, teachers from both sides of divisive conflict came together cooperatively to plan a program promoting the values inherent in their collaborative process: conflict resolution, tolerance of diverse perspectives, and mutual respect for the human rights of others.

FURTHERING ACTIVITIES OF THE UN FOR THE MAINTENANCE OF PEACE

The Peace-Building Handbook

In 2003, scholars at the Columbia University Center for the Study of Human Rights (CSHR) published a ground-breaking and highly specialized planning and evaluation handbook sponsored by the United States Institute of Peace.

---

25. See www.mnadvocates.org
26. See Ilana Felsenthal and Israelit Rubinstein, "Democracy, School, and Curriculum Reform: The 'Rules of the Game' in Israel," in Roberta S. Sigel and Marilyn Hoskin, eds., *Education for Democratic Citizenship: A Challenge for Multi-Ethnic Societies* (Hillsdale, N.J.: Lawrence Erlbaum, 1991), 87–102, at 92.
27. Ibid., 95.

Human Rights Education for Peace Building is a multi-authored research project reflecting several years of brainstorming and fieldwork by J. Paul Martin, Tania Bernath, Tracey Holland, and Loren Miller.[28] The CSHR authors gathered educational materials and conducted interviews in post-conflict areas such as El Salvador, Guatemala, Mexico, Liberia, and Sierra Leone where the international community sought to restore peace. The resulting manual is replete with lessons drawn from these zones of conflict and presented to help future planners, administrators, and teachers in implementing HRE in violence-ridden areas where peace-building programs are targeted. Martin and colleagues give human rights practitioners a detailed *vade mecum* on how, under challenging conditions, to conceive, plan, and implement HRE programs in their cognitive, attitudinal, behavioral, and skill-building components. The handbook presents a rich mix of theoretical wisdom and anecdotal and practical prescriptions for advancing reconstruction and transitions to peace with educational components. The contribution of human rights in such environments lies in the vision of living without violence it offers to the powerless arguing for long-term educational projects that present a conceptional alternative to violence as a means of social action. With strong analytical guidance, the book shows that HRE objectives may be appropriate at one level of peace-building but not at another. HRE planners are guided by a "stage approach" model on the peace-conflict continuum suggesting variations in HRE objectives suitable for, among other things, the pre-peace and settlement stage, the negotiation stage, and the reconstructive stage. For example, educational objectives for the pre-peace stage are reactive and emphasize monitoring skills and the need for meticulous accuracy in recording violations for possible legal process. As reconstruction activities develop, HRE programs become pro-active and forward looking, focusing on expanded notions of human rights beyond legal claims and to norms for everyday living, including nondiscrimination, empathy, and respect for everyone's human dignity. In answer to the question: how does HRE differ from other peace-building activities? the CSHR authors write:

> In the eye of the storm, where everything seems negotiable and thus subject to the fiat of the most powerful, HRE can provide both structure and standards. HRE introduces an alternative, namely a set of laws or codes as defined by the international community away from the heat of the crisis as a way towards preventing human right abuses. This was precisely the motivation of the world's states after the horrors of the world war when in 1948 they approved the UN Declaration on Human Rights.[29]

Philippine HRE for Military and Police

The Republic of the Philippines has long experienced turmoil, but it is the turmoil of life, not death, of people in search of a more human and humane way of developing their society and political community. After the fall of the dictatorship of Ferdinand Marcos in 1986, they survived a post-conflict transition and inaugurated a human rights respecting constitutional system. The new government of President Corazon Aquino impaneled a constitutional convention one of whose accomplishments was to give birth to the only regime in the world in which all educators are constitutionally bound to teach human rights.

Since 1987 when the new Constitution mandated the teaching of human rights, police, military, and teacher training in the island nation, HRE has been implemented with varying degrees of success. For lack of well-planned models, efforts to implement HRE requirements were initially shaky and notably uncertain.[30] For example, the military made seven coup d'état attempts against the new government within three years until a Philippine Senate Committee focused sharply on the need for stronger discipline supplemented by education "with teeth." The Committee concluded: "A more effective education program is needed for the military and government personnel in order for them to have a better understanding of their duties and

28. J. Paul Martin, Tania Bernath, Tracey Holland, and Loren Miller, *Human Rights Education for Peace Building: A Planning and Evaluation Handbook* (New York: Columbia University Center for the Study of Human Rights, 2003).

29. Ibid., 5.

30. Richard Pierre Claude, "Civil-Military/Police Relations," in Richard Pierre Claude, *Educating for Human Rights: The Philippines and Beyond* (Quezon City: University of the Philippines Press, 1996), ch. 5.

responsibilities in the protection and promotion of human rights in accordance with the Constitution, laws, and internationally accepted human rights norms and standards."[31] The demand for the restoration of domestic peace served as a rebuke to the National Human Rights Commission because it is constitutionally responsible for HRE for the military and police.

After several failed attempts at implementing HRE, and in response to the Senate's criticism, fresh efforts to gain military acceptance of effective human rights education were launched under the leadership of the Human Rights Commission's education officer, Dr. Amancio. S. Donato, whose ideas partially relied on Johan Galtung and Anders Helge Wirak's "Human Needs and Human Rights," published in 1977.[32] Under the new program he planned with the help of social scientists and law professors, thousands of police and military officers began undergoing periodic eight-day "conscientization programs" on human rights, constitutional law, and humanitarian law. The "teeth in the programs" derived from Presidential orders specifying that promotions and pay increases should be withheld from officers failing to pass the required course on human rights and international humanitarian law.

In 1995, recognizing the importance of HRE program evaluation, the university-based Development Academy of the Philippines designed an assessment program focusing on police and military training at two levels. First, at the individual level, an attitude and skills survey instrument helped to evaluate psychological behavior norms. Second, a community-level impact assessment canvassed the incidence of increases and decreases in human rights violations among those who have gone through the program of human rights education and training. Professionals conducting HRE programs recognize that critical evaluation is always important to ensure that long-term programs adjust to changing circumstances and meet their stated objectives.

GLOBAL RESOURCES AND SUPPORT FOR HUMAN RIGHTS EDUCATION

By many standards, the original UN Decade for Human Rights Education (1995–2004) was a success. By the end of the Decade, HRE programs could be found in the majority of countries worldwide. Many were

- facilitated by UN and regional support and technical assistance;
- funded by international agencies;
- converted into long-term programs with the aid of university certificates and teacher training; and
- supplemented by creative popular education projects of NGOs targeting specialized groups such as women and children, the disabled, the rural poor, and those unreached by the formal school systems.

The supporting structure at the international level includes UNESCO's Division of Human Rights, Democracy, Peace and Tolerance, which provides strategies for teaching human rights on an international and regional level. Also from the United Nations, the UN Cyber School Bus is an attractive website to facilitate infusing classroom activities with human rights information and materials.[33] Further, international and national funding agencies have favored the use of HRE, among them being the European Human Rights Foundation, the Canadian Human Rights Foundation, the United States Agency for International Development, and many private foundations, including the Ford Foundation, Redd/ Barna/Norway, the Fredrick Neuman Foundation (Germany), the Dutch Foreign Ministry, the Asia Foundation, and many others.[34]

A new step was taken at the level of international financial institutions when the Asia Development Bank, not traditionally known for progressive initiatives, assessed the region's legal systems at the beginning of the twenty-first century as "plagued by corruption and interests vested in maintaining the status quo."[35] The Bank

31. Ibid., 73.

32. Johan Galtung and Anders Helge Wirak, "Human Needs and Human Rights—A Theoretical Approach," *Bulletin of Peace Proposals* 8 (1977): 251–58.

33. See http://www.un.org/Pubs/CyberSchoolBus/humanrights. The site includes an interactive Universal Declaration of Human Rights, a "plain language version of the Universal Declaration"; Questions and Answers; definitions of human rights terms appropriate for primary and secondary school classes; and an ingenious "Global Atlas of Student Activities."

34. Funding agencies supporting human rights education are listed in Frank Elbert, ed., *Human Rights Education Resource Book* (Cambridge: Human Rights Education Associates, 2000).

35. Asian Development Bank, *Legal Literacy for Supporting Governance*, RETA 5856 (Manila: Regional Technical Assistance Study, 1999).

concluded that their funded development projects would benefit by including programs of "legal literacy training," a term less controversial to Asian governments than "popular human rights education." Linked to development projects, "legal literacy" training, according to the Bank, should promote improved governance based on "citizen knowledge of rights, demands for accountability, and participation in decision-making" to foster a "legal system's responsiveness to the needs of the disadvantaged."

There are many Internet sites established to support HRE programs, and they are especially useful to classroom teachers and NGOs undertaking educational projects for the first time. A few notable examples suggest the range and diversity of such resources. Amnesty International USA supports a Human Rights Education site offering a monthly e-mail newsletter for human rights educators. BBC World Service's "I Have a Right to . . ." supplies case studies used to teach students about the Universal Declaration of Human Rights. The Council of Europe's "All Different, All Equal" includes curriculum to promote inter-cultural education. Other sites with substantial HRE materials are hosted by the Human Rights Education Associates (HREA), Human Rights Internet (HRI), Partners in Human Rights Education (PHRE), The People's Movement for Human Rights Education (PDHRE), etc. PDHRE sponsors "Human Rights Cities," a unique project to build sustainable human rights friendly communities.[36]

No group-specific educational program has attracted more organizing activity than women's rights. A good example of a high quality culturally sensitive curricular design is "Sisterhood Is Global," a program for the human rights education of women in Muslim societies, with two texts, "Claiming our Rights," and "Safe and Secure," on violence against women.[37] In the United States, an excellent text is *Women's Human Rights: Step by Step*, published by two collaborating groups: Women, Law and Development International, and the Women's Rights Project of Human Rights Watch.[38] The book uses plain language to describe the content of human rights law, enforcement mechanisms, and implementation strategies useful to women seeking social change.

CONCLUSION

Many observers, activists, and educators now perceive the beginnings of an international movement in support of human rights education. It is more viable for having globally available UN resources in combination with a burgeoning international network of cooperating public and private groups. The vision shared by those involved is directed to constructing a "universal culture of human rights," no longer a utopian fancy but now a challenge for a globalizing world in need of shared positive values. We are faced with the obligation at the international, national, local, and personal levels to implement effective programs of human rights education and to employ methodologies that ensure that the task is well done, consistent with the goals of world peace and respect for human rights everywhere. To reinforce our responsibilities to support HRE, a poignant comment by Eleanor Roosevelt is apt. As if speaking to us today, she said in 1948:

> It will be a long time before history will make its judgment on the value of the Universal Declaration of Human Rights, and the judgment will depend, I think, on what the people of different nations do to make this document familiar to everyone. If they know it well enough, they will strive to attain some of the rights and freedoms set forth in it, and that effort on their part is what will make it of value in clarifying what was meant in the Charter in the references to human rights and fundamental freedoms.[39]

36. People's Movement for Human Rights Education, "The Human Rights Cities" project: http://pdhre.org/projects/hrcommun.html

37. Mahnaz Afkhami and Haleh Vaziri, *Claiming Our Rights: A Manual for Women's Human Rights Education in Muslim Societies* (Bethesda, Md.: Sisterhood Is Global Institute, 1998).

38. Women, Law and Development International/Women's Rights Project of Human Rights Watch, *Women's Human Rights Step by Step* (New York: Women, Ink, 1997).

39. Eleanor Roosevelt, speech.

QUESTIONS FOR REFLECTION AND DISCUSSION

1. What does the human right to education have to say about equality of access to education? Children in North America and Western Europe typically have access to far greater educational opportunity (measured both in average length of education and in average per-pupil expenditures) than their counterparts in Africa, Asia, and Latin America, where, in the poorest countries especially, children are often forced to work to enhance family income. Does such inequality constitute a *per se* abrogation of the right to education among the children of the latter three regions? Many states in the United States have attempted to combat town-by-town differences in education opportunity by requiring wealthier communities to send money to poorer communities for education. Does the fulfillment of the human right to education require a similar approach globally?

2. Do parents violate the human right to education (and possibly other rights as well) by insisting that they have a right to the fruits of their children's labor? If it means denying their children access to formal education? If their children are able to attend school for part of the year? If the children do so voluntarily, lovingly? What do the 1989 Convention on the Rights of the Child and 1999 ILO Convention (No. 182) Concerning the Prohibition and Immediate Elimination of the Worst Forms of Child Labour (each referenced in Documentary Appendix B) have to say about this issue? For keen insight, see Susan L. Bissell, "Earning and Learning: Tensions and Compatibility," in Burns H. Weston, ed., *Human Rights and Child Labor: Making Children Matter* (Boulder, Colo.: Lynne Rienner, 2005), ch. 15.

3. It is well known that educational facilities in U.S. inner-city schools pale in comparison to schools in more affluent suburbs. Often this disparity parallels racial divisions. Is it correct to conclude that in this regard the United States is not living up to its international legal obligations relative to the right to education? Never having ratified the 1966 International Covenant on Economic, Social and Cultural Rights (reprinted and referenced in Documentary Appendix A) and not likely to do so any time soon, does the United States have any international legal obligation to ensure a right to education for all its citizenry? Does it have a constitutional obligation to do so? If so, in each case, on what theory? If not, in each case, why not?

4. Increasingly state legislatures in the United States are reducing funding of higher education, such that college tuition and other costs at U.S. public universities is approaching, at least for nonresident students, the tuition and other costs of private colleges and universities in the United States. Consider this trend in light of the common European practice to fund public higher education through general taxation, leaving students with essentially nominal costs to bear once admitted to their university of choice. Does the U.S. trend constitute another possible breach of international legal obligation on the part of the United States? Consider your answers to Question 3 when answering this question.

5. The famous U.S. Supreme Court decision *Brown v. Board of Education*, 347 U.S. 483 (1954), overturning the doctrine of "separate but equal" in American schools, is more than a half-century old. Yet American schools continue to be more separate than equal when it comes to the education of African Americans. Why? Does the answer lie in the fact that American society, almost 150 years after the American Civil War, is "still a residentially segregated society." See Douglas S. Massey and Nancy A. Denton, *American Apartheid: Segregation and the Making of the Underclass* (Cambridge, Mass.: Harvard University Press, 1993), 1. How is this state of affairs to be overcome? Is the United States obligated to do so under U.S. constitutional law? International law? The U.S. is a party to the 1965 International Convention on the Elimination of All Forms of Racial Discrimination (referenced in Documentary Appendix B). Does this make a difference?

6. Some of Richard Claude's case studies suggest that education is a prerequisite for individual empowerment, echoing the "capabilities approach" to human rights pioneered by Martha Nussbaum (Reading 2 in Chapter 1 of this volume) and Nobel laureate Amartya Sen. Does this comport with your experience in the country in which you grew up? Can people be truly empowered without education? Does the answer differ in different societies? How would Martha Nussbaum answer each of these questions?

7. Do you agree with the view expressed by a UDHR framer that education is a preventive measure against "any attempt at a revival of fascism"? Is education inherently

aligned with (or opposed to) particular ideologies? What is the difference between education and indoctrination?

8. In the course of fulfilling the human right to education, is it appropriate or desirable for governments to fund explicitly religious education? Why? Why not? Do you think a system of universally available education vouchers, expendable at either secular or sectarian schools, would fulfill the human right to education? Consider in this regard the U.S. Supreme Court in *Zelman v. Simmons-Harris*, 536 U.S. 639 (2002), holding that a state-sponsored voucher program does not violate the First Amendment "establishment clause." Do you agree with the Court's judgment?

9. Many advocates of faith-based education as well as advocates of education generally believe that with education comes understanding, tolerance, and friendship. Is education necessarily synonymous with teaching understanding, tolerance, and friendship? Might not education lead as easily to the spread of pernicious ideologies as of humane ones? What was the German educational system like during the era of Adolph Hitler? How does one guard against such education?

10. Consider, on the one hand, a totalitarian regime interested in satisfying its people's human right to education; on the other, a "Third World," largely agrarian democracy interested in doing the same. How will their approaches likely differ? In the former case, does the very nature of totalitarian rule imply that the right to education has been abrogated? Has North Korea fulfilled its people's right to education? Did the Soviet Union? Does China?

11. In the United States, the controversy over whether evolution or creationism (or both) should be taught in schools has continued for over a half-century. Does the idea that there is a human right to education shed any light on that debate? Does the human right to education imply only a right to *some sort of* education, or does it imply a right to a *particular* education? In either case, who decides which education people should receive?

12. Is the human right to education simply a means to expose people to Western values in the guise of providing values-neutral access to universal truths? What might a human rights activist interested in furthering access to education have to say to, for example, the American Amish, who withdraw their children from school at about age 13 since any classroom education beyond that is, in their view, "worldly" and useless as preparation for the Amish agrarian life? The United States Supreme Court has ruled that the Amish, alone among minority religious groups, may lawfully withdraw their children from school before others (*Wisconsin v. Yoder*, 406 U.S. 205 (1972)). Does this comport with your view of the right to education? Should Amish children have a choice in whether to continue attending school? Why? Why not?

13. Should human rights education (HRE) receive the same emphasis as education in general? Less? More? Why? Why not? Is a certain level of general education necessary before educational authorities provide human rights instruction? Why? Why not? Is a certain level of HRE for educational authorities necessary before human rights instruction is provided? If so, how much and of what sort? If not, why not?

14. Imagine that you are an advisor to the UN High Commissioner for Human Rights tasked to suggest recommendations the High Commissioner might propose for reforming the human rights treaty reporting system relative to the right to education. The High Commissioner hands you the following proposal and asks for your opinion: "The High Commissioner recommends that human rights treaty bodies, when examining reports of states parties, devote attention specifically to HRE so that they can make recommendations as to how such education can contribute to national capacity-building aimed at strengthening national human rights protection mechanisms." What arguments would you make for or against this proposal?

15. Imagine further that you are a policy advisor in a ministry of education in your country or of the department of education in which you reside. Your office has made a commitment to promote HRE in the public school system. You have been asked to make a presentation on whether HRE should or should not also be promoted beyond the formal education system (for example, in government bureaus, military installations, police departments, corporate board rooms, union halls, and elsewhere that adults meet). If HRE should be promoted, should the recommended educational goals go beyond the development of cognitive and analytical skills to include attitude and behavior change? Why? Why not?

16. In his Declaration on "The Human Right to Peace" of 1 January 1997 (available at http://unesdoc.unesco.org/images/0010/001055/105530e.pdf; reprinted in Weston and Carlson, 3: III.S.3), former UNESCO Director-General Frederico Mayor appealed to the world community as follows:

> At the dawn of the new millennium, our ideal must be to put [human rights] into practice, to add to them, to live and breathe them, to relive them, to revive them with every new day! . . . Human rights can neither be owned nor given, but must be won and deserved afresh with every passing day. Nor should they be regarded as an abstraction, but rather as practical guidelines for action which should be part of the lives of all men and women and enshrined in the laws of every country. . . .

The statement suggests that human rights should be approached as *a way of life*. Should HRE reflect such an approach? Is it appropriate to teach human rights as a way of life? What is the difference between HRE thus approached and indoctrination? What precautions would you take, if any? How should it manifest itself?

17. Richard Claude notes that the 1987 Philippine Constitution calls for HRE at all levels and in all fields of education. Imagine that you are an expert consultant to constitutional framers drafting a new basic law for a country in transition to democracy. Would you recommend that HRE be constitutionally required? Why and to what extent? Or why not?

18. Does the introduction of HRE from Western to non-Western cultures smack of cultural imperialism? If so, what is to be done about it? If not, why not? What would Richard Claude say?

19. The next reading in this volume is "The Right to Take Part in Cultural Life." As you read that essay by Stephen A. Hansen, consider the possible ways in which the right to education, insofar as it militates for a changed way of life for young people, may conflict with the right to take part in cultural life. How should such conflicts, if you think there are any, be resolved? Should the right to education always trump the right Hansen advocates? Vice versa? Should the decision be left up to the discretion of local governments? National governments? Consider these questions also with reference to HRE specifically. Would your answers differ? Why? Why not?

18. STEPHEN A. HANSEN *The Right to Take Part in Cultural Life*

In what way or ways are cultural rights violated? A quick answer to this question is summarized from the "concluding observations" of the treaty bodies ("committees") charged to uphold the 1966 International Covenant on Economic, Social and Cultural Rights (ICESCR) and the 1966 International Covenant on Civil and Political Rights (ICCPR) and, as well, the 1965 International Convention on the Elimination of Racial Discrimination (ICERD), the 1979 Convention on the Elimination of All Forms of Discrimination against Women (CEDAW), and the1989 Convention on the Rights of the Child (CRC).[1] Thus:

- Failure to respect the other rights and freedoms necessary for the enjoyment of cultural rights, or interference with these rights and freedoms when exercised.

- Failure of a state to recognize officially the existence of distinct minority groups within its borders. The identification of minority groups and subsequent analysis of their political, economic and social status are preconditions for determining the difficulties that minority groups may be facing, whether and how these difficulties may be the result of discrimination, and whether any special programs would be effective in

Reprinted with changes from Stephen A. Hansen, "The Right to take Part in Cultural Life: Toward Defining Minimum Core Obligations Related to Article 15(1)(a) of the International Covenant on Economic, Social and Cultural Rights," in Audrey Chapman and Sage Russell, eds., *Core Obligations: Building a Framework for Economic, Social and Cultural Rights* (Antwerp: Intersentia, 2002), 279–303. Reprinted by permission.

1. The ICESCR and ICCPR, each concluded Dec. 16, 1966, are reprinted and referenced in Documentary Appendix A. ICERD (concluded Dec. 21, 1965), CEDAW (concluded Dec. 18, 1979), and CRC (concluded Nov. 2, 1989) are referenced in Documentary Appendix B.

improving the situation of specific groups identified.

- Failure to take corrective measures to ensure that persons belonging to minority groups and the groups themselves are adequately represented in political and public life, as reflected in their representation among the voting public and holders of public office. Inadequate representation and participation by these groups may be the result of nation-building policies, leading to the weakening of policies to protect minorities and their identities. This in turn could aggravate the relations between communities.
- Persistence of structural discrimination toward indigenous populations at various levels of the political, economic, and social life of the country. Such discrimination may affect their political participation, educational and occupational possibilities, access to basic public services, health, housing, and land ownership and use.
- Failure to take measures to bridge cultural gaps between mainstream society and minority groups. The result is that members of these groups may be unable or unwilling to participate in the national culture, or political systems, or to take advantage of their rights to education, public health care, and social services, to name a few.
- Failure of a government to engage in a public campaign conducted through the media, the schools, and other means at its disposal, to attempt to change traditional prejudices against minorities, and to convey messages of tolerance. Governments should provide instruction on international human rights standards and norms in schools and conduct training programs for persons engaged in the administration of justice, including judges, police officers, and lawyers.
- Failure to enact or enforce legislation against manifestations of all forms of discrimination, including racism, acts of violence, the propagation of racist speech, and discriminatory employment practices.
- Failure to implement adequate government programs to address difficulties experienced by groups in preserving their culture and in teaching their language.
- Lack of effective implementation of policies aimed at guaranteeing indigenous communities control of the quality of their environment, and the exploitation of their territories and natural resources. This includes issues of land ownership and distribution, which

are crucial because land is the means of subsistence and even survival for many of these groups.

- Development-related activities that lead to the displacement of indigenous peoples against their will from their traditional territories and environment, often denying them access to their means of subsistence.

It is interesting to note that the majority of violations or "areas of concern" (the term used by the committees) fall into the category of failure to take action to protect the cultural rights of minorities. A complementary observation is that the less ethnically and culturally diverse the society in the reporting state, the fewer the violations found by the treaty-committee responsible.

THE LEGAL FRAMEWORK

Article 15(1)(a) of the ICESCR, proclaims the right of everyone "to take part in cultural life." Subsequent provisions of the same article state that: "[t]he steps to be taken by the States Parties to the present Covenant to achieve the full realization of this right shall include those necessary for the conservation, the development and the diffusion of science and culture" [art. 15(2)]; that "The States Parties to the present Covenant undertake to respect the freedom indispensable for scientific research and creative activity" [art. 15(3)]; and that "The States Parties to the present Covenant recognize the benefits to be derived from the encouragement and development of international contacts and cooperation in the scientific and cultural fields" [art. 15(4)].

Provisions of other international human rights instruments also mention culture, cultural development, and cultural life. Most frequently noted is Article 27 of the Universal Declaration of Human Rights (UDHR),[2] stating that "everyone has the right freely to participate in the cultural life of the community, to enjoy the arts and to share in scientific advancement and its benefits." Also noteworthy are provisions that address cultural rights in via the right to self-determination and the protection of minorities. Common Article 1 of the ICESCR and the ICCPR states that "all peoples have the right of self-determination" and that "[b]y virtue of that right they freely determine their political status and freely pursue

2. Adopted Dec. 10, 1948, reprinted and referenced in Documentary Appendix A.

their economic, social and cultural development." Article 27 of the ICCPR specifically addresses the cultural rights of minorities: "In those States in which ethnic, religious or linguistic minorities exist, persons belonging to such minorities shall not be denied the right, in community with the other members of their group, to enjoy their own culture, to profess and practice their own religion, or to use their own language."

References to the right to participate in cultural life and pursue cultural development appear on the global plane also in the Charter of the United Nations;[3] the UNESCO Constitution and Declaration on the Principles of International Cultural Cooperation;[4] the ICERD, and CEDAW. With perhaps most far-reaching effect in view of its near universal adherence, they appear also in the CRC.

On the regional plane, echoing the UDHR and ICESCR, are found, among other legal assurances, Article 15 of the American Declaration on the Rights and Duties of Man and Article 14 of the Additional Protocol to the American Convention on Human Rights in the Area of Economic, Social and Cultural Rights:[5] "Every person has the right to take part in the cultural life of the community, to enjoy the arts, and to participate in the benefits that result from intellectual progress, especially scientific discoveries." And at the national level, many states have incorporated aspects of cultural rights into their constitutions.[6]

Not to be overlooked, finally, are large numbers of theoretically non-binding declarations, statements, drafts, and working documents, referenced throughout this essay, that address cultural rights. These instruments often echo aspects of cultural rights that appear in other instruments and address and clarify problems of interpretation, gaps in applicability and coverage, and governmental obligations (especially as they concern minority cultures).

SOME CONCEPTUAL ISSUES RELATING TO CULTURAL RIGHTS

Despite their established presence in treaty and customary international law, and even

though they are components of many other human rights, cultural rights appear to be among the least understood and developed of all human rights, both conceptually and legally. Issues include the nature and scope of culture within a human rights context, individual and collective rights, and the recognition of unique cultural groups with special needs. Much of the focus is on minority cultures, as it is with these groups that many issues concerning cultural rights are most prominently demonstrated. This essay, working within existing international human rights standards, discusses some minimum state obligations necessary to ensure the right to take part in cultural life.

It is not possible to discuss all the issues here. I have chosen, therefore, some of the most significant issues that have impeded the conceptualization and implementation of the right of everyone "to take part in cultural life."

A central issue, of course, is to define what we mean by "cultural rights." Another is the need to adopt an approach to culture which, in a human rights context, applies equally to everyone in all societies regardless of ethnic heritage, status, etc. Yet another issue concerns determining to whom, how, and to what extent the right to participate in cultural life applies. Can there be a uniform set of human rights standards that apply to all cultures, or do some require different standards and/or additional protections to guarantee this right? As a human right, the right to participate in cultural life applies to everyone on an equal basis; however, several issues concerning the nature of these rights have limited their full enjoyment by many groups. These issues include recognizing the collective nature of some rights, and reconciling cultural diversity and international human rights standards.

APPROACHES TO CULTURAL RIGHTS

One reason why cultural rights are still so undefined and difficult to implement is the lack of a consistent approach to them. Traditionally, universal human rights concerning culture have

---

3. See arts. 1, 13, and 55, reprinted in Documentary Appendix A.
4. Adopted Nov. 4, 1966, referenced in Documentary Appendix B.
5. The American Declaration (adopted Mar. 30-May 2, 1948) and the Additional Protocol (concluded Nov. 17, 1988) are referenced in Documentary Appendix B.
6. For example, Article 30 of the Bill of Rights of the Constitution of the Republic of South Africa (Act 108 of 1996), as amended, states that "everyone has the right to use the language and to participate in the cultural life of their choice."

focused almost exclusively on *rights relating to culture* or rights concerning creativity, including the visual arts, literature, music, dance, and theater, and representing the highest intellectual and artistic achievements of a group.[7] In Western society where the arts continue to be the most readily recognized expression of creativity, products of culture or their expressions— e.g., the graphic arts, literature, music—are commonly viewed as capital, as having commercial value, such that the financial interests of their creators are seen to need protection. Access to culture often must be purchased, as in purchasing a ticket to see a play or purchasing a recording to hear a performance. Generally, any given individual in society has equal rights of access to this culture, subject to their individual economic limitations. Individuals are free to participate in or consume this culture and are equally free not to participate. They also are free to choose and reject specific elements of the culture.

Another, but not totally distinct, approach to cultural rights focuses on *rights to a culture*.[8] This approach emphasizes rights to the conservation and preservation of culture as well as the right to have access to and participate in cultural life. According to Article 2(a) of UNESCO's Recommendation on Participation by the People at Large in Cultural Life and their Contribution to It,[9] access to culture means "opportunities available to everyone, in particular through the creation of the appropriate socio-economic conditions, for freely obtaining information, training, knowledge and understanding, and for enjoying cultural values and cultural property." Article 2(b) defines participation in cultural life itself as the "concrete opportunities guaranteed for all— groups or individuals—to express themselves freely, to act, and engage in creative activities with a view to the full development of their personalities, a harmonious life and the cultural progress of society."

Lyndel Prott, formerly UNESCO's Heritage Director, suggests yet another approach to cultural rights which involves enhancing or enabling the survival of a culture.[10] Although the existence of a culture is obviously the prerequisite for a right to a culture, the guaranteed survival of any given culture cannot be deemed a right per se. As Prott argues, however, many other human rights, which include "freedom of assembly, freedom of the person, the right to participate in the political process, and nondiscrimination are critical to the survival of minority cultures."[11]

The *rights to a culture* approach generates a need to conceptualize and broaden the meaning of culture within social, political, and human rights contexts beyond the traditional Western focus on creativity to one that is more anthropological in scope. Anthropologist Marshall Sahlins has stated that "a great deal of confusion arises . . . when culture in the humanistic sense is not distinguished from "culture" in its anthropological senses, notably culture as the total and distinctive way of life of a people or society."[12]

Recently, anthropological concepts of culture have been applied to cultural rights utilizing social science techniques to better address the two major approaches to cultural rights—*rights relating to culture* and the *right to a culture*. But new dangers are created; some of these approaches to culture and human rights may end up being just as limiting as focusing only on the creative aspects of culture. Older anthropological approaches to culture tended to view culture as a homogeneous, static, and coherent entity. One shortcoming of applying older concepts of culture to human rights is that once culture is treated as a static and bounded entity, it can result in an "us" versus "them" dichotomy, reinforcing the concept of cultural relativism and its related human rights issues. Another shortcoming of anthropological approaches to culture and human rights is that they may emphasize or promote the rights of collectivities ("collective rights") over the rights of the individual.

But for many years now, anthropological thought has addressed the reality that culture is in fact not static, that it is, rather, in constant state of change and adaptation. Therefore, any

7. See, e.g., Lyndel Prott, "Understanding One Another on Cultural Rights,"in Halina Niec, ed., *Cultural Rights and Wrongs: A Collection of Essays in Commemoration of the 50th Anniversary of the Universal Declaration of Human Rights* (Paris: UNESCO, 1998), 164–65.
8. Ibid., 165.
9. Adopted Nov. 26, 1976 by the General Conference of UNESCO at its19th session in Nairobi.
10. Prott, "Understanding One Another," note 7, at 165.
11. Ibid.
12. Quoted in World Commission on Culture and Development, *Our Creative Diversity: Report of the World Commission on Culture and Development* (Paris: UNESCO, July 1996), Introduction.

approaches to culture as the "sum total" or a distinct "whole" way of life do not adequately reflect the reality of culture. Anthropologist Frederick Barth was an early opponent of such cohesive models of culture, claiming that they do not adequately reflect the reality of culture and fail to take into account social processes, and the interactions, social roles, relationships, decisions, and innovations of individuals operating against a context of social constraints.[13] According to Barth, people's realities are culturally constructed and they "participate in multiple, more or less discrepant, universes of discourse; they construct different, partial and simultaneous worlds in which they move; their cultural construction of reality springs not from one source and is not of one piece."[14] Thus, culture does not present itself as a predefined and limited set of options for human behavior. It has open boundaries and individuals create their own realities and act based on influences from within and outside their own culture.

This more modern approach is better suited to developing a workable human rights approach to culture, as it addresses the dynamic aspects of culture and the continuous influences of both internal and external factors on any given culture. Within this context, culture should be viewed as a framework within which individual and collective decisions are made and actions taken, and where human rights can serve to guide these decisions, actions and cultural change itself.

THE EQUAL ENJOYMENT OF CULTURAL RIGHTS

The enjoyment of cultural rights belongs equally to everyone. But discussions of cultural rights invariably turn to discussions of the rights of members of special groups, especially indigenous groups and other cultural minorities. Members of these groups should enjoy the same level of cultural rights as members of a majority, no more and certainly no less than is set out in the UDHR and human rights treaties to which states are party. But cultural minorities require special attention when examining cultural rights; their cultural rights tend to be not as effectively implemented and protected as they are for the majority, such that their entire way of life, including their means of subsistence, their natural wealth and resources, and ultimately their cultural identities, can be severely degraded.

Although human rights are universal and apply to all, were cultural rights originally meant to be all-inclusive and to cover all groups equally? When the UDHR was being drafted (1946–48), some states wanted to include specific provisions on the cultural rights of minorities to ensure that their unique situations and requirements were addressed. The prominent view at the time was that this was not a general human rights issue but relevant to a limited number of specific, multicultural societies. According to Eleanor Roosevelt, minority rights were a purely European matter and had no relevance to human rights in general. It was assumed at the time that the principles of nondiscrimination and equality were sufficient to ensure equal enjoyment of all rights by everybody, whether civil and political or economic, social, and cultural, therefore avoiding the need to address differences in cultures and values.[15] It was not until almost 45 years later, in 1992, that the UN General Assembly, in its Declaration on the Rights of Persons Belonging to National or Ethnic, Religious and Linguistic Minorities, called upon states to "protect the existence and the national or ethnic, cultural, religious and linguistic identity of minorities within their respective territories, and encourage conditions for the promotion of that identity."[16]

For minority cultures to be assured equal enjoyment of their cultural rights, they must be recognized as distinct groups entitled to respect

---

13. Frederick Barth, "Transactionalism," in Kenneth McLeish, ed., *Bloomsbury Guide to Human Thought* (London: Bloomsbury, 1993), available at http://www.bloomsbury.com/ARC/detail.asp?entryid=103016&bid=2&mscssid=938SA2M4PJ5V8L5XQB8NXLH14GDA2VP8

14. Frederick Barth, "The Analysis of Culture in Complex Societies," *Ethnos* 3–4 (1989): 120.

15. The American Anthropological Association has argued that the UDHR was conceived only in terms of prevalent Western European and American values and proposed that a statement of the right to live in terms of one's own traditions be incorporated into the proposed UDHR. Declaration on Anthropology and Human Rights, Anthropological Association, June 1999, available at http://www.aaanet.org/stmts/humanrts.htm

16. Adopted Dec. 18, 1992 (hereinafter "UN Minorities Declaration (1992)"), art. 1, referenced in Documentary Appendix B.

for their unique cultural traditions. The United Nations has been reluctant to address the cultural rights and issues of specific groups, and when it does inconsistencies in terminology are often confusing or misleading. It has never differentiated between, nor offered a definition for, its use of the terms "people" or "peoples," which appear in the Preamble to the UN Charter and in the ICESCR and ICCPR. Until recently, with the adoption of ILO Convention (No. 169) Concerning Indigenous and Tribal Peoples in Independent Countries (ILO C169),[17] indigenous groups have been most often covered by the terms "minority" or "populations." Generally the term "peoples" is used to describe nations.

In addition to ICCPR Article 27, the only other legally binding UN instrument referring to minorities as distinct cultural groups is the Convention on the Prevention and Punishment of the Crime of Genocide.[18] Although this convention addresses genocide specifically, it indirectly recognizes the right of specific groups (national, ethnic, racial, or religious) to exist as groups, which, according to Thomas Buergenthal, is the most fundamental of all cultural rights.[19] ILO C169 takes a further step, defining both indigenous and tribal peoples and affirming their self-identification as indigenous or tribal as a fundamental criterion for determining the groups to which the provisions of the Convention apply. In addition, the 1993 Vienna Declaration and Program of Action,[20] while referring to indigenous "people" rather than "peoples," is perceived by many to have significant political ramifications for indigenous populations. The UN Draft Declaration of the Rights of Indigenous Peoples,[21] which is being discussed in the UN Human Rights Commission, recognizes the existence and rights of indigenous "peoples."

UNESCO's Mexico City Declaration on Cultural Policies declares that "the assertion of cultural identity . . . contributes to the liberation of peoples [and that] any form of domination constitutes a denial or an impairment of that identity."[22] When governments recognize and promote only a national culture through a policy of "nation-building," in which governments determine a people's culture, allowing one group to dominate others and seeking to make all groups homogeneous, then violations of cultural rights occur. These violations may consist of actions taken with the intent of depriving groups of their integrity as distinct peoples (their cultural values and ethnic identities), dispossessing them of their lands and resources, or forcing their assimilation or integration into the dominant culture. Often this process is referred to as ethnocide or cultural genocide.

The assertion of cultural identity, UNESCO argues, should not result in the formation of isolated groups.[23] But often it does. When a government fails to recognize distinct groups, or favors or discriminates against groups on the basis of ethnicity, race, or religion, this can lead to the politicization of culture, in which groups turn to their cultural distinctiveness to resist external threats to their integrity, prosperity, and survival.[24] Once one group begins this practice, others are encouraged to do so also, a process that is likely to destroy the goals of nation-building and make it impossible for states to realize the potential benefits of a pluralistic society.

ISSUES OF CULTURAL DIVERSITY AND COLLECTIVE RIGHTS

Many aspects of cultural rights are collective in nature, as they can exist only when they are practiced with other members of a group. The freedom to participate in cultural life may therefore require the recognition of some collective aspects of the right as well as individual rights. But many argue against the validity of collective rights, as they are perceived to have the potential to override some individual rights. Others accept the concept of collective rights as long as they represent only the voluntary practicing together of individual rights. But such concerns cannot negate the requirement of a collective

17. Adopted June 27, 1989, referenced in Documentary Appendix B.
18. Concluded Dec. 9, 1958, referenced in Documentary Appendix B.
19. Thomas Buergenthal, *International Human Rights* (St. Paul, Minn.: West Publishing, 1988), 49.
20. Adopted June 25, 1993, referenced in Documentary Appendix B.
21. Referenced in Documentary Appendix B.
22. UNESCO, The Mexico City Declaration on Cultural Policies, adopted by the World Conference on Cultural Policies, Mexico City, July 26-Aug. 6, 1982, Principle 2.
23. UNESCO Recommendation, note 9.
24. World Commission, *Our Creative Diversity*, note 12, at 20.

approach to specific rights in the International Bill of Human Rights, which include self-determination, economic, social and cultural development, communal ownership of property, disposal of wealth and natural resources, and moral and material (intellectual property) rights. In relation to the cultures of indigenous peoples, the UN Special Rapporteur on the Realization of Economic, Social and Cultural Rights has stated that without such collective rights as the right not to be assimilated and the right to cultural autonomy, protections offered for other human rights would have no significance at all.[25]

Although the recognition and protection of collective rights are essential to the realization of cultural rights, at the same time a state cannot accept or overlook certain traditional practices under the umbrella of collective rights that are contrary to accepted universal human rights norms.[26] Many cultural traditions violate individual rights, particularly women's rights to non-discrimination in areas such as rites of passage, marriage, divorce, and inheritance which often are denied on cultural grounds. Asbjørn Eide has stated that while states cannot prohibit groups from developing their culture, as long as such developments are not contrary to international standards, groups cannot demand preservation and protection of those aspects of culture and identity that are incompatible with universal human rights norms.[27] This leads to the dilemma that any forced discontinuation of such practices on the part of the state or other dominant culture may be perceived to be in violation of the collective right of peoples to participate in their own culture. There are groups and even countries which claim that a woman's subordination is a cornerstone of their culture and/or religion, and that requiring them to implement all articles of certain international human rights instruments such as CEDAW would violate their religious, ethnic, group, or collective cultural rights. For example, several Islamic countries, including Libya, Malaysia, and Morocco, have entered general reservations to several articles in CEDAW that prohibit discrimination on the basis of gender, in situations in which it could pose a conflict with the Islamic religious law Shari`a. Shari`a, which has a stated goal to maintain balance between the spouses to preserve coherence of Islamic family life, governs all marital and family relations and confers the right of divorce on a woman only by decision of a Shari`a judge.

The conflict between universal human rights standards and cultural relativism or specificity is reflected in contradictory provisions in human rights law. For example, the 1993 Vienna Declaration and Program of Action states that "the significance of national and regional particularities and various historical, cultural, and religious backgrounds must be borne in mind" while at the same time calling for, e.g., "the eradication of any conflicts which may arise between the rights of women and the harmful effects of certain traditional or customary practices, cultural prejudices and religious extremism."[28] The 1992 UN Minorities Declaration[29] calls for minority groups themselves to discontinue practices that are in direct conflict with international law and in violation of universal human rights, but does not mention any obligation on the part of the state to intervene.

Because in fact culture is not static but, rather, constantly changing and adapting, some scholars have argued for a replacement approach according to which practices that violate human rights are replaced with new and culturally acceptable practices that do not, yet nonetheless may serve the same social or cultural function as the offending practice. For this replacement approach to be successful, however, it must be initiated from within the culture itself. One progressive example is the initiative in Uganda called REACH (Reproductive, Educative, and Community Health Program) to replace the practice of "female genital mutilation" (FGM) with another rite of passage ritual that still allows for the

25. Danilo Turk, "The Full Realization of Economic, Social and Cultural Rights," *Final Report of the Special Rapporteur of the Sub-Commission on the Prevention of Discrimination and Protection of Minorities,* UN ESCOR, Commission on Human Rights, 48th Sess., Agenda Item 8, UN Doc. E/CN.4/Sub.2/1992/16 (1992), 198.
26. On cultural relativism versus universality in human rights, see Reading 3 by Burns Weston in Chapter 1 of this volume.
27. Asbjørn Eide, *Peaceful and Constructive Resolution of Situations Involving Minorities* (Oslo: Norwegian Institute of Human Rights, 1994).
28. Vienna Declaration, note 20, pt. I(5) and pt. II(38).
29. UN Minorities Declaration (1992), note 16.

formal recognition of the entrance of girls into womanhood.[30] A pilot project developed by Ugandans in 1996, REACH was financially supported by the United Nations Population Fund, and its work included the holding of "culturally sensitive" seminars to educate Sabiny community leaders about the consequences of FGM. It also helped to establish "Culture Day," which coincided with the opening of the traditional circumcision period. One of the goals of Culture Day was to celebrate the positive aspects of many Sabiny traditions and to affirm their culture, while at the same time exploring culturally suitable ways to replace the FGM practice.

States must find and promote suitable means to encourage and support changes in such cultural practices, but at the same time, be sensitive to the fact that change must come from within the culture itself. Culture is often an individual or group's sole frame of reference and does not always allow the option of ignoring or refusing to participate in harmful cultural practices. Without movement from within society itself, it is difficult for customs such as FGM, which are deeply embedded in a culture, to be changed as a result of external pressure alone.

[*Eds.*—The author next discusses extensively "the right to participate in cultural life as it relates to other rights in the ICESCR." The enjoyment of the right to culture, he points out, "is often the result of the enjoyment of other rights and is closely related to, or is a fundamental component of, other rights." He then proceeds to demonstrate "how inextricable interwoven cultural life relates to other rights," in this case other rights in the ICESCR: the right to self-determination and to economic, social, and cultural development (art. I(1)); the right to freely dispose of natural wealth and resources and means of subsistence (art. I(2)); the right to work, to just and favorable working conditions and to vocational guidance and training (arts. 6, 7); the rights to protection and assistance to the family (art. 10); the right to an adequate standard of living (including housing and food) (art. 11); the right to the enjoyment of the highest attainable standard of physical and mental health (art. 12); the right to education (art. 13); the right to protection of moral and material interests (art.

15(1)); the right to conservation, development, and diffusion of science and culture (art 15(2)); freedom indispensable for research and creative activity (art. 15(3)); and recognition of the benefits from the encouragement and development of international contacts and cooperation in the scientific and cultural fields (art 15(4)). The author then continues:]

MINIMUM CORE OBLIGATIONS FOR THE RIGHT TO PARTICIPATE IN CULTURAL LIFE

Article 15(2) of the ICESCR states that the steps necessary to achieve the full realization of the right to participate in cultural life include those necessary for the conservation, development and diffusion of science and culture. While the Covenant appears to address realizing the right progressively by delineating the steps to be taken, some of the obligations on the part of the state necessary to conserve culture should be considered core obligations and subject to immediate implementation.

Conservation of culture entails several obligations, one of which is respect for cultural practices and traditions. It involves respect for the freedom of individuals to choose, express, and develop their culture. This freedom stems from other fundamental rights and freedoms, including freedom of assembly, freedom of the person (life, liberty, and security), the right to participate in the political process, and non-discrimination. Other equally important freedoms underpinning the right to participate in cultural life include freedom of thought, conscience, and religion, freedom to choose and/or establish educational institutions, freedom to use one's own language, and freedom of expression. These rights are central to participating in cultural life and allow individuals and groups of people to follow, adopt, or create a way of life of their choice. But of these rights central to cultural freedom, the ICESCR itself addresses only two: freedom from discrimination [Article 2(2)] and the right to choose and/or establish educational institutions [Article 13(3)]

The obligation to conserve culture requires a state to recognize the identity and existence of all cultures within its jurisdiction and to recognize

30. See Sara Horsfall and Rebecca Salonen, "Female Genital Mutilation and Associated Gender and Political Issues Among the Sabiny of Uganda" (March 2000), available at Rising Daughters Arise, http://www.stopfgm.org/stopfgm/doc/EN/90.pdf

that they all form and contribute to a national and global culture. This entails respecting the self-identification of individuals and groups as minorities, indigenous, or tribal and guaranteeing the equal treatment of these cultures at all levels and without discrimination. To ensure that individuals have the freedom to choose their culture, states are obliged to remove immediately any obstacles inhibiting or limiting access to one's own and other cultures, without distinction or discrimination. Therefore, states must ensure particularly that minorities have full opportunities for gaining access to and participating in the national and global culture, while safeguarding their right to preserve their own cultural identities as well.

Religion and language are fundamental components of a culture; therefore, respect for language and religion must be considered a core minimum obligation. Both language and religion are covered by the right to freedom of expression and are addressed specifically in the ICCPR. Both instruments declare that the choice and use of language are not to be subject to discriminatory actions, and ICCPR Article 27 states that minority groups have the right to use their own language. Although the ICESCR does not address language, except in terms of nondiscrimination as enunciated in its Article 2(2), human rights scholar Fons Coomans asks whether the right to be educated in the language of one's choice constitutes a core minimum obligation under the right to education.[31] He cites the *Belgian Linguistic Case* (1968),[32] which stated that it benefits the individual to be educated in the national language and that an individual cannot claim a right to state-funded education in the language of his or her own choice. However, though not obliged to provide funding, states do have the obligation to respect teaching in minority languages in non-state schools or other institutions outside the public education system. Coomans therefore concludes that the right to be educated in the language of one's choice does belong to the core content of the right to education. In this sense, the right also belongs to the core content of the right to participate in cultural life.

Religion embodies and expresses a culture's ethics, values, explanation for existence, relationship to the environment, and relationships and responsibilities to members within and outside the community. The right to religious freedom, as addressed in UDHR Article 18 and ICCPR Article 18, includes the rights to have, adopt, profess, and practice one's own religion. Religion also plays a role in the right to education and, unlike with choice of language, ICESCR Article 13(3) does declare an obligation on the part of the state to respect the liberty of parents to choose schools other than those established by the public authorities to ensure the religious and moral education of their children in conformity with their own convictions.

To protect the right to participate in cultural life, states have an obligation to create the necessary conditions or correct their regional and national political and legal systems to ensure the representation or direct participation of cultural groups in the political process. Central to this obligation is ensuring the general rights of citizenship for all individuals regardless of their cultural group or affiliation. States should also adopt progressive measures to assure democratic and adequate representation of minority groups in government and actively involve cultural minorities in the formulation of laws and policies that affect them. While UDHR Article 21(1) declares the right of everyone to take part in the government of his own country, not all political systems are structured to allow for the full or partial formal representation of all minority groups or cultures within their jurisdictions. According to the CESCR, the ICESCR is neutral with regard to forms of government and economic systems and recognizes that the rights in the ICESCR are susceptible to realization within the context of a wide variety of economic and political systems.[33] In situations in which formal political representation may not be possible, states should determine other effective ways for groups to take part in the political process, allowing them to exercise control over matters and decisions directly affecting their communities such as those affecting their environment, access to and use of

31. Fons Coomans, "In Search of the Core Elements of the Right to Education," in Audrey Chapman and Sage Russell, eds., *Core Obligations: Building A Framework for Economic, Social and Cultural Rights* (Antwerp: Intersentia, 2002), 217–46.
32. *Case Relating to Certain Aspects of the Law on the Use of Languages in Education in Belgium*, July 23, 1968, Eur. Ct. Hum. Rts., Series A, Vol. 6, at 31.
33. CESCR (5th Sess., 1990), General Comment No. 3, UN Doc. E/1991/23, Annex III, ¶ 8.

natural resources, cultural development, children, and families.

CONCLUSIONS

Although there are several references to culture in the ICESCR, the instrument intended to protect cultural rights, the emphasis to date has been on economic and social rights. When discussions are turned toward cultural rights specifically, these rights are often quickly dismissed, due to historic Western conceptions of culture, the complexity of the issues associated with culture and human rights, or as the interests of minority groups.

The application of a broader concept of culture within a human rights context, one that goes beyond the traditional focus on creativity and the arts, demonstrates the inextricability of culture from all aspects of human life. Within this context, cultural rights apply not only to aspects of creativity, but to a much wider set of human rights concerns, ranging from food procurement to intellectual property protections. Failure to develop and adapt this broader concept of culture within the human rights context will perpetuate the a lack of conceptualization of these rights themselves, as well as threaten the equal enjoyment and cultural adequacy of most other human rights. This broader approach to cultural rights finds support in the current legal framework, in which many of the fundamental components necessary to protect and promote the right to participate in cultural life are addressed. Therefore, any conceptualization of the right to participate in cultural life, as declared but not defined in the ICESCR, must include an examination of these international human rights instruments as well.

Some unresolved issues, which to date have impeded a more complete conceptualization of cultural rights, do not lend themselves to immediate, uniform, or global solutions under universal human rights standards. For example, while certain cultural practices that violate human rights must stop, states need to be sensitive to the fact that such changes should be initiated from within a culture itself, while finding and promoting suitable ways to encourage and support successful changes of these cultural practices. While solutions to such issues may take additional time to implement, they should not stand in the way of the protection of other fundamental rights and freedoms necessary for individuals and groups to participate freely in their cultural lives. The time is long overdue for cultural rights to take an equal place along side the other rights in the ICESCR, as well as serve as one of the fundamental components in the consideration and protection of the other rights declared in it.

QUESTIONS FOR REFLECTION AND DISCUSSION

1. It has been suggested that, at this time in history, in the wake of international debates on indigenous and minority rights in global forums such as the UN and the EU and through the influence of Western-based NGOs and Western-born or Western-trained international lawyers, advancing culture-based claims to rights requires a reductive, "essentialist" description of culture. For example, anthropologists Rachel Sieder and Jessica Witchell have found that the recognition of indigenous rights in the 1995 peace accord in Guatemala took place at the price of trivializing the complex social realities of post-conflict indigenous culture. The indigenous movement's leaders saw the need to project "an essentialized, idealized, and atemporal indigenous identity" that conformed to "dominant [Western] legal discourses, especially those of international human rights law and multiculturalism" as a means to securing collective rights. "Advancing Indigenous Claims Through the Law: Reflections on the Guatemalan Peace Process," in Jane K. Cowan, Marie-Bénédicte Dembour, and Richard A. Wilson, eds., *Culture and Rights: Anthropological Perspectives* (Cambridge: Cambridge University Press, 2001), 201–25, at 201. Sieder and Witchell are concerned that the settlement will not increase the political voice of indigenous Guatemalans and might limit access to justice for the conflict's victims. Is there a "right" and "wrong" way to claim rights in the name of culture? Does familiarity with rights discourse determine how cultural identity is experienced and politicized? Does it matter that international legal standards, NGOs, and Western-educated elites shape the cultural identities that are asserted in pursuit of rights? Is human rights discourse a minority's only available

way out of marginalization, abuse, and disenfranchisement? How might Hansen answer these questions?

2. According to David Scott, "Culture in Political Theory," *Political Theory* 32, no. 1 (Feb. 2003): 92–115, post-Cold War liberal democracies are faced with "non-Western peoples coming to the West in large numbers and making material claims on its institutions and resources" (94). Does this suggest that for cultural minorities the value of cultural recognition and its attendant human rights discourse is now less important than the value of economic redistribution and its attendant human rights discourse? The reverse? In *Justice Interruptus: Critical Reflections on the "Postsocialist" Condition* (New York: Routledge, 1997), Nancy Frazer argues that "claims for the recognition of group difference . . . in the recent period . . . [have been] eclipsing claims for social equality" (2). "The context for these developments," she suggests, is "a resurgent economic liberalism" which displaces the focus of political debate from "redistribution" to "recognition." Claims to cultural rights have emerged, she asserts, as the old "egalitarian commitments appear to recede" and a "globalizing wall-to-wall capitalism is increasingly marketizing social relations, eroding social protections and worsening the life-chances of millions" (3). Does all this imply that there is now a moral urgency for discourse concerning the rights of cultural minorities? If so, should that discourse be focused more on claims for distinctive recognition than equal distribution? The reverse? How might Hansen respond to these questions? How might Rhoda Howard-Hassmann (Reading 4 in Chapter 1 of this volume)? And you?

3. Culture comes into play, Hansen observes, when minority groups seek greater autonomy or self-rule. But who decides which minorities deserve autonomy and which do not? For penetrating discussion, see Sonia Lucarelli, *Europe and the Breakup of Yugoslavia* (The Hague: Kluwer Law International, 2000). Lucarelli analyzes Germany's early push for international recognition of Croatian and Slovenian claims to self-determination *qua* secession which, they suggest, was driven by Germany's own recent experience of reunification and a consequent susceptibility to Croatian and Slovenian claims of cultural and religious affinity with Europe in contrast to the supposed Eastern-Asiatic identity of the then other Yugoslav republics. By maneuvering EU decision-making processes and European rivalries, Germany succeeded in having Croatia's and Slovenia's secessionist demands recognized, thus fueling, as many believe, the subsequent explosion of interethnic violence in Yugoslavia. Is James Tully justified in arguing, in *Strange Multiplicity: Constitutionalism in an Age of Diversity* (Cambridge: Cambridge University Press, 1995), that Western constitutionalism is trapped in the assumption that "every culture worthy of recognition is a nation, and every nation should be recognized as an independent nation-state" (8)?

4. Yael Tamir uses the notion of the "right to culture" to reclaim nationalism in the political language of liberalism. See Yael Tamir, *Liberal Nationalism* (Princeton, N.J.: Princeton University Press, 1993). Tamir distinguishes between traditional culture and national culture, arguing that the second is an individual right and therefore entitled to protection. Unlike ethnic, tribal, and other kinds of communal identities, national identity, Tamil argues, is freely chosen as a matter of conscious decision on a personal level. It is a voluntary association whose primary purpose is the public expression and reaffirmation of a culture, and therefore the nation is entitled to self-determination in a cultural sense as a means of realizing the "right to culture" proclaimed in international law. Tamir's aim is of course to discourage liberals from surrendering the concept of nationalism to chauvinist, racist, and otherwise crabbed expressions of culture and to see nationalism as affirming communal membership and as a quest for cultural recognition and self-respect. But are there not severe dangers lurking in this viewpoint? What happens when the nation (a cultural concept) is also a state (a political concept) and the nationalism of the governing elite is culturally antithetical to a given minority? History is replete with tragic answers. Consider, for one conspicuous example, the cooptation of culture by German nationalism during the Third Reich. Can you think of other examples? How does one facilitate Tamir's purpose without severe risk?

5. Gender is a highly controversial issue in cultural rights discourse. Polygamy, forced marriage, female genital cutting, punishing women for being raped, differential access for men and women to health care and education, unequal rights of ownership—these and other practices and traditions are standard in many parts of the world, but in our commitment to respect other cultures are we bound to respect them at the expense of gender

equity? If so, are we not making them more likely to continue and to spread to liberal democracies? In Susan Moller Okin, *Is Multiculturalism Bad for Women?* ed. Joshua Cohen, Matthew Howard, and Martha Nussbaum (Princeton, N.J.: Princeton University Press, 1999), at 9, Okin expresses a common concern: "what should be done," she asks, "when the claims of minority cultures or religions clash with the norm of gender equality that is at least formally endorsed by liberal states . . .?" She illustrates her concern by noting the French government's giving thousands of male immigrants special permission to bring multiple wives into the country despite French laws against polygamy and the wives' own opposition to the practice. She argues that if we agree that women should not be disadvantaged because of their sex, we should not accept group rights that permit practices oppressive to women on the grounds that they are fundamental to the self-conception or even existence of other cultures. Do you agree? Disagree? Why? Consider William Barbieri, "Group Rights and the Muslim Diaspora," *HRQ* 21 (1999): 907–26, who argues that religious freedom is a fundamental human right (ranking higher than mere cultural or group rights) and that by virtue of this right Muslims in non-Muslim countries are entitled to "collective rights, such as the right to wear headscarves even in self-consciously laicized public schools, the right to take time off from work to engage in prayer and the celebration of holy days, and the right to polygamous marriage." These rights, Barbieri contends, are "rights of self-determination." Who is right, Okin or Barbieri? Is there a solution to this cross-cultural dilemma? In this connection, see Reading 3 by Burns H. Weston in Chapter 1 of this volume.

6. In many countries today there is concern that national cultures are being eroded by globalization and economic migration just as minority cultures were once eroded by national cultures. For some, globalization is synonymous with cultural as well as economic Americanization. Others worry that the influx of foreign workers in countries whose national identity is not defined, as in the United States, in terms of the immigrant experience will erode the shared bond embodied in the national culture. National cultures or identities represent entire worldviews—unique perspectives on economics, education, politics, and society generally that have evolved over centuries. Are they not entitled to protection on the international level in the same or similar way that minority cultures are? What would Hansen say?

Chapter Four

Community or Solidarity Rights—Group Rights

I N this chapter, we continue the focus of Chapter 3 connecting human needs with human rights and understanding them as security rights. Here, however, we concentrate not on individual rights but on "third generation" rights, that is group rights that are sometimes called "community rights," sometimes "solidarity rights." Presaged in Article 28 of the Universal Declaration of Human Rights (UDHR)[1]—proclaiming that "everyone is entitled to a social and international order in which the rights and freedoms set forth in this Declaration can be fully realized"—these include, but are not limited to, the right to self-determination, the right to development, the right to a clean and sustainable environment, and the right to peace, each topics we address in this chapter.

THE HUMAN RIGHT TO SELF-DETERMINATION

The first selection, "The Right to Self-Determination in the Twenty-First Century" (Reading 19), is by international human rights law scholar Hurst Hannum. Giving people a say in their own fate and future is central to the achievement of all rights, of course, but it is the very essence of the right to self-determination.[2] Proclaimed in the 1966 International Covenant on Economic, Social, and Cultural Rights (ICESCR) and International Covenant on Civil and Political Rights (ICCPR),[3] it is identified by Galtung and Wirak as a collective right designed to realize group security.[4] Hannum observes that, though adherence to the

1. Adopted Dec. 10, 1948, reprinted and referenced in Documentary Appendix A.
2. For an extensive, sensitive treatment of the right to self-determination, see Hurst Hannum, *Autonomy, Sovereignty, and Self-Determination: The Accommodation of Conflicting Rights* (Philadelphia: University of Pennsylvania Press, 1989). See also Lung-chu Chen, "Self-Determination as a Human Right," in W. Michael Reisman and Burns H. Weston, eds., *Toward World Order and Human Dignity: Essays in Honor of Myres S. McDougal* (New York: Free Press, 1976), 198–261.
3. Reprinted and referenced in Documentary Appendix A, each of these instruments was concluded Dec. 16, 1966.
4. See generally Johan Galtung and Anders Helge Wirak, "Human Needs, Human Rights and the Theories of Development," in Johan Galtung and R. G. Cant, eds., *Indicators of Social and Economic Change and Their Applications*, Reports and Papers in Social Science 37 (Paris: UNESCO, 1976), 7–34. See also, by the same authors, "Human Needs and Human Rights—A Theoretical Approach," *Bulletin of Peace Proposals* 8 (1977): 251–58. See also text accompanying notes 5–13 in Reading 2 by Martha Nussbaum in Chapter 1 of this volume.

right has been widely proclaimed, its genuine realization has been limited largely to post-colonial situations but otherwise left to international vagaries of one sort or another. Thus the independence of the Baltic states of Estonia, Latvia, and Lithuania—diplomatically recognized in 1991—did not depend upon their long standing assertion of the right so much as it did upon the changing constellation of power that year in the wake of the dissolution of the Union of Soviet Socialist Republics, their former overlord.

Is the right to self-determination a viable right only when applicable under politically determined circumstances, such as the sufferance of superior force or when it is strategically important to great powers? The intense—indeed, often vituperative and violent—nature of the debate over conflicting Palestinian claims to self-determination and the claims of Israel advanced as a collective right are, perhaps, not so much a remedy for a problem as a statement of the problem itself. Hurst Hannum's essay reveals several such troubling inconsistencies in the conceptualization of the right to self-determination of peoples. As a corollary, he notes that the right is less likely to be pressed by minorities and others in a genuinely democratic rights-respecting regime where people are not prone to leave it. He also opines, relatedly, that "even when self-determination is purportedly the issue, it is better to try to address denials of human rights before trying to address the denial of so-called self-determination." All of which implies that, as a practical matter, nongovernmental organizations or human rights activists are "more likely to be able to influence a government by focusing on respect for human rights than by entering the quagmire of self-determination and secession." Of course, you, the reader, must be the judge.

THE HUMAN RIGHT TO DEVELOPMENT

In "The Theory and Practice of the Right to Development" (Reading 20), widely respected Indian economist Arjun Sengupta concedes that international law is ambiguous in its recognition of the collective right to development. He argues that the cause of global social justice would be significantly advanced by a right to development more carefully articulated or defined than it has been up to now. Thus he offers this definitional guidance: "The right to development refers to a process of development which leads to the realization of each human right and of all of them together and which has to be carried out in a manner known as rights-based, in accordance with the international human rights standards, as a participatory, non-discriminatory, accountable and transparent process with equity in decision-making and sharing of the fruits of the process."

Sengupta's definition is both instrumentalist, seeing development as a means to promote other rights, and a good in itself, consistent with basic human needs and human dignity.[5] In explaining the components of this definition, the author notes that the 1986 Declaration on the Right to Development[6] places primary responsibility for implementation on the states with individuals as the beneficiaries. Additionally, he observes, corresponding responsibilities are shared by the international community, including programs of development assistance by donor states[7] and international financial institutions.[8] In either case, the

---

5. See Henry J. Steiner, "Social Rights and Economic Development: Converging Discourses?" *Buffalo Human Rights Law Review* 4 (1998): 25–42.
6. Adopted Dec. 4, 1986, referenced in Documentary Appendix B.
7. See Jan Schulkin and Paul Kleindorfer, "Equity Decisions: Economic Development and Environmental Prudence," *HRQ* 17, no. 2 (May 1995): 382–97; Peter Uvin, *Human Rights and Development* (Bloomfield, Conn.: Kumarian Press, 2004).
8. See Daniel D. Bardlow and Claudio Grossman, "Limited Mandates and Intertwined Problems: A New Challenge for the World Bank and the IMF," *HRQ* 17, no. 3 (August 1995): 411–42.

purpose of introducing human rights issues into international development assistance programs should be taken into account so as to prevent maldevelopment—the remedy for which is participation in decision-making by those affected. Aid programs should seek to promote indigenous rather than imported policies, to strengthen grassroots movements, and to encourage popular participation, thereby giving life to the collective right to development.

Since 1990, the annual Reports of the United Nations Development Program (UNDP) have significantly influenced the ways we now perceive development. The Reports have become ever more insistent about the need to correct the "mismeasure of human progress by economic growth alone." Instead, and especially recently, they draw upon the "capabilities" approach of Amartya Sen and Martha Nussbaum to supply more complex indicators of development, emphasizing that development programs must be "people-centered, equitably distributed and environmentally and socially sustainable."[9] In this spirit, the UN *Human Development Report 2004* wisely provides a humane context for the presentation of a massive array of pertinent statistics:

> The range of capabilities that individuals can have, and the choices that can help to expand them, are potentially infinite and vary by individual. However, public policy is about setting priorities, and two criteria are helpful in identifying the most important capabilities for assessing meaningful global progress in achieving human well being. . . . First the capabilities must be universally valued. Second, they must be basic to life, in the sense that their absence would foreclose many other choices.[10]

For these reasons, human development measures presented in the UNDP *Report* and used by policy makers in planning to satisfy the right to development include three variables: (1) life expectancy, (2) educational attainment, and (3) income.[11] In the language of the human capabilities approach, these variables represent, respectively, the capability to lead a long and healthy life; the capability to be knowledgeable; the capability to have access to the resources needed for a decent standard of living; and, thereby, the capability to participate in the life of the community. Unfortunately, even these human development measures fall short of capturing the full dimensions of the constituent human rights because—important to human rights analysis—they do not tell us who is left out and what groups are underserved. That is, the data are not disaggregated to show how significantly human development differs relative to age, ethnicity, gender, race, and so on.[12] Partly to rectify this problem, the *Report* has in recent years added indices looking specifically at gender (the gender-related development index and gender empowerment measure[13]) and poverty (the human poverty index[14]).

9. For pertinent discussion, see Reading 2 in Chapter 1 of this volume by Martha Nussbaum. See also Amartya Sen, "Capability and Well-Being," in Martha Nussbaum and Amartya Sen, eds., *The Quality of Life*, Studies in Development Economics (New York: Oxford University Press, 1993), 30–53.
10. United Nations, *Human Development Report 2004* (New York: United Nations Development Program, 2004), 127 (hereafter *UNDP Report 2004*).
11. The Human Development Index (HDI) is a composite index that measures the average achievement in a country in three basic dimensions of human development: a long and healthy life as measured by life expectancy at birth; knowledge as measured by the adult literacy rate and the combined gross enrollment ratio for primary, secondary and tertiary schools; and a decent standard of living as measured by GDP per capita in purchasing power parity (PPP; U.S. dollars). "The index is constructed using indicators that are currently available globally, and a methodology that is simple and transparent," 137.
12. See Richard Pierre Claude, "Statistics in the Service of Human Rights," in Richard Pierre Claude, *Science in the Service of Human Rights* (Philadelphia: University of Pennsylvania Press, 2002), 112–20.
13. Ibid., Table 25, at 221–24.
14. Ibid., Human and Income Poverty, Developing Countries, Table 3, at 147–49.

The reason why activists and students of human rights concerned with third-generation rights and cognate economic, social, and cultural rights should be interested in data-based approaches to related fields of public policy should be clear: the indicators give us an understanding of forward motion or backsliding over time. Moreover, the complex interconnections among such rights become more evident as we understand how the UNDP annual reports have come to envision economic and social and political development in referents compatible with human rights analysis. The development policy-maker will understand that improving the nutrition, health, and education of workers leads to gains in worker productivity. Particularly does primary education enhance such productivity. But the human rights analyst will also appreciate that these relationships are not the only justification for social investment in fields like food, health, and education. As policy analysts and human rights analysts now increasingly agree, "the development of human capabilities," in the words of the UNDP *Human Development Report 1996,* "is an end in itself."[15]

THE HUMAN RIGHT TO A SUSTAINABLY HEALTHFUL ENVIRONMENT

In addition to the long-standing debate over the scope and meaning of the right to self-determination (reaching back into the nineteenth century) and to the debate over both the existence of a right to development and how best to make and measure progress toward its full realization, there is also debate, relatively recent, over whether there is or should be a right to a sustainably healthful environment and, if so, what its meaning and scope should be. Nuclear and other hazardous waste disposal, loss of biological diversity, ozone depletion and deforestation—all these issues and more direct our attention to the necessity for planetary or intergenerational rights; to ensure a viable environment for future generations, we need freshly conceptualized intergenerational rights.[16]

That some countries are saddled with environmental pollution (commonly involving the various by-products of poverty) to the benefit of other countries more favorably situated in the global political economy is a fact that must be evaluated in human rights terms, contends Puerto Rican law professor Luis E. Rodriguez-Rivera in "Is the Human Right to Environment Recognized Under International Law?" (Reading 21). As he observes, there is now a broad consensus among at least developed nations recognizing that global ecological interdependence mandates a coordinated international response to the serious environmental problems threatening all of humanity; and out of this consensus, he notes, has resulted, over the last quarter century, a veritable cornucopia of instruments addressing specifically global and regional environmental concerns that signal, he argues, the emergence of a new human right, aggregated and otherwise, to a sustainably healthful environment: over 350 multilateral treaties, 1,000 bilateral treaties, and hundreds of intergovernmental instruments in the form of law-making declarations, resolutions, and programs of action.

One formulation bundling human rights and the environment has been articulated in, for example, the Draft Declaration of Principles on Human Rights and the Environment (1994) of the UN Sub-Commission on Prevention of Discrimination and Protection of Minorities (now Sub-Commission on the Promotion and Protection of Human Rights):

---

15. United Nations, *Human Development Report 1996* (New York: United Nations Development Program, 1996), 75.
16. See Edith Weiss Brown, *In Fairness to Future Generations: International Law, Common Patrimony and Intergenerational Equity* (Dobbs Ferry, N.Y.: Transnational Publishers, 1988).

1. Human rights, an ecologically sound environment, sustainable development and peace are interdependent and indivisible.
2. All persons have the right to a secure, healthy and ecologically sound environment. This right and other human rights, including civil, cultural, economic, political and social rights, are universal, interdependent and indivisible.
3. All persons shall be free from any form of discrimination in regard to actions and decisions that affect the environment.
4. All persons have the right to an environment adequate to meet equitably the needs of present generations and that does not impair the rights of future generations to meet equitably their needs.[17]

Additionally, we may consult UDHR Article 28, which proclaims everyone's entitlement to an "international order in which the rights and freedoms set forth in this Declaration can be fully realized," thereby implying that a sense of global equity must be brought to bear, delineating not only rights but also obligations—of governments and citizens, both—to guarantee, at the very least, life itself. More recently, the 1992 Rio Declaration on Environment and Development[18] advances the cause of environmental rights in saying, in its Principle 1, that "human beings . . . are *entitled* to a healthy and productive life in harmony with nature" (emphasis added) and, in its Principle 10, enjoining states to "encourage public awareness" and ensure "access to judicial and administrative proceedings, including redress and remedy" to safeguard that entitlement.

In the face of acid rain, deforestation, desertification, reduction in the world's biodiversity, and export of hazardous wastes, Rodriguez-Rivera is understandably impatient with the state of normative development in terms of what he calls "soft international law"—aspirational resolutions, draft declarations, guiding principles—arguing that our needs today require stronger resolve and greater clarity regarding the sources of environmental rights and their vindication. To this end, via careful analysis, he clarifies three broad categories of ecologically oriented rights: the right *to* environment, the right *of* environment, and environmental rights. He evaluates how each category is inextricably linked to a more expansive articulation of the human right to environment which he argues bridges evident gaps better filled by his version of "the expansive right to environment."

The need for an expansive, holistic concept of such rights becomes more compelling when we consider its opposite, an anarchic international system inattentive to the total human environment. This baleful specter is the subject of the famous essay by biologist Garrett Hardin, "The Tragedy of the Commons."[19] In this much celebrated essay, Hardin describes British cattle-grazing practices during the nineteenth century, wherein each cattle owner sought to maximize his individual well-being by adding to the total number of cattle on the finite grazing areas or "commons." A series of these uncoordinated decisions by the individual owners ultimately resulted in the demise of all of them because of the permanent destruction of the commons. In his analysis of historical experience, Hardin extended the notion of the "commons" to include the open seas, the earth's atmosphere,

---

17. "Draft Principles on Human Rights and the Environment," in Final Report of Mrs. Fatma Zohra Ksentini, Special Rapporteur, UN ESCOR Commission on Human Rights, Sub-Commission on Prevention of Discrimination and Protection of Minorities, 46th Sess., UN Doc. E/CN.4/Sub.2/1994/9 (1994), Annex I. For analysis of the Draft Declaration, see Neil A. F. Popovic, "In Pursuit of Environmental Human Rights: Commentary on the Draft Declaration of Principles on Human Rights and the Environment," *Columbia Human Rights Law Review* 27 (1996): 487–603.
18. Adopted June 13, 1992, referenced in Documentary Appendix B.
19. Garrett Hardin, 'The Tragedy of the Commons,' *Science* 162 (1968): 1243–48, reprinted in over 100 anthologies and widely accepted as a fundamental contribution to ecology, population theory, economics, law, and political science.

and the space around the planet. His conclusion: that maximization of states' interests relative to the consumption of nonrenewable resources, environmental pollution, and population policy sorely requires some kind of global coordination that closely heeds the interrelation of rights and needs consistent with the collective security of all.

This compelling vision of the world as a commons and the perspective of a global population of interconnected human beings should prompt us to think of human rights not only in terms of individual rights, such as the right to food and to personal security, but in terms also of collective or group rights such as a sustainably healthy environment—or the equitable distribution of food, shelter, and medical care. The needs of entire groups of people must be seen as connected to human rights just as the rights of individuals are so connected. And to this viewpoint must be added, perhaps uniquely in the case of the environment, the proposition that group rights include intergenerational rights, i.e., taking the rights of future generations into account.[20] Also to be noted: the concept of planetary rights does not compete with existing human rights, but complements them.

THE HUMAN RIGHT TO PEACE

The interconnection of environmental rights with other human rights is becoming increasingly evident to policy-makers, activists, and scholars. Indian lawyer Clarence J. Dias, president of the International Center on Law and Development in New York City, insists that the rights to development, the environment, and the right to peace are all linked. In succinct, consequentialist terms, he specifies the connections thus: "There is no peace where human rights are systematically violated and where there is no development to bring about poverty elimination. The absence of peace creates conditions that make development difficult and that breeds massive and widespread violations of human rights. Respect and promotion of human rights, however, create an environment favorable to both development and peace.[21]

In the concluding essay in this chapter, "Peace: A Sacred Right" (Reading 22), Canadian Senator Douglas Roche, O.C., approaches the ideal of a humane international order from a related but different angle: the human right to peace, conceptualized not only as a collective security right in the Galtung-Wirak universe but as the *sine qua non* for the realization of all human rights. With supreme irony, though often justified by a concern to prevent or limit the cruelties of war, arms manufacturing, stockpiling, and trading have strengthened the ability of governments to violate human rights in the most fundamental sense. Moreover, preparations for war and war itself divert resources that could alleviate poverty, homelessness, hunger, and disease. Making coercion and conscription a way of life more often than not, they also threaten civil liberties. Decisions shrouded in military secrecy behind the arras of "national security" erode what potential exists for expanding constitutional democracy, including in so-called "advanced democracies."

Of course, if what is done in fear of the possibility of war is bad, what is done in war itself is far worse. Wars are no longer the local affairs they once were, fought strictly among

20. See, e.g., Brown, *In Fairness to Future Generations*, note 16. See also Alan E. Boyle, "The Role of International Human Rights Law in the Protection of the Environment," in Alan E. Boyle and Michael R. Anderson, eds., *Human Rights Approaches to Environmental Protection* (Oxford: Clarendon Press, 1996), 43–69.
21. Clarence J. Dias, "Human Rights, Development, and Environment," in Yael Danieli, Elsa Stamatopoulou, and Clarence J. Dias, eds., *The Universal Declaration of Human Rights: Fifty Years and Beyond* (Amityville, N.Y.: Baywood, 1999), 395–401, at 395. See also Robert J. Muscat, *Investing in Peace: How Development Aid Can Prevent or Promote Conflict* (Armonk, N.Y.: M.E. Sharpe, 2002).

combatants; they typically engulf entire regions and peoples. Unconventional wars (guerrilla and terrorist), which are waged on behalf of many causes, deprive states of what was once their exclusive monopoly on belligerence. Venerable distinctions between combatants and civilians have been obliterated by new weapons and tactics. Wars of "liberation" and global campaigns of terror, characteristic of recent decades and increasingly messianic in character, inexorably conflict with the right to peace. Not even the prohibition on first use is sacrosanct any more, the line between preemptive and preventive warfare having become severely blurred. And while important international institutions have been created and numerous arms control and arms reduction treaties and resolutions proclaimed "to save succeeding generations from the scourge of war," to quote the Preamble to the UN Charter, still we have made grossly insufficient progress to ensure the survival of the "commons." Senator Roche's essay takes on many of these disturbing facts, explores the nature and specifications of existing obligations in the name of the right to peace, and enlarges our perspectives with the broad vision of a culture of peace that stems from "a global ethic toward life in full vibrancy" and that rejects the culture of war that offers mostly "the prospect of misery and annihilation."

The history of the last 100 years offers clear instruction on the importance of peace. War in our time has not only killed millions of people, it also has killed, more often than not, the infant processes of democracy and human rights that affirm human dignity. We ask: how can peace be maintained? The first essential step in answer to this question is to take seriously the Preamble of the Universal Declaration of Human Rights declaring that "the inherent dignity of the equal and inalienable rights of all members of the human family is the foundation of freedom, justice and peace in the world."

The foundation is fragile. On September 11, 2001, the twin towers of New York's World Trade Center and the Pentagon complex of the U.S. Department of Defense were attacked by terrorists with terrible loss of thousands of innocent civilian lives.[22] Within 24 hours, the UN Security Council approved Resolution 1368 (2001) stating that "any act of international terrorism [is] a threat to international peace and security."[23] It recognized the right of victim states to collective self-defense under the UN Charter and called on all states "to work together urgently to bring to justice the perpetrators, organizers and sponsors of these terrorist attacks," stressing that "those responsible for aiding, supporting or harbouring the perpetrators, organizers and sponsors of these acts will be held accountable." Thereafter, along with other countries, the United States launched an armed assault on military targets in Afghanistan because that country's Taliban regime had failed to take action against the putative perpetrator, Osama bin Laden, and his associates. The "Allied" view was that such failure effectively amounted to state tolerance of atrocious acts, human rights violations, and crimes against humanity.

To the bane of us all, the dogs of war have been unleashed over recent decades in many forms. First, during the Cold war we faced catastrophic damage, technologically feasible on a monstrous scale and at a moment's notice. Although that conflict is over and nuclear warfare did not happen, the weapons of mass destruction, nuclear, chemical, and biological, all remain. Second, the 1990s witnessed the challenge of episodic chaos, largely ethnically based, as embodied in situations such as Somalia, Rwanda, Kosovo, Bosnia, Sierra Leone, and Liberia. With the violence of those conflicts ended (at least temporarily), we

---

22. For the official account, see *The 9/11 Commission Report: Final Report of the National Commission on Terrorist Attacks upon the United States* (Washington, D.C.: U.S. Government Printing Office, 2004).
23. UN Security Council Resolution 1368, On Threats to International Peace and Security Caused by Terrorist Acts, Sept. 12, 2001, SC Res. 1368, UN SCOR, 56th Sess., 4370th mtg., UN Doc. S/RES/1368 (2001), reprinted in *ILM* 40 (2001): 1277 and 2 Weston and Carlson 2: II.F.28.

are nonetheless left with no consensus on a doctrine of humanitarian intervention suitable to guide the world community in its rapid and effective response to such violent indulgence, ethnic cleansing, and genocide.[24] Third, the twenty-first century confronts and confounds us with organized terrorism and global insurgency prompted by sectarian zealotry and private individuals bringing death and destruction to innocent victims throughout the world. The legacy of these three models of lawless hostility remain: we still have weapons of mass destruction, conceptual chaos prevails in respect of armed humanitarian intervention; and dominant approaches to globalized terrorism are preemptively put in place with unilateral impetuousness and, too often, sacrifice of human rights.[25]

In light of these conditions, complex as they are, we would do well to return to the post-World War II vision of the framers of the Universal Declaration of Human Rights. On the theory that respect for people's rights and liberties reduces the prospects of hostility, human carnage, destruction, and war, world leaders meeting to design the United Nations sought to introduce human rights into the international commitments of member states. Their hypothesis was simple, elegant, and promising: governments that respect human rights do not make war on other human rights respecting regimes.[26] The problem is that the theory remains insufficiently tested. In the name of the human right to peace, Senator Roche implores us to try.

24. For confirmation of this conclusion, see Reading 30 by Richard Falk in Chapter 7 of this volume.
25. See Jeffrey Hopkins, ed., *The Art of Peace: Nobel Peace Laureates Discuss Human Rights, Conflict, and Reconciliation* (New York: Snow Lion, 2000); Michael Ignatieff, *The Lesser Evil: Political Ethics in an Age of Terror* (Princeton, N.J.: Princeton University Press, 2004).
26. R. J. Rummel, *Power Kills: Democracy as a Method of Nonviolence* (New Brunswick, N.J.: Transaction Publishers, 2004); Michael W. Doyle, "Three Pillars of Liberal Peace," *APSR* 99 (Aug. 2005): 463–66.

19. HURST HANNUM *The Right of Self-Determination in the Twenty-First Century*

One can address the right of self-determination from a number of different perspectives. For example, the exercise of this right in the past decade has had a dramatic effect on theories of international organizations, the role of force, and conflict resolution. Claims of self-determination led in part to the destruction of the former Yugoslavia, and the specter of secessionist movements has magnified the attention given to the rights of minorities and indigenous peoples.

In the following discussion, I link self-determination to human rights in two different ways. First, I explore self-determination as a human right, addressing issues of content and definition. Second, I discuss the impact of self-determination claims on other human rights.

SELF-DETERMINATION AS A HUMAN RIGHT

Self-determination is a human right. Although there are many hortatory references to self-determination in General Assembly resolutions and elsewhere, the only legally binding documents in which the right of self-determination is proclaimed are the two international covenants.[1] The first paragraph of common article 1 states: "All peoples have the right of self-determination. By virtue of that right they freely determine their political status and freely pursue their economic, social and cultural development."

Although the quoted language fails to answer several questions, at least some aspects of the right have become clear through subsequent

Reprinted with changes from Hurst Hannum, "The Rights of Self-Determination in the Twenty-First Century," *Washington & Lee Law Review* 55 (Summer 1998): 773–80. Reprinted by permission.

1. International Covenant on Civil and Political Rights (Dec. 19, 1966), art. 1 (hereinafter ICCPR) and International Covenant on Economic, Social and Cultural Rights (Dec. 16, 1966), art. 1 (hereinafter ICESCR), each reprinted and referenced in Documentary Appendix A.

reflection and interpretation. The first clarification is that self-determination is a right that belongs to collectivities known as "peoples," not to individuals. Thus, the Human Rights Committee has consistently made clear that claims that the right of self-determination has been violated cannot be raised under the First Optional Protocol, which applies only to individuals.[2] I think that the Committee is probably wrong to exclude self-determination claims automatically from the scope of individual complaints, but its jurisprudence has been consistent on this point.

It also is clear that self-determination is a right that belongs to peoples, but not to minorities.[3] This truism may only shift the debate to definitions and semantics, but the distinction between minorities and peoples remains an article of faith for states and international bodies concerned with monitoring human rights.

There are numerous problems in defining both "peoples" and what they are entitled to "determine." Without reviewing the entire history of self-determination, let me just outline how the concept has passed through at least two distinct phases and is now entering a third one. Initially, meaning perhaps the middle of the nineteenth century when the phrase "self-determination" came into common usage, self-determination was not a right but was a principle. It was a principle that first allowed disparate people who spoke the same language, such as Germans and Italians, to group themselves together and form a new state. This "grouping," of course, did not occur without coercion and, in some cases, a good deal of violence. A bit later, at the end of World War I, the principle of self-determination provided a guiding principle or rationale for dismembering the defeated Austro-Hungarian and Ottoman empires.

As a political principle, but not a right under international law, self-determination in this period was subject to many limitations. The most obvious limitation, consistent with realpolitik concerns, was that the successful exercise of self-determination required the support of the victorious powers if there had been a war or the support of major powers even absent a war. Philosophically, "external" self-determination or independence would be rejected if the resulting state would not be economically and politically viable. Self-serving political restrictions made the principle of self-determination applicable to Europe, for instance, but not to colonial empires; thus to Poland, but not to Ireland.

Following a somewhat confused period between the two world wars, the adoption of the United Nations Charter in 1945 marked the beginning of the second phase. This second phase began, as did the first phase, by identifying self-determination as a principle rather than as a right.[4] Self-determination was proclaimed in a manner that did not necessarily require the dismemberment of colonial empires; if it had included such an understanding, Britain, France, and Belgium simply would not have adhered to the Charter. Yet, at the same time, use of the word "peoples" must have implied that self-determination meant more than simply a reaffirmation of the sovereign equality of states.

This situation gradually changed, and I think that one of the great contributions of the United Nations to international law was in promoting the shift from proclaiming a principle of self-determination in the Charter to recognizing a right of self-determination some twenty years later. The problem is that, during this transition, the United Nations continued to refer rhetorically to the right of all peoples to self-determination, when what it really meant was the right of colonial territories to independence.[5] And those are two very different concepts.

Self-determination from 1960 on, at least as articulated by the United Nations, had nothing to do with ethnicity, language, or culture. Although there were some exceptions such as the division of British India, Rwanda-Burundi, and a few others, the accepted mantra was that colonial territories would become independent. It did not matter how many "peoples" were found within them, although obviously each

---

2. See, e.g., Human Rights Committee's General Comment 23 on art. 27 (50th Sess. 1994), reprinted in *Compilation of General Comments and General Recommendations adopted by Human Rights Treaty Bodies,* UN Doc. HRI/GEN/1/Rev. 3 (1997), ¶ 3.1, at 39.
3. Ibid.
4. See UN Charter arts. 1(2), 55 (discussing "respect for the principle of equal rights and self-determination of peoples"), reprinted in Documentary Appendix A.
5. See, e.g., UN General Assembly Declaration on the Granting of Independence to Colonial Countries and Peoples (Dec. 14, 1960), referenced in Documentary Appendix B.

contained many different peoples, nations, and ethnic groups. Thus, in general, territories, not peoples, enjoyed the right to independence.

It was also clear during this period that, although there were other theoretical options (for example, Hawaii and Alaska exercised their right to self-determination by becoming part of the United States), the international preference was for independence. This result could, and often was, achieved with only minimal preparation or even consultation with the colony concerned, although any option other than independence, such as free association or full integration, required the full and informed consent of the people involved.[6]

Thus, in the second half of the twentieth century, a territorial right to independence for former colonies replaced the nineteenth-century principle of allowing ethnic, linguistic, or religious groups to form various kinds of political units that might or might not become independent states. In the postcolonial period,[7] what I would identify as the third phase of self-determination, some are attempting to join those two principles in order to create a new right in international law: the right of every people defined ethnically, culturally, or religiously to have its own independent state.

Although this new position has its adherents, it is clear that international law has not yet recognized such a new paradigm. One reason for this is that, because practically all of the world's surface is now divided among sovereign states, self-determination defined as the right to create a new state would necessarily imply a right to secession. However, no state, no foreign ministry, and very few disinterested writers or scholars suggest that every people has the right to a state, and they implicitly or explicitly reject a right to secession.

This is the current state of international law, whether one is talking about popular groups like Tibetans or unpopular groups like Tamils in Sri Lanka. There simply is no right of secession under international law, nor has there been even preliminary agreement on the criteria that might be used in the future to determine when secession should be supported. Of course, there is no prohibition in international law against secession, either. If a country disintegrates as the result of a civil war, international law poses no barrier to recognition of the two or more succeeding states. That is, however, a quite different position than recognizing the right of a group to secede from an existing state.

Cementing the world's frontiers forever is an overly conservative position, however, and I would like to suggest at least two exceptions to the no-right-to-secession rule. The first exception would recognize a right of secession when there have been massive and discriminatory human rights violations that approach genocide. The violations need not constitute genocide under the technical definition of that term, but I do believe that they must be both massive and discriminatory. So-called "cultural genocide," for example, in which a culture may be radically affected by modernization or by a surrounding dominant culture but not otherwise subjected to human rights violations, would not justify secession. Rather, this category seeks to provide a remedy in those rare situations in which there is an explicit attempt to destroy a culture or people. One could argue, although one would have to look at the facts very closely, that the repression of Kurds in Iraq and conceivably Tibetans might be among the situations that would fall into this exception.

The other and more difficult exception might arise when a group, community, or region has been systematically excluded from political and economic power or when a minimum level of minority rights or a reasonable demand for self-government has been consistently denied. I want to emphasize that this exception would not apply when a central government refuses to agree to whatever the minority or the region wants. Rather, it would apply only when the central government has been so intransigent that, for example, it refuses to allow the minority to speak its own language, it excludes minority members from participation in the parliament, or it refuses to accede to demands for minimal local or regional power-sharing.

Leaving aside these two possible exceptions to the rule, I now return to the basic proposition

6. See Principles Which Should Guide Members in Determining Whether or Not an Obligation Exists to Transmit the Information Called For Under Article 73e of the Charter, GA Res. 1541 (XV), UN GAOR, 4th Comm., 15th Sess., Supp. No. 16, at 29–30, UN Doc. A/4684 (1960).
7. There are today somewhat less than 20 non-self-governing territories recognized by the United Nations, most them small islands controlled by the United Kingdom or the United States.

that self-determination today does not mean either independence or secession. If that is correct, is there any reason that we still talk about self-determination as a human right? Is there anything left of it? I would suggest that there is. What is left in the contemporary content of self-determination reflects the right's position in the two covenants and offers an opportunity to ensure that it continues to have meaning and validity into the next century.

Here, too, I am suggesting what the law should be, rather than describing what I think it is at present. First, we should keep in mind that self-determination, except in the narrow context of decolonization, is not absolute. This point should not be surprising, because there are very few absolute rights. Recognizing that one has a right to self-determination does not imply that one can always exercise the right to its maximum extent any more than exercising the right to free expression means that one is absolutely free to say whatever one wants under all conceivable circumstances.

I suggest that we can find meaningful content to self-determination by looking at two other human rights, or at least aspects of two human rights, on which there is a much greater degree of consensus than is the case if one focuses on self-determination per se. These related rights are as follows: (1) the protection of the cultural, religious, linguistic, and ethnic identity of individuals and groups; and (2) the right of individuals and groups to participate effectively in the economic and the political life of the country.

Protecting the identity of groups is not very popular in the United States or in some other countries, such as Sweden. It is clear, however, that, particularly during the past decade, greater attention is being given to the issues of minority and indigenous rights, reflecting what I believe is a consensus on the importance of preserving one's identity both as an individual and as a member of a group. Related to this is a growing consensus that diversity and pluralism are, in themselves, worthwhile goals to pursue. Thus, there is room to include protection of identity in a contemporary understanding of self-determination.

The second aspect, participation, is derived to some extent from economic development discussions, in which the right of popular participation in decision-making was identified as a way of ensuring that assistance received by states would better serve the purpose for which it was intended. This concept was extraordinarily subversive, because, once one effectively participates in economic decision-making, a need to participate effectively in all sorts of other decision-making processes almost inevitably follows.

More recently, the belief that a new democratic era has arrived has reinforced this notion of participation. Participation, however, goes beyond democracy.[8] Determining what is and what is not effective participation is, of course, difficult. Ensuring participation opens up a whole range of possibilities, ranging from representation in the central government to different forms of federalism, consociationalism, and autonomy. As a principle, however, it is not inherently less manageable than due process or fair trial, even if the answer to whether the people in a particular region or group participate effectively in governing themselves, both through the central government and locally, is not always immediately apparent. The idea of effective participation identifies another component of self-determination that should not be overly threatening to the states that are expected to implement it.

A final suggestion in defining self-determination for the twenty-first century is to impose a limit or a price on its exercise by requiring that any ethnic group that succeeds in establishing a new state based on principles of ethnicity, religion, language, or culture should be willing to grant to other groups within the new state the same right of self-determination and secession that it has just exercised. Pursuant to this principle, Serbs would have had a right to secede from Croatia and Bosnia-Hercegovina, and Crees would be able to leave an independent Quebec. Such a principle might cause potential secessionists to think more carefully about the consequences of their actions and would give newly trapped minorities a way out without resorting to violence.

8. I [am] disturbed by the fact that the Clinton Administration decided to rename the Bureau of Human Rights the Bureau of Democracy, Human Rights and Labor. This suggests that neither democracy nor labor is included in human rights or that democracy and labor are somehow more important than human rights. Both are dangerous positions to maintain.

Even with, or perhaps because of, the exceptions and the nuances I outline, self-determination as a human right remains relatively vague. Unfortunately, it is unlikely that any existing human rights mechanism or even a new mechanism will be of much assistance in defining the right in the foreseeable future, because few states are willing to allow an international forum to judge a situation that might, if a claim to self-determination and secession is upheld, result in the destruction of the state itself. Some things are too important to be left to lawyers, and I think that self-determination might be one of those issues.

IMPACT OF SELF-DETERMINATION CLAIMS ON OTHER HUMAN RIGHTS

The situation in Kosovo and statements by U.S. [governmental officials] demanding that Serbia recognize the "legitimate rights" of the people of Kosovo raise several questions: What are those rights? Do they have anything to do with human rights? Does the United States support the political goal of an independent Kosovo or a Kosovo united with Albania? Do Kosovo Albanians have a right to autonomy? Do they have a right to return to the status they enjoyed in Yugoslavia in 1989, even though we certainly are not returning anything else to its 1989 position? The obvious danger is that, whenever self-determination is involved, a destructive confusion of political goals, basic human rights norms, and humanitarian issues may make it more difficult to deal with any of these aspects successfully.

The other potential impact of self-determination claims is to encourage violent conflict. Although it is a truism, it needs to be reiterated that more human rights are violated during wars than at any other time. If policy-makers do not arrive at a better understand-ing of how to respond to claims for self-determination, such claims are likely to increase. It is very likely that the number of violent conflicts will increase as well, and increased conflict will have a direct impact on the entire gamut of international human rights.

At the same time, I think that if we reverse the lens and look at "ordinary" human rights first, and if we can imagine that all the human rights that we want to have protected are protected, violence is much less likely to ensue.

Disputes over self-determination will not disappear, but they will be resolved by countries such as Canada, the United Kingdom, and Belgium, as opposed to being decided by countries such as Russia or Yugoslavia. If one creates a genuinely democratic rights-respecting regime, it is less likely that people will want to leave it. If, however, they do leave it, it is also more likely that any separation will occur peacefully.

This approach suggests that, even when self-determination is purportedly the issue, it is better to try to address denials of human rights before trying to address the denial of so-called self-determination. As a practical matter, a non-governmental organization or human rights activist is more likely to be able to influence a government by focusing on respect for human rights than by entering the quagmire of self-determination and secession. I think that one is also more likely to protect what we would all agree are human rights—for example, physical integrity, use of language, and protection of culture without confusing those rights with political goals. Even if we may share some of the latter goals, it is essential to keep them distinct from the universally recognized and legally articulated provisions of international human rights law.

CONCLUSION

For better or for worse, self-determination will not disappear as an issue that has the potential to create serious conflict in the future. Self-determination is not a new issue, however. Self-determination claims did not start at the end of the Cold War, as numerous conflicts in Africa and Asia remind us. But we do need to guard against the usurpation of the slogan and the symbol of self-determination and its use as a purely partisan political tool by both governments and disaffected groups. Because self-determination is such an emotional concept, appeals by "ethnic entrepreneurs" are always likely to create an atmosphere in which violence and greater violations of human rights are more, rather than less, likely. This position may be relatively conservative, but I believe that it is a solid human rights position. As the immortal Mick Jagger said, "You can't always get what you want / But if you try sometimes, you just might find / You get what you need."[9]

9. Mick Jagger/Keith Richards, "You Can't Always Get What You Want."

QUESTIONS FOR REFLECTION AND DISCUSSION

1. Hannum asserts that the right to self-determination belongs to "'peoples,' not individuals," but he also asserts that it "is probably wrong to exclude self-determination claims automatically from the scope of individual complaint." Do you think individuals should be able to advance the claim to self-determination? If so, in what capacity? What types of problems would be created, if any? In what circumstances would it be beneficial for an individual to be able to make a claim to self-determination?

2. Hannum also asserts that "It . . . is clear that self-determination is a right that belongs to peoples, but not to minorities." He calls this a "truism." Why? What is "a people"? What is "a minority"? In "Self-Determination Under International Law: Validity of Claims to Secede," *Case Western Reserve Journal of International Law* 13 (1981): 257–80, at 276, Ved P. Nanda suggest how to define "a people." He writes:

> the emphasis should be on the subjective factors of a group's identity and a common destiny, for it is that group's own values and preferences which lie at the basis of their claim to have the power to decide their future course. Accordingly, psychological perceptions and not tangible attributes, such as racial characteristics, should determine whether the group seeking secession meets the threshold requirement.

Do you agree with Nanda? Could not the same thing be said of "a minority"? Aside from Nanda's deemphasis of "tangible attributes, such as racial characteristics," what distinguishes African Americans (commonly considered a minority) from Native Americans (commonly considered a people)? Is it merely an accident of history?

3. One of the most painful reminders of the difficulty of achieving agreement on what constitutes "a people" has been the ongoing Israeli-Palestinian conflict. Commentators sympathetic to the Palestinian cause have no trouble seeing Palestinians as "a people." Commentators sympathetic to Israel tend to dissent from "the myth that Jews in Palestine unjustly displaced 'the Palestinian People' [given that] official documents before 1947 generally spoke of 'Arabs in Palestine,' not a 'Palestinian people.'" Michael Curtis, "International Law and the Territories," *HILJ* 32 (1991): 457–95, at 457. With which viewpoint do you agree? Why? Might there be an intermediate position? For extensive treatment of this and related issues, see Richard A. Falk and Burns H. Weston, "The Relevance of International Law to Palestinian Rights in the West Bank and Gaza: In Defense of the Intifada," *HILJ* 32 (1991): 129–57 and, by the same authors, "The Israeli-Occupied Territories, International Law, and the Boundaries of Scholarly Discourse: A Reply to Michael Curtis," *HILJ* 33 (1992): 191–204.

4. It often has been observed that, though first authoritatively advocated by U.S. President Woodrow Wilson, the principle of self-determination became a widespread clarion call for the dismantling of colonial empires in the years following World War II. Hannum traces the historical evolution of self-determination from a principle to a right. Do you think self-determination enjoys the legal status of a right or is it still a principle? Do you think the successful exercise of self-determination requires a certain measure of political power or, as Hannum puts it, "support of major powers"? If so, how do you reconcile the demise of colonialism and the former colonies demands for self-determination? Was this merely an exercise done with the consent and support of the major powers? Or was this a struggle, sometimes bloody?

5. Given its historical antecedents and the fact that colonies and non-self-governing trust territories are now few in number, has the principle of self-determination essentially outlived its usefulness? Or does the principle extend to noncolonial contexts? If so, which ones? If not, why not? What is Hannum's view?

6. Hannum observes that from a "nineteenth-century principle of allowing ethnic, linguistic, or religious groups to form various kinds of political units that might or might not become independent states" and a post-World War II "territorial right to independence for former colonies," a "third phase of self-determination" now involves the creation of "the right of every people defined ethnically, culturally, or religiously to have its own independent state." Does the right to self-determination today embrace under international law a general right of groups to secede from the states of which they are a part? Hannum says not. Should international law recognize this claimed right? If so, what are the consequences,

both good and bad, of doing so, of recognizing the right to secession? And subject to what conditions, if any?

7. Hannum proffers two scenarios when a right to self-determination *qua* secession should be recognized: (a) where there is a history of "massive and discriminatory human rights violations that approach genocide"; (b) when "a group, community, or region has been systematically excluded from political and economic power or when a minimum level of minimum rights or a reasonable demand for self-government has been consistently denied." Are these reasonable exceptions? Are they practical? Should the right to secession take into account any other factors, such as the ability of the group or region to function as a state? Should the state's right to territorial integrity outweigh a group's right to secede? Consider Chechnya, which claims Russia is committing a genocide on its people while Russia claims that it is trying to maintain its "territorial integrity" and to control a hotspot for terrorism. Should Chechnya be allowed the right to secede from Russia? Does the fact that Chechnya, if granted independence, would be surrounded on all sides by Russian territory influence your decision? What about the ramifications of Chechnya's secession for other minorities living in Russia who might also seek independence?

8. And then there are Taiwan and Tibet. Does either of Hannum's scenarios fit them? Assuming their ability to do so, should they be allowed to secede from China? Should the world community actively encourage their secession?

9. Do statistics support the fear that an unchecked right to self-determination might lead to disintegration of the state being challenged? Or do you think that Hannum's suggestion that the exercise of the right be subject to a caveat that any new state carved out of another state must be willing to allow other groups to do the same would constitute a deterrent sufficient to prevent abuse of the right?

10. If the right to self-determination is not a general right to secession, what is it? What does Hannum say? What does Maivân Clech Lâm (Reading 12 in Chapter 2 of this volume) say it is? What do you think it comprises? In "The Capacity of International Law to Advance Ethnic or Nationality Rights Claims," *Iowa Law Review* 75 (1990): 837–44, at 842, Professor (and Native American) S. James Anaya argues:

> self-determination should not be equated with a right to independent statehood. Under a human rights approach, the concept of self-determination is capable of embracing much more nuanced interpretations and applications, particularly in an increasingly interdependent world in which the formal attributes of statehood mean less and less. Self-determination may be understood as a right of cultural groupings to the political situations necessary to allow them to exist and develop according to their distinctive characteristic. The institutions and degree of autonomy, necessarily, will vary as the circumstances of each case vary. And in determining the required conditions for a claimant group, decisionmakers must weigh in the human rights of others. While not precluded, independent statehood will be justified only in rare instances.

What might be the result of a successful exercise of the right of self-determination if not the achievement of independent statehood? Can you give concrete examples? Does Maivân Clech Lâm's essay suggest any answers?

11. In *Autonomy, Sovereignty, and Self-Determination: The Accommodation of Conflicting Rights* (Philadelphia: University of Pennsylvania Press, 1989), at 458, Hurst Hannum, its author, concludes that issues common in conflicts over autonomy include conflicts relating to language, education, access to governmental civil service (including police and security forces, and social services), land and natural resources, and representative government structures. Does this list of issues suggest any answers to Questions 8 and 10? What other issues might be added to the list? What issues would you remove? How are these issues related to other human rights?

12. Hannum asserts that "if one creates a genuinely democratic rights-respecting regime, it is less likely that people will want to leave it. If, however, they do leave it, it is also more likely that any separation will occur peacefully." Do you agree? Are there any examples to support this conclusion? Conversely, are there any examples showing the reverse is true? Do you think that denials of human rights are at the heart of self-determination claims and that if these issues were seriously and thoughtfully addressed by the jurisdictional sovereign there would be little or no need to discuss the right to self-determination?

13. In *Self-Determination and International Law* (Hamden, Conn.: Archon Books, 1972), 192, U. O. Umozurike identifies the "basic characteristics" of self-determination as "(1) government according to the will of the people; (2) the absence of internal or external domination; (3) the free pursuit of economic, social, and cultural development; (4) the enjoyment of fundamental human rights and equal treatment; and (5) the absence of discrimination on grounds of race, color, class, caste, creed, or political conviction." Given these standards, do you think many peoples enjoy full self-determination in today's world? Do peoples of color and other minorities in the United States?

20. ARJUN SENGUPTA *The Right to Development*

THE RIGHT TO DEVELOPMENT IN THEORY

DEFINITION AND CONTENT OF THE RIGHT TO DEVELOPMENT

The adoption by the United Nations in 1986 of the Declaration on the Right to Development[1] ("the Declaration") was the culmination of a long process of international campaigning for human rights. Several countries abstained and the United States cast the single dissenting vote, even though the Declaration was, in effect, an attempt to revive the immediate postwar consensus about human rights developed by U.S. President Roosevelt, based on four freedoms—including the freedom from want. The world was still divided between those who denied that economic, social, and cultural rights could be regarded as human rights, and those who believed that economic, social, and cultural rights were not only fully justifiable human rights but were essential, even necessary, to realize civil and political rights. However, a new consensus emerged in Vienna at the Second UN World Conference on Human Rights in 1993, which even the United States supported. The Vienna Declaration[2] reaffirmed "the right to development, as established in the Declaration, as a universal and inalienable right and an integral part of fundamental human rights." The world got back, so to speak, to the mainstream of the human rights movement from which it was deflected for several decades by Cold War politics.

As a result of this consensus, there is no more room for promoting one set of rights as against another, or putting forward some rights, such as economic and social, to be fulfilled prior to or in violation of civil and political rights, or vice versa. All rights have to be fulfilled together and the violation of one would be as offensive as that of another. The international community, instead, has moved on to examine the question of implementation of those rights as a part of the right to development and ensuring the realization of the right to development has become a major concern of the member Governments of the United Nations. . . .

The Right to Development as a Human Right

There has been considerable debate as to whether the right to development can be regarded as a human right. This issue can now be taken as settled, after the achievement of consensus for the Vienna Declaration and Programme of Action in 1993. We must distinguish between recognizing the right to development as a human right—which is an undeniable fact—and the creating of legally binding obligations relating to that right—which requires a more nuanced explanation. In the early history of the

Reprinted with changes from Arjun Sengupta, "On the Theory and Practice of the Right to Development," *HRQ* 24 (1998): 837–89. Reprinted by permission.

1. Adopted Dec. 4, 1986, referenced in Documentary Appendix B.
2. Vienna Declaration and Programme of Action, adopted June 25, 1993, referenced in Documentary Appendix B.

human rights movement, this binary matching of rights with duties was understood too inflexibly. Rights would be acceptable only if they were realizable, and that would require matching rights claims with corresponding duties that had identifiable methods of carrying out the obligations by the duty-holder. Over time, this inflexible view of rights has given way to a broader understanding of the rights-duty relationship in terms of what Sen describes as the Kantian view of "imperfect obligations." Instead of perfectly linking rights to exact duties of identified agents, as Sen puts it, "the claims are addressed generally to anyone who can help," and the rights become "norms" of behavior or action of the agents, such as other individuals, the state or the international community, who can contribute to the fulfillment of those rights.[3]

Feasibility in principle does not automatically lead to actual realization. Realization would depend on the agreement of the duty-holders to work together according to a program and some binding procedures to honor the agreement. Legislation that converts an "in-principle valid" right into a justiciable "legal" right is one such procedure, but it need not be the only one. There are many other ways of making an agreement binding among different duty-holders. This is particularly true if the duty-holders are different states parties and the imperfect obligations cannot be reduced to legal obligations. Even if a right cannot be legislated, it can still be realized if an agreed procedure for its realization can be established. In other words, such an agreed procedure, which can be legally, morally, or by social convention binding on all the parties, would be necessary to realize a valid right, that is, a right that is feasible to realize through interaction between the holders of the right and of the obligations.

Content of the Right to Development

The right to development refers to a process of development which leads to the realization of each human right and of all of them together and which has to be carried out in a manner known as rights-based, in accordance with the international human rights standards, as a participatory, nondiscriminatory, accountable and transparent process with equity in decision-making and sharing of the fruits of the process.

Equity—which is associated with fairness or the principles of a just society—is basic to that process. Secondly, the objectives of development should be expressed in terms of claims or entitlements of right-holders, which duty-bearers must protect and promote. The identification of the corresponding obligation at the national and the international level is essential to a rights-based approach. As the Declaration on the Right to Development itself points out, the primary responsibility for implementing the right to development belongs to states. The beneficiaries are individuals. The international community has the duty to cooperate to enable the states to fulfill their obligations. Thirdly, to make the right to development a valid, concrete right, procedures have to be worked out so that the rights can be realized through appropriate social arrangement.

The content of the right to development can be analyzed on the basis of the Declaration on the Right to Development. Article 1(1) of the Declaration states, "The right to development is an inalienable human right by virtue of which every human person and all peoples are entitled to participate in, contribute to, and enjoy economic, social, cultural and political development, in which all human rights and fundamental freedoms can be fully realized." Development is defined in the preamble of the Declaration as a "comprehensive economic, social, cultural and political process, which aims at the constant improvement of the well-being of the entire population and of all individuals, on the basis of their active, free and meaningful participation in development and in the fair distribution of benefits resulting therefrom." The process of development that is recognized as a human right is the one, "in which all human rights and fundamental freedoms can be fully realized," consequent to the constant improvement of well-being that is the objective of development. According to Article 2 (3), such a development process would be the aim of national development policies that the states have the right and duty to formulate. Article 8 states more specifically that in taking steps to realize the right to development, states shall ensure "equality of opportunity for all in their access to basic resources, education, health services, food, housing, employment and the fair distribution of

---

3. Amartya Sen, *Development as Freedom* (New York: Knopf, 1999), 227–31.

income," and take effective measures to ensure "that women have an active role in the development process," as well as carrying out "appropriate economic and social reforms with a view to eradicating all social injustices."

The Right to Development as the Right to a Process of Development

Several articles in the Declaration elaborate the point that the right claimed as a human right is the right to a particular process of development. A closer analysis of these articles reveals a number of important features of that process. A country, it may be noted, can develop by many different processes. There may be a sharp increase in gross domestic product (GDP) with the "richer groups" becoming increasingly prosperous and the "poorer sections" lagging behind. There may be some industrialization without the increased income spreading over all the sectors, with the small-scale and informal sectors getting increasingly marginalized. There may be an impressive growth of the export industries with increased access to global markets, but without integrating the economic hinterland into the process of growth and not breaking the structure of a dual economy. All these may be regarded as development in the conventional sense. However, they will not be regarded as objects of [human rights] claims so long as these are not accompanied by a process where equal opportunities were provided. Economic growth, attended by increased inequalities or disparities and rising concentrations of wealth and economic power, and without any improvement in human rights standards and associated with violation of civil and political rights, cannot fulfill the human right to development.

The nature of this process of development is centered around the concept of equity and justice, with the majority of the population, who are currently poor and deprived, having their living standards raised and capacity to improve their position strengthened, leading to the improvement of the well-being of the entire population. The concept of well-being in this context extends well beyond the conventional notions of economic growth to include the expansion of opportunities and capabilities to enjoy those

opportunities, captured in the indicators of social and human development, which in turn expand their substantive freedoms.

It is important to appreciate the full significance of this point. The Declaration on the Right to Development is founded on the notion that the right to development implies a claim for a social order based on equity. Several of its articles call for equality of opportunity, equality of access to resources, equality in the sharing of benefits and fairness of distribution, and equality in the rights to participation. In short, considerations of equity and justice determine the whole structure of development [according to the right to development].

Indeed, to go beyond looking at development simply in terms of growth of income or opulence and to capture the quality of growth in terms of social and human development and the notion of equity based on a fair distribution of the benefits and meaningful participation by all concerned [is], in a way, introducing a paradigmatic shift in the thinking about development, built up by the Human Development Reports of the United Nations Development Programme (UNDP) and articulated by Amartya Sen in his writings on development. Expansion of well-being equated with the expansion of "substantial freedoms," is what Sen describes as the development process and identifies with expansion of "capabilities of persons to lead the kind of lives they value or have reasons to value."[4] These freedoms, as Sen points out, should be seen as both the "primary end" and the "principal means" of development, both in a "constitutive role" and in the "instrumental role."[5] The freedom to achieve valuable functionings is called "capability" and "functionings" are defined as things we value doing or being, such as being in good health, being literate or educated, being able to participate in the life of the community, and so on. In that sense development becomes the expansion of capabilities or the substantive freedoms to allow people to lead the kind of life they value. But then capabilities are also instrumental to further expansion of these capabilities. Being educated and healthy permits them, for example, to enjoy their freedoms. The free agency of people who enjoy civil and political rights is essential for that process.

4. Sen, *Development as Freedom*, note 3, at 24–25.
5. Ibid., 36.

The right to development builds upon the notion of human development and can be described as the right to human development, defined as a development process that expands substantive freedoms and thereby realizes all human rights. However, when human development is claimed as a human right, it becomes a qualitatively different approach. It is not just achieving the objectives of development, but also the way they are achieved that becomes essential. The objective is fulfilling human rights and the process of achieving this is also a human right, respecting the notion of equity and participation, not violating human rights, including a clear specification of obligations and responsibilities, establishing culpability and having a mechanism for monitoring and correcting the failures of the process.

Duties and Obligations

This takes us to another feature of the process related to designing the social arrangement, public action, and individual duties and assigning responsibilities to the different agents. For the realization of any right, the assignment of duties must be carried out so as to establish accountability. The Declaration assigns these responsibilities.

Article 2(2) stipulates that all human beings, individually and collectively, have a responsibility for securing the right to development, "as well as their duties to the community" with full respect for human rights and fundamental freedoms. States, according to Article 3, have "the primary responsibility for the creation of national and international conditions favourable to the realization of the right to development." The responsibility of states, which is complementary to that of individuals, is basically to create the conditions for realizing the right to development, and not necessarily for actually realizing development. The actions that states need to adopt to create such conditions are elaborated in the different articles in terms of both national and international operations. At the national level, in Article 2(3), it is pointed out that "States have the right and the duty to formulate appropriate national development policies." According to Article 8, "States should undertake, at the national level, all necessary measures for the realization of the right to development," and

"should encourage popular participation in all spheres." In addition, in Article 6, states are required to take steps "to eliminate obstacles to development resulting from failure to observe civil and political rights as well as economic, social, and cultural rights."

The national development policies that states have a duty to formulate, according to Article 2(3), will have two characteristics: (a) they must be participatory ("on the basis of their active, free and meaningful participation") and (b) equitable ("the fair distribution of benefits"). Further, states have the right to adopt these policies, implying that if states acting on their own are unable to formulate and execute those policies, they have the right to claim cooperation and help from other states and international agencies. Articles 3 and 4 elaborate on the nature of that international cooperation. According to Article 3(3), states have the duty "to cooperate with each other in ensuring development and eliminating obstacles to development" and should fulfill their duties in such a manner as to promote a new international economic order based on sovereign equality, interdependence, and mutual interest. Article 4 declares quite categorically that states have the duty, individually and collectively, to formulate international development policies to facilitate the realization of the right to development. It recognizes that sustained action is required to promote rapid development, and that as a complement to the efforts of developing countries, "effective international cooperation is essential in providing these countries with appropriate means and facilities to foster their comprehensive development."

To appreciate fully the emphasis that the Declaration puts on international cooperation, Article 4 should be read in conjunction with the opening sentences of the preamble [which refers to "the purposes and principles of the Charter of the United Nations relating to the achievement of international cooperation in solving international problems of an economic, social, cultural and humanitarian nature, and in promoting and encouraging respect for human rights and fundamental freedoms."] The Vienna Declaration of 1993 reaffirms the solemn commitment of all states to fulfill these obligations in accordance with the Charter (¶ 1) and provides: that states should cooperate with each other in ensuring development and eliminating obstacles to development, and that the international community should promote effective international cooperation for the realization of the right to development (¶ 10); that progress towards the implementation of the right to development requires a favorable as well as equitable international economic environment (¶ 10), and that the international community should make all efforts to alleviate specific problems such as the external debt burden of developing countries to supplement the efforts of the governments of these countries.

In sum, the primary responsibility for implementing the right to development [belongs] to states. The beneficiaries are individuals. The international community has the duty to cooperate to enable the states parties to fulfill those obligations. When the right to development is seen not as realizing a few rights in isolation but as implementing all or most rights in a planned manner in tandem with an appropriately high and sustainable growth of the economy and change in its structure, the importance of international cooperation becomes even more evident.

Steiner and Alston enumerate the duties of the states parties in terms of five obligations: (a) respect the rights of others, (b) create institutional machinery essential to realization of rights, (c) protect rights and prevent violations, (d) provide goods and services to satisfy rights and (e) promote rights.[6] The Maastricht Guidelines on Violations of Economic, Social and Cultural Rights address the obligations to respect, protect, and fulfill, and lay down enforceable remedies.[7] In the nature of things, the right to development largely entails obligations to fulfill or to promote and provide which in general are "imperfect obligations." That will not, however, make the right to development invalid or unrealizable. It still is possible to specify a program of action, where all parties, particularly the states and the international community, have clear roles to play in helping realize the right to development. These roles can be translated into obligations with provisions for corrective action and enforceable remedies if the obligations are not fulfilled. Since these policies or programs involve the action of

a number of agents and are vulnerable to exogenous developments and uncertainties, they can be evaluated only in terms of a probability of success, and therefore the rights may remain unrealized or unfulfilled. But still these programs can be designed, with a high probability that the right will be delivered with a clear assignment of roles and obligations of all the parties concerned.

Controversies Regarding the Right to Development

Once the right to development is seen as a human right derived from an implicit social contract binding civil society that identifies duty-holders—primarily the nation-states, but also the international community, individuals, and groups operating in civil society—with the obligation to deliver this right, it should not be difficult to understand the controversies surrounding this right.

[*Eds.*—The author next discusses the following seven controversial themes: "Human Rights as Natural Rights"; "Justiciability"; "Monitoring of Implementation"; "Collective Rights vs. Individual Rights"; "Resource Constraints"; "Interdependence of Rights and the Process of Development"; and "Value Added of the Right to Development as a Process." Most of these themes are addressed above in at least preliminary fashion. Space limitations compel us to restrict this discussion, therefore, to the following four.]

Human Rights as Natural Rights

The traditional argument against economic, social, and cultural rights, and hence the right to development, has been that they are not human rights because they cannot be identified with natural rights. As Donnelly puts it, in the Universal Declaration "human rights are clearly and unambiguously conceptualized as being inherent to humans and not as the product of social cooperation. These rights are conceptualized as being universal and held equally by all;

---

6. Henry J. Steiner and Philip Alston, *International Human Rights in Context: Law, Politics, Morals,* 2nd ed. (New York: Oxford University Press, 2000), 182–84.
7. "The Maastricht Guidelines on Violations of Economic, Social and Cultural Rights," *HRQ* 20 (1998): 691–704.

that is, as natural rights."[8] In that paradigm, human rights are only personal rights, based on negative freedom whereby the law prohibits others from killing, imprisoning, or silencing an individual who has a claim to such freedoms. Economic and social rights are, however, associated with positive freedoms, which the state has to secure and protect through positive action. They are not natural rights; therefore, according to this view, they are not human rights. The right to development is seen as linked to collective rights, which are more than just the sum of individual or personal rights, and to positive economic rights, and therefore it would not be regarded as a human right.

All these arguments have been substantially repudiated in the literature. The Universal Declaration has many elements going beyond the principles of natural rights. In fact, it is firmly based on a pluralistic foundation of international law with many elements of economic and social rights, considering an individual's personality as essentially molded by the community. Logically, there is no reason to take the rights of a group or a collective (people or nation, ethnic or linguistic groups) to be fundamentally different in nature from an individual's human rights, so long as it is possible to define the obligation to fulfill them and for duty-holders to secure them. Even personal rights can be taken as rights to be protected for individuals and groups. Furthermore, it is well established that the identification of civil and political rights with negative rights and economic, social, and cultural rights with positive rights is too superficial because both require negative as well as positive actions.

Collective Rights vs. Individual Rights

There is a different type of criticism, which has been most persistently leveled against the right to development, in particular, which is applicable to all rights other than the civil and political rights. The right to development was promoted both by the Third World protagonists and First World critics as a collective right of states and of peoples for development. We have

argued that it is perfectly logical to press for collective rights to be recognized as human rights. Indeed there are legal institutional agreements and covenants that have recognized and built upon collective rights, and the Declaration on the Right to Development itself has recognized the collective right of peoples in Article 1 which states that every human person and all peoples are entitled to the human right to development and also the right to self-determination, which includes "the exercise of their inalienable right to full sovereignty over all their natural wealth and resources." But these collective rights are not opposed or superior to the right of the individual. The Declaration states categorically (Article 2) "the human person is the central subject of development and should be the active participant and beneficiary of the right to development."

One of the most articulate defenders of the Third World position regarding collective rights, Georges Abi-Saab, a Professor at the Graduate Institute of International Studies in Geneva, suggests two possible definitions of collective rights. the first is a sum-total of double aggregation of the rights and of the individuals.[9] This, as Abi-Saab says, has the intent of highlighting the link between the rights of an individual and the rights of the collectivity. The second definition of collective rights is seen as a right from the collective perspective, "(without going through the process of aggregating individual human rights) by considering it either in the economic dimensions of the right of self-determination, or alternatively as a parallel right to self-determination."[10]

Both these definitions build on the rights of individuals. Indeed, the right to self-determination gives nations "the full sovereignty over all their natural wealth and resources," but that has to be exercised for the benefit of all individuals. In the case of an individual, the right-holder is also the beneficiary of the exercise of the right. In the case of collective right, such as that to self-determination, the right-holder may be a collective such as a nation, but the beneficiary of the exercise of the right has to be the individual. There may of course be some occasion when the right of a particular individual may come

---

8. Jack Donnelly, "Human Rights as Natural Rights," *HRQ* 4 (1982): 391–405, at 401.
9. Georges Abi-Saab, "The Legal Formulation of a Right to Development," in René-Jean Dupuy, ed., *The Right to Development at the International Level* (Alphen aan den Rijn: Sijthoff and Noordhoff, 1980), 159–75, at 164.
10. Ibid.

into conflict with the right of a collective. It is also quite possible that different rights or different individuals enjoying a right may come into conflict in some specific situations. It would be necessary to institute some transparent procedures to resolve these conflicts. But such procedural restrictions do not detract from the nature and importance of the collective right built on individual rights. Indeed, in many cases individual rights can be satisfied only in a collective context, and the right of a state or a nation to develop is a necessary condition for the fulfillment of the rights and the realization of the development of individuals. Collective rights were never meant to disregard the primacy of individual rights. Those who detract from the significance of the right to development by arguing that it is a collective right in conflict with the individual rights foundations of the human rights tradition are, more often than not, politically motivated.

Resource Constraints

A related issue is the question of resources—financial, physical, and institutional, at both the national and the international level—which would put a constraint on the speed and the coverage of the realization of the right to development and of the individual rights recognized in the two International Covenants on Human Rights [i.e., the ICESCR and ICCPR]. There was earlier a view that civil and political rights had a greater claim to being regarded as human rights, because they could be protected immediately by law. Economic, social, and cultural rights, on the other hand, required positive action over time, which would consume resources, and since resources were always limited, the realization of these rights would naturally be constrained. According to this view, if certain rights cannot be fully realized and protected within a limited time, they cannot be regarded as human rights. This argument, however, does not hold because many of the civil and political rights also require as much positive action as economic and social rights, thereby consuming many resources.

Indeed, the existence of the rights should not depend on the availability of resources or the methods of realizing them, but should, once they are recognized as human rights, guide the determination of the methods of their realization depending upon the objective conditions in the states parties (including the availability of resources) and the international environment. The human rights instruments themselves recognize the importance of resource constraints quite explicitly.

International lawyers and human rights agencies have been debating the implications of such resource constraints and the Limburg Principles, formulated at the University of Limburg (Maastricht, The Netherlands), by a group of distinguished experts in international law, laid down the principles for dealing with them.[11] The Principles state, *inter alia*, that

> the obligation to achieve progressively the full realization of the rights requires States parties to move as expeditiously as possible towards the realization of the rights. Under no circumstances shall this be interpreted as implying for States the right to defer indefinitely efforts to ensure full realization. On the contrary all States parties have the obligation to begin immediately to take steps to fulfill their obligations under the Covenant.

Further: "Progressive implementation can be effected not only by increasing resources, but also by the development of societal resources necessary for the realization by everyone of the rights recognized." Similarly: "The obligation of progressive achievement exists independently of the increase in resources; it requires effective use of resources available." The Principles define the term, "its available resources" as referring to "both the resources within a State and those available from the international community through international cooperation and assistance."

The approach in all these has been based on the principle that all states parties must make "the best endeavour" to fulfill their obligations and that the monitoring mechanisms of the treaty bodies would have the jurisdiction to examine and pronounce on whether that best endeavour has been exercised. Included in that process are those measures that can be adopted immediately and without much expenditure of resources, such as prohibiting discrimination in

---

11. Limburg Principles on the Implementation of the International Covenant on Economic, Social and Cultural Rights, adopted Jan. 8, 1987; referenced in Documentary Appendix B.

the access to available services and benefits and adopting legislation and administrative measures to redress the violation of the obligations. If all states parties follow the Limburg Principles, it would go a long way towards the realization of economic, social, and cultural rights which, together with civil and political rights, form an essential basis for the right to development.

There would still remain the issue of prioritization, which cannot be ignored if the realization of these rights requires expenditure of resources, the supply of which remains limited. The problem should not be blown out of proportion or used as a pretext for avoiding action. Most of the activities needed to fulfill these rights do not require many financial resources. Also, resource constraints affect different countries differently. For the very poor countries the institutional constraints may be so important that unless they are removed little can be done to use financial and other resources efficiently to realize the rights. For other developing countries, it may be the fiscal resources of the Government rather than the overall savings that are more crucial. For many others, the infrastructure services, like roads, communication, transportation, electricity, or water supply, may turn out to be the binding constraints.

Whatever the resource constraints, the minimum obligations must be satisfied. The only way to decide on these "minimum obligations" or "basic rights" of preferred incremental change of some rights, is, in a human rights framework, through public discussion. It should be based genuinely on public choice through a participatory process of consultation with the beneficiaries or in a democratic forum of a state.

Interdependence of Rights and the Process of Development

The right to development as the right to a process of development is not just an umbrella right or the sum of a set of rights. It is the right to a process that expands the capabilities or freedom of individuals to improve their well-being and to realize what they value (i.e., a value added right and process). The right to development as a right to a particular process of development can be best described as a "vector" of all the different rights and freedoms. Each element of the vector is a human right just as the vector

itself is a human right. They all will have to be implemented following fully the human rights standards. Furthermore, all the elements are interdependent; the realization of one right, for example the right to health, depends on the level of realization of other rights, such as the right to food, or to housing, or to liberty and security of the person, or to freedom of information. Similarly, realization of all these rights in a sustainable manner would depend upon the growth of GDP and other resources, which in turn would depend upon the realization of the rights to health and education, as well as to freedom of information given the initial stock of human, material, and institutional assets. Looking at the right to development as a vector of rights essentially means not violating if not actually improving rights such as civil and political rights and improving all other rights such as economic, social, and cultural rights by promoting and providing the goods and services that are enjoyed in those rights, respecting the principles of equity, nondiscrimination, participation, accountability, and transparency that constitute the basic human rights standards. In a practical program, the interrelation between the different rights and the provision of goods and services associated with them should be fully taken into account, both at the present time and over the future.

THE RIGHT TO DEVELOPMENT IN PRACTICE

INTERNATIONAL COOPERATION

The movement for the right to development was initiated by the developing countries as a claim of the developing countries on the international community. It was associated with the 1970s movement for establishing a New International Economic Order when the world was largely divided between the [industrialized] North and the [developing] South, with the countries in the Soviet bloc generally supporting the South from the sidelines. The right to development, besides being a claim on equitable treatment in all international transactions of the developing countries, became concerned mostly with the transfer of resources and the favorable treatment of those countries in international trade and finance.

Much of the language used by the developing countries at that time has lost its relevance today.

But despite the considerable differences in the interests of different developing countries, arising from their different levels of development, the essential nature of their dependence on international cooperation has not changed. Except in the case of a few newly industrialized economies, most developing countries are still short of resources. They require a substantial transfer of resources from the industrial countries to supplement their domestic resources and much more such as debt relief, commodity price stabilization, or preferential access to markets. The structure of the international financial system still discourages private capital flows to most low-income countries, and any external shock can generate panic in the international capital market, resulting in the flight of capital from most developing countries. Developing countries still require international cooperation to enable them to cope with such problems.

For a great number of countries, making more effective use of existing resources may be more important than the additional flow of resources. For many projects implemented with a rights-based approach to development, the resulting transparency, accountability, increased equity, and empowerment may be cost-effective in terms of public expenditure and may substantially reduce the need for a large injection of foreign aid. But this does not mean that there is no need to increase the transfer of resources: the resource gap is still very large for most developing countries, especially in those poorer countries which are bypassed by private capital. In addition, international cooperation will have to take many different forms to tackle the problems mentioned above, such as solving the debt problem, decreasing the instability of commodity prices and export earnings, reducing the protectionism in developed countries, and dealing with the inadequacies of the international financial system.

However, the overall responsibility of developing countries themselves in implementing the right to development, following the human rights approach, is not diminished even if international cooperation is not forthcoming to the extent desired. The states' responsibility remains absolute. They must enact legislation, adopt appropriate measures, engage in public actions, formulate schemes that empower the beneficiaries at the grass-roots level, allocate investment and restructure production to promote a process of development with equity and sustainable growth with whatever resources they have. If the level of international cooperation improves, they will be able to do the job more effectively. But states cannot simply wait for that increase while not doing all that they can to implement the right to development.

The duty of the international community to cooperate in order to implement the right to development is also absolute, and it is imperative that a consensus is created around a framework for international cooperation enabling the states parties, with the help of civil society, to realize the right to development for all the people of the developing countries. As the realization of the right to development is a process, it can be done step by step, creating a framework and taking up areas progressively in accordance with the availability of financial, technical, and institutional resources.

Such international cooperation would usually have two dimensions. First, cooperation measures should be conceived and executed internationally in a multilateral process in which all developed countries, multilateral agencies and international institutions could participate by providing facilities to which all qualifying developing countries could have access. Second, bilateral facilities or country-specific arrangements would deal with problems requiring measures adapted to particular contexts. There are now a number of multilateral facilities and arrangements dealing with the debt problems of developing countries; structural adjustment, concessional financing facilities of international financial institutions, world trade organizations and developed industrial countries' programs of providing market access, and restructuring of the international financial system to solve the many problems of inadequacy and instability of financial flows of developing countries. All of these require intensive review from the point of view of meeting the obligations of international cooperation with different states trying to realize the right to development. In a human rights framework such international cooperation should not only be transparent and nondiscriminatory but also equitable and participatory, both in the decision-making and in the benefits-sharing. The quid pro quo for the industrial countries and the international institutions of accepting this human rights framework is that their obligation is matched by the obligation of the developing countries to facilitate the realization of the right to development of their people.

With regard to bilateral facilities and country-specific arrangements, it is possible to operationalize them to realize the right to development in a step-by-step manner. Indeed, both the multilateral and bilateral dimensions of international cooperation open up new possibilities for realizing the right to development in a human rights framework. This can radically transform international economic relations, especially between the developed and developing countries. The human rights approach to the realization of the right to development provides scope for building up a cooperative relationship between the developed and developing countries on the basis of partnership rather than the confrontation of earlier years.

[*Eds.*—The author next discusses in considerable detail the benefits and burdens of "official development assistance" (foreign aid, market access through preferential trade liberalization, increased investment flows, technology transfers, debt forgiveness, emergency assistance) and "development compacts" (mutual commitments between donors and recipient countries to fulfill conditions for implementing development programs mutually agreed upon). He then outlines the implementing elements for rights-based development programs.]

ELEMENTS FOR A PROGRAM TO IMPLEMENT THE RIGHT TO DEVELOPMENT

The basic characteristics of any program for realizing the right to development can be summarized as follows:

(a) The implementation of the right to development should be seen as an overall plan or program of development where some or most of the rights are realized while no other rights are violated. In addition, there should be sustained overall growth of the economy, with increased provision of resources for the realization of those rights and with improved structure of production and distribution.

(b) Implementation of any of the rights cannot be an isolated exercise, and plans or projects for the implementation of the other rights should be designed taking into account time and cross-sectoral consistency.

(c) The overall plan must be carried out with transparency, accountability, and in a non-discriminatory and participatory manner and with equity and justice. In practice, this means that the schemes should be formulated and implemented at the grass-roots level with the beneficiaries participating in the decision-making and implementation, as well as sharing equitably in the benefits.

(d) A process of development associated with human development and expanding opportunity with equity and justice will often require a fundamental change in [national and international] institutions.

(e) While the holders of the right to development are peoples and individuals in developing countries, the duty-bearers are primarily the states and the international community and the other members of national and international civil society. It would therefore be necessary to specify the policies [which duty-bearers] must carry out to implement those rights.

Although not clearly identified as an abiding principle in human rights instruments, the motivation of the human rights approach to development guides one along the lines of protecting the worst-off, the poorest, and the most vulnerable. This could be regarded as the minimal principle of equity, over which there may be not much difficulty in generating a universal consensus. Poverty is the worst form of violation of human rights. If it is possible to generate greater consensus on international cooperation for poverty eradication, that might be most useful for realizing the right to development.

Poverty has at least two dimensions. The first is income poverty, which relates to what percentage of a country's population subsists below a minimum level of income or consumption. The second is related to the capability of the poor to come out of poverty in a sustainable manner by having increased access to facilities like health, education, housing, and nutrition. In that context, pursuing policies to realize some of the other basic rights, such as the right to food, the right to health, and the right to education in a framework of international cooperation would be wholly consistent with a program for the reduction of income poverty.

From the perspective of realizing human rights, the concept of poverty goes much beyond just income poverty. It signifies an unacceptable level of deprivation of well-being, a level that a civilized society considers incompatible with human dignity. Amartya Sen claims that poverty must be seen as deprivation of basic capabilities rather than merely as low incomes.[12] Capabilities are essentially related to human rights, giving individuals expanded freedom to be and do things that they value. Capabilities are not limited to basic education and health care, although they are undoubtedly important not just as values but also in raising the capacity of individuals to increase their income and well-being. Several studies that asked poor people in different countries what they considered to be basic characteristics of poverty found that income mattered, but so too did other aspects of well-being and the quality of life—health, security, self-respect, justice, access to goods and services, family, and social life.

So, for a program for the eradication of poverty, it is necessary to look at a number of indices of well-being or social indicators together, and an approach based on the right to development implies considering improvement in each of the indices through a rights-based approach and as a part of a coordinated program of growth and development. The rights-based approach, where the beneficiaries are empowered to participate in the decision-making and in executing the different schemes, transparently and accountably, and sharing the benefits equitably, is not just an end in itself, realizing the human right to development. Such an approach also improves the outcome of the schemes that increase the value of the different social indicators. The rights-based approach would then also be instrumental to the realization of the right to development.

[*Eds.*—The author concludes with a discussion of the "illustrative elements" of a rights-based development program and of the importance of "economic growth."]

QUESTIONS FOR REFLECTION AND DISCUSSION

1. Sengupta considers development to be a human right. Do you agree? If so, how would you define it? Is it anything more than the achievement of all the economic, social, and cultural rights enumerated in, say, the Universal Declaration of Human Rights (reprinted and referenced in Documentary Appendix A)? If not, why speak of it as a separate human right? If so, what else is it, specifically? What does Sengupta say?

2. Sengupta considers the right to development to be a third generation right. Is it? Is it anything more than a second generation right writ large? What is Sengupta's argument? Do you agree with it? Why? Why not?

3. The UN Commission on Human Rights has described the right to development as the right to the "realization of the potentialities of the human person in harmony with the community," UN Doc. E/CN.4/1334, para. 27 (1979). How does this compare with Sengupta's view?

4. In May 2002, at the World Summit for Sustainable Development in Johannesburg, UN Secretary-General Kofi Annan proposed the WEHAB frameworks for development. These five frameworks for action propose guidelines for sustainable development in respect of water, energy, health, agriculture, and biodiversity (hence "WEHAB"). Do you think that a proper understanding of development necessarily implies sustainability in the five areas listed above? Would you add any others? Is sustainability in these areas compatible with the economic growth that the right to development also encompasses? What does *un*sustainable development look like?

5. The World Bank has articulated several Millennium Development Goals and dozens of subsidiary targets and progress indicators (see http://devdata.worldbank.org/wdi2005) based on the UN's Millennium Declaration of September 8, 2000 (referenced in Documentary Appendix B). The Millennium Declaration, a core UN General Assembly resolution, commits member states to creating a secure and peaceful world conducive to human development. According to the World Bank, "The Millennium Development Goals embody that commitment and set quantified targets for reducing poverty, educating all children, improving the status of women, combating disease and reducing premature deaths, ensuring

12. Sen, *Development as Freedom*, note 3.

environmental sustainability, and establishing an effective partnership between rich countries and developing countries." How does this compare to Sengupta's use of the word "development"? What is meant by "an effective partnership between rich countries and developing countries"? Does it mean anything more than the right to participate in the world economy? If not, is the right to development truly beneficial to those in the "developing" world, whose participation in that economy is often based on radically imbalanced relationships with the world's richer nations and business enterprises?

6. Article 2(3) of the International Covenant on Economic, Social, and Cultural Rights (reprinted and referenced in Documentary Appendix A) states that "Developing countries, with due regard to human rights and their national economy, may determine to what extent they would guarantee the economic rights recognized in the present covenant to non-nationals." Why was this provision included in the Covenant? What are its implications? What is likely to happen as countries become more developed?

7. It has been argued often that it is sometimes necessary to restrict civil and political rights for the sake of development. In *Human Rights and Foreign Policy* (Oxford: Pergamon Press, 1981), 19, the late Evan Luard observed that

> human rights [for poor countries] begin with breakfast. What matters to them is that people should have enough to eat and to house and to clothe their families. The civil and political liberties to which Western countries attach such importance, therefore, are a luxury and an irrelevance which have little meaning for such countries.

Is there any logical or practical foundation for this contention? Should a trade-off be accepted as at least a possible necessity? How does Sengupta address this issue?

8. The United Nations has repeatedly affirmed the interdependence of economic, social, and cultural rights with civil and political rights, as well as the inherent importance of all such rights. Is this claimed interdependence valid? The late Julius Nyerere, former President of Tanzania, has commented: "Freedom and development are as completely linked as chickens and eggs. Without chickens, you get no eggs, and without eggs, you soon have no chickens. . . . Without freedom you get no development; and without development you soon lose your freedom." Julius K. Nyerere, *Freedom and Development* (Dar es Salaam: Oxford University Press, 1973), 60. Is Nyerere's statement helpful? Would Sengupta agree with it? Is it an effective response to Luard in Question 7, above. How? How not?

9. Sengupta asserts that "equity," "fairness," and "the principles of a just society" are basic to the realization of the right to development. When, in particular cases, these individual considerations clash with the needs of the nation as a whole, which should yield? Consider the case of the Pak Moon Dam in rural Thailand. The dam was built to provide electric power, primarily to urban areas, and resulted in the destruction of a way of life for thousands of fishing-dependent villagers both upstream and downstream from the dam. Such projects are often justified with development language; how does this comport with your view of development? With Sengupta's? With the WEHAB framework? With the World Bank's? With Nyerere's?

10. N. J. Udombana proposes that dictatorships are inherently incompatible with development. "The Human Right to Development: Between Rhetoric and Reality," *HRQ* 22 (2002): 753–87. Does democracy actually promote development, or is the former simply a necessary precondition for the latter? Can you imagine a dictatorship in which the human right to development has been fully or substantially realized? What about North Korea? China? Is the right to a particular political process part of the right to development?

11. The King of Bhutan has proposed the notion of Gross National Happiness (GNH) as the "next evolution in indicators for sustainable development," reflecting Bhutan's Buddhist vision on the purpose of human life which puts the individual's self-cultivation at the center of the nation's developmental goals, a primary priority for Bhutanese society as a whole as well as for the individual concerned. See, e.g., *Gross National Happiness: Discussion Papers* (Thimphu, Bhutan: Centre for Bhutan Studies, 1999). Compare the GNH approach with the United Nations Human Development Index, reflected in the UN Human Development Reports (available at http://hdr.undp.org) and which purports to measure quality of life rather than simple economic development. To what extent does the Human Development Index reflect Western prejudices about "the good life"? Does development as Sengupta defines it always correspond with individual happiness? Does it always correspond with the average happiness of all the individuals in a given society?

12. Can developing states realistically take responsibility for their own development in the absence of significant debt relief? In the absence of disarmament by stronger, richer nations? In the absence of stronger global corporate governance? In the absence of democracy?

13. Should former colonial powers bear any special duty toward their former colonies when it comes to the right to development? What might be the rationale for such a duty? What form might such duty take? Would monetary reparations be enough? Technology transfers? Debt forgiveness? Land transfers from members of the former colonial power to the indigenous people? What problems, from a development perspective, are associated with these strategies?

14. What is a *developed* country? What is a *developing* country? Are these terms anything more than euphemisms for "rich" and "poor"? Are not all countries developing countries? Why do we shy from the terms "rich" and "poor"? Does our tendency to do so retard the development of poor countries? Does it retard our understanding and acceptance of the right to development? Is there not a human right not to be poor? See, e.g., Sigrun I. Skogly, "Is There a Right Not to Be Poor?" *Human Rights Law Review* (University of Nottingham) 2 (2002): 59–80.

15. In "World Poverty and Human Rights," *Ethics & International Affairs* (Carnegie Council on Ethics and International Affairs) 19, no. 1 (Spring 2005): 1–7, philosopher Thomas Pogge asserts that affluent countries are "guilty of the largest crime against humanity ever committed, to wit, condemning billions of human beings to life-long severe poverty." Do you agree with Pogge? Why? Why not?

21. LUIS E. RODRIGUEZ-RIVERA *Is the Human Right to Environment Recognized Under International Law?*

For nearly three decades, the international community has aggressively responded to the ever-increasing recognition that environmental problems require a comprehensive international approach. Depletion of the ozone layer, global warming, acid rain, deforestation, desertification, reduction in the world's biodiversity, and export of hazardous wastes all prove the obvious: the environmental problematique does not respect, and is not contained within, national boundaries. In this context, a broad consensus has developed among nations recognizing that global ecological interdependence mandates a coordinated international response to serious environmental problems.

The international community has accepted this challenge proactively by taking steps to protect the quality of the global biosphere and its ecosystems, as well as the quality of its local environments. The main incentive behind this concerted action is apparent—namely, to safeguard the life and health of present and future generations. Thus, the last 30 years have witnessed a proliferation of international instruments specifically addressing global and regional environmental concerns. Over 350 multilateral treaties, 1,000 bilateral treaties, and hundreds of intergovernmental declarations, resolutions, and programs of action addressing a plethora of environmental issues have been adopted during that period.

The substantive, procedural, and institutional norms derived from these international instruments, together with juridical principles found in customary international law, have blossomed into a body of law commonly referred to as international environmental law (IEL).[1] A subpart of general international law, IEL "involves questions

Reprinted with changes from Luiz E. Rodriguez-Rivera, "Is the Human Right to Environment Recognized Under International Law? It Depends on the Source," *Colorado Journal of International Environmental Law and Policy* 12 (2001): 1–45. Reprinted by permission.

1. See, e.g., Philippe Sands, *Principles of International Environmental Law* (Cambridge: Cambridge University Press, 1995), vol. 1; Jonathan C. Carlson, Sir Geoffrey R. W. Palmer, and Burns H. Weston, eds., *International Environmental Law and World Order: A Problem-Oriented Coursebook*, 3rd ed. (St. Paul, Minn.: West Group, 2006).

of sovereignty, jurisdiction, regulation, and state responsibility and liability. It can also involve individuals' responsibility under municipal laws and decisions of national courts."[2] In this complex setting, it has made significant contributions to general international law through innovative approaches such as the effective use of framework or umbrella conventions (whereby environmental standards are provided for with technical specificity in subsequent protocols) and the extensive use of non-binding/soft law documents (in which consensus is reached on matters where global environmental protection conflicts with states' economic and developmental interests).

While the development of IEL has been lauded as a remarkable achievement, the mere application of traditional international principles to environmental problems is insufficient for its further development given the complexity and heterogeneity of the international community.

[*Eds.*—The author next quotes several scholars who have noted that the mere rote application of general principles of traditional international law will not suffice to regulate the complex world of environmental harms with which IEL must concern itself. Those general principles are problematic for several reasons, including but not limited to their lack of remedies, their assumption of simple bilateral relations, problems of proof and causation, and the no-longer-tenable assumption that harms are generated and felt only locally.]

Due to the limitations inherent in the application of general customary international law principles to present global environmental problems, the international community has adopted international regulation as its main approach to addressing environmental protection. This has been accomplished through international cooperation in the face of the growing environmental common interest of humankind.

Despite the impressive corpus of IEL developed during the last three decades, we cannot conclude that its development has resulted in a significant improvement in the quality of the global environment. Among the many reasons for this reality, identified in the literature, is that "There is no effective legal framework to help halt the degradation. . . . There is no institutional machinery to evaluate gaps that may be found in the international framework of agreements or to develop means of assigning priorities among competing claims for attention."[3] Thus, the environmental problematique still represents a serious threat to humankind, and the need to continue expanding current principles and developing new norms to safeguard human life and health persists. It therefore is important to attempt to fill the gaps present in current IEL.

One obvious gap not covered by IEL involves the protection of human life and dignity from threats associated with environmental degradation, especially when such threats result from actions or inactions by an individual's own national government. This is the area of international law where international human rights issues overlap with international and national environmental issues.

CONTENT OF THE HUMAN RIGHT TO ENVIRONMENT

The articulation of a human right to environment encompasses a compendium of rights constructed in an effort to protect the environment, as well as human life and dignity. Three broad categories of rights addressed by scholars in the context of a human right to environment include: right to environment, right of environment, and environmental rights. Each of these categories are inextricably linked to a more expansive articulation of the human right to environment which I propose and to which I refer generally as the expansive right to environment.

RIGHT TO ENVIRONMENT

For the purposes of this essay, I refer to the right to environment as a human right to live in an environment of such a minimum quality as to allow for the realization of a life of dignity and well-being. The right to environment is the substantive component of the expansive right to environment proposed in this essay.

[*Eds.*—The author next acknowledges the difficulty, in a context of scientific uncertainty, of

---

2. Patricia W. Birnie and Alan E. Boyle, *International Law and the Environment* (New York: Oxford University Press, 1992), 9.

3. Geoffrey Palmer, "New Ways to Make International Environmental Law," *AJIL* 86 (1992): 259–83, at 263.

establishing "a precise minimum standard of environmental quality that allows for a life of dignity and well-being" even while accepting that "ambiguity has not been an obstacle in the implementation and enforcement of recognized human rights." Defining the right to environment as "the right to conserve, protect, and improve the current environment" and "as incorporating such economic, social, and cultural rights as the right to a standard of living adequate for health and well-being, the right to the highest attainable standard of mental and physical health, and the right to safe and healthy working conditions" are too vague, he says. He endorses, however, an approach suggested by Dinah Shelton which, he asserts, "overcomes the uncertainty."]

Shelton, borrowing from the strategy used in reference to recognized economic entitlements, observes that individual states take varying measures according to changing economic indicators, needs, and resources when implementing the rights to an adequate standard of living and to social security. For instance, the use of general provisions in framework treaties allows individual states to define and amend the standards to be implemented. In turn, these local standards are drafted in protocols to the applicable framework treaties, and evaluated by the supervising bodies of these treaties. Shelton therefore proposes that

> A similar approach should be utilized to give meaning to a right to environment. Both the threats to humanity and the resulting necessary measures are subject to constant change based on advances in scientific knowledge and models of the environment. Thus, it is impossible for a human rights instrument to specify precisely the products which should not be used or the chemical composition of air which must be maintained. These matters will vary in the same way that the economic situations of communities change. The necessary measures to implement the right to environment will thus be determined by reference to independent environmental findings and regulations capable of rapid amendment. . . . The fact that the right to environment will be implemented in varying ways in response to different threats over time and place does

not undermine the concept of the right, but merely takes into consideration its dynamic character.[4]

Accepting that specific environmental qualitative standards can be derived from vague, ambiguous, and abstract general terms, this essay recognizes that national and international tribunals have historically provided substantive specificity to equally abstract terms found in both local and international legal systems. Of course, in determining the minimum qualitative standards contained in the right to environment, tribunals will have to weigh conflicting visions and values of human life. But this is precisely the role of courts in interpreting and enforcing rights generally, and human rights specifically. Moreover, tribunals are today in a position to effectively articulate the content of the right to environment given "that there presently exists in the public conscience a clear image of an environment which should be preserved and from which each person should benefit."[5]

RIGHT OF ENVIRONMENT

The right of environment is founded upon the notion that the environment possesses rights derived from its own intrinsic value, separate and distinct from human use of the environment. Proponents of the right of environment argue that an anthropocentric approach to the protection of the environment is inherently flawed, and that the best approach to protect the environment is by conferring rights directly upon the environment:

Policy analysts typically operate within a social, political, and intellectual tradition that regards the satisfaction of individual human wants as the only defensible measure of the good, a tradition that perceives the only legitimate task of reason to be that of consistently identifying and then serving individual appetite, preference, or desire. * * * By treating individual human need and desire as the ultimate frame of reference, and by assuming that human goals and ends must be taken as externally "given" . . . rather than generated by reason, environmental policy makes a value judgment of enormous significance. And, once that judgment has been

---

4. Dinah Shelton, "Human Rights, Environmental Rights, and the Right to Environment," *Stanford Journal of International Law* 28 (1991): 103–38, at 136–37.
5. Alexandre Kiss and Dinah Shelton, *International Environmental Law* (Ardsley, N.Y.: Transnational Publishers, 1991), 24.

made, any claim for the continued existence of threatened wilderness areas or endangered species must rest on the identification of human wants and needs which would be jeopardized by a disputed development. As our capacity increases to satisfy those needs and wants artificially, the claim becomes tenuous indeed.[6]

Taken textually, the right to environment (in its narrow/anthropocentric formulation) and the right of environment are incompatible concepts. However, legal scholars have proposed that a human right to environment may be so constructed as to recognize the intrinsic value of the environment. Alexandre Kiss and Dinah Shelton propounded that:

> The intrinsic value of the biosphere is not rejected but is integrated with a recognition that man makes up part of the universe and cannot exist without conservation of the biosphere and the ecosystems which comprise it. In this perspective all sectors of the environment have a value not only in their short-term utility to humans . . . , but also as indispensable elements of an interrelated system which must be protected to ensure human survival. While this ultimate aim of human survival remains anthropocentric, humans are not viewed as apart from or above the natural universe, but as an interlinked and interdependent part of it. It follows that because all parts of the natural web are linked, they must each be protected and conserved. It is in this sense that "intrinsic value" may be understood.[7]

Thus, the right of environment, or at least the emphasis it places on the intrinsic value of the environment, can be interpreted as a fundamental element in the expansive right to environment. The expansive right to environment links human rights (with its inherently anthropocentric emphasis) with the right of environment (with its emphasis on the environment's intrinsic value).

ENVIRONMENTAL RIGHTS

Environmental rights encapsulate the procedural human rights necessary for the implementation of the substantive rights that are part of the expansive right to environment and include access to environmental information, participation in the decision-making process of environmental policies, availability of legal remedies to redress environmental harm, and due process rights in general. The legal community has been much more willing to recognize the existence of environmental rights in the international legal order than that of its substantive counterpart because the former are based on established civil and political human rights. The expansive right to environment links procedural and substantive human rights.

In sum, the expansive right to environment includes: qualitative environmental standards intrinsic value of the environment, and procedural guarantees. It is to this expansive formulation of the human right to environment that I refer when evaluating the existence of a new or emerging human right to environment (hereinafter also expansive right to environment).

CONSTRUCTION OF THE HUMAN RIGHT TO ENVIRONMENT: AN OVERVIEW OF ITS SOURCES

Three main strategies have been formulated by legal scholars in constructing a human rights approach to environmental protection: (a) the reinterpretation or expansion of existing human rights to include environmental protection; (b) the emergence of a right to environment within the context of a third generation of rights or solidarity rights; and (c) the development of an expansive right to environment or, in the alternative, of environmental rights (procedural guarantees). Before evaluating each of these strategies, it is appropriate to expound on the international document that triggered the discussion of a human rights approach to environmental protection: the 1972 Stockholm Declaration on the Human Environment.[8]

The Stockholm Declaration was the first international instrument to incorporate a human rights approach to environmental protection. Principle 1 proclaims: "Man [sic] has the fundamental right to freedom, equality and adequate conditions of life, in an environment of a quality that permits a life of dignity and well-being,

---

6. Laurence H. Tribe, "Ways Not to Think About Plastic Trees: New Foundations for Environmental Law," *Yale Law Journal* 83 (1974): 1315–48, at 1325–26.
7. Kiss and Shelton, *International Environmental Law*, note 5, at 11.
8. Adopted June 16, 1972, referenced in Documentary Appendix B.

and he bears a solemn responsibility to protect and improve the environment for present and future generations." The Declaration's Preamble states: "Both aspects of man's environment, the natural and the man-made, are essential to his well-being and to the enjoyment of basic human rights—even the right to life itself." Additionally, the works of the Preparatory Committee of the United Nations Conference on the Human Environment reveal that the draft of the Stockholm Declaration "was based on the recognition of the rights of individuals to an adequate environment."[9] Nonetheless, there is wide consensus that the Declaration fell short of establishing the existence of a human right to environment.

Thus, since the Declaration, legal scholars have grappled with the concept of treating environmental protection within the human rights framework. This essay analyzes, in chronological order, the three strategies formulated by legal scholars to construct a human rights approach to environmental protection, with special attention to the sources used in constructing the same.

THE RE-INTERPRETATION AND EXPANSION OF EXISTING HUMAN RIGHTS

The approach of re-interpreting and expanding existing human rights to incorporate environmental protection finds its foundation in a narrow reading of the Stockholm Declaration. The reasoning behind this strategy is that an adequate measure of environmental protection can be obtained by the reformulation of existing human rights, thus taking advantage of existing international and regional monitoring and enforcement mechanisms.

Both civil and political rights, and economic, social, and cultural rights include rights which could be reformulated to include environmental protection. The civil and political rights which may be expanded include: the right to life; the right against cruel, inhuman, or degrading treatment; the right to liberty and security of person; the right to privacy; the right to freedom of thought, conscience, and religion; the right to freedom of expression; the right to peaceful assembly; the right of the child; the right against discrimination and to the equal protection of the law; cultural and indigenous rights; the right to political participation; the right to information; and the right to legal redress. In turn, the following economic, social, and cultural rights may be expanded to incorporate environmental protection: the right to safe and healthy working conditions; the right to an adequate standard of living and the continued improvement of living conditions; the right to food; the right to highest attainable standard of physical and mental health; the right to improvement of all aspects of environmental and industrial hygiene; the right to education; the right to enjoy benefits of scientific progress; and the right to participate in cultural life. Although the above human rights are recognized with reference to the inherited international legal order, "existing rights must be reinterpreted with imagination and rigor in the context of environmental concerns which were not prevalent at the time existing rights were first formulated."[10]

The expansion of the right to life, for example, has been proposed as including the traditional protection against intentional or arbitrary deprivation of life, as well as an obligation on the part of states to ensure that every individual within its boundaries has access to the means of survival. This expansive conception of the right to life would protect individuals from all possible threats, including environmental threats. However, as former Deputy High Commissioner for Human Rights B. G. Ramcharan has indicated, the environmental protection afforded under this expansive formulation would extend only to those "environmental hazards which involve direct risks of immediate loss of life if the hazard is not removed."[11]

Given the scientific uncertainty surrounding environmental problems, such a reformulation of the right to life would add little toward resolving the environmental problematique from a human rights perspective. The same limitations

9. Preparatory Committee for the United Nations Conference on the Human Environment, UN Doc. A/Conf.48/PC/17 (1972), para. 77.
10. Michael R. Anderson, "Human Rights Approaches to Environmental Protection: An Overview," in Alan E. Boyle and Michael Anderson, eds., *Human Rights Approaches to Environmental Protection* (Oxford: Clarendon Press, 1996).
11. B. G. Ramcharan, "The Concept and Dimension of the Right to Life," in B. G. Ramcharan, *The Right to Life in International Law* (The Hague: Nijhoff, 1985), 13.

would exist if the right to health, for example, were reformulated to extend only to situations where direct risks to health were present. The evidentiary standard in both cases would be too high for individuals, or communities, to prove that a particular right was violated or threatened by a particular environmental threat. It is worth noting that courts in India, Pakistan, and several Latin American countries have expanded the rights to life and health afforded under their national constitutions to incorporate a right to a safe environment. Hence, it is conceptually possible that air, water, and soil pollution could be effectively tackled through this human rights approach to environmental protection. However, it seems unlikely that even the most expansive reformulation of international human rights would suffice to address such global environmental problems as climate change, threats to biodiversity, and protection of the environment based on its own intrinsic value.

EMERGENCE OF THE RIGHT TO ENVIRONMENT AS A SOLIDARITY RIGHT

The concept of solidarity rights or a third generation of rights, first articulated in 1979, is characterized as individual and collective rights or aspirations that require for their realization cooperation or solidarity from the individual, the state, public and private bodies, and the international community.[12] The following six areas were proposed as emerging solidarity rights: "environment, development, peace, the common heritage, communication, and humanitarian assistance."[13]

Regarding the right to environment, Stephen Marks identified it as the most "classical" case for a solidarity right because all the features of a third-generation right were present—namely, the "elaboration of a specialized body of law, an easily identifiable international legislative process, incorporation of the right as a human right within municipal legal systems, and need for concerted efforts of all social actors."[14] The content of the right to environment under the solidarity rights approach is two-fold: first, an individual

right for the victim of an environmental harm or threat to enjoin and obtain reparation for the harmful or threatening activity; and second, a collective right obligating the state to resolve environmental problems through international cooperation. The sources of the solidarity right to environment, as identified by Marks, include the Stockholm Declaration, subsequent (albeit unsuccessful or non-binding) attempts to obtain international recognition of the right to environment, the development and growth of IEL, acceptance by states of the right to environment as reflected in the express adoption of the same in state constitutions, and the conclusions of numerous scientific and nongovernmental meetings on the subject.

[*Eds.*—The author next notes that "traditionalist legal scholars" have rejected the generations approach to human rights, but argues that the third generation approach has served, at the very least, to "liberate" the human right to environment from a formerly static traditionalist framework.]

DEVELOPMENT OF THE RIGHT TO ENVIRONMENT

The expansive right to environment (which incorporates the substantive right to environment, the intrinsic value of the environment, and procedural environmental rights) derives explicitly and implicitly from numerous international, regional, and national legal instruments. This discussion identifies the sources most frequently referred to by legal scholars.

First, several international human rights instruments implicitly support the expansive right to environment. The Universal Declaration of Human Rights (UDHR) contains several applicable rights and entitlements: article 3 (right to life, liberty, and security of the person); article 22 (entitlement to the realization of the economic, social, and cultural rights indispensable for dignity and the free development of personality); article 24 (right to rest and leisure); article 25 (right to standard of living adequate for health and well-being, including food and housing);

12. For brief exposition of solidarity or third generation rights, see Reading 1 by Burns Weston in Chapter 1 of this volume. For extended treatment, see Stephen P. Marks, "Emerging Human Rights: A New Generation for the 1980s?" *Rutgers Law Review* 33 (1981): 435–52.
13. Marks, "Emerging Human Rights," note 12, at 441.
14. Ibid., 442–43.

and article 28 (entitlement to social and international order in which human rights can be fully realized). The International Covenant on Economic, Social and Cultural Rights (ICESCR), in articles 1 (right to self-determination and right to freely dispose of natural wealth and resources), 7 (right to decent living, safe and healthy working conditions, and rest and leisure), 11 (right to adequate standard of living, including food and housing, and to the continuous improvement of living conditions), 12 (right to health, including to improvement of all aspects of environmental and industrial hygiene), and 15 (right to cultural life and to benefits of scientific progress and its applications), contains implicit support for the right to environment. The International Covenant on Civil and Political Rights (ICCPR) also supports implicitly the right to environment in: article 1 (right to self-determination and right to freely dispose of natural wealth and resources); article 6 (right to life); article 7 (protection from cruel, inhuman, or degrading treatment); article 17 (right to privacy); and article 20 (prohibition of propaganda for war).[15] Of course, international instruments covering specific environmental problems, as well as human rights which are linked to environmental protection, also can be interpreted as implicitly supporting the expansive human right to environment.[16]

The UN General Assembly has not expressly recognized a human right to environment, but it has emphasized on several occasions the link between environmental protection and the realization of human rights. In 1990, it explicitly recognized "that all individuals are entitled to live in an environment adequate for their health and well-being."[17] That same year, the UN Commission on Human Rights reiterated the link between the preservation of the environment and the promotion of human rights, and welcomed the decision made by the Sub-Commission on Prevention of Discrimination and Protection of Minorities (hereinafter Sub-Commission)[18] to study the problems of the environment and their relation to the realization of human rights.

[*Eds.*—The author goes on to report that the Sub-Commission ultimately issued a Final Report (the Ksentini Final Report)[19] and a Draft Declaration of Principles,[20] both of which recognized the right to environment.]

More recently, UNESCO and the United Nations High Commissioner for Human Rights organized the International Seminar of Experts on the Right to the Environment, which on February 12, 1999, issued the Bizkaia Declaration on the Right to the Environment.[21] Article 1 of the Bizkaia Declaration states that "[e]veryone has the right, individually or in association with others, to enjoy a healthy and ecologically balanced environment . . . [which] may be exercised before public bodies and private entities, whatever their legal status under national and international law."

Two regional instruments also expressly recognize a human right to environmental protection. Article 24 of the African Charter on Human and Peoples' Rights[22] declares that "all peoples shall have the right to a generally satisfactory environment favourable to their development."

---

15. The UDHR (Dec. 10, 1948), ICESCR (Dec. 16, 1966), and ICCPR (Dec. 16, 1966) are reprinted and referenced in Documentary Appendix A.
16. For an in-depth analysis of international human rights and IEL instruments which implicitly support the right to environment, see Final Report Prepared by Mrs. Fatma Zohra Ksentini, Special Rapporteur, UN ESCOR Commission on Human Rights, Sub-Commission on Prevention of Discrimination and Protection of Minorities, 46th Sess., UN Doc E/CN.4/Sub.2/1994/9 (1994), at 238 [hereinafter Ksentini Final Report]; Sierra Club Legal Defense Fund, "Human Rights and the Environment: The Legal Basis for a Human Right to Environment," *Report to the United Nations Sub-Commission on the Prevention of Discrimination and the Protection of Minorities* (April 1992).
17. Adopted Dec. 14, 1990, referenced in Documentary Appendix B.
18. The Sub-Commission is now known as the Sub-Commission on the Promotion and Protection of Human Rights.
19. See note 16.
20. Draft Declaration of Principles on Human Rights and the Environment, in Ksentini Final Report, note 16, Annex I (hereinafter Draft Declaration). For an in-depth analysis of the Draft Declaration, see Neil A.F. Popovic, "In Pursuit of Environmental Human Rights: Commentary on the Draft Declaration of Principles on Human Rights and the Environment," *Columbia Human Rights Law Review* 27 (1996): 487–603.
21. UNESCO Declaration of Bizkaia, Referenced in Documentary Appendix B.
22. Concluded June 27, 1981, referenced in Documentary Appendix B.

The 1988 San Salvador Protocol,[23] article 11, states: "Everyone shall have the right to live in a healthy environment. . . . The States Parties shall promote the protection, preservation and improvement of the environment." The European Union has not recognized expressly a human right to environment; however, "[p]rovisions of EC secondary legislation do . . . give rise to rights of information, participation and legal remedies regarding the environment"[24] (previously referred to as procedural environmental rights). Moreover, in *Lopez Ostra v. Spain*,[25] the European Court of Human Rights afforded a remedy for an environmental cause of action, albeit under article 8 of the European Convention for the Protection of Human Rights and Fundamental Freedoms (right to respect for private and family life and home).[26]

Numerous international and regional environmental law instruments also indirectly support the proposition that the expansive right to environment is an existing international human right.[27] At a minimum, the vast body of international and regional environmental law instruments complement the expansive right to environment by providing procedural and institutional mechanisms (environmental rights) to implement the substantive right to environment and by incorporating to it the intrinsic value of the environment (right of environment). However, it is more appropriate to view the proliferation of international and regional environmental law instruments as flowing directly from the existence of the expansive right to environment; these instruments reflect the expansion of the human right to environment. This is evidenced by the international community's overwhelming commitment to safeguard the same in both its individual and collective construction.

The national recognition of the expansive right to environment further reflects its existence. The Ksentini Final Report elaborates on this issue by pointing to the fact that over sixty national constitutions have incorporated specific provisions relating to the environment, and many more states have developed national legislation to ensure the realization of the human right to environment. Moreover, the proliferation of IEL instruments during the last three decades must be explained by something more than a mere assertion that state participation in this process has been motivated by economic or political self-interest. Most IEL instruments do not offer states obvious economic or political gains. On the contrary, most of these instruments impose economic and political liabilities, which are the inevitable trade-offs associated with global environmental protection. States are not in the practice of entering into international legal instruments that limit their sovereignty in the absence of recognized legal or moral duties to do so. Therefore, the exponential growth of IEL instruments, in and of itself, evinces the existence of the expansive right to environment.

A second category of sources often used to substantiate the existence of the expansive right to environment is the philosophical or moral claim for a secure, healthy, and ecologically balanced environment. Although moral duties, by themselves, do not create international legal obligations, "they are today the driving force behind the emergence of new principles of international law."[28] The value of human rights is not derived merely from the duties and obligations imposed on states through their recognition in international law, but from the moral principles and ideals which human rights embody: care and compassion in dealing with other human beings, their dignity, and their interests; respect for persons as persons; recognition of the destructive qualities of pain, suffering, and deprivation; and a concern for individuality, autonomy, and the development of a person's fruitful potentialities. The moral claim behind the human right to

---

23. Additional Protocol to the American Convention on Human Rights in the Area of Economic, Social and Cultural Rights (Nov. 17, 1988), referenced in Documentary Appendix B.

24. Sionaidh Douglas-Scott, "Environmental Rights in the European Union—Participatory Democracy or Democratic Deficit?" in Boyle and Anderson, eds., *Human Rights Approaches*, note 10, 109–28, at 109.

25. 20 Eur. Ct. H.R. (Ser. A) at 277 (1994).

26. Concluded Nov. 4, 1950, referenced in Documentary Appendix B.

27. Since hundreds of international and regional environmental legal instruments can be interpreted to support indirectly the existence of the right to environment, they are not listed here. For a compilation of such documents, see Patricia W. Birnie and Alan E. Boyle, eds., *Basic Documents on International Law and the Environment* (Oxford: Clarendon Press, 1995). See also Weston and Carlson, vols. 3, 5.

28. Roland Y. Rich, "The Right to Development as an Emerging Human Right," *VJIL* 23 (1983): 287–328, at 289. See also Reading 20 by Arjun Sengupta in this chapter.

environment is both logical (supported by reason) and essential (driven by human necessity).

The strategic importance of recognizing the expansive right to environment as an existing human right can be best understood in the context of the "trumping" effect of rights in our society.[29] An example of the application of this "trumping" effect in the context of the expansive right to environment is as follows:

> Although rights are a part and not the whole of morality, having rights is significant in at least two ways. First, if I can show that I have a moral right to, say, a clean environment I have something which has to be taken into account in any discussion of the moral aspects of environmental policy. I am, so to speak, a player in the morality game. Secondly, and perhaps more important, such is the value that attaches to rights that if I am a rights-holder I am not just a player, but a serious, indeed a privileged player in the game. That is to say my right will tend to pre-empt not only preferences and other non-moral considerations, but other moral considerations as well. What is true of moral rights is true *a fortiori* of legal rights. Thus having environmental rights, for example, incorporated in a constitution or recognized in international law cannot guarantee that the putative rights-holder will be successful in every dispute in which the right may be relevant, but certainly creates a situation in which not only must the right always be considered, but very good reasons will be needed for denying it effect.[30]

Thus, when the expansive right to environment is used as a "trump" card, "[t]he effect is to demand a response rather than a silence and a response which must be formulated in a way which takes account of the content of the right."[31]

In practical terms, an expansive right to environment provides individuals and communities with judicial remedies and processes through which they may seek redress when their governments do not provide such judicial forums or access thereto. "An environmental right may serve as the ultimate 'safety net' to catch legitimate claims which have fallen through the

procedural cracks of public and private law."[32] Moreover, the recognition of a human right to environment may result in increased political activism at the grass-roots level, an essential element for the effective enforcement of international human rights.

However, the fundamental question is whether the moral or philosophical claim to an expansive right to environment is presently just a general social value or whether it has achieved the status of a recognized legal principle under international law. This question must be asked in light of the legal and moral sources discussed in this section.

[*Eds.*—The author next observes that there has been widespread resistance among "traditionalist legal scholars" to the very existence of a right to environment, even narrowly defined. These objections, he notes, have been founded in large part on what he considers a too-narrow definition of the acceptable sources of international law; this is one facet, the author contends, of a detached formalism that has resulted all too often in the failure of Western scholars to take seriously emerging human rights norms. The author further argues that the formalists' contention that the right to environment will distract attention from other, more productive methods of protecting the environment, is simply untrue. All avenues, the author forcefully contends, *must* be pursued if global environmental problems are to be solved. Finally, the author notes that the formalists' strongest objection is that the right to environment's proponents have not yet produced sufficient evidence from acceptable sources that the right exists.]

THE HUMAN RIGHTS/ENVIRONMENTAL PROTECTION/SOURCES DOCTRINE CONUNDRUM: A PROBLEM AT THE HEART OF MODERN INTERNATIONAL LAW

The formal sources of international law are understood as those that are outlined in Article

---

29. See Ronald Dworkin, *Taking Rights Seriously* (London: Duckworth, 1977).
30. J. G. Merrills, "Environmental Protection and Human Rights: Conceptual Aspects," in Boyle and Anderson, eds., *Human Rights Approaches*, note 10, 25–41, at 26–27.
31. Wade Mansell and Joanne Scott, "Why Bother About a Right to Development?" *Journal of Law and Society* 21 (1994): 171–92, at 179.
32. Michael R. Anderson, "Human Rights Approaches to Environmental Protection: An Overview," in Boyle and Anderson, eds., *Human Rights Approaches*, note 10, at 21–22.

38(1) of the Statute of the International Court of Justice:[33]

    (a) international conventions, whether general or particular, establishing rules expressly recognized by the contesting States;

    (b) international custom, as evidence of a general practice accepted as law;

    (c) the general principles of law recognized by civilised nations; [and]

    (d) . . . judicial decisions and the teachings of the most highly qualified publicists of the various nations, as subsidiary means for the determination of the rules of law.

This traditional enumeration of sources corresponds to what we have referred to alternatively as a positivist, neo-positivist, or statist (collectively, "traditionalist") approach to the construction of international law. Under the traditionalist approach, "[i]nternational law is about the real policies and commitments of governments, it is not about the incantations of secular or religious morality."[34] In turn, the states' consent or commitments are evidenced through the traditional sources of international law.

Traditionalists hesitate to add other sources to the traditional list; instead, they evaluate whether the proposed new sources (e.g., acts of international institutions) fit within the classic forms. However, this attitude is inconsistent with the evolution of modern international law, and does not reflect the activities that contribute to the development of new norms, such as those derived from acts of international institutions. More importantly, the traditionalist approach to the sources doctrine of international law has the effect of curtailing *a priori* the recognition of new human rights. Thus, when discussing the existence of the expansive right to environment, I propose two questions: (1) what are the sources of international human rights; and (2) in light of the evolution of modern international law, which non-traditional sources, if any, should be considered in assessing the development of previously unrecognized human rights?

SOURCES OF INTERNATIONAL HUMAN RIGHTS

Commentators generally consider the rights contained in the UDHR, the ICCPR, and the ICESCR as authoritative enunciations of the human rights recognized under traditional international law because they possess the consent of the international community. But is this a finite list of rights or may the list be expanded? The answer, of course, "depends upon one's perception of what constitutes a human right."[35] Although there are no objections to the category of human rights within international law, no general agreement exists as to the nature, definition, sources, or basic moral principles on which human rights rest.[36]

Traditionalist legal scholars are of the view that human rights "must take into account the matrices of customary or general international law." Therefore, the human rights complainant must establish that the matter disputed is subject to international law and not within the state's area of discretion or sovereignty. When commentators recognize a human rights claim, state sovereignty on that matter yields to international law. But, once again, what is a human right?

Maurice Cranston defined a human right as "a universal moral right, something which all men [sic] everywhere, at all times ought to have, something of which no one may be deprived without a grave affront to justice, something which is owing to every human being simply because he [sic] is human."[37] Since human rights flow directly from the integrity and dignity of the human being, "[t]hey are thus rights that cannot be given or withdrawn at will by any

---

33. Concluded June 26, 1945, 33 UNTS 993, reprinted in Weston and Carlson, 1: I.H.2.

34. Ian Brownlie, "The Rights of Peoples in Modern International Law," in James Crawford, ed., *The Rights of Peoples* (Oxford: Clarendon Press, 1992), 1–16, at 15.

35. Rosalyn Higgins, *Problems and Process: International Law and How We Use It* (Oxford: Clarendon Press, 1994), 104.

36. See Eugene Kamenka, "Human Rights, Peoples' Rights," in Crawford, ed., *The Rights of Peoples*, note 34, 127–39, at 137; also James Crawford, "The Rights of Peoples: Some Conclusions," 159–75, at 162. But see the other readings in this volume, especially Reading 1 by Burns Weston in Chapter 1. See also Burns H. Weston and Mark B. Teerink, "Rethinking Child Labor: A Multidimensional Human Rights Problem," in Burns H. Weston, ed., *Child Labor and Human Rights: Making Children Matter* (Boulder, Colo.: Lynne Rienner, 2005), ch. 1.

37. Maurice Cranston, *What Are Human Rights?* (London: Bodley Head, 1973), 36. See also Reading 1 by Burns Weston in Chapter 1 in this volume.

domestic legal system."[38] In light of the universality of human rights, the traditionalists' emphasis on state consent in discussing human rights
is misplaced. The source of human rights is not
the will of states, but the will of humanity. This
reality still leaves the problem of how to establish the will of the people. Clearly, one method
is the traditionalists' consensual approach. However, other methods, such as the international
response to a specific human right claim, may
also be effective indicators of the people's will.
Of course, the non-classical or non-traditional
sources are more difficult to prove, but such is
the nature of the sources of human rights.

EXPANSION OF SOURCES DOCTRINE IN MODERN
INTERNATIONAL LAW: THE DEBATE

Traditionalist sources rhetoric divides sources
into two general categories: hard law and soft
law. Hard law is understood as representing
states' consent, thus the international community considers it more persuasive. Commentators see soft law, such as resolutions, declarations,
principles, and other international and regional
instruments, as relying on an extra-consensual
notion of justice, thus making it less persuasive.
However, as David Kennedy has recognized,
"there is no *a priori* reason to divide either the
'sources' of law or persuasive reasons for compliance into these two categories."[39]

Regardless of the normativity objection to the
international recognition of soft law principles,
the role of international organizations and of
non-governmental organizations has gained
importance in the formulation of international
norms. Further, it is undeniable that soft law
instruments have become [a] preferred legislative approach in the international community,
particularly in the field of human rights. The
factors that explain the exponential growth of
soft law instruments in modern international law
must be considered.

The attractiveness of soft law instruments
stems from the flexibility they provide. The form
of these instruments is not the important element; what is important is "the manner in which

the obligations, if any, created by them are expressed."[40] Soft law instruments are generally
produced by lengthy, and often controversial,
negotiations. The fact that states are careful in
the drafting of soft law documents is evidence
that these "are perceived to have political consequences of a serious sort."[41] States may continue to defend their actions under the doctrine
of sovereignty, but it is clear by the proliferation
of soft law documents that states understand
that mutual interdependence in the world order
necessitates cooperation. Global cooperation, in
turn, requires the narrowing of the sovereignty
doctrine.

In assessing the importance of soft law instruments in modern international law, Sir Geoffrey
Palmer has noted that, since formal rules tend
to lag behind the contemporary reality, law-
making methods should recognize this new reality.[42] Christine Chinkin writes:

> The international legal order is an evolving
> one that requires a wide range of modalities
> for change and development, especially into
> new subject areas . . .. Labelling these instru-
> ments as law or non-law disguises the reality
> that both play a major role in the devel-
> opment of international law and both are
> needed for the regulation of States' activities
> and for the creation of expectations. Soft law
> instruments allow for the incorporation of
> conflicting standards and goals and provide
> States with the room to manoeuvre in the
> making of claims and counterclaims.[43]

She concludes: "While this process inevitably
causes normative confusion and uncertainty in
terms of the traditional sources of international
law, it is probably the inevitable consequence of
unresolved pressures for change in international
law."[44]

More recently, Edith Brown Weiss has propounded a new approach to the sources doctrine conundrum: "The common assumption is
that countries comply much better and more
fully with binding international agreements
than with nonbinding legal instruments. Experience suggests an alternative hypothesis: that

38. Higgins, *Problems and Process*, note 35, at 96.
39. David Kennedy, *International Legal Structures* (Baden-Baden: Nomos, 1987), 99.
40. Palmer, "New Ways to Make International Environmental Law," note 3, at 269.
41. Ibid., 270.
42. Ibid., 271.
43. Christine M. Chinkin, "The Challenge of Soft Law: Development and Change in International Law,"
ICLQ 38 (1989): 850–66, at 866.
44. Ibid.

countries under some circumstances may comply with legally nonbinding instruments as well as they do with binding ones."[45] Under this new approach, the determinative factor is the degree to which international actors comply with soft law instruments. This new approach stems from a realization that "[t]he emerging international system consists of networks of states, international organizations, non-state actors and millions of individuals."[46]

Thus, it is necessary to recognize that some non-binding legal instruments are indeed sources of international norms. Several scholars suggest frameworks in which to apply this new approach to the sources doctrine. They argue that a majority of international actors comply with a significant number of non-binding or soft law instruments in several modern international law subject areas. In the context of international economic law, Joseph Gold has written, "the essential ingredient of soft law is an expectation that the states accepting these instruments will take their content seriously and will give them some measure of respect."[47]

To expect new international norms to derive exclusively from binding or hard law instruments is, in effect, to oversimplify the dynamics of modern international law. An expansion or a redefinition of the sources of international norms is required to conform with the evolution of modern international law. This expansion mandates a re-evaluation of the persuasive weight to be afforded to soft law evidence as sources of international human rights, particularly of the expansive right to environment.

CONCLUSION: IS THERE AN EXISTING HUMAN RIGHT TO ENVIRONMENT? IT DEPENDS ON THE SOURCE

As discussed, the strongest argument against the existence of the expansive right to environ-

ment is the evidentiary objection that the human right to environment "has not found express affirmation in any binding or effective international legal instrument."[48] This objection is based on a traditionalist approach to the sources of international norms. It rejects as unpersuasive the accumulation of soft law instruments that directly or indirectly support the expansive right to environment. However, there are many instruments that serve as sources for the recognition of the human right to environment in the international legal order, including: thousands of international environmental soft law instruments; many national constitutions and legislative acts; dozens of international, regional, and national court decisions; the hundreds of non-governmental international organizations; thousands of local or "grass-roots level" community organizations, and, more importantly, the overwhelming and sweeping transformation in the valoration of environmental concerns in all levels of society. To ignore this voluminous evidence of the will of the people would be to ignore the evolution of international law during the last half-century. The fields of international human rights law and IEL have been the two areas of modern international law that have experienced the most prolific growth during the last thirty years. Are we to ignore this fact? Traditionalists must accept the challenge made by Prott regarding the elaboration of new rights: "If we really care for the texture of international law and its intellectual integrity, we should do something solid about the practical problems that are encouraging its distortion, and not simply spend our time lamenting it."[49]

Soft law instruments are necessary in the development of IEL given the technical complexities and the conflicting values involved in addressing global environmental problems. But the response to the question of whether the human right to environment is recognized under

---

45. Edith Brown Weiss, "Introduction," in Edith Brown Weiss, ed., *International Compliance with Nonbinding Accords* (Washington, D.C.: American Society of International Law, 1997), 1.
46. Ibid., 2.
47. Joseph Gold, "Strengthening the Soft International Law of Exchange Arrangements," *AJIL* 77 (1983): 443–89, at 443. Gold adds: "Certain other elements are postulated. First, a common intent is implicit in the soft law as formulated, and it is this common intent, when elucidated, that is to be respected. Second, the legitimacy of the soft law as promulgated is not challenged. Third, soft law is not deprived of its quality as law because failure to observe it is not in itself a breach of obligation. Fourth, conduct that respects soft law cannot be deemed invalid."
48. Gunter Handl, "Human Rights and Protection of the Environment: A Mildly 'Revisionist' View," in Antônio Augusto Cançado Trindade et al., eds., *Derechos humanos, desarrollo sustentable y medio ambiente /*

international law is: It depends! If the sources of international law are expanded to conform to the evolution of modern international law, thus recognizing that the will of the people may be evidenced persuasively through sources other than the classical sources propounded by traditionalist legal scholars, then the response is a definite yes. But, if the international legal community persists in restricting the evolution of the sources doctrine, then the response is "not yet."

QUESTIONS FOR REFLECTION AND DISCUSSION

1. Does a human right to environment—i.e., a *good* environment—exist? On the basis of what sources does Rodriguez-Rivera suggest that it does exist? Treaties? Customary international law? Other? Do you agree with him? Why? Why not? Is there agreement about the source or sources of the claimed right?

2. After reading Rodriguez-Rivera's essay, do you think you could determine whether, in a given factual situation, the human right to a good environment was fulfilled or abrogated? Consider, as one example, the case of the people living in and around Bhopal, India, site of the well-known and tragic leak of the poison gas methyl isocyanate in 1984. The leak has resulted in more than 20,000 deaths and has afflicted over 100,000 people with health ailments of various sorts. In 1999, nearby municipal water supplies were found to contain dangerously elevated levels of, among other things, mercury. What, if anything, does the human right to environment Rodriguez-Rivera advocates add to the vindication of the human rights of those who live near Bhopal? Would other human rights, if adequately enforced, provide sufficient protection, or does Rodriguez-Rivera's "expansive right to environment" provide more?

3. It has often been pointed out that the right to a good environment can be protected through national constitutions and laws. What advantage is there, if any in basing the right to a good environment in international human rights law in contrast to domestic law? How does Rodriguez-Rivera answer this question?

4. Assuming the human right to a good environment exists, should it and laws drawn up to implement it aim to protect the environment itself or to protect humans from environmental degradation? What does Rodriguez-Rivera think? Is there a substantive difference in outcome depending on which approach is chosen? Which approach has the United States government taken (in particular the U.S. Environmental Protection Agency)?

5. Again assuming the human right to a good environment exists, who are its rights-holders? Who are its duty-bearers? Is it, like the right to development and the right to peace, a third-generation collective or solidarity right? Or is it simply an individual right?

6. In *In Fairness to Future Generations: International Law, Common Patrimony, and Intergenerational Equity* (Dobbs Ferry, N.Y.: Transnational Publishers, 1988), 95–117, author Edith Brown Weiss has argued that "Enforcement of planetary rights is appropriately done by a guardian or representative of future generations as a group, not of future individuals, who are of necessity indeterminate." Do you think the right to environment is such a planetary right? Why? Why not? What are the practical consequences of deciding that a human right is held by a group rather than by individuals? Which type of right is easier to enforce? To get states to recognize?

7. On final analysis, irrespective of future generations, is the human right to a good environment a justiciable right or merely an aspirational one? Either way, what evidence substantiates your viewpoint?

8. Can you think of situations in which the right to a good environment might clash with other rights (e.g., the right to development, the right to a decent standard of living, the right to food and water)? If so, which should carry the day? Can you think of situations in which the right to a good environment actually has clashed with other rights? If so, which did carry the day? Do you think it is possible to construct a world order such that inter-right conflicts would never arise? How? What systemic changes would be required? What changes to individual behavior?

Human Rights, Sustainable Development and Environment, 2nd ed. (San José: Instituto Interamericano de Derechos Humanos: Banco Interamericano de Desarrollo, 1995), 117–42, at 122.
49. Lyndel V. Prott, "Cultural Rights as Peoples' Rights in International Law," in Crawford, ed., *The Rights of Peoples*, note 34, 93–106, at 106.

9. The United States has a notoriously complex, comprehensive legal regime governing human interactions with the environment. The Endangered Species Act (16 U.S.C. § 460 et seq.), the Clean Water Act (33 U.S.C. § 1251 et seq.), the Clean Air Act (42 U.S.C. § 7401 et seq.), the Comprehensive Environmental Response, Compensation, and Liability Act (42 U.S.C. § 9601 et seq.), and the Resource Conservation and Recovery Act (42 U.S.C. § 6901 et seq.) combine with other federal and state statutory and regulatory schemes to provide a range of protections for the environment itself, and for the human needs directly impacted by environmental quality. Unfortunately, the complexity of the environmental regulatory environment has resulted, some say, in the abrogation of the very rights it is designed to protect. At the very least, it is clear that its complexity renders it less useful than it might be for those whose health and well-being are most commonly impacted negatively by environmental problems of all sorts. How might environmental laws be made both more simple and effective? Would the widespread recognition of a human right to a good environment help in this regard? How? How not?

10. The United States is not a party to the December 10,1997, Kyoto Protocol to the United Nations Framework Convention on Climate Change (FCCC/CP/1997/7/Add.1, reprinted in *ILM* 37 (1998): 32 and Weston and Carlson 5: V.E.20d), which commits states parties to reducing their emissions of the gases known to contribute to global warming (carbon dioxide, methane, nitrous oxide, hydrofluorocarbons, perfluorocarbons, and carbon hexafluoride). The United States is responsible, according to the U.S. Environmental Protection Agency, for about 24 percent of the global total emissions of such gasses. Should the states parties to the UNFCCC and the Kyoto Protocol have a legal recourse against the United States if, due to its continued emissions, the global climate changes in ways that adversely impact people in those states? What form should that recourse take?

11. Many have observed that the gravest threat to the natural environment is nuclear war and the nuclear testing that is required for it. Yet the United States has refused to ratify the September 10, 1996, Comprehensive Nuclear Test Ban Treaty (GA Res. 50/245, UN GAOR, 50th Sess., Supp. No. 49, at 14, UN Doc. A/50/1027 (1996), reprinted in Weston and Carlson 2: II.C.33d) banning *all* nuclear explosions. Do individual and whole societies have a human right to be free of pollution of the land, sea, and atmosphere that nuclear weapons cause when tested and used? If not, why not? If so, how?

12. Rodriguez-Rivera cites with approval Dinah Shelton's proposal that individual states should be able to implement the right to environment differently based on local conditions which may change too rapidly for global governance to keep up. Do you agree with Shelton and Rodriguez-Rivera that such a high level of local control would not undermine the human right to a good environment?

13. Which countries are most eager to embrace the right to environment? Which are the most reluctant? Why? How would the world be different today if a recognized, justiciable human right to a good environment had existed in 1700? 1800? 1900? Today?

14. Rodriguez-Rivera notes that "the last 30 years have witnessed a proliferation of international instruments specifically addressing global and regional environmental concerns." Do you think that such agreements will, to borrow a phrase from Rhoda Howard-Hassmann (Reading 4 in Chapter 1 of this volume), result in demands from those whose rights have been least respected for their place at the head of the line? What form might such demands take? Are there any procedural barriers to such claims being heard?

22. DOUGLAS ROCHE *Peace: A "Sacred Right"*

The work already accomplished in the UN system to develop the concept of the human right to peace is one of the world's best-kept secrets. The culture of war so pervades public opinion that it has drowned out voices asserting that the human right to peace is a fundamental right of every human being and is, in fact, the major precondition for all human rights. The time has come to emphasize that the peoples of the world have a sacred right to peace.

That very concept—"the peoples of our planet have a sacred right to peace"—was inserted into the first operative paragraph in the Declaration on the Right of Peoples to Peace, adopted by the UN General Assembly on November 12, 1984."[1] One does not need to be reminded of the countless deaths in wars that have occurred in the two decades following. Such a recounting does not invalidate the UN Declaration, it only underlines the point that this right needs to be better understood before procedures are developed to enforce it under the rule of law.

The intimate linkage between human rights and peace was first recognized in the Preamble and in Articles 1 and 55 of the UN Charter; in Article 28 of the Universal Declaration of Human Rights; and in the Covenant on Civil and Political Rights, and the Covenant on Economic, Cultural, and Social Rights.[2] The Preamble to the Charter, in stirring language evoked by the ashes of World War II, affirms that the peoples of the UN are determined "to practice tolerance and live together in peace with one another as good neighbours." Article 1 proclaims as the first purpose of the UN the maintenance of international peace and security. Written a few years later, the Preamble to the Universal Declaration of Human Rights states, "The recognition of the inherent dignity and the equal and inalienable rights of all members of the human family is the foundation of freedom, justice and peace in the world." These documents affirm the right of states to peace through a "peace system" with the primary goal being the preservation of peace and a respect for human rights as essential to the development of friendly relations among nations.

Taken together, these documents provide a basis for the human right to peace, but it was not until 1978, when the UN General Assembly adopted the Declaration on the Preparation of Societies for Life in Peace,[3] that the right to peace began to take shape in a more formal way. The Declaration states:

> . . . every human being, regardless of race, conscience, language or sex, has the inherent right to life in peace. Respect for that right, as

well as for the other human rights, is in the common interest of all mankind and an indispensable condition of advancement of all nations, large and small, in all fields.

The Declaration calls upon countries to ensure that their international and national policies are directed toward achieving life in peace, especially with regard to younger generations. This emphasis on national duty and youth would become the central element in later elaborations of the right to peace.

The Declaration was given a boost with the 1981 African Charter on Human and Peoples' Rights,[4] which proclaimed that all peoples have the right to national and international peace and security. Article 3 declared firmly: "Human beings are inviolable. Every human being shall be entitled to respect for his life and the integrity of his person. No one may be arbitrarily deprived of this right."

Like its 1978 counterpart adopted by the General Assembly, the African Charter places the onus for ensuring the right to peace on governments, but also emphasizes the individual citizen's duty to work toward the right to peace.

Subsequently, the UN General Assembly adopted the Declaration on the Right of Peoples to Peace in 1984. After affirming the principle that "the peoples of our planet have a sacred right to peace," the resolution declares that the preservation of the right of peoples to peace "constitute[s] a fundamental obligation of each State." The Declaration goes on to state that the exercise of this right demands "the elimination of the threat of war" particularly nuclear war. (It was undoubtedly this reference to the elimination of the threat of nuclear war that caused multiple abstentions by Western states. Although the vote was 92 in favour and none opposed, there were 34 abstentions and the Declaration could not be implemented.) Although the Declaration does not explicitly declare the right to peace as a "human right," it can be argued that its intent was just that. This is clear in the assertion that:

---

1. Referenced in Documentary Appendix B.
2. Except for the UN Charter, of which only select provisions are reprinted in Documentary Appendix A, each of the three remaining instruments noted—the UDHR (Dec. 10, 1948), the ICCPR (Dec. 16, 1966), and the ICESCR (Dec. 16, 1966)—are reprinted in full and likewise referenced in Documentary Appendix A.
3. Adopted Dec. 15, 1978, referenced in Documentary Appendix B.
4. Concluded June 27, 1981, referenced in Documentary Appendix B.

. . . life without war serves as the primary international prerequisite for the material well-being, development and progress of countries, and for the full implementation of the rights and fundamental human freedoms proclaimed by the United Nations. . . .

In this statement, the right to peace is considered the fundamental prerequisite for the fulfillment of other basic rights. For instance, the Declaration understands that economic development is only possible in the presence of peace. It links human rights, development, and peace as three conditions that cannot exist in isolation from one another. Simply stated, without peace every other right is illusory. Thus—and in retrospect—even in 1984 the UN was responding to a changing international environment with the kind of innovative thinking needed to lift up humanity to confront the challenges of globalization.

A MAJOR DIPLOMATIC EFFORT

Only with the end of the Cold War in the 1990s did work toward the right to peace grow from a few sentences in international agreements into a major diplomatic effort. This new push was, in part, a product of the hopeful climate surrounding the end of the superpower rivalry. However, the 1997 Declaration of a Human Right to Peace by UNESCO's Director-General, Federico Mayor,[5] was very much a response to the many conflicts that had consumed one society after another earlier in the decade. The wars in Iraq, Somalia, Yugoslavia, Rwanda, and elsewhere left a sense that the international community had taken a wrong turn after the end of the Cold War and was missing a golden opportunity to build a better foundation for peace. This window of opportunity was the driving force behind the UNESCO Director-General's call to get back on track and build the lasting conditions for peace within two or three years.

Mayor's Declaration was different from past elaborations of the right to peace in that it not only confirmed the importance of peace as the precursor of all other rights, but also laid out a strategy to achieve it. The plan called for energies to be refocused on the systemic and root causes of conflict so that conflicts can be tackled in the early stages and the kind of out-of-control bloodletting that had characterized recent conflicts may be avoided.

Of course, to achieve the right to peace, it is first necessary to make the transition from a culture of war to a culture of peace. Mayor's Declaration realizes that the international community cannot simultaneously absorb the cost of war and the cost of peace. The Declaration is thus a wake-up call of sorts in that it puts the spotlight on a dangerously flawed international order and calls upon us to do what is necessary to build a more peaceful one. Not only is this necessary for our very survival, but since peace is "a prerequisite for the exercise of all human rights and duties," it is also our right.

The means to achieve this right are divided in the Declaration into two concurrent strategies. First, the Declaration calls for immediate action on urgent issues such as poverty, environmental destruction, and international justice, and it calls upon the international community to provide the UN system with the necessary resources and power to tackle these challenges. In other words, countries need to reduce their investment in arms and militarism and reinvest in the construction of peace. The second strategy involves a massive education campaign focused on youth and designed to foster an understanding and tolerance of other cultures as well as an understanding of the value of peace and justice.

In hindsight, and especially in the wake of September 11, these goals and their suggested time line seem perhaps overly optimistic. But the Declaration nonetheless ignited a flurry of interest and activity among governments and civil society. It was quickly followed in 1997 by a meeting of experts organized by the University of Las Palmas, the Tricontinental Institute of Parliamentary Democracy and Human Rights, and UNESCO that was held in Las Palmas, Spain. The participants included Mohammed Bedjaoui, President of the International Court of Justice. The meeting recognized the intimate link between peace and human rights and called for a formal Declaration on the Human Right to Peace, which would be ready for the 50th anniversary of the Universal Declaration on Human Rights in 1998.

5. Issued Jan. 1, 1997, referenced in Documentary Appendix B.

THE OSLO DECLARATION

In 1997, the Norwegian Institute of Human Rights convened a meeting in Oslo to prepare a draft Declaration for UNESCO's General Conference later that year. The aim of the Declaration was to broaden the human dimension of peace and to divide the right to peace into three inter-related components. The first defines peace as a human right, understanding that all human beings have a right to peace inherent to their humanity. War and violence of any kind, including insecurity, are considered "intrinsically incompatible" with the human right to peace. The section calls on states and members of the international community to ensure its implementation without discrimination.

The second section elaborates on this task by making it a "duty" for all global actors, including individuals, to "contribute to the maintenance and construction of peace" and to prevent armed conflicts and prevent violence in all its manifestations.

The third section elaborates the "Culture of Peace" the means by which the right to peace is to be achieved. As we have seen, the culture of peace is a strategy that seeks to root peace in people's minds through education, communication, and a set of ethical and democratic ideals.

Draft Oslo Declaration on the Human Right to Peace

Article 1: Peace as a human right
- Every human being has the right to peace, which is inherent in the dignity of the human person. War and all other armed conflicts, violence in all its forms and whatever its origin, and insecurity also are intrinsically incompatible with the human right to peace;
- The human right to peace must be guaranteed, respected and implemented without any discrimination in either internal or international contexts by all states and other members of the international community;

Article 2: Peace as a duty
- Every human being, all states and other members of the international community and all peoples have the duty to contribute to the maintenance and construction of peace, and to the prevention of armed conflicts and of violence in all its forms. It is incumbent upon them notably to favour disarmament and to oppose by all legitimate means acts of aggression and systematic,

massive and flagrant violations of human rights which constitute a threat to peace;
- As inequalities, exclusion and poverty can result in the disruption of peace both at the international level and internally, it is the duty of states to promote and encourage social justice both on their own territory and at the international level, in particular through an appropriate policy aimed at sustainable human development;

Article 3: Peace through the culture of peace
- The culture of peace, whose aim is to build the defenses of peace in the minds of human beings every day through education, science and communication, must constitute the means of achieving the global implementation of the human right to peace;
- The culture of peace requires recognition and respect for -and the daily practice of-a set of ethical values and democratic ideals which are based on the intellectual and moral solidarity of humanity.

In essence, the right to peace is a global ethic of nonviolence and reverence for all life and offers a blueprint for identifying the roots of global problems and for addressing conflicts early. It is an attempt to move beyond the day-today crises that make the headline news and to address their deep-seated causes.

The power of this draft declaration is in its challenge to the hypocrisy dominating the world order today and it was here that the codification of the right to peace came to a temporary halt. A remarkable debate on the Oslo Draft Declaration took place in UNESCO's General Conference on November 6, 1997. One European country after another either attacked or expressed reservations about the right to peace and accused Mayor of overstepping his mandate. Countries from the South struck back, accusing the North of wanting to protect their arms industries. At the end, Paraguay stated, "This rich discussion shows that the culture of peace is the central issue . . . and that the Human Right to Peace is needed for individuals and states." Noting that the debate split North and South, Paraguay added, "Perhaps peace is a greater concern in the South where scarce resources are being diverted to war."

Failing to achieve a consensus, Mayor did not press further with the issue. Skepticism about the human right to peace continued to echo for years after. In the informal discussions at the UN in 1999 that concerned the Draft Declaration and Programme of Action on a Culture of Peace,[6] the U.S. delegate stated. "Peace should not be elevated to the category of human right, otherwise it will be very difficult to start a war." Whether the speaker was aware of the irony of this statement or not, he had put his finger precisely on why a human right to peace is needed.

Efforts are continuing at the UN, but they still lack the necessary Western backing.[7] In 2002 the UN Social, Humanitarian and Cultural Committee adopted a resolution calling for the promotion of the right to peace. The resolution would have the UN affirm that the peoples of the planet have a sacred right to peace, and resources released through disarmament measures should be devoted to the economic and social development of all peoples, particularly those in developing countries. Although the resolution had 90 votes in favour, a hefty 50 negative votes (mostly Western countries and the new East European members of NATO) were cast against it, and 14 abstentions were registered. Such division renders the resolution practically inoperable.[8]

Some states are still arguing that the "right to peace" has not been negotiated at a sufficiently high level of international relations. Denmark, speaking for the European Union, said the issue should be dealt with in other forums (the same argument that was used in UNESCO meetings). Canada—speaking on behalf of the U.S., New Zealand, and Australia—expressed opposition because the resolution focused more on relations between states, as opposed to states' obligations to their peoples. The fact that Cuba was the main sponsor alienated many Western states. Nonetheless, an objective reading of the text does not provide any reason for rejection— unless a state wants to keep its options for warfare open. If the peoples of the states that voted against the resolution knew what their governments were doing, the governments would not be able to slide away so easily from their responsibility to build the structural basis for the right to peace.

When language is softer, the idea of moving away from war as a means of resolving conflict meets less resistance. For example, in 2003, the UN General Assembly concluded five months of negotiations by adopting by consensus a resolution on the prevention of armed conflict.[9] The resolution called on parties to a dispute threatening international peace to make the most effective use of existing and new methods for peacefully settling disputes, including arbitration, mediation, other treaty-based arrangements, and the International Criminal Court, thus promoting the role of international law in international relations. It reaffirmed the primary responsibility of the Security Council for the maintenance of international peace and security. And it called on Member States to support poverty eradication measures and enhance the capacity of developing countries to comply with treaties on arms control, nonproliferation and disarmament; and to strengthen their international verification instruments and eradicate illicit trade in small arms and light weapons. The resolution was hailed as a landmark in efforts to move the world body from a culture of reacting to crises to one of preventing them reaching critical mass.

Though shying away from any implication that the prevention of armed conflict sets the stage for a full-scale discussion of the "right to peace," the resolution contains important elements of the culture of peace. Far from being anodyne or just another resolution, it is infused with an obligation to the victims of violence and challenges states to move from rhetoric to reality in preventing violence. It is a significant step forward by the UN in preparing the way for the right to peace.

Meanwhile, attention in UNESCO has shifted back from a right to peace to the culture of peace. This was easier to digest for those who did not want their right to make war impeded. Everyone, after all, could be for peace in general, and especially in the abstract. UNESCO showed its wisdom by treading slowly. It developed the concept of the culture of peace into a series of programs that would, at least in the minds of those who truly understood the dimensions of the culture of peace, prepare the groundwork for a later acceptance of the human right to peace.

6. See Consolidated Report Containing a Draft Declaration and Programme of Action on a Culture of Peace, 53rd Sess., Provisional Agenda Item 31, UN Doc. A/53/370 (Sept. 2, 1998).
7. See, e.g., Commission on Human Rights Resolution 2001/69 on Promotion of the Right of Peoples to Peace (2001), adopted by a roll-call vote of 29-16-7, referenced in Documentary Appendix B.
8. The resolution was nevertheless subsequently adopted by the UN General Assembly in Res. 57/216 on the Promotion of the Right of Peoples to Peace, referenced in Documentary Appendix B.
9. GA Res. 57/337, adopted July 2, 2003, referenced in Documentary Appendix B.

A THIRD GENERATION OF RIGHTS

To fully grasp the potential of the human right to peace to change human conduct, is it necessary to consider the evolving nature of human rights.

[*Eds.*—The author summarizes the more extensive treatment of the evolution of first, second, and third generation of human rights recounted in Reading 1 of Chapter 1 this volume. He then elaborates on third generation rights.]

Essentially, third-generation rights call for the redistribution of power and resources, and consider the current international system ineffective in its attempts to resolve contemporary issues. Third generation rights include: the right to political, economic, and cultural self-determination; the right to economic and social development; the right to participate in and benefit from the common heritage of mankind; the right to a healthy environment; the right to humanitarian relief, and the right to peace. The key characteristic of these rights is that they are fundamentally collective in nature and require international cooperation for their achievement. A clean environment cannot be achieved by the actions of one country since pollution does not recognize national frontiers. Likewise, it is difficult for a country to raise its gross national product when other countries' tariffs prevent it from selling its goods to raise revenue that could be put toward social services.

More generally third-generation rights provide an essential ingredient lacking in first and second generation rights. Largely based on the individual, first and second generation rights are permeated by an atmosphere of selfishness that sees the individual as the primary concern. But this focus neglects the fact that, more than ever, society is a system of competing groups and individuals and that, for society to achieve its full potential, it is necessary to participate cooperatively, within the community. Achieving this demands major changes from the individualistic attitude that prevails in Western democracies.

The challenges inherent in globalization make such an approach vitally necessary The very nature of the dilemmas the third generation of rights seeks to address—namely the right to a clean environment, development, and peace—are issues that today pertain to humanity's very survival. The world has rapidly compressed through a breathtaking combination of popultion growth, technological and economic advancement and interdependence. Combining these with a readily available supply of deadly weapons and easily transmitted contagion of hatred and incitement to violence makes it essential and urgent to find ways to prevent disputes from turning massively violent.

In reality more than a new generation, third generation rights are perhaps better thought of as an awakening. World problems can no longer be solved by the actions of one state alone. Keeping the peace, protecting the environment, and fostering sustained and equitable development require cooperative and determined action at the international level. Lacking this, states cannot fulfill their first- and second-generational obligations.

Human rights are thus indivisible and interdependent. One set of human rights cannot be realized in a world where others are absent or violated. Framed this way, the metaphor for successive "generations" of rights is somewhat misleading since, although they coexist, generations actually succeed each other in the true sense of the term. In reality, the international community has approached human rights in a top-down fashion. Just as it was realized that taking the first generation of human rights seriously necessitated fulfilling the second, achieving the first and second generations of human rights in a globalized world requires realizing the third set of rights. Although at a nascent stage and thus not as established as its "ancestors;" this new generation of rights offers a blueprint for confronting and managing the pressing challenges posed by globalization.

The most important among these newly emerging rights is the human right to peace. Often regarded as just another third-generation right in the human rights literature, the right to peace is unique. It transcends all other rights, enables their exercise, and offers the innovation needed to lift up society and allow it to achieve its full potential in an interconnected world. Indeed, without basic security of the person, other human rights are but an illusion. What use is the right to vote, or the right to medical care, in a society torn apart by armed conflict?

[*Eds.*—The author next notes that some human rights scholars, in particular Professor David P.

Forsythe in his book *Human Rights and Peace*,[10] have argued that the human right to peace and other third-generation rights do not rise to the level of "rights" since they have "no specific meaning" and impose no "specific duties." In riposte, the author notes that first and second generation rights may at one time have suffered the same defect, but over time evolved to have very specific content and consequences. Third generation rights, the author contends, must be given the same opportunity to evolve. He then continues:]

Human rights are a product of their times, and such is the case with first and second generation rights. One group of rights is not meant to outdate or ascend another, but rather to expand upon and supplement others. This is clear in the international community's continually expanding conception of what it considers to be human rights and the strides that have been made to formalize them. New aspects of life, new situations, and new types of conflict that cannot be foreseen are continually pushing the definition of human rights beyond old limits. This is a normal legal process that has been adopted by national legal systems the world over, and it should be no surprise that the same process is becoming evident in an increasingly interconnected world.

Such is the case with the right to peace, which is the product of a paradigm shift at the international level. Rights that focus solely on the relationship between the state and the individual are not sufficient in responding to a globalized world in which problems are no longer defined purely in national terms. The same global circuitry that fuels transportation, information, finance, and organization has also increased the power of the arms trader, the warlord, the religious fanatic, the deranged political leader, the human trafficker, and the terrorist. There is, thus, a technological burden with which the other two generations of human rights were never designed to cope, and the right to peace is an attempt to respond to the perils of the modern interconnected world. Dismissing the right to peace as vague and declaring that it offers nothing new is an exercise that misses the mark. The right to peace is innovative and addresses a whole swath of new and interconnected global challenges.

Obviously, the world community has much work to do before the "right to peace" is codified in the same way that political, civil, economic, and social rights have been codified in the covenants to the Universal Declaration of Human Rights. But the fact that so much progress has been made in recognizing, defining, and implementing the right to peace is a sign of the advance of civilization. Those who wish to maintain the war culture and divert yet more precious resources to prosecute wars must not be permitted to use the terrorist attacks of September 11 as an excuse. This will not get at the systemic causes of the problems faced by the international community today.

Only when we fully understand our own potential to make the human right to peace the ruling norm in society will the international community have fulfilled the promise it made in 1945. This promise was to construct the defenses of peace in the minds of all the peoples of the Earth and finally "save succeeding generations from the scourge of war."

"HUMAN RIGHTS HAVE COME A LONG WAY"

In considering the difficulties of enshrining the human right to peace in law, it is helpful to consider the overall progress made on the human rights agenda. The whole field of human rights has taken centre stage starting with the Universal Declaration and followed by the covenants; the various conventions on women's and children's rights; and such instruments as the Anti-Personnel Landmines Treaty,[11] the Rwanda and Yugoslav tribunals, and the International Court of Justice. As Mary Robinson, former UN High Commissioner for Human Rights (and former President of Ireland), puts it: "Human rights have indeed come a long way." Even though many governments do not necessarily observe human rights standards, most at least acknowledge that human rights have a role to play.

There is no question that the development process was spurred by the UN's assertion in 1986

10. David P. Forsythe, *Human Rights and Peace: International and National Dimensions* (Lincoln: University of Nebraska Press, 1993).
11. Concluded Sept. 18, 1997, referenced in Documentary Appendix B.

of the "Right to Development." The resolution emphasized that "the human person is the central subject of development," and inspired development planners who then began to place more emphasis on education and health in funding development projects. The resolution stated that elimination of threats of war would enhance the development process and that resources released by disarmament should be devoted to the economic and social development of peoples. This contributed significantly to an understanding that development requires the presence of peace, and peace cannot endure without the conditions of development.[12]

The Declaration on the Right to Development and the Declaration on the Right of Peoples to Peace (adopted during the same time period) broaden the basis of human rights to consider both peace and development. Both underscore the key idea that all human rights are "indivisible and interdependent." Human rights are inherent in each human being. They are not conferred by the state, but states do have the obligation to uphold and enforce the application of human rights.

Like the right to peace, the right to development is criticized because it cannot be enforced. When is a person "developed"? When is there "peace"? These objections are invalid, since the declaration of rights, carried out with the consensus of humanity through international institutions, is meant to set norms for human conduct. These norms, at their extreme end, can be enforced. The state has an obligation to provide food to a starving child. The state has an obligation to protect civilians during warfare. Only when more sophisticated interpretations of rights are called for does consensus begin to break down. How much Official Development Assistance should be provided by a state to help developing countries? At what point does a state's level of weaponry exceed its needs for defense and become a threat to its neighbour? These questions, the stuff of the political process, must be dealt with on a daily basis. Ongoing debates must stand on principles, and those principles are expressed in the human rights conventions.

The forward-minded nature of the UN's work on the delineation and implementation of human rights is seen particularly in the Convention on the Rights of the Child,[13] the first legally binding international instrument to incorporate the full range of human rights—civil and political rights as well as economic, social, and cultural rights. By ratifying this instrument, national governments have committed themselves to protecting and ensuring children's rights, and they have agreed to hold themselves accountable before the international community. Every country in the world has ratified it except two: the U.S. and Somalia.

In considering to what the child is entitled so that he or she can live in minimum economic and social standards, is it too much of a leap to state that the first thing the child needs to grow up safely is a peaceful environment? Children must have peace in order to develop in a way that is consistent with the inherent human rights they possess. Peace is their right. But it cannot yet be formally articulated in ways that guarantee that the processes of sustainable development will nor be destroyed by the ravages of war. The political system has not yet sufficiently matured.

Nonetheless, the subject of the human right to peace has clearly entered circles of discussion at the UN. Some hold that it is already a component of developing international law. This is a signal moment because a full discussion of the right to peace puts a new spotlight on the age-old question of the abolition of war itself. In the new era of weapons of mass destruction, the viability of war as a legal means to resolve disputes is clearly over. War today can lead to the obliteration of humanity. Unfortunately, the world community, held in check by the forces of the culture of war, is a long way from outlawing war. The debate on the human right to peace, therefore, is a step forward. As it is pursued, it will force the political system to face up to its responsibility to at least avoid war.

The debate inevitably will centre on the deeply controversial question of the future of nuclear weapons. The International Court of Justice has already given its view on this matter: it says nations have a legal obligation to get rid of them.[14] While the abolition of nuclear weapons

12. On the Declaration and the right to development, see Reading 20 by Arjun Sengupta in this chapter.
13. Concluded Nov. 2, 1989, referenced in Documentary Appendix B.
14. *Legality of the Threat or Use of Nuclear Weapons*, 1996 I.C.J. General List No. 95 (July 8, 1996). For a somewhat less sanguine reading of this decision, see Burns H. Weston, "Nuclear Weapons and the World Court: Ambiguity's Consensus," *TLCP* 7 (1997): 371–99.

will not by itself guarantee peace, it is an elementary fact of the twenty-first century that as long as nations brandish nuclear weapons there can be no peace. Indeed, P. N. Bhagwati, former Chief Justice of the Supreme Court of India, argues that "the main function of the right to peace is the promotion and protection of the right to life through peaceful settlement of disputes, by the prohibition of the threat or use of force in international relations, by the prohibition of the manufacture, use and deployment of nuclear weapons, and by total disarmament."[15]

The proponents of nuclear weapons do indeed know which way the debate on the human right to peace is headed. That is why they will use every argument they can think of, every political device they can find, and every form of intimidation they can invent to try to derail the debate. They effectively disrupted the debate in UNESCO. They have rendered inoperative nuclear weapons abolition resolutions at the UN.

They have used the tragedy of September 11 to scare the populace into believing that only gigantic amounts of weaponry can head off the terrorism of the future. They have already caused an erosion of civil liberties in the guise of combating terrorism.

These proponents of militarism as the route to peace appear to operate today from the commanding heights of public opinion. But against this insidious thinking that war equals peace is rising a new army, not of soldiers but of highly informed, dedicated, and courageous citizens of all countries who do see the perils ahead. There is a blossoming of both understanding and action in the new phenomenon of an alert civil society calling governments to account for paying only lip service to their human rights commitments. Buttressed by the dynamic means of electronic communication, they are bringing new energy to the global quest for peace.

QUESTIONS FOR REFLECTION AND DISCUSSION

1. A principal purpose of the United Nations, as stated in UN Charter Article 1(1), is "To maintain international peace and security" and, to this end, "to bring about by peaceful means . . . adjustment or settlement of international disputes or situations which might lead to a breach of the peace." But what does "peace" mean? In "Nonterritorial Actors and the Problem of Peace," in Saul H. Mendlovitz, ed., *The Creation of a Just World Order* (New York: Free Press, 1975), 151–88, at 151–52, political scientist Johan Galtung defines "peace" as the absence of "structural" as well as "direct" violence. What is "structural" violence? Galtung writes that, "reproduced in the agricultural, industrial, commercial , and administrative sectors of society," it is the "way that surplus is extracted from the lower levels [of society] and transferred upwards, making the higher levels richer at the expense of he lower levels, producing the famous 'gaps' in development [and resulting in] often highly differential morbidity and mortality rates between rich and poor countries, districts, and individuals." Clearly the UN Charter's use of the word "peace" addresses *direct* violence. Does it also address *structural* violence? Should it? For the purpose of defining the right to peace, is it helpful or unhelpful to define "peace" to mean not only the absence of hostilities ("negative peace") but also the presence of social justice ("positive peace")? Should the human right to peace encompass both meanings? Why? Why not? Note in this connection that the English word "peace" has two Arabic counterparts: *sulah*, meaning the end of hostilities or a truce; and *salaam*, meaning an enduring nonviolent relationship based on mutual respect. Is *sulah* possible without *salaam*? Why? Why not? Which is present in international relations today? Which is present in the internal economic ordering of your home country? In your personal relationships? Which should the human right to peace encompass? How would Roche answer these questions? For pertinent discussion, see Burns H. Weston, "The Role of Law in Promoting Peace and Violence: A Matter of Definition, Social Values, and Individual Responsibility," in W. Michael Reisman and Burns H. Weston, eds., *Toward World Order and Human Dignity: Essays in Honor of Myres S. McDougal* (New York: Free Press, 1976), 114–31.

2. The many armed conflicts since the UN's founding, now including the 2003 U.S. military invasion of Iraq, bear witness that the UN has been largely unable to achieve the goal

---

15. *Eds.*—The author gives no reference for this quotation.

of "international peace and security" for which, in major part, it was established. Why? Might it be more accurate to say that UN member states, especially the major powers, have made it impossible for the UN to achieve the goals? Do your answers to these questions affect your judgment about the existence of the right to peace? Are you persuaded by Roche that a right to peace exists? Why? Why not?

3. U.S. President George W. Bush designated May 28, 2001 as a "day of prayer for permanent peace." In his speech announcing the designation, the President spoke exclusively of the sacrifices of the veterans of the United States military. Is war a legitimate means of pursuing peace? Have the actions of the militaries of the world, at an aggregate expense of approximately $1 trillion in 2003 alone, contributed to or detracted from peace? Would the absence of militaries contribute to peace? How might the money spent on the military be redirected to promote the "permanent peace" the President wishes U.S. citizens to pray for?

4. Are there economic barriers to peace? Who profits from a lack of peace? Consider the question John Somerville posed in his classic *The Peace Revolution: Ethos and Social Process* (Westport, Conn.: Greenwood Press, 1975), 150:

> What would be the probable effect of a law which provided that whenever the government waged war, and drafted the youth, all industry and capital would become public property for the duration, that private profit and private dividends would cease (be socialized), and all salaries would be limited to the scale of military pay? What proportion of the public would accept the moral principle that, if lives are drafted, property should also be drafted?

Can you think of any wars that would not have been waged if Somerville's moral principle had been accepted at the time? If so, should this principle be viewed as integral to the right to peace?

5. How is peace best promoted in the context of ongoing armed conflicts? Consider, as a non-exhaustive list of possibilities, the methods of parties external to the conflict intervening under the banner of, for example, the Nonviolent Peaceforce (www.nonviolentpeaceforce.org): "witnessing (i.e., monitoring and reporting on conflicts as they happen to render violence politically unfeasible)"; "protective accompaniment (i.e., accompanying vulnerable leaders and negotiators in combat zones to ensure their safety)"; "international presence (i.e., placing large numbers of Peaceforce members in vulnerable towns or villages to protect them from attack)"; and "interpositioning (placing oneself between warring parties to prevent escalation)." All of these methods, like all methods of violent intervention, place their practitioners at risk of harm. Do you think that risk is increased or decreased, in the case of the Nonviolent Peaceforce, by their lack of weapons, even in the face of other armed parties to the underlying conflict?

6. In "Peace as a Human Right," *Bulletin of Peace Proposals Journal* 11, no. 4 (1980): 319–30, Philip Alston contended that absent "drastic transformation of the existing international system" it is highly unlikely that an effective mechanism for peace enforcement will ever exist. Do you agree? Disagree? Why? How might the structure of the United Nations be changed to better protect the right to peace? Is Alston's statement tantamount to saying that there exists no human right to peace?

7. Do you agree with Roche that the international political process has not yet sufficiently matured to formally articulate the right to peace "in ways that guarantee that the processes of sustainable development will not be destroyed by the ravages of war"? Do you think that the right to peace will ever be so completely achieved as to "guarantee" anything?

Part II
ACTION

Chapter Five

International Human Rights: Action Overviews

IN this chapter, we move beyond the many human rights issues introduced in Part I of this volume and turn to discussion of the essential elements of human rights action, focusing especially on the enforcement of international human rights. To provide context for the understanding of some guiding principles and some of the many forms of human rights action we see and in which we participate in our modern era, the chapter begins with Burns H. Weston's comprehensive and panoramic historical review of human rights institution-building. His presentation, ranging over several centuries, ultimately confronts us with distinctively contemporary efforts to take action against needless inhumanity and to grapple with human suffering in its many human-made forms. Focusing further on institutions, Anne F. Bayefsky writes critically on the inadequacy of human rights treaty regimes, providing a strong indictment of United Nations institutions but doing so realistically and in such a way as to invite discussion about appropriate reforms and institutional changes to enhance efforts to deal with abridgements of human rights and to promote effective remedial action. Nicely balancing Bayefsky's views on UN shortcomings is Harold Koh's work on human rights enforcement. His work raises our horizon line to a positive vision of what is humanly possible, and he does this in an analytically skillful sorting out of the "whys and wherefores" of implementing, protecting, and enforcing human rights today, laying out a framework that helps to answer the question: "How Is International Human Rights Law Enforced?" In so doing, he illustrates our contemporary multi-layered field of struggle, transactional intercourse, and global action. The scope of his presentation clarifies the fact that many human rights are implemented, not by official programs of centralized authority and enforcement, but by people conscientiously responding to the values of human rights. That such value-based behavior can be projected on a larger global scale is the broad topic of Part II of this book, which concerns intergovernmental, national, nongovernmental, and individual action in support of internationally defined human rights.

PRINCIPLES OF ACTION: MUTUAL SELF-INTEREST AND RESPECT FOR HUMAN DIGNITY

Burns H. Weston's essay, "Human Rights: Prescription and Enforcement" (Reading 23) begins, appropriately, by referencing some of the historical antecedents of modern human rights law.[1] He notes that, prompted by the vision of the Swiss humanitarian Jean Henri Dunant (one of two laureates for the first Nobel Peace Prize in 1901), and under the guiding hand of the International Committee of the Red Cross (ICRC), the "laws of war" traverse many decades of the modern era, becoming formalized first in the Geneva and Hague conventions of the mid- to late nineteenth century and currently defined by the four Geneva conventions of 1949, their two additional protocols of 1977,[2] the statutes for the ad hoc war crimes tribunals for the former Yugoslavia and Rwanda,[3] and the Statute of the newly established (without U.S. participation) International Criminal Court.[4] The term "laws of war" seems ironic because war is the ultimate form of social violence. As such, it is difficult to apprehend the notion that war could be restrained by specific rules seeking to limit violent activities in the field of battle. Improbable as it may seem, this is exactly what the laws of war do, or what they are supposed to do. The fundamental principles of action underlying "humanitarian law" (as the humanitarian rules of armed conflict are today called) are essentially the same as those undergirding international human rights law, but with important and therefore noteworthy exceptions.

That a regulatory system limiting war works at all is due less to the existence of enforcement institutions and a century's history than to its acceptance based on mutual utility and the perceived self-interest of states. Instructive on this point is the first modern agreement among states to limit the effects of armed conflict ending the Crimean War in 1853.[5] The parties to the 1856 Declaration of Paris, the concluding peace treaty, agreed that maritime warfare thereafter should require warring parties to recognize and respect neutral ships and their immunity from attack. The signers reasoned that wanton assault on ships not involved in armed conflict resulted in no wartime partisan gain—a strictly utilitarian calculation tied not to notions of human dignity or respect for property so much as to ordering the winning of wars efficiently, without needless waste of resources.

The neutral-ships rule relies on the elemental dynamics of mutual self-interest based upon the same premise that supports much of contemporary deterrence theory (and, for that matter, law itself). Its foundational axiom is that if no party stands to gain and all parties stand to lose by breaking a given rule, then reciprocity makes the rule realistic, supplying a workable principle of enforcement. Thus, a neutral ship, unless of course it is carrying enemy goods, should not be a wartime target. That would waste weaponry, and its destruction is not justified by the objective of winning a war to settle a power struggle. Mutual self-interest of the parties serves as a guide for action and promotes the survival of the rule.

Generalizing beyond the neutral ships example, it is well accepted among scholars of international law that the mutual self-interest of states is a long-standing principle guiding action in world affairs and sustaining international law and, indeed, law generally. It is

---

1. Reading 23 by Burns H. Weston is a continuation of his essay in Chapter 1 of this volume, Reading 1. The reader may wish to review Reading 1, in particular its preliminary pre-World War II history of human rights ("Historical Development"), before undertaking Reading 23.
2. The four Geneva conventions were concluded Aug. 12, 1949, and Protocol Additional I and Protocol Additional II were concluded June 8, 1977. All are referenced in Documentary Appendix B. See Geneva Convention (No. I) for the Amelioration of the Wounded and Sick in Armed Forces in the Field; Geneva Convention (No. II) for the Amelioration of the Wounded and Sick and Shipwrecked Members of Armed Forces at Sea; Geneva Convention (No. III) Relative to the Treatment of Prisoners of War; Geneva Convention (No. IV) Relative to the Protection of Civilian Persons in Time of War; Protocol Additional (No. I) Relating to the Protection of Victims of International Armed Conflicts; and Protocol Additional (No. II) Relating to the Protection of Victims of Non-International Armed Conflicts.
3. Adopted May 23, 1993 and Nov. 8, 1994, respectively, each is referenced in Documentary Appendix B.
4. Adopted July 17, 1998, referenced in Documentary Appendix B.
5. Dietrich Schindler and Jiri Toman, *The Laws of Armed Conflict* (Dordrecht: Nijhoff, 1988), 787.

instructive, as Burns Weston writes, "to think upon law in functional rather than institutional terms, and from this perspective to acknowledge its invention, its application, and its appraisal both within and beyond the formal corridors of power."[6] He continues:

> Law does not live by executives and legislators and judges alone. It lives also by individual human beings such as ourselves, pushing and pulling through reciprocal claim and mutual tolerance in our daily competition for power, wealth, respect, and other cherished values. To turn a phrase, law is legitimized politics—a Hydra-headed process of social decision, involving persons at all levels and from all walks of public and private life who, with authority derived both explicitly and implicitly from community consensus or expectation, and supported by formal and informal sanction, effect those codes or standards of everyday conduct by which we plan and go about our lives.[7]

When defining "law," Weston emphasizes, it is not just helpful in a theoretical sense but important in a practical sense "to avoid transforming the mere *characteristics* of the popular model into the *prerequisites* of a comprehensive theory about law."[8] In this way, he observes—with obvious relevance for international human rights law—"[we] avoid the allegation that law is not, or that it cannot be, the expression of the will of all or most of the people."

Thus, like the nineteenth-century rules on the senseless destruction of neutral vessels, modern "laws of war" (now known as "humanitarian law," as mentioned above) continue to depend for enforcement on expectations or mechanisms of reciprocity. In the absence of strong institutions for enforcement, reciprocity among the states of the world remains at the root of the international legal system.

However, the expectation of reciprocity in a purely utilitarian sense of crass self-interest does not explain the existence of all the rules. Over the century and a half of its development, the legal substratum of humanitarian law has added rules of ethics and related humane perspectives, including most notably lessons drawn from experience with the horrors of mid-twentieth century fascism,[9] which prompted actors in the world of international affairs to think beyond the limits of utility and instrumental practicality. For example, in 1945 a Charter was drafted by the World War II allied powers to establish the Nuremberg Tribunal, giving it jurisdiction over crimes against peace, war crimes and crimes against humanity.[10] In Article 6(b) it identified "war crimes" in terms that continue to be accepted today:

> Such violations shall include, but not be limited to, murder, ill-treatment or deportation to slave labour or for any other purpose of civilian population of or in an occupied

6. Burns H. Weston, "The Role of Law in Promoting Peace and Violence: A Matter of Definition, Social Values, and Individual Responsibility," in W. Michael Reisman and Burns H. Weston, eds., *Toward World Order and Human Dignity: Essays in Honor of Myres S. McDougal* (New York: Free Press, 1976), 114–31, at 116.
7. Ibid., 16–17.
8. Ibid., 16.
9. Ingrid Detter de Lupis, *The Laws of War* (Cambridge: Cambridge University Press, 1987), 339. See generally also Judith Gardam, ed., *Humanitarian Law* (Aldershot: Ashgate, 1999); Michael Howard, George J. Andreopoulos, and Mark R. Shulman, eds., *The Laws of War: Constraints on Warfare in the Western World* (New Haven, Conn.: Yale University Press, 1994); W. Michael Reisman and Chris T. Antoniou, eds., *The Laws of War: A Comprehensive Collection of Primary Documents on International Laws Governing Armed Conflict* (New York: Vintage, 1994); Jean S. Pictet, *Humanitarian Law and the Protection of War Victims* (Leyden: Sijthoff, 1975). But see also M. Cherif Bassiouni, "The Normative Framework of International Humanitarian Law: Overlaps, Gaps and Ambiguities," *TLCP* 8, no. 2 (1998): 199–275.
10. Concluded Aug. 8, 1945, referenced in Documentary Appendix B. For a historical accounting, see Joseph E. Persico, *Nuremberg: Infamy on Trial* (New York: Penguin, 1994).

territory, murder or ill-treatment of prisoners of war or persons on the seas, killing of hostages, plunder of public or private property, wanton destruction of cities, towns or villages, or devastation not justified by military necessity.

Notice the last phrase exposing the operative utility value and specifying the instrumental means-ends link embedded in the caution to avoid cruelty not required by "military necessity" (by which is meant, of course, winning the battle or war). The drafters of the 1948 Universal Declaration of Human Rights (UDHR),[11] meeting at the same time as the Nuremberg proceedings, closely followed developments in the post-war criminal trials of Nazi officials. They forthrightly premised their newly formulated human rights standards, however, on a concept of human dignity rather than utility.[12]

Consider a very specific and revealing example. The value placed on human dignity influenced the debate on how or whether to connect human rights, health, and medicine in the UDHR.[13] In unqualified language, UDHR Article 5 rebukes the cruelty attested at Nuremberg and suffered by millions during the war years saying that "No one shall be subject to torture or to cruel, inhuman or degrading treatment or punishment." The rationale for this restriction was not utilitarian; rather, as the UDHR Preamble states explicitly, the UDHR's provisions were formulated in major part to affirm the dignity and worth of the human person and to express humankind's "outraged conscience" over "barbarous acts" resulting from "disregard and contempt for human rights"[14]—a moral perspective later unmistakably confirmed in Article 7 of the International Covenant on Civil and Political Rights (ICCPR),[15] which prohibits not only torture but also medical experimentation without informed consent. If utility were the only fundamental ethical principle, there would be no need to obtain informed consent from research subjects when the research is likely to yield great benefits to future patients while posing little risk of harm to the patients themselves.[16] In other words, principles of Immanuel Kant permeate the UDHR's Preamble, ICCPR Article 7, and other human rights provisions. His moral teaching of respect for the person is unambiguously present, and evident in two respects: first, that individuals should be treated as autonomous agents; second, that the capacity of human beings to decide knowledgeably about their own welfare must be respected and protected. A utilitarian

11. Adopted Dec. 10, 1948, reprinted and referenced in Documentary Appendix A.
12. See Theo C. van Boven, "Reliance on Norms of Humanitarian Law by United Nations Organs," in Astrid J. M. Delissen and Gerard J. Tanja, eds., *Humanitarian Law of Armed Conflict: Challenges Ahead—Essays in Honour of Frits Kalshaven* (Dordrecht: Nijhoff, 1991), 495, 509–13. See also Fereydoun Hoveyda, "The Universal Declaration and Fifty Years of Human Rights," *TLCP* 8, no. 2 (1998): 429–36.
13. In November 1947, the War Crimes Commission said its report "was designed to serve the specific purpose of contributing to the task of the Commission on Human Rights in preparing an international bill of human rights." United Nations Commission on Human Rights Drafting Committee, UN Doc E/CN.4/W.20, at vi. That it was so received is evidenced by René Cassin's statement to fellow UDHR Drafting Committee members that he understood the Article 5 prohibition of torture to include a rule that doctors have no "right to inflict suffering and pain on other human beings without their consent, even for ends that may appear 'good.'" UN Doc E/CN4/AC.1/SR.3, at 13.
14. On the principle that human beings should be treated by each other as ends not means, the UDHR Preamble is unequivocal in emphasizing that international human rights are premised on the "recognition of the inherent dignity and . . . the equal and inalienable rights of all members of the human family."
15. Concluded Dec. 16, 1966, reprinted and referenced in Documentary Appendix A.
16. Ruth Macklin, "Which Way Down the Slippery Slope? Nazi Medical Killing and Euthanasia Today," in Arthur L. Caplan, ed., *When Medicine Went Bad: Bioethics and the Holocaust* (Totowa, N.J.: Humana, 1992), 173–200. The two principles that individuals should be treated as autonomous agents, and that persons with diminished autonomy are entitled to protection are incorporated in the U.S. National Commission for the Protection of Human Subjects of Biomedical and Behavioral Research, *The Belmont Report: Ethical Principles and Guidelines for the Protection of Human Subjects of Research* (Washington, D.C.: U.S. Government Printing Office, 1979), 4.

action guide does not suffice for those acquainted with the Nuremberg "Doctors' Trials" which presented ghastly images of physicians trained in the pseudo-science of eugenics and undertaking concentration camp experiments on unwilling prisoners.[17]

For present purposes, however, what is perhaps most significant about these important internationally defined norms is that they did not remain the province of governmental duty-bearers and decision-makers alone. In 1947, soon after the Doctors' Trials were publicized, the newly founded World Medical Association (WMA) promulgated a new elaboration of the Hippocratic Oath, reformulated and expanded the International Code of Medical Ethics, and later identified medical doctors and other health professionals as "duty-bearers" or "enforcers" of internationally defined standards prohibiting torture. Article 1 of the WMA Declaration of Tokyo (1975) states that doctors "shall not countenance, condone or participate in the practice of torture or other forms of cruel, inhuman or degrading procedures, whatever the offense of which the victim of such procedures is suspected, accused or guilty, and whatever the victim's beliefs or motives, and in all situations, including armed conflict and civil strife."[18]

The lesson to learn from these intertwined events bears importantly on our thematic concern: human rights action and enforcement. It is a lesson well developed in Harold Hongju Koh's essay (Reading 24) entitled "How Is International Human Rights Law Enforced?" Beyond nation-states, he sketches a variety of groups and entities whose programs and initiatives are addressed to human rights enforcement but whose actions are not consistent with a model of centralized coercive governmental or intergovernmental policing. Echoing Burns Weston's definition of legal process, Koh describes what he calls a "vertical" array of "values entrepreneurs"—the International Committee of the Red Cross (ICRC) fostering humanitarian law since the nineteenth century, and the World Medical Association inserting human rights norms into their code of professional ethics exemplified by the torture provisions of the Declaration of Tokyo.

In Koh's analysis, the "vertical" strain to norm-consistency among diverse nongovernmental groups is an important component of human rights enforcement in world affairs. The examples of the ICRC and WMA illustrate a complex field of action contributing to human rights enforcement, though seldom recognized as such by those who assume law enforcement to be restricted to governmental policing bureaucracies according to some conceptually narrow model of domestic law, a category that Koh nonetheless characterizes, appropriately, as "horizontal" enforcement institutions. Indeed, as we turn to this field of "horizontal" action and the enforcement model it reflects, the picture is all too disappointing. The difficulties of such state-to-state enforcement are legion. As Koh asserts, "the overall picture of this standard enforcement story is one of impotence, ineffectiveness, of a horizontal system where the key actors are nation-states and intergovernmental organizations, the key forums are governmental forums, and the key transactions are transactions between states and other states."

Unfortunately, this statement serves to characterize several of the institutions discussed in Anne F. Bayefsky's essay entitled "Making the Human Rights Treaties Work" (Reading 25).[19] While she does not use Koh's vocabulary, her concern is with "horizontal enforcement"

17. Robert N. Proctor, "Nazi Doctors, Racial Medicine, and Human Experimentation," in George J. Annas and Michael A. Grodin, eds., *The Nazi Doctors and the Nuremberg Code: Human Rights in Human Experimentation* (New York: Oxford University Press, 1992), 17–31.
18. World Medical Association, Declaration of Tokyo (1975), reprinted in Alfred Heijder and Herman Van Geuns, eds., *Professional Codes of Ethics* (London: Amnesty International, 1976), 28. Also available at http://www1.umn.edu/humanrts/instree/tokyo.html
19. For this reason, instructors (and others) may find it pedagogically useful to review Reading 25 by Anne Bayefsky before Reading 24 by Harold Koh.

which she finds all too inefficient in the case of most of the UN treaty committees (or "treaty bodies" as they often are called) responsible for monitoring the compliance of states parties. Her essay supplies diverse examples of shortcomings leading to her baleful conclusion that, by and large, the treaty committee regime does not work well. Problems of inefficiency in reaching stated goals are multiple from the point of view of the public: some committees rely on excessively complicated procedures for lodging complaints; disappointed complainants learn too late about the lack of satisfactory enforcement powers; and, from the point of view of the committees, huge backlogs of reports go untended for too long and committee work is hobbled by severely limited budgets, staff, and resources.[20]

For example, the Committee on Economic, Social and Cultural Rights (CESCR), the treaty body established to enforce the International Covenant on Economic, Social, and Cultural Rights (ICESCR),[21] requires substantive, analytical, expert research support because the issues they address are complex. The Committee is an 18-member body of experts empaneled to study periodic reports required of contracting states. The pattern has been for the Committee members to discuss the reports with representatives of the governments concerned. Its comments aim to help them in their duty to implement social, economic, and cultural rights, as well as to bring to their attention deficiencies in reports and procedures. Yet the Committee has a very small staff and an historically low budget. Ergo, the CESCR members complain of inadequate supporting research to provide an independent basis on which to conduct critical assessments of state reports.

To fill the gap, NGO participation in the activities of the Committee has come to be important. Today, under the terms of the state reporting system of the ICESCR, NGOs regularly file "shadow reports," addressing critical challenges to the Committee to draw offending governments into a process of query and response to explain or defend their short-comings.[22] In 1993, the CESCR sought more active NGO participation, saying that it "reiterates its long-standing invitation to NGOs to submit to it in writing, at any time, information regarding any aspect of its work."[23] To the extent that NGO critiques of state reports reflect careful independent research, the Committee's work can become more effective.

An example of external assistance to the CESCR involves the Science and Human Rights Program of the American Association for the Advancement of Science (a nongovernmental membership society) which has provided consulting services to the Committee, advising it on such matters as information systems, data management, and technical issues relating to human rights such as intellectual property and privacy associated with information technology. In 1996, Osman El-Hajjé presented a Working Paper to the UN calling for an annual report to the General Assembly designed to keep the organization and the public's eye on human rights issues adversely affected by technological developments.[24] The recommendation was constructive, certainly, but it presupposed an institutional capacity to

20. For confirmation, see William F. Felice, "The UN Committee on the Elimination of All Forms of Racial Discrimination: Race and Economic and Social Human Rights," *HRQ* 24 (2002): 205–36.
21. Concluded Dec. 16, 1966, reprinted and referenced in Documentary Appendix A.
22. See Christof Heyns and Frans Viljoen, "The Impact of the United Nations Treaties on the Domestic Level," *HRQ* 23, no. 3 (August 2001): 483–535, at 507.
23. UN Committee on Economic, Social and Cultural Rights, "NGO Participation in Activities of the Committee," 8th Sess., UN Doc E/C.12/1993/WP.14 (May 10–28 1993). See also Fausto Pocar and Cecil Bernard, "National Reports: Their Submission to Expert Bodies and Follow-Up," in *Manual on Human Rights Reporting Under Six Major International Human Rights Instruments* (New York: United Nations, 1991), 25–28.
24. UN Commission on Human Rights, Sub-Commission on Prevention of Discrimination and Protection of Minorities, 49th Sess., Item 11, "Potentially Adverse Consequences of Scientific Progress and its Applications for the Integrity, Dignity and Human Rights of the Individual" (working paper prepared by Mr. Osman El-Hajjé in conformity with Sub-Commission decision 1996/110).

receive, critically assess, and act on such information. Unfortunately, UN use of science knowledge historically has been problematic as attested by Calestous Juma, a Harvard University specialist on science policy who argues that most UN agencies are not well organized to tap into advisory services and independent sources of information on science and technology.[25] He noted the particular needs of treaty committees to provide opportunities for NGO participation as a way of rallying the input of the scientific and technological community to the benefit of the UN goals. It follows that NGOs, scientific associations and other nonstate knowledge-based organizations must become more alert and prepared to offer treaty committees the benefits of their technical expertise.[26] Such external technical support is essential lest the treaty committees suffer a crisis of legitimacy by virtue of the ineffectiveness and inefficiency Bayefsky attributes to some of them.

Independent scholars like Bayefsky are not the only sharp critics of the UN Treaty Committee system. Committee members themselves also complain that their work sometimes fails to command the respect of the states obliged to report to them. According to Philip Alston, the former CESCR Committee Chair, the process historically has not been auspicious.[27] He noted wryly the delinquency record among reporting states who simply ignore their obligations as if they were an illegitimate intrusion of state sovereignty (Bayefsky calls them "rejectionist states"), as well as the substantial record of past experience that "shows that there is a tendency for reports to list a few pieces of legislation and some international exchange agreements and assume that the reporting requirements are thereby satisfied." Such selective games of "show and tell" hardly constitute a process of accountability. Thus the problems are twofold: committees lacking the time and resources to be effective, and states sometimes showing they do not believe in the importance of their reporting tasks and do not take their related duties seriously.

A core normative principle in modern political theory holds that the legitimacy of any governing regime has to do with the quality of authoritativeness, bindingness, or rightness attached to a political order by those affected. Institutions that lack authoritativeness, whose decisions are not seen as binding, and whose advice is ignored as not rightful, not only face problems of legitimacy but of effectiveness as well. In an important essay, "The Effectiveness of International Institutions," Oran R. Young states that "An institution is effective to the extent that its operation impels actors to behave differently than they would if the institution did not exist or if some other institutional arrangement were put in its place."[28] Bayefsky does not go so far in her critical observations about the UN treaty bodies as to say that they face a legitimacy crisis, but she may as well have done so. She writes: "the veneer of consensus removed, the United Nations human rights regime reveals a front of rejection as solid as the resistance that prevailed before November 1989 and the fall of the Berlin Wall. The terminology has changed and so have the players, but the fundamental rift in the United Nations system simply metastasized. * * * The newest form of rejectionist politics has successfully stymied the effective implementation of global international human rights law."

25. Calestous Juma, "The UN's Role in the New Diplomacy," *Issues in Science and Technology* 17, no. 1 (Fall 2000): 37–38.
26. Richard Pierre Claude, *Science in the Service of Human Rights* (Philadelphia: University of Pennsylvania Press, 2002).
27. Philip Alston, "The International Covenant on Economic, Social and Cultural Rights," in *Manual on Human Rights Reporting*, note 23, 39–78, at 70.
28. Oran R. Young, "The Effectiveness of International Institutions: Hard Cases and Critical Variables," in James N. Rosenau and Ernst-Otto Czempiel, *Governance Without Government: Order and Change in World Politics*, Cambridge Studies in International Relations 20 (Cambridge: Cambridge University Press, 1992), 160–94, at 161.

All this might make a most discouraging situation were it not for two positive developments. First, the Office of the UN High Commissioner for Human Rights (OHCHR) has taken these issues seriously, proposing many reforms such as "consolidated state reports" relieving states of the need, in many cases, to file six separate treaty reports."[29] Second, and significant for those interested in improving the effectiveness of the United Nations, Canadian law professor Anne Bayefsky has acted upon her own critical perspectives with a most constructive initiative. Consulting her website (http://www.Bayefsky.com), one finds multiple resources to promote active public interest in improving the effectiveness and credibility of the UN treaty system. For example, the website supplies up-to-date descriptions of the working methods of the UN treaty system; includes the text of human rights treaties; publishes documents by reporting states; offers instructions on "how to complain about human rights treaty violations"; and so forth. The purpose of the website is to generate constructive responses to the criticisms and concerns her essay in this chapter sets out and also, uniquely, to mobilize the participation of the public in developing improvements in our international human rights system. In doing so, her work is a model of accomplishment for the scholar-activist and her lesson should be clear: if you see institutional deficiencies in the field of human rights, study them, get the facts straight, analyze them, and then take action.

If the goal of effective action is ever achieved, despite countervailing political and sectarian forces, it is because human rights groups, activists, and scholars as well as the general public support open debate and freely exchanged ideas as essential to the success of holding states accountable for human rights violations and progress in overcoming obstacles to the goal we all seek: a global human rights respecting society. Part II of this volume is dedicated to this end.

29. Office of the United Nations High Commissioner for Human Rights, "Effective Functioning of Human Rights Mechanisms Treaty Bodies," Note to the Commission on Human Rights of the Economic and Social Council, UN Doc E/CN.42003/126 (Feb. 26, 2003).

23. BURNS H. WESTON *Human Rights: Prescription and Enforcement*

DEVELOPMENTS BEFORE WORLD WAR II

Ever since ancient times, but especially since the emergence of the modern state system, the Age of Discovery, and the accompanying spread of industrialization and European culture throughout the world, there has developed, for economic and other reasons, a unique set of customs and conventions regarding the humane treatment of foreigners. This evolving International Law of State Responsibility for Injuries to Aliens, as these customs and conventions came to be called, represents the beginning of active concern—however much they served the interests of colonial expansion—for human rights on the international plane. The founding fathers of international law—particularly Francisco de Vitoria, Grotius, and Emmerich de Vattel—were quick to observe that all persons, outlander as well as other, were entitled to certain natural rights, and they emphasized, consequently, the importance of according aliens fair treatment.

With the exception of occasional treaties to secure the protection of Christian denominations,

Reprinted with changes from Burns H. Weston, "Human Rights," in *Encyclopædia Britannica*, 15th rev. ed. (2002), available from *Encyclopædia Britannica Online* at http://www.britannica.com/eb/article?tocId= 219350. Copyright © 2002 Encyclopædia Britannica, Inc. Reprinted by permission. This reading concludes the essay begun in Reading 1 in Chapter 1 of this volume.

it was not until the start of the nineteenth century, however, that active international concern for the rights of nationals began to make itself felt. Then, in the century and a half before World War II, several noteworthy efforts to encourage respect for nationals by international means began to shape what today is called the International Law of Human Rights (which for historical but no theoretically convincing reasons was treated separately from the International Law of State Responsibility for Injuries to Aliens).

Throughout the nineteenth and early twentieth centuries, numerous military operations and diplomatic representations, not all of them with the purest of motives but performed nonetheless in the name of "humanitarian intervention" (a customary international law doctrine), undertook to protect oppressed and persecuted minorities in the Ottoman Empire, Syria, Crete, various Balkan countries, Romania, and Russia. Paralleling these actions, first at the Congress of Vienna (1814–15) and later between the two world wars, a series of treaties and international declarations sought the protection of certain racial, religious, and linguistic minorities in central and eastern Europe and the Middle East. During the same period, the movement to combat and suppress slavery and the slave trade found expression in treaties sooner or later involving the major commercial powers, beginning with the Treaty of Paris (1814)[1] and culminating in the International Slavery Convention (1926).[2]

In addition, beginning in the late nineteenth century and continuing well beyond World War II, the community of nations, inspired largely by persons associated with what is now the International Committee of the Red Cross, concluded a series of multilateral declarations and agreements designed to temper the conduct of hostilities, protect the victims of war, and otherwise elaborate the humanitarian law of war (now commonly referred to as International Humanitarian Law). At about the same time, first with two multilateral labour conventions concluded in 1906 and subsequently at the initiative of the International Labour Organization (ILO; established in 1919), a reformist-minded international community embarked upon a variety of collaborative measures directed at the promotion of human rights. These measures addressed not only concerns traditionally associated with labour law and labour relations (e.g., industrial health and safety, hours of work, and annual paid holidays), but also—mainly after World War II—such core human rights concerns as forced labour, discrimination in employment and occupation, freedom of association for collective bargaining, and equal pay for equal work.

Finally, during the interwar period, the covenant establishing the League of Nations (1919)—though not formally recognizing "the rights of Man" and failing to lay down a principle of racial nondiscrimination as requested by Japan (owing mainly to the resistance of Great Britain and the United States)—nevertheless committed its members to several human rights goals: fair and humane working conditions, the execution of agreements regarding trafficking in women and children, the prevention and control of disease in matters of international concern, and the just treatment of indigenous colonial peoples. Also, the victorious powers—who as "mandatories" were entrusted by the League with the tutelage of colonies formerly governed by Germany and Turkey—accepted responsibility for the well-being and development of the inhabitants of those territories as "a sacred trust of civilization." This arrangement was later carried over into the trusteeship system of the United Nations.

As important as these efforts were, however, it was not until after the war—and the Nazi atrocities accompanying it—that active concern for human rights truly came of age internationally. In the proceedings of the International Military Tribunal at Nürnberg in 1945–46 (the Nürnberg trials), German high officials were tried not only for "crimes against peace" and "war crimes," but also for "crimes against humanity" committed against civilian populations, even if the crimes were in accordance with the laws of the country in which they were perpetrated. Although the tribunal, whose establishment and rulings subsequently were endorsed by the UN General Assembly, applied a cautious approach to allegations of crimes against humanity, it nonetheless made the treatment by a state of its own citizens the subject of international criminal process. The ad hoc international criminal tribunals established in 1993–94 for the prosecution of serious violations of International Humanitarian Law in

1. Concluded May 30, 1814, available at http://www.napoleonseries.org/reference/diplomatic/paris1.cfm
2. Concluded Sept. 25, 1926, referenced in Documentary Appendix B.

the former Yugoslavia and Rwanda were its first heirs on the international plane. Both courts were empowered to impose sentences of life imprisonment (though not the death penalty), and both focused their efforts, with some success, on political leaders who had authorized human rights abuses. Most conspicuous was the arrest and detention in June 2001 of former Yugoslav president Slobodan Milosevic by the International Criminal Tribunal for Yugoslavia, representing the first time a former head of state has been placed in the physical custody of an international judicial authority. The tribunal charged him with war crimes and crimes against humanity allegedly committed by Serbian forces in Kosovo in 1999 and subsequently with the crime of genocide allegedly committed by Serbian forces during the war in Bosnia and Herzegovina in 1992–95.

Also heir to the Nürnberg tribunal is the International Criminal Court, authorized by the adoption by 160 countries of the Rome Statute of the International Criminal Court in July 1998.[3] The statute creates a permanent international criminal court whose jurisdiction includes crimes against humanity, crimes of genocide, war crimes, and crimes of "aggression" (pending the adoption of an acceptable definition of that term). However, the creation of the court, which depends on the ratification of the statute by at least 60 signatory states, was resisted by some countries, notably the United States, on the ground that it would unduly infringe upon their national sovereignty. The long-term future of the court is therefore uncertain.

HUMAN RIGHTS IN THE UNITED NATIONS

The Charter of the United Nations (1945) begins by reaffirming a "faith in fundamental human rights, in the dignity and worth of the human person, in the equal rights of men and women and of nations large and small." It states that the purposes of the UN are, among other things: "to develop friendly relations among nations based on respect for the principle of equal rights and self-determination of peoples . . . [and] to achieve international co-operation . . . in promoting and encouraging respect for human rights and for fundamental freedoms for all

without distinction as to race, sex, language, or religion."

In addition, in two key articles, all members "pledge themselves to take joint and separate action in cooperation with the Organization" for the achievement of these and related purposes. It must be noted, however, that a proposal to ensure the protection as well as the promotion of human rights was explicitly rejected at the Charter-drafting San Francisco conference establishing the UN. Also, the Charter expressly provides that nothing in it "shall authorize the United Nations to intervene in matters which are essentially within the domestic jurisdiction of any state," except upon a Security Council finding of a "threat to the peace, breach of the peace, or act of aggression." Furthermore, though typical of major constitutive instruments, the Charter is conspicuously given to generality and vagueness in its human rights clauses, among others.

Thus, not surprisingly, the reconciliation of the Charter's human rights provisions with the history of its drafting and its "domestic jurisdiction" clause has given rise to legal and political controversy. Some authorities have argued that, in becoming parties to the Charter, states accept no more than a nebulous promotional obligation toward human rights and that, in any event, the UN has no standing to insist on human rights safeguards in member states. Others have insisted that the Charter's human rights provisions, being part of a legally binding treaty, clearly involve some element of legal obligation; that the "pledge" made by states upon becoming party to the Charter consequently represents more than a moral statement; and that the domestic jurisdiction clause does not apply because human rights no longer can be considered a matter "essentially within the domestic jurisdiction" of states.

When all is said and done, however, it is clear from the actual practice of the UN that the problem of resolving these opposing contentions has proved less formidable than the statements of governments and the opinions of scholars would suggest. Neither the Charter's drafting history nor its domestic jurisdiction clause—nor, indeed, its generality and vagueness in respect of human rights—has prevented the UN from investigating, discussing, and evaluating specific human rights situations. Nor have they prevented

---

3. Concluded July 17, 1998, referenced in Documentary Appendix B.

it from taking concrete action in relation to them—at least not in the case of "a consistent pattern of gross violations," as in the Security Council's imposition of a mandatory arms embargo against South Africa in 1977 and its authorization of the use of military force to end human rights abuses in Somalia and Haiti in the early 1990s. Of course, governments usually are protective of their sovereignty, or domestic jurisdiction. Also, the UN organs responsible for the promotion and protection of human rights suffer from most of the same disabilities that afflict the UN as a whole, in particular the absence of supranational authority, the presence of divisive power politics, and the imposition of crippling financial constraints by member states (most notably the United States). Hence, it cannot be expected that UN actions in defense of human rights will be, normally, either swift or categorically effective. Indeed, many serious UN efforts at human rights implementation have been deliberately thwarted by the major powers. In 1999, for example, opposition by China and Russia prevented the Security Council from agreeing on forceful measures to end the persecution by Serbia of ethnic Albanians in the province of Kosovo, prompting the United States and other members of the North Atlantic Treaty Organization (NATO) to take matters into their own hands through a massive bombing campaign against Serbian targets. Nevertheless, assuming some political will, the legal obstacles to UN enforcement of human rights are not insurmountable.

Primary responsibility for the promotion and protection of human rights under the UN Charter rests in the General Assembly and, under its authority, in the Economic and Social Council (ECOSOC), the Commission on Human Rights, and the UN High Commissioner for Human Rights (UNHCHR). The UN Commission on Human Rights, an intergovernmental subsidiary body of ECOSOC that met for the first time in 1947, serves as the UN's central policy organ in the human rights field. The UNHCHR, a post created by the General Assembly in 1993, is the official principally responsible for implementing and coordinating UN human rights programs and projects, including overall supervision of the UN's Geneva-based Centre for Human Rights, a bureau of the UN Secretariat.

THE UN COMMISSION ON HUMAN RIGHTS AND ITS INSTRUMENTS

For the first 20 years of its existence (1947–66), the UN Commission on Human Rights concentrated . . . on setting human rights standards, believing itself unauthorized to deal with human rights complaints. Together with other UN bodies such as the ILO, . . . UNESCO, the UN Commission on the Status of Women, and the Commission on Crime Prevention and Criminal Justice, it . . . drafted standards and prepared a number of international human rights instruments. Among the most important [were] the Universal Declaration of Human Rights (1948), the International Covenant on Economic, Social and Cultural Rights (1966), and the International Covenant on Civil and Political Rights (1966) together with its Optional Protocols (1966, 1989).[4] Collectively known as the "International Bill of Human Rights," these three instruments serve as touchstones for interpreting the human rights provisions of the UN charter. Also central . . . [were] the International Convention on the Elimination of All Forms of Racial Discrimination (1965), the Convention on the Elimination of All Forms of Discrimination against Women (1979), the Convention against Torture and Other Cruel, Inhuman or Degrading Treatment or Punishment (1984), and the Convention on the Rights of the Child (1989), each of which elaborates on provisions of the International Bill of Human Rights.[5]

The commission continue[d] to perform this standard-setting role [for the next four decades. Beginning in 1967, however, when it was authorized to deal with violations of human rights, its work became highly investigatory, evaluative, and advisory in character. Each year it established working groups to consider and make recommendations concerning alleged "gross violations" of human rights referred to it by the commission's Sub-Commission on the Promotion and Protection of Human Rights based on both "communications" from individuals and groups and investigations by the Sub-Commission. Also, on an ad hoc basis, it appointed Special Rapporteurs and other envoys to examine human rights situations—both country-oriented and thematic—and report back on the basis of trustworthy

---

4. Each of these instruments is reprinted and referenced in Documentary Appendix A.
5. Each of these instruments is referenced in Documentary Appendix B.

evidence.] These fact-finding and implementation mechanisms and procedures were the focus of the commission's attention during the 1970s and '80s. In the 1990s, it turned increasingly to economic, social, and cultural rights, including the right to development and the right to an adequate standard of living. Increased attention [was] paid also to the rights of minorities, indigenous peoples, women, and children. [In June 2006, the 53-member commission was replaced by a 47-member UN Human Rights Council (HRC), established by the UN General Assembly with a larger mandate that includes all the best elements of the commission's investigatory, evaluative, and advisory functions.[6] In a sudden reversal of policy regarded as unfortunate by many, the United States declined to seek election to it.]

The UN High Commissioner on Human Rights

Appointed by the secretary-general in a regular rotation of geographic regions and approved by the General Assembly, the UNHCHR serves a fixed term of four years with the possibility of renewal for an additional four-year term. The first high commissioner, José Ayala Lasso of Ecuador, took office in April 1994, and Mary Robinson, formerly president of Ireland, became the second high commissioner in September 1997. Among other duties, the high commissioner is charged by the General Assembly to promote and protect all civil, political, economic, social, and cultural rights; to provide advisory services and technical and financial assistance in the field of human rights to states that request them; to coordinate human rights promotion and protection activities throughout the UN system, including education and public-information programs; and otherwise to enhance international cooperation for the promotion and protection of human rights—all within the framework of the International Bill of Human Rights.

The Universal Declaration of Human Rights (UDHR)

The catalog of rights set out in the UDHR, which was adopted without dissent by the General Assembly on December 10, 1948, is scarcely less than the sum of most of the important

traditional political and civil rights of national constitutions and legal systems, including equality before the law; protection against arbitrary arrest; the right to a fair trial; freedom from ex post facto criminal laws; the right to own property; freedom of thought, conscience, and religion; freedom of opinion and expression; and freedom of peaceful assembly and association. Also enumerated are such economic, social, and cultural rights as the right to work, the right to form and join trade unions, the right to rest and leisure, the right to a standard of living adequate for health and well-being, and the right to education.

The Universal Declaration, it should be noted, is not a treaty. It was meant to proclaim "a common standard of achievement for all peoples and all nations" rather than enforceable legal obligations. Nevertheless, the Universal Declaration has acquired a status juridically more important than originally intended, and it has been widely used, even by national courts, as a means of judging compliance with human rights obligations under the UN Charter.

The International Covenant on Civil and Political Rights (ICCPR) and Its Optional Protocols

The civil and political rights guaranteed by the ICCPR, which was opened for signature on December 19, 1966, and entered into force on March 23, 1976, incorporate almost all those rights proclaimed in the Universal Declaration, including the right to nondiscrimination but excluding the right to own property and the right to asylum. The Covenant also designates several rights that are not listed in the Universal Declaration, among them the right of all peoples to self-determination and the right of ethnic, religious, and linguistic minorities to enjoy their own culture, to profess and practice their own religion, and to use their own language. To the extent that the Universal Declaration and the Covenant overlap, however, the latter is understood to explicate and to help interpret the former.

In addition, the Covenant calls for the establishment of a Human Rights Committee, comprising persons serving in their individual expert capacities, to study reports submitted by the states parties on measures they have adopted to give

---

6. The HRC replaced the commission as this book went to press. For details, see http//www.un.org/News/Press/docs/2006/ga10449doc.htm and http//www.ohchr.org/english. See also the introduction to Chapter 6 in this volume at 330–31.

effect to the rights recognized in the Covenant. For states parties that have expressly recognized the competence of the committee in this regard, the committee also may respond to allegations by one state party that another state party is not fulfilling its obligations under the Covenant. If the committee is unable to resolve the problem, the matter is referred to an ad hoc conciliation commission, which eventually reports its findings on all questions of fact, plus its views on the possibilities of an amicable solution. States parties that become party to the covenant's first Optional Protocol[7] further recognize the competence of the Human Rights Committee to consider and act upon communications from individuals claiming to be victims of covenant violations. Other treaty-based organs within the UN system that are empowered to consider grievances from individuals in quasi-judicial manner are the Committee on the Elimination of Racial Discrimination and the Committee on Torture, under the 1965 race discrimination and the 1984 torture conventions, respectively.

Also noteworthy is the Covenant's Second Optional Protocol,[8] which is aimed at abolishing the death penalty worldwide. Adopted in 1989 and entered into force in 1991, it has been favorably received in most of the countries of western Europe and many countries in the Americas, though not in the United States.

The International Covenant on Economic, Social and Cultural Rights (ICESCR)

Just as the International Covenant on Civil and Political Rights elaborates upon most of the civil and political rights enumerated in the Universal Declaration of Human Rights, so the International Covenant on Economic, Social and Cultural Rights elaborates upon most of the economic, social, and cultural rights set forth in the Universal Declaration: the right to work, the right to just and favourable conditions of work, trade union rights, the right to social security, rights relating to the protection of the family, the right to an adequate standard of living, the right to health, the right to education, and rights relating to culture and science. Unlike its companion agreement, the International Covenant on Civil and Political Rights, however, generally

this Covenant, sometimes called a "promotional convention," is not intended for immediate implementation, the states parties having agreed only "to take steps" toward "achieving progressively the full realization of the rights recognized in the . . . Covenant," and then subject to "the maximum of [their] available resources." One obligation, however, is subject to immediate application: the prohibition of discrimination in the enjoyment of the rights enumerated on grounds of race, colour, sex, language, religion, political or other opinion, national or social origin, property, and birth or other status. Also, the international supervisory measures that apply to the Covenant oblige the states parties to report to the UN Economic and Social Council on the steps they have adopted and on the progress they have made in achieving the realization of the enumerated rights.

OTHER UN HUMAN RIGHTS CONVENTIONS AND DECLARATIONS

Numerous other human rights treaties drafted under UN auspices address a broad range of concerns, including the prevention and punishment of the crime of genocide; the humane treatment of military and civilian personnel in time of war; the status of refugees; the protection of stateless persons; the abolition of slavery, forced labour, and discrimination in employment and occupation; the suppression and punishment of the crime of apartheid; the elimination of discrimination in education; the promotion of the political rights of women; the protection of minorities and indigenous peoples; and the promotion of equality of opportunity and treatment among migrant workers. In addition to overseeing human rights treaties, the UN also adopts declarations, in the form of resolutions, aimed at promoting human rights. Although technically not binding on member states in the sense of a treaty or a resolution of the Security Council, such declarations—particularly when they enunciate principles of great and solemn importance—may nevertheless create strong expectations about authority and control. Perhaps the best-known examples subsequent to the Universal Declaration are the Declaration on the Granting of Independence to Colonial Countries and Peoples (1960)

---

7. Referenced in Documentary Appendix B.
8. Referenced in Documentary Appendix B.

and the Declaration on Principles of International Law concerning Friendly Relations and Co-operation among States in accordance with the Charter of the United Nations (1970),[9] which affirms, among other things, "the duty of all states to refrain from organizing, instigating, assisting or participating in . . . terrorist acts."

Other declarations have addressed the rights of disabled persons; the elimination of all forms of intolerance and discrimination based on religion or belief; the right of peoples to peace; the right to development; the rights of persons belonging to national, ethnic, religious, and linguistic minorities; and the elimination of violence against women.

HUMAN RIGHTS AND THE HELSINKI PROCESS

After World War II, international concern for human rights was evident at the global level outside the UN as well as within it, most notably in the proceedings and aftermath of the Conference on Security and Co-operation in Europe (CSCE), convened in Helsinki, Finland, on July 3, 1973, and concluded there (after continuing deliberations in Geneva) on August 1, 1975. Attended by representatives of 35 governments —including the NATO countries, the Warsaw Pact nations, and 13 neutral and nonaligned European states—the conference had as its principal purpose a mutually satisfactory definition of peace and stability between East and West, previously made impossible by the Cold War. In particular, the Soviet Union wished to gain recognition of its western frontiers as established at the end of World War II (which ended without the conclusion of an omnibus peace treaty). The West, with no realistic territorial claims of its own, sought concessions primarily on security requirements and human rights, largely in that order.

The Final Act of the conference,[10] also known as the Helsinki Accords, begins with a Declaration on Principles Guiding Relations between Participating States, in which the participating states solemnly declare "their determination to respect and put into practice," alongside other "guiding" principles, "respect [for] human rights and fundamental freedoms, including the freedom of thought, conscience, religion or belief"

and "respect [for] the equal rights of peoples and their right to self-determination." It was hoped that this declaration, the importance of which is reflected in its having been signed by almost all of the principal governmental leaders of the day, would mark the beginning of a liberalization of authoritarian regimes.

From the earliest discussions, however, it was clear that the Helsinki Final Act was not intended as a legally binding instrument. The expression "determination to respect" and to "put into practice" were seen as moral commitments only, the Declaration of Principles was said not to prescribe international law, and nowhere did the participants provide for enforcement machinery. On the other hand, the Declaration of Principles, including its human rights principles, was always viewed as being at least consistent with international law, and in providing for periodic follow-up conferences, it made possible a unique negotiating process ("the Helsinki process") to review compliance with its terms, thus creating normative expectations concerning the conduct of the participating states. In these ways it proved to be an important force in the fall of the Iron Curtain and the transformation of eastern Europe in 1989–90.

The Helsinki process, involving long-running "follow-up," "summit," and other meetings, served also to establish a mechanism for the evolution of the CSCE from a forum for discussion to an operational institution, beginning with the adoption of the Charter of Paris for a New Europe in 1990. In 1994 the CSCE was renamed the Organization for Security and Co-operation in Europe (OSCE), and its principal organs and bureaus now include an Office for Democratic Institutions and Human Rights (in Warsaw), a Conflict Prevention Centre (in Vienna), a High Commissioner on National Minorities (in The Hague), and a Court of Conciliation and Arbitration (in Geneva). These offices have been increasingly pressed into service to alleviate major deprivations of human rights, particularly those arising from ethnic conflicts. In addition, the Vienna Human Dimension Mechanism and the Moscow Human Dimension Mechanism provide a preliminary formal means of raising and seeking to resolve disputes about violations of human rights commitments, including the possibility of on-site investigation by independent experts. All

9. Each of these General Assembly declarations is referenced in Documentary Appendix B.
10. Adopted Aug. 1, 1975, referenced in Documentary Appendix B.

these mechanisms, however, bespeak an essentially interstate process; neither individuals nor nongovernmental organizations (NGOs) have access to them except indirectly as suppliers of information and conveyors of political pressure. They thus contrast markedly with the individual complaint procedures that are available within the UN and in regional human rights systems.

REGIONAL DEVELOPMENTS

Action for the international promotion and protection of human rights has proceeded at the regional level in Europe, the Americas, Africa, the Middle East, and, to a minor extent, Asia. Only the first three of these regions, however, have created enforcement mechanisms within the framework of a human rights charter.

EUROPEAN HUMAN RIGHTS SYSTEM

On November 4, 1950, the Council of Europe agreed to the European Convention for the Protection of Human Rights and Fundamental Freedoms,[11] the substantive provisions of which are based on a draft of what is now the International Covenant on Civil and Political Rights. Together with its 11 additional protocols, this convention, which entered into force on September 3, 1953, represents the most advanced and successful international experiment in the field to date. Over the years, the enforcement mechanisms created by the Convention have developed a considerable body of case law on questions regulated by the Convention, which the states parties typically have honoured and respected. In some European states the provisions of the Convention are deemed to be part of domestic constitutional or statutory law. Where this is not the case, the states parties have taken other measures to make their domestic laws conform with their obligations under the Convention.

Notwithstanding these successes, a significant streamlining of the European human rights regime took place on November 1, 1998, when Protocol No. 11 to the Convention entered into force. Pursuant to the protocol, two of the enforcement mechanisms created by the convention—the European Commission of Human Rights and the European Court of Human Rights—were merged into a reconstituted court, which now is empowered to hear individual (as opposed to interstate) petitions or complaints without the prior approval of the local government. The decisions of the court are final and binding on the states parties to the Convention.

A companion instrument to the European Convention—similar to but preceding the International Covenant on Economic, Social and Cultural Rights—is the European Social Charter (1961) and its additional protocol (1988).[12] In contrast to the adjudicatory enforcement procedures of the European Convention, the Charter's provisions are implemented through an elaborate system of control based on progress reports to the various committees and organs of the Council of Europe. In July 1996 the Revised Social Charter,[13] which modernizes its forebear's substantive provisions and strengthens its enforcement capabilities, entered into force. Both charters have suffered from a notable lack of public awareness, however, and this fact, together with an increased emphasis on market-oriented economic policies in many European countries, threatens not only the ratification of the 1996 charter, but, as well, the political commitment to the several and joint aims of each treaty.

INTER-AMERICAN HUMAN RIGHTS SYSTEM

In 1948, concurrent with its establishment of the Organization of American States (OAS), the Ninth Pan-American Conference adopted the American Declaration on the Rights and Duties of Man,[14] which, unlike the Universal Declaration of the UN adopted seven months later, set out the duties as well as the rights of individual citizens. Subsequently, in 1959, a meeting of the American Ministers for Foreign Affairs created the Inter-American Commission on Human Rights, which has since undertaken important investigative activities in the region. Finally, in 1969, the Inter-American Specialized Conference on Human Rights adopted the American

---

11. Referenced in Documentary Appendix B.
12. Concluded Oct. 18, 1961 and May 5, 1988, respectively, each referenced in Documentary Appendix B.
13. European Social Charter (Revised), concluded May 3, 1996, referenced in Documentary Appendix B.
14. Adopted Mar. 30–May 2, 1948, referenced in Documentary Appendix B.

Convention on Human Rights,[15] which, among other things, after entering into force in July 1978, made the existing Inter-American Commission an organ of the convention and established the Inter-American Court of Human Rights, which sits in San José, Costa Rica. In November 1988, the OAS adopted the Additional Protocol to the American Convention on Human Rights in the Area of Economic, Social and Cultural Rights.[16] Of the 26 Western Hemispheric states that so far have signed the convention, only the United States has yet to ratify it. Nor is the United States a party to the additional protocol, which entered into force in November 1999.

The core structure of the inter-American human rights system is similar to that of its European counterpart. Nevertheless, some noteworthy differences exist, and three stand out in particular. First, as noted above, the American Convention, reflecting the influence of the American Declaration, acknowledges the relationship between individual duties and individual rights. Second, the American Convention reverses the priorities of the European Convention prior to Protocol No. 11 by guaranteeing individual petitions while making interstate complaints optional. Finally, both the Inter-American Commission and the Inter-American Court operate beyond the framework of the American Convention. The Commission is as much an organ of the OAS Charter as of the American Convention, with powers and procedures that differ significantly depending on the source of the Commission's authority. The Court, while primarily an organ of the Convention, nonetheless has jurisdiction to interpret the human rights provisions of other treaties, including those of the OAS Charter.

AFRICAN HUMAN RIGHTS SYSTEM

In 1981, the Eighteenth Assembly of Heads of State and Government of the Organization of African Unity (OAU) adopted the African Charter on Human and Peoples' Rights.[17] Also known as the "Banjul Charter" for having been drafted in Banjul, Gambia, it entered into force on Octo-

ber 21, 1986, and boasts the vast majority of the states of Africa as parties.

Like its American and early European counterparts, the African Charter provides for a human rights commission, which has both promotional and protective functions. There is no restriction on who may file a complaint with it. In contrast to the European and American procedures, however, concerned states are encouraged to reach a friendly settlement without formally involving the investigative or conciliatory mechanisms of the commission. Also, the African Charter does not, at present, call for a human rights court. African customs and traditions, it has been said, emphasize mediation, conciliation, and consensus rather than the adversarial and adjudicative procedures that are common to Western legal systems. Nevertheless, owing largely to political changes wrought by the end of the Cold War, planning for an African Court of Human Rights was begun in the late 1990s. As envisioned, the Court would not replace the Commission but would supplement and reinforce its mandate.

Four other distinctive features of the African Charter are noteworthy. First, it provides for economic, social, and cultural rights as well as civil and political rights. In this respect it resembles the American Convention and differs from the European Convention. Second, in contrast to both the European and American Conventions, it recognizes the rights of groups in addition to the family, women, and children. The aged and the infirm are accorded special protection also, and the right of peoples to self-determination is elaborated in the right to existence, equality, and non-domination. Third, it uniquely embraces two third-generation, or "solidarity," rights: the right to economic, social, and cultural development and the right to national and international peace and security. Finally, it is to date the only treaty instrument to detail individual duties as well as individual rights—to the family, society, the state, and the international African community. Nevertheless, in view of the turmoil that beset northern and sub-Saharan Africa at the end of the twentieth century, it is fair to say that the African human rights system is still in its infancy.

15. Concluded Nov. 22, 1969, referenced in Documentary Appendix B.
16. Concluded Nov. 17, 1988, referenced in Documentary Appendix B.
17. Concluded June 27, 1981, referenced in Documentary Appendix B.

MIDDLE EASTERN AND ASIAN HUMAN RIGHTS
SYSTEMS

The Permanent Arab Commission on Human
Rights, founded by the Council of the League of
Arab States in September 1968, has been preoccupied primarily with the rights of Arabs living
in Israeli-occupied territories. Functioning more
to promote than to protect human rights, at the
end of the 1990s it had yet to bring a proposed
Arab Convention on Human Rights to a successful conclusion. Nevertheless, work by other
intergovernmental and nongovernmental bodies manifested a continuing desire to establish
human rights protection mechanisms in the Middle East. Building on the Universal Islamic Declaration of Human Rights (1981)[18] and the Cairo
Declaration on Human Rights in Islam (1990),[19]
the League of Arab States approved an Arab
Charter on Human Rights in September 1994.[20]
The charter provides for periodic reports to the
league's Human Rights Committee by states parties and for an independent Committee of Experts apparently empowered to request and study
reports and submit its own findings to the Human Rights Committee. No other institutions or
procedures for monitoring human rights are specified in the charter, however. More so than in
most other regions of the world (except Asia),
the states of the Middle East were greatly divided
over the need to enforce human rights law and
the desirability of achieving a true regional system for the promotion and protection of human
rights.

In Asia, despite efforts by NGOs and the United
Nations, the states of the region have been at best
ambivalent—and at worst hostile—to human
rights concerns, thus precluding agreement on
almost all regional human rights initiatives.
In early 1993, anticipating the Vienna World
Conference on Human Rights later that year,
a conference of Asia-Pacific NGOs adopted an
Asia-Pacific Declaration of Human Rights, and
in 1997 another meeting of NGOs adopted an
Asian Human Rights Charter. Both of these initiatives supported the universality and indivisibility of human rights. However, whereas the

first initiative called for the creation of a regional
human rights regime, the second—seemingly in
deference to the cultural diversity and vastness
of the region—urged instead the establishment
of national human rights commissions and so-
called "People's Tribunals," which would be based
more on moral and spiritual foundations rather
than on legal ones. The states of Asia were slow
to respond to these recommendations. Their positions were indicated at a UN-sponsored workshop in 1996, where the 30 participating states
concluded that "it was premature . . . to discuss
specific arrangements relating to the setting up
of a formal human rights mechanism in the Asian
and Pacific region." The same states agreed, however, to "[explore] the options available and the
process necessary for establishing a regional
mechanism."[21] It remains to be seen whether
the economic and political crises that beset Asia
at the end of the twentieth century will stimulate efforts to ensure greater respect for human
rights through regional cooperation.

INTERNATIONAL HUMAN RIGHTS IN DOMESTIC COURTS

Using domestic courts to clarify and safeguard
international human rights is a new and still
evolving approach to human rights advocacy. In
addition to the inevitable interpretative problems involved in applying norms that are fashioned in multicultural settings, controversial
theories about the interrelation of national and
international law, as well as many procedural
difficulties, burden the human rights claimant
in this setting. To be sure, considerable progress
has been made, as perhaps best evidenced in the
far-reaching decision handed down by the U.S.
Court of Appeals for the Second Circuit in *Filártiga v. Peña-Irala* (1980), in which the court held
that the international prohibition of torture, because it is unequivocally established in customary international law and applies regardless of
the nationality of the victim or the perpetrator
(at least in the case of private litigants), must
be honoured in U.S. courts.[22] More recently, in

18. Concluded Sept. 19, 1981, referenced in Documentary Appendix B.
19. Concluded Aug. 5, 1990, referenced in Documentary Appendix B.
20. Concluded Sept. 15, 1994, referenced in Documentary Appendix B.
21. Report to the Fourth Workshop on Regional Human Rights Arrangements in the Asian and Pacific
Region, Kathmandu, Feb. 26–28, 1996, E/CN/1996/46/Add.1
22. 630 F. 2d 876 (2d Cir., 1980).

1998–99, the United Kingdom's highest tribunal, the Law Lords of the British House of Lords, captured international attention when, in response to an extradition request by a Spanish court, it upheld the arrest in England of former Chilean President Augusto Pinochet on charges of torture and conspiracy to commit torture in violation of international treaty law. Although Pinochet was later returned to Chile and declared by a Chilean court to be mentally unfit to stand trial,[23] the Law Lords' ruling established the precedent that former heads of state do not enjoy immunity from prosecution, at least for systematic human rights crimes.

HUMAN RIGHTS AT THE TURN OF THE 21ST CENTURY

Whatever the current attitudes and policies of governments, the reality of popular demands for human rights, including both greater economic justice and greater political freedom, is beyond debate. A deepening and widening concern for the promotion and protection of human rights on all fronts, hastened by the ideal of self-determination in a postcolonial era, is now unmistakably woven into the fabric of contemporary world affairs.

Substantially responsible for this progressive development has been the work of the UN, its allied agencies, and such regional organizations as the Council of Europe, the OAS, and the OAU. Also contributing to this development, particularly since the 1970s and '80s, have been five other salient factors: (1) the public advocacy of human rights as a key aspect of national foreign policies, made initially legitimate by the example of U.S. President Jimmy Carter; (2) the emergence and spread of civil society on a transnational basis, primarily in the form of activist nongovernmental human rights organizations such as Amnesty International, Interights, and Human Rights Watch, the International Commission of Jurists, and diverse faith-based and professional groups; (3) a worldwide profusion of teaching and research devoted to the study of human rights in both formal and informal settings; (4) the proliferation of large UN conferences in areas such as children's rights, population, social development, women's rights, human settlements, and food production and distribution; and (5) a mounting feminist intellectual and political challenge regarding not only the rights of women worldwide, but also what feminists consider the paternalistic myths and myth structures that purport to define humane governance generally.

To be sure, because the application of international human rights law depends for the most part on the voluntary consent of nations, formidable obstacles attend the endeavours of human rights policy-makers, activists, and scholars. Human rights conventions continue to be undermined by the failure of states to ratify them and by emasculating reservations and derogations, by self-serving reporting systems that outnumber objective complaint procedures, and by poor financing for the implementation of human rights prescriptions. In short, the mechanisms for the enforcement of human rights are still in their infancy. Nevertheless, it is certain that, out of necessity no less than out of realism, a palpable concern for the advancement of human rights is here to stay.

QUESTIONS FOR REFLECTION AND DISCUSSION

1. Weston discusses the institutionalization of human rights on the international plane in the years preceding World War II. What principal human rights developments took place prior to World War II? Did any of them survive? Did any of them foreshadow events to come?

2. Weston discusses briefly the role of the UN in promoting and protecting human rights. For detailed discussion, see Reading 26 by Stephen P. Marks in Chapter 6 of this volume. Weston also summarizes the role of regional systems in promoting and protecting human rights. For detailed discussion, see Reading 27 by Dinah Shelton in Chapter 6 of this volume.

3. Weston notes that the Helsinki Process diverged from the UN and regional human rights systems because "neither individuals nor nongovernmental organizations have access to them except indirectly as suppliers of information and conveyors of political pressure."

23. On Dec. 14, 2004, Chilean appeals court Judge Guzmán Tapia reversed this ruling and declared General Pinochet fit to stand trial.

Which type of system is more effective in addressing human rights? What types of problems do you anticipate follow from an individual complaint procedure? What is the advantage of allowing NGOs more than an information-providing role, such as, for example, bringing claims of abuses on behalf of individuals? The disadvantages?

4. As of this writing, there is no regional human rights system in Asia or the Middle East. Why not? What would it take to establish human rights systems in these regions? What would be the principal problems? The principal benefits?

5. The United States has long been a self-proclaimed champion of human rights. It also has played a direct part in drafting many of the human rights treaties and declarations developed under the auspices of the United Nations and the Inter-American human rights system. Why, then, has the U.S. so far failed to ratify such major human rights conventions as the International Covenant on Economic, Social and Cultural Rights (ICESCR), the two additional protocols to the International Covenant on Civil and Political Rights (ICCPR), the Statute of the International Criminal Court (ICC), the American Convention on Human Rights (ACHR), the Convention on the Elimination of All Forms of Discrimination against Women (CEDAW), and Convention on the Rights of the Child (CRC)?

6. Weston concludes by stating that "Human rights conventions continue to be undermined by the failure of states to ratify them and by emasculating reservations and derogations, by self-serving reporting systems that outnumber objective complaint procedures, and by poor financing for the implementation of human rights prescriptions. In short, the mechanisms for the enforcement of human rights are still in their infancy. Nevertheless, it is certain that, out of necessity no less than out of realism, a palpable concern for the advancement of human rights is here to stay." Given these inadequacies, what is the use of human rights? Why are they important? Why does Weston say that they are "here to stay"?

7. In "The International Human Rights Movement: Part of the Problem?" *HHRJ* 15 (2002): 101–25, at 110, Harvard law professor David Kennedy writes:

> The strong attachment of the human rights movement to the legal formalization of rights and the establishment of legal machinery for their implementation makes the achievement of these forms an end in itself. Elites in a political system—international, national—which has adopted the rules and set up the institutions will often themselves have the impression and insist persuasively to others that they have addressed the problem of violations with an elaborate, internationally respected and "state of the art" response. This is analogous to the way in which holding elections can come to substitute for popular engagement in the political process. These are the traditional problems of form: form can hamper peaceful adjustment and necessary change, can be over- or under-inclusive. Is the right to vote a floor—or can it become a ceiling? The human rights movement ties its own hands on progressive development.

What is your reaction to Kennedy's statement? Do you find it overly critical, on target, or something in between? Do you believe he articulates a legitimate danger of the human rights movement? For an important critique, see Hilary Charlesworth, "Author! Author! A Response to David Kennedy," *HHRJ* 15 (2002): 127–31.

24. Harold Hongju Koh *How Is International Human Rights Law Enforced?*

I wouldn't be surprised if many were to give a pessimistic answer [to the question that is the title of this lecture]: international human rights law is not enforced, you might say. Just take a look at the massive human rights violations in Bosnia, violations that have gone unredressed in Cambodia; the continuing crises in the Congo, Sierra Leone, Algeria, and Burundi. Look at indicted war criminals, like Radovan Karadzic in Republika Srpska, who continue to flout the

Reprinted with changes from Harold Hongju Koh, "How Is International Human Rights Law Enforced?" Addison C. Harris Lecture at Indiana University-Bloomington, Jan. 21, 1998, *Indiana Law Journal* 74 (Fall 1999): 1397–1417. Copyright © 1999 Trustees of Indiana University and Harold Hongju Koh. Reprinted by permission.

jurisdictions of the Bosnian war crimes tribunal. Look, you might say, at the world's willingness to overlook human rights violations committed by more powerful nations, such as Russia's activities in Chechnya, or China's continuing repression after Tiananmen Square. International human rights law is not enforced, you might say, because human rights norms are vague and aspirational, because enforcement mechanisms are toothless, because treaty regimes are notoriously weak, and because national governments lack the economic self-interest or the political will to restrain their own human rights violations. So if the question is "how is international human rights law enforced?" many of you might answer: "not at all, or hardly at all." If you hold to this common, skeptical view of human rights enforcement, you would say that international human rights law is not enforced, like "real" domestic law; instead, it is only occasionally "complied with," by nation-states acting out of transparent convenience or self-interest.

Let me take a somewhat different tack, asking first, "What do we mean when we say that any laws are enforced?" Are any laws perfectly enforced? Even here in Bloomington, Indiana, the height of civilization, are the parking laws or burglary laws perfectly enforced? Of course, you would concede, parking violations occur here in Bloomington, and burglaries occur, perhaps even daily; sometimes egregiously. But those facts alone hardly mean that there is no enforcement of laws against parking violations or burglary. Here in Indiana, the laws against burglary may be underenforced, they may be imperfectly enforced, but they are enforced, through a well-understood domestic legal process of legislation, adjudication, and executive action. That process involves prosecutors, statutes, judges, police officers, and penalties that interact, interpret legal norms, and work to internalize those norms into the value sets of citizens like ourselves.

But if we are willing to give that answer to the question "how is domestic law enforced?," why not similarly answer the question whether international human rights law is enforced? In much the same way, these international norms of international human rights law are underenforced, imperfectly enforced; but they are enforced through a complex, little-understood legal process that I call transnational legal process. As I have elaborated in other writing, transnational

legal process can be thought of in three phases: the institutional interaction whereby global norms of international human rights law are debated, interpreted, and ultimately internalized by domestic legal systems. To claim that this complex transnational legal process of enforcing international human rights law via interaction, interpretation, and internalization exists is not to say that it always works or even that it works very well. As I will be the first to concede, this process works sporadically, and we often most clearly see its spectacular failures, as in Cambodia, Bosnia, and Rwanda. But the process of enforcing international human rights law also sometimes has its successes, which gives us reason not to ignore that process, but to try to develop and nurture it. Just as doctors used early successes in addressing polio to push our understanding of how the prevention and healing process works, lawyers can try to globalize the lessons of human rights enforcement. So if the question is "how is international human rights enforced?" my short answer is through a transnational legal process of institutional interaction, interpretation of legal norms, and attempts to internalize those norms into domestic legal systems.

With that introduction, let me divide the balance of these remarks into two parts: First, how, in theory, does transnational legal process promote national obedience of international human rights law? Second, how does transnational legal process—this process that I call "interaction, interpretation, and internalization"—work in real cases?

THE THEORY OF TRANSNATIONAL LEGAL PROCESS

The first question, why do nations obey international human rights law, is really a sub-set of a much broader question: why do nations obey international law of any kind? That timeless question . . . has troubled thinkers over historical eras dating back to the Roman Empire.

FROM COMPLIANCE TO OBEDIENCE

Let us start by asking what it means to "obey" international law at all. Imagine four kinds of relationships between rules and conduct: coincidence, conformity, compliance, and obedience.

For example, I have lived my whole life in the United States; but a few years ago, I took a sabbatical year in England. While there, I noticed that everybody drives on the left side of the road, as a matter of both practice and of law. Yet what is the relationship between the law and the observed practice?

One remote possibility is coincidence. It could be coincidence that the law is that everyone must drive on the left and that in practice everybody follows that norm. Yet coincidence might explain why one person follows a rule, but not why millions of people throughout the country do the same. That suggests a second possibility: conformity. If people know of the rule that you must drive on the left, they may well choose to conform their conduct to that rule when convenient; but feel no obligation to do so when inconvenient. (Perhaps some Scots, for example, swerve over and drive on the right, in remote unpopulated areas of the Hebrides.) But, is there a third possibility, compliance? Perhaps people are both aware of the rule and accept the rule for a variety of external reasons, for example, to get specific rewards, to receive insurance benefits, or to avoid certain kinds of bad results, such as traffic tickets, or getting hit by an oncoming car. These are instrumental reasons why someone might decide to comply with a rule even if they felt no moral obligation to obey it. Finally, there is a fourth possibility, obedience: the notion that a person or an organization adopts the behavior that is prescribed by the rule because he or it has somehow internalized that rule and made it a part of their internal value system.

Notice that as we move down this scale from coincidence to conformity to compliance to obedience, we see an increase of what I will call "norm-internalization." As you move from grudgingly accepting a rule one time only to habitually obeying it, the rule transforms from being some kind of external sanction to becoming an internal imperative. We see this evolutionary process regularly in our daily lives: when you put on a bicycle helmet; when you snap on your seatbelt; when you recycle a tin can; when you do not smoke in the cafeteria. All of these are examples of people moving from conformity with a rule to compliance and gradually obedience, which is driven by a sense of an internalized norm. There is a further point as well: the most effective form of law-enforcement is not the imposition of external sanction, but the inculcation of internal obedience. Most traffic laws, litter laws, tax laws, and the like are enforced primarily not by enforcement officers but by the social internalization of norms of obedience! Indeed, enforcement is maximized when a norm is so widely obeyed that external sanctions become virtually unnecessary.

THE RELATIONSHIP BETWEEN ENFORCEMENT AND OBEDIENCE

Five distinct explanations have emerged to answer the question "why nations obey?": power; self-interest or rational choice; liberal explanations based on rule-legitimacy or political identity; communitarian explanations; and legal process explanations at the state-to-state level ("horizontal" or "international legal process" explanations) and from the international-to-national level ("vertical" or "transnational legal process explanations").

In their current form, each of these five approaches gives their own short answer to the question "how is international human rights law enforced?" Let me start with the realists, who date back to Thomas Hobbes, but include such modern-day theorists as George Kennan, Hans Morgenthau, and Henry Kissinger. To the question "why do nations obey international law?" their short answer is power: nations never truly "obey" international law, they only comply with it, because someone else makes them. Why, for example, did Iraq ultimately respect the borders of Kuwait? In the end, because the other nations of the world came in and drove Saddam out! Under this view, nations can be coerced or bribed to follow certain rules, or even induced to bargain in the shadow of such incentives. But in the end, the critical factor is neither altruistic nor normative, only the realist values of power and coercion.[1] Thus, the familiar power explanation traces back to Thucydides: the strong

---

1. The "power" rationale is captured in a famous joke often told about Henry Kissinger, who after he ceased to be the Secretary of State, reportedly went to work as a zoo keeper. After the first day, zoo patrons noticed an amazing phenomenon: that after all these centuries, the lion was finally lying down with the lamb. The patrons ran excitedly to Dr. Kissinger, and asked, "How have you achieved this miraculous result?" The famous realist replied, "It's simple. A lamb a day!"

states do what they can, the weak states suffer what they must, but in the end there is no real "obedience" of international law, only such coincidence between national conduct and international rules that results from power and coercion.

There is a second, kinder and gentler explanation, based on the self-interest rationales favored by the vibrant school of "rational choice" theory. Under this explanation, nations may choose rationally to follow certain global rules out of a sense of self-interest. After participating in game-theoretic discussions, to avoid multi-party prisoners' dilemma, nations may decide to cooperate around certain rules, which lead them to establish what international relations theorists call "regimes": governing arrangements in which certain governing norms, rules, and decision-making procedures come to predominate because the nations in their long-term self-interests have calculated that they should follow a presumption favoring compliance with such rules.

This "self-interest" rationale helps explains why, for example, complex global rules have emerged in a whole variety of international areas in which nations have established regimes structured around legal rules born of self-interested cooperation. Talented international relations scholars such as Robert Keohane, Duncan Snidal, and Oran Young have applied increasingly sophisticated rational choice techniques to argue for such an instrumental, interest-based view of international law.[2] Recently, a number of legal scholars, most prominently Kenneth Abbott, Alan Sykes, and John Setear, have espoused a similar, "rationalistic" legal vision.[3] Under the rationalist account, participants in a given issue area will develop a set of governing arrangements, along with a set of expectations, rules, and decision-making procedures—in other words, a regime—both to restrain the participants and to provide means for achieving their common aims. Within these regimes, international law stabilizes expectations and promotes compliance by reducing transaction costs, providing dispute-resolution procedures, performing signaling functions, triggering negative responses, and promoting information disclosure.

Recently, more sophisticated instrumentalists have begun to disaggregate the state into its component parts, to introduce international institutions and transnational actors, to incorporate long-term self-interest, and to consider the issue within massively iterated multi-party games. The rationalists recognize nonstate actors as players in the transnational system, but too often ignore them because of the complexity their inclusion adds to their game-theoretic analysis. Their chosen issue areas thus tend to be areas like trade and arms control, where nation-states remain the primary players and traditional realist assumptions still largely prevail. Such rationalistic, state-centric theories thus work less well, for example, in such areas as human rights, debt restructuring, or international commercial transactions, where nonstate actors abound, pursue multiple goals in complex non-zero-sum games, and interact repeatedly within institutions nested within broader informal regimes. Rationalists see law as regulating behavior by changing incentives, not altering interests or identities. In effect, they see international law as a kind of mechanical device, a switching mechanism, which facilitates the interactions of autonomous states, not as a communal decision-making structure that helps generate options, modify preferences, and build a normative interpretive community.

In short, my major complaint about the self-interest explanation is that it does not take account of what I consider to be an important factor—the "vertical" internalization of international norms into domestic legal systems. For the rationalists, the decision to obey the law remains perpetually calculated, never internally felt. Compliance always remains an instrumental computation, never an internalized normative imperative.

This brings me to a third possible explanation for why international human rights laws are enforced, so-called "liberal" theories, which I divide into those scholars who follow principles of "rule legitimacy" and those who focus on national "political identity." Both sets of theorists derive their analysis from Immanuel Kant's pamphlet in 1795, Perpetual Peace. Rule-legitimacy theorists, led by Thomas Franck, argue that nations do feel some sort of internal "compliance

2. See, e.g., Robert O. Keohane, "When Does International Law Come Home?" *Houston Law Review* 35 (1998): 699–713.

3. See, e.g., Kenneth W. Abbott, "Modern International Relations Theory: A Prospectus for International Lawyers," *YJIL* 14 (1989): 335–411.

pull" toward certain rules that they feel are legitimate; for example, the rules against genocide or the rules favoring diplomatic immunity. When nations perceive that rules are legitimate, either because they meet some procedural standard of legitimacy or some substantive notion of due process or distributive justice, they will obey that rule because they are "normatively pulled" toward that rule by its legitimacy.[4]

In my view, this rule-legitimacy approach is problematic because it claims to draw its power from the legitimacy of rules themselves, rather than from communitarian and legal process pressures. In fact, most of us do not litter when others are watching, but not because the no-littering rule itself has such compliance pull, but because of a combination of internal impulse and felt peer pressure. In the same way, Franck's rule-legitimacy ends up being another way of saying that a state obeys a norm because it has been both internalized, and is being enforced by "communitarian peer pressure" (which, I will argue below, is really a form of transnational legal process).

A second view, pressed strongly by other members of this liberal school, argues that whether or not nations comply with international law depends crucially on the extent to which their political identity is based on liberal democracy. This approach derives from a branch of international relations literature known as the "Democratic Peace" literature, pioneered by Michael Doyle, Bruce Russett, and many others who have sought to verify a basic tenet of Kant's writing that liberal democracies do not go to war with each other. The many adherents of this view include President Clinton, who in October 1995 opined that promoting democracies that participate in the new global marketplace is the right thing to do because we know that these democracies are less likely to go to war.

Transposing this basic maxim to international law, Anne-Marie Slaughter and Andrew Moravcsik have flipped this maxim, arguing not so much that democracies do not fight each other, but rather, that democracies are more inclined to "do law" with one another.[5] For these analysts, the key variable for whether a nation

will or will not obey international law is whether it can be characterized as "liberal" in identity, i.e., having certain democratic attributes such as a form of representative government, civil and political rights, and an independent judicial system dedicated to the rule of law. Not surprisingly, many liberal scholars focus on European Union law, noting that the European system of human rights works because it is largely composed of liberal democracies, who share reasons for collective obedience. This helps explain why, for example, the embryonic African human rights system—a collection of democracies and authoritarian systems—does not work nearly as well.

What is troubling about this view is that it suggests that liberal states interact mainly in a zone of law, while liberal and illiberal states interact in a zone of politics. But in my view, any analysis that treats a state's identity as somehow exogenously or permanently given is overly essentialist. National identities, like national interests, are socially constructed products of culture, ideology, learning, and knowledge. As we have witnessed, nations transition back and forth from dictatorship to democracy [and] democratization has powerful international dimensions, potentially spreading from one country to another by contagion, control, or consent. Liberal identity analysis does not directly address the impact of compliance on democratization, and thus leaves unanswered a critical, constructivist question: to what extent does compliance with international law itself help constitute the identity of a state as law-abiding, and hence, as "liberal" or not? The notion that "only liberal states do law with one another" can be empirically falsified, particularly in such areas as international commercial law, where even rogue states tend to abide fastidiously by private international law rules on letters of credit without regard to whether they are representative democracies. Finally, like the "cultural relativist" argument in human rights, the claim that nonliberal states somehow do not participate in a zone of law denies the universalism of international law and effectively condones dealing with nonliberal states within a realist world of power politics.

4. Franck calls this the "compliance pull" of particular international legal rules. See generally Thomas M. Franck, *The Power of Legitimacy Among Nations* (New York: Oxford University Press. 1990).
5. See, e.g., Anne-Marie Slaughter, "International Law in a World of Liberal States," *EJIL* 6: 503; Andrew Moravcsik, "Taking Preferences Seriously: A Liberal Theory of International Politics," *International Organization* 51 (1997): 516–24, at 513.

A fourth possible explanation—"communitarian" reasons—can be found in the English "International Society" school of International Relations, particularly in the work of Martin Wight and Hedley Bull, who traced their international origins back to the Dutch international law scholar Grotius. These theorists argue that nations obey international law because of the values of the international society of which they are a part. So, for example, the Czech Republic, Poland, and Hungary now feel peer pressure to obey international law because of their community ties as NATO nations. The idea is that one's membership in a community helps to define how one views the obligations of that community. When someone becomes a member of a church, they decide they will conduct their lives differently because they now view themselves as Catholic, Jewish, or Muslim. Similarly, the governments of Russia, Ukraine, and Turkey should all feel communitarian pressure to obey the European Convention on Human Rights—the "rules of their church"—because they have all now become members of the Council of Europe.

Unlike a liberal approach, this communitarian, constructivist approach at least recognizes the positive transformational effects of a state's repeated participation in the legal process. At the same time, however, the approach gives too little study to the vertical "transmission belt" whereby the norms created by international society infiltrate into domestic society. The existence of international community may explain the horizontal pressures to compliance generated among nation-states on the global plane, but it does not clarify the vertical process whereby transnational actors interact in various fora, generate and interpret international norms, and then seek to internalize those norms domestically, as future determinants of why nations obey.

Fifth and finally, there are so-called "legal process" explanations for why nations obey international law. Let me distinguish here between what I call "international legal process" or horizontal reasons for compliance, which tend to function at a government-to-government level, and the so-called "vertical" explanation, which focuses on the relationship between the international and the domestic legal systems. Suppose, for example, that the government of Canada wishes to urge Japan to join the global land mine treaty. Initially, the two governments will engage in government-to-government discussions at the "horizontal" nation-state level within an intergovernmental process organized by the United Nations. But at the same time, there is also a "vertical," transnational process whereby governments, inter-governmental organizations, nongovernmental organizations, and private citizens argue together about why nations should obey international human rights law. Through this vertical dynamic, international rules that are developed at a government-to-government level gradually work their way down and become internalized into domestic legal structure.

My broader point, simply speaking, is that all five explanations—power, self-interest, liberal theories, communitarian theories, and legal process explanations—work together to help explain why nations obey international law. These five explanatory strands work together as complementary conceptual lenses to give a richer explanation of why compliance with international law does, or does not, occur in particular cases.

To clarify, let me ask the parallel question, how is domestic law enforced? What is the explanation, for example, for why we now buckle our seatbelts, even though nobody wore seatbelts only a quarter of a century ago? First, because after the seatbelt rule issued, a lot of tickets were given out and I felt coerced to comply: a power explanation. A second factor: self-interest. People calculated that it is more rational to wear your seatbelt to avoid injury, sanction, or to gain insurance benefits. Third, the seatbelt rule acquired "rule-legitimacy" and over time developed a compliance pull. Over time, this became part of one's sense of personal identity. Individuals calculated: "If I am a law abiding person, I ought to obey the seatbelt laws." Partly, the rationale was communitarian. Authorities exhorted people with slogans such as "Seatbelts Save Lives." And fifth and finally, the seatbelt rule was inculcated via legal process. Seatbelts were required by state laws, required by federal highway standards; incorporated into federal automotive standards and became part of the way the automobiles were made.

So in short, how are seatbelt laws enforced? Not by any one of these factors acting alone, but by all of them acting in combination. As we move through the five explanations—from power to legal process—we also move from external enforcement of legal rules to internal obedience with legal rules. True compliance is not so much the result of externally imposed sanctions so much as internally felt norms. In other words, as we move from external to internal factors, we also move from coercive to constitutive behavior. As always, the best way to enforce legal norms is not to coerce action, not to impose sanctions, but to change the way that people think about themselves: whether as teetotalers, safe drivers, or regular taxpayers. In short, our prime way to enforce the law is to encourage people to bring rules home, to internalize rules inside themselves, to transform themselves from lawless into law-abiding individuals.

What does this have to do with international human rights law? I would argue that in the international arena, we are seeing the exact same process at work; a process by which norms and rules are generated and internalized and become internal rules, normative rules, and rules that constitute new nations. The best example we have is South Africa; a country which for many years was an outlaw, was subjected to tremendous external pressure and coercive mechanisms over a long period of time. Through a gradual process, South Africa has converted itself into a country that has undergone a fundamental political transformation. It has now reconstituted itself as a law-abiding country that through its constitutional processes has internalized new norms of international human rights law as domestic law.

In the same way, if the United States is attempting to encourage China to follow norms of international human rights law, the analysis above suggests the need to act at all five levels: at the level of power and coercion, to apply external and political sanctions; at the level of self-interest, to develop carrots that can be offered to China in terms of trade benefits or other kinds of economic incentives; at the level of liberal theory, to encourage Hong Kong's liberal legal identity to bubble up to the Beijing government; at the level of communitarian values, to seek to encourage China to ratify the International Covenant on Civil and Political Rights[6] and other multilateral international human rights [treaties]; and finally, from a legal process perspective, to seek to engage the Chinese people and groups in civil society in a variety of international interactions that will cause them to internalize norms of international human rights law. As with the seat belt example, our goal is not simply to coerce conduct. More fundamentally, we seek to encourage a change in the nature of the Chinese political identity to reconstitute China as a nation that abides by core norms of international human rights law. In short, a theory of transnational legal process seeks to enforce international norms by motivating nation-states to obey international human rights law—out of a sense of internal acceptance of international law—as opposed to merely conforming to or complying with specific international legal rules when the state finds it convenient.

HOW IS INTERNATIONAL HUMAN RIGHTS LAW ENFORCED?

Against this background, how should we now understand the recent history of international human rights enforcement? Let me contrast what I will call the horizontal story of enforcement with what I prefer: the vertical, transnational story of human rights enforcement.

THE "HORIZONTAL" STORY

The conventional "horizontal" story about international human rights law enforcement is that international human rights law was born about fifty years ago, the product of the UN Charter,[7] the Nuremberg and Tokyo war crimes trials, and the Universal Declaration of Human Rights.[8] Under this view, the principal enforcers of human rights law have always been nation-states, who have always interacted with one another on an interstate, government-to-government level. The UN Charter introduced into this picture UN organizations and UN norms, which soon led to regional human rights systems as well:[9] in Europe, the Strasbourg (Council of Europe) and the Helsinki (Organization of Security and Cooperation in Europe) process; in the Americas, the Inter-American Commission and Court of Human Rights; and far less well

---

6. Concluded Dec. 16, 1966, reprinted and referenced in Documentary Appendix A.
7. Concluded June 26, 1945, excerpted in Documentary Appendix A.
8. Adopted Dec. 10, 1948, reprinted and referenced in Documentary Appendix A.
9. See Reading 27 by Dinah Shelton in Chapter 6 of this volume.

developed regional human rights systems in Africa, the Middle East, and Asia.

In this postwar order, an international regime developed in which governments and intergovernmental organizations began to put pressure on each other—always at a horizontal, intergovernmental level—to comply with human rights, invoking such universal treaty norms as the international covenants on civil and political and economic, social, and cultural rights. UN organizations, such as the UN Human Rights Commission, and treaty-based organizations, such as the UN Human Rights Committee, participated as intergovernmental actors in this horizontal international regime, which addressed all manner of global issues: worker rights, racial discrimination, the rights of children, women, and indigenous peoples. As we soon saw, the difficulties of this horizontal, state-to-state enforcement mechanism were legion: the rules were largely declaratory and precatory, and the few mechanisms created had virtually no enforcement. Occasionally new mechanisms would be created: judicial fora, such as the Yugoslav and Rwandan War Crimes Tribunals, or new executive actors, such as the UN High Commissioner on Human Rights, or new quasi-legislative fora, such as the Vienna Conference on Human Rights or the 1995 Beijing Women's Conference. Despite these occasional advances, the overall picture of this standard enforcement story is one of impotence, ineffectiveness, of a horizontal system where the key actors are nation-states and intergovernmental organizations, the key fora are governmental fora, and the key transactions are transactions between states and other states.

The "Vertical" Story

If one accepts the horizontal story as the entire picture of human rights enforcement, than the glass is indeed more than half empty. But what is the vertical picture? The "vertical" story of human rights enforcement, I would argue, is a much richer picture: one that focuses on a transnational legal process that includes a different set of actors, fora, and transactions. The key agents in this transnational legal process are transnational norm entrepreneurs, governmental norm sponsors, transnational issue networks, interpretive communities and law-declaring fora, bureaucratic compliance procedures, and issue linkages among issue areas.

Many efforts at human rights norm-internalization are begun not by nation-states, but by "transnational norm entrepreneurs," private transnational organizations or individuals who mobilize popular opinion and political support within their host country and abroad for the development of a universal human rights norm. Such norm entrepreneurs first became prominent in the 19th century, when activists such as Lord William Wilberforce and the British and Foreign Anti-Slavery Society pressed for treaties prohibiting the slave trade, Jean-Henri Dunant founded the International Committee of the Red Cross, and Christian peace activists, such as America's William Ladd and Elihu Burritt promoted public international arbitration and permanent international criminal courts. Modern-day entrepreneurs have included individuals as diverse as Eleanor Roosevelt, Jesse Jackson, the Dalai Lama, Aung Sang Suu Kyi, and Princess Diana. These nongovernmental actors seek to develop transnational issue networks to discuss and generate political solutions among concerned individuals at the domestic, regional, and international levels, among government and intergovernmental organizations, international and domestic academics, and private foundations. Moreover, these norm entrepreneurs seek national government officials and bureaucracies concerned with the same issue areas and seek to enlist them as allies in their transnational cause. These governmental norm sponsors—UN Human Rights Commissioner Mary Robinson, Presidents Oscar Arias of Costa Rica, Jimmy Carter of the United States, and the Pope, to take just a few prominent ones—use their official positions to promote normative positions. These transnational actors then seek governmental and nongovernmental fora competent to declare both general norms of international law (e.g., treaties) and specific interpretation of those norms in particular circumstances (e.g., particular interpretations of treaties and customary international law rules). Such law- declaring fora thus include treaty regimes; domestic, regional, and international courts; ad hoc tribunals; domestic and regional legislatures; executive entities; international publicists; and nongovernmental organizations: law-declaring fora that create an "interpretive community" that is capable of defining, elaborating, and testing the definition of particular norms and their violation.

The next vertical step is for national governments to internalize norm-interpretations issued by the global interpretive community into their domestic bureaucratic and political structures. Within national governments and intergovernmental organizations, for example, in-house lawyers and legal advisers acquire institutional mandates to ensure that the government's policies conform to international legal standards that have become imbedded in domestic law. Such institutional mandates to justify noncompliance with international legal norms may be found within the legal advising apparatus of national governments, in the Executive Branch, (e.g., the Legal Adviser's Office at the U.S. State Department), the legislature, as well as intergovernmental organizations (e.g., the United Nations, the OAS, etc.).

In the same way as corporations develop standard operating procedures to address new domestic mandates regarding corporate sentencing guidelines, occupational health and safety, and sexual harassment, domestic institutions adopt standard operating procedures and other internal mechanisms to maintain habitual compliance with the internalized international norms. These institutions evolve in path-dependent routes that avoid conflict with the internalized norms. Thus, over time, domestic decision-making structures become "enmeshed" with international legal norms, so that institutional arrangements for the making and maintenance of an international commitment become entrenched in domestic legal and political processes. Gradually, legal ideologies come to prevail among domestic decision-makers so that they seek to avoid perceptions that their actions will be perceived as domestically unlawful. Finally, strong process linkages exist across issue areas. Thus, when the United States adopts a twelve-mile limit in the ocean law area, for example, it is bound by it when dealing with refugees sailing toward U.S. shores. Because international legal obligations tend to be closely interconnected, even a single deviation tends to lead noncompliant nations into vicious cycles of treaty violation. These institutional habits soon lead nations into default patterns of compliance. These patterns act like riverbeds, which channel conduct along compliant pathways. When a nation deviates from that pattern of presumptive compliance, frictions are created.

By so saying, I do not mean to suggest that international legal violations never occur. I merely suggest viewing human rights enforcement through vertical, "transnational legal process" lenses can help explain why, in Louis Henkin's famous phrase, "almost all nations observe almost all principles of international law almost all of the time."[10] To avoid such frictions in its continuing interactions, a nation's bureaucracies or interest groups may press their leaders to shift over time from a policy of violation into one of compliance. Thus it is through this repeated cycle of interaction, interpretation, and internalization—this transnational legal process—that international law acquires its "stickiness," and that nations come to "obey" international human rights law out of a perceived self-interest that becomes institutional habit.

CONCLUSION

Let me close with two thoughts. First, the foregoing analysis teaches something about our duty, as citizens, to participate in transnational legal process. It is sometimes said that someone who, by acquiring medical training, comes to understand the human body acquires as well a moral duty not just to observe disease, but to try to cure it. In the same way, I would argue, a lawyer who acquires knowledge of the body politic acquires a duty not simply to observe transnational legal process, but to try to influence it. Once one comes to understand the process by which international human rights norms can be generated and internalized into domestic legal systems, one acquires a concomitant duty, I believe, to try to influence that process, to try to change the feelings of that body politic to promote greater obedience with international human rights norms.

In that effort, every citizen counts. To this, many Americans might say, "What can one person really do? Isn't such influence beyond the capacity of any one person?" But [could not have] Aung San Suu Kyi, Jody Williams, Nelson Mandela, and Martin Luther King, Jr., said the same thing? In response, many might say: "But surely, I am not such a world historical figure," to which I would answer, "You don't need to be a Nobel Prize winner to make a difference. Just look at Rosa Parks, or Linda Brown, or Fred

10. Louis Henkin, *How Nations Behave*, 2nd ed. (New York: Praeger, 1979), 47.

Korematsu, ordinary people who simply said that they would not go to the back of the bus, or attend a segregated school, or live in a Japanese internment camp." In short, we need look no further than those individuals who have triggered these legal processes in our own lifetime to promote the enforcement of human rights norms.

The struggle of these individuals reminds us again of the remarkable words of Robert Kennedy, which are etched on his grave in Arlington Cemetery:

> Each time a man stands up for an ideal, or acts to improve the lot of others, or strikes out against injustice, he sends forth a tiny ripple of hope, and crossing each other from a million different centers of energy and daring, those ripples build a current that can sweep down the mightiest walls of oppression and resistance.

What he is talking about, in the end, is the need for individuals to activate transnational legal process. As proof that what he says is indeed possible, one need look only at the country in which he said those words: South Africa, in 1966, a country which only three decades later has now been totally transformed by international human rights law.

So, in closing, if my question is "how is international human rights law enforced?" my answer is simple. International human rights law is enforced not just by nation-states, not just by government officials, not just by world historical figures, but by people like us, by people with the courage and commitment to bring international human rights law home through a transnational legal process of interaction, interpretation, and internalization.

QUESTIONS FOR REFLECTION AND DISCUSSION

1. Yale law professor (now Dean) Harold Koh asks, "How is international human rights law enforced?" He answers: "not just by nation-states, not just by government officials, not just by world historical figures, but by people like us." Who are "people like us"? How is it possible for "people like us"—most of "us" being without official position or legal standing—to *enforce* international human rights law? And just how well do "people like us"—and government officials and world historical figures and others—enforce international human rights law? According to Koh, not very well. He writes: "International human rights law is not enforced . . . because human rights norms are vague and aspirational, because enforcement mechanisms are toothless, because treaty regimes are notoriously weak, and because national governments lack the economic self-interest or political will to restrain their own human rights violations." What explains this negative state of affairs, and what if anything can be done to reverse it? Perhaps more importantly, who is going to take the initiative? Us? How?

2. Koh focuses on two key questions: "First, how, in theory, does transnational legal process promote national obedience of international human rights law? Second, how does transnational legal process—this process that I call 'interaction, interpretation, and internalization'—work in real cases?" What are Koh's answers to these two questions? Do you agree with him? Disagree? Why?

3. Koh offers five explanations as to why states obey international law. What are they? Which explanation is the most convincing? None? Some? All? What does Koh say?

4. What does Koh mean by the "interaction, interpretation, and internalization" of international human rights law? In particular, what does he mean by "internalization"? Is it possible for "internalization" of international human rights to take place in authoritarian societies? In democratic societies where citizens, in the words of political philosopher Giorgio Agamben (Question 10 in Reading 11 in Chapter 2 of this volume) "divest themselves of their citizenship by withdrawing from political life into apathy"?

5. If there is no "internalization" of a human rights doctrine, principle, or rule, does this mean that persons living in a country where "internalization" does not take place have no rights in respect of such norm? No enforceable rights? Which? Does the distinction matter? Is a human right without a domestic remedy a human right at all? What about a human right without *any* remedy—for example, China in respect to various civil and political rights (e.g., the right to speak freely or to vote in national elections) or the United States in respect of various economic, social, and cultural rights (e.g., the right to

education or the right to health)? What does Koh say? What does Burns Weston say in Reading 1 of Chapter 1 of this volume? What do you say? Why?

6. On final analysis, is Koh saying that international human rights law is not worth the paper it is written on unless it is absorbed into and made a part of national law and policy? Regardless, do you agree with that view? Why? Why not?

7. Koh concludes by discussing the "duty" of citizens to participate in the generation and internalization of international human rights law, stating that "Once one comes to understand the process by which international human rights norms can be generated and internalized into domestic legal systems, one acquires a concomitant duty . . . to try to influence that process, to try to change the feelings of that body politic to promote greater obedience with international human rights norms." In contrast, in "The International Human Rights Movement: Part of the Problem?" *HHRJ* 15 (2002): 101–25, at 117–18, Harvard law professor David Kennedy writes:

> human rights offers itself as the measure of emancipation. This is its most striking—and misleading—promise. Human rights narrates itself as a universal/eternal/human truth and as a pragmatic response to injustice—there was the holocaust and then there was the genocide convention, women everywhere were subject to discrimination and then there was CEDAW. This posture makes the human rights movement itself seem redemptive—as if doing something for human rights was, in and of itself, doing something against evil. It is not surprising that human rights professionals consequently confuse work on the movement for emancipatory work in society. But there are bad consequences when people of good will mistake work on the discipline for work on the problem. . . . We routinely underestimate the extent to which the human rights movement develops in response to political conflict and discursive fashion among international elites, thereby overestimating the field's pragmatic potential and obscuring the field's international dynamics and will to power.

Do you share Koh's or Kennedy's worldview? Why? Is there a way to reconcile these two views? How? Do you think Koh overestimates the ability of everyday people to effect human rights change in a society via transnational legal process? Is Kennedy's cynicism about the ability of the human rights movement's ability to effect change convincing? For helpful insight, see Hilary Charlesworth, "Author! Author! A Response to David Kennedy," *HHRJ* 15 (2002): 127–31.

8. Do you believe you personally have a duty to participate in the enforcement of international human rights law? If so, in what way or ways might you perform that duty? If not, why not?

25. ANNE F. BAYEFSKY *Making the Human Rights Treaties Work*

INTRODUCTION

The regime of the major international human rights treaties and the operation of the concomitant monitoring bodies have been called the cornerstone of the United Nations human rights program. It is a regime that has functioned since the adoption of the International Convention on the Elimination of All Forms of Racial Discrimination (ICERD) in 1965.[1] This was followed by the adoption in 1966 of the International Covenant on Civil and Political Rights (ICCPR), the Optional Protocol to the International Covenant on Civil and Political Rights, and the International Covenant on Economic, Social and Cultural Rights (ICESCR), the Convention on the Elimination of All Forms of Discrimination against Women (CEDAW) in 1979, the

Reprinted with changes from Anne F. Bayefsky, "Making the Human Rights Treaties Work," in Louis Henkin and John Lawrence Hargrove, eds., *Human Rights: An Agenda for the Next Century* (Washington, D.C.: American Society of International Law, 1994), 229–55. Copyright © 1994 American Society of International Law. Reprinted by permission.

1. Concluded Dec. 21, 1965, referenced in Documentary Appendix B.

Convention against Torture and Other Cruel, Inhuman or Degrading Treatment or Punishment (CAT) in 1984, and the Convention on the Rights of the Child (CRC) in 1989.[2]

The treaty bodies have operated for varying lengths of time, beginning with the Racial Discrimination Committee (CERD), which first met in 1970. Since then five similar bodies have been created. The Human Rights Committee (the ICCPR Covenant) first met in 1977; the Committee on Economic, Social and Cultural Rights (the ICESCR Covenant) in 1987, the Committee on the Elimination of Discrimination Against Women (CEDAW) in 1983, the Committee against Torture (CAT) in 1988 and the Committee on the Rights of the Child (CRC) in 1991.

As the list of treaties and monitoring bodies grew, so did the scope of the regime [as evidenced by the number of states parties, the number of their reports, the amount of time their treaty bodies have met, the various general comments on the meaning of the treaties, and the number of cases decided or otherwise disposed of by those treaty bodies having the capacity to consider individual complaints]. There is no doubt that in terms of quantity, the system has expanded significantly. But international lawyers must ask another question. What is the relationship between, on the one hand, the increase in standard-setting and the workload of the treaty bodies and on the other hand, respect for international law or the actual protection of human rights?

Overall, few states take issue either with the principle that protection of human rights is not merely a matter of domestic jurisdiction, or with the doctrine that human rights limit the scope of state sovereignty. And, since the end of the Cold War, there is agreement on the "indivisibility" of these rights.

Nevertheless, the veneer of consensus removed, the United Nations human rights regime reveals a front of rejection comparable to what prevailed before November 1989 and the fall of the Berlin Wall. The terminology has changed and so have the players, but the fundamental rift in the United Nations system simply metastasized. The conflict of priorities is now formulated in terms of cultural particularity versus universality and democracy versus development.

The rejectionists display enthusiasm for standard-setting and the newest Vienna Declaration and Programme of Action, while serious efforts at implementation and behavioral changes are thwarted at every opportunity.

The newest form of rejectionist politics has inhibited the effective implementation of global international human rights law. The current mechanisms for implementing human rights treaties were devised at a time when the power of the argument about interference in domestic jurisdiction was at its peak. Those mechanisms remain as relics of the past. They contain gigantic loopholes that are taken up with new zeal by large numbers of holdouts.

THE RECORD

The major human rights treaties do not have identical implementation schemes. For example, while all rely primarily on a scheme of state reporting, several but not all (e.g., the Convention on the Rights of the Child) incorporate a procedure for handling individual complaints of treaty violations. The treaty bodies exhibit quite a few variations, both mandated by their respective treaties and adopted themselves.

When the human rights treaties were first written, enforcement was intended largely to depend on a system of state reporting. According to the original rationale, state reports could further human rights protection in two ways. The process of drafting the state report could serve as an exercise of internal self-analysis and soul-searching, which in itself could prompt improvements in national laws and practices. Second, the subsequent scrutiny of those reports by independent expert bodies would expose human rights violations and such exposure would encourage change.

On the first score, the experts say state reports are "quintessentially government reports." In practice, the process of drafting state reports is almost never conducted in consultation with the individuals or the nongovernmental organizations most closely concerned with the terms of the treaty. Their preparation is generally understood—with some few exceptions—as a bureaucratic exercise or diplomatic chore and not as an opportunity for self-analysis and the

---

2. The ICCPR and the ICESCR, each concluded Dec. 16, 1966, are reprinted and referenced in Documentary Appendix A. The ICCPR Optional Protocol (Dec. 16, 1966), CEDAW (Dec. 18, 1979), CAT (Dec. 10, 1984), and CRC (Nov. 2, 1989) are referenced in Documentary Appendix B.

amendment of national laws or practices. As for after-the-fact discussion, domestic interest in another self-congratulatory government publication has been, and will continue to be, minimal at best.

But even that assumes the report is available to the public. In some states, it is not translated into the languages citizens understand. In others, it is a classified document. In still others, citizens cannot get the report and must obtain it from international sources. And in other states, even copies of the treaties are not available.

The idea that governments will take the opportunity to present their internal human rights situation to international forums in self-critical or negative terms is illusory. The treaty bodies euphemistically refer to the effort to encourage states to expose their shortfalls as reporting on the "factors and difficulties impeding the application of the treaty." The predictable response from so many of the most culpable states, year after year, is to claim that the treaty obligations are all satisfied. For example, the Libyan report to the Human Rights Committee, dated May 4, 1993, states:

> Following the revolution of 1 September 1969, sovereignty has been exercised by the people . . . Libya is a free and democratic Arab republic. . . . Since the revolution . . . [Libya] has shown concern for basic human rights. Its fundamental and supreme objective is to promote the health, social and cultural aspects of human welfare. . . . The . . . law in the Jamahiriya . . . meets the standards set in the most modern and progressive constitutions and laws anywhere in the world.[3]

This is not to say that the treaty bodies themselves fail to perceive either the inadequacies of the preparation, internal distribution, and discussion of state reports, or the close relationship between these procedural inadequacies and the degree of seriousness with which the state takes the substantive terms of the treaty. But it is quite clear that what was supposed to be the secondary role for international monitors has turned out to be the primary hope for the victims of human rights abuses.

On the second score, however, the exposure anticipated from the scrutiny of the treaty bodies, as statistical evidence alone reveals, is grossly inadequate.

There are an extremely large number of overdue reports. Furthermore, these overdue reports emanate from a large percentage of states parties. Of those reports that are overdue, many have been outstanding for considerable lengths of time. Significant numbers of even initial reports are overdue. This circumstance cannot be explained by an overloading of the state through some internal backlog. Such an excuse tends to be a favorite alibi of defaulting states. This neglect of the basic obligation to produce state reports clearly indicates that for a large number of states ratification has become an end in itself. It is appearance, rather than compliance, that has become important. Among those states having the greatest number of overdue reports are some of the world's most notorious human rights violators.

When states parties do produce reports, the treaty bodies spend minimal amounts of time considering them. The time the treaty bodies allot to considering state reports relates to the amount of meeting time that is permitted during the year. This varies widely. The normal number of weeks per year, without budget cuts or additional sessions, ranges from four to six total. Some of this time is used for activities other than the examination of state reports. In general, a state party will be required to account orally for the implementation of each human rights treaty for roughly three hours minimum to ten hours maximum. This procedure will be repeated in each treaty body every four to five years, and probably even less frequently in light of the backlogs. Obviously this time allotment for public scrutiny is minimal.

If one combines the time each treaty body devotes to the consideration of state reports with the current number of overdue reports, the time it would take to consider all the overdue reports if they were to be submitted can be calculated. In the case of four of five of the human rights treaties, it would take six to nine and one-half years to consider all the overdue reports if submitted, and if considered one by one.

The system of state reporting was intended to be the primary means of enforcing the human rights treaties, but not the only means. In several cases, as noted above, provision was made also for individual complaints of treaty violations. These would be made directly to

3. Report to the Human Rights Committee, Libyan Arab Jamahiriya, CCPR/C/28/Add. 16, May 4, 1993, p. 2, ¶ 7, p. 3, ¶ 10.

the treaty bodies. The strongest form of the right of individual petition is found in the Optional Protocol to the Covenant on Civil and Political Rights.

If states do not voluntarily adhere to treaty obligations or participate in a viable state reporting scheme, it might be expected that individual victims would serve to activate the system. However, rejectionist governments continue to stand between right and remedy, and suppress the potential for individuals to bring forward claims of treaty violations. About 1.5 billion people live in countries which allow individual complaints (under one or more of the treaties), but only about 200–300 complaints are registered each year.

Most importantly, a great many of the states parties to the Covenant on Civil and Political Rights, the Racial Discrimination Convention, and the Convention Against Torture fail to ratify the accompanying individual complaint mechanisms! Furthermore, even in the context of the widely ratified Optional Protocol, there are a surprising number of states parties that have never been the subject of a communication. In some cases, an explanation can be found in the preference for regional human rights complaint procedures or the recent date of ratification of the Optional Protocol. But in many cases, neither of these explanations is relevant. In addition, the number of cases placed before the Human Rights Committee is not significantly increasing, despite the increasing number of ratifications of the Optional Protocol.

In general, the ICCPR's Human Rights Committee is more likely to find situations disclosing gross human rights abuses to be in violation of the Covenant. Situations involving more subtle human rights claims are more likely to be dismissed. Perhaps not surprisingly, a mechanism that is intended to service the global community, as opposed to a regional instrument servicing generally democratic countries like the European Convention on Human Rights, is a relatively blunt instrument even where it is permitted to operate.

ATTRIBUTING FAULT

The failures of the current mechanisms for implementing the human rights treaties can be attributed to three sources: (1) the states parties, (2) the treaty bodies, and (3) the General Assembly or the larger corpus of states.

THE STATES PARTIES

The states parties themselves carry primary responsibility for the failures of the largely voluntary state reporting system. In large numbers, they fail to produce timely reports, do not engage in reform activities in the course of producing reports, author inadequate reports, send uninformed representatives to the examination of reports by the treaty bodies, fail to respond to questions during the examinations, discourage greater media attention of the examination of reports, fail to disseminate reports and the results of examinations within the state, elect government employees rather than independent persons to treaty body membership, make reservations that are incompatible with the object and purpose of the treaties, fail to object to reservations, and fail to challenge reservations by additional means. When states do report, they frequently recite intolerable situations without any recognition of a human rights abuse, or any state responsibility to prevent the violation.

As for the length of reports, short ones are not uncommon. Frequently, reports do little more than recite the laws of the state (contrary to guidelines) and then often on a selected basis and in the words of the author of the report. The laws themselves, including constitutions, civil codes, and codes of criminal procedure, may be submitted as annexes. But they are submitted in the local language and are not translated. Therefore, the original materials or the principal legislative texts are frequently not available in a readable form to the treaty bodies.

When treaty body members put questions to state representatives, they are very often left unanswered. When the questions are not entirely ignored, responses of state representatives are often ridiculous. State representatives quite simply often lie. They frequently will say anything they think the treaty body members want to hear.

States that do report and appear before the treaty bodies to engage in what is euphemistically referred to as a "constructive dialogue" often do not anticipate much public interest in the spectacle. Nor do states encourage such interest, either on the part of the international media and international nongovernmental organizations, or on the part of local media and national non-governmental organizations. Radio and TV crews rarely show up. Most often, however, such interest in the proceedings of the treaty bodies does not exist. There usually are very few outside observers of the treaty body sessions.

The resistance of states parties to implementing the terms of the human rights treaties is also evident from the quality of the members that they nominate and elect to serve on the treaty bodies. All of the human rights treaties call for members of the treaty bodies to be elected to serve in their personal capacity. Yet an examination of the curriculum vitae that have been submitted to the states parties for the purposes of the election of the members of the six treaty bodies reveals that approximately 45 percent to 65 percent were employed in some capacity by their nominating governments.

Reservations are another obvious indicator of the authenticity of a state's professed willingness to adhere to the treaty obligations. Although the substance of reservations and declarations is central to evaluating the real limits placed on the scope of a treaty, the large number of reservations and declarations to the human rights treaties emanating from a sizeable proportion of states parties is in itself of concern.

At a substantive level the situation is also disturbing. For example, Islamic states that have ratified the human rights treaties often only do so with the caveat that assumed obligations must be compatible with Islamic law, the Shari`a. Such reservations negate the treaty's central purpose of identifying overriding, universal international human rights standards. The Vienna Convention on the Law of Treaties and provisions in the ICERD Convention, the CEDAW Convention, and the Convention on the Rights of the Child provide that states are not permitted to make reservations "incompatible with the object and purpose of the treaty."[4] Nevertheless, states parties have done virtually nothing to challenge these kinds of reservations. States parties have also failed to explore the idea of requesting judicial determination of their validity. Furthermore, states parties have not encouraged the treaty bodies to take a greater role in supervising or monitoring this threat to the system's integrity.

Most limitations upon the individual complaint mechanisms of the treaties also rest squarely with the states parties. As indicated earlier, many states sign on to the treaties as standard-setting instruments without accepting the full range of concomitant enforcement mechanisms. Even among those states that allow the right of individual petition, many fail to do enough to ensure adequate accessibility to the international remedy by possible victims. Furthermore, when the right has been exercised, a significant number of states have failed to remedy findings of violations.

The Treaty Bodies

Although the treaty bodies have undertaken significant reforms of their practices over the years, and continue to do so on a regular basis, they bear some measure of responsibility in any overall account of the shortcomings of implementation. The boldness and innovativeness of the treaty bodies are not uniform and there are inherent limitations arising from the different allotted meeting times. Nevertheless, while a detailed comparison of their methodology is beyond the scope of this chapter, it is possible to identify failings, to varying degrees, across the system.

First, treaty bodies sometimes fail to point out the inadequacies of oral responses by state representatives. They frequently fail to follow up the deficiencies (either oral or written) by demanding further information, scheduling further hearings based on that information (rather than waiting for the next state report), or publishing in a separate section of annual reports an account of specific requests for further information and the responses received.

On occasion, treaty body members are quite forthright about the quality of state representative's answers. Nevertheless, most frequently treaty bodies are prepared to accept that answers to their questions be included in the next report of the state party.

Second, the treaty bodies often fail to issue direct and forceful conclusions about the adequacy of state reports, and about the human rights situation in states. The work of the treaty bodies is very uneven in this regard, but it is not

---

4. Vienna Convention on the Law of Treaties, concluded May 23, 1969 (entered into force Jan. 27, 1980), 1155 UNTS 331, art. 19(c).

uncommon for treaty bodies to adopt very weak language representing a minimum common denominator when adopting final comments on a state report.

Third, the treaty bodies generally fail to request unscheduled state reports where conditions warrant.

Fourth, the treaty bodies have frequently failed to examine the implementation of the treaty obligations in states that have not reported. The procedure, even when invoked, however, has been hampered by the inability of the treaty bodies to familiarize themselves with the situation in a country in the absence of a report. They also have been often unwilling to issue forceful conclusions in these circumstances.

Fifth, the treaty bodies have not sufficiently isolated and criticized states with long overdue reports.

Sixth, the treaty bodies are reluctant to comment on the inadequacy of state representatives sent to appear before them.

Seventh, the treaty bodies often do not sufficiently press states on the authorship of reports, the involvement of nongovernmental sources in producing and/or providing critiques of reports, the details of the dissemination of the state report, and the dissemination of the comments of the treaty body within the state. Such information is not included in most state reports, and its omission is not followed up.

Eighth, the treaty bodies have often failed to identify and promote alternative ways of obtaining information about a state in the absence of cooperation.

Ninth, the treaty bodies have often failed actively to encourage participation by informed and reliable nongovernmental organizations—both national and international—in their work They have frequently not engaged in pro-active attempts to solicit information from appropriate nongovernmental organizations and to advise national nongovernmental organizations of forthcoming examinations of state reports.

Tenth, the treaty bodies have failed to foster relationships with the world press, both national and international, failed to develop opportunities for news conferences, and failed to pay attention to the newsworthiness of press releases.

Eleventh, where the right of individual petition exists, the treaty bodies have neglected the actual remedy obtained, and have not done enough to follow up findings of violations.

Twelfth, the treaty bodies have failed to advertise in an appropriate manner, within the relevant states, the availability of the right of petition.

Thirteenth, the treaty bodies have taken insufficient steps to attempt to ensure that the exercise of the right of petition is not inhibited by state interference, particularly in relation to those states which have ratified the Optional Protocol and yet are the subject of either very few or no complaints.

Fourteenth, the treaty bodies have failed to take steps to develop the expertise to handle more subtle human rights situations raised in democracies, in addition to gross human rights violations.

THE GENERAL ASSEMBLY

The treaty bodies currently operate within severe externally imposed limitations. Those limitations are perpetuated by the complicity of the General Assembly. In general, the system is forced to function with inadequate financial resources. Financial resources are needed to improve weaknesses of the treaty body regime such as the lack of an adequate information base, available to treaty body members, on the human rights conditions within each state party.

Such an information base would involve a central collection of information on a state-by-state basis, including any reports by, or on, states parties to UN bodies, any records of decision on a state party by a UN body, information provided by reliable nongovernmental organizations, and reports or judgments produced in the context of regional human rights bodies. Greater financial resources are also needed to increase the meeting time for treaty bodies, to improve support services for the treaty bodies, and to provide appropriate emoluments for treaty body members.

The General Assembly also fails to support the work of the treaty bodies in other ways. It does little to promote the dissemination of state reports, the annual reports of the treaty bodies, and the summary records of the examination of states by the treaty bodies. Action tends to be limited to making reports of states parties and summary records of the discussion with the treaty bodies available in United Nations Information Centers. But such centers exist in only [77] of the [191] countries in the world. Countries like Angola, China, Cuba, and Jamaica simply do not have one. Even where they do exist, as one commentator has pointed out:

> United Nations Information Centres . . . have generally been reduced to a discreet silence and do not have sufficient resources at their disposal. . . .. The Information Centres usually suffer from an acute shortage of staff . . . the Centres . . . do not properly play their information and public relations role in regard to human rights.[5]

The General Assembly does not do enough to ensure adequate publicity or media coverage of the examination of reports. It also fails to follow up treaty body conclusions, particularly concerning failures to abide by the obligation to report, the submission of inadequate reports, or evidence of treaty violations by states parties. The General Assembly tends to content itself with passing resolutions in which it "again urges States parties to make every effort to meet their reporting obligations and to contribute, individually and through meetings of States parties, to identifying ways of further streamlining and improving reporting procedures."

The whole issue of reservations is also one upon which the General Assembly has done very little. The General Assembly passes vague, general exhortations in which, for example, it "[a]ppeals to States parties to the Convention that have made reservations to review the compatibility of their reservations with article 51 of the Convention and other relevant rules of international law."[6] The General Assembly has not, for instance, attempted to explore the possibility of requesting an advisory opinion from the International Court of Justice on the validity and legal effect of any of the reservations to the human rights treaties.

[*Eds.*—The author concludes her essay with an extended discussion of the future of human rights treaty implementation, including a "catalogue of proposals" derived from "the recommendations of a number of studies or reports," designed "to cure the ills of the human rights treaty regime," and directed at the states parties to the multilateral human rights treaties, the treaty bodies, and "all states, the General Assembly, the Commission on Human Rights," and ECOSOC." On www.Bayefsky.com ("The United Nations Human Rights Treaties"), with support from the Ford Foundation, the Andrew W. Mellon Foundation, and other funding sources, she has continued her commitment to "enhancing the implementation of the human rights legal standards of the United Nations." Uniquely illustrative is her important study, *The UN Human Rights Treaty System: Universality at the Crossroads*, done in collaboration with the Office of the High Commissioner for Human Rights and published in 2001 by Kluwer Academic Publishers (hardbound) and Transnational Publishers (softbound). The most in depth study ever done on the treaty bodies, it is available free of charge at http://www.bayefsky.com/tree.php/id/9250. Professor Bayefsky writes on her website: "Accessibility to UN human rights norms by individuals everywhere is fundamental to their successful realization. The information provided herein encompasses a range of data concerning the application of the UN human rights treaty system by its monitoring treaty bodies since their inauguration in the 1970s."]

QUESTIONS FOR REFLECTION AND DISCUSSION

1. What sorts of sanctions do you think are required to stop the apparently endemic failure of states parties to human rights treaties to abide by the treaty terms? Does the UN need bigger enforcement "teeth" in the form of, say, a global sheriff? Absent such a step, how can or will the UN guarantee widespread adherence to the terms of its human rights treaties? What does Bayefsky recommend? Do you agree? Disagree? Why?

2. To what extent do you agree with Bayefsky's separate allocation of blame to states, UN treaty bodies, and the UN General Assembly? Are the three truly distinct? After all,

5. Maxime Tardu, *The Effectiveness of United Nations Methods and Mechanisms in the Field of Human Rights: A Critical Overview*, commissioned by the United Nations Centre for Human Rights for the World Conference on Human Rights. A/CONF157/PC/60/Add.S, April 1, 1993, p. 39, ¶ 209, p. 45, ¶¶ 251 and 252.

6. General Assembly in Resolution 47/112 on the Implementation of the Convention on the Rights of the Child, Dec. 16, 1992, GA Res. 47/112, UN GAOR, 47th Sess., Supp. No. 49, at 194, UN Doc. A/RES/47/112 (1992).

UN treaty bodies and the General Assembly are, ultimately, just different groupings of UN member states. Considered in this light, are the thirteen indictments Bayefsky levels against the treaty bodies simply a reflection of states parties' selfish interests in nonenforcement? Similarly, what is the ultimate source of the General Assembly's widely noted paucity of funding and support? Does allocating blame separately to the three entities serve a rhetorical purpose? A practical one?

3. Bayefsky is troubled by the practice of Islamic states becoming party to treaties subject to the reservation that those treaties will be enforced only insofar as they do not conflict with Shari`a law. Do you agree with Bayefsky that such reservations constitute a "threat to the [treaty] system's integrity"? Are not such reservations consistent with the right to culture (see Reading 18 by Stephen A. Hansen in Chapter 3 of this volume)? On the other hand, how does the allowance of such reservations fit with the principle of universality? Also, is it possible to have a functioning system of international treaties with standards that vary from nation to nation?

4. In "On the Margins of the Human Rights Discourse: Foreign Policy and International Welfare Rights" (Sleeping Under Bridges Project, Oct. 9, 2003 Draft, available at http://www.unl.edu/polisci/faculty/forsythe/SUB_1932C7.pdf), David P. Forsythe and Eric A. Heinze have noted that, especially among liberal democracies, contemporary state policy concerning welfare rights (i.e., those falling under the enforcement umbrella of the ICESCR) is directed primarily at narrow legal issues such as adjudication methods, treaty wording, violation definitions, and treaty-monitoring mechanisms, rather than at more practical (and potentially effective) matters like enforcement and programming. Why do you think this is so? Is such a focus a reflection of distaste for economic, social, and cultural (ESC) rights? A way of deflecting attention away from their own questionable human rights records? Is their behavior any different from that of Islamic countries when they subordinate their human rights treaty commitments Shari`a law (see Question 3, above)?

5. Forsythe and Heinze (see Question 4) note that U.S. opposition to welfare rights seems to have crossed some Rubicon by the end of Eisenhower's first administration (1952–56) when "big business, the Republican Party, and . . . other sectors . . . such as the medical profession," all of them opposed to "nationalized health care," coalesced to oppose U.S. commitments to international welfare rights. To what extent do you think the same groups remain the leaders in that opposition? How would you answer the following question posed by Forsythe and Heinze: "What if American society had been able to debate specific subsistence rights, like national health care, on their merits in the 1940s and 1950s free from the taint of the cold war, McCarthyism, and the red scare?"

6. When a person lacks a civil or political right (i.e., one falling under the aegis of the ICCPR)—for example, freedom of speech—it often is quite obvious who has abrogated that right; it has been taken away or denied by some affirmative act. When, however, a person lacks a welfare right (i.e., one falling under the aegis of the ICESCR)—for example, the right to universal health care—it is much less clear that something has been taken away; rather, something has simply not been provided. Is this to say that ESC rights are more problematic to enforce and therefore less likely to become universally available? Or have we simply posed a false dichotomy? Is there a meaningful difference between taking a right away and failing to take affirmative steps to protect a nascent right? What would Bayefsky say? On ESC rights, see Reading 13 by Asbjørn Eide in Chapter 3 of this volume.

7. Chapter VII of the UN Charter anticipates that one method of effectively enforcing compliance with UN treaties is through military action taken in conjunction with individual member states or organizations of member states. Was this strategy an effective way to "make the human rights treaties work" in Liberia in the 1990s? Consider reading Kenneth L. Cain, "The Rape of Dinah: Human Rights, Civil War in Liberia, and Evil Triumphant," *HRQ* 21 (1999): 229–55 for a wrenching account of the strategy's failure. Cain posits that the litany of human rights abuses perpetrated by the Economic Community of West African States (ECOWAS) Monitoring Group (ECOMOG) were carried out with the tacit approval of a UN incapable of preventing them. What might the UN do differently if and when it is faced with a similar situation again? Is Cain right to assert that the UN was "derelict" in its duty to protect human rights? Or was it the member states who make up the UN and, in particular, those who at the time governed the UN Security Council (alone

under the UN Charter with authority to impose military sanctions) who were derelict (perhaps most especially those with veto power)?

8. Professor Bayefsky's website is devoted, in part, to providing free access to information about UN human rights treaties. Do you think more widespread access to treaties will have a significant impact on the effectiveness of the treaties? What tactics are the countries which oppose full implementation likely to employ in the face of more widespread dissemination of treaty information? Will the truth about human rights treaties, if it becomes universally available, have beneficial effects?

Chapter Six

International Approaches to Human Rights Implementation

I N this chapter, we consider international approaches to the implementation of human rights, first through the United Nations, second via the regional human rights regimes of Europe, the Americas, and Africa. The chapter features essays by two experienced senior scholars who are renowned in the fields about which they write here. "The United Nations and Human Rights: The Promise of Multilateral Diplomacy and Action" by Stephen P. Marks reminds the reader that the status of human rights as a UN concern was based on a theory of peace "according to which respect for human rights and fundamental freedoms was a necessary condition for peace within and among nations." Dinah Shelton on "The Promise of Regional Human Rights Systems," explains that regional systems began as the global human rights system was developing and were inspired by the agreed-upon United Nations norms, but took shape reflecting the fact that each region "had its own issues and concerns."

THE UNITED NATIONS

The United Nations is an intergovernmental organization that seeks to foster friendly relations among nations, helps to maintain international peace and security, and works to facilitate economic, social, and cultural cooperation and development. Additionally, as set forth in Article 1 of its Charter,[1] one of the United Nations' principal purposes is "to achieve international cooperation . . . in promoting and encouraging respect for human rights and for fundamental freedoms for all without distinction as to race, sex, language, or religion."

The linkage of human rights with more familiar UN goals is no accident of the UN Charter. It reflects a connection that U.S. President Franklin D. Roosevelt saw between peace and freedom and between international security and human rights. In a message to Congress on January 26, 1941, Roosevelt enunciated "four freedoms": freedom of speech and expression, freedom of worship, freedom from want (meaning economic security), and

1. Pertinent provisions of the UN Charter, concluded June 26, 1945, are reprinted in Documentary Appendix A.

freedom from fear (meaning a worldwide reduction of armaments and international peace).[2] These freedoms—especially in the wake of systematic genocide before and during World War II—were perceived as essential world concerns that mandated international cooperation and participation.

On the basis of this perception, the 1945 San Francisco conference that drafted the UN Charter sought not only to continue the struggle against tyranny begun during World War II, but, as well, to initiate the creation of effective norms, institutions, and procedures addressed to broadly defined human rights issues. The aim was not to fashion a world government; that would have been idealism run amok. The purpose was to achieve, step by step, a world community capable of securing the UN Charter's goals of peace and social justice—a golden-age image, perhaps, but one toward which, since the San Francisco conference, some ordered progress actually has been made.[3]

Since 1945, the United Nations has taken three interrelated steps toward the advancement of human rights: (a) the prescription (definition, formulation) of international norms of behavior regarding human rights; (b) the promotion (advocacy) of human rights through information dissemination, education, and training about human rights at all levels of social organization; and (c) the protection (application, implementation) of human rights norms through the design and creation of relevant institutions and procedures. Each of these steps—prescription, promotion, protection—merits brief attention.

PRESCRIBING (DEFINING, FORMULATING) HUMAN RIGHTS

The initial step of defining and formulating international human rights norms was taken soon after the United Nations was organized.[4] When the UN General Assembly first met in London in 1946, it transmitted to its Economic and Social Council a draft Declaration of Fundamental Human Rights and Freedoms "for reference to the Commission on Human Rights in its preparation of an international bill of rights."[5] In 1947, the UN Commission decided to apply the term "International Bill of Human Rights" to a declaration of human rights, a convention on human rights (to be called "The Covenant on Human Rights"), and measures of implementation. This decision led, in turn, to the adoption and proclamation of the Universal Declaration of Human Rights on December 10, 1948 as the first of these

2. Address to Congress by President Roosevelt, 87th Cong. Rec. 44 (1944), excerpted as "Four Human Freedoms," *HRQ* 6 (1984): 384–85. The most succinct statement connecting the global values of rights with international security was John F. Kennedy's maxim that "peace, in the last analysis, is a matter of human rights." Quoted in Arthur J. Goldberg, "Our Concern for Human Rights," *Congress Bi-Weekly* 32, no. 13 (Nov. 15, 1965): 8, at 9. The philosophy is elaborated in the context of a normative theory of world order explained by Samuel S. Kim, *The Quest for a Just World Order* (Boulder, Colo.: Westview Press, 1984).
3. See Michael Barnett and Martha Finnemore, *Rules for the World: International Organizations in Global Politics* (Ithaca, N.Y.: Cornell University Press, 2004); Emanuel Adler, Beverly Crawford, and Jack Donnelly, "Defining and Conceptualizing Progress in International Relations," in Emanuel Adler and Beverly Crawford, eds., *Progress in Postwar International Relations* (New York: Columbia University Press, 1991), 1–42. With an eye to potential future progress, see B. G. Ramcharan, "Reforming the United Nations to Secure Human Rights," in Saul H. Mendlovitz and Burns H. Weston, eds., *Preferred Futures for the United Nations* (Ardsley, N.Y.: Transnational Publishers, 1995), 193–219.
4. See Mary Ann Glendon, *A World Made New: Eleanor Roosevelt and the Universal Declaration of Human Rights* (New York: Random House, 2001); Louis B. Sohn, "A Short History of United Nations Documents on Human Rights," in Commission to Study the Organization of Peace, *The United Nations and Human Rights*, 18th Report (Dobbs Ferry, N.Y.: Oceana, 1968), 39–186.
5. Feb. 16, 1946, ECOSOC Res. 1/5, UN Doc. E/CN/AC.1/3. The draft declaration is reproduced as Annex A of UN Doc. E/CN.4/21. See John Humphrey, "The Universal Declaration of Human Rights: Its History, Impact and Juridical Character," in B. G. Ramcharan, ed., *Human Rights: Thirty Years After the Universal Declaration of Human Rights* (The Hague: Nijhoff, 1979), 21–40.

projected instruments.[6] However, instead of one international covenant on human rights, there emerged, in 1966, two such covenants: the International Covenant on Economic, Social and Cultural Rights (ICESCR) and the International Covenant on Civil and Political Rights (ICCPR).[7] Each contains a plan for international supervision of the rights it addresses and for resolution of complaints by one state against another. In addition, the first Optional Protocol to the ICCPR[8] provides important international machinery for dealing with claims from individuals regarding alleged state violations of the rights guaranteed in that Covenant.

The drafting of human rights standards that are universally acceptable is necessarily an awesome task because the words must be carefully chosen if, in our multicultured world, they are to be understood and taken seriously. In 1977, the late Allard K. Lowenstein, United States Representative to the UN Thirty-Third Commission on Human Rights, paid tribute to Eleanor Roosevelt, who chaired the committee responsible for the drafting of the UDHR. Arguing that "words matter," he stated: "Mrs. Roosevelt's . . . efforts to get agreement about what was meant by the words 'human rights'. . . was the toughest semantic job of all, and the fact that the job eventually got done makes the complexities that still exist somehow more manageable. We have developed over thirty years' time a body of precedents and of common usages of words, and that is a formidable influence on what governments have to say they are trying to measure up to."[9]

PROMOTING (ADVOCATING) HUMAN RIGHTS

A second UN task is the promotion of human rights, by which is meant campaigns to "market" or "sell" human rights, to increase knowledge (educate) about, and secure public support for, international human rights instruments such as the two covenants and the many more specialized conventions and declarations promulgated since. UN efforts to promote human rights include information exchanges, educational training courses, the establishment of fellowships for human rights scholars, programs of the United Nations University in Tokyo, and the advisory services of human rights experts to aid member states with human rights problems and issues.[10] Additionally, the United Nations has undertaken many special human rights studies—on the "disappeared," freedom of religion, freedom of movement across national boundaries, and threats to human rights posed by advances in technology, to mention but a few.

Particularly popular have been the worldwide and regional human rights conferences and seminars on diverse specialized topics, open to private individuals and organizations. Examples include: human rights in developing countries (Nicosia, 1968); human rights and scientific and technological development (Vienna, 1972); women, equality, development, and peace (Copenhagen, 1980); human rights teaching (Malta, 1987). Such human rights conferences attended by private persons only, when sponsored by the United Nations, can inform public opinion globally and thereby promote human rights standards as a basis

6. Reprinted and referenced in Documentary Appendix A. December 10 of each year is now officially Human Rights Day throughout the world.
7. Each of these instruments is reprinted and referenced in Documentary Appendix A.
8. Concluded Dec. 16, 1966, referenced in Documentary Appendix B.
9. "Review of the UN 33rd Commission on Human Rights," House Committee on Foreign Affairs, Subcommittee on Human Rights and International Organizations, *Hearing*, 95th Cong, 1st Sess., May 19, 1977, at 19.
10. See, e.g., Evan Luard, "Promotion of Human Rights by UN Political Bodies," in Evan Luard, ed., *The International Protection of Human Rights* (New York: Praeger, 1967), 132–59.

for judging governments. Moreover, international conferences involving state participants along with parallel NGO meetings have been extraordinarily influential, e.g., the World Conference on Human Rights (Vienna, 1993) and the World Conference on Women (Beijing, 1995). Such conferences are important not only because they attract government delegations together with interested NGOs and private parties from throughout the world, but also because they promote networking opportunities and supply fora for penetrating discussions of the deeper issues of injustice underlying human rights abuses. Scholars and other private persons in educational seminars are more free than governmentally instructed UN representatives to debate the information, research, and education needed to analyze the unjust conditions under which human rights are denied and to eradicate the root causes for their denial. In addition, such conferences, relying on widely accepted standards of human rights, can assess human rights progress from country to country. While it is true that technically no state is bound by an international human rights instrument until it has ratified or otherwise approved the instrument according to its own constitutional processes, still, in the sunlight of open international discussions, no state can escape scrutiny regarding its adherence to international human rights norms.

Formulating and promoting human rights are important tasks, but by themselves do not actually vindicate rights, remedy violations, or punish transgressors. Codification, though impressive, often involves, as Stephen Marks says in Reading 26, "the establishment largely of paper rights and of studies and public information useful but at the same time innocuous to governments who considered their freedom to mistreat their population as an attribute of sovereignty." Rights without protection, while not completely without value, have much diminished practical value.

PROTECTING (APPLYING, ENFORCING) HUMAN RIGHTS

In principle, international human rights conventions leave the task of directly enforcing their standards to the states parties; the states parties are themselves expected to enact the legislation and other measures that are necessary for implementation. But UN organs typically play a supervisory role in such implementation, and, as may be inferred from Stephen Marks' essay, they can be graded from "weak" to "strong" depending upon how directly and swiftly they respond to complaints.[11]

The weakest, most indirect form of UN supervision of human rights is the requirement of government reporting, especially since, as in numerous human rights treaties, the requirement involves merely the ritual filing of reports with few questions asked. For example, states that are party to the International Convention on the Elimination of All Forms of Racial Discrimination (ICERD)[12] are obliged by Article 9 to report every two years to the UN Secretary-General on national measures taken to implement the agreement. Detailed reporting requirements are contained as well in Part 4 of the ICESCR. However, as Bayefsky notes in Reading 25 of preceding Chapter 5, the delinquency rates for the states bound by these instruments are unfortunately all too high, suggesting that the procedure is regarded less seriously than was intended by the drafters.[13]

11. See Sir Nigel Rodley, "United Nations Treaty Bodies and Special Procedures of the Commission on Human Rights—Complementarity or Competition?" *HRQ* 25, no. 4 (2003): 882–908.
12. Concluded Dec. 21, 1965, referenced in Documentary Appendix B.
13. See A. Glenn Mower, Jr., "Reports from State Parties," in Mower, *International Cooperation for Social Justice, Global, and Regional Protection of Economic/Social Rights* (Westport, Conn.: Greenwood Press, 1985), 39–40.

On the other hand, the promise of stronger UN supervision exists in the treaty-based reporting systems that contain potential for specific legal accountability. One example is ICCPR Article 40 which, when read in conjunction with Article 2, obliges the states parties to report the extent to which they have (a) adopted legislative or other measures to implement the rights recognized in the covenant, (b) ensured that persons whose rights and freedoms are violated have had access to effective remedies from competent judicial, administrative, or legislative authorities, and (c) guaranteed that competent authorities have enforced such remedies when granted. These reports are submitted to, and carefully scrutinized by, the Human Rights Committee established under the Covenant to supervise its implementation. Further, when a state becomes a party to the ICCPR's first Optional Protocol, it automatically recognizes, as stated in Optional Protocol Article 1, "the competence of the [Human Rights] Committee to receive and consider communications from individuals . . . who claim to be victims of a violation by that State Party." While not empowered to supply a remedy directly, the Committee is authorized by Optional Protocol Article 4(2) to demand of the accused state "written explanations or statements clarifying the matter and the remedy, if any, that may have been taken by that State," thus offering some recourse to individuals whose rights have been violated.

The Committee has earned a positive reputation by becoming increasingly active in challenging governments to hold them to their treaty promises.[14] As Cindy A. Cohn has shown, states parties to the Optional Protocol have tried in many different ways to bring their respective laws into harmony with the Covenant by establishing national agencies that check prospective laws for compliance before enactment.[15] This increasingly active role of the Human Rights Committee is consistent with the general trend of UN activity in the protection of human rights. As Marks points out in Reading 26, the role of the United Nations in the international protection of human rights has developed from that of a rudimentary receptacle for human rights complaints to that of a more active intermediary seeking to promote compliance with human rights norms and standards.

Another example is the older non-treaty-based "1503 Procedure," so-called because of UN Economic and Social Council Resolution 1503 of May 1970 that gave birth to it.[16] Involving "the entire hierarchy of the UN's human rights organs"[17]—the General Assembly, the Economic and Social Council, the Commission on Human Rights, and its Sub-Commission on Prevention of Discrimination and Protection of Minorities (now the Sub-Commission on the Promotion and Protection of Human Rights)—the procedure differs from that under the ICCPR's first Optional Protocol in two important ways. First, it allows for communications from nongovernmental organizations and other interested groups as well as from individual victims and their representatives. Second, being a confidential procedure by design, it neither exposes the states complained of publicly nor condemns offending states publicly, but, rather, considers situations of widespread, massive violations of human rights and helps concerned states to cease committing or allowing the

14. See, e.g., A. H. Robertson, "Individual Communications: The Optional Protocol," in A. H. Robertson, *Human Rights in the World: An Introduction to the Study of the International Protection of Human Rights*, 2nd ed. (Manchester: Manchester University Press, 1982), 54–60. See also Kirsten A. Young, *The Law and Process of the U.N. Human Rights Committee* (Ardsley, N.Y.: Transnational Publishers, 2002).
15. Cindy A. Cohn, "The Early Harvest: Domestic Legal Changes Related to the Human Rights Committee and the Covenant on Civil and Political Rights," *HRQ* 13 (1991): 295–321.
16. ECOSOC Resolution 1503, adopted May 27, 1970, referenced in Documentary Appendix B.
17. Dinah L. Shelton, "Individual Complaint Machinery Under the United Nations 1503 Procedure and the Optional Protocol to the International Covenant on Civil and Political Rights," in Hurst Hannum, ed., *Guide to International Human Rights Practice* (Philadelphia: University of Pennsylvania Press, 1984), 60.

commission of the violations in question—all essentially in secret, purportedly to facilitate communications without political or personally endangering repercussions.[18]

Procedures for managing and processing complaints are cumbersome, and their short-comings are explained by diverse factors, including the inability of states to reach agreement on how and even whether to protect human rights. In Reading 26, Stephen Marks acknowledges the difficulties and shows how multiple UN organs are occasionally effective but more often uncoordinated and ill-equipped to pressure an offending regime. Of course, politics enters the picture as well.

That politics enter the picture is perhaps nowhere more evident than in the functioning of the UN Commission on Human Rights (UNCHR). While the Commission can take credit for formulating the International Bill of Rights and other important human rights instruments, it has a well-deserved reputation for being openly political. Unlike the UN human rights treaty-bodies which are made up of independent experts, the Commission's 53 member states name their representatives to Commission membership who then act under government instruction. Accordingly, the Commission has been routinely subject to criticism. Harvard human rights specialist Samantha Power has sharply reproached the Commission as a "politicized farce," reasoning that, because the Commission allocates its seats on a regional basis, the occasional result is that "some of the world's most vicious regimes are members"[19]—including, for example, the reelection of Sudan to Commission membership at the very time it was "busy ethnically cleansing hundreds of thousands of Africans in Darfur," a grotesque anomaly prompting Power's conclusion that "Until membership comes with responsibilities, the commission will shelter too many human rights abusers and condemn too few." Thus, it came as no surprise when, in an address to the UN General Assembly on March 21, 2005[20] in which he advocated major UN reforms as detailed in a draft report (including a strengthened Office of the UN High Commissioner for Human Rights),[21] Secretary-General Kofi Annan took direct aim at the UNCHR himself. Observing that the Commission included countries with histories of rights violations that sought Commission membership "not to strengthen human rights, but to protect themselves against criticism, or to criticize others" and that, as a result, the Commission had "been increasingly undermined by its declining credibility and professionalism," he proposed the creation of a smaller "Human Rights Council" to replace the Commission whose members would be appointed by the General Assembly and whose members would "undertake to abide by the highest human rights standards."[22]

Consequently, during the 2005 World Summit, over 150 heads of state and government took the historic step of mandating the establishment of the Human Rights Council (HRC). Thereafter, on March 15, 2006, the General Assembly, voting 170-4-3 (Israel, the Marshall Islands, Palau, and the United States voting against), adopted Assembly President Jan Eliasson's plan prescribing the membership, purpose, functions, and procedures of the new body,[23]

18. Because of the confidentiality of the 1503 Procedure, its effectiveness is difficult to evaluate. Theo C. van Boven writes that the 1503 Procedure at first appeared very promising, but the time consumed by its technicalities, secrecy, and the reluctance of the UN Commission on Human Rights to act effectively turned high expectations to disappointment. "A Peoples' Commission," in *People Matter: Views on International Human Rights Policy* (Amsterdam: Meulenhoff Nederland, 1981): 59–67.
19. Samantha Power, "Business as Usual at the UN," *Foreign Policy* 144 (Sept./Oct. 2004): 38–39, at 39.
20. See The Secretary-General, *Statement to the General Assembly*, Mar. 21, 2005, available at http://www.un.org/largerfreedom/sg-statement.html
21. Report of the Secretary-General of the United Nations for Decision by three Heads of State and Government in September 2005, in *Larger Freedom: Towards Development, Security and Human Rights for All*, available at http://www.un.org/largerfreedom.
22. As quoted in Colum Lynch, "Annan Drafts Changes for UN," *Washington Post*, Mar. 20, 2005, at A01.
23. UN General Assembly Resolution 60/251 (A/RES/60/251), formalizing General Assembly Draft

including a broad mandate to scrutinize human rights abuses worldwide on the basis of periodic reviews of every country's human rights performance. Guided by "the principles of universality, impartiality, objectivity and non-selectivity, constructive international dialogue and cooperation," it is authorized to investigate violations of human rights (gross and systematic violations included), make recommendations, and even arrange for technical assistance to implement programs of remediation. Enlarged responsibility is facilitated by the HRC's creation as a standing body of the General Assembly, with year-round presence in Geneva, that can respond promptly to human rights emergencies as they arise. Minimally, it meets three times and for at least ten weeks each year. A positive carryover from the earlier Commission is the continued participation of NGOs in the work of the Council and in other forms of cooperation with UN human rights investigative initiatives.

Of course, the effectiveness of the HRC depends on its membership, reduced from the Commission's 53 to 47. Membership is open to all states subject to equitable geographic distribution, taking into account their commitment and contribution to the promotion and protection of human rights and refusing membership to states found guilty of gross and systematic violations of human rights. Winning a seat on the HRC requires an absolute majority vote of the General Assembly's total membership (191 members at this writing). Under terms meant to restrict rights abusers from membership, candidates are voted on individually rather than as a regional group and by secret ballot. States elected to the Council must uphold the highest standards in the promotion and protection of human rights and their rights records are subject to mandatory periodic review.

Some of the best of the former Commission's institutional innovations are retained and charged in general terms to serve as fora for continuing dialogue on all kinds of thematic issues of human rights and fundamental freedoms, positioning them to make recommendations to the General Assembly for the further development of international human rights law and policy. Under the earlier Commission, this task was ingeniously undertaken by the invention of the thematic offices. Examples include the Working Group on Involuntary Disappearances (1980) and special investigators called "rapporteurs," such as the Special Rapporteur on Torture (1985), the Special Rapporteur on Indigenous People (2001), and more recently, the Special Rapporteur on the Sale of Children, Child Prostitution, and Child Pornography (2002). Generally, these thematic offices have had a mandate of three years, at which point their work finishes with reports and recommendations that typically produced resolutions and pronouncements from the UNCHR to help keep human rights standards "up-to-date," providing NGOs with issues on which to focus as they monitor human rights. For example, while the International Bill of Rights nowhere stipulates a "right to a healthful environment," the Commission, in 1998, accepted the report of a special rapporteur on issues related to developing countries and responded by "categorically condemning the increasing rate of dumping of toxic and dangerous products in poor countries which adversely affects the human rights to life and health of individuals in those countries"; and on the basis of that statement supplied the standard by which the NGO, Human Rights Watch, later condemned dumping by a Taiwan Corporation of mercury-laced waste on Cambodian beaches resulting in the illness and death of children who played there.[24]

With its government representatives and complex formula of election designed to ensure membership from all regions, the UNCHR was necessarily a political body and, as noted,

---

Resolution 60/L48 of September 2005 submitted by the President of the General Assembly to the Assembly for its adoption.

24. Human Rights Watch, *Toxic Justice: Human Rights and Toxic Waste in Cambodia* (New York: Human Rights Watch, 1999).

often controversial. Yet in Reading 26, Stephen Marks does not hesitate to emphasize the positive features of the UN record and positive potential for UN diplomacy and action on such critically important issues as women's human rights, civil society, peace operations, and so forth.

There is, indeed, much to applaud in the gradual development of the UN's protective approaches. The development of specialized task forces, such as the many Working Groups (comprehensively listed on the website of the UN High Commissioner for Human Rights[25]), the increasing reliance on special rapporteurs, "urgent messages," country visits, and reports "requiring immediate action" all involve innovations at the international level that reflect creative even if too often uncoordinated efforts. At another level, among such disparate efforts are increasing indications of human rights progress within various countries where internationally defined human rights standards increasingly influence domestic law.[26]

This phenomenon was noted approvingly by the UN High Commissioner for Human Rights, Louise Arbour, soon after the Canadian Supreme Court Justice and former Chief Prosecutor for the International Criminal Tribunals for the former Yugoslavia and for Rwanda was appointed in 2004 to her post of UN High Commissioner for Human Rights. Reaffirming her faith in the rule of law, she stated:

> One objection that is sometimes raised with respect to international human rights law is that it is incapable of effective enforcement. I think this criticism is less valid than it once was. To start with, we should be proud of our collective achievements in turning human rights ideals into legal obligations that most States now voluntarily accept at both the international and national levels. Through the ratification of human rights treaties and their incorporation into domestic constitutional and legal systems, individuals are increasingly able to assert and claim their rights. We have seen inspiring judgments from courts at all levels in all continents that turn human rights into a reality for ordinary people across the globe.[27]

Commissioner Arbour concluded: "These are not small accomplishments."

The post of High Commissioner for Human Rights, an appointee of the UN Secretary General, was created in 1994 in large measure in response to demands made by NGOs at the World Conference on Human Rights in Vienna in 1993. The High Commissioner for Human Rights is the principal UN official with responsibility for human rights and is accountable to the Secretary-General. The Office of the High Commissioner for Human Rights (OHCHR) is based at the Palais Wilson in Geneva, Switzerland, with an office at United Nations Headquarters in New York.

The first Commissioner was José Ayala Lasso (Ecuador), succeeded in 1997 by Mary Robinson, former President of Ireland. While on duty in 2003, the service of her successor,

25. See http://www.ohchr.org/english.
26. See, e.g., *Roper v. Simmons*, U.S. Sup. Ct. Docket No. 03-633 (Mar. 1, 2005), wherein Justice Anthony M. Kennedy, writing for the 5-4 majority to outlaw juvenile (under 18) executions, stated: "It is proper that we acknowledge the overwhelming weight of international opinion against the juvenile death penalty, resting in large part on the understanding that the instability and emotional imbalance of young people may often be a factor in the crime. . . . The opinion of the world community, while not controlling our outcome, does provide respected and significant confirmation for our own conclusions."
27. Louise Arbour, United Nations High Commissioner for Human Rights, "Activities of the Office of the United Nations High Commissioner for Human Rights: Achievements and Challenges," Tokyo, United Nations University, Nov. 9, 2004, available at http://www.unhchr.ch/huricane/huricane.nsf/view01/3EE6AE0C10AA80C1C1256F4D0058AFD5?opendocument; cf. Christof Heyns and Frans Viljoen, "The Impact of the United Nations Human Rights Treaties on the Domestic Level," *HRQ* 23, no. 3 (2001): 483–535.

the late Sergio deMello (Brazil), was tragically cut short when he was killed in Iraq. At present, since 2004, Louise Arbour (Canada) occupies the office, bringing to her tasks considerable energy and a willingness to try new initiatives.

Several tasks are assigned to the High Commissioner and new ones have been proposed to enhance the position in order to strengthen the international human rights regime:

- *Leadership.* The High Commissioner makes frequent public statements on human rights crises as a moral authority and voice for victims and travels widely to ensure that the human rights message is heard everywhere—engaging in dialogue and building constructive cooperation with Governments to strengthen national human rights protection; and working with NGOs, academic institutions, and the private sector to instill commitment to human rights as widely as possible, e.g., speaking out on trafficking in people, HIV/AIDS, and human rights issues associated with biotechnology, and the effects of globalization.

- *Mainstreaming Human Rights in the United Nations.* The High Commissioner is charged with integrating human rights thinking and standards throughout the work of the Organization, coordinating with UN programs on peace and security, economic and social affairs, development cooperation and humanitarian affairs. In 2004, the Secretary General's High-Level Panel on Threats, Challenges and Change proposed that the Security Council request the High Commissioner's participation in their meetings to implement the human rights related provisions of Council resolutions, "thus enabling focused, effective monitoring of these provisions."[28]

- *Supporting International Human Rights Bodies.* The High Commissioner seeks to offer high quality research, expertise, advice, and administrative services to the main UN human rights bodies. The OHCHR provides support for the meetings of the United Nations Human Rights Council and its Sub-Commission and follow-up to their deliberations. Its staff, including UN fellows and interns, assist experts appointed by these bodies in investigating and reporting on human rights issues.

- *Improving In-Country and Regional Programs.* The High Commissioner encourages links between national, regional, and international groups and organizations. To foster those links, the OHCHR has appointed regional representatives and advisers and set up field offices in troubled countries such as Cambodia. The High Commissioner has encouraged the formation in Southeast Asian countries of National Human Rights Commissions.[29]

- *Promoting Human Rights Education.* The High Commissioner disseminates information on human rights and promotes human rights education worldwide. The OHCHR maintains a website that makes all official documents and information on international human rights developments accessible to millions (www.unhchr.ch) and in that vein, published reports on countries' progress in meeting the goals of the UN Decade of Human Rights Education, 1995–2004.

As if these responsibilities were not enough, the Secretary General's High-Level Panel on UN reform proposed, in 2004, that the High Commissioner take on a far-reaching new responsibility recommending that he/she "prepare an annual report on the situation of

---

28. Report of the High-Level Panel on Threats, Challenges and Change, "A More Secure World: Our Shared Responsibility," UN Doc. A/59/565 (2 December 2004), 75.
29. E.g., the Philippine Human Rights Commission plays several roles to implement and enforce human rights. They monitor and report on violations throughout the country. The National Commission trains the military and police on human rights, ensures that violators are punished and that those not passing human rights examinations are not promoted or given salary increases. For discussion, see Richard Pierre Claude, *Educating for Human Rights: The Philippines and Beyond* (Quezon City: University of the Philippines Press, 1996), chap. 5, "Civil-Military/Police Relations."

human rights worldwide. This could then serve as a basis for a comprehensive discussion with the Human Rights Council. The report should focus on the implementation of all human rights in all countries, based on information stemming from the work of treaty bodies, special mechanisms and any other sources deemed appropriate by the High Commissioner."[30]

The OHCHR has taken on an expanded reach and extended the scope of its human rights implementation efforts. By 2004, the Office was engaged operationally in some 40 countries, through its own offices, through United Nations peace missions, or in connection with technical cooperation projects. From training law enforcement officials to strengthening national human rights institutions, from mapping past human rights violations to denouncing current violations, the OHCHR has shown an increasing willingness to undertake bold initiatives in a wide range of activities designed to enhance and protect universal human rights. Soon after taking her UN post, Judge Arbour told a Japanese audience that "the operations dimension, is, in many ways, the apex of our work: endeavoring to ensure that we adopt the best approach, and have the commensurate means, to remedy or reverse situations of human rights violations, when and where they occur.[31]

REGIONAL SYSTEMS OF HUMAN RIGHTS IMPLEMENTATION

A strong argument can be made that the most promising prospects for human rights institution-building are at the regional rather than the global level. Support for this view lies in the "functional theories" developed to explain successful examples of international integration, such as the Council of Europe, organized in 1950. According to functional integration theory, successful regional or international organizations initially perform relatively nonpolitical technical activities that are mutually beneficial to all parties, for example, trade or defense. From this shared experience, people learn cooperative and extranational attitudes. Says one expert, Hidetoshi Hashimoto: "Functionalists argue that because problems confronting the world today (e.g., gross human rights violations, environmental degradation) can no longer be solved solely within national boundaries, international cooperation has become imperative."[32] When this tipping point is reached, he explains, we see the crux of functional theory at work in the phenomenon of "spillover," whereby "the development of collaboration in one field leads to collaboration in other fields." Clovis C. Morrisson, Jr., another functional theorist, says that when such collaboration reaches a high level of comprehensiveness "final transfers of political and legal relationships can take place." Morrisson concluded on this basis that "the European Human Rights Convention can be viewed . . . as a regional functional institution."[33]

In Reading 27, Dinah Shelton assesses "The Promise of Regional Human Rights Systems"

---

30. High-Level Panel, note 28, at 75.
31. Arbour, note 27.
32. Hidetoshi Hashimoto, *The Prospects for a Regional Human Rights Mechanism in East Asia* (New York: Routledge, 2004), 2–3, citing the original articulation of this view by David Mitrany, "The Functional Approach to World Organization," *International Affairs* (July 1948): 350–63. For a critical contemporary exposition, see Craig N. Murphy, "The Functional Approach, Organization Theory and Conflict Resolution," in Lucian M. Ashworth and David Long, eds., *New Perspectives on International Functionalism* (New York: St. Martin's Press, 1999), 84–104.
33. Clovis C. Morrisson, Jr., "The European Human Rights Convention System as a Functional Enterprise," *Universal Human Rights* 1 (Oct.-Dec. 1979): 81–92, at 82. This perspective also guided the analysis of Ernst Haas, *Human Rights and International Action: The Case of Freedom of Association* (Stanford, Calif.: Stanford University Press, 1970); see also his "Turbulent Fields and the Theory of Regional Integration," *International Organization* 30 (Winter 1976): 173–213.

and concludes that the European Convention on Human Rights and Fundamental Freedoms[34] has given birth to the most effective and advanced international system for the interpretation and protection of human rights currently in existence. For example, the European Court in Strasbourg has declared that the Austrian Government should pay damages to a criminal defendant who had been held too long before trial.[35] It has ruled that the United Kingdom violated the European Convention in forbidding the *London Sunday Times* from publishing an article on the thalidomide tragedy while civil litigation involving children whose birth defects were allegedly due to the drug was pending.[36] In addition, it has decided privacy cases involving abortion, telephonic eavesdropping, and homosexual activity. The Court and the related Committee of Ministers of the Council of Europe have confirmed rulings of the German Constitutional Court that liberalization of abortion and German wiretap laws did not violate the European Convention on Human Rights, but that an 1861 Irish sodomy law did violate human rights according to a ruling in 1988.[37]

European human rights institutions have also supplied a framework for effective multilateral diplomacy regarding human rights. For example, after a military coup in Greece in 1967, the Benelux and Nordic members of the Council of Europe produced a report condemning human rights abuses in that country. The report raised the specter of the expulsion of Greece from the Council, but, before that happened, Greece withdrew. In 1973, however, Greece was readmitted to the institutions of the European Convention and the Council of Europe after its government moved to comply with the Council's conditions, including the lifting of a declared state of emergency, the release of all political detainees, the restoration of human rights, and the holding of elections under "a genuinely democratic constitution."[38] Such achievements in the resolution of human rights disputes reflect a high degree of regional integration, realistic implementation measures, and effective supranational institutional development. A similar process unfolded in the early part of this twenty-first century as Turkey sought to join the European community.[39]

The Inter-American Court of Human Rights and the Inter-American Commission are based in San José, Costa Rica. As Shelton notes, they have been rather weak institutions, partly because the United States has refused to play a participatory role. It never has ratified

34. Concluded Nov. 4, 1950, referenced in Documentary Appendix B. In addition to Shelton's essay below, see her *Remedies in International Human Rights Law*, 2nd ed. (New York: Oxford University Press, 2001).

35. *Ringeisen v. Austria*, 15 Eur. Ct. H.R. (ser. A) (1972) and 16 Eur. Ct. H.R. (ser. A) (1973). See Alastair R. Mowbray, *Development of Positive Obligations Under the European Convention and the European Court of Human Rights* (Oxford: Hart, 2004).

36. *Times Newspapers Ltd. v. United Kingdom*, 30 Eur. Ct. H.R. (ser. A) (1979) and 38 Eur. Ct. H.R. (ser. A) (1981).

37. On the abortion issue, see *Bruggeman and Scheuten v. Federal Republic of Germany*, Application 5959175, Committee of Ministers, Resolution DH(78)1 (adopted Mar. 17, 1978). On the wiretap issue, see *Case of Klass and Others*, 28 Eur. Ct. H.R. (ser. A) (1978). The right to respect for private life was the basis for a ruling favorable to David Norris, an Irish homosexual rights advocate; he contested nineteenth-century laws setting a maximum penalty of life imprisonment for homosexual acts, even if carried out in private between consenting adults. *Norris v. Ireland*, 38 Eur. Ct. H.R. (1988).

38. *The Greek Case*, European Commission of Human Rights, *Report of the Commission* (adopted Nov. 5, 1969), Council of Europe, Doc. 15, 707/1, vol. 1, pt. 1 at 5–11; also Consultative Assembly of the Council of Europe, Res. 558, Jan. 22, 1974. These cases are regularly reported in the monthly *Human Rights Law Journal* (Kehl, Strasbourg, and Arlington, Va.: N.P. Engel). See also Mark W. Janis and Richard S. Kay, eds., *European Human Rights Law* (Hartford: University of Connecticut Law School Foundation Press, 1990).

39. See Zornitsa M. Stoyanova-Yerburgh, "Turkey and the European Union: One Step Closer" (Sept. 26, 2004), available at http://www.worldpress.org. Cf. the negative EU view in 1989 based on human rights performance: Commission of the European Communities, "Commission Opinion on Turkey's Request for Accession to the Community," Brussels (Dec. 20, 1989), available at http://www.europa. eu.int/comm/enlargement/ turkey/pdf/sec89_2290f_en.pdf

the Inter-American system's constitutive treaty, the American Convention on Human Rights (ACHR),[40] notwithstanding that the ACHR prescribes a human rights code paralleling that of the ICCPR to which the United States is a party. Article 4 gives everyone "the right to have his [sic] life respected" and proclaims that "No one shall be arbitrarily deprived of . . . life." Article 5 forbids torture. And Article 7 prohibits "arbitrary arrest or imprisonment." It is useful to note that the Inter-American Court is not set up to protect human rights through criminal prosecutions of states or state officials.[41]

But a significant breakthrough for the system occurred in 1988, implicating these provisions. In the famous *Velásquez Rodríguez* case, the Court demonstrated its interpretive capabilities, its concern to ensure real enforcement capacity among participating states, and its willingness to provide for the civil reparation of damages resulting from the acts of ACHR states parties, thus setting an important precedent.[42] Arising out of a period of political turmoil and violence in Honduras, the case started with a petition against Honduras received by the Inter-American Commission on Human Rights in 1981, alleging that Angel Manfredo Velásquez Rodríguez and others were arrested without warrant by members of the Honduran armed forces dressed in civilian clothes who abducted him, subjected him to torture, and caused his disappearance along with others in violation of ACHR Articles 4, 5, and 7. Noting that he and those originally accompanying him were still missing in 1986, and receiving no cooperation from the Government of Honduras, the Commission referred the case to the Court. Testimony showed that during 1981–84 about 130 persons were "disappeared," many after beatings, electric shock, drugging, and sexual abuse. A former member of the military unit notorious for such action testified that he knew the victims, including Velásquez Rodríguez, and said that, after being tortured, they were dismembered and buried in ways to confuse any later investigation and hide the crimes. The Commission presented testimony that between 1981 and 1984 the Honduras courts were inadequate, unwilling, and unable to protect human rights, some judges themselves being arrested and "disappeared." The Inter-American Court held the Government of Honduras in breach of its duties under the ACHR for the torture and killing of the "disappeared" Velásquez Rodriguez and ordered it to pay compensation to the victim's relatives, later revealed to be about $80,000. Honduras paid after several years of delay, but nevertheless ultimately paid. The supranational authority and applicability of the ACHR was thus established in the prosecution of Convention violations—at least in civil cases. In ordering remedies, as Michael Scharf has pointed out, the Court "did not direct the Honduran government to institute criminal proceedings against those responsible for the disappearance of Velásquez Rodríguez, notwithstanding the fact that the lawyers for the victims' families and the Inter-American Commission had specifically requested such injunctive relief."[43] Still, the case was a breakthrough.

Will the European example be followed elsewhere and will other regional systems gain strength to remedy past wrongs as in *Velásquez Rodríguez*? Article 52 of the UN Charter

40. Concluded Nov. 22, 1969, referenced in Documentary Appendix B.
41. See David J. Harris and Stephen Livingstone, *The Inter-American System of Human Rights* (Oxford: Clarendon Press, 1998); Jo M. Pasqualucci, *The Practice and Procedures of the Inter-American Court of Human Rights* (Cambridge: Cambridge University Press, 2003).
42. 4 Inter-Am. C.H.R. (ser. C) No. 4, ¶ 174 (July 29, 1988) (Judgment), reprinted in Neil J. Kritz, ed., *Transitional Justice: How Emerging Democracies Reckon with Former Regimes* (Washington, D.C.: United States Institute of Peace Press, 1995), 3: 586.
43. Michael Scharf, "The Letter of the Law: The Scope of the International Legal Obligation to Prosecute Human Rights Crimes," *Law and Contemporary Problems* 59 (Autumn 1996): 41–61, at 50–51. "Indeed," Scharf continues, "although the court said that '[s]tates must prevent, investigate and punish any violation of the rights recognized by the Convention,' it did not specifically refer to criminal prosecution as opposed to other forms of disciplinary action or punishment" (51).

encourages regional bodies within the UN system to make every effort to achieve pacific settlement of local disputes. Shelton compares the institutionally developed but still fledgling Inter-American human rights system and the new, more weakly integrated African system with the relatively mature European system. Her essay analyzes the enforcement machinery of the three systems in terms of the scope of the rights proclaimed and the accessibility of the institutions charged with implementing them. While observing that the jury is still out, she expresses optimism.

THE HELSINKI PROCESS

While not represented in our readings below, it is important to note the Organization for Security and Co-operation in Europe (OSCE), an outgrowth of the 1975 Final Act of the Conference on Security and Co-operation in Europe (also known as the "Helsinki Agreement" or "Helsinki Accords"),[44] an unusual instrument not comparable to other regional instruments for the promotion and protection of human rights. The end-product of a concerted effort by the former Soviet Union and its allies to secure official recognition and acceptance of their post-World War II European frontiers (the Second World War having ended without a omnibus peace treaty), the Final Act was adopted after two years of negotiation in Helsinki at the level of heads of state and/or government by 35 governments—including all the European states except Albania, but including the principalities of Liechtenstein, Monaco, and San Marino, plus Canada, the United States, and the Holy See—participating on a basis of formal equality. The West sought concessions primarily in relation to security requirements and human rights, largely in that order, and it was expressly stated that the Final Act as not to be a legally binding instrument. However, as Louis Henkin has argued, it "clearly preclude[d] any suggestion that matters it deals with are within domestic jurisdiction and beyond the reach of appropriate inquiry and recourse."[45] Henkin concludes: "Gentlemen's agreements," such as the Helsinki Final Act, "and other non-binding political and moral undertakings are established instruments in international relations, and their violation brings important political and moral consequences."[46]

Highlights of the fascinating history of this "toothless agreement" show how words do matter because they serve as the first step in a political process that may, indeed, lead to action. The political undertaking of what came to be known as the Helsinki Process involved recognition of the terms under which World War II was concluded, the postwar boundaries of Germany and Poland being of special concern. The moral undertaking was the acknowledgment that fundamental standards of human rights are prominent in the foundation of a durable peace. "In the field of human rights and fundamental freedoms," Principle I(a)(vii) of the Final Act proclaims "the participating States will act in conformity with the purposes and principles of the Charter of the United Nations and with the Universal Declaration of Human Rights. They will also fulfill their obligations as set forth in the international declarations and agreements in this field, including *inter alia* the International Covenants on Human Rights by which they may be bound."

The Final Act thus legitimizes the principle that human rights protection is an essential ingredient of security and cooperation. Recognition of this principle is embodied in an

44. Adopted Aug. 1, 1975, referenced in Documentary Appendix B.
45. Louis Henkin, "Human Rights and Domestic Jurisdiction," in Thomas Buergenthal, ed., with Judith R. Hall, *Human Rights, International Law, and the Helsinki Accord* (Montclair, N.J.: Allanheld, Osmun/Universe, 1977), 21–40, at 29.
46. Ibid.

agreement to continue the multilateral process initiated by the conference with follow-up meetings featuring the "thorough exchange of views" regarding the tasks defined by the Final Act—Principle I(b)(ii). On the other hand, the Final Act has no enforcement mechanisms. It provides only for periodic reviews of progress by representatives of the state signatories; thus it is long on promise and short on implementation. However, as Virginia Leary observes, this "vacuum" in implementation has been "filled by government spokesmen, intergovernmental organizations, parliamentary commissions, informal monitoring groups, and religious organizations, which have undertaken to investigate the implementation of the Final Act."[47] Indeed, as it turned out, the Final Act, in its human rights component especially, proved to be an important force in the collapse of the Iron Curtain and the transformation of Eastern Europe. As Professor (now Judge) Thomas Buergenthal wrote in 1992:

> The Solidarity movement in Poland, the Charter 77 in Czechoslovakia, the Helsinki Watch committees in the Soviet Union all trace their genesis to the [Helsinki Final Act]. This instrument and the publicity its adoption generated gave the Walesas, the Havels, the Sharanskys, and many others in the East political legitimacy. . . . By being reprinted in the government newspapers of all Iron Curtain countries, [it] gained an official imprimatur that greatly enhanced its value as a moral and political tool in the struggle for human rights.[48]

Buergenthal added: "This phenomenon, not fully grasped at the time by the Communist leadership, [is] pregnant with the ironies of a propaganda that backfired. It also demonstrates the political impact of ideas whose time has come."

Because Helsinki kindled new hopes in the 1970s and provoked human rights interest throughout the 35 countries involved—even *Pravda* and *Izvestia* published the text of the Final Act—it fostered monitoring groups to develop information on compliance with human rights standards. On May 12, 1977, the Russian physicist Yuri Orlov announced the formation of the Public Group to Promote Observation of the Helsinki Accords in the Soviet Union, commonly called the Helsinki Watch Group. The Moscow group planned, among other things, to "accept directly from Soviet citizens written complaints of human rights violations" and pledged to forward such complaints "to all Heads of States signatory to the Final Act and [to] inform the public at large of the substance of the complaints."[49] Thereafter, such groups sprang up in the then Soviet areas of the Armenia, Georgia, Lithuania, and the Ukraine. Several other groups adopted the Helsinki principles in monitoring human rights violations: for instance, the Working Commission on Psychiatric Abuse and various religious committees for the defense of believers in the Soviet Union. In all cases, authorities responded by acts of persecution ranging from threats of violence and loss of employment to imprisonment, forced emigration, and incarceration in psychiatric hospitals.[50]

During the early 1980s, in the follow-up meetings in Belgrade and Madrid, the Soviet Union and other East European signatories to the Final Act generally took the view that

47. Virginia Leary, "The Implementation of the Human Rights Provisions of the Helsinki Final Act: A Preliminary Assessment, 1975–1977," in Buergenthal, ed., *Human Rights, International Law, and the Helsinki Accord*, note 45, 111–60, at 113.
48. Thomas Buergenthal, "The Helsinki Process: Birth of a Human Rights System," in Richard Pierre Claude and Burns H. Weston, eds., *Human Rights in the World Community: Issues and Action*, 2nd ed. (Philadelphia: University of Pennsylvania Press, 1992), 256–68, at 256–57.
49. For a history of Orlov's role, see the English language page of the Moscow Helsinki Group (Public Group for the Assistance of the Implementation of Helsinki Accords in the USSR, Moscow Group "Helsinki"), available at http://www.mhg.ru/english/18E49C2
50. "Basket III: Implementation of the Helsinki Accords," *Hearings Before the Commission on Security and Cooperation in Europe* (Washington, D.C.: U.S. Government Printing Office, 1977), vols. 2–3.

discussion of specific cases and charges of human rights abuses constituted interference in the domestic affairs of sovereign states. However, at the third review Conference on Security and Co-Operation in Europe (CSCE), which opened in Vienna in 1986, the Soviet Union and its Warsaw Pact allies, after coming under concerted and concentrated attack for their human rights abuses, largely abandoned this tactic. They turned, instead, to a more activist strategy involving talk of a shift in their human rights policies consistent with the newly proclaimed "glasnost" or posture of "openness," and a counterattack against alleged instances of human rights violations in the West. On January 16, 1989, at the close of the Vienna Conference, 35 countries, including Canada, the United States, the Soviet Union, and all other European states exclusive of Albania (which did not become a full member of CSCE until 1991), approved a new agreement for the further protection of human rights, including freedom of association, religion, travel, emigration, and special protection of individuals and organizations who monitor human rights conditions in the countries where they reside.[51] The new CSCE agreement also called for better conditions for East-West business ventures, improved barter deals, and freer exchanges of enhanced economic statistics. Perhaps most importantly, however, for the first time since the Helsinki Process began with the adoption of the Helsinki Accords in 1975, a formal CSCE mechanism was approved pursuant to which a signatory state must reply if another signatory state requests information about suspected abuses of human rights. Participating governments also were empowered to demand bilateral meetings to discuss such abuses and to notify the other CSCE states about such cases formalized under a program titled the CSCE Human Dimension Mechanism.

By the 1990s, the Helsinki Process had undergone substantial change reflecting the political sea-change in Eastern Europe. A Paris summit and resultant Charter that year publicly recognized the end of the Cold War and created new CSCE institutions. For example, the Charter of Paris,[52] which offers democracy as "the only system of government of our nations," set up an Office of Free Elections in Warsaw. In the spirit of this innovation, in a meeting in Copenhagen in 1991, the CSCE states committed themselves to hold genuinely free elections. This plan was predicated on the view that democracy is supportive of human rights and on the axiom that one of the basic purposes of government is the protection of human rights and fundamental freedoms.

At the 1994 Budapest Summit Meeting and reflecting the substantial evolution of the Helsinki Process, the Conference on Security and Co-operation in Europe (CSCE) was renamed the "Organization on Security and Co-operation in Europe" (OSCE). Its principal organs, bureaus, and bodies now include the following:

Structures and Institutions

1. Chairman-in-Office (the Minister of Foreign Affairs of an OSCE participating state, rotating each year)
2. Parliamentary Assembly
3. Secretariat (headquartered in Prague and headed by a Secretary General who, as chief administrative officer, acts under the political guidance of the rotating Chairman-in-Office who is responsible for coordinating the fulfillment of the OSCE objectives)
4. Office for Democratic Institutions and Human Rights (situated in Warsaw; formerly the "Office for Free Elections")

51. Concluding Document of the Vienna Meeting 1986 of Representatives of the Participating States of the Conference on Security and Co-operation in Europe (Jan. 17, 1989), referenced in Documentary Appendix B.
52. Adopted Nov. 21, 1990, referenced in Documentary Appendix B.

5. High Commissioner on National Minorities (located in The Hague)
6. Representative on Freedom of the Media (based in Vienna)
7. Court of Conciliation and Arbitration (established in Geneva, for OSCE participating states that are party to a 1992 Convention on Conciliation and Arbitration Within the CSCE[53])
8. Arms Control and Confidence- and Security-Building Measures

Negotiating and Decision-Making Bodies

1. The Permanent Council
2. The Forum for Security Co-operation
3. The Senior Council/Economic Forum (replacing the original Committee of Senior Officials)
4. Summits
5. Ministerial Council (formerly the "CSCE Council of Ministers for Foreign Affairs")

As of this writing, 55 states are members of the OSCE, including all the republics of the former Soviet Union. As stated in Paragraph 3 of the 1992 Budapest Summit Declaration,[54] the OSCE is "the security structure embracing States from Vancouver to Vladivostok." On the whole, despite relatively low-level material support and physically scattered institutions, its increased membership and infrastructural enhancement have been welcomed by most observers. U.S. President Bill Clinton commented at a plenary session of the Budapest Summit Meeting in 1992 that the OSCE should be "our first flexible line of defense against ethnic and regional conflicts. Its rules can guard against the assertion of hegemony or spheres of influence. It can help nations come together to build prosperity. And it can promote Europe's integration."[55]

At the beginning of the twenty-first century, the Human Dimension Implementation meetings continued, supplying a useful mechanism for members to discuss sundry issues, note irritants in interstate relations, and maintain ongoing conversations on priority matters including human rights issues affecting several member countries. For example, the U.S. Mission to the OSCE noted that in 2003 President George W. Bush condemned "human trafficking" across international borders in a speech at the United Nations where he pledged $50 million dollars in additional funds to support organizations that rescue men, women, and children from bondage labor, prostitution, and sex trafficking, including the heinous practice of child sex tourism. In the "give and take" of OSCE meetings, the U.S. Mission complained to European counterparts that 44 OSCE States are among the 140 countries of origin, transit, or destination for a "significant number of victims" and adopted a scolding tone in asserting that the anti-trafficking efforts of eleven OSCE countries in particular (mostly East European) "have to be strengthened in the coming months."[56]

All of this signals a remarkable turn of events. The mechanism, initially dismissed on the one hand as a temporary vestige of the Cold War and, on the other, labeled with

53. Concluded Dec. 15, 1992, entered into force Dec. 5, 1994. Reprinted in *ILM* 32 551 (1993): 551 and Weston and Carlson, 1: I.H.12. An outgrowth of CSCE meetings on the peaceful settlement of disputes, the Convention's substantive jurisdiction extends to disputes concerning a state's territorial integrity, national defense, title to sovereignty over land territory, or competing claims with regard to jurisdiction over other areas. It is not intended, at least at present, for the protection of human rights.
54. Adopted Dec. 6, 1994, referenced in Documentary Appendix B.
55. Remarks of President Clinton (Dec. 5, 1994), reprinted in *U.S. Dep't State Dispatch* (1994), 5: 813, 814.
56. United States Mission to the OSCE, "Statement on Trafficking in Persons," delivered by Kelly Ryan, Deputy Assistant Secretary for Population, Refugees and Migration, Warsaw: Human Dimension Implementation Meeting, October 8, 2004, available at http//osce.usmission.gov

hubris as "an embryo of a human rights court for all Europe,"[57] has taken on a quality of permanent soft diplomacy. The Human Dimension Implementation meetings of the North American and European participants have evolved constructively into a program for an on-going cooperative interstate conversation, a kind of diplomatic "chat room" where healthy candor and constructive criticism are normal and routine.

As the twenty-first century unfolds, the gradual and successful construction of international institutions and procedures for the promotion and protection of human rights cannot be taken for granted. The obstacles to progressive development are many and the task, if taken seriously, calls attention to the need for both visionary idealism (as in the case of the Helsinki Process) and hard-headed realism (as in initiatives of the Office of the High Commissioner for Human Rights) in devising international human rights institutions and procedures that will be valid and effective.[58] The Marks and Shelton essays make clear that institutions must have sufficient regional or global support to gain acceptance by states and peoples so the norms and mechanisms they create to implement human rights are perceived as correct and appropriate. To be effective, international mechanisms must be able to implement their objectives indirectly through education, dialogue, and supervision, and/or directly through diplomatic action and other measures, rarely through supranational directives. Of course, if we accept these standards of validity and effectiveness in assessing international implementation, we are met with the substantial challenge of directing responsible attention and constructive thought toward developing international human rights institutions and procedures in which people can believe and from which people can expect results.

57. So described by British chief delegate Lawrence O'Keeffe, *Washington Post*, Jan. 16, 1989, at A1, col. 6.
58. The literature on balancing idealistic-visionary and "hard-headed-realistic" perspectives on international human rights is substantial. See Michael Ignatieff, *The Lesser Evil: Political Ethics in an Age of Terror* (Princeton, N.J.: Princeton University Press, 2004); Robert J. Drinan, S.J., *The Mobilization of Shame: A World View of Human Rights* (New Haven, Conn.: Yale University Press, 2001).

26. STEPHEN P. MARKS *The United Nations and Human Rights*

INTRODUCTION: THE "SPIRIT OF OUR AGE"

The principal institutional framework for furthering human rights is the United Nations, the only structure with a general mandate for realizing all human rights in all countries. In the coming decades, its role as a force for the realization of human rights will be determined by three world order dimensions that are both constraining and liberating.

First, the *neoliberal paradigm* (i.e., the general acceptance of the neoliberal premise that free markets go hand-in-hand with a free society) is constraining because it tends to leave the realization of economic, social, and cultural rights to the vagaries of market forces. It is liberating insofar as democratic modes of exercising power allow demands for social justice to be heard and acted upon in the legislative and political process.

The second dimension—*the dominant role of a single superpower*—limits much of the potential of other nations and of popular movements to achieve change in the interests of human rights unless the change is consistent with U.S. national interest and capacity, which frequently has proved to be contrary to the human rights of many people in the U.S. (immigrants, prisoners, minorities) and abroad (victims of repressive regimes strategically allied with the U.S. and people suffering from deprivation due to practices of multinational corporations and international financial institutions supported by U.S. policy). At the same time, human rights continues to be a U.S. foreign policy objective, making it sometimes possible for people's human rights movements and enhanced mandates of international institutions to receive official support from the U.S. government.

The third dimension characterizing post-Cold War international relations is the *weakening of the state*. The first principle guiding the action of the UN and its members is "the sovereign equality of all its Members."[1] Today, the principle of state sovereignty has been challenged not only by secessionist nationalism and religious fundamentalism but also by the vast power of multinational business interests. The potential for effective human rights progress through the UN is thus limited to the extent that multinational business interests wield power superior to many states and act in the interests of return on investment, which is indifferent at best to human rights concerns and often hostile to them. Nonstate actors who seek the destruction of the state out of religious or nationalistic zeal similarly jeopardize efforts to guarantee human rights. The state thus remains an indispensable agency for human rights. At the same time, the interests of the state are less important and often contrary to those within civil society who would base legitimacy of those who govern on the degree to which they respect and protect the rights of the governed. The emergence of a global civil society, embracing nongovernmental organizations (NGOs) of all kinds and capable of collaborating or contending with states and intergovernmental structures has proved to be the most prominent influence on the progressive development of human rights norms and action in international relations. From this perspective,

the Leviathan state must be resisted and constantly held in check by a global movement of peoples pursuing the human interest.

These, then, are among the most salient dimensions of world order that determine the potential for UN diplomacy and action at the present time. A major consequence of them is the persistent impoverishment of much of Africa, Asia, Latin America, and especially the former Soviet Union, as well as increased inequality in the U.S. with predictable implications for human rights.

Also noteworthy, however, is the status of human rights as a UN concern from the UN's beginnings. The founders of the United Nations, not content merely to add human rights as one among many common objectives for UN members, articulated a theory of peace according to which respect for human rights and fundamental freedoms was a necessary condition for peace within and among nations. Yet they did not apply it to the political power arrangement of the Charter. Instead, the human rights provisions are relegated to the authorization of nonbinding studies and recommendations of the General Assembly and to the setting up by the Economic and Social Council (ECOSOC) of a commission—the UN Commission on Human Rights—to promote human rights.[2] The Charter language was deliberately weak, emphasizing "promotion" (as opposed to "protection"), which can be limited to rhetoric. The real power was vested in the Security Council, authorized to render binding decisions and require states to modify their aggressive behavior under threat of enforcement action, including the use of armed force.

No such power was envisaged to promote, much less "protect" (or enforce) human rights. Articles 55 and 56 of the Charter stipulate that the member states "pledge themselves to take joint and separate action in cooperation with the Organization" to "promote . . . universal respect for and observance of human rights." This "pledge" (a legally ambiguous term) remains the core human rights obligation of member states. While resulting today in a considerable and impressive body of international human rights law, it involved the establishment largely of paper

---

1. UN Charter art. 2(1), reprinted in Documentary Appendix A.
2. *Eds.*—On March 15, 2006, the UN General Assembly adopted Resolution 60/251, abolishing the Commission and replacing it with a smaller, standing Human Rights Council as a subsidiary body of the General Assembly.

rights and of studies and public information useful but at the same time innocuous to governments who considered their freedom to mistreat their population as an attribute of sovereignty.

The aim of this essay is to reexamine the potential for UN action in the field of human rights in light of the limitations on that action since the end of the Cold War. Borrowing from Upendra Baxi's apt distillation of the 1993 Vienna Declaration on human rights,[3] I ask the following questions: Has the end of the Cold War created new opportunities for the UN to act in new ways "in the spirit of our age" (i.e., people's solidarity)? Has it placed new constraints on the Organization to take greater account of "the realities of our times" (i.e., state power)? After reflecting on these questions, I identify some priority issues for UN action in the field of human rights as the dawn of a new millennium breaks. Finally, I consider the means and methods for making this action more effective.

CONSTRAINTS ON UN HUMAN RIGHTS DIPLOMACY AND ACTION IN THE POST-COLD WAR ERA

Four trends characteristic of the post-Cold War period limit the potential for United Nations action in the field of human rights. All are characteristic of international relations in these times in general, but raise particular problems and opportunities in the post-Cold War era.

A Fragile Consensus on the Content of Human Rights

Throughout the Cold War, the terms "democracy," "freedom," and "human rights" were employed in the West in opposition to communism. Until the early 1990s, the human rights policy of the United States was officially described as part of the struggle against communism as opposed to expressing any intrinsic value. With the end of the Cold War and the de-linking of human rights and ideology, words took on new meaning and a new consensus became possible.

Thus, in spite of its shortcomings, the Vienna Declaration, adopted at the conclusion of the World Conference on Human Rights in June 1993, confirmed the universality of human rights standards as defined by the UN and by and large rejected the counterclaims of cultural relativism.[4] The consensus reached there was a fragile bridging of the very real divide between perceptions of human rights by different governments and peoples' movements. Many Western countries, chiefly the United States, do not take economic, social, and cultural rights seriously, and countries that have moved rapidly from communist-party states and planned economies to multiparty democracies with market economies are discovering the extreme social dislocations and hardship that follow the abandonment of these rights. States whose societies value respect for authority at all levels tend to equate their economic prosperity with the virtues of authoritarian rule, challenge human rights as Western-imposed, and seek to define their own approach to democracy and human rights.

The idea of human rights is, I submit, falsely perceived by some as an exclusively Western cause. There is no doubt that, for reasons related to educational opportunities, legal capacity to operate independently of governments, access to means of mass communication and transportation, NGOs tend to be located in Western capitals and to draw upon Western methods of mobilizing civil society. However, the rapidly expanding networks of human rights NGOs based outside of the West and involvement of persons from non-Western cultures in major human rights NGOs and in UN human rights work are creating a more accurate image of the common human rights struggle across cultures.

The Persistence of the "Domestic Jurisdiction" Limitation

The inclusion of human rights among the purposes and principles of the United Nations appears to contradict the principle of nonintervention by the UN "in matters which are essentially within the domestic jurisdiction of any

3. See Upendra Baxi, "The Spirit of Our Age, the Realities of Our Time: The Vienna Declaration on Human Rights," in Upendra Baxi, *Mambrino's Helmet? Human Rights for a Changing World* (Delhi: Har Anand, 1994). The Vienna Declaration is referenced in Documentary Appendix B.
4. For a new approach to the debate between the universality of human rights and cultural relativism, see Reading 3 by Burns H. Weston in Chapter 1 of this volume.

state."[5] A simple way of illustrating the shifting trend over the last fifty years is to note the changing perception of the tension between the principles of human rights and nonintervention. The range of action by the UN to respond to human rights situations without violating the "domestic jurisdiction" clause has expanded over time in three directions.

The first, which I call "soft intervention," is rendered possible by the contraction of the scope of Article 2(7) and the expansion of that of the Article 56 obligation of every member state to cooperate with the UN to achieve universal respect for and observance of human rights for all. Numerous actions by the UN that would have been deemed "intervention" by most states a few decades ago, such as investigation of abuse, adoption of resolutions explicitly denouncing countries by name, sending special envoys and rapporteurs, and addressing complaints to a government, are now common practices of the General Assembly and the Commission on Human Rights. This "soft intervention" is based on the consent of the accused state obtained under the political pressure that the Commission, the General Assembly, individual governments, and NGOs are willing to bring to bear.

The second significant evolution has to do with "hard intervention"—that is, the use of coercive or enforcement measures pursuant to Chapter VII of the Charter.[6] Such enforcement action, through economic sanctions or use of military force, is an explicit exception to the prohibition of intervention in domestic affairs when there is a "threat to the peace, breach of the peace, or act of aggression."[7] Therefore, when, for example, the Security Council authorized "Member States to form a multinational force under unified command and control and . . . to use all necessary means to facilitate the departure from Haiti of the military leadership,"[8] it was acting under Chapter VII and fell within this exception to the rule against intervention. Although the authorizing resolution stressed the "unique character" of the Haitian situation, it

was, nevertheless, a precedent for military intervention to redress a humanitarian crisis due to an antidemocratic coup and massive human rights violations.

A third UN response to the domestic jurisdiction obstacle to human rights action is *intrusive action based on invitation or consent* by the territorial state to carry out tasks designed to restore or establish the conditions for a peaceful society—in UN parlance, "peacekeeping" and "peacebuilding." When consent is given by the territorial state to a multicomponent peace operation, the role of the UN is couched in terms of "cooperation" with whatever is left of a sovereign state rather than "intervention." But the form of action—despite consent to the agreement and to the presence of the international military and civilian personnel—is clearly an intrusive one. As defined by former Secretary-General Boutros Boutros-Ghali, "peace-building" refers to "comprehensive efforts to identify and support structures which will tend to consolidate peace and advance a sense of confidence and well-being among people"; it involves "disarming the previously warring parties and the restoration of order, the custody and possible destruction of weapons, repatriating refugees, advisory and training support for security personnel, monitoring elections, advancing efforts to protect human rights, reforming or strengthening governmental institutions and promoting formal and informal processes of political participation."[9] The potential impact of the UN's efforts is considerable, whether through an explicit human rights program or through the promotion of the rule of law and good governance.

Thus, "intervention " by the UN in human rights situations, where normal rules of state sovereignty would otherwise preclude it, has been resorted to, and in such a manner, as Richard Falk has put it, that the "basic social contract between States and the United Nations is . . . being rewritten."[10] Acceptance by the international community of these encroachments constitutes a major shift in international relations

---

5. UN Charter, art. 2(7).
6. Regarding "hard intervention" mostly outside the terms of the UN Charter, see Reading 30 by Richard Falk in Chapter 7 of this volume.
7. UN Charter, art. 39.
8. SC Res. 940, UN SCOR, 49th Sess., Supp. No. 49, at 51, UN Doc. S/INF/50 (1994).
9. Boutros Boutros-Ghali, *An Agenda for Peace: Preventive Diplomacy, Peacemaking, and Peace-Keeping* (New York: United Nations, 1992), 32.
10. Richard A. Falk, "The United Nations and the Rule of Law," *TLCP* 4 (1994): 611–42, at 630.

that enhances considerably opportunities for the UN to investigate and improve human rights situations inside member states, although that capacity has proved of little effect when confronted with xenophobic nationalism and ethnic conflict.

NATIONALISM AND ETHNIC CONFLICT

One of the most dangerous features of post-Cold War politics is the challenge to the sanctity of the principle of sovereignty of the nation-state and the resurgence of ethnic nationalism. For the United Nations human rights agenda, this development is full of contradictions. Self-determination had attained the status of a peremptory norm during the period of decolonization and was attached to the international bill of human rights as common Article 1 of the two international covenants of 1966[11] which constitute the basic catalogue of internationally recognized human rights. It was in the name of self-determination that colonial empires were dissolved and the majority of the UN's members gained independence and admission to the Organization. And it was in its name that the Baltic states attained or regained independence, followed by nations whose claims overturned the presumption in favor of the integrity of existing states. The passion of the principle's basic premise overran this traditional state-centric limitation and produced the breakup of the Soviet Union and the Yugoslav Federation. The international human rights system had not anticipated this development any more than the international security system had done, and was ill prepared to respond to it, whether the massive human rights violations perpetrated by the Serbs in Bosnia and Kosovo and the Russians in Chechnya, or the even more massive atrocities resulting from the breakdown of all authority in Somalia, Rwanda, Zaire/Congo, Sierra Leone, and elsewhere.

Whether, against this backdrop, the UN can find an acceptable meaning of "self-determination" for the twenty-first century is doubtful. The tragedy of the Balkans is likely to provoke serious hesitation before recognizing similar claims in the future.

BUREAUCRATIC CONSTRAINTS

Alongside these external ideological and political constraints on United Nations human rights diplomacy action are internal constraints resulting from the nature of the bureaucracy and the pressures placed on it by member states. These constraints have an impact on leadership, the quality and morale of staff, and on the availability of resources.

After the Vienna Conference in 1993, there occurred a major breakthrough with the creation of the post of UN High Commissioner for Human Rights.[12] The post was long an ideal of NGO activists and visionary government delegates who saw in it a high-level figure with potential for effective intervention on behalf of victims of human rights violations. The idea may be traced back to a proposal from René Cassin of France to establish a position of Attorney-General for Human Rights. Secretary-General Boutros Boutros-Ghali appointed as the first UN High Commissioner for Human Rights Mr. Jost Ayala Lasso, the Ecuadorian diplomat who had successfully chaired the working group that found the compromise language for the High Commissioner's mandate.

[*Eds.*—The author then notes that "leadership was problematic" from the start, due largely to conflicting personalities and policy differences, but as well to a difficult mandate that called upon the High Commissioner simultaneously "to respect the sovereignty, territorial integrity and domestic jurisdiction of States" and "to promote and protect the effective enjoyment by all of all civil, cultural, economic, political and social rights" and also "play an active role in removing the current obstacles and in meeting the challenges to the full realization of all human rights and in preventing the continuation of human rights violations throughout the world." Calling for a person who is "less a diplomat and more a highly visible and pro-active world figure" to fill

11. See International Covenant on Economic, Social and Cultural Rights (ICESCR) and International Covenant on Civil and Political Rights (ICCPR), each concluded Dec. 16, 1966 and reprinted and referenced in Documentary Appendix A.
12. See the website of the OHCHR (Office of the High Commissioner for Human Rights) at http://www.ohchr.org/english

the post of High Commissioner, the author comments: "The issue for the future is how the High Commissioner will interpret this 'active role.'" Thereafter, he notes favorably the appointment as High Commissioner on June 12, 1997, by then new Secretary-General Kofi Annan of Ireland's President, Mary Robinson: "By naming a woman with a reputation for courage and integrity who also knows a great deal about human rights," he writes, "Mr. Annan gave the post of High Commissioner a higher profile than before. She changed the name to the Office of the High Commissioner for Human Rights (OHCHR), absorbed the Centre for Human Rights into it, and benefitted from Kofi Annan's reform, which upgraded the New York office of the High Commissioner and placed her on all four executive committees (dealing with peace and security; economic and social affairs; development cooperation; humanitarian affairs)." As this book goes to press, the position is held by the Honorable Louise Arbour, former Justice of the Supreme Court of Canada and former chief prosecutor of the Yugoslav and Rwandan war crimes and genocide tribunals established in the 1990s.]

THE POTENTIAL FOR UN HUMAN RIGHTS DIPLOMACY AND ACTION

Four challenges merit priority attention to enhance the effectiveness of the UN as the principal instrument for multilateral diplomacy and action to advance human rights.

LISTENING TO NEW VOICES

While it is true that the claim of universality of human rights draws on both international law and the experience of peoples, the UN political organs began only a few decades ago to take seriously the voices of those who are not represented in diplomatic circles, where mainly men from dominant social groups working for governments draft texts and determine policies. Today, the struggle by women and indigenous peoples—to name but two significant examples—for recognition of their rights have made

inroads into multilateral diplomacy at the UN. In addition, the democratization of the UN through the increased involvement of "global civil society" in the UN's decision-making and implementation processes is gaining strength. As argued by Upendra Baxi, these and other voices need to be heard if the UN's human rights agenda is to be responsive to the new challenges of coming decades.

[*Eds.*—The author then discusses the UN record "on improving the status of women and protecting their rights" which is, "like human rights generally, one of timid beginnings and immense potential." He thereafter does the same with "indigenous peoples."[13] *In the case of women*, he highlights the role played by the UN Commission on the Status of Women (a functional commission of ECOSOC) in the drafting of the 1979 Convention on the Elimination of All Forms of Discrimination against Women (CEDAW)[14] and other key women's rights conventions. His call for an "effective complaints procedure" to make good on CEDAW has since been realized in the Committee on the Elimination of Discrimination against Women. *In the case of indigenous peoples*, he highlights the creation in 1992 of the Working Group on Indigenous Populations under the aegis of the UN Sub-Commission on Prevention of Discrimination and Protection of Minorities (now the Sub-Commission on the Promotion and Protection of Human Rights). He also notes the active role of the International Labour Organization (ILO) regarding its Convention (No. 169) Concerning Indigenous and Tribal Peoples in Independent Countries of 1989[15] and the significant impact on indigenous peoples of development projects by other UN specialized agencies and the international financial institutions. Finally, he joins others in calling for the transformation of the Trusteeship Council, its original mission accomplished, into a council responsible for minorities and indigenous peoples so as to assure them "system wide action." He then turns to the UN's relationship to civil society. While some of this discussion is treated in Reading 31 by Richard Claude, certain aspects of the author's commentary bear special notice.]

13. For pertinent detail, see Reading 12 by Maivân Clech Lâm in Chapter 2 and Reading 19 by Hurst Hannum in Chapter 4 of this volume.
14. Concluded Dec. 18, 1979, referenced in Documentary Appendix B.
15. Concluded June 27, 1989, referenced in Documentary Appendix B.

Civil Society

The meaning of "civil society" has evolved in the history of Western political thought and has been used in post-Cold War political discourse to refer to those organizations and movements that stand between society and the state and seek to define and monitor the norms by which the latter may be held accountable to the former. In recent years, though they have animated the human rights movement since the founding of the UN, independent human rights groups have contributed in significant measure to the end of centralized authoritarian regimes, whether in the pre-1989 right-wing militaristic model of Central and South America and South Africa or the communist police states of East Central Europe.

In fact, the rights of NGOs have been on the agenda of the Commission on Human Rights since 1984, when a working group was established to draft a declaration on human rights defenders. After almost a decade and a half of laborious and often stalled negotiations, the Commission's working group on the Declaration finished its work in Winter 1998 and the Commission adopted it on March 4, 1998. In spite of its weakness, the text was welcomed by NGOs and was adopted by the General Assembly on December 9, 1998.[16]

[Eds.—The author goes on to detail efforts to bring NGO efforts to bear more broadly on UN activities outside ECOSOC, to which the Charter assigned NGO liaison responsibility. These efforts, the author notes, have been "motivated by the best of intentions," but have been largely frustrated by resistance from the U.S. and other powerful countries. The introduction of NGOs into other UN organs, the author is careful to point out, is not entirely unproblematic, as it raises the specter of powerful nonstate actors creating sham NGOs to gain entry to the UN. Nevertheless, the author contends that "the process of listening to the voices of . . . global civil society, including those of women and indigenous peoples, is gaining momentum and will be a prominent feature of the UN human rights agenda in the future."[17]]

PEACE OPERATIONS

The entry of human rights into the UN's mandate in international peace and security has been one of the most promising of post-Cold War developments, although fraught with risks and political misgivings. The most dramatic human rights link with peace and security has been the use of enforcement powers for expanded human rights purposes, including prosecution of individuals responsible for genocide, crimes against humanity, and war crimes. The second salient dimension of this link has been the creation of human rights components of multidimensional peace operations. The third aspect—related to, but different from, the second—is the human rights dimension of post-conflict peace-building, including human rights field operations.

Peace Enforcement

The Gulf War brought human rights into the purview of the Security Council when it characterized internal repression as a threat to international peace and security. The willingness of Russia and China to let such a determination pass was a major turning point. A determination of the existence of such a threat is a precondition for Security Council action under its peace enforcement powers,[18] and the Council concluded, per Resolution 688, that the consequences of the repression of the Kurds had that effect, and this was enough for it to demand that Iraq allow access by international humanitarian organizations and to appeal to member states to contribute to this humanitarian effort.[19] The resolution was interpreted by the U.S., UK, and French governments as providing the basis

16. UNGA Declaration on the Rights and Responsibilities on the Rights and Responsibilities of Individuals, Groups and Organs of Society to Promote and Protect Universally Recognized Human Rights and Fundamental Freedoms, adopted Dec. 9, 1998, referenced in Documentary Appendix B.
17. For further discussion about human rights NGOs, see Reading 31 by Richard Pierre Claude in Chapter 8 in this volume.
18. See UN Charter, art. 39, reprinted in Documentary Appendix A.
19. SC Res. 688, UN SCOR, 46th Sess., 2082nd mtg., at 31, UN Doc. S/INF/47 (1993).

for them to station troops in, and send NATO aircraft over, northern Iraq to protect the Kurdish population from further abuse by Baghdad authorities. Baghdad, in turn, agreed to let the UN set up "humanitarian centres" in the Kurdish region of the north and the Shiite region of the south with UN guards. Human rights made an ambiguous entry into UN peace enforcement.

[*Eds.*—The author goes on to review the next major precedents of Security Council authorizations of multilateral military force—in Haiti to secure the departure of the *de facto* military regime there and the return of democratically elected President Aristide; and in Bosnia to create the conditions required for an overall settlement of the Yugoslav crisis. The avoidance of human rights language in the first instance and the absence of a human rights mandate in the second, he observes, led to ambiguous and troubling results. He continues:]

The enforcement function of the UN without a human rights dimension can be disastrous for human rights. When the Security Council decided to establish the "safe areas" in eastern Bosnia, military advisors determined that 34,000 troops would be needed to enforce them. After weeks, only a few thousand were authorized and fewer still actually deployed. Bosnian Serbian forces are said to have slaughtered some 8,000 unarmed Muslims in July 1995, while the UN forces were outnumbered and powerless. On July 10, when the UN military observers warned that air strikes alone could prevent the impending massacre, the Force Commander rejected the advice. As a result, massive human rights violations, constituting war crimes, were committed, and vastly outnumbered Dutch peacekeepers did nothing to prevent it.

[*Eds.*—The author additionally notes that "In Bosnia, Somalia, and elsewhere, not only was the UN unable to protect human rights, but some of its forces actually committed human rights violations themselves." He thus recommends that, in addition to an international legal duty of troop-contributing countries to train every soldier to respect humanitarian law and to discipline them when they do not, "the UN should require that everyone serving the UN must know, respect, and ensure respect by others of UN human rights standards."]

Human Rights Components of Multidimensional Peace Operations Rights

It requires a humanitarian emergency and intense diplomatic pressure before the Security Council will use its enforcement powers, and as a consequence the Council has moved in fits and starts to use those powers for human rights purposes. The Council is much more willing to support deployment of UN personnel in the context of a comprehensive political settlement to a long-festering conflict, and the doctrine applicable in such cases has been called "second generation" or "expanded" peacekeeping. The first such mission was the United Nations Advisory Group in Namibia. The peace agreements in Cambodia and El Salvador built upon this experience. In all these cases, the UN painstakingly engineered peace negotiations towards the conclusion of a comprehensive political settlement, in which human rights was an integral part, and the relative success of the UN Transitional Authority in Cambodia (UNTAC) and the UN Observer Mission in El Salvador (ONUSAL) influenced the setting up of human rights components in Haiti, Rwanda, and Angola. However, the lessons of previous missions are not always well-studied.

[*Eds.*—Next, therefore, the author cites favorably a 1995 Aspen Institute study[20] that recommended standardized terms of reference for human rights missions; more careful advanced missions; collaboration with other components; early and more professional recruitment; improved staff training and advanced briefing; a code of conduct for mission staff; standard reporting formats; improved security; public reporting; the building into peace agreements of human rights protection and verification, as well as long-term institution-building, legal reform, and human rights education; and the UN creation of a "specialized unit to coordinate and institutionalize human rights field work in the context of peacekeeping operations."]

---

20. Alice Henkin, ed., *Honoring Human Rights and Keeping the Peace: Lessons from El Salvador, Cambodia, and Haiti; Recommendations for the United Nations* (New York: Aspen Institute, 1995).

Democratic Institution-Building and Constitutionalism

Beyond the investigative and educational tasks of human rights components of peacekeeping, UN field operations are called upon to contribute to the institutionalization of key democratic institutions, without which progress to ensure human rights during a peace operation will be short-lived. Judicial reform, constitution drafting, professionalization and demilitarization of the police—all are tasks that the UN has been given and about which its capacity to produce lasting results has not been adequately tested.

The UN's role is this area has to be seen in a broader context of trends towards democratization, although the General Assembly has been somewhat schizophrenic on the question of democracy. On the one hand, it asserts that elections and democratization are the sole prerogative of the state, and, on the other, it asserts that all states must have periodic and genuine elections. Many members resist the push for internationally supervised elections, holding firm to the view, justified in traditional international law, that the way they govern is purely an internal matter.

The building of democratic societies, it is true, is a task of generations. However, there is a window of opportunity during UN multicomponent peace operations and their aftermath where many processes can receive a "kick-start." Since the decline of peacekeeping in the mid-1990s, many of these human rights tasks have been pursued by field operations under the responsibility of the High Commissioner for Human Rights. These offices operate under difficult conditions with inadequate resources. More effective and better-supported offices would make a significant difference in the extent to which societies in transition benefit from international support in integrating human rights into their institutions and political culture and thereby consolidate democracy. The positive experiences of Cambodia and El Salvador deserve to be improved upon and adapted elsewhere.

RESPONDING TO VIOLATIONS

Responses to human rights violations have always been the cutting edge between absolute state sovereignty and international accountability.

While the long-term, preventive strategy calls for the creation of a culture in which rights are respected as a matter of course, the curative strategy requires that human rights violations be detected, that victims be protected, and that the perpetrators be held accountable. The UN can improve the effectiveness of all of its procedures for dealing with human rights violations in the coming years, whether treaty-based or Charter-based.

Treaty-Based Procedures for Dealing with Violations of Human Rights

Of the sixty or so major UN human rights treaties, six have functioning monitoring bodies that examine states parties' reports on progress made and problems encountered: the 1966 ICESCR and ICCPR, the 1965 International Convention on the Elimination of All Forms of Racial (ICERD), the 1979 Convention on the Elimination of All Forms of Discrimination against Women (CEDAW), the 1984 Convention against Torture and Other Cruel, Inhuman or Degrading Treatment or Punishment (CAT), and the 1989 Convention on the Rights of the Child (CRC).[21] Four of these (the ICCPR, ICERD, CAT, and CEDAW) have procedures for handling individual complaints of alleged violations. The three principal concerns for the effectiveness of the treaty system are (1) universal ratification without crippling reservations; (2) timely presentation and proper consideration of reports with follow-up on recommendations; and (3) availability of a complaints procedure for individual cases of violation of human rights treaties.

1. Universal Ratification. Universal ratification has been endorsed as a major objective of the High Commissioner. The dilemma of universal ratification is that, at the drafting stage, the norms risk dilution in order to accommodate countries that might hesitate to ratify high standards and, at the accession stage, as countries impose reservations to avoid the higher standards. Reservations, understandings, and declarations by the U.S. upon ratification of human rights treaties, particularly the ICCPR, reservations by Islamic countries upon ratification of CEDAW, the purported (although illegal) withdrawal from the ICCPR by North Korea, and the

21. ICERD (Dec. 21, 1965), CEDAW (Dec. 18, 1979), CAT (Dec. 10, 1984), and the CRC (Nov. 2, 1989) are referenced in Documentary Appendix B.

denunciation by Jamaica of the first optional protocol to the ICCPR are significant cases of backsliding on the universality of the treaty regime.

At the request of the General Assembly in 1988, the Secretary-General solicited detailed recommendations to achieve universal ratification, to resolve the problem of overdue reports and delays in submitting and processing reports, and to improve public information, including some valuable reform options: consolidated reports, creation of a single treaty body, treaty amendments, and the creation of special bureaus on ratification with the High Commissioner's office. The effectiveness of the treaty system would be greatly enhanced if they were fully implemented.

2. The Reporting Process. The second weakness of the treaty monitoring system is the failure of states parties to submit their reports on time, if at all, and to utilize the process as an opportunity to rethink and reform national policies. The public is rarely involved in the process of preparing and reviewing national reports. The treaty monitoring bodies themselves are not always willing to point out deficiencies in reports and to keep after governments that either fail to provide adequate information or fail to take the committee's recommendations seriously.

[*Eds.*—The reader is here referred to Reading 25 in this volume, which explores this subject in extensive detail.]

To cope with a serious backlog of reports, it has been proposed to consolidate the six committees into one mega-committee or super-committee which would examine all reports. The disadvantage is that such a committee would not be able to give the same level of attention or provide the same degree of expertise as the current six committees. A possible solution would be to constitute a committee of the whole, consisting of all six committees, subdivided into six chambers. Thus, the "Child Rights Chamber" would meet to examine special reports on child rights, and so on for each committee/treaty. While the creation of such a large body of over one hundred members would be admittedly cumbersome, a more streamlined version would be possible, with the larger committee being a pool from which general meetings to examine consolidated reports would be constituted by a limited number selected by each committee. Whether such an arrangement is made or not, it is urgent that the idea of consolidated reports and rescheduling of overdue reports be implemented.

3. Individual Complaints Procedures. The third area in which the human rights treaty system could be strengthened is with regard to the availability of individual complaints procedures. As noted above, four human rights treaties have such procedures: the 1965 ICERD, 1966 ICCPR, 1979 CEDAW, and 1984 CAT. Under the Optional Protocol to the ICCPR,[22] the Human Rights Committee examines and expresses its final views on individual cases brought to it by alleged victims of violations occurring within states parties to the protocol. The Committee on Economic, Social and Cultural Rights has prepared a draft optional protocol for the ICESCR.[23] Scholars familiar with the Committee on the Rights of the Child have proposed such a protocol for the 1989 CRC.[24]

Charter-Based Procedures for Dealing with Violations of Human Rights

The procedures for dealing with violations that are based on the UN Charter rather than separate treaties include complaints procedures and special procedures.

1. Complaints Procedures. . . . The UN has had two non-treaty procedures for dealing with complaints or petitions addressed to it and alleging human rights violations. The first is the so-called "public" procedure, which has existed since 1967. In appropriate cases, the Commission was authorized, per ECOSOC Resolution 1235, to "make a study of situations which reveal a consistent pattern of violations of human rights, as exemplified by the policy of apartheid . . . and racial discrimination . . . and report, with recommendations thereon, to the Economic

---

22. Concluded Dec. 16, 1966, referenced in Documentary Appendix B.
23. See UN Doc. E/CN.4/1997/105 (Annex).
24. See, e.g., Burns H. Weston and Mark B. Teerink, "Abolishing Child Labor: A Multifaceted Human Rights Solution," in Burns H. Weston, ed., *Child Labor and Human Rights: Making Children Matter* (Boulder, Colo.: Lynne Rienner, 2005).

and Social Council."[25] Although conceived as a means of attracting attention to apartheid in southern Africa and other situations characterized by colonialism and racism, the "1235 Procedure" (as it has come to be called) is now used to examine all types of situations and usually involves appointing a Special Rapporteur to visit the country under scrutiny. The Rapporteur's report of relevant findings is the basis for the Commission's resolution on that country.

The second extra-conventional complaints procedure is a "confidential procedure" for examining petitions sent by victims or their representatives that reveal a pattern of violations in any country in the world. In 1970, the Commission, pursuant to ECOSOC Resolution 1503, adopted a procedure now known as the "1503 Procedure" to examine in closed session complaints revealing "a consistent pattern of gross and reliably attested violations of human rights."[26] These complaints may be referred to the Commission by the Sub-Commission, both of which have established working groups to deal with such violations. The Commission "received" its first situations in 1974; in 1978, the Chair of the Commission began announcing the countries under discussion; and in 1984 the Chair began providing the names of countries kept under consideration and those that had been dropped. While the 1503 Procedure was reformed during the 56th session of the Commission on Human Rights in 2000, this confidential, cumbersome, and inconclusive procedure has been justly criticized by NGOs and by independent scholars and diplomats. Philip Alston has concluded that the procedure should be either radically reformed or abolished since "its shortcomings are so considerable, its tangible achievements so scarce, the justifications offered in its favour so modest, and the need for an effective and universally applicable petition procedure so great. . . ."[27]

2. Special Procedures of Thematic and Country Rapporteurs. Since 1980, the Commission on Human Rights has appointed numerous working groups or Special Rapporteurs, Representatives, and Experts to examine a general phenomenon (theme) of particular significance to ensuring respect for human rights. These "thematic mechanisms" include special procedures to collect information directly from victims and to communicate with governments—not only to request a clarification of the situation concerning the alleged victim but also to apply an "urgent action" or "prompt intervention" procedure when necessary to protect the treatment of the victim, her or his family, witnesses, or NGOs involved, and to facilitate on-site visits. The reports of the Special Rapporteurs constitute a mode of accountability that many governments take quite seriously. The list of thematic mechanisms in operation as of November 2004 includes mandates on the whole litany of contemporary human rights issues—from adequate housing to child prostitution, to involuntary disappearances, to extreme poverty, to the right to food, to freedom of opinion and expression, to the independence of judges and lawyers, to the human rights of migrants, to contemporary forms of racism, to the effects of structural adjustment policies and foreign debt, to the protection of fundamental freedoms while countering terrorism, to the adverse effects of the dumping of toxic and dangerous products and wastes, to violence against women, and so forth.

Similar special procedures have developed for the country rapporteurs, who have also developed the practice of communicating with victims, their representatives, NGOs, and governments. The effectiveness of these special procedures has been enhanced by annual meetings of the special rapporteurs, representatives, experts, and chairpersons of working groups since 1993. By the fourth meeting, the Special Rapporteurs had formulated an impressive set of recommendations, but the Chairperson of the meeting expressed considerable frustration and irritation at the lack of follow-up by the OHCHR.

The problems for the special procedures are in part technical, including the need for better coordination of missions and for changing the structure of the OHCHR so that support for

25. Adopted June 6, 1967, referenced in Documentary Appendix B. The Commission has since been replaced by the UN Human Rights Council.
26. Adopted May 27, 1970, referenced in Documentary Appendix B. The Commission has since been replaced by the UN Human Rights Council.
27. Philip Alston, "The Commission on Human Rights," in Philip Alston, ed., *The United Nations and Human Rights: A Critical Appraisal* (Oxford: Clarendon Press; New York: Oxford University Press, 1992), 126–210, at 151.

special procedures may be separated from the technical cooperation role of that office. The special rapporteurs have expressed concern over the lack of coordination of visits and appeals between the High Commissioner, the thematic rapporteur, and the country rapporteur when all three are dealing with the same country.

These difficulties are easier to remedy than the political ones. Countries seeking to avoid international scrutiny of their own practices have pursued initiatives to weaken these procedures and, in the name of "rationalization" and of avoiding duplication, challenged the special procedures through resolutions on nonselectivity, impartiality, and objectivity. The legitimate concern with efficiency and effectiveness must not be allowed, however, to justify ending the mandate of rapporteurs or working groups whose investigations or urgent appeals would not be covered adequately by other mechanisms. Indeed, the political clout of special rapporteurs needs to be raised so that people of high caliber do not resign in disgust, that their recommendations do not remain dead letters, and that governments do not sue them. More publicity and political attention should be paid to the recommendations of the truly independent and courageous country rapporteurs, and thematic rapporteurs need far more human and financial resources (especially for research and site visits to locations of large-scale violations), revised mandates allowing them to examine country situations on their own initiative, and wide publicity relative to the failure of governments to respond to requests for information as well as other forms of noncooperation.

The innovation of the special procedures stands as one of the most valuable human rights achievements of the political organs of the UN and the NGOs that have lobbied them. The threats against them are not a reaction to a "Western" agenda or approach, since many of them were initiatives of developing countries. They are more the result of certain governments clinging to a state-centered mode of multilateral diplomacy and action rather than one that seeks to preserve and protect human beings from abuses committed by states.

[Eds.—The author next discusses "the human rights approach to the development gap." The reader is referred to Reading 20 in this volume, which explores this subject in extensive detail.]

CONCLUSIONS

The observations contained in this essay only scratch the surface of the complex web of UN institutions and bodies and their vast potential to contribute, through multilateral diplomacy and action, to the realization of human rights. The human rights movement in the UN began with an educational mission whose revolutionary potential has been and still is generally underestimated.

I have outlined a few of the new opportunities and new challenges facing the UN's human rights agenda as we go forward in a new century and millennium. These may be summarized as follows:

1. State sovereignty is less than ever an insurmountable obstacle to UN action to pursue the Charter objective of universal respect for human rights. The traditional limitations based on Article 2(7) are receding. As a result, the margin of action by the UN has expanded.

2. Transitions to democracy in former communist-party states and in former military dictatorships, as well as through UN peacebuilding and democratic empowerment, have released the potential for the participation of civil society in transformative processes and in the consolidation of democracy. The UN can capture and nurture this trend by recognizing greater participation of NGOs in its work, providing more voice to representative groups, and supporting various forces of the civil society "on the ground."

3. The principal structural innovation in the UN human rights world is the OHCHR. While coming of age due to the well-deserved reputation of its recent leadership and the sincere and politically effective support of the Secretary-General, it is nevertheless a fragile institution not yet endowed with resources sufficient to the tasks it has been mandated to fulfill. The renewed hopes in that Office risk being disappointed if rhetorical commitment is not transformed into a significant commitment of resources.

4. The nature of conflict in the post-Cold War era has created radically new challenges for the UN's human rights program. Massive violations occur in the course of internal armed conflict, especially when fed by ethnic nationalism. Two UN responses show promise. First, the international community

seems willing, for the first time since the Nuremberg and Tokyo trials, to hold perpetrators and their commanders criminally responsible. Second, UN preventive diplomacy and peacemaking have demonstrated the value of integrating the human rights dimension into comprehensive peace agreements, a consequence in part of the High Commissioner for Human Rights now serving as a member of the Secretary-General's Executive Committee on peace and security.

5. The creation of a "human rights culture," long a UN rhetorical appeal, was given a significant, tangible boost by the UN's launching of its Decade for Human Rights Education in 1994. The potential value of human rights education to democratic empowerment cannot be over-stressed. In the broader sense, it is the key to the creation of a political culture based on human rights. Military defense will continue to lay claim to the resources of nations and to provide the primary strategic option. A new doctrine of human security based on a holistic approach to human rights deserves to capture the imagination of people who can think beyond the military option. The UN is necessarily the principal framework for the development and expansion of this idea.

6. A major challenge to the UN is to give practical meaning to economic, social, and cultural rights and the right to development.

Today, Central and Eastern European countries have embraced civil and political rights and market economy, and suffer the most rapid rise in social inequalities, organized crime, unemployment, and general deterioration of social conditions of any region in the world. Ordinary people are paying a high price for the abandonment of the economic, social, and cultural rights provided by their previous communist governments. The U.S. has been particularly impervious to these rights, failing to acknowledge these rights are legitimate claims of people against the harmful consequences of free market economies. Through multilateral diplomacy, the UN should be the leader in promoting wider acceptance of these rights and, through multilateral action, in pursuing exemplary ways of defining and implementing a human rights-based approach to development. Without such diplomacy and action these concepts are likely to remain little more than pious aspirations.

These are but a few of many challenges facing the UN in its human rights program. The deeper question is whether the UN, as an intergovernmental institution, can be expected to make any meaningful contribution in this area that so challenges state prerogatives. If so, hundreds of millions of people stand to benefit in this new century.

QUESTIONS FOR REFLECTION AND DISCUSSION

1. Stephen Marks states that "The founders of the United Nations, not content merely to add human rights as one among many common objectives for UN members, articulated a theory of peace according to which respect for human rights and fundamental freedoms was a necessary condition for peace within and among nations. Yet they did not apply it to the political power arrangement of the Charter." Why do you think human rights was delegated a promotional role in the UN Charter? Does this undercut the importance of human rights in the UN's mission to secure peace and security in the state system? Why? Why not? And why only a "pledge" by member states to promote human rights? Is this the language of obligation, aspiration, or something else? Do you think the role of human rights in the UN has evolved since the Charter? If so, has this evolution been for the better or for the worse? Why?

2. Marks cites the "fragile consensus on the content of human rights" as one of the limits on the UN's ability to act on human rights issues. This discussion hearkens back to the debate between universalism and cultural relativism (see Reading 3 by Burns H. Weston in Chapter 1 of this volume). Do you think there needs to be one, universally shared understanding of what constitutes human rights? Are there any advantages to not having one shared definition? Do you agree with Marks that the lack of a universal definition is an impediment to the UN? Does a universal understanding necessarily have to be a Western understanding?

3. Despite the UN's long-term contribution to the promotion and protection of human

rights via the preparation and adoption of many standard-setting human rights treaties that, by definition, are intended to be binding on the states parties to them, widespread violations of even the most fundamental human rights continue more or less unabated. To minimize further damage to the UN's already fragile authority and prestige, might it be better for the UN to propose, instead, model laws that can be later enacted into national legislation? Indeed, might not a model-laws approach serve the cause of human rights more effectively because it would obviate the need for ratifications and because it could adapt to local idiosyncracies from the highest to the lowest of domestic jurisdictions? What arguments might weigh against this idea?

4. Of the three principal concerns for the effectiveness of UN human rights treaties—universal ratification without crippling reservations; timely presentation and proper consideration of reports with follow-up recommendations; and availability of a complaints procedure for individual cases—which one do you consider to be the most pressing? The most feasible? The most likely? Why?

5. Marks discusses the desire for universal ratification of human rights treaties and how reservations, understandings, and declarations made by ratifying states often undercut the purpose of these treaties. Is a push for universal ratification desirable? Practical? What are the benefits? Do reservations have any beneficial use in promoting human rights or do they merely provide ratifying states a means to derogate from their treaty obligations?

6. Is there anything to prevent the incorporation into local law of the substantive provisions of UN-adopted human rights treaties? Precisely such an approach has been adopted in the State of Iowa, where city councils, first in Burlington and later in Iowa City, made the substantive provisions of the 1965 International Convention on the Elimination of All Forms of Racial Discrimination (ICERD) part of the human rights ordinances of the two cities. Following the first such initiative in Burlington in 1986, the *Burlington Hawkeye* editorialized that "The idea of turning international conventions into local ordinances will constitute a national endorsement which the [U.S.] Senate will be under pressure to recognize" ("City Shows Local Issues Have Global Roots," *Burlington Hawkeye*, Sept. 21, 1986). It quotes Burns Weston, who helped to inspire the movement, as saying that "This will force judges in local jurisdictions to pay attention to international justice. . . . [I]t is a case of thinking globally and acting locally." Would the UN be well advised to reconsider the uses to which its many proposed or minimally ratified human rights treaties might be put? Are you prepared to work for the same thing in your home town? On behalf of ICERD? On behalf the Convention on the Elimination of All Forms of Discrimination against Women (CEDAW)? Some other human rights treaty? If not, why not?

7. What is the role of the UN Commission on Human Rights? Of its Sub-Commission on the Promotion and Protection of Human Rights? Are these organs effective? How might they be improved? Remember that on March 22, 2005, UN Secretary-General Kofi Annan proposed strengthening the UN's human rights mechanisms by abolishing the Commission and replacing it with a smaller, standing Human Rights Council. Is this a good idea? Why? Why not?

8. Marks describes the 1235 Procedure and the 1503 Procedure. What are these? What functions do they serve? How do they differ?

9. Marks also discusses "treaty bodies." What are they and what do they do? Which are the most effective? Least effective? How do they compare to the 1235 and 1503 Procedures?

10. What, according to Marks, are the three ways in which the UN has moved away from the nonintervention principle? Has this been a positive or negative development? Why? For only one type of intervention or all three? Under what human rights scenario do you believe the UN should be authorized to intervene into a sovereign state's affairs? Using what type of intervention? Diplomatic? Military? Economic? Reactive? Preemptive? Preventive? Is a state's prevention of a minority group from going to school or owning property sufficient? What about a military coup that results in the death and disappearance of thousands?

11. Marks notes that one of the challenges facing the UN is introducing new voices into the organization. How might the UN encourage participation from those most harmed and/or threatened by human rights abuses, such as minority groups, women, and children? What role do NGOs play in the UN human rights framework? What role should

they play? Might it be a good idea to extend formal UN participation to human rights NGOs? If so, what preconditions would have to be met? Also, what might the formal status be and what might be the consequences of formalizing that status?

12. Given the mixed record of UN peacekeeping missions, should the UN be involved in them? If not the UN, then who? Or should anyone? If you were an adviser to the U.S. Representative to the United Nations, what changes would you suggest the UN undertake to strengthen peacekeeping missions? Should the UN put its efforts only into democratic institution-building and let its member states (e.g, the United States) or other international organizations (e.g., NATO) use force to respond to human rights abuses?

13. One of the biggest complaints about human rights treaties is the failure of states to meet their reporting requirements. Given the lack of compliance by states in submitting timely reports, do you think the idea of the reporting system is a good one or is it time to develop a new scheme to monitor state compliance with treaty obligations? Also, how reliable are state reports when they come from the state itself? Would it be more beneficial and reliable to have independent observers compile these reports? Why? Why not? How might this be accomplished? Are there alternatives?

14. After reading Marks's essay, what in your view is the biggest challenge facing the UN relative to the promotion and protection of human rights? How would you propose that the UN meet this challenge?

15. On balance, has the United Nations done a good or a bad job in *promoting* human rights? In *protecting* human rights? What are your reasons for concluding as you do? What does Marks say?

27. DINAH SHELTON *The Promise of Regional Human Rights Systems*

A human rights system can be said to consist of (1) a list or lists of internationally-guaranteed human rights; (2) permanent institutions; and (3) compliance or enforcement procedures. This essay evaluates the promise of regional human rights systems to contribute to respect for human rights in the coming decades. A brief survey of the reasons behind the creation of regional systems and their stated aims precedes this discussion.

THE ORIGINS OF REGIONAL SYSTEMS

The promise of regional systems can be understood initially by considering why regional systems exist. First, regional systems are a product of the global concern for human rights that emerged at the end of the Second World War. Given the widespread movement for human rights that followed, it should not be surprising

that regional organizations created or reformed after the war should have added human rights to their agendas. All of them drew inspiration from the human rights provisions of the United Nations Charter and the Universal Declaration of Human Rights (UDHR).[1]

Second, historical and political factors encouraged each region to focus on human rights issues. The Americas had a tradition of regional approaches to international issues, including human rights, that grew out of regional solidarity developed during the movements for independence. Pan American Conferences had taken action on several human rights matters well before the creation of the United Nations and this history led the Organization of American States to refer to human rights in its Charter and to adopt the American Declaration on the Rights and Duties of Man,[2] some months before the United Nations completed the UDHR.

Reprinted with changes from Dinah Shelton, "The Promise of Regional Human Rights Systems," in Burns H. Weston and Stephen P. Marks, eds., *The Future of International Human Rights* (Ardsley, N.Y.: Transnational Publishers, 1999), 351–98. Copyright © 1999 Transnational Publishers. Reprinted by permission.

1. Adopted Dec. 10, 1948, reprinted in Documentary Appendix A.
2. Both the Charter of the OAS (Apr. 30, 1948) and the American Declaration (Mar. 30–May 2, 1948) are referenced in Documentary Appendix B.

Europe had been the theater of the greatest atrocities of the Second World War, and felt compelled to press for international human rights guarantees as part of European reconstruction. Faith in western European traditions of democracy, the rule of law, and individual rights inspired the belief that a regional system could be successful in avoiding future conflict and stemming post-war revolutionary impulses supported by the Soviet Union.

Somewhat later, in Africa, claims to self-determination became a recognized part of the human rights agenda as African states emerged from colonization and continued struggles for national cohesion. Resistance to human rights abuses in South Africa also contributed to regional efforts for all of Africa.

A third impulse to regionalism came from frustration at the long-stalled efforts of the United Nations to produce a human rights treaty that would complete the international bill of human rights—indeed, it took nearly two decades to finalize and adopt the two United Nations covenants.[3] During the process, it became clear that the compliance mechanisms at the global level would not be strong and that any judicial procedures to enforce human rights would have to be on the regional level. As a result, beginning with Europe, regional systems focused on the creation of procedures of redress, establishing control machinery to supervise the implementation and enforcement of the guaranteed rights.

Regional systems have elements of uniformity and diversity in their origins. All began as the global human rights system was developing and each was inspired by the agreed universal norms. At the same time, each region had its own issues and concerns. As the systems have evolved, the universal framework within which they began, together with their own interactions, have had surprisingly strong influence, leading to converging norms and procedures in an overarching interdependent and dynamic system. In many respects they are thinking globally and acting regionally. Each uses the jurisprudence of the other systems and amends and strengthens its procedures with reference to the experience of the others. In general, their mutual influence is highly progressive, both in normative development and institutional reform.

REGIONAL HUMAN RIGHTS SYSTEMS

As noted, regional human rights systems exist in Europe, the Americas, and Africa. The Arab League has assisted a nascent system in the Middle East. Continuing efforts are underway to create a regional system or systems within the Asia-Pacific region.[4] All of the systems have experienced important recent changes in membership and enacted new normative instruments and procedural reforms.

THE EUROPEAN SYSTEM

The European system, the first to be fully operational, began with the creation of the Council of Europe by ten Western European states in 1949. It has since expanded to include Central and Eastern European countries, bringing the total membership to forty-five (as of Apr. 1, 2005). Article 3 of the Council's Statute provides that every member state must accept the principles of the rule of law and of the enjoyment by all persons within its jurisdiction of human rights and fundamental freedoms; membership in the Council is conditioned de facto upon adherence to the European Convention on Human Rights and Fundamental Freedoms (ECHR) and its eleven protocols.[5]

As the first of its kind, the ECHR began with a short list of civil and political rights, to which additional guarantees have been added over time. The European system was the first to create an international court for the protection of human rights and to create a procedure for individual denunciations of human rights violations. But the jurisprudence of the European Court of Human Rights has been relatively conservative compared to that of other systems, reflecting an

3. The two covenants—the International Covenant on Economic, Social and Cultural Rights (ICE-SCR), and the International Covenant on Civil and Political Rights (ICCPR)—were concluded Dec. 16, 1966 and, together with the UDHR (note 1), comprise the "international bill of human rights." All three instruments are reprinted in Documentary Appendix A.
4. See Vitit Muntarbhorn, "Asia, Human Rights, and the New Millennium: Time for a Regional Human Rights Charter?" *TLCP* 8 (1998): 407–21, at 413.
5. Concluded Nov. 4, 1950, referenced in Documentary Appendix B.

early concern for maintaining state support in light of the innovations of the European system and the then-optional nature of the Court's jurisdiction. The role of the victim was initially very limited and admissibility requirements were stringent. As the system has matured, however, the institutional structures and normative guarantees have been considerably strengthened. Although most of the changes result from efforts to improve the effectiveness of the system and add to its guarantees, some of the evolution reflects a responsiveness to the activities of other regional organizations both within and outside Europe, while still other changes have resulted from the impact of expanding membership in the Council of Europe.

The evolution of the European system is characterized by the adoption of numerous treaties and protocols. Through its Parliamentary Assembly, the Council has drafted a series of human rights instruments. The most significant of these are the 1950 ECHR and its twelve protocols, the 1961 European Social Charter (ESC) with its protocols and as revised in 1996, the 1987 European Convention for the Prevention of Torture and its protocols, the European Charter for Regional or Minority Languages, the 1995 Framework Convention for the Protection of National Minorities, and the 1997 Convention on Human Rights and Biomedicine, with its protocol banning human cloning.[6] Together these instruments form a network of mutually reinforcing human rights protections in Europe.

THE INTER-AMERICAN SYSTEM

The Inter-American system began with the transformation of the Pan American Union into the Organization of American States (OAS), the Charter of which proclaims the "fundamental rights of the individual" as one of the Organization's basic principles.[7] The 1948 American Declaration on the Rights and Duties of Man[8] gives definition to the Charter's general commitment to human rights. Over a decade later, in 1959, the OAS created a seven member Inter-American Commission of Human Rights with a mandate to further respect for human rights among the OAS member states. In 1965, the Commission's competence was expanded to accept communications, request information from governments, and make recommendations to bring about the more effective observance of human rights. In 1969, the American Convention of Human Rights,[9] which entered into force in 1978, conferred additional competence on the Commission to oversee compliance with the Convention.

The Commission's jurisdiction extends to all thirty-five OAS member states.[10] The 25 states that have ratified the Convention are bound by its provisions, while other member states are held to the standards of the American Declaration. Communications may be filed against any state; the optional clause applies only to interstate cases. Standing for non-state actors to file communications is broad. The Commission may also prepare country reports and conduct on-site visits to examine the human rights situations in individual countries and make recommendations to the government in question. Country reports have been prepared on the Commission's own initiative and at the request of the country concerned. The Commission may also appoint special rapporteurs to prepare studies on hemisphere wide problems.

The American Convention also created the Inter-American Court of Human Rights. The Court has jurisdiction over contentious cases submitted against states that accept its jurisdiction and it may issue advisory opinions.

Like the European system, the Inter-American system has expanded its protections over time through the adoption of additional human rights prescriptions. The major instruments are: the 1985 Inter-American Convention to Prevent and Punish Torture; the 1988 Additional Protocol to the American Convention on Human Rights in the Area of Economic, Social and Cultural Rights; the 1990 Second Additional Protocol to the

6. Each of the several European instruments mentioned is referenced in Documentary Appendix B.
7. Note 2.
8. Note 2.
9. Concluded Nov. 22, 1969, referenced in Documentary Appendix B.
10. Virtually the entire Western Hemisphere is included: Antigua and Barbuda, Argentina, The Bahamas, Barbados, Belize, Bolivia, Brazil, Canada, Chile, Colombia, Costa Rica, Cuba, Dominica, Dominican Republic, Ecuador, El Salvador, Grenada, Guatemala, Guyana, Haiti, Honduras, Jamaica, Mexico, Nicaragua, Panama, Paraguay, Peru, St. Kitts and Nevis, Saint Lucia, Saint Vincent and the Grenadines, Suriname, Trinidad and Tobago, the United States, Uruguay, and Venezuela.

American Convention on Human Rights to Abolish the Death Penalty; the 1994 Inter-American Convention on the Prevention, Punishment, and Eradication of Violence against Women; the 1994 Inter-American Convention on the Forced Disappearance of Persons; and the [1999 Proposed American Declaration of the Rights of Indigenous Populations].[11]

THE AFRICAN SYSTEM

The regional promotion and protection of human rights in Africa is established by the African Charter on Human and Peoples' Rights (African Charter),[12] designed to function within the framework of the Organization of African Unity (OAU) [reconstituted as the African Union (AU)]. The OAU Assembly of Heads of State and Government adopted the African Charter on 27 June 1981, since ratified by all 53 OAU member states.

The African Charter differs from other regional human rights treaties in its inclusion of "peoples' rights." It also includes economic, social, and cultural rights to a greater extent than either the European or the American conventions. Like its European and American counterparts, however, it establishes a human rights commission, the African Commission on Human and Peoples' Rights (comprising eleven independent members elected for a renewable period of six years) and, as of January 15, 2004, the African Court on Human and Peoples' Rights. The functioning European and Inter-American courts are among the great contributors to the protection of human rights by regional systems. A 1998 protocol to the African Charter created the court in the African system, thus adding to the regional protections.[13]

The Charter confers four functions on the Commission: promotion of human and peoples' rights; protection of those rights; interpretation of the Charter; and performance of other tasks that may be entrusted to it by the OAU Assembly of Heads of State and Government. In addition, the Commission may undertake studies, perform training and teaching functions, convene conferences, initiate publication programs, disseminate information, and collaborate with national and local institutions concerned with human and peoples' rights. Unlike the other regional systems, the African system envisages not only interstate and individual communications procedures, but also a special procedure for the handling of gross and systematic violations of human rights.

THE NASCENT MIDDLE EAST SYSTEM

On September 15, 1994, building on earlier texts adopted by regional nongovernmental and inter-governmental organizations, the League of Arab States, which did not mention human rights in its founding charter, approved an Arab Charter on Human Rights.[14] The Charter requires acceptance by seven states before it will enter into force; until then there are no Middle Eastern regional institutions or procedures for monitoring human rights. The Charter foresees the election by its states parties of a seven-member independent Committee of Experts. Article 41 foresees periodic reporting by the states parties and implies that the Committee may request a report by submitting inquiries to a state party, with the Committee studying the reports and distributing its own report to the Human Rights Committee of the Arab League. No other functions of human rights promotion or protection are specified in the Charter. The emerging Middle East system is marked probably more than other regional systems by the great division among its states in their willingness to accept and give effect to international human rights law. These divisions have slowed progress in achieving a true human rights system.[15]

11. Each of the several inter-American instruments mentioned is referenced in Documentary Appendix B.
12. Concluded June 27, 1981, referenced in Documentary Appendix B.
13. Protocol to the African Charter on Human and Peoples' Rights on the Establishment of the African Court on Human and Peoples' Rights, concluded June 9, 1998, referenced in Documentary Appendix B.
14. Adopted Sept. 15, 1994, referenced in Documentary Appendix B.
15. According to the Office of the High Commissioner for Human Rights (OHCHR), the Arab Summit held in Tunis, May 22–23, 2004, adopted a "modernized" version of the Arab Charter, the outcome of a "process of revision" begun in 2003 with the help of the OHCHR in cooperation with the Permanent Arab Human Rights Commission. According to the OHCHR, "The purpose of the exercise was to bring the Charter into conformity with internationally-accepted human rights standards." *Respect—The Human Rights Newsletter* (Office of the High Commissioner for Human Rights, June 2004), 1:6, available at http://www.ohchr.org/english/about/publications/docs/issue1.pdf

ASIA

No human rights system exists in Asia, despite efforts by nongovernmental organizations and the United Nations to create one. In 1993, over one hundred Asia-Pacific nongovernmental organizations adopted an Asia-Pacific Declaration of Human Rights supporting the universality of human rights and the creation of a regional system,[16] but governments have been slow to respond. At a 1996 UN-sponsored workshop on the issue, the thirty participating governments concluded that "it was premature, at the current stage, to discuss specific arrangements relating to the setting up of a formal human rights mechanism in the Asian and Pacific region." The participating governments agreed, however, to explore "the options available and the process necessary for establishing a regional mechanism."[17]

There are many hurdles to creating an Asian-Pacific regional system. First, there is far greater diversity of language, culture, legal systems, religious traditions, and history in the Asia-Pacific region than in other regions of the world. Second, the geographic limits of the region are as unclear as they are vast. These two factors suggest that the region may be better served by "sub-regional" mechanisms that could be more easily and quickly developed on the basis of the closer ties and geographic proximity of states in smaller areas. A third factor hindering the development of an Asian regional system is that, in general, governments in the region have been unwilling to ratify human rights instruments, a reluctance that makes it unlikely that an effective regional system can garner widespread support in the near future.

Finally, economic crises in Asia have put additional pressures on governments trying to survive in the wake of growing unrest; the crises create risks of repression in the short term. "Asian values," observes Thai human rights scholar Vitit Muntarbhorn, may become even more "a tool of some authoritarian regimes to suppress individual rights, especially freedom of expression and association which are at the heart of democratic aspirations."[18] On the other hand, the regional economic and political crises have led many to question the concept of "Asian values" as a means to progress. Political movements and nongovernmental organizations have renewed efforts to ensure greater respect for human rights in the region. If the economic justification often given for limiting civil and political rights disappears, the opportunity to create a regional system may improve quickly and dramatically, as it did in Central and Eastern Europe.

UNIVERSALITY AND REGIONAL DIVERSITY

The seemingly endless debate over universality and diversity in human rights law is inescapable when evaluating regional systems.[19] The issue of normative diversity is complex. Virtually all the legal instruments creating the various regional systems refer to the UDHR and to the Charter of the United Nations, providing a measure of uniformity and reinforcement of the universal character of the Declaration. Also, the rights contained in the regional human rights treaties reflect the norms set forth in global declarations and conventions, in particular the ICESCR and its companion ICCPR. In addition, as each successive system has been created, it has looked to the normative instruments and jurisprudence of the systems founded earlier; and this jurisprudential cross-referencing, with the help of provisions regarding choice of law and canons of interpretation, has led, despite differences, to a mutual influence that is producing some convergence in fundamental human rights principles.

In fact the various regional instruments not only mention the global instruments, they contain similar guarantees and in many instances use language identical to that contained in other instruments. The economic, social, and cultural

16. Bangkok Declaration on Human Rights (Asian Cultural Forum on Development), Mar. 29–Apr. 3, 1993, UN Doc. A/CONF/93, reprinted in *Human Rights Law Journal* 14 (1993): 370. The support of the universality of human rights was equivocal, however.
17. United Nations, *Fourth Workshop on Regional Human Rights Arrangements in the Asian and Pacific Region,* IIR/PUB/96/3 (1996).
18. Vitit Muntarbhorn, "Protection of Human Rights in Asia and the Pacific: Think Universal, Act Regional?"in Yael Danieli, Elsa Stamatopoulou, and Clarence J. Dias, eds., *The Universal Declaration of Human Rights: Fifty Years and Beyond* (Amityville, N.Y.: Baywood, 1999), 295–308, at 297.
19. On the universalist-relativist debate generally, see Reading 3 by Burns Weston in Chapter 1 of this volume.

rights proclaimed in the UDHR are found also in the American Declaration and in the African and Arab charters. The Arab Charter and the African Charter include the principle of self-determination from Article 1 of the two UN covenants, a right perhaps understandably omitted from their European and American counterparts. In the Arab Charter, virtually all of the rights contained in the ICCPR are included, in some cases with more or less detail. The Arab Charter also iterates ICCPR articles 2(1) and 3 in its affirmation of the duty of the states parties to ensure the guaranteed rights without discrimination, including as between men and women. It further echoes the Article 27 minority rights provision of the ICCPR in its Article 37. The duties of individuals, included in Article 29 of the UDHR are found in the African Charter, the American Declaration, and the American Convention.

At the same time, while basing themselves on universal norms, regional instruments also contain different guarantees and emphases; indeed the preambles of all the regional instruments refer to their regional heritages. The European Convention focuses on civil rights, especially due process. The American system is strongly concerned with democracy and the rule of law, having experienced repeated military coups in the region. Its preamble begins with a reference to democratic institutions and its guarantees emphasize the right to participate in government and the right to judicial protection. The Arab Charter is deistic, taking religion as its starting point, referring in its preamble to God, monotheistic religions, the Islamic Shari`a and "other divine religions." It refers both in its Preamble and in its Article 1 to rejecting racism and Zionism and to the close link between human rights and world peace. The Preamble to the African Charter contains similar language on racism and Zionism. The African Charter focuses on economic development, calling it essential to pay particular attention to the right to development. It also is unique in its inclusion of peoples' rights, although the Preamble suggests that they are viewed as instrumental to the achievement of individual rights rather than goals in and of themselves, recognizing "that the reality and respect of peoples' rights should necessarily guarantee human rights."

Among the pronounced differences, the Arab Charter is unique in omitting explicit mention of slavery, although it prohibits forced labor which could be intended to include slavery, and it has few guarantees of political rights, leaving out the right to free and fair elections and specifying only the right of citizens to occupy public office. The Arab Charter is also less protective of the rights of aliens, limiting to citizens the right to leave and not to be expelled, the right of political asylum, the right to private property, the right to freedom of assembly and association, the right to work and to social security, the right to equal opportunity in employment and equal pay for equal work, political rights, and the right to education. However, the Arab Charter expands on the right of political asylum, adding that "political refugees shall not be extradited," and in its regulation of the death penalty it uniquely prohibits the execution of a nursing mother until two years have passed from the date of the birth of her child. Additionally, the prohibition on torture specifies that it extends to both physical and psychological torture and mandates criminal penalties for performing or participating in an act of torture.

Other regional systems, since their inception, have added rights, and in no case has a right been limited or withdrawn by a later instrument. Regional systems appear to have added new rights in a kind of feedback process of mutual inspiration, including such specific guarantees as abolition of the death penalty, action to combat violence against women, the right to a satisfactory environment, and strengthened guarantees of economic, social, and cultural rights.

All the regional instruments contain limitations clauses, using similar language, based on the UDHR. Limitations clauses allow states parties to restrict the exercise of guaranteed rights, but specify the legal grounds and requirements for valid restrictions. Regional instruments also contain "clawback" clauses that are similar to limitations clauses insofar as they permit national law to specify the scope of the right guaranteed. However, "clawback" clauses are less constraining of the state's discretion. Article 8 of the European Convention, for example, allows a state to limit by law the right to respect for privacy and family life, home and correspondence if "necessary in a democratic society in the interests of national security, public safety or the economic well-being of the country, for the prevention of disorder or crime, for the protection of health or morals, or for the protection of the rights and freedoms of others." In contrast, the right to marry and to found a family proclaimed in Article 12 is subject to a "clawback" clause that subsumes it unreservedly "to the national laws governing the exercise of this right." The African and Arab charters contain extensive "clawback" clauses that could undermine the effectiveness of both systems, although the developing jurisprudence of the African system is encouraging in insisting on the effective enjoyment of the rights prescribed.

Some of the greatest differences among the regional instruments are found in their derogations provisions, which govern the exercise of rights during periods of national emergency. The bases for derogating differ, as do the lists of nonderogable rights. Article 15 of the European Convention limits the grounds for suspending rights to "time of war or other public emergency threatening the life of the nation," making it hard to justify a suspension of rights. In contrast, according to Article 27 of the American Convention, states may suspend guarantees "in times of war, public danger, or other emergency that threatens the independence or security" of the state, making it easier to do so. On the other hand, the list of nonderogable rights is much longer in the Inter-American system, so that the ease of derogation is balanced by greater human rights protections in periods of emergency. Africa has no general derogation clause, but "clawback" provisions may make it unnecessary. Article 4 of the Arab Charter is close to the language of the ICCPR, referring to public emergencies which threaten the life of the nation and requiring that the measures be "strictly required by the circumstances," but the nonderogable rights in the Arab Charter are unusual, applying to the right to be free from torture and degrading treatment, the right to return to one's country, the right of political asylum, the right to trial, a prohibition on double jeopardy, and "the principle of the legality of the crime and punishment." It is unclear if the reference to trial would include due process guarantees, but the emphasis on the rule of law suggests that it might.

The protections of the various legal instruments are further enhanced by canons of interpretation or choice of law principles that call for states and tribunals to apply the rule most favorable to the individual. Article 15(1) of the European Convention affirms that measures taken by a state in derogation of the Convention cannot be "inconsistent with [that state's] other obligations under international law." Article 1 of Protocol 1 contains a similar reference to international law, which the European Court of Human Rights apparently considers to embrace the traditional rules of customary international law on state responsibility. More generally, Article 60 of the European Convention provides that nothing in the Convention "shall be construed as limiting or derogating from any of the human rights and fundamental freedoms which may be ensured under the laws of any High Contracting Party or under any other agreement to which it is a Party."

The American Convention, implicitly referring to customary as well as conventional international law, is particularly broad. Article 29 provides that no provision of the Convention can be interpreted to restrict a right recognized in the national or international law applicable to a state party. Article 60 of the African Charter mandates its Commission to "draw inspiration from international law on human and peoples' rights," explicitly citing the UN Charter, the UDHR, and other instruments adopted by the UN and its specialized agencies. Article 61 then lists "subsidiary measures to determine principles of law," thus indicating the primary nature of international human rights law as a source of law for interpreting and applying the Charter. Also, the African court is directed in Protocol Article 7 to apply the provisions of the African Charter and "other human rights instruments." Finally, the Arab Charter specifies that there can be no restriction of any basic human right that is recognized in any state party "by virtue of law, treaties or custom" and, according to Article 3(A), nothing in the Charter can be used to derogate from these guarantees.

In sum, there is diversity within diversity. The basic texts of each regional system can be read to reaffirm the universal norms. Yet there are sufficient references to regional divergences that the states and the supervisory organs of each system could choose to focus on their differences instead of their similarities. Thus it is important to study the normative evolution of the systems as it is reflected in the jurisprudence of the regional commissions and courts.

NORMATIVE EVOLUTION

The dynamic reading given human rights guarantees by the regional supervisory organs has prevented a rigid formalism from reducing the relevance of regional systems as circumstances change and new problems arise. The character of human rights conventions, written in general terms, gave ample scope for judges and commissioners to apply and creatively interpret their provisions.

All of the systems have a growing case law detailing the rights and duties enunciated in the basic instruments which has become, in turn, a major source of human rights law. In many instances, this case law reflects a convergence of different substantive protections in favor of broad human rights protections. In other instances, differences in treaty terms or approach have resulted in a rejection of precedent from other systems. In general, however, the judges and commissioners have been willing to substantiate or give greater authority to their interpretations of the rights guaranteed by referencing not only their own case law but the decisions of other regional and even global bodies.

Some decisions cross-reference specific articles of other regional and global instruments. Best known is the Soering case, wherein the Court found implicit in Article 3 of the European Convention the obligation of Article 3 of the UN Torture Convention[20] not to extradite someone who might face torture.[21]

The Inter-American Court frequently uses other international decisions and human rights instruments to interpret and apply inter-American norms. It has referred to the European Convention, the ICCPR and other United Nations treaties, and to decisions of the European Human Rights Commission and the Court. It has stated explicitly that it will use cases decided by the European Court and the ICCPR Human Rights Committee when their value is to augment rights protection, and has indicated a commitment to the nonincorporation of restrictions from other systems.

The decisions of the African Commission also show the influence of other regional systems, having adopted several doctrines established in European and Inter-American case law: presumption of the truth of the allegations from silence of government, the notion of continuing violations, continuity of obligations despite a change of government, state responsibility for failure to act, and the presumption that states are responsible for custodial injuries. The African Commission, like the Inter-American Court, emphasizes the need for independence of the judiciary and the guarantees of a fair trial, having called attacks on the judiciary "especially invidious, because while it is a violation of human rights in itself, it permits other violations of rights to go unredressed."[22]

While the mutual influence of the systems is clear, there are regional differences in the nature of cases filed that have limited the relevance of precedents from other systems. In Europe, until recently, virtually all cases raised questions of law on agreed facts. In addition, a large percentage concerned procedural guarantees in civil and criminal proceedings. In contrast, nearly all of the Inter-American cases have concerned factual determinations of state responsibility for the death, disappearance, or other mistreatment of individuals. The result has been an Inter-American focus on issues of standard of proof and burden of proof that have arisen in the European system only rarely. The Inter-American Commission also has had to be concerned with widespread civil strife and internal armed conflicts in the region. As a result, it has begun to document human rights violations by non-state actors, making an important contribution to international human rights law. Matters submitted in Africa thus far have involved varied issues, including trade union freedoms, arbitrary detention, killings, and the right to health.

There also is divergence in treaty interpretation. One evident difference is found in the law concerning derogations from enunciated rights and the protection of nonderogable rights. The relative conservatism of the European Court of Human Rights is particularly evident in this regard. Where national interests are at stake, the Court appears to be concerned that a state condemned for wrongfully suspending rights might withdraw from the Convention. Another difference in interpretation can be seen in the approach each institution takes to the issue of its implied or inherent powers to create remedies for violations

20. Convention against Torture and Other Cruel, Inhuman or Degrading Treatment or Punishment (Dec. 10, 1984), referenced in Documentary Appendix B.
21. *Soering v. United Kingdom*, 161 Eur. Ct. H.R. (set. A) ¶ 88 (1989).
22. Comm. 129/94, *Civil Liberties Organization v. Nigeria*, in *Ninth Annual Activity Report of the African Commission on Human and Peoples' Rights*, Annex VIII, at 17.

of human rights. In contrast to the European Court's restrictive view, the African and Inter-American Commissions, and the American Court, have often used doctrines of implied powers.

Despite the differences in treaty interpretation and norm application, there is a progressive convergence in these respects and it is in large part stimulated by the victims and their lawyers. They submit memorials that draw attention to the relevant case law of other systems and help to expand human rights protections by obtaining a progressive ruling in one system, then invoking it in another, a pattern that is enhanced by the liberal standing rules of the Inter-American and African systems. Many complaints are filed by nongovernmental organizations (NGOs) familiar with, and operating in, more than one system. All of which strongly suggests that no human rights lawyer should rely solely on the jurisprudence of a single system in pleading a case.

PROCEDURAL AND INSTITUTIONAL EVOLUTION

Regional human rights procedures and institutions have evolved perhaps to an even greater extent than have substantive human rights guarantees. While some changes result from amendments to the basic legal instruments, at least as much change is due to regional bodies developing their own implied powers. A serious commitment to giving effect to regional protections is evident in the evolution of the functions and procedures of regional human rights bodies.

INDIVIDUAL COMPLAINTS PROCEDURES

One of the greatest contributions of the regional systems is the establishment of individual complaint mechanisms for judicial or quasi-judicial redress of human rights violations. Europe was the first to create a commission and court that could hear such complaints, followed by the Americas and now Africa. In Europe, a slow evolution toward individual standing first allowed individuals to appear before the court in the guise of assistants to the Commission. A protocol later permitted them to appear by right. Individual complainants now have sole standing.

From its creation in 1960, the Inter-American Commission on Human Rights interpreted its powers broadly to include the ability to make general recommendations to each individual state as well as to all of them, and to include the power to take cognizance of individual petitions and use them to assess the human rights situation in a particular country, based on the normative standards of the American Declaration. The Inter-American system was thus the first to make the complaints procedure mandatory against all member states. Additionally, restructuring of the case system in the Inter-American system has involved greater use of provisional measures, registration of petitions, creating chambers for hearings, and more on-site visits to gather evidence.

The African system has evolved quickly through the African Commission's interpretation of its powers and revision of its rules of procedure. The African Commission, like the Inter-American Commission, may give its views or make recommendations to governments and it has read this mandate to include the formulation of principles and rules for the resolution of human rights problems in specific states.

All of the regional systems have enhanced their complaints procedures by providing for greater participation by victims and their representatives. In most cases, these changes have occurred through action by the supervisory bodies rather than through amending the basic texts.

OTHER FUNCTIONS AND POWERS

The exercise of implied powers has not only improved complaint procedures, but has strengthened other functions of regional institutions, especially in the case of Africa. The ability of the African Commission to write its own rules of procedure has enhanced its functioning and allowed it to expand its role considerably. They allow it to hold sessions anywhere and to convene extraordinary as well as regular sessions. They also provide the greatest openness and transparency of proceedings among the regional bodies (e.g., authorizing publication of the Commission's proceedings). Nongovernmental organizations may submit items for inclusion in the Commission's agenda and they must be informed of the provisional agenda of each session. According to its Rule 72, the Commission may invite any informed organization or persons to participate in its deliberations without voting rights. NGOs with observer status may appoint representatives to participate in public sessions of the Commission and its subsidiary bodies. Also, the African Commission has developed a periodic reporting system to match the procedure followed by the UN Human Rights Committee, although many reports are more than ten years overdue and many of the states parties have not submitted any reports. On the other hand, ironically, the lack of reports probably has enhanced the effectiveness of the African Commission, given its limited resources and meeting time, by leaving it more time to focus on individual communications and situations of gross and systematic violations.

The Inter-American and African Commissions have adopted, in addition, the procedure of thematic rapporteur, giving them broad mandates to address problems specific to their regions. In 1998, the Inter-American Commission had rapporteurs studying women's rights, indigenous populations, migrant workers, prison conditions, and freedom of expression. The African Commission has appointed rapporteurs on extrajudicial executions, prisons, and women.

The evolution of the regional systems demonstrates their dynamic nature and their ability to respond to new demands, through cases brought, through NGO pressure, and through inter-regional meetings. In some instances, the need for change has been sudden, in the face of an unexpected crisis. The Inter-American system's action in Haiti, where it cooperated with the United Nations to restore the democratically-elected government, is a case in point. The smaller size of the regional systems relative to the UN system may make the change easier to achieve than at the UN, where bureaucratic inertia often seems overwhelming.

On-Site Visits

The trust and cooperation that develops in regional systems can lead to highly effective mechanisms apart from the individual communications procedures. The ability to make on-site visits to study the human rights situation in member states is particularly significant. The Inter-American Commission has long claimed this power and exercised it frequently. More recently, the European Committee for the Prevention of Torture and Inhuman or Degrading Treatment was given the power to visit prisons and other places of detention, making both periodic visits for which it gives notice and ad hoc visits which are not announced but made whenever the Committee deems it necessary on the basis of information supplied by nongovernmental organizations.

The technique of the on-site visit is an invaluable instrument in human rights protection and promotion. On-site visits enable regional bodies to gather information and verify information. At the same time, they allow governments to indicate the context and complexities of situations, giving officials as well as private persons the opportunity to be heard, and increase public knowledge of the regional system. Finally, they can deter violations by the mere presence of an outside human rights group. As such, a principal advantage to on-site visits is preventive. On-site visits are particularly important in avoiding regression during periods of transition and in dealing with gross and massive violations of rights where it may be impracticable to open individual cases. It is not surprising that the Inter-American Commission has visited the large majority of OAS member states and that the practice of on-site visits is becoming the rule, not the exception, in Africa.

Institutional Changes

The regional systems have in recent years undertaken major changes in their institutional structures. This is particularly true of the European and African systems.

In Europe, rather than continue to make *ad hoc* incremental changes in procedure to improve the functioning of the complaints process, the institutional structure has been reworked entirely. A new full-time Court of Human Rights replaces the former Commission and Court and consists largely of new judges. The full-time nature of the court precludes judges from holding any other office, a mandatory retirement age of 70 has been added, and the time in office has been reduced from nine to six years. In a substantial change, a merit selection process has been instituted, requiring all judicial candidates to appear before a panel of the Parliamentary Assembly for an individual interview and evaluation prior to the election of the judges.

Additionally, fundamental changes in procedures give individuals direct access to the Court to bring actions against any state party to the Convention—that is, acceptance of individual communications is no longer optional. In addition, a limited appellate procedure has been introduced.

In Africa, dramatic change is seen in the establishment in January 2004 of the African Court on Human and Peoples' Rights.[23] The Court has jurisdiction over all cases and disputes submitted to it concerning the Charter, the Protocol, and, in the words of the Protocol, "any other applicable African human rights instrument." Cases can be submitted by the Commission or a state party involved in a case as complainant or defendant, but Article 6 of the Protocol, highlighting the "leapfrogging" effect of regional systems, provides for broader standing by opening the African Court also to public interest litigation by individuals and by NGOs with observer status, including litigation in cases involving serious, systematic, or massive violations of human rights against states that file a declaration accepting Article 6. The Protocol is progressive also in giving the African Court the broadest remedial jurisdiction of any human rights tribunal. If the court finds that there has been a violation of a human or people's right, then, as stated in Protocol Article 24, "it shall make appropriate orders to remedy the violation, including the payment of fair compensation or reparation." No other court is expressly given the power to issue orders, although the Inter-American Court has directed the release of a prisoner held in violation of the Convention. Additionally, those who appear before the African Court are entitled to legal representation. Free representation may be provided where the interests of justice require, something also provided in the European system, but not in the Inter-American system.

CHANGING MEMBERSHIPS AND CHANGING PROBLEMS

All the regional systems have seen dramatic changes in their geopolitical environments, especially from democratic transitions in South Africa, Central and Eastern Europe, and much of Latin America. There has been a breakdown of authoritarian, repressive regimes and a resulting dramatic decrease in the worst governmental abuses: disappearances, summary executions, and other forms of brutal repression. New member states have joined all the regional systems, bringing with them both new possibilities and new problems. Regional systems also face unprecedented problems from the resurgence of minority nationalism and ethnic tensions, often leading to massive violations of human rights by non-state as well as state actors. Still, the response of regional institutions suggest a "mainstreaming" of human rights, as regional bodies are occupied increasingly with issues of democracy, armed conflict, transnational crime, environmental protection, economic development, science and technology, and, indeed, the full range of human activities. In Europe, this "mainstreaming" may be seen in the proliferation of intra-regional institutions concerned with human rights, a development that has had an impact on regional norms and procedures.

CHANGES IN MEMBERSHIP

Efforts to strengthen human rights protections on the regional level have succeeded in large part because of the cultural, geographic, economic, and historical proximity of the states involved. Such relative homogeneity has fostered a sense of trust among the member states that has made them sometimes less sensitive to criticism of their human rights performance.

Changes in membership in the regional systems, which have been significant, are not altogether positive to regional cohesion. For example, with its expansion into Central and Eastern Europe, some have questioned whether the European system can continue to be successful. The reconstituted European Court will likely face unprecedented situations of widespread violations where factual determinations of responsibility will be crucial; future European cases may be comparable to those found in the Inter-American and the African systems. Both the character of the system and its effectiveness will be challenged. There is a risk that the new Court may narrow the interpretation of the principles embedded in the Convention and that the new states may disregard prior jurisprudence, deliberately or from lack of knowledge.

23. See note 13 above and accompanying text.

INSTITUTIONAL PROLIFERATION

In contrast to the other regions, Europe is faced also with an institutional proliferation that creates problems and possibilities for advancing human rights protections. In addition to the European system that was created by the Council of Europe, the Organization on Security and Cooperation in Europe (OSCE) and the European Community (EC) are engaged in human rights activities. Their existence and work constitute a fundamental change in the European human rights environment and have helped to transform the region in relation to the promotion and protection of human rights.

The 1975 Helsinki Final Act,[24] which is at the origin of the OSCE, brought human rights into the context of peace and security in the region, and the various follow-up meetings to the Helsinki Conference have helped to strengthen human rights protections, sometimes adding details not found in other regional or global instruments. The OSCE has tended to focus on human rights issues primarily through diplomatic intervention for conflict-prevention and mediation and, in this context, various meetings have made specific references to and commitments regarding national minorities. The OSCE has been engaged also in developing regional democracy, linking it with human rights. An Office for Democratic Institutions and Human Rights, established in Warsaw, assists the democratization process in OSCE states and monitors the implementation of OSCE commitments regarding "the human dimension." Parallel to the OSCE efforts, the Council of Europe created a program in 1990 to strengthen genuine democracy and to facilitate the integration of new member states into the Council of Europe.

The European Community (EC), in its transformation into the European Union, has also been concerned with human rights, although it was comprised originally of institutions of economic integration. Since the 1970s, the European Court of Justice has held that respect for basic rights is an integral part of Community law.[25] Over time, both the basic legal instruments and the jurisprudence of the Court have evolved to expand the rights of individuals not just in the economic field, but with respect to political rights as well, referring to the European Convention in its jurisprudence. Other Community institutions also act in regard to human rights. The EC signs OSCE documents through its president and EC employees sometimes participate in OSCE meetings as delegation members. In 1989, the European Parliament adopted a Declaration of Fundamental Rights and Freedoms,[26] which has broader guarantees than the European Convention. In addition, the Parliament's Human Rights Sub-Committee produces an annual report on human rights in countries throughout the world.

The result of multiple regional institutions can be both positive and negative. On the positive side, the mutual influence that can be seen inter-regionally also can occur intra-regionally, leading to greater human rights protections. Under the influence of the Helsinki Process, for example, which has set high standards for minority protections, the Council has taken action to meet the challenges of ethnic tensions in the region (important since the enlargement of the Council of Europe) by adopting new treaties to protect minority rights. Also, multiple regional institutions can manifest areas of specialization. More generally, the various regional bodies can reinforce the views and messages of the others provided there is good cooperation and careful coordination to avoid forum shopping by governments and contradictory messages from European institutions. On the other hand, multiple institutions can lead to divergent jurisprudence, which is more problematic within a region than between regions because it places states in a position of conflicting obligations. In addition, the competition between institutions can create a risk of diluting human rights protections.

MAINSTREAMING OF HUMAN RIGHTS:
OLD AND NEW PROBLEMS

All the regional systems are expanding their efforts to consider issues of democracy, conflict

---

24. Final Act on Security and Co-Operation in Europe (Aug. 1, 1975), referenced in Documentary Appendix B.
25. *Case I 1/70, International Handelsgcsellschaft mbH v Einfuhr-and Vorratsstelle fur Getreide and Futtermittel*, 1970 E.C.R. 1125.
26. Adopted May 16, 1989, referenced in Documentary Appendix B.

prevention and resolution, environmental protection, and other problems related to human rights. Ethnic conflicts are a particular concern. Increasingly, the regional systems are similarly facing problems of wide disparity of economic development, civil war or repeated military coups, and terrorists and organized criminal associations. Coordination, cooperation, and competition among them may help produce some solutions to these seemingly intractable issues.

Threats to Regional Systems

The regional systems suffer from expanding work and diminishing resources. Their success is in part responsible for the difficulties they face. Beginning in the early 1980s, the caseload of the European system began to double every five years on average. The caseload is not likely to decrease; dissemination of knowledge about the Convention has encouraged more frequent recourse to the regional system. The question is whether even a full-time court can cope. The Inter-American Commission's caseload is also expanding, and in Africa the Commission has repeatedly complained of shortages of staff and equipment.

There is also the risk of "backsliding." In the Caribbean, in 1999, Barbados, Guyana, Jamaica, and Trinidad intend to establish a Caribbean Court of Justice in large part out of disagreement with Inter-American standards on due process in death penalty cases. On May 26, 1998, Trinidad and Tobago denounced the Inter-American Convention on Human Rights, the only state ever to do so. It also denounced the Optional Protocol to the ICCPR. In January 1998, Jamaica withdrew from the ICCPR Optional Protocol on the death penalty and Barbados announced that it was considering denouncing the American Convention. While these events challenge both regional and global standards, the regional system can continue to supervise the states' behavior. So long as the states remain members of the OAS, they are bound by regional norms and subject to the jurisdiction of the Inter-American Commission.

CONCLUSIONS

The evolution in regional norms and procedures does not address the fundamental question of whether regional systems actually have had a positive impact on respect for human rights, but there can be little doubt in this regard. While compliance is not as good as it should be and while much remains to be done, there is considerable evidence that states have responded to judgments of the regional tribunals, changing their laws and practices as a result. Even without undertaking a detailed empirical analysis, it is clear that the regional systems contribute to the functioning and improvement of the global human rights system.

Human rights law has been enhanced through the developing jurisprudence and evolution of regional human rights systems, wherein the various systems reinforce global norms while responding to the particular problems of each region. In particular, regional systems continue to reaffirm the UDHR on which each of them is based. The convergence of regional jurisprudence confirms the universality of the rights proclaimed in the Declaration and the wisdom of its authors. Through the participation of NGOs in various ways and through their own interactions, regional systems learn from each other about the meaning of the Declaration and its ongoing relevance to regional human rights instruments, enhancing the legitimacy of their decisions by relying on it and on precedents from other systems.

Regional systems thus are interconnected with each other, with the larger global system of which they are components, and with smaller systems of which they are products. They also are engaged in constant exchanges with their geopolitical and technological environments and thus never reach equilibrium. As a result, their operations never will be completely consistent with their goals; there almost always will be some malfunction or inefficiency in the process. Nonetheless, it is possible to seek reform and greater efficiency to achieve the aim of promoting and protecting international human rights. That is the promise of the regional systems.

QUESTIONS FOR REFLECTION AND DISCUSSION

1. At around the time of its founding, the United Nations questioned the development of regional human rights systems. Why might it have done so? What role, if any, should the UN now play in the development of regional human rights systems? Might it assist in the still-needed development of regional adjudication and enforcement machinery in Asia and the Middle East? If so, how? What factors have impeded—and might continue to impede—the establishment of effective human rights systems in those regions? Are they culturally homogeneous in the way that the European and Inter-American systems are culturally homogenous? Or are they more like Africa? If so, does the experience of the African human rights system offer any guidance? What about the possibility of sub-regional systems in Asia and the Middle East? Would that make sense? Why? Why not? What does Shelton say?

2. How are the European, Inter-American, and African human rights systems the same? How do they differ? What historical and contemporary conditions or factors have given them shape and how? What are their comparative strengths? Their comparative weaknesses?

3. Shelton points out that the African system "differs from other regional human rights bodies in its inclusion of 'peoples' rights.'" This is a good example of the heterogeneity that is expressed in the regional systems. What are the benefits and dangers of this capacity for (and tolerance of) regional relativism?

4. Shelton highlights the strengths of the existing three regional systems, noting that regional bodies are simultaneously well-established and flexible. Regional systems, she says, are therefore adept intermediaries between state violators and the far-removed global system of human rights standards, often able to provide redress for individual victims where neither national government nor global actors are able to do so. Based on Shelton's analysis, do you think the money currently expended on the global enforcement system would be better spent on regional enforcement bodies? Consider also Anne Bayefsky's cogent critique of global treaty enforcement (Reading 25 in Chapter 5 of this volume); why not simply divert those perhaps-wasted resources to the more-effective regional bodies?

5. Shelton notes that many of the regional systems have adopted language used in other regional systems and have cited judicial precedent from other systems in their own judicial proceedings. To what extent might these twin processes contribute to the development of more fully functional regional systems in Asia and the Middle East? Given the well-documented—and, perhaps, growing—mistrust felt by those in those two regions for the institutions of the West, do you think such contributions will be welcomed?

6. Do you think there is a "critical mass" of states necessary for a regional human rights enforcement system to be effective? Is there an upper limit beyond which the system begins to suffer the same maladies as the global enforcement system?

7. As of this writing, the United States has yet to become a party to the 1969 American Convention on Human Rights (referenced in Documentary Appendix B). The U.S. is not a party either to the two protocols to the Convention, the first of which provides for protection of second generation rights, and the second of which is dedicated to the abolition of the death penalty. Why do you think the United States is not a party to the Convention and its protocols? Compare the obligations incurred by mere membership in the OAS with the obligations incurred by becoming a party to the Convention and protocols. Will the U.S. ever become a party to the latter two instruments?

8. In August 1975, 33 European states, along with the U.S. and Canada, concluded their Conference on Security and Cooperation in Europe (CSCE) by signing what has come to be known as the Helsinki Final Act (HFA). The HFA contained, among other things, a list of Guiding Principles, which included Principle VII, entitled "Respect for Human Rights and Fundamental Freedoms, Including Freedom of Thought, Conscience, Religion, or Belief," and Principle VIII, titled "Equal Rights and Self-Determination of Peoples." These two Principles, along with other provisions of the HFA, were, according to Thomas Buergenthal, "The Helsinki Process: Birth of a Human Rights System," in Richard P. Claude and Burns H. Weston, eds., *Human Rights in the World Community: Issues and Action*, 2nd ed. (Philadelphia: University of Pennsylvania Press, 1992), 256–68, "propaganda that backfired" when the human rights language therein was used by the Solidarity movement in Poland, the Helsinki Watch committees in the former Soviet Union, and Charter 77 in the

former Czechoslovakia to discredit their national governments. Has the ultimate downfall of those governments resulted in an increase in the welfare of the mass of their citizens? Do you think the drafters of the HFA contemplated such a result? Was the change necessary in order to fulfill the HFA provisions?

9. Buergenthal points out that the HFA and the later CSCE documents associated with it are not treaties. Why is it, then, that states adhere to them as if they were law? Does this mean that in fact they have become law, part of international law and not just international politics? Refer briefly to Reading 24 by Harold Koh in Chapter 5 of this volume for pertinent background.

Chapter Seven

National Approaches to Human Rights Implementation

THE implementation of human rights is a responsibility of individual nations as well as of international institutions. Anchored in the many human rights treaties to which states have become party, in customary state practice, and in the general principles of law recognized by the world's different legal systems, it is a responsibility that is made explicit in the UN Charter. According to Articles 55 and 56 of the Charter, all UN member states "pledge themselves to take joint and separate action in cooperation with the (United Nations)" to promote "universal respect for, and observance of, human rights and fundamental freedoms for all without distinction as to race, sex, language or religion."[1]

One significant way in which this state responsibility for the promotion and protection of human rights is exercised is by the adoption of international human rights principles and standards in the national constitutions and basic laws that help to fix the structure of governments. Over one-half of all nations, especially those emerging from colonialism after World War II, have modeled their fundamental rights provisions on the Universal Declaration of Human Rights (UDHR),[2] proclaimed by the UN General Assembly in 1948 as a "foundation for justice and peace in the world."[3] And increasingly states are taking responsibility for promoting internationally defined human rights. Article 7 of the 2003 Constitution of Afghanistan, for example, provides that "the state shall abide by the UN Charter, international treaties and international human rights conventions that Afghanistan has signed and the Universal Declaration of Human Rights." Given that Afghanistan became a party to the 1979 Convention on the Elimination of All Forms of Discrimination

---

1. These and other pertinent provisions of the UN Charter are reprinted in Documentary Appendix A.
2. Adopted Dec. 10, 1948, reprinted and referenced in Documentary Appendix A.
3. See Egon Schwelb, "The Influence of the Universal Declaration of Human Rights on International and National Law," *Proceedings of the 53rd Annual Meeting of the American Society on International Law* (1959): 217–29, at 222–23; and *UN Seminar on the Experience of Different Countries in the Implementation of International Standards of Human Rights*, June 20-July 1, 1983, St/HR/SER.A/15. See also John Humphrey, "The Universal Declaration of Human Rights: Its History, Impact and Juridical Character," in B. G. Ramcharan, ed., *Human Rights: Thirty Years After the Universal Declaration* (The Hague: Nijhoff, 1979): 21–40.

Against Women (CEDAW)[4] in March 2003[5]—indeed, without reservation or other qualification—discrimination against women is thus prohibited in that country. Likewise, the new South African Constitution ties its constitutional rights standards to international norms.[6] Like many others in the post-Cold War era, this new constitution was the result of open processes featuring high levels of grassroots participation. In 1994, for example, the South African Constitutional Assembly invited the involvement of first-time voters with the widely advertised maxim: "You've made your mark, now have your say"—a call that elicited 2 million submissions from individuals as well as groups throughout South African civil society. President Nelson Mandela signed the resulting human rights-rich instrument in 1996.[7] Thus, international human rights principles and standards have become not only matters of constitutional obligation but, as well, matters of increasingly universal expectation—a consequence that, over time, makes the goal of worldwide humane governance more than a utopian dream.

Two innovative examples of national constitutions supporting internationally defined human rights merit special notice. The 1983 Constitution of The Netherlands contains a comprehensive modern bill of rights. Also, it takes notice of international human rights responsibilities and acknowledges them as national obligations. Article 93 of the 1983 Constitution stipulates that "provisions of treaties and of international instruments, which may be binding on all persons by virtue of their contents, shall become binding after they have been published,"[8] a constitutional reflection of the Dutch "monistic" view of the relationship between national and international law holding that the two are part of the same legal order and that the former is subservient to the latter. The operative consequence of this perspective is dramatic. In their study titled "A Statistical Analysis of Dutch Human Rights Case Law," Manfred Nowak and Herman von Hebel show that, today, Dutch lawyers increasingly invoke human rights treaty provisions in national courts, and conclude that "it is more and more the International Bill of Rights adopted by the United Nations and the Council of Europe which determines the human rights position of the Dutch people."[9]

The Philippines Constitution, promulgated in February 1987 with the plebiscite support of 78 percent of Filipino voters is a much celebrated (even if not always respected) example of a government charter influenced by internationally articulated human rights principles and standards. In an innovative provision, it commands that "All educational institutions shall include the study of the Constitution . . . [and] shall . . . foster love of humanity, respect for human rights . . . and teach the rights and duties of citizenship."[10]

The adoption of international human rights norms, principles, and standards in national constitutions and basic laws is of course but one way in which states exercise their

4. Concluded Dec. 19, 1979, referenced in Documentary Appendix B.

5. Regarding Afghanistan's adherence to human rights treaties, CEDAW included, see Mir Hermatullah Sadat, "The Implementation of Constitutional Human Rights in Afghanistan," *Human Rights Brief* 11, no. 3 (Spring 2004): 48–50, at 71.

6. See, e.g., Lucrecia Seafield, "South Africa: The Interdependence of All Human Rights," in Abdullahi Ahmed An-Na`im, ed., *Human Rights Under African Constitutions: Realizing the Promise for Ourselves* (Philadelphia: University of Pennsylvania Press, 2003), 295–341, at 306–7.

7. Vivien Hart, *Democratic Constitution-Making*, Special Report 103 (Washington, D.C.: United States Institute of Peace, 2003), 8–9.

8. The Netherlands Constitution is reproduced in Robert L. Maddex, *Constitutions of the World* (Washington, D.C.: Congressional Quarterly, 1995), 183–86.

9. Manfred Nowak and Herman von Hebel, "A Statistical Analysis of Dutch Human Rights Case Law," in Thomas B. Jabine and Richard P. Claude, eds., *Human Rights and Statistics: Getting the Record Straight* (Philadelphia: University of Pennsylvania Press, 1991), 313–27.

10. The Constitution of the Republic of the Philippines, art. 14, §3(1)(2), is reprinted in Fernand de Varennes, *Asia-Pacific Human Rights Documents and Resources* (Boston: Nijhoff, 2000), 2: 333–49, at 346–67.

international legal responsibility to promote and protect human rights. While seldom with explicit acknowledgment of legal obligation, increasingly the promotion and protection of human rights has become a fixture of modern-day diplomacy and foreign policy as well. Indeed, in countries with significant foreign aid programs—e.g., Canada, the Netherlands, Norway, Sweden, the United States—human rights advocacy and enforcement has become the province not only of foreign policy-makers but also of legislators dealing with foreign economic assistance and development. Additionally, albeit still on a limited scale (especially in the United States among Western countries), international human rights are implemented by way of litigation in domestic courts.

The readings in this chapter explore these nationally based human rights realms in acutely targeted terms, largely through the prism of United States policy and practice. In Reading 28 ("No Exceptions? The United States Pick-and-Choose Approach to Human Rights"), Michael Ignatieff addresses the ambivalence and exceptionalism which, American popular wisdom to the contrary notwithstanding, has marked official human rights practices in U.S. domestic and foreign policy generally. In Reading 29 ("Civil Remedies for Gross Human Rights Violations"), Michael Ratner turns our attention to the persuasive arts of legal advocacy and decision by assessing the U.S. judicial enforcement of human rights standards based on legislation such as the Alien Tort Claims Act (1789) and the Torture Victims Protection Act (1987). Finally, in Reading 30 ("Humanitarian Intervention: Imperatives and Problematics"), Richard Falk, moving us from persuasive to key coercive strategy, invites reconsideration of the long-time controversial doctrine of "humanitarian intervention," made the more controversial by U.S. President George W. Bush's *preventive*—not *preemptive*—post-9/11 attack against Saddam Hussein's Iraq on March 20, 2003. Previous to his essay, Falk commented in *The Nation* in July 2003 that "the Bush Administration has been doing its best to wreck world order as it had been evolving, and that part of the wreckage is the abandonment of legal restraints on the use of international force, the heart and soul of the UN Charter."[11]

FOREIGN POLICY AND HUMAN RIGHTS

Because of American "superpower" status, U.S. foreign policy produces many ripple effects around the world. A case in point is the Philippines. Before the election of President Carter in 1976, public discussion of human rights in Ferdinand Marcos's Philippines was suspect, as was all political talk. With the advent of Carter's human rights rhetoric in U.S.-Filipino diplomacy during the martial law years of the late 1970s, however, Filipinos became newly emboldened to question their government. As one attorney in Manila stated in 1977, "since so much can now be said and done in the name of 'human rights' which was previously forbidden, it is not surprising that there is much curiosity about these human rights."[12] National human rights NGOs such as the Task Force Detainees-Philippines, at considerable risk, documented human rights abuses throughout the island nation, particularly detailing the incidence of torture in multiple detention camps. Their reports, secreted out of the country, were delivered to sympathetic human rights groups overseas such as the International Commission of Jurists and Amnesty International. They in turn pressured

11. "Humanitarian Intervention: A Forum," *The Nation* 277, no. 2 (July 14, 2003): 11–20, Richard Falk at 12.
12. Quoted in Richard P. Claude, "Human Rights in the Philippines and U.S. Responsibility," in Peter G. Brown and Douglas MacLean, eds., *Human Rights and U.S. Foreign Policy: Principles and Applications* (Lexington, Mass.: Lexington Books, 1979), 229–54, at 247.

the Carter Administration on grounds of human rights violations to threaten to cut off security assistance to the Marcos government.

The process of indigenous NGOs networking with sympathetic overseas groups to effect external sanctions and diplomatic pressure is an important phenomenon in modern human rights politics. Identified as the "boomerang effect" by political scientists Margaret Keck and Kathryn Sikkink, this transnational channel is sometimes effective.[13] Indeed, widespread concern about abuses of human rights was one of the decisive factors that finally tumbled the Marcos tyranny in 1986. There is thus good reason to believe that the Carter Administration's concern for human rights in the Philippines (and elsewhere) helped to make talk of human rights among tyrannized populations legitimate and ultimately to come back to hit the abusive target.[14]

Of course, the effect of the boomerang process depends on diverse circumstances, including world opinion, the sympathetic foreign policy of various pressuring governments, and their respective leverage over the offending regime. Much depends, as well, on the posture of response taken by the violator government.

Thomas Risse, Stephen Ropp, and Kathryn Sikkink have categorized the responsive postures of such governments in terms of five phases:[15]

first, repressive regimes seek to squelch the dissemination of information about their transgressions so as to impede the activation of a human rights response;

second, violator states will deny that allegations are true and that pressure from overseas is legitimate, a ruse sometimes successful in stirring up nationalistic resentment to "outside interference";

third, when "shaming and blaming" initiatives from outside are effective, violator states may make tactical concessions as if to "buy off" the external pressure,[16] concessions that may serve actually to expand human rights activism and, in the estimate of Risse and Sikkink, result in "self-entrapment" also—for example, when the Marcos government denied the use of torture in detention camps, Solicitor General Estelito Mendoza, under challenge by visiting diplomats and relying on bluff, made the boastful but fatal mistake of saying that international human rights groups could interview detainees at random, thereby opening the door to a process that, with popular consciousness attuned to excessive human rights violations, contributed to Filipinos taking to the streets of Manila and ultimately bringing down the Marcos regime in a bloodless "peoples power" revolution in 1986;

fourth, by now chastized and as typified by the new successor government of President Corazon Aquino, governments will enter into a "prescriptive status" wherein they will

13. Margaret E. Keck and Kathryn Sikkink, *Activists Beyond Borders: Advocacy Networks in International Politics* (Ithaca, N.Y.: Cornell University Press, 1998), 12–13. See also Sikkink, *Mixed Signals: U.S. Foreign Policy and Latin America* (Ithaca, N.Y.: Cornell University Press, 2004). Cf. Shale Horowitz and Albrecht Schnabel, eds., *Human Rights and Societies in Transition: Causes, Consequences, Responses* (New York: United Nations University Press, 2004).
14. Claude, "Human Rights in the Philippines," note 12, at 228–54.
15. See Thomas Risse, Stephen Ropp, and Kathryn Sikkink, *The Power of Human Rights: International Norms and Domestic Change* (Cambridge: Cambridge University Press, 1999), 20.
16. The "shaming and blaming effect" with a "self entrapment bonus" is illustrated by Harry G. Barnes, Jr., in "U.S. Human Rights Policies and Chile," saying that without U.S. pressure during the Carter Administration "the DINA [secret police] would probably have continued its previous murderous practices, but . . . perhaps the greatest . . . benefit of the Carter human rights emphasis was the encouragement it gave to the democratic opposition and to the work of groups like the Catholic Church's Vicariate of Solidarity." Jack Donnelly and Debra Liang-Fenton, "Introduction," in Debra Liang-Fenton, ed., *Implementing U.S. Human Rights Policy: Agendas, Policies, and Practices* (Washington, D.C.: United States Institute of Peace Press, 2004), 299–330, at 307.

offer explicit acceptance of human rights standards as legitimate and pledge to cooperate in their promotion and protection, though by dint of the transitional process implement them imperfectly[17]—for example, while the Aquino regime's new Constitution of 1987 proclaimed adherence to internationally defined human rights standards and encouraged human rights dialogue, local NGOs continued to report unacceptably high rates of military and police violence randomly directed at the citizenry; and

fifth, compliance with internationally defined human rights norms enforced habitually on the basis of rule of law.

In analyzing the potential effect of foreign policy on human rights internationally, the Risse-Ropp-Sikkink analysis can be helpful as an analytical and policy tool that takes on refinement and nuance when put in "real world" diplomatic context.

In this regard the diplomatic experience of the late British political scientist Evan Luard in pressing for human rights is noteworthy.[18] He argued that, by relying on diplomacy to nudge regimes toward human rights compliance, there always is the possibility of direct as well as indirect positive consequences. Changes may be induced even within the government itself when officials who favor a more humane policy (partly because of its foreign policy effects) prevail to some extent over those who favor a repressive policy (some Filipino torturers under the repressive Marcos regime faced military disciplinary action, for example). Even if these direct effects are minimal and symbolic, Luard avers, "it is the international climate as a whole which will be altered by expressions of concern in such matters."[19] Hopefully, the expectations that are placed on all members of the international community are slowly changed.

Luard's analysis of human rights diplomacy is taken a step further by R. J. Vincent, who argues that, in addition to the indirect and more obvious consequences of placing diplomacy in service to human rights, "there is also a deeper sense in which human rights have arrived in foreign policy than that which observes the presence in foreign offices of desks bearing that title."[20] Vincent continues:

> Human rights now play a part in the decision about the legitimacy of a state (and of other actors and institutions) in international society, about whether what it is or what it does is sanctioned or authorized by law or right. It's not now enough for a state to be, and to be recognized as, sovereign. Nor is it enough for it to be a nation-state in accordance with the principle of self-determination. It must also act domestically, in such a way as not to offend against the basic rights of individuals and groups within its territory.[21]

Self-styled "realists," on the other hand, dismiss interest in human rights worldwide as a short-term fad. William F. Buckley, Jr., for one, once called the promotion of human rights through foreign policy a kind of naive evangelism bound to founder on the rocks of international political reality.[22] Such "realist" skepticism, however, seems belied by the long-term

17. The "prescriptive status in a transitional country" is further illustrated in "Getting It Right: U.S. Policy in South Africa." Pauline H. Baker says, "Unlike many other societies in conflict, South Africa experienced a successful transition in part because it did not actually collapse as a state." Donnelly and Fenton, 85–114, at 100. See also generally Carla Hesse and Robert Post, eds., *Human Rights in Political Transitions: Gettysburg to Bosnia* (Cambridge, Mass.: Zone Books, MIT Press, 1999).
18. See Evan Luard, *Human Rights and Foreign Policy* (Oxford: Pergamon Press, 1981), 1–38.
19. Ibid., 37.
20. R. J. Vincent, *Human Rights and International Relations* (Cambridge: Cambridge University Press, 1986), 130.
21. Ibid.
22. William F. Buckley, Jr., "Human Rights and Foreign Policy: A Proposal," *Foreign Affairs* 58 (1980): 775–96.

commitments that many governments clearly have made, including the United States, to institutionalize their human rights programs.

But of course questions remain. Is it not true that shaping foreign policy is often made difficult by the inevitable tension between, on the one hand, demand for the sovereign independence of states and, on the other, demand for the expansion of freedom and democracy? Noninterference can, in effect, be the equivalent of tolerating oppression; urging freedom and human rights upon others can create international tension.

Whether this dilemma is real or only apparent is a topic of ongoing debate in the United States and elsewhere, and the outcome is by no means clear. Former Secretary of State Henry A. Kissinger, who dominated foreign policy in the Nixon and Ford administrations, regularly argued against "linking" human rights issues to foreign policy decisions claimed not to be of human rights character, fearing "excessively moralistic" policy may "turn quixotic or dangerous."[23] Kissinger said he supported human rights but that American commitments abroad had to be based not upon moral judgments primarily but upon a realistic assessment of national security priorities. According to Kissinger, neither public threats against violator-regimes nor "grandstand" condemnations of one country by another are likely to produce significant human rights gains. Human rights, he maintained, should be factored into foreign policy, if at all, by means of "quiet diplomacy."

Kissinger's "one size fits all" prudential judgment favoring "quiet diplomacy" was shaped in the icy climate of the Cold War. Since that time, however, it has been displaced by accumulated U.S. Department of State experience, from the Gerald Ford and Jimmy Carter Administrations to those of William Jefferson Clinton and George W. Bush—and made clear in a wide-ranging study of the intervening presidencies published by the U.S. Institute of Peace in 2004. In *Implementing U.S. Human Rights Policy*, political scientists Jack Donnelly and Debra Liang-Fenton summarized 25 years of historical experience and concluded that seven tools have been most commonly used by the United States to respond to human rights concerns abroad:

- *Private diplomacy*: confidential representations between government officials.
- *Public diplomacy*: statements made in the target countries, the United States and international forums by officials of varying seniority that praise, condemn, or otherwise address human rights practices.
- *Cultural, scholarly, and other exchanges and contacts*: increasing or decreasing the range or frequency of sponsored, encouraged, or permitted formal or informal transnational interaction between citizens and private organizations of the United States and the target countries.
- *Economic and political sanctions*: restricting, extending, or threatening to alter access to U.S. resources and official contacts, including diplomatic, political, or military contacts, foreign assistance, debt servicing, investment insurance, trade and arms sales.
- *Democracy promotion*: strengthening civil society and political parties in the target country.
- *Country Reports on Human Rights Practices*: a congressionally mandated annual report produced by the U.S. Department of State, that examines national human rights practices, with special attention to violations or deficiencies and change in behavior, in more than 190 countries.
- Congressional action: hearings, legislation, and nonbinding resolutions that encourage or require the executive branch to act in a particular way.[24]

23. Henry Kissinger, U.S. Secretary of State, *Department of State Bulletin* 69, no. 1792 (Oct. 29, 1973): 527–52.
24. Donnelly and Liang-Fenton, "Introduction," note 16, 3–25, at 10–11.

While this toolbox is large and the tools within it varied, Donnelly and Liang-Fenton conclude, critically, that "we must be aware that sometimes none are employed."[25] They continue: "Often the key foreign policy action of the United States is the decision not to act," such as in the case of Rwanda where the failure of the Clinton Administration in 1994 to call for or undertake humanitarian intervention enabled genocide to take place in that country.[26]

Whether the instruments available for the conduct of foreign policy on behalf of human rights are used well or badly or whether the consequences of any given action or inaction has helped as intended involve important questions. Insofar as the United States is concerned, a presidential administration may fairly be judged in this regard by its choice of goals, instruments, and methods, or at least so argues Michael Ignatieff in his essay: "No Exceptions? The United States Pick-and-Choose Approach to Human Rights" (Reading 28). Persons without appreciation for irony might take this essay as justification for a policy that says "Do what I say, not what I do." But in setting out many examples of apparent inconsistency, the author's larger intent is directed at explanation, much of which boils down to his proposition that America's politics are "significantly to the right of its allies in other liberal democracies . . . on issues like the death penalty, abortion, and welfare, and [its] human rights culture reflects this." The question is: what, if anything, should be done about it? Surely human rights education on a widespread basis, is potentially one answer.[27] But more legislative and judicial sensitivity to human rights among sundry initiatives and projects, including a humane foreign policy that responds with simultaneously cooperative and effective dispatch to prevent or mitigate human rights crises, are part of the answer as well.

LEGISLATIVE IMPLEMENTATION OF HUMAN RIGHTS

In *Liberal America and the Third World*, Robert Packenham shows how, since the 1940s, the United States has sought to use foreign aid legislation to achieve various social and political aims in recipient countries—for example, free enterprise and trade unionism.[28] More recently, these aims have come to include the promotion of "internationally recognized human rights," utilizing especially economic strategies to do the job.[29] Beginning in the 1970s, at the initiative of then Minnesota Representative Don Fraser and Iowa Representative (now Senator) Tom Harkin, Congress sought to influence overseas development policy by attaching several human rights amendments to the Foreign Assistance Act of 1961, for example, in Section 116 (also known as the "Harkin Amendment"):

> No assistance may be provided . . . to the government of any country which engages in a consistent pattern of gross violations of internationally recognized human rights, including torture or cruel, inhuman, or degrading treatment or punishment, prolonged detention without charges, causing the disappearance of persons by the abduction and clandestine detention of those persons or other flagrant denial of the right to life, liberty, and the security of person, unless such assistance will directly benefit the needy people in the country.[30]

25. Ibid., 11.
26. On humanitarian intervention, including in genocidal contexts, see Reading 30 by Richard Falk in this chapter.
27. On human rights education, see Reading 17 by Richard Pierre Claude in Chapter 3 of this volume.
28. Robert Packenham, *Liberal America and the Third World: Political Development Ideas in Foreign Aid and Social Science* (Princeton, N.J.: Princeton University Press, 1973).
29. See generally David Cortright and George A. Lopez, eds., *Smart Sanctions: Targeting Economic Statecraft* (Lanham, Md.: Rowman and Littlefield, 2002).
30. 22 U.S.C. § 2151 (1982).

But Congress did not limit itself to restrictions on development aid for roads, schools, hospital construction projects, and the like. It restricted foreign military assistance as well, seeking, in Section 502B of the Foreign Assistance Act,[31] to cut off arms and military aid to any country engaging in "a consistent pattern of gross violations of human rights . . . unless the President certifies in writing . . . that extraordinary circumstances exist warranting provision of such assistance."

Political scientist David P. Forsythe, who has studied the multiple legislative efforts made by the U.S. Congress to influence foreign aid and foreign policy since 1973, concludes (with co-author Susan Welch) that, by and large, the legislative branch has lacked "the attention span, the will power, and the consensus for effective oversight that would implement the original congressional intent."[32] Effectively carried out or not, however, these legislative developments in the United States since the 1970s have spurred a lively debate over the linking of foreign aid with human rights standards. Supporting the view that the link is essential are the arguments (a) that U.S. foreign aid, since its inception, has been not a gesture of international charity but a tool of foreign policy associated with specific goals consistent with U.S. values; (b) that foreign policy, to be durable, must reflect the values of its constituent people;[33] and (c) that a country that annually appropriates billions of dollars to more than 80 countries cannot deny a sense of purpose or be blind to the consequences of its aid.[34] Additionally, linkage strategy is seen to associate U.S. human rights policy with that of like-minded countries.[35] Canada, the Netherlands, Norway, and Sweden all link their programs of foreign aid with the human rights record of recipient countries. In all of these countries, the term "conditionality" has been added to the jargon of international politics, with legislators debating the merits of making financial and military aid to governments conditional on their respect for human rights.

Whatever the justification for conditional legislation, however, the debate over the appropriate place for ethical considerations in implementing foreign aid policy has the allure of an impressionist painting. From a distance we can discern the features of the painting quite clearly, but when we move closer to analyze the component elements, the image dissolves and we wonder why it seemed so clear. The analogy seems to characterize the approaches of Carter and Reagan to integrating human rights into their foreign policy. According to David Carleton and Michael Stohl, if one moves from the human rights rhetoric of these two administrations to the empirical details of the implementation of their policy, some of the most apparent differences blur;[36] while their rhetoric contrasts sharply, the two administrations were remarkably similar in the implementation of their respective aid distribution programs. Both leaned heavily on the exception clauses in the human rights statutes and neither "acted in accordance with the established human rights package."[37] Consistent with Ignatieff's thesis on "American exceptionalism," President Clinton likewise waived requirements—for example, in respect of the amendment to the 1997

31. 22 U.S.C. § 2304 (1982).
32. Susan Welch and David P. Forsythe, "Foreign Policy Attitudes of American Human Rights Supporters," *HRQ* 5 (1983): 491–509, at 506.
33. See, e.g., Tom Harkin, "Human Rights and Foreign Aid: Forging an Unbreakable Link," in Brown and MacLean, *Human Rights and U.S. Foreign Policy*, note 12, at 15–26.
34. See Henry Shue, "Some Principles for U.S. Foreign Policy," in Shue, *Basic Rights: Subsistence, Affluence, and U.S. Foreign Policy* (Princeton, N.J.: Princeton University Press, 1980), 155–74.
35. David P. Forsythe, "Human Rights and Foreign Policy in Comparative Perspective," in Forsythe, *Human Rights in International Relations* (New York: Cambridge University Press, 2000), 139–62.
36. David Carleton and Michael Stohl, "The Foreign Policy of Human Rights: Rhetoric and Reality from Jimmy Carter to Ronald Reagan," *HRQ* 7 (1985): 205–29.
37. Ibid., 227.

Foreign Operations Appropriations Act of Vermont Senator Patrick Leahy ("the Leahy Law') that would have the Colombian government meet certain human rights conditions before security assistance could be released.[38]

JUDICIAL ENFORCEMENT OF HUMAN RIGHTS

In the United States, the judiciary's role in implementing international human rights principles and standards has been cast in a minor role. A case decided in 1952 by the Supreme Court of California, *Sei Fujii v. State of California*,[39] propounded the doctrine that the human rights provisions of the UN Charter, though a binding treaty informed by the UDHR, were nevertheless not "self-executing"—that is, they "do not purport to impose legal obligations on the individual member nations or to create rights in private persons."[40] Technically this precedent was binding only on the courts of California (no federal court, including the U.S. Supreme Court, ever having ruled on the precise issue to date), and for this and other reasons litigants in later years[41] made efforts to invoke the UN Charter and the Universal Declaration to challenge such national actions as the United States' involvement in the Vietnam war[42] and U.S. support "aiding the forces of racial repression in Southern Africa."[43] However, as the late Richard Lillich thoroughly documented in 1978, such efforts in state and federal courts, while well intentioned, have commonly proved abortive.[44] True, as documented in footnote 44, Lillich's evaluation was formulated during the last half of the Carter Administration. However, it was tempered with hope and a consequent plea. Lillich wrote:

> To date the cases that have been litigated before the United States courts have not been winners, at least in the traditional sense, but they have achieved the not inconsiderable result of calling increased attention to the issue of implementing international human rights law. At the very least, they have raised the consciousness of lawyers,

38. See Debra Liang-Fenton, "Conclusion, What Works?" in Liang-Fenton, *Implementing U.S. Human Rights Policy*, note 16, 435–61, at 441–42. See also the Human Rights Watch website at http://66.102. 9.104/search?q=cache:DbNLc7aoX9MJ:www.hrw.org/worldreport99/americas/colombia3.html+leahy+ amendment&hl=en. The Leahy Law's jurisdiction has expanded since it first appeared as part of the 1997 Foreign Operations Appropriations Act (FOAA), P.L. 104–208. Initially, the law applied only to the State Department International Narcotics Control Program. In 1998 it was broadened to include all security assistance programs funded through the FOAA, and in 1999 was extended to include training programs authorized under the Defense Department appropriations bill. In the 2001 FOAA, the Leahy Law (Sec. 563 of P.L. 106–429) states that "None of the funds made available by this Act may be provided to any unit of the security forces of a foreign country if the Secretary of State has credible evidence that such unit has committed gross violations of human rights, unless the Secretary determines and reports to the Committees on Appropriations that the government of such country is taking effective measures to bring the responsible members of the security forces unit to justice."
39. 38 Cal.2d 718, 242 P.2d 617 (1952).
40. 38 Cal.2d at 722; 242 P.2d at 620–21. The California Supreme Court reversed the state District Court of Appeals insofar as the district court had based its decision on the UN Charter and the UDHR. However, it proceeded to hold the Alien Land Law invalid on the grounds that it violated the equal protection clause of the Fourteenth Amendment to the U.S. Constitution. On "self-executing" and "non-self-executing" agreements, see Burns H. Weston, "Treaty Power," in Leonard W. Levy, Kenneth L. Karst, and Dennis J. Mahoney, eds., *Encyclopedia of the American Constitution*, 2nd ed. (New York: Macmillan, 1986), 6: 2721–22.
41. Cf. Bert B. Lockwood, Jr., "The United Nations Charter and United States Civil Rights Litigation: 1946–1955," *Iowa Law Review* 69, no. 4 (1984): 901–56.
42. See, e.g., *Mitchell v. United States*, 386 U.S. 972 (1967).
43. See, e.g., *New York Times Co. v. City of New York, Commission on Human Rights*, 41 N.Y. 2d 345; 361 N.E. 2d 63 (1977).
44. Richard B. Lillich, "The Role of Domestic Courts in Promoting International Human Rights Norms," *New York Law School Law Review* 24 (1978): 153–78.

judges, government officials and the general public—both in the United States and abroad—to the existence and, perhaps more importantly, to the potential of this body of law. Human rights advocates should continue to use the courts not only to seek relief or establish useful precedent, but also to marshal public opinion against governments, including that of the United States, which violate human rights.[45]

As it happens, Lillich's hope and plea have borne fruit. The situation of human rights in American courts has not changed greatly since he wrote, but it has changed in some very important ways, particularly in relation to the use of U.S. federal courts by non-U.S. nationals seeking redress for "gross" human rights abuses in their native lands.

"National courts, such as those of Spain and Belgium," writes Michael Ratner in Reading 29 in this chapter, "are beginning to employ the concept of universal jurisdiction and the Convention Against Torture[46] to bring perpetrators of human rights violations to justice." In the United States, he observes, "It all began . . . with the landmark 1980 decision of the United States Court of Appeals for the Second Circuit, *Filártiga v. Peña-Irala*,"[47] a civil suit filed in Brooklyn by Paraguayan nationals against a former Paraguayan police official in 1979 that succeeded where previous cases had failed, and thus revealed the potential in U.S. courts for international human rights law. Ratner, Director of the Center for Constitutional Rights (CCR) in New York City which brought the suit on behalf of the Filártigas, describes the development and outcome of the case wherein, initially, a federal district court judge ruled that the family of a seventeen-year-old Paraguayan youth who had been tortured and murdered in Paraguay was entitled to $10.4 million in damages from the former Paraguayan police official who was responsible for his torture and death and who had later moved to New York. The decision rested on the Alien Tort Claims Act of 1789 (ATCA), granting jurisdiction to U.S. Federal Courts over "any civil action by an alien for a tort only, committed in violation of the law of nations or a treaty of the United States."[48] Lawyers for the CCR claimed that the ATCA gave U.S. courts jurisdiction to hear claims stemming from injuries inflicted abroad if the wrongdoer later was found in the United States. On appeal from the District Court, the Court of Appeals accepted that argument and permitted the survivors of Joelito Filártiga to sue former Police Chief Américo Peña, then living in Brooklyn. In awarding damages on remand in 1984, Judge Eugene H. Nickerson ruled in part that the acts of torture described in the case were "so monstrous as to make Peña an outlaw around the globe" under the tenets of customary international law.[49]

Filártiga v. Peña-Irala marks the first time that the U.S. courts ventured into an area traditionally reserved for the executive and legislative branches of government, branches that often are too constrained by political interests to take effective action in halting or remedying human rights violations. The case is of more than academic interest because it foreshadowed similar suits against torturers and death-squad members from Argentina,[50] the Philippines,[51] and elsewhere who have sought refuge in the United States. It provides a

45. Ibid., 177.
46. Convention against Torture and Other Cruel, Inhuman or Degrading Treatment or Punishment (Dec. 10, 1984), referenced in Documentary Appendix B.
47. 630 F. 2d 876 (2d Cir., 1980). The case is presented in compelling and highly readable terms by historian Richard Alan White, *Breaking Silence: The Case That Changed the Face of Human Rights* (Washington, D.C.: Georgetown University Press, 2004).
48. 28 U.S.C. § 1350 (1976).
49. 577 F.Supp. 860 (E.D.N.Y., 1984).
50. *Forti v. Suarez-Mason*, 672 F. Supp. 1531 (N.D.Cal. 1987), on reconsideration, 694 F.Supp. 707 (N.D. Cal. 1988), resulting in a $21 million award to the plaintiffs.
51. *Sison v. Marcos*, 103 F.3d 789 (9th Cir., 1997).

glimpse of a world community in which states establish themselves as advocates and defenders of universal human rights principles in the more or less objective atmosphere of their court rooms.

That hopeful prospect notwithstanding, the U.S. Department of Justice in 2004 asked the Supreme Court to sweep the ATCA cases off the books because using American courts to settle torture cases in other countries "interferes with the conduct of U.S. foreign policy." At least that's what the George W. Bush Administration said in the brief it filed in the case of *Sosa v. Alvarez-Machain.*[52] The case involved a former Mexican policeman, José Sosa, whom the U.S. Drug Enforcement Agency (DEA) persuaded to kidnap Dr. Alvarez-Machain, a Mexican citizen in Mexico. The DEA thought the doctor helped to kill one of its agents. Sosa did the DEA's bidding and forcibly detained and brought Alvarez-Machain from Mexico to California in 1990 to stand trial for the murder. In 1992, however, a trial judge acquitted him, finding that the government's case was based on "hunches" and the "wildest speculation." Dr. Alvarez-Machain then sued his kidnapper in a California federal court and won. The Ninth Circuit Court of Appeals upheld this decision, and Sosa appealed to the U.S. Supreme Court. The U.S. Department of Justice and Department of State filed a brief in support of the kidnapper, Sosa, seeking to eliminate the use of ATCA by survivors of human rights violations. Before the U.S. Supreme Court in that case, the Deputy Solicitor General argued that the ATCA, passed in 1789, was never designed to be used in human rights cases, but simply to protect the rights of ambassadors in foreign countries.[53]

In a complicated cluster of opinions, with Justice David Souter writing the "opinion of the Court," the Supreme Court rejected Dr. Alvarez-Machain's claim for relief based on his arbitrary arrest and detention in Mexico, concluding that his particular treatment "violates no norm of customary international law sufficiently well defined as to support the creation of a federal remedy." However, it also rejected the government's anti-ATCA arguments and upheld the fundamental reasoning of recent ATCA cases, beginning with *Filártiga v. Peña-Irala* in 1980 and carefully distinguishing between ATCA claims where the international legal norms are "specific, universal, and obligatory" and claims such as the arbitrary arrest suffered by Dr. Alvarez-Machain that fail to meet this test.[54] It is noteworthy, too, that the Court chose to strengthen its reasoning by referring positively to the 1992 Torture Victims Protection Act[55] which legislatively endorses the use of civil suits to vindicate torture victims' rights and extends such rights to citizens and not just aliens. Also noteworthy, in closing, is the fact that the Justice Department drew the Supreme Court's attention, approvingly, to George Washington's Farewell Address counsel that "no nation has a right to intermeddle in the internal concerns of another"—ironically at the very time the United States was involved in military intervention in Iraq, claimed *post hoc* to be humanitarian.

---

52. *Sosa v. Alvarez-Machain,* 540 U.S. 1160 (2004).

53. The Bush Administration's lawyers argued as well that, if the Supreme Court did not disable this ancient statute, then, as a result of war in Afghanistan and Iraq, some of the inmates at the U.S. naval base at Guantánamo Bay might be enabled to file a suit against the United States. Two days after oral argument, the famous photos of U.S.-sponsored torture at Abu Ghraib were published. Whether the photos and the weakness of the government's arguments played any role in the Supreme Court's negative reaction is publicly unknown, but the decision ignored the administration's policy arguments.

54. Parts I and III of the opinion were decided unanimously. Part II was joined by Chief Justice Rehnquist, and Justices Stevens, O'Connor, Scalia, Kennedy, and Thomas. Part IV was joined by Justices Stevens, O'Connor, Kennedy, Ginsburg, and Breyer. Justice Scalia filed an opinion concurring in part and concurring in the judgment, in which Chief Justice Rehnquist and Justice Thomas joined. Justice Ginsburg filed an opinion concurring in part and concurring in the judgment in which Justice Breyer joined. Justice Breyer filed an opinion concurring in part and concurring in the judgment.

55. 28 U.S.C. §1350 (1992).

HUMANITARIAN INTERVENTION

The war in Iraq, begun in 2000, has challenged thoughtful people everywhere with difficult moral and legal questions. The explosion of critical literature on this topic is one indication of serious concern.[56] The editors of *The Nation*, for example, opened their pages to a twelve-person debate under the title "Humanitarian Intervention: A Forum."[57]

Richard Falk, author of Reading 30 in this chapter, weighed into this debate recounting that George W. Bush came into the White House in 2000 arguing against "nation building" and "generally skeptical of the entire humanitarian agenda, opposing any connection with the International Criminal Court and seeking to minimize the relevance of the UN."[58] In Falk's view, the doctrine of humanitarian intervention constituted a "post hoc rationalization for uses of force otherwise difficult to reconcile with international law." With the U.S. invasion of Iraq, American policy "morphed into an imperial war," Falk argued, hiding its true character "in the fog of moralizing rhetoric." Against the background of this critical perspective, Falk's essay in this chapter ("Humanitarian Intervention: Imperatives and Problematics") explores the historical and normative status of arguably justifiable interventionary goals as matters stood before the U.S. invasion of Iraq. The legal dimension of his essay invokes precedents and advances legal arguments that might justify humanitarian intervention in extreme cases. "What makes this subject-matter challenging from a normative perspective of law and ethics," he argues against the relatively recent backdrop of Rwanda (1994) and Kosovo (1999), "is that it is neither beneficial to give a green light to all interventionary diplomacy that proclaims humanitarian goals nor to absolutize the norm of non-intervention by posting a red light that prohibits humanitarian encroachments on sovereignty altogether."

When talking about the unilateral use of superpower force, it is well to be at least skeptical of the sincerity of those who invoke the doctrine of humanitarian intervention, a point of view strongly endorsed by Will D. Verwey, a Dutch professor of international law, and shared by many others.[59] Verwey argues that such action, when not authorized by the United Nations, presumptively "reflects, in essence, power politics on a hegemonical basis, not a legal right of any kind."[60] He proposes, instead that any state or group of states using the label "humanitarian intervention" to justify the use of armed force should be prepared to submit evidence to the UN that meets seven conditions or tests of international legality: (1) that the intervening state has a "relative disinterest" in the situation, in the sense that its overriding concern is the protection of human rights; (2) that there is an emergency situation in which fundamental human rights of a non-political nature are being violated or are about to be violated on a massive scale; (3) that only a last-resort armed action can

56. See, e.g., Michael C. Davis, Wolfgang Dietrich, Bettina Scholdan, and Dieter Sepp, eds., *International Intervention in the Post-Cold War World: Moral Responsibility and Power Politics* (Armonk, N.Y.: M.E. Sharpe, 2004); Martha Finnemore, *The Purpose of Intervention: Changing Beliefs About the Use of Force* (Ithaca, N.Y.: Cornell University Press, 2003); William J. Lahneman, ed., *Military Intervention: Cases in Context for the Twenty-First Century* (Lanham, Md.: Rowman and Littlefield, 2004); Anthony F. Lang, Jr., ed., *Just Intervention* (Washington, D.C.: Georgetown University Press, 2003); Anne Orford, *Reading Humanitarian Intervention: Human Rights and the Use of Force in International Relations* (New York: Cambridge University Press, 2003). See also "Agora: Future Implications of the Iraq Conflict," *AJIL* 97, no. 3 (2003): 553–642; "Agora (continued): Future Implications of the Iraq Conflict," *AJIL* 97, no. 4 (2003): 803–72.
57. "Humanitarian Intervention: A Forum," note 11.
58. Ibid., 12.
59. See Will D. Verwey, "Humanitarian Intervention," in Antonio Cassese, ed., *The Current Legal Regulation of the Use of Force* (Dordrecht: Nijhoff, 1986), 57–78.
60. Ibid., 70.

save the actual or potential victims; (4) that there is not enough time to await action by the United Nations or UN action has proved ineffectual; (5) that the impact on the authority structure of the target state will be minimal; (6) that military action is proportional to the requirements of the rescue mission; and (7) that the action does not threaten to incur more human losses than it seeks to prevent.[61] While Falk's jurisprudential premises differ from Verwey, he is not at odds with Verwey's seven tests, as evidenced by the compatible eleven "threshold" and "contextual" principles propounded in 2000 by the Kosovo Commission in which he played an important creative part.

In 2004, the UN Secretary General's High-level Panel on Threats, Challenges and Change, without explicitly referencing American initiatives in the Middle East, assessed current threats to international peace and security and stated that the fact that force *can* legally be used, does not always mean that, as a matter of good conscience and good sense, it *should* be used. Avoiding "Security Council positivism"—whatever the Security Council decides is sufficient to justify the use of force—the Panel formulated five criteria for legitimate humanitarian intervention similar to those advanced by Verwey and Falk (i.e., seriousness of threat, proper purpose, last resort, proportional means, and balance of consequences). In deciding on whether or not to authorize or apply military force, it said, the Security Council and anyone else involved in such decisions should always consider these guidelines. While they "will not produce agreed conclusions with push-button predictability," the Panel observed, they should "significantly improve the chances of reaching international consensus on what have been in recent years deeply divisive issues."[62]

Many commentators have pointed out that, in a world made up of countries pledged to the objectives of the UN Charter, caution, restraint, and skepticism are called for in response to any effort to excuse the use of armed force in the name of human rights. As Thomas Franck and Nigel Rodley observed with irony over three decades ago, "nothing would be a more foolish footnote to man's [sic] demise than that his [sic] final destruction was occasioned by a war to ensure human rights."[63]

61. Ibid., 74–75.
62. Report of the High-level Panel on Threats, Challenges and Change, "A More Secure World: Our Shared Responsibility," UN Doc. A/59/565 (Dec. 2, 2004), 53–58, at 57.
63. Thomas M. Franck and Nigel S. Rodley, "After Bangladesh: The Law of Humanitarian Intervention by Military Force," *AJIL* 67 (1973): 275–305, at 300.

28. MICHAEL IGNATIEFF *No Exceptions? The United States Pick-and-Choose Approach to Human Rights*

American don't see it this way, but the country with the most puzzling human rights record in the world is their own. The global ascendancy of human rights would not have happened without American leadership, yet the United States refuses to comply with important international rights covenants. Even as it criticizes the human rights records of dozens of countries, the United States resists when its own human rights performance—on capital punishment, for example—is called into question.

This is the hypocrisy that America is often accused of, by its foes and sometimes by its friends. For most Americans the charge is insulting: Why should the land of Thomas Jefferson and Abraham Lincoln allow others to lecture it about rights? Others dismiss the charge as irrelevant: As long as the United States is the sole superpower and can impose its will on notorious human rights violators, what does it matter if critics say it doesn't practice what it preaches? To most of its citizens, America is exceptional, and it's only natural that it should take exception to certain international standards.

Yet the question of whether hypocrisy actually costs the United States something needs to be addressed. And, since America's relationship to human rights is at the core of much of the foreign critique of its behavior abroad, it is important for America to explain why it is exceptional, first to itself and then to the rest of the world.

We need a clear sense of just how different America is. The United States exempts itself from international rights standards in several important ways.

First, the government refuses to sign some international agreements, like the Mine Ban Treaty,[1] that have been signed by Canada, Australia, almost all the countries of the European Union, and Latin American democracies like Chile, Brazil, and Colombia.

Then, the U.S. Senate refuses to ratify other agreements like the Rome Statute[2]—which created the International Criminal Court and is supported by most of its allies—and the Convention on the Rights of the Child,[3] which every other country except Somalia has agreed to.

Next, even when the United States does sign and ratify agreements, it fails to pass the legislation that would give them the force of law. Or the United States imposes so many caveats about particular provisions that the treaties' effect on American law is nil. One example is the International Covenant on Civil and Political Rights (ICCPR),[4] which the United States ratified with reservations to shield its laws allowing for the death penalty and protecting free speech under the First Amendment.

In addition, the United States has refused to comply with obligations that it has agreed to under the United Nations Charter requiring payment of UN dues, under the Vienna treaty mandating that police inform foreign prisoners (including those accused of capital crimes) that they have a right to seek help from their consulates, and under the Geneva Convention governing the status of wartime prisoners[5] like those at Guantánamo Bay in Cuba.

Finally, the United States is indifferent to legal decisions of other countries. In the words of the Supreme Court Justice Antonin Scalia, "We think such comparative analysis inappropriate to the task of interpreting a constitution, though it was of course quite relevant to the task of writing one." America's European allies, by contrast, have signed on to the European Convention on Human Rights and a European court with power to review national legislation under that convention. While most American judges look inward, the judiciaries of other countries increasingly look to each other: Israeli judges survey Canadian precedents on cases about the rights of linguistic and religious minorities, and the South African Constitutional Court studies German cases to interpret claims.

As international rights conventions proliferate and states like South Africa and Canada create new human rights charters, the Bill of Rights in the U.S. Constitution stands out in ever sharper relief as a late 18th-century model surrounded by late 20th-century ones—a grandfather clock in a shop window of Swatches. As the metaphor implies, newer is not necessarily better, and the grandfather clock is still keeping good time. But what once was a symbol of America's eminence as a rights protector is now out of sync with the constitutions of other states.

The roots of America's exceptionalism lie in the United States' distinctive history and legal tradition—a mix of democratic principles from the Enlightenment and the struggle for self-determination against British colonialism, which left in its wake a lingering distrust of the state as guardian of individual rights.

The Bill of Rights makes no reference to socioeconomic rights—the entitlements to food, shelter, health care, and unemployment insurance

---

1. Convention on the Prohibition of the Use, Stockpiling, Production and Transfer of Anti-Personnel Mines and on Their Destruction, concluded Sept. 18, 1997, referenced in Documentary Appendix B.
2. Rome Statute of the International Criminal Court, concluded July 17, 1998, referenced in Documentary Appendix B.
3. Concluded Nov. 2, 1989, referenced in Documentary Appendix B.
4. Concluded Dec. 16, 1966, reprinted and referenced in Documentary Appendix A.
5. Geneva Convention (III) Relative to the Treatment of Prisoners of War, concluded Aug. 12, 1949, referenced in Documentary Appendix B.

that are standard in international agreements and in the laws of post-World War II European states and emerging democracies like Poland and the Czech Republic.

Instead of defining rights as positive entitlements, the Constitution defines them as negative protections against government intrusion, for example by ordering that "Congress shall make no law" limiting free speech. And it protects rights, like the right to bear arms, that other modern constitutions don't mention at all. American rights are distinctive, then, both for what they include and for what they exclude.

American law is also distinctive in how it interprets rights that other countries try to protect as well. Consider three examples: free speech, protection against cruel and unusual punishment, and the right to life. First Amendment law affords more protection to the rights of speakers than the laws of most other liberal democratic states. Canada, France, Germany, and Switzerland permit the punishment of Holocaust deniers. New Zealand treats inciting racial hatred as a crime. The International Covenant on Civil and Political Rights, supported by 147 countries, says that free speech may be trumped if the speech threatens public order; defames a religious or racial group and thus incites discrimination, hostility, or violence; or promotes war propaganda. In almost all cases, U.S. law does none of these things.

At the same time, 110 nations around the world have abolished the death penalty, while in the United States, 38 states and the federal government continue to execute adults . . . despite the constitutional ban on cruel and unusual punishment. This is the example of American exceptionalism most criticized in Europe. Finally, other countries like Canada, Britain, and France give a woman's right to choose some legal priority, providing for at least early-term abortion, while in the United States fetal rights are more contested because of the right-to-life movement.

In other words, America is an exception in most cases because its politics is significantly to the right of its allies in other liberal democracies. Americans are more conservative on issues like the death penalty, abortion, and welfare, and their human rights culture reflects this.

And there is the weight of racial segregation in America's past. After World War II, the chief opposition to American approval of international human rights covenants came from conservative southern senators who feared that ratification would weaken states' rights and strengthen the power of the federal government to strike down segregation. Meanwhile, leaders like Dr. Martin Luther King, Jr., explicitly linked their national struggle for racial equality to the battle of colonized peoples for freedom.

Where American conservatives once resisted human rights because of race, they now fight the Convention on the Rights of the Child and the Convention on the Elimination of All Forms of Discrimination Against Women as threats to traditional ideas about gender roles and family.

On the other side, liberals who want the U.S. to abolish the death penalty and promote women's and gay rights also want the government to ratify international accords. The force of American exceptionalism is a consequence of the weakness of American liberalism since the 1960s.

As Andrew Moravcsik, a political scientist at Harvard University, has shown, no international rights agreement has a chance of Senate ratification unless that body has a hefty Democratic majority. Since the 1960s, this has rarely happened. Quirks of the American political system also come into play here—the United States requires the votes of two-thirds of senators present for ratification of international treaties, a fact that all by itself gives conservative senators leverage disproportionate to their electoral power.

America's unique nationalism also helps explain its lack of attention to international standards. No other country, with the possible exception of France, defines its identity so exclusively in terms of the rights and freedoms that its own constitution provides. At the same time, the U.S. doesn't share the historic or geographic incentives that propel other countries to embrace international rights. Postwar West Germany adopted new basic laws and the European Convention on Human Rights out of shame about Nazism. The United States, by contrast, feels no need to cleanse its shameful past by signing international covenants. France and Britain have allowed the European Court of Human Rights power to review their own national legislation at least in part to anchor European stability in an institution with transnational authority that is strong enough to prevent the recurrence of German fascism. Meanwhile, the U.S. position as a continental empire, safe between two oceans and with friendly neighbors to the north and south, gives it no strategic reason to seek such covenants.

Instead, American history and geography have created a strong link among self-sufficiency, national pride, and democratic self-government. Paul W. Kahn, a Yale Law School professor, has identified the core of American exceptionalism: deep attachment to popular sovereignty.[6] Behind American suspicion of international human rights law is the belief that Americans should obey only laws that their own representatives have written. What strikes Europeans and Canadians as arrogance, narcissism, or isolationism may be a commitment to law as an expression of national sovereignty. Other countries may care as much about their national sovereignty, but again with the exception of France, they do not believe that their democracy is the best in the world.

The most controversial issue at stake, the death penalty, illustrates this point. If the people of Texas conscientiously believe that the death penalty deters crime, eliminates dangerous offenders, and expresses the values that ought to hold Texas society together—as polls indicate they do, though recently with reservations—then why, Texans might ask, should international preferences trump domestic ones? Rights created by a society's own founders, and interpreted by its own judges, are more legitimate than those written by the unelected legal experts who seek to make abolition of the death penalty universal.

Americans are also sometimes reluctant to embrace international human rights because they are not convinced that these guarantees are superior to their own. The obvious example is free speech: It is not obvious that the International Covenant on Civil and Political Rights favoring public order over free-speech rights is better than American First Amendment law. The issue of how much free speech to allow is infinitely contestable, and is best resolved through national courts and politics. So when the United States ratified the ICCPR, it was wise to exempt itself from the provisions that could require it to pass laws that would conflict with American court decisions. If American rights may sometimes be superior to international ones, and if they have the legitimacy of national sovereignty

though they may not be superior, is it really a problem for America to exempt itself from international standards when it chooses? American exceptionalism may not hinder the United States in promoting human rights abroad. By signing on to international human rights pacts with reservations and exemptions, or by refusing to be bound by some agreements at all, the U.S. manages to maintain leadership in global human rights with the least possible restraint on its own margin of maneuver as the world's sole superpower. Exceptionalism, then, achieves a balance: The United States remains within the framework of international human rights law, but on its own terms. The choice for the rest of the world is to concede or reckon with these exceptional terms, or see the United States stand aside, becoming ever more unilateralist and isolationist.

This defense of the United States does not, however, address the charge of hypocrisy. If America wants to be a human rights leader, the argument goes, it must obey the rules it seeks to champion. Leadership depends on legitimacy, and legitimacy requires consistency. But it's not clear that the effective use of American power in fact depends on being consistent, or on being seen by others as legitimate. Perceived legitimacy eases but it isn't essential to the exercise of power. Being seen as hypocritical or double-dealing may impose some costs on a superpower, but these costs are rarely prohibitive. America has faced a storm of protest about its treatment of the Guantánamo Bay prisoners—a storm that has led the Bush Administration to concede that the Geneva Convention should determine which protections Taliban prisoners (though not Al Qaida ones) receive. At the same time, the prisoners remain, and are likely to remain, in American custody and subject to American justice.

In another example, Slobodan Milosevic [was] in detention in The Hague, thanks in large measure to the pressure of the United States on the Serbian government. America could exert that pressure despite resisting the creation of a permanent criminal court with the power to try American citizens. [*Eds.*—Until his death in 2006, Milosevic claimed he was casualty of victor's justice.] And again, as a matter of equity and ethics, it may be undesirable for the United States to

6. See, e.g., Paul W. Kahn, "Exceptionalism, Popular Sovereignty, and the Rule of Law," in *American Exceptionalism and Human Rights* (Princeton, N.J.: Princeton University Press, 2005), 198–2002.

support international tribunals for others but not for its own citizens. It is less clear, however, that this prevents American support for these tribunals from being effective.

If the hypocrisy of exceptionalism doesn't prevent the U.S. from promoting human rights abroad, then what's really at stake is American identity. Those who wish that America didn't except itself, or excepted itself less often, want the United States to be a certain kind of good international citizen. They want it to be bound, despite its unique power, by international definitions of a state's responsibility to its own people. This identity is supposed to make the U.S. more effective by winning over more friends. But it's really about making America more attractive to itself, a benevolent empire that voluntarily restricts its own sovereignty for the sake of the greater global good.

The problem here is that this benevolent ideal has limited appeal to the American electorate. To most voters, it makes little sense to say, "Why can't you be more like the Europeans?" or less plausibly, "Why can't you be more like the Canadians?" In addition, the identity that internationalists envision is decidedly more liberal than most Americans are comfortable with: against the death penalty, in favor of a woman's right to choose, in favor of allowing American citizens to be tried in international courts.

The point here is not to regard the conservative character of American culture as a fixed feature of the political landscape. Defining the right wing as the permanent center of gravity leaves out fundamental moments in recent history like Franklin Delano Roosevelt's New Deal and Lyndon Johnson's Great Society, both of them national commitments to help the disadvantaged. If we know anything about American politics, it is that the landscape of possibility

shifts, sometimes rapidly. Views on capital punishment are a good example. In the 1960s, only a minority of Americans supported the death penalty—a 1966 Gallup poll showed 42 percent in favor, a 50-year low—and the number of executions dropped sharply. But a complex set of causes, including sharply rising crime rates, reversed the trend by the end of the decade. Now a moratorium on the death penalty in Illinois, along with rising evidence that capital punishment is sometimes inflicted arbitrarily and with racial bias, may again shift American opinion away from executions.

There is an important message here for American human rights activists who are troubled by the hypocrisy of U.S. exceptionalism. Domestic debate and politics, not international pressures, will have much greater impact on America's relationship to international standards. Instead of insisting that the U.S. subscribe to values because most of the world endorses them, human rights activists need to win favor by engaging directly in American politics. They need to focus on the support that America's own traditions about rights lend to the adoption of international standards and to mass that support for the cause of human rights.

Just as it was the authentic American language of freedom—civil rights and blacks' religious faith—that struck down Jim Crow in the South, so it will be national discussion of fair process and legal equality that will change America's standards of punishment. Americans will not believe any truths to be self-evident to which their own men and women of greatness haven't committed themselves. International human rights will have its place, as it had in Martin Luther King, Jr.'s strikingly international conception of his own struggle, but these rights will become strong in America only when their advocates speak in the American vein.

QUESTIONS FOR REFLECTION AND DISCUSSION

1. In *Human Rights and Foreign Policy* (Oxford: Pergamon Press, 1981), 26–27, the late Evan Luard discusses the means of human rights policy. In so doing, he lists "the main types of action which a government can take to influence other states on such matters, in ascending order of urgency: (a) confidential representations to the government concerned; (b) joint representations made with other governments; (c) public statements of concern in parliament or elsewhere; (d) support for calls in such bodies as the UN Commission on Human Rights for investigation of the situation; (e) direct initiation of such action in international bodies; (f) cancellation or postponement of ministerial visits; (g) restraints on cultural and sporting contacts; (h) embargoes on arm sales; (i) reduction in aid programs;

(j) withdrawal of an ambassador; (k) cessation of all aid; (l) breaking of diplomatic relations; (m) trading sanctions." In your view, which of these are most characteristic of U.S. human rights policy and why? Which are the most easily instituted? Why? The most difficult? Would any of them have been adequate to prevent the genocide of more than one million Cambodians during the Pol Pot regime of the mid-1970s? The Tutsis in Rwanda in 1994? Are any of them sufficient to prevent the crimes against humanity taking place in Darfur as this book goes to press? Why? Why not? Note that Luard did not list a show of armed force, military intervention, or other military sanctions. Why? Note also that there is little mention of multilateral action through the United Nations or regional organizations. Why? Is it because he was writing in 1981? That, as a former minister in the British Foreign Office, he was skeptical about a too aggressive policy in support of human rights? To what extent, if at all, should one be concerned about being too aggressive in the pursuit of a human rights policy?

2. Can you think of situations in which some or all of the policy options listed by Evan Luard in Question 1, above, have been utilized by the United States for human rights purposes? If so, have they been more or less successful? More or less unsuccessful? Why? To what extent, historically, has the United States proceeded unilaterally in respect of these options? Multilaterally? In defense of human rights, is it better for the United States and other countries to act unilaterally or multilaterally? Why?

3. Is acting unilaterally the same thing as acting exceptionally? Michael Ignatieff says that the United States tends to act exceptionally in the conduct of its foreign policy, especially in relation to human rights. Do you agree? Disagree? What's the historical evidence? Does the United States act any more exceptionally than any other country in these respects?

4. Ignatieff cites U.S. reluctance to ratify human rights treaties as one form of American exceptionalism. The refusal of the United States to ratify the 1989 Convention on the Rights of the Child (referenced in Documentary Appendix B) is a case in point. So also is the U.S. withdrawal from the Rome Statute of the International Criminal Court (also referenced in Documentary Appendix B). However, while many states ratify human rights treaties many also have no intent of following through on their commitments. Does this fact minimize the exceptionality of U.S. behavior? Does it excuse it? In any event, what, in principle, is wrong with refusing to become party to a human rights treaty? Is it not possible that a treaty may be contrary to a state's perceived self-interests or that it might be poorly crafted?

5. Ignatieff notes also that certain members of the U.S. Supreme Court (e.g., Justice Antonin Scalia) believe the U.S. should not use human rights or other decisions of foreign courts to inform the Court's decisions on issues of American constitutional law, even though other countries engage in precisely this kind of comparative interworking. Do you agree with Justice Scalia that comparative human rights analysis is inappropriate? Why? Why not? Is Justice Scalia's American exceptionalism appropriate or helpful? Inappropriate or unhelpful? Why? Why not? Does it exert a negative effect on the struggle for human rights worldwide? Positive? Something in between? Why?

6. "Behind American suspicion of international human rights law," Ignatieff writes, "is the belief that Americans should obey only laws that their own representatives have written. What strikes Europeans and Canadians as arrogance, narcissism, or isolationism may be a commitment to law as an expression of national sovereignty. Other countries may care as much about their national sovereignty, but again with the exception of France, they do not believe that their democracy is the best in the world." Do you think it is exceptional behavior to trust in your own government's laws? Is it exceptional to believe your democracy is the best in the world? What is it about these behaviors that is exceptional, if anything? What is at the core of American exceptionalism? Citing Yale law professor Paul Kahn, Ignatieff says it is "deep attachment to popular sovereignty." If this is accurate, how will it ever be possible to change the mainstream American outlook toward international human rights? Is it a hopeless task? Or is there something useful that can be done? If so, what?

7. Ignatieff states that the way to change America's exceptional behavior is to engage in domestic politics. For example, Ignatieff says that "national discussion of fair process and legal equality . . . will change American standards of punishment." In 2005, the U.S. Supreme Court struck down state laws prescribing the death penalty for juvenile offenders,

citing a change in contemporary societal attitudes as one of the reasons for this change. Does this make Ignatieff's argument more plausible? Do you think there is any other way to change America's exceptional behavior outside of domestic politics? What about a massive commitment to human rights education both within and outside the classroom? Desirable? Possible? Why? Why not?

8. Ignatieff discusses mainly the negative consequences of American exceptionalism. Harold Koh, however, in "On American Exceptionalism," *Stanford Law Review* 55 (2003): 1479–1527, at 1487–88, argues that American exceptionalism can have a positive face:

> Having focused until now on the negative faces of American exceptionalism, I must address a fifth, much-overlooked dimension in which the United States is genuinely exceptional in international affairs. Looking only at the half-empty part of the glass, I would argue, obscures the most important respect in which the United States has been genuinely exceptional, with regard to international affairs, international law, and promotion of human rights, namely, in its exceptional global leadership and activism. To this day, the United States remains the only superpower capable, and at times willing, to commit real resources and make real sacrifices to build, sustain, and drive an international system committed to international law, democracy, and the promotion of human rights. Experience teaches that when the United States leads on human rights, from Nuremberg to Kosovo, other countries follow. When the United States does not lead, often nothing happens, or worse yet, as in Rwanda and Bosnia, disasters occur because the United States does not get involved.

What are some other examples of "positive" American exceptionalism? Is this what Ignatieff is talking about when he asks, provocatively, "No Exception?" Overall, do you believe American exceptionalism exerts a negative, positive, or middling influence on the world community? Why?

9. Does American exceptionalism weaken or strengthen the U.S. role as the world's only superpower? Or, as the only superpower, does the U.S. have a higher moral leadership role to fulfill that is negated by acts of American exceptionalism?

10. In "U.S. Foreign Policy and Enlarging the Democratic Community," *HRQ* 22, no. 4 (2000): 988–1010, at 1009, David P. Forsythe and Barbara Ann J. Reiffer state:

> U.S. support for democracy abroad may exist mostly to allow Americans to maintain their self-image as an exceptionally good people who stand for personal freedom. Still, it is on balance better to have such an orientation than not, as long as we mean support for liberal democracy and not the type of illiberal democracies that have existed in places like Iran, rump Yugoslavia, and Tudjman's Croatia. U.S. contributions to liberal democracy abroad, in conjunction with others, might make some difference at the margins, at least in some situations over time.

In contrast, in "The Interplay of Domestic Politics, Human Rights and U.S. Foreign Policy," in Thomas G. Weiss, Margaret E. Crahan, and John Goering, eds., *Wars on Terrorism and Iraq: Human Rights, Unilateralism and U.S. Foreign Policy* (London: Routledge, 2004), 29–60, at 47, Tom Farer writes:

> A crusade for democracy, even full-blown liberal democracy, overlaps but is not synonymous with a crusade for human rights. Moral criteria for evaluating the exercise of power stretch into the remote past. So does the idea of possessing rights in relationship to power holders. But the idea of rights held in common not just by all members of the same class, profession, guild, race, religion, or nation but by every human being simply by virtue of being human, now that is a modern idea. And just as it is not synonymous with liberal democracy, it is not synonymous with general human welfare.

Both authors are discussing the merits of U.S. foreign policy activities that attempt to spread human rights by spreading liberal democracy. Which authors' argument is more persuasive? Why? Should the U.S. be involved in exporting liberal democracy? Is this the best way for the U.S. to promote human rights abroad?

11. To what extent should human rights be a cornerstone of U.S. foreign policy? Should human rights be promoted all the time? Only when it serves U.S. economic and strategic interests? Never?

29. MICHAEL RATNER *Civil Remedies for Gross Human Rights Violations*

INTRODUCTION

Over the last few years many in the human rights community have focused on criminal remedies for pursuing individual human rights abusers.[1] United Nations sponsored criminal courts are trying those who committed abuses in Rwanda and Bosnia and the International Criminal Court (ICC) will soon be a reality. National courts, such as those of Spain and Belgium, are beginning to employ the concept of universal jurisdiction and the Convention Against Torture[2] to bring perpetrators of human rights violations to justice. These are all very important developments, but even once there is an operating ICC, there will still be a need for additional international remedies. Only a few of the worst abusers will be tried by the ICC or by national courts; and international law's primary enforcement mechanisms are likely to remain weak. The simple fact is that even with the institutional improvements represented by the UN tribunals and the ICC, the vast majority of violators will not be brought to justice nor will their victims be compensated for their injuries.

Criminal cases on both the national and international level require the cooperation of officials. While some such cases can be initiated by individuals, they cannot be fully prosecuted without prosecutors and/or investigating judges. All too frequently political or other concerns will prevent any prosecutions from going forward.

For these reasons civil remedies have an important role to play as a means of enforcing human rights norms. Courts in the United States have pioneered the use of civil remedies to sue human rights violators. Litigation under the Alien Tort Claims Act [ATCA or sec.1350][3] and the Torture Victim Protection Act [TVPA][4] have resulted in billions of dollars in judgments, and

have had an important impact on plaintiffs and human rights both in the United States and internationally. Such cases do not require official approval; they can be brought by individuals who have control over the lawsuits and thus are less subject to political vagaries.

Civil remedies include damage awards for injuries and punitive damages meant to deter future abusive conduct as well as send a message to others that such conduct is unacceptable. In addition to any money that can be collected, these cases are important to the victims and their families. Plaintiffs are allowed to tell their stories to a court, can often confront their abusers, and create an official record of their persecutions. Filing these civil suits can empower the victims and give them a means for fighting back. It can also help them heal. One person who was in a center for torture victims described the importance to his psychological health of the filing of a civil suit against his torturer. Civil suits can also have consequences for the defendants aside from a monetary judgment. Héctor Gramajo, a Guatemalan general, was barred from the United States after a court found him responsible for summarily executing and torturing Guatemalan Indians. The lawsuit may have also dashed his hopes to run for president of Guatemala. He has nowhere to hide.

An important aspect of civil suits is the annunciation of legal norms through courts declaring that torture and other abuses are violations of international law. These decisions have their effect internationally. A number of the Law Lords in the Pinochet decisions relied on ATCA and TVPA precedents.

The success of these civil suits is a remarkable chapter in American law. In 2004, in *Sosa v.*

Reprinted with changes from Michael Ratner, "Civil Remedies for Gross Human Rights Violations," in David Barnhizer, ed., *Effective Strategies for Protecting Human Rights* (Burlington, Vt.: Ashgate-Dartmouth, 2001), 249–62. Copyright © 2001 Michael Ratner and Ashgate Publishing Company. Reprinted by permission.

1. I am addressing here the trials of perpetrators outside their home countries where the crimes were committed. Often national courts are unwilling for a variety of reasons to try their own nationals.
2. Convention against Torture and Other Cruel, Inhuman or Degrading Treatment or Punishment, concluded Dec. 10, 1984, referenced in Documentary Appendix B.
3. Alien Tort Claims Act of 1789 (ATCA), 28 U.S.C. §1350 (1988).
4. 28 U.S.C. §1350 n. (1992).

Alvarez-Machain,[5] the Supreme Court affirmed the principles underlying these cases. They have opened great future possibilities for the enforcement of international law and the bringing to justice of human rights abusers. To date, however, no other country appears to have adopted these civil remedies as a means of suing rights violators. Hopefully, the success of these cases in the United States will encourage others and civil remedies against abusers will become commonplace.

FILARTIGA AND ITS PROGENY: FROM PERPETRATOR TO COMMANDER

It all began in the United States with the landmark 1980 decision of the United States Court of Appeals for the Second Circuit, *Filártiga v. Peña-Irala*.[6] *Filártiga* dealt with the 1976 torture and murder of Joelito Filártiga by a Paraguayan police official. The official fled to the United States where the family of the victim was able to track him down. The Filártigas came to the Center for Constitutional Rights [in New York City] and asked if they could sue the torturer and bring him to justice.

At the time there was no precedent for such a suit. It would involve a suit by an alien plaintiff against an alien in the United States for torture that had taken place in Paraguay. It was not exactly a case that U.S. courts could be expected to treat hospitably. The U.S. had little or no connection to the case; it might raise foreign policy concerns as the defendant was an official at the time of the crime, and the courts were not familiar with applying international law. In fact, the Second Circuit had held in two relatively recent cases that international law did not apply to a country's treatment of its own citizens. The court followed the old rule that international law applied only as between countries or to a country's treatment of foreigners. So there seemed little hope.

On the other hand, there was a statute containing plain language that seemed to fit the case. The ATCA stated that U.S. courts had jurisdiction over suits by aliens for torts committed in violation of the law of nations or what is commonly referred to as customary international laws Although the statute had been rarely

applied, the *Filártiga* case seemed like an ideal test. President Carter was then emphasizing international human rights, and a number of statutes had been enacted limiting U.S. aid to countries violating human rights. There was also a strong argument that the Second Circuit precedents were wrong. The Nuremberg and Tokyo war crimes trials, the United Nations Charter, the ratification of various human rights treaties and numerous UN resolutions were contributing to a new consensus that international law did govern a state's treatment of its own citizens and that a person had a right to be free from torture even in his home country.

Initially the federal district court dismissed the case, finding that it was bound by the appeals court decisions that international law did not govern a state's treatment of its own citizens. On appeal, President Carter's Departments of Justice and State filed a brief in support of the plaintiffs, arguing that this was no longer true and that torture was one of a handful of international law violations that gave rights to individuals against their own states. The appeals court agreed and gave a resounding victory to the Filártigas. The principles set forth in that decision were to guide similar litigation over the next two decades and have a major influence on the development of international law both in the United States and throughout the world.

The *Filártiga* decision held that "deliberate torture perpetrated under color of official authority violates universally accepted norms of the international law of human rights, regardless of the nationality of the parties." In other words, torture is prohibited by the law of nations or customary international law and, significantly, international law "confers fundamental rights upon all people vis-à-vis their own governments." The court had overruled its earlier precedents and permitted the Filártigas to sue their own government.

The court also found that it was appropriate for a court in the United States to hear the case, even though the occurrence and the parties had no substantial connection to the U.S. In part this was based on the concept of universal jurisdiction and that the right to be free from torture had been universally proclaimed by all nations. With stirring language, the court emphasized that a torturer could be brought to justice where

5. Docket No. 03-339, decided June 29, 2004.
6. *Filártiga v. Peña-Irala*, 630 F2d 876 (2d Cir. 1980).

found even for civil liability: "Indeed, for purposes of civil liability, the torturer has become—like the pirate and slave trader before him—*hostis humani generis*, an enemy of all mankind."

Eventually, the defendant Peña-Irala was deported back to Paraguay and the case continued without him. At a damage hearing, damages including punitive damages of over $10 million were awarded to the plaintiffs, i.e., the father and sister of the deceased.

Over the next two decades a series of cases following *Filártiga* made a number of important advances in establishing the civil liability of those responsible for human rights violations. In *Filártiga*, the actual perpetrator had been sued; in future cases the range of defendants was expanded. Those who ordered or authorized the violations or those persons with command responsibility who knew, or should have known, and failed to stop violations were also found liable. A series of cases were brought against General Guillermo Suárez-Masón, an Argentine general in charge of Buenos Aires and responsible for the torture, murder, and disappearances of hundreds of Argentinian citizens during the "dirty war."[7] He, like the defendant in *Filártiga*, had come into the United States where he was served with legal process. The suits resulted in over $80 million in judgments and expanded the *Filártiga* holding to a commanding officer and not just the torturer.

Likewise in *Xuncax v. Gramajo*[8] eight Kanjobal Indians, refugee survivors of what many human rights advocates alleged was genocide against the Indians of Guatemala in the early 1980s, sued the general they claimed was responsible. General Héctor Gramajo was in the U.S. at the time studying for a degree at Harvard's Kennedy School of Government. Although the general did not personally commit the murders and torture, he was held liable under the doctrine of command responsibility, the court finding that he "devised and directed the implementation of an indiscriminate campaign of terror against civilians such as plaintiffs and their relatives." Subsequent to this decision General Gramajo was barred from the U.S. under provisions of its immigration laws.

Numerous other cases have now reaffirmed the responsibility and civil liability of commanders and those in authority for the actions of their troops and subordinates. In *Todd v. Panjaitan*, the Indonesian general with authority over the soldiers involved in the 1991 Dili massacre in East Timor was found liable for the death of a young student-activist; in *Paul v. Avril*, the dictator-president of Haiti was held liable for the torture of five political opponents; and in a series of cases against the estate of the former dictator-president of the Philippines, Ferdinand Marcos, the jury imposed liability of hundreds of millions of dollars on behalf of at least 10,000 victims. The major recent case affirming such liability is *Kadic v. Karadzic*,[9] a suit against the leader of the Bosnian-Serbs on behalf of the victims of the war in Bosnia-Herzegovina. Plaintiffs alleged that Karadzic possessed ultimate command authority over the Bosnian-Serb military forces, and that their injuries were committed as part of a pattern of systematic human rights violations directed by him and carried out by military forces under his command. Not only did the Second Circuit permit the suit to go forward, but a jury imposed a $4.5 billion judgment against him. As a result of these cases it is now well established in U.S. courts that those who oversee murder, torture, and other human rights violations are civilly liable to their victims.

In addition to suits against individual defendants, two cases have sued groups involved in human rights violations. In *Belance v. FRAPH* (Revolutionary Front for Advancement and Progress in Haiti), a Haitian woman who had been almost macheted to death by a defendant paramilitary group brought suit against a branch of the organization operating in New York. In *Doe v. Islamic Front* (FIS) nine women and men filed a lawsuit against the Islamic Salvation Front charging them with committing crimes against humanity.

Not only did these cases expand the category of defendants that could be sued, but the courts found that a number of other violations of customary international law were actionable. In *Forti v. Suarez-Mason*, the court found that prolonged arbitrary detention and disappearances[10]

---

7. See, e.g., *Forti v. Suarez-Mason*, 672 F. Supp. 1531 (N.D.Cal. 1987), on reconsideration, 694 F.Supp. 707 (N.D. Cal. 1988).
8. *Xuncax v. Gramajo*, Civ. No. 91-11564 (D. Mass., Apr. 12, 1995).
9. *Kadic v. Karadzic*, 70 F.3d 232 (2d Cir. 1995).
10. The *Forti* court defined disappearances as constituting two elements: "(a) abduction by a state

constituted violations of customary international law and met the ATCA requirements. The court set out a test that many of the courts hearing ATCA cases now employ: to establish a norm of customary international law actionable under the ATCA the prohibition violated must be "definable," "universal," and "obligatory." These criteria are similar to those articulated in *Filártiga*. By "universal" the court explained that the norm required an international consensus: "definable" meant the norm was clear and unambiguous; and "obligatory" meant that it was nonderogable. In *Suarez-Mason* the court determined that cruel, inhuman, and degrading treatment (CIDT) was not definable and did not have universal consensus.

But in *Xuncax*, decided subsequently to *Suarez-Mason*, and after ratification of the Convention Against Torture (CAT), the court found that cruel, inhuman, and degrading treatment did constitute a norm of customary international law actionable under the ATCA. But it did so with a limitation. By the time *Xuncax* was decided, the U.S. and most other countries had ratified the CAT which contained a prohibition on cruel, inhuman, and degrading treatment (CIDT), and the court had little trouble finding that the prohibition was universal as well as obligatory. In addition, when the Senate ratified CAT, one of its reservations was that the scope of CIDT would be the same as the cruel, unusual, and inhumane treatment or punishment prohibited by the Fifth, Eighth, and Fourteenth Amendments to the U.S. Constitution. While the customary norm of CIDT may be broader than the U.S. Constitution's prohibitions, this did give the court a comfort level with CIDT's definability. For ATCA cases, CIDT was to be defined according to the U.S. Constitution, a definition with which U.S. courts are comfortable. The *Xuncax* court also added summary execution or extrajudicial execution and arbitrary detention (as differentiated from prolonged arbitrary detention) to the list of torts cognizable under the ATCA.

KARADZIC: OPENING THE DOOR TO NONSTATE ACTORS

A major breakthrough in the law with regard to cognizable international law violations for ATCA purposes came with the Second Circuit's opinion in *Kadic v. Karadzic*. The problem plaintiffs faced was that the court might find that Karadzic, an unrecognized foreign leader, was not acting on behalf of the state when he authorized or approved massive human rights abuses. These included a campaign of murder, rape, forced impregnation, and other forms of torture against Bosnian Muslims and Croats. Although the issue had not been raised directly, *dicta*[11] in some of the earlier ATCA cases appeared to require that norms of international law required some form of state action; in other words violations of international law could not be committed by private persons acting without some form of state involvement. For example, torture committed solely by a person acting without such involvement does not constitute a violation of international law; nor do disappearances or summary executions. However, plaintiffs' lawyers determined that certain international law violations could be committed by individuals without any involvement by the state; these included genocide, crimes against humanity, and war crimes. Thus, while an individual could commit a single murder and not violate the international law prohibition on summary executions, he would violate international law if he committed such murders on a large scale or in a preconceived and systematic way. That would be a crime against humanity. It is likewise with genocide; the Convention Against Genocide[12] does not require state action if the elements of genocide are met. This was a key element to the plaintiffs' arguments in the Second Circuit.

This question had never been decided previously by a U.S. court and it was unclear if the Circuit would uphold plaintiffs' arguments. However, in a remarkable opinion, the court held that "certain forms of conduct violate the law of nations whether undertaken by those acting

---

official or by persons acting under state approval or authority; and (b) refusal by the state to acknowledge the abduction and detention." 694 F. Supp. at 710 (citations omitted).

11. A judge's (or court's) statement of legal opinion that is not directly relevant to the case being heard and therefore deemed theoretically nonbinding.

12. Convention on the Prevention and Punishment of the Crime of Genocide, concluded Dec. 9, 1948, referenced in Documentary Appendix B.

under auspices of a state or only as private individuals." The court found that both genocide and war crimes were included in these "forms of conduct" by individuals that violated the law of nations. As the court said, "genocide is a crime under international law that is condemned by the civilized world, whether the perpetrators are private individuals, public officials or statesmen." For its conclusion the court relied upon, *inter alia*, the Convention Against Genocide and the Genocide Convention Implementation Act of 1987,[13] both of which make acts of genocide illegal without regard as to whether the offender is acting under color of law. With regard to war crimes the court relied upon the law of the Nuremberg trials and Common Article 3 of the Geneva Conventions which it found bound the parties to a conflict whether or not they were recognized countries or "roving hordes of insurgents." The court had no difficulty in finding that the type of atrocities alleged were violations of the customary laws of war and applied to Karadzic whether or not he was an official of a recognized state.

Subsequent to the Circuit's decision, the district court held a jury trial to assess damages (Karadzic defaulted). At the trial a number of his victims testified and the jury came back with a $4.5 billion verdict.

THE TORTURE VICTIM PROTECTION ACT

While most of the above-described cases were brought under the ATCA, a few of the cases utilized a 1992 statute, the Torture Victim Protection Act.[14] This statute was passed primarily to permit U.S. victims of certain human rights violations to proceed in U.S. courts in a similar manner as aliens were permitted to do under ATCA. However, the TVPA is not restricted to citizens; aliens can use it as well. Some of the TVPA's proponents also believed that it was important for Congress to pass a contemporary statute that would reinforce *Filártiga*'s interpretation of the ATCA in the courts. The legislative history of the TVPA is clear on this point stating that the ATCA has "important uses and should not be replaced."

However, the TVPA in certain respects is more limited than the ATCA. The TVPA grants a cause of action for only two international law violations: torture and extrajudicial killing. Thus, the TVPA cannot be used as ATCA was, for example in *Forti*, for disappearances, or as ATCA was in *Karadzic* for war crimes and genocide. The TVPA also requires that the defendant act under the authority or law of a foreign nation; thus suits against U.S. officials are prohibited unless somehow they are acting under foreign law, a very unlikely scenario. The TVPA contains a ten-year statute of limitation which is helpful in the ATCA cases where courts have struggled with determining the appropriate limitation period.

The TVPA was first employed in *Ortiz v. Gramajo*, a companion case to Xuncax. Diana Ortiz was an American citizen nun tortured and sexually abused while in Guatemala. As a citizen she could not use the ATCA and had to rely on the TVPA. She sued Gramajo under the statute arguing that it was retroactive to the time of her torture. (The statute was passed in 1992; Ortiz was tortured in 1989.) The court agreed with Ortiz and found that the TVPA could be applied retroactively. It reasoned that torture had been universally condemned prior to Ortiz's ordeal and thus there was no compromise of Gramajo's substantive rights nor manifest injustice in applying the statute to his conduct. A number of courts have agreed with this analysis.

One other important point to recognize regarding the TVPA is that its language employs the term "individual"' in referring to defendants. Not only might this limit suits against groups and organizations, but suits against corporations may also not come within the statute's terms.

ATTEMPTS TO SUE U.S. OFFICIALS

While ATCA and TVPA suits against foreign human rights violators have been very successful, it is a different story with regard to suing U.S. officials for human rights violations committed overseas. To date, the courts have been hostile to this type of litigation. The key case in the area is *Sanchez-Espinoza v. Reagan*,[15] a suit by victims of the *contras* in Nicaragua against various U.S.

---

13. Convention against Genocide and Genocide Convention Implementation Act of 1987, 18 U.S.C. §1091 (1988).
14. 28 U.S.C. §1350 (1992).
15. *Sanchez-Espinoza v. Reagan*, 770 F.2d 202 (D.C. Cit. 1985).

officials, including President Reagan, the director of the CIA, and others responsible for funding and directing the war against the Nicaraguan government. The plaintiffs alleged that the U.S. officials had knowingly assisted in the financing and directing of the *contras* in carrying out a plan of terror against civilians that included torture, rape, and summary execution. In an opinion that cannot be justified legally, the D.C. Circuit dismissed the case, holding that the law of domestic sovereign immunity immunized the defendants. The court reasoned, and that is a charitable use of the word, that as the actions were official, the suit was in essence one challenging official actions of the United States. As there was no waiver of sovereign immunity, the case was dismissed.

Obviously, the suit involved officials acting under color of federal law, but that should not have meant they were immune. The defendants may have acted under color of law, but the suit alleged they were acting illegally under international law and therefore acting outside the law in a manner that was unauthorized.[16] Just as the court had acknowledged that foreign officials are not protected in that situation (the court said its decision did not conflict with *Filártiga*), neither should U.S. officials be immune.

The court, however, distinguished the two classes of defendants by stating that the "doctrine of foreign sovereign immunity is quite distinct from the doctrine of domestic sovereign immunity," the former being based on comity and the latter on separation of powers. Presumably, by this the court was addressing the fact that foreign affairs powers are an executive function that should not be intruded upon by the judicial branch. But judicial abstention is inappropriate when those powers are employed to torture people. One would have assumed that the opposite result was more likely to ensue. In suits against U.S. officials for violations such as torture, judicial scrutiny would cause less interference with foreign affairs than suits against foreign officials. The latter action would appear to have greater potential to interfere with our relations with foreign countries. Unfortunately, the chances of overruling *Sanchez* are remote.

Two of the three judges in the Circuit Court are now Justices of the Supreme Court: Scalia and Ginsberg.

In the one major case filed, plaintiffs have fared better when they have sued U.S. officials for violations of international law in the United States. In a precedent setting decision a federal district court held that U.S. officials, U.S. corporations acting pursuant to government contract, and their employees could be sued for violating customary international human rights law in the United States. In *Jama v. United States*[17] the plaintiffs were political asylum seekers housed in an Immigration and Naturalization Service (INS) contract detention facility. They alleged that they were being subjected to physical, sexual, and psychological abuse by the defendants. As the plaintiffs were excludable aliens, they were unsure of their right to be free from such conduct under the U.S. Constitution. However, they were protected by international law prohibiting cruel, inhuman, and degrading treatment and brought suit under the ATCA upon that basis. The *Jama* decision is the first case to recognize that U.S. officials can be sued for violating customary international law for abuses committed in the United States. It opens great opportunities for victims who have suffered abuses in the U.S.

A series of cases regarding the Guantánamo detainees relied on the ATCA to sue U.S. officials for prolonged arbitrary detention as well as torture. These cases are both to enjoin these officials from their illegal conduct as well as to obtain damages. The Supreme Court in *Rasul v. Bush*[18] upheld the right of the Guantánamo detainees to sue regarding their conditions. At this writing, the cases are pending.

SUING [FOREIGN] COUNTRIES FOR HUMAN RIGHTS VIOLATION

Although it was argued in a number of cases that the ATCA permitted suits against [foreign] countries despite the bar of the Foreign Sovereign Immunities Act (FSIA),[19] this effort was unsuccessful. In *Argentine Republic v. Amerada Hess Shipping Corp.*,[20] plaintiff shipping company

16. In fact, many civil rights suits brought in U.S. courts are based upon this precise reasoning.
17. *Jama v. U.S. Immigration and Naturalization Service*, 22 F. Supp. 2d 353 (D. N.J. 1998).
18. Docket No. 03-334, decided June 28, 2004.
19. 28 U.S.C. 28 U.S.C. §§1330, 1332(a), 1391(f), and 1601–1611 (1976).
20. *Argentine Republic v. Amerada Hess Shipping Corp.*, 488 U.S. 428 (1989).

claimed that one of its oil tankers was bombed by defendants during the Malvinas-Falklands war in violation of the customary international laws of war. The U.S. Supreme Court ruled that the FSIA was the sole basis for obtaining jurisdiction over a foreign country. Unless a case fit within one of FSIA's exceptions, a court did not have subject matter jurisdiction. The exceptions are relatively narrow and include commercial disputes torts within the United States and waivers of immunity by the country concerned. Thus, in general, suits for human rights abuses can only be brought against the officials involved.

There is, however, one narrow but important exception to immunity passed by Congress in 1996, 28 U.S.C. §1605(a)(7), the so-called terrorist state exception. Under this exception nationals of the United States are permitted to sue foreign countries for international law violations, including torture and extrajudicial execution. The limitation is that the exception only applies to countries designated as "state sponsors of terrorism." Only six countries have been so designated as of February 19, 2005: Iran, Sudan, Libya, Cuba, North Korea, and Syria. As a result of this provision, which has been retroactively applied a handful of cases have been filed against certain of the designated countries. Among the most well known is *Alejandre v. Cuba*,[21] a suit filed by the families of pilots belonging to the organization Brothers to the Rescue. Three of the pilots were shot down by the Cuban Air Force in what the court deemed was an extrajudicial execution. Cuba did not contest the case and it resulted in a default judgment of 187 million dollars.

Whatever one thinks of the merits of these cases, there is a striking difference between them and the ATCA cases. The ATCA cases can be brought against officials of any country, and permission to sue is not required from the U.S. Department of State. On the other hand, these so-called terrorist state cases can only be brought if the State Department has designated the state as terrorist. This highly politicizes the bringing of these human rights cases and undercuts their legitimacy. In the last annual designation of Cuba as a terrorist state, it was practically admitted that Cuba did not belong on the list and was not engaging in acts of terrorism. In fact, the designation appears to be for domestic U.S. political

reasons. Countries that should be on the list are not: Turkey, despite its abuses against the Kurds, is not included because it is too close an ally to the U.S.

THE POST-*KARADZIC* CASES: SUING CORPORATIONS

The most fruitful recent development emerging from the *Karadzic* decision are the corporate ATCA cases. These are cases brought against corporations allegedly involved in human rights abuses outside the United States. The *Karadzic* decision opened up the possibility of suing such entities as a result of its holding that certain international law violations could be committed by private parties. Jurisdiction over the corporation is obtained either because the corporation is headquartered in the U.S. or is otherwise doing business in the U.S. One of the more significant cases is *Doe v. Unocal*.[22] Plaintiffs alleged that Unocal was complicit in forced labor, forced relocation and torture, carried out by the Burmese military in the building of the Yadana natural gas pipeline. Plaintiffs argued that as a result of Unocal's joint venture with a state-owned entity, Unocal was acting under color of law with regard to the human rights violations. Alternatively, it was argued that at least two of the international law violations—forced labor and forced relocation—could be committed by private parties. The case involved extensive discovery and eventually motions by the defendants for summary judgment.

The District Court Judge granted the motion for summary judgment, but made a number of favorable factual findings in favor of the plaintiffs. He found that the evidence demonstrated that Unocal knew that the Burmese military utilized forced labor and benefitted from it in connection to the pipeline. However, he decided that Unocal itself did not use the forced labor and therefore could not be held liable. Even this loss demonstrates the importance of these cases. Plaintiffs were able to prove that a major oil corporation knew about and benefitted from forced labor. The case also sent shockwaves through the global corporate community. Not only could business enterprises no longer hide their human rights practices, they might even be held liable

---

21. *Alejandre v. Republic of Cuba*, 996 F. Supp. 1239 (S.D. Fla. 1997).
22. *Doe v. Unocal*, 110 F.Supp. 2d 1294 (C.D. Cal 2000).

for abuses committed by their partners as well, a possibility that in fact became very real when, on September 18, 2002, the U.S. Court of Appeals for the Ninth Circuit reversed the District Court's decision and allowed the plaintiffs to go forward to trial to demonstrate Unocal's complicity.[23] In 2004, however, the case was settled out of court "in principle," with reaffirmations of commitment by Unocal as well as the plaintiffs to the principle of respect of human rights included.[24]

A second important corporate case is *Wiwa v. Royal Dutch Petroleum*,[25] a case charging defendants with complicity in the 1995 hanging of Ken Saro-Wiwa and John Kpuinen, two Nigerian activists. International law claims include extrajudicial execution and torture, and allegations that the defendants conspired with the Nigerian government in the killings. *Wiwa* demonstrates the global reach of human rights law and the willingness of U.S. courts to hear these cases. The killings occurred in Nigeria, and the defendants were headquartered in the UK and the Netherlands and are the corporate owners of Shell Nigeria. Jurisdiction was obtained as a result of the activities of an investor relations office set up by Shell's subsidiary in New York. In an extremely important decision, the Second Circuit unanimously agreed that there was jurisdiction over the defendants and that the case could be tried in New York. In doing so the court emphasized that Congress, by its passage of both the ATCA and the TVPA, had stated the importance of U.S. courts hearing these human rights cases.

A third case, *Manzanarez-Tercero v. C & Y Sportswear, Inc.*,[26] is another case that is forging new ground in the efforts to hold multinational corporations responsible for their human rights abuses overseas. It is the first of the ATCA cases to address the many abuses that occur in textile assembly plants overseas. The plaintiffs are fired workers and union leaders formerly of Chentex, a Nicaraguan factory that manufactures jeans for department stores in the U.S., such as Kohl's. The international law claim they are raising is the right to associate as workers and form a union: they are arguing that this is a right protected by customary international law. Jurisdiction was obtained over the Taiwanese parent owner of Chentex through a subsidiary in California. If this case can be won, it will be a major step in both the scope of ATCA litigation and offer some hope toward improving conditions in overseas sweatshops.

These cases give some sense of the future possibilities offered by suits for civil remedies against corporations. Suits against classic human rights abusers—those for torture, extra judicial execution and the like—continue to be important. The world is still filled with individual evildoers. However, the lawsuits brought against them are generally for past conduct committed when the abusers are out of power. In addition, actually collecting the damages can be very difficult. On the other hand, suits against corporations are generally for abuses that are continuing: those suits present the possibility of actually modifying current conduct. Even the filing of such lawsuits

---

23. A three-judge panel held that the District Court was wrong in concluding that the plaintiffs had to show that Unocal controlled the Burmese military's actions in order to establish Unocal's liability. It held that the plaintiffs had only to prove that Unocal knowingly assisted the military in perpetrating the abuses. Under this standard, the court determined that the plaintiffs had presented enough evidence to go to trial.

24. In February 2003, the Ninth Circuit Court decided to rehear the appeal before an eleven-judge en banc panel. Prior to decision in that case, a settlement was reached the terms of which remain confidential until the details are resolved. On December 13, 2004, the parties issued the following statement regarding the settlement:

> The parties to several lawsuits related to Unocal's energy investment in the Yadana gas pipeline project in Myanmar/Burma announced today that they have reached a settlement in principle of their suits. Although the terms are confidential, the settlement in principle will compensate plaintiffs and provide funds enabling plaintiffs and their representatives to develop programs to improve living conditions, health care and education and protect the rights of people from the pipeline region. These initiatives will provide substantial assistance to people who may have suffered hardships in the region. Unocal reaffirms its principle that the company respects human rights in all of its activities and commits to enhance its educational programs to further this principle. Plaintiffs and their representatives reaffirm their commitment to protecting human rights.

25. *Wiwa v. Royal Dutch Petroleum*, 226 F. 3d 88 (2d. Cir. 2000).
26. *Manzanarez Tercero v. C&Y Sportswear, Inc.*, Case No. CV 00-12715 NM (Ct.) (filed C.D. Calif., Dec. 2000).

spotlights the egregious behavior of some of these multinational corporations and can lead to positive changes. Corporations can also pay judgments, thus giving some remuneration to victims. That also means the defendants can and do pay major law firms to represent them, requiring that increased resources be made available on the plaintiffs' side if the lawsuits are to have a chance at success. Such litigation also raises more alarm bells in the establishment. Taking on a known evildoer is generally not very controversial: taking on the big oil companies is.

It is hoped that the success of the suits against individual abusers and the newer corporate cases will encourage litigators in other countries to attempt similar suits or try to have laws passed to permit such litigation. The great advantage of this litigation is that it is not controlled by governments, but is a remedy available to anyone who was a victim of abuse. And cases can be brought outside the country of the abuse, thus lending a margin of safety not often available in the home state. If these civil remedies become widely used, they could have a real impact on making this world a better place.

QUESTIONS FOR REFLECTION AND DISCUSSION

1. "Courts in the United States," Michael Ratner writes, "have pioneered the use of civil remedies to sue human rights violators." Given the reluctance of the United States to ratify human rights treaties (as recorded in Reading 28 by Michael Ignatieff in this chapter), is this not a surprising fact? What explains it? Is it the difference between elected term legislators in the U.S. Senate and unelected lifetime appointees to U.S. federal courts? Something else? Perhaps that American citizens are generally exempt from international human rights scrutiny (neither the ATCA nor the TVPA applies to human rights abuses perpetuated by U.S. officials outside U.S. territory)? And why is it that, according to Ratner, other countries do not offer civil remedies in their courts similar to those available under the Alien Tort Claims Act (ATCA) and the Torture Victim Protection Act (TVPA)? Might it have anything to do with the fact that many countries have little to no real interest in promoting and protecting human rights, defying popular wisdom about the global reach of human rights? Or, to the contrary, that some countries (for example those in Africa, Europe, and Latin America) are party to regional human rights systems whereas the United States is not? Other reasons?

2. What message do ATCA and the TVPA send to the American people? To other nations and peoples? What is to be made of the fact that neither the ATCA nor the TVPA apply to human rights abuses perpetuated by U.S. officials outside U.S. territory? Should they? Does it suggest a double standard in the U.S. application of human rights law, another example of American exceptionalism when it comes to the enforcement in contrast to the proclamation of human rights policy? Consider that the United States is not a party to the First Optional Protocol to the International Covenant on Civil and Political Rights (referenced in Documentary Appendix B), the consequence of which is to thwart human rights claims by or against U.S. citizens before the ICCPR Human Rights Committee? Does this influence your answer?

3. In *The Paquete Habana*, 175 U.S. 677 (1900), at 700, the U.S. Supreme Court stated that

> where there is no treaty, and no controlling executive or legislative act or judicial decision, resort must be had to the customs and usages of civilized nations; and, as evidence of these, to the works of jurists and commentators, who by years of labor, research and experience, have made themselves peculiarly well acquainted with the subjects of which they treat. [These works] are trustworthy evidence of what the law really is.

This famous passage is often quoted to explain the incorporation of customary international law—including customary international human rights law—into U.S. domestic law, no such language having been included in the U.S. Constitution. What, exactly, does it mean? Is customary international human rights law part of domestic U.S. law? What does *Filártiga* say?

4. Judge Irving R. Kaufmann's opinion in *Filártiga*, rendered four years before the Convention against Torture and Other Cruel, Inhuman or Degrading Treatment or Punishment

(referenced in Documentary Appendix B), included the following statement at 630 F.2d 882:

> although there is no universal agreement as to the precise extent of the "human rights and fundamental freedoms" guaranteed to all by the [UN] Charter, there is at present no dissent from the view that the guarantees include, at a bare minimum, the right to be free from torture. This prohibition has become part of customary law, as evidenced and defined by the Universal Declaration of Human Rights . . . which states, in the plainest terms, "no one shall be subjected to torture." The General Assembly has declared that the Charter precepts embodied in this Universal Declaration "constitute basic principles of international law."

In light of the U.S. treatment of prisoners at Abu Ghraib and Guantánamo in the early 2000s, could Judge Kaufmann say today that "there is at present no dissent from the view that the guarantees include, at a bare minimum, the right to be free from torture"? See Reading 6 by Lisa Hajjar in Chapter 2 of this volume. Regardless, this statement is jurisprudentially significant. Why?

5. The ATCA provides that "The district courts shall have original jurisdiction of any civil action by an alien for a tort only, committed in violation of the law of nations." Assuming the *Filártiga* court was correct in deciding that torture violates customary international law, might there be other conduct that courts would find similarly violative of the law of nations? Consider *Flores v. S. Peru Copper Corp.*, 343 F.2d 140 (2d Cir. 2003). In this ruling, the U.S. Court of Appeals for the Second Circuit affirmed the dismissal of a complaint under the ATCA by Peruvian residents against a U.S. mining company for pollution at its mine in Peru that allegedly caused severe lung disease and thereby violated the plaintiffs' human rights to life and health. The court held that the rights to life and health articulated in the Universal Declaration of Human Rights (UDHR), the two Covenants (ICESCR and ICCPR), the Convention on the Rights of the Child (CRC), the American Convention on Human Rights (ACHR), the American Declaration of the Rights and Duties of Man, and UN General Assembly resolutions did not set forth specific rules. Some of these instruments, it added (the first three reprinted and referenced in Documentary Appendix A, the remainder referenced in Documentary Appendix B), were not treaties, some were treaties not ratified by the U.S., and others were non-self-executing—and thus not legitimate sources of customary international law. How does *Flores* shape your answer to the question posed above? Was it correctly decided? Why? Why not? Was it consistent with *Filártiga*? Why? Why not?

6. Assuming *Filártiga* was correctly decided, how might or should a U.S. court , operating under the ACTA, decide a claim against an individual (or group of individuals) acting without state authority or color of state authority and accused of, say, torture of known or presumed terrorists? See *Hanoch Tel-Orfen v. Libyan Arab Republic*, 726 F.2d 774 (D.C. Cir., 1984), *cert. denied* 470 U.S. 1003 (1985).

7. Is the ATCA a useful tool to further the principle of corporate responsibility for human rights abuses abroad? An appropriate one? Is it stretching the ATCA's purposes too far? Why? Why not? Should U.S. courts be more willing to hear ATCA cases involving U.S. corporations than those involving U.S. officials involved in human rights abuses abroad? Why? Why not?

8. In "The Key Human Rights Challenge: Developing Enforcement Mechanisms," *HHRJ* 15 (2002): 183–203, at 202–3, Terry Collingsworth discusses some of the limitations of the ATCA:

> The other major limitations are simply practical. By definition, ATCA cases involve human rights violations in countries that allow such things to happen; in most cases, the government itself is involved in the wrongful acts. Victims in these cases are often terrified of making claims, and are not likely to have access to lawyers unless they are discovered by local organizations with U.S. connections. Further, given the conditions that often lead to human rights violations, it is often extremely difficult for lawyers to gather evidence and interview witnesses in the places where violations have occurred. In the Unocal case, for example, the plaintiffs' lawyers were not able to travel to Burma to interview witnesses because they could not get visas. Even if they could have traveled to Burma, they would have risked arrest or physical harm. Finally, the costs and

time involved in bringing an ATCA case require that it be viewed as an extraordinary remedy, not lightly undertaken. The Unocal case is in its sixth year, and attorneys for plaintiffs have donated millions of dollars in legal fees to date, in addition to spending several hundreds of thousands of dollars in costs.

Do these limitations signal a need to change and/or clarify some of the ways the ATCA can be used? Or do they signify the true limits of the Act and the need to develop other mechanisms to deal with these limitations? If so, what other mechanisms would you suggest?

9. The *act of state doctrine* in U.S. courts is a rule of judicial deference that prohibits judging the validity of a foreign act of state ostensibly to avoid embarrassing the Executive Branch in its conduct of foreign policy. The *doctrine of sovereign immunity*, which permits domestic courts to decline jurisdiction because of the sovereign status of a defendant state, serves much the same purpose. So, too, does the so-called *political questions doctrine*, pursuant to which the judiciary finds an issue to be constitutionally delegated to one or both of the other "political" branches of government. How might a domestic court surmount these barriers to justiciability to enable adjudication of human rights cases brought against foreign states? How should domestic courts draw the line between foreign policy and international human rights law? The ACTA and TVPA offer one answer. Can you think of others?

10. In *Sei Fujii v. California*, 217 P.2d 481 (1950), a California District Court of Appeals held invalid a state statute forbidding aliens ineligible for citizenship to "acquire, possess, enjoy, use, cultivate, occupy, and transfer" real property in California on the grounds that the statute conflicted with the UN Charter and the Universal Declaration of Human Rights (UDHR). On appeal, the California Supreme Court held the statute invalid under the Fourteenth Amendment to the U.S. Constitution but expressly rejected the lower court's view that the UN Charter provisions on human rights had become part of the "supreme law of the land." 38 Cal.2d 713, 242 P.2d 617 (1952). Chief Justice Gibson, referring to UN Charter articles 1(3), 55, and 56, stated in part, at 38 Cal.2d 724, 242 P.2d 621–22:

> The fundamental provisions in the charter pledging cooperation in promoting observance of fundamental freedoms lack the mandatory quality and definitiveness which would indicate an intent to create justiciable rights in private persons immediately upon ratification. Instead, they are framed as a promise of future action by member nations.

What legal obligations, whether or not "self-executing," actually are imposed by Charter articles 1(3), 55, and 56? If a case raising the question of whether or not these provisions are "self-executing" came before the U.S. Supreme Court, which so far it has not, how do you think the Supreme Court would rule? Why? Would it make any difference what type of human rights violation was at issue? Or is it all really just a matter of politics?

11. What is the proper role of domestic courts in the struggle for internationally guaranteed human rights? Consider Richard A. Falk, *The Role of Domestic Courts in the International Legal Order* (Syracuse, N.Y.: Syracuse University Press, 1964), xi–xii:

> Two sets of considerations dominate my interpretation of the proper role for domestic courts to play. First, international law exists in a social system that possesses weak central institutions. As a result, international tribunals are not consistently or conveniently available to resolve most disputes involving questions of international law. Domestic courts can help to overcome this structural weakness in the international legal system. Also, since no international institution is endowed with legislative competence, it is difficult to change old rules in response to changes in the composition and character of international society. If international law is to develop into a universal basis of order, then it is necessary that divergent attitudes toward the content of law be treated with respect. . . . Domestic courts in the older states can help adapt international law to the modern world by developing principles that express tolerance for diverse social and economic systems.
>
> Second, domestic courts must struggle to become their own masters in international law cases. The executive must not be allowed, and must certainly not be invited, to control the outcome of judicial proceedings by alleging the presence of foreign policy considerations. The courts are not good vehicles for the promotion of foreign policy; moreover, the independence of courts from national political control is essential if international legal order is to be upheld and developed. A legal tradition depends upon

the autonomy of its method and the saliency of its governing principles. Only an independent judiciary can establish a tradition.

Do you agree with Falk? Was his proposal realistic when written? Why? Why not? Is it realistic now, nearly a half-century later? Why? Why not? Do not international human rights guarantees rest on such a precarious basis that proposals such as this one must be seen as absolutely necessary, however realistic or unrealistic?

30 RICHARD FALK *Humanitarian Intervention: Imperatives and Problematics*

Many developments account for the intensity of the recent debate concerning humanitarian intervention: the rise of humanitarian consciousness reinforced by an evolving sense of international accountability for political leaders; a post-Westphalian realisation that ideas about territorial sovereignty need to be reconsidered in light of the various dimensions of globalisation; suspicions that dominant countries, especially the United States and its coalition partners, are using humanitarian pretexts to pursue otherwise unacceptable geopolitical goals and to evade the non-intervention norm and legal prohibitions on the use of international force; a series of high-profile instances (including Somalia, Bosnia, Rwanda, Kosovo, Darfur-Sudan) in which controversy arose about whether the international community was unacceptably doing too little or too much about a severe humanitarian emergency; and the post-hoc rationalisation of the Iraq War as allegedly justified on humanitarian grounds, rescuing the Iraqi people from tyranny, despite the absence of any prior authorisation by the United Nations Security Council and the opposition of world public opinion. Additionally, the contextualisation of global security in relation to the American-led struggle against mega-terrorism tends to erode claims of sovereignty on the part of states seen as havens for anti-Western political extremism, but also gives rise to normative explanations of this erosion as achieving humanitarian benefits (e.g., liberating women from an oppressive Taliban regime in Afghanistan).

This series of developments has stimulated two sets of responses pertaining to the legal, ethical, and political status of humanitarian intervention: a statist response highlighted by reports of commissions composed of eminent persons; and a civil society response highlighted by case-by-case advocacy and criticism of action and inaction by the international community, and by various expressions of suspicion directed at self-serving accounts of motives on the part of intervening actors, particularly the United States, with its claimed right to initiate wars in pursuit of its security without obtaining "a permission slip" from the United Nations (a phrase first used by President George W. Bush in his January 2004 State of the Union address to Congress). It is not possible, especially in light of the Iraq War, to disentangle the US government's claim of right to wage pre-emptive war from the diplomacy of the last decade or so associated with humanitarian intervention. The inhibitions on intergovernmental initiatives or on bodies constituted by "eminent persons," that is, persons prominently associated with governmental and intergovernmental careers, are such that they can address these issues only indirectly if at all.[1] This leaves the delicate task of disentangling geopolitics from humanitarianism to independent critical voices of opinion in global civil society.

THE INTERVENTION QUANDARY

What makes this subject matter challenging from a normative perspective of law and ethics is that it is beneficial neither to give a green light to all interventionist diplomacy that proclaims humanitarian goals, nor to make absolute the

1. For discussion of the political constraints on such international commissions, see Richard Falk, "Liberalism at the Global Level: Solidarity vs. Cooperation," Eivind Hovden and Edward Keene, eds., *The Globalization of Liberalism* (New York: Palgrave, 2002), 75–98.

norm of non-intervention by posting a red light that altogether prohibits humanitarian encroachments on sovereignty. What seems appropriate is the yellow light of caution, recognising both the danger of allowing intervention to proceed under the humanitarian banner, and the corresponding danger of insisting on non-intervention despite the existence of a humanitarian emergency.

Such a cautious approach would seem to depend on an adminstering role for the United Nations, especially the Security Council. A precondition for a valid instance of humanitarian intervention is some explicit prior authorisation by the Security Council. But suppose it is not forthcoming despite a severe, unfolding humanitarian catastrophe? Can the UN General Assembly or a regional organisation play a residual authorising role? Can a coalition of the willing? Or in an extreme case of unfolding genocide or massive crimes against humanity would there not be a tacit approval regionally and globally that amounted to authorisation, or at least acquiescence?

This was the case when India entered East Pakistan (now Bangladesh) in 1971 to stop Pakistani atrocities, Vietnam entered Cambodia in 1978 to end the reign of terror by the Khmer Rouge, and Tanzania entered Uganda in 1979 to depose the Idi Amin dictatorship. Each of these examples involved an intervention by a neighbouring country which seemed to act on the basis of strategic interests, but also appeared to be motivated by genuine humanitarian concerns. Such a setting—mingling self-interest with humanitarianism—arouses suspicions about the true intentions of the intervention, but if a humanitarian catastrophe really is unfolding, it also should strengthen confidence that the intervention will be effective. In effect, realist incentives reinforce the humanitarian rationale for violating sovereign rights. To assess whether this rationale is but a pretext for intervention, consideration should also be given to factors such as whether the intervening state withdraws shortly after the humanitarian emergency has ended, whether it insists on establishing strategic bases and a long-term military presence in the target country, or whether it shows respect for the latter's right of self-determination.

To grasp the contours of the contemporary debate, as a prelude to recommending an approach, the next two sections will consider, first, the perspectives of the official bodies appointed to set forth guidelines and resolve conceptual and doctrinal tensions; and second, the less consensual civil society perspectives that reflect the spectrum of views on how to balance deference to sovereign rights and concerns about geopolitical manipulations against the moral imperative to prevent or mitigate an unfolding humanitarian catastrophe caused by political developments as distinct from natural disasters.

The issue is complicated legally by the disposition in 1945 to reassure states joining the United Nations that the new organisation would not intervene in matters "essentially within domestic jurisdiction" (Article 2.7 of the UN Charter), a provision widely understood to encompass abuses of a citizenry by its own government and even instances of civil strife and insurgency. Obviously, if the United Nations was denied the right to intervene, then states and regional actors had no such legal authority to use non-defensive force for such a purpose. Article 51 of the UN Charter creates an exception to the prohibition on recourse to force, but only with respect to preserving the right of self-defence, and then appearing to limit this right to occasions where the state invoking self-defence has experienced a prior attack. In effect, humanitarian intervention appeared to be outlawed by the UN Charter as initially drafted.

But the charter is a constitutional document that evolves as community values change and patterns of practice shape new understandings of the balance between the Westphalian autonomy of states and the global governance role of the international community. Integral to this shift in the direction of interventionist authority has been the unexpected rise of international human rights, and supportive notions and institutions of implementation, accountability, and even enforcement. The establishment in 2002 of the International Criminal Court is an institutional milestone in this process, although how far it will be able to realise its promise is uncertain, especially as it currently faces implacable opposition from the United States.

OFFICIAL BODIES

The Kosovo War of 1999 was undertaken by NATO in reaction to an unfolding scenario of acute human rights violations, a massive exodus of refugees, and a plausible prospect of ethnic cleansing. The Albanian 90 per cent majority population of Kosovo seemed at the mercy of the Serb minority, and given the then recent experience of the war in Bosnia, culminating in the 1995 Srebrenica massacre of about seven thousand Muslim males, it seemed reasonable to insist on humanitarian intervention despite the absence of support from permanent members of the UN Security Council. NATO did represent the leading countries in Europe, but it was not a true regional organisation, and in any event lacked authority to engage in any kind of enforcement action without Security Council approval. Also present were undisclosed strategic motivations, such as a desire to demonstrate NATO's credibility in the aftermath of the Cold War, and possibly to show that the United States would continue to provide leaderhsip on European security despite the absence of any external threat.

THE KOSOVO COMMISSION

It was this combination of circumstances that generated a highly visible debate about whether the Kosovo War should be regarded as a positive precedent for humanitarian intervention. (I leave aside legal and moral criticisms of the war relating to the tactical reliance on high-altitude bombing, and the failure of occupying forces to avoid reverse ethnic cleansing and other abuses of the Serb minority, especially immediately following the cessation of hostilities.) On the one side was concern about setting a precedent that allowed recourse to war outside the scope of the right of self-defence and in the absence of a mandate to intervene from the United Nations. On the other side was the moral and political desirability of acting effectively in the face of a humanitarian emergency, confirmed by a welcoming population and the rapid return of most of the Kosovo Albanian refugees. Shortly after the war, an "Independent International Commission on Kosovo" was established by the Swedish government, acting in consultation with the UN Secretary-General, to address these issues, as well as to consider the future of Kosovo.

The basic effort of the Kosovo Commission, which issued its report in 2000, was to offer an approach to addressing the doctrinal tension identified above. The report suggested, first of all, that the Kosovo War was "legitimate, although illegal." In effect, this meant an acceptance of the argument that a humanitarian emergency existed, making it morally and politically justified, and hence legitimate, to intervene militarily to protect the vulnerable Kosovar population. At the same time, the intervention was illegal because it involved a non-defensive use of international force that had not been authorised in advance by the United Nations.[2]

This circumstance of "legitimate, although illegal" was acknowledged to be confusing and unfortunate, but it seemed highly unlikely in the near future that the United Nations would formally revise its conceptions on the legality of force so as to overcome this tension. And yet it also seemed important for the international community to act in the face of an unfolding humanitarian emergency as it had in Kosovo.

One viewpoint that gained some attention at the time was to pronounce the law of the UN Charter to be essentially obsolete, and to leave the decision to intervene, as in Kosovo, to coalitions of the willing. Such an assessment, in effect, prematurely gives up on the charter effort to prohibit non-defensive wars of choice, a viewpoint that would exempt the invasion and subsequent occupation of Iraq from legal condemnation as a war of aggression. This "adjustment" unnecessarily concedes too much ground to geopolitical opportunism.

An alternative adjustment would involve the suspension of the veto enjoyed by permanent members of the Security Council, either by formal arrangement or informal patterns of practice, in instances of humanitarian emergency of the Kosovo or Darfur variety. This adjustment would be beneficial, and would have enabled the Kosovo intervention to receive Security Council authorisation, circumventing the expected vetoes of China and Russia. This adjustment is not politically acceptable at present as the trade-off between sovereignty and humanitarianism is understood and interpreted differently by permanent members of the Security Council. At play are not only differing degrees of attachment to sovereign rights, but the suspicion that humanitarian claims are often pretexts for the pursuit of grand strategy by hegemonic actors including

2. See Independent International Commission on Kosovo, *The Kosovo Report: Conflict, International Response, Lessons Learned* (Oxford: Oxford University Press, 2000).

pursuit of imperial ambitions. In effect, diminishing the relevance of the veto is also an unlikely adjustment under present world conditions.

Slightly less unlikely would be the evolution of a practice that allowed authorisation to come from the UN General Assembly in those instances where a positive recommendation of humanitarian intervention was blocked solely because of negative votes by one or two permanent members with veto powers.

The Kosovo Commission, acknowledging these difficulites, sought to endow the legitimate-but-illegal approach with a principled framework that would test a claim of legitimacy. The commission's report sets forth eleven principles, divided into threshold principles and contextual principles that determine whether and to what extent the contention of legitimacy associated with the intervention is persuasive. There are three threshold principles, the first of which is that there are two sets of triggering curcumstances: acute violations of human rights or of international humanitarian law; and state failure that exposes a population to mass suffering. The other two threshold principles insist that the intervention be undertaken for "the direct benefit of the victimised population" and that the method of intervention must be "reasonably calculated" to end the catastrophe as rapidly as possible and in a manner that protects civilians as a whole.

There are eight further contextual principles: war must be the last resort; efforts to gain UN authorisation must be undertaken; efforts to resolve the conflict peacefully must be undertaken; some degree of multilateralism must guide the whole process; there should not exist a formal censure of the proposed intervention by either the Security Council or the International Court of Justice; the laws of war must be strictly upheld; the intervening states should obtain no territorial or economic rewards, and should show a readiness to withdraw as soon as normalcy is restored; and sufficient resources should be made available in the post-conflict phases to facilitate economic, social, and political reconstruction.

Such checklist of principles is meant to provide guidelines for policy and appraisal, and is obviously subject to wide variations of interpretation in specific circumstances. Whether such considerations help to identify occasions for legitimate intervention and to shape its implementation remains to be seen. Of course, as

inaction in response to the unfolding and deepening humanitarian crisis in Sudan's Darfur region illustrates, as Rwanda did in 1994, no matter how legitimate the case for humanitarian intervention, without political will on the part of those actors with the capacity to intervene an effective international response will not be forthcoming. Paradoxically, it is one of the shadows cast upon claims of legitimacy—namely, the presence of strategic motives alongside humanitarian considerations—that makes it more likely that *effective* action will be taken only in situations where the moral and political case for humanitarian intervention is reinforced by strategic incentives. In this sense, vulnerable peoples exposed to abuse and state failure in sub-Saharan Africa are not nearly as likely to be protected by an international initiative as those being victimised in regions that enjoy high geopolitical priorities.

ICISS

A similar although distinctive tack on interventionist diplomacy was taken by the Canadian initiative that led to the establishment of the International Commission on Intervention and State Sovereignty (ICISS), which issued an influential report in 2001 under the title of *The Responsibility to Protect*. The report seeks to circumvent the controversy surrounding humanitarian intervention partly by adopting a different language, and shifting the locus of inquiry from the victimised population to the role of the international community in such circumstances. In this spirit, it abandons the terminology of "humanitarian intervention" as unnecessarily provocative in so frontally posing issues of sovereign rights and the use of force by the most powerful states. The aim is that by substituting the language of responsibility and protection, hot-button issues associated with interventionist diplomacy, evoking many bad memories of colonialism, can be circumvented, or at least mitigated.

The Responsibility to Protect frames the undertaking by reference to four basic objectives:

- to establish clearer rules, procedures and criteria for determining whether, when and how to intervene;
- to establish the legitimacy of military intervention when necessary and after all other approaches have failed;

- to ensure that military intervention, when it occurs, is carried out only for the purposes proposed, is effective, and is undertaken with proper concern to minimize the human costs and institutional damage that will result; and
- to help eliminate, where possible, the causes of conflict while enhancing the prospects for durable and sustainable peace.[3]

As with the Kosovo Commission's eleven principles, these objectives of ICISS seem intended as guides to policy and assessment rather than as reinforcements of the red lines of international law. The engagement of national and international responsibility is inevitably related to political will, which is itself shaped by strategic interests, public opinion, media attention, and short-term memories of success and failure associated with prior interventions. In the 1990s, the perceived failure of the U.S.-led mission in Somalia contributed significantly to the refusal to support UN action in Rwanda, despite the transparency of the genocidal dangers. This refusal reflected both the absence of strategic interests in sub-Saharan Africa perceived by the dominant states and the realisation that intervention could be costly in lives and resources. In contrast, Kosovo in 1999 generated the combination of an American sense of strategic stakes, a shift of tactics to diminish the risk of casualties for the intervening side, memories of impotence arising from the feeble role of the United Nations in Bosnia a few years earlier, and the impulse to show that a regional military alliance, NATO, was far more effective as an intervening actor than the United Nations had been.

ICISS was also intent on suggesting that responsibility be substituted for rights when it comes to the understanding of sovereignty, rendering a state that fails to protect its citizenry "irresponsible" and no longer entitled to unqualified deference. Such a rhetorical move is explained as necessary to incorporate the rise of human rights and to support the then emergent perspective on security that involved thinking less about that of the state (national security) and more about that of people (human security). The

report also urges that the main organs of the United Nations take steps to endorse this approach and to act accordingly, seeking to shape the political climate of opinion by formalising at intergovernmental and institutional level the consensus reached by the commission, which was composed of eminent persons representative of the world as whole, many of whom had enjoyed prominent careers in the governments of their respective countries.

THE UN's HIGH-LEVEL PANEL

The ICISS report attracted considerable attention when issued, partly because of the energy of ICISS's co-chair, Gareth Evans, former foreign minister of Australia, and partly because it made a successful effort to find a less threatening, yet sensible and clear, way to discuss humanitarian intervention. Its approach has been adopted by the report of the UN Secretary-General's High-Level Panel on Threats, Challenges and Change, *A More Secure World*, issued with considerable fanfare in November 2004. Two elements may be highlighted. The first is the explicit abridgement of the non-intervention norm:

> The principle of non-intervention in internal affairs cannot be used to protect genocidal acts or other atrocities, such as large-scale violations of international humanitarian law or large-scale ethnic cleansing, which can properly be considered a threat to international security and as such provoke action by the Security Council.[4]

A More Secure World recommends against any effort to alter the language of the UN Charter to accommodate this approach, contending that it is unnecessary and probably not politically feasible.

The second element is the claim that sovereignty is no longer operative as a shield for oppressive governments. The report suggests that "successive humanitarian disasters" in Somalia, Bosnia, Rwanda, Kosovo, and Darfur "have concentrated attention not on the immunities of

---

3. ICISS, *The Responsibility to Protect* (Ottawa: International Development Research Centre, 2001), 11, para. 2.3. ICISS also sets forth its own set of guidelines that resembles in most respects the eleven principles listed by the *Kosovo Report*, and that borrows from the language and approach used in the just war tradition: see xii–xiii.

4. Secretary General's High-Level Panel on Threats, Challenges and Change, *A More Secure World: Our Shared Responsibility* (New York: United Nations, 2004), 65, para. 200.

sovereign Governments but their responsibilities, both to their own people and to the wider international community."[5] In this regard, "responsibility" has a dual face, upwards to impose duties of protection on the organised international community, and downwards to confirm obligations of territorial governance on the sovereign state. Of course, given the nature of international society, as well as its normative framework, major states are essentially exempted from such obligations, being too large to be held accountable.

SHORTCOMINGS

These developments await further incidents to determine whether their impact is mainly on the *style* of diplomatic language or whether they also affect *behaviourial patterns of response*. What is excluded in these inquiries by credible individuals is the relevance, some would say the dominance, of geopolitics that seems crucial to the formation of political will, which in turn determines whether there is a strong prospect of an effective effort to insist on responsible behaviour by governments and the United Nations. The effects on the global policy agenda of the September 11, 2001 attacks, the dithering response to Darfur, and the apparent hostility of the current U.S. leadership to "humanitarian" nation-building (as contrasted with its enormous efforts in pursuit of strategic goals in Afghanistan and Iraq), combine to give the impression that humanitarian concerns and an ethos of human solidarity do not enjoy strong support from leading governments. Whether the epic natural disaster caused by the south Asian tsunami of December 2004 will result in a more hopeful picture of the extent of humanitarian concerns remains to be seen. From a realist perspective, the appeal of responding to a natural disaster is that costs and risks can be fixed with relative certainty in advance, and no loss of life on the intervening side is likely. It is also worth noting that the list of "humanitarian disasters" in the UN High-Level report mentions neither Afghanistan nor Iraq, despite the efforts of the United States, especially in Iraq, to justify its use

of force after the fact by reference to the undoubtedly oppressive conditions existing in both countries prior to the U.S. interventions there.

What is also missing, owing to the eminence of the membership of these elite bodies, which tend towards a concern with the credibility of their findings and recommendations in mainstream intergovernmental circles, is any kind of critical bite. There is a reluctance to name names, whether of states or individuals, and an unwillingness to address the distorting selectivity of geopolitics or to discuss the hidden motivations of the parties. The UN High-Level Panel went further than usual, perhaps too far as regards institutional etiquette, when it included in its report a somewhat disguised criticism of U.S. pretensions to provide for global security: "There is little evident international acceptance of the idea of security being best preserved by a balance of power, or by any single—even benignly motivated—superpower."[6] To find less veiled criticism or more ardent support for humanitarian intervention one must turn to civil society perspectives, especially those shaped by independent scholars who benefit from academic freedom. Conversely, those academic voices associated with think tanks and the like tend to reproduce the views of the blue-ribbon commissions, or even more narrowly, to tailor their recommendations to the viewpoints held by current power-wielders or their own major donors.

CIVIL SOCIETY PERSPECTIVES

MAINSTREAM MORALISTS

Throughout the extensive literature on humanitarian intervention, almost all of it written by scholars living in the countries that do the intervening, either directly or through the agency of international institutions, there is encountered a self-serving, moralistic rhetoric and tone. Michael Walzer has long served as a leading exponent of geopolitically conservative moralistic advocacy, including with respect to humanitarian intervention. In this spirit he writes, "Whenever the filthy work can be stopped, it

---

5. Ibid., para. 201.
6. Ibid., 62, para. 186. The scepticism relating to balance of power appears to be an elliptical repudiation of the realist approach to world order, and when combined with the rejection of hegemonic or imperial geopolitics appears to imply support for a norm-based, UN-centred approach.

should be stopped. And if not by us, the supposedly decent people of this world, then by whom?"[7]

Another stalwart mainstream moralist, Michael Ignatieff, who is even more explicitly supportive than Walzer of the moral claims of the the the leading political actors in the current world order, holds that criticism should be mostly directed at the reluctance to intervene, rather than at the supposedly incidental harm done by intervention.[8]

Such views by independent scholars provide invaluable aid and comfort to the United States and the former colonial powers, casting them in the role of moral saviours of peoples trapped in barbaric circumstances. What such apologists for imperial prerogatives uniformly ignore is the historical record of cruel criminality on the part of these self-appointed, post-colonial guardians of world order. They also ignore the latter's post-intervention record of irresponsible withdrawal or engagement with exploitative forms of reconstruction that ensure strategic control and economic benefits by way of lucrative investment contracts.

CRITICAL VOICES

Fortunately, the balance sheet on humanitarian intervention has been redrawn recently by several scholars who write from a critical perspective.[9] Anne Orford's *Reading Humanitarian Intervention* is a major contribution along these lines.[10] She effectively demonstrates the extent to which the perils of the present for societies experiencing humanitarian catastrophes are directly attributable to the legacy of colonial rule. The brunt of her trenchant analysis of humanitarian intervention focuses on the harm done to the society that is supposedly being helped to recover from atrocious circumstances, contending that this harm is neither collateral nor peripheral to the rescue operations. Orford shows that in the name of reconstruction, a capitalist set of

constraints is imposed on a broken society that impairs its right of self-determination and prevents its leadership from adopting an approach to development that benefits the people of the country rather than makes foreign investors happy. The essence of her position is that "legal narratives" justifying humanitarian intervention have had the primary effect of sustaining "an unjust and exploitative status quo."[11]

The deepest criticism of humanitarian intervention as legal narrative is that it operates to revalidate violence by the strong and dominant against the weak and subordinate. In Orford's provocative words,

> the international community shares something with those fantasized others against which it constitutes itself. It shares a commitment to the wounding and excluding of marked others as its founding act. This fact helps to explain the vehemence with which those who identify with the international community come to disavow the leaders of "rogue" or "failed" national or tribal communities as less than human. This disavowal is necessary precisely because these communities in fact share that which the international community rejects as illegitimate: an originary violence deployed against those marked out on the grounds of race, ethnicity and gender. The attempts to disavow this lead to more violence.[12]

Orford urges that rather than accepting explanations of state failure and abuse based on ethnic tensions, extremist religion, and micronationalist and tribal rivalries, attention be devoted to the strains imposed by the brutalising submission of labour and inequitable distribution of resources brought about by the disciplinary influence of neo-liberal capitalism. The further contention here is that legal narratives of development and material progress, even human rights, are relied upon to mask unjust structural divisions based on class, gender, and race that are being deliberately perpetuated by power-wielders, assisted in this dirty work at every stage by international lawyers.

7. Michael Walzer, *Arguing About War* (New Haven, Conn.: Yale University Press, 2004), 81.
8. Michael Ignatieff, "The Burden," *New York Times Magazine*, Jan. 5, 2003, 22–27, 50–54.
9. As with so much critical writing in international relations, Noam Chomsky has authored the seminal text repudiating the humanitarian claims of the United States. See Chomsky, *The New Military Humanism: Lessons from Kosovo* (Monroe, Maine: Common Courage Press, 1999).
10. Anne Orford, *Reading Humanitarian Intervention: Human Rights and the Use of Force in International Law* (Cambridge: Cambridge University Press, 2003).
11. Ibid., 11.
12. Ibid., 68.

Again, it is useful to reflect upon Orford's carefully chosen words: "The imperial desire to know and to access 'other' peoples and territories is transformed through the practice of international law into a sense of expertise and authorization to speak about those who can be constructed as in need of 'our' help."[13] Such an analysis encourages us to explore the hidden infrastructure of violent undertakings that proclaim their humanitarian credentials. This hidden infrastructure of economic and strategic self-interest manifests itself in a number of ways: by abandoning a society in shambles once the strategic objective of the intervener has been achieved (for example, Afghanistan in 1989); by sustaining an occupation without investing sufficiently in reconstruction (Bosnia since 1995, Kosovo since 1999); by seeking to establish strategic bases and economic privileges in a ravaged society (Iraq, 2003); and by imposing a new leadership and a capitalist developmental template on the occupied country, thereby obstructing the right of self-determination and setting the stage for future political violence (almost every country that has been the site of humanitarian intervention since 1990).

All of this contributes to sustaining a sort of "collective day-dream," as Edward Said describes the Orientalist process of visioning the other, which in the setting of humanitarian intervention allows the exploitative dominant side to preserve the illusion of moral distance between itself and evil out there at a remove. By so doing, Orford argues, the intervening states, or their constructed "international community," represent themselves by contrasting images arising from being "sovereign, civilized, autonomous, powerful and humane."[14] Such thinking as Orford's is definitely a needed corrective to patterns of naïve and uncritical liberal advocacy that have dominated mainstream discussions of humanitarian diplomacy, but does it go too far? When wirting and speaking from the margins it is generally necessary to exaggerate to be heard at all, but then supercilious voices from the centre respond knowingly that the criticism is "polemical," "utopian," and "irresponsible." At a minimum, it is important to listen carefully

to criticism from the margins, and then decide whether to correct for exaggeration.

Orford recognises the anguishing dilemma posed by the choice between inhumane action and inhumane inaction, specifically in the face of the terrifying 1999 crisis in East Timor when the Indonesian military engaged in and fomented massacres of the helpless civilian society that had been brutally colonised for the previous twenty-four years. Her point is that narrowing the issue to such a choice between action and inaction distorts the challenge facing analyst and advocate alike. Instead of evolving rationalisations for humanitarian intervention at the boiling point, it should be the work of international lawyers to point to the deforming legacies of colonial rule and hegemonic aspirations, and even more so to suggest alternative paths to development that will avoid the onset of catastrophe for a society and to shape post-catastrophe reconstruction in ways that produce a just and sustainable social, political, and economic order. The lens of intervention, pro or contra, is too narrow to encompass the relevant terrain for a genuine humanitarian undertaking.

A parallel critique of conventional understandings of humanitarian intervention is offered by Ikechi Mgbeoji with specific reference to sub-Saharan Africa, focusing on Liberia as a case that illuminates a far wider pattern of instability afflicting the post-colonial destiny of much of the continent.[15] Mgbeoji locates the source of contemporary African troubles in the crude colonialist machinations of European states, culminating in the carving up of African natural communities into a series of artificial colonies at the 1884–1885 Berlin Conference. This resulted in a dynamic of emergence from the colonial experience with artificial polities that were vulnerable to disruption and had populations unprepared for the exercise of constructive leadership. Mgbeoji also attributes blame to the kind of opportunistic African elites that took power in so many of these countries, often with the connivance of the former colonial overlords, disclosing an overall pattern of co-responsibility:

I argue that the corrosion of the African psyche and the mutilation of precolonial African

---

13. Ibid., 79.
14. Ibid., 204.
15. Ikechi Mgbeoji, *Collective Insecurity: The Liberian Crisis, Unilateralism, and Global Order* (Vancouver: UBC Press, 2003).

political structures laid the basis for the modern crises afflicting the continent. Beyond the pernicious legacy of European imperialism coupled with myopic, selfish, and impoverished leadership of the African elite, it seems clear that the solution to African political instability lies in a structural rearrangement of the African polity for the purpose of legitimate governance of African peoples.[16]

In sum, the boundaries of the post-colonial state should not be treated as sacrosanct, especially when their effect is to bisect communities of solidarity. Mgbeoji shows how much the tragedy of Liberia is a product of this heritage of artificial boundaries that disregard the ethnic and tribal contours of peoples. Unlike Orford, he gives less significance to predatory capitalism, except as a by-product of this unholy alliance between the colonialist background and a corrupt indigenous foreground. But like Orford, Mgbeoji repudiates the moralistic aura of Western interventionist diplomacy that purports to be an antidote to African primitiveness and barbarism.

Mgbeoji is worried about the loosening of the bonds of international law in African initiatives designed to address humanitarian catastrophes. He is not very positive about enstrusting African regional actors with peace-keeping missions unsupervised by the United Nations, citing the troubling experience of Liberia to bolster a wider argument. In the end, Mgbeoji believes that so long as the underlying conditions in Africa are based on artificial ideas of statehood, humanitarian catastrophes will recur, and interventionist undertakings, even if properly guided, can do no more than provide temporary relief to a beleaguered society.

Overcoming this circumstance of what he calls "collective insecurity" will require a much more comprehensive approach that gets at the roots of conflict and hostility: "the practice of a holistic concept of collective security and distributive social justice secured by legitimate state boundaries and good governance is the antidote to the civil conflicts ravaging the continent."[17] Mgbeoji makes it clear that part of the problem is the international practice of associating legitimate governance with control of the capital city by the leader and with an electoral process that often has only ritualistic significance, thereby circumventing the more fundamental sources of legitimacy that lie in genuine political loyalty by the people and a corresponding commitment by the leaderhsip to achieve social justice for the totality of the society. Such goals cannot be realised within the parameters of present African statehood, giving Mgbeoji's argument a certain utopian edge, despite the power of his compelling assessment of the African situation, which includes the judgement that a fire-fighting mentality about the continent's underlying crisis is totally inadequate.

CONCLUDING OBSERVATIONS

The subject matter of humanitarian intervention has been foregrounded by the rise of the issue of human rights in a globalising world. At the same time, the practices of rescuing populations raises a variety of *proximate* concerns associated with justification and effectiveness. It also raises more *fundamental* concerns associated with the causal onset of humanitarian emergencies and the impact of reconstructive efforts. There are two sets of responses that have been noted; the first comes from those who represent the established order, and seek to reconcile a sensitivity to the rights of independent states with actions designed to bring relief and rescue to peoples entrapped within oppressive or anarchic circumstances. These perspectives seek to make humanitarian intervention acceptable and operational, revising international law along the way, but without questioning underlying conditions or the motives of the interveners.

The second set of responses comes from critics of the established order who regard humanitarian intervention as a hypocritical exercise in post-colonial imperialism that not only fails to address basic issues generative of mass suffering, but may aggravate and intensify such suffering by diverting attention from real causes and available cures.

This whole setting of debate has been complicated by the September 11 attacks on the United States, and the American response that has fused a new generation of real concerns about domestic security with a militarist push for global dominance by a Western power. In

16. Ibid., 1.
17. Ibid., 142.

this latter context, as seen in Iraq since the U.S. invasion of 2003, the humanitarian intervention argument is invoked as a cover for aggressive warfare and a prolonged hostile occupation. At the same time, the massive humanitarian catastrophe festering in Darfur has evoked widespread concern internationally, but only minimalist protective action, again confirming that where strategic interests are weak, the necessary political will for protective action will not be forthcoming, no matter how grave and massive the unfolding tragedy and no matter how the intervention is sanitised by the language of protection. Rwanda *redux*.

The way forward is to proceed on complementary lines. Despite the difficulties and ambiguities of practice, it remains beneficial to counsel effective action in response to instances of ethnic cleansing, genocide, and crimes against humanity. It may be feasible to bring into being a volunteer, professional capability under the auspices of the United Nations that would be entrusted with the implementation of humanitarian diplomacy with reduced geopolitical interference. At the same time, it is essential to disseminate beyond academic circles the sorts of critical perspective developed so powerfully by Orford and Mgbeoji, widening the orbit of understanding to encompass the *causes* of humanitarian catastrophe and the *effects* of both humanitarian intervention and adherence to the norm of non-intervention.

QUESTIONS FOR REFLECTION AND DISCUSSION

1. What constitutes humanitarian intervention? A speech in the United Nations critical of another country's mistreatment of its own or other citizens? A transboundary radio or television broadcast for the same purpose? The termination of diplomatic relations in protest of mistreatment of citizens or others? A trade embargo? Deployment of armed forces to the offending nation's border? One writer once stated that "intervention may be anything from a speech of Lord Palmerston's in the House of Commons to the partition of Poland." P. H. Winfield, "The History of Intervention in International Law," *British Yearbook of International Law* 3 (1922–23): 130–49, at 130. Would Falk agree? How does he define the concept of unilateral humanitarian intervention? Is Winfield's definition simply an anachronism, reflective of a world in which nations were still largely able to exist in isolation and in which something so seemingly minor as a speech represented an unusual encroachment on another nation's sovereignty?

2. Falk notes that the Kosovo Commission suggested that the Kosovo War was "legitimate, although illegal." Does this formulation have any real meaning? Is a legal system in which an act is simultaneously legitimate and illegal a coherent system? Would it not be more coherent—and honest—to say "illegal, although pardonable"? Is not the etymological derivation of "legitimate" and "legal" more or less identical? Or is the Kosovo Commission distinguishing between morality and law or between justice and law? If so, how is it possible to have a war or other event that is moral or just but illegal? Does this make the formulation any more coherent? Why? Why not?

3. Assuming that the international law doctrine of unilateral humanitarian intervention means, at a minimum, the right of State A to use force against State B for the purpose of protecting the inhabitants of State B from inhumane treatment by State B, what factors should State A be required to take into account when seeking to justify a right to unilateral humanitarian intervention? What constitutes lawful unilateral humanitarian intervention? Unlawful intervention? What criteria might help to distinguish between the two? Consult articles 2(4), 51, 55, and 56 of the UN Charter. Also the eleven principles of the Kosovo Commission. Do they present an adequate test of legitimacy?

4. Falk argues that both the eleven principles of the Kosovo Report and the four basic objectives announced in *The Responsibility to Protect* "seem intended as guides to policy and assessment rather than as reinforcements of the red lines of international law." Do you think this is a sign of deficiency or pragmatism? Do you think the "red lines" need changing? Or simply obeying?

5. U.S. President George W. Bush claimed as a partial justification for the war in Iraq begun in 2003 that he was acting to prevent further human rights violations against the Iraqi people by Saddam Hussein. In particular, Bush and the rest of the U.S. administration made much of the unquestionably horrific atrocities visited on the Kurds of northern

Iraq in the decade preceding the first Gulf War. Should there be a statute of limitations on justifications for purportedly "humanitarian" interventions? If one were to grant that the United States was justified in intervening in Iraq on humanitarian grounds, how would the methods used fare based on the principles Falk enunciates? Research briefly the costs, human and environmental, of the war in Iraq. For an impressionistic glimpse, see Human Rights Index (Winter 2004–5) of The University of Iowa Center for Human Rights, *The Iowa Review* 34, no. 3 (Winter 2004–5): v–vi, available at http://www.uichr.org/Activities. Are the costs "incidental" as Ignatieff might argue? What would Anne Orford say?

6. Do you agree that humanitarian intervention is a "hypocritical exercise in post-colonial imperialism"? Is it so in all cases? Consider the case of Kosovo: who were the colonizers and who the colonized? Who were the hypocrites?

7. In "Interpretation and Change in the Law of Humanitarian Intervention," in J. L. Holzgrefe and Robert O. Keohane, eds., *Humanitarian Intervention: Ethical, Legal, and Political Dilemmas* (Cambridge: Cambridge University Press, 2003), 204–31, Thomas Franck argues, at 206, that "the [UN] Charter *is* what the principal organs *do*." Franck notes that the diplomats who serve in the UN are deeply conscious that their actions *make* law. Do you think this is true? Do you think it is just? Are the actions of all the diplomats equal? The actions of all nations? Is Franck right to assert that this does not amount to the "law of the jungle"? What is the "law of the jungle"?

8. The Canadian Commission on Intervention and State Sovereignty noted in its 2001 report, *The Responsibility to Protect*, that there is currently a "gulf between outdated concepts of peacekeeping [i.e., the UN strategies crafted "for an era of war between states"] and full-scale military operations that may have deleterious impacts on civilians." Do you agree that the UN strategies are outdated? If so, what has rendered them obsolete? Does it matter? What does the Commission advocate to replace them?

9. Can a stable international order ever result from continuing to meet atrocities with violence? Does violent intervention always produce a "loser" who will likely not be satisfied with the regime resulting from the intervention? What recourse does that loser have? Consider, in this regard, the violence in Sudan's Darfur province ongoing at this writing. Will that violence end by the application of violent remedies? What would nonviolent remedies look like? Would they work? Does the following thought from David McReynolds offer any guidance? "Non-violence means an effort to do battle with injustice without risking the destruction of our opponents, both because we cannot be absolutely certain we are right . . . and because our opponents are as unique as ourselves." *The Philosophy of Non-Violence*, available at http://www.nonviolence.org. If we were truly to recognize our opponents as unique (i.e., as worth preserving), would we necessarily have to place ourselves at more risk in order to avoid endangering them?

10. Many commentators on humanitarian intervention argue strenuously that proportionality between the harm sought to be prevented and the methods employed is crucial to the legitimacy and/or legality of an intervention. This is one of the few grounds for consensus among many of these thinkers. But consider Howard Zinn's counterpoint: "It seems that however moral is the cause that initiates a war (in the minds of the public, in the mouths of the politicians), it is in the nature of war to corrupt that morality until the rule becomes 'An eye for an eye, a tooth for a tooth,' and soon it is not a matter of equivalence, but indiscriminate revenge." Howard Zinn, "Just and Unjust War," in *The Zinn Reader: Writings on Disobedience and Democracy* (New York: Seven Stories Press, 1997), 229–66, available at http://co.quaker.org/Writings/JustAndUnjustWar.htm. Do you agree? What contains a war besides the good faith of the winner?

11. In "Humanitarian Intervention and American Foreign Policy: Law, Morality and Politics," *Journal of International Affairs* 37 (1984): 311–28, political scientist Jack Donnelly, no friend of unilateral military intervention and in thoughtful search of proportionality, proposes the alternative of "positive nonintervention," i.e., "thorough noninvolvement with regimes guilty of massive violations of human rights" or "non-support for major human rights violators," not as a matter of right but as a matter of international legal duty, a form of obligatory shunning familiar to the Amish and other religious sects. Would such a policy be significantly less debilitating to the people of the target state than military sanctions? Than economic sanctions? In "American Intervention in Cuba and the Rule of Law," *Ohio State Law Journal* (Summer 1961): 546–85, Richard A. Falk argues that the withdrawal

from Cuba by the administration of U.S. President Eisenhower of a preferential quota for Cuban sugar imports by the United States, ostensibly in protest of Cuban human rights violations, amounted to an unlawful unilateral intervention since Cuba's economy was then dependent on the U.S. market. Frank Dawson and Burns H. Weston make the same point in *"Banco Nacional de Cuba v. Sabbatino*: New Wine in Old Bottles," *University of Chicago Law Review* 31 (1963): 63–102, at 94. Would Donnelly agree? Comparing Falk's 1961 assessment with his essay here, can it be said that his position has changed? If so, how, and are you persuaded? In any event, how would a policy of "positive nonintervention" be effectively implemented? In a fractious global community, could it be effectively implemented multilaterally? Would not its potential effectiveness be restricted to essentially powerful states acting more or less unilaterally? If so, would that be any more healthy an outcome for the international system?

12. Articles 19, 20, and 21 of the Charter of the Organization of American States (referenced in Documentary Appendix B) provide as follows:

Article 19. No State or group of States has the right to intervene, directly or indirectly, for any reason whatever, in the internal or external affairs of any other State. The foregoing principle prohibits not only armed force but also any other form of interference or attempted threat against the personality of the State or against its political, economic, and cultural elements.

Article 20. No State may use or encourage the use of coercive measures of an economic or political character in order to force the sovereign will of another State and obtain from it advantages of any kind.

Article 21. The territory of a State is inviolable; it may not be the object, even temporarily, of military occupation or of other measures of force taken by another State, directly or indirectly, on any grounds whatever. No territorial acquisitions or special advantages obtained either by force or by other means of coercion shall be recognized.

Review Question 11, above, in light of these provisions. Is unilateral humanitarian intervention or even "positive nonintervention" ever legally permissible among the member states of the OAS?

13. Louis Henkin argued in "Kosovo and the Law of 'Humanitarian Intervention,'" *AJIL* 93 (1999): 824–28, at 826, that "the law is, and ought to be, that unilateral intervention by military force by a state or group of states is unlawful unless authorized by the Security Council." Is this view now as anachronistic as the 80-year-old language quoted in Question 1, above? Or is Henkin standing on legal bedrock? What are the *legal* foundations of the more permissive views held by others and outlined by Professor Falk?

14. What do you make of Article 2(4) of the UN Charter, which states that "All Members shall refrain in their international relations from the threat or use of force against the territorial integrity or political independence of any state." Does this language create a blanket prohibition against State A sending troops or projectiles into State B for *any* purpose? Or, rather, does it merely prohibit the use of military force for conquering another state? Consider also the language of Article 51, which states that "Nothing in the present Charter shall impair the inherent right of individual or collective self-defence if an armed attack occurs against a Member of the United Nations." Following the terrorist attacks of September 11, 2001, against whom would Article 51 have justified military action by the United States? Would any of the other UN Member states who lost nationals in the attacks have been similarly justified?

Chapter Eight

Private Sector Approaches to Human Rights Implementation

ADDRESSING the enforcement of human rights, legal scholar Louis Henkin has written that it was "the early assumption [of the founders of the United Nations] that states might be prepared to scrutinize other states and be scrutinized by them."[1] This optimism has not stood the test of time in any energetic way, however. There is a discernible lack of commitment on the part of many governments to protect human rights in their own countries and through international institutions at the global level as well. Except for the Netherlands and the Scandinavian countries, which consistently champion human rights, there has been little "horizontal" enforcement of the sort suggested by Henkin. Instead, the defense of human rights has been left largely to private groups and individuals at the grass roots.

Communications media daily draw to our attention private initiatives on behalf of human rights: international wire services carried Vaclav Havel's message that "if freedom and dignity are threatened somewhere in the world they are in jeopardy everywhere"— uttered by the Czech playwright and human rights activist in 1989 on the occasion of his popular election as President of the Czech and Slovak Republic; in 1991, *Prime Time Live* featured a TV interview of Sister Dianna Ortiz describing her rape and torture by Guatemalan government security forces outraged by the nun's human rights work with indigenous peoples; since 2001, Migrants Assistance Program (MAP, Thailand) has had weekly broadcast radio programs in the Karen language on health and human rights to persecuted ethnic Karens in Myanmar.

Such expressions of private concern for human rights have multiplied around the globe and now characterize post-Cold War political life as key aspects of what has come to be called "the worldwide human rights movement." According to Saul H. Mendlovitz and R. B. J. Walker, world movements—constituting social patterns of non-statist political participation in international affairs, are increasing. In our time, they write, "political life has been marked by a renewed resurgence of social movements . . ., peace movements, human rights movements, environmental movements, urban movements, movements of

1. Louis Henkin, *The Rights of Man Today* (Boulder, Colo.: Westview Press, 1980), 94.

indigenous people and movements for alternative forms of economic life. Massive popular movements have challenged authoritarian regimes and demonstrated opposition to specific policies."[2] They add: "Grass-roots movements have sprung up everywhere. . . . While it is possible to interpret their character and significance in different ways, it is not possible to ignore them—no analysis of modern political life can leave them out."[3]

Occasionally the exemplars of such movements are accorded international approval, as illustrated by the annual Jan Palach Human Rights Award conferred on Vaclav Havel in 1983 or the annual Eclipse Award conferred in 2001 on Dianna Ortiz by the Center for the Victims of Torture. With publicity and fanfare, individual heroics and group service on behalf of human rights are formally recognized also through the presentation of awards by, to name a few, the Martin Luther King, Jr. Foundation, the Reebok Human Rights Foundation, the Robert F. Kennedy Memorial Fund, and Front Line, an Irish NGO honoring "human rights defenders working at considerable risk." The public symbolism involved in these awards lends credibility and strength to individual initiative. When Kenyan human rights activist and environmental advocate Wangari Maathai or Iranian lawyer and human rights defender Shirin Ebadi speak up against government abuses, the voices of the two women are enhanced by their status as Nobel Laureates (2003 and 2004 respectively).

Indeed, the recent willingness of the Nobel Committee to award its Peace Prize to such persons for their courageous work in defense of human rights not only "says volumes about the intimate connection between the advancement of important human values and the establishment of peaceful societies"[4] but also speaks well of the important role that private individuals and groups can play in support of human rights on the international plane. It is significant, writes political scientist Lynn Miller, "that several Nobel awards have gone to private individuals or organizations whose efforts often have run directly counter to the practices of governments or important political parties. In a world where such recognition is possible, governments and their spokesmen no longer are without effective gadflies from within their societies to push them toward the fuller enhancement of the rights of human beings."[5] Among the most conspicuous nongovernmental human rights organizations to which Miller refers is, of course, Amnesty International (AI), recipient of the Nobel Peace Prize in 1977. After AI won its award, its profile and activities shot up. The same can be said of the Campaign to Ban Landmines 20 years later, led by Jody Williams. The publicity brought by such awards translates into adherents and donations.

HUMAN RIGHTS NGOS

By and large, nongovernmental organizations (NGOs)[6] have been significant catalysts relative to the promotion and protection of internationally recognized human rights.[7] Their development germinated in the origins of the Universal Declaration when, according to

2. Saul H. Mendlovitz and R. B. J. Walker, *Towards a Just World Peace: Perspectives from Social Movements* (London: Butterworths, 1987), 9.
3. Ibid.
4. Lynn H. Miller, *Global Order: Values and Power in International Relations* (Boulder, Colo.: Westview Press, 1985), 173.
5. Ibid.
6. Borrowing from Stephen Marks, we use the term "nongovernmental organizations"(NGOs) "because it is used in the UN Charter and is the most common way of referring to associations independent of the state that animate civil society. However, more positive appellations have been proposed, such as People's Movements, Voluntary Independent Movements, Civil Society Associations, and Voluntary Civil Societies." Stephen P. Marks, "The United Nations and Human Rights: The Promise of Multilateral

William Korey, NGOs played an important role in the formulation of international human rights norms.[8] His book, *NGOs and the Universal Declaration of Human Rights*, meticulously documents the encouragement and support tendered UDHR framers by such groups as the American Federation of Labor, the American Jewish Committee, the Federal Council of Churches, and others, to make human rights a core commitment of the new United Nations.

The subtitle of Korey's book, *A Curious Grapevine*, derives from Mrs. Eleanor Roosevelt's reference to NGOs when she presciently told the *New York Times* on December 8, 1948 that: a "curious grapevine" will carry word of the Declaration throughout the world whereby information "may seep in even when governments are not so anxious for it."[9] Indeed, validating Mrs. Roosevelt's prescience, the "curious grapevine" over the decades since 1948 has come to be essential for raising public consciousness about human rights, for monitoring violations, and for shaming human rights violators. Human rights groups have created a legacy of achievement in trying to influence governments to rectify human rights violations. In so doing they characteristically fight an uphill battle in which human rights values often are sacrificed by government officials to Realpolitik: the need for economic markets, favoring military allies, or preserving entrenched elites. Jerome Shestack compares the nongovernmental organizations dedicated to the human rights struggle to the mythical Sisyphus who resolutely pushed a weighty stone up a steep mountain. Says Shestack, "the pinnacle may never be reached. Still, while traveling the upward road, obstructions are overcome; the path is made smoother for others."[10] Like Sisyphus, the NGOs do what they must. The very struggle itself takes on a symbolic meaning, enhancing human dignity. "When all is said and done," Shestack concludes, "there is no other human course to pursue."[11]

In Reading 31 in this chapter, Richard Pierre Claude answers the question: "What Do Human Rights NGOs Do?"—presenting examples to explain the roles NGOs play in national and international politics for the promotion and protection of one or more internationally recognized human rights. Probably the most famous such group is Amnesty International (AI) which, in 2005, claimed more than 1.8 million members in over 150 countries.[12] AI, headquartered in London, seeks the release of persons detained arbitrarily anywhere—for their beliefs, for example—provided such persons have not used or advocated violence. AI terms these people "prisoners of conscience."[13] Also noteworthy, not least because it is an outgrowth of the Helsinki Process that led ultimately to the collapse of the Soviet Union, is Human Rights Watch (HRW). Headquartered in New York City, HRW shares with AI the distinction of being one of only two international human rights organizations that operate worldwide in most situations of severe repression or abuse.[14]

Diplomacy and Action," in Burns H. Weston and Stephen P. Marks, eds. *The Future of International Human Rights* (Ardsley, N.Y.: Transnational Publishers, 1999), 291–350, at 292 n. 5.

7. See, e.g., Henry F. Carey and Oliver P. Richmond, eds., *Mitigating Conflict: The Role of NGOs* (Portland, Ore.: Frank Cass, 2003).

8. William Korey, *NGOs and the Universal Declaration of Human Rights: "A Curious Grapevine"* (New York: St. Martin's Press, 1998), 48.

9. Ibid., 48, quoting from the *New York Times*, Dec. 8, 1948, at 13.

10. Jerome J. Shestack, "Sisyphus Endures: The International Human Rights NGO," *New York Law School Law Review* 24 (1978): 89–123, at 20.

11. Ibid., 89. See also Sidonie Smith and Kay Schaffer, *Human Rights and Narrated Lives: The Ethics of Recognition* (New York: Palgrave, Macmillan, 2004).

12. See AI's website at http://www.amnesty.org

13. See Ann Marie Clark, *Diplomacy of Conscience: Amnesty International and Changing Human Rights Norms* (Princeton, N.J.: Princeton University Press, 2001).

14. See the HRW website at http://www.hrw.org

VARIETIES OF NGOS

Unlike AI and HRW, not all human rights NGOs are international in membership or universal in scope. But among those with comparable range are the International Commission of Jurists (ICJur, headquartered in Geneva),[15] the International Helsinki Federation for Human Rights (IHFHR, Vienna),[16] the International League for Human Rights (ILHR, New York),[17] and the Minority Rights Group (MRG, London).[18] Like AI and HRW, these four groups are international in the sense that they have a contributing membership base and affiliates from throughout the world. The International Committee of the Red Cross (ICRC), deriving its international status from its unique role as guardian of the Geneva Conventions on the humanitarian rules of armed conflict, is a special case because its membership is wholly Swiss.[19]

International human rights NGOs such as AI, HRW, ICJur, IHFHR, ILHR, and MRG have special "consultative status" with the United Nations. As a result, they have direct access to the UN Commission on Human Rights, its Subcommission on the Promotion and Protection of Human Rights, the International Labour Organization (ILO), and the United Nations Educational, Scientific and Cultural Organization (UNESCO). Whenever the item "Violations of Human Rights" is taken up by the UN Commission on Human Rights, the most courageous and outspoken champions of human rights usually are these and other NGOs in their consultative status.

A special category of private human rights activity is found in the work of religious organizations[20] and professional groups—often called "transnational organizations"—whose membership and concerns transcend national boundaries.[21] In recent years, international professional associations have established human rights units or committees to support colleagues who, despite political pressure, follow professional ethical standards or who speak out critically about public policy. Lawyers, having a stake in the rule of law, were among the first to organize international collegial support. For example, the Committee on International Human Rights of the American Bar Association Section on Individual Rights and Responsibilities publishes "network mailings" urging lawyers to write letters of support for counterparts overseas. When Dr. Vu Quoc Thong, former Dean of the University of Saigon Law School, was forbidden by the new Vietnamese government to practice law and also was barred from emigration, attorneys elsewhere wrote on his behalf to the Ministry of Justice of the Socialist Republic of Vietnam.

15. See the ICJur website at http://www.icj.org
16. See the IHFHR website at http://www.ihf-hr.org/index.php
17. See the ILHR website at http://www.ilhr.org
18. The MRG develops information on oppressed ethnic, linguistic, and religious groups worldwide. See Minority Rights Group, *World Directory of Minorities* (Chicago: St. James Press, 1990). See also the MRG website at http://www.minorityrights.org
19. See David P. Forsythe, *The Humanitarians: The International Committee of the Red Cross* (Cambridge: Cambridge University Press, 2005); John F. Hutchinson, *Champions of Charity: War and the Rise of the Red Cross* (Boulder, Colo.: Westview Press, 1996). See also the ICRC web site at http://www.icrc.org
20. The literature on religious groups and human rights is substantial. See, e.g., David Hollenbach, S.J., *The Global Face of Public Faith: Politics, Human Rights, and Christian Ethics* (Washington, D.C.: Georgetown University Press, 2003); Peter Juviler, ed., *Religion and Human Rights: Competing Claims?* (Armonk, N.Y.: M.E. Sharpe, 1998); Milton Ridvas Konvitz, *Judaism and Human Rights* (New Brunswick, N.J.: Transaction Publications, 2001); Wayne L. Proudfoot and J. Paul Martin, eds., *Religious Diversity and Human Rights* (New York: Columbia University Press, 1996); Ahmed E. Soovaiaia, *Human Rights and Islam: The Divine and the Mundane in Human Rights Law* (New York: Universe, 2003); Desmond Tutu, *God Has a Dream: A Vision of Hope for Our Time* (New York: Doubleday, 2004).
21. See, e.g., Richard Pierre Claude, *Science in the Service of Human Rights* (Philadelphia: University of Pennsylvania Press, 2002). Churches, like professions, are transnational organizations. See also Robert O. Keohane, *Transnational Relations and World Politics* (Cambridge, Mass.: Harvard University Press, 1972).

In another professional field, PEN, an international association of poets, playwrights, essayists, editors, and novelists (hence the acronym), pledges responsibility for writers silenced by repressive governments and focuses attention on their plight by mobilizing assistance, dispatching letters to officials, and occasionally sending representatives to foreign capitals to obtain information on imprisoned writers. Comparable groups include Article 19, based in London and taking its name from that provision of the UDHR that proclaims "the right to freedom of opinion and expression (which includes) freedom to hold opinions without interference and to seek, receive and impart information and ideas through any media and regardless of frontiers"; and Canadian Journalists for Free Expression (CJFE) which has created an electronic mail system for an Action Alert Network linking scores of media organizations from more than 20 countries to monitor human rights and freedom of expression abuses of journalists, writers, and academics around the world— a crisis-oriented initiative that has saved numerous people from imprisonment and death.[22] Also noteworthy for like reasons is the Network of Cities of Asylum established on the initiative of Salman Rushdie and Wole Soyinka in 1994 as the International Parliament of Writers in response to an appeal launched in 1993 by 300 writers from around the world following an upsurge in assassinations of writers in Algeria. The Network strives to provide protected working environments for writers, journalists, editors, and publishers active in theater, music, the media, and so forth from around the world and also regularly publishes *Autodafe—The Journal of the International Parliament of Writers* that aims to be "a place for debate and experimentation" where writers, silenced by censorship, join voices with world-renowned writers to reflect on the "social and political realities of the world, censorship, the interdict of language, and the effects of globalization among others."[23] Similarly, though not restricted to writers and artists, the Scholars at Risk Network (SAR), an international network of universities and colleges founded in 2000 and based in New York City, works to promote academic freedom and to defend the human rights of scholars worldwide.[24] Many of these organizations are affiliated by their membership in International Freedom of Expression Exchange (IFEX), founded in 1992 when many of the world's leading freedom of expression organizations came together in Montreal to discuss how best to further their collective goals.[25]

Scientists, too, have acted collectively for international human rights. The Human Rights Committee of the National Academy of Science (Washington, D.C.) has taken up the cause of Somali, Syrian, and Chinese scientists since the 1990s. The Human Rights Program of the American Association for the Advancement of Science has issued reports on the abuse of Russian nuclear whistle-blowers, Belarus scientists, and Cuban technicians. In Europe, the International Council of Scientific Unions (Paris) has a Committee on the "Safeguard of the Pursuit of Science," documenting cases of scientists who have been seriously restricted in the pursuit or communication of their research. The work of Physicians for Human Rights (PHR, Boston) began in 1988, when it sent Dr. John Constable, the Harvard Medical School burn specialist, to Chile to attend to Rodrigo Rojas and Carmen Quintana after police in Santiago tried to incinerate them for engaging in a protest demonstration against the Pinochet regime. PHR sponsors a forensics anthropology program which, in the *Journal of the American Medical Association*, published the results of its exhumation of a mass grave in Iraq that harbored evidence of the horrendous slaughter of Iraqi citizens by the regime

22. See the CJFE website at http://www.cjfe.org
23. "Description," *Autodafe* 1 (Spring 2001), available at http://www.sevenstories.com/Book/index.cfm?GCOI =58322100398870
24. See the SAR website at http://scholarsatrisk.nyu.edu/index.htm
25. See the IFEX website at http://www.ifex.org

of Saddam Hussein.[26] The forensic application of scientific methods to human rights problems is described by Christopher Joyce and Eric Stover in *Witnesses from the Grave: The Story Bones Tell*,[27] a book the *Washington Post* described as a "human rights thriller."

Another category of human rights organizations are "solidarity groups" that focus on human rights in a particular country or region.[28] An example is the Tibet Centre for Human Rights and Democracy, whose monthly *Update* publishes details on the current human rights situation in Tibet.[29] Drawing primarily on the testimonies of Tibetans who have recently arrived in exile, the newsletters highlight the individual experience of Tibetans in Chinese-occupied Tibet. Since the first issue in November 1996, the readership has greatly expanded and copies are sent around the world to relevant human rights organizations, Tibet support groups, embassies, and individual subscribers.

The largest number of human rights NGOs are domestically oriented groups concerned with human rights in their own societies—the first such group being, historically, the French League for Human Rights, established in 1902. With the support of the great French writer, Victor Hugo, the League organized in reaction to the Dreyfus case and attendant French anti-semitism. The French example was imitated by other domestically based groups in Western Europe and likewise by the American Civil Liberties Union (ACLU) in the United States, which grew out of the National Bureau of Civil Liberties, organized in 1919, to oppose arbitrary deportations of both naturalized citizens and disfavored aliens. The European leagues and the ACLU have followed similar patterns of growth. While formed in response to specific conflict situations, they soon pursued a broad range of activities in defending individual civil liberties and expanding democratic governance. The Philippine Civil Liberties Union was specifically founded on the model of the ACLU. Because of their heroic defiance of "martial law" and their protest of the suspension of habeas corpus during the 1970s, some of its members paid dearly with their health and lives.

DEFENDING NGOS ON THE FRONT LINE

The founder of the Philippine Civil Liberties Union, Senator Jovito Solanga, was crippled for life by armed retribution for speaking out against the imposition of martial law. His misfortune did not prevent him and his associates from continuing their work as human rights defenders during a period of political repression (1972–1986). The dangers faced by human rights defenders worldwide continue no less today. Both Amnesty International and Human Rights First (formerly the Lawyers Committee for Human Rights)[30] make the defense of human rights NGO members and other human rights defenders major parts of their programs. Human Rights Watch likewise has a program in support of vulnerable NGO activists who, because of their work, may become the victims of "disappearances," political killings, arbitrary arrest, torture and intimidation—the very violations from which they have struggled to protect others.

Examples of the heroic risks taken by human rights defenders are now legion and well

26. See Eric Stover, William D. Haglund, and Margaret Samuels, "Exhumation of Mass Graves in Iraq: Considerations for Forensic Investigations, Humanitarian Needs, and the Demands of Justice," *Journal of the American Medical Association* 290 (2003): 663–66.
27. Christopher Joyce and Eric Stover, *Witnesses from the Grave: The Stories Bones Tell* (Boston: Little Brown, 1991).
28. Sarah E. Mendelson and John K. Glenn, eds, *The Power and Limits of NGOs: A Critical Look at Building Democracy in Eastern Europe* (New York: Columbia University Press, 2002).
29. See the Centre's website at http://www.tchrd.org
30. See the web site for Human Rights First at http://www.humanrightsfirst.org/index.html

documented.[31] In China, Rebiya Kadeer was imprisoned in 1999 on politically motivated charges stemming from her work on behalf of women's rights and the rights of the predominantly Muslim Uighur population in Xinjiang Uighur Autonomous Region. In 2002, Kimy Pernia, a well-known indigenous human rights activist in Columbia, was "disappeared" at a time when his country was, for citizens wishing to speak out for their rights, one of the most dangerous places in the world. In 2004, Russian journalist and environmentalist Grigory Paski was finally freed on parole after serving three years of his four-year sentence for criticizing government policies. Amnesty International, whose Defend the Defenders Program had publicized his case for years, reported Paski's view that his early release was attributable "to the millions of people who campaigned tirelessly on his behalf."[32]

The cause of protecting those at risk for carrying out legitimate human rights activities advanced significantly in 1998 with the adoption by the UN General Assembly of the Declaration on the Rights and Responsibilities of Individuals, Groups and Organs of Society to Promote and Protect Universally Recognized Human Rights and Fundamental Freedoms.[33] To the relief of those "on the front line" helping victims, the Declaration is a milestone for several reasons. It is the first UN instrument to emphasize that everyone has the right to promote, protect, and defend human rights on the national and international planes. In so doing, it enumerates the specific duties of states to guarantee the rights of human rights defenders to promote, protect, and implement human rights in law and in practice, as well as their duty to take all necessary measures to protect human rights defenders from violence and arbitrary action. It specifies, too, that states have the obligation to carry out investigations in cases of alleged violations of human rights, including those contained in the Declaration.

Of special importance to NGOs, the Declaration reaffirms and clarifies the existing rights of human rights defenders that are most often challenged by governments, e.g., the right to meet and assemble peacefully; to form, join, and participate in NGOs; to hold and publish information about human rights; to complain about the policies and actions of officials and government bodies; and to enjoy unhindered access to international bodies. Moreover, the Declaration incorporates the right to receive and obtain funding for human rights activities, a right not otherwise articulated in any existing human rights instrument or standard. One of the most innovative aspects of the Declaration is its affirmation that everyone is entitled to enjoy the rights of human rights defenders "individually and in association with others." In this regard, the Declaration makes an important contribution to the development of the right to freedom of association, a right traditionally neglected in international law insofar as it relates to NGOs.

For NGOs to function effectively, the safety of human rights defenders must be secured, of course. But so also must be the integrity of their fact-finding reports. Because the reliability of NGOs disseminating human rights information depends upon the careful gathering and evaluation of such information, the accuracy and credibility—ergo integrity—of NGO fact-finding missions must be ensured; and to this end procedural rules have been developed and proposed, to wit, the Minimal Rules of Procedure for International Human Rights Fact-Finding Missions, agreed to at a meeting of the International Law Association

---

31. Kerry Kennedy with Eddie Adams, ed. Nan Richardson, *Speak Truth to Power: Human Rights Defenders Who are Changing Our World* (New York: Crown Books, 2004).
32. On results achieved by NGOs, see Claude E. Welch, Jr., ed., *NGOs and Human Rights: Promise and Performance* (Philadelphia: University of Pennsylvania Press, 2001), especially Morton Winston, "Assessing the Effectiveness of International Human Rights NGOs: Amnesty International" (25–54) and David L. Cingranelli and David L. Richards, "Measuring the Impact of Human Rights Organizations" (225–37).
33. Adopted Dec. 9, 1998, referenced in Documentary Appendix B.

in Belgrade in 1980.[34] The need for such rules reflects widespread agreement that the documentation of human rights violations can be strengthened and made less haphazard by the adoption of more nearly uniform standards for collecting information.[35] As it is, the reports of human rights groups often cannot be readily compared owing to the variation among NGOs in their information gathering, evaluation, and reporting techniques.

CORPORATIONS

In addition to human rights NGOs, one must take into account also the work and impact of business enterprises—as, for example, foreign (often multinational) corporations in formerly apartheid South Africa. Though most multinational corporations operating in that context "really had not given the topic of international human rights a lot of thought," writes J. Frederick Truitt, "until forced to it by organizations as diverse as the American Friends Service Committee, Resist, the Interfaith Center for Corporate Responsibility, and the Institute for Sport and Social Analysis,"[36] still the business community could not escape the challenge of human rights, at least not in southern Africa before the abolition of apartheid in 1991.

Reading 32 in this chapter ("Multinational Corporations and the Ethics of Global Responsibility") raises the question of whether or not multinational corporations (MNCs) should be legally or at least morally obligated to protect human rights. The authors, Mahmood Monshipouri, Claude E. Welch, Jr., and Evan T. Kennedy acknowledge that international human rights conventions hold only *states* liable for human rights abuses—in keeping with the classical international law distinction between the "subjects" (states and international governmental organizations) and "objects" (private persons and groups) of international law that grants "legal standing" in the international legal order only to the former, not the latter. From a rights-based perspective, however, the authors argue that, in the context of neoliberal globalization, the wrongdoers actually are often corporations and that therefore it is important to consider the possibility of an outside governing body to hold in check unfettered global capitalism and to bring to account MNC policies that are socially detrimental for being violative of human rights. The argument is meritorious. As Burns Weston and Mark Teerink have written, in the context of holding private business enterprises accountable under international law for child labor that violates the human rights of children, "theories are but intellectual paradigms, prototypes of thought that define not only what we look at but also how we go about looking at what we look at. They do not necessarily mirror reality. So when the facts of life no longer fit the theory, it is time, as Copernicus taught us, to change the theory."[37] Weston and Teerink go on to point out that, in addition to UDHR Article 30 which, they note emphatically, provides that "Nothing in this

34. See "Draft Minimal Rules of Procedure for International Human Rights Fact-Finding Missions," *Report of the Subcommittee on Equal Application of Human Rights Laws and Principles of the International Committee on Human Rights*, 59th Congress held at Belgrade, Aug. 17, 1980 (London: International Law Association, 1982).
35. See Hans Thoolen and Berth Verstappen, *Human Rights Missions: A Study of the Fact-Finding Practice of Non-Governmental Organizations*, sponsored by SIM, The Netherlands Institute of Human Rights (Dordrecht: Nijhoff, 1986). See also Randy B. Reiter, M. V. Zunzungegui, and José Quiroga, "Guidelines for Field Reporting of Basic Human Rights Violations," *HRQ* 8, no. 4 (1986): 628–53 (part of a symposium on Statistical Issues in the Field of Human Rights).
36. J. Frederick Truitt, "The Improbable Alliance: Human Rights, Prosperity and International Business," *Worldview* 23 (May 1980): 24–27, at 24.
37. Burns H. Weston and Mark B. Teerink, "Rethinking Child Labor: A Multidimensional Human Rights Problem," in Burns H. Weston, ed., *Child Labor and Human Rights: Making Children Matter* (Boulder, Colo.: Lynne Rienner, 2005).

Declaration may be interpreted as implying for any State, *group or person* any right to engage in any activity or to perform any act aimed at the destruction of any of the rights and freedoms set forth herein," there exists also the plain fact that, "Expressly or by implication, many of the most fundamental human rights instruments recognize human rights obligations on the part of private actors per se, while others and cognate treaties require states parties to ensure and enforce the rights enumerated against violations by private perpetrators."[38] Further, they cite Resolution 2003/16 of the UN Sub-Commission on the Promotion and Protection of Human Rights on Norms on the Responsibilities of Transnational Corporations and Other Business Enterprises with Regard to Human Rights,[39] and, in addition, the report of the Office of the High Commissioner for Human Rights (OHCHR) submitted to the UN Commission on Human Rights in February 2005 on Responsibilities of Transnational Corporations and Related Business Enterprises with regard to Human Rights.[40]

Human rights violations by multinational corporations occur despite widespread agreement that they should respect human rights; not collaborate with abusive governments; refrain from interfering in internal policy; avoid acting as political vehicles; and respect the employment, environmental, and socioeconomic policy of the host country.[41] Attempts to impose regulations on MNCs have generally foundered, although in 2000, the British government commissioned a "white paper" that called for progress. Published by the Department for International Development, the policy study focused on the implications of economic globalization and development. In recent years, it noted, public interest in corporate social responsibility had exposed problems of abusive and exploitative child labor, corruption, human rights, labor standards, and the environment. The corporate interests of global businesses sometimes entail trading in technology that subjects people to harm to health and life. British courts have begun to respond favorably to complaints about UK-based multinationals, allowing South African and Namibian victims of mercury poisoning, uranium ore radiation, and asbestos to file indemnification suits against Thor Chemicals, Rio Tinto, and Cape Industries.[42] The report called for corporate self-reform, noting that by applying "best practices" in the areas complained of, business can play an increased role in reducing poverty and sustaining development. Finally, the report concluded that "Many companies have also realized important commercial benefits in terms of reputation, risk-management and enhanced productivity" by respecting internationally defined human rights, labor, and environmental standards.[43]

The British study precisely paralleled views gaining strength in the Office of the Secretary-General of the United Nations. In January 1999, at the World Economic Forum in Davos, Switzerland, Secretary-General Kofi Annan challenged business leaders to join in a "global compact of shared values and principles" and give globalization a humane face.[44] He argued that, unless the global market, like national markets, was held together

---

38. Ibid., 15.

39. Adopted Aug. 13, 2003, referenced in Documentary Appendix B.

40. See the OHCHR website at http://www.ohchr.org/english/issues/globalization/business/reportbusiness.htm

41. See generally Jedrzej George Frynas and Scott Pegg, eds., *Transnational Corporations and Human Rights* (New York: Palgrave Macmillan, 2003).

42. Richard Meeran, "Accountability of Transnationals for Human Rights Abuses," *New Law Journal* 148 (November 1998):1686–87, 1706–7.

43. To similar effect, see Elliott J. Shrage, *Promoting International Worker Rights through Private Voluntary Initiatives: Public Relations or Public Policy?* (A Report to the U.S. Department of State on behalf of The University of Iowa Center for Human Rights, Jan. 2004), available from The University of Iowa Center for Human Rights at http://www.uichr.org

44. "UN Launches New Effort on Global Business Compact," Press Release, World Economic Forum, Jan. 28, 2001, available online at http://www.weforum.org/pressreleases.nsf

by shared values, it would be exposed to backlashes from protectionism, populism, nationalism, ethnic chauvinism, fanaticism, and terrorism. Calling for a pro-active approach, Annan asserted that in addition to the efforts of the UN and other international agencies to promote human rights, the corporate sector must directly tackle issues linking business enterprise with internationally defined human rights. He urged them to "use these universal values as the cement binding together your global corporations, since they are values people all over the world will recognize as their own."[45] He also cautioned business executives to "make sure that in your own corporate practices you uphold and respect human rights, and that you are not yourselves complicit in human rights abuses."

Over the next two years, Mr. Annan's warning to international business leaders that globalization was more fragile than they realized became prophetic as serious rioting disrupted meetings of trade organizations and international financial institutions. The demonstrators are demanding that international financial institutions and multinational corporations clean up the dehumanizing face of globalization.[46] These popular pressures have given rise to a constructive UN initiative. To enlist the help of the private sector and to give institutional shape to the Secretary-General's proposal, a Global Compact Office (GCO) has been established in the UN, working with other agencies such as the Office of the High Commissioner for Human Rights (OHCHR) and the International Labour Organization (ILO). As a first step toward full participation, the GCO requires a letter of support from a company's chief executive officer which is taken as a declaration of intent at the highest corporate level.[47] One of the attractions of the Global Compact—initially endorsed by companies such as British Petroleum, Daimler-Chrysler, Unilever, Deutsche Bank, Ericsson, and Novartis—is that it operates from a baseline of clear international standards. These companies unquestionably open themselves to sharp criticism if they fall short, having announced their intentions to accept the Compact's nine principles formulated thus:

In the field of *human rights*, the Secretary-General asked world business to:

1. support and respect the protection of international human rights within their sphere of influence; and
2. make sure their own corporations are not complicit in human rights abuses.

In the field of *labor*, the Secretary-General asked world business to uphold:

3. freedom of association and the effective recognition of the right to collective bargaining;
4. the elimination of all forms of forced and compulsory labor;
5. the effective abolition of child labor; and
6. the elimination of discrimination in respect of employment and occupation.

In the field of *the environment*, the Secretary-General asked world business to:

7. support a precautionary approach to environmental challenges;
8. undertake initiatives to promote greater environmental responsibility; and
9. encourage the development and diffusion of environmentally friendly technologies.

At a Global Compact Leaders Summit in 2004, a tenth principle against corruption was added, together with a list of participating companies on the Compact website.[48]

45. Ibid.
46. Alan Pike, "Seattle Has Given Both Political and Business Leaders Good Reason to Pause for Thought," *Financial Times*, Jan. 25, 2001, at 3. See also Donatella Delia Porta and Sidney Tarrow, eds., *Transnational Protest and Global Activism: People, Passions, and Power* (Lanham, Md.: Rowman and Littlefield, 2005); Robert J. S. Ross, *Slaves to Fashion: Poverty and Abuse in the New Sweatshops* (Ann Arbor: University of Michigan Press, 2004).
47. UN Website at http://www.unglobalcompact.org./gc/UNWeb.nsf/content/thenine.htm
48. See http://www.unglobalcompact.org

Putting the Secretary-General's ten principles into practice through a "learning forum," and using a "soft" educational approach, the GCO does not assess performance but, rather, seeks to identify and promote good practices.[49] One way it does this is by developing and disseminating individual case studies to provide the basis for sharing experiences among participants, promoting complementary research findings resulting in an information bank of "good practices." Thus, companies supporting the Compact will post specific examples of progress on the Global Compact web site. The GCO also encourages the growing trend of companies to publish social reports—in which they account for their social, ethical, and environmental as well as their financial activities—allowing the reports to be verified externally. As positive as these developments appear, it must be noted that there is no UN oversight mechanism and, from the point of view of NGOs, there is no clear way of contesting a company's membership with the result that they might inappropriately use their affiliation to the Global Compact merely for public relations purposes.

Disseminating the results of any external review has become easier in light of new efforts to define standards for judgment. For example, Amnesty International's business unit has drafted proposed human rights standards for corporations,[50] and the International Labor Organization has done so as well.[51] As the Internet has moved to the center of the social responsibility arena, issues are quickly engaged. For example, Christopher L. Avery's "Business and Human Rights in a Time of Change," an important manifesto on corporate responsibility, first appeared as an Internet publication sponsored by British Amnesty International in 1999.[52] In our global age of instant communication, monitors scrutinizing large corporations use websites to present critical assessments and performance evaluations, and even mount attacks on corporate behavior calling for boycotts and demonstrations. Companies, in turn, have begun using their own sites to promote examples of responsible corporate citizenship.

INDIVIDUALS

Finally, it is to be noted that even the individual has an important role to play in redressing human rights injustices; for, if left unopposed, governments and other social institutions will succeed in their disregard of simple human respect if individuals themselves do not join the human rights struggle. Happily, history is replete with examples of such opposition (today called "activism"), whether championed by individuals or groups of individual "dissidents." The heroic action of Andrei Sakharov in founding the human rights movement in the Soviet Union, for example, ranks him with historic figures such as Thomas Paine, Mohandas Gandhi, Martin Luther King, Jr., and 2005 Nobel Laureate Dr. Wangari Muta Maathai. Each of these defiant dissidents was a dauntless proponent of the human spirit in the face of serious repression. Each, at great personal risk, was successful in pursuing human rights thought by opponents and adherents alike at the time to stand for revolutionary ideas.

In the last essay of this chapter and volume (Reading 33), international lawyer Jordan

49. See "Twenty Questions on the UN Global Compact: What Companies Need to Know," available on the UN website at http://www.unglobalcompact.org./gc/UNWeb.nsf/content/questions.htm
50. Amnesty International, *Human Rights: Is It Any of Your Business?* (London: Amnesty International-UK, 2000).
51. ILO Tripartite Declaration of Principles Concerning Multinational Enterprises and Social Policy, Nov. 17, 2000, adopted by the Governing Body of the ILO, 204th Sess. (Nov. 1977), as amended at its 279th Sess. (Nov. 17, 2000). *Official Bulletin* 83 (2000), available at http://www.ilo.org/public/english/ employment/ multi/download/ english.pdf
52. See http://www.Amnesty.org.uk.

J. Paust raises the question of whether revolutionary modes of action are ever appropriate to secure a public order of human dignity and whether one may cogently and coherently speak of "a human right to revolution." Some argue that two standards must be met to justify its invocation: first, that the resistance or revolution must be taken up on the authority and in the interest of the majority of the people and not simply an aggrieved minority; second, that it must be taken up against a state that oppresses its citizenry by political or economic means. For international human rights purposes, one may look for guidance to the Preamble of the UDHR: "it is essential," it says, " if man [sic] is not to be compelled to have recourse, as a last resort, to rebellion against tyranny and oppression, that human rights should be protected by the rule of law."

Exploring the connections between rights and revolution beyond the Universal Declaration, it should be clear that ours is a time of crisis. It is a time that juxtaposes, on the one hand, common demands for dignity from Soweto to Srebrenica to Jerusalem to Tianamen Square to Swainsboro (Georgia) to Kiev to Beirut, and, on the other hand, the operational code of too many governments that in practice deliver the opposite of human rights. Professor Paust observes that it is thus, on the basis of a denial of fundamental human rights that a viable theory of legitimate resistance may be mounted.[53]

Whatever the criteria that may be said to apply to any asserted right of resistance, the fact is that the peoples of the world, whatever the differences in their cultural traditions and institutional practices, are increasingly demanding to participate in the shaping of the world in which they live. These demands stem from the enduring elements of most of the world's great religions and philosophies. However, what used to be a dream of uncertain promise now is emerging as a necessary reality of world order, and as a result it can safely be predicted that the contemporary global human rights movement will continue to gain in strength. For the foreseeable future, the sinews of that strength will derive substantially from individual and nongovernmental action undertaken and organized in resistance to injustice on behalf of all who suffer at the hands of oppressive and repressive governments and societies.

53. See in this connection, for example, Richard A. Falk and Burns H. Weston, "The Relevance of International Law to Palestinian Rights in the West Bank and Gaza: In Legal Defense of the Intifada," *HILJ* 32 (Winter 1991): 129–57; Richard A. Falk and Burns H. Weston, "The Israeli-Occupied Territories, International Law, and the Boundaries of Scholarly Discourse: A Reply to Michael Curtis," *HILJ* 33 (1992): 191–204.

31. RICHARD PIERRE CLAUDE *What Do Human Rights NGOs Do?*

INTRODUCTION

Human rights nongovernmental organizations (NGOs) are private associations devoted to promoting and protecting human rights. They pursue these goals at many levels: international, regional, national, and local. They also have attracted the attention of many political scientists.[1]

In *Human Rights in International Relations*, political scientist David Forsythe says that, in

Reprinted with changes from Richard Pierre Claude, "NGO Activism in Science, Technology, and Health" in *Science in the Service of Human Rights*" (Philadelphia: University of Pennsylvania Press, 2002), 146–61. Copyright © 2002 University of Pennsylvania Press. Reprinted by permission.

1. See, e.g., Ann Marie Clark, *Diplomacy of Conscience: Amnesty International and Changing Human Rights Norms* (Princeton, N.J.: Princeton University Press, 2001); Claude E. Welch, Jr., *NGOs and Human Rights, Promise and Performance* (Philadelphia: University of Pennsylvania Press, 2001); Laurie Wiseberg, *Protecting Human Rights Defenders: The Importance of Freedom of Association for Human Rights NGOs* (Montreal:

2000, there were about 250 private organizations with worldwide operations devoted to the full time advocacy of human rights.[2] The files of the Human Rights Internet (Ottawa) indicate that, counting part-time and strictly national groups (e.g., the Cambodian Project Against Domestic Violence or the Chad Association for Human Rights), such NGOs number over 5,000, many of them local and regional.[3] Dean Joseph Nye of the Kennedy School of Government estimates the number of public interest groups (not just those concerned with human rights) at over 26,000 worldwide.[4] Those that specialize in human rights are able to maximize the free flow of information across borders, spreading the word on human rights violations around the globe. They all use the politics of information-gathering and advocacy, and they perform many other tasks as well.

NGOs have a good reputation and are widely trusted, according to a 2001 international survey conducted by Strategy One in Australia, France, Germany, the United Kingdom, and the United States, canvassing 1,100 opinion leaders.[5] In each country Strategy One asked about attitudes on the reliability of information from NGOs, particularly on issues concerning human rights, health, and the environment. The survey revealed that NGOs such as Amnesty International and Greenpeace command far greater trust among the public in industrialized countries than do governments, corporations, and the media. In Europe, almost a third of the respondents trusted NGOs to do the right thing "in shaping a better world" compared to only a fifth who trusted government, 15 percent business, and 11 percent the media. In the U.S., 70 percent of those surveyed were positive about the role NGOs play in shaping a better world, compared to 11 percent who trusted government and business. In France, Amnesty International and the World Wildlife Fund were held in higher esteem (73 percent and 60 percent respectively) than Air

France and Microsoft (37 percent and 34 percent respectively). In Australia, twenty-two times as many respondents as those trusting corporations said they turn to NGOs for information on human rights issues; thirteen times more for information on the environment.

NGOs come from a wide range of political, social, cultural, and financial environments. Some operate in relative freedom and enjoy high prestige, others are brutally repressed. All are independent of the state and seek no political power for themselves. They play an important role in the growth of civil society in virtually every country in the world. Their myriad functions become clear when we answer the question: what do NGOs do?

- they *monitor* human rights violations
- they undertake programs of information-sharing and *public education*
- they sponsor programs of *technical training*
- they undertake and demonstrate the utility of rigorous technical analysis
- they engage in *lobbying* activities to influence public policy
- they organize *advocacy campaigns* to promote rights and redress wrongs
- they build *solidarity* with other domestic and international NGOs
- they perform *service functions* and provide humanitarian support
- they protect and vindicate human rights in *litigation*

MONITORING VIOLATIONS

The tragic case of Joelito Filártiga, the seventeen-year-old son of Paraguay's most famous physician, illustrates the work of Amnesty International (AI) in monitoring human rights violations, including the right not to suffer government sponsored torture.

For decades, Dr. Joel Filártiga has run a clinic for the 50,000 impoverished people in the Ybycuí Valley of Paraguay, a small landlocked country in South America. Because Dr. Filártiga was

International Centre for Human Rights and Democratic Development, 1993). See also law professor Julie A. Mertus, "Human Rights and the Promise of Transnational Civil Society," in Burns H. Weston and Stephen P. Marks, eds., *The Future of International Human Rights* (Ardsley, N.Y.: Transnational Publishers, 1999), 433–56.

2. David P. Forsythe, *Human Rights in International Relations* (New York: Cambridge University Press, 2000), 163.

3. See the HRI website at http://www.hri.ca

4. Joseph S. Nye, Jr., "Defining National Interests in an Information Age," *Morgenthau Memorial Lecture* (New York: Carnegie Council on Ethics and International Affairs, 1989).

5. Strategy One, *Institutional Trust: A Five Country Survey* (New York: Edelman Public Relations Worldwide, 2001).

an outspoken critic of General Alfredo Stroessner's dictatorship and its derelict public health policy, and because he gave free medical care to the *campesinos*, the police suspected him of leftist sympathies and subversive activities. In 1976, his teenage son Joelito Filártiga was abducted by police Inspector Américo Peña-Irala, who assumed the boy could be forced to betray his father. Instead, he died of cardiac arrest during a hideous torture interrogation. Thereafter, Dr. Filártiga and his family cooperated with AI human rights workers in Paraguay. Richard Alan White, a historian then visiting from the University of California, Los Angeles, documented the case in Asunción and transmitted information about the politically motivated torture-murder to AI's research headquarters in London.[6] The Amnesty Secretariat took an interest in the murdered boy's case because AI is dedicated to acting on behalf of those prisoners of conscience who suffer torture in violation of the Universal Declaration of Human Rights.[7]

As in all cases, AI double-checked the facts, making sure that the Filártigas were not advocates of violence, that the boy was taken as a prisoner of conscience, and tortured for political reasons. They then organized a worldwide campaign, issuing reports and urgent action memos calling on members to pressure the Paraguayan and other governments to take action. Soon the dictator buckled under the intense international outcry and suspended Peña-Irala who, while visiting the United States, was tracked down by Dr. Filártiga and his daughter Dolly in New York and subsequently apprehended by U.S. immigration authorities.

Thereafter, Dolly Filártiga and her father filed a wrongful death action in the federal District Court for the Eastern District of New York under the 1789 Alien Tort Statute alleging that in 1976 Police Inspector Peña-Irala kidnaped and tortured Joelito Filártiga to death. The district court dismissed the Filártigas' complaint for lack of subject matter jurisdiction.

In 1980, however, the U.S. Court of Appeals for the Second Circuit reversed, recognizing the emergence of a universal consensus that international law affords substantive rights to individuals and places limits on a state's treatment of its citizens.[8] From these circumstances emerged the landmark case of *Filártiga v. Peña-Irala*, marking for the first time a U.S. Federal Court accepting jurisdiction in a civil suit against torture committed in a foreign country. Peña-Irala's responsibility for the human rights offense supplied the basis on which the court ruled that officially sanctioned torture is a violation of international law. The Court said: "Like the pirate and slave trader before him, the torturer has become the enemy of all mankind." In 1984, on remand to the District Court and on the basis of expert testimony from four medical specialists, Judge Eugene Nickerson announced a total judgment against Peña-Irala amounting to $10.3 million. The *Filártiga* case has become important as a precedent, having many progeny including some directed at corporations for human rights violations.[9]

PUBLIC EDUCATION AND INFORMATION-SHARING

B'Tselem is the Hebrew name popularly used by The Israeli Center for Human Rights in the Occupied Territories. It was established in 1989 by a group of prominent academics, attorneys, journalists, and Knesset members. The Hebrew word means "in the image of," and is used also as a synonym for human dignity as reflected in Genesis 1:27: "And God created humans in his image. In the image of God did He create him." The group seeks to document and educate the Israeli public and policy-makers about human rights violations in the Occupied Territories and to combat the phenomenon of denial they say is prevalent among the Israeli public. Ultimately the educational objective is to create a human rights culture in Israel in compliance with Israel's obligations under international law.

In 1989 in Atlanta, the Carter-Menil Award for Human Rights was presented to B'Tselem in recognition of its important work and its consistent and careful accuracy in reporting. They ensure the reliability of information by conducting

---

6. Richard Alan White, *Breaking Silence: The Case That Changed the Face of Human Rights* (Washington, D.C.: Georgetown University Press, 2004), provides a unique participant-observer's account of *Filártiga v. Peña-Irala*, 630 F. 2d 876 (2d Cir., 1980).
7. Adopted Dec. 10, 1948, reprinted and referenced in Documentary Appendix A.
8. See White, *Breaking Silence*, note 6.
9. See Reading 29 by Michael Ratner in Chapter 7 of this volume. See also Ann Marie Slaughter and David Bosco, "Plaintiff's Diplomacy," *Foreign Affairs* 79 (Sept.–Oct. 2000): 102–16.

their own fieldwork and research and thoroughly cross-checking with relevant documents, official government sources, and information from other sources, among them Israeli, Palestinian, and other human rights organizations. The scores of B'Tselem reports, called "Information Sheets," cover most kinds of human rights violations that have occurred in the Occupied Territories, e.g., torture, fatal shootings by security forces, restriction on movement, expropriation of land, discrimination in planning and building in East Jerusalem, administrative detention, and settler violence. Reports are supplemented by press conferences and educational outreach programs in Israel relying on volunteers who set up information stands, distribute printed material, and participate in protests in the Occupied Territories.

In their 2004 Information Sheet entitled, *Not All it Seems*, B'Tselem documented and analyzed the consequences of the Israeli "Separation Barrier"—a wall preventing Palestinians access to their own lands beyond the barrier. The report concedes that a state is entitled to deny this right if it has proper justification. However, B'Tselem concluded that "the barrier severely infringed the human rights of tens of thousands of Palestinians in the West Bank" in violation of their "freedom of movement" based on Article 12 of the International Covenant on Civil and Political Rights.[10] According to *Not All It Seems*, the system of permits set up in 2003 forbids Palestinians to move about freely in their villages and on their land unless they supply sufficient justification to warrant their movement. All Palestinians must have permits but settlers living in the area or Jews from anywhere in the world are allowed to move in the same area freely and without the need for a permit of any kind. The educational report thus concluded that "[t]he permit system has resulted in hundreds of Palestinians being prohibited from enjoying the benefits of their private property or from their right to work and support their families— rights enshrined in articles 17 and 23 of the Universal Declaration of Human Rights."

B'Tselem's educational objective of sharing information is designed to provide the Israeli public with a basis for taking action and making choices. Their regularly published Information Sheets proclaim that readers of their publications may decide to do nothing, but they cannot say "We didn't know."

TECHNICAL TRAINING

Training, as distinct from the broader field of education, is directed at teaching others to become proficient in a particular task or field of technical operations. A program of technical training is now underway, for example, to implement the International Labor Organization's (ILO) Convention No. 169 concerning the rights of "tribal peoples in independent countries."[11] The Convention stresses the vital importance to human rights of "tribal peoples" of the ownership and possession of the lands they traditionally occupy and their right to participate in the management and conservation of these resources. Such participation rights play an important role in the work of the Center for the Support of Native Lands working in Central and South America and responsible for remarkable examples of technology transfer promoted by the non-profit conservation group.[12] The NGO responds to initiatives by the indigenous peoples themselves seeking to gain social and political advantage from detailed and long-standing knowledge of their environmental heritage. Professional ethno-cartographers lend a technical helping hand to train Indian community workers. As a result, the Bolivian indigenous "people of the Izozog" have learned the methodologies of mapping techniques which they have used effectively in an area encompassing over 19,000 square kilometers.

With the support of the Bolivian Ministry of Sustainable Development and with training by Native Lands' ethnocartographers, surveyors, and draftsmen, Indian leaders enthusiastically took on responsibility to handle the mapping project, managing all the field activities. The "para-cartographers" meticulously documented the locations of their traditional homeland, settlements, temporary structures, soils, trees, water, forests, and other treasured natural resources

---

10. B'Tselem, *Not All It Seems* (Jerusalem: Israeli Information Center for Human Rights in the Occupied Territories, Information Sheet, June 2004), 22.
11. Concluded June 27, 1989, referenced in Documentary Appendix B.
12. See the Center's website at http://www.nativelands.org. See also Mac Chapin and William Threlkeld, *Indigenous Landscapes: A Study in Ethnocartography* (Alexandria, Va.: Center for the Support of Native Lands, 2001).

such as sites where honey and medicinal plants can be found. Displacing official maps that showed enormous swaths of land as "uninhabited," the new map resulted in the naming of many physical features and renaming some landmarks from Spanish back to the original Guarani names.

In addition to the empowerment objectives of the project, a major outcome was the national development of a plan to establish the Gran Chaco National Park and Integrated Management Area, a 3.4 million hectare tract extending to the Paraguayan border. To be administered by the Izoceños, it is the largest territorial protected area in Tropical America. In September 1995, the area was legally established by presidential decree, and a year later an agreement was signed giving the Indian Assembly administrative control over the area.

TECHNICAL ANALYSIS

Each violation of human rights and fundamental freedoms deserves individual attention and universal condemnation. No one seriously interested in applying statistical science to monitoring human rights violations would argue that "if you can't count them they don't count." However, those who work in the field of human rights know that fixing the responsibility for violations requires an assessment of how, how much, and why human freedoms are curtailed or endangered.

The Science and Human Rights Program of the American Association for the Advancement of Science (AAAS) has a distinguished history of initiating helpful and technically cutting edge methods for the promotion, analysis, and implementation of internationally defined human rights. A model of excellence in analyzing large scale human rights violations is the AAAS report titled *State Violence in Guatemala, 1960–1996.*[13] The report combines historical analysis with statistics from the International Center for Human Rights Investigations (CIDH) to present a compelling history of the deliberate and sustained violence committed by state forces during Guatemala's domestic armed conflict. Subtitled "A Quantitative Reflection," it relies on a database meticulously assembled covering 43,070 violations

against 16,265 victims, of whom 13,527 are victims whose full identity is known. The statistics present a clear picture of the period, decades of unrelenting Guatemalan state reliance on extrajudicial violence to maintain political control in a divided nation. Data analysis by the authors credibly supports the view that state terror over time expanded in both intensity and in the scope of its victims, from selective assassinations of militants in the armed insurgency to an everwidening attack on members of the political opposition. The report also inquires into the methods and agents of violence, including the Government's use of civilians to attack other civilians, a policy which contributed to the longterm militarization of Guatemalan society. Analysis of data-based information shows how violence rose and fell across all presidential regimes, military and civilian. Human rights violations are analyzed by the gender, ethnicity, and age of the victims, and regional differences show the ever increasing penetration of violence into rural areas.

The statistical profile of such violence shows that a record number of over 800 killings and disappearances per month took place during 17 months of President José Efrain Rios Montt's incumbency (1978–1982). Nevertheless, because of increased state censorship and intimidation of the media by killings of journalists and attacks on media offices and equipment at that time, fewer government killings were reported during his regime. The press blackout coincided with Reagan Administration lobbying to restore military aid to Guatemala cut off by the U.S. Congress in 1977. Thus, the question of how people do or do not get timely information about human rights violations has a strong bearing on how they can respond to such abuses, both where the violations take place and among attentive groups in other countries as well.

LOBBYING

Sometimes human rights NGOs influence public policy through the standard methods of political lobbying. An example of such work under the sponsorship of Physicians for Human Rights (USA) took place in July 2000 when over 75 activists from 26 states gathered in Washington, D.C., to participate in the first U.S.

13. Patrick Ball, Paul Kobrak, and Herbert F. Spirer, *State Violence in Guatemala, 1960–1996: A Quantitative Reflection* (Washington, D.C.: American Association for the Advancement of Science, 1999).

Campaign to Ban Landmines (USCBL).[14] As a grassroots and legislative action coalition (including medical school students, health professionals, and others), they met with hundreds of members of Congress or their aides, gaining the immediate support of over 40%, and actively urged the President to join the 1997 Ottawa Convention Banning Land Mines.[15] Calling for a total ban on the use, manufacture, stockpiling, and transfer of antipersonnel landmines, it was ratified by 144 countries as of January 11, 2005, including all NATO nations except the United States. The treaty seeks to reduce needless human suffering by increasing resources for mine clearance, mine awareness, and mine assistance.

In 2000, U.S. Representative Jim McGovern from Maine and others circulated a "Dear Colleague" sign-on letter in the House that urged President Clinton to take steps toward joining the treaty. Physicians for Human Rights, the coordinator of the USCBL, also organized an action and information-packed conference with over 200 participants. In turn, growing out of the USCBL, the young people who attended launched their own initiative, "Students Against Landmines." To motivate the participants, Nobel Laureate Jody Williams spoke at the event, and USCBL distributed a new Human Rights Watch report, "Clintons' Landmines Legacy" along with the Watch Committee's website address.[16] Further solidarity came from representatives of the Bahá'í, Buddhist, Catholic, Jewish, Lutheran, Methodist, and Muslim communities who participated in an inter-faith prayer service to remind everyone that the heart and soul behind the ban betokened the tens of thousands of innocent civilians killed and maimed by landmines.

The failure of the Clinton Administration to sign on to the landmine treaty did not deter PHR from its lobbying activities under the succeeding Bush Administration. Since lobbying involves the effort to influence decision-making elites, PHR wisely added a professional elite component to their campaign in 2003 asking prominent health professionals (deans of medical schools, hospitals heads, directors of health-related organizations, etc.) to endorse a letter to all the 2004 presidential candidates urging them to support the landmine treaty and associate themselves with the campaign and PHR's "sign-on" letter accessible on the Internet.[17]

ADVOCACY

Advocacy by NGOs in the form of campaigns of persuasion and pressure is conventionally directed at units of government, but also sometimes at private groups and corporations. Advocacy campaigns have become a routine concern of ever more public interest groups. The work of Médicins sans frontiers (Doctors Without Borders), an NGO monitoring and reporting on pharmaceutical companies and their response to the AIDS pandemic, is illustrative. It has undertaken heroic work in Africa and played an important role in raising international consciousness about the need there for HIV/AIDS treatment.

By 2003, nearly two-thirds of the 30 million people afflicted with human immune deficiency virus lived in sub-Saharan Africa, five million residing in the Republic of South Africa. South African health professionals have been most vocal in international fora, complaining that very few can afford the drugs that have enabled richer countries to convert the malady from a killer to a manageable illness.

In the United States, sympathetic NGOs, including gay and lesbian organizations and human rights groups, have pressured pharmaceutical companies to cease all efforts to block access to generic drugs where branded medications are not available or are priced out of the reach of people with HIV/AIDS. In a remarkable essay, Dr. William Prusoff explained that, in a Yale University pharmacology laboratory, he and his late colleague, Dr. Tai-shun Lin, developed d4t, an important antiretroviral drug[18] that forms a critical part of a "cocktail" used beneficially by people with HIV and AIDS. As the patent holder,

14. Physicians for Human Rights (USA), "PHR Steps Up Efforts to Get U.S. to Join Mine Ban Treaty," *Record* 13 (Apr. 2000):1–4, at 4.
15. Officially known as the Convention on the Prohibition of the Use, Stockpiling, Production and Transfer of Anti-Personnel Mines and on Their Destruction, concluded Sept. 18, 1997, referenced in Documentary Appendix B.
16. See www.hrw.org
17. See www.banminesusa.org
18. William Prusoff, "The Scientist's Story," *New York Times*, Mar. 6, 2001, 4. See also Sarah Joseph, "Pharmaceutical Companies and Access to Drugs: The Fourth Wave of Corporate Human Rights Scrutiny," *HRQ* 25, no. 2 (May 2003): 425–52.

Yale University leased usage to the Bristol-Myers Squibb drug company for clinical trials, development, and marketing. Prusoff states that the prompting of the French-based physicians advocacy group Médicins sans Frontières made all the difference, convincing Bristol-Myers Squibb to cut the cost of the antiretroviral drug. The NGO's demands on the drug company convinced the Yale administration, pressured by law students and the school newspaper, to join the cause. Forgoing substantial profits, the company's vice president announced their cooperation "to energize a groundswell of action" to fight AIDS in Africa. Bristol-Myers Squibb reduced the cost of the Yale patented drug Zerit to 15 cents for a daily dose, or 1.5 percent of the cost to an American patient. Professor Prusoff writes: "Something has to be done, the African problem is so acute." On the basis of his experience, he concluded that nothing less would do than a well organized international advocacy effort.

BUILDING SOLIDARITY

Building solidarity distinctively calls for an explicit manifesting of sympathetic concern for the causes and concerns of others. In our global society, it becomes an ever more important function for nongovernmental organizations which mobilize moral and material transnational political support across national boundaries among themselves and others to achieve human rights for the marginalized and oppressed. Efforts at solidarity-building necessarily involve interaction and networking. In *Activists Beyond Borders*, Margaret E. Keck and Kathryn Sikkink ably analyze the development of networks of environmental NGOs.[19] The "common advocacy position," they say, is more likely to produce mutually supportive concrete results. Moreover, the very process of networking promotes a search for common ground and solidarity.

Consider the case of Alexandr Nikitin, a nuclear safety inspector, former Soviet navy submarine captain, and environmental activist. In February 1996, he was arrested by Russian authorities and charged with divulging "state

secrets" to the Bellona Foundation, a Norwegian environmental organization that exposed dangers of nuclear waste disposal practices posed by deteriorating nuclear submarines of the Russian Navy in the Barents Sea region in and near Murmansk. Captain Nikitin was held in pre-trial detention for ten months, and then released only under the condition that he not leave St. Petersburg. In 1998, after several attempts by the St. Petersburg Procuracy and the Russian security service to produce a viable indictment, Nikitin's first trial ended inconclusively, with the judge sending the case back for further investigation. He was finally acquitted in December 1999, and that decision was upheld by the Russian Supreme Court in April 2000. It noted that the Russian Constitution clearly states that "everyone has the right to a favorable environment, reliable information about its state, and compensation for damages inflicted on his health and property by ecological violations." Further, the Constitution prohibits employing unpublished laws in prosecuting citizens, a tactic that the Russian Federal Security Service tried to use against Nikitin. The Supreme Court Presidium of the Russian Federation finally closed the case by rejecting the General Prosecutors' protest against the St. Petersburg verdict.[20]

These developments were monitored by the Commission on Security and Cooperation in Europe (the Helsinki Commission) before which Captain Nikitin testified in 2000 that, as the Russian people have increasingly become aware of their rights, environmental NGOs have emerged as among the strongest and most popular of organized groups—albeit not to the liking of President Vladimir Putin who ominously singled out environmental groups as fronts for international espionage. Nikitin is the founder of the Environmental Rights Center in St. Petersburg, which addresses issues at the intersection of environmental and human rights and in turn works with the Coalition for Environment and Human Rights consisting of over 40 grassroots NGOs in Russia. Nikitin freely acknowledged that, as a defensive measure, the groups with which he is linked work cooperatively and in solidarity with others, networking their efforts

---

19. Margaret E. Keck and Kathryn Sikkink, "Environmental Advocacy Networks," in *Activists Beyond Borders, Advocacy Networks in International Politics* (Ithaca, N.Y.: Cornell University Press, 1998), 121–63.
20. Case Number 476p2000pr, *Decision of the Supreme Court Presidium of the Russian Federation*, Sept. 13, 2000, examining the General Prosecutor Deputy's protest against the verdict of the St. Petersburg City Court, Dec. 29, 1999.

at national and international levels to enhance their efficacy (and security). Moreover, the Norwegian Bellona Foundation enjoys international solidarity links fostered by the Sierra Club, which in 2000 awarded him and the Bellona Foundation its highest international honor, the Earthcare Award in defense of the survival of a livable global environment.

SERVICE AND HUMANITARIAN RELIEF

By the start of the millennium, nearly 39 million people worldwide had been uprooted from their homes by war, including seven million displaced in 1999 alone. Medical assistance frequently is critically important to persons victimized by armed conflict, torture, cruel and inhumane treatment and punishment, and other egregious human rights deprivations. Forensic medicine used for legal investigations is a uniquely pertinent humanitarian service valuable in modern human rights cases. Its utility was dramatically illustrated relative to the Balkan wars of the 1990s in the former Yugoslavia which brought terrible suffering to East Central Europe and caused enormous human carnage and dislocations. War, ethnic cleansing, the persecution of minorities, indiscriminate attacks on civilians, lack of respect for humanitarian principles, and deliberate targeting of aid workers were some of the trademarks of the conflict in Bosnia in the early 1990s. That catastrophe exacted a substantial cost in lives and human health, and in the aftermath of hostilities forensic work was critically important.

The story of its most tragic episode, involving the Muslim enclave of Srebrenica, is brilliantly recounted from a physician's point of view by Dr. Sheri Fink, in *War Hospital,* a gripping account of medical service, surgery, and survival.[21] For almost the entire month of April 1993, Serbian forces surrounding the town obstructed all convoys of humanitarian supplies. Members of the armed militia violated standards of humanitarian law with a medical blockade excluding health professionals from entering. During the siege, denial of humanitarian assistance meant that Srebrenica was left with a single doctor for over 40,000 people, of whom some 30,000 were

refugees, resulting in the death of thousands of civilians. In the years that followed, the surviving women of Srebrenica joined together to find out what happened to their families, and in 2000, at a new morgue facility in the northern Bosnian town of Tuzla, investigators tried to uncover the answer. Dozens of international experts worked for months, digging up 2,028 bodies and finding another 2,500, spread over more than a score of sites. In their cold storage facilities, they assembled the disinterred remains.

The International Commission for Missing Persons, in coordination with Physicians for Human Rights (USA), provided state of the art technology for the forensic pathologists identifying the remains. The mitochondrial DNA sequencers donated by the California-based "PE Biosystems" made possible matching DNA from the victims' bones with blood samples from a relative. Appropriately, the fit served two purposes. The process informed the surviving families of the fate of their missing loved ones. It also established evidence useful in proceedings at the International Criminal Tribunal for the former Yugoslavia in The Hague, making it possible for the court (along with the International Criminal Tribunal established to judge the 1994 genocide in Rwanda which likewise has made use, though less so, of such forensic evidence) to cross an historic threshold because such evidence was not produced during the trials in Nuremberg and Tokyo following World War II.

On August 2, 2001, the Yugoslav Tribunal found former general Radislav Krstic guilty of genocide for his role in the systematic execution of more than 7,000 unarmed Muslim men and boys near Srebrenica in 1995.[22] He was sentenced to 46 years imprisonment. Prosecutors said that Krstic's trial was the first international trial where forensic evidence played such a crucial role. Presiding Judge Almiro Rodriques said: "By deciding to kill all the men of fighting age, a decision was taken to make it impossible for the Muslim people of Srebrenica to survive." He concluded, "what was ethnic cleansing became genocide."[23] Bringing humanitarian aid as well as some promise of justice to the victims of Srebrenica encompassed the work of many organizations.

21. Sheri Fink, M.D., *War Hospital: A True Story of Surgery and Survival* (New York: Public Affairs, 2003).
22. Marlise Simmons, "Tribunal in Hague finds Bosnia Serb Guilty of Genocide," *New York Times*, Aug. 3, 2001, 1, 8.
23. Ibid.

LITIGATION

NGOs in the United States lead the world in reliance on litigation for the protection and vindication of human rights. Such groups include the Center for Constitutional Rights (New York),[24] Global Rights-Partners for Justice (Washington, D.C.), Rights First (New York), and the Southern Center for Human Rights (SCHR, Atlanta). The SCHR director, Stephen Bright, believes that because prison inmates have no political power, lawsuits on their behalf are necessary. He asserts that in all too many cases in the United States, "the human rights of prisoners are dependent upon the order of federal judges." An NGO such as the SCHR which operates like a law firm must wait to receive grievances from potential plaintiffs because, under traditional standards of legal ethics, they cannot initiate lawsuits on their own. In 1999, the Southern Center acted on serious complaints they received, suing the Fulton County jail on behalf of HIV-positive jail inmates.[25] Many of these unfortunate people in Georgia's largest jail were awaiting trial on minor charges and had not been convicted of any crime. They said that 23 inmates died in the Fulton County jail for lack of proper medical care in the preceding two years. Defendants in the suit included Correctional Healthcare Solutions, Inc, the contractor responsible for inmates' health and medical care. Filed in Federal District Court in Atlanta in early 2000, the suit alleged that the contractor withheld timely medication and was otherwise careless, causing hundreds of inmates infected with HIV and AIDS to suffer excruciating and unnecessary pain, develop resistance to life-saving medication, and risk premature death. The Southern Center reports their case docket on their Internet website.[26]

In the Fulton County case, Judge Marvin Shoob ordered that inmates be screened for HIV, TB, and other diseases upon admission to the jail. Also, a new health care contractor provides an HIV specialist at the jail to diagnose, prescribe, and provide medication for and monitor those who are HIV positive. The judge appointed Robert Greifinger, MD, the former chief medical officer of the New York Department of Corrections, to evaluate improvements over time. On the occasion of his first visit, he found dental equipment dumped in a sink and hardly cleaned before being used on the next patient. His general conclusion was that "the medical staff at the County Jail had not learned the basic hygienic lessons of the nineteenth century." Under Judge Shoob's orders, however, Greifinger soon found conditions "remarkably better," but he insisted after ten months that "they're still not at a point yet where these new systems will continue without, quite frankly, the supervision of the court."[27] Such judicial oversight is critically important in the United States, which leads the world in the number of prison inmates. Litigation on behalf of their human rights is essential because they otherwise have little or no influence through conventional political processes to assure minimal humane living conditions.

CONCLUSIONS

Throughout the world, the recognition of internationally defined human rights and the need for adherence by public authority to domestic and international law are acknowledged. They are also often ignored as governments give higher priority to perceived national security needs, economic gain, and political advantage. These perennial forces within our global political economy will not change on the basis of mere appeals to conscience or excessive trust in new international rules and institutions. To keep such negative forces in check, people must organize to pursue common objectives, fashion new modes of humane governance, and work out human rights respecting accommodations to conflicting interests. This means, among other actions, vindicating human rights via NGOs persistently telling truth to power; heroic grassroots level action by individuals advocating social justice and asserting their human rights; the vigilance of professionals demanding the political space necessary to exercise their commitments to professional responsibility; and the willingness of technically trained people to offer their expertise when needed in the service of human rights wherever they are endangered.

24. See Reading 29 by Michael Ratner in Chapter 7 of this volume.
25. See *Ruben Foster et al. v. Fulton County, Georgia et al.*, No.1:99-CV-0900(MHS), 1999.
26. See http://www.schr.org
27. Ibid.

Increasingly, NGOs serve as catalysts in the promotion and protection of internationally recognized human rights. As their numbers proliferate and a global division of labor sets in, the capacity, efficacy, and legitimacy of NGOs increases, prompting them to take on diverse functions, particularly in the mutually reinforcing work of monitoring, educating and training, analyzing, lobbying, advocating, providing humane service, building solidarity, and litigating on behalf of human rights.

QUESTIONS FOR REFLECTION AND DISCUSSION

1. Why are human rights NGOs important actors in the international human rights movement? What purpose or purposes do they serve? Are they more effective than states or intergovernmental organizations in promoting and protecting human rights? What are their comparative advantages? Their comparative weaknesses? What does Claude say?

2. Of the nine NGO functions discussed by Claude, which does Claude think are the most important? Which do you think are most important? Why?

3. For maximum effectiveness in promoting and protecting human rights, is it better for human rights NGOs to concentrate on influencing a target country's domestic policy or the foreign policies of their home countries? Why? Suppose the target country were Belarus, China, Colombia, Congo, Cuba, Egypt, Indonesia, Iran, Moldova, Myanmar (Burma), North Korea, Saudi Arabia, Sudan, or Zimbabwe. Does your answer depend on the country selected? Why? Why not?

4. Often it is difficult for a human rights NGO to resolve whether it is useful or not to take action in a particular country or on a particular issue. As observed in David Weissbrodt, "The Contribution of International Nongovernmental Organizations to the Promotion and Protection of Human Rights," in Theodor Meron, ed., *Human Rights in International Law* (Oxford: Clarendon Press, 1984), 403–29, at 409, a human rights NGO must answer several key questions each time:

> Might intervention help or hurt the victims? What sort of intervention would be most effective? Have interventions in [the target] country or with respect to [the given] type of problem been successful in the past? Are the officials of the country receptive to initiatives from outsiders? Are the facts sufficiently well established to permit diplomatic intervention or publicity? Which NGO would be most effective in raising the issues?

How would/should one answer these questions? How would Claude?

5. Similarly, how does an NGO decide whether to accept a case or file a complaint on behalf of a victim of a human rights abuse? What criteria would aid the NGO in determining whether it would be the best organization to handle the case? Should the choice be based on political judgments or strictly legal ones? Why? Why not?

6. What are the moral/ethical responsibilities of professionals and professional associations relative to international human rights? How should professional associations—in, say, law, medicine, or journalism—operate in relation to human rights abuses in their areas of specialization? Should they undertake human rights missions? In fields unrelated to their areas of expertise? How might they have the most impact in promoting and protecting human rights?

7. Some people argue that professionals sometimes have a duty to be or appear to be neutral in the face of human rights abuse—for example, journalists who may need access to authoritative information. Do you accept this argument? Can you think of situations in which it might be made by lawyers? Doctors? Is there not a danger of cooptation? After all, lawyers, doctors, and scientists contributed to genocidal activities in Nazi Germany, did they not? What are the limits beyond which professionals should not go? For example, a doctor or lawyer administering to a tortured prisoner at the behest of the torturing authorities? See, e.g., Jacobo Timerman, *Prisoner Without a Name, Cell Without a Number*, trans. Toby Talbot (New York: Knopf, 1981).

8. Given that most NGOs operate to advance specific human rights interests, is there any danger that they may offer information skewed toward their specific interest? Is there a reliability issue with NGOs? Are there other dangers that might be posed by over-reliance on NGOs?

Min. wage low
countries too vulnerable
harm to environment
low pay to red
oil spills
overwork

9. Human rights NGOs have at various times been criticized for being fragmented, inadequately coordinated, redundant, and the like. Is this a problem and, if so, is there a solution to it? Should the United Nations and/or regional human institutions play a coordinating role? If you were charged to recommend a central body to coordinate NGOs, what would you propose to ensure that no human rights complaint gets overlooked and that minimal overlap in cases or complaints is the rule rather than the exception? Should these be priority goals? Why? Why not?

10. Typically NGOs are financially strapped, making it difficult for them to carry out their important functions. Mostly they are funded via private charitable contributions and project-oriented foundation grants. Are there other means of financial support that should be considered? For example, should states and or intergovernmental organizations, regional as well as global, be required to make, say, annual contributions? Why? Why not?

11. Should the role of human rights NGOs be strengthened? If so, how? If not, why not? Should they be represented in UN and/or regional bodies? If so, given that not all NGOs can participate, by what criteria would they be chosen and by whom? Might a global peoples assembly, representing global civil society, within or independent of the UN, prove beneficial? Along these lines, see Richard A. Falk and Andrew Strauss, "On the Creation of a Global Peoples Assembly: Legitimacy and the Power of Popular Sovereignty," *Stanford Journal of International Law* 36 (2000): 191–220.

32. MAHMOOD MONSHIPOURI, CLAUDE E. WELCH, JR., AND EVAN T. KENNEDY
Multinational Corporations and the Ethics of Global Responsibility

The global economy and forces of globalization have become prominent characteristics of current world politics. In this context, the political spotlight has rested on the balancing claims and criticisms of the multinational, or transnational, corporation (MNCs or TNCs). What makes MNCs a pertinent subject is their dynamic growth and influence; they affect the life chances of millions of people around the world.

Human rights groups and organizations insist that free trade and its rules, or lack thereof, are insufficient to promote a fair game and that the push for greater social responsibility of the MNCs is necessary given their increasing influence and the trend toward further privatization. Because MNCs have gained powers traditionally vested only in states, they should arguably be held to the same standards that international law presently imposes upon states. As Garth Meintjes has put it, "the idea of a corporation as a legal fiction without responsibilities is no more sacred or accurate than the idea of unfettered state sovereignty."[1]

The MNCs' power to control international investment, especially portfolio investments, has had enormous bearing on the economies of developing countries. Faced with pressures to attract such investments, governments in the South have had little or no alternative but to be receptive to the terms of MNCs, a lack of leverage that has meant, for example, that the minimum wage has been set unrealistically low in developing countries to attract foreign investment. A related criticism of MNCs is that their overall strategy to relocate from the North has kept wages and living conditions down and resulted in the expansion of sweatshops in the South. This has led to the view that "globalization" is a euphemism for "sweatshop global economy."

Critics argue that the current neoliberal global economy allows MNCs to utilize Southern workers as cheap labor and to exploit lower standards on working conditions, basic worker rights, and environmental regulations. MNCs have provoked considerable debate around the

1. Garth Meintjes, "An International Human Rights Perspective on Corporate Codes," in Oliver F. Williams, ed., *Global Codes of Conduct: An Idea Whose Time Has Come* (Notre Dame, Ind.: University of Notre Dame Press, 2000), 83–99, at 87.

conflicting issues of "efficiency" and "fairness," and the resultant balance of economic growth and social injustice. The simultaneous surge in economic growth and inequity has led to serious implications for human rights in the developing world. The MNCs' advocates, in contrast, regard them as benign engines of prosperity—enhancing local living conditions by generating employment, income, and wealth, as well as by introducing advanced technology to the developing world.

There are three emerging perspectives that inform corporate social responsibilities. First is the so-called "reputation capital" view that sees corporate social responsibility as a strategy to reduce investment risks and maximize profits. The second view, referred to as the "eco-social" view, considers social and environmental sustainability crucial to the sustainability of the market. The third perspective is the "rights-based" view, which underscores the importance of accountability, transparency, and social/environmental investment as key aspects of corporate social responsibility.

Using a rights-based perspective, we argue that in the human rights domain the responsible party is generally the state, and that, especially in the context of neoliberal globalization, the wrongdoers are often corporations. Some experts have argued that states are not and should not be the sole target of international legal obligations and that reliance on state duties alone may not be sufficient to broadly protect human rights.[2] A consensus has emerged that certain corporate behavior is detrimental to internationally recognized norms of human rights.

This essay examines the possibility of an outside governing body to hold in check unfettered global capitalism and to bring accountability to MNC policies that are socially detrimental. While we leave open the argument as to where this governing body should be located institutionally, we argue that restructuring international organizations, such as the World Trade Organization (WTO), might be a good place to start. It is also worth mentioning that the United Nations may provide an appropriate base for mobilizing support for a code of conduct. For now, however, private actions, media exposure, and lawsuits based on civil law seem to be the only practical way to put pressure on MNCs to consider observing global standards.

THE GLOBALIZATION-HUMAN RIGHTS INTERSECTION

Although there is no broadly accepted definition of the term "globalization," it is about the way in which the world is changing.[3] A simple description is offered by Allan Cochrane and Kathy Pain: "Cultures, economies and politics appear to merge across the globe through the rapid exchange of information, ideas and knowledge, and the investment strategies of global corporations."[4]

Some popular interpretations of globalization include the view that it is "an evolutionary process of change driven by technological and scientific progress in the modern era."[5] A force behind this definition is the recent communication and information technology revolution, from which corporations operate in a world market outside of national boundaries.

Another popular definition of globalization maintains that it magnifies and intensifies the level of interaction and interdependence among nation-states and societies. As markets become available on a worldwide level, once-separate societies deepen their relationships, politically and economically. From a realist perspective, globalization is a new hegemonic system upheld by the world's major capitalist economies to promote their own political and economic interests, a tool of the wealthy nations used to maintain their economic dominance.

Finally, some scholars see globalization as a paradigm shift, in which values, lifestyles, tolerance for diversity, and individual choice are simultaneously undergoing transformations on a global scale. Globalization as such relates not only to an increased interconnectedness between markets, but also to a shared culture, often effecting a social shift away from some traditional ideas and values.

2. We have borrowed the assumption developed in the seminal work of Steven R. Ratner, "Corporations and Human Rights: A Theory of Legal Responsibility," *Yale Law Journal* 111 (2001): 461–546.
3. On the intersection of globalization and human rights, see also Reading 4 in Chapter 1 of this volume.
4. Allan Cochrane and Kathy Pain, "A Globalizing Society," in David Held, ed., *A Globalizing World? Culture, Economics, Politics* (London: Routledge in association with Open University, 2000), 5–21, at 6.
5. Mahmood Monshipouri and Reza Motameni, "Globalization, Sacred Beliefs, and Defiance: Is Human Rights Discourse Relevant in the Muslim World?" *Journal of Church and State* 42 (2002): 709–36, at 712.

At both local and global levels, the protection and promotion of human rights have been caught up in this globalization process. As more institutions function at the global level, organizations such as MNCs, the IMF, and the European Commission of the European Union have rarely, if ever, been held to the standard of democratic accountability. The language of human rights has increasingly arisen to counter neoliberal globalization, and an emerging normative consensus has begun to take shape on the realization of some fundamental human rights.

We are nevertheless far from creating a single moral universe. Rather, what has happened through globalization is that the fate of communities throughout the world has become linked. Although there still are varying conceptions of what constitute "rights" and what priorities should be assigned to varying types of rights, the philosophical and political debate underlying these disagreements is itself conducted in a global context.

Because MNCs are not equipped to deal with questions of international ethics themselves, they need the help of human rights NGOs and others to deal with various human rights concerns. The key to this process is making corporations realize the benefits social responsibility will bring to them. Understandably, businesses have other concerns, such as profits and obligations to shareholders, that must be taken into account when discussing human rights issues. But the true means to develop a sustainable global economy is to integrate the concerns of business and human rights. They are not necessarily in opposition.

By emphasizing their mutual concerns, both communities may find themselves better positioned to concurrently advance their objectives. In this context, several questions must be raised. How will MNCs react to the rising tide of global human rights? What implications will lie ahead if MNCs choose to bypass such normative standards in the name of economic rationality and efficiency? Can MNCs be subject to some form of international regulation or litigation? Will mandatory/legal compliance work better than a voluntary approach to achieving corporate social responsibility?

THE POWER OF CAPITAL

Because MNCs have a direct impact on the economic, political, and social landscape of the countries in which they operate, their activities have considerable effect on individuals and human rights, both positively and negatively. Steven R. Ratner, who sees limits to holding states solely accountable for human rights violations, asserts that "corporations may have as much or more power over individuals as governments."[6] Corporations control a great amount of capital, generating about one-fifth of the world's wealth. Only six nations (the United States, Germany, Japan, United Kingdom, Italy, and France) have tax revenues larger than the nine largest MNCs' sales. Wal-Mart, which is not one of the top ten revenue-earning MNCs, still profits more per year than the Canadian government's annual tax revenues, while relying on developing countries' labor to produce many of its products.

Some studies on MNCs argue that their presence in Third World economies is beneficial, leading to increased life expectancy and reductions in illiteracy and infant mortality, along with increases in first- and second-generation rights as a whole. Despite evidence that corporate activities in the developing world improve human rights standards, it is still fair to say that MNCs often react to human rights concerns slowly and callously.

MNCs have consistently argued that the responsibility to improve the socioeconomic standards of living in Third World countries is that of the local government, not of corporations. The chasm between maximizing economic self-interest and promoting human rights, which has separated the operations of MNCs from those of human rights activists, characterizes the existing tensions between the two. In the second half of the twentieth century, writes David P. Forsythe, "the globalization of the economy and the globalization of human rights concerns developed separately from each other . . . ."[7]

MNC activity in the Third World has enhanced the inequitable tendencies of the market and further widened the gap between the rich and the poor. MNCs have also become the principal sites of economic and political power

---

6. Ratner, "Corporations and Human Rights," note 2, at 461.
7. David P. Forsythe, *Human Rights in International Relations* (Cambridge: Cambridge University Press, 2000), 197.

in the developing world. One Asian expert has argued that the removal of barriers to trade as well as to the movement of capital has given MNCs "enormous flexibility in the organization of production and has made them 'footloose,' able to exploit economic opportunities around the world."[8]

Many other factors contribute to the increase in the power of corporations. These include international protection of their property and their prominent role in international institutions that regulate trade, such as the World Trade Organization (WTO). It is important to bear in mind the mounting power of corporations in the context of international trade. Throughout the world, trade, investment, and information technology are constraining governments' ability to provide social safety nets and public services to cushion the negative consequences of globalization.

The power of capital is changing the relationship between states and the market. States are forced to lower their tax rates to entice capital to their economies, and are sacrificing public expenditures to do so. To invest in an area, the state has to provide conditions that the corporation prefers over those offered by other countries. States are inclined to do so because they see the opportunities for employment and revenues as investments in the future—not merely opportunities to skim off bribes. To the extent that the state has become increasingly subordinated to international capital, policy-making has often been dictated by the exigencies of capital movement. The ability of MNCs to coerce states into lowering labor standards highlights the inequities of the global market.

CORPORATE HUMAN RIGHTS ABUSES

Corporations frequently infringe on human rights indirectly, but sometimes they are directly complicit in abuses. Steven R. Ratner argues that MNCs have the responsibility—"complicity-based duties"—to avoid any situation that would lead to abuse.[9] The duties of corporations are directly linked to their capacity to harm human dignity. In some cases, private actors prevent their employees from leaving the country,

as evidenced by the problem of forced prostitution. Likewise, corporations are liable if they fail to exercise due diligence over their agents, including by not attempting corrective measures after the fact.

Given the close connection between economic development and socioeconomic rights, it is argued, MNCs' operations in the developing world are likely to enhance human rights. To the extent that MNCs create jobs, bring new capital and new technology, and provide such employee benefits as health care, they advance economic and social rights. The difficulty with such logic is that it overlooks the issue of uneven development. MNCs' operations usually accentuate existing inequalities, both in terms of income and wealth, by simultaneously creating pockets of poverty and wealth, development as well as underdevelopment.

Perhaps the most troubling aspect of MNCs' operations in the new global economy is the inordinate importance attached to portfolio investment as compared to foreign direct investment (FDI). Critics claim that MNCs' preference for portfolio investment has had devastating impacts on the economies of developing countries. It is liquid capital, flies by night, is largely driven by profit, often resulting in crony capitalism, and spurs purely speculative economic activities such as arbitrage, causing further economic corruption and disruption. Furthermore, the geographic flexibility that MNCs enjoy—mostly in the form of plant relocation—leaves local communities that are dependent on them for employment increasingly vulnerable [to many forms of exploitation].

William Meyer's study on the effects of MNCs' involvement in the Third World gets to the essence of the ambivalent effect they have on Third World countries. While acknowledging that some corporations have a history of human right abuses, he nevertheless maintains that MNCs have a "net beneficial impact" on rights.[10] It is of course easy to prove that a Wal-Mart factory in Honduras, for example, lowers unemployment in the region, providing jobs for persons that would not have them without such a factory. But this improvement does not mean that the hypothetical Wal-Mart operation is in compliance

---

8. Ibid., 251.
9. Ratner, "Corporations and Human Rights," note 2, at 512.
10. William H. Meyer, *Human Rights and International Political Economy in Third World Nations: Multinational Corporations, Foreign Aid, and Repression* (Westport, Conn.: Praeger, 1998), 198.

with universally accepted standards of human rights. As of yet, there is no universal protocol or method to weigh the benefits and drawbacks of MNCs' activity in the Third World.

Meyer cites specific examples of MNC operations that violate second- and third-generation rights in the Third World:[11] the Bhopal environmental disaster in India; *maquiladoras* (export-oriented factories) in Mexico, Honduras, and El Salvador; and Nike sweatshops in Indonesia and Pakistan are prime examples of human rights violations. Meyer asserts that "some MNCs try to destroy labor unions and many MNCs do harm to the environment." Currently, however, there are no [formally binding] guidelines that the international community can use to regulate corporate activity. Some have expressed a fear that MNCs, if left without regulation, will "opt for short-term profits at the expense of human dignity for many persons affected directly and indirectly by their practices."[12] The evidence to support this claim comes through increasing media coverage of human rights abuses in the developing world, especially "sweatshop" factories used by such companies as Nike, Wal-Mart, Gap, and Reebok. One situation often studied and cited is Nike's operation in Indonesia. There, workers are paid approximately $37 per month, enough to purchase two basic meals per day and only the most basic necessities, even when working up to 30 hours of overtime per week.

Companies other than Nike also find themselves under intense scrutiny from human rights organizations and other forces. Wal-Mart factories in China and Honduras have been found in violation of certain human rights in their operations. In Honduras, workers in *maquiladoras* have reported working up to twenty hours a day making only thirty-one cents an hour; and in China, a factory used by Wal-Mart set up a phony workshop that was up to Chinese labor code to mask conditions of illegally low pay and forced overtime.

Human rights abuses are not limited to Asian and Latin American factories set up by Western mercantilists, evidenced by the charges against the Unocal Oil Corporation and its operations in Myanmar (formerly Burma). A group of Burmese citizens, in conjunction with some human rights organizations, say that in building a gas pipeline through Myanmar to Thailand, Unocal participates in a project that includes "slave labor, the forced relocation of entire villages, and, in some cases, torture, rape, and murder by Burmese soldiers."[13] The pipeline is estimated to generate about $200 million a year in revenue, money that Unocal is not likely to turn away because of a few isolated human rights concerns.

In a similar case, European Union member states have consistently acted through the European Parliament to embarrass British Petroleum (BP) over its policies in Colombia that allegedly led to the repression of labor rights through brutal actions by the Colombian army in constructing a BP pipeline.

The case of Royal Dutch/Shell in Nigeria is another vivid example. In 1958, Royal Dutch/Shell began its oil operation in one of the most densely populated regions of Nigeria, an area in the Niger River Delta named Ogoni after the region's dominant ethnic group. Though oil production dramatically increased Nigeria's GNP, this growth, experts note, came at a horrendous cost to the 6 million people living in the Niger River Delta. The region suffered severe environmental damage related primarily to massive pollution from oil spills, and the inhabitants of the Ogoni lands who protested were subjected to systematic violent repression at the hands of the military dictatorship. Shell denied any involvement but admitted that it had imported arms for the Nigeria military. Shell refused to intercede with the Nigerian government to object to acts of violence against the Ogoni people.

DEVELOPING A REGIME OF CORPORATE RESPONSIBILITY

Perhaps due to a growing list of human rights abuses attributable to corporate activity in the developing world, a movement for a code of conduct for MNCs is gaining momentum internationally. The idea for a code of conduct for MNCs dates back to the mid-1970s, with the first meetings of the UN Commission on Transnational Corporations. This commission considered, among other things, whether the code

11. Ibid., 198–99, 202–3.
12. Forsythe, *Human Rights in International Relations*, note 7, at 199.
13. *Eds.*—See Rachel Chambers, "The Unocal Settlement: Implications for the Developing Law on Corporate Complicity in Human Rights Abuses," *Human Rights Brief* 13, 1 (Fall 2005): 14–16, 36.

should be mandatory or voluntary, and whether or not MNCs/TNCs were significant enough actors in international economic and political relations to warrant such a code.

With the increased international attention on corporate human rights abuses in the 1990s, the international community, headed by the United Nations, addressed the issue again in the form of the Global Compact, proposed by UN Secretary-General Kofi A. Annan at the World Economic Forum on 31 January 1999.[14] With roots in the 1948 Universal Declaration of Human Rights,[15] the fundamental principles and rights of the International Labour Organization, and with the environmental backing of the Earth Summit's Agenda, the Global Compact has a prestigious basis of literature supporting it.

The Compact sets out guidelines for corporate practices in its nine principles.[16] The first two principles deal with human rights in a general sense, asking corporations to support the protection of universal human rights and ensure that they are not complicit in human rights abuses. Corporations that commit themselves to the human rights cause would ensure and adhere to human rights practices not only in the workplace, but also condemn violations in the wider community. The Compact advocates safe and healthy working conditions, rights to basic health, education, and housing, and an end to forced and child labor.[17] The Compact asserts that in the wider community corporations should prevent forced migration, protect the local economy, and most importantly, contribute to the public debate—MNCs have both the right and the responsibility to express their views on matters that affect their operations in the community.

Principles three through six deal exclusively with labor issues. In these principles, Secretary-General Annan asked MNCs to support workers' freedom of association and right to unionize, to eliminate forced labor (such as mandatory overtime), to abolish child labor, and to eliminate discrimination in the workplace. This proclamation argues that unions allow for increased dialogue between workers and managers, and lead to more efficient and effective problem solving. It also condemns discriminatory practices, as they restrict the pool of workers available to a corporation and generally promote social fractionalization.

Principles seven through nine of the Compact address environmental issues. These three principles emphasize that MNCs should promote environmental responsibility, encourage the development of environmentally friendly technologies, and support a "precautionary approach" to environmental challenges. A precautionary approach to environmental protection suggests that companies take early preventive actions to ensure that irreparable environmental damage does not occur instead of waiting until the damage is done before addressing the problem. Doing this, the Compact suggests, is more cost-effective and also protects the corporation's public image.

THE CASE FOR SYSTEMATIC REGULATION

Will codes of conduct offer a role for MNCs in promoting the human rights of their workers? It is generally believed that MNCs are profit-maximizing and profit-seeking corporations that use codes as public relations tools, not for the benefit of workers. Urging corporate self-regulation is a false proposition: "it is untenable to expect companies to enforce their codes voluntarily."[18] Governments and international bodies should ultimately control the workers' rights by regulating companies through both national and international legislation. Medea Benjamin, executive director of Global Exchange, notes that "[i]t is important to talk more about international codes rather than codes that each company designs. Most codes of conduct are based on

14. See *The Global Compact: Corporate Citizenship in the World Economy* (United Nations Global Compact Office, Sept. 2004), available at http://www.unglobalcompact.org/irj/servlet/prt/portal/prtroot/com. sapportals.km. docs/ ungc html_content/AboutTheGC/EssentialReadings/GC%20brochure_master.pdf
15. Adopted Dec. 10, 1948, reprinted and referenced in Documentary Appendix A.
16. *Eds.*—A tenth principle added to the Global Compact since the original publication of this essay and focusing on "anti-corruption" asks businesses to "work against all forms of corruption, including extortion and bribery."
17. On human rights and child labor, see Burns H. Weston, ed., *Child Labor and Human Rights: Making Children Matter* (Boulder, Colo.: Lynne Rienner, 2005).
18. "An Interview with Medea Benjamin," *Human Rights Dialogue* (Carnegie Council on Ethics and International Affairs) 2 (2000): 7–9.

internationally recognized rights, on the ILO's own standards. These codes have been forced on companies. The companies did not want to have the codes, so the code itself is not the companies' agenda."[19]

Cynicism about international codes and instruments is widespread. At present, the standards by which the conduct of MNCs should be judged are neither uniform nor effective. Strategies that human rights NGOs have employed against governments may, therefore, be the best hope for confronting irresponsible MNCs. Although the Global Compact does represent a step toward curtailing human rights abuses by MNCs, the fact remains that it is voluntary and does not hold corporations accountable by way of penalties or sanctions for violating its principles. In its own words, the Compact is not a code of conduct.[20]

Human Rights Watch maintains that three obstacles stand in the way of the Compact's effectiveness: "The lack of legally enforceable standards, the lack of a monitoring and enforcement mechanism, and a lack of clarity about the meaning of the standards themselves."[21] It follows that the UN may be tarnishing its image as a protector of universal human rights by issuing a document with broad definitions of complicity that fall far short of enforcing stricter guidelines or establishing a monitoring body to ensure corporate compliance with the human rights agenda.

To guard against the Compact becoming a forum for hypocrisy, the UN should also develop a mechanism for monitoring and evaluating corporate compliance. In the absence of such a mechanism, there is a troubling possibility that the guidelines could be misinterpreted, misapplied, or ignored. That would result in corporations being given what they might claim is a "UN Seal of Approval" without having taken meaningful steps to implement the Compact's standards.

A similar view echoes this concern: the UN should never align itself with MNCs that violate the human rights that the organization holds dear. "By embracing multinationals," it is argued, "the UN has tarnished its reputation and abdicated its role as a protector of human rights. . . . The United Nations should be establishing itself as a tough, independent monitor. Instead, it's jumped into bed with some of the most notorious companies in the world."[22] By embracing MNCs through the Global Compact, the UN is sending a message that companies will voluntarily abide by the principles of the Compact, even though history has proven otherwise.

Corporations, however, are increasingly realizing that they cannot continue to ignore human rights concerns. There is an increasing realization among executives of large MNCs that in order for their companies to thrive, the communities in which they do business must prosper as well. British Petroleum, for instance, invested in computer technology in Vietnam for flood-related damage control, provided refrigerators in Zambia for the storage of anti-malaria vaccines, and has helped to replant a forest destroyed by fire in Turkey, to name a few examples. This blossoming movement is likely to help transform the human rights practices of MNCs. The challenge remains, however, to find the most effective way (voluntary or coercive) to promote corporate social responsibility. Some experts have pointed to voluntary adoption of socially responsible policies as a vital component of running a business. They have sought ways in which to modify corporations' internal cultures. The key here, they argue, is to create an environment conducive to moving beyond the legal to the ethical realm of corporate social responsibility. Such a voluntary approach to code formation and enforcement, they note, "would minimize the need for further governmental regulation, which is invariably more expensive and less efficient."[23]

---

19. Ibid., 9.

20. *Eds.*—In its own words: "The Global Compact is not a regulatory instrument—it does not 'police,' enforce or measure the behavior or actions of companies. Rather, the Global Compact relies on public accountability, transparency and the enlightened self-interest of companies, labour and civil society to initiate and share substantive action in pursuing the principles upon which the Global Compact is based." *The Global Compact*, note 14.

21. Letter from Kenneth Roth, Executive Director, Human Rights Watch, to Kofi Annan, Secretary-General of the United Nations, July 28, 2000, available at http://www.hrw.org/advocacy/corporations/index.htm

22. Anonymous, "The UN Sells Out," *Progressive* (Sept. 2000), available at http://proquest.umi.com

23. S. Prakash Sethi, "Corporate Codes of Conduct and the Success of Globalization," *Ethics & International Affairs* 16, no. 1 (2002): 89–106, esp. 106

Some have looked to the United Nations and its Global Compact, contending that the most encouraging part of the Compact is its emphasis on the social responsibility of corporations, an aspect critical to the protection of human rights. MNCs, according to the Compact, have a responsibility not only to obey the laws of the host communities, but also to contribute to the vitality of those communities. Judgments regarding MNCs operations are directly linked to their transparency and good governance.

The first principle of the Compact asks that MNCs support and respect internationally proclaimed human rights "within their sphere of influence." While the language is vague, the Compact makes it clear that corporations' responsibilities to protect human rights do not stop at the doorsteps of their factories. MNCs have a wider responsibility to promote human rights interests in the surrounding community. Within this guideline, there are some suggestions for how companies can help to promote a human rights agenda. The Compact's recommendations include MNCs taking the lead in protecting the rights of unions, especially in countries with tight labor restrictions such as China, providing medical care for laborers who have fallen ill as a result of their work, raising awareness in the community about child labor, and providing education and training for working children.

The mere adoption of a code of conduct is only the first step in a long process. International law has to protect these rights by holding corporations liable if they do not comply with universally accepted human rights standards, such as those outlined in the Global Compact. By focusing solely on the economic effects of the MNCs, international law has yet to hold these companies accountable for the social effects they have on developing countries.

International regulation and transnational litigation, also known as "foreign direct liability," is gaining momentum and poses a real challenge for the MNCs' operations. The 1789 Alien Tort Claims Act is an example.[24] Legal recourse is based on allegations of corporate complicity in violations of fundamental human rights or principles of international environmental law. Several cases against U.S. multinationals for alleged violations occurring in other countries have been heard in U.S. courts. The victims of India's Bhopal disaster sued Union Carbide in U.S. courts. Texaco was sued by indigenous Amazonians for environmental damage in Ecuador.

There are signs that MNCs are realizing the importance, and value, of social responsibility. U.S.-based corporations used to hold more of a "hands-off" policy toward human rights abuses abroad, claiming they could not be held responsible for abuses undertaken in foreign factories. With increased human rights activism, sharper media scrutiny, and the intensive communications made possible by information technology, U.S. corporations find it immensely difficult and costly to sustain the old hands-off policies. Mounting pressure has compelled them to accept responsibility for the labor practices and human rights abuses of their foreign subcontractors.

FILLING THE ENFORCEMENT GAP

The preceding discussion has revolved around four key points: (1) that companies cannot be trusted to monitor their own compliance to human rights standards; (2) that there are no existing international legal obligations that require corporate social responsibility, let alone an effective legal regime to enforce such obligations; (3) that the Global Compact has made great contributions, both in terms of setting standards and monitoring compliance; (4) that the lack of enforcement mechanisms and reliance on self-monitoring should not detract from the value of the Global Compact as a first step to developing and monitoring codes of conduct.

There is a need for a monitoring system outside of the corporations themselves. In the past, some MNCs have themselves contracted factory monitoring firms to check out their overseas operations; firms such as PriceWaterhouseCoopers (PWC), which performs more than 6,000 factory inspections per year for corporations such as Nike. When the corporation itself hires the firm to examine its Third World factories, however, the odds are high that the inspecting firm will return a favorable review. PWC came under fire by various study groups and human rights NGOs for its conflicted role in these types of deals.

Certainly a cosmopolitan body to adjudicate corporate wrongdoing will not spring up overnight, nor will it ever develop without finding a

---

24. On the Alien Tort Claims Act, see Reading 29 by Michael Ratner in Chapter 7 of this volume.

balance between corporate concerns and human rights concerns. Once the international community reaches a consensus on the need for such a system, the focus should turn to finding a balance between corporate and human rights concerns, and how to give the court the power it needs to hold corporations accountable. As noted above, the issue is where will the power for this international court come from—should it have its basis in the United Nations or should it be independent of all corporate, political, and nongovernmental organizations (NGOs)?

[*Eds.*—The authors go on to recount a series of proposals for "a cosmopolitan body to adjudicate corporate wrongdoing," some within the UN system, others outside of it. In the latter category they note the IMF, the World Bank, and, perhaps most prominently, the WTO. They also note, however, that the WTO "is widely regarded 'as a preserve of powerful and rich nations.' Many developing countries simply lack the resources, including money or expertise, to fight drawn-out legal battles in Geneva. Almost one quarter of the members of the WTO cannot even afford representation in Geneva." They then turn their attention to NGOs.]

WHAT ROLE FOR THE NGOS?

Debate continues as to what impact NGOs may have on strengthening the democratic accountability of such international organizations as the WTO. Some experts insist that NGOs' direct influence on policy should be channeled through national governments, because governments usually are more accountable to their citizens. Others argue that, although NGOs are self-selected and not democratically elected, they can play a positive role in increasing transparency in international organizations and thus deserve an observer status and a voice, but not a vote. Still others observe that, given the pluralistic and multidimensional nature of social responsibility, neither NGOs nor governments have the wisdom or the right to lay down what corporations must do.

Many critics of international organizations have challenged the notion that the WTO as presently constituted can be reformed, arguing that as long as power resides in the hands of large transnational corporations and the big

powers that support them, the WTO is unreformable. It is thus essential that NGOs pressure the WTO into observing labor, environmental, and human rights standards. Pressure for progressive change coming from private actions, civil society, media exposure, and lawsuits based on civil law can endanger corporate brand names and profit margins by exposing the MNC Achilles' heels, and evidence suggests that corporate behavior has been increasingly influenced by such public stigmatization. As a result, more companies may seek to avoid negative exposures by adopting and enforcing internationally recognized human rights codes of conduct before they have been targeted. Ultimately, however, it is the responsibility of national governments to enact and implement global labor, environmental, and human rights standards for the MNCs.

CONCLUSION

Given the many questions and controversies surrounding the operations of MNCs, a case can be made for holding MNCs accountable to human rights standards and for pressuring MNCs to reorient their policies and practices. Two broad conclusions can be drawn.

First, MNCs have thus far shown meager interest in sociocultural welfare or human rights of the vast majority of the people living in host countries. MNCs are under no legal—much less ethical—obligations to the governments of the countries within which they operate, even as their policies and actions affect hundreds of millions of people. Conversely, it is states that are accountable to the transnational business forces and economic private regimes set by the MNCs. In the absence of international regulatory agencies, MNCs have been entirely free to devise their own rules, creating an environment less hospitable or indifferent to human rights.

Second, corporate policies and practices are arguably subject to constant evolution, as are corporate responsibilities and obligations. MNCs have an inherent responsibility to provide for their workers and the good of the community as a whole. Workers in developing countries' factories have the same inherent human rights as the company's shareholders, and need to be treated with the same dignity and respect. The urgency of "growth" and "efficiency" need not detract from the importance of preserving the human rights and dignity of laborers in the developing world. In the future, growth will be problematic if it further exacerbates existing disparities.

Notwithstanding the recent surge in the rhetoric of social responsibility, many corporations will not apply human rights agendas to their developing countries' operations without an outside monitoring agent or structure enforcing standards. The lack of consensus between states and the absence of leadership among MNCs have prevented the emergence of coherent and effective standards to assess the operation of the MNCs. The UN Global Compact is unlikely to completely end MNCs' misconduct, but it is a step in the right direction. The standards addressed therein necessitate a substantial supportive system to gain merit in the international community. Corporate codes of conduct are useful to the extent that they are an integral part of the employment contracts and the right to organize. Such codes, however, lack mechanisms for implementation and external monitoring.

Whether the answer lies in restructuring international organizations, linking their strengths, enhancing private actions and media exposure, or creating a single intermediary institution, or regional or global governance, the case for the MNCs' self-policing is utterly unpersuasive. In the current global economy, MNCs and their shareholders are able to reap enormous benefits, and use their power to take advantages of workers and governments alike. If they can benefit from this increasingly interdependent global economy, it is only fair that they accept the responsibilities that go along with these economic gains.

QUESTIONS FOR REFLECTION AND DISCUSSION

1. Should multinational corporations and other transnational business enterprises be involved in promoting and protecting internationally recognized human rights, or should they stick to that for which they are constituted—producing goods and services, expanding markets, and making profits? Why? Why not? Shortly before the lifting of South African apartheid, W. Michael Reisman, with corporate enterprise in mind, described structural problems in governmental enforcement of human rights norms in terms of "institutional elasticity"—i.e., "the extent to which institutions created and still used for other purposes can be 'stretched' in order to get them to perform human rights functions." "Through or Despite Governments: Differentiated Responsibilities in Human Rights programs," *Iowa Law Review* 72 (1987): 391–400, at 395. To what extent, if at all, is it appropriate or just to stretch institutions created for one purpose to perform another, such as the promotion and protection of human rights? How would you answer this question with reference to China today? Myanmar (Burma) today? Sudan? Zimbabwe? Others?

2. Do multinational corporations and other transnational business enterprises have any comparative advantages relative to other entities or groups in promoting and protecting internationally recognized human rights? If so, what are they? If not, why not? Consider, on the one hand, Wal-Mart with global annual revenues exceeding $250 billion and, on the other, Chile with a GDP of approximately $160 billion. Which is better positioned to safeguard human rights? Which, under traditional international law, is under the more stringent obligation to safeguard them? Are there sound reasons for this state of affairs or is it a matter merely of inertia? Should international law remedy the apparent imbalance? Why? Why not?

3. Do multinational corporations or other transnational business enterprises have a responsibility to the citizens of their host countries when the host countries commit human rights violations against their own people? Why? Why not? What if the host country violation affects essentially one or two people only—for example, the arrest and detention of one or two political dissidents? What if the violation is gross in character—for example, the arrest, detention, torture, and perhaps even "disappearance" of hundreds of political dissidents or the systematic discrimination or even slaughter of ethnic minorities? Should multinational corporations or other transnational business enterprises be allowed or encouraged to do "business as usual" under either of these circumstances? What do Monshipouri, Welch, and Kennedy say? Do you agree? Disagree? Why? Why not?

4. Do multinational corporations or other transnational business enterprises have a responsibility to the citizens of their host countries when they cause or commit human

rights violations themselves directly? What about violations that impact the general population—for example, the negligent release of toxic chemicals causing thousands of deaths? What about violations against their own employees only—for example, the maintenance of unsafe workplace conditions or the abuse and exploitation of children working for them? What do Monshipoori, Welch, and Kennedy say? Do you agree? Disagree? Why? Why not?

5. Do multinational corporations or other transnational business enterprises have a responsibility to the citizens of their host countries when they operate in such a way as to threaten or deprive host country citizens of their human rights more or less indirectly? For example, it is commonly noted that multinational corporations, largely unfettered by international law, are able to move production facilities (and, to lesser degree, management) freely from country to country. This often has resulted, as many have noted, in a "race to the bottom," i.e., where impoverished governments desperate to increase tax revenues and employment rates offer multinationals increasingly lax human rights standards. Witness as one concrete example the infamous *maquiladoras* in the cities of northern Mexico where U.S.-based multinationals find, *inter alia*, cheaper labor, fewer environmental regulations, and lower import duties on raw materials. What does or can international human rights law do to recognize the obvious dilemma that results: on the one hand, the Mexican people may want the factories because of limited employment alternatives; on the other hand, traditional domestic industry is likely to shrivel to nothing once *maquiladora* work becomes available in a given area. Both sides of this coin implicate the right to livelihood and many other rights. Which should win out? Should the citizens of a host country be permitted to decide what they will and will not allow, irrespective of the future harms that others in the international community may think will follow? Or should international human rights law create a clear set of baseline labor standards? If so, should the baseline be minimalist in kind? Maximalist in kind? Somewhere in between?

6. Suppose that a multinational corporation or other transnational business enterprise were to lend financial or other support to a repressive host government and get tax breaks, a relaxation of environmental or workplace standards, or other favors beneficial to its entrepreneurial pursuits? It happens often as a result of corrupt host country bribes imposed as a condition of doing business within its territorial jurisdiction. Commonly the ultimate loser is the host country citizen. Should such behavior be allowed under international law? What do Monshipouri, Welch, and Kennedy say? Do you agree? Disagree? Why? Why not?

7. Assuming that multinational corporations and other transnational business enterprises have some responsibility to uphold human rights, is that obligation a legal one? A moral one? If it be a legal obligation, then by what logic or according to what theory? How is it possible to hold legally accountable private actors that have, at least in theory, no standing in the international legal order? What do Monshipouri, Welch, and Kennedy say? Do you agree? Disagree? Why? Why not?

8. The Office of the UN High Commissioner for Human Rights (OHCHR), in a report titled *Business and Human Rights: A Progress Report* and available at http://www.unhchr.ch/business.htm, asserts that "Businesses are increasingly focused on the impact they have on individuals, communities, and the environment." Do you agree? Why? Why not? If so, why do you think businesses have adopted this new, seemingly altruistic, focus? Does respecting human rights help a business' bottom line? Does the "bottom line" improve because respecting human rights is an efficient way to do business? Because consumers are more willing to buy products from a company they respect?

9. In February 2005, the UN Sub-commission on the Promotion and Protection of Human Rights released its *Report of the UNHCHR on the responsibilities of transnational corporations and related business enterprises with regard to human rights* (UN Doc. E/CN.4/2005/91, Feb. 15, 2005). That report, issued after a consultative process involving member states, transnational corporations, NGOs, and others, concluded that there are "gaps in understanding the . . . responsibilities of business with regard to human rights," and recommended further study of the following issues in particular:

> the concepts of "sphere of influence" and "complicity"; the nature of positive responsibilities on business to "support" human rights; the human rights responsibilities of business in relation to their subsidiaries and supply chain; questions relating to jurisdiction and protection of human rights in situations where a State is unwilling or unable to protect human rights; sector specific studies identifying the different challenges

faced by business from sector to sector; and situation specific studies, including the protection of human rights in conflict zones.

Amnesty International welcomed the report and urged states to encourage the UNHCHR to further develop universal human rights standards for business. Based on the above-quoted language, do you think such universality is likely to result from the process the UNHCHR is pursuing? Does the involvement of businesses, along with the involvement of the International Chamber of Commerce, affect your perception of the legitimacy of the process? Compare the attempts to define the human rights responsibilities of businesses with the similar, but earlier, attempts to define the responsibilities of states. Are they different? If so, how? What are their similarities? Does the comparison suggest a *de facto* revision of international legal theory relative to the standing of private actors in the international legal order?

33. JORDAN J. PAUST *The Human Right to Revolution*

This country, with its institutions, belongs to the people who inhabit it. Whenever they shall grow weary of the existing government, they can exercise their constitutional right of amending, or their revolutionary right to dismember or overthrow it.[1]

These are the words not of a twentieth-century revolutionary or even an eighteenth-century founder of our Republic, but of a nineteenth-century Republican President at the beginning of a long and destructive civil war in the United States. What Abraham Lincoln recognized was the fundamental democratic precept that authority comes ultimately from the people of the United States, and that with this authority there is retained a "revolutionary right to dismember or overthrow" any governmental institution that is unresponsive to the needs and wishes of the people.

The right of revolution recognized by President Lincoln has, of course, an early foundation in American history. Both the Declaration of Independence (1776) and the Declaration of the Causes and Necessity of Taking Up Arms (1775) contain recognitions of this right, and several state constitutions within the United States consistently recognized the right of the people "to reform, alter, or abolish government"' at their convenience. Indeed, the American Republic was founded on revolution.

The American Revolution served as a precursor for numerous others in the Americas, Europe, and elsewhere, even into the twentieth century. Today, it is common to recognize that all peoples have a right to self-determination[2] and, as a necessary concomitant of national self-determination, a right to engage in revolution. Yet, it is not as widely understood that, under international law,

Reprinted with changes from Jordan J. Paust, "The Human Right to Participate in Armed Revolution and Related Forms of Social Violence: Testing the Limits of Permissibility," *Emory Law Journal* 32 (1983): 545–81. Copyright © Emory University School of Law and Jordan J. Paust. Reprinted by permission.

1. Abraham Lincoln, "First Inaugural Address" (Mar. 4, 1861), in *Lincoln's Stories and Speeches*, ed. Edward F. Allen (New York: New York Books, 1900), 212. In this essay, the right of "revolution" refers to the right fundamentally to change a governmental structure or process within a particular nation-state, thus including the right to replace governmental elites or overthrow a particular government. Such a change can occur slowly or quickly, peacefully or with strategies of violence. Thus defined, one might distinguish "revolution" from claims for minority protection, claims to be free from external oppression, and claims to secession. It is worth emphasizing that this paper is concerned with the legal propriety (under domestic and international law) of revolutionary social violence and does not address moral propriety or "justness" as such. However, in contrast to some writers, it does recognize that civil disobedience might, in a given case, involve a repudiation of the general authority of a constituted government. But "civil disobedience" can, under certain circumstances, involve revolutionary claims, strategies, or effects. One author argues realistically that disobedience limited to particular matters, which "does not, in fact, challenge the existence of the larger society, only its authority in this or that case," is "not revolution but civil disobedience," adding that "unlimited and uncivil disobedience" is "revolution." Michael Walzer, "The Obligation to Disobey," in Edward Kent, ed., *Revolution and the Rule of Law* (Englewood Cliffs, N.J.: Prentice-Hall, 1971), 111, 119, 125.

2. See Reading 12 by Maivân Clech Lâm in Chapter 2 and Reading 19 by Hurst Hannum in Chapter 4 in this volume.

there are limits to the permissibility of armed revolution and the participation of individuals in revolutionary social violence.

The purpose of this essay is to clarify the nature and scope of the right of revolution. In doing so, it will be necessary to identify the relationship between the right of revolution and the international legal precepts of authority, self-determination, and more general norms of human rights. With these interrelations in mind, one can also identify and clarify relevant legal constraints on armed revolution and the participation of individuals in such a process.

Such a focus should inform choice with regard to permissibility, but a realistic and policy-serving decision about the legality of any particular strategy of armed revolution (or of social violence in general) must also hinge upon adequate inquiry into the actualities of circumstance or contextual analysis. Realistic and policy-serving choice concerning the permissibility or impermissibility of a particular coercive process engaged in by private individuals or groups must be guided by an awareness of community expectations about the process of authority as well as an awareness of all relevant domestic and international legal policies at stake, actual trends in authoritative decision, relevant features of past and present context, and probable future effects that might condition the serving or thwarting of legal policies in the future.

With such a focus, one should discover that private individuals and groups can and do engage in numerous forms of permissible violence. It is too simplistic to say, therefore, that authoritative violence can only be engaged in by "the government"' or by governmental elites and functionaries. The useful question is not whether private violence is permissible, but what forms of private violence are permissible, when, in what social context, and why. As Professor Reisman argues: "[I]nsistence on non-violence and deference to all established institutions in a global system with many injustices can be tantamount to confirmation and reinforcement of those injustices. In certain circumstances, violence may be the last appeal or the first expression of demand of a group or unorganized stratum for some measure of human dignity."[3] Of course, such an injunction can also have particular relevance concerning the question of revolutionary social violence. Here, as elsewhere, no facile "rule"' or simplistic prohibition will do.

GENERAL LEGAL POLICIES AT STAKE

Natural Law, Authority of the People, and the American Revolution

Early in American history, we appealed to natural law and the "rights of man"' to affirm the right of revolution. Two historic declarations provide an inventory of the forms of oppression thought to justify armed revolution. The American Declaration of Independence proclaimed to the world the expectation that all governments are properly constituted in order "to secure" the inalienable rights of man, that governments derive "their just powers from the consent of the governed," and that "it is the Right of the People to alter or abolish" any form of government which "becomes destructive of these ends." More specifically, the American people denounced the King of England as a tyrant who was "unfit to be the ruler of a free People" because, among other things, he invaded "the rights of the people," dissolved representative governmental bodies, obstructed the administration of justice, failed to control the depredations of the military, and engaged in numerous other strategies of tyranny and oppression. The Declaration of the Causes and Necessity of Taking Up Arms had also denounced Parliament's "cruel and impolitic purpose of enslaving the colonial Americans . . . by violence . . .," the British government's "intemperate rage for unlimited domination," acts of "cruel aggression," and numerous "oppressive measures" that had reduced our ancestors "to the alternative of choosing an unconditional submission to the tyranny of irritated ministers, or resistance by force."

It is important to note two primary aspects of the right of revolution claimed in these two Declarations. First, the claim was made in a situation in which a ruler and a government sought to subject a people to despotism through various forms of political and economic oppression. Second, and most importantly, the Declaration of Independence was proclaimed "in the Name, and by authority of the . . . People."' Thus, although the framers of these Declarations

---

3. W. Michael Reisman, "Private Armies in a Global War System: Prologue to Decision," *VJIL* 14 (1973): 1–55, at 32–33.

appealed to natural law and inalienable rights, including the right to be free from governmental oppression and to alter or abolish oppressive forms of government, the primary justifying criterion was the proclaimed authority of the people.

Since the dawn of U.S. constitutional history, the Supreme Court has consistently recognized that the primary source of authority in the United States is the people of the United States. As the Court early declared, "their will alone is to decide."[4] Thus, necessarily, any criterion of permissibility under United States domestic law must ultimately be compatible with the will of the people of the United States. The "authority of the people" is the peremptory criterion; and, under domestic law, their will alone is to decide.

For this reason, the right of revolution is in the nation as a whole and is not a right of some minority of an identifiable people. In Locke's view, the right of revolution was a right of the majority of a community. This view was shared by many of the founders of the American Republic as well as many others, and is reflected in early U.S. state constitutions.

In view of the above, one can also recognize the propriety of a claim by the government, when representing the authority of the people, to regulate certain forms of revolutionary violence or, when reasonably necessary, "incitement to violence" engaged in by a minority of the people of the United States and without their general approval. Indeed, several Supreme Court cases document the permissibility of such a claim, although a few others seem to go too far. If, however, the right of revolutionary violence is engaged in by the predominant majority of the people, or with their general approval, the government (or a part of thereof) would necessarily lack authority, and governmental controls of such violence or incitements to violence would be impermissible. Thus, for example, it would be constitutionally improper to allege that "incitement to violence" is always a justification for governmental suppression of such conduct even if violence is imminent. Permissibility does not hinge upon violence as such, but ultimately upon the peremptory criterion of authority— i.e., the will of the people generally shared in the community.

In the United States, loyalty is owed to the Constitution as such and not to any particular government. Even some of the earlier cases that affirmed a broad power to regulate the advocacy of social violence mentioned a "danger to organized government," "existing Government," or "representative government" and thus, implicitly, to the American form of constitutional government. Also of primary concern was the need for the government to "be responsive to the will of the people . . . so that changes, if desired, may be obtained by peaceful means."[5]

Cases such as *Dennis v. United States*, *Yates v. United States*, and *Scales v. United States*[6] addressed the advocacy of violent revolution by members of the Communist Party of the United States who, as a small and disfavored minority, were hardly representing the general will and authority of the people of the United States at those periods in time. Thus, although mere advocacy is permissible today, the Communist Party, if it still represents a disfavored minority, would not have a right to initiate an armed revolution against the government of the United States.

In an unusual case, a United States circuit court responded to an alien's claim that "the right of revolution is inherent in every individual" by remarking: "That right, if it exists, depends upon where such individual attempts to operate. . . ," adding that "revolution presupposes an antagonism between a government and its nationals, not between a government and aliens. As a citizen of Denmark, appellant has no right of revolution as against the United States."[7] It is certainly not the point of the circuit court that all forms of outside participation in revolution are unlawful, especially in view of the well-known assistance of foreign participants to the American colonials during the Revolutionary War. Rather, the court held that foreign persons do not have a right of revolution against the government of the United States. In that sense, the decision was consistent with the view that a right of revolution can be exercised by a majority of the people of the United States, but not by a mere minority of the people or by nonresident aliens who are considered to form no part of the people of this nation.

4. *Ware v. Hylton*, 3 U.S. (3 Dall.) 199, 237 (1796); see also 236.
5. *Keyishian v. Board of Regents*, 385 U.S. at 602 (quoting *De Jonge v. Oregon*, 299 U.S. 353, 365 (1937)).
6. *Dennis*, 341 U.S. 494 (1951); *Yates*, 354 U.S. 298 (1957); *Scales*, 367 U.S. 203 (1961).
7. *Kjar v. Doak*, 61 F.2d 566, 569 (7th Cir. 1932).

In summary, numerous cases either affirm or are consistent with a distinction between permissible forms of violence approved by the authority of the people and unlawful violence, especially violence engaged in contrary to the authority of the people. Perhaps in recognition of such a distinction, Justice Black has stated:

> Since the beginning of history there have been governments that have engaged in practices against the people so bad, so cruel, so unjust and so destructive of the individual dignity of men and women that the "right of revolution" was all the people had left to free themselves. . . . I venture the suggestion that there are countless multitudes in this country, and all over the world, who would join [the] belief in the right of the people to resist by force tyrannical governments like those.[8]

As the next section demonstrates, there are apparently "countless multitudes . . . all over the world" who would recognize the permissibility of such a right of revolution by a people.

Permissibility Under International Law

It is doubtful whether Justice Black had in mind specific portions of the Universal Declaration of Human Rights (UDHR)[9] when he recognized the seemingly wide approval of a general right of revolution, but he could have. The preamble to the Universal Declaration declares, for instance, that "it is essential, if man is not to be compelled to have recourse, as a last resort, to rebellion against tyranny and oppression, that human rights should be protected by the rule of law." As one commentator has noted, the UDHR preamble actually supports the right of revolution or rebellion, and it reflects the growth of acceptance of that right at least from the time of the American Declaration of Independence, an acceptance so pervasive as to allow text writers to conclude that "the right of a people to revolt against tyranny is now a recognized principle of international law."[10] Indeed, prior to the American and French Revolutions of the eighteenth century, the right of revolution had been accepted in several human societies. Scholars have identified related expectations, for example, among the early Greeks and Romans; in Germanic folk law; among naturalist theorists such as Thomas Aquinas in medieval Western Europe; and in the writings of early international scholars such as Grotius and Vattel.

Today, the right of revolution is an important international precept and a part of available strategies for the assurance both of the authority of the people as the lawful basis of any government and of the process of national self-determination. Under international law, the permissibility of armed revolution is necessarily interrelated with legal precepts of authority and self-determination, as well as with more specific sets of human rights. For example, the right to change a governmental structure is necessarily interrelated with the question of the legitimacy of that structure in terms of the accepted standard of authority in international law and with the precept of self-determination, both of which are interrelated and are also interconnected with the human rights of individuals to participate in the political processes of their society." As recognized in numerous international instruments and by the International Court of Justice, all peoples have the right to self-determination and, by virtue of that right, to freely determine their political status.[11] Similarly it is recognized "that the application of the right of self-determination requires a free and genuine expression of the will of the peoples concerned."[12] Political self-determination, in fact, is a dynamic process involving the genuine, full and freely expressed will of a given people, that is, a dynamic aggregate will of individuals. The "will of the people" is actually the dynamic outcome of such a process and reflects an equal and aggregate participation by individuals and groups in a process of authority.

Furthermore, there is a significant consistency among the precept of self-determination, the human right to individual participation in

---

8. *In re Anastaplo*, 366 U.S. 82, 113 (Black, J., dissenting).

9. Adopted Dec. 10, 1948, reprinted and referenced in Documentary Appendix A.

10. Gerald Sumida, "The Right of Revolution: Implications for International Law and Order," in Charles A. Barker, ed., *Power and Law: American Dilemma in World Affairs* (Baltimore: Johns Hopkins University Press, 1971), 130, 134.

11. *Western Sahara Advisory Opinion*, 1975 ICJ 12, 31–33, 36, citing several international instruments including the authoritative Declaration on Principles of International Law, GA Res. 2625, 25 UN GAOR Supp. (No. 28) at 121, UN Doc. A/8028 (1970).

12. Ibid., 32, ¶ 55.

the political process, and the only standard of authority recognized in international law. Self-determination and human rights both demand that the only legitimate basis of the authority of any government is the dynamic process of self-determination and authority noted above.

The first two paragraphs of Article 21 of the Universal Declaration recognize the rights of every person "to take part in" the governmental processes of one's country and to "equal access to public service." The more significant content of Article 21, however, is set forth in paragraph 3 that states: "The will of the people shall be the basis of the authority of government; this will shall be expressed in periodic and genuine elections which shall be held by secret vote or by equivalent free voting procedures." A legitimate government, the Declaration affirms, is one in which the "will of the people" is the basis of authority. The authority of a government exists lawfully on no other basis, in no other form. Indeed, the only specific formal reference to the concept of authority that one finds among all of the major international legal documents is the reference to the authority of the people of a given community.

Many interrelated norms from the Universal Declaration, when taken together, tend to confirm the clear and unswerving criterion of authority contained in the third paragraph of Article 21. When one considers how individuals acting within a political process are to exercise their rights, affirmed in the Declaration, to take part in governmental processes and to obtain equal access to public service in a manner that is consistent with the rights of each and every person to equality, dignity, and the equal protection and enjoyment of law, it seems clear that participation should be on the basis of one person, one voice. Stated differently, an equally weighted "will" of each individual conjoined in a so-called "will of the people" or common expression is the only formula that allows equal individual participation in a political process. Having this in mind, it is understandable why Article 21 contains other references to what one might term the related aspects of a process of authority. There is a great deal of illuminating consistency within the Article, evidencing that the people of a given community have the right to alter, abolish, or overthrow any form of government that becomes destructive of the process of self-determination and the right of individual

participation. Such a government, of course, would also lack authority and, as a government representing merely some minority of the political participants, it could be overthrown by the majority in an effort to ensure authoritative government, political self-determination, and the human rights of all members of the community equally and freely to participate.

Thus, as mentioned, the right of revolution supported by the preamble to the Universal Declaration and accepted by text writers as a principle of international law is a concomitant precept and a part of available strategies for the securing of the authority of the people and national self-determination. Importantly also, the international precepts of authority and self-determination provide criteria relevant to our inquiry into the permissibility of individual participation in armed revolution. As in the case of domestic standards, the right of revolution is necessarily a right of the majority against, for example, an oppressive governmental elite. Furthermore, the authority of the people is the only legitimate standard. Although the process of authority is dynamic and individuals might engage in violence with the approval of the people, the right of revolution is not a right of only some minority of the people or to be utilized in an effort to oppress the authority of the people. Indeed, in view of the many interrelated international legal precepts noted above, an oppression of the authority of the people is a form of political slavery that is not only violative of human rights but also constitutes a treason against humanity.

THE CONCEPT OF REVOLUTION AND CRITERIA OF PERMISSIBILITY

When one considers further the use of the concept of revolution in American legal history, one is struck by the fact that many conceptual categorizations have been utilized. The right of revolution has been described variously as "the great and fundamental right of every people to change their institutions at will;" a "legal right" of the people; "the reserved right" of a people; "an original right" of the people; a "natural right;" "a most sacred right;" "an indubitable, inalienable, and indefeasible right" of the community; and a "revolutionary right."

Perhaps some of these are useful, but they

seem merely to supplement the general points noted above that this right is that of the people, it is their right to change their institutions at will, and the peremptory criterion of permissibility remains the authority of the people. Even the United States Supreme Court has added little to clarify the criteria or the policies at stake in differing social contexts.

Although some have recognized that armed revolution is a form of "self-defense" for an oppressed people and others seek to limit the right of revolution to cases of a reasonably necessary defense against political oppression, the principles of necessity and proportionality should apply only to the strategies of violence utilized during revolution and are not needed for the justification of a revolution. Indeed, according to Lincoln, Jefferson, and so many of the founders, revolution is justified whenever the people generally so desire.

The "necessity" test endorsed by some writers might actually relate to another question, the question of when a defense of right arises because of oppression of an individual's right to participate in the political process. It might be argued that an individual or group has a right to use strategies of violence when reasonably necessary and proportionate to the effectuation of a human right to participate. If so, such a use of violence is not to be engaged in to deny participation by others or to oppress others politically, and such a use of violence might not have as its aim the achievement of an authoritative revolution by the people as a whole. Nevertheless, permissible revolution might be stimulated by such a strategy, and governmental elites that deny a relatively full and free sharing of power might themselves be denied some form of participation temporarily in order to effectuate the fuller and freer sharing and shaping of power by all participants.

It is important to reiterate here that the right of revolution as such is not vested in some minority of an identifiable society. Violence as a right of political failures is incompatible with any objective conception of self-determination of a people and contravenes domestic and international standards of authority as well as the human right of other persons to participate.

In the turbulent 1960s, Professor Charles Black identified a related question—whether disobedience of state laws is compatible with the authority of a federal constitutive process.[13] He argued that a revolutionary movement using massive "civil disobedience" mounted against "the very structure of state power" is not necessarily unconstitutional or "incompatible with federal allegiance." He also suggested that we are not "bound to hold up the wax hand of the effigy of state law" in such a circumstance where state power "cannot and will not fulfill its basic obligations to federal law and human justice." Thus, he argues that certain forms of revolutionary activity can result in revolutionary change within a part of the overall constitutive process and that a higher, overall authority reflected in "federal law and human justice" can provide a useful criterion for choice about permissibility. Actually, as Black noted, such a movement within a federal union can be supported by federal authority and constitute "a mere claim of legal right, asserted against what only seems to be law." Others seem to agree that such a claim is permissible and go so far as to suggest that it is not a claim to engage in civil "disobedience," but is actually an appeal to supreme federal law within a federal union. It is, at least, a claim to disobey one set of putative laws under a claim of deference to another.

Even in times of relative tranquility, the decisions of official elites are constantly subject to a process of review. All persons are participants in such a process whether or not they are aware of that fact, even if they participate through an apathetic or hostile inaction that can function as a form of passive acceptance of official elite decisions or allow more active participants to play a more effective role in the review of decisions. As McDougal, Lasswell, and Reisman remarked in another context:

> Most of us are performing . . . these . . . roles without being fully aware of the scope and consequences of our acts. Because of this, our participation is often considerably less effective than it might be. Every individual cannot, of course, realistically expect or demand to be a decisive factor in every major decision. Yet the converse feeling of pawn-like political impotence, of being locked out of effective decision, is an equally unwarranted orientation. The limits of the individual's role . . . [are] as much a function of his

13. See Charles Black, "The Problem of the Compatibility of Civil Disobedience with American Institutions of Government," *Texas Law Review* 43 (1965): 492–506.

passive acquiescence and ignorance of the potentialities of his participation as of the structures of the complex human organizations of the contemporary world.[14]

Such a recognition is profound. It can redirect attention to the fact of private participation in the creation, shaping, and termination of law as well as private participation in the overall process of authority. Whether actively or passively, individuals do play a role even in a revolutionary process during which other participants make contending claims about authority and even clash in arms.

There is an unavoidable need, therefore, to address the question of the legality of various forms of private participation. Since the declarations of even authoritatively constituted official elites are not determinative, what jurisprudential orientations offer the most useful guidance concerning the permissibility of various forms of private participation? As noted above, only a jurisprudential orientation that is sufficiently realistic and policy-serving will suffice. Such an orientation must be sufficiently contextual and attentive to all relevant legal policies at stake, including awareness of actual trends in decision, relevant features of past and present context, and probable future effects.

For this reason, no easy, mechanistic test of permissibility concerning strategies or tactics of private violence will suffice. As several writers recognize, an adequate analysis of strategies or tactics of revolution or "civil disobedience" demands consideration of all relevant features of context, including, of course, an examination of the larger social process in which such strategies or tactics operate.

One of the more involved contextual approaches to the ethics of revolution generally is that offered by the philosopher Herbert Marcuse.[15] Marcuse noted that " violence per se has never been made a revolutionary value by the leaders of historical revolutions." What should be considered, he argued, are the goals sought to be achieved and predictable social outcomes. Rational criteria can aid in what he termed an "historical calculus" of the "chances of a future society as against the chances of the existing society with respect to human progress." For Marcuse, a rational historical calculus

> must, on the one side, take into account the sacrifices exacted from the living generations on behalf of the established society, the established law and order, the number of victims made in defense of this society in war and peace, in the struggle for existence, individual and national. The calculus would further have to take into account the intellectual and material resources available to the society and the manner in which they are actually used with respect to their full capacity of satisfying vital human needs and pacifying the struggle for existence. On the other side, the historical calculus would have to project the chances of the contesting revolutionary movement of improving the prevailing conditions, namely, whether the revolutionary plan or program demonstrates the technical, material, and mental possibility of reducing the sacrifices and the number of victims.[16]

At the same time, Marcuse was quick to identify a peremptory limit to revolutionary "means." As he explained,

> No matter how rationally one may justify revolutionary means in terms of the demonstrable chance of obtaining freedom and happiness for future generations, and thereby justify violating existing rights and liberties and life itself, there are forms of violence and suppression which no revolutionary situation can justify because they negate the very end for which the revolution is a means. Such are arbitrary violence, cruelty, and indiscriminate terror.[17]

From a legal perspective, Marcuse's statement about the means of violence is equally relevant. Under international law, including the law of human rights, there are certain forms of violence that are impermissible per se. Included here are strategies and tactics of arbitrary violence, cruelty, and indiscriminate terror. International law also prohibits the use of violence against certain targets, and permissible uses of force are conditioned generally by the principles of necessity and proportionality.

---

14. Myres S. McDougal, Harold D. Lasswell, and W. Michael Reisman, "Theories About International Law: Prologue to a Configurative Jurisprudence," *VJIL* 8 (1968): 188–299, at 193.
15. See, e.g., Herbert Marcuse, "Ethics and Revolution," in Richard T. DeGeorge, ed., *Ethics and Society: Original Essays on Contemporary Moral Problems* (New York: Doubleday, 1966) 133–47. This is, of course, a different focus from one addressing the legality of revolution.
16. Ibid., 52.
17. Ibid., 53.

Thus, with regard to questions of legality concerning targets, tactics, and strategies of social violence, international law already provides normative guidance. A realistic and policy-serving jurisprudence would integrate relevant principles of international law into appropriate analysis and choice about the permissibility of a particular method or means of violence in a given social context, using tools of phase and value analysis for empirical inquiry and choice.

CONCLUSION

Here, an effort has been made to identify and clarify the nature and scope of the right to revolution in both United States domestic and international law. As noted, the right of revolution is a right of the people. It is to be exercised in accordance with a peremptory precept of authority documentable in both United States constitutional and international law, the will of the people expressed through a dynamic process involving an aggregate will of individuals. Revolution is actually one of the strategies available to a people for the securing of authority, national self-determination and a relatively free and equal enjoyment of the human right of all persons to participate in the political processes of their society.

With regard to the separate question of the legality of various means of furthering revolution, numerous sets of domestic and international law already proscribe certain forms of social violence. For example, international law, including human rights law, prohibits tactics of arbitrary violence, cruelty, and indiscriminate terror; the targeting of certain persons (such as children) and certain things; and generally any unnecessary death, injury, or suffering.

Accordingly, normative guidance exists concerning the permissibility of strategies and tactics, but refined, realistic and policy-serving inquiry or choice concerning such methods of social violence must be guided by a jurisprudential orientation that is sufficiently contextual and policy-attentive for such a task.

Finally, those who are rightly concerned about the evils of any form of violence and the threat that domestic violence can pose to human dignity and international peace might also consider the warning of former President John F. Kennedy: "[T]hose who make peaceful evolution impossible make violent revolution inevitable."[18]

QUESTIONS FOR REFLECTION AND DISCUSSION

1. Why is Jordan Paust's essay the last in this book? Is it because violence is the ultimate weapon of the disenfranchised or otherwise marginalized? Or is it that private violence—particularly revolutionary private violence—never should be used in the first instance or in an early stage of political struggle? Perhaps both? Either way, do you agree with these two propositions? Why? Why not?

2. Is not resort to violence in defense of human rights inherently contradictory? However much or little the right to revolution may be legally sanctioned, what about the proposition that the taking of life, if not also the large-scale destruction of property (as in New York City on September 11, 2001, for example) never can be morally justified no matter what the purpose? What would Paust say? What does Falk say in Reading 30 in the volume? If you believe that resort to violence never can be morally justified, would your answer change if you were the victim of human rights abuse? Suppose you had been a Kurd, a Palestinian, or a black South African when the rights of Kurds, Palestinians, and black South Africans were being systematically ignored. Would you not have resisted violently, even if only with stones? What did Samuel Adams do in Boston Harbor in 1773?

3. In *Why Men Rebel* (Princeton, N.J.: Princeton University Press for Center of International Studies, 1970), Ted Robert Gurr reasons that "Relative deprivation, defined as perceived discrepancy between value expectations and value capabilities," is among the prime explanations of collective violence. Gurr goes on to consider "three other concepts frequently

---

18. Address by John F. Kennedy at Punta del Este, quoted in M. Cherif Bassiouni, ed., *The Law of Dissent and Riots* (Springfield, Ill.: Thomas, 1971), vii. President Kennedy also declared, "Is not peace, in the last analysis, basically a matter of human rights?" Address by John F. Kennedy at American University (June 10, 1963), quoted in Myres S. McDougal, Harold D. Lasswell, and Lung-chu Chen, *Human Rights and World Public Order: The Basic Policies of an International Law of Human Dignity* (New Haven, Conn.: Yale University Press, 1980), 236 n. 229.

employed in the analysis of disruptive collective behavior that are not directly analogous [to relative deprivation] but that appear to be alternatives to it: dissonance, anomie, and conflict." *Dissonance*, he says, is "a concept widely used in individual psychology" that refers to "inconsistency between two cognitive elements or clusters of elements . . .that people . . . are motivated to reduce or eliminate." *Anomie*, he explains, "Is specifically a sociological concept" that refers to "a breakdown of social standards governing social behavior" which, in turn, can lead to "widespread deviant behavior and the establishment of alternative norms." And *conflict* he defines as a condition in which "the source of [relative deprivation] is another group competing for the same values" or as a process of "interaction between groups in their respective attempts to alleviate" relative deprivation. What bearing does this theorizing have on the revolutionary use of force in defense of human rights? Do social systems that produce relative deprivation, dissonance, anomie, and/or conflict forfeit legitimacy in the Kantian sense, and, instead, legitimate such use of force?

4. Is there a human right to revolution? Note that the Preamble to the Universal Declaration of Human Rights (UDHR, reprinted and referenced in Documentary Appendix A) says that "it is essential, if man [sic] is not to be compelled to have recourse a last resort to rebellion against tyranny and oppression, that human rights should be protected by the rule of law." Does this clause represent recognition of the principle that people have a right to revolt against tyranny and oppression? Or is it meant simply to warn states how best to avoid rebellion? Note that UDHR contains no provision expressly providing for the right to revolution.

5. If there is a right to revolution, when is it permissible? Impermissible? Paust argues that two standards must be met: first, the resistance or revolution must be taken up on the authority and interest of the majority of the people, not simply an aggrieved minority; second, it must be taken up against a state that oppresses its citizenry by political or economic means. Do you agree with Paust? Disagree? Why?

6. If there is a right to armed rebellion, what level of violence is permissible? Do human rights proponents have any legal or moral obligation to use only that proportion of violence that is necessary to defend their interests? If so, how do you measure proportionality? May the violence permissibly result in the death of innocent victims? In this connection, Paust quotes Herbert Marcuse:

> No matter how rationally one may justify revolutionary means in terms of the democratic chance of obtaining freedom and happiness for future generations, and thereby justify violating existing rights and liberties and life itself, there are forms of violence and suppression which no revolutionary situation can justify because they negate the very end for which the revolution is a means. Such are arbitrary violence, cruelty and indiscriminate terror.

Do you agree with Marcuse (and by implication Paust)? Do not the ends ever justify the means? Is not this precisely what the administration of U.S. President George W. Bush has been contending *post hoc* to justify the U.S. invasion of Iraq in March 2002?

7. Does violence or the threat of violence provide organized minorities with bargaining power they might not otherwise possess? Is it possible that violence or the threat of violence is an important element in maintaining democratic forms of governance? If so, what does this signify for Paust's view that the right to resistance or revolution should not be available to an aggrieved minority? Is it possible that Paust's formulation, presupposing individual rights and liberal democracy, is too Western or bourgeois to be universally applicable? Or can it be universally applied?

8. In "The Right to Rebel," *Oxford Journal of Legal Studies* 8 (1988): 34–54, at 46, Tony Honoré suggests that if there is a right to revolution it should be conditioned on the exhaustion of nonviolent remedies, e.g., constitutional methods, recourse to the legal system, political propaganda, peaceful protests, civil disobedience, passive resistance, and so forth. Do you agree? Are there not instances when it is not possible to exhaust peaceful remedies or when the exhaustion of peaceful remedies would be known to be futile?

9. Herbert Marcuse has argued that violence is incorporated in oppressive institutions and that it is possible that logic and language will not suffice to reform, transform, or eliminate them. In *Counterrevolution and Revolt* (Boston: Beacon Press, 1972), 132–33, Marcuse writes:

The Slogan "let's sit down and reason together" has rightly become a joke. Can you reason with the Pentagon on any other thing than the relative effectiveness of killing machines—and their price? The Secretary of State can reason with the Secretary of the Treasury, and the latter with another Secretary and his [sic] advisers, and they all can reason with Members of the Board of the great corporations. This is incestuous reasoning; they are all in agreement about the basic issue: the strengthening of the established power structure. Reasoning "from without" the power structure is a naive idea. They will listen only to the extent to which the voices can be translated into votes, which may perhaps bring into office another set of the same power structure within the same ultimate concern.

The argument is overwhelming. Bertolt Brecht noted that we live at a time where it seems a crime to talk about a tree. Since then, things have become worse. Today, it seems a crime merely to *talk* about change while one's society is transformed into an institution of violence, terminating in Asia [and now Africa] the genocide which began with the liquidation of the American Indians. Is not the sheer power of this brutality immune against the spoken and written word which indicts it? And is not the word which is directed against the practitioners of this power the same they use to defend their power?

Is there a level on which even incautious and reckless action against oppressive and/or tyrannical social structures seems justified?

10. In "Young India," *New Delhi Newspaper*, July 27, 1924, Mohandas K. Gandhi made the following assertion:

They say "means are after all [just] means." I would say "means are after all everything." As the means, so the end. Violent means will give violent [results]. . . . There is no wall of separation between means and ends. . . . I have been endeavoring to keep the country [India] to means that are purely peaceful and legitimate.

Does Gandhi's view supply a workable axiom applicable to the pursuit of human rights? Why does he link "peaceful" means with "legitimate" means? Do you agree with Gandhi's objection to violence because, as he wrote in "Young India," *New Delhi Newspaper*, on May 21, 1925, "when [violence] appears to be good, the good is only temporary, the evil it does is permanent"?

11. In "'Looking and Thinking' About Human Rights and Revolution," *Human Peace* 8, no. 1 (Spring 1990): 6–10, Winston P. Nagan questions how effectively the right to revolution can further human rights goals:

To what extent should counterelites forgo the right of self-defense for the even higher moral precept that the oppressed are themselves transformed by the suffering of struggle; that in effect, "true" struggle against injustice transforms both victim and interlocutor? Did Gandhi, Luthuli, and King set a standard too lofty in their protest, to man's conscience, that violent solutions to human problems are obscene and degrading? Or as we make an inventory of the cost of reactionary and revolutionary violence, do we discover somewhat cynically that leopards only change their spots when they move from one spot to another?

In other words, the "true" realists were the Kings, the Luthulis, the Gandhis, and the Tutus of the world because they see more clearly than most that violence is generally a high-cost nonsolution to difficult problems of coexistence, peace, and justice. Implicit in the message of Gandhi, King, Luthuli, and Tutu is a message about the integrity of the struggle as well as the integrity of the objectives of the struggle for justice, respect, and dignity. A further implication in this perspective is a message of restoration and hope, the capacity for moral growth in the human species and a pervasive optimism that a public order comitted to the dignity of man is not a far-fetched idea.

Do you agree with Nagan? Disagree? Why? Are there not times when violence is the only choice? Or is it true that violence only begets more violence?

12. Nagan, "Looking and Thinking'" (Question 11) also states that "we are all, in a general sense, moral agents and responsible—yes—accountable for what we do, or do not do." Do you agree that the responsibility of which Nagan speaks extends to everyone on earth who is the victim of human rights abuse, that we are our brothers' and sisters' keepers everywhere? Why? Why not?

Postscript: Human Rights and Humane Governance

LIFE is a journey. In its present-day collective form, it is called "globalization," and, though a journey on which we are all embarked, too few of us understand that we are its map-makers and pilots as well as its passengers. It is unparalleled in human history.

Of course, the process of globalization is not new. It has been with us in forms economic and political for centuries—since at least the fourth century when, ten centuries before the European "Age of Exploration," Alexander the Great's empire extended to what we now call India and, a few hundred years later, the Han Dynasty of China and the Roman Empire regularly traded with one another and even exchanged diplomats. Nevertheless, in its current form, globalization presents the most daunting challenge to international cooperation ever known to humankind. Since the Treaty of Westphalia in 1648, we have been guided by an essentially two-dimensional map according to which interstate relations travel by the compass of an international law system that, in defense of competing sovereignties and territories, looks upon interstate warfare and economic disparity as inevitable ingredients of any political order that lacks a governmental center—the law of geopolitics. Today, we need minimally a three-dimensional map for multilayered relations and interdependencies among diverse forms of authority (qua governments, markets, individual citizens) and diverse doctrines, principles, and rules (qua treaties, laws, social norms) as we move ever more rapidly toward a new world order that compels us to work together, however haltingly but at our peril if we do not, toward new common objectives and new, humane modes of governance—the law of humanity.

Governance is not the same as government. When we think of legislation, law enforcement, and adjudication, typically we think of governments that perform these functions backed by the coercive police powers of the state. Governance is a broader, more inclusive term. Political scientists define governance as a network of cooperative and integrative norms, institutions, and procedures that may or may not issue from formally constituted state power.[1] Relying on consensus and consent more than coercion—indeed, commonly to

1. See, e.g., Oran R. Young, *Governance in World Affairs* (Ithaca, N.Y.: Cornell University Press, 1999); also, by the same author, "Rights, Rules and Resources in International Society," in Susan Hanna, Carl Folke, and Karl-Göran Möle, eds., *Rights to Nature: Ecological, Economic, Cultural, and Political Principles of Institutions for the Environment* (Washington, D.C.: Island Press, for Beijer International Institute of Ecological Economics, Royal Swedish Academy of Sciences, 1996), 245–63. See also Michael Edwards, *Future Positive: International Co-operation in the 21st Century* (London: Earthscan, 1999).

the exclusion of coercion—it is more about process than bureaucracy and includes within its embrace nongovernmental entities such as corporations, NGOs, and professional associations serving informally (though increasingly formally) as actors, claimants, and decision-makers alongside state and state-dominated intergovernmental institutions. "The State remains focal for many purposes; but, overall, non-State actors, territorial socioeconomic forces, and globally organized media and communications networks are exerting a defining influence on large-scale social behavior."[2]

In his presidential address to the American Political Science Association in 2000, Robert O. Keohane observed that globalization can be good or bad depending on the cultivation of appropriate and effective governance and that if we earnestly want a benign globalized world we need to think in ethical, humane terms about our future.[3] Good governance depends on ethically humane visions of the decision-making norms, institutions, and procedures—local to global, formal and informal—that shape our lives.

In recent times, however, globalization has gotten a bad name, the result of overbearing market forces, fundamentalist agendas, and hegemonic impulses that prompt the strong to subdue the weak. Largely this is due to the interstate system remaining stuck in the logic and time warp of geopolitics, the central focus of which is "a global security system in which the leadership and management role is played by a few dominant States and in which recurrent conflict tends to be resolved through wars and their outcomes."[4] At the same time, however, new modes of national, regional, and global governance are emerging, albeit hesitatingly and with some distressing backsliding,[5] to alleviate worldwide harm because people everywhere are capable of envisioning the more noble quest for national and transnational justice—the global rule of just law and policy, the law of humanity. Beyond governmental agreements to adhere to human rights norms, we see now a striving for justice in other layers of authoritative and increasingly controlling decision-making. The energetic work of NGOs, the adoption of corporate codes and compacts, newly defined developmental and environmental rights, and the incorporation of human rights into codes of professional ethics—each of these and more testify to the acceptance of interrelated humane principles of governance and the emergence of an holistic vision for human and world survival.[6] Of course, formal acceptance of a new ethos of species identity and solidarity is not enough. The principles that inform humane governance and the ethos that gives them direction must be made truly to influence attitudes and behavior for the better. That is the vision and program of *humane governance*, "a type of governance that is people- and human rights-oriented rather than statist and market-oriented."[7]

Using the concept of humane governance, international law and world order scholar Richard Falk has called for a global order that can secure essential human rights by transforming the world's order as it now exists. His preliminary objective, shared by the editors

---

2. Saul H. Mendlovitz and Burns H. Weston, "The United Nations at Fifty: Toward Humane Global Governance," in Saul H. Mendlovitz and Burns H. Weston, *Preferred Futures for the United Nations* (Ardsley, N.Y.: Transnational Publishers, 1995), 3–20, at 17.

3. Robert O. Keohane, "Governance in a Partially Globalized World," Presidential Address, American Political Science Association, 2000, *American Political Science Review* 95 (Mar. 2001):1–13, at 1. For insightful elaboration on this theme, see Reading 4 by Rhoda Howard-Hassmann in Chapter 1 of this volume.

4. Mendlovitz and Weston, note 2, at 17.

5. See, e.g., Richard A. Falk, *The Declining World Order: America's Imperial Geopolitics* (New York : Routledge, 2004).

6. See generally, for example, Saul H. Mendlovitz and Burns H. Weston, "From Geopolitics to Humane Governance: Transition Steps," in Mendlovitz and Weston, note 2, at 361–79.

7. Weston and Mendlovitz, note 2, at 18.

of this volume, is to stimulate debate for the purpose of extending the boundaries of human rights beyond those set by the dictates of the still prevailing state system (and its operative codes linked to exclusive sovereignty and territoriality).[8] Indeed, the template for humane governance is implied by Article 28 of the Universal Declaration of Human Rights (UDHR)[9] which proclaims that "everyone is entitled to a social and international order in which the rights and freedoms set forth in this Declaration can be fully realized." In these terms, humane governance refers to the right of every individual and group to live in societies that realize or conscientiously attempt to realize the overarching values that inform the International Bill of Rights—the 1948 UDHR, the 1966 International Covenant on Economic, Social and Cultural Rights (ICESCR), and the 1966 International Covenant on Civil and Political Rights (ICCPR).[10] Thereby, humane governance draws attention to the universal duty—the duty of everyone—to assist the realization of these values both alone and cooperatively, pursuing politics in the human interest and participating in the struggle for global justice.

The prospects for global justice, however, have so far been considered "under the nonideal conditions of the established world order."[11] Veiled by the failings of persistent geopolitics, Falk asserts, they therefore may or may not lead humanity toward a beneficial form of global governance.[12] But the prospects for global justice are veiled, too, by the failings of human foresight and imagination. Who among us foresaw the end of the Cold War or the dismantling of the racist apartheid regime of South Africa? Implicitly, there are grounds for optimism.[13] As sentient beings we have the capacity to envision and act upon a better future, a future premised on a culture of human rights, human rights as a way of life.

Indeed, for the sake of future generations, we have a duty to do so. As stated by the People's Movement for Human Rights Education in its "Global Appeal for Human Rights Education" in December 2004 (on the close of the 1995–2004 United Nations Decade for Human Rights Education),

> All people must know their human rights in order to live together in justice and dignity; to become agents of transformation and establish human rights as a way of life. Humanity—standing on the brink of devastation, with millions of people mired in poverty, environmental destruction, violence and oppression—aspires to live in a world of human dignity, freedom, and social and economic justice. . . . To secure this vision, all people must learn and act according to our universal human rights, which define a shared moral and legal framework for living in dignity within our varied communities. . . , a shared global culture of human rights."[14]

At a high-level communications conference in 1997, UN Secretary-General Kofi Annan put it this way: "what we must offer is a vision of human rights that is foreign to none

---

8. See, e.g., Richard Falk, *On Humane Governance: Toward a New Global Politics—The World Order Models Project of the Global Civilization Initiative* (University Park: Pennsylvania State University Press, 1995); Richard Falk, *Human Rights and State Sovereignty* (New York: Holmes and Meier, 1981), esp. 180–3; Richard A. Falk, *Human Rights Horizons: The Pursuit of Justice in a Globalizing World* (New York: Routledge, 2000), esp. 19–20, 34–35. See also Saul H. Mendlovitz, *On the Creation of a Just World Order* (New York: Free Press, 1975).
9. Adopted Dec. 10, 1948, reprinted and referenced in Documentary Appendix A.
10. Each of these landmark instruments is reprinted and referenced in Documentary Appendix A.
11. Falk, *Human Rights Horizons*, note 8, at 34.
12. Ibid. See also Falk, *The Declining World Order*, note 5.
13. Falk demurs: "We do not understand political reality well enough to be pessimistic, or for that matter optimistic." *Human Rights Horizons*, note 8, at 34.
14. For the complete Appeal, its history, and an opportunity to endorse it, see the website of the People's Movement at http://www.pdhre.org/global-appeal.html

and native to all."[15] The stakes are simply too high not to treat human rights as an indispensable way of life.

And this, in essence, is what humane global governance is all about. Humane governance and a social order accountable to human rights are, on final analysis, the same thing. All that is needed is a belief in the possible and a willingness, despite the odds, to hazard the initiatives that can make it happen. No small task, we concede. But what other conceivable way is there to affirm our own, our children's, and our grandchildren's futures?

Robert F. Kennedy, in his June 6, 1966 "Day of Affirmation" speech at the University of Cape Town when South Africa was fully in the grip of an evil and seemingly invincible racist regime, put it this way:

> Let no one be discouraged by the belief there is nothing one man [or one woman] can do against the enormous array of the world's ills—against misery and ignorance, injustice and violence. . . . Few will have the greatness to bend history itself; but each of us can work to change a small portion of events, and in the total of all those acts will be written the history of this generation.
>
> It is from numberless diverse acts of courage and belief that human history is shaped. Each time a man [or woman] stands up for an ideal, or acts to improve the lot of others, or strikes out against injustice, he [or she] sends a tiny ripple of hope, and crossing each other from a million different centres of energy and daring those ripples build a current which can sweep down the mightiest walls of oppression and resistance.[16]

It is this message of everyday heroism on behalf of humane governance—"Not occasional heroism, a remarkable instance of it here and there, but constant heroism, systematic heroism, heroism as governing principle"[17]— that we hope this volume passes on to our companion travelers of the twenty-first century, every man, woman, and child who yearns for a human rights respecting world.

15. Kofi Annan, "Ignorance, Not Knowledge, Makes Enemies of Man," Statement by Secretary-General Kofi Annan, delivered Oct. 18, 1997 to the Communications Conference of the Aspen Institute, Colorado, UN Doc. SG/SM/6366 (Oct. 20, 1997).
16. As quoted in Arthur M. Schlesinger, Jr., *Robert Kennedy and His Times* (Boston: Houghton Mifflin, 1978), 745–46.
17. Russell Banks, *Continental Drift* (New York: Harper and Row, 1985), 40.

Documentary Appendix A: Select Instruments

1. CHARTER OF THE UNITED NATIONS.* Signed at San Francisco, June 26, 1945. Entered into force, Oct. 24, 1945. 1976 YBUN 1033; available also at http://www.unhchr. ch/udhr/ lang/eng.htm

PREAMBLE

WE THE PEOPLES OF THE UNITED NATIONS DETERMINED

to save succeeding generations from the scourge of war, which twice in our lifetime has brought untold sorrow to mankind, and

to reaffirm faith in fundamental human rights, in the dignity and worth of the human person, in the equal rights of men and women and of nations large and small, and

to establish conditions under which justice and respect for the obligations arising from treaties and other sources of international law can be maintained, and

to promote social progress and better standards of life in larger freedom,

AND FOR THESE ENDS

to practice tolerance and live together in peace with one another as good neighbours, and

to unite our strength to maintain international peace and security, and

to ensure, by the acceptance of principles and the institution of methods, that armed force shall not be used, save in the common interest, and

to employ international machinery for the promotion of the economic and social advancement of all peoples,

HAVE RESOLVED TO COMBINE OUR EFFORTS TO ACCOMPLISH THESE AIMS

Accordingly, our respective Governments, through representatives assembled in the city of San Francisco, who have exhibited their full powers found to be in good and due form, have agreed to the present Charter of the United Nations and do hereby establish an international organization to be known as the United Nations.

CHAPTER I. PURPOSES AND PRINCIPLES

Article 1

The Purposes of the United Nations are:

1. To maintain international peace and security, and to that end: to take effective collective measures for the prevention and removal of threats to the peace, and for the

---

* Selected provisions bearing on contemporary human rights issues only.

suppression of acts of aggression or other breaches of the peace, and to bring about by peaceful means, and in conformity with the principles of justice and international law, adjustment or settlement of international disputes or situations which might lead to a breach of the peace;

2. To develop friendly relations among nations based on respect for the principle of equal rights and self-determination of peoples, and to take other appropriate measures to strengthen universal peace;

3. To achieve international co-operation in solving international problems of an economic, social, cultural, or humanitarian character, and in promoting and encouraging respect for human rights and for fundamental freedoms for all without distinction as to race, sex, language, or religion; and

4. To be a centre for harmonizing the actions of nations in the attainment of these common ends.

Article 2

The Organization and its Members, in pursuit of the Purposes stated in Article 1, shall act in accordance with the following Principles.

1. The Organization is based on the principle of the sovereign equality of all its Members.

3. All Members shall settle their international disputes by peaceful means in such a manner that international peace and security, and justice, are not endangered.

4. All Members shall refrain in their international relations from the threat or use of force against the territorial integrity or political independence of any state, or in any other manner inconsistent with the Purposes of the United Nations.

7. Nothing contained in the present Charter shall authorize the United Nations to intervene in matters which are essentially within the domestic jurisdiction of any state or shall require the Members to submit such matters to settlement under the present Charter; but this principle shall not prejudice the application of enforcement measures under Chapter Vll.

CHAPTER II. MEMBERSHIP

Article 4

1. Membership in the United Nations is open to all other peace-loving states which accept the obligations contained in the present Charter and, in the judgment of the Organization, are able and willing to carry out these obligations.

Article 5

A Member of the United Nations against which preventive or enforcement action has been taken by the Security Council may be suspended from the exercise of the rights and privileges of membership by the General Assembly upon the recommendation of the Security Council. The exercise of these rights and privileges may be restored by the Security Council.

Article 6

A Member of the United Nations which has persistently violated the Principles contained in the present Charter may be expelled from the Organization by the General Assembly upon the recommendation of the Security Council.

CHAPTER III. ORGANS

Article 7

    1. There are established as the principal organs of the United Nations:
    a General Assembly
    a Security Council
    an Economic and Social Council
    a Trusteeship Council
    an International Court of Justice
    a Secretariat
    2. Such subsidiary organs as may be found necessary may be established in accordance with the present Charter.

Article 8

    The United Nations shall place no restrictions on the eligibility of men and women to participate in any capacity and under conditions of equality in its principal and subsidiary organs.

CHAPTER IV. THE GENERAL ASSEMBLY

Article 9

    1. The General Assembly shall consist of all the Members of the United Nations.

Article 10

    The General Assembly may discuss any questions or any matters within the scope of the present Charter or relating to the powers and functions of any organs provided for in the present Charter, and, except as provided in Article 12, may make recommendations to the Members of the United Nations or to the Security Council or to both on any such questions or matters.

Article 13

    1. The General Assembly shall initiate studies and make recommendations for the purpose of:
    a. promoting international co-operation in the political field and encouraging the progressive development of international law and its codification;
    b. promoting international co-operation in the economic, social, cultural, educational, and health fields, and assisting in the realization of human rights and fundamental freedoms for all without distinction as to race, sex, language, or religion.
    2. The further responsibilities, functions and powers of the General Assembly with respect to matters mentioned in paragraph 1 (b) above are set forth in Chapters IX and X.

CHAPTER V. THE SECURITY COUNCIL

Article 23

    1. The Security Council shall consist of fifteen Members of the United Nations. The Republic of China, France, the Union of Soviet Socialist Republics, the United Kingdom of Great Britain and Northern Ireland, and the United States of America shall be permanent

members of the Security Council. The General Assembly shall elect ten other Members of the United Nations to be non-permanent members of the Security Council, due regard being specially paid, in the first instance to the contribution of Members of the United Nations to the maintenance of international peace and security and to the other purposes of the Organization, and also to equitable geographical distribution.

Article 25

The Members of the United Nations agree to accept and carry out the decisions of the Security Council in accordance with the present Charter.

Article 27

1. Each member of the Security Council shall have one vote.

2. Decisions of the Security Council on procedural matters shall be made by an affirmative vote of nine members.

3. Decisions of the Security Council on all other matters shall be made by an affirmative vote of nine members including the concurring votes of the permanent members; provided that, in decisions under Chapter VI, and under paragraph 3 of Article 52, a party to a dispute shall abstain from voting.

CHAPTER VII. ACTION WITH RESPECT TO THREATS TO THE PEACE, BREACHES OF THE PEACE, AND ACTS OF AGGRESSION

Article 39

The Security Council shall determine the existence of any threat to the peace, breach of the peace, or act of aggression and shall make recommendations, or decide what measures shall be taken in accordance with Articles 41 and 42, to maintain or restore international peace and security.

Article 40

In order to prevent an aggravation of the situation, the Security Council may, before making the recommendations or deciding upon the measures provided for in Article 39, call upon the parties concerned to comply with such provisional measures as it deems necessary or desirable. Such provisional measures shall be without prejudice to the rights, claims, or position of the parties concerned. The Security Council shall duly take account of failure to comply with such provisional measures.

Article 41

The Security Council may decide what measures not involving the use of armed force are to be employed to give effect to its decisions, and it may call upon the Members of the United Nations to apply such measures. These may include complete or partial interruption of economic relations and of rail, sea, air, postal, telegraphic, radio, and other means of communication, and the severance of diplomatic relations.

Article 42

Should the Security Council consider that measures provided for in Article 41 would be inadequate or have proved to be inadequate, it may take such action by air, sea, or land forces as may be necessary to maintain or restore international peace and security. Such action may include demonstrations, blockade, and other operations by air, sea, or land forces of Members of the United Nations.

Article 51

Nothing in the present Charter shall impair the inherent right of individual or collective self-defence if an armed attack occurs against a Member of the United Nations, until the Security Council has taken measures necessary to maintain international peace and security. Measures taken by Members in the exercise of this right of self-defence shall be immediately reported to the Security Council and shall not in any way affect the authority and responsibility of the Security Council under the present Charter to take at any time such action as it deems necessary in order to maintain or restore international peace and security.

CHAPTER IX. INTERNATIONAL ECONOMIC AND SOCIAL COOPERATION

Article 55

With a view to the creation of conditions of stability and well-being which are necessary for peaceful and friendly relations among nations based on respect for the principle of equal rights and self-determination of peoples, the United Nations shall promote:

a. higher standards of living, full employment, and conditions of economic and social progress and development;

b. solutions of international economic, social, health, and related problems; and international cultural and educational cooperation; and

c. universal respect for, and observance of, human rights and fundamental freedoms for all without distinction as to race, sex, language, or religion.

Article 56

All Members pledge themselves to take joint and separate action in co-operation with the Organization for the achievement of the purposes set forth in Article 55.

CHAPTER X. THE ECONOMIC AND SOCIAL COUNCIL

Article 61

1. The Economic and Social Council shall consist of fifty-four Members of the United Nations elected by the General Assembly.

Article 62

1. The Economic and Social Council may make or initiate studies and reports with respect to international economic, social, cultural, educational, health, and related matters and may make recommendations with respect to any such matters to the General Assembly to the Members of the United Nations, and to the specialized agencies concerned.

2. It may make recommendations for the purpose of promoting respect for, and observance of, human rights and fundamental freedoms for all.

3. It may prepare draft conventions for submission to the General Assembly, with respect to matters falling within its competence.

4. It may call, in accordance with the rules prescribed by the United Nations, international conferences on matters falling within its competence.

2. UNIVERSAL DECLARATION OF HUMAN RIGHTS. Adopted by the UN General Assembly, Dec. 10, 1948. GA Res 217A, UN GAOR, 3d Sess., Pt. I, Resolutions, at 71, UN Doc A/810 (1948), reprinted in Weston and Carlson, 3: III.A.1; available also at http://www.unhchr.ch/udhr/lang/eng.htm.

PREAMBLE

Whereas recognition of the inherent dignity and of the equal and inalienable rights of all members of the human family is the foundation of freedom, justice and peace in the world,

Whereas disregard and contempt for human rights have resulted in barbarous acts which have outraged the conscience of mankind, and the advent of a world in which human beings shall enjoy freedom of speech and belief and freedom from fear and want has been proclaimed as the highest aspiration of the common people,

Whereas it is essential, if man is not to be compelled to have recourse, as a last resort, to rebellion against tyranny and oppression, that human rights should be protected by the rule of law,

Whereas it is essential to promote the development of friendly relations between nations,

Whereas the peoples of the United Nations have in the Charter reaffirmed their faith in fundamental human rights, in the dignity and worth of the human person and in the equal rights of men and women and have determined to promote social progress and better standards of life in larger freedom,

Whereas Member States have pledged themselves to achieve, in cooperation with the United Nations, the promotion of universal respect for and observance of human rights and fundamental freedoms,

Whereas a common understanding of these rights and freedoms is of the greatest importance for the full realization of this pledge,

Now, therefore,

THE GENERAL ASSEMBLY,

Proclaims this Universal Declaration of Human Rights as a common standard of achievement for all peoples and all nations, to the end that every individual and every organ of society, keeping this Declaration constantly in mind, shall strive by teaching and education to promote respect for these rights and freedoms and by progressive measures, national and international, to secure their universal and effective recognition and observance, both among the peoples of Member States themselves and among the peoples of territories under their jurisdiction.

Article 1

All human beings are born free and equal in dignity and rights. They are endowed with reason and conscience and should act towards one another in a spirit of brotherhood.

Article 2

Everyone is entitled to all the rights and freedoms set forth in this Declaration, without distinction of any kind, such as race, colour, sex, language, religion, political or other opinion, national or social origin, property, birth or other status.

Furthermore, no distinction shall be made on the basis of the political, jurisdictional or international status of the country or territory to which a person belongs, whether it be independent, trust, non-self-governing or under any other limitation of sovereignty.

Article 3

Everyone has the right to life, liberty and security of person.

Article 4

No one shall be held in slavery or servitude; slavery and the slave trade shall be prohibited in all their forms.

Article 5

No one shall be subjected to torture or to cruel, inhuman or degrading treatment or punishment.

Article 6

Everyone has the right to recognition everywhere as a person before the law.

Article 7

All are equal before the law and are entitled without any discrimination to equal protection of the law. All are entitled to equal protection against any discrimination in violation of this Declaration and against any incitement to such discrimination.

Article 8

Everyone has the right to an effective remedy by the competent national tribunals for acts violating the fundamental rights granted him by the constitution or by law.

Article 9

No one shall be subjected to arbitrary arrest, detention or exile.

Article 10

Everyone is entitled in full equality to a fair and public hearing by an independent and impartial tribunal, in the determination of his rights and obligations and of any criminal charge against him.

Article 11

1. Everyone charged with a penal offence has the right to be presumed innocent until proved guilty according to law in a public trial at which he has had all the guarantees necessary for his defence.

2. No one shall be held guilty of any penal offence on account of any act or omission which did not constitute a penal offence, under national or international law, at the time when it was committed. Nor shall a heavier penalty be imposed than the one that was applicable at the time the penal offence was committed.

Article 12

No one shall be subjected to arbitrary interference with his privacy, family, home or correspondence, nor to attacks upon his honour and reputation. Everyone has the right to the protection of the law against such interference or attacks.

Article 13

1. Everyone has the right to freedom of movement and residence within the borders of each State.

2. Everyone has the right to leave any country, including his own, and to return to his country.

Article 14

1. Everyone has the right to seek and to enjoy in other countries asylum from persecution.

2. This right may not be invoked in the case of prosecutions genuinely arising from non-political crimes or from acts contrary to the purposes and principles of the United Nations.

Article 15

1. Everyone has the right to a nationality.

2. No one shall be arbitrarily deprived of his nationality nor denied the right to change his nationality.

Article 16

1. Men and women of full age, without any limitation due to race, nationality or religion, have the right to marry and to found a family. They are entitled to equal rights as to marriage, during marriage and at its dissolution.

2. Marriage shall be entered into only with the free and full consent of the intending spouses.

3. The family is the natural and fundamental group unit of society and is entitled to protection by society and the State.

Article 17

1. Everyone has the right to own property alone as well as in association with others.

2. No one shall be arbitrarily deprived of his property.

Article 18

Everyone has the right to freedom of thought, conscience and religion; this right includes freedom to change his religion or belief, and freedom, either alone or in community with others and in public or private, to manifest his religion or belief in teaching, practice, worship and observance.

Article 19

Everyone has the right to freedom of opinion and expression; this right includes freedom to hold opinions without interference and to seek, receive and impart information and ideas through any media and regardless of frontiers.

Article 20

1. Everyone has the right to freedom of peaceful assembly and association.

2. No one may be compelled to belong to an association.

Article 21

1. Everyone has the right to take part in the government of his country, directly or through freely chosen representatives.

2. Everyone has the right to equal access to public service in his country.

3. The will of the people shall be the basis of the authority of government; this will shall be expressed in periodic and genuine elections which shall be by universal and equal suffrage and shall be held by secret vote or by equivalent free voting procedures.

Article 22

Everyone, as a member of society, has the right to social security and is entitled to realization, through national effort and international co-operation and in accordance with the organization and resources of each State, of the economic, social and cultural rights indispensable for his dignity and the free development of his personality.

Article 23

1. Everyone has the right to work, to free choice of employment, to just and favourable conditions of work and to protection against unemployment.

2. Everyone, without any discrimination, has the right to equal pay for equal work.

3. Everyone who works has the right to just and favourable remuneration ensuring for himself and his family an existence worthy of human dignity, and supplemented, if necessary, by other means of social protection.

4. Everyone has the right to form and to join trade unions for the protection of his interests.

Article 24

Everyone has the right to rest and leisure, including reasonable limitation of working hours and periodic holidays with pay.

Article 25

1. Everyone has the right to a standard of living adequate for the health and well-being of himself and of his family, including food, clothing, housing and medical care and necessary social services, and the right to security in the event of unemployment, sickness, disability, widowhood, old age or other lack of livelihood in circumstances beyond his control.

2. Motherhood and childhood are entitled to special care and assistance. All children, whether born in or out of wedlock, shall enjoy the same social protection.

Article 26

1. Everyone has the right to education. Education shall be free, at least in the elementary and fundamental stages. Elementary education shall be compulsory. Technical and professional education shall be made generally available and higher education shall be equally accessible to all on the basis of merit.

2. Education shall be directed to the full development of the human personality and to the strengthening of respect for human rights and fundamental freedoms. It shall promote understanding, tolerance and friendship among all nations, racial or religious groups, and shall further the activities of the United Nations for the maintenance of peace.

3. Parents have a prior right to choose the kind of education that shall be given to their children.

Article 27

1. Everyone has the right freely to participate in the cultural life of the community, to enjoy the arts and to share in scientific advancement and its benefits.

2. Everyone has the right to the protection of the moral and material interests resulting from any scientific, literary or artistic production of which he is the author.

Article 28

Everyone is entitled to a social and international order in which the rights and freedoms set forth in this Declaration can be fully realized.

Article 29

1. Everyone has duties to the community in which alone the free and full development of his personality is possible.

2. In the exercise of his rights and freedoms, everyone shall be subject only to such limitations as are determined by law solely for the purpose of securing due recognition and respect for the rights and freedoms of others and of meeting the just requirements of morality, public order and the general welfare in a democratic society.

3. These rights and freedoms may in no case be exercised contrary to the purposes and principles of the United Nations.

Article 30

Nothing in this Declaration may be interpreted as implying for any State, group or person any right to engage in any activity or to perform any act aimed at the destruction of any of the rights and freedoms set forth herein.

3. INTERNATIONAL COVENANT ON ECONOMIC, SOCIAL AND CULTURAL RIGHTS (exclusive of concluding Part V except for art. 28). Concluded at New York, Dec. 16, 1966. Entered into force, Jan. 3, 1976. 993 UNTS 3, reprinted in Weston and Carlson, 3: III.A.2; available also at http://www.unhchr.ch/udhr/lang/eng.htm

PREAMBLE

THE STATES PARTIES TO THE PRESENT COVENANT,

Considering that, in accordance with the principles proclaimed in the Charter of the United Nations, recognition of the inherent dignity and of the equal and inalienable rights of all members of the human family is the foundation of freedom, justice and peace in the world,

Recognizing that these rights derive from the inherent dignity of the human person,

Recognizing that, in accordance with the Universal Declaration of Human Rights, the ideal of free human beings enjoying freedom from fear and want can only be achieved if conditions are created whereby everyone may enjoy his economic, social and cultural rights, as well as his civil and political rights,

Considering the obligation of States under the Charter of the United Nations to promote universal respect for, and observance of, human rights and freedoms,

Realizing that the individual, having duties to other individuals and to the community to which he belongs, is under a responsibility to strive for the promotion and observance of the rights recognized in the present Covenant,

Agree upon the following articles:

PART I

Article 1

1. All peoples have the right of self-determination. By virtue of that right they freely determine their political status and freely pursue their economic, social and cultural development.

2. All peoples may, for their own ends, freely dispose of their natural wealth and resources without prejudice to any obligations arising out of international economic co-operation, based upon the principle of mutual benefit, and international law. In no case may a people be deprived of its own means of subsistence.

3. The States Parties to the present Covenant, including those having responsibility for the administration of Non-Self-Governing and Trust Territories, shall promote the realization of the right of self-determination, and shall respect that right, in conformity with the provisions of the Charter of the United Nations.

PART II

Article 2

1. Each State Party to the present Covenant undertakes to take steps, individually and through international assistance and co-operation, especially economic and technical, to the maximum of its available resources, with a view to achieving progressively the full realization of the rights recognized in the present Covenant by all appropriate means, including particularly the adoption of legislative measures.

2. The States Parties to the present Covenant undertake to guarantee that the rights enunciated in the present Covenant will be exercised without discrimination of any kind as to race, colour, sex, language, religion, political or other opinion, national or social origin, property, birth or other status.

3. Developing countries, with due regard to human rights and their national economy, may determine to what extent they would guarantee the economic rights recognized in the present Covenant to non-nationals.

Article 3

The States Parties to the present Covenant undertake to ensure the equal right of men and women to the enjoyment of all economic, social and cultural rights set forth in the present Covenant.

Article 4

The States Parties to the present Covenant recognize that, in the enjoyment of those rights provided by the State in conformity with the present Covenant, the State may subject such rights only to such limitations as are determined by law only in so far as this may be compatible with the nature of these rights and solely for the purpose of promoting the general welfare in a democratic society.

Article 5

1. Nothing in the present Covenant may be interpreted as implying for any State, group or person any right to engage in any activity or to perform any act aimed at the destruction of any of the rights or freedoms recognized herein, or at their limitation to a greater extent than is provided for in the present Covenant.

2. No restriction upon or derogation from any of the fundamental human rights recognized or existing in any country in virtue of law, conventions, regulations or custom shall be admitted on the pretext that the present Covenant does not recognize such rights or that it recognizes them to a lesser extent.

PART III

Article 6

1. The States Parties to the present Covenant recognize the right to work, which includes the right of everyone to the opportunity to gain his living by work which he freely chooses or accepts, and will take appropriate steps to safeguard this right.

2. The steps to be taken by a State Party to the present Covenant to achieve the full realization of this right shall include technical and vocational guidance and training programmes, policies and techniques to achieve steady economic, social and cultural development and full and productive employment under conditions safeguarding fundamental political and economic freedoms to the individual.

Article 7

The States Parties to the present Covenant recognize the right of everyone to the enjoyment of just and favourable conditions of work which ensure, in particular:

(a) Remuneration which provides all workers, as a minimum, with:

(i) Fair wages and equal remuneration for work of equal value without distinction of any kind, in particular women being guaranteed conditions of work not inferior to those enjoyed by men, with equal pay for equal work;

(ii) A decent living for themselves and their families in accordance with the provisions of the present Covenant;

(b) Safe and healthy working conditions;

(c) Equal opportunity for everyone to be promoted in his employment to an appropriate higher level, subject to no considerations other than those of seniority and competence;

(d) Rest, leisure and reasonable limitation of working hours and periodic holidays with pay, as well as remuneration for public holidays

Article 8

1. The States Parties to the present Covenant undertake to ensure:

(a) The right of everyone to form trade unions and join the trade union of his choice, subject only to the rules of the organization concerned, for the promotion and protection of his economic and social interests. No restrictions may be placed on the exercise of this right other than those prescribed by law and which are necessary in a democratic society in the interests of national security or public order or for the protection of the rights and freedoms of others;

(b) The right of trade unions to establish national federations or confederations and the right of the latter to form or join international trade-union organizations;

(c) The right of trade unions to function freely subject to no limitations other than those prescribed by law and which are necessary in a democratic society in the interests of national security or public order or for the protection of the rights and freedoms of others;

(d) The right to strike, provided that it is exercised in conformity with the laws of the particular country.

2. This article shall not prevent the imposition of lawful restrictions on the exercise of these rights by members of the armed forces or of the police or of the administration of the State.

3. Nothing in this article shall authorize States Parties to the International Labour Organisation Convention of 1948 concerning Freedom of Association and Protection of the Right to Organize to take legislative measures which would prejudice, or apply the law in such a manner as would prejudice, the guarantees provided for in that Convention.

Article 9

The States Parties to the present Covenant recognize the right of everyone to social security, including social insurance.

Article 10

The States Parties to the present Covenant recognize that:

1. The widest possible protection and assistance should be accorded to the family, which is the natural and fundamental group unit of society, particularly for its establishment and while it is responsible for the care and education of dependent children. Marriage must be entered into with the free consent of the intending spouses.

2. Special protection should be accorded to mothers during a reasonable period before and after childbirth. During such period working mothers should be accorded paid leave or leave with adequate social security benefits.

3. Special measures of protection and assistance should be taken on behalf of all children and young persons without any discrimination for reasons of parentage or other conditions. Children and young persons should be protected from economic and social exploitation.

Their employment in work harmful to their morals or health or dangerous to life or likely to hamper their normal development should be punishable by law. States should also set age limits below which the paid employment of child labour should be prohibited and punishable by law.

Article 11

1. The States Parties to the present Covenant recognize the right of everyone to an adequate standard of living for himself and his family, including adequate food, clothing and housing, and to the continuous improvement of living conditions. The States Parties will take appropriate steps to ensure the realization of this right, recognizing to this effect the essential importance of international co-operation based on free consent.

2. The States Parties to the present Covenant, recognizing the fundamental right of everyone to be free from hunger, shall take, individually and through international co-operation, the measures, including specific programmes, which are needed:

(a) To improve methods of production, conservation and distribution of food by making full use of technical and scientific knowledge, by disseminating knowledge of the principles of nutrition and by developing or reforming agrarian systems in such a way as to achieve the most efficient development and utilization of natural resources;

(b) Taking into account the problems of both food-importing and food-exporting countries, to ensure an equitable distribution of world food supplies in relation to need.

Article 12

1. The States Parties to the present Covenant recognize the right of everyone to the enjoyment of the highest attainable standard of physical and mental health.

2. The steps to be taken by the States Parties to the present Covenant to achieve the full realization of this right shall include those necessary for:

(a) The provision for the reduction of the stillbirth-rate and of infant mortality and for the healthy development of the child;

(b) The improvement of all aspects of environmental and industrial hygiene;

(c) The prevention, treatment and control of epidemic, endemic, occupational and other diseases;

(d) The creation of conditions which would assure to all medical service and medical attention in the event of sickness.

Article 13

1. The States Parties to the present Covenant recognize the right of everyone to education. They agree that education shall be directed to the full development of the human personality and the sense of its dignity, and shall strengthen the respect for human rights and fundamental freedoms. They further agree that education shall enable all persons to participate effectively in a free society, promote understanding, tolerance and friendship among all nations and all racial, ethnic or religious groups, and further the activities of the United Nations for the maintenance of peace.

2. The States Parties to the present Covenant recognize that, with a view to achieving the full realization of this right:

(a) Primary education shall be compulsory and available free to all;

(b) Secondary education in its different forms, including technical and vocational secondary education, shall be made generally available and accessible to all by every appropriate means, and in particular by the progressive introduction of free education;

(c) Higher education shall be made equally accessible to all, on the basis of capacity, by every appropriate means, and in particular by the progressive introduction of free education;

(d) Fundamental education shall be encouraged or intensified as far as possible for those persons who have not received or completed the whole period of their primary education;

(e) The development of a system of schools at all levels shall be actively pursued, an adequate fellowship system shall be established, and the material conditions of teaching staff shall be continuously improved.

3. The States Parties to the present Covenant undertake to have respect for the liberty of parents and, when applicable, legal guardians to choose for their children schools, other than those established by the public authorities, which conform to such minimum educational standards as may be laid down or approved by the State and to ensure the religious and moral education of their children in conformity with their own convictions.

4. No part of this article shall be construed so as to interfere with the liberty of individuals and bodies to establish and direct educational institutions, subject always to the observance of the principles set forth in paragraph 1 of this article and to the requirement that the education given in such institutions shall conform to such minimum standards as may be laid down by the State.

Article 14

Each State Party to the present Covenant which, at the time of becoming a Party, has not been able to secure in its metropolitan territory or other territories under its jurisdiction compulsory primary education, free of charge, undertakes, within two years, to work out and adopt a detailed plan of action for the progressive implementation, within a reasonable number of years, to be fixed in the plan, of the principle of compulsory education free of charge for all.

Article 15

1. The States Parties to the present Covenant recognize the right of everyone:
   (a) To take part in cultural life;
   (b) To enjoy the benefits of scientific progress and its applications;
   (c) To benefit from the protection of the moral and material interests resulting from any scientific, literary or artistic production of which he is the author.

2. The steps to be taken by the States Parties to the present Covenant to achieve the full realization of this right shall include those necessary for the conservation, the development and the diffusion of science and culture.

3. The States Parties to the present Covenant undertake to respect the freedom indispensable for scientific research and creative activity.

4. The States Parties to the present Covenant recognize the benefits to be derived from the encouragement and development of international contacts and co-operation in the scientific and cultural fields.

PART IV

Article 16

1. The States Parties to the present Covenant undertake to submit in conformity with this part of the Covenant reports on the measures which they have adopted and the progress made in achieving the observance of the rights recognized herein.

2. (a) All reports shall be submitted to the Secretary-General of the United Nations, who shall transmit copies to the Economic and Social Council for consideration in accordance with the provisions of the present Covenant;

(b) The Secretary-General of the United Nations shall also transmit to the specialized agencies copies of the reports, or any relevant parts therefrom, from States Parties to the present Covenant which are also members of these specialized agencies in so far as these reports, or parts therefrom, relate to any matters which fall within the responsibilities of the said agencies in accordance with their constitutional instruments.

Article 17

1. The States Parties to the present Covenant shall furnish their reports in stages, in accordance with a programme to be established by the Economic and Social Council within one year of the entry into force of the present Covenant after consultation with the States Parties and the specialized agencies concerned.

2. Reports may indicate factors and difficulties affecting the degree of fulfilment of obligations under the present Covenant.

3. Where relevant information has previously been furnished to the United Nations or to any specialized agency by any State Party to the present Covenant, it will not be necessary to reproduce that information, but a precise reference to the information so furnished will suffice.

Article 18

Pursuant to its responsibilities under the Charter of the United Nations in the field of human rights and fundamental freedoms, the Economic and Social Council may make arrangements with the specialized agencies in respect of their reporting to it on the progress made in achieving the observance of the provisions of the present Covenant falling within the scope of their activities. These reports may include particulars of decisions and recommendations on such implementation adopted by their competent organs.

Article 19

The Economic and Social Council may transmit to the Commission on Human Rights for study and general recommendation or, as appropriate, for information the reports concerning human rights submitted by States in accordance with articles 16 and 17, and those concerning human rights submitted by the specialized agencies in accordance with article 18.

Article 20

The States Parties to the present Covenant and the specialized agencies concerned may submit comments to the Economic and Social Council on any general recommendation under article 19 or reference to such general recommendation in any report of the Commission on Human Rights or any documentation referred to therein.

Article 21

The Economic and Social Council may submit from time to time to the General Assembly reports with recommendations of a general nature and a summary of the information received from the States Parties to the present Covenant and the specialized agencies on the measures taken and the progress made in achieving general observance of the rights recognized in the present Covenant.

Article 22

The Economic and Social Council may bring to the attention of other organs of the United Nations, their subsidiary organs and specialized agencies concerned with furnishing technical assistance any matters arising out of the reports referred to in this part of the present Covenant which may assist such bodies in deciding, each within its field of competence, on the advisability of international measures likely to contribute to the effective progressive implementation of the present Covenant.

Article 23

The States Parties to the present Covenant agree that international action for the achievement of the rights recognized in the present Covenant includes such methods as the conclusion of conventions, the adoption of recommendations, the furnishing of technical assistance and the holding of regional meetings and technical meetings for the purpose of consultation and study organized in conjunction with the Governments concerned.

Article 24

Nothing in the present Covenant shall be interpreted as impairing the provisions of the Charter of the United Nations and of the constitutions of the specialized agencies which define the respective responsibilities of the various organs of the United Nations and of the specialized agencies in regard to the matters dealt with in the present Covenant.

Article 25

Nothing in the present Covenant shall be interpreted as impairing the inherent right of all peoples to enjoy and utilize fully and freely their natural wealth and resources.

PART V

Article 28

The provisions of the present Covenant shall extend to all parts of federal States without any limitations or exceptions.

4. INTERNATIONAL COVENANT ON CIVIL AND POLITICAL RIGHTS (exclusive of concluding Part VI except for art. 50). Concluded at New York, Dec. 16, 1966. Entered into force, Jan. 3, 1976. 993 UNTS 3, reprinted in Weston and Carlson, 3: III.A.2; available also at http://www.unhchr.ch/udhr/lang/eng.htm

PREAMBLE

THE STATES PARTIES TO THE PRESENT COVENANT,

Considering that, in accordance with the principles proclaimed in the Charter of the United Nations, recognition of the inherent dignity and of the equal and inalienable rights of all members of the human family is the foundation of freedom, justice and peace in the world,

Recognizing that these rights derive from the inherent dignity of the human person,

Recognizing that, in accordance with the Universal Declaration of Human Rights, the ideal of free human beings enjoying civil and political freedom and freedom from fear and want can only be achieved if conditions are created whereby everyone may enjoy his civil and political rights, as well as his economic, social and cultural rights,

Considering the obligation of States under the Charter of the United Nations to promote universal respect for, and observance of, human rights and freedoms,

Realizing that the individual, having duties to other individuals and to the community to which he belongs, is under a responsibility to strive for the promotion and observance of the rights recognized in the present Covenant,

Agree upon the following articles:

PART I

Article 1

1. All peoples have the right of self-determination. By virtue of that right they freely determine their political status and freely pursue their economic, social and cultural development.

2. All peoples may, for their own ends, freely dispose of their natural wealth and resources without prejudice to any obligations arising out of international economic co-operation, based upon the principle of mutual benefit, and international law. In no case may a people be deprived of its own means of subsistence.

3. The States Parties to the present Covenant, including those having responsibility for the administration of Non-Self-Governing and Trust Territories, shall promote the realization of the right of self-determination, and shall respect that right, in conformity with the provisions of the Charter of the United Nations.

PART II

Article 2

1. Each State Party to the present Covenant undertakes to respect and to ensure to all individuals within its territory and subject to its jurisdiction the rights recognized in the present Covenant, without distinction of any kind, such as race, colour, sex, language, religion, political or other opinion, national or social origin, property, birth or other status.

2. Where not already provided for by existing legislative or other measures, each State Party to the present Covenant undertakes to take the necessary steps, in accordance with

its constitutional processes and with the provisions of the present Covenant, to adopt such laws or other measures as may be necessary to give effect to the rights recognized in the present Covenant.

3. Each State Party to the present Covenant undertakes:

(a) To ensure that any person whose rights or freedoms as herein recognized are violated shall have an effective remedy, notwithstanding that the violation has been committed by persons acting in an official capacity;

(b) To ensure that any person claiming such a remedy shall have his right thereto determined by competent judicial, administrative or legislative authorities, or by any other competent authority provided for by the legal system of the State, and to develop the possibilities of judicial remedy;

(c) To ensure that the competent authorities shall enforce such remedies when granted.

Article 3

The States Parties to the present Covenant undertake to ensure the equal right of men and women to the enjoyment of all civil and political rights set forth in the present Covenant.

Article 4

1. In time of public emergency which threatens the life of the nation and the existence of which is officially proclaimed, the States Parties to the present Covenant may take measures derogating from their obligations under the present Covenant to the extent strictly required by the exigencies of the situation, provided that such measures are not inconsistent with their other obligations under international law and do not involve discrimination solely on the ground of race, colour, sex, language, religion or social origin.

2. No derogation from articles 6, 7, 8 (paragraphs 1 and 2), 11, 15, 16 and 18 may be made under this provision.

3. Any State Party to the present Covenant availing itself of the right of derogation shall immediately inform the other States Parties to the present Covenant, through the intermediary of the Secretary-General of the United Nations, of the provisions from which it has derogated and of the reasons by which it was actuated. A further communication shall be made, through the same intermediary, on the date on which it terminates such derogation.

Article 5

1. Nothing in the present Covenant may be interpreted as implying for any State, group or person any right to engage in any activity or perform any act aimed at the destruction of any of the rights and freedoms recognized herein or at their limitation to a greater extent than is provided for in the present Covenant.

2. There shall be no restriction upon or derogation from any of the fundamental human rights recognized or existing in any State Party to the present Covenant pursuant to law, conventions, regulations or custom on the pretext that the present Covenant does not recognize such rights or that it recognizes them to a lesser extent.

PART III

Article 6

1. Every human being has the inherent right to life. This right shall be protected by law. No one shall be arbitrarily deprived of his life.

2. In countries which have not abolished the death penalty, sentence of death may be imposed only for the most serious crimes in accordance with the law in force at the time of the commission of the crime and not contrary to the provisions of the present Covenant and to the Convention on the Prevention and Punishment of the Crime of Genocide. This penalty can only be carried out pursuant to a final judgement rendered by a competent court.

3. When deprivation of life constitutes the crime of genocide, it is understood that nothing in this article shall authorize any State Party to the present Covenant to derogate in any way from any obligation assumed under the provisions of the Convention on the Prevention and Punishment of the Crime of Genocide.

4. Anyone sentenced to death shall have the right to seek pardon or commutation of the sentence. Amnesty, pardon or commutation of the sentence of death may be granted in all cases.

5. Sentence of death shall not be imposed for crimes committed by persons below eighteen years of age and shall not be carried out on pregnant women.

6. Nothing in this article shall be invoked to delay or to prevent the abolition of capital punishment by any State Party to the present Covenant.

Article 7

No one shall be subjected to torture or to cruel, inhuman or degrading treatment or punishment. In particular, no one shall be subjected without his free consent to medical or scientific experimentation.

Article 8

1. No one shall be held in slavery; slavery and the slave-trade in all their forms shall be prohibited.

2. No one shall be held in servitude.

3. (a) No one shall be required to perform forced or compulsory labour;

(b) Paragraph 3 (a) shall not be held to preclude, in countries where imprisonment with hard labour may be imposed as a punishment for a crime, the performance of hard labour in pursuance of a sentence to such punishment by a competent court;

(c) For the purpose of this paragraph the term "forced or compulsory labour" shall not include:

(i) Any work or service, not referred to in subparagraph (b), normally required of a person who is under detention in consequence of a lawful order of a court, or of a person during conditional release from such detention;

(ii) Any service of a military character and, in countries where conscientious objection is recognized, any national service required by law of conscientious objectors;

(iii) Any service exacted in cases of emergency or calamity threatening the life or well-being of the community;

(iv) Any work or service which forms part of normal civil obligations.

Article 9

1. Everyone has the right to liberty and security of person. No one shall be subjected to arbitrary arrest or detention. No one shall be deprived of his liberty except on such grounds and in accordance with such procedure as are established by law.

2. Anyone who is arrested shall be informed, at the time of arrest, of the reasons for his arrest and shall be promptly informed of any charges against him.

3. Anyone arrested or detained on a criminal charge shall be brought promptly before

a judge or other officer authorized by law to exercise judicial power and shall be entitled to trial within a reasonable time or to release. It shall not be the general rule that persons awaiting trial shall be detained in custody, but release may be subject to guarantees to appear for trial, at any other stage of the judicial proceedings, and, should occasion arise, for execution of the judgement.

4. Anyone who is deprived of his liberty by arrest or detention shall be entitled to take proceedings before a court, in order that that court may decide without delay on the lawfulness of his detention and order his release if the detention is not lawful.

5. Anyone who has been the victim of unlawful arrest or detention shall have an enforceable right to compensation.

Article 10

1. All persons deprived of their liberty shall be treated with humanity and with respect for the inherent dignity of the human person.

2. (a) Accused persons shall, save in exceptional circumstances, be segregated from convicted persons and shall be subject to separate treatment appropriate to their status as unconvicted persons;

(b) Accused juvenile persons shall be separated from adults and brought as speedily as possible for adjudication. 3. The penitentiary system shall comprise treatment of prisoners the essential aim of which shall be their reformation and social rehabilitation. Juvenile offenders shall be segregated from adults and be accorded treatment appropriate to their age and legal status.

Article 11

No one shall be imprisoned merely on the ground of inability to fulfil a contractual obligation.

Article 12

1. Everyone lawfully within the territory of a State shall, within that territory, have the right to liberty of movement and freedom to choose his residence.

2. Everyone shall be free to leave any country, including his own.

3. The above-mentioned rights shall not be subject to any restrictions except those which are provided by law, are necessary to protect national security, public order (ordre public), public health or morals or the rights and freedoms of others, and are consistent with the other rights recognized in the present Covenant.

4. No one shall be arbitrarily deprived of the right to enter his own country.

Article 13

An alien lawfully in the territory of a State Party to the present Covenant may be expelled therefrom only in pursuance of a decision reached in accordance with law and shall, except where compelling reasons of national security otherwise require, be allowed to submit the reasons against his expulsion and to have his case reviewed by, and be represented for the purpose before, the competent authority or a person or persons especially designated by the competent authority.

Article 14

1. All persons shall be equal before the courts and tribunals. In the determination of any criminal charge against him, or of his rights and obligations in a suit at law, everyone shall be entitled to a fair and public hearing by a competent, independent and impartial

tribunal established by law. The press and the public may be excluded from all or part of a trial for reasons of morals, public order (ordre public) or national security in a democratic society, or when the interest of the private lives of the parties so requires, or to the extent strictly necessary in the opinion of the court in special circumstances where publicity would prejudice the interests of justice; but any judgement rendered in a criminal case or in a suit at law shall be made public except where the interest of juvenile persons otherwise requires or the proceedings concern matrimonial disputes or the guardianship of children.

2. Everyone charged with a criminal offence shall have the right to be presumed innocent until proved guilty according to law.

3. In the determination of any criminal charge against him, everyone shall be entitled to the following minimum guarantees, in full equality:

(a) To be informed promptly and in detail in a language which he understands of the nature and cause of the charge against him;

(b) To have adequate time and facilities for the preparation of his defence and to communicate with counsel of his own choosing;

(c) To be tried without undue delay;

(d) To be tried in his presence, and to defend himself in person or through legal assistance of his own choosing; to be informed, if he does not have legal assistance, of this right; and to have legal assistance assigned to him, in any case where the interests of justice so require, and without payment by him in any such case if he does not have sufficient means to pay for it;

(e) To examine, or have examined, the witnesses against him and to obtain the attendance and examination of witnesses on his behalf under the same conditions as witnesses against him;

(f) To have the free assistance of an interpreter if he cannot understand or speak the language used in court;

(g) Not to be compelled to testify against himself or to confess guilt.

4. In the case of juvenile persons, the procedure shall be such as will take account of their age and the desirability of promoting their rehabilitation.

5. Everyone convicted of a crime shall have the right to his conviction and sentence being reviewed by a higher tribunal according to law.

6. When a person has by a final decision been convicted of a criminal offence and when subsequently his conviction has been reversed or he has been pardoned on the ground that a new or newly discovered fact shows conclusively that there has been a miscarriage of justice, the person who has suffered punishment as a result of such conviction shall be compensated according to law, unless it is proved that the non-disclosure of the unknown fact in time is wholly or partly attributable to him.

7. No one shall be liable to be tried or punished again for an offence for which he has already been finally convicted or acquitted in accordance with the law and penal procedure of each country.

Article 15

1. No one shall be held guilty of any criminal offence on account of any act or omission which did not constitute a criminal offence, under national or international law, at the time when it was committed. Nor shall a heavier penalty be imposed than the one that was applicable at the time when the criminal offence was committed. If, subsequent to the commission of the offence, provision is made by law for the imposition of the lighter penalty, the offender shall benefit thereby.

2. Nothing in this article shall prejudice the trial and punishment of any person for any act or omission which, at the time when it was committed, was criminal according to the general principles of law recognized by the community of nations.

Article 16

Everyone shall have the right to recognition everywhere as a person before the law.

Article 17

1. No one shall be subjected to arbitrary or unlawful interference with his privacy, family, home or correspondence, nor to unlawful attacks on his honour and reputation.

2. Everyone has the right to the protection of the law against such interference or attacks.

Article 18

1. Everyone shall have the right to freedom of thought, conscience and religion. This right shall include freedom to have or to adopt a religion or belief of his choice, and freedom, either individually or in community with others and in public or private, to manifest his religion or belief in worship, observance, practice and teaching.

2. No one shall be subject to coercion which would impair his freedom to have or to adopt a religion or belief of his choice.

3. Freedom to manifest one's religion or beliefs may be subject only to such limitations as are prescribed by law and are necessary to protect public safety, order, health, or morals or the fundamental rights and freedoms of others.

4. The States Parties to the present Covenant undertake to have respect for the liberty of parents and, when applicable, legal guardians to ensure the religious and moral education of their children in conformity with their own convictions.

Article 19

1. Everyone shall have the right to hold opinions without interference.

2. Everyone shall have the right to freedom of expression; this right shall include freedom to seek, receive and impart information and ideas of all kinds, regardless of frontiers, either orally, in writing or in print, in the form of art, or through any other media of his choice.

3. The exercise of the rights provided for in paragraph 2 of this article carries with it special duties and responsibilities. It may therefore be subject to certain restrictions, but these shall only be such as are provided by law and are necessary:

(a) For respect of the rights or reputations of others;

(b) For the protection of national security or of public order (ordre public), or of public health or morals.

Article 20

1. Any propaganda for war shall be prohibited by law.

2. Any advocacy of national, racial or religious hatred that constitutes incitement to discrimination, hostility or violence shall be prohibited by law.

Article 21

The right of peaceful assembly shall be recognized. No restrictions may be placed on the exercise of this right other than those imposed in conformity with the law and which are necessary in a democratic society in the interests of national security or public safety, public order (ordre public), the protection of public health or morals or the protection of the rights and freedoms of others.

Article 22

1. Everyone shall have the right to freedom of association with others, including the right to form and join trade unions for the protection of his interests.

2. No restrictions may be placed on the exercise of this right other than those which are prescribed by law and which are necessary in a democratic society in the interests of national security or public safety, public order (ordre public), the protection of public health or morals or the protection of the rights and freedoms of others. This article shall not prevent the imposition of lawful restrictions on members of the armed forces and of the police in their exercise of this right.

3. Nothing in this article shall authorize States Parties to the International Labour Organisation Convention of 1948 concerning Freedom of Association and Protection of the Right to Organize to take legislative measures which would prejudice, or to apply the law in such a manner as to prejudice, the guarantees provided for in that Convention.

Article 23

1. The family is the natural and fundamental group unit of society and is entitled to protection by society and the State.

2. The right of men and women of marriageable age to marry and to found a family shall be recognized.

3. No marriage shall be entered into without the free and full consent of the intending spouses.

4. States Parties to the present Covenant shall take appropriate steps to ensure equality of rights and responsibilities of spouses as to marriage, during marriage and at its dissolution. In the case of dissolution, provision shall be made for the necessary protection of any children.

Article 24

1. Every child shall have, without any discrimination as to race, colour, sex, language, religion, national or social origin, property or birth, the right to such measures of protection as are required by his status as a minor, on the part of his family, society and the State.

2. Every child shall be registered immediately after birth and shall have a name.

3. Every child has the right to acquire a nationality.

Article 25

Every citizen shall have the right and the opportunity, without any of the distinctions mentioned in article 2 and without unreasonable restrictions:

(a) To take part in the conduct of public affairs, directly or through freely chosen representatives;

(b) To vote and to be elected at genuine periodic elections which shall be by universal and equal suffrage and shall be held by secret ballot, guaranteeing the free expression of the will of the electors;

(c) To have access, on general terms of equality, to public service in his country.

Article 26

All persons are equal before the law and are entitled without any discrimination to the equal protection of the law. In this respect, the law shall prohibit any discrimination and guarantee to all persons equal and effective protection against discrimination on any ground such as race, colour, sex, language, religion, political or other opinion, national or social origin, property, birth or other status.

Article 27

In those States in which ethnic, religious or linguistic minorities exist, persons belonging to such minorities shall not be denied the right, in community with the other members of their group, to enjoy their own culture, to profess and practise their own religion, or to use their own language.

PART IV

Article 28

1. There shall be established a Human Rights Committee (hereafter referred to in the present Covenant as the Committee). It shall consist of eighteen members and shall carry out the functions hereinafter provided.

2. The Committee shall be composed of nationals of the States Parties to the present Covenant who shall be persons of high moral character and recognized competence in the field of human rights, consideration being given to the usefulness of the participation of some persons having legal experience.

3. The members of the Committee shall be elected and shall serve in their personal capacity.

Article 29

1. The members of the Committee shall be elected by secret ballot from a list of persons possessing the qualifications prescribed in article 28 and nominated for the purpose by the States Parties to the present Covenant.

2. Each State Party to the present Covenant may nominate not more than two persons. These persons shall be nationals of the nominating State.

3. A person shall be eligible for renomination.

Article 30

1. The initial election shall be held no later than six months after the date of the entry into force of the present Covenant.

2. At least four months before the date of each election to the Committee, other than an election to fill a vacancy declared in accordance with article 34, the Secretary-General of the United Nations shall address a written invitation to the States Parties to the present Covenant to submit their nominations for membership of the Committee within three months.

3. The Secretary-General of the United Nations shall prepare a list in alphabetical order of all the persons thus nominated, with an indication of the States Parties which have nominated them, and shall submit it to the States Parties to the present Covenant no later than one month before the date of each election.

4. Elections of the members of the Committee shall be held at a meeting of the States Parties to the present Covenant convened by the Secretary General of the United Nations at the Headquarters of the United Nations. At that meeting, for which two thirds of the States Parties to the present Covenant shall constitute a quorum, the persons elected to the Committee shall be those nominees who obtain the largest number of votes and an absolute majority of the votes of the representatives of States Parties present and voting.

Article 31

1. The Committee may not include more than one national of the same State.

2. In the election of the Committee, consideration shall be given to equitable geographical distribution of membership and to the representation of the different forms of civilization and of the principal legal systems.

Article 32

1. The members of the Committee shall be elected for a term of four years. They shall be eligible for re-election if renominated. However, the terms of nine of the members elected at the first election shall expire at the end of two years; immediately after the first election, the names of these nine members shall be chosen by lot by the Chairman of the meeting referred to in article 30, paragraph 4.

2. Elections at the expiry of office shall be held in accordance with the preceding articles of this part of the present Covenant.

Article 33

1. If, in the unanimous opinion of the other members, a member of the Committee has ceased to carry out his functions for any cause other than absence of a temporary character, the Chairman of the Committee shall notify the Secretary-General of the United Nations, who shall then declare the seat of that member to be vacant.

2. In the event of the death or the resignation of a member of the Committee, the Chairman shall immediately notify the Secretary-General of the United Nations, who shall declare the seat vacant from the date of death or the date on which the resignation takes effect.

Article 34

1. When a vacancy is declared in accordance with article 33 and if the term of office of the member to be replaced does not expire within six months of the declaration of the vacancy, the Secretary-General of the United Nations shall notify each of the States Parties to the present Covenant, which may within two months submit nominations in accordance with article 29 for the purpose of filling the vacancy.

2. The Secretary-General of the United Nations shall prepare a list in alphabetical order of the persons thus nominated and shall submit it to the States Parties to the present Covenant. The election to fill the vacancy shall then take place in accordance with the relevant provisions of this part of the present Covenant.

3. A member of the Committee elected to fill a vacancy declared in accordance with article 33 shall hold office for the remainder of the term of the member who vacated the seat on the Committee under the provisions of that article.

Article 35

The members of the Committee shall, with the approval of the General Assembly of the United Nations, receive emoluments from United Nations resources on such terms and conditions as the General Assembly may decide, having regard to the importance of the Committee's responsibilities.

Article 36

The Secretary-General of the United Nations shall provide the necessary staff and facilities for the effective performance of the functions of the Committee under the present Covenant.

Article 37

1. The Secretary-General of the United Nations shall convene the initial meeting of the Committee at the Headquarters of the United Nations.

2. After its initial meeting, the Committee shall meet at such times as shall be provided in its rules of procedure.

3. The Committee shall normally meet at the Headquarters of the United Nations or at the United Nations Office at Geneva.

Article 38

Every member of the Committee shall, before taking up his duties, make a solemn declaration in open committee that he will perform his functions impartially and conscientiously.

Article 39

1. The Committee shall elect its officers for a term of two years. They may be re-elected.

2. The Committee shall establish its own rules of procedure, but these rules shall provide, inter alia, that:

(a) Twelve members shall constitute a quorum;

(b) Decisions of the Committee shall be made by a majority vote of the members present.

Article 40

1. The States Parties to the present Covenant undertake to submit reports on the measures they have adopted which give effect to the rights recognized herein and on the progress made in the enjoyment of those rights:

(a) Within one year of the entry into force of the present Covenant for the States Parties concerned;

(b) Thereafter whenever the Committee so requests.

2. All reports shall be submitted to the Secretary-General of the United Nations, who shall transmit them to the Committee for consideration. Reports shall indicate the factors and difficulties, if any, affecting the implementation of the present Covenant.

3. The Secretary-General of the United Nations may, after consultation with the Committee, transmit to the specialized agencies concerned copies of such parts of the reports as may fall within their field of competence.

4. The Committee shall study the reports submitted by the States Parties to the present Covenant. It shall transmit its reports, and such general comments as it may consider appropriate, to the States Parties. The Committee may also transmit to the Economic and Social Council these comments along with the copies of the reports it has received from States Parties to the present Covenant.

5. The States Parties to the present Covenant may submit to the Committee observations on any comments that may be made in accordance with paragraph 4 of this article.

Article 41

1. A State Party to the present Covenant may at any time declare under this article that it recognizes the competence of the Committee to receive and consider communications to the effect that a State Party claims that another State Party is not fulfilling its obligations under the present Covenant. Communications under this article may be received

and considered only if submitted by a State Party which has made a declaration recognizing in regard to itself the competence of the Committee. No communication shall be received by the Committee if it concerns a State Party which has not made such a declaration. Communications received under this article shall be dealt with in accordance with the following procedure:

(a) If a State Party to the present Covenant considers that another State Party is not giving effect to the provisions of the present Covenant, it may, by written communication, bring the matter to the attention of that State Party. Within three months after the receipt of the communication the receiving State shall afford the State which sent the communication an explanation, or any other statement in writing clarifying the matter which should include, to the extent possible and pertinent, reference to domestic procedures and remedies taken, pending, or available in the matter;

(b) If the matter is not adjusted to the satisfaction of both States Parties concerned within six months after the receipt by the receiving State of the initial communication, either State shall have the right to refer the matter to the Committee, by notice given to the Committee and to the other State;

(c) The Committee shall deal with a matter referred to it only after it has ascertained that all available domestic remedies have been invoked and exhausted in the matter, in conformity with the generally recognized principles of international law. This shall not be the rule where the application of the remedies is unreasonably prolonged;

(d) The Committee shall hold closed meetings when examining communications under this article;

(e) Subject to the provisions of subparagraph (c), the Committee shall make available its good offices to the States Parties concerned with a view to a friendly solution of the matter on the basis of respect for human rights and fundamental freedoms as recognized in the present Covenant;

(f) In any matter referred to it, the Committee may call upon the States Parties concerned, referred to in subparagraph (b), to supply any relevant information;

(g) The States Parties concerned, referred to in subparagraph (b), shall have the right to be represented when the matter is being considered in the Committee and to make submissions orally and/or in writing;

(h) The Committee shall, within twelve months after the date of receipt of notice under subparagraph (b), submit a report:

(i) If a solution within the terms of subparagraph (e) is reached, the Committee shall confine its report to a brief statement of the facts and of the solution reached;

(ii) If a solution within the terms of subparagraph (e) is not reached, the Committee shall confine its report to a brief statement of the facts; the written submissions and record of the oral submissions made by the States Parties concerned shall be attached to the report. In every matter, the report shall be communicated to the States Parties concerned.

2. The provisions of this article shall come into force when ten States Parties to the present Covenant have made declarations under paragraph I of this article. Such declarations shall be deposited by the States Parties with the Secretary-General of the United Nations, who shall transmit copies thereof to the other States Parties. A declaration may be withdrawn at any time by notification to the Secretary-General. Such a withdrawal shall not prejudice the consideration of any matter which is the subject of a communication already transmitted under this article; no further communication by any State Party shall be received after the notification of withdrawal of the declaration has been received by the Secretary-General, unless the State Party concerned has made a new declaration.

Article 42

1. (a) If a matter referred to the Committee in accordance with article 41 is not resolved to the satisfaction of the States Parties concerned, the Committee may, with the prior consent of the States Parties concerned, appoint an ad hoc Conciliation Commission (hereinafter referred to as the Commission). The good offices of the Commission shall be made available to the States Parties concerned with a view to an amicable solution of the matter on the basis of respect for the present Covenant;

(b) The Commission shall consist of five persons acceptable to the States Parties concerned. If the States Parties concerned fail to reach agreement within three months on all or part of the composition of the Commission, the members of the Commission concerning whom no agreement has been reached shall be elected by secret ballot by a two-thirds majority vote of the Committee from among its members.

2. The members of the Commission shall serve in their personal capacity. They shall not be nationals of the States Parties concerned, or of a State not Party to the present Covenant, or of a State Party which has not made a declaration under article 41.

3. The Commission shall elect its own Chairman and adopt its own rules of procedure.

4. The meetings of the Commission shall normally be held at the Headquarters of the United Nations or at the United Nations Office at Geneva. However, they may be held at such other convenient places as the Commission may determine in consultation with the Secretary-General of the United Nations and the States Parties concerned.

5. The secretariat provided in accordance with article 36 shall also service the commissions appointed under this article.

6. The information received and collated by the Committee shall be made available to the Commission and the Commission may call upon the States Parties concerned to supply any other relevant information.

7. When the Commission has fully considered the matter, but in any event not later than twelve months after having been seized of the matter, it shall submit to the Chairman of the Committee a report for communication to the States Parties concerned:

(a) If the Commission is unable to complete its consideration of the matter within twelve months, it shall confine its report to a brief statement of the status of its consideration of the matter;

(b) If an amicable solution to the matter on tie basis of respect for human rights as recognized in the present Covenant is reached, the Commission shall confine its report to a brief statement of the facts and of the solution reached;

(c) If a solution within the terms of subparagraph (b) is not reached, the Commission's report shall embody its findings on all questions of fact relevant to the issues between the States Parties concerned, and its views on the possibilities of an amicable solution of the matter. This report shall also contain the written submissions and a record of the oral submissions made by the States Parties concerned;

(d) If the Commission's report is submitted under subparagraph (c), the States Parties concerned shall, within three months of the receipt of the report, notify the Chairman of the Committee whether or not they accept the contents of the report of the Commission.

8. The provisions of this article are without prejudice to the responsibilities of the Committee under article 41.

9. The States Parties concerned shall share equally all the expenses of the members of the Commission in accordance with estimates to be provided by the Secretary-General of the United Nations.

10. The Secretary-General of the United Nations shall be empowered to pay the expenses of the members of the Commission, if necessary, before reimbursement by the States Parties concerned, in accordance with paragraph 9 of this article.

Article 43

The members of the Committee, and of the ad hoc conciliation commissions which may be appointed under article 42, shall be entitled to the facilities, privileges and immunities of experts on mission for the United Nations as laid down in the relevant sections of the Convention on the Privileges and Immunities of the United Nations.

Article 44

The provisions for the implementation of the present Covenant shall apply without prejudice to the procedures prescribed in the field of human rights by or under the constituent instruments and the conventions of the United Nations and of the specialized agencies and shall not prevent the States Parties to the present Covenant from having recourse to other procedures for settling a dispute in accordance with general or special international agreements in force between them.

Article 45

The Committee shall submit to the General Assembly of the United Nations, through the Economic and Social Council, an annual report on its activities.

PART V

Article 46

Nothing in the present Covenant shall be interpreted as impairing the provisions of the Charter of the United Nations and of the constitutions of the specialized agencies which define the respective responsibilities of the various organs of the United Nations and of the specialized agencies in regard to the matters dealt with in the present Covenant.

Article 47

Nothing in the present Covenant shall be interpreted as impairing the inherent right of all peoples to enjoy and utilize fully and freely their natural wealth and resources.

PART VI

Article 50

The provisions of the present Covenant shall extend to all parts of federal States without any limitations or exceptions.

Documentary Appendix B: Select References

Additional Protocol to the American Convention on Human Rights in the Area of Economic, Social and Cultural Rights (Protocol of San Salvador), Nov. 17, 1988 (entered into force Nov. 16, 1999), OASTS 69, reprinted in 28 *ILM* 156 (1989) and 3 Weston and Carlson III.B.25; available also at http://www.oas.org/juridico/english/treaties/a-52.html

Additional Protocol to the European Convention for the Protection of Human Rights and Dignity with Regard to the Application of Biology and Medicine on the Prohibition of Cloning Human Beings, Jan. 12, 1998 (entered into force Mar. 1, 2001), ETS 168, reprinted in 36 *ILM* 145 (1997), and 3 Weston and Carlson III.K.7; available also at http://conventions.coe.int/treaty/en/ treaties/html/ 168.htm

Additional Protocol to the European Social Charter, May 5, 1988 (entered into force Sept. 4, 1992), ETS 128, reprinted in 3 Weston and Carlson III.B.12; available also at http://conventions.coe.int/ treaty/en/treaties/html/128.htm

Affirmation of the Principles of International Law Recognized by the Charter of the Nuremberg Tribunal, Dec. 11, 1946, GA Res. 95, UN GAOR, 1st Sess., at 1144, UN Doc. A/236 (1946); available also at http://www.un.org/documents/ga/res/1/ares1.htm

African Charter on Human and Peoples' Rights (Banjul Charter), June 27, 1981 (entered into force Oct. 21, 1986), OAU Doc. CAB/LEG/67/3 Rev 5, reprinted in 21 *ILM* 58 (1982) and 3 Weston and Carlson III.B.1; available also at http://www.africa-union.org/Official_Documents/Treaties_% 20Conventions_%20 Protocols/Banjul%20Charter.pdf

Agreement for the Prosecution and Punishment of the Major War Criminals of the European Axis Powers and Charter of the International Military Tribunal, Aug. 8, 1945 (entered into force Aug. 8, 1945), 82 UNTS 279, reprinted in 2 Weston and Carlson II.E.1; available also at http://www.icrc. org/ihl.nsf/0/59e5a3f 396d98cc3c125641e00405ea7

American Declaration of the Rights and Duties of Man, Mar. 30-May 2, 1948, OAS Res. XXX, OAS Off. Rec OEA/Ser.L/V/I.4 Rev, reprinted in 3 Weston and Carlson III.B.23; available also at http:// www.oas.org/juridico/english/ga-Res98/Eres1591.htm

American Convention on Human Rights (ACHR), Nov. 22, 1969 (entered into force July 8, 1978), 1114 UNTS 123, OASTS 36, reprinted in 3 Weston and Carlson III.B.24; available also at http:// www. oas.org/juridico/english/treaties/b-32.htm

Arab Charter on Human Rights, Sept. 15, 1994 (not in force as of May 1, 2006), Council of the League of Arab States, 102nd Sess., Res. 5437, reprinted in 3 Weston and Carlson III.B.27; available also at http://www1.umn.edu/humanrts/instree/arabhrcharter.html

Budapest Summit Declaration and Decisions, Dec. 6, 1994, reprinted in 34 *ILM* 764 (1995) and 1 Weston and Carlson I.D.18; available also at http://www.osce.org/documents/mcs/ 1994/12/ 4048_ en.pdf

Cairo Declaration on Human Rights in Islam, Aug. 5, 1990, UN GAOR World Conf. on Human Rights, 4th Sess., Agenda Item 5, UN Doc.4/CONF.157/PC/62/Add.18(1993) (English transl.)

Charter of Fundamental Rights of the European Union, Dec. 7, 2000, C364 OJEC 8, reprinted in 40 *ILM* 266 (2001) and 3 Weston and Carlson III.B.16f; available also at http://www.europarl.eu.int/ charter/ pdf/text_en.pdf

Charter of Paris for a New Europe and Supplementary Document to Give Effect to Certain Provisions Contained in the Charter of Paris for a New Europe, Nov. 21, 1990, reprinted in 30 *ILM* 190

(1991) and 1 Weston and Carlson I.D.13; available also at http://www.osce.org/documents/mcs/ 1990/11/4045_ en.pdf

Charter of the Organization of American States, Apr. 30, 1948 (entered in to force Dec. 13, 1951), 119 UNTS 3; OASTS 1 and 61, PAULTS 23, reprinted in 1 Weston and Carlson I.B.14; available also at http://www.oas.org/juridico/english/charter.html

Charter of the United Nations, June 26, 1945 (entered into force Oct. 24, 1945), 1976 YBUN 1033, reprinted in 1 Weston and Carlson I.A.1, available at http://www.un.org/aboutun/charter

Commission on Human Rights Resolution 2001/69 on Promotion of the Right of Peoples to Peace, 78th mtg., April 25, 2001, available at http://www.unhchr.ch/HuriDocda/HuriDoca.nsf/0/ 332f19eff55bc6f5c1256 a4500391692

Concluding Document of the Vienna Meeting 1986 of Representatives of the Participating States of the Conference on Security and Co-operation in Europe, Held on the Basis of the Provisions of the Final Act Relating to the Follow-up to the Conference (Vienna Concluding Document), Jan. 17, 1989, reprinted in 28 *ILM* 527 (1989) and 1 Weston and Carlson I.D.11; available also at http://www.osce.org/ documents/mcs/1986/11/4224_en.pdf and http://www1.umn.edu/human rts/peace/docs/oscevienna.html

Convention against Torture and Other Cruel, Inhuman or Degrading Treatment or Punishment, Dec. 10, 1984 (entered into force June 26, 1987), 1465 UNTS 85, reprinted in 24 *ILM* 535 (1985) and 3 Weston and Carlson III.K.2; available also at http://untreaty.un.org/ENGLISH/bible/ englishinternetbible/partI/ chapterIV/ treaty14.asp and http://www.ohchr.org/english/law/cat.htm

Convention for the Suppression of the Traffic in Persons and of the Exploitation of the Prostitution of Others (with Final Protocol), Mar. 21, 1950 (entered into force July 25, 1951), 96 UNTS 271, reprinted in 3 Weston and Carlson III,C,7; available also at http://untreaty.un.org/ENGLISH/ bible/englishinternetbible/partI/chapterVII.asp

Convention Governing the Specific Aspects of the Refugee Problem in Africa, Sept. 10, 69 (entered into force June 20, 1974), 1001 UNTS 45, reprinted in 8 *ILM* 1288 (1969); available also at http://www.africa-union.org/Official_Documents/Treaties_%20Conventions_%20Protocols/ Refugee_Convention.pdf

Convention on Biological Diversity, June 5, 1992 (entered into force Dec. 29, 1993), 1760 UNTS 79, reprinted in 31 *ILM* 818 (1992) and 5 Weston and Carlson V.H.22 ; available also at http://www. biodiv.org/Doc/legal/cbd-en.pdf

Consent to Marriage, Minimum Age for Marriage and Registration of Marriages, Dec. 10, 1962 (entered into force Dec. 9, 1964), 521 UNTS 231, reprinted in 3 Weston and Carlson III.C.11; available also at http://untreaty.un.org/ENGLISH/bible/englishinternetbible/partI/chapterVII.asp and http://www.ohchr.org/english/law/convention.htm

Convention on the Elimination of All Forms of Discrimination against Women (CEDAW), Dec. 18, 1979 (entered into force Sept. 3, 1981), 1249 UNTS 13, reprinted in 19 *ILM* 33 (1980) and 3 Weston and Carlson III.C.13; available also at http://untreaty.un.org/ENGLISH/bible/english internetbible/ partI/ chapterIV/treaty10.asp and http://www.un.org/womenwatch/daw/cedaw/text/econvention. htm

Convention on the Non-Applicability of Statutory Limitations to War Crimes and Crimes against Humanity, Nov. 26, 1968 (entered into force Nov. 11, 1970), 754 UNTS 73, reprinted in 8 *ILM* 68 (1969) and 2 Weston and Carlson II:E.6; available also at http://www.ohchr.org/english/law/ warcrimes.htm

Convention on the Prevention and Punishment of the Crime of Genocide, Dec. 9, 1948 (entered into force Jan. 12, 1951), 78 UNTS 277, reprinted in 3 Weston and Carlson III.J.1; available also at http://untreaty. un.org/ENGLISH/bible/englishinternetbible/partI/chapterIV/treaty1.asp and http:// www.unhchr.ch/ html/menu3/b/p_genoci.htm

Convention on the Prohibition of the Use, Stockpiling, Production and Transfer of Anti-Personnel Mines and on Their Destruction, Sept. 18, 1997 (entered in to force March 1, 1999), reprinted in 36 *ILM* 1507 (1997) and 2 Weston and Carlson II.C.11b; available also at http://www.un.org/millennium/ law/ xxvi-22.htm

Convention on the Reduction of Statelessness, Aug. 30, 1961 (entered into force Dec. 13, 1975), 989 UNTS 175; available also at http://www.ohchr.org/english/law/statelessness.htm

Convention Relating to the Status of Refugees, July 28, 1951 (entered into force Apr. 22, 1954), 189 UNTS 150, reprinted in 3 Weston and Carlson III.G.4; available also at http://untreaty.un.org/ ENGLISH/bible/englishinternetbible/partI/chapterV/treaty2.asp and http://www.unhchr.ch/html/ menu3/b/o_c_ref.htm

Convention on the Rights of the Child, Nov. 2, 1989 (entered into force Sept. 2, 1990), 1577 UNTS 3, reprinted in 28 *ILM* 1448 (1989) and 3 Weston and Carlson III.D.3; available also at http://untreaty.un.org/ENGLISH/bible/englishinternetbible/partI/chapterIV/treaty19.asp and http://www.unhchr.ch/html/menu3/b/k2crc.htm

Durban Declaration and Programme of Action of the 2001 United Nations World Conference against Racism, Sept. 8, 2001, Office of the United Nations High Commissioner for Human Rights website at http://www.unhchr.ch/pdf/Durban.pdf (last visited Jan. 1, 2005), reprinted in 3 Weston and Carlson III.I.9

ECOSOC Resolution (No. 1235) Concerning Questions of the Violation of Human Rights and Fundamental Freedoms, Including Policies of Racial Discrimination and Segregation and of *Apartheid*, in All Countries, with Particular Reference to Colonial and Other Dependent Countries and Territories, June 6, 1967, ESC Res. 1235, UN ESCOR, 42nd Sess., 1479th mtg., Supp. No. 1, at 17, UN Doc. E/4393 (1967), reprinted in 3 Weston and Carlson III.T.3

ECOSOC Resolution (No. 1503) Concerning Procedures for Dealing with Communications Relating to Violations of Human Rights and Fundamental Freedoms, May 27, 1970, ESC Res. 1503, UN ESCOR, 48th Sess., Supp. 1A, at 8, UN Doc. E/4832/Add.1 91970), reprinted in 3 Weston and Carlson III.T.6

European Agreement on the Abolition of Visas for Refugees, Apr. 20, 1959 (entered into force Apr. 9, 1960), ETS No. 31; available also at http://conventions.coe.int/treaty/commun/ListeTraites.asp.MA=14&TI=Agreement+on+the+abolition+of+visas+for+refugees&LO=999&AO=1959&AV=&CRM=2&CL=ENG

European Agreement on Transfer of Responsibility for Refugees, Oct. 16, 1980 (entered into force Dec. 1, 1980), ETS No. 107; available also at http://conventions.coe.int/treaty/commun/ListeTraites.asp.MA=14&TI=Transfer+of+responsibility+for+refugees&LO=999&AO=1980&AV=&CM=2&CL=ENG

European Charter for Regional or Minority Languages, Nov. 5, 1992 (entered in to force Mar. 1, 1998), ETS 148; available also at http://conventions.coe.int/treaty/en/treaties/html/148.htm

European Convention for the Prevention of Torture and Inhuman or Degrading Treatment or Punishment, Nov. 26, 1987 (entered into force 1 Feb 1989), ETS 126, reprinted in 3 Weston and Carlson III.K.4; available also at http://conventions.coe.int/treaty/en/treaties/html/126.htm

European Convention for the Protection of Human Rights and Dignity of the Human Being with Regard to the Application of Biology and Medicine: Convention on Human Rights and Biomedicine, Apr. 4, 1997 (entered into force Dec. 1, 1999) : ETS CE Doc. DIR/JUR (97) Jan. 1, 1997); 3 Weston and Carlson III.K.6; 36 *ILM* 817 (1997) available also at http://conventions.coe.int/treaty/en/treaties/html/164.htm

European Convention on Human Rights and Biomedicine, Apr. 4, 1997 (entered into force Dec. 1, 1999), ETS No. 164; available also at http://conventions.coe.int/treaty/commun/ListeTraites.asp.MA=9&TI=biomedicine&LO=999&AO=1959&AV=&CRM=2&CL=ENG

European Convention on Human Rights and Fundamental Freedoms, Nov. 4, 1950 (entered into force Sept. 3, 1953), 213 UNTS 221, ETS 5, reprinted in 3 Weston and Carlson III.B.2; available also at http://www.europarl.eu.int/charter/ Docs/pdf/a2_0003_89_en_en.pdf

European Convention on the Legal Status of Migrant Workers, Nov. 24, 1977 (entered into force May 1, 1993), ETS No. 93; reprinted in 16 *ILM* 1381 (1977); available also at http://conventions.coe.int/treaty/commun/ListeTraites.asp?CM=9&TI=biomedicine&LO=999&AO=1959&AV=&CRM=2&CL=ENG

European Framework Convention for the Protection of National Minorities (provisional text), Feb. 1, 1995 (entered into force Feb. 1, 1998), ETS 157, reprinted in 34 *ILM* 351 (1994) and 3 Weston and Carlson III.I.7; available also at http://www.europarl.eu.int/charter/Docs/pdf/a2_0003_89_en_en.pdf

European Parliament Declaration of Fundamental Rights and Freedoms, May 16, 1989, C120 OJEC. 51, Doc. A 2-3/89, reprinted in 3 Weston and Carlson III.B.13; available also at http://www.europarl.eu.int/ charter/Docs/pdf/a2_0003_89_en_en.pdf

European Social Charter, Oct. 18, 1961 (entered into force Feb. 26, 1965), 529 UNTS 89, ETS 35, reprinted in 3 Weston and Carlson III.B.4; available also at http://conventions.coe.int/treaty/en/treaties/html/ 035.htm

European Social Charter (Revised), May 3, 1996 (entered into force July 1, 1999), ETS 163, reprinted in 3 Weston and Carlson III.B.16d; available also at http://conventions.coe.int/treaty/en/treaties/html/163. htm

Final Act on Security and Co-Operation in Europe (Helsinki Final Act), Aug. 1, 1975, 73 USDSB 323 (1975), reprinted in 14 *ILM* 1292 (1975) and 1 Weston and Carlson I.D.9; available also at http://www.osce. org/Docs/english/1990–1999/summits/helfa75e.htm

Final Act of the United Nations International Conference on Human Rights at Teheran, May 13, 1968, in Human Rights: A Compilation of International Instruments 43 (1988), reprinted in 3 Weston and Carlson III.U.1; available also at http://www.unhchr.ch/html/menu3/b/b_tehern.htm

Geneva Convention (No. I) for the Amelioration of the Condition of the Wounded and Sick in Armed Forces in the Field, Aug. 12, 1949 (entered into force Oct. 21, 1950), 75 UNTS 31, reprinted in 2 Weston and Carlson II.B.11; available also at http://www.icrc.org/Web/Eng/siteeng0.nsf/html/genevaconventions

Geneva Convention (No. II) for the Amelioration of the Condition of the Wounded and Sick and Shipwrecked Members of Armed Forces at Sea, Aug. 12, 1949 (entered into force Oct. 21, 1950), 75 UNTS 85, reprinted in 2 Weston and Carlson II.B.12; available also at http://www.icrc.org/Web/Eng/siteeng0.nsf/html/genevaconventions

Geneva Convention (No. III) Relative to the Treatment of Prisoners of War, Aug. 12, 1949 (entered into force Oct. 21, 1950), 75 UNTS 135, reprinted in 2 Weston and Carlson II.B.13; available also at http://www.icrc.org/Web/Eng/siteeng0.nsf/html/genevaconventions and http://www.ohchr.org/english/law/prisonerwar.htm

Geneva Convention (No. IV) Relative to the Protection of Civilian Persons in Time of War, Aug. 12, 1949 (entered into force Oct. 21, 1950), 75 UNTS 287, reprinted in 2 Weston and Carlson II.B.14; available also at http://www.icrc.org/Web/Eng/siteeng0.nsf/html/genevaconventions and http://www.ohchr.org/english/law/civilianpersons.htm

Helsinki Final Act. *See* Final Act on Security and Co-Operation in Europe.

ILO Convention (No. 29) Concerning Forced or Compulsory Labour, June 28, 1930 (entered into force May 1, 1932), 39 UNTS 55, reprinted in 3 Weston and Carlson III.H.2; available also at http://www.ilo.org/ilolex/english/convdisp1.htm and http://www.unhchr.ch/html/menu3/b/31.htm

ILO Convention (No. 87) Concerning Freedom of Association and Protection of the Right to Organise, July 9, 1948 (entered into force July 4, 1950), 68 UNTS 17, reprinted in 3 Weston and Carlson III.O.1; available also at http://www.ilo.org/ilolex/english/convdisp1.htm and http://www.unhchr.ch/html/ menu3/b/j_ilo87.htm

ILO Convention (No 97) Concerning Migration for Employment (Revised), July 1, 1949 (entered into force Jan. 22, 1952), 120 UNTS 71; available also at http://www.ilo.org/ilolex/english/ convdisp1.htm

ILO Convention (No. 98) Concerning the Application of the Principles of the Right to Organise and to Bargain Collectively, July 1, 1949 (entered into force July 18, 1951), 96 UNTS 257, reprinted in 3 Weston and Carlson III.O.2; available also at http://www.ilo.org/ilolex/english/convdisp1.htm and http://www. unhchr.ch/html/menu3/b/j_ilo98.htm

ILO Convention (No. 100) Concerning Equal Remuneration for Men and Women Workers for Work of Equal Value, June 29, 1951 (entered into force May 23, 1953), 165 UNTS 303, reprinted in 3 Weston and Carlson III.O.3; available also at http://www.ilo.org/ilolex/english/convdisp1.htm and http://www.unhchr.ch/ html/menu3/b/d_ilo100.htm

ILO Convention (No. 105) Concerning the Abolition of Forced Labour, June 25, 1957 (entered into force Jan. 17, 1959), 320 UNTS 291, reprinted in 3 Weston and Carlson III.H.4; available also at http://www. ilo.org/ilolex/english/convdisp1.htm and http://www.unhchr.ch/html/menu3/b/32. htm

ILO Convention (No. 107) Concerning the Protection and Integration of Indigenous and Other Tribal and Semi-Tribal Populations in Independent Countries, June 26, 1957 (entered into force June 2, 1959), 328 UNTS 247, reprinted in 3 Weston and Carlson III.F.1; available also at http://www.ilo. org/ilolex/cgi-lex/ convde.pl?C107

ILO Convention (No. 111) Concerning Discrimination in Respect of Employment and Occupation, June 25, 1958 (entered into force June 15, 1960), 362 UNTS 31, reprinted in 3 Weston and Carlson III.O.4; available also at http://www.ilo.org/ilolex/english/convdisp1.htm and http://www.unhchr.ch/html/ menu3/b/d_ilo111.htm

ILO Convention (No. 138) Concerning Minimum Age for Admission to Employment, June 26, 1973 (entered into force June 19, 1976), 1015 UNTS 297 (revising ILO conventions nos. 5, 7, 10, 15, 33, 58, 59, 60, 112, and 123, supra), reprinted in 3 Weston and Carlson III.O.5; available also at http://www.ilo.org/ilolex/english/convdisp1.htm and http://www.ilo.org/ilolex/cgi-lex/convde. pl?C138

ILO Convention (No. 143) Concerning Migrations in Abusive Conditions and the Promotion of Equality of Opportunity and Treatment of Migrant Workers, June 24, 1975 (entered into force Dec. 9, 1978), 1120 UNTS 323; available also at http://www.ilo.org/ilolex/english/convdisp1.htm

ILO Convention (No. 169) Concerning Indigenous and Tribal Peoples in Independent Countries, June 27, 1989 (entered into force Sept. 5, 1991), ILO Off. Bull., Ser. A, No. 2, at 59, reprinted in 28 *ILM* 1382 (1989) and 3 Weston and Carlson III.F.2; available also at http://www.ilo.org/ilolex/english/convdisp1. htm and http://www.unhchr.ch/html/menu3/b/62.htm

ILO Convention (No. 182) Concerning the Prohibition and Immediate Elimination of the Worst Forms of Child Labour, June 17, 1999 (entered into force Nov. 19, 2002), reprinted in 38 *ILM* 1207 (1999) and 3 Weston and Carlson III.D.4; available also at http://www.ilo.org/ilolex/english/convdisp1.htm and http://www. ohchr.org/english/law/child labour.htm

ILO Declaration on Fundamental Principles and Rights at Work, June 18, 1998, reprinted in 37 *ILM* 1233 (1998) and 3 Weston and Carlson III.O.7; available also at http://www.ilo.org/public/english/standards/ relm/ilc/ilc86/com-dtxt.htm

Inter-American Convention on Diplomatic Asylum, Mar. 28, 1954 (entered into force Dec. 29, 1954), OASTS 18, reprinted in 3 Weston and Carlson III.G.5; available also at http://www.oas.org/juridico/english/treaties/a-57.htm

Inter-American Convention on the Forced Disappearance of Persons, Jun. 9, 1994 (entered into force Mar. 12, 1996), OAS/Ser.L/V/I.4 Rev 7 (Jan. 2000), reprinted in 33 *ILM* 1529 (1994); available also at http://www.oas.org/juridico/english/Treaties/a-60.html

Inter-American Convention on International Traffic in Minors, Mar. 18, 1994 (entered into force Aug. 15, 1997), OASTS 79, reprinted in 33 *ILM* 721 (1994); available also at http://www.oas.org/juridico/english/treaties/b-57.html

Inter-American Convention on the Nationality of Women, Dec. 26, 1933 (entered into force Aug. 29, 1934), OASTS 4; available also at http://www.oas.org/juridico/spanish/tratados/a-33.htm

Inter-American Convention on the Prevention, Punishment and Eradication of Violence against Women, Jun. 9, 1994 (entered into force Mar. 5, 1995), OAS/Ser.L/V/I.4 Rev (Jan 2000), reprinted in 33 *ILM* 1534 (1994); available also at http://www.oas.org/juridico/english/ treaties/ a-61.htm

Inter-American Convention to Prevent and Punish Torture, Dec. 9, 1985 (entered into force Feb. 28, 1987), OASTS 67 reprinted in 25 *ILM* 519 (1986) and 3 Weston and Carlson III.K.3; available also at http://www.oas.org/juridico/english/treaties/a-51.html

Inter-American Convention on Territorial Asylum, Mar. 28, 1954 (entered into force Dec. 29, 1954), OASTS 19, reprinted in 3 Weston and Carlson III.G.6; available also at http://www.oas.org/juridico/english/treaties/a-47.html

International Convention against *Apartheid* in Sports, Dec. 10, 1985 (entered into force Apr. 3, 1988), 1500 UNTS 161, reprinted in 3 Weston and Carlson III.I.4; available also at http://untreaty.un.org/ENGLISH/bible/englishinternet/partI/chapterIV/treaty18.asp

International Convention on the Elimination of All Forms of Racial Discrimination (ICERD), Dec. 21, 1965 (entered into force Jan. 4, 1969), 660 UNTS 195, reprinted in 3 Weston and Carlson III.I.1; available also at http://untreaty.un.org/ENGLISH/bible/englishinternetbible/partI/chapterIV/treaty2.asp and http:// www.unhchr.ch/html/menu3/b/d_icerd.htm

International Convention on the Protection of All Migrant Workers and Their Families, Dec. 18, 1990 (entered into force July 1, 2003), GA Res. 45/158 (Annex), UN GAOR, 45th Sess., Supp. No. 49, at 262, UN Doc. A/45/49 (1991), reprinted in 30 *ILM* 1517 (1991) and 3 Weston and Carlson III.O.6; available also at http://www.un.org/Depts/dhl/res/resa45.htm

International Convention on the Suppression and Punishment of the Crime of Apartheid, Nov. 30, 1973 (entered into force July 18, 1976), 1015 UNTS 243, reprinted in 13 *ILM* 50 (1974) and 3 Weston and Carlson III.I.2; available also at http://untreaty.un.org/ENGLISH/bible/englishinternetbible/partI/ chapterIV/treaty9.asp and http://www.unhchr.ch/html/menu3/b/11.htm

International Covenant on Civil and Political Rights (ICCPR), Dec. 16, 1966, (entered into force Mar. 23, 1976), 993 UNTS 171, reprinted in 3 Weston and Carlson III.A.3 and Documentary Appendix A; available also at http://untreaty.un.org/ENGLISH/bible/englishinternetbible/partI/chapterIV/treaty6.asp and http:// www.unhchr.ch/html/menu3/b/a_ccpr.htm

International Covenant on Economic, Social and Cultural Rights (ICESCR), Dec. 16, 1966 (entered into force Jan. 3, 1976), 993 UNTS 3 (hereinafter ICESCR), reprinted in 3 Weston and Carlson III.A.2 and Documentary Appendix A; available also at http://untreaty.un.org/ ENGLISH/bible/englishinternetbible/partI/chapterIV/treaty5.asp and http://www.unhchr.ch/html/menu3/b/a_cescr.htm

Limburg Principles on the Implementation of the International Covenant on Economic, Social and Cultural Rights, adopted Jan. 8, 1987, UN ESCOR, Comm'n on Hum. Rts., 43d Sess., Agenda Item 8, UN Doc. E/CN.4/1987/17/Annex (1987), reprinted in *HRQ* 9 (1987): 122–35; available also at http://www2.law. uu.nl/english/sim/instr/limburg.asp

Maastricht Guidelines on Violations of Economic, Social and Cultural Rights, reprinted in *HRQ* 20, no. 1 (1998); in *Netherlands Quarterly of Human Rights* 15, no. 2 (1997); and in SIM Special No. 20 (Utrecht: Netherlands Institute of Human Rights, 1998); available also at www.uu.nl/content/20-01.pdf

Montreal Protocol on Substances that Deplete the Ozone Layer, Sept. 16, 1987 (entered into force Jan. 1, 1989), 1522 UNTS 3, reprinted in 26 *ILM* 1541 (1987) and 5 Weston and Carlson V.E.9; available also at http://www.unep.org/ozone/pdfs/Montreal-Protocol2000.pdf

Norms on the Responsibilities of Transnational Corporations and Other Business Enterprises with Regard to Human Rights, Aug. 13, 2003, UN Sub-Commission on the Promotion and Protection of Human Rights, Res. 2003/16, UN Doc. E/CN.4/Sub.2/2003/12/Rev.2 (2003); reprinted in 3 Weston and Carlson III.T.25

Optional Protocol to the Convention on the Elimination of all Forms of Discrimination against Women, Oct. 19, 1999 (entered into force Dec. 22, 2000), GA Res. 54/4, UN GAOR, 54th Sess., Supp. No. 49, at 4, UN Doc. A/54/4(1999), reprinted in 39 *ILM* 281 (2000) and 3 Weston and Carlson III.C.16; available also at http://www.un.org/Depts/dhl/resguide/r54.htm

Optional Protocol (No. 1) to the International Covenant on Civil and Political Rights, Dec. 16, 1966 (entered into force Mar. 23, 1976), 999 UNTS 171, 999 UNTS 302, reprinted in 6 *ILM* 383 (1967) and 3 Weston and Carlson III.A.4; available also at http://untreaty.un.org/ENGLISH/bible/englishinternetbible/partI/ chapterIV/treaty7.asp and http://www.unhchr.ch/html/menu3/b/a_opt.htm

Optional Protocol (No. 2) to the International Covenant on Civil and Political Rights Aiming at the Abolition of the Death Penalty, Dec. 15, 1989 (entered into force July 11, 1991), 1644 UNTS 414, reprinted in 29 *ILM* 1464 (1990) and 3 Weston and Carlson III.A.5; available also at http://untreaty.un.org/ENGLISH/bible/englishinternetbible/partI/ chapterIV/treaty24.asp

Protocol Additional (No. I) to the Geneva Conventions of August 12, 1949, and Relating to the Protection of Victims of International Armed Conflicts, June 8, 1977 (entered into force Dec. 7, 1978), 1125 UNTS 3, reprinted in 16 *ILM* 1391 (1977) and 2 Weston and Carlson II.B.20; available also at http://www.unhchr. ch/html/menu3/b/93.htm

Protocol Additional (No. II) to the Geneva Conventions of August 12, 1949, and Relating to the Protection of Victims of Non-International Armed Conflicts, June 8, 1977 (entered into force Dec. 7, 1978), 1125 UNTS 609, reprinted in 16 *ILM* 1442 (1977) and 2 Weston and Carlson II.B.21; available also at http://www.unhchr.ch/html/menu3/b/94.htm

Protocol Amending the European Social Charter, Oct. 21, 1991 (not in force as of May 1, 2006), ETS 142, reprinted in 31 *ILM* 155 (1992) and 3 Weston and Carlson III.B.15; available also at http://conventions. coe.int/treaty/en/treaties/html/142.htm

Protocol to the African Charter on Human and Peoples' Rights on the Establishment of the African Court on Human and Peoples' Rights, June 9, 1998 (entered into force Jan. 15, 2004) OAU/LEG/MIN/AFCHPR/PROT 1, rev.2 (1997), reprinted in 3 Weston and Carlson III.B.1a; available also at http://www.africa-union.org/Official_Documents/Treaties_%20Conventions_%20Protocols/africancourt-humanrights.pdf

Protocol to the American Convention on Human Rights to Abolish the Death Penalty, June 8, 1990 (in force among each state party depositing instrument of ratification), OASTS 73, reprinted in 29 *ILM* 1447 (1990) and 3 Weston and Carlson III.B.25a; available also at http://www.oas.org/main/main.asp?sLang=EandsLink=../../Documents/eng/Documents.asp

Protocol to the Convention Relating to the Status of Refugees, Jan. 31, 1967 (entered into force Oct. 4, 1967), 606 UNTS 267, reprinted in 6 *ILM* 78 (1967) and 3 Weston and Carlson III.G.8; available also at http://untreaty.un.org/ENGLISH/bible/englishinternetbible/partI/chapterV/treaty5.asp and http://www. unhchr.ch/html/menu3/b/o_p_ref.htm

Rio Declaration on Environment and Development, June 13, 1992, UN Doc. A/CONF.151/26 (vol I) (1992), reprinted in 31 *ILM* 874 (1992) and 5 Weston and Carlson V.B.16; available also at http://www.un.org/ Documents/ga/conf151/aconf15126-1annex1.htm

Rome Declaration on World Food Security and World Food Summit Plan of Action, adopted by the World Food Summit, Rome, Italy, Nov. 13–17, 1996, FAO, *Rome Declaration on World Food Security and World Food Summit Plan of Action* (Rome: FAO, 1996), reprinted in 3 Weston and Carlson III.N.3; available also at http://www.fao.org/wfs/index_en.htm

Rome Statute of the International Criminal Court, UN Doc. A/CONF.183/9, July 17, 1998 (entered into force July 1, 2002), reprinted in 37 *ILM* 199 (2004) and 3Weston and Carlson III.J.1; available also at http://www.un.org/law/icc/statute/romefra.htm

Slavery Convention, Sept. 25, 1926 (July 7, 1955), 60 LNTS 253, 212 UNTS 17 (consolidated with the 1953 Protocol), reprinted in 3 Weston and Carlson III.H.1; available also at http://untreaty.un.org/ENGLISH/ bible/englishinternetbible/partI/chapterXVIII/treaty2.asp and http://www.unhchr.ch/html/menu3/b/f2sc. htm

Statute of the International Tribunal (for the Prosecution of Persons Responsible for Serious Violations of Humanitarian Law Committed in the Territory of the Former Yugoslavia since 1991), May 3, 1993 (entered into force May 25, 1993), Annex to the *Secretary-General's Report on Aspects of Establishing an International Tribunal for the Prosecution of Persons Responsible for Serious Violations of Humanitarian Law Committed in the Territory of the Former Yugoslavia*, UN Doc. S/25704 (May 3, 1993), reprinted in 31 *ILM* 1159 and 2 Weston and Carlson II.E.10; available also at http://www.un.org/icty/basic/ statut/stat2000.htm

Stockholm Declaration of the United Nations Conference on the Human Environment, June 16, 1972, UN Doc. A/CONF.48/14/Rev.1 at 3 (1973), UN Doc. A/CONF.48/14 at 2–65 and Corr. 1 (1972), reprinted in 11 *ILM* 1416 (1972) and 5 Weston and Carlson V.B.3; available also at http://www.unep.org/Documents/Default.asp?DocumentID=97andArticleID=1503

Supplementary Convention on the Abolition of Slavery, the Slave Trade, and Institutions and Practices Similar to Slavery, Sept. 7, 1956 (entered into force Apr. 30, 1957), 266 UNTS 40, reprinted in 3 Weston and Carlson III.H.3; available also at http://untreaty.un.org/ENGLISH/ bible/english internetbible/partI/chapterXVIII/treaty4.asp and http://www.ohchr.org/english/law/slavetrade.htm

UNESCO Convention on Discrimination in Education, Dec. 14, 1960 (entered into force May 22, 1962), 429 UNTS 93, reprinted in 3 Weston and Carlson III.P.1; available also at http://www.unesco.org/ education/pdf/DISCRI_E.pdf

UNESCO Declaration of Bizkaia on the Right to the Environment, Feb. 12, 1999, UN Doc. 30C/INF.11; available also at http://unesDoc.unesco.org/images/0011/001173/117321e.pdf

UNESCO Declaration of the Principles of International Cultural Co-operation, Nov. 4, 1966, reprinted in 3 Weston and Carlson III.P.2; available also at http://portal.unesco.org/en/ev.php- URL_ID= 13147andURL_ DO=DO_TOPICandURL_SECTION= 201.html

UNESCO Director-General Declaration on the Human Right to Peace (UNESCO, Jan. 1, 1997), reprinted in 3 Weston-Carlson III.S.3; available also at http://unesDoc.unesco.org/images/0010/001055/105530e.pdf

United Nations Convention on Biological Diversity, June 5, 1992 (entered into force Dec. 29, 1993), 1760 UNTS 79, reprinted in 31 *ILM* 818 (1992) and 5 Weston and Carlson V.H.22; available also at http://www.biodiv.org/Doc/legal/cbd-en.pdf

United Nations Convention on the Nationality of Married Women, Feb. 27, 1957 (entered into force Aug. 11, 1959), 309 UNTS 65, reprinted in 3 Weston and Carlson III.C.10; available also at http://untreaty.un.org/ENGLISH/bible/englishinternetbible/partI/chapterXVI/treaty2.asp and http://www.unhchr.ch/html/menu3/b/78.htm

United Nations Convention on the Political Rights of Women, Mar. 31, 1953 (entered into force July 7, 1954), 139 UNTS 135, reprinted in 3 Weston and Carlson III.C.9; available also at http://untreaty.un.org/ENGLISH/bible/englishinternetbible/partI/chapterXVI/treaty1.asp and http://www.un.org/womenwatch/asp/user/list.asp?ParentID=10741

United Nations Draft Declaration on the Rights of Indigenous Peoples, UN Doc. E/CN.4/1995/2; E/CN.4/Sub.2/1994/56 (Oct. 28, 1994), reprinted in 34 *ILM* 541 (1995) and 3 Weston and Carlson III.F.4; available also at http://www.unhchr.ch/huriDocda/huriDoca.nsf/(Symbol)/E.CN.4.SUB.2.Res1994.45.En:OpenDocuments

United Nations Framework Convention on Climate Change, May 9, 1992 (entered into force Mar. 21, 1994), 1771 UNTS 107, reprinted in 31 *ILM* 849 (1992) and 5 Weston and Carlson V.E.19; available also at http://unfccc.int/files/essential_background/background_publications_html.pdf/application/pdf/conveng.pdf

United Nations General Assembly Code of Conduct for Law Enforcement Officials, Dec. 17, 1979, GA Res. 34/169 (Annex), UN GAOR, 34th Sess., Supp. No. 46, at 186, UN Doc. A/RES/34/169 (1993); available also at http://untreaty.un.org/ENGLISH/bible/englishinternetbible/partI/ chapterXXVII/treaty32.asp and http://www.unhchr.ch/html/menu3/b/h_comp42.htm

United Nations General Assembly Declaration of Basic Principles of Justice for Victims of Crime and Abuse of Power, Nov. 29, 1985: GA Res. 40/34, UN GAOR, 40th Sess., Supp. No. 53, at 213, UN Doc. A/40/53 (1986); available also at http://www.un.org/Depts/dhl/res/resa40.htm and http://www.unhchr. ch/html/ menu3/b/h_comp49.htm

United Nations General Assembly Declaration on Principles of International Law Concerning Friendly Relations and Co-operation among States in Accordance with the Charter of the United Nations, Oct. 24, 1970, GA Res. 2625, UN GAOR, 25th Sess., Supp. No. 28, at 121 UN Doc. A/8028 (1971), reprinted in 9 *ILM* 1292 (1970) and 1Weston and Carlson I.D.7; available also at http://www.un. org/Documents/ ga/res/25/ares25.htm

United Nations General Assembly Declaration on the Elimination of All Forms of Intolerance and of Discrimination Based on Religion or Belief, Nov. 25, 1981, GA Res. 36/55, UN GAOR, 36th Sess., Supp. No. 51, at 171, UN Doc. A/36/51 (1981), reprinted in 21 *ILM* 205 (1982) and 3 Weston and Carlson III.I.3; available also at http://www.un.org/Depts/dhl/res/resa36.htm and http://www.unhchr.ch/ html/menu3/ b/d_intole.htm

United Nations General Assembly Declaration on the Granting of Independence to Colonial Countries and Peoples, Dec. 14, 1960, GA Res. 1514, UN GAOR, 15th Sess., Supp. No. 16, at 66, UN Doc. A/4684 (1961), reprinted in 3 Weston and Carlson III.Q.2; available also at http://www.un. org/Documents/ ga/res/15/ares15.htm and http://www.unhchr.ch/html/menu3/b/c_coloni.htm

United Nations General Assembly Declaration on the Need to Ensure a Healthy Environment for the Well-being of Individuals, Dec. 14, 1990, GA Res. 45/94, UN GAOR, 45th Sess., Supp. No. 49A, at 178, UN Doc. A/45/749 (1990); available also at http://www.un.org/Depts/dhl/res/resa45.htm

United Nations General Assembly Declaration on the Preparation of Societies for Life in Peace, Dec. 15, 1978, GA Res. 33/73, UN GAOR, 33rd Sess., Supp. No. 45, at 55, UN Doc. A/33/45 (1978), reprinted in 3 Weston and Carlson III.S.1; available also at http://www.un.org/documents/ga/res/33/ares33.htm

United Nations General Assembly Declaration on the Protection of All Persons from Being Subjected to Torture and Other Cruel, Inhumane or Degrading Treatment or Punishment, Dec. 9, 1975, GA Res. 3452, UN GAOR, 30th Sess., Supp. No. 34, at 91, UN Doc. A/RES/10034 (1976); available also at http://www.un.org/documents/ga/res/30/ares30.htm and http://www.unhchr. ch/html/menu3/ b/h_comp 38.htm

United Nations General Assembly Declaration on the Right of Peoples to Peace, Nov. 12, 1984, GA Res. 39/11 (Annex), UN GAOR, 39th Sess., Supp. No. 51, at 22, UN Doc. A/39/51 (1985), reprinted in 3 Weston and Carlson III.S.2; available also at http://www.un.org/Depts/dhl/ res/resa39. htm and http://www.unhchr.ch/html/menu3/b/73.htm

United Nations General Assembly Declaration on the Right to Development, Dec. 4, 1986, GA Res. 41/128 (Annex), UN GAOR, 41st Sess., Supp. No. 53, at 186, UN Doc. A/41/53 (1987), reprinted in 3 Weston and Carlson III.R.2; available also at http://www.un.org/Depts/dhl/res/resa41.htm and http://www. unhchr.ch/html/menu3/b/74.htm

United Nations General Assembly Declaration on the Rights and Responsibilities of Individuals, Groups and Organs of Society to Promote and Protect Universally Recognized Human Rights and Fundamental Freedoms, Dec. 9, 1998, GA Res. 53/144, UN GAOR, 53rd Sess., Supp. No. 49, at 261, UN Doc.A/RES/53/144 (known unofficially as the UN Declaration on Human Rights), reprinted in 3 Weston and Carlson III.T.21; also available at http://www.un.org/Depts/dhl/resguide/ r53.htm

United Nations General Assembly Declaration on the Rights of Persons Belonging to National or Ethnic, Religious and Linguistic Minorities, Dec. 18, 1992, GA Res. 47/135, UN GAOR, 46th Sess., Supp. No. 49, at 210, UN Doc. A/RES/47/135 (1993), reprinted in 3 Weston and Carlson III.I.5; available also at http://www.un.org/Depts/dhl/res/resa46.htm and http://www.unhchr.ch/ html/ menu3/b/d_minori.htm

United Nations General Assembly Resolution on the Elimination of All Forms of Racial Discrimination, Nov. 10, 1975: GA Res. 3379, UN GAOR, 30th Sess., Supp. No. 34, at 83, UN Doc. A/30/83 (1975); available also at http://www.un.org/documents/ga/res/30/ares30.htm

United Nations General Assembly Resolution on the Prevention of Armed Conflict, July 3, 2003, GA Res. 57/337, UN GAOR, 57th Sess., Supp. No. 49, Vol. 3at 13, UN Doc. A/RES/57/337 (2003); available also at http://www.un.org/Depts/dhl/resguide/r57.htm

United Nations General Assembly Resolution on the Promotion of the Right of Peoples to Peace, Dec. 18, 2002, GA Res. 57/216, UN GAOR, 57th Sess., Supp. No. 49, Vol. 1 at 421, UN Doc. A/RES/57/216 (2002); available also at http://www.un.org/Depts/dhl/resguide/r57.htm

United Nations General Assembly Resolution on the United Nations Decade for Human Rights Education, Dec. 23, 1994, GA Res. 49/184, UN GAOR, 49th Sess., Supp. No. 49, at 202, UN Doc. A/RES/49/184 (1994); available also at http://www.un.org/Depts/dhl/res/resa49.htm

United Nations Millennium Declaration, Sept. 8, 2000, GA Res. 55/2, UN GAOR, 55th Sess., Supp. No. 49, at 4, UN Doc. A/55/49 (2000), reprinted in 3 Weston and Carlson III.U.4; available also at http://www.un. org/Depts/dhl/resguide/r55.htm

United Nations Security Council Resolution 955 (On Establishing the International Tribunal for Rwanda), Nov. 8, 1994, SC Res. 955, UN SCOR, 49th Sess., 3453d mtg., at 15, UN Doc. S/RES/955 (1994), reprinted in 33 *ILM* 1958 (1994) and 2 Weston and Carlson II.E.12; 33; available also at http://www.un.org/Docs/scres/1994/scres94.htm and http://www.un.org/ictr/statute.html

United Nations Standard Minimum Rules for the Treatment of Prisoners, Aug. 30, 1955, UN Doc. A/CONF/611(Annex I), ESC Res. 663C, 24 UN ESCOR Supp. No. 1, at 11, UN Doc. E/3048 (1957), amended ESC Res. 2076, 62 UN ESCOR Supp. No. 1, at 35, UN Doc. E/5988 (1977), reprinted in 3 Weston and Carlson III.M.1; available also at http://www.unhchr.ch/html/ menu3/b/h_comp34. htm

Universal Declaration of Human Rights, GA Res. 217A, UN GAOR, 3d Sess., Pt. I, Resolutions, at 71, UN Doc. A/810 (1948) (UDHR), reprinted in 3 Weston and Carlson III.A.1 and Documentary Appendix A; available also at http://www.un.org/documents/ga/res/3/ares3.htm and http://www. un.org/Overview/ rights.html

Universal Declaration on the Eradication of Hunger and Malnutrition, Nov. 16, 1974, UN Doc. E/CONF65/20, Ch. IV (1974), reprinted in 3 Weston and Carlson III.N.1; available also at http:// www.unhchr.ch/html/ menu3/b/69.htm

Universal Islamic Declaration of Human Rights, Sept., 19, 1981, 4 EHRR 433 (1982), reprinted in 3 Weston and Carlson III.B.26; available also at http://www.alhewar.com/ISLAMDECL.html

Vienna Declaration and Programme of Action (Vienna Declaration), adopted by the UN World Conference on Human Rights, June 25, 1993, UN Doc. A/CONF.157.24 (pt. I), (1993), at 20, reprinted in 32 *ILM* 1661 (1993) and 3 Weston and Carlson III.U.2; available also at http://www.unhchr. ch/huri Docda/huriDoca.nsf/(Symbol)/A.CONF.157.23.En

World Charter for Nature, Oct. 28, 1982, GA Res. 37/7 (Annex), UN GAOR, 37th Sess., Supp. No. 51, at 17, UN Doc. A/37/51 (1983), reprinted in 22 *ILM* 455 (1983) and 5 Weston and Carlson V.B.11; available also at http://www.un.org/Documents/ga/res/37/a37r007.htm

Select Bibliography

Adler, Emanuel and Beverly Crawford, eds. *Progress in Postwar International Relations*. New York: Columbia University Press, 1991.

Afkhami, Mahnaz and Haleh Vaziri. *Claiming Our Rights: A Manual for Women's Human Rights Education in Muslim Societies*. Bethesda, Md.: Sisterhood Is Global Institute, 1998.

Aga Khan, Sadruddin. *Study on Human Rights and Massive Exoduses*. New York: United Nations Commission on Human Rights, 38th Session, 1981.

Agamben, Giorgio. *Homo Sacer: Sovereign Power and Bare Life*. Trans. Daniel Heller-Roazen. Stanford, Calif.: Stanford University Press, 1998.

Agosín, Marjorie, ed. *Women, Gender, and Human Rights: A Global Perspective*. New Brunswick, N.J.: Rutgers University Press, 2001.

Ahed, George T. and Sanjeev Gupta, eds. *Governance, Corruption, and Economic Performance*. Washington, D.C.: International Monetary Fund, 2002.

Aikio, Pekka and Martin Scheinin, eds. *Operationalizing the Right of Indigenous Peoples to Self-Determination*. Turku/Åbo: Åbo Akademi University Institute for Human Rights, 2000.

Alston, Philip, ed. *The United Nations and Human Rights: A Critical Appraisal*. Oxford: Clarendon Press; New York: Oxford University Press, 1992.

Alston, Philip and Katarina Tomaševski, eds. *The Right to Food*. The Hague: Nijhoff, 1984.

Amnesty International. *Codes of Professional Ethics*. 2nd ed. New York: Amnesty International USA, 1984.

———. *Disappearances: A Workbook*. New York: Amnesty International, 1981.

———. *Human Rights: Is It Any of Your Business?* London: Amnesty International UK, 2000.

———. *Reasonable Fear: United States Refugee Policy*. New York: Amnesty International USA, 1990.

An-Na`im, Abdullahi Ahmed, ed. *Human Rights in Cross Cultural Perspectives: A Quest for Consensus*. Philadelphia: University of Pennsylvania Press, 1991.

———. *Human Rights Under African Constitutions: Realizing the Promise for Ourselves*. Philadelphia: University of Pennsylvania Press, 2003.

An-Na'im, Abdullahi and Francis M. Deng, eds. *Human Rights in Africa: Cross Cultural Perspectives*. Washington, D.C.: Brookings Institution, 1990.

Anderson, Benedict R. *Imagined Communities: Reflections on the Origin and Spread of Nationalism*. London: Verso, 1991.

Andreopolous, George J., ed., *Genocide: Conceptual and Historical Dimensions*. Philadelphia: University of Pennsylvania Press, 1994.

Andreopolous, George J. and Richard Pierre Claude, eds. *Human Rights Education for the Twenty-First Century*. Philadelphia: University of Pennsylvania Press, 1997.

Annas, George J. and Michael A. Grodin, eds. *The Nazi Doctors and the Nuremberg Code: Human Rights in Human Experimentation*. New York: Oxford University Press, 1992.

Arat, Zehra F. *Democracy and Human Rights in Developing Countries*. Boulder, Colo.: Lynne Rienner, 1991.

Archibugi, Daniele and David Held and Martin Kohler, eds. *Re-Imagining Political Community: Studies in Cosmopolitan Democracy*. Stanford, Calif.: Stanford University Press, 1998.

Askin, Kelly D. and Dorean M. Koenig, eds. *Women and International Human Rights Law*. 3 vols. Ardsley, N.Y.: Transnational Publishers, 1999.

Ashworth, Lucian M. and David Long, eds. *New Perspectives on International Functionalism*. New York: St. Martin's Press, 1999.

Australian Branch of the International Law Association. *The International Status of Human Rights Non-governmental Organizations*. Sidney: Butterworths, 1978.

Bailey, Peter. *Human Rights: Australia in an International Context*. Sydney: Butterworths, 1990.

Ball, Patrick, Paul Kobrak, and Herbert F. Spirer. *State Violence in Guatemala, 1960–1996: A Quantitative Reflection*. Washington, D.C.: American Association for the Advancement of Science, 1999.

Banks, Russell. *Continental Drift*. New York: Harper and Row, 1985.

Barker, Charles A., ed. *Power and Law: American Dilemma in World Affairs*. Baltimore: Johns Hopkins University Press, 1971.

Barnard, Catherine, Simon Deakin, and Gillian S. Morris, eds. *The Future of Labour Law*. Oxford: Hart, 2004.

Barnett, Michael. *Eyewitness to Genocide: The UN and Rwanda*. Ithaca, N.Y.: Cornell University Press, 2002.

Barnett, Michael and Martha Finnemore. *Rules for the World: International Organizations in Global Politics*. Ithaca, N.Y.: Cornell University Press, 2004.

Barnhizer, David, ed. *Effective Strategies for Protecting Human Rights*. Burlington, Vt.: Ashgate-Dartmouth, 2001.

Bassiouni, M. Cherif. *Crimes Against Humanity in International Criminal Law*. Dordrecht: Nijhoff, 1992.

————, ed. *The Law of Dissent and Riots*. Springfield, Ill.: Thomas, 1971.

Bauer, Joanne R. and Daniel A. Bell. *The East Asia Challenge for Human Rights*. Cambridge: Cambridge University Press, 1999.

Baxi, Upendra. *Mambrino's Helmet? Human Rights for a Changing World*. Delhi: Har Anand, 1994.

Bayefsky, Anne F. *How to Complain to the UN Human Rights Treaty System*. Ardsley, N.Y.: Transnational Publishers, 2002.

————. *The UN Human Rights Treaty System: Universality at the Crossroads*. Ardsley, N.Y.: Transaction Publishers, 2001.

Beaglehole, Robert, ed. *Global Public Health: A New Era*. Oxford: Oxford University Press, 2003

Beigbeder, Yves. *International Public Health: Patients' Rights vs. the Protection of Patents*. Aldershot: Ashgate, 2004.

Bennett, Gordon. *Aboriginal Rights in International Law*. London: Royal Anthropological Institute of Great Britain and Ireland, Survival International, 1978.

Berting, Jan et al., eds. *Human Rights in a Pluralist World: Individuals and Collectivities*. Westport, Conn.: Meckler, 1990.

Birnie, Patricia W. and Alan E. Boyle, eds. *Basic Documents on International Law and the Environment*. Oxford: Clarendon Press, 1995.

————. *International Law and the Environment*. New York: Oxford University Press, 1992.

Blaustein, Albert P., Roger S. Clark, and Jay A. Sigler, eds. *Human Rights Sourcebook*. New York: Paragon House, 1987.

Bloed, Arie and Pieter Van Dijk, eds. *Essays on Human Rights in the Helsinki Process*. Boston/Dordtrecht/London: Nijhoff, 1985.

Boutros-Ghali, Boutros. *An Agenda for Peace: Preventive Diplomacy, Peacemaking, and Peace-Keeping*. New York: United Nations, 1992.

Boyle, Alan E. and Michael R. Anderson, eds. *Human Rights Approaches to Environmental Protection*. Oxford: Clarendon Press, 1996.

Boyle, Kevin. *Article 19 World Report 1991: Information, Freedom, and Censorship*. New York: Times Books, 1991.

Breum, Martin and Art Hendriks, eds. *AIDS and Human Rights: An International Perspective*. Copenhagen: Akademisk Forlag, 1988.

British Medical Association. *The Medical Profession and Human Rights: Handbook for a Changing Agenda*. London: Zed Books with the BMA, 2001.

Broomhall, Bruce. *International Justice and the International Criminal Court: Between Sovereignty and the Rule of Law*. New York: Oxford University Press, 2004.

Brosted, Jens, ed. *Native Powers: The Quest for Autonomy and Nationhood of Indigenous Peoples*. Bergen: Universitetsforlegt, 1985.

Brown, Edith Weiss. *In Fairness to Future Generations: International Law, Common Patrimony and Inter-generational Equity*. Dobbs Ferry, N.Y.: Transnational Publishers, 1988.

Brown, Michael E., ed. *Grave New World: Security Challenges in the 21st Century*. Washington, D.C.: Georgetown University Press, 2003.

Brown, Peter and Douglas MacLean, eds. *Human Rights and U.S. Foreign Policy: Principles and Applications.* Lexington, Mass.: Lexington Books, 1979.

Brownlie, Ian, ed. *Basic Documents on Human Rights.* 2nd ed. New York: Oxford University Press, 1981.

Brysk, Alison, ed. *Globalization and Human Rights.* Berkeley: University of California Press, 2002.

Brzezinski, Zbigniew. *The Choice: Global Domination or Global Leadership.* New York: Basic Books, 2004.

B'Tselem. *Not All It Seems.* Jerusalem: Israeli Information Center for Human Rights in the Occupied Territories, Information Sheet, June 2004.

Buergenthal, Thomas A. *International Human Rights.* St. Paul, Minn.: West, 1988.

Buergenthal, Thomas A., ed., with Judith R. Hall. *Human Rights, International Law, and the Helsinki Accord.* Montclair, N.J.: Allanheld Osmun/Universe, 1977.

Buergenthal, Thomas A., Robert Norris, and Dinah Shelton. *Protecting Human Rights in the Americas.* 2nd ed. Keil, Germany; Arlington, Va.: Engel, 1986.

Campbell, Tom et al., eds. *Human Rights: From Rhetoric to Reality.* New York: Blackwell, 1986.

Cançado Trindade, Antônio Augusto et al., eds. *Derechos humanos, desarrollo sustentable y medio ambiente / Human Rights, Sustainable Development and Environment.* 2nd ed. San José: Instituto Interamericano de Derechos Humanos: Banco Interamericano de Desarrollo, 1995.

Caplan, A. L., ed. *When Medicine Went Bad: Bioethics and the Holocaust.* Totowa, N.J.: Humana, 1992.

Caporoso, James A., ed. *Continuity and Change in the Westphalian Order.* Malden, Mass.: Blackwell, 2000.

Carey, Henry F. and Oliver P. Richmond, eds. *Mitigating Conflict: The Role of NGOs.* Portland: Frank Cass, 2003.

Carlson, Jonathan C., Sir Geoffrey R.W. Palmer, and Burns H. Weston, eds. *International Environmental Law and World Order: A Problem-Oriented Coursebook.* 3rd ed. St. Paul, Minn.: West, 2006.

Cassese, Antonio, ed. *The Current Legal Regulation of the Use of Force.* Dordrecht: Nijhoff, 1986.

———. *Human Rights in a Changing World.* Cambridge: Polity Press, 1990.

———, ed. *UN Law/Fundamental Rights.* Alphen aan den Rijn: Sijthoff and Noordhoff, 1979.

Cassin, René. *La Pensée et l'action.* Paris: Centre National de la Recherche Scientifique, 1981.

Castberg, Frede. *The European Convention on Human Rights.* Dobbs Ferry, N.Y.: Oceana Publications, 1974.

Chan, Steve and James R. Scarritt. *Coping with Globalization: Cross-National Patterns in Domestic Governance and Policy Performance.* Portland: Frank Cass, 2002.

Chapin, Mac and William Threlkeld. *Indigenous Landscapes: A Study in Ethnocartography.* Alexandria, Va.: Center for the Support of Native Lands, 2001.

Chapman, Audrey R. and Sage Russell, eds. *Core Obligations: Building a Framework for Economic, Social and Cultural Rights.* Antwerp: Intersentia, 2002.

Charnovitz, Steve. *Trade Law and Global Governance.* London: Cameron, 2002.

Chomsky, Noam. *The New Military Humanism: Lessons from Kosovo.* Monroe, Me.: Common Courage Press, 1999.

Chua, Amy. *World on Fire: How Exporting Free Market Democracy Breeds Ethnic Hatred and Global Instability.* New York: Anchor Books, 2004.

Chuter, David. *War Crimes: Confronting Atrocity in the Modern World.* Boulder: Lynne Rienner, 2003.

Cingranelli, David Louis, ed. *Human Rights and Measurement.* London: Macmillan, 1988.

Clark, Ann Marie. *Diplomacy of Conscience: Amnesty International and Changing Human Rights Norms.* Princeton, N.J.: Princeton University Press, 2001.

Clark, Ian. *Globalization and International Relations Theory.* Oxford: Oxford University Press, 1999.

Claude, Richard Pierre. *The Bells of Freedom—With Resource Materials for Facilitators of Non-Formal Education and 24 Human Rights Echo Sessions.* Addis Ababa: Action Professionals Association for the People, 1996.

———. *Educating for Human Rights: The Philippines and Beyond.* Quezon City: University of the Philippines Press, 1996.

———. *Popular Education for Human Rights: 24 Participatory Exercises for Facilitators and Teachers.* Cambridge, Mass.: Human Rights Education Associates, 2001.

———. *Science in the Service of Human Rights.* Philadelphia: University of Pennsylvania Press, 2002.

Cohen, Stanley. *States of Denial: Knowing About Atrocities and Suffering.* Cambridge: Polity Press, 2001.

Commission to Study the Organization of Peace. *Fundamentals of the International Organization, Fourth Report.* Vol. 4, *International Safeguard of Human Rights.* New York: the Commission, 1944.

———. *The United Nations and Human Rights.* 18th Report. Dobbs Ferry, N.Y.: Oceana, 1968.

Cook, Rebecca J., ed. *Human Rights of Women: National and International Perspectives.* Philadelphia: University of Pennsylvania Press, 1994.

Coomaraswamy, Radhika. *Reinventing International Law: Women's Rights as Human Rights in the International Community*. Cambridge, Mass.: Human Rights Program, Harvard Law School, 1997.

Cortright, David and George A. Lopez, eds. *Smart Sanctions: Targeting Economic Statecraft*. Lanham, Md.: Rowman and Littlefield, 2002.

Council on Foreign Relations 1980s Project. *Enhancing Global Human Rights*. New York: McGraw-Hill, 1979.

Cowan, Jane K., Marie-Bénédicte Dembour, and Richard A. Wilson, eds. *Culture and Rights: Anthropological Perspectives*. Cambridge: Cambridge University Press, 2001.

Coyle, Andrew, Allison Campbell, and Rodney Neufeld. *Capitalist Punishment: Prison Privatization and Human Rights*. London: Zed Books, 2003.

Crahan, Margaret E., ed. *Human Rights and Basic Needs in the Americas*. Washington, D.C.: Georgetown University Press, 1982.

Cranston, Maurice. *What Are Human Rights?* London: Bodley Head, 1973.

Crawford, James, ed. *The Rights of Peoples*. Oxford: Clarendon Press, 1992.

Cristescu, Alfredo. *The Right to Self-Determination*. New York: United Nations, 1981.

Danieli, Yael, Elsa Stamatopoulou, and Clarence J. Dias, eds. *The Universal Declaration of Human Rights: Fifty Years and Beyond*. Amityville, N.Y.: Baywood, 1999.

Danner, Mark. *Torture and Truth: America, Abu Ghraib, and the War on Terror*. New York: New York Review of Books, 2004.

Davis, Michael C., Wolfgang Dietrich, Bettina Scholdan, and Dieter Sepp, eds. *International Intervention in the Post-Cold War World: Moral Responsibility and Power Politics* Armonk, N.Y.: M.E. Sharpe, 2004.

DeGeorge, Richard T., ed. *Ethics and Society: Original Essays on Contemporary Moral Problems*. New York: Doubleday, 1966.

De Greiff, Pablo and Ciaran Cronin, eds. *Global Justice and Transnational Politics*. Cambridge, Mass.: MIT Press, 2002.

de Soto, Hernando. *The Mystery of Capital*. Twenty-First Morgenthau Memorial Lecture on Ethics and Foreign Policy. New York: Carnegie Council on Ethics and World Affairs, 2002.

de Varennes, Fernand. *Asia-Pacific Human Rights Documents and Resources*. Boston: Nijhoff, 2000.

Delissen, Astrid J. M. and Gerard J. Tanja, eds. *Humanitarian Law of Armed Conflict: Challenges Ahead, Essays in Honour of Frits Kalshaven*. Dordrecht: Nijhoff, 1991.

Dershowitz, Alan. *Rights from Wrongs: The Origin of Human Rights in the Experience of Injustice*. New York: Basic Books, 2004.

Detter de Lupis, Ingrid. *The Laws of War*. Cambridge: Cambridge University Press, 1987.

Donnelly, Jack. *Human Rights and World Politics*. Boulder, Colo.: Westview Press, 1991.

———. *Universal Human Rights*. 2nd ed. Ithaca, N.Y.: Cornell University Press, 2002.

Douzinas, Costa. *The End of Human Rights: Critical Legal Thought at the Turn of the Century*. Oxford: Hart, 2000.

Downing, Theodore E. and Gilbert Kushner with Human Rights Internet, eds. *Human Rights and Anthropology*. Cambridge, Mass.: Cultural Survival, 1988.

Drinan, Robert J., S.J. *The Mobilization of Shame: A World View of Human Rights*. New Haven, Conn.: Yale University Press, 2001.

Du Bois, W. E. B. *Color and Democracy: Colonies and Peace*. 1945. Intro Herbert Aptheker. Millwood, N.Y.: Kraus, 1975.

Dunér, Bertil. *The Global Human Rights Regime*. Lund: Studentlitterature, 2002.

Dunne, Tim and Nicholas J. Wheeler, eds. *Human Rights in Global Politics*. Cambridge: Cambridge University Press, 1999.

Dupuy, René-Jean, ed. *The Right to Development at the International Level*. Alphen aan den Rijn: Sijthoff & Noordhoff, 1980.

Dworkin, Ronald. *Taking Rights Seriously*. London: Duckworth, 1977.

Dwyer, Kevin. *Arab Voices: The Human Rights Debate in the Middle East*. Berkeley: University of California Press, 1991.

Eckersley, Richard, Jane Dixon, and Bob Douglas, eds. *The Social Origins of Health and Well-Being*. Cambridge: Cambridge University Press, 2001.

Edkins, Jenny. *Whose Hunger? Concepts of Famine, Practices of Aid*. Minneapolis: University of Minnesota Press, 2000.

Edwards, Michael. *Future Positive: International Co-operation in the 21st Century*. London: Earthscan, 1999.

Ehrenreich, Barbara and Arlie Russell Hochschild. *Global Woman: Nannies, Maids, and Sex Workers in the New Economy*. New York: Metropolitan, 2003.

Eide, Asbjørn. *Peaceful and Constructive Resolution of Situations Involving Minorities*. Oslo: Norwegian Institute of Human Rights, 1994.

Eide, Asbjørn, Catarina Krause, and Allan Rosas, eds. *Economic Social, and Cultural Rights*. 2nd rev. ed. Dordrecht: Nijhoff, 2001.

Eide, Asbjørn et al., eds. *Food as a Human Right*. Tokyo: United Nations University Press, 1984.

Ehrenreich, Barbara and Arlie Russell Hochschild. *Global Woman: Nannies, Maids, and Sex Workers in the New Economy*. New York: Metropolitan, 2003.

Elbert, Frank, ed. *Human Rights Education Resource Book*. Cambridge: Human Rights Education Associates, 2000.

A Fair Globalization Creating Opportunities for All. Report of the World Commission on the Social Dimension of Globalization. Geneva: International Labour Organization, 2004.

Falk, Richard A. *The Declining World Order: America's Imperial Geopolitics*. New York : Routledge, 2004.

———. *The Great Terror War*. New York: Olive Branch Press, 2002.

———. *Human Rights and State Sovereignty*. New York: Holmes and Meier, 1981.

———. *Human Rights Horizons: The Pursuit of Justice in a Globalizing World*. New York: Routledge, 2000.

———. *On Humane Governance: Toward a New Global Politics—The World Order Models Project of the Global Civilization Initiative*. University Park: Pennsylvania State University Press, 1995.

———. *Predatory Globalization: A Critique*. Cambridge: Polity Press, 1999.

———. *The Role of Domestic Courts in the International Legal Order*. Syracuse, N.Y.: Syracuse University Press, 1964.

Falk, Richard A., Samuel S. Kim, and Saul H. Mendlovitz, eds. *The United Nations and a Just World Order*. Boulder, Colo.: Westview Press, 1991.

FAO. *Declaration of the World Food Summit: Five Years Later*. Rome: FAO, 2002.

———. *Explanatory Notes/Reservation to the Declaration of the World Food Summit: Five Years Later*. Rome: FAO, 2002.

Farer, Tom J., ed. *Toward a Humanitarian Diplomacy: A Primer for Policy*. New York: New York University Press, 1980.

Fawcett, James E. S. *The Application of the European Convention on Human Rights*. Oxford: Clarendon Press, 1969.

Fein, Helen. *Accounting for Genocide: National Responses and Jewish Victimization During the Holocaust*. New York: Free Press, 1979.

Fields, A. Belden. *Rethinking Human Rights for the New Millennium*. New York: Palgrave Macmillan, 2003.

Fink, Sheri, M.D. *War Hospital: A True Story of Surgery and Survival*. New York: Public Affairs, 2003.

Finnemore, Martha. *The Purpose of Intervention: Changing Beliefs About the Use of Force*. Ithaca, N.Y.: Cornell University Press, 2003.

Fitzgerald, Ross, ed. *Human Needs and Politics*. Rushcutters Bay, NSW: Pergamon Press, 1977.

Flaherty, David I. *Protecting Privacy in Surveillance Societies*. Chapel Hill: University of North Carolina Press, 1989.

Flanagan, Robert J. and William B. Gould, IV, eds. *International Labor Standards: Globalization, Trade, and Public Policy*. Stanford, Calif.: Stanford University Press, 2003.

Flanz, G. H. *Comparative Women's Rights and Political Participation in Europe*. Dobbs Ferry, N.Y.: Transnational Publishers, 1983.

Fogel, Robert William. *The Escape from Hunger and Premature Death, 1700–2100: Europe, America, and the Third World*. New York: Cambridge University Press, 2004.

Forsythe, David P., ed. *Human Rights and Development: International Views*. London: Macmillan, 1989.

———. *Human Rights and Peace: International and National Dimensions*. Lincoln: University of Nebraska Press, 1993.

———. *Human Rights and World Politics*. 2nd ed. Lincoln: University of Nebraska Press, 1988.

———. *Human Rights in International Relations*. New York: Cambridge University Press, 2000.

———. *The Humanitarians: The International Committee of the Red Cross*. Cambridge: Cambridge University Press, 2005.

Fowler, Michael Ross. *Thinking About Human Rights: Contending Approaches to Human Rights in U.S. Foreign Policy*. Lanham, Md.: University Press of America, 1987.

Franck, Thomas M. *Human Rights in the Third World*. 3 vols. Dobbs Ferry, N.Y.: Oceana Publishers, 1982.

———. *The Power of Legitimacy Among Nations*. New York: Oxford University Press, 1990.

Frazer, Nancy. *Justice Interruptus: Critical Reflections on the "Postsocialist" Condition*. New York: Routledge, 1997.

Freeman, Michael. *Human Rights: An Interdisciplinary Approach*. Cambridge: Polity Press, 2002.

Freire, Paulo. *Pedagogy of the Oppressed*. New York: Seabury Press, 1973.

Friedman, Lawrence M. *The Republic of Choice: Law, Authority, and Culture*. Cambridge, Mass.: Harvard University Press, 1990.

Frynas, Jedrzej George and Scott Pegg, eds. *Transnational Corporations and Human Rights*. New York: Palgrave Macmillan, 2003.

Galtung, Johan. *Human Needs as the Focus of the Social Sciences*. Oslo: University of Oslo Press, 1977.

———. *Human Rights in Another Key*. Cambridge: Polity Press, 1994.

Galtung, Johan and R. G. Cant, eds. *Indicators of Social and Economic Change and Their Applications*. Reports and Papers in Social Science 37. Paris: UNESCO, 1976.

Gardam, Judith, ed. *Humanitarian Law*. Aldershot: Ashgate, 1999.

Gearon, Liam, ed. *Human Rights and Religion*. Brighton: Sussex Academic Press, 2002.

Giddens, Anthony. *Runaway World: How Globalization Is Reshaping Our Lives*. New York: Rouledge, 2003.

Gilligan, Carol. *In a Different Voice: Psychological Theory and Women's Development*. Cambridge, Mass.: Harvard University Press, 1982.

Glendon, Mary Ann. *A World Made New: Eleanor Roosevelt and the Universal Declaration of Human Rights*. New York: Random House, 2001.

Glennon, Michael J. *Limits of Law, Prerogatives of Power: Interventionism After Kosovo*. New York: Palgrave, 2001.

Glover, Jonathan. *Humanity: A Moral History of the Twentieth Century*. New Haven, Conn,: Yale University Press, 1999.

Gould, Carol C. *Globalizing and Democracy and Human Rights*. Cambridge: Cambridge University Press, 2004.

Gray, Ian and Moira Stanley. *A Punishment in Search of a Crime: Americans Speak Out Against the Death Penalty*. New York: Avon for Amnesty International USA, 1990.

Grimshaw, Katie Holmes and Marilyn Lake, eds. *Women's Rights and Human Rights: International Historical Perspectives*. New York: Palgrave, 2001.

Gross, James A. *Workers' Rights as Human Rights*. Ithaca, N.Y.: Cornell University Press, 2003.

Gross National Happiness: Discussion Papers. Thimphu, Bhutan: Centre for Bhutan Studies, 1999.

Gupta, Sanjeev, Mark Plant, Benedict Clements, Thomas Dorsey, Emanuele Baldacci, Gabriela Inchauste, Shamsuddin Tareq, and Nita Thacker. *Is the PRGF Living Up to Expectations? An Assessment of Program Design*. Occasional Paper 216. Washington, D.C.: International Monetary Fund, September 2002.

Gurr, Ted Robert. *Why Men Rebel*. Princeton, N.J.: Princeton University Press for Center of International Studies, 1970.

Gutman, Roy and David Rieff, eds., Kenneth Anderson, legal ed. *Crimes of War: What the Public Should Know*. New York: W.W. Norton, 1999.

Gutmann, Amy, ed. *Multiculturalism and the "Politics of Recognition"*. Princeton, N.J.: Princeton University Press, 1992.

Haas, Ernest B. *Human Rights and International Action: The Case of Freedom of Association*. Stanford, Calif.: Stanford University Press, 1970.

Hamilton, Charles V. *Beyond Racism: Race and Inequality for Brazil, South Africa and the United States*. Boulder, Colo.: Lynne Reinner, 2001.

Hanna, Susan, Carl Folke, and Karl-Göran Möle, eds. *Rights to Nature: Ecological, Economic, Cultural, and Political Principles of Institutions for the Environment*. Washington, D.C.: Island Press, for Beijer International Institute of Ecological Economics, Royal Swedish Academy of Sciences, 1996.

Hannum, Hurst. *Autonomy, Sovereignty, and Self-Determination: The Accommodation of Conflicting Rights*. Philadelphia: University of Pennsylvania Press, 1989.

———, ed. *Guide to International Human Rights Practice*. 4th ed. Ardsley, N.Y.: Transnational Publishers, 2004.

Hannum, Hurst and Dana D. Fischer, eds. *U.S. Ratification of the International Covenants on Human Rights*. Washington, D.C.: American Society of International Law, 1993.

Harff, Barbara and T. R. Gurr. *Ethnic Conflict in World Politics*. 2nd ed. Boulder, Colo.: Westview Press, 2004.

Harris, David J. and Stephen Livingstone. *The Inter-American System of Human Rights*. Oxford: Clarendon Press, 1998.

Hart, Vivien. *Democratic Constitution-Making*. Special Report 103. Washington, D.C.: United States Institute of Peace, 2003.

Hashimoto, Hidetoshi. *The Prospects for a Regional Human Rights Mechanism in East Asia*. New York: Routledge, 2004.

Havel, Václav. *The Power of the Powerless: Citizens Against the State in Central-Eastern Europe*. Armonk, N.Y.: M.E. Sharpe, 1985.

Hazon, Winnie. *The Social and Legal Status of Women: A Global Perspective*. Westport, Conn.: Greenwood Press, 1990.

Hegarty, Angela and Siobhan Leonard, eds. *Human Rights: An Agenda for the 21st Century*. London: Cavendish, 1999.

Heijder, Alfred and Herman Van Geuns, eds. *Professional Codes of Ethics*. London: Amnesty International, 1976.

Held, David, ed. *A Globalizing World? Culture, Economics, Politics*. London: Routledge in association with the Open University, 2000.

Henkin, Alice, ed. *Honoring Human Rights and Keeping the Peace: The Peace Lessons from El Salvador, Cambodia, and Haiti; Recommendations for the United Nations*. New York: Aspen Institute, 1995.

Henkin, Louis. *The Age of Rights*. New York: Columbia University Press, 1990.

———. *How Nations Behave*. 2nd ed. New York: Praeger, 1979.

———, ed. *The International Bill of Rights: The Covenant on Civil and Political Rights*. New York: Columbia University Press, 1981.

———. *The Rights of Man Today*. Boulder, Colo.: Westview Press, 1980.

Henkin, Louis and John Lawrence Hargrove, eds. *Human Rights: An Agenda for the Next Century*. Washington, D.C.: American Society of International Law, 1994.

Hennelly, Alfred and John Langan. *Human Rights in the Americas: The Struggle for Consensus*. Washington, D.C.: Georgetown University Press, 1982.

Henrad, Kristin. *Minority Protection in Post-Apartheid South Africa: Human Rights, Minority Rights and Self Determination*. Westport, Conn.: Praeger, 2002.

Hesse, Carla and Robert Post, eds. *Human Rights in Political Transitions: Gettysburg to Bosnia*. Cambridge, Mass.: Zone Books, MIT Press, 1999.

Hevener, Natalie Kaufman. *International Law and the Status of Women*. Boulder, Colo.: Westview Press, 1983.

Hick, Steven, Edward F. Halpin, and Eric Hoskins, eds. *Human Rights and the Internet*. New York: St. Martin's Press, 2000.

Higgins, Roslyn. *Problems and Process: International Law and How We Use It*. Oxford: Clarendon Press, 1994.

Hixon, Richard F. *Privacy in a Public Society: Human Rights in Conflict*. New York: Oxford University Press, 1989.

Hollenbach, David, S.J. *The Global Face of Public Faith: Politics, Human Rights, and Christian Ethics*. Washington, D.C.: Georgetown University Press, 2003.

Holzgrefe, J. L. and Robert O. Keohane, eds. *Humanitarian Intervention: Ethical, Legal and Political Dilemmas*. Cambridge: Cambridge University Press, 2003.

Hopkins, Jeffrey, ed. *The Art of Peace: Nobel Peace Laureates Discuss Human Rights, Conflict, and Reconciliation*. New York: Snow Lion, 2000.

Horowitz, Shale and Albrecht Schnabel, eds. *Human Rights and Societies in Transition: Causes, Consequences, Responses*. New York: United Nations University Press, 2004.

Howard, Bradley Reed. *Indigenous Peoples and the State: The Struggle for Native Rights*. De Kalb: Northern Illinois University Press, 2003.

Howard, Michael, George J. Andreopoulos, and Mark R. Shulman, eds. *The Laws of War: Constraints on Warfare in the Western World*. New Haven, Conn.: Yale University Press, 1994.

Howard-Hassmann, Rhoda E. *Human Rights and the Search for Community*. Boulder, Colo.: Westview Press, 1995.

Hovden, Eivind and Edward Keene, eds. *The Globalism of Liberalism*. New York: Palgrave, 2002.

Human Rights Watch. *Criminal Injustice: Violence Against Women in Brazil*. New York: Human Rights Watch, 1991.

———. *Toxic Justice: Human Rights and Toxic Waste in Cambodia*. New York: Human Rights Watch, 1999.

Hutchinson, John F. *Champions of Charity: War and the Rise of the Red Cross*. Boulder, Colo.: Westview Press, 1996.

Ignatieff, Michael. *The Lesser Evil: Political Ethics in an Age of Terror*. Princeton, N.J.: Princeton University Press, 2004.

Independent International Commission on Kosovo. *The Kosovo Report: Conflict, International Response, Lessons Learned*. Oxford: Oxford University Press, 2000.

Institut International des Droits de l'Homme. *Commerce mondial et protection des droits de l'homme/World Trade and the Protection of Human Rights*. Bruxelles: Bruylant, 2001.

International Commission of Jurists. *Development, Human Rights and the Rule of Law*. Oxford: Pergamon Press, 1981.

International Commission on Intervention and State Sovereignty. *The Responsibility to Protect*. Ottawa: International Development Research Centre, 2001.

International Institute of Human Rights. *Universality of Human Rights in a Pluralistic World: Proceedings of the Colloquy Organized by the Council of Europe in Co-operation with the International Institute of Human Rights, Strasbourg, 17–19 April 1989*. Arlington Va.: N.P. Engel, 1990.

International Law Association. *Report of the Fifty-Third Conference Held at Buenos Aires, August 25th to August 31st, 1968*. London: the Association, 1969.

Irvine of Lairg, Alexander, Baron. *Human Rights, Constitutional Law and the Development of the English Legal System*. Oxford: Hart, 2003.

Ishay, Micheline R. *The History of Human Rights: From Ancient Times to the Era of Globalization*. Berkeley: University of California Press, 2004.

Jabine, Thomas B. and Richard P. Claude, eds. *Human Rights and Statistics: Getting the Record Straight*. Philadelphia: University of Pennsylvania Press, 1992.

Jacobs, Francis G. *The European Convention on Human Rights*. Oxford: Oxford University Press, 1975.

Janis, Mark W. and Richard S. Kay, eds. *European Human Rights Law*. Hartford: University of Connecticut Law School Foundation Press, 1990.

Jefferson, Thomas. *Writings of Thomas Jefferson*. Ed. Paul Leicester Ford. 10 vols. New York: Putnam, 1892–99.

Jones, Dorothy V. *Toward a Just World: The Critical Years in the Search for International Justice*. Chicago: University of Chicago Press, 2002.

Joyce, Christopher and Eric Stover. *Witnesses from the Grave: The Stories Bones Tell*. Boston: Little Brown, 1991.

Joyce, James Avery. *The New Politics of Human Rights*. New York: St. Martin's Press, 1978.

Juviler, Peter, ed. *Religion and Human Rights: Competing Claims?* Armonk, N.Y.: M.E. Sharpe, 1998.

Kahn, Paul W. *American Exceptionalism and Human Rights*. Princeton, N.J.: Princeton University Press, 2005.

Kallen, Evelyn. *Label Me Human: Minority Rights of Stigmatized Canadians*. Toronto: University of Toronto Press, 1989.

Karis, Thomas and Gwendolen Carter, eds. *From Protest to Challenge: A Documentary History of African Politics in South Africa, 1882–1990*. 4 vols. Stanford, Calif.: Hoover Institution Press, 1977.

Kavass, Igor I., Jacqueline Paquin Granier, and Mary Frances Dominick, eds. *Human Rights, European Politics, and the Helsinki Accord: The Documentary Evolution of the Conference on Security and Cooperation in Europe, 1973–1975*. 3 vols. Buffalo, N.Y.: Hein, 1981.

Kawachi, Ichiro and Bruce Kennedy. *The Health of Nations: Why Inequality Is Harmful to Your Health*. New York: New Press, 2002.

Keck, Margaret E. and Kathryn Sikkink. *Activists Beyond Borders: Advocacy Networks in International Politics*. Ithaca, N.Y.: Cornell University Press, 1998.

Kennedy, David. *The Dark Side of Virtue: Reassessing International Humanitarianism*. Princeton, N.J.: Princeton University Press, 2004.

——. *International Legal Structures*. Baden-Baden: Nomos, 1987.

Kennedy, Kerry with Eddie Adams, ed. Nan Richardson. *Speak Truth to Power: Human Rights Defenders Who Are Changing Our World*. New York: Crown Books, 2004.

Kent, Edward, ed. *Revolution and the Rule of Law*. Englewood Cliffs, N.J.: Prentice-Hall, 1971.

Kent, George. *Freedom from Want: The Human Right to Adequate Food*. Washington, D.C.: Georgetown University Press, 2005.

Keohane, Robert O. *Transnational Relations and World Politics*. Cambridge, Mass.: Harvard University Press, 1972.

Kim, Samuel S. *The Quest for a Just World Order*. Boulder, Colo.: Westview Press, 1984.

Kingfisher, Catherine, ed. *Western Welfare in Decline: Globalization and Women's Poverty*. Philadelphia: University of Pennsylvania Press, 2002.

Kiss, Alexandre and Dinah Shelton. *International Environmental Law.* Ardsley, N.Y.: Transnational Publishers, 1991.

Kommers, Donald P. and Gilburt D. Loescher, eds. *Human Rights and American Foreign Policy.* Notre Dame, Ind.: Notre Dame University Press, 1979.

Konvitz, Milton Ridvas. *Judaism and Human Rights.* New Brunswick, N.J.: Transaction Publications, 2001.

Korey, William. *NGOs and the Universal Declaration of Human Rights: "A Curious Grapevine".* New York: St. Martin's Press, 1998.

Korn, David. *Human Rights in Iraq.* New Haven, Conn.: Yale University Press for Middle East Watch, 1990.

Kramer, Daniel C. *Comparative Civil Rights and Liberties.* Lanham, Md.: University Press of America, 1982.

Kritz, Meil J., ed. *Transitional Justice: How Emerging Democracies Reckon with Former Regimes.* 3 vols. Washington, D.C.: United States Institute of Peace Press, 1995.

Kunnie, Julian. *Is Apartheid Really Dead? Pan-Africanist Working-Class Cultural Critical Perspectives.* Boulder, Colo.: Westview Press, 2000.

Kuper, Leo. *Genocide: Its Political Use in the Twentieth Century.* New Haven, Conn.: Yale University Press, 1981.

Landman, Todd. *Protecting Human Rights: A Comparative Study.* Washington, D.C.: Georgetown University Press, 2005.

Lahneman, William J., ed. *Military Intervention: Cases in Context for the Twenty-First Century.* Lanham, Md.: Rowman and Littlefield, 2004.

Lang, Anthony F., Jr. *Just Intervention.* Washington, D.C.: Georgetown University Press, 2003.

Laqueur, Walter and Barry Rubin, eds. *The Human Rights Reader.* Updated ed. New York: Penguin, 1990.

Larson, Egon. *The Flame in Barbed Wire: The Story of Amnesty International.* New York: Norton, 1979.

Lasswell, Harold D. and Abraham Kaplan, *Power and Society: A Framework for Political Inquiry.* New Haven, Conn.: Yale University Press, 1950.

Lauren, Paul Gordon. *The Evolution of International Human Rights: Visions Seen.* 2nd ed. Philadelphia: University of Pennsylvania Press, 2003.

Lauterpacht, Hersch. *International Law and Human Rights.* New York: Garland, 1973.

LeBlanc, L. T. *The OAS and the Promotion and Protection of Human Rights.* The Hague: Nijhoff, 1977.

Lemkin, Raphael. *Axis Rule in Occupied Europe.* Washington, D.C.: Carnegie Endowment for International Peace, 1944.

Lerner, Natan. *Group Rights and Discrimination in International Law.* Boston: Nijhoff, 1991.

———. *The UN Convention on the Elimination of All Forms of Racial Discrimination.* 2nd ed. Alphen aan den Rijn: Sijthoff and Nordhoff, 1980.

Lernoux, Penny. *Cry of the People: The Struggle for Human Rights in Latin America—The Catholic Church in Conflict with U.S. Policy.* New York: Penguin, 1988.

Levenstein, Aaron. *Escape to Freedom: The Story of the International Rescue Committee.* Westport, Conn.: Greenwood Press, 1983.

Levy, Leonard W., Kenneth L. Karst, and Adam Winkler, eds. *Encyclopedia of the American Constitution.* 6 vols. 2nd ed. New York: Macmillan, 2000.

Liang-Fenton, Debra, ed. *Implementing U.S. Human Rights Policy: Agendas, Policies, and Practices.* Washington, D.C.: United States Institute of Peace Press, 2004.

Lifton, Robert Jay and Eric Markusen. *The Genocidal Mentality: Nazi Holocaust and Nuclear Threat.* New York: Basic Books, 1990.

Lillich, Richard B. *The Human Rights of Aliens in Contemporary International Law.* Manchester: Manchester University Press, 1984.

———, ed. *U.S. Ratification of the Human Rights Treaties With or Without Reservations?* Charlottesville: University Press of Virginia, 1981.

Lincoln, Abraham. *Lincoln's Stories and Speeches.* Ed. Edward F. Allen. New York: New York Books, 1900.

Livezey, Lowell W. *Nongovernmental Organizations and the Ideas of Human Rights.* Princeton, N.J.: Princeton University Center of International Studies, 1989.

Luard, Evan. *Human Rights and Foreign Policy.* Oxford: Pergamon Press, 1981.

———, ed. *The International Protection of Human Rights.* New York: Praeger, 1967.

Lucarelli, Sonia. *Europe and the Breakup of Yugoslavia.* The Hague: Kluwer Law International, 2000.

———, ed. *The International Protection of Human Rights.* New York: Praeger, 1967.

Lutheran World Federation. *Theological Perspectives on Human Rights: Report of an LWF Consultation on Human Rights*. Geneva: Lutheran World Federation, 1977.

Lutz, Ellen L., Hurst Hannum, and Kathryn J. Burke, eds. *New Directions in Human Rights*. Philadelphia: University of Pennsylvania Press, 1989.

Lyons, Gene M. and James Mayall, eds. *International Human Rights in the 21st Century: Protecting the Rights of Groups*. Lanham, Md.: Rowman & Littlefield, 2003.

Macfarlane, L. T. *The Theory and Practice of Human Rights*. London: Temple Smith, 1985.

MacKinnon, Catherine. *Feminism Unmodified: Discourses on Life and Law*. Cambridge, Mass.: Harvard University Press, 1987.

Maddex, Robert L. *Constitutions of the World*. Washington, D.C.: Congressional Quarterly, 1995.

Madison, G. B. *The Political Economy of Civil Society and Human Rights*. New York: Routledge, 1998.

Mahoney, Kathleen A. and Paul Mahoney, eds. *Human Rights in the Twenty-First Century: A Global Challenge*. Dordrecht: Nijhoff, 1993.

Malik, Charles. *These Rights and Freedoms*. Lake Success, N.Y.: United Nations Department of Public Information, 1950.

Mann, Jonathan M., Sofia Gruskin, Michael A. Grodin, and George J. Annas, eds. *Health and Human Rights: A Reader*. New York: Routledge, 1999.

Maran, Rita. *Torture: The Role of Ideology in the French-Algerian War*. New York: Praeger, 1989.

Marcuse, Herbert. *Counterrevolution and Revolt*. Boston: Beacon Press, 1972.

Martin, J. Paul, Tania Bernath, Tracey Holland, and Loren Miller. *Human Rights Education for Peace Building: A Planning and Evaluation Handbook*. New York: Columbia University Center for the Study of Human Rights, 2003.

Massey, Douglas S. and Nancy A. Denton. *American Apartheid: Segregation and the Making of the Underclass*. Cambridge, Mass.: Harvard University Press, 1993.

Mastny, Vojtech and Jan Zielonka, eds. *Human Rights and Security: Europe on the Eve of a New Era*. Boulder, Colo.: Westview Press, 1991.

McCaffrey, Stephen C. and Robert E. Lutz, eds. *Environmental Pollution and Individual Rights: An International Symposium*. Devanter: Kluwer, 1978.

McDougal, Myres S., Harold D. Lasswell, and Lung-chu Chen. *Human Rights and World Public Order: The Basic Policies of an International Law of Human Dignity*. New Haven, Conn.: Yale University Press, 1980.

McKean, Warwick. *Equality and Discrimination Under International Law*. Oxford: Clarendon Press, 1983.

McLeish, Kenneth, ed. *Bloomsbury Guide to Human Thought*. London: Bloomsbury, 1993.

Mendelson, Sarah E. and John K. Glenn, eds. *The Power and Limits of NGOs: A Critical Look at Building Democracy in Eastern Europe*. New York: Columbia University Press, 2002.

Mendlovitz, Saul H., ed. *On the Creation of a Just World Order*. New York: Free Press, 1975.

Mendlovitz, Saul H. and R. B. J. Walker, *Towards a Just World Peace: Perspectives from Social Movements*. London: Butterworths, 1987.

Mendlovitz, Saul H. and Burns H. Weston, eds. *Preferred Futures for the United Nations*. Ardsley, N.Y.: Transnational Publishers, 1995.

Merali, Isfahan and Valerie Oostrveld, eds. *Giving Meaning to Economic, Social, and Cultural Rights*. Philadelphia: University of Pennsylvania Press, 2001.

Meron, Theodor. *Human Rights and Humanitarian Norms in Customary Law*. Oxford: Clarendon Press, 1989.

———, ed. *Human Rights in International Law: Legal and Polity Issues*. 2 vols. New York: Oxford University Press, 1984.

Merrills, J. G. *The Development of International Law by the European Court of Human Rights*. 2nd ed. New York: St. Martin's Press, 1993.

Mertus, Julie A. *Bait and Switch: Human Rights and U.S. Foreign Policy*. New York: Routledge, 2004.

Meyer, Mary K. and Elisabeth Prügl, eds. *Gender Politics in Global Governance*. Lanham, Md.: Rowman and Littlefield, 1999.

Meyer, William H. *Human Rights and International Political Economy in Third World Nations: Multinational Corporations, Foreign Aid, and Repression*. Westport, Conn.: Praeger, 1998.

Mgbeoji, Ikechi. *Collective Insecurity: The Liberian Crisis, Unilateralism, and Global Order*. Vancouver: UBC Press, 2003.

Miller, Lynn H. *Global Order: Values and Power in International Relations*. Boulder, Colo.: Westview Press, 1985.

Minority Rights Group. *World Directory of Minorities*. Chicago: St. James Press, 1990.

Minow, Martha. *Making All the Difference: Inclusion, Exclusion and American Law*. Ithaca, N.Y.: Cornell University Press, 1990.

Mohanty, Chandra Talpade, Ann Russo, and Lourdes Torres, eds. *Third World Women and the Politics of Feminism*. Bloomington: Indiana University Press, 1991.

Monshipouri, Mahmood, Neil A. Englehart, Andrew J. Nathan, and Kavita Philip, eds. *Constructing Human Rights in the Age of Globalization*. Armonk, N.Y.: M.E. Sharpe, 2003.

Morsink, Johannes. *The Universal Declaration of Human Rights: Origins, Drafting, and Intent*. Philadelphia: University of Pennsylvania Press, 1999.

Mowbray, Alastair.R. *Development of Positive Obligations Under the European Convention and the European Court of Human Rights*. Oxford: Hart, 2004.

Mower, A. Glenn, Jr. *The Convention on the Rights of the Child: International Law Support for Children*. Westport, Conn.: Greenwood Press, 1997.

———. *Human Rights and American Foreign Policy: The Carter and Reagan Experiences*. New York: Greenwood Press, 1987.

———. *International Cooperation for Social Justice, Global, and Regional Protection of Economic/Social Rights*.Westport, Conn.: Greenwood Press, 1985.

———. *Regional Human Rights: A Comparative Study of the West European and Inter-American Systems*. New York: Greenwood Press, 1991.

———. *The United States, the United Nations, and Human Rights: The Eleanor Roosevelt and Jimmy Carter Eras*. Westport, Conn.: Greenwood Press, 1979.

Muscat, Robert J. *Investing in Peace: How Development Aid Can Prevent or Promote Conflict*. Armonk, N.Y.: M.E. Sharpe, 2002.

Mutua, Makau. *Human Rights: A Political and Cultural Critique*. Philadelphia: University of Pennsylvania Press, 2002.

Nanda, Ved P., James R. Scarritt, and George W. Shepherd, Jr. *Global Human Rights: Public Policies, Comparative Measures, and NGO Strategies*. Boulder, Colo.: Westview Press, 1981.

Narayan-Parker, Deepa with Raj Patel et al. *Can Anyone Hear Us!* Voices of the Poor. New York: Oxford University Press for World Bank, 2000.

Neier, Aryeh. *Taking Liberties: Four Decades in the Struggle for Rights*. New York: Public Affairs, 2003.

Newberg, Paula R. *The Politics of Human Rights*. New York: New York University Press, 1981.

Newman, Frank C. and David S. Weissbrodt. *International Human Rights: Law, Policy, and Process*. Cincinnati, Oh.: Anderson, 1990.

Newsom, David D. *The Diplomacy of Human Rights*. Lanham, Md.: University Press of America for Institute for the Study of Diplomacy, 1986.

Nickel, James W. *Making Sense of Human Rights: Philosophical Reflections on the Universal Declaration of Human Rights*. Berkeley: University of California Press, 1987.

Niec, Helena, ed. *Cultural Rights and Wrongs: A Collection of Essays in Commemoration of the 50th Anniversary of the Universal Declaration of Human Rights*. Paris: UNESCO, 1998.

Niezen, Ronald. *The Origins of Indigenism: Human Rights and the Politics of Identity*. Berkeley: University of California Press, 2003.

The 9/11 Commission Report: Final Report of the National Commission on Terrorist Attacks upon the United States. Washington, D.C.: U.S. Government Printing Office, 2004.

Novak, Michael. *This Hemisphere of Liberty: A Philosophy of the Americas*. Washington, D.C.: American Enterprise Institute, 1990.

Nunca Más! (Never Again): A Report by Argentina's National Commission on Disappeared People. London: Faber and Faber, 1986.

Nussbaum, Martha C. *Hiding from Humanity: Disgust, Shame, and the Law*. Princeton, N.J.: Princeton University Press, 2004.

———. *Sex and Social Justice*. New York: Oxford University Press, 1999.

———. *Women and Human Development: The Capabilities Approach*. Cambridge, New York: Cambridge University Press, 2001.

Nussbaum, Martha and Amartya Sen, eds. *The Quality of Life*. Studies in Development Economics. New York: Oxford University Press, 1993.

Nye, Joseph S., Jr. *Defining National Interests in an Information Age*. Morgenthau Memorial Lecture. New York: Carnegie Council on Ethics and International Affairs, 1989.

Nyerere, Julius K. *Freedom and Development*. Dar es Salaam: Oxford University Press, 1973.

Okin, Susan Moler. *Is Multiculturalism Bad for Women?* Ed. Joshua Cohen, Matthew Howard, and Martha Nussbaum. Princeton, N.J.: Princeton University Press, 1999.

O'Manique, John. *The Origins of Justice: The Evolution of Morality, Human Rights, and Law*. Philadelphia: University of Pennsylvania Press, 2003.

Orford, Anne. *Reading Humanitarian Intervention: Human Rights and the Use of Force in International Law*. Cambridge: Cambridge University Press, 2003.

Owen, David. *Human Rights*. London: Jonathan Cape, 1978.

Packenham, Robert. *Liberal America and the Third World: Political Development Ideas in Foreign Aid and Social Science*. Princeton, N.J.: Princeton University Press, 1973.

Pasqualucci, Jo M. *The Practice and Procedures of the Inter-American Court of Human Rights*. Cambridge: Cambridge University Press, 2003.

Persico, Joseph E. *Nuremberg: Infamy on Trial*. New York: Penguin, 1994.

Peter, Chris Maina. *Human Rights in Africa: A Comparative Study of the African Human and Peoples' Rights Charter and the New Tanzanian Bill of Rights*. New York: Greenwood Press, 1990.

Peters, Julie and Andrea Wolper, eds. *Women's Rights, Human Rights: International Feminist Perspectives*. New York: Routledge, 1995.

Pictet, Jean S. *Humanitarian Law and the Protection of War Victims*. Leyden: Sijthoff, 1975.

Polanyi, Karl. *The Great Transformation: The Political and Economic Origins of Our Time*. Boston: Beacon Press, 1944.

Pollis, Adamantia and Peter Schwab, eds. *Human Rights: Cultural and Ideological Perspectives*. New York: Praeger, 1979.

Pomerance, Michla. *Self-Determination in Law and Practice: The New Doctrine in the United Nations*. The Hague: Nijhoff, 1982.

Porta, Donatella Delia and Sidney Tarrow, eds. *Transnational Protest and Global Activism: People, Passions, and Power*. Lanham Md.: Rowman and Littlefield, 2005.

Power, Jonathan. *Against Oblivion: Amnesty International's Fight for Human Rights*. London: Fontana, 1981.

Power, Samantha. *"A Problem from Hell": America and the Age of Genocide*. New York: Basic Books, 2002.

Proudfoot, Wayne L. and J. Paul Martin, eds. *Religious Diversity and Human Rights*. New York: Columbia University Press, 1996.

Ramcharan, B. G. *The Concept and Present Status of the International Protection of Human Rights*. Boston: Nijhoff, 1989.

———, ed. *Human Rights: Thirty Years After the Universal Declaration of Human Rights*. The Hague: Nijhoff, 1979.

———. *Humanitarian Good Offices in International Law*. The Hague: Nijhoff, 1983.

———, ed. *International Law and Fact-Finding in the Field of Human Rights*. The Hague: Nijhoff, 1982.

———. *The Right to Life in International Law*. The Hague: Nijhoff, 1985.

Randall, Glenn R. and Ellen L. Lutz. *Serving Survivors of Torture: A Practical Manual for Health Professionals and Other Service Providers*. Washington, D.C.: American Association for the Advancement of Science, 1991.

Randall, Kenneth C. *Federal Courts and the International Human Rights Paradigm*. Durham, N.C.: Duke University Press, 1990.

Ratner, Michael and Ellen Ray. *Guantánamo: What the World Should Know*. Adlestrop, UK: Arris Books, 2004.

Ratner, Stephen R. *Accountability for Human Rights Atrocities in International Law: Beyond the Nuremberg Legacy*. 2nd ed. New York: Oxford University Press, 2001.

Rawls, John. *A Theory of Justice*. Cambridge, Mass.: Belknap Press of Harvard University Press, 1971.

Reilly, Kevin, Stephen Kaufman, and Angela Bodino, eds. *Racism: A Global Reader*. Armonk, N.Y.: M.E. Sharpe, 2003.

Reisman, W. Michael and Chris T. Antoniou, eds. *The Laws of War: A Comprehensive Collection of Primary Documents on International Laws Governing Armed Conflict*. New York: Vintage, 1994.

Reisman, W. Michael and Burns H. Weston, eds. *Toward World Order and Human Dignity: Essays in Honor of Myres S. McDougal*. New York: Free Press, 1976.

Renteln, Alison Dundes. *International Human Rights: Universalism Versus Relativism*. Newbury Park, Calif.: Sage, 1990.

Risse, Thomas, Stephen Rapp, and Kathryn Sikkink. *The Power of Human Rights: International Norms and Domestic Change*. Cambridge: Cambridge University Press, 1999.

Robertson, A. H. and J. G. Merrills. *Human Rights in the World: An Introduction to the Study of the International Protection of Human Rights*. 4th ed. Manchester, Manchester University Press, 1996.

Rodley, Nigel R. *The Treatment of Prisoners Under International Law.* Oxford: Clarendon Press, 1986.

Roht-Arriaza, Naomi. *The Pinochet Effect: Transnational Justice in the Age of Human Rights.* Philadelphia: University of Pennsylvania Press, 2005.

Rose, David. *Guantánamo: America's War on Human Rights.* London: Faber and Faber, 2004.

Rosenau, James N. and Ernst-Otto Czempiel. *Governance Without Government: Order and Change in World Politics.* Cambridge Studies in International Relations. Cambridge: Cambridge University Press, 1992.

Rosenbaum, Alan S., ed. *The Philosophy of Human Rights: International Perspectives.* London: Aldwych Press, 1980.

Ross, Fiona C. *Bearing Witness: Women and the Truth and Reconciliation Commission in South Africa.* London: Pluto Press, 2003.

Ross, Robert J. S. *Slaves to Fashion: Poverty and Abuse in the New Sweatshops.* Ann Arbor: University of Michigan Press, 2004.

Rueschemeyer, Dietrich, Evelyne Huber Stephens, and John D. Stephens, *Capitalist Developnent and Democracy.* Chicago: University of Chicago Press, 1992.

Rummel, R. J. *Power Kills: Democracy as a Method of Nonviolence.* New Brunswick, N.J.: Transaction Publishers, 2004.

Russell, Ruth B. *History of the United Nations Charter: The Role of the United States, 1940–1945.* Washington, D.C.: Brookings Institution, 1953.

Sachs, Jeffrey D. *The End of Poverty: Economic Possibilities for Our Time.* New York: Penguin, 2005.

Sands, Philippe. *Principles of International Environmental Law.* 2 vols. Cambridge: Cambridge University Press, 1995.

Santa Cruz, Hernán. *Racial Discrimination.* Rev. ed. New York: United Nations, 1977.

Sarkhaov, A. D. *Progress, Co-Existence and Intellectual Freedom.* Harmondsworth: Penguin, 1976.

Schindler, Dietrich and Jiri Toman. *The Laws of Armed Conflict.* Dordrecht: Nijhoff, 1988.

Schlesinger, Arthur M., Jr. *Robert Kennedy and His Times.* Boston: Houghton Mifflin, 1978.

Schoultz, Lars. *Human Rights and United States Policy Toward Latin America.* Princeton, N.J.: Princeton University Press, 1981.

Schultz, William F. *In Our Own Interest: How Defending Human Rights Benefits Us All.* Boston: Beacon Press, 2002.

Schwab, Peter and Adamantia Pollis, eds. *Toward a Human Rights Framework.* New York: Praeger, 1982.

Secretary-General's High-Level Panel on Threats, Challenges and Change. *A More Secure World: Our Shared Responsibility.* Report of the High-Level Panel on Threats, Challenges, and Change. New York: United Nations, 2004.

Sen, Amartya Kumar. *Development as Freedom.* New York : Knopf, 1999.

———. *Poverty and Famines: An Essay on Entitlement and Deprivation.* Oxford: Oxford University Press, 1981.

Shelton, Dinah L. *Remedies in International Human Rights Law.* 2nd ed. Oxford: Oxford University Press, 2001.

Shepherd, George W., Jr. and Ved P. Nanda, eds. *Human Rights and Third World Development.* Westport, Conn.: Greenwood Press, 1985.

Shue, Henry. *Basic Rights: Subsistence, Affluence, and U.S. Foreign Policy.* Princeton, N.J.: Princeton University Press, 1980. 2nd ed. 1996.

Siegel, Richard Lewis. *Employment and Human Rights: The International Dimension.* Philadelphia: University of Pennsylvania Press, 1994.

Sieghart, Paul. *The International Law of Human Rights.* Oxford: Clarendon Press, 1983.

Sigel, Roberta S. and Marilyn Hoskin, eds. *Education for Democratic Citizenship: A Challenge for Multi-Ethnic Societies.* Hillsdale, N.J.: Lawrence Erlbaum, 1991.

Sikkink, Kathryn. *Mixed Signals: U.S. Foreign Policy and Latin America.* Ithaca, N.Y.: Cornell University Press, 2004.

Simmons, Alan B., ed. *International Migration, Refugee Flows and Human Rights in North America: The Impact of Free Trade and Restructuring.* New York: Center for Migration Studies, 1996.

Singer, Peter. *One World: The Ethics of Globalization.* New Haven, Conn.: Yale University Press, 2002.

Slaughter, Anne-Marie. *A New World Order.* Princeton, N.J.: Princeton University Press, 2004.

Smillie, Ian and Larry Minear. *The Charity of Nations: Humanitarian Action in a Calculating World.* Bloomfield, Conn.: Kumarian Press, 2004.

Smith, Sidonie and Kay Schaffer. *Human Rights and Narrated Lives: The Ethics of Recognition.* New York: Palgrave Macmillan, 2004.

Somerville, John. *The Peace Revolution: Ethos and Social Process.* Westport, Conn.: Greenwood Press, 1975.

Soroos, Marvin S. *Beyond Sovereignty: The Challenge of Global Policy*. Columbia: University of South Carolina Press, 1987.

Soovaiaia, Ahmed E. *Human Rights and Islam: The Divine and the Mundane in Human Rights Law*. New York: Universe, 2003.

Steiner, Henry J. and Philip Alston, eds. *International Human Rights in Context: Law, Politics, Morals*. 3rd ed. New York: Oxford University Press, 2006.

Stiglitz, Joseph E. *Globalization and Its Discontents*. New York: Norton, 2002.

Stover, Eric and Elena O. Nightingale, eds. *The Breaking of Bodies and Minds: Torture, Psychiatric Abuse and the Health Professions*. New York: W.H. Freeman, 1985.

Strategy One. *Institutional Trust: A Five Country Survey*. New York: Edelman Public Relations Worldwide, 2001.

Svensson, Marina. *Debating Human Rights in China: A Conceptual and Political History*. Lanham, Md.: Rowman and Littlefield, 2002.

Tamir, Yael. *Liberal Nationalism*. Princeton, N.J.: Princeton University Press, 1993.

Thoolen, Hans and Berth Verstappen. *Human Rights Missions: A Study of the Fact-Finding Practice of Non-Governmental Organizations*, sponsored by SIM, The Netherlands Institute of Human Rights. Dordrecht: Nijhoff, 1986.

Timerman, Jacobo. *Prisoner Without a Name, Cell Without a Number*. Trans. Toby Talbot. New York: Knopf, 1981.

Tolley, Howard, Jr. *The UN Commission on Human Rights*. Boulder, Colo.: Westview Press, 1987.

Tomaševski, Katarina. *Development Aid and Human Rights: A Study for the Danish Center of Human Rights*. New York: St. Martin's Press, 1989.

Tomuschat, Christian, ed. *Modern Law of Self-Determination*. Dordrecht: Martinus Nijhoff, 1993.

Tully, James. *Strange Multiplicity: Constitutionalism in an Age of Diversity*. Cambridge: Cambridge University Press, 1995.

Tutu, Desmond. *God Has a Dream: A Vision of Hope for Our Time*. New York: Doubleday, 2004.

Uildriks, Niels and Piet van Reenen. *Policing Post-Communist Societies: Police-Public Violence, Democratic Policing and Human Rights*. New York: Open Society Institute, 2003.

Umozurike, U. O. *Self-Determination and International Law*. Hamden, Conn.: Archon Books, 1972.

UNESCO. *Human Rights in Urban Areas*. Paris: UNESCO, 1983.

UNESCO. *Statement on Race and Racial Prejudice*. Paris: UNESCO, 1967.

United Nations, Office of the High Commissioner for Human Rights. *International Human Rights Instruments*. New York: United Nations Publications, 2004.

United Nations, Office of the UN High Commissioner for Refugees. *Handbook on Procedures and Criteria for Determining Refugee Status Under the 1951 Convention and the 1967 Protocol Relating to the Status of Refugees*. Rev. ed. Geneva: UNHCR, 1992.

United Nations Centre for Human Rights. *Manual on Human Rights Reporting Under Six Major International Human Rights Instruments*. New York: United Nations, 1991.

United Nations Department of Public Information. *The United Nations and Human Rights*. New York: United Nations, 1984.

United Nations Information Organization. *Documents of the United Nations Conference on International Organization, San Francisco, 1945*. 22 vols. London: United Nations Conference on International Organization, 1946–55.

U.S. Department of State. *Foreign Relations of the United States, 1945*. 9 vols. Washington, D.C.: Government Printing Office, 1966.

U.S. House of Representatives, Subcommittee on International Organizations. *Human Rights in the International Community and in U.S. Foreign Policy, 1945–76*. Washington, D.C.: Government Printing Office, 1977.

U.S. National Commission for the Protection of Human Subjects of Biomedical and Behavioral Research. *The Belmont Report: Ethical Principles and Guidelines for the Protection of Human Subjects of Research*. Washington, D.C.: U.S. Government Printing Office, 1979.

Uvin, Peter. *Human Rights and Development*. Bloomfield, Conn.: Kumarian Press, 2004.

Valentino, Benjamin A. *Final Solutions: Mass Killing and Genocide in the 20th Century*. Ithaca, N.Y.: Cornell University Press, 2004.

Van Boven, Theo C. *People Matter: Views on International Human Rights Policy*. Amsterdam: Menlankoff, 1982.

Van Dijk, Pieter and G. J. H. van Hoof. *Theory and Practice of the European Convention of Human Rights.* Boston: Kluwer Law, 1984.

Van Dyke, Vernon. *Human Rights, Ethnicity and Discrimination.* Westport, Conn.: Greenwood Press, 1985.

Vasak, Karel, ed., rev. and ed. for the English edition Philip Alston. *The International Dimensions of Human Rights.* 2 vols. Westport, Conn.: Greenwood Press for UNESCO, 1982.

Vincent, R. J., ed. *Foreign Policy and Human Rights: Issues and Responses.* New York: Cambridge University Press in association with the Royal Institute of International Affairs. 1986.

———. *Human Rights and International Relations.* Cambridge: Cambridge University Press, 1986.

Vogelgesang, Sandy. *American Dream, Global Nightmare: The Dilemma of U.S. Human Rights Policy.* New York: Norton, 1981.

Walden, Raphael. *Racism and Human Rights.* Amsterdam: Nijhoff Law Special, 2004.

Walker, Samual. *In Defense of American Liberties: A History of the ACLU.* New York: Oxford University Press, 1990.

Walzer, Michael. *Arguing About War.* New Haven, Conn.: Yale University Press, 2004.

Waters, Malcolm. *Globalization,* New York: Routledge, 1995.

Weiss, Edith Brown. *In Fairness to Future Generations: International Law, Common Patrimony, and Intergenerational Equity.* Dobbs Ferry, N.Y.: Transnational Publishers, 1988.

———, ed. *International Compliance with Nonbinding Accords.* Washington, D.C.: American Society of International Law, 1997.

Weiss, Thomas G., Margaret E. Crahan, and John Goering, eds. *Wars on Terrorism and Iraq: Human Rights, Unilateralism and U.S. Foreign Policy.* London: Routledge, 2004.

Weissbrodt, David, ed. *International Compliance with Nonbinding Accords.* Washington, D.C.: American Society of International Law, 1997.

Weitz, Eric D. *A Century of Genocide: Utopias of Race and Nation.* Princeton, N.J.: Princeton University Press, 2003.

Welch, Claude E., Jr., ed. *NGOs and Human Rights: Promise and Performance.* Philadelphia: University of Pennsylvania Press, 2002.

Welch, Claude E., Jr. and Virginia A. Leary, eds. *Asian Perspectives on Human Rights.* Boulder, Colo.: Westview Press, 1990.

Welch, Claude E., Jr. and Ronald I. Meltzer, eds. *Human Rights and Development in Africa.* Albany: State University of New York Press, 1984.

Weschler, Lawrence. *A Miracle, a Universe: Settling Accounts with Torturers.* New York: Pantheon, 1990.

Weston, Burns H., ed. *Child Labor and Human Rights: Making Children Matter.* Boulder, Colo.: Lynne Rienner, 2005.

Weston, Burns H. and Jonathan C. Carlson, eds. *International Law and World Order: Basic Documents.* 5 vols. Ardsley, N.Y.: Transnational Publishers, 1994–.

Weston, Burns H. and Stephen P. Marks, eds. *The Future of International Human Rights.* Ardsley, N.Y.: Transnational Publishers, 1999.

Wheaton, Bernard and Karen Zdenek. *The Velvet Revolution: Czechoslovakia, 1988–1990.* Boulder, Colo.: Westview Press, 1991.

Wheeler, Nicholas J. *Saving Strangers: Humanitarian Intervention in International Society.* Oxford: Oxford University Press, 2000.

Whitaker, Ben, ed. *The Fourth World: Victims of Group Oppression.* New York: Schocken, 1972.

White, Richard Alan. *Breaking Silence: The Case That Changed the Face of Human Rights.* Washington, D.C.. Georgetown University Press, 2004.

Williams, Oliver F., ed. *Global Codes of Conduct: An Idea Whose Time Has Come.* Notre Dame, Ind.: University of Notre Dame Press, 2000.

Williams, Paul, ed. *The International Bill of Human Rights.* Glen Ellen, Calif.: Entwhistle Books, 1981.

Wippman, David. *International Law and Ethnic Conflict.* Ithaca, N.Y.: Cornell University Press, 1998.

Wiseberg, Laurie. *Protecting Human Rights Defenders: The Importance of Freedom of Association for Human Rights NGOs.* Montreal: International Centre for Human Rights and Democratic Development, 1993.

Women, Law, and Development International/Women's Rights Project of Human Rights Watch. *Women's Human Rights Step by Step.* New York: Women, Ink, 1997.

World Bank. *A User's Guide to Poverty and Social Impact.* Washington, D.C.: World Bank, 2003.

World Commission on Culture and Development. *Our Creative Diversity: Report of the World Commission on Culture and Development.* Paris: UNESCO, July 1996.

Woodwiss, Anthony. *Making Human Rights Work Globally.* London: Cavendish, 2003.

Young, Kirsten A. *The Law and Process of the U.N. Human Rights Committee*. Ardsley, N.Y.: Transnational Publishers, 2002.

Young, Oran R. *Governance in World Affairs*. Ithaca, N.Y.: Cornell University Press, 1999.

Zalaquett, José. *The Human Rights Issue and the Human Rights Movement*. Geneva: Commission of the Churches on International Affairs, World Council of Churches, 1981.

Zinn, Howard. *The Zinn Reader: Writings on Disobedience and Democracy*. New York: Seven Stories Press, 1997.

Select Filmography

CHAPTER 1: ISSUES OVERVIEW

Anne Frank Remembered. Jon Blair. UK: BBC, 1995. 117 min. DVD/video. Documentary offers the most complete telling of one of the most famous victims of the Holocaust, Anne Frank. Provides a detailed account of the living conditions that Frank and others endured while hiding in an Amsterdam attic during World War II.

For Everyone Everywhere: The Making of the Universal Declaration of Human Rights. United Nations, 1998. 60 min. Video. Out of the tragedy of World War II, one of the most noble ideals of humankind was born: the Universal Declaration of Human Rights. This canonical document overcame language and cultural differences to create a definitive standard for human rights. Includes archival footage from four different continents during the drafting of the document.

Human Rights. Thames Television, producer. UK: Media Guild, 1984; 120 min. Video. British television documentary traces the development of human rights since the 1948 adoption of the UN Universal Declaration of Human Rights. Interviews with diplomats, human rights advocates, and victims of violations around the world who attempt to discuss the concept of universal and inalienable human rights.

Judgment at Nuremberg. Stanley Kramer, director. USA: CBS/Fox, 1961. 178 min., color; DVD/video. A powerful dramatization of the trials of Nazi war criminals at Nuremberg following World War II. Reveals the extent of the atrocities committed, which, in turn, set in motion the movement to draft the international Bill of Rights. Stars Marlene Dietrich, Burt Lancaster, Maximillian Schell, and Spencer Tracy.

Life Is Beautiful. Roberto Benigni. Italy. Miramax, 1997. 122 min. DVD/video. This tragicomedy follows an Italian husband, wife, and child as they are imprisoned in a concentration camp during World War II. To shelter his son, the father goes to extraordinary lengths to portray the Holocaust as a lighthearted contest with prizes at the end of the "game."

Mein Krieg (My War). Harriet Eder and Thomas Kufus, directors. German: Kanguruh-Film, Berlin, Germany, 1990. 90 min. Winner of the Peace Prize in the 1990 Berlin Film Festival. Guns and cameras at the warfront—six German veterans from World War II recount their memories of battle through the examination of their own amateur film footage shot during the German invasion of the Soviet Union.

Memory of Justice. Marcel Ophuts, producer. France: Films Inc., 1976. 278 min., color. French (English subtitles); 16 mm. Landmark documentary of the Nazi war crimes trials at Nuremberg. Filmmaker Ophuls traveled throughout Germany searching for people's attitudes about the past and about other atrocities of war, probing the questions of guilt and responsibility.

Night and Fog. Alain Resnais, director. France: Argos/Como/Cocinor, 1955. 31 min., color & bw; 16 mm. Michigan Media or University of California Extension Media, Berkeley. A documentary film that contrasts color footage of Auschwitz as it appeared in the 1950s with black and white footage of the horrors that took place within its walls during the Holocaust.

The Pianist. Roman Polanski. Poland/UK/France/Germany: Focus Film, 2002. 148 min. DVD/video. Dramatization of the life of an affluent Polish Jew in Warsaw before and during World War II. Film illustrates the rising threat of Nazi aggression and the false sense of security felt by many European Jews. Roman Polanski, the director, grew up in Nazi-occupied Poland.

Prisoners of the Sun. Stephen Wallace. Australia: Greater Union Film Distributors, 1991. 109 min. DVD/ video. Courtroom dramatization of the discovery of Australian POWs tortured and murdered at the hands of Japanese guards. A showdown develops between Australian justice, American politics, and the Japanese "warrior code."

Schindler's List. Steven Spielberg. USA: Universal, 1993. 200 min. DVD/video. Epic telling of the life of Oskar Schindler, Nazi-collaborator turned savior. Schindler employed Jews at his factories in Poland as a means to keep them away from concentration camps. One of the best films about the Holocaust.

Sophie's Choice. Alan J. Pakula. USA: CBS/Fox, 1982. 150 min., color. DVD/video. Meryl Streep won an Academy Award for "best actress" for her extraordinary portrayal of a survivor of a Nazi concentration camp.

Welcome to Womanhood. Charlotte Metcalf. TVE and BBC, 1998. 14 min. In the remote Kapchorwe region of Uganda, "female circumcision" ceremonies occur among the Sabiny people every two years. This documentary illustrates how the United Nations Population Fund's REACH efforts are trying to end this practice.

CHAPTER 2: BASIC DECENCIES/PARTICIPATORY RIGHTS

Against the Tide of History: Landmines in Casamance. Moussa Bocoume. Senegal/USA: WITNESS, 2004. 27 min. Video. Documentary addresses the longest lasting danger of Senegal's civil war: landmines. Told through the voices of landmine victims, community efforts and government programs have done little to help victims or defuse the minefields.

American History X. Tony Kaye. USA: Turman-Morrissey Company, 1998. 118 min. Gripping story of an American white supremacist family and the effects of hatred. Edward Norton plays a bigot, imprisoned for killing a black man, who realizes the nuances of race while serving time in prison.

Balsaro. Carles Bosch and Josep M. Domenech. Spain: Seventh Art Releasing, 2002. Video. Documents seven Cuban economic refugees as they flee to the U.S. via homemade rafts. Rescued at sea and temporarily sent to a refugee camp, the asylum-seekers eventually get to America, only to discover that the standard of living is not what they had hoped.

La Boca del lobo. Francisco José Lombardi. Madrid: José Manuel Espinosa, Dept. de Trafico TVA S.A., 1988. 122 min. Peru's best known filmmaker, Francisco José Lombardi, dramatically explores the horrors of the 1983 massacre of forty-seven men, women, and children in a small Andean village. The film examines the power of paranoia and its effect on the relationship between the soldiers and villagers.

Breaking Barriers. Simone di Bagno. United Nations Films, 1989. 28 min., color. 16 mm. There are more than five hundred million people in the world with disabilities. For many societies they are an untapped resource, or even considered a burden. But throughout the world people with physical and mental disabilities have a great deal to give to their societies. They are demanding equal rights and equal opportunities. Filmed in China, Ivory Coast, Thailand, Austria, and the United States, the UN film shows how disabled people everywhere are breaking down the barriers that have prevented them from enjoying the rights and duties, hopes and dreams, that are common to us all.

Cambodia: Year Zero. American Friends Service Committee, producer. 1979. 60 min., color. The incredible story of Cambodia from 1975 to 1979. The brutality of the Pol Pot years is starkly portrayed, but within a sound historical and political context.

Chain of Tears. Central Independent TV, producer. California Newsreel, 1988. 52 min., color. Video. Documents the effects of apartheid politics and civil war on the children of Angola, Mozambique, and South Africa.

Deadline. Katy Chevigny and Kirsten Johnson. USA: Big Mouth Productions, New York, 2003. 90 min. Video. After a group of Northwestern University law students uncovered evidence that exonerated some death row inmates, long time conservative governor Jack Ryan commuted the death sentences of the entire Illinois death row. This documentary reports on this incident and questions the credibility of capital punishment in the United States.

Death Squadrons: The French School. Mari-Monique Robin. France. First Run/Icarus Films, 2003. 60 min. Video. In English, French, and Spanish with English subtitles. Documentary examines how the French military taught torture techniques to Operation Condor, an international criminal organization formed by South American dictatorships to target political opposition.

An Evening of Forbidden Books. PEN American Center, producer. USA: PEN, 1982. 60 min., bw. VHS or 3/4-in. Video. Selected readings by well-known authors from forbidden books—those not allowed to be used or distributed in the U.S. at various points in recent history; includes a short history of book banning in America presented by Nat Hentoff.

Everyman: Iraq, Enemies of the State. John Blake. London: BBC Enterprises, John Blake Associates, 1990. 36 min. Video. Journalist Charles Glass presents a documentary that reveals the human rights record of Saddam Hussein's Iraq. The program was updated on the day of transmission to take into account the execution of British-based journalist Farzad Bazoft.

Eyes of the Birds. Gabriel Auer, producer. France: Facets, 1982. 80 min., color. French (English subtitles); 16 mm. Dramatization of an International Red Cross delegation visit to Libertad Prison, Uruguay, a so-called model prison in which they discover the effects of physical and psychological torture of prisoners.

Farmingville. Carlos Sandoval and Catherine Tambini. USA: Camino Bluff Productions, 2004. 78min. DVD/video. As more economic migrants illegally enter the US, tension builds within communities. Reports on the killing of two Mexican immigrants in an average American suburb and the community activism, and vigilantism, that followed.

The Flute Player. Jocelyn Glatzer. USA: Jocelyn Glatzer, 2003. 50 min. Video. Documentary. The Khmer Rouge campaign of death was directed at educated Cambodians and led to the killing of 90 percent of Cambodia's musicians. Arn Chorn Pond, the subject of this documentary, is an internationally recognized musician and human rights activist who survived the massacre.

For a Place Under the Heavens. Sabiha Sumar. Pakistan: Women Make Movies, 2003. 53 min. Video. Documentary. In English and Urdu with English subtitles. Tracing the role of Islam in Pakistan since its formation in 1947, this film examines how Pakistani women cope with Islamic fundamentalism and the struggle toward liberalism.

The Forgotten Genocide. Michael Hagopian, producer. USA: Atlantic, 1976. 28 min., color. 16 mm. Story of the genocide of the Armenian people in 1915 told with the intent to show that such events do occur and threaten all humanity.

Forgotten Prisoners: The Amnesty Files. Robert Greenwald. Los Angeles: Turner Network Television/ Washington, D.C.: Amnesty International USA, 1990. 93 min., color. Video. A contemporary, political thriller about a volunteer lawyer working for Amnesty International.

Get a Life. Joao Canijo. France/Portugal: Gemini Films, 2001. 115min. 35mm. This drama is one of the first to address the three million Portuguese immigrants living in France. Extremely conservative and alienated from present day Portugal, these immigrants have a rocky relationship with French culture.

Good Husband, Dear Son. Heddy Honigmann. Netherlands: Ideale Audience Internationale, 2001. 50 min. Video. During the war in the former Yugoslavia, Serbian soldiers killed every man in the small village of Ahatovici. This film commemorates these men by interviewing their families and examining photos and personal items.

Goodbye Hungaria. Jon Nealon. USA/Hungary, 2003. 56 min. Video. Documentary, English and Arabic with English subtitles. A Palestinian refugee and an American volunteer act as translators and advocates in a Hungarian refugee camp. Teeming with asylum seekers, the camp is populated by people from all over the world who are trafficked via underground smuggling rings.

Hiroshima: A Document of the Atomic Bombing. Michigan Media, 1970. 28 min., color. One of the best documentations of the bomb's effects on Hiroshima.

Hiroshima-Nagasaki! August 1945. Museum of Modern Art Circulating Film Program, 1970. 17 min., b&w. Uses Japanese film withheld from the public for twenty years, to show the results of the bombing.

The Hooded Men. Canadian Broadcasting Corporation, producer. Canada: Facets, 1982. 60 min., color. 3/4-in. Beta or VHS video. Documentary. Examines torture in many countries, including Argentina, Nicaragua (pre-1981), Northern Ireland, and South Africa, through the eyes of a sensory deprivation researcher and former torturers and torture victims.

Hotel Rwanda. Terry George. South Africa/USA: Lions Gate Entertainment, 2004. 121 min. Dramatization of Paul Rusesabagina, a hotel owner who refuses to provide shelter to those being slaughtered in the Rwandan Genocide in 1994. As the conflict escalates, Rusesabagina is appalled by the senseless violence and transforms his hotel into a make shift refugee camp, saving countless lives.

How Nice to See You Alive. Lucia Murat, producer and director. Brazil: Women Make Movies, New York, 1989. 100 min. Video. Blending fiction and documentary, this film provides a searing record of life during Brazil's military dictatorship in the 1970s. Murat interviews women who, like herself, were imprisoned and tortured because of their political convictions.

Inside Burma. David Munro. Carlton UK, 1997. 51 min. Video. In-depth look at the history and brutality of Burma, home to one of the world's most repressive regimes. Murder, torture, forced relocations, and slavery are just some of the things the people of Burma have endured under a military regime.

Interrogation. Richard Bugajski. Film Polski. Poland: Kino International Corporation, New York, 1982. 118 min. 16 mm or 35 mm. Originally banned in Poland, *Interrogation* is a grim but powerful story about a cabaret singer detained for interrogation by Polish secret police. A five-year Kafkaesque torture unfolds. Krystyna Janda was named best actress for her performance at the 1990 Cannes Film Festival.

In the Shadow of the City. Jean Khalil Chamoun. France/Lebanon: Arab Film Distribution, 2000. 100 min. 35mm. Drama addresses Lebanon's decade-and-a-half civil war from the perspective of a twelve-year-old Lebanese boy. The boy and his family move from the countryside to Beirut, but struggle with unemployment and the disappearance of loved ones.

In This World. Michael Winterbottom. United Kingdom: Sundance Channel, 2002. 89 min. DVD. Drama follows two young Afghan refugees who put themselves at the mercy of underground smugglers. Their journey takes them through Iran, Turkey, and France as they try to reach the United Kingdom.

Jiyan. Jano Rosebiani. Iraqi Kurdistan: Media Luna Entertainment, 2002. 94 min. 35mm. Drama illustrates the lasting physical and emotional effects of Saddam Hussein's infamous chemical attack on Halabja in Iraqi Kurdistan. Many of the residents are still scarred, emotionally and physically, by the chemical agents.

Juvies. Leslie Neale. USA: Chance Films, 2004. 66 min. Video. This documentary questions the validity of sentencing American youth to decades-long prison sentences for crimes they may or may not have committed. Objections are also made to the growing trend of sentencing juvenile offenders in the adult court system.

The Killing Fields. Roland Joffe, producer. USA: WHV, 1984. 142 min., color. Beta or VHS video. An uncompromising film about two men who find themselves caught up in the Khmer Rouge revolution in Cambodia. Based on a true story and starring Sam Waterston and Haing S. Ngor, the film presents a vivid demonstration of modern-day genocide.

Kurdistan, the Last Colony. Great Britain: Independent Filmmakers. Landmark Films, Falls Church, Va., 1990. 40 min. Video. A vivid documentary examining the plight of the Kurdish people during and after the Iran/Iraq war. Includes interviews with refugees in Turkey and other countries.

Land of Fear, Land of Courage. NBC News, producer. USA: CC Films, 1983. 60 min., color. Video. Documentary filmed in South Africa features Bishop Desmond Tutu, leader of the nonviolent struggle against apartheid, who discusses the time bomb of racial politics and the fears behind both sides of the color bar. Narrated by Edwin Newman.

The Last Just Man. Steven Silver. Canada: Barna-Alper Productions, 2001. 70 min. Beta SP video. Canadian General Romeo Dallaire oversaw the worst human rights disaster since World War II: the massacre of 800,000 Rwandans in 1994. In this documentary, Dallaire questions whether he could have done more to prevent the disaster.

Leila. Dariush Mehrjui. Iran: First Run Features, New York, 1999. 129 min. 35mm. Farsi with English subtitles. Story of a young Iranian couple examines changes in Iranian society and the role of women.

Liberia: An Uncivil War. Jonathan Stack and James Brabazon. USA: Gabriel Films, 2004. 90 min. Video. Documentary. This film criticizes America's weak response to preventing a bloody civil war in Liberia during summer 2003. Includes a series of exclusive interviews with Charles Taylor, the corrupt former president of Liberia who was indicted for war crimes.

Missing. Costa-Gavras. USA: MCA, 1982. 122 min., color. DVD/video. A young American journalist mysteriously disappears during a violent military coup in a South American country. When his wife (Sissy Spacek) and father (Jack Lemmon) attempt to find him, they are confronted with a deeply disturbing political discovery, the horrifying reality of the "disappeared." A 1982 Cannes Film Festival Award winner.

The Mission. Roland Joffé. UK: Warner Brothers, 1986. 125 min. DVD/video. Eighteenth-century idealistic missionaries and greedy slave traders vie for control of the indigenous peoples of South America, backed by the Vatican, resulting in genocide.

Namibia: A Trust Betrayed. United Nations, producer. UN: IL Films, 1974. 27 min., color. 16 mm. Namibia, previously known as South-West Africa, instead of progressing toward independence was swallowed up into South Africa in defiance of the United Nations and the International Court of Justice. Despite the termination of the mandate, South Africa refused to relinquish the mineral rich country. The South African apartheid race system was applied in the territory where 90 percent of the population are black.

Nobody Listened. Nestor Almendros and Jorge Ulia, producers and directors. USA: Direct Cinema Limited, Santa Monica, CA, 1988. Two versions, 117 min. and 60 min. 35 mm or video. Direct, humorous, and moving testimonies by twenty-five Cubans on the human rights situation in their country during the past thirty years. Many of them were imprisoned by the Castro regime; many also fought the previous Batista dictatorship.

Not My Living Self. Jet Homoet and Simon Wilkie, directors. Beaconsfield, England: The National Film and Television School, 1991, 68 min. This film interviews Somalis, Sri Lankans, and West Africans who have fled their homelands in search of freedom and a better life in Holland. The result is a dramatic look at life in exile.

One of Us. Uri Barbash, director. Israel: Israfilm, 1990. 110 min. An Israeli soldier investigates the death of a Palestinian in an Israeli detention center. Through his investigation, he uncovers the real causes behind the death and new truths about his friends and fellow soldiers.

One Shot. Nurit Kedar, Israel, 2004. 60 min. Video. Hebrew with English subtitles. Since the beginning of the second intifada, Israeli snipers have been frequently used to perform targeted killings. This documentary shows perceptions of these snipers as both heroes and cold-blooded killers.

Persons of Interest. Alison Maclean and Tobias Perse. USA: First Run/Icarus Films, 2003. 63 min. Video. Since September 11, secret detentions, arbitrary arrest, and prisoners held incommunicado have drastically increased among Muslim immigrants in the United States. This documentary uses interviews with these targeted immigrants to expose how the U.S. legal system has changed.

Prisoners of Conscience. Noel Fox, producer. Great Britain: Facets/Cinema Guild, 1980. 30 min., color. 16 mm. Film that illustrates the work of the human rights organization Amnesty International by tracing efforts to achieve the release of two prisoners, a Russian and an Argentine. Follows AI's actions on behalf of each from the London research department to an adoption group working to obtain the prisoners' freedom.

Prisoner Without a Name, Cell Without a Number. Linda Yellin, producer. USA: Yellin, 1983. 100 min., color. Video. Dramatization of the story of Jacobo Timmerman, exiled Argentine newspaper editor who was imprisoned and tortured by the military regime for being Jewish and for publishing editorials asking for an account of the "disappeared" in Argentina.

Repatriation. Dong-won Kim. South Korea: Indie Story, 2003. 149 min. 35mm. Documentary. During the cold war, North Korean spies captured in South Korea underwent conversion schemes in prison that involved torture. This film follows two such spies that refused to renounce their beliefs.

Romero. John Duigan. USA: Four Seasons Entertainment, 1989. 102 min. DVD/video. Oscar Arnulfo Romero was a conservative archbishop of El Salvador who initially supported the corrupt Salvadorian government. After learning of government torture and soldiers shooting into crowds of protestors, Romero denounced the government and became an outspoken advocate of human rights.

Saints and Sinners. Abigail Honor and Yan Vizinberg. USA: Avator Films, New York, 2004. 71 min. Video. Documents a gay couple's attempt to be married in a Catholic church in America.

Secret Ballot. Babak Payami. Iran. Sony Pictures Classics, 2001. 123 min. 35mm. A female election pollster is sent to a remote region of Iran to encourage voting but is escorted by an Iranian soldier determined to prevent voter registration. With a sense of humor, the film shows how Iranians are adapting to democracy.

Skins. Chris Eyre. USA: First Look Media, 2001. 86 min. DVD/video. Dramatization of a Native American policeman trying to shed the stereotype of Native Americans being apathetic alcoholics, an image that his brother flaunts.

Through the Wire. Nina Rosenblum, producer, director. USA: Daedalus Productions, Fox/Lorber Home Video., 1990. 77 min., color. VHS video. Documents the shutting down of the Female High Security Unit in Lexington, Kentucky, following Amnesty International and ACLU investigations of mistreatment of three women inmates.

To Kill a Mockingbird. Alan Pakula, producer. USA: Universal, 1962. 130 min. Video. A widowed attorney with two young children accepts the significant challenge of defending a black man wrongly accused of rape in their racially divided Southern U.S. town.

Torture Victims Speak. Amnesty International/USA, producer. USA: Facets, 1984. 30 min., color. Video. Three victims of torture speak of their experiences in this video produced at Amnesty International/USA's June 1984 meeting. Alicia Portnoy, Argentina, Lee Shin-Bom, South Korea, and Reverend Simon Farisani, South Africa are featured.

Tulia, Texas: Scenes from the Drug War. Emily Kunstler and Sarah Kunstler. USA: William Moses Kunstler

Fund for Racial Justice, 2002. 26 min. The small rural community of Tulia, Texas, was hit hard by a federally funded sting operation. Over 10 percent of the African-American population were questionably imprisoned.

The Tree That Remembers. Masoud Raouf. Canada. National Film Board of Canada, 2002. 50 min. Video. Iranians overthrew the Shah with hopes that an Islamic Republic would offer a more humane government. This optimism was dashed when the new regime turned out to be equally repressive and murderous. Using interviews with Iranian dissidents and archival footage, this documentary shows how the Iranian diaspora cope with exile and express hope for the future of Iran.

U.S./U.S.S.R. Peace Walk in Ukraine: Interview with Ukrainian Dissidents. USA: Americans for Human Rights in Ukraine (AHRU), 1989. Video. This video was made during the U.S./U.S.S.R. Peace Walk in Ukraine, which took place August 16-September 16, 1988. It consists of interviews with Ukrainian dissidents in Kiev, members of the Ukrainian Helsinki Union, who discuss the impact of "russification" on Ukrainian society and the emergence of protest since the beginning of glasnost.

Voices from Gaza. Britain: First Run/Icarus Films, New York, 1989. 51 min., color. 16 mm or video. Living conditions for Palestinian refugees on the Gaza strip are documented. Aspects of the Israeli occupation, confrontations between both sides, and the refugees' efforts to obtain rights and services are described.

Welcome to Hadassah Hospital. Ramón Gieling. The Netherlands: Netherlands Public Broadcasting, 2002, 50 min. Video. Victims and perpetrators of sucide attacks in Israel are treated with equal care (and sometimes in the same room) at Hadassah Hospital. This documentary focuses on the hospital staff and their compassion for human life.

What Right Has a Child. United Nations, producer. Univ IL Films, 1968. 15 min., color. 16 mm. Classic film of children's art from around the world; commentary is by children talking about the UN Declaration of Rights of the Child.

When the Storm Came. Shilpi Gupta. USA: Veritas Films/Shilpi Productions, 2003. 24 min. Video. Documentary shows that in the conflict for Kashmir, civilian women are targeted by soldiers. Using rape as a weapon of war, soldiers violate Kashmiri women to escalate tension.

When the War Is Over. Francois Verster. South Africa: Seventh Art Releasing, 2002. 52 min. Video. Bonteheuwel Military Wing (BMW), a militant teenage self-defense unit, fought to end apartheid in South Africa during the 1980s. Interviews with surviving members illustrate the lasting effect of war and racism on South African freedom fighters.

Who Will Cast the First Stone? Ahmed A. Jamal and Sabiha Sumar. New York: Cinema Guild, , 1989. 52 min. Video. Filmed secretly in Pakistan showing how General Zia al-Haq's regime manipulated the legal system and devalued Pakistani women. This film focuses on three women accused of adultery, which is considered a crime against the state, punishable by stoning.

Z. Costa-Gavras, producer. USA: RCA-COL, 1969. 128 min., color. Beta or VHS video. An Oscar-winning foreign film based on actual events of political repression during the time of the Greek junta in the late 1960s. Reveals details of the political assassination of a deputy, "Z," and the shocking aftermath of the crime. Stars Yves Montand, Irene Papas, and Jean-Louis Trintignant.

CHAPTER 3: BASIC HUMAN NEEDS/SECURITY RIGHTS

And the Dish Ran Away with the Spoon. Christopher Laird and Anthony Hall. Banyan Limited/BBC, 1992. 49 min. Video. By contrasting Caribbean poetry and music with imported sitcoms, this documentary shows Caribbean cultures that are saturated with American and French television. Viewing the world through television has created distorted perceptions of the world and alienated people from their native cultures.

And Who Shall Feed This World? Films, Inc., 1975. 47 min., color. Does the United States have an obligation to provide food for the rest of the world? This film tries to answer that question.

The Big Village. United Nations, producer. Barr/Univ IL Films, 1979. 25 min., color. 16 mm. A view of the relations between the "rich" and "poor" nations from a Third World perspective; film questions why there are persistent inequities and how the resources and bounty of the earth can be shared.

Born into Brothels. Zana Briski and Ross Kauffman. USA Red Light Films, 2003. 85 min. Video. The filmmakers of this documentary spent several years in Calcutta recording the plight of the children of prostitutes. Winner of the 2004 Sundance Documentary Audience Award.

Bottle Babies. Peter Krieg, producer. USA: New Time/Ecufilm, Michigan Media/CC Films, 1976. 26 min., color. 16 mm. Film explores the alarming increase in malnutrition in Third World infants due to consumption of imported powdered formula. Investigates one probable cause—the massive advertising campaigns of multinational companies that sell these products.

Celso and Cora. Gary Kildea, producer. Australia: Philippine Resource, 1983. 109 min., color. 16 mm. Tagalog (English subtitles). Portrait of a young couple with children living in a squatter settlement in Manila; follows their attempts to survive economically and as a family unit as they face daily life and confront the greater sociopolitical forces surrounding them.

Children of Fire. Mai Masri and Jean Chamoun, producers. Great Britain: American-Arab Anti-Discrimination Committee, Washington, D.C., 1990. 70 min. Video. The story of the Israeli occupation in the West Bank through the eyes of Palestinian children.

City of God. Kátia Lund and Fernando Meirelles. Brazil: Miramax, 2002. 131 min. DVD/video. Gripping story of impoverished Brazilian youths who grow up to become ruthless gangsters. Driven by violence, drugs, and wealth, these hoods battle to control the lucrative drug racket of Rio de Janeiro.

The Eye of the Day. Leonard Retel Helmrich. Netherlands: Scarabeefilms, 2001. 92 min. 35mm. In 1998, a political and economic crisis forced the Indonesian ruling government of 32 years to step down. This documentary focuses on the transition to democracy and political prisoners, including the director of this film.

The Face of Famine. Films, Inc., 1982. 75 min., color. Shows how enormous quantities of grain are used to feed livestock in the West and the repercussions of such a system on starving people all over the world.

Field of Genes. Janet Thomson. CBC, 1997. 44 min. Video. Genetically altered crops offer an opportunity to increase production and feed more of the world's starving population. But citing expensive modified seed and lackluster yields, this documentary questions how well this optimistic forecast happens in practice.

Fragile Harvest. Robert Lang. Canada: National Film Board of Canada, 1987. 49 min. Video. Documentary examines a growing crisis in world agriculture: genetically-altered crops that are successful in one area fail to produce in another area. This results in farmers driven from their land, increased dependence on agrichemicals, and the elimination of indigenous adapted varieties of food crops.

In the Light of Reverence. Christopher McLeod. USA: Sacred Land Film Project of Earth Island Institute, 2001. 73 min. DVD/video. Across the U.S., Native Americans are struggling to protect their sacred places. Strip mining, disrespectful tourists, and new developments are threatening the culture of Native Americans. This documentary questions to what degree the U.S. government follows through on its promise to protect the religion of its people.

A Kind of Childhood. Susan Bissell and Tareque Masud. Canada: Xingu Films/Audiovision, 2003. 51 min. Video. Documents the harsh realities of child labor in India. Focusing on several children over the course of six years, this documentary shows real examples of child labor—ranging from children supporting their parents, dreams of education squashed, and upward mobility perpetually out of reach.

Life by the Tracks. Ditsi Carolino. UK/Philippines: Ditsi Carolino, 2002. 70 min. Video. Illustrates one family's struggle to live in makeshift housing dangerously close to railroad tracks. The landlord threatening eviction only adds to the family's other problems of poverty and alcoholism.

The Migrants. Films, Inc., 1980. 52 min., color. Documents the fact that the plight of America's itinerant farm workers has improved very little since 1970.

The Navigators. Ken Loach. UK: First Look Media, 2001. 96 min. 35mm. Drama illustrates how rail workers must take cuts in pay and benefits during the privatization of British Rail. The options are slim: lose the benefits or lose your job.

Poison. Giuseppe Petitto, Enrico Pizianti, and Gianluca Pulcini. Italy/Thailand: Karousel Films, 2001/2002. 27 min. Documents the questionable sport of Thai kickboxing, in which contestants are as young as seven years old. The sport is touted as a means to keep kids out of trouble, but is also surrounded by a seedy gambling racket.

The Seattle Syndrome. Steve Bradshaw. USA: Television Trust for the Environment, 2000. 25 min. Video. Questions the validity of liberal and protectionist protestors who view free trade as exploitation. Includes footage of protestors who rioted during the WTO summit in Seattle.

Seeing Is Believing. Christopher Walker. Television Trust for the Environment, 2002. 27 min. DVD/video. This film explains Zambia's multi-pronged plan to increase the vitamin A intake of its malnourished citizens. Genetically modified palm oil and vitamin supplements are just some of the methods being used to increase the health of the nation.

Shelter for the Homeless. United Nations Films, 1987. 27 min., color. 16 mm. Roughly one quarter of the world's population lack adequate housing and live in appalling conditions. The film describes the One Million Homes Programme in Sri Lanka, which enables families living below the poverty level to build their own homes with minimum government spending. It also focuses on a new policy of land tenure in Rio de Janeiro to help shantytowns (favelas) become functioning neighborhoods, and looks at the change in attitude toward homeless children in Brazil.

The Sixth Section. Alex Rivera. USA: Subcine, Los Angeles, 2003; 26 min. Video. Documentary examines a positive aspect of the global economy; Grupo Union, a transnational labor union created by Mexican immigrants now living in upstate New York, who collectively send American dollars to Mexico to rebuild their home town.

South Africa Belongs to Us. C. Austin, P. Chappell, and R. Weiss, producers. USA: Icarus/So. Africa Media/ Ecufilm/Michigan Media, 1980. 57 min., color. 16 mm or video. Portrait of five Black women in South Africa depicts their struggle for human dignity in the face of apartheid, for homes and food for their children, and for the liberation of the Black people; an in-depth focus on the economic and emotional burdens borne by Black women in South Africa.

State of Denial. Elaine Epstein. USA: California Newsreel, 2002, 86 min. Video. Documentary examines how South Africans are dealing with the AIDS epidemic, without the help of the government of South Africa.

Stolen Childhoods. Len Morris-Producer and Robin Romano. Kenya/Indonesia/Brazil/India/Mexico/ USA: Galenfilms, 2003. 86 min. DVD/video. Examining child labor on a global scale, this documentary explains why child labor happens and how it contributes to global insecurity. Education is presented as a means to liberate child laborers from toiling in mines, fields, and brothels. Includes interviews with Senator Tom Harkin and leading human rights advocates for children.

Super-Companies. Boyce Richardson. Canada: National Film Board of Canada, 1989. 57 min. Video. A scathing look at the effects the aluminum industry has on its workers. From Jamaica to Australia, pollution and the world market lower aluminum industry workers' standard of living.

The Cost of Living. Toni Strasburg. Television Trust for the Environment, 2000. 24 min. Video. Documentary exposes the high cost of HIV/AIDS drugs due to patent protection; examines how Thailand and South Africa legally make their own generic forms of patent-protected HIV/AIDS drugs.

The Water of Ayole. United Nations Development Program, 1988. 28 min., color. 16 mm or video. Documentary about the efforts to bring clean water to the villages of Togo, West Africa, where the water supply is threatened by the guinea worm.

Witches in Exile. Allison Berg. Ghana/USA: Satellite Pictures, 2004. 79 min. Video. In Ghana, woman accused of practicing witchcraft are banished from their communities and forced to live in isolation. This documentary shows the Ghanaian government unsuccessfully trying to abolish these "witch camps," but the age-old tradition continues.

CHAPTER 4: COMMUNITY/GROUP/SOLIDARITY RIGHTS

Argentina—Hope in Hard Times. Mark Dworkin and Melissa Young. Moving Images Video. Project, 2005. 74 min. Video. An economic meltdown in Argentina wipes out people's savings and jump-starts a grassroots democracy movement. This documentary illustrates how economic downturn can effect all levels of society.

Armed to the Teeth. Niels von Kohl. United Nations, 2000. 55 min. Video. There are enough small arms on the planet to arm one twelfth of the global population. This UN-produced documentary focuses on the worldwide illegal trade of small arms and pays special attention to small arms use by children.

Banking on Disaster. Adrian Cowell. Nomad Films, 1988. 78 min. Video. In hopes of promoting economic growth, the World Bank financed a road that cut through the Amazon rainforest. This road caused great disruptions to the environment and the indigenous people. The planners intended the road to allow farmers to prosper from access to new land, but ironically, even they have not benefited due to poor soil and dense jungle that cannot be cleared. This poor planning resulted in an expensive lose-lose situation.

Barizogon. Watanabe Fumiki. Japan: Malpaso Productions, 1996. 114 min. Video. Dramatization of a whistler-blower who exposes corrupt campaigning that results in the coverup of an unsafe nuclear plant. Crony politics endangers the lives of everyone in the town.

Big Spuds, Little Spuds. Christoph Corves and Delia Castiñeira. Germany: SHK, 1999. 52 min. BetaSP. Documents the correlation between climate change and food production. Rising temperatures, genetically modified foods, and the spread of disease and wildlife can have extremely detrimental effects on communities that depend on food production.

Black Sea: Voyage of Healing. Peter Davis. 1998. 54 min. Video. Documents the Black Sea region's difficult situation: polluted by European rivers, a depleting food source depended on by many, and ideologically bankrupt since the fall of the Soviet Union. Includes interviews with environmentalists and religious leaders.

Black Triangle. Nick Davidson, director. London: Central Television Enterprises, 1990. 60 min. Video. Interweaving interviews with mine workers and environmental experts, this documentary examines the daily life and culture of the people who work and live in the "black triangle," the most polluted region in Europe, where Poland, Czechoslovakia, and Germany meet.

Chemical Weapons: A Monster Tamed. United Nations, 1994. 47 min. Video. Tracing chemical weapons from their birth in Word War I to the present, this UN film documents the proliferation and destruction of these lethal weapons. Following the UN ban on chemical weapons in 1993, there is now a worldwide ban on the creation and stockpiling of chemical weapons. Includes rare footage of a Soviet chemical weapons lab, Japan's chemical weapons program, and the destruction of such weapons by UN personnel in Iraq.

Crapshoot: The Gambling with Our Wastes. Jeff McKay. Canada/India/Italy/Canada/USA: National Film Board of Canada, 2003. 52 min. DVD/video. Documentary questions whether modern sewer systems protect communities or just condense waste. Shows examples of poor sewer systems leading to health problems and environmental degradation.

Discordia. Ben Addelman and Samir Mallal. Canada: National Film Board of Canada, 2004. 71 min. Video. News that former Israeli Prime Minister Benjamin Netanyahu was going to speak at Montreal's Concordia University sparked heated debate between the school's pro-Israel and pro-Palestinian students. Documentary addresses how race, religion, and world politics affect college students' lives.

Farming the Seas. Steve Cowan and Barry Schienberg. USA: Bullfrog Films, 2003. 56 min. Video. Argues that the seas are being overfished for short-term gains; also addresses debate between communities and fisheries experts regarding the socioeconomic, environmental, and food safety concerns of "fish farming."

The Golf War. Jen Schradie and Matt DeVries. Anthill Productions, 2000. 39 min. Video. Conflict begins when the Philippine government tries to convert ancestral farmland into a tourist resort. Contrasting economic development with community rights, this documentary includes the opinions of the natives, the developers, and even Tiger Woods.

In the Reign of Twilight. Kevin McMahon. Primitive Features, 1994. 87 min. Video. The Inuits of Alaska were untouched by the U.S until the cold war began. To counter a potential Russian missile attack, the U.S. government built an array of military installations that forced the Inuits from the stone age to the space age. With their old way of life destroyed, the Inuits are finding ways to cope with the intrusions of the modern world.

Kurdistan, the Last Colony. Great Britain: Independent Filmmakers. Landmark Films, Falls Church, Va., 1990. 40 min. Video. A vivid documentary examining the plight of the Kurdish people during and after the Iran/Iraq war. Includes interviews with refugees in Turkey and other countries.

The On Going Story. Steve Bradshaw. Television Trust for the Environment, 2000. 24 min. Video. Questions how strong the international community's commitment is to link social development with economic development and human rights. Includes interviews with the World Bank president, Nobel Prize winner Amartya Sen, and Noam Chomsky.

The Palestinian People Do Have Rights. Icarus Films, 1979. 48 min., color. Presents a comprehensive examination of the Palestinian-Israeli conflict.

Rising Waters: Global Warming and the Fate of the Pacific Islands. Andrea Torrice. Independent Television Service and Pacific Islanders in Communications, 2000. 57 min. Video. For the seven million people living on thousands of tiny islands in the Pacific Ocean, global warming is a very real threat. This documentary shows the cultural and environmental effects already being caused by global warming.

The Road from Rio. Steve Bradshaw. Television Trust for the Environment, 2002. 27 min. DVD/video. The World Summit on Sustainable Development opened on August 26, 2002 with a broad question: what can be done to raise the standard of living of the poor. Includes footage from the summit and interviews with prominent guest speakers.

The Summit. Steve Bradshaw. Television Trust for the Environment, 2000. 24min. Video. The UN 1995 Copenhagen Social Summit and the 2000 "Justice Summit" both had aspirations of reducing poverty and inequality, but have seen little progress. This documentary examines both summits and includes interviews with UN representatives from both developed and developing nations.

Thirst. Alan Snitow and Deborah Kaufman. Bolivia/India/USA: Bullfrog Films, 2004. 62 min. DVD/video. By showing examples of water privatization plans that turn communities against corporations, this documentary questions whether water is a human right or just another commodity to be sold.

Ticket to Development. United Nations Films, 1990. 24 min. 16 mm or video. This third film in the series of Developmental Magazines was filmed on location in Costa Rica, at a fish farm where Brazilian fish are being cultivated; in Nairobi, Kenya, at a women's cooperative that is being visited by urban planners; and in Jaipur, India, where a group of Nicaraguan technicians learn the art of making low-cost prostheses. These are but a few of the projects taking place in the ever-increasing exchange of technical expertise among developing countries.

The Trade Trap. Steve Bradshaw. Television Trust for the Environment, 2002. 27 min. DVD/video. Documentary illistrates the effects of free trade on rural Ghanaian farmers. Includes interviews with those who feel free trade is rigged in favor of developed nations and those that see free trade as a means to reduce poverty.

Unconquering the Last Frontier. Robert Lundahl. Evolution Film, 2002. 57 min. Video. Documents how a hydroelectric dam was illegally built on the Olympic River and destroyed the food source of the Elwha Klallam, the native people of the area. After 90 years of lobbying the government, the Elwha Klallam got the dam removed.

Up in Smoke. Martin Otanez and Christopher Walker. Television Trust for the Environment, 2003. 27 min. DVD/video. Malawi's number one money-maker is tobacco, but the majority of tobacco farmers live in poverty. This documentary questions whether the tobacco industry is really helping these people.

Uranium. Magnus Isacsson. Canada: National Film Board of Canada, 1991. 48 min. Video. Filled with unforgettable images, this film documents the lasting health effects on communities that mine uranium. Since much of Canada's uranium is located on land belonging to indigenous peoples, the mining operations trample the rights of Canada's native population.

The West Bank: Whose Promised Land? Esti Marpet, producer. USA: Electronic Arts, 1984. 30 min., color. Video. Documentary looks at the strained and often volatile day-to-day life of Israelis and Palestinians in the occupied West Bank; residents of the region, Jewish and Arab, express a range of sentiments and political views on the status of the territory.

CHAPTER 5: ACTION OVERVIEW

Going Home. Emily Marlow. Television Trust for Environment, 1998. 31 min. Video. This film evaluates the success of the Guinean government and the UN High Commission for Refugees (UNHCR) in protecting the rights of children forced to fight in Sierra Leone's and Liberia's bloody civil wars. Children as young as ten were forced to carry heavy equipment, act as servants to adult soldiers, and torture other child soldiers who stepped out of line.

Three Kings. David O. Russell. USA. Atlas Entertainment, 1999. 115 min. DVD/video. Dramatization of U.S. soldiers involved in the 1991 UN-sanctioned Iraq war. After seeing a civilian shot in cold blood, the group took a stand to protect Iraqi civilians from the Iraqi army.

The World Stopped Watching. Peter Raymont and Harold Crooks. Canada: First Run/Icarus, 2003. 56 min. Video. During the 1980s, Nicaragua experienced a media circus surrounding the Sandinista/Contra struggle. This film shows how the world press stopped reporting on Nicaragua in the 1990s, even though the same problems continued.

CHAPTER 6: INTERNATIONAL ENFORCEMENT ISSUES

About the United Nations: Decolonization. United Nations, 1992. 18 min. Video. Documentary addresses how the United Nations has influenced decolonization and provides examples of indigenous people living under colonial rule.

Bolivian Blues. Rosalind Bain. Television Trust for the Environment, 2000. 24 min. Video. Among the poorest nations in Latin America, Bolivia has extremely low per capita incomes and a very shoddy education system. Efforts by the International Monetary Fund and International Development

Fund have substantially reduced inflation and better coordinated foreign aid to reduce poverty. This film illustrates that foreign aid organizations can do great good for the poor.

Forgive Us Our Debt. Karen Pascal. Canada: Canadian International Development Agency, 2001. 50 min. DVD/video. The IMF and World Bank aim to reduce poverty by giving loans to nations. Some argue that debt-wracked nations can never get ahead, and the only remedy is to drop the current debt. This documentary addresses advocates for dropping the debt as a means to fostering economic development.

The Long Shadow of War. United Nations, 2001. 56 min. Video. Decades of war in Afghanistan have crippled development and forced families from their homes. For the last fifteen years, aid workers from several UN agencies—UNHCR, UNICEF, and WFP—have been trying to rebuild the nation. This documentary includes eighteen segments that show persistent problems, such as landmines and refugee camps, but also optimism and economic development.

Namibia: Independence (The Elections). United Nations Films, 1990. 28 min. Video. The citizens of Namibia can, for the first time in their country's history, exercise the right to vote. The United Nations Transition Assistance Group (UNTAG) was sent to supervise a fair and free election process. This documentary reviews the historic events leading to Namibia's independence from voter education to registration to elections.

Namibia: Independence (The First Phase). United Nations Films, 1989. 27 min. Video. Namibia, formerly South-West Africa, the last colony on the African continent, became an independent nation in 1990. The United Nations Security Council created the UN Transition Assistance Group (UNTAG) to ensure Namibia's independence through UN-supervised free and fair elections. This operation, one of the largest of its kind, is captured in this historic film, which shows the arrival and deployment of the initial contingent of UNTAG personnel in Namibia and describes the operation through the eyes of the participants, the military, the police, and the civilians. It concludes with the return of the first group of excited Namibians.

NATO Today. NATO, 1997. 20 min. Video. Documentary outlines the basic structure and goals of NATO. This is a useful introduction to the institution that was the bulwark of the free world during the cold war, and that currently performs humanitarian interventions.

No Place to Hide. United Nations, 1995. 50 min. Betacam. There is much ambivalence in regard to the role of UN peacekeepers. Addressing both the history and future of the blue-helmeted UN peacekeepers, this documentary includes archival footage and interviews with diplomats, journalists, and peacekeepers.

Paying the Price: Killing the Children of Iraq. Alan Lowery. Carlton International, 2000. 74 min. Video. The UN sanctions on Iraq did not unseat Saddam Hussein, but they did contribute to the death of millions of undernourished Iraqi children and diminished the nation's standard of living. Documents the visit of Denis Halliday, former Assistant Secretary-General of the United Nations, as he assesses the crippled nation.

A Place to Stand. United Nations, 1995. 15 min. Video. Examines the history and accomplishments of the United Nations in regard to global security, peacekeeping, refugee assistance, sustainable development, and environmental protection. Over half a century after the drafting of the UN charter, the organization continues to address global issues.

The United Nations: Working for Us All. Ingrid Kasper. United Nations Films, 2004. 14 min. Video. Narrated by Michael Douglas, this documentary shows the vast scope of the United Nations agencies, including weather forcasting, humanitarian relief, and fighting the AIDS epidemic. Also includes interviews with prominent UN officials, including Kofi Annan.

World Action Against Apartheid. Richard Sydenham, producer. United Nations Films, 1990. 27 min., color. Video. This film begins with a brief history of apartheid in South Africa and then documents the actions that the world community and the United Nations have taken to put pressure on the South African government to abolish apartheid and free all political prisoners. Footage reveals solidarity demonstrations around the world, consumer boycotts, a UN oil embargo, economic sanctions, and boycotts by members of the arts community.

CHAPTER 7: NATIONAL/DOMESTIC ENFORCEMENT ISSUES

American Justice: War Crimes. A&E/The History Channel. VHS. Unflinchingly documents American war crimes tribunals, including when Americans are being tried. Coverage includes World War II and Vietnam era tribunals.

El Barco de la Paz. E. Katz, D. Halleck, and H. Kipnis, producers. USA: Fellowship of Reconciliation, 1984. 28 min., color. 3/4-in. or VHS video. Documentary about the 1984 sailing of the Peace Ship to Nicaragua, sponsored by Norway and Sweden to provide humanitarian aid and demonstrate the potential for nonviolent alternatives to the threat of war in Central America; includes interviews with Nobel Peace Prize Laureates and Nicaraguan people to emphasize the importance of international attention to the issues of peace.

Black Hawk Down. Ridley Scott. USA: Columbia Pictures, 2001. 144 min. DVD/video. Dramatization of a failed operation during the U.S. intervention in Somalia in 1993. While trying to kidnap a warlord, American forces are pinned down in urban street fight, leaving 18 Americans and hundreds of Somalis dead.

Devils Don't Dream! Andreas Hoessli. Switzerland: First Run/ Icarus Films, 1996. 90 min. Video. Jacobo Arbenz Guzman was a wildly popular and fairly elected president of Guatemala in the 1950s. This documentary reports how the U.S. mistook Arbenz for a communist, used military force to overthrow the Guatemalan government, and installed a puppet regime.

The Fog of War. Errol Morris. Sony Pictures Classics, 2003. 105 min. DVD/video. Gripping interview with former Secretary of Defense Robert MacNamara, architect of the Vietnam War. With pride and regret, MacNamara explains the successes and failures throughout his career as both secretary of defense and president of the World Bank. This moving documentary puts a human face on a very controversial American leader.

Full Metal Jacket. Stanley Kubrick. UK/USA: Warner Brothers, 1987. 116 min. DVD/video. Dramatization of a group of marines' tragic experience in boot camp and Vietnam, raising serious questions about the validity of the Vietnam war. the men are torn down in boot camp and later sent into a chaotic war in Vietnam that involved killing civilians.

GACACA, Living Together Again in Rwanda? Anne Aghion. France/US: First Run/Icarus Films, 2002. 55 min. Video. Documents GACACA, a citizen-based justice tribunal that aims to bridge the gap between Hutus and Tutsis since the Rwandan genocide. A bold experiment in reconciliation.

In Whose Interest? David Kaplowitz. USA, 2002. 27 min. Using eyewitness accounts, photographs, and archive footage, this documentary examines the dark side of U.S. foreign interventions over the last fifty years.

Kosovo: Rebuilding the Dream. Chris Jeans. Television Trust for the Environment, 2003. 27 min. DVD/video. The Albanians and Serbs of the former Yugoslavia broke out in brutal fighting several times during the 1990s, resulting in a NATO intervention. This documentary examines the success of NATO in stopping the ethnic violence and bringing the nations back to normalcy.

Legacies of War. Ingrid Kasper. United Nations, 1994. 43 min. Video. When a war ends, the effects are still felt for years to come. This UN documentary addresses the lasting effects of wars, ranging from landmines to psychological trauma. Efforts by the UN and other organizations are documented in this film.

Not the Numbers Game: Fight Back. Nadja Mehmedbasic. Television Trust for the Environment, 1996. 9 min. Video. The civil war in Bosnia and NATO intervention devastated the entire population, but women especially. After her two sons were killed during a bombing, Hilada coped with her loss by forming an organization of bereaved women. These women provide support for each other by sharing their stories of losing loved ones and caring for maimed family members.

Presumed Guilty. Pamela Yates. USA: Skylight Pictures, 2002. 115 min. Video. Documents three lawyers in the San Francisco Public Defender's Office who are driven to promote justice.

A Question of Conscience. Ilan Ziv, director. USA: Icarus Films international, New York, 1990. 47 min., Video. In 1989, six Jesuit priests were brutally murdered in El Salvador. This film looks at the political climate at the time of the murders and examines actions and reactions of the United States.

Traffic. Steven Soderbergh. USA: USA Films, 2000. 147 min. DVD/video. Award-winning dramatization of America's international war on drugs. The U.S. government ineptly deals with treating drug addicts, is unknowingly allied with violent drug cartels, and fails to prevent the proliferation and transport of illicit drugs. Creates the impression that policy makers are out of touch with the reality of drug abuse.

The Trial of Henry Kissinger. Alex Gibney and Eugene Jarecki. US/UK/Chile: First Run/Icarus Films, 2002. 80 min. DVD/video. This documentary labels Henry Kissinger a war criminal for his involvement in world affairs ranging from Chile to Cambodia. Holding American foreign policy to standard justice, Kissinger is portrayed as the architect of policies that have no regard for human rights.

Triumph over Terror: Where Truth Lies. Mark J. Kaplan. New Vision Production, 1998. 30 min. Video. The

South African Truth and Reconciliation Commission aims to end the impunity of apartheid-era human rights abusers. This documentary examines the commission's investigation of the brutal slaying of two youths at the hands of South Africa's notorious security police.

CHAPTER 8: PRIVATE SECTOR ENFORCEMENT ISSUES

The Arab and the Israeli. Steve York, producer. USA: PBS Video, 1984. 60 min., color. Video. Documentary on 1984 speaking tour of (expelled) Palestinian mayor Mohammed Milhem and Israeli Knesset member Mordechai Bar-On, former army officer and activist in the peace movement, who traveled together to the United States to speak publicly about mutual recognition and the dialogue for peace in the Middle East.

Citizen Bishara. Simone Bitton. France. Cineteve, 2001. 52 min. Video. Documentary focuses on Azmi Bishara, a Palestinian member of Israel's Knesset. Bishara is a brilliant political figure who has fought for the equality of Israel's Arab citizens.

The Corporation. Mark Achbar and Jennifer Abbot. Canada: Zeitgeist Films, 2003. 145 min., 35mm. Winner of the Documentary Audience Award at the 2004 Sundance Film Festival, this documentary traces the growth of corporations and their effect on the welfare of their workers. Includes interviews with Michael Moore, Noam Chomsky, and Howard Zinn.

For Export Only. Richter Productions, 1982. 112 min., color. This film shows how products banned or restricted in the West, because of their danger to humans, are knowingly exported to the Third World by multinational corporations.

It Takes a Village. Ashley Bruce. Television Trust for the Environment, 2002. 23 min. DVD/video. Documents how a devastating cyclone spurred the construction of an experimental health clinic in Bangladesh. For the first time, this conservative Muslim community was forced to pull together and control their own health administration.

Justifiable Homicide. Jon Osman and Jonathan Stack. USA: Reality Films, 2001. 86 min. Video. Documents the corrupt investigation and public outcry over the murder of two Puerto Rican men at the hands of the New York City police. The event turned the mother of one of the men into a community activist who vowed to hold the police accountable.

McLibel: Two Worlds Collide. Franny Armstrong. UK: One-Off Productions, 2003. 53 min. DVD/video. Struggling to defend themselves in the longest trial in English history, two activists take a stand against McDonalds in regard to the environment, labor, advertising, and freedom of speech. The pair must deal with corporate spies, clandestine meetings with executives, and a visit from Ronald McDonald.

Missing Young Woman. Lourdes Portillo. Mexico/U.S.: Women Make Movies, 2001. 75 min. Video. Addresses the vast number of unsolved murders of Mexican woman working in factories across from the U.S. border. Who is responsible? multinational corporations, street gangs, American nationals, and narco-traffickers are all suspect.

My Mother Built This House. Toni Strasburg. Television Trust for the Environment, 2002. 27 min. DVD/video. Homelessness in South Africa is out of control: nearly one million people in Cape Town live in squatter communities. The Homeless People's Federation was formed by homeless people to build housing for the homeless. This documentary focuses on three woman squatters and how the Homeless People's Federation helped them.

The New Rulers of the World. Alan Lowery. UK Bullfrog Films, 2004. 53 min. Video. Documentary presents a case study on globalization: foreign investment in Indonesia creates sweatshops and eventually an economic meltdown. Multinational corporations are singled out as being greedy, heartless, and extremely influential.

Promises to Keep. USA: Durrin Productions, 1988. 57 min., color. 16 mm or video. Documents the efforts of the late Mitch Snyder, homeless activist, to establish a shelter for the homeless in Washington, D.C.

Rainmakers: Season Two—Tina Machida in Zimbabwe. Robbie Hart. Adobe Productions, 1999. 26 min. Video. Tina Machida is a gay rights advocate who, despite death threats, pushes for social reform in Zimbabwe. Tina's parents attempted to "cure" her homosexuality by having her raped, a violent act that only emboldened her struggle for the fair treatment of homosexuals. These reforms are slow going considering that Robert Mugabe, dictator of Zimbabwe, characterizes gays and lesbians as "dogs and pigs."

Rainmakers: Season Two—Tsuyoshi Inaba in Japan. Luc Côté. Adobe Productions, 1999. 26 min. Video. Documents how Japan, a nation without homeless shelters, has homeless populations living near the busiest subway stations. Tsuyoshi Inaba works to empower the homeless to get jobs and homes instead of freezing on the streets of Tokyo.

Resistencia: Hip-Hop in Colombia. Tom Feiling. UK: Faction Films, 2002. 51 min. Video. Chronicles the opinions and actions of Colombian rappers, djs, and break dancers in regard to Colombia's long running civil war.

Super-Companies. Boyce Richardson. Canada: National Film Board of Canada, 1989. 57 min. Video. A scathing look at the effects the aluminum industry has on its workers. From Jamaica to Australia, pollution and the world market lower aluminum industry workers' standard of living.

Talk Mogadishu. Judy Jackson. USA. Judy Films, 2003. 50 min. DVD/video. Following the disastrous U.S. intervention on Somalia, three Somali-Canadians created HornAfrik, the first TV and radio station among war and chaos. Documentary illustrates how popular and provocative this station is.

A Tribe of His Own: The Journalism of P. Sainath. Joe Moulins. Moulins Media, 2002. 50 min. DVD/video. Documents how journalist Palagummi Sainath aggressively and consistently reported on the poverty of India in an attempt to bring about action. Sainath aims to make journalism "for people, not shareholders."

Index